The I-Series

Microsoft® Office System 2003

Volume II

The I-Series

Microsoft® Office System 2003

Volume II

Stephen Haag
University of Denver

James Perry
University of San Diego

Merrill Wells
University of Denver

Paige Baltzan
University of Denver

Amy Phillips
University of Denver

Technology Education

Boston   Burr Ridge, IL   Dubuque, IA   Madison, WI   New York   San Francisco   St. Louis
Bangkok   Bogotá   Caracas   Kuala Lumpur   Lisbon   London   Madrid   Mexico City
Milan   Montreal   New Delhi   Santiago   Seoul   Singapore   Sydney   Taipei   Toronto

Technology Education

THE I-SERIES: MICROSOFT® OFFICE SYSTEM 2003, VOLUME 2

Published by McGraw-Hill Technology Education, a business unit of The McGraw-Hill Companies, Inc., 1221 Avenue of the Americas, New York, NY, 10020. Copyright © 2005 by The McGraw-Hill Companies, Inc. All rights reserved. No part of this publication may be reproduced or distributed in any form or by any means, or stored in a database or retrieval system, without the prior written consent of The McGraw-Hill Companies, Inc., including, but not limited to, in any network or other electronic storage or transmission, or broadcast for distance learning.
Some ancillaries, including electronic and print components, may not be available to customers outside the United States.

This book is printed on acid-free paper.

1 2 3 4 5 6 7 8 9 0 WEB/WEB 0 9 8 7 6 5 4

ISBN 0-07-283051-4

Editor-in-chief: *Bob Woodbury*
Publisher: *Brandon Nordin*
Senior sponsoring editor: *Donald J. Hull*
Developmental editor: *Jennie Yates*
Editorial assistant: *Alaina Grayson*
Marketing manager: *Andy Bernier*
Executive producer, Media technology: *Mark Christianson*
Lead project manager: *Mary Conzachi*
Senior production supervisor: *Rose Hepburn*
Lead designer: *Pam Verros*
Senior supplement producer: *Rose M. Range*
Senior digital content specialist: *Brian Nacik*
Cover design: *Asylum Studios*
Interior design: *Mary Christianson*
Typeface: *10.5/12 Minion*
Compositor: *GAC Indianapolis*
Printer: *Webcrafters, Inc.*

Library of Congress Control Number: 2004101585

www.mhhe.com

MCGRAW-HILL TECHNOLOGY EDUCATION

At McGraw-Hill Technology Education, we publish instructional materials for the technology education market, in particular computer instruction in post-secondary education—from introductory courses in traditional four-year universities to continuing education and proprietary schools. McGraw-Hill Technology Education presents a broad range of innovative products—texts, lab manuals, study guides, testing materials, and technology-based training and assessment tools.

We realize that technology has created and will continue to create new mediums for professors and students to use in managing resources and communicating information to one another. McGraw-Hill Technology Education provides the most flexible and complete teaching and learning tools available, and offers solutions to the changing world of teaching and learning. McGraw-Hill Technology Education is dedicated to providing the tools for today's instructors and students that will enable them to successfully navigate the world of Information Technology.

- **McGraw-Hill/Osborne**. This division of The McGraw-Hill Companies is known for its best-selling Internet titles, Harley Hahn's *Internet & Web Yellow Pages*, and the *Internet Complete Reference*. For more information, visit Osborne at www.osborne.com.

- **Digital Solutions**. Whether you want to teach a class online or just post your "bricks-n-mortar" class syllabus, McGraw-Hill Technology Education is committed to publishing digital solutions. Taking your course online doesn't have to be a solitary adventure, nor does it have to be a difficult one. We offer several solutions that will allow you to enjoy all the benefits of having your course material online.

- **Packaging Options**. For more information about our discount options, contact your McGraw-Hill sales representative at 1-800-338-3987 or visit our Web site at www.mhhe.com/it.

McGraw-Hill Technology Education is dedicated to providing the tools for today's instructors and students

THE I-SERIES PAGE

By using the I-Series, students will be able to learn and master applications skills by being actively engaged—by *doing*. The "I" in I-Series demonstrates Insightful tasks that will not only Inform students, but also Involve them while learning the applications.

How Will the I-Series Accomplish This for You?

Thorough, relevant, real-world chapter opening cases.

Tasks throughout each chapter incorporating steps and tips for easy reference.

Alternative methods and styles of learning to keep the student involved.

Rich, end-of-chapter materials that support what the student has learned.

I-Series Titles Include:

Computer Concepts

Computing Concepts, 2e, Introductory

Computing Concepts, 2e, Complete

Microsoft Office Applications

Microsoft Office 2003, Volume I

Microsoft Office 2003, Volume II

Microsoft Office Word 2003 (Brief, Introductory, Complete Versions) 11 Total Chapters

Microsoft Office Excel 2003 (Brief, Introductory, Complete Versions) 12 Total Chapters

Microsoft Office Access 2003 (Brief, Introductory, Complete Versions) 12 Total Chapters

Microsoft Office PowerPoint 2003 (Brief, Introductory Versions) 8 Total Chapters

Microsoft Office Outlook 2003 (Brief, Introductory Versions) 8 Total Chapters

Microsoft Office FrontPage 2003 (Brief Version) 4 Total Chapters

Microsoft Office XP, Volume I

Microsoft Office XP, Volume I Expanded (with Internet Essentials bonus chapters)

Microsoft Office XP, Volume II

Microsoft Word 2002 (Brief, Introductory, Complete Versions) 12 Total Chapters

Microsoft Excel 2002 (Brief, Introductory, Complete Versions) 12 Total Chapters

Microsoft Access 2002 (Brief, Introductory, Complete Versions) 12 Total Chapters

Microsoft PowerPoint 2002 (Brief, Introductory Versions) 8 Total Chapters

Microsoft Internet Explorer 6.0 (Brief Version) 5 Total Chapters

Microsoft Windows

Microsoft Windows 2000 (Brief, Introductory, Complete Versions) 12 Total Chapters

Microsoft Windows XP (Brief, Introductory, Complete Versions) 12 Total Chapters

For additional resources, visit The I-Series Online Learning Center at www.mhhe.com/i-series

GOALS/PHILOSOPHY

The I-Series applications textbooks strongly emphasize that students learn and master applications skills by being actively engaged—by *doing*. We made the decision that teaching how to accomplish tasks is not enough for complete understanding and mastery. Students must understand the importance of each of the tasks that lead to a finished product at the end of each chapter.

Approach

The I-Series chapters are subdivided into sessions that contain related groups of tasks with active, hands-on components. The session tasks containing numbered steps collectively result in a completed project at the end of each session. Prior to introducing numbered steps that show how to accomplish a particular task, we discuss why the steps are important. We discuss the role that the collective steps play in the overall plan for creating or modifying a document or object, answering students' often-heard questions, "Why are we doing these steps? Why are these steps important?" Without an explanation of why an activity is important and what it accomplishes, students can easily find themselves following the steps but not registering the big picture of what the steps accomplish and why they are executing them.

I-Series Applications for 2003

The I-Series offers three levels of instruction. Each level builds upon knowledge from the previous level. With the exception of the running project that is the last exercise of every chapter, chapter cases and end-of-chapter exercises are independent from one chapter to the next, with the exception of Access. The three levels available are

Brief   Covers the basics of the Microsoft application and contains Chapters 1 through 4. The Brief textbooks are typically 200 pages long.

Introductory   Includes chapters in the Brief textbook plus Chapters 5 through 8. Introductory textbooks typically are 400 pages long and prepare students for the Microsoft Office Specialist (MOS) Core Exam.

Complete   Includes the Introductory textbook plus Chapters 9 through 12. The four additional chapters cover advanced-level content and the textbooks are typically 600 pages long. Complete textbooks prepare students for the Microsoft Office Specialist (MOS) Expert Exam. The Microsoft Office User Specialist program is recognized around the world as the standard for demonstrating proficiency using Microsoft Office applications.

In addition, there are two compilation volumes available.

Office I   Includes introductory chapters on Windows and Computing Concepts followed by Chapters 1 through 4 (Brief textbook) of Word, Excel, Access, and PowerPoint. In addition, material from the companion Computing Concepts book is integrated into the first few chapters to provide students with an understanding of the relationship between Microsoft Office applications and computer information systems.

Office II   Includes introductory chapters on Windows and Computing Concepts followed by Chapters 5 through 8 from each of the Introductory-level textbooks including Word, Excel, Access, and PowerPoint. In addition, material from the companion Computing Concepts book is integrated into the introductory chapters to provide students with a deeper understanding of the relationship between Microsoft Office applications and computer information systems. An introduction to Visual Basic for Applications (VBA) completes the Office II textbook.

STEPHEN HAAG

Stephen Haag is a professor and Chair of Information Technology and Electronic Commerce and the Director of Technology in the University of Denver's Daniels College of Business. Stephen holds a B.B.A. and M.B.A. from West Texas State University and a Ph.D. from the University of Texas at Arlington. He has published numerous articles appearing in such journals as *Communications of the ACM, The International Journal of Systems Science, Applied Economics, Managerial and Decision Economics, Socio-Economic Planning Sciences,* and the *Australian Journal of Management.*

Stephen is also the author of 20 other books including *Interactions: Teaching English as a Second Language* (with his mother and father), *Case Studies in Information Technology, Information Technology: Tomorrow's Advantage Today* (with Peter Keen), and *Excelling in Finance.* He is also the lead author of the accompanying I-Series *Computing Concepts* text, released in both an Introductory and a Complete version. Stephen lives with his wife, Pam, and their four sons—Indiana, Darian, Trevor, and Elvis—in Highlands Ranch, Colorado.

JAMES PERRY

James Perry is a professor of Management Information Systems in the University of San Diego's School of Business. He holds a B.S. in mathematics from Purdue University and a Ph.D. in computer science from The Pennsylvania State University. Jim has published several journal and conference papers. He is the co-author of 60 other textbooks and trade books including *Using Access with Accounting Systems, Building Accounting Systems, Understanding Oracle, The Internet,* and *Electronic Commerce.* His books have been translated into Chinese, Dutch, French, and Korean. Jim teaches both undergraduate and graduate courses at the University of San Diego and has worked as a computer security consultant to various private and governmental organizations including the Jet Propulsion Laboratory. He was a consultant on the Strategic Defense Initiative ("Star Wars") project and served as a member of the computer security oversight committee. Jim lives with his wife, Nancy, in San Diego, California. He has three grown children: Jessica, Stirling, and Kelly.

PAIGE BALTZAN

Paige Baltzan is a professor of Information Technology and Electronic Commerce in the University of Denver's Daniels College of Business. Paige holds a B.S.B.A. from Bowling Green State University and an M.B.A. from the University of Denver. Paige's primary concentration focuses on object-oriented technologies and systems development methodologies. She has been teaching Systems Analysis and Design, Telecommunications and Networking, Software Engineering, and The Global Information Economy at the University of Denver for the past three years. Paige has contributed materials for several McGraw-Hill publications including *Using Information Technology* and *Management Information Systems for the Information Age.*

Prior to joining the University of Denver Paige spent three years working at Level(3) Communications as a Technical Architect and four years working at Andersen Consulting as a Technology Consultant in the telecommunications industry. Paige lives in Lakewood, Colorado, with her husband, Tony, and her daughter, Hannah.

AMY PHILLIPS

Amy Phillips is a professor of Information Technology and Electronic Commerce in the University of Denver's Daniels College of Business. She holds a B.S. degree in environmental biology and an M.S. degree in education from Plymouth State College. Amy has been teaching for more than 18 years: 5 years in public secondary education and 13 years in higher education. She has also been an integral part of both the academic and administrative functions within the higher educational system.

Amy's main concentration revolves around database driven Web sites focusing on dynamic Web content, specifically ASP and XML technologies. Some of the main core course selections that Amy teaches at the University of Denver include Analysis and Design, Database Management Systems, Using Technology to Communicate, and Using Technology to Manage Information. Her first book, *Internet Explorer 6.0,* written with Stephen Haag and James Perry, was published in September 2002.

MERRILL WELLS

Merrill Wells is a professor of Information Technology and Electronic Commerce in the University of Denver's Daniels College of Business. Merrill holds a B.A. and M.B.A. from Indiana University. Although her goal was to teach and write, she followed the advice of her professors and set out to gain business experience before becoming a professor herself.

Merrill began her nonacademic career as a business systems programmer developing manufacturing, accounting, and payroll software using relational databases. Throughout her first career Merrill worked in the aerospace, manufacturing, construction, and oil and gas industries. After years of writing technical manuals and training end users, Merrill honored her original goal and returned to academia to become an active instructor of both graduate and undergraduate technology courses.

Merrill is the author of several online books including *An Introduction to Computers, Introduction to Visual Basic,* and *Programming Logic and Design.* Merrill lives with her husband, Rick, in Denver, Colorado. They have four children—Daniel, Dusty, Victoria (Tori), and Evan—and foster twins Connor and Gage.

Each textbook features the following:

Did You Know   Each chapter has six or seven interesting facts—about both high-tech and other topics.

Sessions   Each chapter is divided into two or three sessions.

Chapter Outline   Provides students with a quick map of the major headings in the chapter.

Chapter and Microsoft Office Specialist Objectives   At the beginning of each chapter is a list of 5 to 10 action-oriented objectives. Any chapter objectives that are also Microsoft Office Specialist objectives indicate the Microsoft Office Specialist objective number.

Chapter Opening Case   Each chapter begins with a case. Cases describe a mixture of fictitious and real people and companies and the needs of the people and companies. Throughout the chapter, the student gains the skills and knowledge to solve the problem stated in the case.

Introduction   The chapter introduction establishes the overview of the chapter's activities in the context of the case problem.

Another Way and Another Word   Another Way is a highlighted feature providing a bulleted list of steps to accomplish a task, or best practices—that is, a better or faster way to accomplish a task such as pasting a format onto an Excel cell. Another Word, another highlighted box, briefly explains more about a topic or highlights a potential pitfall.

Step-by-Step Instructions   Numbered step-by-step instructions for all hands-on activities appear in a distinctive color. Keyboard characters and menu selections appear in a **special format** to emphasize what the user should press or type. Steps make clear to the student the exact sequence of keystrokes and mouse clicks needed to complete a task such as formatting a Word paragraph.

Tips   Tips appear within a numbered sequence of steps and warn the student of possible missteps or provide alternatives to the step that precedes the tip.

Task Reference and Task Reference Summary   Task References appear throughout the textbook. Set in a distinctive design, each Task Reference contains a bulleted list of steps showing a generic way to accomplish activities that are especially important or significant. A Task Reference Summary at the end of each chapter summarizes a chapter's Task References.

Microsoft Office Specialist Objectives Summary   A list of Microsoft Office Specialist objectives covered in a chapter appears in the chapter objectives and the chapter summary.

Making the Grade   Short answer questions appear at the end of each chapter's sessions. They test a student's grasp of each session's contents, and Making the Grade answers appear at the end of each chapter so students can check their answers.

Rich End-of-Chapter Materials   End-of-chapter materials incorporating a three-level approach reinforce learning and help students take ownership of the chapter. Level One, Review of Terminology, contains fill in the blank, true/false, and multiple choice questions that enforce review of a chapter's key terms. Level Two, Review of Concepts, contains review questions and a Jeopardy-style create-a-question exercise. Level Three contains Hands-On Projects (see the paragraph following this one). Level Four, Analysis, contains short questions that require students to step back from the details of what they learned and think about higher level concepts covered in the chapter.

Hands-On Projects   Extensive hands-on projects engage the student in a problem-solving exercise from start to finish. There are seven clearly labeled categories that each contain one or two questions. Categories are Practice, Challenge!, E-Business, On the Web, Around the World, and a Running Project that carries throughout all the chapters.

We understand that, in today's teaching environment, offering a textbook alone is not sufficient to meet the needs of the many instructors who use our books. To teach effectively, instructors must have a full complement of supplemental resources to assist them in every facet of teaching, from preparing for class to conducting a lecture to assessing students' comprehension. The **I-Series** offers a complete supplements package and Web site that is briefly described below.

INSTRUCTOR'S RESOURCE KIT

The Instructor's Resource Kit is a CD-ROM containing the Instructor's Manual in both MS Word and .pdf formats, PowerPoint Slides with Presentation Software, Brownstone test-generating software, and accompanying test item files in both MS Word and .pdf formats for each chapter. The CD also contains figure files from the text, student data files, and solutions files. The features of each of the three main components of the Instructor's Resource Kit are highlighted below.

Instructor's Manual Featuring:

- Chapter learning objectives
- Chapter key terms
- Chapter outline and lecture notes
  - Teaching suggestions
  - Classroom tips, tricks, and traps
  - Page number references
- Additional end-of-chapter practice projects
- Answers to all Making the Grade and end-of-chapter questions
- Text figures

PowerPoint Presentation

The PowerPoint presentation is designed to provide instructors with comprehensive lecture and teaching resources that will include

- Chapter learning objectives followed by source content that illustrates key terms and key facts per chapter
- FAQ (frequently asked questions) to show key concepts throughout the chapter; also lecture notes, to illustrate these key concepts and ideas

- End-of-chapter exercises and activities per chapter, as taken from the end-of-chapter materials in the text
- Speaker's Notes, to be incorporated throughout the slides per chapter
- Figures/screen shots, to be incorporated throughout the slides per chapter

Test Bank

The I-Series Test Bank, using Diploma Network Testing Software by Brownstone, contains over 3,000 questions (both objective and interactive) categorized by topic, page reference to the text, and difficulty level of learning. Each question is assigned a learning category:

- Level 1: Key Terms and Facts
- Level 2: Key Concepts
- Level 3: Application and Problem-Solving

The types of questions consist of 20 percent Multiple Choice, 50 percent True/False, and 30 percent Fill-in-the-Blank Questions.

ONLINE LEARNING CENTER/ WEB SITE

To locate the I-Series OLC/Web site directly, go to www.mhhe.com/i-series. The site is divided into three key areas:

- **Information Center** Contains core information about the text, the authors, and a guide to our additional features and benefits of the series, including the supplements.
- **Instructor Center** Offers instructional materials, downloads, additional activities and answers to additional projects, answers to chapter troubleshooting exercises, answers to chapter preparation/post exercises posed to students, relevant links for professors, and more.
- **Student Center** Contains chapter objectives and outlines, self-quizzes, chapter troubleshooting exercises, chapter preparation/post exercises, additional projects, simulations, student data files and solutions files, Web links, and more.

RESOURCES FOR STUDENTS

SimNet

SimNet is a simulated assessment and learning tool for either Microsoft® Office XP or Microsoft® Office 2003. SimNet allows students to study MS Office skills and computer concepts, and professors to test and evaluate students' proficiency, within MS Office applications and concepts. Students can practice and study their skills at home or in the school lab using SimNet, which does not require the purchase or installation of Office software. SimNet includes:

Structured Computer-Based Learning SimNet offers a complete computer-based learning side that presents each skill or topic in several different modes. *Teach Me* presents the skill or topic using text, graphics, and interactivity. *Show Me* presents the skill using an animation with audio narration to show how the skill is used or implemented. *Let Me Try* allows you to practice the skill in SimNet's robust simulated interface.

Computer Concepts Coverage! SimNet includes coverage of 60 computer concepts in both the Learning and the Assessment side.

The Basics and More! SimNet includes modules of content on:

Word	Windows 2000
Excel	Computer Concepts
Access	Windows XP Professional
PowerPoint	Internet Explorer 6
Office XP Integration	FrontPage
Outlook	

More Assessment Questions! SimNet includes over *1,400* assessment questions.

Practice or Pre-Tests Questions! SimNet has a separate pool of over *600* questions for Practice Tests or Pre-Tests.

Comprehensive Exercises! SimNet offers comprehensive exercises for each application. These exercises require the student to use multiple skills to solve one exercise in the simulated environment.

Simulated Interface! The simulated environment in **SimNet** has been substantially deepened to more realistically simulate the real applications. Now students are not graded incorrect just because they chose the wrong submenu or dialog box. The student is not graded until he or she does something that immediately invokes an action—just like the real applications!

DIGITAL SOLUTIONS FOR INSTRUCTORS AND STUDENTS

PageOut PageOut is our Course Web Site Development Center that offers a syllabus page, URL, McGraw-Hill Online Learning Center content, online exercises and quizzes, gradebook, discussion board, and an area for student Web pages. For more information, visit the PageOut Web site at www.pageout.net.

Online Courses Available OLCs are your perfect solutions for Internet-based content. Simply put, these Centers are "digital cartridges" that contain a book's pedagogy and supplements. As students read the book, they can go online and take self-grading quizzes or work through interactive exercises.

Online Learning Centers can be delivered through any of these platforms:

McGraw-Hill Learning Architecture (TopClass)

Blackboard.com

College.com (formerly Real Education)

WebCT (a product of Universal Learning Technology)

CHAPTER

one

01

Creating Worksheets for Decision Makers

Did You Know?

A unique presentation of text and graphics introduce interesting and little-known facts.

did you
know?

one-third *of online shoppers abandon their electronic shopping carts before completing the checkout process.*

goldfish *lose their color if they are kept in a dim light or if they are placed in a body of running water such as a stream.*

electric *eels are not really eels but a type of fish.*

in *1963, baseball pitcher Gaylord Perry said, "They'll put a man on the moon before I hit a home run." Only a few hours after Neil Armstrong set foot on the moon on July 20, 1969, Perry hit the first and only home run of his career.*

Chapter Objectives

- Start Excel and open a workbook
- Move around a worksheet using the mouse and arrow keys
- Locate supporting information (help)—MOS XL03S-1-3
- Select a block of cells
- Type into worksheet cells text, values, formulas, and functions—MOS XL03S-2-3
- Edit and clear cell entries—MOS XL03S-1-1
- Save a workbook
- Add a header and a footer—MOS XL03S-5-7
- Preview output—MOS XL03S-5-5
- Print a worksheet and print a worksheet's formulas—MOS XL03S-5-8
- Exit Excel

Chapter Objectives

Each chapter begins with a list of competencies covered in the chapter.

Task Reference

Provides steps to accomplish an especially important task.

---

task *reference*　　　　**Opening an Excel Workbook**

- Click **File** and then click **Open**
- Ensure that the Look in list box displays the name of the folder containing your workbook
- Click the workbook's name
- Click the **Open** button

SESSION 1.1

Making the Grade

Short-answer questions appear at the end of each session, and answers appear at the end of each chapter.

making the grade

1. A popular program used to analyze numeric information and help make meaningful business decisions is called a _____ program.

2. _____ analysis is observing changes to spreadsheets and reviewing their effect on other values in the spreadsheet.

3. An Excel spreadsheet is called a(n) _____ and consists of individual pages called _____.

4. Beneath Excel's menu bar is the _____ toolbar, which contains button shortcuts for commands such as Print, and the _____ toolbar containing button shortcuts to alter the appearance of worksheets and their cells.

5. The _____ cell is the cell in which you are currently entering data.

Modifying the left and right margins:

1. With the Print Preview window still open, click the **Setup** button. The Page Setup dialog box opens

2. Click the **Margins** tab and double-click the **Left spin control box** to highlight the current left margin number

3. Type **0.5** to set the left margin to one-half inch

4. Double-click the **Right spin control box** to highlight the current right margin number

5. Type **0.5** to set the right margin to one-half inch

6. Click **OK** to close the Page Setup dialog box

tip: If you still cannot see the entire worksheet on one page, you can force the worksheet to fit by clicking the **Page** tab in the Page Setup dialog box and then click the **Fit to** option button in the Scaling section of [t]... it fits on a single page

7. Click the **Close** butto[n] ...nd return to the wo[rksheet]

Step-by-Step Instruction

Numbered steps guide you through the exact sequence of keystrokes to accomplish the task.

Tips

Tips appear within steps and either indicate possible missteps or provide alternatives to a step.

---

hands-on projects

practice

LEVEL THREE · CHAPTER ONE

1. Creating an Income Statement

Carroll's Fabricating, a machine shop providing custom metal fabricating, is preparing an income statement for its shareholders. Betty Carroll, the company's president, wants to know exactly how much net income the company has earned this year. Although Betty has prepared a preliminary worksheet with labels in place, she wants you to enter the values and a few formulas to compute cost of goods sold, gross profit, selling and advertising expenses, and net income. Figure 1.26 shows an example of a completed worksheet.

1. Open the workbook **ex01Income.xls** in your student disk in the folder Ch01

2. Click **File** and then click **Save As** to save the workbook as **Income2.xls** in the folder Ch01

3. Scan the Income Statement worksheet and type the following values in the listed cells: Cell C5, **987453**; cell B8, **64677**; cell B9, **564778**; cell B10, **-43500**; cell B15, **53223**; cell B16, **23500**; cell B17, **12560**; cell B18, **123466**; cell B19, **87672**

4. In cell C10, write the formula =SUM(B8:B10) to sum cost of goods sold

5. In cell C12, type the formula for Gross Profit: **=C5-C10**

6. In cell C19, type the formula to sum selling and advertising expenses: **=SUM(B15:B19)**

7. In cell C21, type the formula **=C12-C19** to compute net income (gross profit minus total selling and advertising expenses)

8. In cell A4, type **Prepared by** <your name>

9. Click the Save button on the Standard toolbar to save your modified worksheet

10. Print the worksheet and print the worksheet formulas

FIGURE 1.26
Income statement

EX 1.41

EXCEL

www.mhhe.com/i-series

Screen Shots

Screen shots show you what to expect at critical points.

End-of-Chapter Hands-On Projects

A rich variety of projects introduced by a case lets you put into practice what you have learned. Categories include Practice, Challenge, On the Web, E-Business, Around the World, and a running case project.

---

another**word**   . . . on Cell Ranges

A SUM function can contain more than one cell range. For example, the function =SUM(A1:A5,B42:B51) totals two cell ranges. Place commas between distinct cell ranges within the SUM function. The collection of cells, cell ranges, and values in the comma-separated list between a function's parentheses is its *argument list*

Another Way/ Another Word

Another Way highlights an alternative way to accomplish a task; Another Word explains more about a topic.

---

task reference **summary**

Task	Location	Preferred Method
Opening an Excel workbook	EX 1.00	• Click **File**, click **Open**, click workbook's name, click the **Open** button
[Enteri]ng a formula	EX 1.00	• Select cell, type =, type formula, press **Enter**
Entering the SUM function	EX 1.00	• Select cell, type =**SUM(**, type cell range, type), and press **Enter**
Editing a cell	EX 1.00	• Select cell, click formula bar make changes, press **Enter**
Saving a workbook with a new name	EX 1.00	• Click **File**, click **Save As**, type filename, click **Save** button
Obtaining help	EX 1.00	Obtaining help

Task Reference Summary

Provides a quick reference and summary of a chapter's task references.

What does this logo mean?

It means this courseware has been approved by the Microsoft, Office Specialist Program to be among the finest available for learning *Microsoft Word 2003, Microsoft Excel 2003, Microsoft PowerPoint 2003, Microsoft Access 2003, Microsoft Outlook 2003.* It also means that upon completion of this courseware, you may be prepared to take an exam for Microsoft Office Specialist qualification. The I-Series Microsoft Office 2003 books are available in three levels of coverage: Brief, Introductory, and Complete. The I-Series Introductory books are approved courseware to prepare you for the Microsoft Office specialist exam. The I-Series Complete books will prepare you for the expert exam.

What is a Microsoft Office Specialist?

A Microsoft Office Specialist is an individual who has passed exams for certifying his or her skills in one or more of the Microsoft Office desktop applications such as Microsoft Word, Microsoft Excel, Microsoft PowerPoint, Microsoft Outlook, Microsoft Access, or Microsoft Project. The Microsoft Office Specialist Program typically offers certification exams at the "Core" and "Expert" skill levels.* The Microsoft Office Specialist Program is the only program in the world approved by Microsoft for testing proficiency in Microsoft Office desktop applications and Microsoft Project. This testing program can be a valuable asset in any job search or career advancement.

More Information:

To learn more about becoming a Microsoft Office Specialist, visit www.microsoft.com/officespecialist.

To learn about other Microsoft Office Specialist approved courseware from McGraw-Hill Technology Education, visit www.mhhe.com/it.

*The availability of Microsoft Office Specialist certification exams varies by application, application version and language. Visit www.microsoft.com/officespecialist for exam availability.

Microsoft, the Microsoft Office Logo, PowerPoint, and Outlook are trademarks or registered trademarks of Microsoft Corporation in the United States and/or other countries, and the Microsoft Office Specialist Logo is used under license from owner.

acknowledgments

The authors want to acknowledge the work and support of the seasoned professionals at McGraw-Hill. Thank you to Bob Woodbury, editor in chief, for his leadership and a management style that fosters creativity and innovation. Thank you to Craig Leonard, associate sponsoring editor. Craig took on the very difficult task of both developmental editor and then sponsoring editor with eagerness and did a splendid job of bringing all the pieces together.

Thank you to Louise Stapleton, a University of San Diego graduate student, who wrote end-of-chapter exercises. Stirling Perry, a graduate student in the English Department at the University of Pittsburgh, wrote end-of-chapter problems and helped with screen captures. Thanks to Jessica Perry for creating photographs that appear in the textbook and in several end-of-chapter exercise data files. We wish to thank our schools, the University of Denver and the University of San Diego, for providing support including time off to dedicate to writing.

If you would like to contact us about any of the books in the I-Series, we would enjoy hearing from you. We welcome comments and suggestions. You can e-mail book-related messages to us at i-series@McGraw-Hill.com. For the latest information about the I-Series textbooks and related resources, please visit our Web site at www.mhhe.com/i-series.

dedication

To my daughter, Kelly Allison Perry:

You say "I will do that," and then you do! What an amazing, bright, and lovely young woman you are. You have taught me more than you realize.

JAMES PERRY

To my wonderful family:

Rick, Daniel, Dusty, Tori, Evan, Connor and Gage

For all that they do to support me when writing isn't easy and to celebrate the times when it goes well.

MERRILL WELLS

To Gus and Marme—the cornerstones of our lives.

PAIGE BALTZAN

To Gabby: My constant companion and wonderful source of energy!

AMY PHILLIPS

brief contents

table of contents

WORD

7 CHAPTER 7
MAINTAINING DATABASES — AC 7.1

8 CHAPTER 8
INTEGRATING WITH OTHER APPLICATIONS — AC 8.1

POWERPOINT

5 CHAPTER 5
CREATING A MULTIMEDIA PRESENTATION — PP 5.1

The I-Series

Microsoft® Office
System 2003

Volume II

Computing Concepts
The Basics

did you
know?

computers *have only been with us for about 50 years. What technology can do and what it can do for you today are truly unbelievable.*

if *other industries had progressed at a similar pace, we would have put someone on the moon six months after the Wright brothers' first flight.*

with *only seven clicks on your mouse, you can use spreadsheet software and turn a table of numbers into a high-quality, revealing graph.*

every *month 750,000 people access the Internet for the first time.*

uproar.com, *a popular gaming site on the Web, receives over three billion visitors each week (many, of course, are repeats).*

after *its inception, it took only five years for 20 percent of U.S. households to be surfing the Web. It took over 40 years before 20 percent of U.S. households owned an automobile.*

write-in *votes for the Academy Awards were disallowed after 1935.*

the *largest jellyfish in the world has a bell that can reach 8 feet across and tentacles that extend over half the length of a football field.*

SESSION 1.1 YOU AND YOUR COMPUTER SYSTEM

A *computer* (or *computer system*) is a set of tools that helps you perform information-related tasks. So your computer is a set of tools that can help you surf the Web, maintain an address book, prepare a report for class, keep a checkbook, create slides for a presentation, and even play video games (the commands you enter for movement and to initiate actions are in fact information to the video game).

Most importantly, your computer is a set of tools (see Figure CC.1). And you need all those tools to work effectively. It's rather like owning a car. It, too, is a set of tools that helps you go from one place to another. You need the steering wheel, the gas pedal, the tires, the engine, and all the other parts of your car to get anywhere. Likewise, all the tools that make up your computer are necessary and important.

Your computer contains two major sets of tools: software and hardware. And within each of those, you can categorize various tools as follows:

- Software
  - Application software
  - System software
- Hardware
  - Input devices
  - Output devices
  - CPU and RAM
  - Storage devices
  - Telecommunications devices
  - Hardware connections

Computers come in a variety of shapes and sizes. In the business world, you can find computers that support the processing needs of thousands of people simultaneously (these are called minicomputers, mainframe computers, and supercomputers). For you personally, there's a wide range of options including desktop computers, notebook computers, and personal digital assistants (see Figure CC.2). Let's focus on your personal computing needs and explore the world of computers.

FIGURE CC.1

Your computer, a set of tools

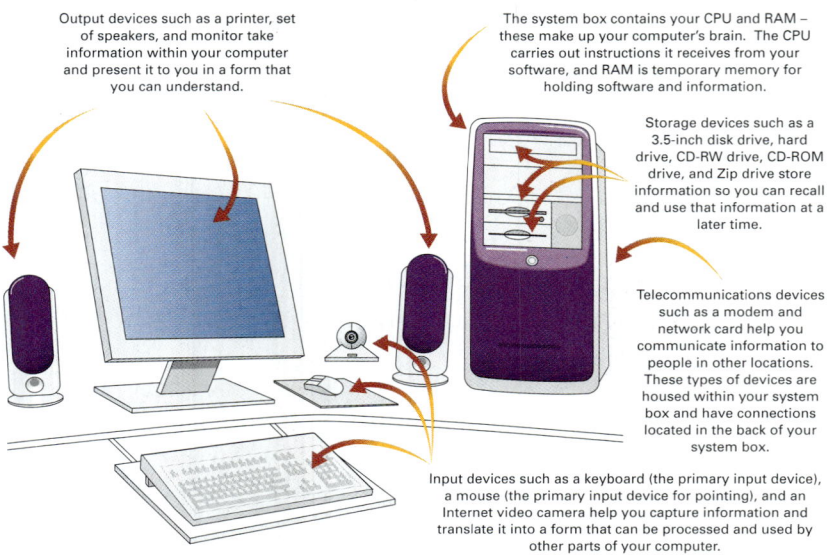

Output devices such as a printer, set of speakers, and monitor take information within your computer and present it to you in a form that you can understand.

The system box contains your CPU and RAM – these make up your computer's brain. The CPU carries out instructions it receives from your software, and RAM is temporary memory for holding software and information.

Storage devices such as a 3.5-inch disk drive, hard drive, CD-RW drive, CD-ROM drive, and Zip drive store information so you can recall and use that information at a later time.

Telecommunications devices such as a modem and network card help you communicate information to people in other locations. These types of devices are housed within your system box and have connections located in the back of your system box.

Input devices such as a keyboard (the primary input device), a mouse (the primary input device for pointing), and an Internet video camera help you capture information and translate it into a form that can be processed and used by other parts of your computer.

SESSION 1.2 SOFTWARE—YOUR INTELLECTUAL INTERFACE

Software is the set of instructions that your computer hardware executes to process information for you. If you make a list of the reasons why you want a computer, those reasons will focus mainly on software. For example, you may say, "I want to keep a home budget, write term papers, generate graphs, and surf the Web." You certainly wouldn't say, "I want to use a mouse." Of course, you may say, "I want to print high-quality documents so I can turn them in for school projects." But you have to create those documents first, and you do that using software. So let's explore software first, and then we'll look at the hardware you might need.

The Two Categories of Software: System and Application

There are two major categories of software: system and application (see Figure CC.3). *System software* is the software that details how your computer carries out technology-specific tasks. These tasks include getting your computer going when you turn it on, writing information to a disk, checking for viruses, and a host of other activities. Because system software deals with technology-specific tasks, we say that it's the layer of software closest to your computer.

FIGURE CC.2

Forms of personal computers

A personal digital assistant (PDA) is a small hand-held computer supporting basic functions such as calendaring, note taking, maintaining "to-do lists," and even surfing the Web.

Notebooks are fully functional computers that you can easily carry with you wherever you go.

Some desktop computers have vertical system boxes called "towers." You can place the tower on your desk or the floor.

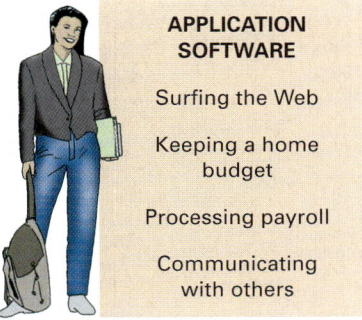

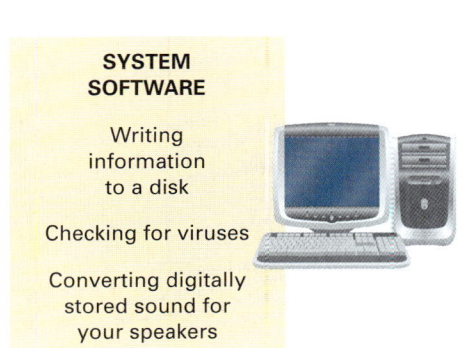

APPLICATION SOFTWARE

Surfing the Web

Keeping a home budget

Processing payroll

Communicating with others

SYSTEM SOFTWARE

Writing information to a disk

Checking for viruses

Converting digitally stored sound for your speakers

FIGURE CC.3

Application and system software

Application software is the software that allows you to perform specific tasks such as writing a term paper, surfing the Web, keeping a home budget, and creating slides for a presentation. Because application software deals with specific information-related tasks you want to perform, we say that it's the layer of software closest to you.

As a personal computer user (and buyer), you'll most often be interested in a subset of application software called personal productivity software. *Personal productivity software* helps you with personal tasks that you can probably perform even if you don't own a computer. Writing a letter, creating slides for a presentation, maintaining your checking account balance, and creating a graph are all examples of these tasks.

Personal Productivity Software

So which personal productivity software do you need? Well, that depends on what you want to do. If you want to write term papers, you need word processing software. If you want to maintain your checking account balance and perhaps pay your bills electronically, you need personal finance software. Figure CC.4 shows the eight categories of personal productivity software.

When you buy personal productivity software, you should consider doing so in a software suite. *Software suites* are "bundles" of related software packages that are sold together. In Figure CC.5, you can see four popular software suites and what they include.

Why buy a software suite? It's simple—price. If you buy each piece of software you need individually, you can expect to pay two to three times as much as you would for a software suite. So, even if you don't need everything in a suite, it's still cheaper to purchase the suite than the exact software you need.

Another important reason to buy a suite is because of the concept of a common user interface. A *common user interface (CUI)* is a consistent look and feel for software

FIGURE CC.4

Selecting your software

What You Want to Do	What Software You Need
Create mainly text (letters, term papers, flyers, etc.)	• Word processing software *or* • Desktop publishing software
Build Web sites	• Web authoring software
Create photos and art	• Graphics software
Build a slide presentation	• Presentation software
Work with numbers, calculations, and graphs	• Spreadsheet software
Manage personal information	• Personal information management software *and/or* • Personal finance software
Communicate with other people	• E-mail software *and/or* • Web browser software
Manage large amounts of logically related information	• Database management software

provided by the same software publisher. In a CUI, the menus and button bars will be similar across all individual pieces of software. So, if you buy Microsoft Office XP Pro, the button for bolding will always be in the same place and represented the same way.

CUIs help you learn software quickly. For example, if you know how to bold an item in Microsoft Word, you also know how to bold an item in Microsoft Excel, Access, PowerPoint, and the other software in Microsoft's software suite.

Basic Personal Productivity Software

For most people, personal productivity software needs include word processing, spreadsheet, presentation, personal information management, and communications software.

Word processing software helps you create papers, letters, memos, and other basic documents. Using word processing software, you can insert photos, create your own drawings, add a table, automatically generate a table of contents, and do many other tasks. You can even check your document for grammar correctness and use the thesaurus function to find alternative words for ones that you have used too many times.

Spreadsheet software helps you work primarily with numbers, including performing calculations and creating graphs. With spreadsheet software, you enter numbers in cells (the intersection of a row and column), and then use the cell identifier or address in formulas and functions to create new information. And, with a few simple clicks, you can turn a table of information into a revealing and high-quality graph. In Figure CC.6, we include a 3-D column graph that shows sales by territory. It took only seven clicks with the mouse to create that graph.

Presentation software helps you create and edit information that will appear in electronic slides. And the information you include can be text, photos, art, tables, graphs, sound, animation, and even video. You can even add links to your slides, giving you the ability to connect to Web sites during your presentation.

Personal information management (PIM) software helps you create and maintain (1) to-do lists, (2) appointments and calendars, and (3) points of contact. Using PIM software, you can easily track your appointments and scheduled activities by the day, week, and even month. Your PIM software even can remind you of an upcoming exam.

Finally, *communications software* is software that helps you communicate with other people through the use of your computer. Communications software mainly includes e-mail software, connectivity software, and Web browser software.

FIGURE CC.5

Variety of personal productivity software suites

	Microsoft Office Standard Edition 2003	Microsoft Office Professional 2003	WordPerfect Office 11 Professional Edition	LotusIBM SmartSuite Millennium 9.8
Word processing	Word 2003	Word 2003	WordPerfect 11	Word Pro
Spreadsheet	Excel 2003	Excel 2003	Quattro Pro 11	1-2-3
Presentation graphics	PowerPoint 2003	PowerPoint 2003	Presentations 11	Freelance Graphics
Desktop publishing		Publisher 2003		
E-mail, personal information management	Outlook 2003	Outlook 2003		Organizer
Database		Access 2003	Paradox 10	Approach

COMPUTING CONCEPTS

FIGURE CC.6

Spreadsheet software and a chart

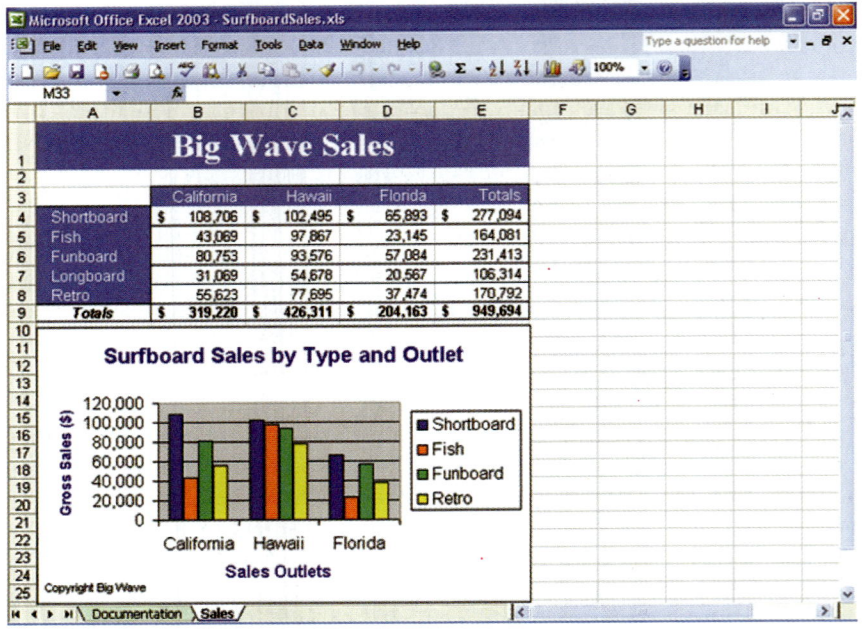

Extended Personal Productivity Software

Once you find out just how "productive" basic personal productivity can help you be, you'll want to extend your computer work into other activities including desktop publishing, Web authoring, graphics, personal finance, and database management software.

Desktop publishing software extends word processing software by including design and formatting techniques to enhance the layout and appearance of a document. This text is a good example. You simply can't create pages that look like these with any word processing software—you must use desktop publishing software.

Web authoring software helps you design and develop Web sites that you publish on the Web. The basic language of Web pages is *HTML (Hypertext Markup Language)*. But you don't have to know how to write HTML to create a Web page. Using Web authoring software, you design the layout of your Web page and include the content. Web authoring software then will generate the HTML for you.

Graphics software helps you create and edit photos and art. Using graphics software, you can crop (adjust) photos to an appropriate size, add captions, change colors, combine photos to create a photo collage, manipulate 3-D images, and even use your computer to create free-hand drawings.

Personal finance software offers you the capabilities of maintaining your checkbook, preparing a budget, tracking investments, monitoring your credit card balances, and perhaps even paying bills electronically (see Figure CC.7). If you can pay your bills electronically with personal finance software, it supports what we call *online banking*—the use of your computer system to interact with your bank electronically, including writing checks, transferring funds, and obtaining a list of your account transactions.

Finally, *database management software* (which also goes by the term *database management system*) is application software that allows you to arrange, modify, and extract data from a database to create information. Database management software allows you to manage and manipulate large amounts of information such as customers, suppliers, and sales orders in an organized fashion.

System Software

Within system software, you'll find two categories of software: operating system and utility software.

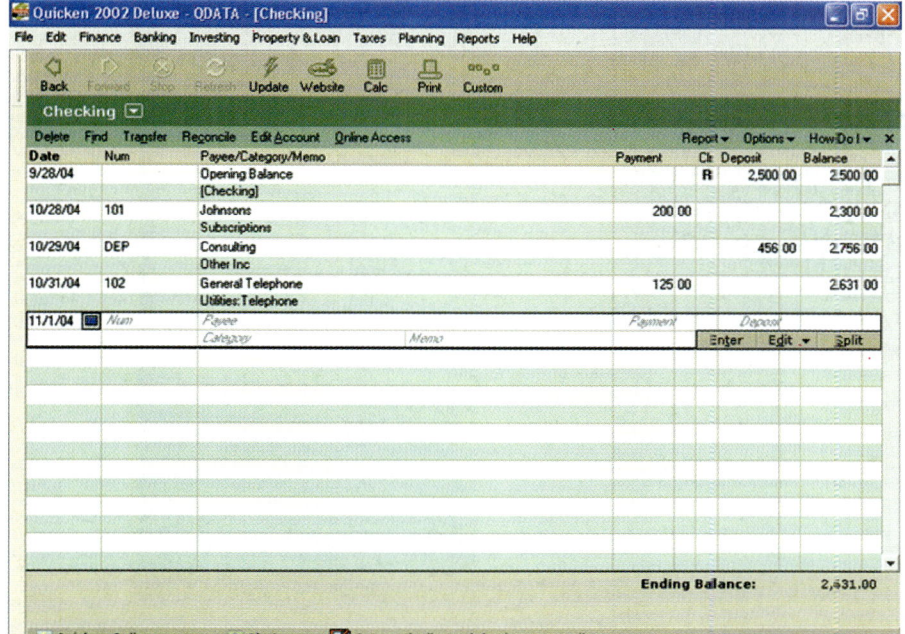

FIGURE CC.7

Personal finance software
example (Quicken Deluxe)

Operating System Software

Operating system software is system software that controls your application software
and manages how your hardware devices work together. Popular personal operating
systems include the Microsoft family (Windows '98, Windows 2000 Me, Windows 2000
Pro, Windows XP Home, and Windows XP Pro), Linux, and Mac OS (the operating
system for Apple computers).

Essentially, your operating system gets your system going and manages all your resources as you use your computer. So, if you want to retrieve a file from a floppy disk,
your operating system checks to make sure the disk is in drive A (the floppy disk drive)
and actually retrieves the file once you specify a file name.

Your operating system also performs a number of other important tasks.
Multitasking is one of them. *Multitasking* allows you to work with more than one piece
of software at a time. In Figure CC.8, you can see that we are using both Word (word
processing software) and Excel (spreadsheet software) at the same time. In this instance, we would use Excel to create the graph and then copy it into our word processing document. The advantage of multitasking is that you don't have to work with one
piece of software, exit it, and then start another piece of software—you can open both
of them at the same time (you can actually open more than two if you wish).

Another important operating system feature is security. When you start your computer, it will ask you for a user name and password. And you must enter them correctly
in order to use your computer. It is your operating system that allows you to maintain
and change your password from time to time, something that we recommend you do
about once a month.

Utility Software

The second category of system software is utility software. *Utility software* is software
that provides additional functionality to your operating system. The most important
piece of utility software today is anti-virus software. *Anti-virus software* is utility software that scans for and often eliminates viruses within your computer (see Figure
CC.9). A *virus (computer virus)* is software that was written with malicious intent to
cause annoyance or damage. Viruses are everywhere today, with 200 to 300 new ones

FIGURE CC.8

Use of multitasking
function

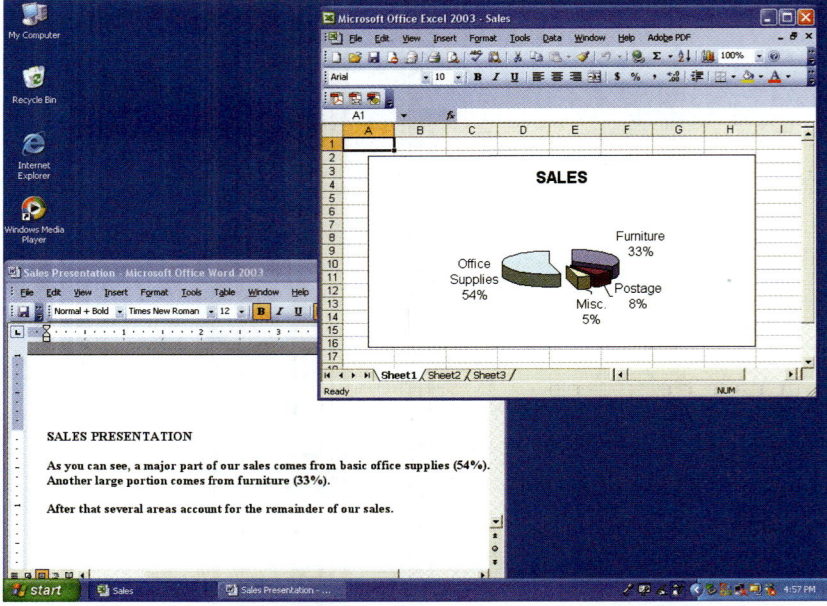

FIGURE CC.9

Anti-virus software

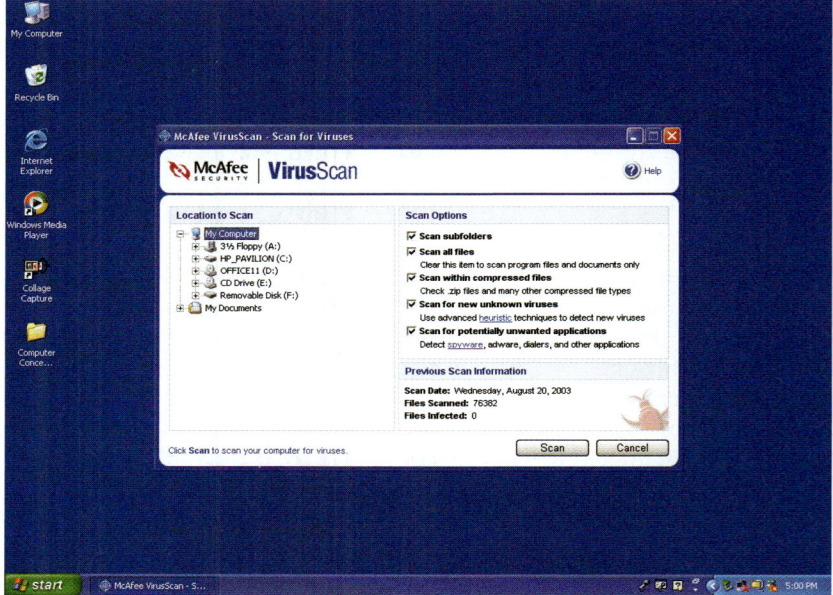

surfacing each month. Viruses can be very destructive to your computer, and you should definitely have anti-virus software to combat them.

Anti-virus software is essential. Beyond that, there's some other utility software you should consider having, including:

- *Crash-proof software*—utility software that helps you save information if your system crashes and you're forced to turn it off and then back on again.

- *Uninstaller software*—utility software that you can use to remove from your hard disk software you no longer want.

- *Disk optimization software*—utility software that organizes your information on your hard disk in the most efficient way.

Now that you know something about the software you'll be using, let's turn our attention to the hardware components of your computer system.

FIGURE CC.10
Variety of input devices

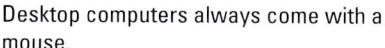

Desktop computers always come with a mouse.

The most common pointing device for notebook computers is a touchpad.

SESSION 1.3 HARDWARE—YOUR PHYSICAL INTERFACE

Hardware includes the physical devices that make up your computer system. You can actually touch these devices (although you shouldn't in some instances). You categorize hardware according to what task it helps you perform. These categories include

1. Input devices—for capturing information you want to use.
2. Output devices—for presenting information you want to see or hear.
3. CPU and RAM—for processing information to create new information.
4. Storage devices—for storing information you want to use later.
5. Telecommunications devices—for communicating information to other people.

Your CPU and RAM are what we refer to as your computer's brain; all of the remaining devices fall into the broad grouping called *peripheral devices*.

Input Devices

An *input device* captures information and translates it into a form that can be processed and used by other parts of your computer. Input devices include a mouse, keyboard, trackball, touchpad, scanner, digital camera, digital video camera, and many others (see Figure CC.10). These devices essentially help you enter information into your computer system so you can use and manipulate it. For example, you would use a keyboard (in conjunction with word processing software) to enter the contents of your term paper. *Keyboards* are the common input device and come in a variety of shapes and sizes.

A *mouse* is a pointing input device that allows you to click on icons or buttons to initiate various tasks. Today's computer systems support a *graphical user interface (GUI),* a graphic or icon-driven interface on which you use your mouse (or other pointing devices) to start software, use that software, and initiate various other functions. As you move a mouse on a flat surface, the pointer on your screen will move accordingly.

A *trackball* is a stationary upside-down mouse on which you move the ball instead of the entire device. Trackballs are a common input device that you'll find on notebook computers. On notebook computers, you'll also find another input device called a touchpad. A *touchpad* is a touch-sensitive input device on which you move or slide your finger to cause your screen pointer to move accordingly. These are now the most common pointing input devices on notebook computers.

As you use your computer system, you're certainly not limited to capturing information that exists in a text or numeric form. You also can capture audio (using a microphone), images, and video (see Figure CC.11). To capture images that already exist on paper, you can use a scanner. A ***scanner*** is an input device that helps you copy or capture images, photos, and artwork that exist on paper. You then can use graphics software to manipulate the image in any way that you see fit.

For capturing live images, you can use a digital camera or digital video camera. A ***digital camera*** is an input device that helps you capture live photos and pictures and transfer them directly to your computer. A ***digital video camera*** is an input device that helps you capture live videos and transfer them directly to your computer. With these two devices, you can easily capture photos and videos and add them to your Web page.

Output Devices

An ***output device*** takes information within your computer and presents it to you in a form that you can understand. The most common output devices are monitors, printers, and speakers. As you might well guess, ***speakers*** are output devices that allow you to hear information. Many of today's computer applications are multimedia-based. ***Multimedia*** is a presentation of information that can include sound, text, graphics, video, and animation and over which you have some sort of control.

Monitors are output devices that display information to you on a screen and come in two basic types: CRT or flat-panel display (see Figure CC.12). ***CRTs*** are the monitors that look like TV sets. ***Flat-panel displays*** are thin, lightweight monitors and take up much less space than CRTs. Of the two, CRTs are still the most common, but that will soon change as more people opt for flat-panel displays. Most flat-panel displays use a technology called LCD. ***LCD (liquid crystal display)*** technology shines a light through a layer of crystalline liquid to make an image.

When you buy a monitor, you need to consider screen size, resolution, and dot pitch. ***Screen size*** defines the viewable area of the screen and is measured from corner to opposite corner. Most people prefer bigger screen sizes, but bigger screens also cost more money.

The ***resolution of a screen*** is the number of pixels it has. ***Pixels (picture elements)*** are the dots that make up the image on your screen. For example, a monitor whose resolution is $1,024 \times 768$ uses 786,432 pixels to create images and text on your screen. That particular screen won't create the sharpness you would get with a monitor whose resolution is $1,280 \times 1,200$ (1,536,000 pixels).

Finally, ***dot pitch*** is the distance between the centers of a pair of like-colored pixels. For example, a monitor with .24-mm dot pitch (.24 millimeters between each pair of pixels) would provide better quality than a monitor with .28 mm as the dot pitch.

A ***printer*** is an output device that creates a hard copy or paper version of the information you want to see. Today's personal computer printers include inkjet and laser

FIGURE CC.11

Additional input devices

printers (see Figure CC.13). You still might find some dot matrix printers in use, but they are quickly fading away.

For both inkjets and lasers, the **resolution of a printer** is the number of dots per inch (dpi) it produces, which is the same principle as the resolution in monitors. The more dots, the better the image, and, usually, the more costly the printer. For example a printer with a resolution of 1,200 × 1,200 produces images using 1,440,000 dots per square inch. That resolution would be higher quality than a printer that uses 1,440 × 720 dpi (1,036,800 dots per inch). Also, an even distribution of dots horizontally and vertically gives you higher-quality output than an uneven distribution of dots.

An **inkjet printer** makes images by forcing ink droplets through nozzles. Most inkjets today can produce images in color using a combination of black, cyan (blue), magenta (purplish pink), and yellow. Some inkjets are specially designed to produce high-quality images and are often advertised as photo printers. These have six colors (a second shade of magenta and cyan) that provide a better range of coloring.

A **laser printer** forms images using an electrostatic process—the same way a photocopier works. Laser printers can be black-only or color. However, most people opt for a laser printer with no color (black-only) as color laser printers cost about $500 or more than a black-only laser printer.

In general, if you need color, you should probably buy an inkjet printer as opposed to a color laser printer. Color inkjet printers sell for as little as $100. However, if you

FIGURE CC.12
CRT and flat-panel display

Flat-panel displays are thin, lightweight monitors.

CRTs are monitors that look like TV sets.

FIGURE CC.13
Inkjet and laser printers

Inkjet printers make images by forcing ink droplets through nozzles.

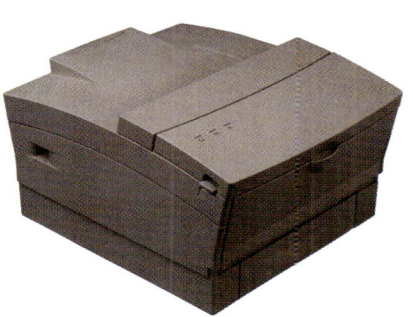

Laser printers form images using an electrostatic process—the same way a photo copier works.

COMPUTING CONCEPTS

want extremely high-quality black-and-white paper prints, you should probably consider buying a laser printer.

CPU and RAM

The original and still most important purpose of your computer is to help you process information. And that's the responsibility of your CPU and RAM—together, they make up what we call your computer's brain (see Figure CC.14). The ***central processing unit (CPU*** or ***processor)*** is the chip that carries out instructions it receives from your software. You'll also hear the CPU referred to as a microprocessor or a CPU chip. The most dominant manufacturer of CPUs is Intel, with its Pentium series.

The most helpful information for comparing CPUs is their relative speeds. CPU speed is usually quoted in megahertz or gigahertz. ***Megahertz (MHz)*** is the number of millions of CPU cycles per second. ***Gigahertz (GHz)*** is the number of billions of CPU cycles per second. The number of CPU cycles per second determines how fast your CPU carries out the software instructions. So, a 1.4 GHz CPU operates at 1.4 billion cycles per second and is faster than an 800 MHz CPU, which operates at 800 million cycles per second.

RAM (random access memory) is temporary memory that holds software instructions and information for your CPU. RAM holds

1. Operating system instructions.
2. Application software instructions.
3. The information you're working with (a Web site or perhaps a document).
4. Keyboard strokes and mouse movements.

The storage capacity of RAM is expressed in terms of the number of bytes it can hold. A byte is equivalent to a character. The following are measures of bytes that you'll see associated with computers:

- ***Kilobyte (KB*** or ***K)***—1,024 bytes.
- ***Megabyte (MB*** or ***M*** or ***Meg)***—roughly 1 million bytes.
- ***Gigabyte (GB*** or ***Gig)***—roughly 1 billion bytes.
- ***Terabyte (TB)***—roughly 1 trillion bytes.

The speed of your CPU and the amount of RAM that you have are critical factors in determining the overall speed and performance of your computer, not to mention price. If you want to perform relatively simple tasks such as creating word processing

FIGURE CC.14
CPU and RAM

Your CPU is the chip that carries out
instructions it receives from your software.

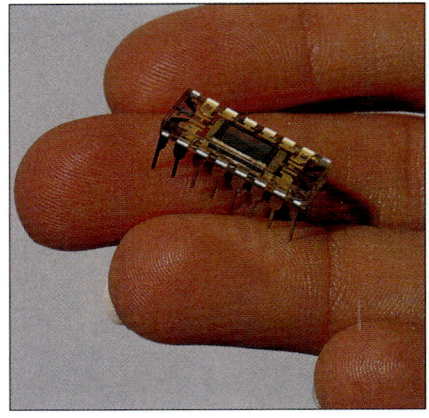

RAM is temporary memory that holds your
information and the software you're using.

documents and surfing the Web for information, you don't need an extremely fast CPU or a great deal of RAM.

On the other hand, if you're a gaming enthusiast or want to view and manipulate video, you'll need a fast CPU and a large amount of RAM. In general, we recommend that you purchase as much RAM as you can—512 MB is our minimum recommendation. The CPU really depends on you and your budget. Top-of-the-line CPUs may be exceeding 3 GHz, but they'll also be the most expensive. If you can't afford that speed, consider going with a 1.8- to 2-GHz CPU.

How Computers Represent Information

From our previous discussion of CPUs and RAM, you can see that people think in terms of characters—that's our smallest unit of meaningful information. Computers, on the other hand, work in terms of bits and bytes. Basically, computers use electricity to function, and electrical pulses have two states: on and off.

A *binary digit (bit)* is the smallest unit of information that your computer can handle. A bit can either be a 1 (on) or a 0 (off). The challenge from a technological point of view is to be able to represent all our characters (0 through 9, A to Z, a to z, and special characters) in binary form. Using ASCII is one way to do this. *ASCII (American Standard Code for Information Interchange)* is the coding system that most personal computers and minicomputers use (see Figure CC.15). In ASCII, a group of eight bits represents one natural language character and is called a *byte*.

For example, if you were to type the word "COOL" on the keyboard, it would change into four bytes—one for each character—that would look like the following so it could be stored in RAM and used by other parts of your computer:

```
01000011    01001111    01001111    01001100
    C           O           O           L
```

There are two important things for you to remember about how a computer works with information. The first is that a character is equivalent to a byte. So 512 MB of RAM can hold roughly 512 million characters. Second, your input devices are largely responsible for converting the information you understand (numbers, characters, and special symbols) into a form with which your other components can work (bits and bytes), and your output devices are largely responsible for converting computer representations of information into a form that you can understand.

FIGURE CC.15

ASCII representations

Special Symbols	ASCII Representation	Letters	ASCII Representation	Numbers	ASCII Representation
Space	00100000	A	01000001	0	00110000
!	00100001	B	01000010	1	00110001
"	00100010	C	01000011	2	00110010
#	00100011	D	01000100	3	00110011
$	00100100	E	01000101	4	00110100
%	00100101	F	01000110	5	00110101
&	00100110	G	01000111	6	00110110
@	01000000	H	01001000	7	00110111

Storage Devices

RAM, which we just discussed, is temporary memory. That is, when you turn your computer off, the contents of RAM are lost. That's why you hear people tell you to be sure and save your work before turning off your computer. And you "save" that information to storage devices. A ***storage device*** stores information so you can recall and use that information at a later time. If you think of RAM as temporary, then storage devices would be "permanent," although you can alter and delete information on most storage devices.

Most current storage devices fall into one of two categories: either magnetic or optical (see Figure CC.16). And in today's world, you need both types. Common magnetic storage devices include 3.5-inch floppy disks, high-capacity floppy disks, and hard disks. Optical storage devices include CDs and DVDs.

Magnetic Storage Devices

The most common storage device is a 3.5-inch ***floppy disk***. Floppy disks hold 1.44 MB of information (roughly 1.44 million characters). To use a floppy disk, you need a floppy disk drive—the device that reads information from and writes information to a floppy disk. Because you can easily swap out floppy disks, we refer to them as removable storage media. Floppy disks are widely used because of their transportability. That is, you can easily copy a file onto a floppy disk and then take it with you or perhaps even give it to a friend. However, we don't expect these traditional floppy disks to be around much longer—they'll soon be replaced by high-capacity floppy disks.

High-capacity floppy disks come in different types and sizes depending on the manufacturer. The two most common ones are the Superdisk and Zip disk. A ***Superdisk***, also known as ***LS 120***, is a high-capacity floppy disk that holds 120 MB of information, much more than a traditional 3.5-inch disk. Like the traditional floppy disk, Superdisks are removable storage media in that you can easily swap out Superdisks as necessary. Superdisk drives also will read from and write to 3.5-inch floppy disks.

FIGURE CC.16

Storage devices: magnetic or optical

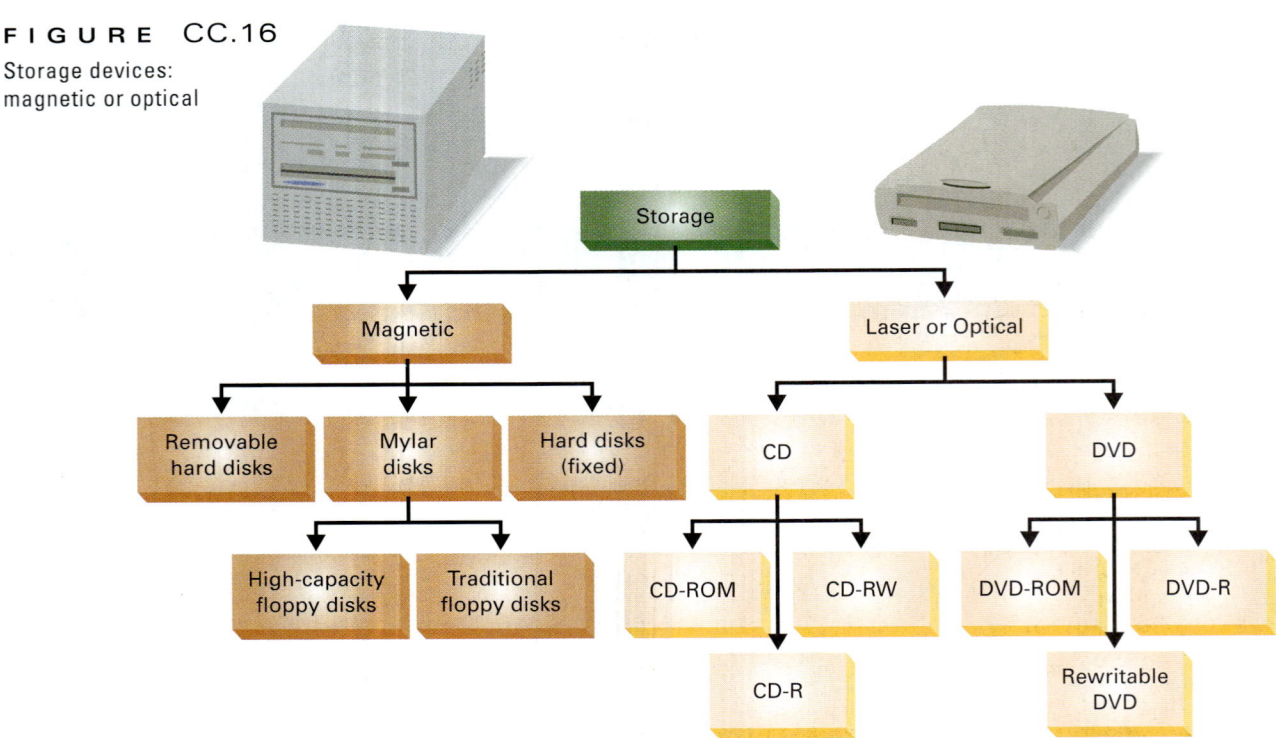

Zip disks are high-capacity floppy disks that come in two sizes: 100 MB and 250 MB. Like the traditional floppy disk and the Superdisk, Zip disks are removable storage media. However, you cannot use a Zip disk drive to read a 3.5-inch disk (or a Superdisk for that matter).

A *hard disk* is a magnetic storage medium, usually fixed inside your system unit, consisting of one or more thin platters or disks that store information (see Figure CC.17). Hard disks can hold much more information than any of the other magnetic storage options. Common hard disks today on personal computers can easily hold 60 GB of information (that's over 60 billion characters).

So, what portable storage devices do you need? A few years ago, we recommended you have a 3.5-inch floppy disk drive. Those are just about obsolete, and many computer manufacturers charge extra for them. The best choice, in our opinion, is a solid state storage device (see Figure CC.20 on page CC 1.17) that plugs into a USB port. All modern microcomputers have at least one USB port, so connecting a solid state storage device, or micro drive as it is sometimes called, is not a problem. Purchase a device with at least 128 MB capacity. Though there are several choices in the 250 MB and larger range too. About the size of a lipstick case, micro drives weigh only a few ounces and fit easily into your shirt pocket or purse. You can use your micro drive to create backups of your most important information.

Finally, you definitely need a hard disk. In fact, you can't buy a computer today without a hard disk. We would recommend that you buy the largest hard disk you can afford. Why? Because your hard disk is where you'll store your operating system software, your application software, and the information you create. After a while, those start to take up a lot of space. You certainly don't want to face having to install a new hard disk because you have no room left on your current one.

Optical Storage Devices

Optical storage devices use a laser to read and write information. Because of this, optical discs can store much more information than their magnetic counterparts. (Note that when we're discussing magnetic disks, the word "disk" ends in "k," and when we're talking about optical discs, the word "disc" ends in "c.") Most software that you buy comes on CDs or DVDs (your two optical storage device options). And these are both removable storage media, so you'll need an appropriate drive to read information from and write information to a CD or DVD.

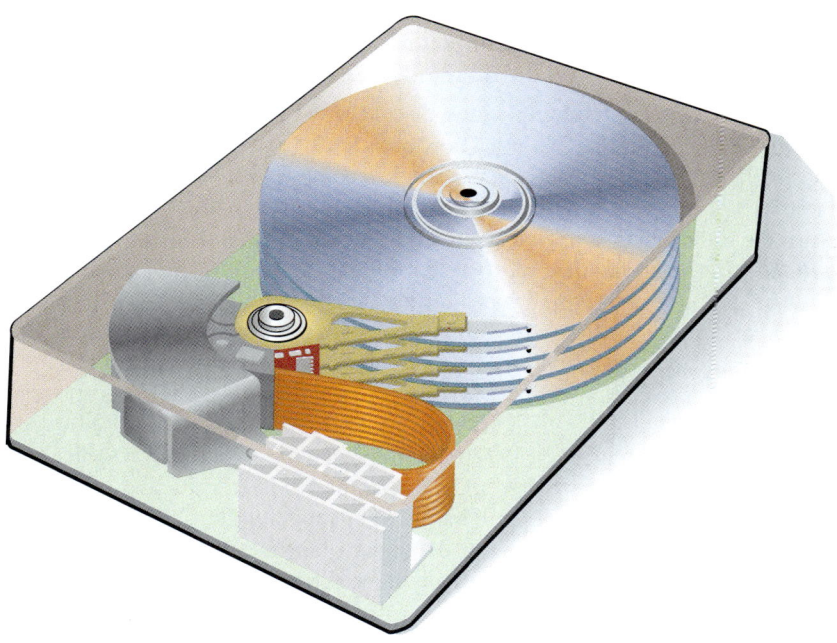

F I G U R E   CC.17

Hard disks

F I G U R E CC.18

CD storage media

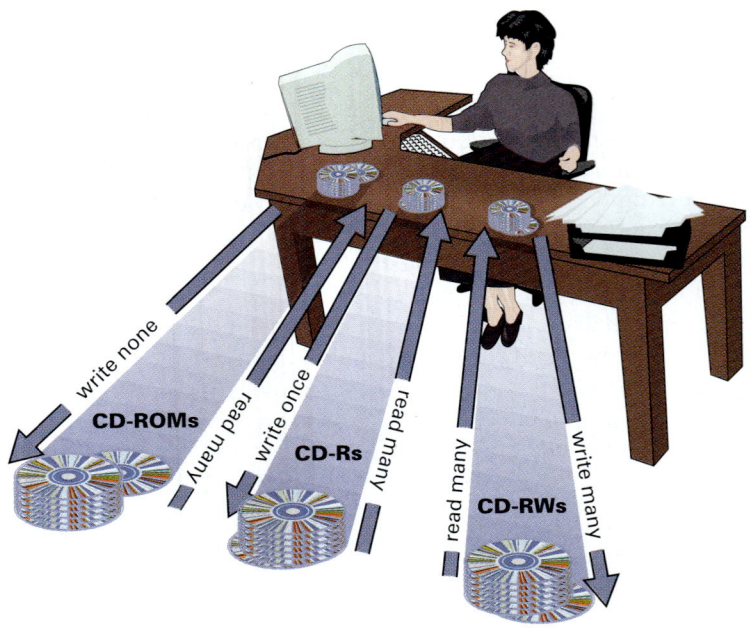

COMPACT DISCS. CD storage media come in three types: CD-ROM, CD-R, and CD-RW (see Figure CC.18). A **CD-ROM (compact disc read-only memory)** is an optical disc whose information cannot be changed once it has been created. This is the type of CD you buy to play in your stereo. A **CD-R (compact disc–recordable)** is an optical disc to which you can write one time only. You would use a CD-R for information that you wanted to keep indefinitely and not change, like your photos. Because you write to them only once but read the information as often as you wish, a CD-R is often referred to as a **WORM (write once, read many)** storage device. On either a CD-ROM or CD-R, you can store about 800 MB of information—that's equivalent to 550 3.5-inch floppy disks.

A **CD-RW (compact disc–rewritable)** is a compact disc storage medium that allows you to save, change, and delete information. CD-RWs are like magnetic storage devices in that they allow you to change and delete existing information. However, they can hold much more information than their magnetic counterparts.

CD-ROMs, CD-Rs, and CD-RWs are all removable storage media.

DIGITAL VIDEO DISCS. DVDs (digital video discs) come in three types: DVD-ROM, DVD-R, and DVD-RW (see Figure CC.19). These are identical to CD-ROM, CD-R, and CD-RW, respectively, except that DVDs have a much greater capacity. While most types of CDs hold 800 MB of information, some DVDs are capable of storing up 17 GB of information. And like their CD counterparts, DVDs are removable storage media.

A **DVD-ROM (digital video disc read-only memory)** is an optical disc whose information can't be changed, but which has a larger capacity than a CD-ROM. This is the type of DVD you rent from the video store or buy from a music store. Again, you can only read information from a DVD-ROM—you cannot write information to it.

A **DVD-R (digital video disc–recordable)** is an optical disc to which you can write one time only and that has a higher capacity than a CD-R. DVD-Rs are WORM (write once, read many) devices. Finally, a **DVD-RW (digital video disc–rewritable**, also called **DVD-RAM** or **DVD+RW** by different manufacturers) is an optical disc that allows you to save, change, and delete files and has a larger capacity than a CD-RW. There are various types of recordable DVDs from different manufacturers, each of which must have its own special drive. This is a relatively new technology, but one that we believe will be the storage of choice in the very near future.

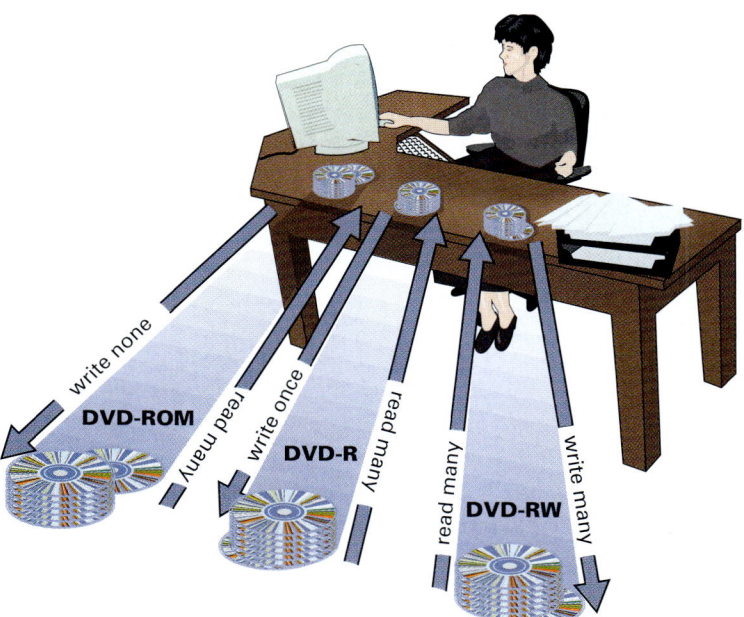

So, what optical storage devices do you need? That's a great question and one that's difficult to answer. You must have an optical storage device, as most software you buy will come on CD or DVD. But you don't need both a CD-ROM and DVD-ROM disc drive. If you have a DVD-ROM drive, you can use it to read CDs. Beyond that, whether or not you want to be able to write to CDs or DVDs is completely up to you.

Solid State Storage Devices

A third type of storage device includes the micro, pen, and thumb drives. These drives are solid state, meaning there are no moving parts (see Figure CC.20). These drives can hold a large amount of information in a very small device. These new storage devices connect using the universal serial bus (USB), enabling them to be moved to any computer that supports USB.

Telecommunications Devices

We certainly live in a networked world. It's hard to find people with a home computer that isn't connected to the Internet. And connecting to the Internet or any other computer network requires some special hardware (and software). Let's talk about connecting to the Internet first.

Connecting to the Internet

You can connect to the Internet in one of five ways:

1. A telephone modem.
2. A digital subscriber line (DSL).
3. A cable modem.
4. A satellite modem.
5. A wireless connection.

A **_telephone modem_** is a device that connects your computer to your phone line, which you use to access your Internet service provider (ISP). Your ISP could be your school or a commercial service such as AT&T's WorldNet or AOL. A telephone modem simply gives you the ability to use your phone line for computer communications.

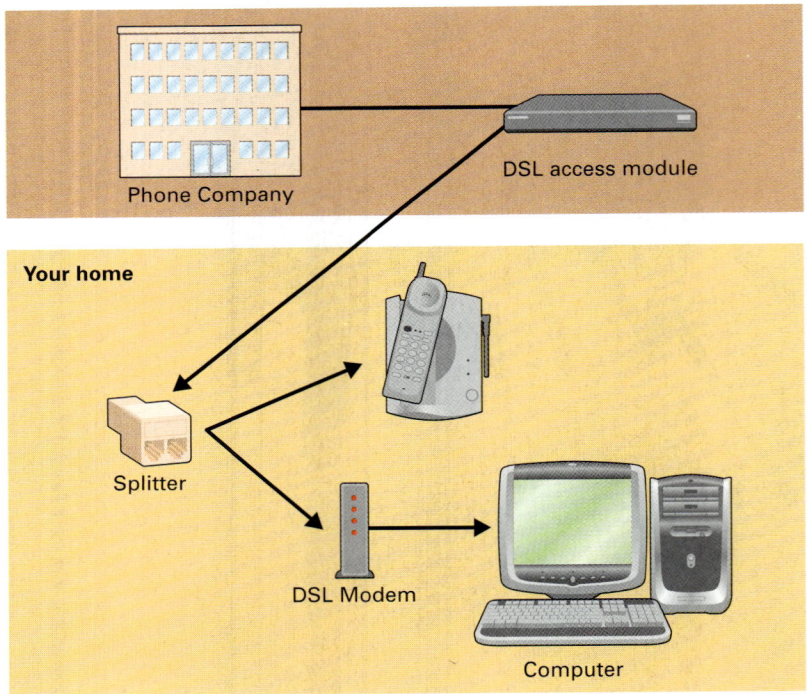

A *digital subscriber line (DSL)* is a high-speed Internet connection using phone lines that allows you to use your phone for voice communication at the same time (see Figure CC.21). A DSL connection basically divides your phone line into separate channels, with one channel dedicated to the Internet and the other for making phone calls. And DSL is up to 100 times faster than a telephone modem.

A *cable modem* is a device that uses your TV cable to deliver an Internet connection (see Figure CC.22). Again, a cable modem creates two separate channels: one you use to receive cable TV programming and one you use to connect to the Internet (simultaneously). Most cable modems are 20 to 100 times faster than a telephone modem.

A *satellite modem* is a modem that allows you to get Internet access using a satellite dish. For this, you'll need the right type of antenna (or satellite dish). You can get an antenna for Internet access alone or one that gives you both Internet access and TV reception.

Finally, you can connect wirelessly to the Internet with a wireless network access point. A *wireless network access point* is a device that allows computers to access a wired network using radio waves. In this instance, you'll also need a wireless ISP. A *wireless Internet service provider (wireless ISP)* does the same job as standard ISPs except that you don't need a wired connection for access. In fact, some ISPs provide both wired and wireless connections.

So how should you connect to the Internet? That depends a lot on you and your chosen ISP. If your school offers free access to the Internet (most do), you may be able to do so only using a standard telephone modem. The advantage is it's free. The disadvantages are speed (which may be fairly slow) and competing with other students for time. If you choose to use a commercial ISP, you may be able to connect using any of the other four methods, depending on the ISP and your local telephone provider. In many areas, you still can't get a DSL connection. And many cable TV providers do not offer cable modem access to the Internet.

The best thing to do is survey all your options. Call your local telephone provider and your cable TV provider. See what they have to offer. And, as always, consider how much money you want to spend to access the Internet. Some options are free; others may cost you as much as $80 per month.

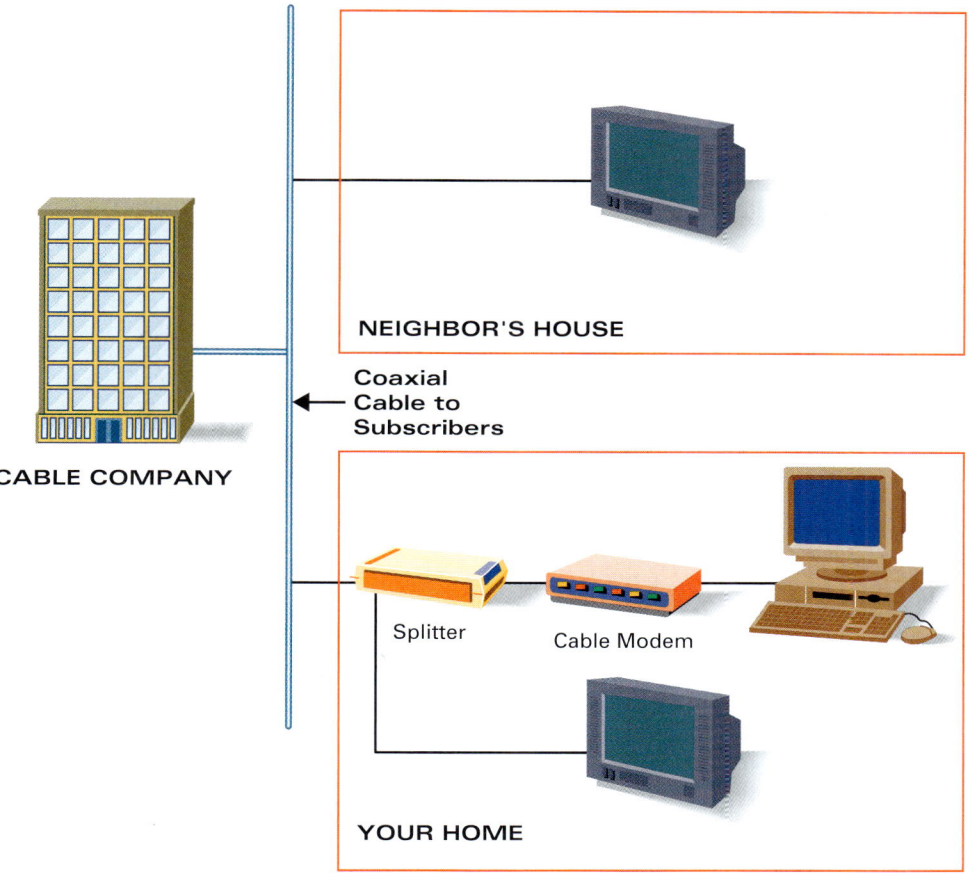

NEIGHBOR'S HOUSE

CABLE COMPANY

Coaxial
Cable to
Subscribers

Splitter   Cable Modem

YOUR HOME

Connecting to Other Networks

If your school has a network and you have a notebook computer, you may be able to directly connect your notebook to your school's computer while you're there. If so, you'll need a network interface card. A *network interface card (NIC)* is an expansion card that connects your computer to a network and allows information to flow between your computer and the rest of the network. An *Ethernet card* is the most common type of network interface card.

In your school's lab, you'll most probably find what is called a local area network. A *local area network (LAN)* is a network of computers that are contained within a small area such as a room or a building or campus. This network is probably also a client/server network. A *client/server network* is a network in which one or more computers are servers and provide services to the other computers, which are called clients (see Figure CC.23). For example, the server could control the use of a color laser printer that everyone shares. Your school probably also has an e-mail server, which would handle incoming and outgoing e-mail messages for the entire campus.

Client/server networks are important in today's business environment for many reasons. The first is control. If you have a client/server network, you can place files of information on a file server and then control who has access to each file. Your school probably does this for registration purposes. As a student, you may be able to view classes and register for them, but you certainly can't add new classes or change the time of existing classes.

Client/server networks also offer economies of scale. Our previous discussion of a shared color laser printer is an example. By creating a client/server network and using only one laser printer, anyone on the network can use the laser printer. That way you don't have to buy each person an expensive piece of equipment.

FIGURE CC.23

Client/server networks

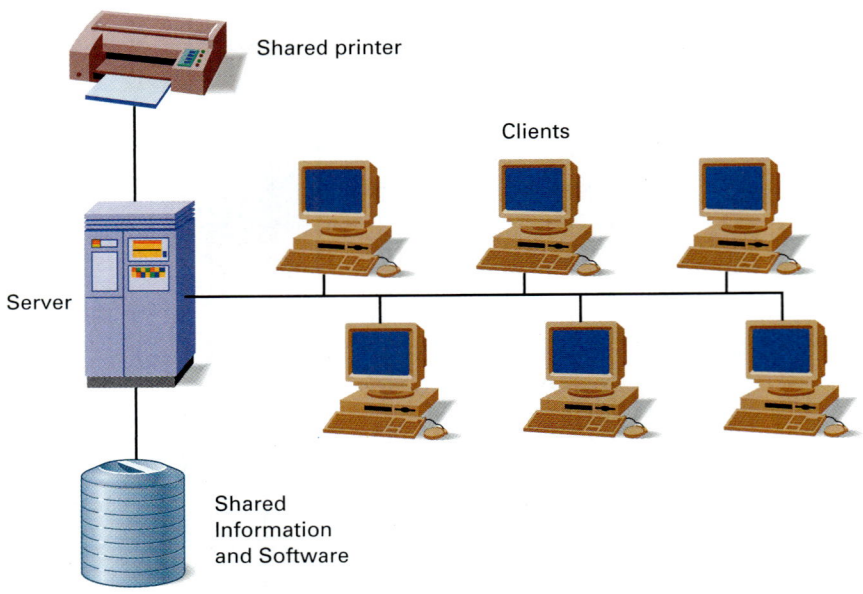

You also can realize software economies of scale in a client/server environment. In this instance, your school would purchase a site license agreement for commonly used software such as Microsoft Office System 2003. Your school would then be able to deploy Office across the entire network of computers. This is much cheaper than buying a separate copy of Microsoft Office for each computer.

Beyond client/server networks in a LAN environment, you can find wide area networks. A *wide area network (WAN)* is a network that covers a large geographical area such as a city, a state, or even the entire world (in the case of the Internet). WANs are basically collections of smaller LANs. Consider the Internet as a WAN. Almost every school and business in this country (and around the world) has connected its LANs to the Internet, making the Internet a large WAN composed of thousands of smaller LANs.

Within each network is one or more network operating systems. A *network operating system (NOS)* is the operating system that runs a network, routing information between computers and managing security and users. NOSs allow network administrators to create new users, define new hardware such as additional lasers printer, and monitor the network for performance. This is critically important operating system software in a network. Although you may not directly use it, it does impact how you use a network, what capabilities you have, and how fast you can move information to other computers and devices within the network.

Hardware Connections

To connect all your hardware components and allow them to communicate with each other, your computer contains a vast infrastructure of buses, expansion cards, connectors, and ports. Let's take a look at these as well as the inside of your computer. Inside your computer, you'll find the motherboard. The *motherboard*, also called the *main board* or *system board*, is the large circuit board inside your system unit that holds the CPU, memory (RAM), and other essential electronic components.

On your motherboard, you have data buses that move or transmit information. There are two primary data buses: the system bus and the expansion bus (see Figure CC.24). The *system bus* consists of electronic pathways that move information between basic components of the motherboard, including between RAM and the CPU. The *expansion bus* forms the highway system to and from connectors and expansion slots that you use to attach devices such as printers and scanners.

FIGURE CC.24
Data bus

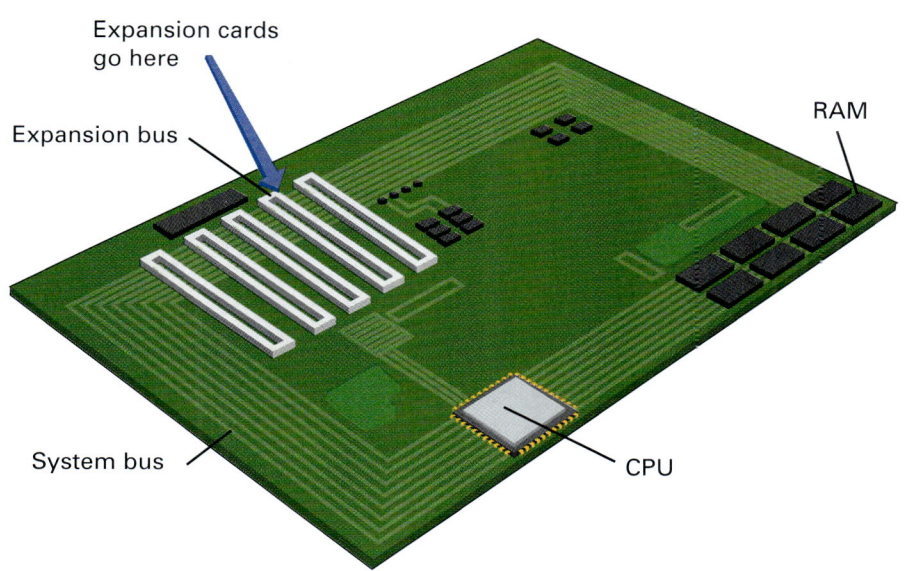

So your complete data bus consists of the system bus that primarily transmits information to and from RAM and your CPU and the expansion bus that connects your peripheral devices to the entire data bus (see Figure CC.24). So all of your peripheral devices must connect to the motherboard via the expansion bus. You connect these types of devices using expansion cards, connectors, and ports.

An *expansion card* or *board* is a circuit board that you plug into the motherboard and connect to a device outside the system unit. A *connector* is that part of the end of the wiring for a peripheral device that you plug into a port. A *port* is the connection portion of an expansion card into which you plug a connector. Let's consider the example of connecting your monitor.

To connect your monitor, you need an expansion card that supports the connection of a monitor (it comes standard on all computers today and will already be installed or entirely integrated into the motherboard). All you do is plug the connector into the appropriate port on the back of your computer, and you're all set.

As you can see in Figure CC.25, there are many different kinds of connectors and ports, namely serial, parallel, and USB. A *serial connector*, which plugs into a serial port, has 9 holes, but may have up to 25, that fit into the corresponding port. Serial connectors are commonly used for mice and modems. A *parallel connector*, which plugs into a parallel port, has 25 pins, which fit into the holes in the corresponding port. Parallel connectors are commonly used for printers, CD drives, and Zip drives.

USB (universal serial bus) connectors and ports are the most popular means of connecting devices to computers. USB connectors (USB 2.0 is the fastest one so far) are used for modems, keyboards, scanners, micro (storage) drives, and a variety of other devices. We believe that someday USB will be the common connection for all devices.

All computers today come with a variety of installed (or integrated) expansion cards and their corresponding ports. As you can see in Figure CC.25, there are ports for a mouse and keyboard, two serial ports, a parallel port (into which you would plug your printer), and two USB ports.

So what do you need to know about expansion cards, connectors, and ports when buying a computer? All you need to know is that your computer will come equipped with everything you need to get up and running. You literally plug all your devices into the appropriate ports and turn on your machine. It's that easy. And your computer will also come equipped with extra ports—you can use these for additional devices such as a scanner or an external storage device (perhaps a Zip disk if the computer you're buying doesn't already have one).

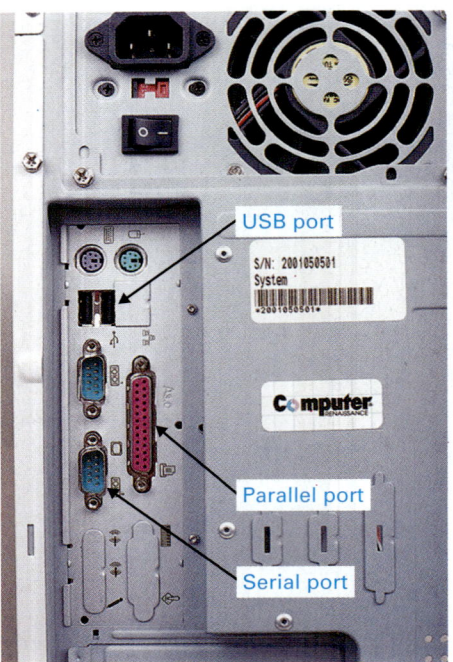

SESSION 1.4 THE INTERNET AND THE WORLD WIDE WEB

As we close our discussion of the basics of your computer system, let's look for a moment at the most visible and explosive technology today—the Internet and the World Wide Web. The **Internet** is a vast network of networked computers (hardware and software) that connects millions of people all over the world. The **World Wide Web (Web)** is the Internet in a linked multimedia form. Most people today use the terms "Internet" and "Web" interchangeably. There is actually a distinct difference between the two, but few people anymore can define that exact difference.

When you connect to your Internet service provider (ISP), you're connecting your computer to one of your ISP's computers that is already connected to the Internet. You then use your **Web browser software** (Internet Explorer and Netscape Communicator are the most popular) to surf the Web. As you surf the Web, you'll be visiting Web sites. A **Web site** is a specific location on the Web where you visit, gather information, and perhaps order products. Each Web site has a Web site address. A **Web site address** is a unique name that identifies a specific site on the Web.

In Figure CC.26, we are using Internet Explorer as our Web browser software to visit the Web site for *USA Today.* Its Web site address is http://www.usatoday.com. Most Web site addresses start with http://www. Then, you'll find the unique part of the address ("usatoday" in this instance), followed by a three-character extension. The three-character extension tells you what type of organization it is. For *USA Today,* it's a commercial for-profit organization, so its three-character extension is "com." Some other extensions include "edu" for educational institutions and "org" for not-for-profit organizations such as the Red Cross.

Now, what you want to do and where you want to go are only limited by your imagination. To read about sports within the *USA Today* site, all you have to do is click on the "Sports" link. A **link** (the technical term is **hyperlink**) is clickable text or an image that allows you to move from one Web site to another or move to different places

FIGURE CC.26

USA Today Web site

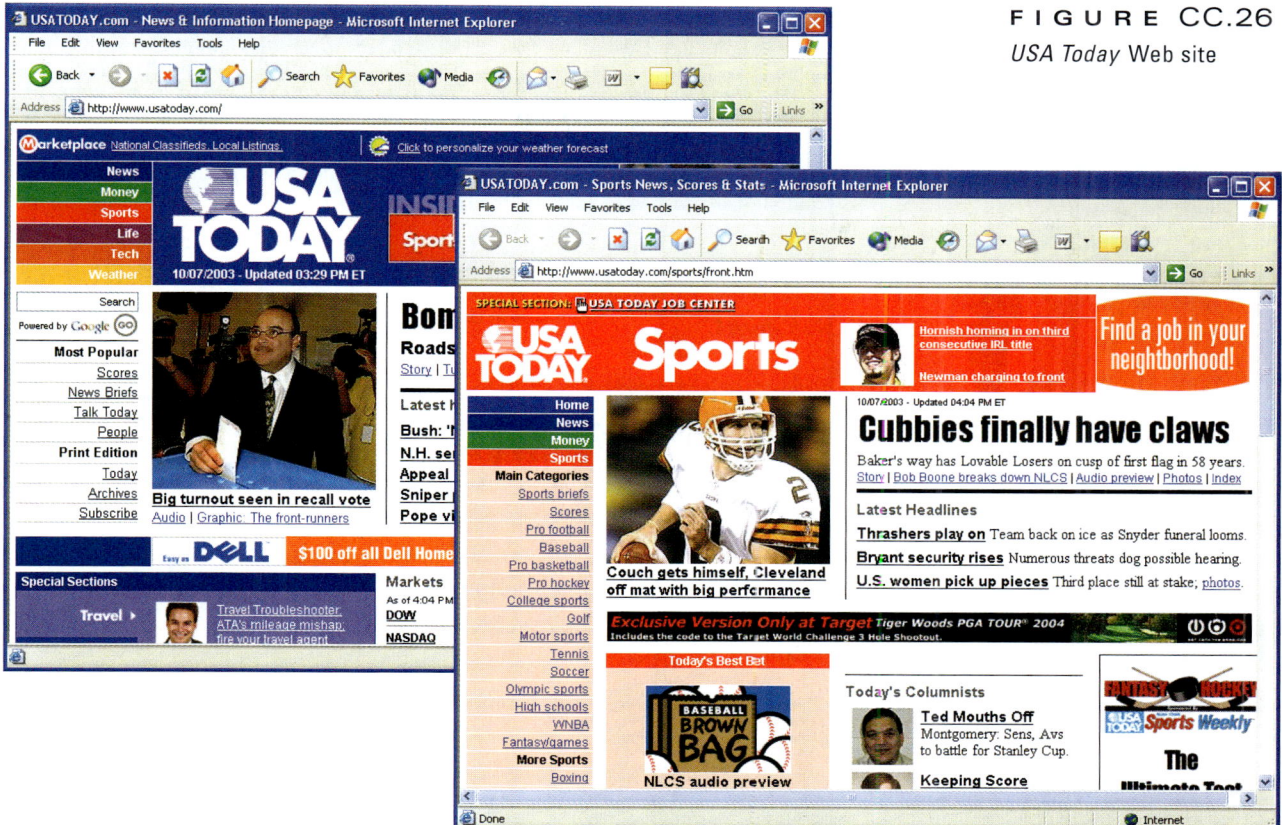

within the same Web site. To go to a completely different Web site, all you do is click somewhere within the Address field, type in a new Web site address (such as http://www.ebay.com to go to eBay, the largest auction house on the Web), and hit the Enter key.

You also can search the Web to find information you need or sites you'd like to visit. To do this, you would use a search engine such as Ask Jeeves (at http://www.askjeeves.com). A ***search engine*** is a facility on the Web that allows you to find Web sites by key word or words. At Ask Jeeves, you simply ask a question for the information you'd like to find. In Figure CC.27, we asked the question, "Who won the Academy Awards in 2003?" As you can see in the second screen, Ask Jeeves then provided a list of Web sites with the information we wanted.

The Web is fun and easy to use. In our brief discussion of it, you already learned how to use Web browser software. You can now visit sites that show video clips of movies (try movies.com at http://movies.go.com), allow you to download free games and screen savers (try Jumbo at http://www.jumbo.com), help you make travel arrangements for a cruise (try Travelocity at http://www.travelocity.com), and find a job (try Monster.com at http://www.monster.com).

You really are only limited by your imagination on the Web.

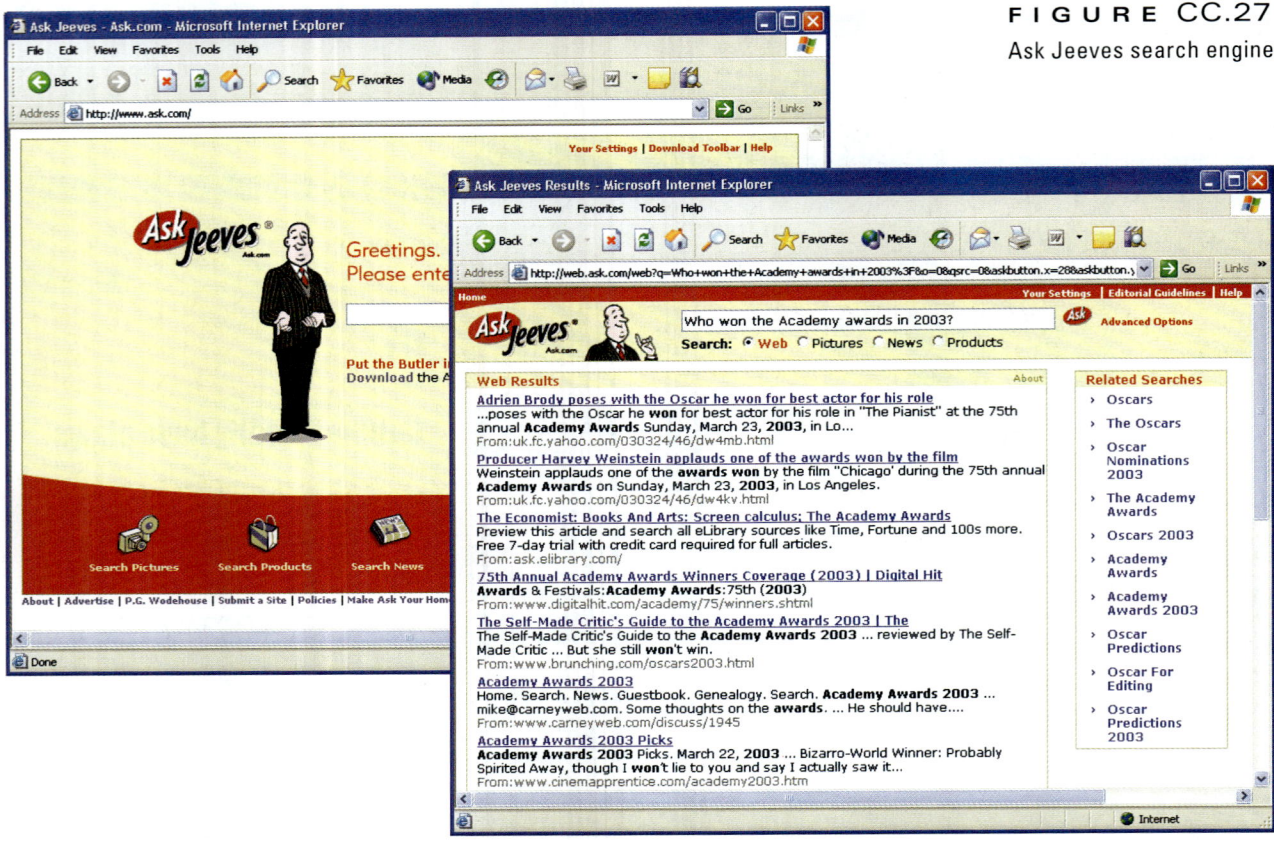

TRUE OR FALSE

1. _____ A CPU is temporary memory.

2. _____ A group of eight bits makes up a byte.

3. _____ The resolution of a screen is measured by the number of pixels it has.

4. _____ A Web address is a unique address for each Web page.

5. _____ The two major sets of tools that your computer contains are software and hardware.

FILL-IN

1. An anti-virus program is an example of _____ _____.

2. Working with more than one software program at a time is known as _____.

3. The _____ is the most commonly used input device.

4. A _____ _____ is a device that uses your TV cable to deliver an Internet connection.

5. A network that covers a large geographical area is known as a _____.

6. Another name for the main board in your computer is _____.

MULTIPLE CHOICE

1. Your computer system includes
   a. CPU and RAM.
   b. storage devices.
   c. input devices.
   d. all of the above.

2. The resolution of a printer is expressed in
   a. dots per inch.
   b. pixels.
   c. bits.
   d. bytes.

3. Temporary memory that holds software instructions and information for your CPU is
   a. a CD.
   b. a DVD.
   c. a hard disk.
   d. RAM.

4. Connectors include
   a. serial.
   b. parallel.
   c. USB.
   d. all of the above.

5. A _____ uses your phone line to enable you to connect your computer to another computer.
   a. network interface card
   b. PC card
   c. modem
   d. cable modem

review of concepts

REVIEW QUESTIONS

1. Describe the concept of multitasking.

2. What is a LAN?

3. Explain what optical storage devices are.

4. Explain why client/server networks are important in today's business environment.

5. Explain a Web site address.

CREATE THE QUESTION

For each of the following answers, create an appropriate, short question.

ANSWER	QUESTION
1. HTML	_____
2. Data bus	_____
3. The keyboard	_____
4. Hardware	_____
5. Megahertz and gigahertz	_____
6. Software suites	_____

practice

1. Getting to Know Your School's Computers

You need to know about the computers you will be using at your school. Go to your school's computer lab and do a little fact finding to answer the following questions:

- What types of computers are in the computer lab: Macs, IBM and compatible PCs, or both?
- If both are present, which one is the main type?
- What is the most common system software in your school's lab?
- What types of application software are available for the computers?

2. Connecting to the Web through Your School

Ask your school's technical support people about how to connect to the Web through your school. Then answer the following questions:

- What connectivity software do you need?
- Does the software needed to connect already reside on your personal computer, or do you need to download it?
- What phone number do you call to make a connection between your computer and your school's computer?
- Is there any time limitation for staying connected to the Web through your school?
- Is ftp software available through your school so that you can download files from the Web?
- Is there any wireless connectivity at your school? If so, what is needed to utilize the wireless network?
- Does your school provide Web space to you for saving files or publishing your own Web site?

hands-on projects

challenge!

1. Using Microsoft Paint

While learning about the OS, you have discovered that it has many built-in accessories that you find helpful. Microsoft Paint is the graphics software that comes with the Microsoft operating system. Click the **Start** button, point to **All Programs**, and then point to **Accessories** and click **Paint**. Experiment with the drawing tools and colors to create a free-hand drawing. What did you draw? How easy was it to learn the basic functions of Paint? Did you use shapes such as rectangle and oval? Add your name to your drawing by using the text tool. Click **File** on the Menu bar, and **Print**, and then click the **Print** button on the Print dialog box.

2. Comparing Personal Computers

Obtain a copy of a recent computer magazine and review the advertisements for desktop personal computers and notebooks. Compare ads for the least and most expensive desktop computers and the least and most expensive notebooks you can find. Using WordPad, create and print a short explanation of your findings. (Hint: You will use almost the same steps to locate and print in WordPad as those outlined in Challenge 1.)

did you
know?

a *pregnant goldfish is called a twit.*

almonds *are members of the peach family.*

human *thigh bones are stronger than concrete.*

in *Tokyo they sell toupees for dogs.*

women *blink nearly twice as much as men.*

bees *beat their wings about 300 times a second.*

Terry's Home Computer

You know someone like Terry. It might be your boss, parent, sibling, favorite relative, or family friend. After years of trying to ignore computers, using them only when it couldn't be avoided, Terry has decided to buy a computer. We are going to take a closer look at the concepts and skills Terry will need to use this new computer.

With the help of family and friends, Terry acquires a new Intel-based personal computer system that uses Windows XP as the operating system. Terry's new computer system is considered a "mid-range" system. It has a 17-inch monitor (TV screen), mouse, ergonomic keyboard, and printer attached to the mini-tower system unit that sits under the desk. The 1.4-MB floppy disk drive is drive A; the hard disk drive is drive C; the removable disk drive is drive D; and the CD-ROM drive is drive E. Drive B is unused.

The library in Terry's house, which had not seen a lot of use in recent years, is now humming with computer power and the potential to improve Terry's quality of life. A new computer desk with a special shelf for the monitor, a comfortable chair, and a small table to hold the printer and extra paper fill the room. A Grateful Dead mouse pad materialized out of nowhere to put the finishing touch on the new computer center.

Terry had bribed a good friend with lunch for help in setting up the new equipment. With the monitor plugged into the system unit and the system unit along with the printer plugged into the surge protector connected to the outlet, Terry is ready to power up. What happens next is what the old-timers call "booting the computer."

After dinner Terry headed to the library to "take the new toy for a spin around the block." Our new computer user waits a little impatiently as the computer goes through its internal circuitry tests and starts looking for a computer program to copy into its memory. At this time the computer first checks to see if there is a floppy disk in drive A. If there is, it will try to use it to start the computer. Normally drive A is empty and the computer finds the necessary program on the hard disk. On Terry's computer this control program, the operating system, is Windows XP. It starts up without a hitch. Since this is the first time the new computer has been turned on, Terry sees the Getting Started with Windows XP box shown in Figure 1.1. Now what?

FIGURE 1.1
Windows XP Welcome screen

SESSION 1.1 GETTING TO KNOW WINDOWS

Windows XP Professional, or just Windows for short, is a *computer program*. In other words, it is a set of instructions a computer follows that work with and control a variety of computer hardware. In this session you will learn to interact with Windows using the keyboard and mouse. These mouse operations are a set of computer skills you will find useful for many years to come.

Starting Windows by turning the computer system on:

1. Make sure there are no removable disks in any disk drives. If a disk is in the floppy disk drive, press the eject button to remove it

tip: *An "Invalid system disk" message appears on the screen if a floppy disk is accidentally left in the computer when it is turned on. If you get this message, remove the disk and press the **Enter** key*

2. Start the computer by turning on the power switch

tip: *A light, usually green, turns on when the hardware is turned on. In some situations, the light needs time to warm up. If no light turns on, try again and then seek assistance*

3. If necessary, turn on the attached monitor and printer

tip: *It takes some time for the computer system to start up. If you are asked to select an operating system, do nothing. The computer will select the best choice*

4. You may be prompted to press Ctrl+Alt+Delete and then enter a user-name and password. Use the keyboard to enter the <Username> given to you and, when necessary, press the **Tab** key to move to the password entry area to enter a password. Whatever the situation, press the **Enter** key when you are ready to continue

tip: *If you just turned the computer on, like Terry, a Welcome screen appears as shown in Figure 1.1*

5. Point to the **appropriate user icon**, in this case Terry, on the Welcome screen by moving the mouse until the mouse pointer rests on the Icon
   Pointing to a log on icon displays a border on the icon and dims the other user icons and names

6. Click the **user icon** by pressing and releasing the left mouse button
   Windows XP highlights the icon and name and prompts you for a password if one has been set

7. Type a **password**, if necessary and click the **Next** button
   The contents of the Welcome screen change to display the word Welcome, on the left side of the screen and the user name, user icon and message Loading your personal settings . . . , on the right side. The screen displays only momentarily and then the background, called the desktop (see Figure 1.2) loads. Your background may be set to display a different color or picture.

FIGURE 1.2

The Windows desktop

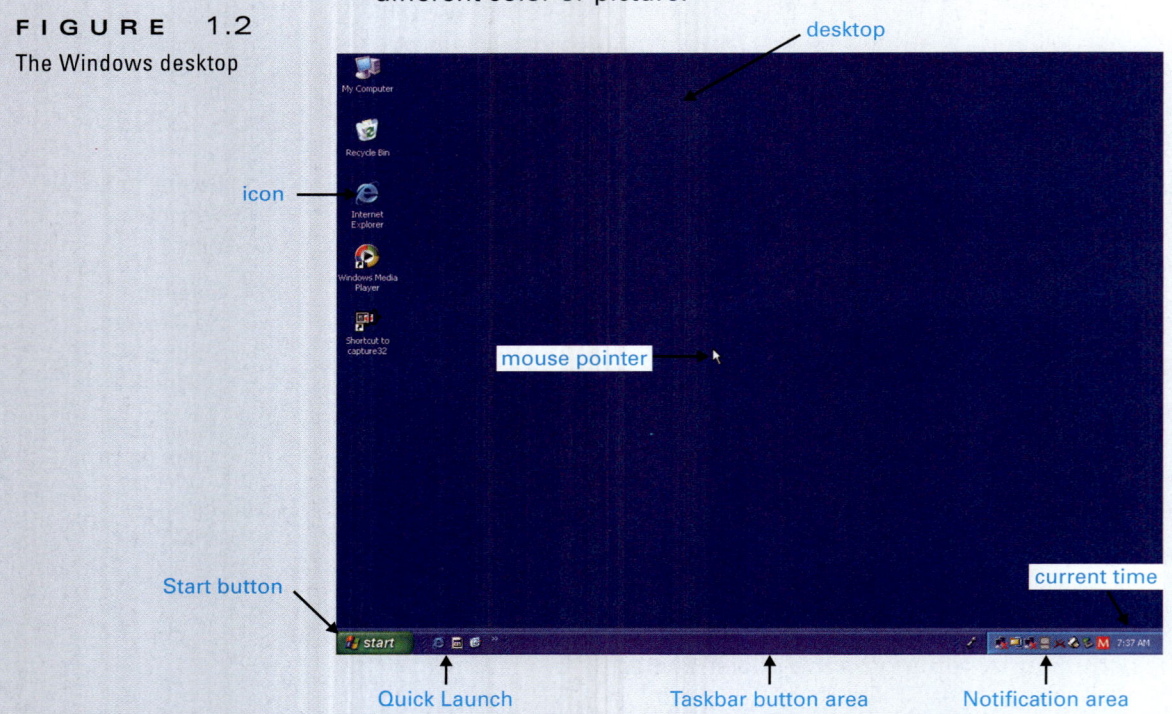

Windows Desktop

There are many variations to the Windows screen you see in Figure 1.2. All of these variations are referred to as the Windows *desktop*. The desktop, through the use of menus, *icons* (pictures), Help screens, and other graphical images, lets you access (interface with) information available on your computer. As a result, the desktop is called a graphical user interface (GUI) or "gooey." Like any workspace, it is customized by everyone to his or her own personal taste. Much of this book focuses on showing you how to personalize your version of Windows and the Windows desktop.

The desktop is aptly named, since you work with images on the screen in the same way that you work with papers, folders, and office tools and supplies laid out on an actual desktop. This desktop metaphor is the basis for all screen displays and processing activities under the control of Windows.

The desktop in Figure 1.2 is the **default** or preset version that is initially installed when Windows is set up on a new computer. It contains the items commonly found on any Windows desktop: icons, Taskbar, and Start button. The icons identify commonly used programs and files. The **Taskbar** along the bottom of the window displays the names of active programs currently running on the computer. Terry uses the **Start button** to run different programs, find files, and change computer settings. The **Notification area** of the Taskbar contains commonly used icons. You will eventually customize the Notification area to include icons for applications needed all the time. The system tray displays icons associated with programs running behind the scenes such as the clock or anti-virus software.

Mouse (Pointing Device) Operations

A mouse is one of several types of **pointing devices** that control the movement of the pointer on the monitor's screen. The **mouse pointer** is usually an arrow that appears on the screen and is controlled by the movement of a pointing device. It is used to open files and start application programs like word processing or games. As you grasp and move the mouse across a flat surface, the movement of the ball rolling under the mouse moves a mouse pointer in a corresponding path around the screen. With other types of pointing devices, like a trackball, you move the ball directly with your hand to control the mouse pointer's movement. We use the term "mouse" in this text to mean any pointing device.

When you work within the desktop, the pointer is shaped like an arrow (see Figure 1.3); however, it changes into other shapes depending on which activity is in progress. You can lift the mouse and set it back down again without changing the location of the pointer on-screen. This action may be necessary if you do not have enough room to move the pointer across the screen in one continuous movement of the mouse.

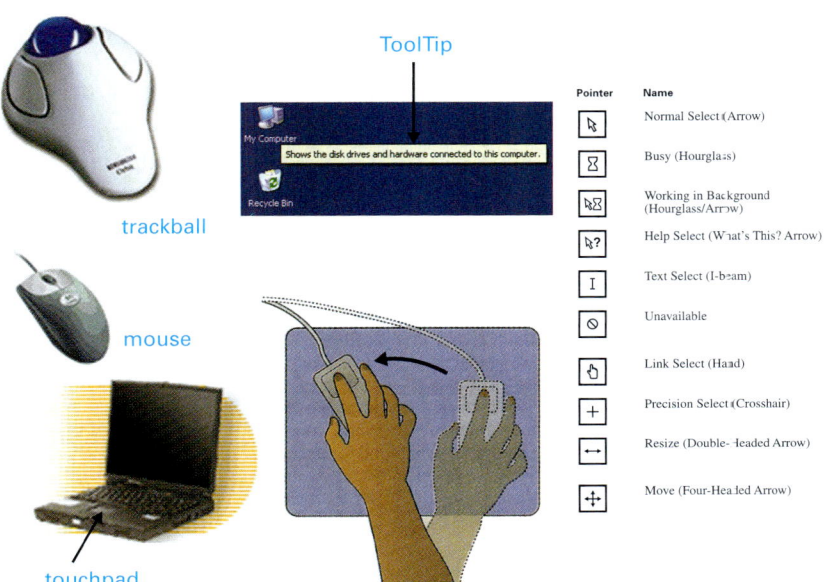

trackball

mouse

touchpad

ToolTip

Pointer	Name
	Normal Select (Arrow)
	Busy (Hourglass)
	Working in Background (Hourglass/Arrow)
	Help Select (What's This? Arrow)
	Text Select (I-beam)
	Unavailable
	Link Select (Hand)
	Precision Select (Crosshair)
	Resize (Double-Headed Arrow)
	Move (Four-Headed Arrow)

FIGURE 1.3

Pointing devices with mouse pointers

Don't worry if you're not familiar with the different icons and objects on the desktop. Windows provides *ToolTips* (see Figure 1.3) that briefly describe the use of each object on the screen. Terry sees these ToolTips when he holds the mouse pointer over the object. Be patient; it takes a split second before the ToolTip is displayed.

Moving the mouse pointer:

1. Move the mouse pointer over the time in the lower-right corner of the screen

tip: *If nothing happens, click on an empty area of the screen and repeat step 1*

2. Move the mouse pointer over the Start button to display the ToolTip

3. Move it over the My Computer icon

tip: *Concentrate on the tip of the pointer when trying to point at an object*

At first, using a mouse may seem awkward. However, this device's operation will soon become second nature. The speed and ease with which you can do things using a mouse will increase your productivity many times over.

Selecting Desktop Objects

The original mouse had only one button. It was pressed or clicked to select the icon or button under the mouse pointer. Typically the mouse that comes with a Windows-based computer system has two buttons: left and right. Both buttons are used when selecting desktop *objects*. Everything on the desktop is an object of one type or another. Applications programs for word processing or video playback appear as icon objects. Documents, music, images, and peripheral hardware such as printers also appear as objects on the Windows desktop. An object is self-contained, has properties, and can perform actions. On the screen it can appear as an icon, bar, or even the desktop itself.

Each object has its own unique set of *properties* (physical attributes). For example, the desktop in Figure 1.4 has properties of color (blue) and the size of the text under icons and on buttons. Actions it can perform include rearranging the icons. Actions other objects might perform include running programs or playing music. These properties and actions are displayed as part of a *shortcut menu* (see Figure 1.4). Terry uses the mouse to open an object's shortcut menu by *right-clicking*, pressing the right mouse button once, with the mouse pointer on the object.

It should go without saying that when you right- (or left-) click, you immediately let go of the button. Holding down the mouse button initiates another type of action, called dragging, which is discussed later. If we want you to right-click, it will be explicitly written.

Right-clicking on objects to display shortcut menu:

1. Right-click on a clear area of the desktop to open the desktop's shortcut menu

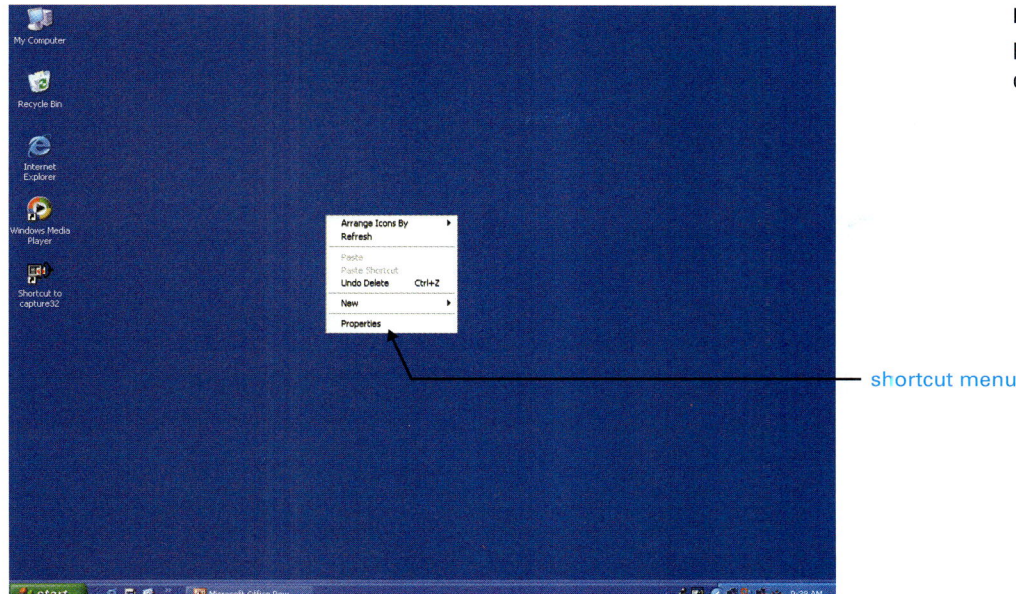

F I G U R E   1.4
Right-clicking on screen
opens a shortcut menu

shortcut menu

---

task *reference*   **Opening Shortcut Menu**

- Right-click on an object

We shorten left-clicking to just clicking because this is the most common means of selecting objects. *Clicking* is used to activate buttons and to select objects, text, or menu options. When a menu is open, clicking on an open area of the screen closes it. You will do this a lot when mousing about Windows.

Left-clicking to select and deselect options:

1. Click a clear area of the desktop to close the menu

2. Right-click the **My Computer** *icon* to open the shortcut menu

3. Click the **Properties** option

tip: *If you accidentally select the wrong menu option, clicking on the **Close** ☒ button in the top-right corner closes the window*

Dialog Boxes

When Terry uses the My Computer shortcut menu's Properties option, Windows opens the System Properties *dialog box* as shown in Figure 1.5. Think of a dialog box as an information delivery system for Windows. The bar at the top of the dialog box is the *Title bar*. It identifies the action being performed or the data being displayed. The ☒ button on the Title bar's far right is the *Close button*. Clicking on the Close or Cancel button removes the dialog box from the screen.

F I G U R E   1.5

System Properties dialog box

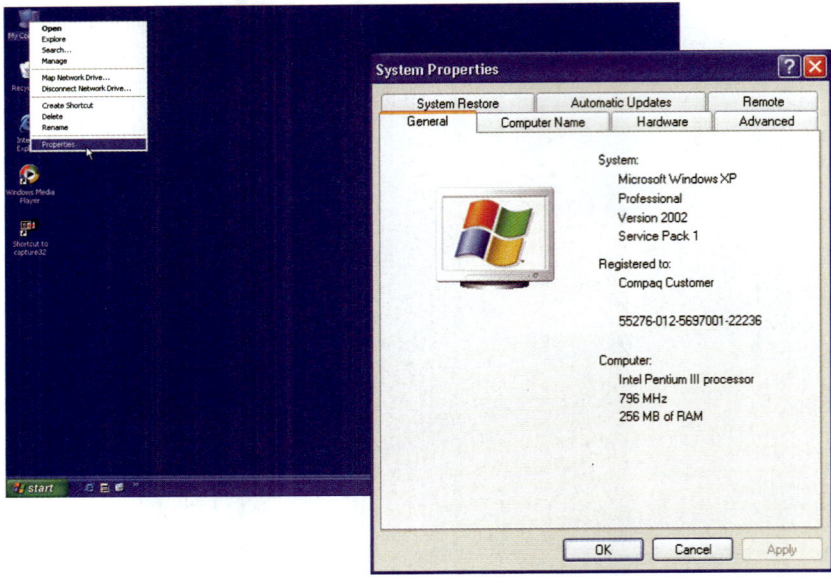

F I G U R E   1.6

Repositioning objects by dragging

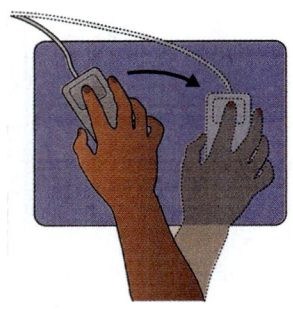

Drag object by holding down mouse button and moving pointer to a new screen location

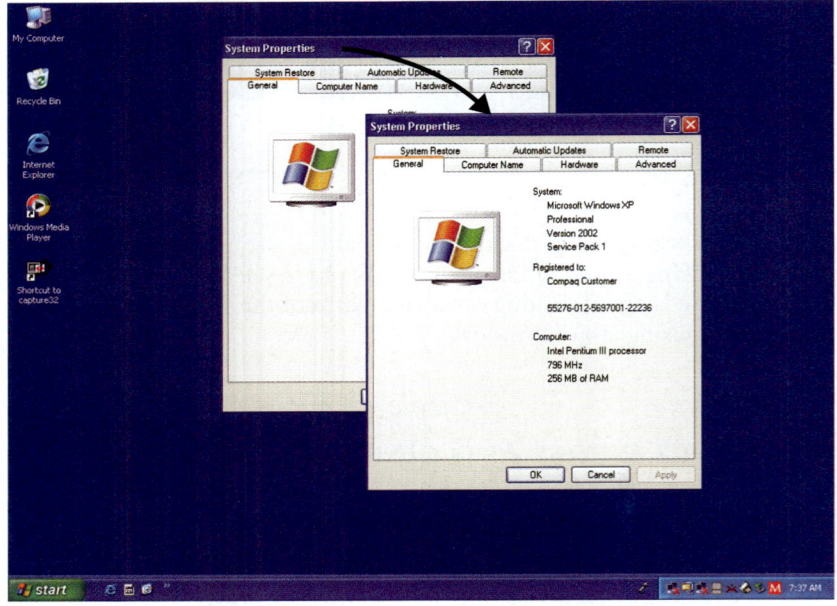

Dragging Objects around the Screen

Another important mouse skill involves moving *(dragging)* objects around the screen as shown in Figure 1.6. Dragging is accomplished by pointing at the desired object, holding down either the left (or right) mouse button and dragging the mouse pointer and object to a new area of the screen before letting go of the button. This action repositions the object on the screen. An easy way to demonstrate this skill is to have you drag the System Properties dialog box to different positions on the desktop.

Dragging using left mouse button:

1. Move the mouse pointer over the dialog box's Title bar

2. Press and hold down the left mouse button

3. With the mouse, drag the dialog box down and to the right

4. Release the left mouse button

tip: *What happens if the dialog box is dragged off the screen? The whole window cannot be completely dragged off the screen. Some part of the Title bar is always visible enough that you can drag it back onto the desktop*

5. Click the **Close** X button to close the dialog box

Windows automatically repositions the dialog box in the screen when using the left mouse button, that is, left-dragging. If an object can move, left-dragging will always reposition it. An extra step is added when using the right mouse button for dragging. As mentioned earlier, using the right button always opens a shortcut menu. When right-dragging, a shortcut menu opens as soon as you let go of the mouse button. Right-dragging is a convenient way to copy objects.

Dragging using right mouse button:

1. Move the mouse pointer over the *My Computer* icon

2. Press and hold down the right mouse button

3. Use the mouse to drag the My Computer icon to an empty area of the desktop

4. Release the left mouse button

tip: *If the icon snaps back into place, then the desktop's AutoArrange feature is active. Continue to the next step*

5. Click the **Cancel** option in the shortcut menu

tip: *If you accidentally create a shortcut (second copy) of My Computer, just drag the copy over the Recycle Bin icon*

Opening Objects

An object is activated or opened in a variety of ways. The fastest and easiest involves moving the mouse pointer over the object and ***double-clicking***—pressing the left mouse button twice in rapid succession. It takes some practice. Give it a try by opening My Computer.

---

anotherword   **. . . for double-clicking**

Two alternative ways to activate an object are

- Right-click on it and select the **Open** option from the shortcut menu
- Click on it and press the **Enter** key

<table>
<tr><td colspan="2">**task** *reference*</td><td>**Mouse Operations**</td></tr>
</table>

- Click (left-click) to select an object
- Click and hold to drag an object
- Double-click to open an object
- Right-click to open an object's shortcut menu
- Right-drag to move or copy an object

Double clicking to open My Computer:

1. Double-click **My Computer** to open the window shown in Figure 1.7

FIGURE 1.7
My Computer window

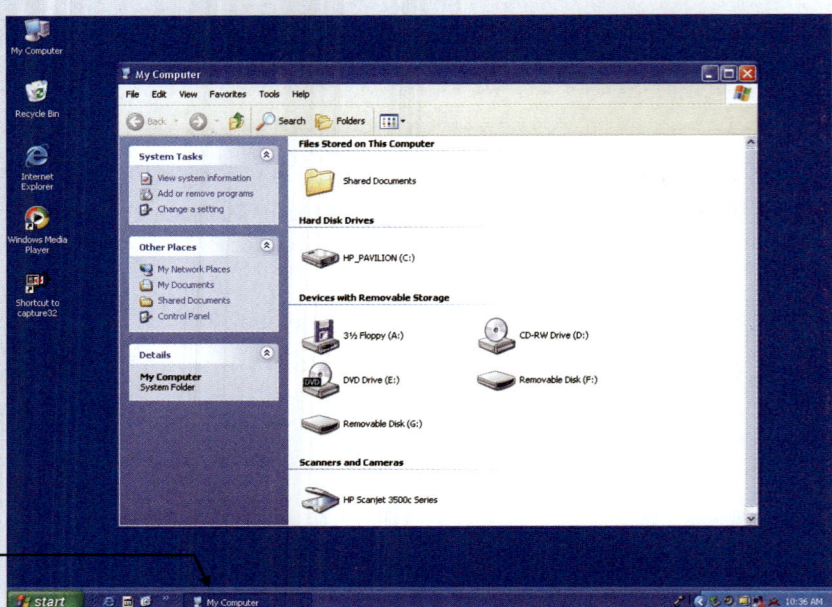

Program button

tip: *If the window fills the screen, double-click on the **Title bar** to restore it back to a window*

tip: *My Computer should appear in the Taskbar, which is usually at the bottom of the screen, as shown in Figure 1.7. If the Taskbar is not visible, move the pointer to the bottom of the screen and around the edges of the screen until the Taskbar appears. When you see it, right-click on an open gray area, select **Properties**, and click on the check in the box in front of Auto hide. This should turn off the checkmark. Click on **OK** to close the dialog box*

<table>
<tr><td colspan="2">**task** *reference*</td><td>**Running Application Software**</td></tr>
</table>

- Click on **Start**, select **All Programs**, and click on desired program from menu

  or
- Classic mode: Double-click on desktop icon

  or
- Web style: Click on desktop icon

Window versus Dialog Box

Double-clicking on My Computer opens a window similar to Figure 1.7. Every program and document is displayed in its own **window**. This is where Windows gets its name. To avoid confusion, we use an uppercase "W" to refer the Microsoft's Windows operating system program. A lowercase "w" is used when writing about a rectangle on the screen that displays information.

How is a window different from a dialog box? An independently running computer program creates a window. Information from an open window's Title bar is displayed as a button in the Taskbar as shown in Figure 1.7. A dialog box is just a request for information from the user by the operating system or some other program. Nothing appears in the Taskbar when a dialog box opens. A quick look at the Taskbar always shows you how many programs are currently running. Clicking on the Close button removes the window from the screen and the related button from the Taskbar.

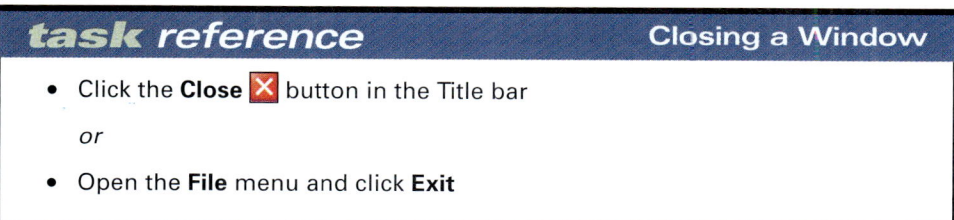

task *reference*   **Closing a Window**

- Click the **Close** ❌ button in the Title bar

   or

- Open the **File** menu and click **Exit**

Menu Bar

The My Computer window displays an icon for each disk drive attached to Terry's computer system along with the Control Panel folder. My Computer and the associated icon appear in the Title bar. Below the Title bar in Figure 1.8 is the **menu bar**, which lists names of various drop-down menus. Although a menu bar does not appear in every window, its presence permits access to menu options containing action the program performs. The My Computer window includes File, Edit, View, Favorites, Tools, and Help as menu names. Drop-down menu options stay hidden in the menu bar until the user clicks on the menu name. When you select a menu, it opens to list program options. Once you select an option, the menu closes.

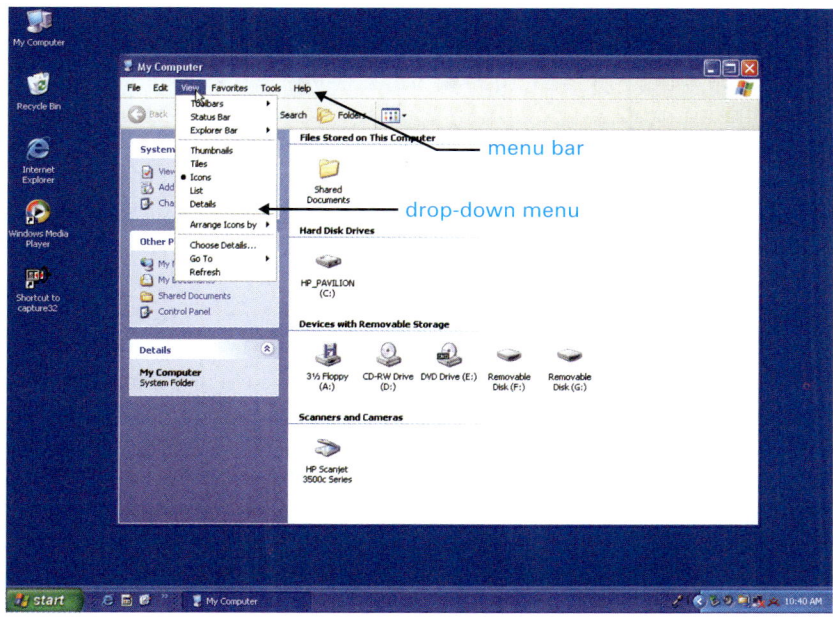

F I G U R E   1 . 8

Menu bar with drop-down menu

Opening menu options:

1. Move the mouse pointer over the File menu name

2. Click and then hold down the left mouse button. Slowly drag the pointer over each menu

3. Move the pointer over the View menu

4. Release the mouse button

5. If necessary, change the view to Icons as shown in Figure 1.8

If you decide not to choose a menu item after you have opened a menu, simply move the pointer outside the menu so that no item is selected and click the mouse button; the menu disappears.

As you open different menus, some of the options appear dimmed. These are menu options that are not available at this time. You cannot select a dimmed option. These items will become available at different times and under other processing circumstances.

Sizing a Window

Terry has complete control over the location and size of each window. Not only can he drag a window around the screen, he can grab the line around the window, called the window frame, and drag it to a new location to change the window's dimensions.

Making a window smaller:

1. Position the pointer at the bottom-right corner of the My Computer window frame and the pointer changes to a double-headed arrow (see Figure 1.9b)

2. As shown in Figure 1.9c, drag the mouse toward the upper-left corner of the screen until at least one icon is not displayed. You will know the screen is small enough when a vertical scroll bar appears

3. Release the mouse

tip: *If the window fills the screen and no window frames are visible, double-click on the* **Title bar**

Scroll Bars

When a window is reduced in size, *scroll bars* appear along the right (vertical) or bottom (horizontal) edges of the window. A *scroll box* within each scroll bar identifies which portion of the window is currently being viewed. Dragging the scroll box or clicking on the *scroll arrows* brings hidden icons into view. Clicking within the scroll bar, but not on the scroll box, moves the scroll box to that area of the scroll bar. You can tell there are hidden icons in a window because of the presence of a scroll bar. When the complete contents of a window are displayed, no scroll bars are present.

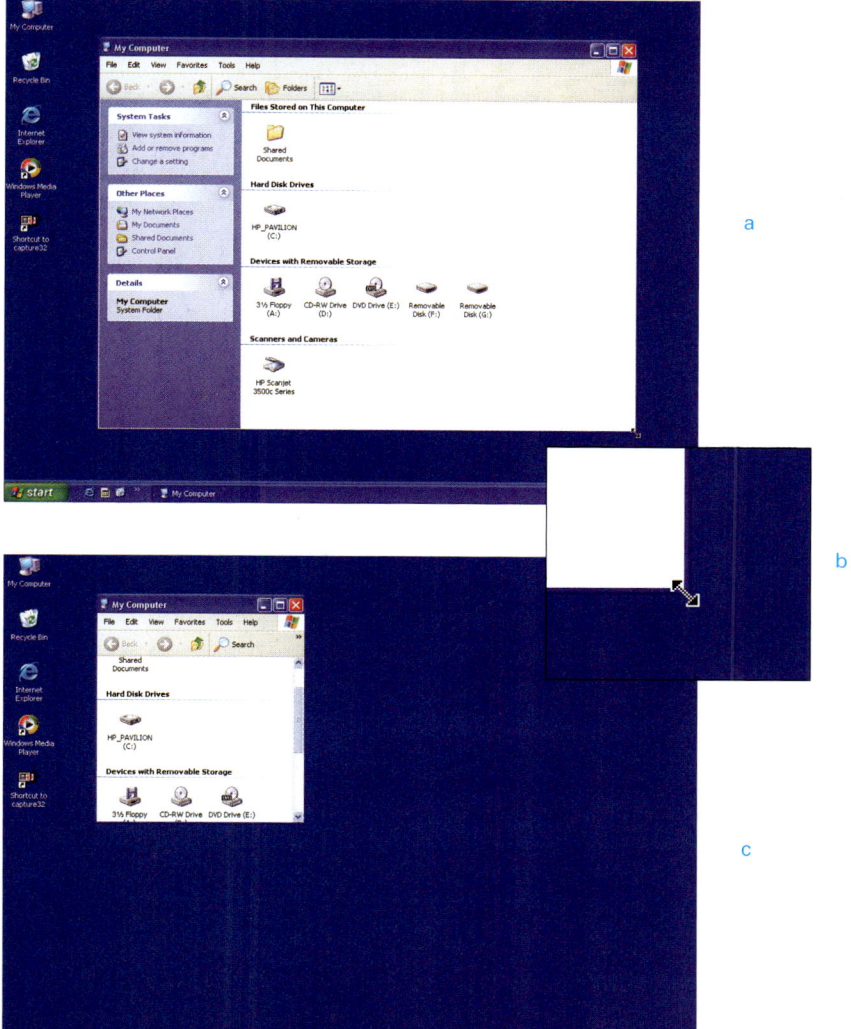

Using the scroll bar:

1. Click the **scroll arrow** that points right (or down)

2. Drag the **scroll bar** back and forth

3. Click within the **scroll bar**, but *not* directly on the scroll box

4. Drag the **window frame** until it accommodates all the icons and the scroll bar disappears

Maximizing and Restoring Window Size

When focused on a specific window, users often enlarge it to fill the screen. By doing so, as much of the window as possible is viewable and usable. Enlarging the window is easily accomplished by using the *Maximize* ▢ *button*. Of the three buttons found in the upper-right corner of the window (see Figure 1.10), it is in the middle. The button appears as a small window with a Title bar. When it is clicked, the window expands to fill

F I G U R E   1.10

Maximizing, minimizing, and restoring the screen

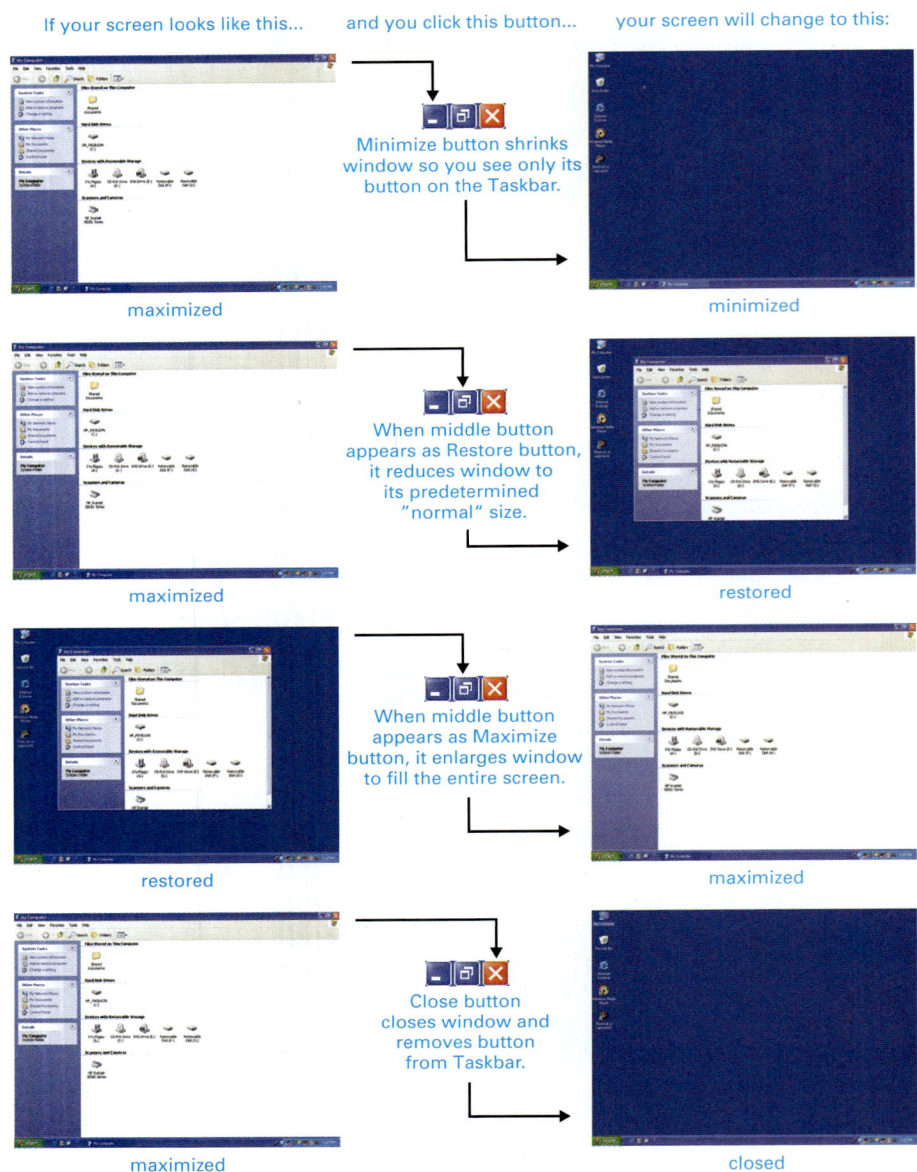

the screen, and the **Restore** button takes its place. When the Restore button is clicked, the window returns to its previous size.

Maximizing and restoring a window:

1. Click the My Computer **Maximize** button to enlarge the window

2. Click the **Restore** button

Desktop Metaphor

Like most workspaces, Terry's computer will help him accomplish several tasks at the same time. The desktop metaphor would be the stacks of paper and file folders that gather on a desk. Each pile represents a different project or task. Once a project is done,

FIGURE   1.11
Both desktops provide a workspace where work gets done

it can be gathered into a file folder and put away in a filing cabinet. The papers taking up the most space are usually the ones currently being used, as illustrated in Figure 1.11.

Minimizing Window Size

Terry's computer desktop can be handled in the same fashion. Maximized windows are the tasks on which you are currently working. When he is finished with a task, Terry closes the window. The ***Minimize*** ▬ ***button*** is used when Terry wants to push a project to the corner of the desk. It is the leftmost of the three buttons in the right corner of the Title bar. The button appears as a horizontal line. Clicking on this button removes the window from the desktop but keeps it active on the Taskbar, as shown in Figure 1.10 (on the previous page). Clicking on the Taskbar button with the window name or associated icon restores the window to the desktop.

Minimizing and restoring a window:

1. Click the My Computer **Minimize** ▬ button

2. Click **My Computer** in the Taskbar to restore the window

3. Close the window to clear the Taskbar

---

task reference   **Sizing a Window**

Maximize window size:
- Click the **Maximize** ▢ button

  or
- Double-click the **Title bar**

Restore window size:
- Click the **Restore** ▣ button

  or
- Double-click the **Title bar**

Change physical size:
- Drag the window's corner or side to a new screen location

Minimize window:
- Click the **Minimize** ▬ button in the Title bar

F I G U R E 1.12

Start button with
Programs, Accessories,
and System Tools menus
open

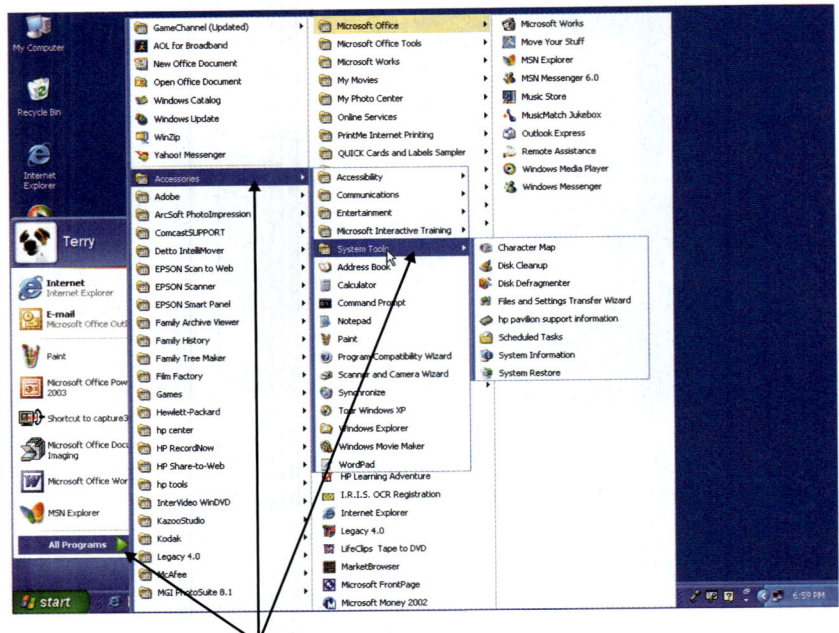

indicates a cascading menu will be open

Start Button

The **Start** *button* is an important desktop object for new Windows users. After years of research, Microsoft finally concluded that people like to have a definitive place to start when using Windows. When in doubt, click on the Start button. It will display available programs, list documents you have used, help you find files, and let you access your computer settings. All of these options are presented as a series of cascading menus as shown in Figure 1.12. A pointing triangle on the right side of the menu option means another menu will open when it is activated.

Selecting program options:

1. Click the **Start** button

2. Point to **All Programs**

   tip: *Follow the menus across the screen when moving the mouse pointer. If you try to take a shortcut across the desktop, the menus close*

3. Point to **Accessories** and the next menu opens

4. Move the pointer over System Tools

5. Click an open area of the desktop to close all open windows

These clicking and dragging techniques are used for other mouse operations besides selecting menu options and moving objects. They are basic techniques for controlling many activities you perform while using Windows and other programs. For example, dragging a program or file icon into the Recycle Bin removes the associated file from the disk.

System Turn Off

When Terry is through for the day, the computer system needs to be turned off. One good rule of thumb is to never turn off a computer while a program is running or a file is open. *Always* use the Start button's Turn Off Computer option before shutting off the computer and associated peripherals. Windows removes temporary files from the hard disk and performs other housekeeping tasks as it shuts down. If Terry just turns off the power, Windows never gets a chance to remove these unwanted files.

Turning off your computer:

1. Take out any removable disks from their disk drives

2. Click the **Start** button

3. Select **Turn Off Computer** [🔘 Turn Off Computer]

4. Click **Turn Off** as shown in Figure 1.13

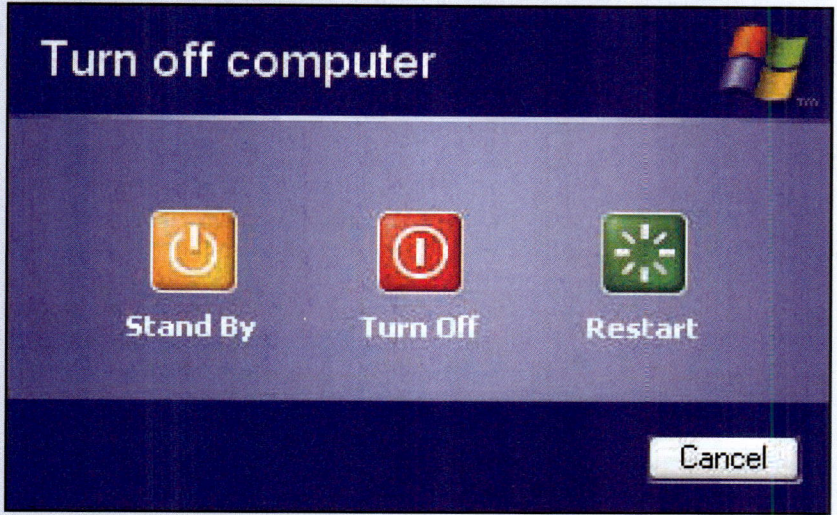

FIGURE   1.13

Turn off computer dialog box

5. Windows logs off and saves your settings before shutting down

task reference	Shutting Down the Computer System

- Click the **Start** button
- Select **Turn Off Computer**
- Click the **Turn Off** button
- You may have to turn off some peripheral devices like printers

SESSION 1.2 RUNNING APPLICATION SOFTWARE

You will need a removable disk to complete this session.

In the last session you learned the basic mouse skills needed to operate a computer running Windows. The best way to get to know the keyboard and other Windows features and skills is to open an application program that uses them. An **application** performs a specific task such as saving and printing words, playing music, drawing pictures, or performing other activities the user needs to do.

Launching a Program (WordPad)

Applications are opened by double-clicking on the associated desktop icon or by using the Start button. Terry's friends had recommended he try using the WordPad application that comes with Windows. WordPad (shown in Figure 1.14) is a word-editing program he can use to save, make changes to, format, and print words and numbers.

To enter text, Terry uses the computer keyboard very much like a typewriter. As he presses a key, the related character appears on the screen in front of a blinking vertical line called the **insertion point**. As he types on the keyboard, words appear and the insertion point moves to the right one position. When Terry makes a mistake while typing, he deletes unwanted characters by pressing the Backspace key, which is the left-arrow key above the Enter key. He then retypes the text.

Another way to delete unwanted characters involves using the Delete or Del key in the following way: Move the insertion point to the immediate left of the character you wish to delete, then press the Delete key to erase unwanted characters to the right of the insertion point. You can then type the correct text.

---

anotherword   . . . on opening a file

A variety of words identify the process by which a computer executes, one by one, a set of instructions called a computer program:

- Activating
- Running
- Launching
- Opening
- Starting
- Initializing
- Bringing it up
- Interfacing with

F I G U R E   1.14

WordPad with example text

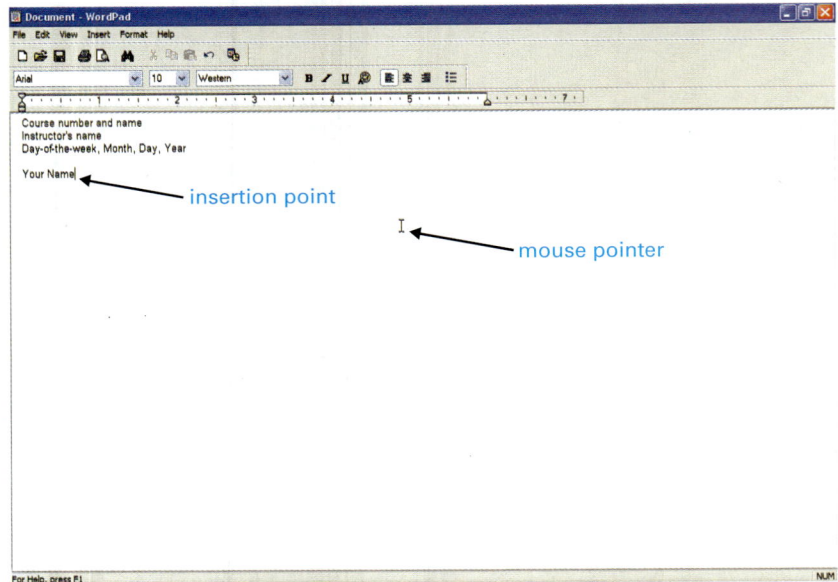

Opening WordPad:

1. If necessary, start your computer
2. Click the **Start** button
3. Point to **All Programs**
4. Point to **Accessories**
5. Click **WordPad**
6. Maximize the window, if necessary

Pressing the Enter key breaks the line and moves the insertion point to the leftmost position, one line down. Pressing the Enter key when the insertion point is on an empty line creates a blank line.

Using WordPad to enter text:

1. Type the <course number> and <name for this class> and press **Enter**
2. Type <your instructor's name> and press **Enter**
3. Click **Insert** on the menu bar
4. Click **Date and Time**
5. Select the option with the day of the week and the date, month first, and click the **OK** button
6. Press the **Enter** key to start a new line
7. Press the **Enter** key to add a blank line
8. Type <your name>

When entering data, you don't want to get very far before saving your data on a disk. We recommend using the "sweaty palm test" when deciding how often to save a file. Ask yourself, "How would I feel if I had to redo everything I've done in the last _____ minutes/hours?" If your palms get sweaty thinking about it, it is time to save your file again!

Saving a File

Most application programs use the File menu's Save option to save the active window's contents. The File menu's Save As option opens a dialog box for identifying where to save the file and the file's name. The *filename* is a unique set of characters given to a file when it is saved. The WordPad information you just typed will be saved in a file named example.rtf. The .rtf extension is automatically given to the filename by the WordPad program, but it is usually not displayed. rtf stands for rich text format.

Common Program Controls

In the process of saving the WordPad document to a disk, Terry uses several new program controls. A *control* is a program feature that allows him to select actions or enter

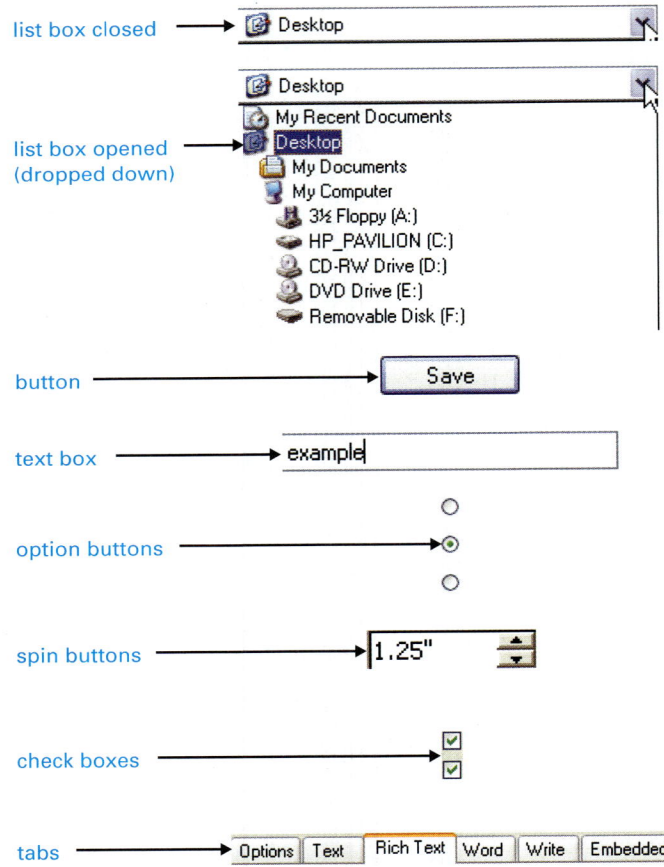

data. A menu is a control feature. So are the OK and Cancel buttons. Common controls are listed in Figure 1.15. Saving a new file involves using a drop-down list box control, **list box** for short, to select a disk drive and a **text box** control to enter the filename. Drop-down list boxes are like drop-down menus in that the options are not displayed until Terry clicks on the down arrow to the right of the list area. When he does, a list of options opens. An item is selected by clicking on it.

Data are entered into a text box using the keyboard. To do so Terry clicks within the text box with the mouse and then starts typing. The insertion point identifies where new text is added as he types. The mouse pointer changes to an I-beam (see Figure 1.3 on page WIN 1.5) when it is inside a text box.

Student Data Disk

From this point forward some type of removable disk must be available to store files needed for working through the tutorials in this book. Combined together these data files require less than 1.4-MB of disk space; therefore, an empty 3.5-inch floppy disk can be used. Whatever removable disk you use, it will be referred to as the *student data disk*. The examples in this session assume you will be putting your student data disk in drive A, usually a floppy disk drive.

Saving a new file to a floppy disk:

1. Insert your disk into its drive
2. Click **File** on the menu bar
3. Click **Save** and the Save As dialog box opens

4. Click the down arrow to the right of the *Save in* list box to view storage options

5. If necessary, select the drive in which you placed your disk

6. Erase *Document* from the File name text box by clicking it and pressing either the **Delete** or **Backspace** key to remove the default filename

7. Type **Example** in the File name text box as shown in Figure 1.16

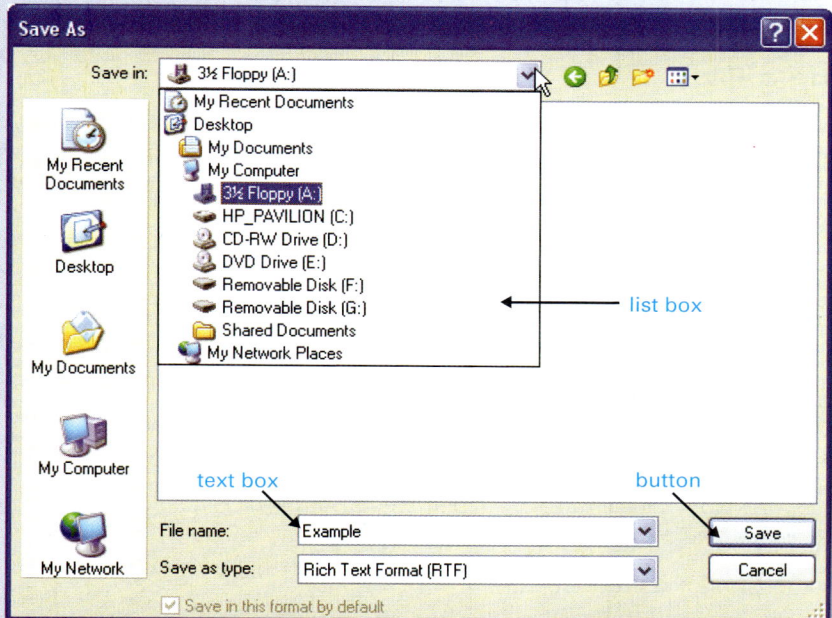

8. If necessary, select **Rich Text Format** in the *Save as type* list box

9. Click the **Save** button

Once a file is saved, the filename appears in the WordPad Title bar. In this case, example is now found in the Title bar on your screen as shown at the top of Figure 1.18 (on page WIN 1.26). A point made earlier now needs further clarification. Although you clicked on the Save option in the File menu, WordPad displayed the Save As dialog box. This happens only the first time a new file is saved. Routinely, Save is used for updating files already on disk, whereas Save As gives the information in memory a new disk location or filename. Windows allows filenames up to 215 characters long, including spaces. If there is room, WordPad adds the three-character filename extension, .rtf in this example, to the end of the filename.

---

task reference   Saving a File with a New Name

- Click the **File** menu and click **Save As**
- Make sure the *Save in* list box contains the name of the folder in which you want to save your file. If not, then use your mouse to navigate to the correct disk and folder
- Change the filename in the *File name* list box
- Click the **Save** button

> ### *another***word**   . . . **on filenames**
>
> Files that need to be compatible with MS-DOS/Windows 3.1 and early versions of Novell networks should be limited to eight characters (no spaces) and three characters in the filename extension.

Your WordPad document is complete. If a printed copy of this valuable information is desirable, you need to know how to use the printer attached to your computer.

Printing a File

To make sure everything looks right before sending a document to the printer, Terry uses WordPad's Print Preview feature. This allows him to check the margins and other document features before using a sheet of paper. Mistakes caught now save him from wasting paper later.

Print preview:

1. Open the **File** menu

2. Click **Print Preview**

tip: *If you want to enlarge an area of the preview, move the magnifying glass pointer over it and click or click on the **Zoom In** button*

3. Click the **Close Preview** button

tip: *If the document looks like it is ready to go, you can print it while previewing by clicking on the Print button*

Windows can connect you to a variety of printers. A personal computer connected to a network can even output to printers in other rooms, buildings, or cities. This can be a problem if you print a document on the wrong printer a long walk away. Using the File menu's Print option opens a dialog box (see Figure 1.17) that lets you print selected pages, print more than one copy, and even change the printer being used.

> ### *task* reference   Print Preview
>
> - Click the **Print Preview** 🔍 button on the Standard toolbar
>
>   *or*
>
> - Open the **File** menu and select **Print Preview**

F I G U R E   1.17
Print dialog box

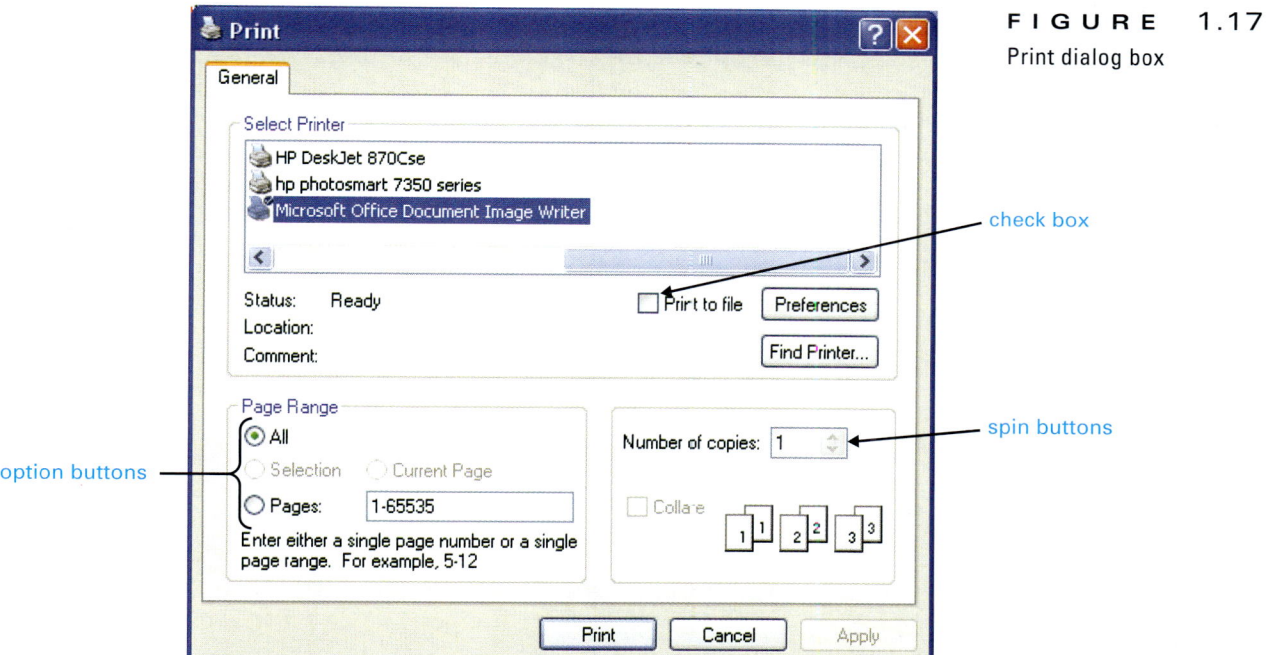

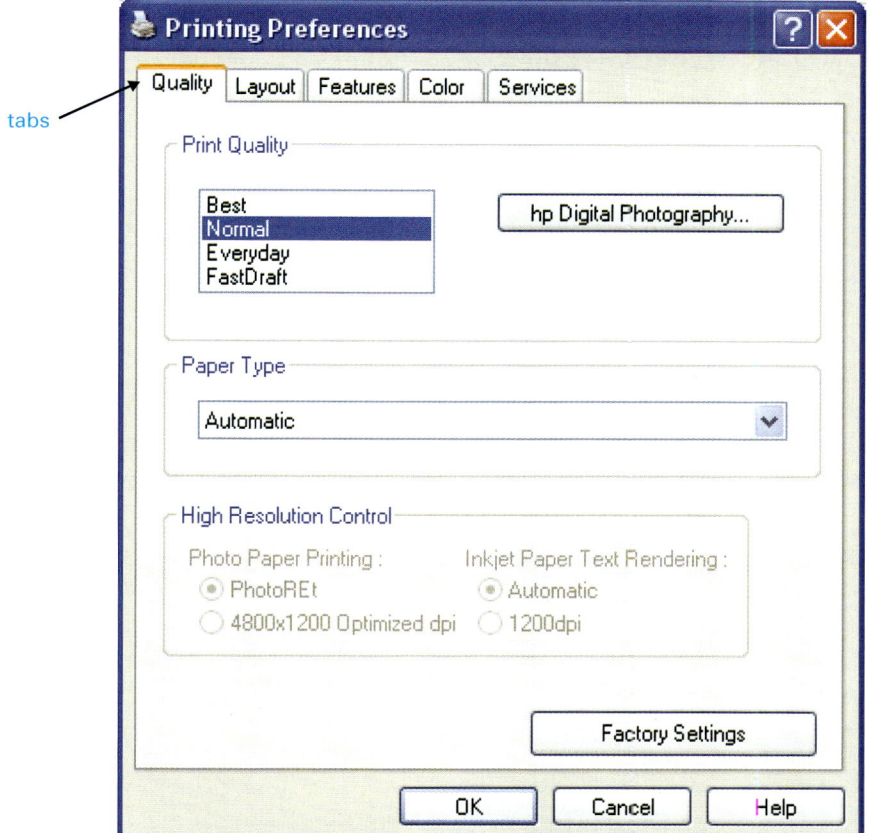

More Program Controls

The Print dialog box also induces new program controls: spin buttons, option buttons, check boxes, and tabs. Examples of popular controls are illustrated in Figure 1.15 (on page WIN 1.20). *Spin buttons* let you increment or decrement a counter by clicking on either up or down arrows. A selected *option button* has a black circle in the middle. Some people call them radio buttons because only one in the group can be selected at a time. This is not the case with *check boxes*. The user can click on as many check boxes as he or she wants. If necessary, every one in a group can be on, which is shown as a √ in the box.

When a dialog box contains many controls, they are often organized under Preferences. Clicking the Preferences button displays a different dialog box with tabs. You will use the Print dialog box to examine these new controls.

Printing data:

1. Verify your computer is connected to a printer and that it is turned on

tip: *Save the file before printing. Should anything go wrong, you can start over by retrieving the file from the disk*

2. Open the **File** menu
3. Click **Print**
4. Click the *Number of copies* spin button up to **3**
5. Click the *Number of copies* spin button down to **1**
6. Clear, if necessary, the **Print to file** check box
7. Click the **Pages** option button
8. Click the **All** option button
9. Click the tab to the right of *General*, but do not change any settings
10. Click the **General** tab to return to the main Print dialog box
11. Click the **Print** button

tip: *Click the **Cancel** button if you don't want to print the example*

tip: *If the printer is unavailable or not working properly, it is possible that a printer error has occurred. To start the troubleshooting, check that the power is on, that paper is available, and that the power cord is firmly plugged into the printer and the power outlet. If Windows displays an error message, write down the contents of the message before talking to a technician*

---

task reference   Printing

- Click the **Print** 🖨 **Print...** button to print one copy of the whole file

  or

- Open the **File** menu and select **Print**

---

*another***word**   . . . on the choices of file formats

WordPad can have the same file format as Microsoft's full-powered word processing program Word. When opening a new WordPad document, you have a choice of which file format to use. In the following steps you will use the rich text format.

This example is complete. At this point you can close WordPad, open another document, or start a new document by using the File menu's New option. Unlike other word processing programs, WordPad can handle only one open document at a time. When you open another document, WordPad will ask if you want to save the currently open document if it has been altered since it was last saved. You have a chance to save it again or just close it. Either way, WordPad closes the document before it can open another.

Opening a new WordPad document:

1. Click **File** on the menu bar
2. Click **New**
3. Click the **OK** button

Opening a File

Since the computer's memory is wiped clean when the power is turned off, files are saved on disk for permanent storage. When saved on a removable disk, inserting the disk into another computer's disk drive allows you to transfer the file to the other system. This is jokingly referred to as a "sneaker net" because the data travels by foot instead of wires. Once a file is saved, it can be opened at any time and on any computer that has software similar to the program that created it.

Opening a file:

1. Click **File** on the menu bar

tip: *The File menu lists recently used files at the bottom, just above the Send option. Clicking the filename opens the file*

2. Click **Open**
3. Use the Look in list box to identify the disk drive with the student data disk
4. Click **Example** in the text area below the Look in list box

tip: *Double-clicking on the filename in the text area automatically opens the file*

5. Click the **Open** button

F I G U R E   1.18

Open dialog box and
WordPad with example
text

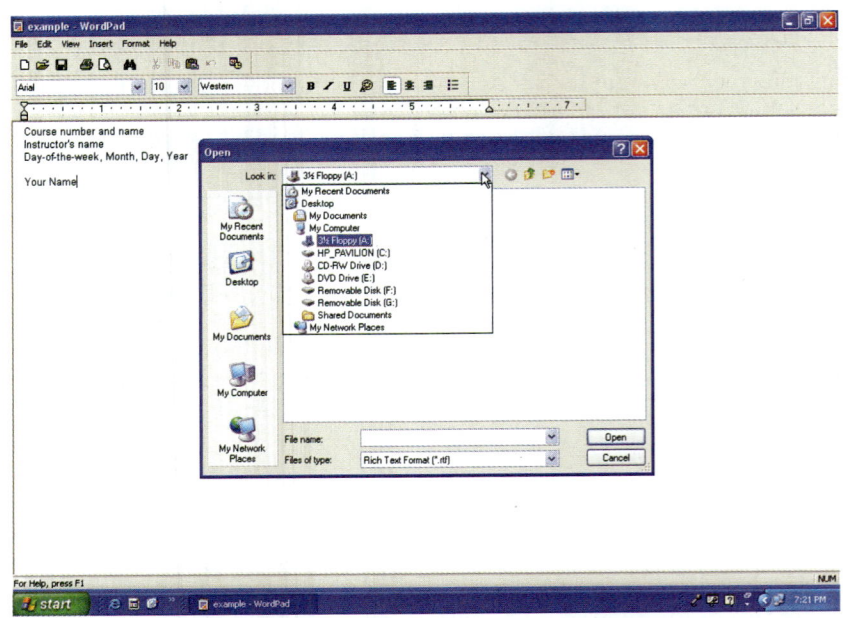

---

task reference   Opening a File

- Click **File** on the menu bar and select **Open**

- Make sure the *Look in* list box contains the name of the folder from which
  you want to open your file. If not, then use your mouse to navigate to the
  correct disk and folder

- Select the desired filename from the display area

- Click the **Open** button

SESSION 1.3 USING HELP

It is easy to be overwhelmed with the options available to you on the desktop or
through the Start button. As a result, Windows provides a set of easy-to-use ***Help and
Support*** windows that answer common user questions or problems. While using these
windows is not the same as asking a friend or your instructor for help, they do provide
a means of getting answers.

Windows Help windows try to be ***context-sensitive***. This means that what you are
doing and the window you currently have open dictate the initial help you get.

Help and Support is available when using Windows XP or when using any application program running under XP.

Help and Support combines the Help features that were available on the previous
versions of Windows (Search, Index, and Favorites) with the online Help features that
can be found on the Microsoft Web site.

Before you can access the Help and Support Center services you must launch Help
and Support. One method of doing this uses the Start menu.

Getting help:

1. Close any open windows

2. Click the **Start** button

3. Select **Help and Support** to open the Help window shown in Figure 1.19

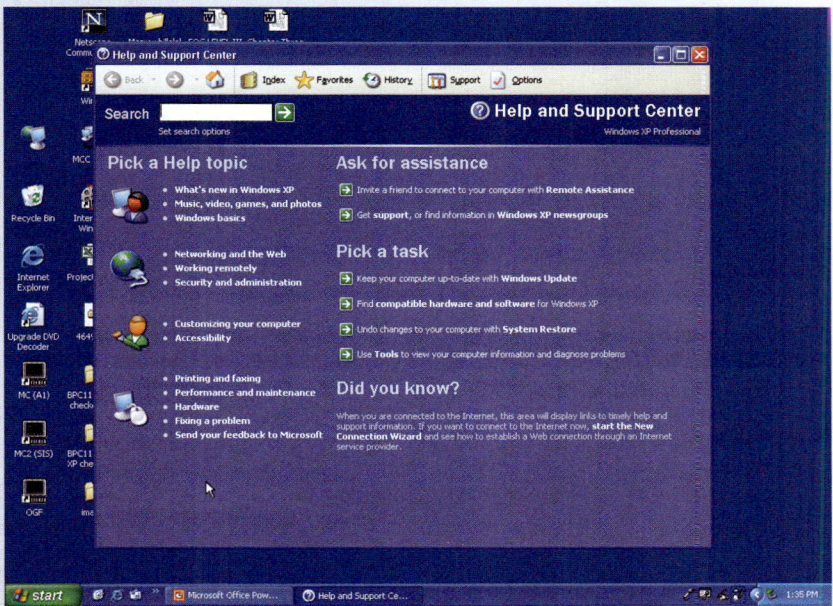

FIGURE　1.19

Windows Help and
Support screen

4. If necessary, maximize the Help window

---

task reference	Initiating Help

- Press **F1** for context-sensitive help

  or

- Click **Start** and click **Help and Support**

  or

- Open **Help and Support** in the menu bar for context-sensitive help

---

The Help and Support navigation toolbar displays below the Title bar and provides you with easy navigation through the Help topics and pages. Eventually Terry will customize Favorites by having it list Help topics he has found to be useful. The area below the toolbar contains the Search text box and Start searching button used to search for help. The table of contents contains four areas: *Pick a help topic* area, *Ask for assistance* area, *Pick a task area,* and *Did you know* area? Helpful information is displayed in the Topic pane as shown in Figure 1.20.

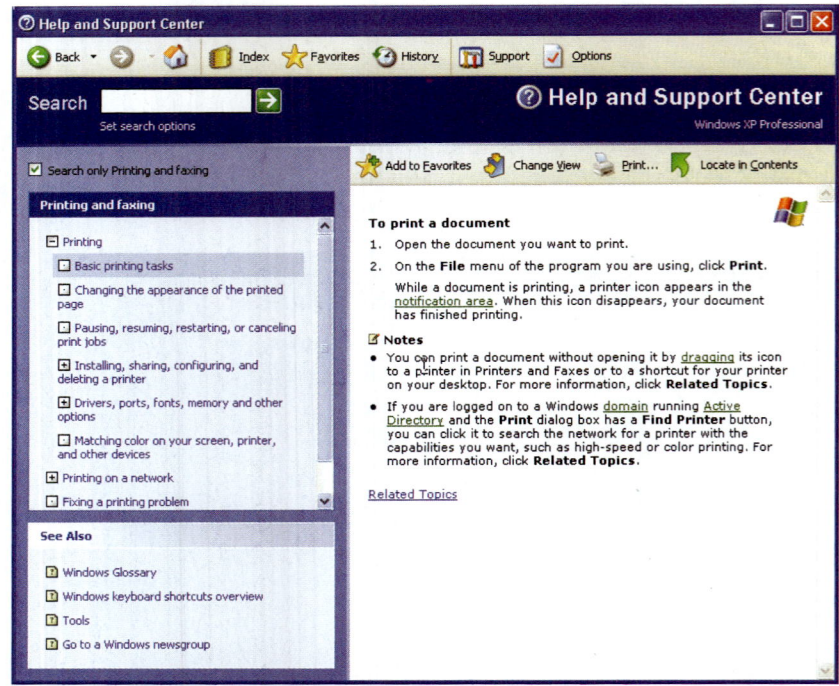

You will find that Help windows are changed to a variety of sizes and shapes so they fit on the screen alongside or overlapping the window with the problem. Not only can you maximize, minimize, and resize the window; you can even hide the Navigation pane. This is particularly useful when the Help window needs to be shrunk down to a very small size.

Hide and unhide the Help and Support window:

1. Click the **Change View** button to remove the full Help and Support window. Only the Help content will display

2. Click the **Change View** button to display the full Help and Support window

Exploring a Help Topic

Topics are either overviews or individual.

Exploring the Contents pane:

1. Select **Printing and faxing**

2. Click the plus to the left of Printing to display individual topics

3. Click **Basic printing tasks** and **Print a document** to display Help information similar to Figure 1.20

4. Select **Related Topics** found in the **Content** pane

5. Click an open area of the Topic pane to close Related Topics

tip: *You may have to scroll down*

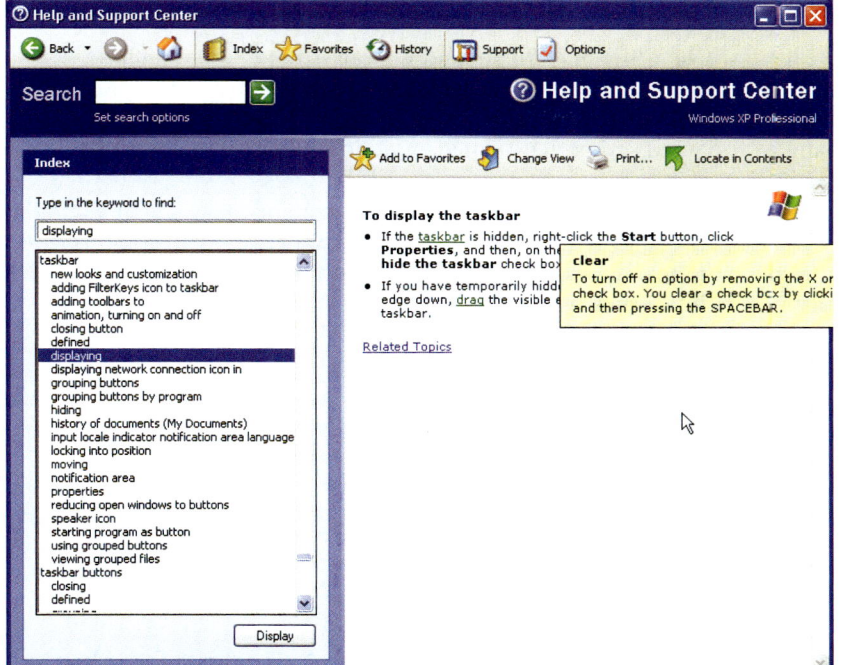

F I G U R E   1.21

Index Help window for
taskbar overview

A variety of situations can bring you to the point where you need to use Windows help. New computer users utilize **Help and Support** to learn about new features and skills. Experienced users might employ it to troubleshoot a problem. Everyone can use it to explore unfamiliar Windows features.

The Index

Users experienced with Windows terminology can utilize the Index to look up Help windows related to specific features. This is done by using keywords such as "taskbar" or "WordPad." The keyword typed into the related text box (see Figure 1.21) is used to display matching topics in the screen area below. Each of these topics has a related Help window. To display the Help window, the user selects the item and clicks on the Display button.

Throughout the help information, you will see underlined words. These words are part of the online glossary of terms. Clicking on these items opens a box with a definition or description. The definition box in Figure 1.21 was opened by clicking on the underlined word "minimize."

Finding help using the index:

1. Click the **Index** button on the Navigation toolbar

2. Type **taskbar** in the *Type in the keyword to find* text box. The display area under the text box displays a variety of Taskbar-related topics as shown in Figure 1.21

3. Select the **displaying** option

4. Click the **Display** button

5. Click the **Taskbar** in the Topic pane

6. Click **Clear** to open the definition box

7. Click an open area of the Content pane to close the definition

Searches

The Search feature works differently from Index. Search looks for matching words within the content of each Help window. If the word or words are found, the related topics are displayed. Be careful; long strings of text create lots of matches because a match with any of the words adds that related topic to the list. If you want an exact match to a long string of words, enclose them in double quotes.

However, using too few words also can create many matches as well. For example, entering **turn off** yields so many matches that a scroll bar appears. If you add one more word, "computer," so the search string is **turn off computer**, the search yields a more manageable list of possible topics, as shown in Figure 1.22.

Searching Help windows for a key term:

1. Click the **Search** ➡ button

2. Type **turn off** in the search text box. So many matches occur that a scroll bar appears in the topics list

3. Type **computer** at the end of the search text box. It should now read: turn off computer

4. Click the **Search** button

5. Select the **Turn off the computer** link. The Content pane should look like Figure 1.22

If you find yourself returning to a Help window more than once, consider printing the information or adding the topics to the Favorites list. A close examination of many desks often will find a printed copy of one Help window or another taped to the side of the screen or a filing cabinet.

FIGURE 1.22

Searches display Help topics that contain matching words

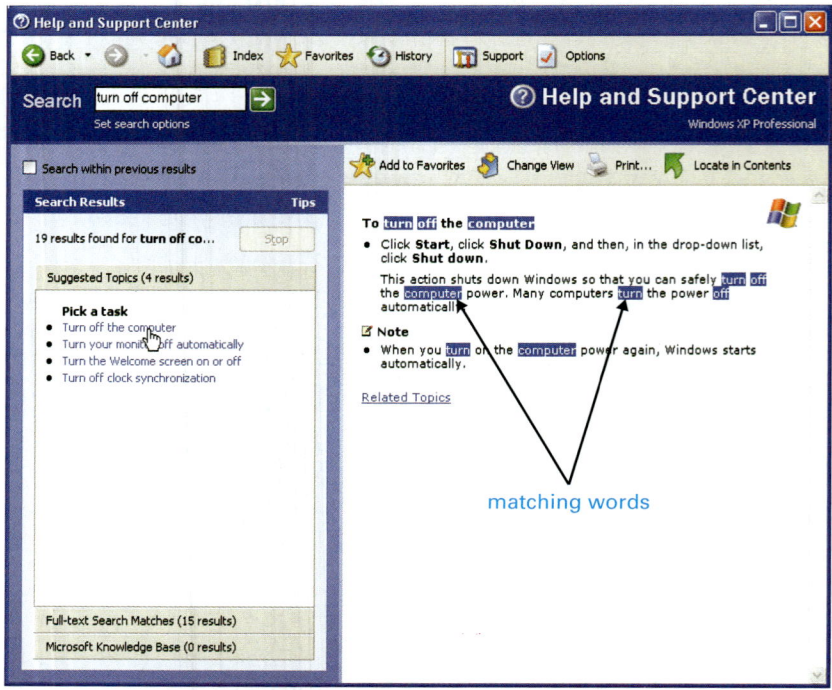

Printing Help information:

1. Make sure the printer is on

2. Select the **Print** ⬚ Print... button to open the Print dialog box

3. Click the **Print** button

Troubleshooting Help

At some point in time, you will need to troubleshoot a problem with your computer on your own. A variety of hardware- and software-related troubleshooting checklists are available. Each screen asks you to identify what the computer is or is not doing. Different answers produce different screens, which help you decide on a course of action. Let's take a quick look at the Printer Troubleshooting windows.

Troubleshooting tutorial:

1. Click the **Home** ⬚ button on the Navigation toolbar

2. Click on the **Fixing a problem** link

3. Click the **Printing problems** link

4. Click on the **Printing Troubleshooter** link in the Contents pane to display the beginning of the Print Troubleshooter shown in Figure 1.23

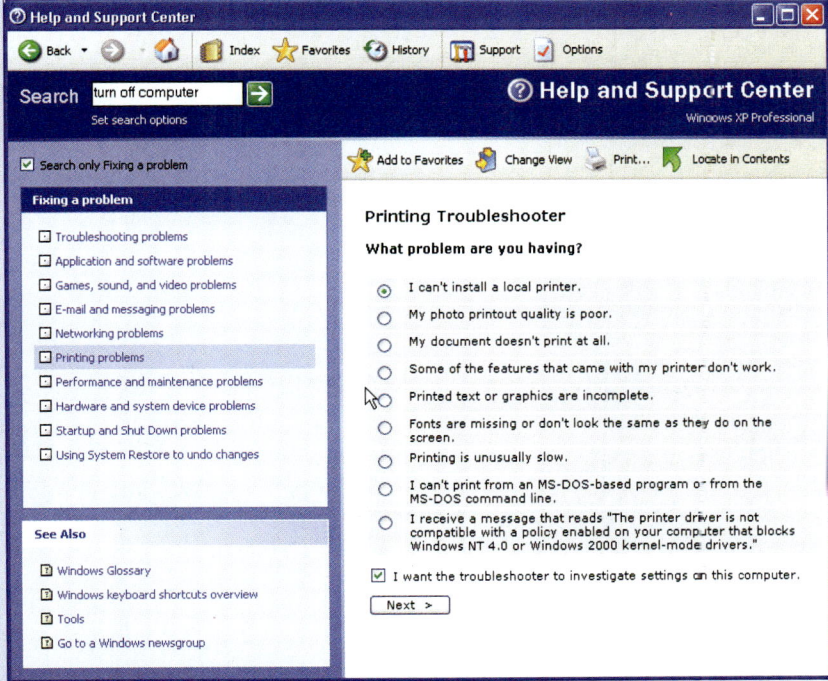

FIGURE 1.23

Help Print Troubleshooter

tip: *You can shut off the tutorial at any time by clicking on the Close* ❌ *button*

WINDOWS

This type of troubleshooting help appeals to Terry's way of doing things. It was useful to him late one lonely weekend night after everyone else had gone to bed. As a matter of fact, it was so useful that he wants to add it to his list of favorite Help topics. The screen Terry really needed to add to Favorites was the list of Windows Troubleshooters one screen back.

The easy way to display this Help window is to use the Back navigation button. Two navigation buttons are located to the right of the Home button. These buttons allow you to backtrack to previously displayed topics with a Back button, while the Forward button displays the Help screen you just came from.

Using the navigation buttons:

1. Click the **Back** [Back] button once to backtrack to the Printing Problems screen

Favorites

Once Terry identifies a Help topic he feels he could use again, it is a simple process to add it to the Favorites list. The easiest way to accomplish this is to display the window and then click the Add to Favorites button. With the desired Help topic displayed in the Content box, he clicks on the Add to Favorites button to include it, as shown in Figure 1.24 (on the next page).

Adding a Help topic to your Favorites list:

1. Click on the **Fixing a printing problem** link in the Content pane
2. Click on the **Add to Favorites** [Add to Favorites] button
3. Click the **OK** button when the Help and Support Center Confirmation box displays
4. Close the dialog box and the Help window

SESSION 1.4 SUMMARY

The Windows desktop is opened when this computer program starts. On it you will see icons and a Taskbar that contains the Start button, Quick Launch area, and Notification area. A pointing device such as a mouse controls the movement of the mouse pointer. Right-clicking when the mouse pointer is over an object opens a shortcut menu, which can be used to view the object's properties and default values. Holding the mouse pointer over an object prompts the display of a ToolTip describing the object.

Application programs are opened using the Start button or double-clicking on an icon. Each application runs in its own window. This window has a Title bar along the top and usually displays the menu bar right underneath. It is enlarged by clicking on the Maximize button and returned to its original size by clicking on the Restore button. The Minimize button is used to remove the window from the desktop while keeping its program button on the Taskbar. Clicking on the Close button removes the window from the desktop and Taskbar.

Adding Fixing a printing problem to Favorites

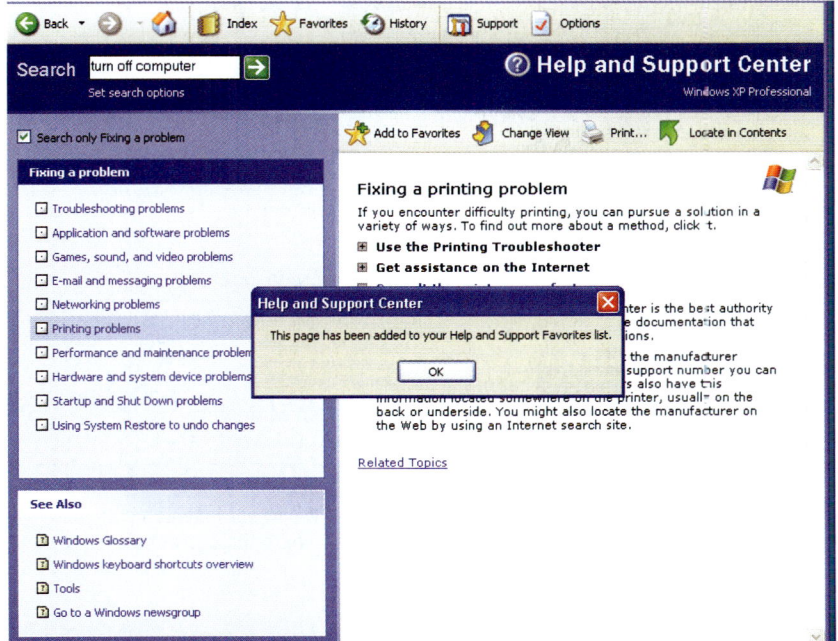

People use a variety of controls to interact with Windows and applications. Controls such as option buttons only allow one selection at a time while any number of check boxes can be active at the same time. Dialog boxes gather data through text boxes that contain insertion points indicating where typed data will appear. Spin buttons allow users to increment or decrement counters while list box options drop down for users to choose. All of these controls are used when opening, saving, and printing files.

Help windows use a Navigation toolbar that lists help topics appearing in the Content pane to provide users with context-sensitive information. Predefined contents, indexes, and search routines are used to identify useful Help topics.

task reference *summary*

Task	Page #	Preferred Method
Opening shortcut menu	WIN 1.7	• Right-click an object
Running application software	WIN 1.10	• Click **Start**, select **All Programs**, and click on desired program from menu *or* • Classic mode: Double-click a desktop icon *or* • Web style: Click a desktop icon
Maximize window size	WIN 1.15	• Click the **Maximize** ⬜ button *or* • Double-click on the Title bar

task reference *summary*

Task	Page #	Preferred Method
Restore window size	WIN 1.15	• Click the **Restore** 🗗 button *or* • Double-click on the **Title bar**
Minimize a window	WIN 1.15	• Click the **Minimize** ▬ button
Sizing a window	WIN 1.15	• Drag the window's corner or frame (side) to a new screen location
Shutting Down the computer system	WIN 1.17	• Click the **Start** button • Click **Turn Off Computer** • Click the **Turn Off** [Turn Off Computer] button • You may have to turn off some peripheral devices such as printers
Saving a file with a new name	WIN 1.21	• Click the **File** menu and click **Save As** • Make sure the *Save in* list box contains the name of the folder in which you want to save your file. If not, then use your mouse to navigate to the correct disk and folder • Change the filename in the *File name* list box • Click the **Save** button
Print preview	WIN 1.22	• Click the **Print Preview** 🔍 button on the Standard toolbar *or* • Open the **File** menu and select **Print Preview**
Printing	WIN 1.24	• Click the **Print** [Print...] button to print one copy of the whole file *or* • Open the **File** menu and select **Print**
Opening a file	WIN 1.26	• Click **File** on the menu bar and select **Open** • Make sure the *Look in* list box contains the name of the folder from which you want to open your file. If not, then use your mouse to navigate to the correct disk and folder • Select the desired filename from the display area • Click the **Open** button
Initiating help	WIN 1.27	• Press **F1** for context-sensitive help *or* • Click **Start** and click **Help and Support** *or* • Open **Help and Support** in the menu bar for context-sensitive help

TRUE OR FALSE

1. _____ The term "drag" means you point to an item, hold down the right mouse button, and copy an item to a desired location.

2. _____ A(n) scroll bar displays when the contents of a pen or window are not completely visible.

3. _____ The Windows XP Welcome screen is the first screen that displays when you turn on the computer.

4. _____ The Minimize button enlarges a window.

5. _____ Only one check box can be checked at a time.

FILL-IN

1. The _____ _____ is the window that you currently are using.

2. A(n) _____ on a menu performs a specific action, such as searching for fields or running an application program.

3. A _____ displays when the mouse pointer is moved to the bottom right corner of an icon displaying on the desktop.

4. _____ the mouse opens up desktop objects.

5. _____ is available if you need assistance in printing a file.

6. A(n) _____ is a user interface that displays graphics in addition to text to the user.

MULTIPLE CHOICE

1. A(n) _____ is a rectangular area in which you can enter text.

   a. text box
   b. dialog box
   c. Taskbar
   d. option button

2. The _____ allows you to launch programs quickly.

   a. Start button
   b. Run Programs button
   c. Command button
   d. Properties button

3. The _____ displays the current time and can contain icons that provide quick access to programs.

   a. Date/Time area
   b. Notification area
   c. Taskbar button area
   d. ToolTip

4. Every item on the Windows XP desktop is considered to be a(n) _____

   a. task.
   b. picture.
   c. object.
   d. command.

5. In WordPad the blinking vertical bar is known as the _____

   a. editing I-beam.
   b. cursor.
   c. pointer.
   d. insertion point.

review of concepts

REVIEW QUESTIONS

1. What type of computer program is Windows?

2. Explain how to display a shortcut menu.

3. Why do some windows not have scroll bars?

4. Why are some menu options dimmed?

5. Why are files saved to a storage device?

CREATE THE QUESTION

For each of the following answers, create an appropriate, short question.

ANSWER	QUESTION
1. Taskbar	_____
2. Left mouse button	_____
3. Menu	_____
4. Start menu	_____
5. Active window	_____
6. Commands	_____

1. Exploring the Hard Disk Drive

To learn more about your computer system, go exploring. Every personal computer has a primary hard drive the computer uses when it starts up. This hard drive, usually drive C, contains a variety of files and programs.

1. Start your computer and enter your username and password if prompted

2. Use the shortcut menu to open My Computer

3. Open the hard drive, usually the C drive

4. Maximize the My Computer window and use the scroll bar if necessary to answer the following questions:

   - How many objects are in the My Computer window?

   - Are there any hidden files? If yes, how many?

   - How many file folders display in the window?

   - What is the drive's name?

2. Writing Notes using WordPad

WordPad provides a quick and convenient way to jot yourself a note or to print a reminder for someone else. It's one of the first computer applications that you can get really comfortable with in a short amount of time. Let's write a quick note, save it, print preview it, and finally print it.

1. Start your computer and Windows if necessary

2. Use the **Start** button and **All Programs** to open **WordPad** on the **Accessories** menu

3. Maximize the WordPad window

4. Enter your name, class, and the current date, each on a separate line

5. Enter the hard drive information you found in Practice 1 into your document

6. Save the note as **<yourname>Win01Info** on your storage device

7. Print preview the note

8. Print the note

9. Close WordPad

challenge!

1. Finding and Using the Calculator

You need to perform some quick math calculations, and you need a calculator to be confident of the answers. Use the desktop resources at your disposal to find and open Windows Calculator. If a complex-looking scientific calculator opens up, click on the **View** menu and select the **Standard** option. Perform the following computations using the calculator:

- Enter the year you were born
- Multiply by 4
- Subtract 50
- Divide by 2
- Add the day you were born
- Write the answer on a piece of paper with your name
- Close the Calculator window

2. Getting Help

You never know when you are going to need help. Questions or trouble happen, so it is good to know how to deal with them. Personal preference and experience play a large role in how you use Help and Support. Create a WordPad file named **<yourname>Win01Answers** to record answers to each of these questions:

- What is the Windows definition of Plug and Play?
- Is your computer set to automatically adjust the clock for daylight savings time changes?
- What is USB?
- What games are installed on the computer you are using?

did you know?

rainbows *are caused by drops of water falling through the air. When sunlight enters a drop of water, it is refracted, or bent, and reflected from the drop so that the light appears as a spectrum of colors. The colors are visible only when the angle of reflection between the sun, the drop of water, and the observer's line of vision is between 40 and 42 degrees.*

Thomas *Cook, the world's first travel agency, was founded in 1850.*

George *Washington and Thomas Jefferson both grew hemp, Ben Franklin owned a mill that made hemp paper, and the U.S. Declaration of Independence was written on hemp paper.*

the *scientific term for the common tomato is lycopersicon lycopersicum, which means "wolf peach."*

the *CD was developed by Philips and Sony in 1980.*

Chapter Objectives

- **Learn about the need for Web browsers**
- **Understand the basic physical components of the Web**
- **Understand the uses of hypertext and hyperlinks**
- **Differentiate between a Web site and a Web page**
- **Understand the uses of a Universal Resource Locator**
- **Learn about the important elements associated with a Web browser**

Exploring the Internet

John Jacobs is a senior in college and approaching graduation. Pursuing a degree in Business Administration—which has led him to use all types of computer applications—John has never had the opportunity or desire to learn about the uses of the Internet, other than to use e-mail. His friends have encouraged him to use the Internet to search for employment when he graduates and to learn about companies and industries, explore potential careers, discover job leads, and investigate geographical areas as well as to assist him in preparing for interviews. John has recently read in the local paper that 17,000 new jobs are posted online each week and that employers and recruiters use the Web to make 48 percent of all hires. Although John knows what a Web browser is, he doesn't feel comfortable using one. Luckily for John, one of his fraternity brothers, Tyler, is a Computer Science major and has installed the latest version of Internet Explorer on John's laptop.

Additionally, Tyler has assisted in bookmarking several Web pages using the Favorites feature in Internet Explorer for John to use in his job search. Some of the resources that John now has in his Favorites folder are direct links to Monster.com, JobDirect.com, OnlineSports.com, and FlipDog.com. Once John becomes more at ease using the Web, he will quickly learn how to navigate around the many resources the Internet has to offer with the use of the browser (see Figure 1.1). He can then create his own Favorites and even post his résumé to some job sites!

FIGURE 1.1

Monster.com

The World Wide Web, or just the Web, is the most popular part of the Internet by far. We need to realize that the Web is not the Internet—they are different. The Web is only a subset of the whole Internet that provides us with a friendly way of organizing and viewing the information available on the Internet—not all the information, but certainly a large portion of it. The Web allows rich and diverse communication by displaying text, graphics, animation, photos, sound, and video. Once you spend time on the Web, you will begin to feel as if there is no limit to what you can discover.

The Web physically consists of your personal computer, Web browser software, a connection to an Internet service provider, computers called servers that host data (i.e., hypertext media), and *routers* and *switches,* which direct the flow of information (see Figure 1.2).

The Web browser contains the basic software you need in order to find, retrieve, view, and send information over the Internet. This includes software that lets you:

- Browse the World Wide Web to find a variety of information
- Send and receive electronic-mail messages
- Read messages from newsgroups (or forums) about thousands of topics where users share information and opinions

SESSION 1.1 BROWSER BASICS

The Web browser is your interpreter to the information and resources that make up the Web. Browsers are designed to read files written in a language called HTML or Hypertext Markup Language. With a browser, you can move from Web page to Web page by selecting hyperlinks (see Figure 1.3), which are more simply known as links. When you select a link on a page, the browser takes you to another page or file at the same location or at a different Web location.

The first browser, called NCSA Mosaic (see Figure 1.4), was developed at the National Center for Supercomputing Applications at the University of Illinois in the early 1990s. The easy-to-use point-and-click interface helped popularize the Web. Although Mosaic is no longer being developed, it most certainly set the tone for Internet Explorer and Netscape, the two most popular browsers available.

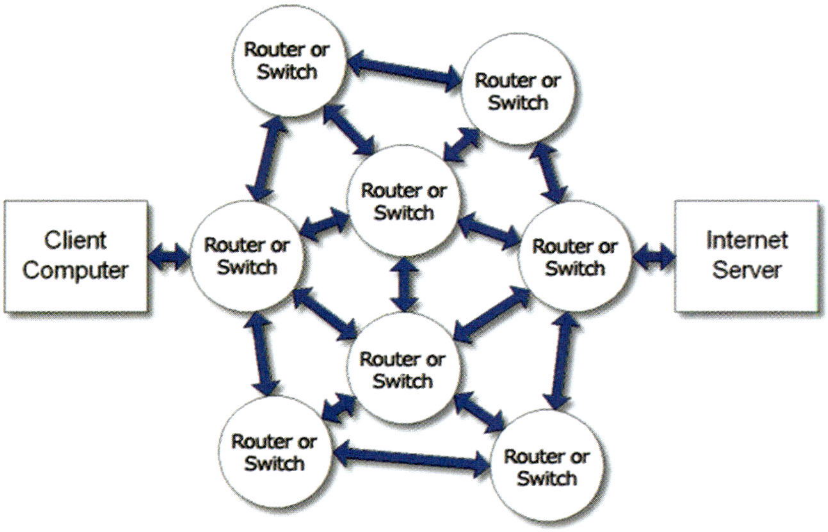

FIGURE 1.2
Routers

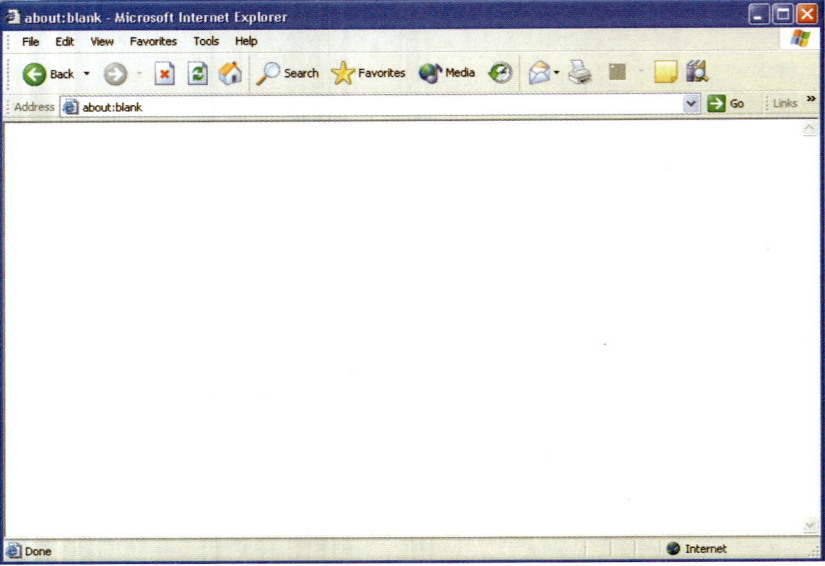

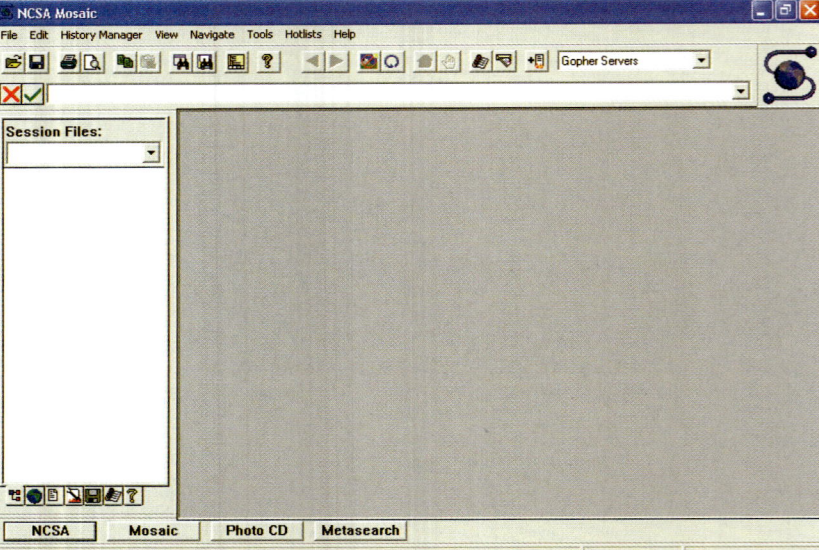

The Anatomy of the World Wide Web

The Web is known as a ***client-server*** system. Your computer is the client; the remote computers that store electronic files, or more specifically Web pages, are the servers. In brief, here's how it works: If you want to visit the ESPN Web site, you must first enter the address or **URL** (Uniform Resource Locator) of the Web site in your Web browser (www.espn.com). Then your browser requests the Web page from the Web server that hosts the ESPN site. The server sends the data over the Internet to your computer. Your Web browser interprets the data, displaying it on your computer screen (see Figure 1.5).

Hypertext and Hyperlinks

The "glue" that holds the Web together is called hypertext and hyperlinks. This feature allows electronic files on the Web to be linked so that you can easily jump between them. On the Web, you navigate through pages of information based on what interests you at that particular moment, commonly known as browsing or surfing the Net.

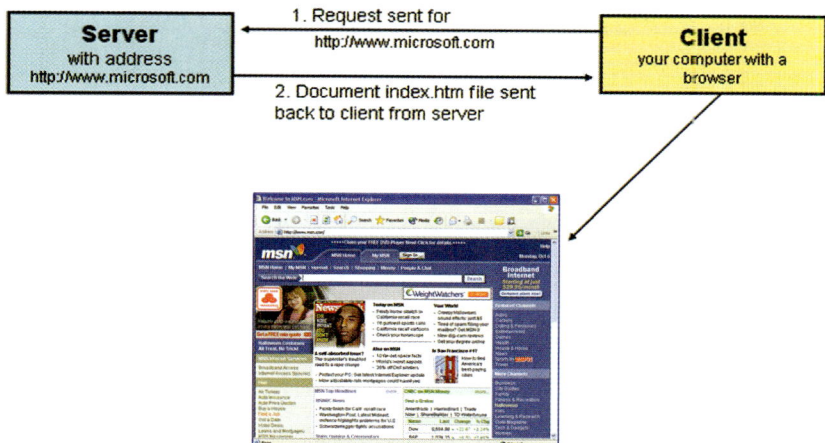

FIGURE   1.5
Client/server

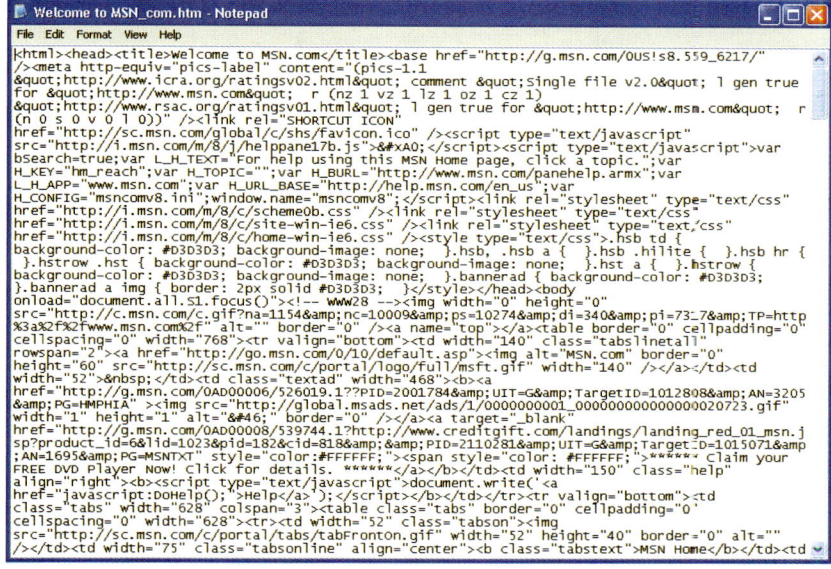

FIGURE   1.6
HTML code in Notepad

To access the Web, you need Web browser software, such as Microsoft Internet Explorer or Netscape Navigator. How does your Web browser distinguish between Web pages and other files on the Internet? The basic HTML page begins with the tag <html> and ends with the tag </html>. In between, the file has two sections—the header and the body (see Figure 1.6). The header, enclosed by the <head> and </head> tags, contains information about a page that won't appear on the page itself, such as the page title. The body, enclosed by <body> and </body>, is where the real action is. Everything that appears on the page is contained within these tags. HTML code puts special marks in a text document to tell browser software how to display the text. For example <FONT FACE=ARIAL COLOR="black"> means to use the font Arial and the color black when displaying the text.

Web Sites and Web Pages

A Web site is a related collection of World Wide Web (WWW) files that includes a beginning file referred to as a home page. A company or an individual tells you how to get to their Web site by giving you the address of their home page. From the home page, you can get to all the other pages on their site. For example, the Web site for Microsoft (see Figure 1.7) has the home page address of http://www.microsoft.com (the home

FIGURE 1.7

http://www.microsoft.com

page address actually includes a specific file name like index.html but, as in Microsoft's case, when a standard default name is set up, users don't have to enter the filename).

Since site implies a geographic place, a **Web site** can be confused with a **Web server**. A server is a computer that stores the files for one or more sites. A very large Web site may be spread over a number of servers in different geographic locations. Microsoft is a good example; its Web site consists of thousands of files spread out over many servers in worldwide locations. A more typical example, however, is probably the site that hosts a school's Web site.

A synonym and less frequently used term for Web site is Web presence. That term seems to better express the idea that a site is not tied to a specific geographic location but is somewhere in cyberspace. However, Web site is used much more frequently.

For a Web user, the home page is the first Web page that is displayed after starting a Web browser. The browser is usually preset so that the home page is the first page of the browser manufacturer, such as www.netscape.com. However, you can set your browser's home page to open to any Web site. For example, you can specify that http://www.yahoo.com be your home page. You can also specify that there be no home page (a blank space will be displayed), in which case you choose the first page from your Favorites or Bookmarks list or enter a Web address, although this is not customary.

Understanding Web Addresses

The Internet is really the interconnection of many individual networks (it's sometimes referred to as an internetwork). Over the years, an open set of standards evolved in support of the Internet called the Transmission Control Protocol/Internet Protocol (or **TCP/IP**) that enables different computers with different operating systems to connect, talk, and share information with one another easily and reliably.

The Internet Protocol (IP) is basically the set of rules for one network communicating with any other network (or occasionally, for broadcast messages, all other networks). Each network must know its own address on the Internet and that of any other network with which it communicates. To be part of the Internet, an organization needs an Internet network number, which it can request from the Internet Network Information Center (InterNIC). This unique network number is included in any data (technically referred to as a **packet**) sent out of the network onto the Internet. In the most widely installed level of the Internet Protocol (IP) today, an IP address is a 32-bit number that identifies each sender or receiver of information that is sent in packets across the Internet. When you request an HTML page or send e-mail, the Internet Protocol part of TCP/IP includes your IP address in the message (actually, in each of the packets if more than one is required) and sends it to the IP address that is obtained by looking up the domain name in the Uniform Resource Locator (URL) you requested or in the e-mail address you're sending to (see Figure 1.8). At the other end, the recipient can see the IP address of the Web page requestor or the e-mail sender and can respond by sending another message using the IP address it received.

Another way to look at IP addressing and packet forwarding (routing) is the snail mail analogy (e.g., postal service). Consider an IP packet to be an envelope containing data and having an address on the front. Every TCP/IP-enabled network interface can be compared to a mailbox. Every mailbox has an IP address. The four bytes of an IP address can be compared to the state, city, street, and house number fields on the front of a snail mail envelope. A router in this analogy is a post office that sorts and forwards mail based on the address on the envelope (packet header). If the address is on the same street, the envelope (packet) is sent directly to the destination mailbox via local courier. If the address is determined to be on another street, or in another city or state, the envelope (packet) is delivered via local courier to the street's post office (router), where the postal workers (routing software) sort and forward mail based on established post office sorting procedures (routing tables).

Because maintaining a central list of domain names and IP addresses would be impractical, the lists of domain names and IP addresses are distributed throughout the Internet in a hierarchy of authority. There is probably a **DNS server** within close geographic proximity to your access provider that maps the domain names in your Internet requests or forwards them to other servers on the Internet. The domain name system (DNS) is the way that Internet domain names are located and translated into IP addresses. A domain name is a meaningful and easy-to-remember "handle" for an Internet address (see Figure 1.9). A domain name locates an organization or other entity on the Internet. For example, the domain name www.denverpost.com locates an Internet address for "denverpost.com" as 63.147.65.205 and a particular **host server** named "www." The "com" part of the domain name reflects the purpose of the organization or entity (in this example, "commercial") and is called the **top-level domain name**. The "denverpost" part of the domain name defines the organization or entity and together with the top level is called the second-level domain name. The **second-level domain name** can be thought of as the "readable" version of the Internet address. The three-letter top-level domains are .com, .net, .org, .edu, .int, mil, and .gov. The first three are operated on commercial principles, while the last four have restrictive conditions on who can register names in those domains (respectively, four-year degree granting institutions in North America, organizations that were established by international treaty, the U.S. military, and the U.S. federal government).

In addition, there are two-letter top-level domains for each country, and a special domain .arpa that currently contains some Internet infrastructure databases. Second-level domain names must be unique on the Internet and registered with one of the ICANN-accredited registrars for the .com, .net, and .org top-level domains. **ICANN** (Internet Corporation for Assigned Names and Numbers, pronounced EYE-can) is the private, nongovernment, nonprofit corporation with responsibility for IP address space allocation, protocol parameter assignment, domain name system management, and root server system management functions—the services previously performed by the Internet Assigned Numbers Authority (IANA). Where appropriate, a top-level domain name can be geographic.

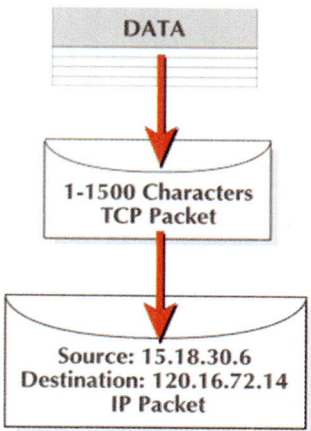

FIGURE 1.8

TCP/IP envelope

FIGURE 1.9

Top-level domain

FIGURE 1.10
URL diagram

A *third-level domain name* can be defined to identify a particular host server at the Internet address. In our example, "www" is the name of the server that handles Internet requests. (A second server might be called "www2.") A third level of domain name is not required. For example, the fully qualified domain name could have been "denverpost.com" and the server assumed.

On the Web, the domain name is that part of the Uniform Resource Locator (URL) that tells a domain name server, using the Domain Name System (DNS,) whether and where to forward a request for a Web page (see Figure 1.10). The domain name is mapped to an IP address (which represents a physical point on the Internet that was described earlier). More than one domain name can be mapped to the same Internet address. This allows multiple individuals, businesses, and organizations to have separate Internet identities while sharing the same Internet server.

The Internet's explosive growth makes it likely that, without some new architecture, the number of possible network addresses using the scheme outlined above will soon be used up. However, a new IP version, *IPv6,* expands the size of the IP address to 128 bits, which will accommodate a large growth in the number of network addresses. Also, there is a proposal to expand the top-level domains, as the current naming structure is nearing capacity. The suggested additional new top-level domains are:

- **.aero** Air-transport industry
- **.biz** Businesses
- **.coop** Cooperatives
- **.info** Unrestricted use
- **.museum** Museums
- **.name** For registration by individuals
- **.pro** Accountants, lawyers, and physicians

Uniform Resource Locators

URLs (pronounced you-are-ell), or Uniform Resource Locators, are the method by which documents or data are addressed in the World Wide Web (see Figure 1.10). The URL contains the following information:

- Internet name of the site containing the resource (file or data)
- Type of service the resource is served by (e.g., HTTP, FTP, Gopher, WAIS)
- Location of the resource in the directory structure of the server

HyperText Transfer Protocol

HTTP (*HyperText Transfer Protocol*), the World Wide Web application protocol that runs on top of the Internet's TCP/IP suite of protocols, brings Web pages to your browser and reduces some of the Web's enormous traffic. Here is a brief summary of how HTTP makes information flow faster:

- Instead of opening and closing a connection for each application request, HTTP provides a persistent connection that allows multiple requests to be pipelined to an output buffer (a midpoint holding place). The underlying Transmission Control Protocol (TCP) layer can put multiple requests (and responses to requests) into one TCP segment that gets forwarded to the Internet

Protocol layer for packet (remember that this terms just means the data) transmission. Because the number of connection and disconnection requests for a sequence of "get a file" requests is reduced, fewer packets need to flow across the Internet. Since requests are pipelined, TCP segments are more efficient. The overall result is less Internet traffic and faster performance for the user

- When a browser that supports HTTP indicates it can decompress HTML files, a server will compress them for transport across the Internet, providing a substantial savings in the amount of data that have to be transmitted (as image files are already in a compressed format, this improvement applies only to HTML and other nonimage data types)

In addition to persistent connections and other performance improvements, HTTP also provides the ability to have multiple domain names share the same Internet address (IP address). This will simplify processing for Web servers that host a number of Web sites in what is sometimes called *virtual hosting*.

making the grade

1. The Internet and the World Wide Web are the same thing. _____
2. _____ is the computer language that Web pages are written in.
3. To navigate to another Web page, you must create a _____.
4. _____ is a valid IP address.
5. Data that travel across the Internet are also known as _____.
6. _____ is an example of a top-level domain name.
7. URL stands for _____ _____ _____.

SESSION 1.2 ELEMENTS OF A WEB BROWSER

Although many different browsers are available, Microsoft Internet Explorer and Netscape Navigator are the two most popular ones (by the way, both are based on NCSA Mosaic). Both Internet Explorer and Navigator are available to download for free from each developer's Web site. Because Internet Explorer and Navigator have more similarities than differences, it is appropriate to outline the benefits and uses of Internet Explorer only.

When you first launch your Web browser, usually by double-clicking on the icon on your desktop, a predefined Web page appears. This page is referred to as your home page or start page. With Internet Explorer, for instance, you may be taken to the Microsoft Network home page (www.msn.com), shown in Figure 1.11, or to a page selected by your Internet service provider. If you choose, you can change your start page, which you will learn about shortly.

Opening Internet Explorer:

1. Click the **Start** button on your Windows Taskbar

2. On the **Start** menu, point to **Programs** and locate **Internet Explorer**

3. From the **Internet Explorer** menu, click **View** and select **Toolbars**. Make sure that **Standard Buttons** and **Address Bar** have a checkmark to the left of their label. If not, make that selection now

F I G U R E   1.11

Browser home page

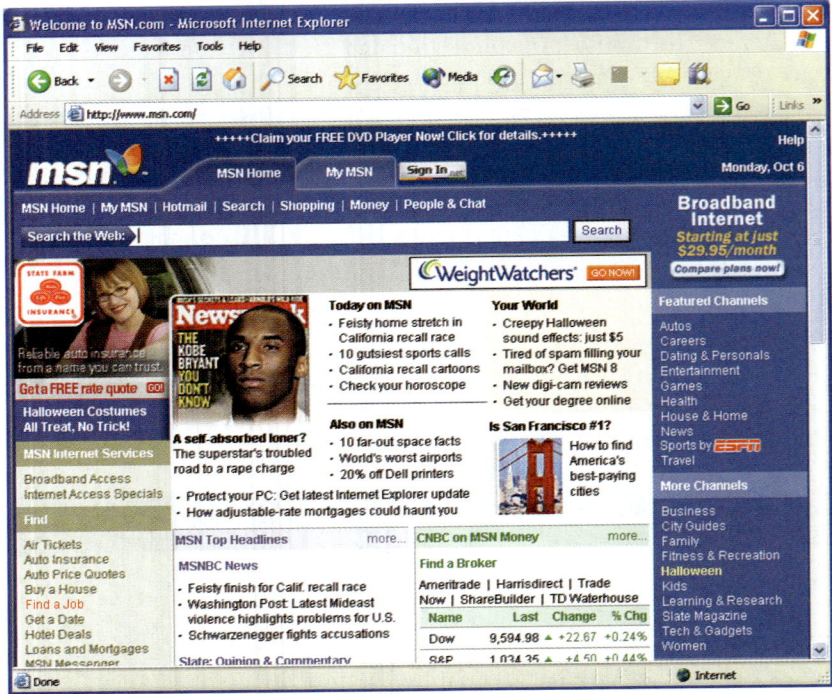

F I G U R E   1.12

Toolbar

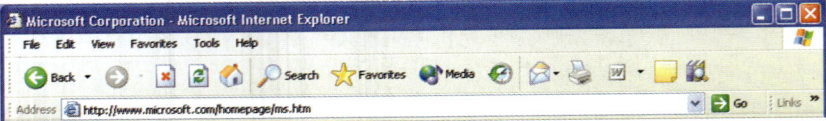

Using Microsoft Internet Explorer

The Toolbar

The row of buttons at the top of your Web browser, known as the toolbar (see Figure 1.12), helps you travel through the web of possibilities, keeping track of where you've been. Here is a summary of what the buttons or the toolbars do:

- The **Back** 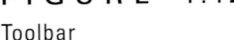 button returns you to the previous page you've visited (one page at a time). However, you can select the small down arrow at the immediate right of the Back button to view the last pages you had traveled to during the current session

- Use the **Forward** button to return to the page you just came from (one page at a time). However, you can select the small down arrow at the immediate right of the Forward button to view the last pages you had traveled to during the current session

- **Home** takes you to whichever home page you've chosen (if you haven't selected one, it will return you to the default home page, usually the Microsoft Network Web site). It is possible to change the home page that loads when you press the Home button

> ### *task reference*   Changing the Default Home Page
>
> - Click **Tools**, and then click **Internet Options**
> - The Internet Options window opens
> - Click the **General** tab
> - Click inside the Address box, and then type in the URL for a new home page
> - Click **OK**

Changing the default home page:

1. Select the **Internet Options** command in the **Tools** pull-down menu (see Figure 1.13)

2. A smaller window opens, offering a number of additional options

3. Select **General** (the first option) and you will see three further subsections: Home Page, Temporary Internet Files, and History (see Figure 1.14). It is only the Home Page section that you are interested in for now

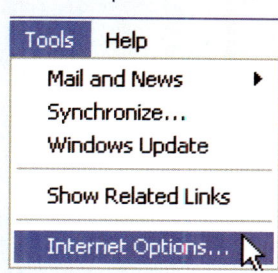

FIGURE 1.13

Internet Options selection

FIGURE 1.14

Internet Options window

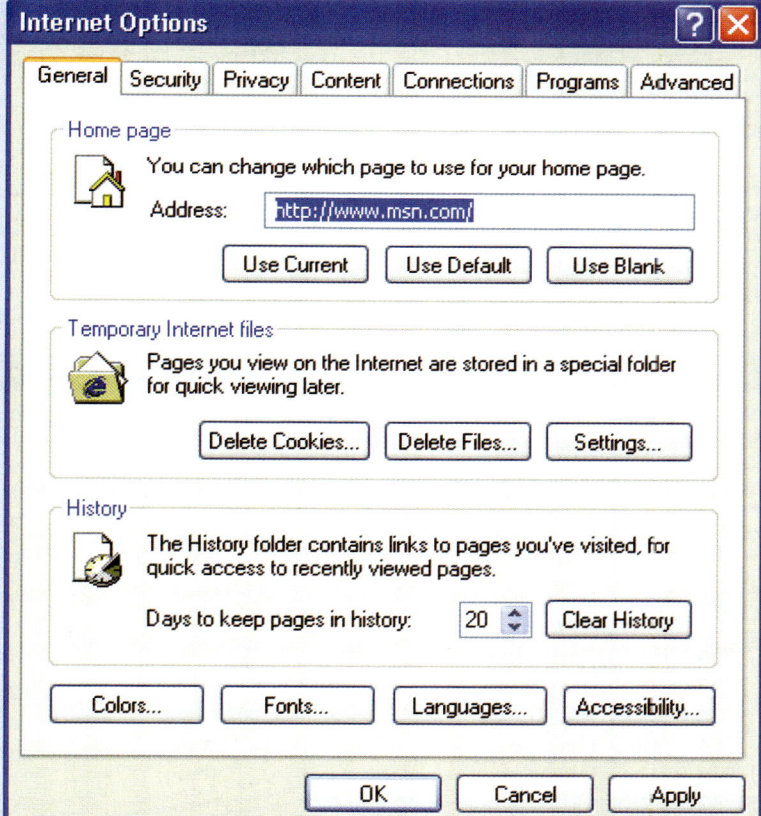

4. You will see an address box under this section containing the URL of your existing default home page. Should you wish to change your default home page, all you need to do is change the URL in the address box

F I G U R E   1.15

Print Menu selection

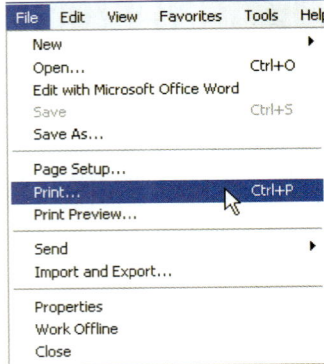

- **Refresh** does just that, it refreshes (or reloads) the Web page again. Why would you want to do this? Sometimes all the elements of a Web page haven't loaded the first time, possibly due to a file transfer that was interrupted. Or, when you download a Web page, the data are cached (pronounced "cashed"), meaning it is stored temporarily in your computer's memory. The next time you want that page, instead of requesting the file from the Web server, your Web browser accesses it from the cache. But if a Web page is updated frequently, as may be the case with news, sports scores, or financial data, you won't get the most current information. By reloading the page, the data are updated directly from the Web server

- **Print** lets you make a hard copy of the current page loaded in your browser. When you print a Web page, the Web address, number of pages, and date on which the page was printed are recorded at the top (or bottom) of the printed page, thus providing you with a hard copy of the Web page or file (see Figure 1.15).

---

task *reference*   **Printing a Web Page**

- Click **File**, and then click **Print**

- Adjust print properties according to preference

- Click **OK**

Printing a Web page:

F I G U R E   1.16

Print dialog box and options

1. You can print the loaded Web page by pressing the **Print** button to open the Print dialog box. Or you can select **Print** from within the **File** pull-down menu on the Main Menu bar. This will open the Print dialog box, allowing you to adjust print properties (see Figure 1.16)

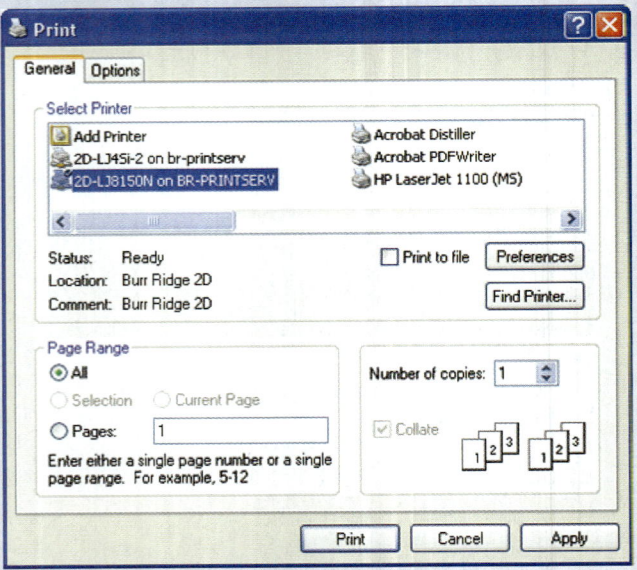

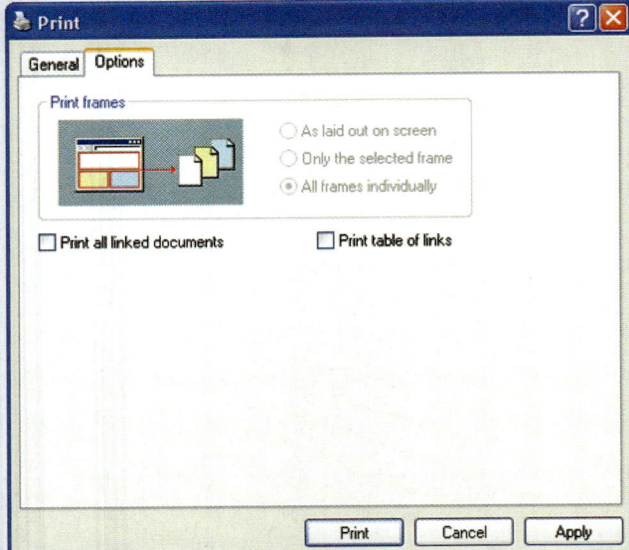

2. By selecting **Page Setup** from the File pull-down menu (Figure 1.17), you can change the page settings (margins, for example, if you want to squeeze more text onto a printed page) (see Figure 1.18)

F I G U R E   1.17
Page Setup

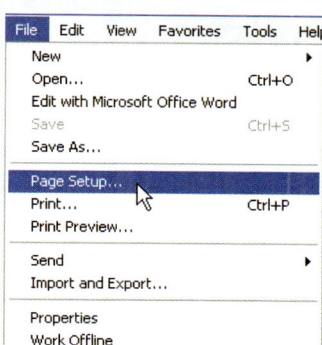

F I G U R E   1.18
Page Setup dialog box

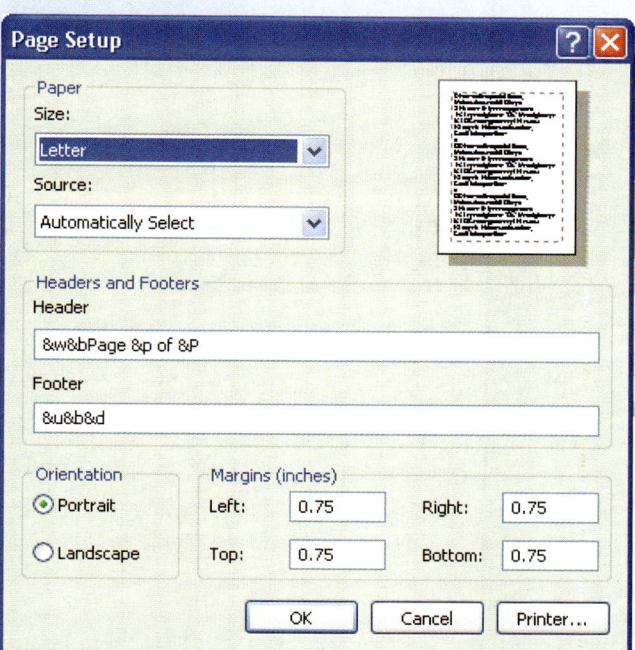

- The **Stop** button stops the browser from loading the current page. It happens quite often that when a page starts downloading, you will decide that either you don't want or don't need the page, or that you have got all the information you want from the first few lines on the page and that there is no need for the page to continue downloading until the end. You would then press the **Stop** button, halting the downloading process

- The **History** button is another useful feature. When you select the History feature, you are presented with a list of Web pages that you have visited. This is different from Favorites, where you decide which Web pages you want to keep track of until you delete them. The History feature is a more transient or temporary feature lasting anywhere from a single session to several weeks based on your choice. It keeps a more comprehensive list of the sites you visit during this period

---

task *reference*   **Using the History Feature**

- Click the **History** button

- The History frame appears on left side of browser

INTERNET ESSENTIALS

Using the History feature:

1. To get to the History feature, you simply select the **History** 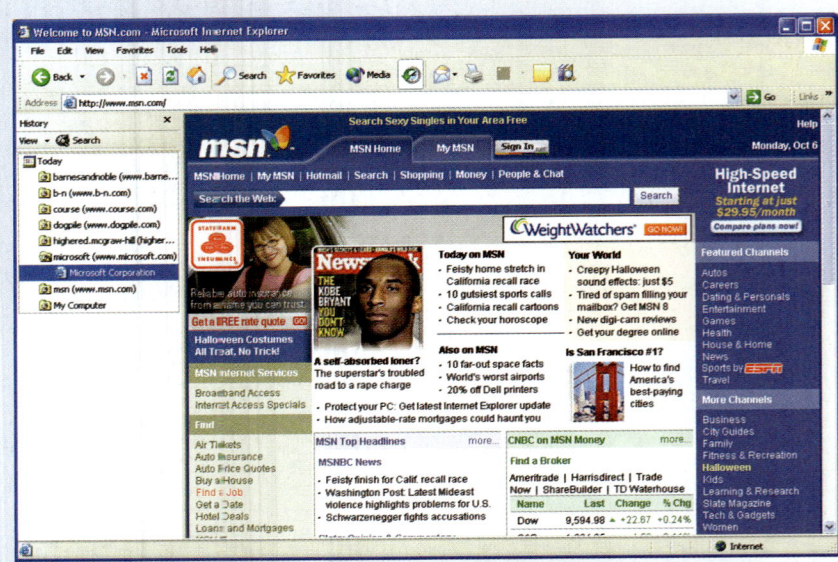 button in the browser window

2. A History frame opens on the left-hand side of the window (see Figure 1.19). You will find a list of the Web pages you have visited during the specific period, organized according to the days involved (2 Weeks Ago, Last Week, Monday, Tuesday, Wednesday, Today, and so on)

FIGURE 1.19

History window

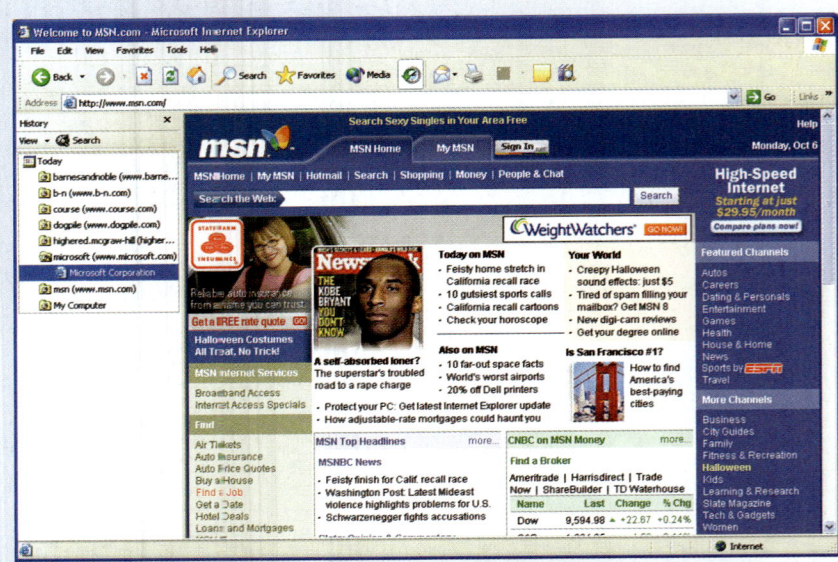

- The **Search** button opens a list of options. You can choose the search tool(s) you want as your default so that you can set your personal preferences for your search experience or just begin your search

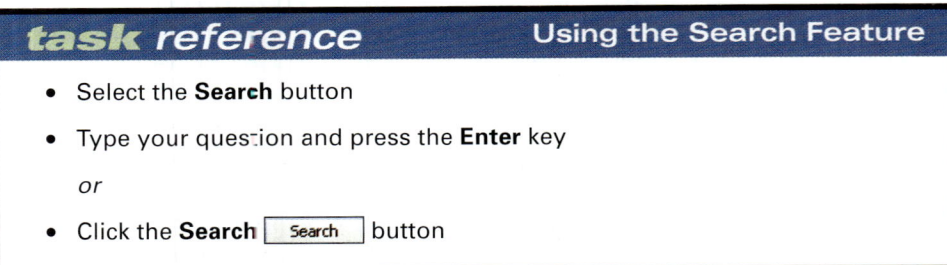

task reference   **Using the Search Feature**

- Select the **Search** button
- Type your question and press the **Enter** key

  or

- Click the **Search** [Search] button

Using the Search feature:

1. Click **Search**, and then type your question and press the **Enter** key

2. If you choose to customize your searching (see Figure 1.20) and select the **Change Preferences** link, you can change many search behaviors, including the **Internet Search Behavior** (see Figure 1.21). This will allow

you to choose to conduct Internet searching with the **Search Companion**, which provides task suggestions and sends your search to other engines, or with your favorite search engine

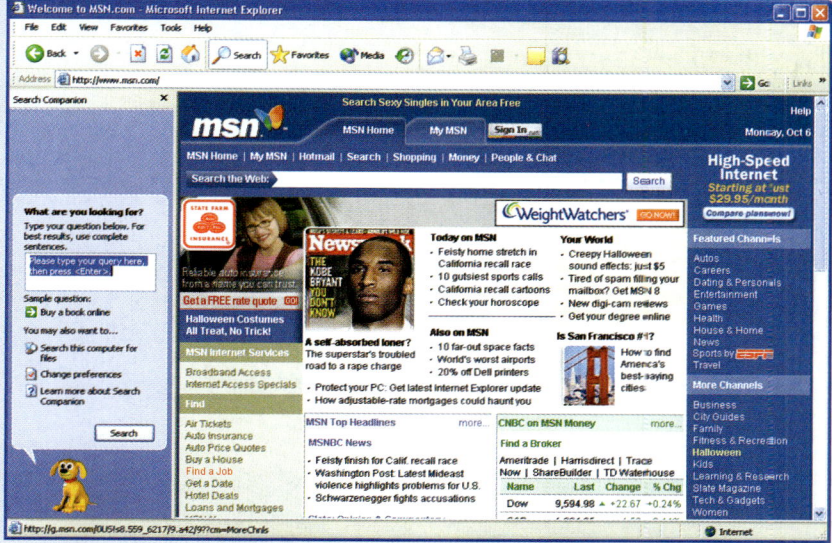

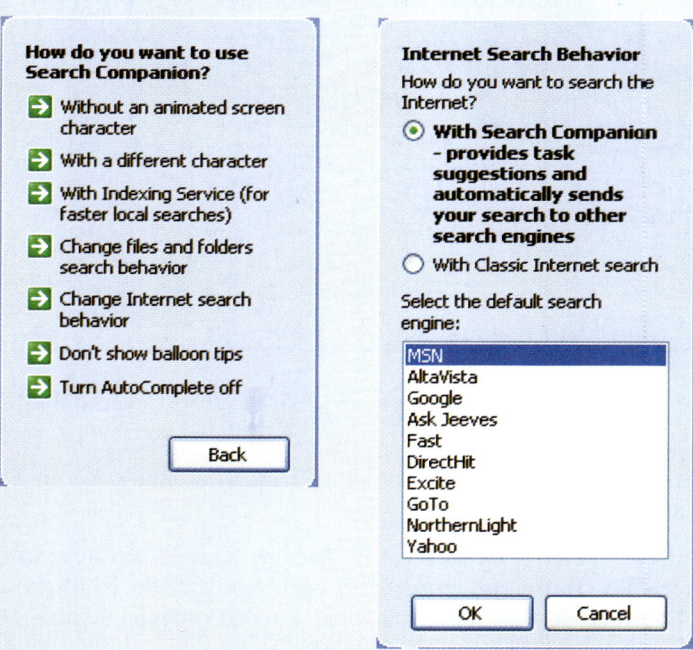

- The **Favorites** option allows you record the addresses of Web sites you want to revisit. Once you add a URL to your list, you can return to that Web page simply by clicking on the link in your list instead of retyping the entire address

task reference	Working with Favorites

- Click the **Favorites** button, and then click **Add**
- Click on **Organize Favorites**, click **Create Folder**, or **Rename**, or **Move Folder**, or **Delete**
- Click **Close** to save

Working with Favorites:

1. To save a Web page, go to the **Favorites** menu or click the **Favorites** icon and select **Add** (see Figure 1.22). When you click the icon again, the title of the page you recorded will appear at the bottom of the list

FIGURE 1.22

Favorites Add selection

2. To revisit the Web page, double-click the hyperlink within the Favorites window

3. To organize your favorites, click the **Favorites** button on the toolbar to open the Favorites window

4. Now click **Organize**. Click the **Create folder** button to create a new folder, and then name it. You might try organizing your bookmarks in folders by subjects, such as Food, Travel, News, Sports, and so on (see Figure 1.23)

5. Click each Favorite once, hold down your left mouse button, and drag the Favorite into the appropriate subject folder (Figure 1.24)

The Location/Address Bar

Just under the toolbar, you will see a box labeled **Address** (see Figure 1.25). This is where you enter the address of a Web site you want to visit. After you enter it, press the **Enter** key to access the site. By clicking the small triangle to the right of the Location

FIGURE 1.23
Organize Favorites

FIGURE 1.24
Organize Favorites drag

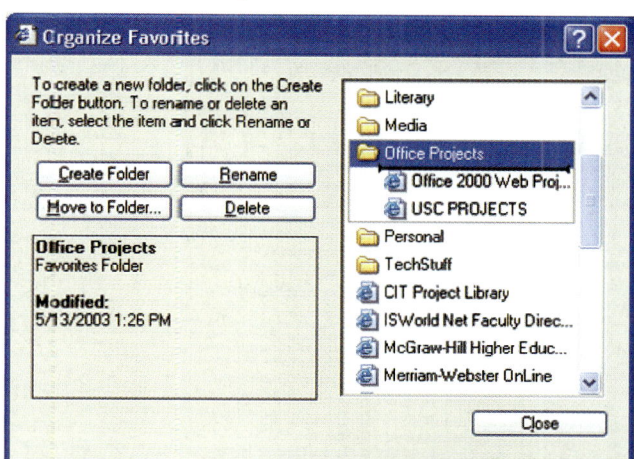

FIGURE 1.25
Location/Address bar

FIGURE 1.26
Location/Address bar
drop-down

FIGURE 1.27
Menu bar

box, you will get a drop-down list of the most recent Web sites you have visited (see Figure 1.26). To revisit a site, just click on the address.

The Menu Bar

Located along the top of the browser window, the menu bar offers a selection of things you can do with a Web page, such as saving it to your hard drive or increasing the size of the text on a page (see Figure 1.27). Many of the choices are the same as the buttons on the toolbar. Click once on a menu bar word to access the drop-down menu, and then click on the appropriate selection you want to make.

The Access Indicator

In the upper right-hand corner of the browser is an image that is animated (typically a very small image of a globe revolving or the ISP provider's logo) when you are requesting a Web page or file. Your browser downloads these remote files to your computer and then displays them on your screen. The speed of this process depends on a number of factors: the method you use to connect to the Internet (i.e., modem, cable, DSL, etc.), your Internet Service Provider's Internet connection speed, the size of the files you are downloading, how busy the server is, and the traffic on the Internet.

INTERNET ESSENTIALS

The Status Bar

At the bottom of the Web browser, you'll find a small window known as a status bar. You can watch the progress of Web page transactions, such as the address of the site you are contacting, whether the host computer has been contacted, and the size and number of the files to be downloaded.

The Scroll Bar

The vertical bar to the right of the browser allows you to scroll up and down a Web page. You can do this by placing your arrow cursor on the up or down arrows and holding down your left mouse button. You can also place the arrow on the slider control, hold down the left mouse button, and drag the slider. If a Web page is too wide to fit your screen, a horizontal scroll bar will appear at the bottom of your browser window. This scroll bar works the same way as the vertical bar. The use of this feature is the same in all Windows applications.

Saving Web Pages

One of the more useful features found with a browser is the ability to save complete Web pages locally. Older versions of Internet Explorer and Netscape have allowed you to view the source HTML code of a page and to save that page as a file on your local drive. However, that didn't save the graphics from the page or any other file used within the page, which meant that if you loaded the file back from the local disk, you would see broken images or dead links. You could save the graphics files separately by right-clicking on a graphic within the browser and choosing Saving picture as . . . , which would save the file to a location you specify.

FIGURE   1.28

Save As

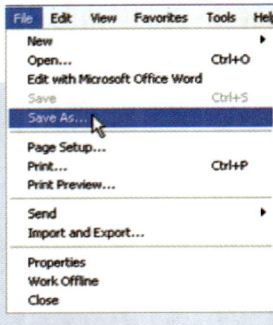

FIGURE   1.29

Save As file types

Saving Web pages locally:

1. If you are viewing a page that you wish to keep, select **File** on the menu bar, and then choose **Save As** (Figure 1.28)

2. The Save As dialog box offers several file types. Saving the page as a different file type will affect how the page is saved (Figure 1.29)

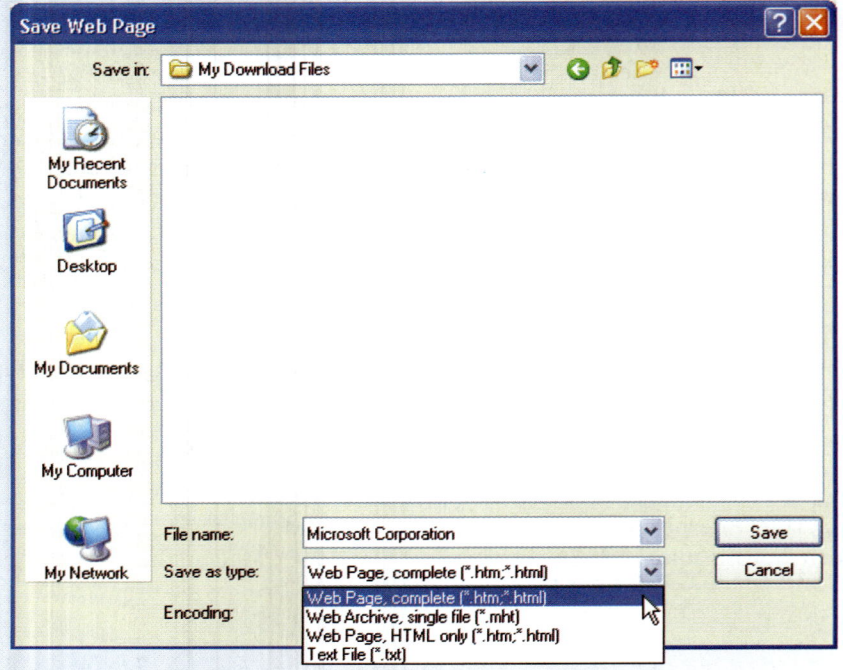

- **Web page, complete (*.htm, *.html)** This is the most common y used feature. It allows you to save the page to a folder on your drive. The browser will save the HTML page, graphics, sounds, and additional files like Java applets or JavaScript files associated with the Web page

- **Single-File web page (*.mht)** This option is available for Internet Explorer 6 and newer. Opera and Netscape cannot render mht files.

- **Web Page, HTML only (*.htm, *.html)** This is the option that has always been available. It will simply save the current page's source HTML to your drive intact. It does not save any external files cr adjust any of the code, as the Web page complete option does

- **Text File (*.txt)** This simply allows you to save the text from the page output. It does not save the HTML code, only the text as displayed in the browser

Copyright

The issue of copyright for Web- and Internet-based materials is still undef_ned, largely because copyright law has not yet caught up with the new medium. Indeed, it will be impossible to give clear and unambiguous guidelines in this area until test cases have been fought.

The information and graphics that your computer down_oads when you view a Web page are like the books you borrow from the library: You do not own them. Material published on the Internet has the same protections against unauthorized use as books, magazines, and newspapers have always had. If the material is copyright written, the author has the right to control how others use the material. Just because you can download and save it does not make it yours!

Some materials that are on the Internet are stated to be free. For example, an artist may create graphics for Web page navigation buttons and backgrounds and offer them for free. Software may also be available as freeware or shareware. Each creator can choose exactly how their creations can be used by others.

Browser Shortcuts

When you use the Internet Explorer browser, you can access everything from the menus using the mouse, although some people prefer to have quick access to certain features through keyboard shortcuts (also known as power keys). Internet Explorer has many shortcuts defined, and you can find a complete list in the Internet Explorer Help file. Here, though, are the most useful ones:

Ctrl+B	Open the Organize Favorites dialog box
Ctrl+D	Add the current page to your Favorites
Ctrl+E	Open/Close the Search Explorer bar
Ctrl+F	Open the Find dialog box to search for text on the current page
Ctrl+I	Open/Close the Favorites Explorer bar
Ctrl+H	Open/Close the History Explorer bar
F5	Refresh/Reload the current page, but only if the time stamp on the Web page on the server is different from that of the version stored/cached on your machine
Ctrl+F5	Refresh/Reload the current page, irrespective of time stamps. This forces a refresh of the page
F11	Toggle between the windowed browser view (standard) and the full screen mode
Alt+Home	Jump back to your home (default) page, as loaded when the browser is first opened
Esc	Stop the current page download

In addition to these general shortcuts you can use in the browser, there are a couple that are useful if you are typing into the Address bar in the browser:

- **F4** Open the Address bar drop-down history menu
- **Alt-D** Select all the text in the Address bar

Internet Options/Control Panel Overview

To change the general preferences used for your browser, you use the Internet Options or Internet Options Control Panel. These are in fact exactly the same, but can be accessed from different locations.

Customizing Internet Options in Internet Explorer:

1. If you don't have a browser open, you can access the Internet Options dialog box from the **Control Panel** folder using the icon labeled **Internet Options**, and if you do, you can simply go to the **Tools** menu and select **Internet Options**

2. The dialog box that opens from either method is the same one, though from the Control Panel the dialog box is labeled **Internet Properties** in its title bar and from inside the browser it is labeled **Internet Options** (see Figure 1.30)

3. The dialog box contains several tabs:

- **General** Change some of the simple browser settings, like the default home page (which you did earlier) and clear the cache from the hard drive

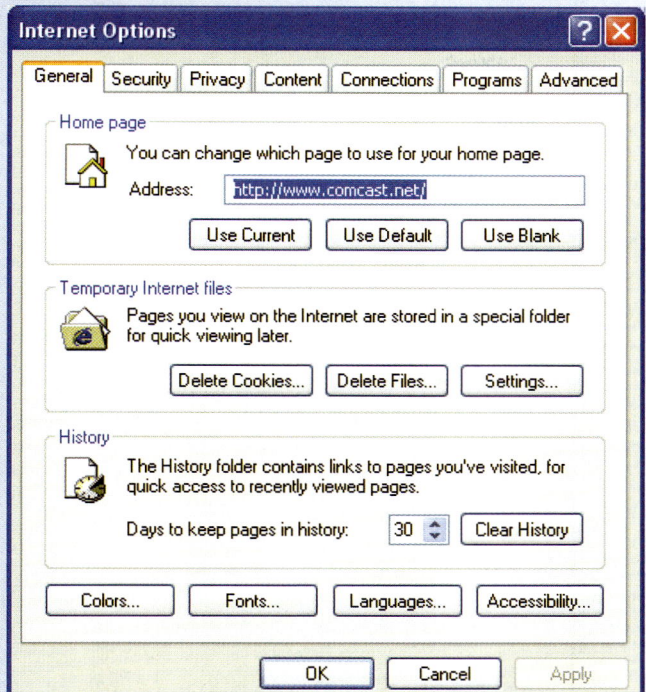

- **Security** Simpler access to the levels of trust you have for content on Web pages accessed from different types of location. The **trust** refers to components on the page that have the ability to affect your computer and files stored on it

- **Privacy** This controls how much information is stored in cookies on your computer. You can move a slider to set values from "Accept All Cookies" to "Low" to "Medium" all the way up to "Block All Cookies"

- **Content** This gives you control over the type of content that you want to allow access to and, to some degree, allows you to exclude offensive material from being displayed

- **Connections** Controls to make your connections easier to manage. It makes dealing with multiple connections you may have on one PC much easier. If you want to add a new connection though, you may be better off using the Internet Connection Wizard

- **Programs** Allows you to decide which programs should be used to deal with certain options in the browser, such as e-mail links or HTML editing

- **Advanced** A host of additional options you simply enable or disable through tick boxes. For most people the default settings will suffice, but if you specifically want to adjust some of the ways the browser works, like Java support or some search facilities, this is where you can do it. More advanced options for security can be set zone by zone in the Security tab that was briefly discussed above

making *the grade*

1. The toolbar in Internet Explorer helps you to _____ on the Web.

2. You use the Refresh button to _____ .

3. The Stop button is used to _____ .

4. The _____ button gives you a list of the Web pages you have visited.

5. Can you customize the Search button in Internet Explorer? _____

6. _____ allows you to save the address of a Web page to use at another time.

7. Copyright issues do not pertain to information on the Internet. _____

SESSION 1.3 SUMMARY

A Web browser is software that enables you to find and view information published on the World Wide Web through a graphical interface. The two most common Web browsers available today are Microsoft's Internet Explorer and Netscape Communicator. Most of the information on the Web is organized into linked pages located on different computers that are connected to the Internet. These networked computers that store and deliver information are called servers. The browser is able to interpret text, pictures, and HTML formatting codes and turns them into something that can be displayed on your computer.

One function of a Web browser is to interpret the address of a piece of information located on the Internet or World Wide Web. These addresses are called URLs or Uniform Resource Locators. Browsers also retrieve requested information. When you access a Web site, the browser actually brings a file called a Web page to your computer, but it only keeps the file temporarily while you view it. Browsers can also save or copy files, pictures, sounds, and software for you to keep. When you type in a URL or click a link, the browser sends a request for that page over the Internet. Your computer uses the URL to find the server that has the Web page and asks for a copy. That server receives the request, finds the page, and then sends a copy of the page over the Internet and back to your computer. Most of the time, this happens in just a few seconds.

World Wide Web pages are written and composed in HTML (HyperText Markup Language) page description language. Browsers read the HTML codes and links (called tags) and display the pages appropriately.

The main toolbar in a browser is composed of different buttons, each with a specific purpose to assist in navigating through Web pages. You are able to add frequently visited Web pages to a Favorites list for easy access, organize your favorite items by using folders, and sort them in the order you want them displayed. Some specific browser features allow you to quickly and easily save Web pages, including images, e-mail pictures, and printing that you find on Web pages. Becoming comfortable working with a Web browser environment unlocks all the possibilities of the Internet!

making the grade *answers*

SESSION 1.1

1. The World Wide Web is a subset of the Internet. The Internet provides the infrastructure upon which the WWW rests.

2. Hypertext Markup Language (HTML)

3. hyperlink

4. 67.68.67.91 (any four part address separated by three dots whose individual values are less than 256)

5. packet(s)

6. com (or .com or .COM); others include .edu, .org, .mil, and so on

7. Uniform Resource Locator

SESSION 1.2

1. go forward, backward, and move to previously visited sites

2. Reload a Web page from the Web, rather than use an older version that could be stored on your computer.

3. Stop the browser from loading the current page.

4. History

5. Yes. You can change many of the search behaviors including the Internet Search Behavior.

6. Click the Favorites button and then click the Add button.

7. False. Nearly everything on the Internet is protected from copyright infringement.

task reference *summary*

Task	Page #	Preferred Method
Changing the default homepage	WEB 1.11	• Click **Tools**, click **Internet Options**, click the **General** tab • Type the new URL for new homepage • Click **OK**
Printing a Web page	WEB 1.12	• Click **File**, click **Print**, click **OK**
Using the History function	WEB 1.13	• Click **History**
Using the Search feature	WEB 1.14	• Select **Search** • Type your question and press **Enter**
Working with Favorites	WEB 1.16	• Click **Favorites**, then Click **Add** • Click **Organize Favorites** • Select **Create Folder, Rename,** or **Move** • Click **Close**

TRUE OR FALSE

1. _____ The Refresh button allows you to reload Web pages.

2. _____ Internet Explorer is the first and only Web browser.

3. _____ Hyperlinks make it easy to navigate from one Web page to another.

4. _____ A server is a remote computer that stores Web pages.

5. _____ You use Favorites to store popular Web page links for quick access.

FILL-IN

1. The two most popular Web browsers are _____ and _____.

2. The _____ feature allows electronic files on the Web to be linked so that they are easily accessible.

3. The _____ page is the first Web page that is displayed after starting a Web browser.

4. The _____ offers a selection of things that you can do with a Web page, and many of the choices are the same as the button on the toolbar.

5. HTTP stands for _____.

6. The _____ is a small icon in the upper right corner of the browser that means your computer is retrieving information.

MULTIPLE CHOICE

1. The interface between the user and the Internet is called
   a. the operating system.
   b. software.
   c. HTML.
   d. the browser.

2. If you decide you don't want to view a certain Web page, use the _____ button.
   a. History
   b. Stop
   c. Forward
   d. Favorites

3. Most Web pages are created and/or saved as
   a. a Visual Basic program.
   b. a Word document.
   c. HTML code.
   d. an Excel spreadsheet.

4. A Web address is also known as a(n)
   a. mail box.
   b. Web site.
   c. URL.
   d. server.

5. A set of standards called _____ enables different computers with different operating systems to connect and share information via the Internet.
   a. Ethernet
   b. TCP/IP
   c. HTML
   d. Netscape

review of concepts

REVIEW QUESTIONS

1. Discuss the advantages of using a Web browser to surf the Web.

2. What is a Uniform Resource Locator used for?

3. Explain the difference between a Web site and a Web server.

4. Discuss how a Web page is routed over the Internet.

5. Explain the issue of copyright as it relates to the Web and Internet-based materials.

CREATE THE QUESTION

For each of the following answers, create an appropriate, short question.

ANSWER	QUESTION
1. You click this button to refresh the current Web page	_____
2. This button lists all the Web pages you have visited	_____
3. Click **Tools** on the menu bar, click **Internet Options**, and select the **General** tab	_____
4. This allows you to save a URL to a Web page in your browser	_____
5. You type in a Web address here	_____
6. You use this to locate information on the Web	_____

practice

1. Creating Favorites

Jane Baylis has just purchased a new computer. She has the task of customizing her desktop and configuring a few applications that she will use frequently. Her first concern is to create her Internet Explorer favorites to allow her to revisit Web pages more quickly. She has asked you to assist with this process because she has never done it before.

1. Open **Internet Explorer**

2. In the **Address** bar of the browser window, type in the URL **www.cnn.com** and press **Enter**

3. Click **Favorites** from the menu bar and then select **Add Favorite**

4. In the Add Favorite dialog box, click the **Create In** button and the **New Folder** button, type in **News** for the folder name, and then click **OK**

5. Click **OK** to close the Add Favorite dialog box

6. In the **Address** bar of the browser window, type in the URL **www.msnbc.com** and press **Enter**

7. Click **Favorites** from the menu bar and then select **Add Favorite**

8. In the **Create in** dialog box, select the folder **News** that you created in the step above and click **OK**

9. In the **Address** bar of the browser window, type in the URL **www.amazon.com** and press **Enter**

10. Click **Favorites** from the menu bar and then select **Add Favorite**

11. In the **Add Favorite** dialog box, click on **New Folder**, type in **Shopping** for the folder name, and click **OK**

12. Click **OK** to close the Add Favorite dialog box

13. In the **Address** bar of the browser window, type in the URL **www.gap.com** and press **Enter**

14. Click **Favorites** from the menu bar and then select **Add Favorite**

15. In the **Create in** dialog box, select the folder **Shopping** that you created in the step above and click **OK**

16. Click on **Favorites** on the toolbar to display your favorites in a window within the browser

2. Search, Save File Option, and Print in Internet Explorer

You have just been hired by the Highlands Ranch Recreation Center to research and report on the types of services being offered by other recreational centers in the Denver area and Colorado region. As part of your inquiry, you will use Internet Explorer to start your research. You will want to save and print the Web pages that you find particularly beneficial to your assignment.

1. Open **Internet Explorer**

2. Click on the **Search** button on the toolbar, and select the Change Preferences link

3. Select the **Change Internet Search behavior** link, select **AltaVista** as the default search engine, and click **OK**

4. On the left side of the Internet Explorer search window type in **Recreation Centers in Colorado**

5. Click on the some of the **hyperlinks** that the search service returned. Locate some information that will assist in your assignment.

6. When you have found some relevant information select **File** on the menu bar, and then select **Print**. Click on the **Print** button

7. You want to also save this page on your computer, to refer to for your report. Select **File** on the menu bar and then select **Save As**. You will want to remember what directory you are saving this file in or modify the **Save In** directory

8. Repeat the steps above (steps 4–7) to search for information on **Recreation Centers in Denver** in order to complete your assignment

hands-on projects

challenge!

1. World Events

Sheryl Rogers is trying to be more knowledgeable about world events and has decided to use the Internet to find foreign newspapers so that she can learn about events that are happening in their countries. Help Sheryl find five headlines or lead stories from five foreign newspapers and add them to a new folder named **Newspapers** in the **Favorites** folder.

2. Internet Job Searching

Based on your current or intended major, use the Internet to find two potential jobs. List the URLs of the site(s) that list the positions, and provide information about each job, such as the organization offering the job, the location, minimum qualifications, benefits, and the salary. Add the site(s) you find to a new folder entitled **Jobs** in the **Favorites** folder.

5

Desktop Publishing

did you know?

in *February 1995, Hiroyuki Goto of Japan recited 42,194 digits of pi from memory in a mere 9 hours and 21 minutes.*

in *1893, white people living in Hawaii organized the overthrow of the Kingdom of Hawaii and waged a successful campaign to bring Hawaii under the control of the United States.*

on *the eve of Halloween in 1938, Orson Welles broadcast a dramatically realistic adaptation of H. G. Wells's War of the Worlds. So authentic was this radio production, that many listeners believed Martians were actually invading Earth.*

recent *research using high-speed films of acorn woodpeckers shows that their heads and brains can endure up to 1,200 gravities of force when their beaks hit the wood.*

when *the Sun acts up—sun storms—it sends streams of electrons and protons toward Earth. These streams cause auroras, electromagnetic disturbances, and damage satellites.*

a *flimflam is a deception, trick, lie, or scam. To flimflam someone is to take advantage of them through a con or swindle.*

Chapter Objectives

- **Apply and format columns—MOS WW03S-3-3**
- **Summarize document content using automated tools—MOS WW03E-2-4**

Creating a Newsletter for HurtinHotSauce.com

Traditionally, most office documents were produced in the single-column format because it was too difficult to produce a document in a multiple-column format. Today, producing multiple-column documents is easy when you are using Word. Multiple-column documents have an advantage over traditional documents because shorter lines of text are easier to read.

Tim Poon works on the help desk at HurtinHotSauce.com. In an effort to reduce help desk calls Tim's team decided to write a series of "how to" newsletters that will feature some of the most common user problems and questions. The newsletters will be mailed to every employee and will be placed on news racks throughout the office. Tim's first newsletter will explain e-mail and provide some tips for using e-mail. Tim's newsletters must be produced in a three-column format. Figures 5.1 and 5.2 display Tim's original and final newsletter.

FIGURE 5.1

Page 1 of Tim's original newsletter

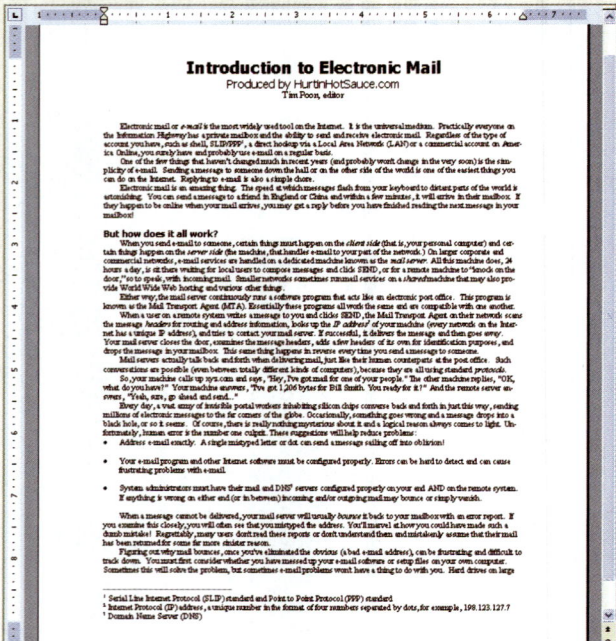

FIGURE 5.2

Page 1 of Tim's final newsletter

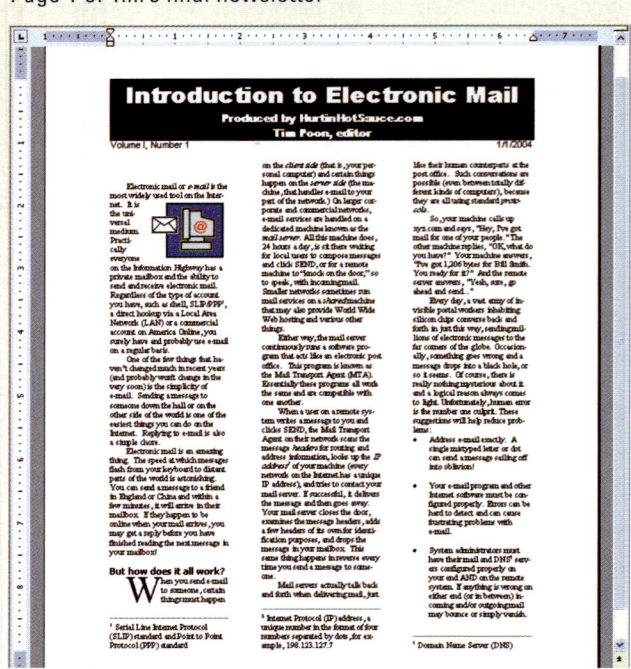

INTRODUCTION

This session is going to teach you how you can produce newsletters and other types of desktop publishing documents using Word. Desktop publishing is one of the more difficult areas you are going to learn in this text; however, once you have mastered this area, you will be able to create high-quality, professional looking, and attractive newsletters. This session will begin with an overview of desktop publishing and then lead into the development of a simple multi-column newsletter. The last session will introduce you to additional tools you can use to enhance your newsletter including graphics and borders and shading.

SESSION 5.1 DESKTOP PUBLISHING— CREATING A NEWSLETTER

What Is Desktop Publishing?

Desktop publishing is the combination of text and graphics to produce a high-quality, professional looking document. Desktop publishing can include such things as newsletters, brochures, and posters. Originally, if a company wanted to produce desktop publishing documents, it had to contract with a desktop publishing company. A company could not produce desktop publishing documents on its own. Today, companies can produce all kinds of professional looking desktop publishing documents by using Word.

Learning and understanding desktop publishing will be invaluable to your career. Not only will you be able to produce professional looking newsletters, but you will also save your company time and money by not having to outsource the development of desktop publishing documents.

Essentials of Desktop Publishing

Throughout this session you will be creating a newsletter for the HurtinHotSauce.com company. Try to keep the following list of desktop publishing essentials in mind when you are creating your newsletter:

- Columns—columns have shorter lines of text making it easier for your reader to understand and comprehend the information
- Multiple fonts—using different font types, sizes, and styles will help guide your reader through the document and emphasize different areas in the document
- Graphics—inserting lines, boxes, pictures, or shading will help to make your document more appealing and guide your reader to different sections of the document
- Clip art—should be used in moderation to catch the reader's eye and draw attention to the text
- Borders and shading—used to emphasize specific areas of text within the newsletter
- *Pull quote*—phrase or sentence pulled out of the main text, enlarged, and typically used to emphasize a key point
- *Dropped-capital letter*—a large capital letter at the beginning of a paragraph used to capture the reader's attention and highlight the associated text
- *Reverse*—light text on a dark background and typically used to highlight specific text

---

anotherword . . . **Use of Desktop Publishing Features**

Be careful not to use too many different fonts, graphics, and clip art when you are creating your newsletter. Documents that have too many different font styles, graphics, and emphasized text tend to distract the reader's eye because they look cluttered and unorganized

---

Elements of a Newsletter

Typography is the style and appearance of printed matter or the arrangement of composed type. Different typographies are used to get the reader's attention, convey information, or create a certain mood. When creating a newsletter you must pay particular attention to the typography in order to ensure you are getting the reader's attention and using the best possible format to provide information. A typical newsletter contains all of the following:

- Headings
- Columns
- Styles
- Graphics
- Borders and shading

A *masthead* is the identifying information found at the top of a newsletter containing information such as the date of publication, title, and volume or number of the newsletter. Tim wants to create the masthead for his newsletter.

Adding a masthead:

1. Open the document **wd05Email.doc**

2. Save the document as **Email1.doc**

3. Insert the cursor on the first blank line following the line containing Tim Poon, Editor

4. Click on the **Table** menu, click **Insert**, and then click **Table**

5. Change the number of columns to **2** and the number of rows to **1**

6. Click **OK**

7. Click in the left column and type **Volume I, Number 1** and ensure the text is left aligned

8. Click in the right column and type **<Current date>** and ensure the text is right aligned

9. Insert the cursor on the first blank line after the table in the masthead

10. Insert a section break by clicking on the **Insert** menu, click **Break**, click Section break type **Continuous**, and click **OK**

11. Compare your work to Figure 5.3 (switch to Normal view, if necessary, to see the section break)

12. Save your document

Introduction to Electronic Mail
Produced by HurtinHotSauce.com
Tim Poon, editor

Volume I, Number 1		1/1/2004

Section Break (Continuous)

Electronic mail or *e-mail* is the most widely used tool on the Internet. It is the universal medium. Practically everyone on the Information Highway has a private mailbox and the ability to send and receive electronic mail. Regardless of the type of account you have, such as shell, SLIP/PPP[1], a direct hookup via a Local Area Network (LAN), or a commercial account on America Online, you surely have and probably use e-mail on a regular basis.

One of the few things that haven't changed much in recent years (and probably won't change very soon) is the simplicity of e-mail. Sending a message to someone down the hall or on the other side of the world is one of the easiest things you can do on the Internet. Replying to e-mail is also a simple chore.

Electronic mail is an amazing thing. The speed at which messages flash from your keyboard to distant parts of the world is astonishing. You can send a message to a friend in England or China and within a few minutes, it will arrive in their mailbox. If they happen to be online when your mail arrives, you may get a reply before you have finished reading the next message in your mailbox!

But how does it all work?

When you send e-mail to someone, certain things must happen on the *client side* (that is, your personal computer) and certain things happen on the *server side* (the machine that handles e-mail to your part of the network). On larger corporate and commercial networks, e-mail services are handled on a dedicated machine known as the *mail server*. All this machine does, 24

FIGURE 5.3

Tim's masthead

Tim has decided to take advantage of the desktop publishing essentials listed above. Tim wants to add a reverse to his masthead so that the title of his newsletter is emphasized.

Adding a reverse to the masthead:

1. Ensure your **Email1.doc** is opened

2. Select the titles **Introduction to Electronic Mail, Produced by HurtinHotSauce.com, Tim Poon, Editor**

3. Select the **Format** menu, click **Borders and Shading**, and click on the **Shading** tab

4. Click the **drop-down arrow** in the **Style** list and select **Solid (100%)** (see Figure 5.4)

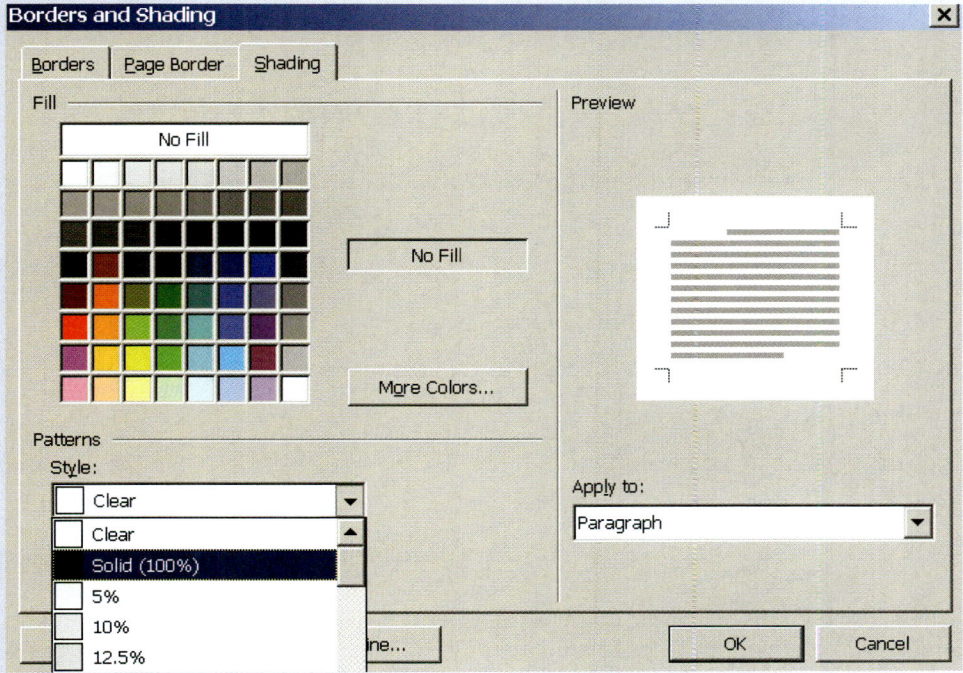

FIGURE 5.4

Border and Shading drop-down list with 100% Solid selected

5. Click **OK**

6. Highlight the table containing the Volume number and date

7. Click on **Format** menu, click **Borders and Shading**, and click the **Borders** tab

8. Select the setting **None** to remove the border around the table

9. Click **OK**

10. Compare your document to Figure 5.5

FIGURE 5.5

Tim's reverse masthead

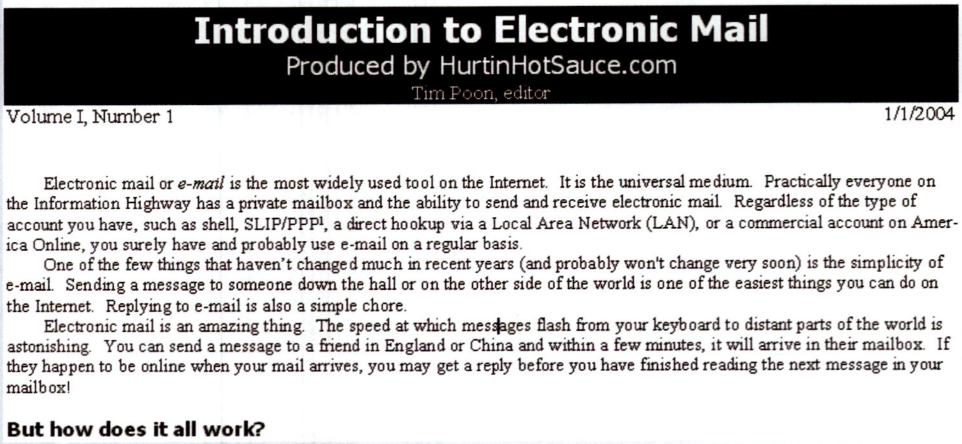

Introduction to Electronic Mail
Produced by HurtinHotSauce.com
Tim Poon, editor

Volume I, Number 1   1/1/2004

Electronic mail or *e-mail* is the most widely used tool on the Internet. It is the universal medium. Practically everyone on the Information Highway has a private mailbox and the ability to send and receive electronic mail. Regardless of the type of account you have, such as shell, SLIP/PPP[1], a direct hookup via a Local Area Network (LAN), or a commercial account on America Online, you surely have and probably use e-mail on a regular basis.

One of the few things that haven't changed much in recent years (and probably won't change very soon) is the simplicity of e-mail. Sending a message to someone down the hall or on the other side of the world is one of the easiest things you can do on the Internet. Replying to e-mail is also a simple chore.

Electronic mail is an amazing thing. The speed at which messages flash from your keyboard to distant parts of the world is astonishing. You can send a message to a friend in England or China and within a few minutes, it will arrive in their mailbox. If they happen to be online when your mail arrives, you may get a reply before you have finished reading the next message in your mailbox!

But how does it all work?

11. Save your document

Tim realizes that he needs to take advantage of different types of typography in order to make his newsletter more appealing. Tim decides to change the font in the heading in order to emphasize the document title.

Changing the font in the masthead:

1. Select the title **Introduction to Electronic Mail**

2. Select **Arial black, 26 point**

3. Select **Produced by HurtinHotSauce.com** and **Tim Poon, Editor**

4. Select **Arial black, 12 point, bold**

5. Select the line containing **Volume I, Number 1** and the **current date**

6. Select **Arial**

7. Compare your document with Figure 5.6

8. Save your document

Tim wants to emphasize some of the key points in the text in order to draw the reader's attention to specific areas. Tim is going to insert pull quotes and dropped-capital letters to help emphasize some of these key points.

FIGURE 5.6

Tim's title with the new fonts

Introduction to Electronic Mail
Produced by HurtinHotSauce.com
Tim Poon, Editor

Volume I, Number 1   1/1/2004

Electronic mail or *e-mail* is the most widely used tool on the Internet. It is the universal medium. Practically everyone on the Information Highway has a private mailbox and the ability to send and receive electronic mail. Regardless of the type of account you have, such as shell, SLIP/PPP[1], a direct hookup via a Local Area Network (LAN), or a commercial account on America Online, you surely have and probably use e-mail on a regular basis.

One of the few things that haven't changed much in recent years (and probably won't change very soon) is the simplicity of e-mail. Sending a message to someone down the hall or on the other side of the world is one of the easiest things you can do on the Internet. Replying to e-mail is also a simple chore.

Electronic mail is an amazing thing. The speed at which messages flash from your keyboard to distant parts of the world is astonishing. You can send a message to a friend in England or China and within a few minutes, it will arrive in their mailbox. If they happen to be online when your mail arrives, you may get a reply before you have finished reading the next message in your mailbox!

But how does it all work?

When you send e-mail to someone, certain things must happen on the *client side* (that is, your personal computer) and certain things happen on the *server side* (the machine that handles e-mail to your part of the network). On larger corporate and commercial networks, e-mail services are handled on a dedicated machine known as the *mail server*. All this machine does, 24 hours a day, is sit there waiting for local users to compose messages and click SEND, or for a remote machine to "knock on the

anotherway
. . . to Apply a Border

You can apply a border by using the Borders and Shading dialog box in the Format menu, or you can highlight the text and select the Borders button on the Formatting toolbar

Inserting a pull quote:

1. Select the first paragraph under the heading **Get it right . . . or don't bother!** on the third page

2. Click on **Center, Times New Roman, 12 point, Italic**

3. On the **Formatting** toolbar, select the **Outside Border** button, and select the **Top Border** button (see Figure 5.7)

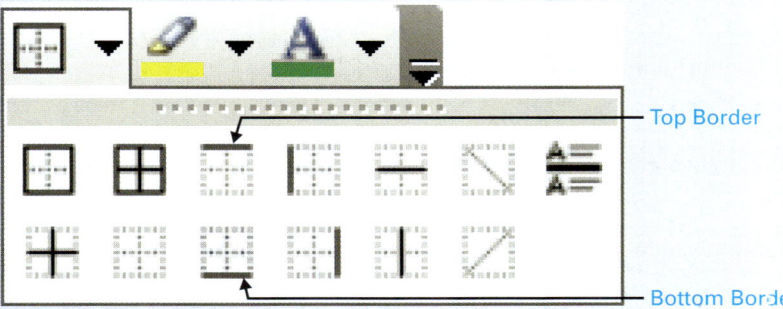

Top Border

Bottom Border

FIGURE 5.7

Top and Bottom Border buttons

4. On the **Formatting** toolbar, select the **Drop-down** button, and select the **Bottom Border** button

5. Compare your work to Figure 5.8

FIGURE 5.8

Pull quote

Get it right ... or don't bother!

If you don't address your message correctly, you might as well not send it at all! It doesn't matter what mail program, browser, or computer you are using. Typing the right e-mail address on the To field is an absolute must.

Every week at the Forrest Hills computing center we receive dozens of messages from people who complain, "Your e-mail addresses aren't working!" And sometimes they're right (mail to a site can bounce for various reasons such as the network being offline, temporary hardware failure, high traffic, or other glitches which can cause e-mail bottlenecks). But more often, when we examine the headers of a bounced message, we find that the sender simply typed the wrong address.

6. Save your document

FIGURE 5.9

Drop Cap dialog box

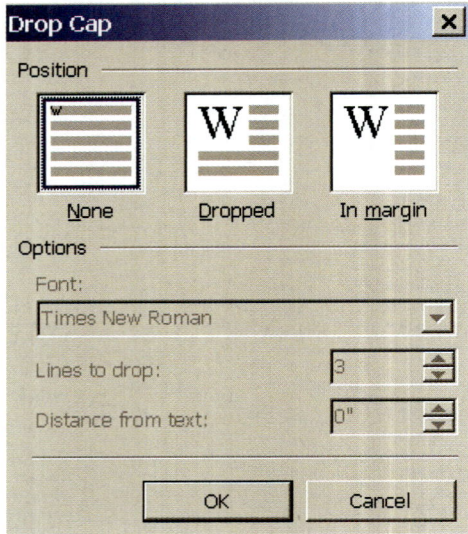

Tim wants his newsletter to jump out at the readers and grab their attention. Tim has decided to add dropped-capital letters to several sections in his newsletter.

---

task reference — Adding a Dropped-Capital Letter

- Click immediately before the text where you want the drop cap to appear
- On the **Format** menu, click on the **Drop Cap** command to view the dialog box displayed in Figure 5.9
- Click the position icon for **Dropped**
- Choose the font, lines to drop, or distance from text
- Click **OK**

Adding a dropped-capital letter to Tim's newsletter:

1. Click immediately before the word **When** under the section **But how does it all work?**

2. Click on the **Format** menu, click **Drop Cap**

3. Click the position **Dropped** and click **OK**

4. Compare your word to Figure 5.10

FIGURE 5.10

Drop cap in Tim's document

But how does it all work?

When you send e-mail to someone, certain things must happen on the *client side* (that is, your personal computer) and certain things happen on the *server side* (the machine that handles e-mail to your part of the network). On larger corporate and commercial networks, e-mail services are handled on a dedicated machine known as the *mail server*. All this machine does, 24 hours a day, is sit there waiting for local users to compose messages and click SEND, or for a remote machine to "knock on the door," so to speak, with incoming mail. Smaller networks sometimes run mail services on a *shared* machine that may also provide World Wide Web hosting and various other things.

Either way, the mail server continuously runs a software program that acts like an electronic post office. This program is known as the Mail Transport Agent (MTA). Essentially these programs all work the same and are compatible with one another.

When a user on a remote system writes a message to you and clicks SEND, the Mail Transport Agent on their network scans the message *headers* for routing and address information, looks up the *IP address*[2] of your machine (every network on the Internet has a unique IP address), and tries to contact your mail server. If successful, it delivers the message and then goes away. Your

---

5. Click immediately before the word **Many** under the section **What's in a Message?** and repeat steps 2 and 3

6. Click immediately before the word **The** under the section **Sound mind, healthy body** and repeat steps 2 and 3

7. Click immediately before the word **On** under the section **Your signature** and repeat steps 2 and 3

8. Click immediately before the word **There** under the section **What's in a name?** and repeat steps 2 and 3

9. Click immediately before the word **Unlike** under the section **Flaming** and repeat steps 2 and 3

10. Click immediately before the word **Most** under the section **Electronic shorthand** and repeat steps 2 and 3

11. Save your document

help yourself *Click the **Ask a Question** combo box, type **Drop cap**, and press **Enter**. Click the hyperlink **Remove a Large Dropped Initial Capital Letter** to display information on how you can remove dropped-capital letters. Click the Help screen **Close** button when you are finished*

Display Readability Statistics

One thing to keep in mind when you are producing a newsletter is your target audience. A newsletter could be read by people of varying ages or by a specific group such as first graders. You can easily check the readability level of your document by turning on the readability statistics feature in Word. The readability statistics feature will analyze your document and tell you the average grade level that will be able to read your document.

---

task reference   Turning on Readability Statistics

- On the **Tools** menu, click **Options**, and then click the **Spelling & Grammar** tab

- Select the **Check grammar with spelling** check box

- Select the **Show readability statistics** check box, and then click **OK**

- On the **Standard** toolbar, click **Spelling and Grammar**

- When Microsoft Word finishes checking spelling and grammar, it displays information about the reading level of the document

---

making the grade

SESSION 5.1

1. A _____ is a phrase or sentence pulled out of the main text, enlarged, and typically used to emphasize a key point.

2. A _____ is an enlarged letter at the beginning of a paragraph used to capture the reader's attention and emphasize the associated text.

3. A _____ is light text on a dark background and is used to call attention to specific text.

4. Desktop _____ is the combination of text and graphics to produce a high-quality, professional looking document.

5. Desktop publishing can include such things as _____, brochures, and posters.

SESSION 5.2 WORKING WITH COLUMNS

Setting Up Columns

As Figure 5.11 illustrates, columns can be used in a variety of ways to improve the readability and overall appearance of a document. Often columns are used to lay out text or a story in newsletters, brochures, and flyers. By using columns you can:

- Create newspaper columns to continue a story in the next column on the same page
- Create linked text boxes to continue a story elsewhere in the same document
- Flow stories in parallel, side-by-side, or in "columns" from page to page
- Specify the number of newspaper columns you want, adjust their width, and add vertical lines between columns
- Add a banner heading that spans the width of the page

The most frequently used columns are newspaper columns that flow the text in the next column on the same page. Tim has decided to change his document to a two-column newspaper style.

---

task reference   **Setting Up Columns**

- Switch to **Print Layout view**
- To format the entire document in columns, click **Select All** on the **Edit** menu

or

- To format part of the document in columns, select the specific text

or

- To format existing sections in columns, click in a section or select multiple sections
- On the Standard toolbar, click **Columns** button
- Drag to select the number of columns you want
- To set exact column widths and spacing, follow the directions in the first two bulleted steps
- Click **Columns** on the **Format** menu, and select the options you want

---

another way
. . . to Apply Columns

You can also apply columns by selecting the Columns item from the Format menu. The columns dialog box is displayed, and you can select the number of columns, width of columns, and area where the columns should be applied

Adding columns to Tim's document:

1. Switch to Normal view, click the **Show/Hide** button on the Standard toolbar if the formatting marks are not currently displayed

2. Press **Ctrl+Home** to move to the top of the document. To create two columns in the entire document click on the first blank line below the Continuous Section Break

FIGURE 5.12

Selecting two columns on the Columns button

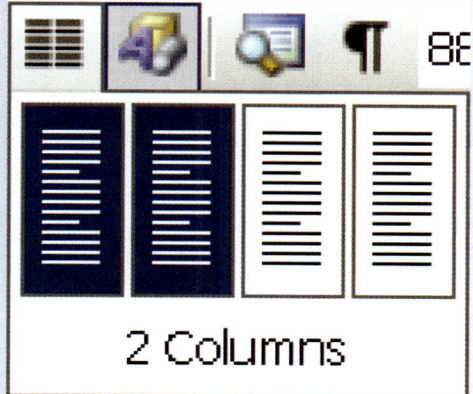

2 Columns

FIGURE 5.13

One page of Tim's document in the two-column format

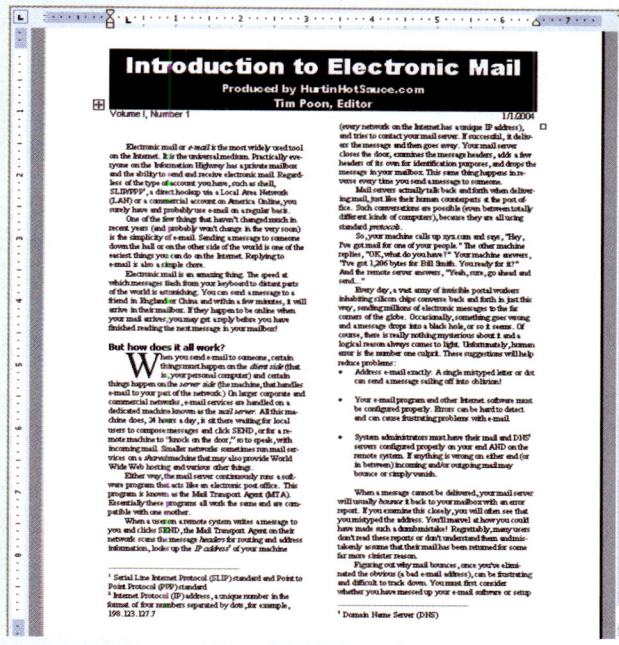

3. Click on the **Columns** button on the Standard toolbar

4. Use the mouse pointer to indicate **two columns** (see Figure 5.12)

5. Compare your results with Figure 5.13

6. Save your document

Adjusting Column Size and Gutter Space

Once you become familiar with columns, you will probably want to change the column size and the gutter space. *Gutter space* is simply the white space between columns.

If the column widths are equal to begin with, all of the columns change as you drag the markers. If the column widths are unequal, only the column you are adjusting changes. To switch between columns of equal and unequal width and specify exact measurements for column widths and spacing, use the Columns command on the Format menu. If you can't widen a column because an adjacent column is in the way, reduce the width of the adjacent column first.

---

task reference   Changing the Width of Columns

- Click on the **Format** menu and click **Columns**
- Set the column widths in the dialog box
- Click **OK**

Changing the width of Tim's columns:

1. Insert the cursor before the first paragraph

2. Click on the **Format** menu, click on Columns

3. Set the 1st column width to **3.5**

4. Click **OK**

5. Compare your work to Figure 5.14

FIGURE 5.14

Tim's newsletter with uneven column widths

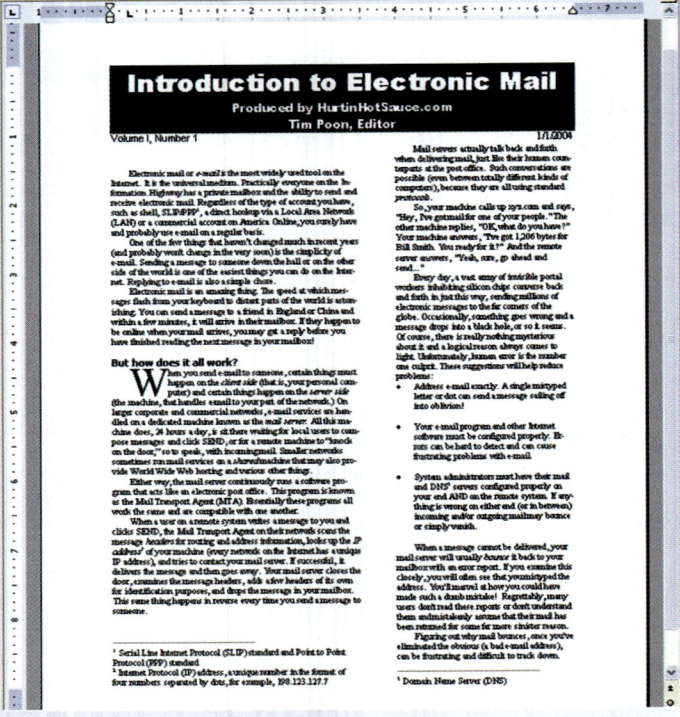

6. Save your document

Inserting Column Breaks

To control columns and to develop the appearance of a document, you will need to force the start of a new newspaper column. When you force the start of a new column, Word moves the text that follows the insertion point to the top of the next column.

---

task reference Forcing the Start of a New Column

- Switch to **Print Layout view**
- Click where you want to start the new column
- On the **Insert** menu, click **Break**
- Click **Column break**

Displaying Multiple Column Format/Same Page

Often a document mixes different column layouts on a single page. For instance, let's assume you have a five-page document and you want to format the center part of page two as three columns. You want the rest of the document to remain a single column. You can overcome this formatting challenge using Word. Word will place selected text into its own section and set it in the number of columns you specified.

task reference — Displaying Multiple Column Format on the Same Page

- Select the text that will appear in the columns
- Choose the **Columns** option from the **Format** menu
- In the **Number of Columns** field, specify the number of columns you desire
- In the **Apply to** box, make sure it says **Selected Text**
- Click your mouse on **OK**

anotherword   . . . Balancing Text in Columns

In order to create a visually appealing document try to ensure you have the same amount of text in each column on a page. For example, try not to have one column full of text and the other column with only a few lines of text. If you run into this problem, you can add more text, more graphics, or try to balance the text between the two columns

help yourself *If you find that one column is full of text and another column only has a few lines of text, you might want to balance the text so that it is evenly distributed between the two columns. Click the **Ask a Question** combo box, type **Columns**, and press **Enter**. Click the hyperlink **Balance newsletter-style column length on a page** to display information on how you can balance the column length on a page. Click the Help screen **Close** button when you are finished*

making the grade   SESSION 5.2

1. Can a document contain columns of varying widths?
2. The Columns button is located on the _____ toolbar.
3. _____ space is the white space between columns.
4. Can you force the start of a new column?
5. To select a Continuous section break, you first select the _____ menu.

SESSION 5.3 CREATING THE NEWSLETTER LAYOUT

Grids

When you first begin working on your newsletter, you need to develop the layout. The *layout* displays how the document is going to look. Most desktop publishers use a grid to define the layout. A *grid* is an invisible set of horizontal and vertical lines that determine the organization of a newsletter (see Figure 5.15). A grid will help to organize your document by displaying the number of columns, widths of the columns, and size of the margins. The most commonly used grid is the three-column grid. Using a grid is a great way to help you organize the content of your newsletter. Once you understand the newsletter grid, or format, you can easily begin to decide where you want particular

F I G U R E   5.15

Three-column grid

F I G U R E   5.16

Tim's document using a three-column grid

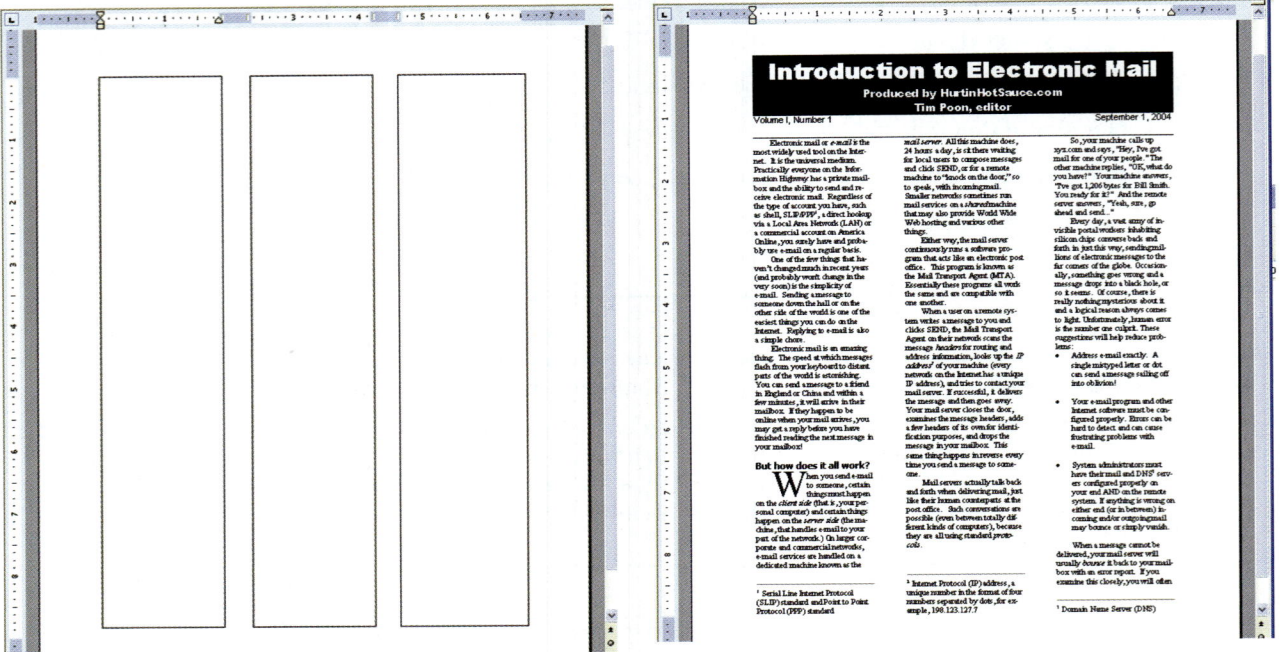

material to be placed. Figure 5.16 displays Tim's document using a three-column grid, Figure 5.17 displays Tim's document using a four-column grid, and Figure 5.18 displays Tim's document using a five-column grid.

help yourself *Click the **Ask a Question** combo box, type **Columns**, and press **Enter**. Click the hyperlink **Change the number of newsletter-style columns** to display information on how you can quickly change the number of columns in a document. Click the Help screen **Close** button when you are finished*

---

another word   . . . **Changing the Number of Columns**

Try changing the number of columns in your grid to add creativity to your document. Having different numbers of columns is a great way to grab your reader's attention

---

task reference   Changing the Number of Columns

- On the **Format** menu, click on **Columns** to view the Columns dialog box (see Figure 5.19)
- Enter in the number of columns
- Click **OK**

Tim has decided to change his newsletter to three columns since this is the most common format for newsletters.

FIGURE 5.17

Tim's document using a four-column grid

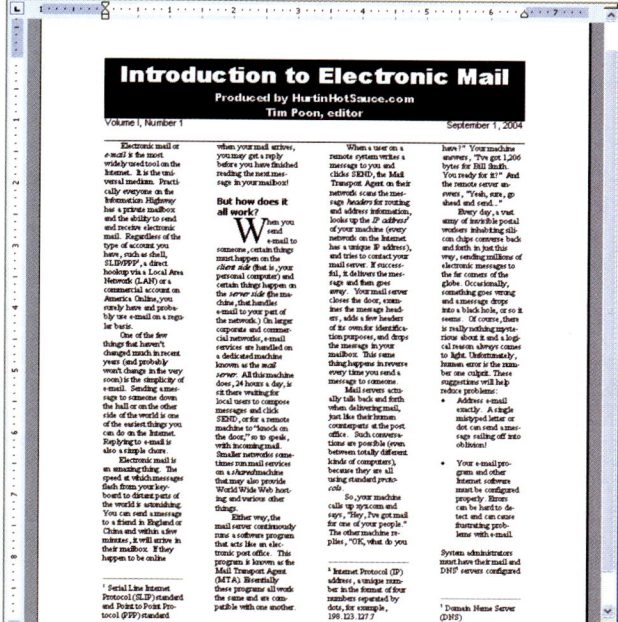

FIGURE 5.18

Tim's document using a five-column grid

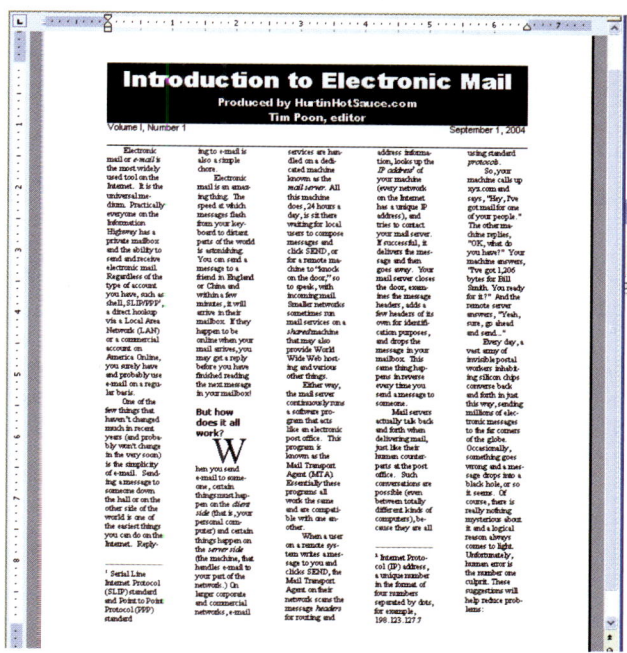

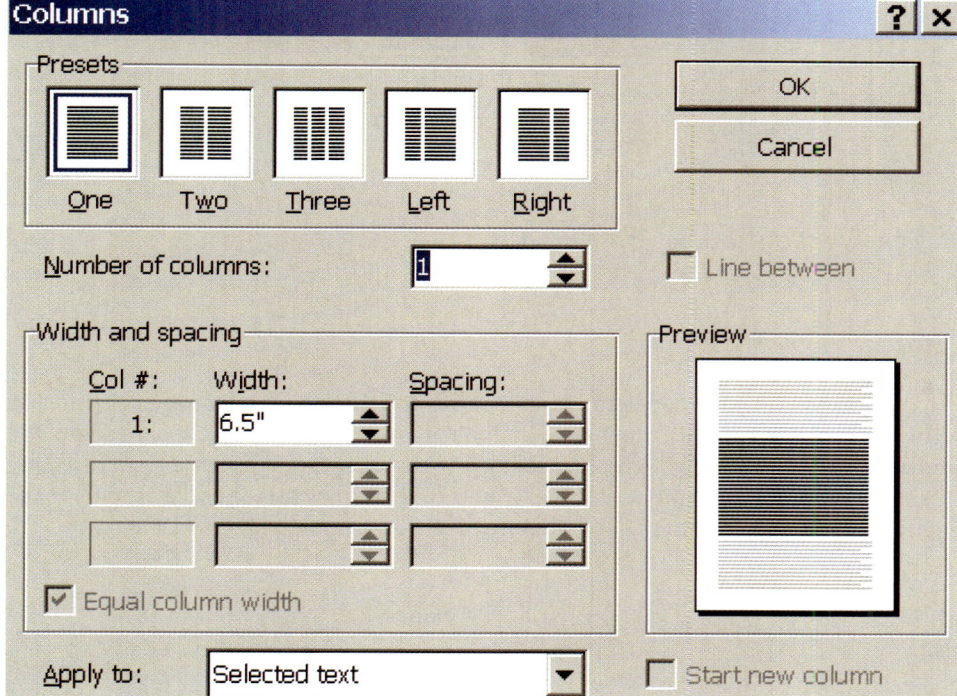

FIGURE 5.19

Columns dialog box

Inserting additional columns in Tim's document:

1. Insert the cursor before the first word in the first paragraph

2. Click on the **Format** menu, and click **Columns**

3. Set the 1st column width to **1.85**

4. Click on the Presets **Three** and put a checkmark in the **Line Between** box

5. Click **OK**

6. Compare your work to Figure 5.20

FIGURE 5.20

Tim's document with three columns and lines between

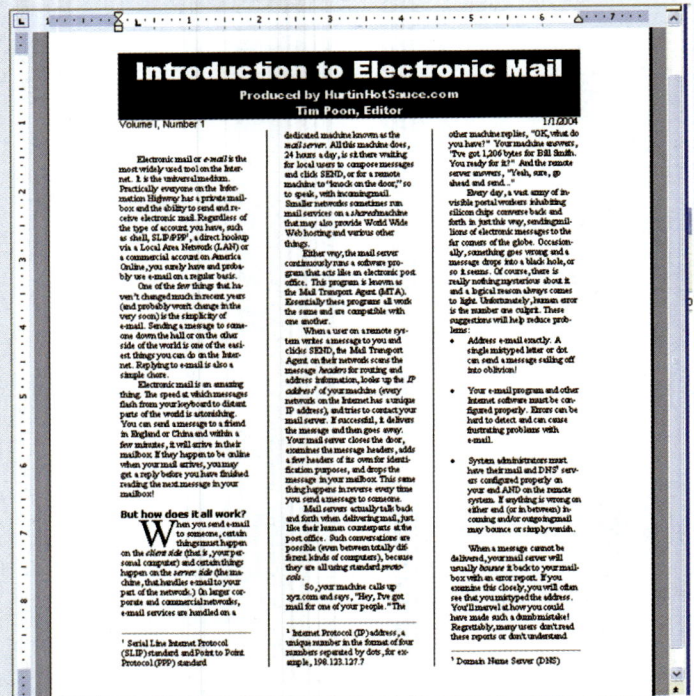

7. Save your document

Inserting Graphics

Placing graphics in your newsletter is a great way to grab your reader's interest and add some creativity in your document. If you look at any magazine or newspaper, you will probably notice lots of great graphics that are used to capture your attention. Inserting clip art or graphics into your newsletter is easy to do. Tim wants to add a graphic to his document to help his readers know that the newsletter is about e-mail.

Inserting a clip art in Tim's document:

1. Insert the cursor at the beginning of the first sentence in the first paragraph

2. Click on the **Insert** menu, click **Picture**, click **Clip Art**

3. Type **e-mail** in the search text section and click **Search**

4. Select an appropriate e-mail graphic

5. Double-click on the graphic to insert it into the first column of the document

6. Compare your work to Figure 5.21 (your graphic might be different)

7. Save your document

FIGURE 5.21

Tim's document with a graphic inserted

Produced

Volume I, Number 1

Elec-
tronic mail or *e-mail* is the most

sona
happ
chine
part
poral
e-ma
dedic
mail
24 h
for 1

Text Wrapping

When you insert a graphic, you can choose if you want the text to wrap around the graphic. **Text wrapping** determines the way text is positioned around a graphic. Tim has decided that he wants to wrap the text around his graphic.

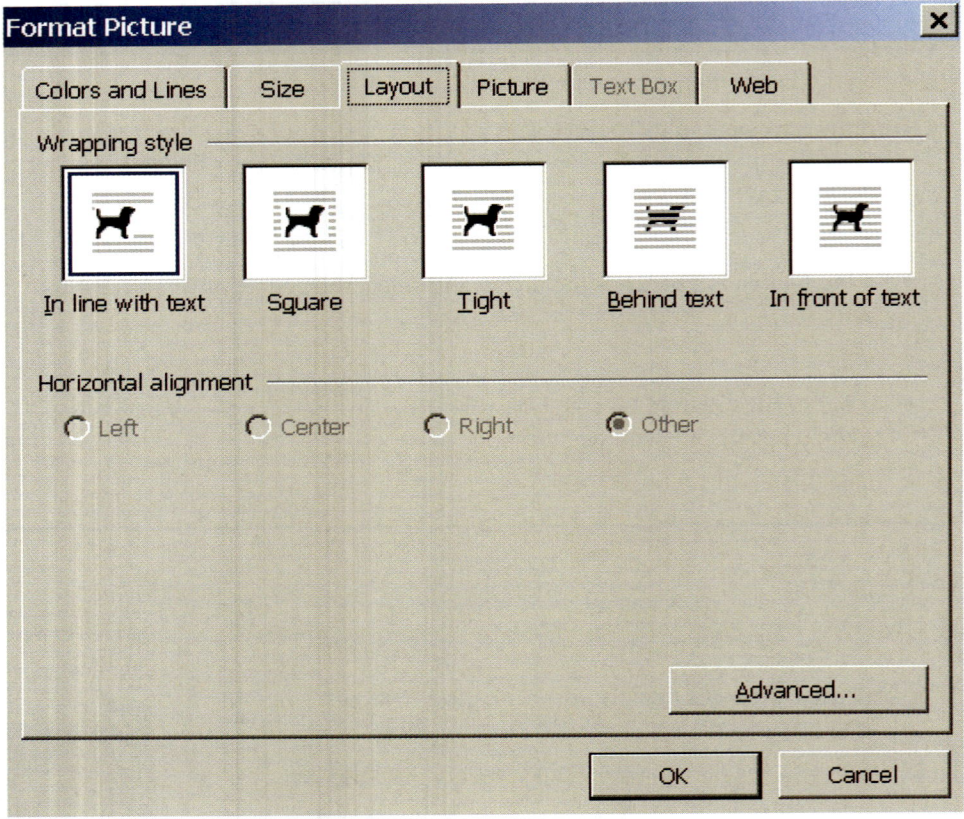

Wrapping text around Tim's graphic:

1. Click on the graphic

2. Click on the **Format** menu, click **Picture**, and click the **Layout** tab

3. Select **Square** wrapping style and **Other** alignment

4. Click **OK**

5. Size the clip art by clicking anywhere on the graphic, which will display the sizing handles

6. Drag a corner handle to change the length and width of the picture while keeping the object in proportion

7. Compare your work to Figure 5.23 (your graphic might be different)

8. Save your document

Inserting Bullets and Numbering

You can insert bullets and numbers into your newsletter exactly the same way as you inserted them into a regular document (see Figure 5.24).

FIGURE 5.23

Tim's document with text wrapped around the graphic

Prod

Volume I, Number 1

Electronic mail or *e-mail* is the most widely used tool on the Internet. It is the universal medium. Practically everyone on the Information Highway  has a private mailbox and the ability to send and receive electronic mail. Regardless of the type of account you have, such as shell, SLIP/PPP[1], a direct hookup via a Local Area

FIGURE 5.24

Bullets in a newsletter

right. Unfortunately, human error is the number one culprit. These suggestions will help reduce problems:

- Address e-mail exactly. A single mistyped letter or dot can send a message sailing off into oblivion!

- Your e-mail program and other Internet software must be configured properly. Errors can be hard to detect and can cause frustrating problems with e-mail.

- System administrators must have their mail and DNS[3] servers configured properly on your end AND on the remote system. If anything is wrong on either end (or in between) incoming and/or outgoing mail may bounce or simply vanish.

When a message cannot be delivered, your mail server will usually *bounce* it back to your mailbox with an error report. If you ex-

---

task reference   Adding Bullets or Numbers

- **Select** the items you want to add bullets or numbers

- On the Formatting toolbar, do one of the following:

- To add bullets, **click** Bullets button

or

- To add numbering, **click** Numbering button

Inserting Borders and Shading

Borders and shading help to enhance the look of any newsletter. Borders and shading can be added to a newsletter in exactly the same way as you would add them to a regular document.

---

task reference   Adding Borders and Shading

- Select the column where you want to apply a border or shading

- On the **Format** menu, click **Borders and Shading**

- Select the **Borders** tab and apply the desired border

or

- Select the **Shading** tab and apply the desired shading

Inserting AutoShapes and Text Boxes

You can also insert AutoShapes and text boxes into your newsletter to enhance its appearance.

task reference	Inserting an AutoShape

- On the Drawing toolbar, click **AutoShapes**, point to a category, and then click the shape you want
- To insert a shape with a predefined size, click the document
- To insert a different size, drag the shape to the size you want
- To maintain the shape's width-to-height ratio, hold down **Shift** while you drag the shape
- To add color, change borders, rotate, add shadow, or 3-D effects select the object, and then use the buttons on the Drawing toolbar

task reference	Creating a Text Box

- On the Drawing toolbar, click the **Text Box** button
- To insert a text box with a predefined size, click the document
- To insert a text box with a different size, drag its sizing handles until the text box is the size you want
- To maintain the text box's width-to-height ratio, hold down **Shift** while you drag the sizing handles
- Position the text box by dragging it to the location you want

Inserting a text box

1. Add a blank line after the last line in the document

2. Click on the **Text box** button in the drawing toolbar

tip: *If the Drawing toolbar is not displayed, select View, Toolbars, Drawing*

3. Insert a text box and size it to take up the additional space in the last column

4. Using **Arial black, 26 point, bold**, type in **For additional comments or questions please contact Tim Poon at x5155**

5. Center the text and use the enter key to arrange the text so the words are not hyphenated

6. Press the **Enter** key **3** times, insert a clip art near the bottom of the text box that is appropriate to the subject (you choose the clip art)

7. Compare your work to Figure 5.25

8. Save your document

FIGURE 5.25

Tim's text box on the last page of his newsletter

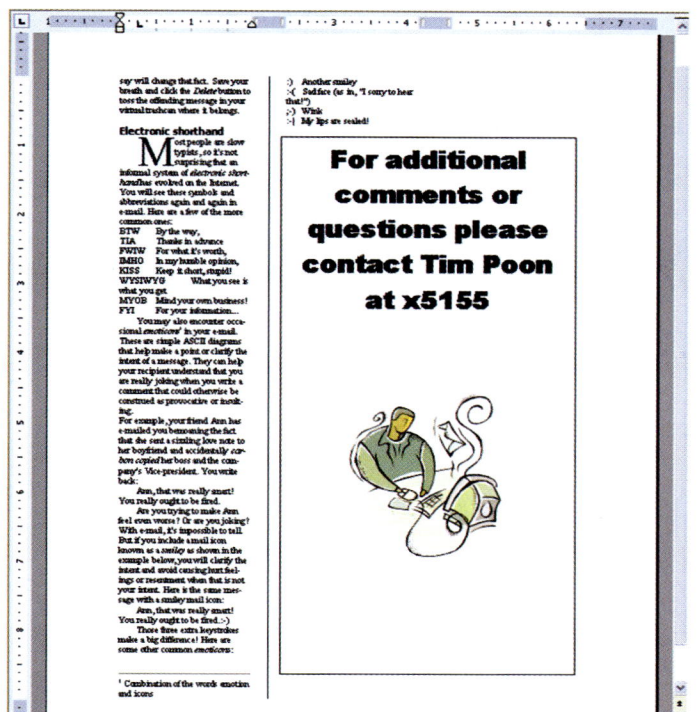

anotherway
. . . to Emphasize Text

You can make it easy for your reader to understand what is important in your newsletter by emphasizing text. You have already learned a number of ways to emphasize text including adding a dropped-capital letter and a pull quote. Don't forget that you can also underline, *italicize*, and **bold** text to help bring your reader's attention to certain areas of your document

---

making *the grade*

SESSION 5.3

1. The _____ displays how the document is going to look.

2. A _____ is an invisible set of horizontal and vertical lines that determine the organization of a newsletter.

3. Can you change the number of columns in a newsletter?

4. Text _____ determines the way text is positioned around a graphic.

5. A _____ is an invisible set of horizontal and vertical lines that determine the organization of a newsletter.

SESSION 5.4 SUMMARY

Desktop publishing is the combination of text and graphics to produce a high-quality, professional looking document. This chapter focused on creating a newsletter. Newsletters are typically produced with multiple columns. With the Columns button on the Standard toolbar, a single-column document or selected text can be quickly converted to multiple columns. A multiple-column document is usually easier for the reader to read because it contains shorter lines of text. You can use such things as different fonts, graphics, clip art, pull quotes, shading, and dropped-capital letters to emphasize text in a newsletter. The masthead is the identifying information found at the top of a newsletter. Creating a reverse masthead helps a newsletter jump out and grab the reader's attention.

MICROSOFT OFFICE SPECIALIST OBJECTIVES SUMMARY

- Apply and format columns—MOS WW03S-3-3
- Summarize document content using automated tools—MOS WW03E-2-4

---

making the grade *answers*

SESSION 5.1

1. Pull quote
2. Dropped-capital
3. Reverse
4. Desktop
5. Newsletters

SESSION 5.2

1. Yes
2. Standard

3. Gutter
4. Yes
5. Insert

SESSION 5.3

1. Layout
2. Grid
3. Yes
4. Wrapping
5. Grid

---

task reference summary

Task	Page #	Preferred Method
Adding a dropped-capital letter	WD 5.8	• Click immediately before the text where you want the drop cap to appear • On the **Format** menu, click on the **Drop Cap** command to view the dialog box • Click the position icon for **Dropped** • Choose the font, lines to drop, or distance from text • Click **OK**
Turning on readability statistics	WD 5.9	• On the **Tools** menu, click **Options**, and then click the **Spelling & Grammar** tab • Select the **Check grammar with spelling** check box • Select the **Show readability statistics** check box, and then click **OK** • On the **Standard** toolbar, click **Spelling and Grammar** • When Microsoft Word finishes checking spelling and grammar, it displays information about the reading level of the document
Setting up columns	WD 5.10	• Switch to **Print Layout view** • To format the entire document in columns, click **Select All** on the **Edit** menu or • To format part of the document in columns, select the text or • To format existing sections in columns, click in a section or select multiple sections • On the Standard toolbar, click **Columns** button • Drag to select the number of columns you want • To set exact column widths and spacing, follow steps 1 and 2 • Click **Columns** on the **Format** menu, and select the options you want
Changing the width of columns	WD 5.11	• Click on the **Format** menu and click **Columns** • Set the column widths in the dialog box • Click **OK**

task reference summary

Task	Page #	Preferred Method
Forcing the start of a new column	WD 5.12	• Switch to **Print Layout view** • Click where you want to start the new column • On the **Insert** menu, click **Break** • Click **Column break**
Displaying multiple column format on the same page	WD 5.13	• Select the text that will appear in the columns • Choose the **Columns** option from the **Format** menu • In the **Number of Columns** field, specify the number of columns you desire • In the **Apply to** box, make sure it says **Selected Text** • Click your mouse on **OK**
Changing the number of columns	WD 5.14	• On the **Format** menu, click on **Columns** to view the columns dialog box • Enter in the number of columns • Click **OK**
Inserting a clip art	WD 5.17	• On the **Insert** menu, point to **Picture**, and click **Clip Art** • In the task pane in the **Search** text box, type a word or phrase that describes the image you want or leave the Search text box blank to display all clip art images or • In the **Search in** box, click the arrow and select the collections you want to search or • In the **Results should be** box, click the arrow and select the check box next to the types of clips you want to find • Click **Search**
Wrapping text	WD 5.17	• Click on the graphic where you want to wrap the text • Click on the Format menu, click Picture • Click on the **Layout** tab and select a Wrapping style • Click **OK**
Adding bullets or numbers	WD 5.19	• **Select** the items you want to add bullets or numbers • On the Formatting toolbar, do one of the following: • To add bullets, **click** Bullets button or • To add numbering, **click** Numbering button
Adding borders and shading	WD 5.19	• Select the column where you want to apply a border or shading • On the **Format** menu, click **Borders and Shading** • Select the **Borders** tab and apply the desired border or • Select the **Shading** tab and apply the desired shading
Inserting an AutoShape	WD 5.20	• On the Drawing toolbar, click **AutoShapes**, point to a category, and then click the shape you want • To insert a shape with a predefined size, click the document • To insert a different size, drag the shape to the size you want • To maintain the shape's width-to-height ratio, hold down **Shift** while you drag the shape • To add color, change borders, rotate, add shadow, or 3-D effects select the object, and then use the buttons on the Drawing toolbar
Creating a Text Box	WD 5.20	• On the Drawing toolbar, click the **Text Box** button • To insert a text box with a predefined size, click the document • To insert a text box with a different size, drag its sizing handles until the text box is the size you want • To maintain the text box's width-to-height ratio, hold down **Shift** while you drag the sizing handles • Position the text box by dragging it to the location you want

TRUE/FALSE

1. Desktop publishing is the combination of text and graphics to produce a high-quality, professional looking document.

2. A dropped-capital letter is a small capital letter at the beginning of a paragraph.

3. Gutter space is simply the white space between columns.

4. A reverse is dark text on a light background.

5. Text wrapping determines the way text is positioned around a graphic.

FILL-IN

1. Desktop publishing is the combination of _____ and _____ to produce a high-quality, professional looking document.

2. A grid is an invisible set of _____ and _____ lines that determine the organization of a newsletter.

3. A _____ is a phrase or sentence pulled out of the main text, enlarged, and typically used to emphasize a key point.

4. _____ is the style and appearance of printed matter or the arrangement of composed type.

5. A _____ displays how the document is going to look.

MULTIPLE CHOICE

1. Which of the following is not included as a type of desktop publishing?
   a. Newsletters
   b. Brochures
   c. Posters
   d. None of the above

2. Which of the following is not a valid column format?
   a. Two-column
   b. Three-column
   c. Five-column
   d. None of the above

3. What is a phrase or sentence pulled out of the main text and enlarged?
   a. Pull quote
   b. Reverse
   c. Dropped-capital letter
   d. None of the above

4. What is a large capital letter at the beginning of a paragraph used to capture the reader's attention and emphasize the associated text?
   a. Pull quote
   b. Reverse
   c. Dropped-capital letter
   d. None of the above

5. What is light text on a dark background and typically used to emphasize specific text?
   a. Pull quote
   b. Reverse
   c. Dropped-capital letter
   d. None of the above

REVIEW QUESTIONS

1. What is a pull quote?

2. Name two different types of desktop publishing materials.

3. Why would you use a grid?

4. What is typography?

5. What is a masthead and why is it important?

CREATE THE QUESTION

For each of the following answers, create an appropriate, short question.

ANSWER	QUESTION
1. Masthead	_____
2. Reverse	_____
3. Typography	_____
4. Layout	_____
5. Grid	_____
6. Desktop publishing	_____

FACT OR FICTION

1. A reverse uses light text on a dark background in order to emphasize specific text and can usually be found in the masthead.

2. Desktop publishing is the combination of text and graphics to produce a high-quality, professional looking document and includes such things as newsletters, brochures, and posters.

3. Desktop publishing essentials include columns, multiple fonts, graphics, clip art, borders and shading, pull quotes, dropped-capital letters, and reverses.

4. A masthead is the identifying information found at the top of a newsletter containing information such as the date of publication, title, and volume or number of the newsletter.

5. A grid is an invisible set of horizontal and vertical lines that determine the organization of a newsletter and can contain anywhere from one column to three columns.

1. Changing the Columns in Tim's Document

You are currently employed at HurtinHotSauce.com and Tim has come to you with his first three-column newsletter. Tim has asked you for your expert opinion on the format of the newsletter. After reviewing Tim's newsletter, you suggest that Tim might want to see how the document looks with a two-column or a four-column format. Help Tim convert his document into different formats.

1. Open the document **Email1.doc**

2. Save the document as **Email2.doc**

3. Insert the cursor before the word *Electronic* in the first sentence

4. Click on the **Format** menu, and click on **Columns**

5. Select Presets **2**, remove the checkmark in the Line Between check box

6. Click **OK**

7. Scroll down to the end of the document and drag the text box up to the right side of the last page

8. With the text box selected, **right click** and **select Format Text Box**, select the **Size** tab, and make the width **3.3** inches

9. Drag the text box to the right to align with the column on the previous page

10. Compare your document to Figure 5.26

11. Save your document

12. Resave the document as **Email3.doc**

13. Insert the cursor before the word *Electronic* in the first sentence

14. Click on the **Format** menu, and click on **Columns**

15. Change to **4** in the Number of columns text box

16. Change the column spacing to **0.35"**

17. Click **OK**

18. Scroll down to the end of the document and drag the text box up to align with the right columns, as done before

19. Compare your document to Figure 5.27

20. Save your document

FIGURE 5.26

Tim's two-column newsletter

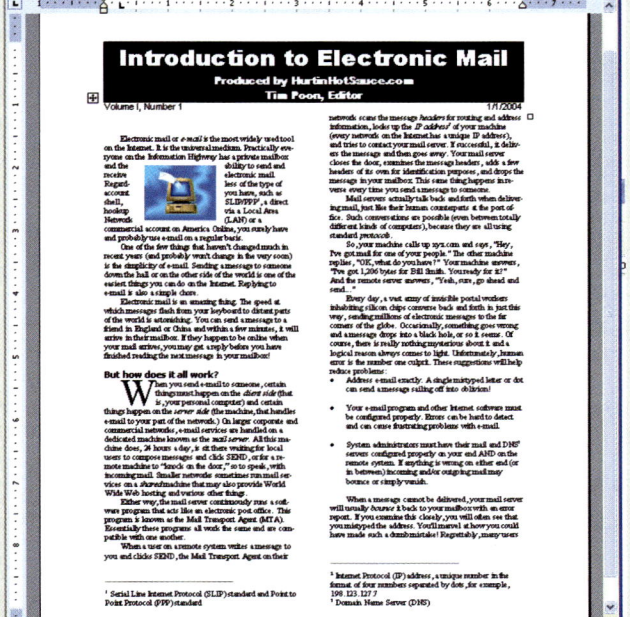

FIGURE 5.27

Tim's four-column newsletter

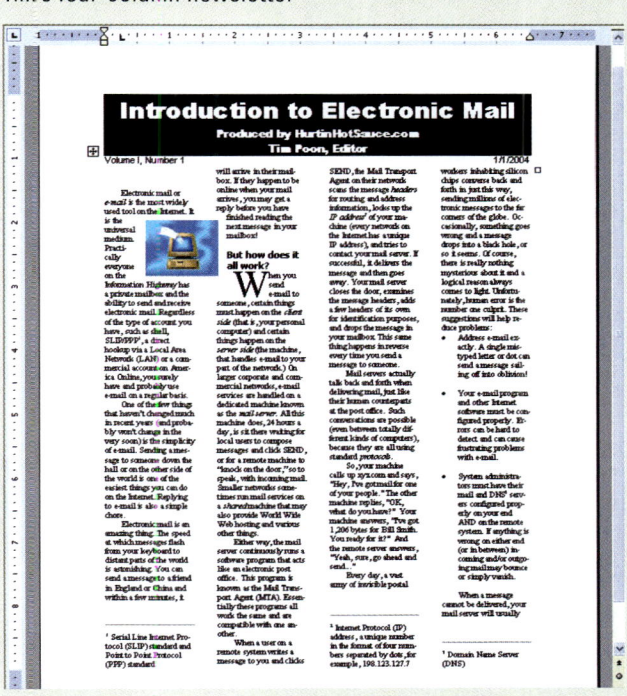

2. Emphasizing Text in a Newsletter

A great way to capture your reader's attention is to try to emphasize text in specific areas of a newsletter. For example, you might use a reverse in the masthead or a pull quote on important information in the first page. You are a volunteer for the Denver Animal Shelter. You are anxious to create a newsletter that highlights all of the different breeds of dogs available at the shelter. The newsletter will be used to help attract people to the shelter to adopt the many different breeds of dogs available. Currently, the Animal Shelter does provide its customers with a document discussing the different types of dogs; however, this document is in a single-column format and contains few graphics (see Figure 5.28). You decide to put your desktop publishing skills to work and help create a new, more attractive newsletter.

1. Open the document **wd05Dogs.doc**

2. Save the document as **Dogs1.doc**

3. Select the heading **Adopting a Dog**

4. Change the font to **Verdana, 18** point, **bold**, and **centered**

5. Click to the right of the line, press enter, and type **YOUR GUIDE TO DOG BREEDS**

6. Select the entire heading and click on **Format, Borders and Shading, Shading** tab, and select **Solid 100%** style and click **OK**

7. Insert the cursor before the first word **Are** in the first sentence and press **Enter**

8. Place the cursor on the blank line directly below the heading and click on **Insert, Break**, select **Continuous**, and click **OK**

9. Insert the cursor before the first word **Are** in the first sentence and select **Format, Columns**, and select **Presets Three** and click **OK**

10. Select **Format, Drop Cap**, select **Dropped**, and click **OK**

11. Compare your work with Figure 5.29

12. Save your document

F I G U R E   5.28

Original Denver Animal Shelter newsletter

ADOPTING A DOG

Are you planning on adding a dog to your family? Adding a dog to your family is a lifetime commitment for the animal. That cute puppy dog you buy for your child's 5th birthday will probably be around for that child's graduation from high school. When deciding which type of breed to adopt be sure to research the breed and make sure there is a good fit between the animal and your lifestyle. The following is a list of breeds we can help you adopt. Please contact us directly with any adoption questions.

WORKING DOGS

Akita
Alaskan Malamute
Anatolian Shepherd
Bernese Mountain Dog
Boxer
Bullmastiff
Doberman Pinscher
Giant Schnauzer
Great Dane
Great Pyrenees
Greater Swiss Mountain Dog
Komondor
Kuvasz
Mastiff
Newfoundland
Portuguese Water Dog
Rottweiler
St. Bernard
Samoyed
Siberian Husky
Standard Schnauzer

HERDING DOGS

Australian Cattle Dog
Australian Shepherd

F I G U R E   5.29

New Denver Animal Shelter newsletter

**ADOPTING A DOG
YOUR GUIDE TO DOG BREEDS**

Are you planning on adding a dog to your family? Adding a dog to your family is a lifetime commitment for the animal. That cute puppy dog you buy for your child's 5th birthday will probably be around for that child's graduation from high school. When deciding which type of breed to adopt be sure to research the breed and make sure there is a good fit between the animal and your lifestyle. The following is a list of breeds we can help you adopt. Please contact us directly with any adoption questions.

WORKING DOGS

Akita
Alaskan Malamute
Australian Shepherd

St. Bernard
Samoyed
Siberian Husky
Standard Schnauzer

HERDING DOGS

Australian Cattle Dog
Australian Shepherd
Bearded Collie
Belgian Malinois
Belgian Sheepdog
Belgian Tervuren
Border Collie
Bouvier des Flandres
Briard
Canaan Dog
Cardigan Welsh Corgi
Collie (smooth/rough)
German Shepherd
Old English Sheepdog
Pembroke Welsh Corgi
Puli
Shetland Sheepdog

TERRIERS

Airedale Terrier
American Staffordshire Terrier
Australian Terrier
Bedlington Terrier

Norwich Terrier
Scottish Terrier
Sealyham Terrier
Skye Terrier
Soft-Coated Wheaten Terrier
Staffordshire Bull Terrier
Welsh Terrier
West Highland White Terrier

TOY DOGS

Affenpinscher
Brussels Griffon
Chihuahua
Chinese Crested
Cavalier King Charles Spaniel
English Toy Spaniel
Havanese
Italian Greyhound
Japanese Chin
Maltese
Miniature Pinscher
Manchester Terrier
Miniature Poodle
Papillon
Pekingese

1. Making a Three-Column Newsletter

Environment 4-Sure is a start-up company that helps save and protect the environment. The company is located outside of Chicago and has 120 employees. You have been hired as the senior publisher. Your first assignment is to revamp the current newsletter.

The data file named **wd05Environment.doc** contains a rough draft of a newsletter from Environment 4-Sure.com. The newsletter needs to be two pages (front and back) in a three-column format with the headings in Arial bold 12-point font. The body text should be Times New Roman in a font size large enough to fill the two pages. The masthead of the newsletter should be composed of the following two lines in Arial 24-point bold, centered:

- **The Environment 4-Sure.com**
- **Volume 1**

Start the columns after the masthead with a horizontal line that runs from the left to right margin. Prevent the bulleted list from breaking between columns. Ensure that Water Uses is at the top of the third column. Add a dropped-capital letter at the beginning of each of the four sections. Add a graphic at the end of the last column to fill in the empty space. Save your work and compare it to the newsletter in Figure 5.30.

FIGURE 5.30

Newsletter for Environment 4-Sure.com

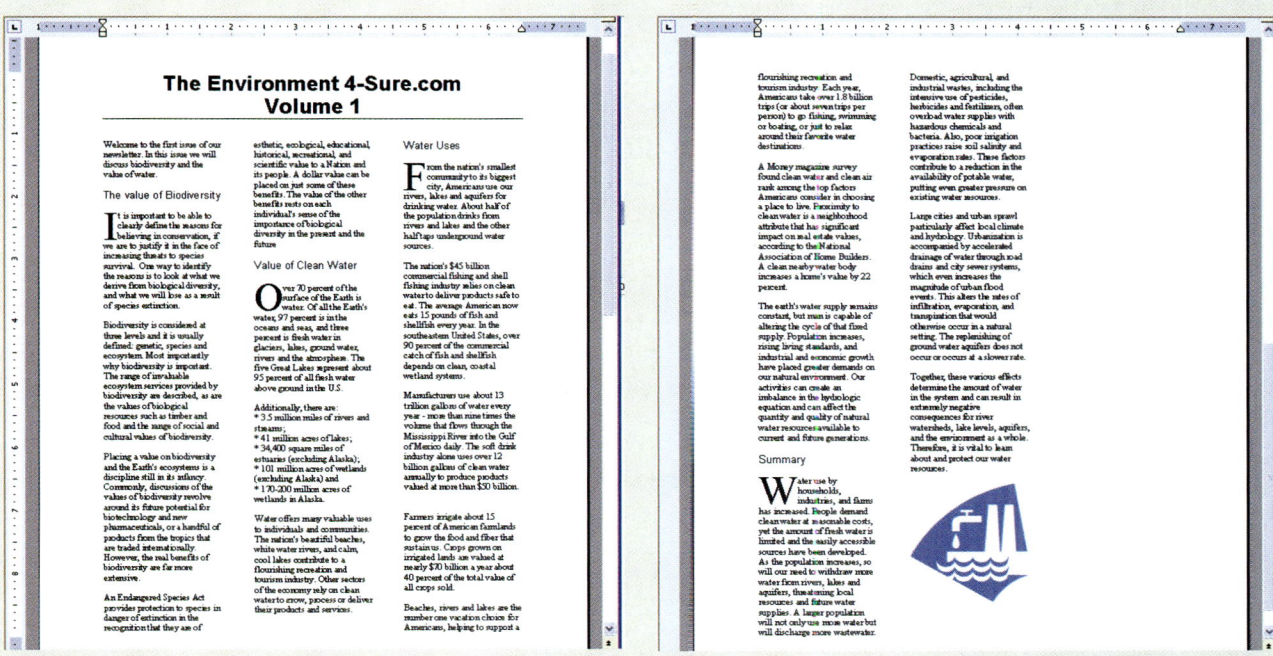

2. Producing a Small Advertising Flyer

You own a small company called Old Pueblo Tours of Tucson. The company takes tour groups around the city to see such exciting sites as the Presidio Park and Old Town Artisans. The local chamber of commerce offers a rack at the visitors' center for local businesses to place their brochures in order to advertise their businesses. Your flyer or brochure is single-sided and only about 3 inches wide. Therefore, to get the most for your printing dollar you decide to put three of your flyers across a page in a landscape orientation. To do this you will use the columns function in Word.

Retrieve the draft copy of the file named **wd05Tours.doc** from your data files. Save the file as **Tours1.doc**. Use your desktop publishing skills to create an attractive flyer. Try to use variations of bold, italic, Arial, and Times New Roman for the fonts. Use pull quotes and dropped-capital letters to emphasize text. Figure 5.31 provides some visual guidelines for your work. Save your work and print out a copy if required.

FIGURE 5.31

Three copies of a single-page flyer for city tours in three columns

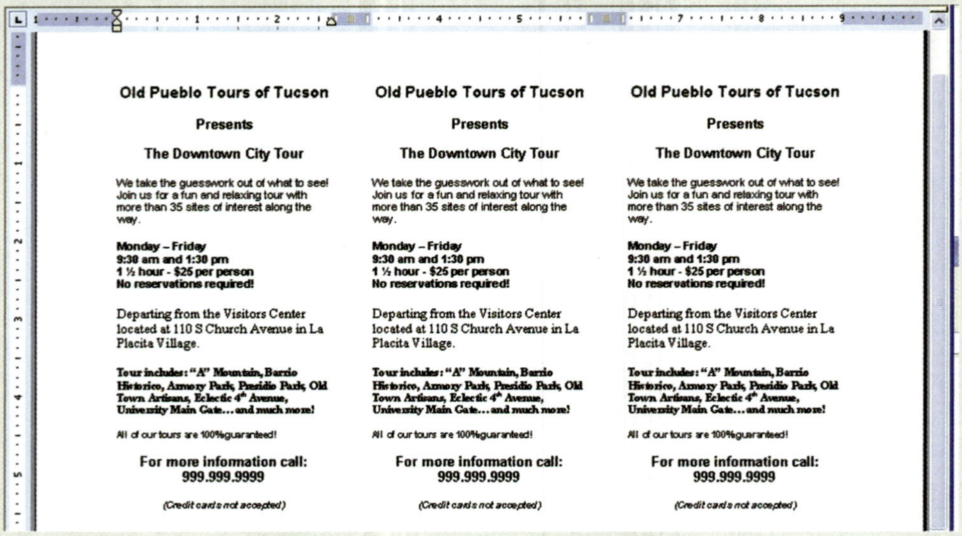

1. CandyHeaven.com

CandyHeaven.com is a new company that is going to buy and sell candy over the Internet. Many of the employees are new to the company and unfamiliar with the different types of candy that the company sells. You have just been hired as the desktop publishing expert at CandyHeaven.com. You are working for Jack Bishop in the Marketing Department. Jack is deeply concerned with the different types of candies that your competitors are going to be offering in the next year. Jack wants to make sure that the employees are thinking of new candies that will beat the competition.

If all of the employees are aware of these different types of candies, then they will be sure to think up new candies that will be competitive. In order to inform all of the other employees about the new candies Jack wants you to create a newsletter discussing all of the different types of candy that is expected to be released over the next year. Jack has already researched the CandyUSA Web site and found the listing of potential new treats. Jack has placed this information in the file named **wd05Candy.doc**. Your job is to transform the document into an attractive newsletter. Figure 5.32 displays a potential format you could use for your newsletter.

FIGURE   5.32

CandyHeaven.com newsletter

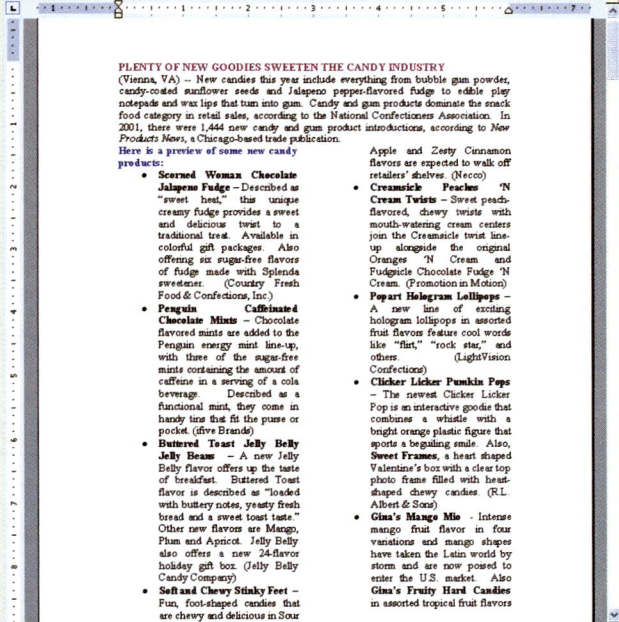

2. Creating a Newsletter for Your School

A newsletter is a great way to transfer information. Your school is currently trying to find new and creative ways to transfer information between the school and the students. You have suggested that the school start a student newsletter. The school is thrilled with your suggestion and has asked you to create the first official student newsletter.

Figure 5.33 displays an example of the student newsletter from Harvard's Web site. You can use this as an example when you are creating your newsletter. Be sure to take advantage of all your desktop publishing skills by including different ways to emphasize text, graphics, and adding clip art. Use different font colors, styles, pull quotes, and dropped-capital letters to help your document appear attractive and easy to read. The content of your newsletter can include anything you want to discuss with your fellow students. Potential topics can include such things as:

- Course schedules
- Upcoming events
- Important dates
- News
- Study tips
- Campus information
- Classifieds
- Personals
- Advertisements

FIGURE   5.33
Sample student newsletter

Lamplighter

The Harvard Extension School Newsletter

Spring 2003   Previous | Next

Mastering the Interview

New Course Enhances Journalism Program

This fall, the Extension School added a course in interviewing to its growing list of journalism courses. Taught by Susan E. Reed, a former Nieman Fellow at Harvard University and an Emmy Award-winning producer for CBS News, the course drew a range of students, including several working journalists seeking to hone their interviewing skills.

Students Delcie Palmer (left) and Ria Riesner (center) discuss writing strategies with instructor Susan E. Reed.

Interviewing, said Reed, is central--not only for students hoping to embark on a career in journalism, but also for anyone who wants to know how to get to "the bottom of things." "The course offers the opportunity to delve deeply into almost any subject, be it a long-time preoccupation with a social problem, a political concern, or a newly discovered career interest," Reed noted. "Over the course of the semester [students] must interview ten sources on one topic. They learn to ask carefully researched questions, listen closely, and, depending on the nature of the story, respond compassionately or challenge the answers. Sometimes they suspect sources of lying or withholding information. Showing students how to cut through such obfuscation is where the challenge begins."

1. Magazines on the Web

Did you know that you can read all kinds of magazines free on the Web? All of the following are magazines available on the Web for free:

- *Forbes*—www.forbes.com
- *Business Week*—www.businessweek.com
- *Rolling Stone*—www.rollingstone.com
- *Automobile Quarterly*—www.autoquarterly.com
- *National Geographic Traveler*—www.nationalgeographic.com/media/traveler
- *Snowboarder*—www.snowboardermag.com
- *Time*—www.time.com
- *Runners World*—www.runnersworld.com

Use the Internet to connect to a few of the online magazines mentioned above. Create a document comparing three of the above-mentioned magazines. Your comparison can include such things as use of graphics, clip art, text emphasis, number of columns, color of text, and so forth. Save your document as **Magazines1.doc**.

2. Creating a Table with Web Site Addresses to Your Favorite Hobbies

As everyone knows, the Internet provides a wealth of information. We all have favorite sites and our reasons for these sites being our favorites. Search the Web and find 10 good sites that give information about your hobbies or interests. Use Word to create a two-column table. In the first column place the site name and in the second column place the site address. Format your table in a professional manner. Save your document as **Favoritesites1.doc**.

FIGURE 5.34

Time magazine Web site

FIGURE 5.35

Rolling Stone magazine Web site

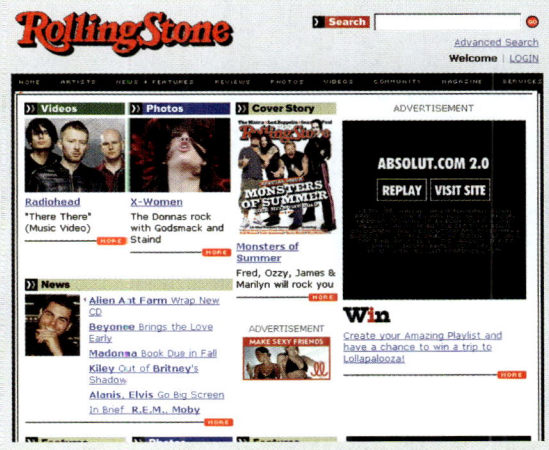

around the world

1. Starting a Travel Brochure

As the owner and operator of Travelight Worldwide Tours you are working on a new travel brochure for a new tour. The new tour offers a seven-day trip around Romania. For now, you are working on the inside two pages of the brochure. The format is two-column, in landscape orientation. From your data files, retrieve the file named **wd05Travelight.doc**. Make the necessary formatting changes to have your document look similar to Figure 5.36. Be certain to prevent any strange breaks in the text as you format it into two-columns. When you have completed your work, save the file as **Travelight1.doc** and compare your work to Figure 5.36.

2. Developing a Directory of International Businesses

Open the document **wd05Directory.doc** and save it as **Directory1.doc**. Search the Web for international e-businesses and choose five that you find interesting and add them to the directory. Include the business name, phone number, country location, and Web site address.

FIGURE 5.36

Inside two pages (columns) of travel brochure

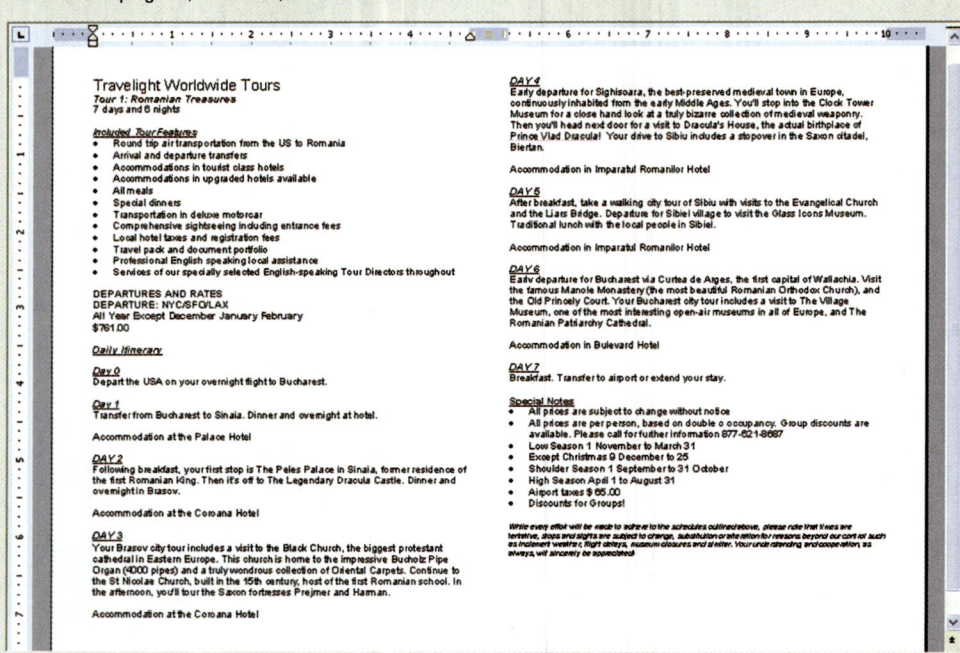

running project

Formatting a Newsletter

The way a page is organized can encourage or discourage readers. Word processing makes enhancements and changes in the organization of pages and documents easy. Consistent use of headings and white space are easily controlled and added with word processing. The Kasota United School District wants to be certain that their newsletter is read and respected.

A two- or three-column document adds to the professionalism and attractiveness of a document. Multiple columns are also desirable because they have shorter lines of text that make them more readable.

The Kasota United School District (KUSD) main office is planning to send out its first ever year-end newsletter to the parents and guardians of all students in the district. This newsletter will be on normal 8½- by 11-inch paper that will be folded

and sent in a legal size envelope. The first draft of the newsletter was put together and submitted to Dr. Alex Trexell, the superintendent, whose letter can be viewed by opening the document **wd05KasotaNewsPrintMe.doc**. Following Dr. Trexell's suggestions the final draft of the newsletter is in a two-column format with all headings in 14-point Arial, bold, underline. The masthead of the newsletter is in 20-point Arial, bold, and the body of the text is in 14-point Times New Roman. Asterisks that were used for bullets are replaced with real bullets. A centered footer at the bottom of each page gives the succinct mission of the district (Quality Education with Standards Educating for the Future). On the second page the $5.00. admission fee is footnoted that in special cases it can be waived. Finally, the spelling is corrected and the file is saved. You can find the original file under **wd05KasotaNews.doc**. Figure 5.37 shows the final newsletter in its completed form.

F I G U R E   5.37

Newsletter in final form

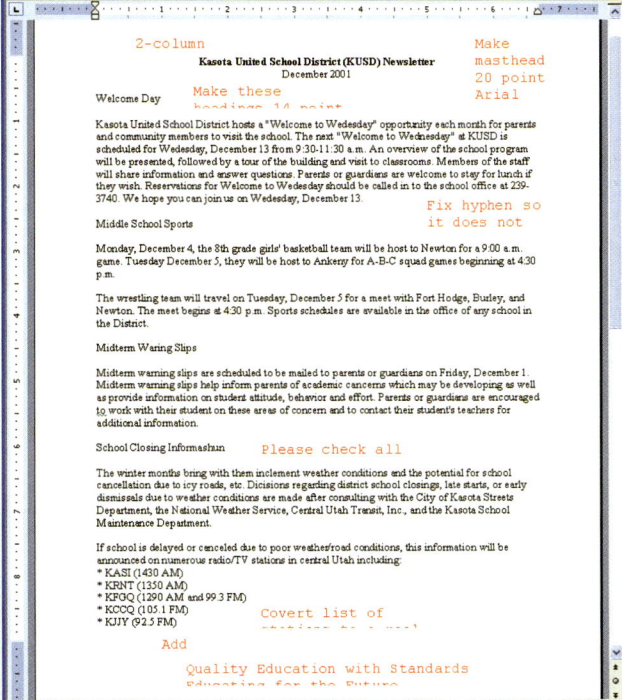

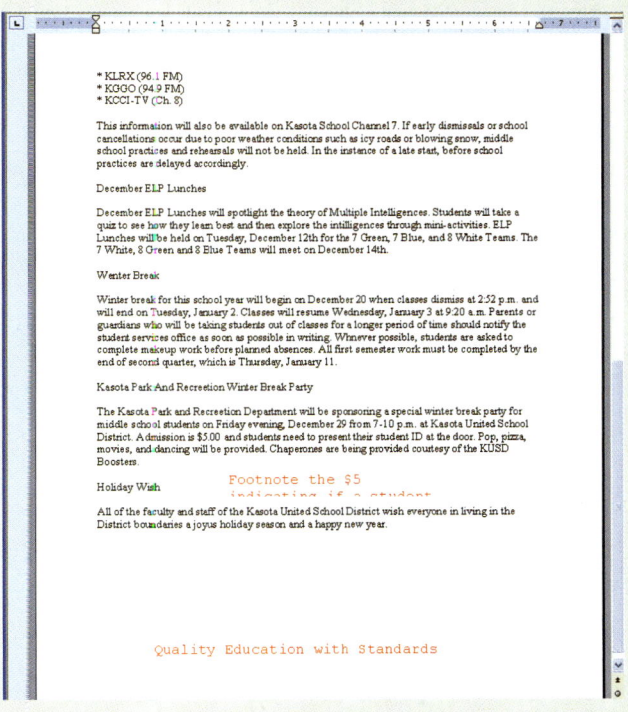

1. Finding Problems in Desktop Publishing

Take a look on the Internet, in a magazine, or around your school and try to find an example of a newsletter that has a bad design. Create a document discussing why the newsletter's design is bad and how you would recommend fixing the design. Be sure to include the original newsletter with your final document.

2. Finding an Online Newsletter

There are numerous newsletters published on the Web. Search the Web for three different newsletters. Discuss the differences between the three different newsletters. Which newsletter did you like the best and why, and which newsletter did you like the least and why?

CHAPTER SIX
6

Merging Documents and Object Linking and Embedding

did you know?

xenon *is one of the noble gases, like helium, neon, and argon. Xenon's symbol is Xe. Although it's present in our atmosphere, its concentrations are below one part per million.*

neon *lighting, discovered and developed by French physicist George Claude, was displayed to the public for the first time at the Paris Motor Show in 1910.*

when *it is closest to the Sun, Pluto is closer than Neptune. But the outer end of its long path is 4.6 billion miles from the Sun. For all but 20 years of its 248-year orbit, Pluto is the outermost known planet in the solar system.*

in *December 1934, U.S. pilot Wiley Post made history when he reached a record altitude of 50,000 feet wearing a pressurized suit that he developed. Post's suit design was essentially the same as that of the space suits worn 35 years later by astronauts.*

on *our heads, individual hairs can grow for up to 10 years. Given the usual growth rate of about 0.013 inch per day, human head hairs might get as long as four feet.*

Chapter Objectives

- **Merge letters with other data sources—MOS WW03E-2-6**
- **Merge labels with other data sources—MOS WW03E-2-7**
- **Insert and modify objects—MOS WW03E-1-4**

Sending Letters to the Membership of NAPE

Marilyn Draper serves as the secretary to a non-profit organization called National Association of Photo Editors (NAPE). The organization has annual membership dues that are paid at the end of each calendar year. In November of each year, Marilyn sends out a membership renewal—the first notice. Then after the first of the new year, about February 1, she sends out a second notice to those members who have not renewed. In years past, she has photocopied a generic letter addressed to "NAPE Member." This year she plans to take a more personal approach, using mail merge to give members a letter addressed to them. Figure 6.1 shows the second notice letter members received.

To send out the letters after they are created, Marilyn will also need to create address labels for the envelopes. Figure 6.2 shows the labels.

After sending out the second notice letter, Clayton William, the president of NAPE, requested a list of those receiving second notices. He wanted the list to include phone numbers so he could give each person a call and encourage them to renew. Fortunately, when Marilyn created the data source for the mail merge, she had also included their phone numbers. Now she could easily create a list with phone numbers as shown in Figure 6.3.

FIGURE 6.1

Second notice letter for NAPE

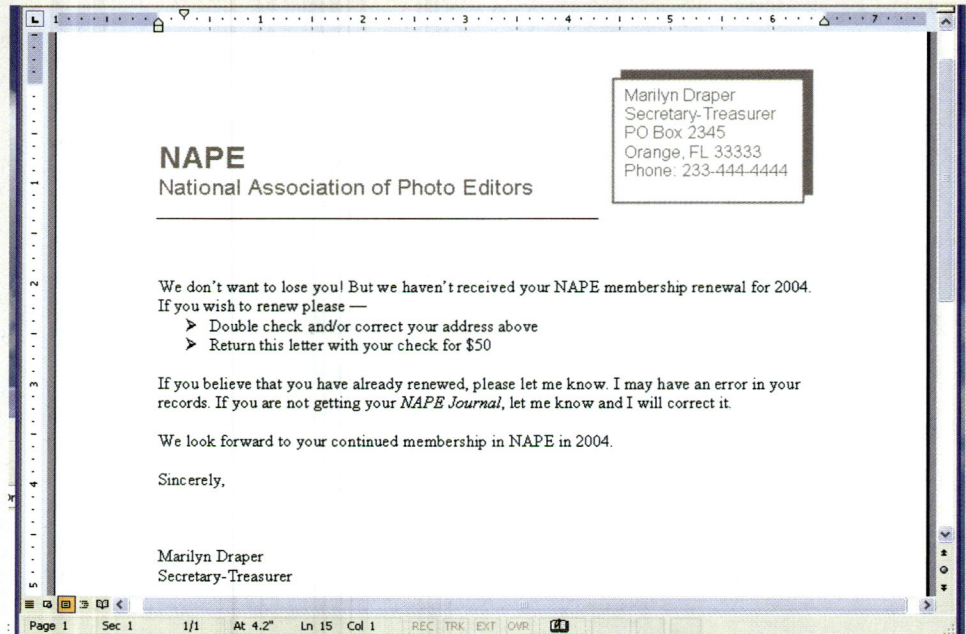

Paul Wehrenberg WC Box 27086 Abilene, TX 79699	Rita Martinez 10 Upper College Drive University Park, IL 14802	Tom Chittick Box C-110 Alpine, VA 79832
Susan Turner 122 Curtiss Hall Ames, WA 50011	JR Pottorff 123 Steiner Rd Fairbanks, MA 01003	Rosa Brandenburg 410 South 3rd St Auburn, MD 36849
LeAnn Marquardt 124 Ag Admin Bldg Laramie, LA 70803	Danny Cook 1180 E Broad St Athens, MO 30602	

Name	Phone
Paul Wehrenberg	354-687-1836
Rita Martinez	797-314-0044
Tom Chittick	886-335-2435
Susan Turner	545-201-2837
JR Pottorff	373-879-3399
Danny Cook	243-786-4738
Rosa Brandenburg	345-275-8694
LeAnn Marquardt	607-449-2257

INTRODUCTION

If you need to send similar, or identical, letters to a group of people, or need to create a list of people who will receive a newsletter or flyer, you will probably want to use the mail merge feature. You might be sending out thank-you letters to people who helped with a workshop or meeting; composing rejection letters at the end of a search process; creating a file of people who will receive monthly mailings during the course of a project; or printing name tags for a conference. In this chapter you are going to learn how to merge letters with a data source in order to produce mail merged documents.

SESSION 6.1 MERGING LETTERS

To merge you need to create two types of documents: (1) a data source and (2) a related form, called the mail merge main document.

- *Data source*: a file that contains the information that varies with each record to be merged into a main document. For example, the list of names and addresses you want to use in a mail merge. You must connect to the data source before you can use the information in it.
- *Main document*: In a mail-merge operation, the document that contains the text and graphics that are the same for each version of the merged document, for example, the return address or salutation in a form letter. It contains the format for the letter, envelope, or mailing list with field references to the data source.

***another*way**
**. . . to Merge
without the Wizard**

You can use the Mail
Merge Wizard, but if
you are familiar with
the concepts of
merging, you can
work outside the
Wizard using the Mail
Merge toolbar. Open
the toolbar by clicking
View, Toolbars, and
selecting Mail Merge.
After clicking the
Main Document
Setup button, a drop-
down list appears
with seven options:
Letters, E-mail
messages, Faxes,
Envelopes, Labels,
Directory, and
Normal Word
document (Figure
6.4). You may change
your selection later if
you plan to use the
data source for more
than one type of
merged document

The main document can be a letter, envelope, mailing label, or another type of document that references the data source. The last step is to combine, or merge, these two documents into a new document. Even if you are sending a similar letter to a unique list of people who you will not need to contact again, it is faster to use the mail merge feature. The alternative—to write one letter, print it, change the address, print the second letter, and so forth—is a time-consuming task. Also, most offices and professionals have a clientele list that is used many times throughout the year or from one year to the next. This is a job for the mail merge feature.

Creating a Main Document

The main document contains the text that will be the same in all of the merged documents. You can create a new main document or use any existing main document. To begin the merge process, open up a new document or have your insertion point at the top of an empty document. The Mail Merge Wizard guides you through all of the steps.

---

task reference   **Using the Mail Merge Wizard**

- To start the Mail Merge Wizard in the task pane, click **Tools, Letters and Mailings, Mail Merge** (Figure 6.5)
- Indicate which type of document by clicking to **select Letters, E-mail messages, Envelopes, Labels**, or **Directory**
- Determine where the document will be found—a new one, a template, or one already saved
- Continue following steps at the bottom of the task pane

---

help yourself *Click the **Ask a Question** combo box, type **Data source**, and press **Enter**. Click the hyperlink **About Mail Merge Data Sources** to display information on how data sources work and how you can connect to different types of data sources. Click the Help screen **Close** button when you are finished*

F I G U R E   6.4

Mail Merge toolbar and
drop-down list of merge
options

click Main Document
Setup button

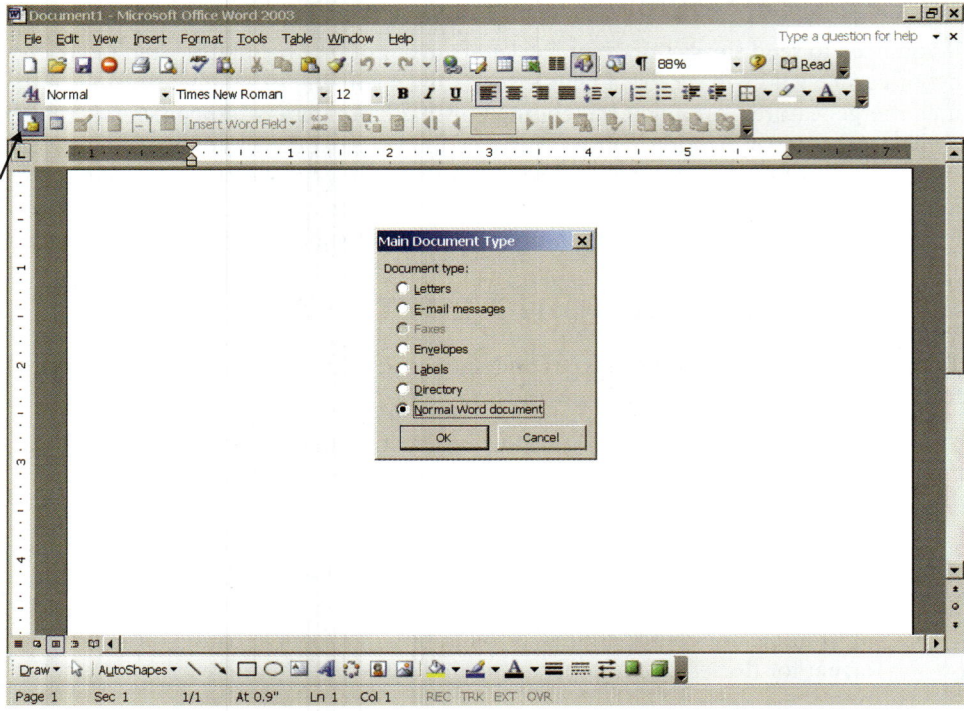

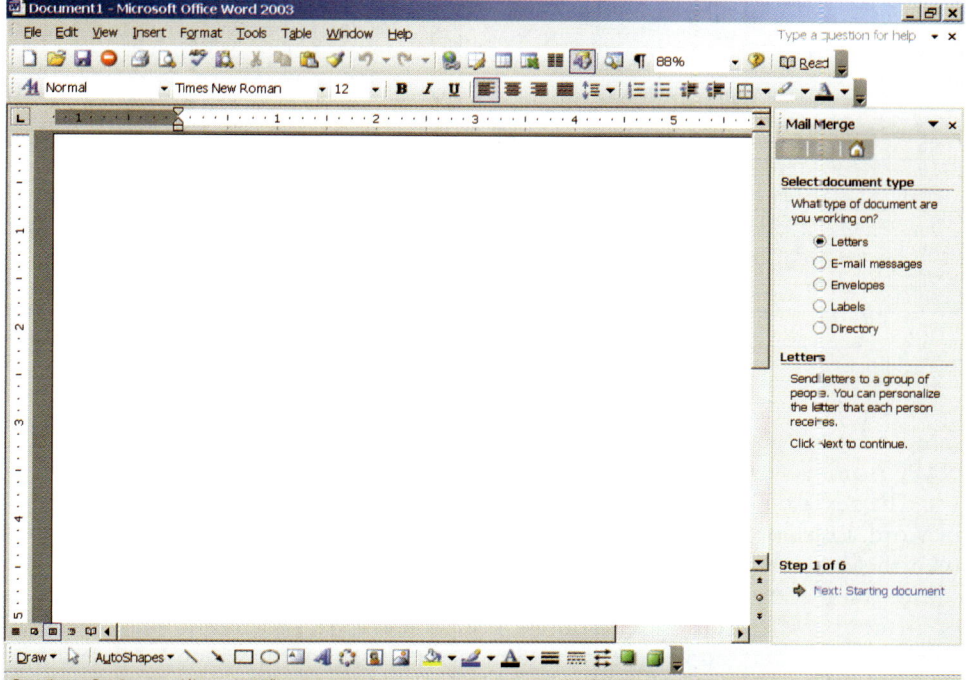

F I G U R E   6.5

Mail Merge Wizard in the task pane

Creating a Data Source

The information that varies from document to document, such as names and addresses for letters, is stored in a document called the data source. The data source is made up of *fields* (data fields), like a person's name, address, and phone number. A related group of fields constitutes a *record*, or *data record*—a group of related information, like information about one person (see Figure 6.6). The first row in a data source is called the *header row* (see Figure 6.7). The header row is made up of a list of field names. When creating a data source, Word provides a list of commonly used field names. You can add or remove names from that list to develop the header row for your data source.

For most of the exercises in this chapter, we will tell you what fields and field names to use, so everyone will be working with the same data source. Figure 6.6 describes a

F I G U R E   6.6

Example of a data source structure

Example of a Data Source Structure

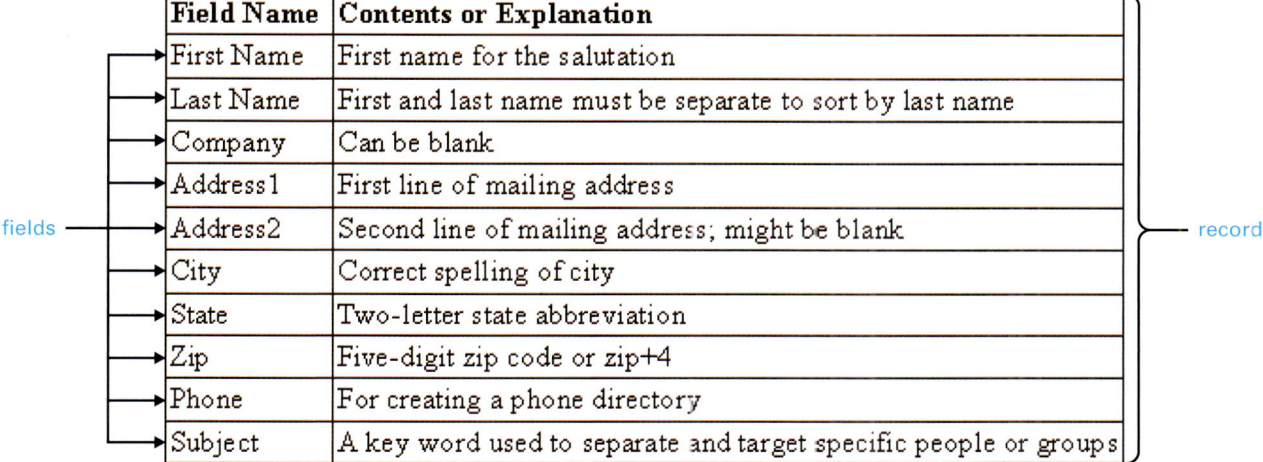

Field Name	Contents or Explanation
First Name	First name for the salutation
Last Name	First and last name must be separate to sort by last name
Company	Can be blank
Address1	First line of mailing address
Address2	Second line of mailing address; might be blank
City	Correct spelling of city
State	Two-letter state abbreviation
Zip	Five-digit zip code or zip+4
Phone	For creating a phone directory
Subject	A key word used to separate and target specific people or groups

fields

record

WORD

F I G U R E   6.7

Data source structure: A short list of NAPE members

First Name	Last Name	Address	City	St	Zip	Phone
Paul	Wehrenberg	WC Box 27986	Abilene	TX	79699	607-449-2257
Rita	Martinez	10 Upper College Dr	University Park	IL	14802	797-314-0044
Tom	Chittick	Box C-110	Alpine	VA	79832	886-335-2435
Susan	Turner	122 Curtiss Hall	Ames	WA	50011	545-201-2837
JR	Pottorff	123 Steiner Rd	Fairbanks	MA	01003	373-879-3399
Danny	Cook	1180 E Broad St	Athens	MO	30602	243-786-4738
Rosa	Brandenburg	410 South 3rd St	Auburn	MD	36849	345-275-8694
LeAnn	Marquardt	124 Ag Admin Bldg	Laramie	LA	70803	607-449-2257

header row →

one record on each row →

each cell represents a field

sample data structure, and Figure 6.7 shows a sample data source structure for the NAPE members used by Marilyn.

The next step is to identify or create the data source. Data for a merge can be saved in Word, Excel, or Access. If the data are not already saved in one of these programs, then the data source needs to be created. Most first-time users will create the data source using Wizard in Word. The Mail Merge Wizard guides you through the process of creating a Microsoft Office Address List. The Wizard provides a form and field names for the data. You will see the field names at the left of the window. These can be customized, added, or deleted (Figure 6.8).

F I G U R E   6.8

Creating a data source using the Mail Merge Wizard in the task pane

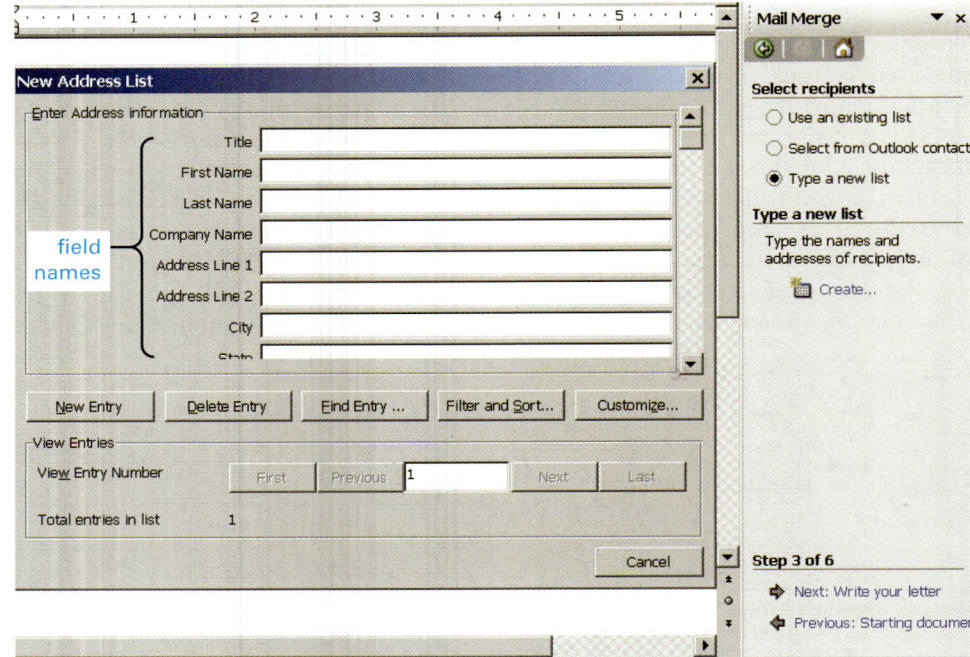

Marilyn is ready to create a small data source of the members of NAPE and then to merge these data into a membership renewal letter. To set up the data source she will type each piece of data in the appropriate window and press Enter or Tab to go to the next field.

task reference
Creating a Data Source with Mail Merge Wizard

- Click **Tools, Letters and Mailings, Mail Merge**
- Select document type
- Click **Next: Starting document**
- Select type of starting document
- Click **Next: Select recipients**
- Select **Type a new list**
- Click **Create**
- Click **Customize** to remove fields
- Enter data
- Click **Close** when all data have been entered into the fields
- Provide filename for data source

Creating a data source and entering data:

1. Open the file named **wd06NapeLetter.doc**

2. Save the file as **NapeLetter1.doc**

3. Type the date two lines below the letterhead, and press **Enter** three times

4. Click **Tools, Letters and Mailings, Mail Merge, Letters**

5. Click **Next: Starting document** at the bottom of the task pane; click **Use the current document**, and click **Next: Select recipients**

6. Click **Type new list**, and click **Create**

7. Click the **Customize** in the New Address List dialog box, and delete the Title, Company Name, Address Line 2, Country, Home Phone, Work Phone, and E-mail Address fields

8. Click **Yes** as each field name is deleted; then click **OK** to return to enter data (see Figure 6.8)

9. Enter the data shown in Figure 6.7 into the boxes to the right of each field name

10. Click **New Entry** as each record is completed

tip: *Figure 6.7 shows a header row of Address; use this information for Address Line 1. Figure 6.7 also lists the phone numbers. Ignore these for now*

11. Click **Close** when all records are entered, and save your document as **NapeNames1**

tip: *The file you just created is saved like an Access file with the extension .mdb and the "key" logo button of Access*

Merging

The actual process of merging consists of inserting *merge fields* in the main document and then merging the data source in the main document. Merge fields specify where you want to insert information from your data source into your main document. Merging the data into the main document creates a unique individual document for each record in the data source.

---

task reference   **Inserting Merge Fields**

- Click **View, Toolbars, Mail Merge**
- On the Mail Merge toolbar, click **Insert Merge Fields** button
- Select the fields and click **Insert**

or

- Using the Mail Merge Wizard, open the **Merge Field dialog box**
- Click **Insert**
- Click **Close**

Marilyn feels that she is ready to merge her letters with the data she has (Figure 6.7); this first time she will rely on the Mail Merge Wizard in the task pane to complete this project.

Note: The next series of steps is a continuation of the merge process. In the first 10 steps above, you set up the data source. You are now ready to add the merge fields to the main document and merge.

Setting up the merge for the NAPE letters:

1. If you have reopened **NapeLetter1.doc**, then click **Tools, Letters and Mailings, and Mail Merge** to open the task pane

2. Click **Next: Write your letter** and select **More items**

tip: *Your document screen should show the **NapeLetter1.doc** as the active document with the current date typed two lines below the letterhead. If you are in Print Layout view, you should see your cursor in front of the third paragraph mark below the date*

3. From the Insert Merge Field dialog box, select the fields and click **Insert** (see Figure 6.9)

tip: *You can insert all of the merge fields and then close the Insert Merge Field dialog box to arrange the fields, as they should appear in box style at the top of the letter. Don't forget to put a comma and space between city and state and a space between the state and the zip code. Your merge fields should look like those in Figure 6.10*

4. Three blank lines below the address block click **More items; Insert** the **First_Name** field from the Insert Merge dialog box; and click **Close**

tip: *Place a colon at the end of the merge field for First_Name and hit **Enter***

5. Compare the placement of your merge fields to Figure 6.10

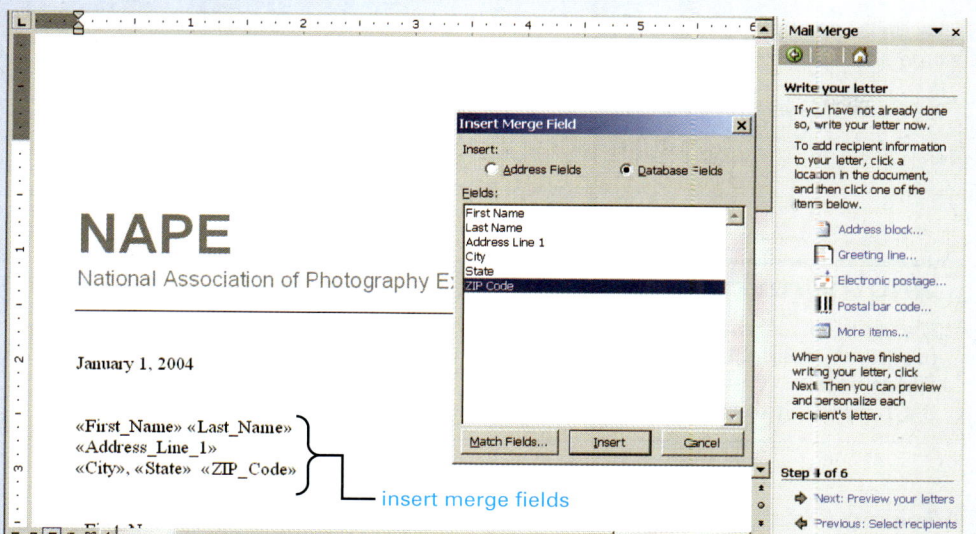

FIGURE 6.9
Insert Merge Field dialog box showing field names with most of the field names inserted in the NAPE letter

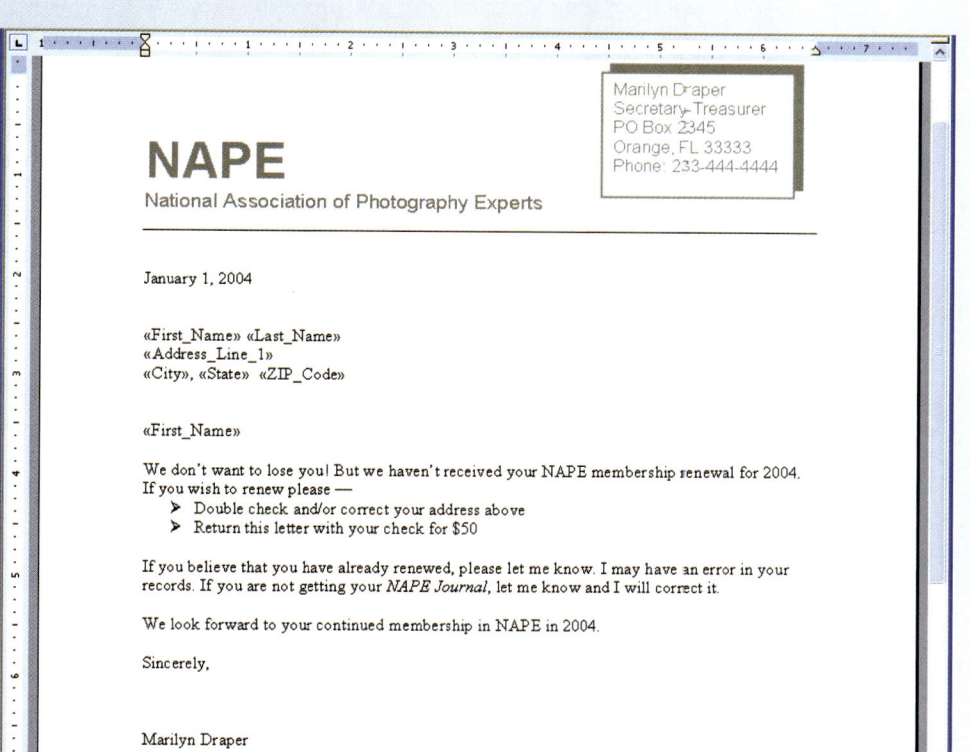

FIGURE 6.10
Merge fields inserted in NAPE letter

6. Preview the letters by clicking on **Next: Preview your letters**

tip: *This shows step 5 of 6 in the lower portion of the task pane*

7. If the merge is correct on the preview, click **Next: Complete the merge**

8. Click **Edit individual letters**, click **Merge** To New Document, and then select **All**, and click **OK**

tip: *If something in the merge is not correct, you can click* **Previous** *in the task pane and fix the problem*

9. Save these merged documents as **My_merge.doc**

10. Close all the documents without saving any changes

---

*another***word**   **. . . on Inserting Merged Fields**

Merge fields can also be inserted into the main document by using the Merge toolbar to open the **Data Source** button and then clicking on the **Insert Merge Fields** button. *Note:* You can't type merge field characters (<<<< >>>>) or insert them by using the Symbol command on the Insert menu

---

Making Changes after the Merge

The new document produced by the merge will reference your data source in appropriate places. As you scroll from letter to letter, you can check the merge to make sure it is correct. You may make changes to individual pages, if you want, without affecting the other letters. As you get comfortable with merging and know your data source, you will not need to keep checking the resulting document.

If each letter has a problem, like no space between the state and zip, do not fix each letter. Instead, close the merged file on your screen without saving. Then, open the form file and make the appropriate changes. Save the form file and try the merge again. This new document can be printed. Once your merged document is printed, you may choose to save it or not. If you choose not to save the merged document, you still have a copy of your data source or source and the main document, and can always merge them again later.

SESSION 6.1

making the grade

1. During the merge process, the main document references the _____ _____ .

2. True or False: Once merged, changes can be made on one document without affecting all the documents in the merge.

3. In the main document, the _____ _____ specify where the data will be placed.

4. List the steps to start the Mail Merge Wizard in the task pane.

5. True or False: The names and the numbers of data fields can be modified.

SESSION 6.2 DATA OPTIONS

The main document, such as letters, envelopes, e-mails, mailing labels, or directories (reference list), are just several examples of forms you can use. The main document that you create depends on the type of data in your data source file and your needs. Other uses of the data could include any of the following and probably many others as you understand the merge process more fully:

- Multiple certificates, by designing a certificate and referencing the name fields

- Name tags for a meeting
- Checklist for attendees at a meeting
- Letters and labels for local, regional, and national committees
- Employee lists and address books
- Solicitations, thank-you letters, and labels for donors and sponsors
- Subscriber lists for newsletters and publication labels
- Data file on expertise and location of resources
- Library catalog by author, title, and subject for a small office
- Once the data source is defined, many uses are apt to be found when combined with the merge function of Word.

Creating Mailing Labels

The ability to print on labels will depend on your printer. Laser and inkjet printers can print on various label forms, which are put in the paper tray. You need labels designed for whatever type of printer you use. The following session assumes you are printing to a laser or inkjet printer.

Basic Label Knowledge

Before creating, you need to know about the labels you will be using. Labels are identified by numbers that will tell the printer what size the labels are and how many are on a page. A common label for laser and inkjet printers is $1 \times 2\frac{5}{8}$ with three per row and 10 rows on an $8\frac{1}{2} \times 11$ page (Avery 5160). Measure your labels, and then pay attention to the label information as you determine which labels you will be printing on. You may need to experiment with measurements and decide which ones you will use. One of the problems with printing labels is having too much text to fit the small label size. Until you complete the merge, you will not know if there is too much text for the label. After merging data into a label format you can scroll through the file, looking for addresses that span more than one label. These will have to be edited to fit the text onto one label. As an alternative, you can also choose a smaller font code to fit more on all the labels.

---

task reference   **Creating Mailing Labels**

- Open a new blank document
- Click **Tools, Letters and Mailings, Mail Merge**
- Select **Labels** as the document type from the merge task pane
- Click **Next: Starting document**, click **Label Options**
- From the Label Products drop-down list of the Label Information section, select the correct label
- Click **OK**
- Click **Next: Select recipients** and select the data source
- Follow the remaining task pane instructions for creating labels

---

Now that Marilyn has printed out all of her second notice letters to the members of NAPE, she needs address labels. To do this she will again use the Mail Merge Wizard in the task pane.

anotherway

. . . to Address Envelopes

If you don't want to use labels for addressing envelopes, you can apply the address directly to the envelope, including your return address. Select the address block in a letter and click Tools, Letters and Mailings, Envelopes and Labels. On the Envelopes and Labels dialog box be certain the Envelopes tab is selected. Using this option, you can change the look of an envelope by specifying the formatting of text, selecting a wide variety of envelope sizes, and adding special text and graphics, for example, a company logo or decorative graphic. Finally, you can print the envelope without saving it. If you want to save the envelope for later editing and printing, you can attach the envelope to a document so that the two are associated. You can also print a whole page of the same label or a single label by using the Labels Tab in the Envelopes and Labels dialog box

Creating mailing labels for letters to NAPE members:

1. Open a new blank document, and click **Tools, Letters and Mailings, Mail Merge**; then select **Labels** as the document type from the merge task pane

2. Click **Next: Starting document**, and then click **Label Options**

3. From the Label Products drop-down list of the Label Information section, select **Avery Standard**; and select the Product number **8160-Address**, and click **OK** (see Figure 6.11)

4. Click **Next: Select recipients**, and select **Use an existing list**; then click **Browse**

5. Click the down arrow in the **Look In** box, and maneuver to the folder where your Student Data files are located

6. Select the **NapeNames1.mdb** file, and click **Open**; then click **OK**

7. Click **Next: Arrange your labels** and then **More items**

8. Insert merge field codes as shown in Figure 6.12

tip: *Be certain to include a space between the first and last name, a comma and a space between the city and state, and at least one space between the state and the zip code. Alternatively, when room is available on the label, the zip code can be on a separate line*

9. Click **Update all labels**; click **Next**

10. Click **Next: Preview Labels**

11. Click **Next: Complete the merge** to merge the data with the label format and compare to Figure 6.13

12. Close the task pane and save as **Labels1.doc**, close the document

Printing a Directory

So far, all of the forms used in the merge have one address per "page" (or envelope or label). If you want to print a continuous list (directory or reference) of names and addresses, without having page breaks, choose the Directory option in the merge function.

help yourself *Click the **Ask a Question** combo box, type **Directory**, and press **Enter**. Click the hyperlink **Create a directory of names, addresses, and other information** to display information on how to arrange and preview the contents of your directory. Click the Help screen **Close** button when you are finished*

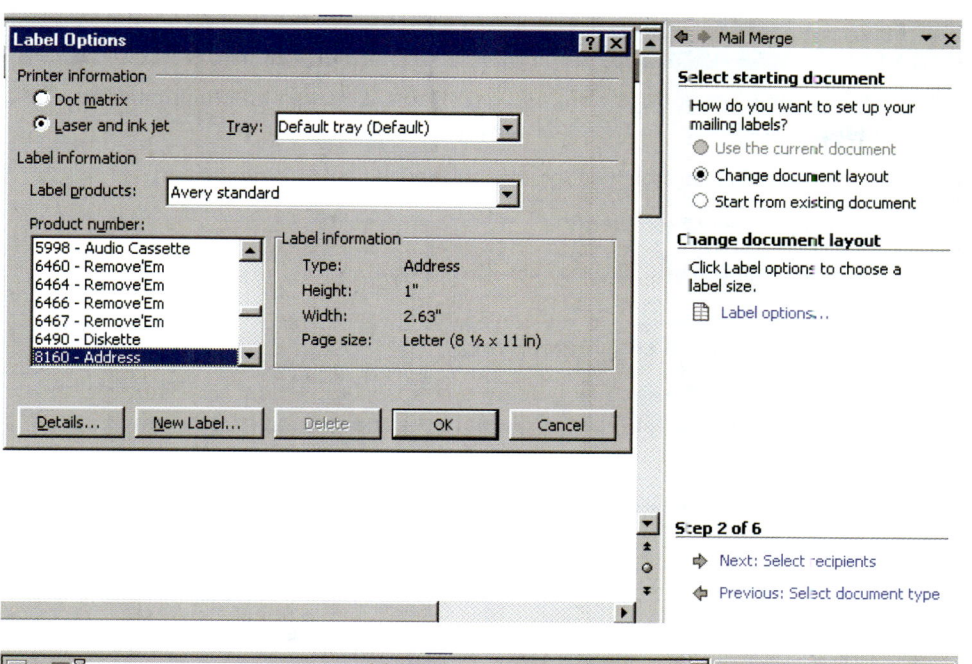

FIGURE 6.11

Completing label options

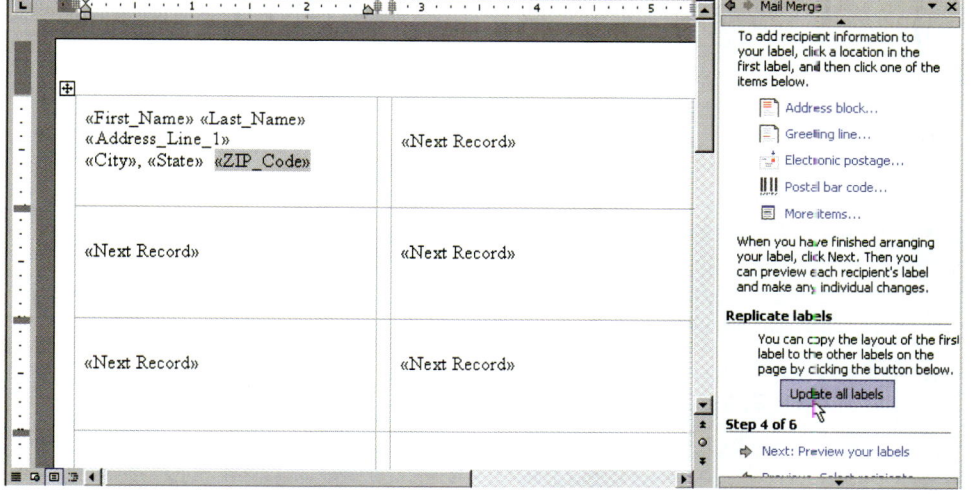

FIGURE 6.12

Merge field codes on labels

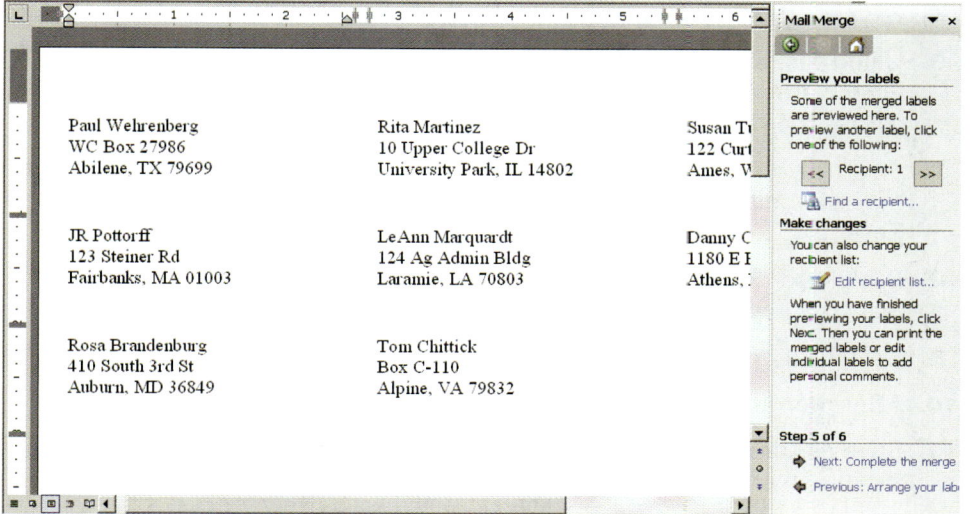

FIGURE 6.13

Names and addresses of NAPE members merged to labels

---

task *reference*   Creating a Directory

- Open a new blank document and click **Tools, Letters and Mailings, Mail Merge, Directory**

- Click **Next: Select starting document; Use the current document**

- Click **Next: Select recipients**

- Click **Use an existing list**, and click **Browse**

- Locate the data source file and click **Open**; click **OK**; click **Next: Arrange your directory**, and click **More items**

- Using the Insert Merge Field dialog box, insert the fields; click **Next: Preview your directory**, click **Complete the merge**, select **To a new document**

- Select **All** on the **Merge** to a **New Document** dialog box

- Click **OK**

Now that the letters and labels are all printed for the second notice mailing to the NAPE members, Marilyn will continue using the merge feature to produce a list or a directory of the names and addresses of individuals who received the mailing. This serves two purposes. She can track who was sent the letter without keeping a copy of a letter to everyone on the list, and she can provide the president of the organization with a list of delinquent members.

Creating a directory:

1. Open a new blank document, and click **Tools, Letters and Mailings, Mail Merge, Directory**

2. Click **Next: Starting document**, select **Use the current document**, and click **Next: Select recipients**

3. Click **Use an existing list**, and click **Browse**

4. Locate the file **NapeNames1.mdb**, click **Open**, and click **OK**

5. Click **Next: Arrange your directory**, and click **More items**

6. Using the Insert Merge Field dialog box, insert the following fields: First_Name, Last_Name, Address_Line_1, City, State, and Zip_Code across the page as shown in Figure 6.14

7. Be sure you put commas and spaces as shown, or tabs between items that will be listed across the page, and after the last merge field press **Enter**

8. Click **Next: Preview your directory**, click **Next: Complete the merge**, select **To a new document**

9. Select **All** on the Merge to a New Document dialog box, and click **OK**

10. After merging compare your results with Figure 6.15

11. Save as **Directory1.doc** and close this file and the other files without saving any changes

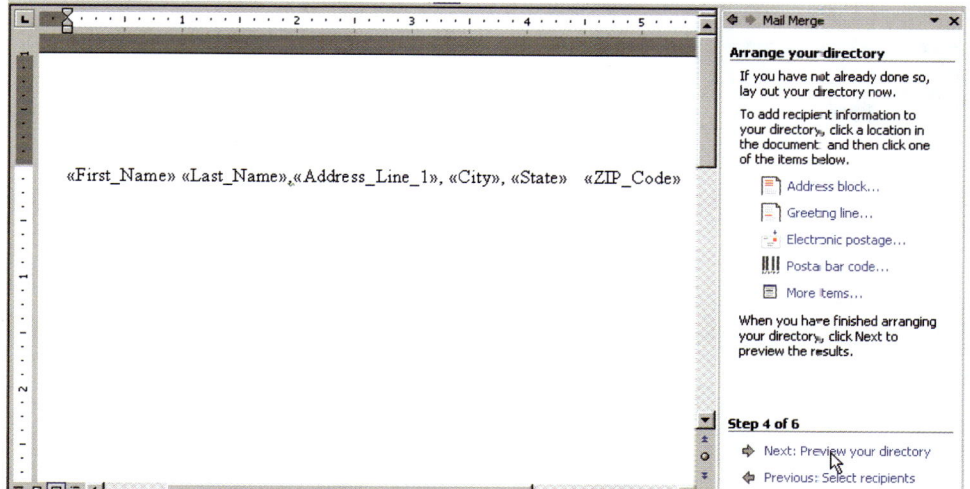

FIGURE 6.14

Merge fields across a page for preparing a directory

Paul Wehrenberg, WC Box 27986, Abilene, TX 79699
Rita Martinez, 10 Upper College Dr, University Park, IL 14802
Susan Turner, 122 Curtiss Hall, Ames, WA 50011
JR Pottorff, 123 Steiner Rd, Fairbanks, MA 01003
LeAnn Marquardt, 124 Ag Admin Bldg, Laramie, LA 70803
Danny Cook, 1180 E Broad St, Athens, MO 30602
Rosa Brandenburg, 410 South 3rd St, Auburn, MD 36849
Tom Chittick, Box C-110, Alpine, VA 79832

FIGURE 6.15

Directory of NAPE mailing

Sorting a Data Source

Like data in any list or in any database, the source data can be sorted. For example, addresses are often sorted by zip code, or lists of names may be sorted alphabetically so people are easier to find. In the following brief exercise, Marilyn will redo her address labels and *sort* them by zip code before merging to address labels.

> **anotherword**   . . . on Directories
>
> After creating a directory from a data source, other text enhancements can be added to the document, just like a regular document. For example, font changes, boldface, titles, and even a table could be created from the text

Sorting by zip code:

1. Open a new blank document, and click **Tools, Letters and Mailings, Mail Merge, Labels**; click **Next: Starting document**, and then click **Label Options**

2. From the Label Products drop-down list of the Label Information section, select the **Avery Standard**, select product number **8160-Address**, and click **OK**

3. Click **Next: Select recipients**, and select **Use an existing list**; then click **Browse**

4. Select the **NapeNames1.mdb** file, and click **Open**; then click **OK**

5. Click **Edit the recipient list**

6. To sort the list by zip code, click **Edit, Filter and Sort**

7. Click the **Sort Records** tab, click Sort by down arrow, scroll down and select **Zip Code**, select **Ascending** if necessary (Figure 6.16)

FIGURE 6.16

Sort Records tab shown during the edit of the recipient list

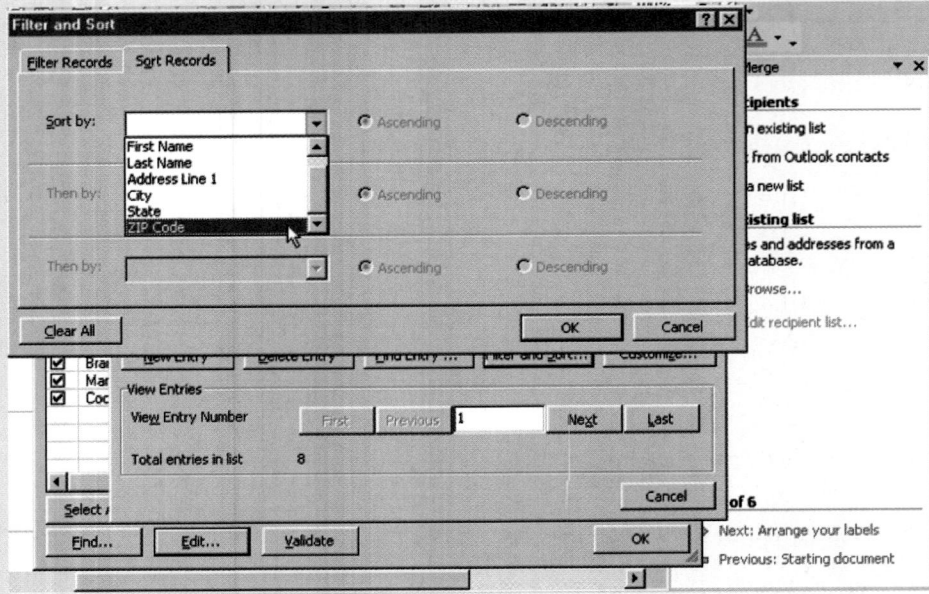

8. Click **OK, Close, OK**, and continue the merge process as for labels

9. Compare your labels to Figure 6.17

FIGURE 6.17

Labels sorted (ascending) by zip code

JR Pottorff 123 Steiner Rd Fairbanks, MA 01003	Rita Martinez 10 Upper College Drive University Park, IL 14802	Danny Cook 1180 E Broad St Athens, MO 30602
Rosa Brandenburg 410 South 3rd St Auburn, MD 36849	Susan Turner 122 Curtiss Hall Ames, WA 50011	LeAnn Marquardt 124 Ag Admin Bldg Laramie, LA 70803
Paul Wehrenberg WC Box 27086 Abilene, TX 79699	Tom Chittick Box C-110 Alpine, VA 79832	

10. Save your sorted labels as **SortedLabels1.doc**, and close your files

SESSION 6.2

making the grade

1. To print a continuous list of information such as names and addresses from a data source, use the _____ option for a main document.

2. When merging data to labels it is important to know the label _____ .

3. What option in the merge feature is used to create an alphabetical list of labels with zip codes in ascending order?

4. True or False: All of the records and all of the fields are used each time a merge takes place.

5. True or False: E-mail messages can reference a data source and be merged.

SESSION 6.3 OBJECT LINKING AND EMBEDDING

Linking and Embedding Objects

You can insert *objects* into a Word document to include information created in Microsoft Office programs or in any program that supports linked objects and embedded objects. In this chapter you will be linking and embedding worksheets from Excel. Worksheet data can be inserted into a Word document three different ways:

1. Copy the data from the worksheet in Excel, and then switch to Word and paste the data in your document
2. Link Excel data to your document
3. Embed the Excel data

The simplest approach to moving Excel worksheet data into a Word document is to copy the data in Excel and then paste the data in Word. This process inserts a plainly formatted table into the Word document. You can apply formatting to the table and change the numbers, but the data will have no connection to the original worksheet. It is a static copy.

When you paste-link worksheet data into your document, you are not just pasting a static copy. In this case, you are pasting a representation of the copied information, which will reflect changes to the original data in Excel. Creating a link in this way saves disk space, since you are pasting a pointer to the data rather than pasting the actual data. For linked data, the source file must remain available to maintain the link.

When you embed Excel data, existing data or data you create using Excel tools from within your Word document can be embedded. Embedding data significantly increases the size of a document. Since the embedded data are independent of the source, the original worksheet does not need to remain accessible.

Copying, linking, and embedding provide tremendous power and flexibility, but trying to figure out which approach to take can be a little intimidating.

help yourself Click the **Ask a Question** combo box, type **Linking objects**, and press **Enter**. Click the hyperlink **Change the appearance of a linked object or an embedded object** and review all the information regarding linked and embedded objects. Click the Help screen **Close** button when you are finished

Linking an Excel Worksheet to Word

To include Excel data in a Word document and to have the information in your document reflect changes made to the data in Excel, take advantage of Word's paste-linking capabilities.

With a *linked object*, information is updated only if you modify the source file. Linked data are stored in the *source file*. The destination file stores only the location of the source file and displays a representation of the linked data. Use linked objects if file size is a consideration.

F I G U R E   6.18

Dialog box for inserting a
linked or embedded object

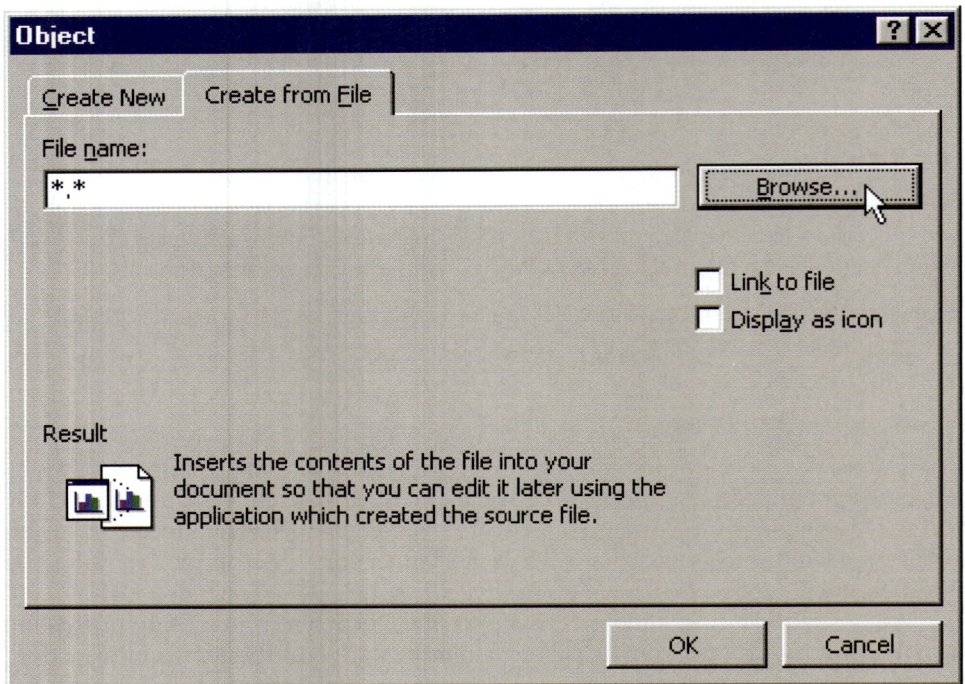

task reference — Creating a Linked Object from an Existing File

- Click in the document where you want to place the linked object
- On the **Insert** menu, click **Object**, and then click the **Create from File** tab (Figure 6.18)
- In the File name box, type the name of the file you want to use to create a linked object, or click **Browse** to select from a list
- Select the **Link to file** check box
- Click **OK**

An ***embedded object*** is created if you don't select the Link to file check box. Select the Display as icon check box to display the linked object as an icon, for example, if others are going to view the document online.

Embedding an Excel Spreadsheet into Word

With an embedded object, information in the destination file does not change if you modify the source file. Embedded objects become part of the destination file, and once inserted, they are no longer part of the source file. To open an embedded object for editing in the Excel program, double-click the embedded object. One of the primary advantages of embedding an object into Word is that you can use the source application tools to make modifications to the embedded documents.

---

task *reference* | Creating an Embedded Object from an Existing File

- Click in the document where you want to place the embedded object
- On the **Insert** menu, click **Object**, and then click the **Create from File** tab
- In the File name box, type the name of the file you want to use to create an embedded object, or click **Browse** to select from a list (make sure there is no checkmark in the **Link to file** check box)
- Click **OK**

Marilyn decides to embed an Excel worksheet that describes the prize amounts awarded for the Photo of the Year contest. The extra page will be added as an attachment to the original document.

Embedding a worksheet into Word:

1. Open the data file **wd06Contest.doc**
2. Save the file as **Contest1.doc**
3. Switch to Print Layout view if necessary. Double-click in the document three lines below the last line in the last paragraph
4. On the **Insert** menu, click **Object**, and then click the **Create from File** tab
5. In the File name box, type **wd06ContestWinners.xls,** or click **Browse** to select it from a list. For this exercise it may be best to Click **Browse** and maneuver to where your student data files are located, and then select **wd06ContestWinners.xls**
6. Click **OK**
7. Compare your results to Figure 6.19
8. Save and close your document

tip: *To make changes in the data, double-click on the embedded spreadsheet to open Excel within Word (the toolbars are Excel, but the Title bar still shows Word). Make the changes, and when done, click outside the spreadsheet*

anotherway
. . . to Link an Excel Worksheet to Word

With a worksheet open in Excel, you can select it and copy it. Then in an open Word document you paste the worksheet just like any other piece of text. After pasting the worksheet, click on the associated Smart Tag and choose Keep Source Formatting and Link to Excel

Still another way to link or embed a worksheet after copying it is to use the Edit, Paste Special and select Paste Link

Creating a Merge from an Excel Worksheet

Before you create a list of names and addresses for a mail merge, you must determine which Office program is best suited to your task. You can use just about any type of data source you want for a mail merge. Some examples include:

- Microsoft Outlook Contact List
- Microsoft Office Address List
- Microsoft Excel worksheet
- Microsoft Access database
- Other database files
- HTML file with a single table
- Microsoft Outlook Address Book
- Microsoft Schedule+ 6.0 Contact List

FIGURE 6.19

Contest prizes embedded into Word

ADVENTURES IN EXTREME SPORTS AND ACTIVITIES CONTEST

Welcome to all who would like to participate in this year's extreme photo contest. Enter the most extreme photo you have taken of a sport or activity in the last year.

There are hundreds of prizes available including a trip to Hawaii, camera gear, and photography lessons. Everyone can enter and be sure your photo is of an extreme sport or activity.

Winners	Prize
5	Trip to Hawaii for two
15	Canon 5100 camera
25	Extreme Photography Lessons
200	Free subscription to Extreme Sports magazine
200	$10 gift certificate to Joe's Camera

- Personal Address Book created for use with Microsoft Exchange Server
- Word document containing a single table, with the first row containing headings and the other rows containing the records
- Text files with data fields

For a small- or medium-size list of names and addresses that you don't expect to make many changes to, you can use the Microsoft Office Address List. For longer lists that you expect to add, delete, and change entries in, or for powerful sorting and searching capabilities, use Microsoft Excel or Access. With Excel, you can select as a data source any worksheet or named range within the workbook. With Access, you can select as a data source any table or *query* defined in the database. A query is a means of finding all the records stored in a data source that fit a set of conditions you specify. Queries can contain operators, quotation marks, wild card characters, and parentheses to help focus your search.

Marilyn has been working on a larger database of NAPE members in Excel (see Figure 6.20). She needs to print a directory (list) with the name (first and last) and phone number of only the individuals whose subject is chemistry.

FIGURE 6.20

NAPE member list in an Excel worksheet

	A	B	C	D	E	F	G	H	I
1	FirstName	LastName	Address1	Address2	City	St	Zip	Phone	Subject
2	Paul	Wehrenberg	Wilmington College	WC Box 27986	Abilene	TX	79699-0001	204-395-1957	Cattle
3	Rita	Martinez	Western II Univ	10 Upper College Dr	University Park	IL	14802-1137	740-106-2963	Physiologist
4	Tom	Chittick	West Virginia University	Box C-110	Alpine	VA	79832-5300	394-850-5016	Mathematics
5	Susan	Turner	Washington State University	122 Curtiss Hall	Ames	WA	50011-0001	207-185-0092	Psychology
6	JR	Pottorff	Vocational School	123 Steiner Rd	Fairbanks	MA	01003-7230	804-175-3760	Horticulture
7	Danny	Cook	University of Missouri	1180 E Broad St	Athens	MO	30602-7502	930-224-5583	Chemistry
8	Rosa	Brandenburg	University Of Maryland	410 South 3rd St	Auburn	MD	36849-5810	407-559-6573	English
9	LeAnn	Marquardt	University Of Louisiana	124 Ag Admin Bldg	Laramie	LA	70803-0001	703-538-2287	Networking
10	Allen	Abaye	Georgia State University	Agriculture Dept	Huntsville	GA	40404-0001	607-449-2257	Animal Science
11	Rosemary	Vaughn	Utah State University	22 Sullivan Road	Berrien Springs	UT	49104-0001	388-334-0087	Social Sciences
12	Raoul	Schmidt	University Of Arizona	1 Big Red Way St	Bowling Green	AZ	42101-5730	725-428-6850	English-ESL
13	Evelyn	Piirto	University Of Alaska	PO Box 172860	Urbana	AK	59717-2860	488-356-7960	Mathematics
14	Danilo	Chrudimsky	Univ Of Wisconsin	101 Fort Ave	Brookings	WI	57007-0001	203-563-2158	Drama
15	Mary	Bollero	Florida Tech University	108 Morrill Hall	Burlington	FL	05405-0106	460-625-3366	Psychology
16	Susan	Elelinger	North Arizona Univesity	Box 898	Canyon	AZ	79016-0001	354-687-1836	English
17	Willis	Jones	Univ Of Maine	654 American Lit Hall	Carbondale	ME	62901-4400	797-314-0044	American Lit
18	Bobba	Fetina	Un Of Virginia At Pine Bluff	9812 Virginia St	Pine Bluff	VA	95929-0001	886-335-2435	Chemistry
19	Murray	Neufville	Three Rivers Com College	101 Barre Hall	Clemson	CA	29634-0001	545-201-2837	Horticulture
20	Lee	Ping	University of Illinois	0 Suny Cobleskill	Cobleskill	IL	12043-1701	373-879-3399	Computer Apps
21	John	Countryman	Texas A & M University	1255 S Range Ave	Lincoln	TX	67701-4099	243-786-4738	Chemistry
22	Leland	Zetzsche	North Dakota Tech University	Computer Applications Dept	College Station	ND	77843-0001	345-275-8694	Computer Apps
23	Dawn	Balaban	Boise Ag & Tech College	2-64 Agriculture Bldg	Boise	NY	65211-7300	615-990-3769	Plant Science
24	TG	Brandt	Stephen F Austin State University	2120 Fyffe Rd	Storrs	MT	43210-1010	292-583-7349	German
25	Eric	Rehkop	Denver University	PO Box 1002	Denver	KS	66901-1002	373-869-0011	Library Science
26	Jacquelyn	McMinnis	Southern Illinois Univ	PO Box 5034	Cookeville	IL	38505-0001	565-794-2344	Business Writing
27	Chao	Wangberg	Scottsdale Community College	864 Kleberg Center	Mesa	OR	97331-8507	280-265-3647	Plant Science
28	Suzanne	Hafer	Nebraska School of Rangeland Mana	RR 3 Box 23A	Fresno	NE	69025-9525	301-757-9922	Chemistry
29	Liam	Kennedy	Pennsylvania School Of Agriculture	700 E Butler Ave	Pierre	PA	18901-2697	707-554-4442	Geology
30	Peter	Jackson	Sam Houston State University	121 Agriculture Hall	East Peoria	MI	48824-1039	828-565-4657	Economics
31	Chris	Reich	Ratcliffe Hicks Business College	Box 2400	Georgetown	WI	61635-0001	909-339-2772	Business

task reference	Creating a Directory by Querying Excel

- Open a new blank document and click **Tools, Letters and Mailings, Mail Merge, Directory**
- Click **Next: Starting document** and click **Use the current document**
- Click **Next: Select recipients** and select **Use an existing list**
- Click **Browse**
- Select the file and click **Open**; click **OK**
- Click **Edit recipient list**; click the arrow next to the appropriate header button
- Click (**Advanced. . .**) and then click the tab for **Filter Records**
- Complete the Field box for comparisons
- Click **Arrange directory**

Creating a directory by querying an Excel worksheet:

1. Open a new blank document, and click **Tools, Letters and Mailings, Mail Merge, Directory**
2. Click **Next: Starting document**, and click **Use the current document**
3. Click **Next: Select recipients**, and select **Use an existing list**; then click **Browse**
4. Select the **wd06Nape.xls** file from your Student Data file folder, and click **Open**; then click **OK**
5. Scroll to the end of the fields. To select only the individuals whose subject is chemistry, click the arrow next to the header button for **Subject**
6. Click (**Advanced. . .**), and then click the tab for **Filter Records** (see Figure 6.21)
7. Click the arrow in the Field: box scroll down and select **Subject**; in the Comparison: box leave in the first option **Equal to**; and in the Compare to: box type **Chemistry**
8. Click **OK**; click **OK**
9. Click **Next: Arrange directory**; select **More items**
10. Add the merge fields for first name; a space; last name; a space; phone; and press **Enter**
11. Continue the merge process by clicking on **Next: Preview your directory**
12. If all is correct, click **Next: Complete the merge**, click **Merge** To New Document and then select **All**, and click **OK**

tip: If something in the merge is not correct, you can click **Previous** in the task pane and fix the problem

13. Compare your directory to Figure 6.22 and save your document as **Chemistry1.doc**. Close your documents

FIGURE 6.21

Dialog box to filter NAPE records for those whose subject is chemistry

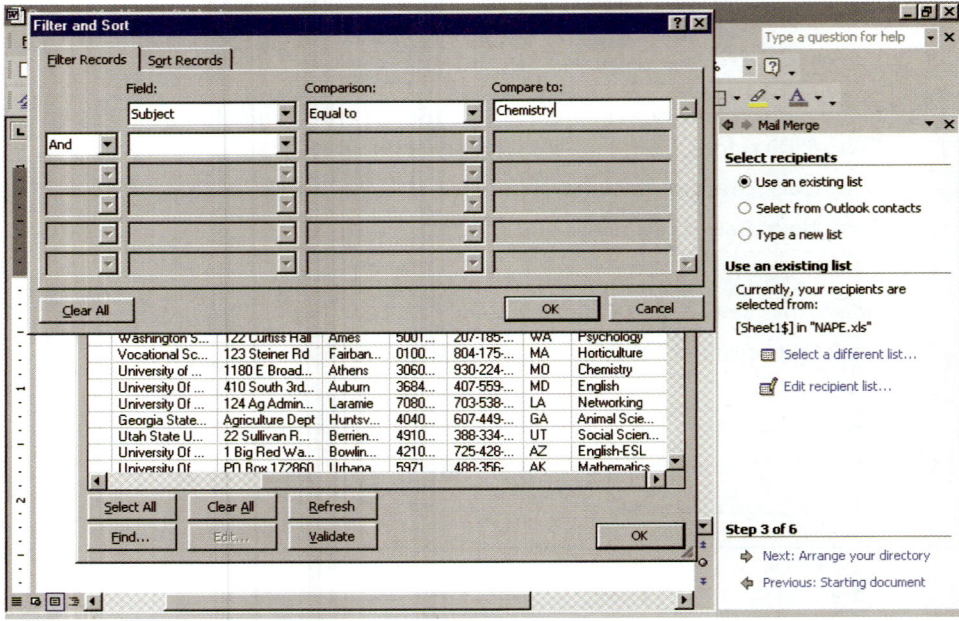

FIGURE 6.22

Phone directory of NAPE members whose subject is chemistry

Name	Phone
John Countryman	243-786-4738
Danny Cook	930-224-5583
Bobba Fetina	886-335-2435
Jacob Jen	454-668-3357
Karla Topliff	310-610-8761
Suzanne Hafer	301-757-9922
JR Pottorff	804-175-3760
Murray Neufville	545-201-2837

Using the power of sorting and querying, Marilyn realizes that she can create a variety of lists, labels, and letters from her NAPE Excel worksheet, even as she adds new members to the worksheet.

---

another**word**   . . . on Using Excel in Merges

While Word has your workbook open to create the mail merge, you can't open the workbook in Excel. If you need to see the data and its column labels, go to step 3 of 5 of the Wizard and click Edit recipient list.

You can continue to use mail merges with Excel data that you created in earlier versions of Word. To open and use these mail merges in Word, you'll need to install Microsoft Query. To create **new** mail merges in Word, Query is no longer required

making *the grade*

1. True or False: Data from Excel or Access can be merged into a Word document.

2. True or False: With Excel you can merge the data from a worksheet or a named range within the workbook.

3. A _____ contains operators, wild cards that help focus a search in a data source.

4. True or False: When merging data from a workbook, the main document must use all of the field names (headers) listed in the worksheet.

5. True or False: While Word has a workbook open to create the mail merge, you can open the workbook in Excel.

6. After creating data in Excel, you must _____ the workbook containing the data and switch to Microsoft Word.

SESSION 6.4 SUMMARY

The mail merge feature is useful when you need to create multiple copies of similar, or identical, documents for many people. Merging is a four-step process:

1. Create or open a main document
2. Create or open a data source file
3. Insert merge fields into the main document
4. Perform the merge

Depending on the comfort level of the person performing a merge, two methods can be used to set up the process: the Mail Merge toolbar or the Mail Merge Wizard in the task pane.

A main document form will use information from the data source. The data source can be developed in Word as an address list where common field names are provided. Alternatively, the data source can be an Excel worksheet, an Access database, or some other database or defined table. Field names are determined by the user, and they are used for selecting and sorting records during the merge process. Once created, the data in the data source can be modified, edited, and added to.

By inserting merge fields into the main document, you control where the data from the data source will be placed during the merging process. It is important not to forget punctuation in the main document. Once you associate your data source with the main document, you can easily reference fields from a list, by clicking to insert merge fields. The records in a merged document are in the same order as the associated data source.

A merge creates a unique individual document for each record in the data source. The results of a merge can be edited, sent to the printer, or saved as a new document. When you print on mailing labels, find the appropriate label type in the listing, check the measurements, and then create the main label document form. If you want to define a form that has more than one record per page, use the Directory option to print multiple records on the same page.

MICROSOFT OFFICE SPECIALIST OBJECTIVES SUMMARY

- Merge letters with other data sources—MOS WW03E-2-6
- Merge labels with other data sources—MOS WW03E-2-7
- Insert and modify object—MOS WW03E-1-4

making the grade answers

SESSION 6.1

1. data source
2. True
3. merge fields
4. Click Tools, Letters and Mailings, Mail Merge
5. True

SESSION 6.2

1. directory
2. size or number
3. Filter or Sort or Sort Records

4. False
5. True

SESSION 6.3

1. True
2. True
3. query
4. False
5. False
6. close

task reference summary

Task	Page #	Preferred Method
Using the Mail Merge Wizard	WD 6.4	• To start the Mail Merge Wizard in the task pane, click **Tools, Letters and Mailings, Mail Merge Wizard** • Indicate which type of document by clicking to **select Letters, E-mail messages, Envelopes, Labels**, or **Directory** • Determine where the document will be found—a new one, a template, or one already saved • Continue following steps at the bottom of the task pane
Creating a data source with Mail Merge Wizard	WD 6.7	• Click **Tools, Letters and Mailings, Mail Merge** • Select document type • Click **Next: Starting document** • Select type of starting document • Click **Next: Select recipients** • Select **Type a new list** • Click **Create** • Click **Customize** to remove fields • Enter data • Click **Close** when all data have been entered into the fields • Provide filename for data source
Inserting merge fields	WD 6.8	• Click **View, Toolbars, Mail Merge** • On the Mail Merge toolbar, click **Insert Merge Fields** button • Select the fields and click **Insert** or • Using the Mail Merge Wizard, open the **Merge Field dialog box** • Click **Insert** • Click **Close**

task reference summary

Task	Page #	Preferred Method
Creating mailing labels	WD 6.11	• Open a new blank document • Click **Tools, Letters and Mailings, Mail Merge** • Select **Labels** as the document type from the merge task pane • Click **Next: Starting document**, click **Label Options** • From the Label Products drop-down list of the Label Information section, select the correct label • Click **OK** • Click **Next: Select recipients** and select the data source • Follow the remaining task pane instructions for creating labels
Creating a directory	WD 6.14	• Open a new blank document and click **Tools, Letters and Mailings, Mail Merge Wizard, Directory** • Click **Next: Select starting document; Use the current document** • Click **Next: Select recipients** • Click **Use an existing list**, and click **Browse** • Locate the data source file and click **Open**; click **OK**; click **Next: Arrange your directory**, and click **More items** • Using the Insert Merge Field dialog box, insert the fields; click **Next: Preview your directory**, click **Complete the merge**, select **To a new document** • Select **All** on the **Merge to a New Document** dialog box • Click **OK**
Creating a linked object from an existing file	WD 6.18	• Click in the document where you want to place the linked object • On the **Insert** menu, click **Object**, and then click the **Create from File** tab • In the File name box, type the name of the file you want to use to create a linked object, or click **Browse** to select from a list • Select the **Link to file** check box • Click **OK**
Creating an embedded object from an existing file	WD 6.19	• Click in the document where you want to place the embedded object • On the **Insert** menu, click **Object**, and then click the **Create from File** tab • In the File name box, type the name of the file you want to use to create an embedded object, or click **Browse** to select from a list (make sure there is no checkmark in the **Link to file** check box) • Click **OK**
Creating a directory by querying Excel	WD 6.21	• Open a new blank document and click **Tools, Letters and Mailings, Mail Merge, Directory** • Click **Next: Starting document** and click **Use the current document** • Click **Next: Select recipients** and select **Use an existing list** • Click **Browse** • Select the file and click **Open**; click **OK** • Click **Edit recipient list**; click the arrow next to the appropriate header button • Click **(Advanced . . .)** and then click the tab for **Filter Records** • Complete the Field box for comparisons • Click **Arrange directory**

TRUE/FALSE

1. To query data is to arrange the data numerically or alphabetically or by some other criteria common to the records.

2. Sorting data is a means of finding all the records stored in a data source that fit a set of criteria you name.

3. An object is a table, chart, graphic, equation, or other form of information.

4. The main document contains the format for the letter or mailing list with field references to the data source.

5. Once merged, changes can be made on one document without affecting all the documents in the merge.

FILL-IN

1. To print a _____ list of information such as names and addresses from a data source, use the Directory option for a main document.

2. When merging data to labels it is important to know the label _____.

3. E-mail messages can reference a data _____ and be merged.

4. With Excel you can merge the data from a worksheet or a _____ range within the workbook.

5. When merging data from a workbook, the main document must use the _____ names (headers) listed in the worksheet.

6. After creating data in Excel, you must _____ the workbook containing the data and switch to Microsoft Word.

7. During the merge process, the _____ _____ references the data source.

MULTIPLE CHOICE

1. Which of the following contains the unique information for each record and merges with the main document to create the customized form letter or mailing list?
   a. Data record
   b. Data source
   c. Data field
   d. Data document

2. Which of the following is a category of information in a data source and corresponds to one column of information in the data source?
   a. Data record
   b. Data source
   c. Data field
   d. Data document

3. Which of the following is a complete set of related information in a data source, and corresponds to one row of information in the data source, for example, all information about one client in a client mailing list?
   a. Data record
   b. Data source
   c. Data field
   d. Data document

4. Which of the following contains a placeholder that is inserted in the main document; for example, <<City>> to have Word insert a city name, such as "New York," that is stored in the City data field in the data source?
   a. Data record
   b. Data source
   c. Directory
   d. Merge field

5. Which of the following contains the text, graphics, and format for the letter or mailing list with field references to the data source?
   a. Data document
   b. Main document
   c. Embedded object
   d. None of the above

review of concepts

REVIEW QUESTIONS

1. Describe a data field and a record. Explain the relationship between the two.

2. What option in the merge feature is used to create an alphabetical list of labels with zip codes in ascending order?

3. List the steps to start the Mail Merge Wizard in the task pane.

4. How do you place the Merge toolbar on your Word screen?

5. What programs can create data that is merged into a Word document?

6. What is a query?

CREATE THE QUESTION

For each of the following answers, create an appropriate, short question.

ANSWER	QUESTION
1. Merge field	_____
2. Data source	_____
3. Query	_____
4. Record	_____
5. Merging	_____
6. Main document	_____
7. Field	_____

FACT OR FICTION

1. A data field is a category of information in a data source. A data field corresponds to one column of information in the data source. The name of each data field is listed in the header row of the data source.

2. A main document is a file containing the text and graphics that stays the same with each version of a mail-merge document, for example, a list of names and addresses for a form letter to send to a list of clients, or in any report in which the information from a database is used.

3. An embedded object is information (the object) inserted into a file (the destination file). Once embedded, the object becomes part of the destination file. When you double-click an embedded object, it opens in the program (source program) it was created in. Any changes made to the embedded object are reflected in the destination file.

4. A query is a means of finding all the records stored in a data source that fit a set of criteria you name. An example of a query could be "list all of the people born before 1982."

5. A data record is a complete set of related information in a data source; corresponds to one row of information in the data source, for example, all information about one client in a client mailing list.

1. Adding Your Name to the NAPE List

You have been taking professional pictures for the last year. You have finally decided to join the National Association of Photography Experts so you can easily learn about new and exciting photographic opportunities and picture-taking techniques. You have not yet paid the $50 fee so you must add your name and address to the data source for the NAPE mailing. Once you have completed that task, you must merge the main document again with the data source in order to print your document.

1. Open the file named **wd06NapeYou.doc**

2. Click **Tools, Letters and Mailings, Mail Merge**

3. If a dialog box appears, click **Find data source** and open **wd06NapeNamesYou.mdb** from your student data files

4. Click **Use the current document**

5. Click **Edit Recipient List**

6. Click on the last line, which contains YourLastName (see Figure 6.23)

7. Click **Edit**, type your information into each field, click **Close**

8. Click **OK**

9. Click **Next: Write your letter**

10. Click **Next: Preview your letters**

11. Click the arrow on the right of the word Recipient 1 until you have a preview of your letter

12. Print the merged letter with your name and address

13. Save your document as **NapeYou1.doc**

FIGURE 6.23

Editing YourLastName in the merged document

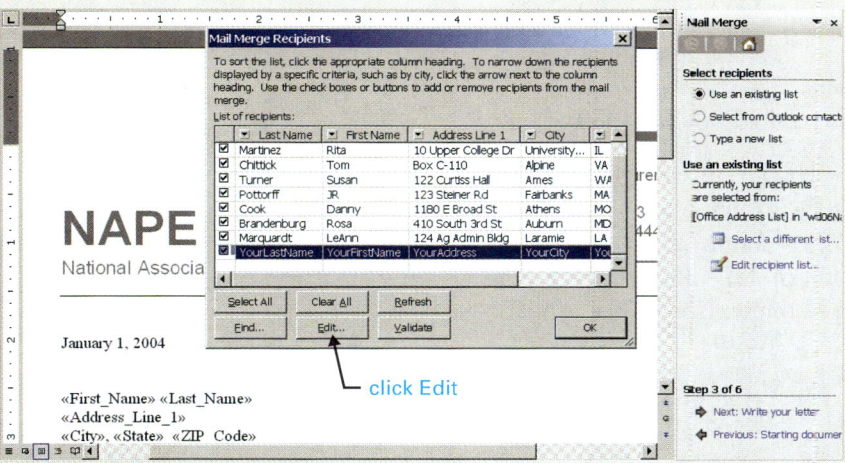

click Edit

2. Printing a Directory with Your Name on the List

Your boss at NAPE has asked you to print a directory of all the individuals in the NAPE database. Print a directory of all the individuals in the **wd06NapeNamesComplete.mdb** database.

1. Open a new blank document and click **Tools, Letters and Mailings, Mail Merge, Directory**

2. Click **Tools**

3. Click **Letters and Mailings**

4. Click **Mail Merge**

5. Click **Directory**

6. Click **Next: Starting document**; for a starting document type **Use the current document**, and click **Next: Select recipients**

7. Click **Use an existing list**, and click **Browse**

8. Locate the file **wd06NapeNamesComplete.mdb**

9. Click **Open**

10. Click **OK**

11. Click **Next: Arrange your directory**

12. Click **More items**

13. Using the Insert Merge Field dialog box, insert the following fields across the page: First_Name, Last_Name, Address_Line_1, City, State, and Zip_Code; click **Close**

14. Put spaces or tabs between items that will be listed across the page

15. After the last merge field, press **Enter**, save your document as **NapeNamesCompleteMain.doc**

16. Click **Next: Preview your directory**

17. Compare your directory with Figure 6.24

18. Click **Complete the merge**, select **To a new document**

19. Select **All** on the Merge to a New Document dialog box, and click **OK**

20. Make sure your name appears on the list, and print the directory

FIGURE 6.24
Directory listing

Paul Wehrenberg WC Box 27986 Abilene, TX 79699
Rita Martinez 10 Upper College Dr University Park, IL 14802
Tom Chittick Box C-110 Alpine, VA 79832
Susan Turner 122 Curtiss Hall Ames, WA 50011
JR Pottorff 123 Steiner Rd Fairbanks, MA 01003
Danny Cook 1180 E Broad St Athens, MO 30602
Rosa Brandenburg 410 South 3rd St Auburn, MD 36849
LeAnn Marquardt 124 Ag Admin Bldg Laramie, LA 70803
Tom Hibbler, 123 South Park, Denver, CO 80210

1. Merging to a Gift Certificate

The Australian Steakhouse has been in business for over 40 years and serves the best steak in all of Maine. You have been hired as the assistant manager. Currently, the Steakhouse manually creates and prints each gift certificate. You have suggested to your boss that they use the mail merge feature in Word to create the gift certificates. Using the mail merge feature will save a great deal of time.

Figure 6.25 displays a list of recipients who will receive gift certificates from the Australian Steakhouse this week. Using the data from Figure 6.25 and the gift certificate format for Rosemary Vaughn (Figure 6.26), create a merge that will create certificates for every recipient in the list. The original gift certificate is saved as **wd06Steakhouse.doc**. Save your main document for the merge as **Steakhouse1Main.doc**. Save the data source for the merge as **Steakhouse1Data.doc**.

tip: When creating the data source the field names cannot contain spaces. You can use an underscore for a space

FIGURE 6.25

Data for creating gift certificates from the Australian Steakhouse

Recipient	Gift From	Amount
Arvela McBride	David White	$100.00
Acyne Stevens	Jeff Fox	$50.00
Jim Knight	Julie Keith	$50.00
Merry Wisall	Dennis Lu	$75.00
Elaine Cantu	Earl Hawkins	$100.00
Char Hannah	Sarah Thomas	$50.00
Lynn Cobb	Rosie Cobb	$45.00
Debbie Fernandez	Lisa Fernandez	$70.00
Kim Skilling	Dave Noble	$100.00
Andrea Giga	Joan Martin	$50.00
Scott Zimmerman	Dave Zimmerman	$50.00
Natalie Part	Noelle Dorr	$100.00
David Friedman	Brynna Friedman	$75.00
John Kruger	Karen Seller	$100.00
Maggie Jordan	Jake Jordan	$50.00

FIGURE 6.26

Original Steakhouse gift certificate

AUSTRALIAN STEAKHOUSE GIFT CERTIFICATE

This certificate entitles Rosemary Vaughn to a dinner valued at $55.00 at the AUSTRALIAN STEAKHOUSE.

A gift from a friend: Bob Lowder

Austin Goldstein
President

2. Merging from Excel

You are working for NAPE as the administrative assistant. Your boss, Jessica Land, has asked you to create a letter informing the NAPE Executive Committee of the upcoming meeting. Use the block format to insert merge fields in the letters so that each letter has the following:

- Current date
- Recipient's address
- Dear <First Name>
- In the body of the letter where you see 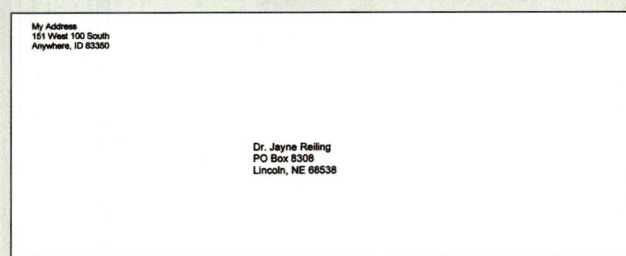, insert a merge field so that each individual will know what time they will take part in the meeting agenda (see Figure 6.27)

Use **wd06NapeExec.xls** for inserting the appropriate fields in both the letters and envelopes. Open the main file named **wd06NapeMeeting.doc** and save it as **NapeMeeting1Main.doc**. Open the data file named **wd06NapeExecs.xls** and save it as **NapeExecs1Data.xls**. Print an envelope for each letter by using the recipient's address that is at the top of each letter. Include your address as the return address for the envelopes (see Figure 6.28).

FIGURE 6.27

NAPE meeting letter with fields

FIGURE 6.28

One envelope for the NAPE Executive Committee mailing

1. Investigating E-Commerce Sites

You are a new instructor at your college and the first course you are going to teach is Introduction to E-Business (BUS 101). For your first assignment you are going to ask your students to create an assignment sheet for visiting Web sites and analyze them based on how they conduct e-business. Each student will receive a personal assignment sheet with a unique Web site address for them to visit (see Figure 6.29).

Using the data file **wd06AssignMain.doc** create a merge document that will merge the data in Figure 6.30 with the individual assignment sheets and unique Web sites. Create a data source from this figure and save it as **Assign1Data.doc**. Save the main document as **Assign1Main.doc** and the final merged document as **Assign1Merge.doc**.

FIGURE 6.29

Assignment 1 for Introduction to E-Business

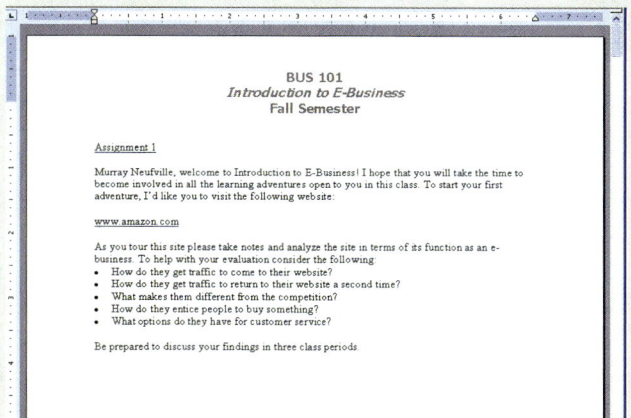

FIGURE 6.30

Students and Web sites for assignment 1

Name	Website
Murry Neufville	www.amazon.com
Lee Ping	www.bn.com
John Countryman	www.half.com
Leland Zetzsche	www.computergeek.com
Dawn Balaban	www.travelocity.com
TG Brandt	www.myseasons.com
Eric Rehkop	ww.sportsmansguide.com
Jacquelyn McMinnis	www.campingworld.com

2. Providing a Regional Sales Report

CampNow is an e-business specializing in the online sale of camping supplies and products. The company has been in business for two years and is located in Huntsville, Ontario. Six of the regional sales representatives manage their own Web sites where customers can purchase equipment. Figure 6.31 shows a letter to one of the sales representatives last quarter. Use this letter (**wd06SalesMain.doc**) to create a merged letter to send out this quarter to each of the representatives with a report of their quarterly sales (see Figure 6.32). Create the data source from this figure and save it as **Sales1Data.doc**. Save the main document as **Sales1Main.doc** and the merged letters as **Sales1Merge.doc**.

FIGURE 6.31

CampNow sales report letter from last quarter

FIGURE 6.32

Sales representatives for CampNow and their total sales for this quarter

FName	LName	Address	City	State	Zip	Sales
Leland	Zetzsche	345 Hilltop Road	Fargo	ND	77843	345,000
Dawn	Balaban	2232 Fairfield Avenue	Boise	NY	65211	305,000
TG	Brandt	2120 Fyffe Rd	Storrs	MT	43210	450,000
Eric	Rehkop	PO Box 1002	Denver	KS	66901	370,000
Jacqueline	McMinnis	PO Box 5034	Cookeville	IL	38505	245,000
Chao	Wangberg	864 Kleberg Center	Mesa	OR	97331	367,800

on the web

1. Requesting Information from Universities

You have been hired as the Web site developer at your school. Your first assignment is to research other college Web sites in order to determine the best way to develop your school's Web site. Search the Internet and review at least 15 different college or university Web sites. For example, Figure 6.33 displays the University of Denver's Web site. Choose five Web sites that you like the best and list them in a table in Word like the one shown in Figure 6.34. Search the Web to find the information necessary to complete the table for at least five colleges or universities. Save your work as **College1.doc** along with the number one college Web site you found.

2. Using Query for Mailing Labels

You are responsible for mailing out information about an upcoming conference on e-business. In the data source file, **wd06NAPEQuery.xls** contains individuals who are involved in computer applications (Subject = Computer Apps). Query this data source, and print a set of address labels for only those individuals involved in computer applications. Save the labels as **NapeComputer.doc**.

FIGURE 6.33

University of Denver's Web site

FIGURE 6.34

Table for collecting contact information from universities

Contact Name	University	E-mail	URL

LEVEL THREE

CHAPTER SIX

1. Inviting People to a World Halloween Party

You are hosting an international Halloween party. Everyone coming to your party has to bring a food unique to a specified country. Your guest list and the country from which they are to bring a food are shown in Figure 6.35.

Create a letter inviting your guests to the party (see Figure 6.36). Merge this letter with the names and addresses shown in Figure 6.35. Also include a line in the invitation for specifying the country from which they are to bring a food. Be sure to merge these data when you merge the letter. Save your main document with the merge fields as **WorldPartyMain.doc** and your data source as **WorldPartyData.mdb**.

Using the same data, create a set of address labels by merging the data with an address label format. Print the addresses on the plain paper, but include your name and section number on the bottom-right of the page.

FIGURE 6.35

List of guests, their address, and the country food representation

Fname	Lname	Address	City	ST	Zip	Country
Liam	Kennedy	700 E Butler Ave	Georgetown	WI	61635	Japan
Peter	Jackson	121 Fort Hall	Georgetown	WI	61635	Hungary
Chris	Reich	Box 2400	Georgetown	WI	61635	Germany
Robert	Turgeon	PO Box 7140	Georgetown	WI	61635	China
Jacob	Jen	PO Box 5435	Georgetown	WI	61635	Indonesia
Walter	Alhashimi	1345 Circle Park	Georgetown	WI	61635	England

FIGURE 6.36

World Halloween Party letter

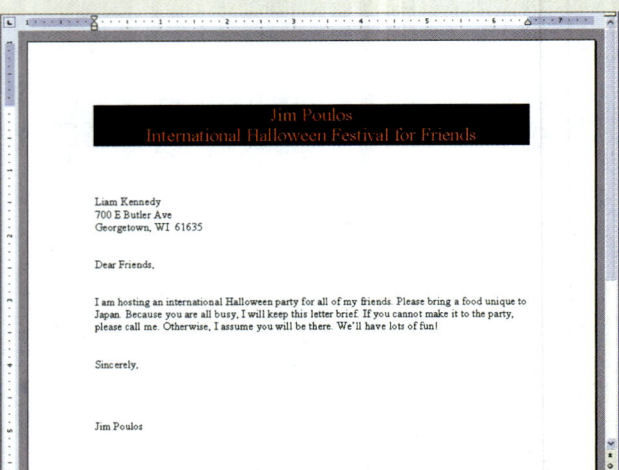

running project

Using Mail Merge to Contact Universities

ElRay Li, senior class counselor at the Kasota High School, sends out a letter each year to a list of colleges and universities to collect current scholarship forms from each. This year for the first time he will use Word to mail merge these letters (Figure 6.37). Include address labels for the envelopes.

ElRay's letter for creating the main document for the merge is saved as **wd06Scholarship.doc**; add the appropriate fields and save the main document as **ScholarshipsMain.doc**. The data he needs for his mailing are contained in an Excel worksheet saved as **wd06ScholarColleges.xls**.

After sending the letter, ElRay will develop a checklist that his student aide will use to check as information is received from the different colleges and universities. The checklist will also include the phone number for any follow-up. The directory feature of mail merge helps generate this list. (*Hint*: Use a tab between Address1, ST, and Phone.) Using the Table feature of Word allowed ElRay to put the list into a checklist as shown in Figure 6.38. Save your table as **ChecklistDirectory.doc**.

FIGURE 6.37

Letter sent to colleges and universities by ElRay Li

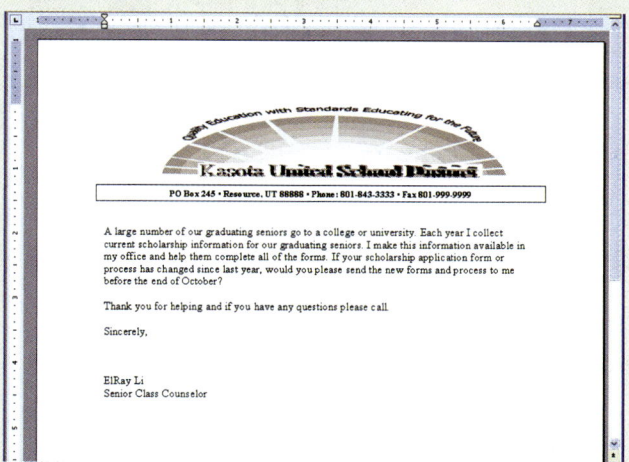

FIGURE 6.38

Checklist for follow-up with colleges and universities

Ck	Name	College	State	Phone
	Evelyn Neswinder	University Of Alaska	AK	488-356-7960
	Raoul Schmidt	University Of Arizona	AZ	725-428-6850
	Susan Jones	North Arizona University	AZ	354-687-1836
	Murray Neufville	Three Rivers Com College	CA	545-201-2837
	Rita Martinez	Western Il Univ	IL	740-106-2963
	Lee Ping	University of Illinois	IL	373-879-3399
	Jacquelyn McMinnis	Southern Illinois Univ	IL	565-794-2344
	Eric Rehkop	Denver University	KS	373-869-0011
	LeAnn Marquardt	University Of Louisiana	LA	703-538-2287
	JR Pottorff	Vocational School	MA	804-175-3760
	Rosa Brandenburg	University Of Maryland	MD	407-559-6573
	Willis Long	Univ Of Maine	ME	797-314-0044
	Peter Jackson	Sam Houston State University	MI	828-565-4657
	Danny Ling	University of Missouri	MO	930-224-5583
	Tom Brandt	Stephen F Austin State University	MT	292-583-7349
	Leland Zetzsche	North Dakota Tech University	ND	345-275-8694
	Suzanne Hafer	Nebraska School of Rangeland Management	NE	301-757-9922
	Dawn Reddeer	Boise Ag & Tech College	NY	615-990-3769
	Jacob Jen	Oklahoma State University	OK	454-668-3357
	Robert Turgeon	Oregon State University	OR	828-332-0091
	Chao Wangberg	Scottsdale Community College	OR	280-265-3647
	Liam Kennedy	Pennsylvania School Of Agriculture	PA	707-554-4442
	Paul Wehrenberg	Wilmington College	TX	204-395-1957
	John Horseman	Texas A & M University	TX	243-786-4738
	Rosemary Vaughn	Utah State University	UT	388-334-0087
	Bobba Fetina	Un Of Virginia At Pine Bluff	VA	886-335-2435
	Tom Chittick	West Virginia University	VA	394-850-5016
	Chris Reich	Ratcliffe Hicks Business College	WI	909-339-2772
	Danilo Chrudimsky	Univ Of Wisconsin	WI	203-563-2158

1. Inserting and Embedding Objects

Explain the advantages of inserting an Excel table instead of creating a table in Word.

2. Multiple Data Sources

Create a document explaining why you would want to create a mail merge with multiple data sources while the main document remains the same. Also explain why you would use the same data source with multiple main documents.

Outlines, PowerPoint, and Web Pages

know? did you

completed *in 1936, the Queen Mary was the largest, fastest, and most luxurious ocean liner of the era. Today the Queen Mary serves as a museum, hotel, and conference center in Long Beach, California.*

when *President James K. Polk gave his annual message to Congress in December 1848, he confirmed that gold had indeed been discovered in California. This "official" announcement triggered the Gold Rush of 1849.*

Albert Einstein's *most famous formula is widely known as $E = mc^2$. According to his formula, the energy of one gram (1/28 ounce) of matter would keep a 100-watt lightbulb glowing for 28,500 years.*

in *Enterprise, Alabama, a monument is dedicated to the boll weevil, one of the worst cotton crop pests ever. The weevil's devastations forced the farmers to try new kinds of crops, including the peanut, which ultimately led to a tripling of profits!*

Bob Keeshan *starred in America's longest-running children's program. In 1955, he joined CBS and started "Captain Kangaroo." The program endured on that network and PBS for nearly 40 years.*

in *1889, an entrepreneur named Louis Glass installed a coin-operated Edison cylinder phonograph in the Palais Royale Saloon in San Francisco—the first jukebox. It cost a nickel to play a single selection from the machine.*

Chapter Objectives

- **Save documents in appropriate formats for different uses— MOS WW03S-2-2**

- **Insert and modify hyperlinks—MOS WW03S-2-3**

- **Create bulleted lists, and numbered lists and outlines— MOS WW03S-5-4**

- **Preview documents and Web pages—MOS WW03S-5-6**

- **Structure documents using XML—MOS WW03E-2-8**

- **Publish and edit Web documents in Word—MOS WW03E-4-2**

- **Use automated tools for document navigation—MOS WW03E-2-5**

Outlines, PowerPoint, and Web Pages for an Animal Nutrition Class

Dr. Jack Schweitzer teaches an introductory animal nutrition class at West Virginia University. He has been teaching this course for 15 years, and with what he knows of Word, he would like to put his lecture notes and readings on the World Wide Web for his students. Dr. Schweitzer plans to use his notes to create PowerPoint slides for his lectures, and he wants to insert hyperlinks to interesting Web sites into his Web page.

During the following sessions you will work with Dr. Schweitzer transferring his lecture outline on nutrition and nutrients to PowerPoint, creating a Web page from a reading on pet nutrition, and embedding bookmarks and hyperlinks into his documents. Figures 7.1 and 7.2 illustrate Dr. Schweitzer's finished products.

F I G U R E 7.1

Thumbnails of PowerPoint slides for nutrition and nutrients lecture

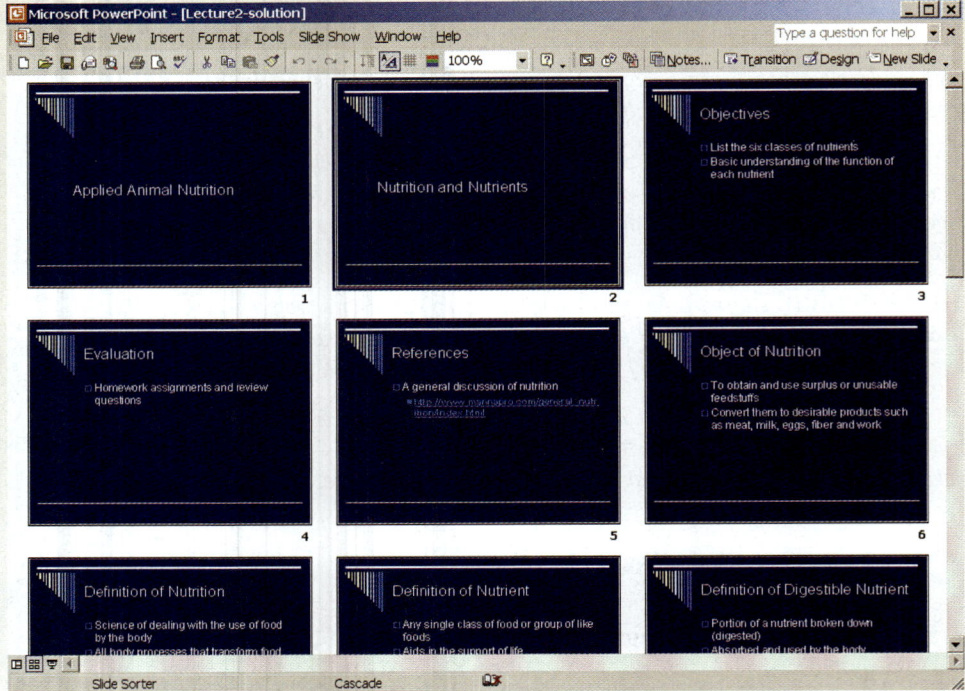

F I G U R E 7.2

Reading on pet nutrition saved as a Web page using Word's Blends theme

Pet Food Labels

Introduction

One pet food company advertises their food as better than others. Wording on pet food labels is sometimes misunderstood, often ignored, and can be confusing. To limit confusion when listing each ingredient in a food, all pet food companies should be required to also use the International Feed Number (IFN) that has been assigned to each feed grade ingredient.

To help you determine what may be in the pet food you are now buying, here are definitions of some words that can be found on most pet food labels today:

By-product

An ingredient produced in the course of making a primary food ingredient; a secondary or incidental product. Feathers are a by-product of poultry meat processing. Feathers that are removed from a carcass during production of poultry meat are then hydrolyzed (pressure cooked with steam until they are an edible gel) which makes them an acceptable feed grade ingredient. Hydrolyzed feathers have been assigned an (IFN) International Feed Number.

Hydrolyzed Poultry By-Products Aggregate is the product resulting from heat treatment, or a combination thereof, of all by-products of slaughter poultry, clean and un-decomposed, including such parts as heads, feet, underdeveloped eggs, intestines, feathers, and blood. Today's regulations allow the entire mix or any part of it to appear on a label as Poultry By-products. A Fish By-product can contain heads, tails, intestines

INTRODUCTION

In general, people seem to avoid outlining. Most of us remember when the skill was taught to us and we were told to use it when we developed a speech or a report. Likely we failed to understand the importance of an outline. A well-developed outline can help you:

- Organize thoughts
- Develop sequence
- Avoid omitting information
- Recognize nonessential facts
- Determine headings
- Make smooth transitions
- Avoid extensive revisions

In this chapter you are going to learn how to create an outline and how to build PowerPoint slides from a Word document. You are also going to learn how to save your document in HTML for use as a Web page.

SESSION 7.1 OUTLINES AND POWERPOINT

Word processing and the ability to outline with a word processor place renewed emphasis on the importance of an outline. After an outline is completed, creating a PowerPoint presentation is easy and convenient.

help yourself *Click the **Ask a Question** combo box, type **Outline**, and press **Enter**. Click the hyperlink **Create an Outline from scratch** to display information on how you can create an outline from scratch. Click the Help screen **Close** button when you are finished*

Creating a Word Outline

Working with an outline helps put information in the proper sequential or chronological order. Outlines help develop comparisons, divisions, classifications, cause-and-effect relationships, and spatial relations. By moving the components of an outline you can develop a report or presentation that runs from the general to the specific, or you can decrease or increase the importance of a topic by changing its level in the outline. When used and understood, outlining is a powerful tool. You can outline a document in three ways (Figure 7.3):

1. Organize a new document
2. Assign outline levels
3. Create an outline-style numbered list

Organizing a New Document with Outlining

When you organize the headings and subheadings of a document as an outline, Word automatically applies built-in heading styles. To make it easier to view and reorganize the document's structure, you can collapse the document (see Figure 7.4) to show just the headings you want. This makes it easy to reorder the headings if necessary.

---

task reference   Organizing a New Document Using the Outline View

- In a new document, switch to **Outline** view; this will open the Outlining toolbar

- Type each heading, and press **Enter** (Word formats the headings with the built-in style Heading 1)

- To assign a heading to a lower level and apply the corresponding heading style, drag the heading's plus (1) or minus (2) or outline symbol to the right (see Figure 7.5)

- To *promote* a heading to a higher level, drag the symbol to the left

- To move a heading to a different location, drag the symbol up or down (the subordinate text under the heading moves with the heading)

- After organizing the outline, switch to **Normal** view or **Print Layout** view to add detailed body text and graphics

F I G U R E   7.3

Three ways to create an outline

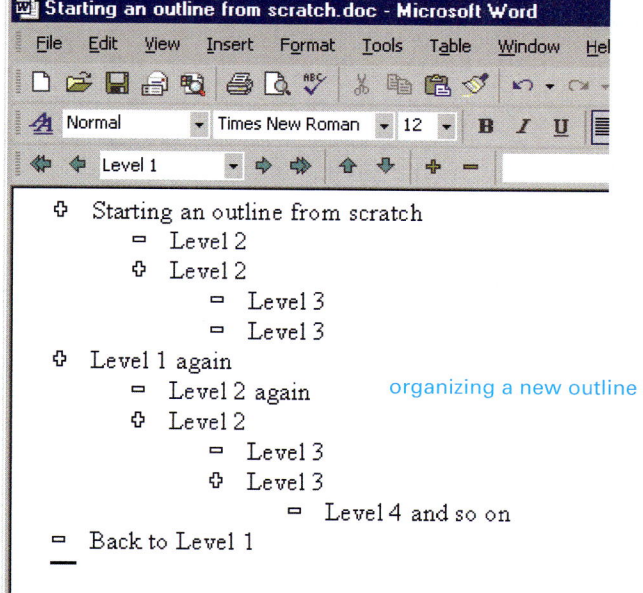

organizing a new outline

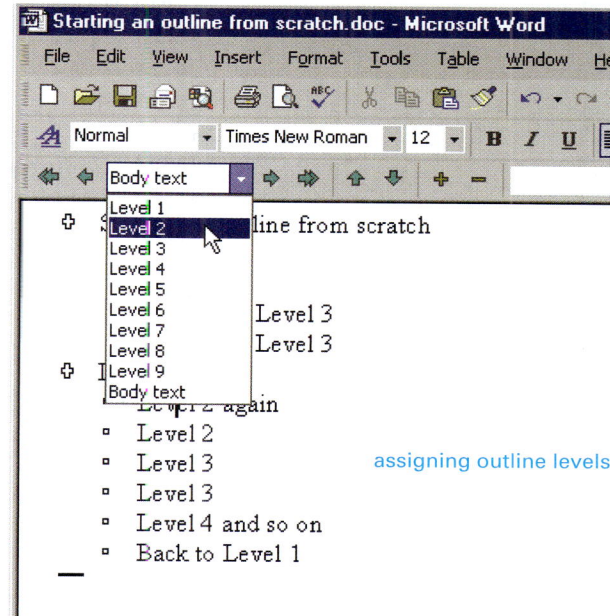

assigning outline levels

creating an outline-style numbered list

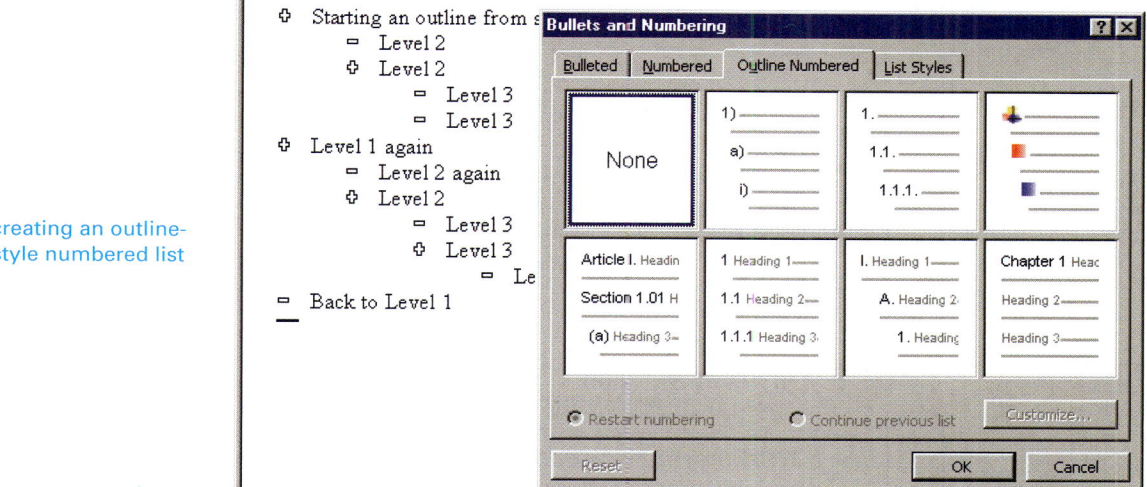

Assigning Outline Levels

You can assign outline levels to your paragraphs if you aren't using the built-in heading styles. This lets you impose a hierarchical structure on your document without having to format your text with the built-in heading styles. Then you can work in the Outline view or the Document Map.

FIGURE   7.4

Expanded and collapsed
outline

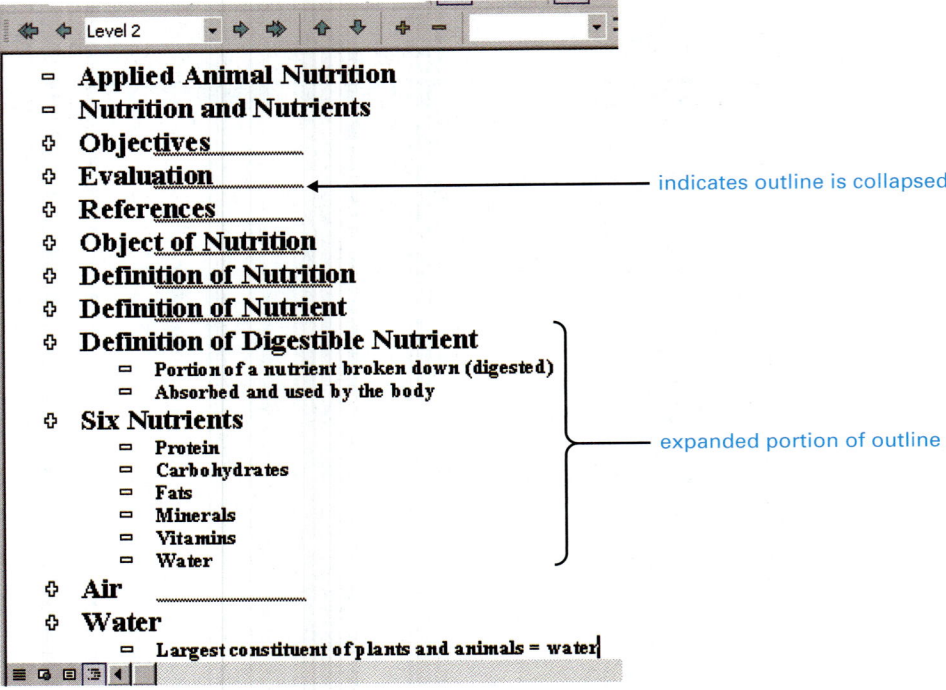

indicates outline is collapsed

expanded portion of outline

FIGURE   7.5

Changing a heading level
by dragging

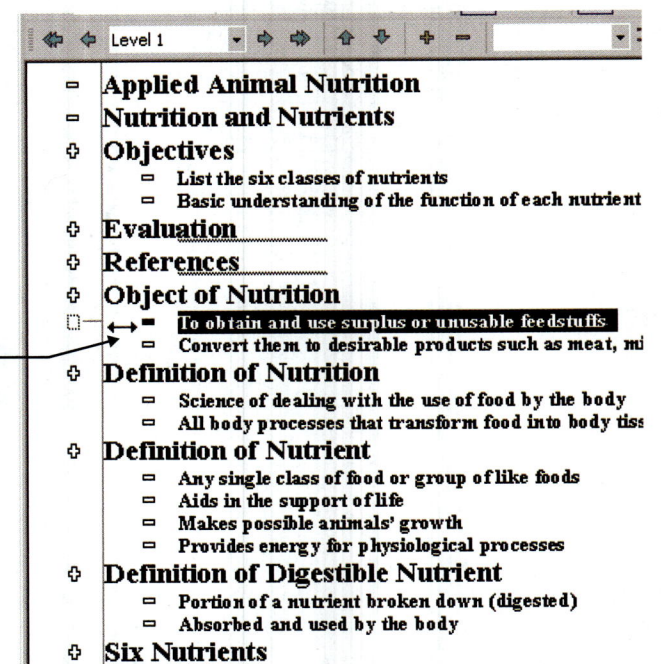

drag to promote or
demote outline level

- Switch to **Print Layout** view

- Select a paragraph you want to assign an outline level to

- On the Format menu, click **Paragraph**, and then click the **Indents and Spacing** tab (Figure 7.6)

- In the **Outline level** box, click the level you want

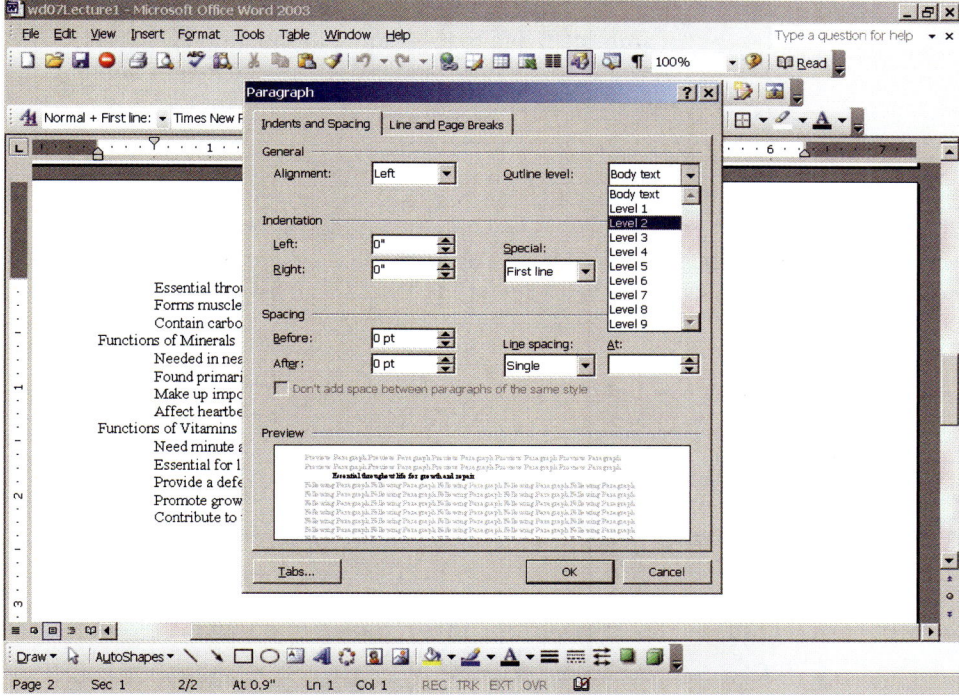

F I G U R E   7.6

Process of applying outline levels paragraphs

Use outline levels when you don't want to change the appearance of your text, since the built-in heading styles apply specific formatting. The outline levels apply an invisible format.

To use the functionality of heading styles without modifying the built-in heading styles, create a new set of custom heading styles that include the outline-level paragraph format. After you create your own heading styles, you can work with them as usual— for example, apply the custom heading styles to text that you want to include in a table of contents.

Outline-Style Numbered Lists

Finally, numbered lists provide an additional method of creating an outline. By typing topics and subtopics in an outline-style numbered list, you can create a hierarchical structure for your document. The text is now formatted with the built-in heading styles. Outline numbered lists can have up to nine levels.

For each numbering level, you can modify the outline numbered list format.

FIGURE 7.7

An outline numbered list

1) This is a numbered list
2) Next line
   a) Demoted one level
      i) Demoted another level
      ii) Second item
   b) Promoted a level

---

task reference — Creating an Outline Numbered List

- On the Format menu, click **Bullets and Numbering**, and then click the **Outline Numbered** tab

- Click a list format that does not contain the text Heading 1, and then click **OK**

- Type the list, pressing **Enter** after each item

- To **demote** the item to a lower numbering level, click anywhere in the item, and click **Increase Indent** on the Formatting toolbar (see Figure 7.7)

- To promote the item to a higher numbering level, click anywhere in the item, and click **Decrease Indent** on the Formatting toolbar

---

Dr. Schweitzer has some outlines that he has used in his applied animal nutrition course. He eventually wants to create PowerPoint slides from them, so he plans to assign outline levels to the topics for each set of lecture notes. After reviewing all the possible ways to outline, he decides to apply outline levels with Heading 1, Heading 2, and so on.

another way

. . . to Change Heading Levels

Heading levels can also be reassigned using the **Tab** and the **Shift+Tab**. To assign a heading to a lower level and apply the corresponding heading style, press **Tab**. To assign a heading to a higher level and apply the corresponding heading style, press **Shift+Tab**

Assigning outline levels to Applied Animal Nutrition lectures:

1. Open file **wd07Lecture.doc**

2. Save the file as **Lecture1.doc**

3. Apply the default style of **Heading 1** to all topics flush with the left margin

4. Apply the default style of **Heading 2** to all topics that are tabbed (indented) once

5. Work through the whole document

6. Apply **Style 2** to the line "A general discussion of nutrition," and **Style 3** to the hyperlink

7. View the document in the **Outline** view, and compare your final results with Figure 7.8

8. Save your document

Creating a PowerPoint Slide Show from a Word Outline

You can use an existing Word document to create a PowerPoint presentation. To do this you send an outline created in Word to PowerPoint. When you send a Word document to PowerPoint, it uses the outline structure from the styles in the document. A Heading 1 becomes a slide title, a Heading 2 becomes the first level of text, and so on. If the document contains no styles, PowerPoint uses the paragraph indentations to create an outline.

- **Applied Animal Nutrition**
- **Nutrition and Nutrients**
- **Objectives**
    - List the six classes of nutrients
    - Basic understanding of the function of each nutrient
- **Evaluation**
    - Homework assignments and review questions
- **References**
    - A general discussion of nutrition
        - http://www.mannapro.com/general_nutrition/index.html
- **Object of Nutrition**
    - To obtain and use surplus or unusable feedstuffs
    - Convert them to desirable products such as meat, milk, eggs, fiber, and work
- **Definition of Nutrition**
    - Science of dealing with the use of food by the body
    - All body processes that transform food into body tissues and activities
- **Definition of Nutrient**
    - Any single class of food or group of like foods
    - Aids in the support of life
    - Makes possible animals' growth
    - Provides energy for physiological processes
- **Definition of Digestible Nutrient**
    - Portion of a nutrient broken down (digested)
    - Absorbed and used by the body
- **Six Nutrients**
    - Protein
    - Carbohydrates
    - Fats
    - Minerals
    - Vitamins
    - Water
- **Air**
    - Sometimes considered the seventh nutrient
- **Water**

You can also insert an outline into an existing presentation. When you import a plain text document, tabs at the starting of paragraphs define the outline structure. The slide master in the current presentation determines the format for the title and text.

---

task reference   Creating a PowerPoint Slide Show

- Open the document with the outline that you want to use to create a PowerPoint presentation

- On the File menu, point to **Send To**, and then click **Microsoft PowerPoint**

When the outline is sent to a new PowerPoint presentation, the slides are blank except for text (see Figure 7.9). From inside PowerPoint you will need to add slide designs, color schemes, graphics, and transitions. Once the slides are created you can add all types of enhancements using what you know and learn about PowerPoint.

Dr. Schweitzer is comfortable with assigning heading levels or outlining; he is ready to send his first outline to PowerPoint.

F I G U R E　7.9

Lecture slides for Applied
Animal Nutrition after
being sent from Word to
PowerPoint

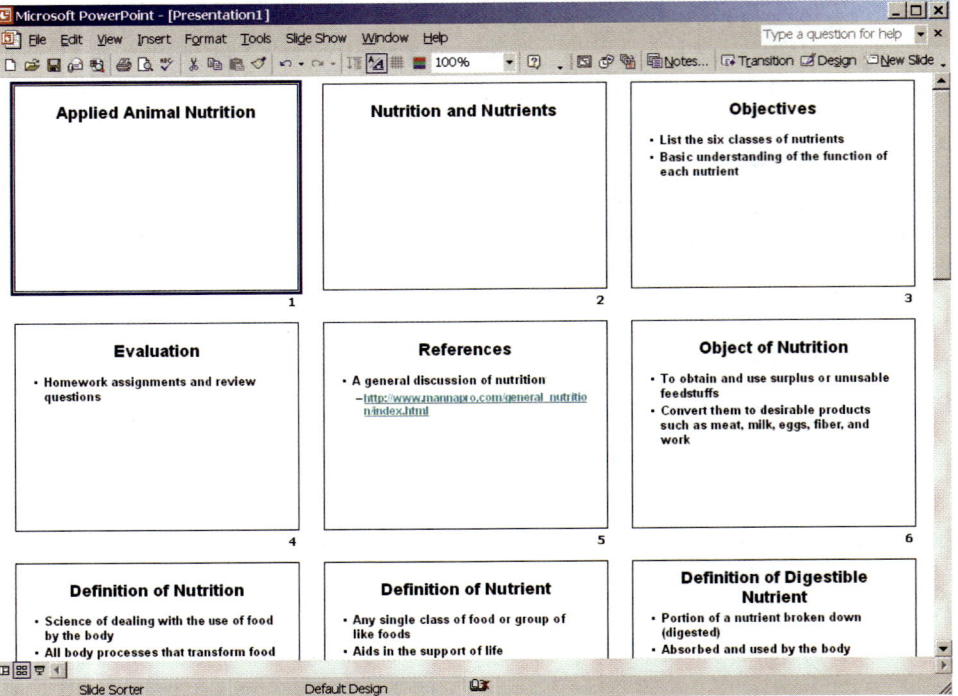

Sending a lecture outline to PowerPoint:

1. Ensure your Lecture1.doc is open

2. Click **File, Send To, Microsoft PowerPoint**

3. View the slides in PowerPoint (see Figure 7.9)

4. Save your document as **Lecture2Slides.ppt**

5. Close PowerPoint and return to Word. Close **Lecture1.doc**

---

another**word**　　　. . . to Create PowerPoint Slides with Word

If you're already working in PowerPoint, you can import a Word document into
PowerPoint. In PowerPoint, click **Open** on the File menu. In the Files of type box,
click **All Files**. In the File name box, enter the filename and location of the Word
document

You can also insert slides from a Word outline into an existing presentation.
In PowerPoint, display the slide you want to insert the new slides after. On the
Insert menu, click **Slides from Outline**, and then select the Word document you
want

making *the grade*

1. Name three types of outlines.

2. True or False: In the Outline view, the 1 collapses an outline.

3. True or False: Each Heading 1 in Word becomes a new slide when an outline is sent to PowerPoint.

4. Name two ways to change the level of an item in an outline.

5. True or False: When an outline is sent to PowerPoint, the resulting slides are automatically assigned a design of white text on a blue background.

SESSION 7.2 FORMATTING AND VIEWING A WEB PAGE

HyperText Markup Language (HTML) tells your browser software how to display text and other objects on the World Wide Web. HTML is used to create Web pages. *HTML tags* contain all the information you'd like to include in your Web page (see Figure 7.10). *Web pages* are text files with HTML code, pictures, and other components capable of being interpreted by a Web browser. A *Web browser* is software that interprets HTML files, formats them into Web pages, and displays them. A Web browser, such as Microsoft Internet Explorer, can follow hyperlinks, transfer files, and play sound or video files that are embedded in Web pages. HTML tells your browser, the software that you use to navigate the World Wide Web, such as Netscape Navigator or Internet Explorer, how to display text and other objects.

FIGURE 7.10

Document showing HTML tags

In order to create Web pages you can either "hard code" or use an HTML editor. To hard code, you can use a simple text editor, such as Notepad, and type the HTML tags or commands (see Figure 7.10) along with the content following the appropriate syntax. This is a lot of work. If you do not "speak" HTML you can still create great looking Web pages using an editor. Many commercial HTML editors are available, but in this session you will concentrate on using Microsoft Word to create HTML files. Using Word, you can easily convert a document into an HTML file.

```
<html>
<head>
<TITLE>A Simple HTML Example</TITLE>
</head>
<body>
<H1>HTML is Easy To Learn</H1>
<P>Welcome to the world of HTML.
This is the first paragraph. While short it is
still a paragraph!</P>
<P>And this is the second paragraph.</P>
</body>
</html>
```

The Web Page

You can use Microsoft Word to create Web pages in the same way you create regular Word documents. To get you started, Word offers some easy ways to start your Web page. You can use the Web Page Wizard, use a Web page template, or create a Web page from an existing document.

Using the Web Page Wizard

A *theme* is a set of unified design elements that provide a look for your document using color, fonts, and graphics. *Link bars* are a collection of graphic or text buttons representing hyperlinks to pages within your Web site and to external sites. A *frame* is the named sub-window of a frames page. The frame appears in a Web browser as one of a number of window regions in which pages can be displayed. The frame can be scrollable and resizable, and it can have a border.

By using the Web Page Wizard, you can create a single Web page or an entire Web site. You can add existing Web pages and Word documents to your Web site, add a theme, insert link bars, and use frames to make Web pages more dynamic and engaging.

help yourself *Click the* **Ask a Question** *combo box, type* **Web Page Wizard**, *and press* **Enter**. *Click the hyperlink* **About creating a Web page** *to display information on how you can create a Web page by using the Web Page Wizard, Web page template, or an existing document. Click the Help screen* **Close** *button when you are finished*

Using a Web Page Template

When you use a Web page template, Word will make features that are not supported by your target browser unavailable so that you don't have to worry about how your formatting will look in a Web browser. Templates allow the addition of a theme, the insertion of link bars, and the use of frames to make Web pages more dynamic and engaging. To apply formatting quickly to several pages, you can attach cascading style sheets. A *cascading style sheet (CSS)* is part of a Web page that defines styles controlling the way a Web page or a part of a Web page appears in a browser. Microsoft Office stores embedded style sheets at the top of each Web page.

F I G U R E   7.11
A Web page template from Word

Main Heading Goes Here

Contents
- Work Information
- Favorite Links
- Contact Information
- Current Projects
- Biographical Information
- Personal Interests

Work Information

Job Title
Type some text.

Key responsibilities
Type some text.

Department or workgroup
Type some text.

Back to top

Favorite Links
- Insert a hyperlink here
- Insert a hyperlink here
- Insert a hyperlink here

Back to top

---

task reference   **Using the Web Page Template**

- On the File menu, click **New**

- In the New Document task pane, under templates, click **On My Computer**

- Click the **Web Page** template (see Figure 7.11)

or

- To create a blank Web page, on the File menu, click **New**

- Under New in the New Document task pane, click **Web Page** (see Figure 7.12)

Creating a Web Page from an Existing Document

Save an existing document as a Web page to quickly get your Word documents ready for copying to the Web or an intranet. An *intranet* is a network within an organization that uses Internet technologies such as the HTTP or FTP protocol. *HyperText Transfer Protocol (HTTP)* is the protocol used by the World Wide Web. HTTP defines how messages are formatted and transferred. *File Transfer Protocol (FTP)* is used to transfer files between computers. By using hyperlinks, you can explore objects, documents, pages, and other destinations on the intranet.

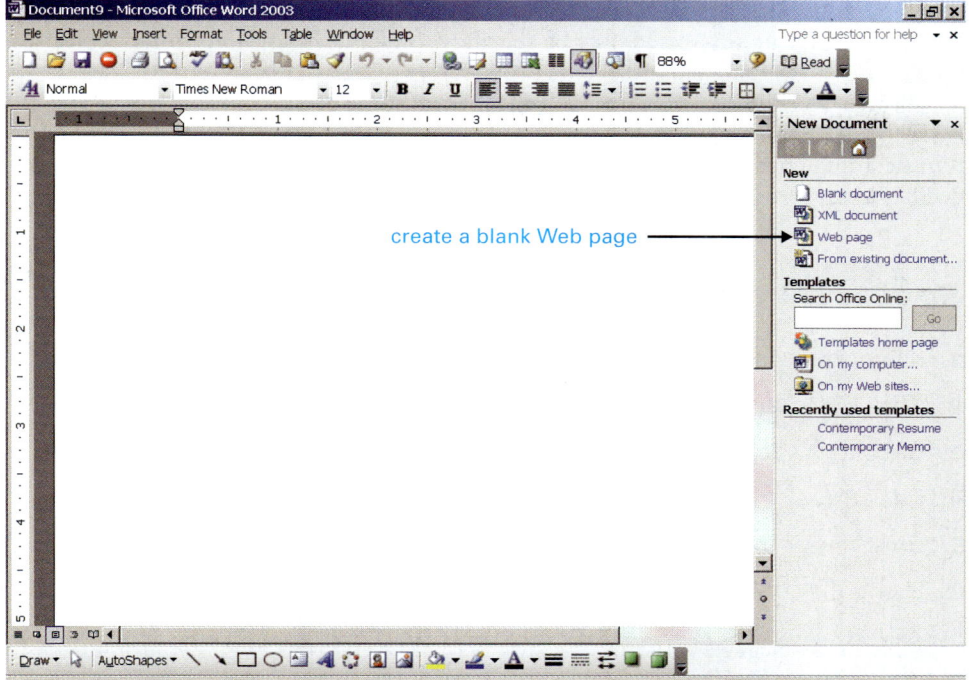

Creating a blank Web page

---

task reference   Saving a Web Page from a Word Document

- On the File menu, click **Save as Web Page**

- If you want to save the document in a different folder, locate and open the folder

- In the File name box, type a name for the document

- Click **Save**

Some formatting that you can use in Microsoft Word may be unsupported by some Web browsers. When you save a Word document as a Web page, Word removes unsupported formatting and applies formatting that Web browsers support. Features that are unsupported in Web browsers include the following:

- Table formatting
- Character formatting
- Paragraph formatting
- Page layout
- Headers and footers
- Tabs (may not align correctly on Web pages)
- Graphic formatting
- Security and document protection
- Asian text formatting
- Combined characters

You can fix this problem if you desire by changing options in Word to create Web pages that use formatting supported only by specific browsers. This option works by clearing the features not supported by specific browsers.

Before Dr. Schweitzer creates Web pages from some of his course materials, he decides to try saving a plain document as a Web page. Recently, a Word file was sent to him detailing computer competencies needed by employees after leaving college. He decides to save this file as a Web page.

Saving a Word document as a Web page:

1. Open your data file **Lecture1.doc**

2. Click **File, Save As Web Page**

3. Save as a Web page using the same filename

4. Click **Save**

5. Check your data files to verify that you have the file Lecture1.htm

6. Using a Web browser, compare your Web page to Figure 7.13

FIGURE 7.13

Lecture 1 saved as a Web page and viewed in a browser

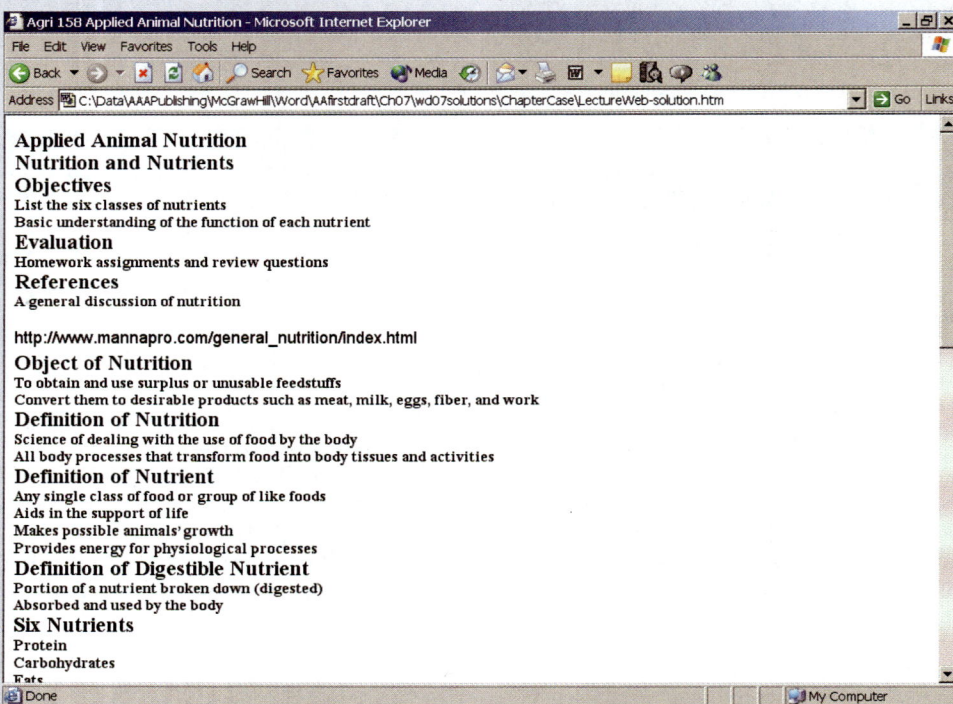

---

anotherword   . . . on **Web Pages from Existing Documents**

Sometimes you may have a number of documents that you would like to use as Web pages. Word allows you to create multiple Web pages from multiple Word documents. Place the documents you want to convert in a single folder. Then in the **New Document** task pane, under New from template, click **General Templates** and click the **Other Documents** tab. At this point double-click **Batch Conversion Wizard** and follow the directions on the screen. If you do not see the Batch Conversion Wizard in the New dialog box, you may need to install it

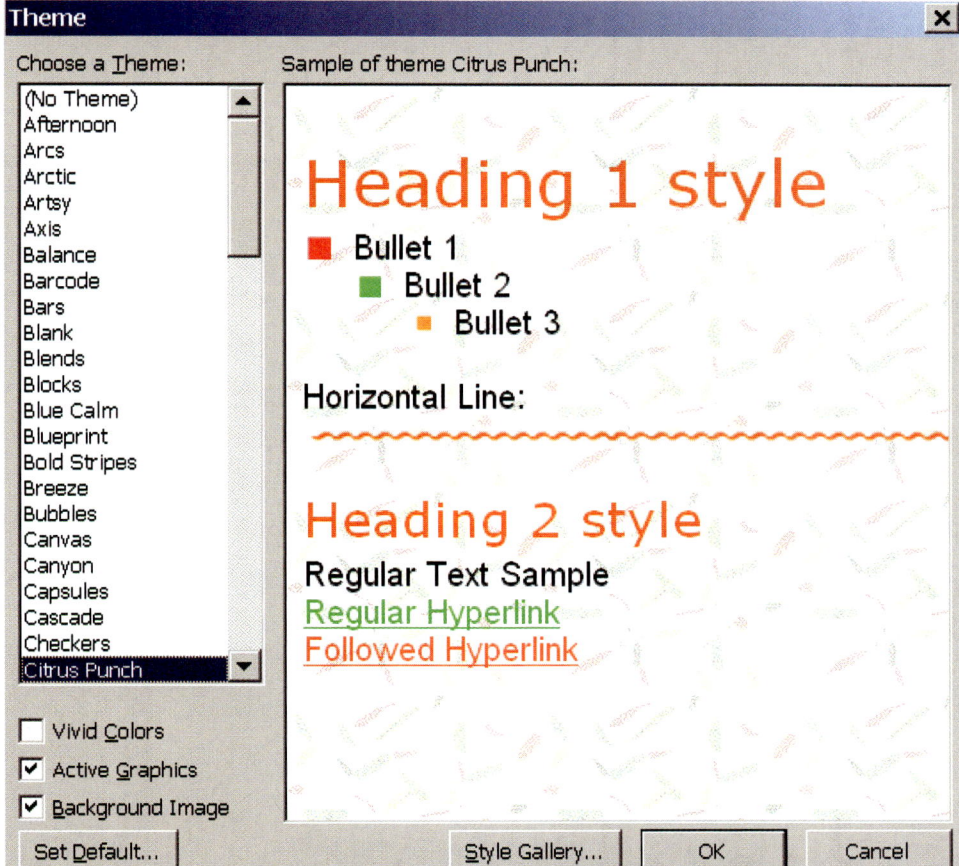

FIGURE 7.14

Theme dialog box in Word showing an example of one of the many themes

Choosing a Theme

A theme is a set of unified design elements and color schemes. A theme helps you easily create professional and well-designed documents for viewing in Microsoft Word, in e-mail, or on the Web (see Figure 7.14).

When you apply a theme to a document, Word customizes the following elements: link bars, background colors or graphics, body and heading styles, lists, horizontal lines, hyperlink colors, and table border colors. Both the single-level and the multiple-level lists are also customized.

To quickly change the appearance of these elements, you can change the theme. Unlike a template, a theme does not provide AutoText entries, custom toolbars, macros, menu settings, or shortcut keys.

You can also select options to apply brighter colors to text and graphics, animate certain theme graphics, or apply a background to your document. To see the animation of theme graphics, view the Web page in a Web browser.

To download additional themes, click Office on the Web on the Help menu. As you work with Web pages and get more comfortable with them, you will probably want to try new things on your Web pages. Most of these you have already learned in Word, such as,

- Formatting text
- Inserting bullets
- Inserting graphics and tables
- Creating hyperlinks

Viewing the Document in a Browser

Work in Web Layout view when you are creating a Web page or a document that is viewed on the screen. In Web Layout view, you can see backgrounds, text is wrapped to fit the window, and graphics are positioned just as they are in a Web browser.

---

task reference   Viewing a Document as a Web Page

- Click on the View menu and select **Web Layout**

or

- Click **Web Layout view** on the buttons in the lower left of the document screen

---

Now that Dr. Schweitzer understands some of the options for creating Web pages, he is ready to practice setting up a new Web page for an article on pet nutrition.

Saving and viewing a Word document as a Web page:

1. Open the file **wd07Petfood.doc**
2. Save the document as **Petfood1.doc**
3. Click **Format, Theme**; choose **Blends** (see Figure 7.15)

FIGURE 7.15

Selecting the Blends theme

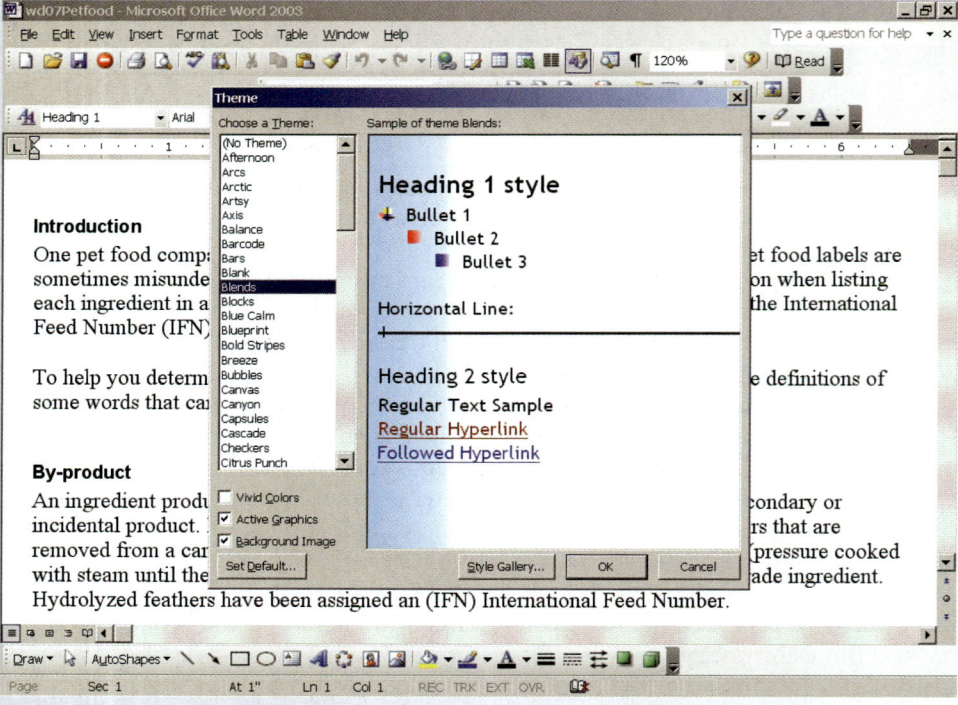

4. Click **OK**
5. Click **File, Save as Web Page**
6. Type **Pet food labels**
7. Click **Save**

8. Compare your results to Figure 7.16

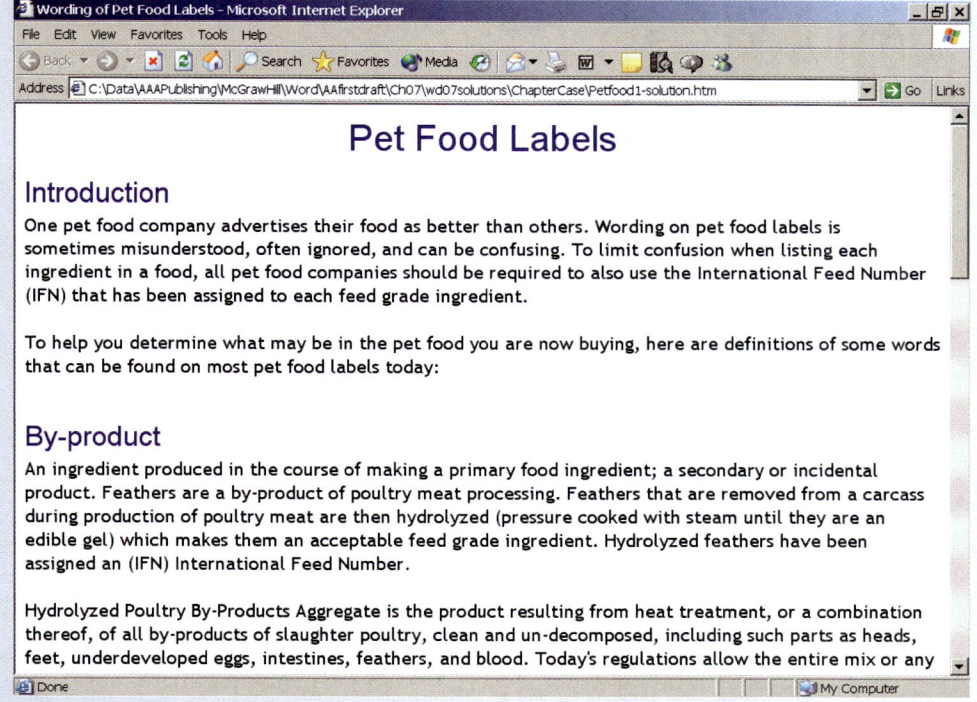

FIGURE 7.16

Pet Food Web page

When you get ready to post Web pages on a file server, you need to remember that when Word creates a Web page, it creates a folder of the same name. This folder contains the graphical elements that are a part of the Web page, and it needs to be placed on a file server with the Web page file that has the .htm extension.

XML Documents in Word

With the increasing demand for the Web, the limitations of HTML became obvious to many programmers. XML stands for Extensible Markup Language and was developed to overcome many of the limitations of HTML. HTML documents are human-readable but are not optimized for computer manipulation, whereas XML is the first language that makes documents both human-readable and computer-manipulable. Word enables you to work with XML documents in two ways:

- *Use Word's schema*: You can create a document in Word and then save it as an XML document. Word uses its own schema to apply XML tags that define the structure of the document, such as paragraph, heading, table, and so on.
- *Use any XML schema*: You can create or open a document in Word, attach any XML schema to it, and apply XML tags to the content of the document. When you save this document as an XML document, the XML tags define the structure of the document in terms of the XML schema that is attached to it.

Whether you use Word's built-in schema for a loosely based structure or attach some other schema for a more specialized structure, any software that can parse XML can read and process the data in a document that you save as an XML document (.xml).

Saving in XML Format

Saving your documents as XML files makes them available to any applications that support XML, not just the Microsoft Office applications.

anotherway
. . . on Saving a Web Page with HTML Filter

You can also save the file as a Web page, filtered (select from the Save as list). If you choose to save the Web page with filtering, this will remove the Microsoft Office–specific tags. This feature is recommended for experienced HTML users who are concerned about the tags that appear in their HTML files. You should only save a Web page in filtered HTML when you're finished editing it in Word

> ### *making the grade*
>
> 1. List three ways to create a Web page in Word.
> 2. Name three items Word can add that make Web pages more dynamic and engaging.
> 3. True or False: Some features of Word are not supported by Web browsers.
> 4. How can the appearance of a Word document as a Web page be checked before being saved as a Web page?
> 5. Themes are found by clicking _____ on the menu bar.

SESSION 7.3 DOCUMENT MAP, BOOKMARKS, AND HYPERLINKS

Being able to move quickly and accurately to locations within a document is essential to reading and editing a large document. Besides using the Find and Go To function to move to specific locations in a document, you can use the Document Map, Bookmarks, and hyperlinks.

- *Document Map*: Outline-type overview of the document's organization, showing the headings arranged hierarchically in a narrow, scrollable pane.
- *Bookmark*: A location or selection of text named for reference purposes. Word marks the location with the name you specify. Bookmarks are more than placeholders. For example, you can use them to create and number cross-references.
- *Hyperlink*: Colored and underlined text or a graphic that you click to go to a file, a location in a file, an HTML page on the World Wide Web, or an HTML page on an intranet.

Document Map

A Document Map is a very useful tool. Document Map provides quick outline-type overview of the document's organization, showing the headings arranged hierarchically in a narrow, scrollable pane on the left side of the screen (see Figure 7.17). You can *expand* or *collapse* any branch of the outline by clicking the little box beside it. Document Map's real value is as a navigation aid. Click a heading, and Word takes you there instantly. However, a heading appears in the Document Map only if it has been assigned a heading level, heading style, or an outline level. You have already learned how to assign heading and outline levels, and heading styles.

> ### *task* reference   Viewing the Document Map
>
> - On the menu bar, click **View, Document Map** to show the Document Map pane
> - To move through the document, click on any titles shown in the Document Map
> - Click **View, Document Map** again to turn off the Document Map

FIGURE   7.17

Document Map

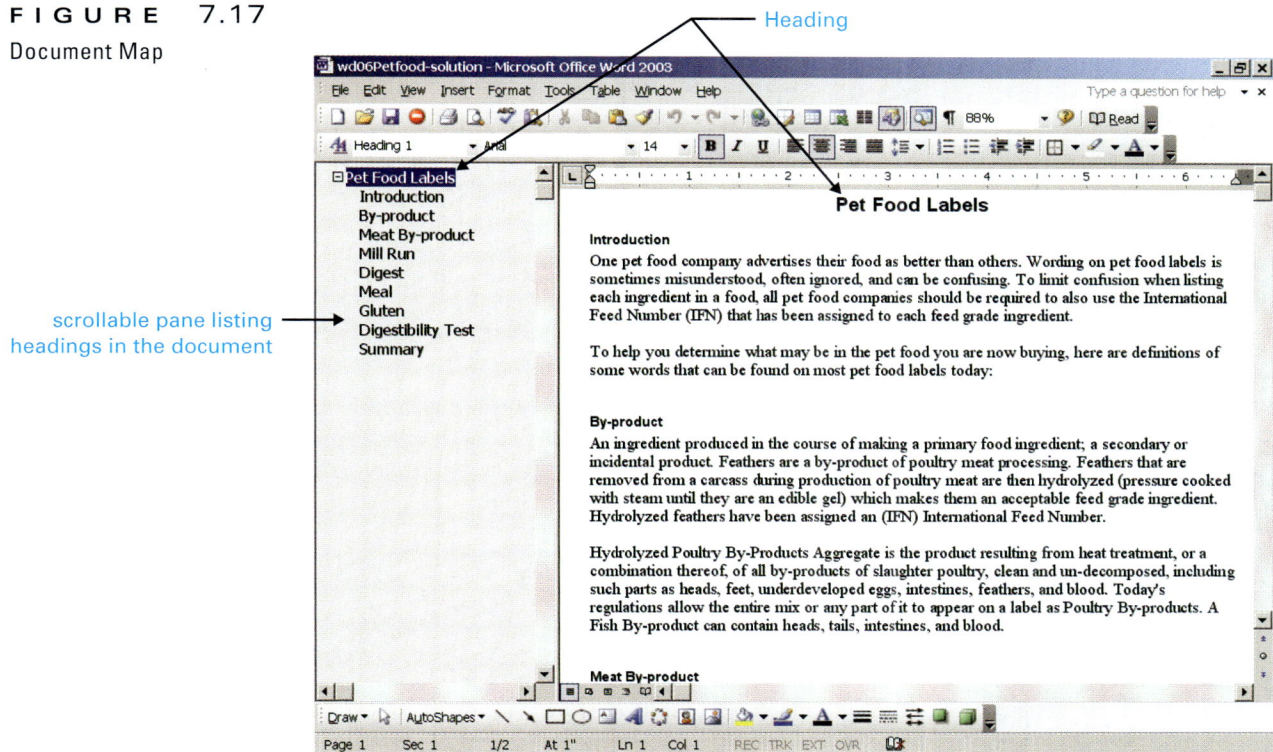

Using the Document Map:

1. Ensure **Petfood1.doc** is open

2. Click **View, Document Map** on the menu bar

3. Click on any of the headings in the Document Map to see how Word moves you to that heading

4. Click **View, Document Map** on the menu bar to turn off the Document Map

Inserting Bookmarks

A Bookmark is an electronic placeholder for Word documents. A Bookmark identifies a location or selection of text that you name and identify for future reference. For example, you might use a Bookmark to identify text that you want to revise at a later time. Instead of scrolling through the document to locate the text, you can go to it by using the Bookmark in the Go To tab of the Find and Replace dialog box.

Bookmarks have a name that identifies them. Bookmark names must start with a letter and can contain numbers but not spaces.

task reference	Adding a Bookmark

- Select an item you want a Bookmark assigned to, or click where you want to insert a Bookmark
- On the Insert menu, click **Bookmark**
- Under Bookmark name, type or select a name
- Click **Add**
- To go to a Bookmark, click **Edit, Go To, Bookmark**, and then select the name of the Bookmark

Dr. Schweitzer needs to be able to quickly and easily update the different portions of the Pet Food Label document. He decides that adding a couple of Bookmarks could help him be more efficient. Specifically, he wants to place one near the end of his document and one near the start.

Adding a Bookmark:

1. Ensure **Petfood1.doc** is opened
2. Click at the end of the heading **Introduction** at the top of the first page
3. On the menu bar, click **Insert, Bookmark** to show the Bookmark dialog box (see Figure 7.18)

FIGURE 7.18

Bookmark dialog box

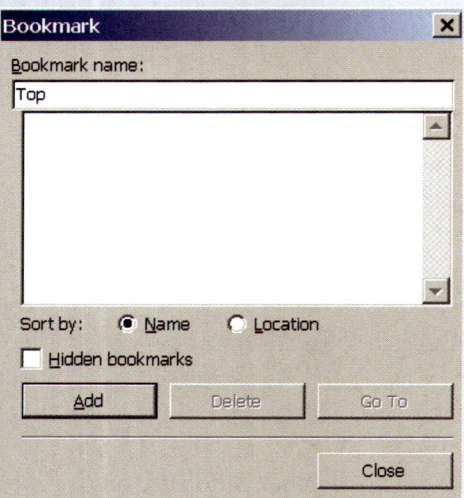

4. In the Bookmark name area type **Top**
5. Click **Add**
6. Find the word **Summary** at the end of the document

tip: *Use the Find function*

7. Click at the end of the word
8. On the menu bar, click **Insert, Bookmark** to show the Bookmark dialog box
9. In the Bookmark name area type **Bottom** and click **Add**

10. To test your Bookmark, click **Edit, Go To** or press **Ctrl+G**

11. Select the **Bookmark** in the **Go to what** box, and select the Bookmark name **Top** from the list of bookmarks found in the Enter Bookmark name text box (see Figure 7.19)

F I G U R E   7.19

Using the Find and Replace dialog box to Go To a Bookmark

12. Click **Go To** and repeat these steps to go to the Bottom Bookmark, click **Close**

Bookmark names must start with a letter and can contain numbers. You can't include spaces in a Bookmark name. However, you can use the underscore character to separate words, for example, "Pet_Food"

Hyperlinks

You can enrich Web pages and Word documents that others read on the screen by inserting hyperlinks, which can be either graphics or text that is colored or underlined. A hyperlink is represented by a "hot" image or display text that the user clicks to go to a different location. The location can be in the document, on your hard disk, on your company's intranet, or on the Internet, such as a page on the World Wide Web. For example, you can create a hyperlink in a Word file that goes to a chart in Excel that provides more detail.

> **another word** . . . **on Maintaining Hyperlinks**
>
> Hyperlinks are useful when you are creating Web pages or documents. Simply clicking on a hyperlink will take your reader straight to another Web site, a document, or another place in a document. However, you must ensure that the Web sites or documents contained in your link are still active. Frequently, Web site addresses are changed or removed completely. Nothing is more frustrating for a user than clicking on an inactive hyperlink. You must continually check your hyperlinks to ensure they are still active

---

task *reference*   **Creating a Hyperlink within a Document**

- Click **Insert** on the menu bar, and select **Hyperlink** or **Ctrl+K**

- In the Insert Hyperlink dialog box (see Figure 7.20), decide what you are linking

- Select the correct **Link to**: Existing File or Web Page, Place in this Document, Create New Document, or E-mail Address

- Choose or type the address text will link to

- Click **OK**

F I G U R E   7.20

Insert Hyperlink dialog box

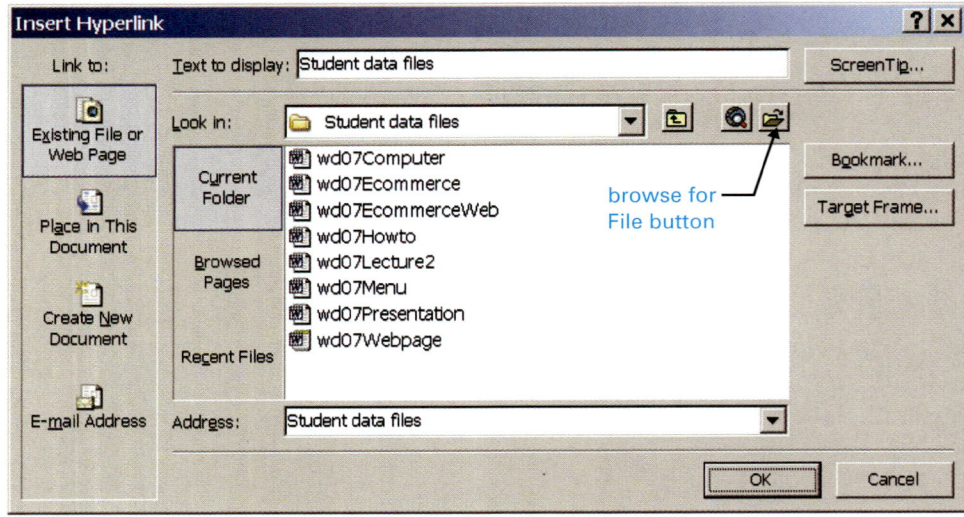

As Dr. Schweitzer plans the Pet Food Labels document, he realizes that electronic versions will be distributed, so he decides to add a hyperlink in the document.

Creating a hyperlink to a different Web site:

1. Ensure your file **Petfood1.doc** is open

2. Insert the cursor at the end of the last sentence

3. Add the following text: **Visit the Animal Protection Institute's Web site for additional information on pet food labels at www.api4animals.org**

4. Select the word **www.api4animals.org**

5. Click **Insert, Hyperlink**

6. In the Address Field type **http://www.api4animals.org** and click **OK** (see Figure 7.21)

F I G U R E   7.21

Hyperlink dialog box for Web site address

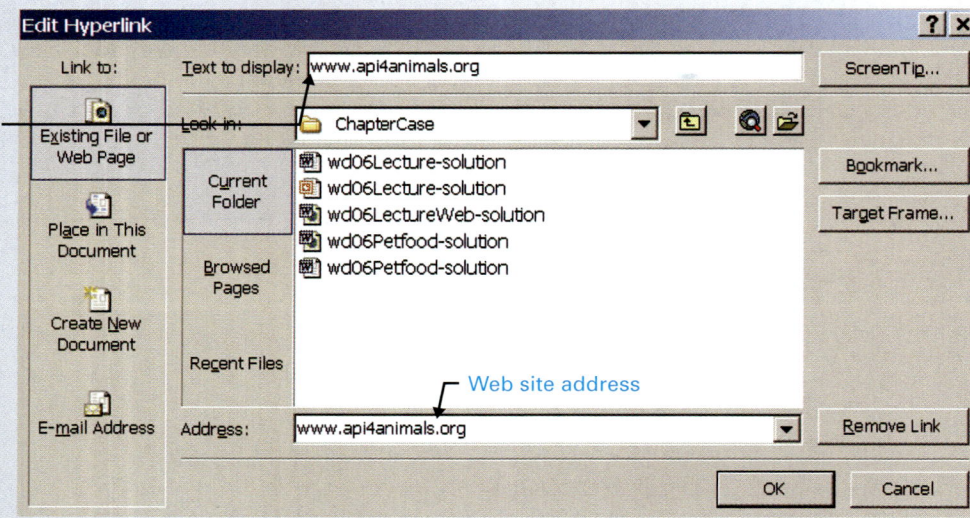

7. Test your hyperlink by clicking on the link

   tip: *Hold down the **Ctrl** key when you hover over a hyperlink to get the graphic hand that allows you to go to the link*

help yourself *Click the **Ask a Question** combo box, type **Hyperlink**, and press **Enter**. Click the hyperlink **Change a hyperlink** to display information on different ways you can view and use hyperlinks. Click the Help screen **Close** button when you are finished*

After creating a hyperlink, you might need to change what it is linked to or even remove the link. This is a simple operation.

---

task reference   **Editing a Hyperlink**

- Right-click on the hyperlink

- Select **Hyperlink, Edit Hyperlink**

- Make changes in the Edit Hyperlink dialog box

- Click **OK**

or

- Click the **Remove Link** button

---

anotherway
. . . to Create a Hyperlink within a Document

If you want to cross-reference a word elsewhere in a document, you can always copy and paste text as a hyperlink. To see how this works, select the word you want to refer to and press **Ctrl+C** to copy it to the Clipboard. Then, select another part of the document and choose **Edit, Paste as Hyperlink**. The pasted text is now highlighted blue, and you can click on the word to jump back to the original text, where you first copied the word to the Clipboard

---

making the grade   **SESSION 7.3**

1. Clicking View, Document Map opens a scrollable _____ on the left side of the screen.

2. Name four ways to quickly move to a specific location in a document.

3. True or False: Bookmarks can be given any name you decide to use.

4. Identify four items that a hyperlink can link to.

5. True or False: Items can be pasted as a hyperlink.

6. To edit or remove a hyperlink, start with a _____ _____ on the hyperlink.

SESSION 7.4 SUMMARY

With Word, outlines are easy to create and to manipulate. Outline levels are built into Word. They can be heading levels or styles, numbered lists, or hidden. Once an outline is created, more or less of the outline and the associated text can be viewed in the Outline view by collapsing or expanding the outline. Levels of individual items can be promoted or demoted in the outline by click and drag or Tab and Shift+Tab.

When the Word outlining feature is used or when tabs are used to specify different levels of an outline, it can be sent to PowerPoint. The outline automatically becomes a presentation, with the items identified as Level 1 or Heading 1 becoming individual slides and the other levels becoming points on the slide.

Word offers several ways of creating Web pages, even for the novice. Word documents can be saved as Web pages. The Web Layout view shows you how your document will look as a Web page and alerts you to some changes in appearance. Word will also help you create Web pages with a Web Page Wizard or Web templates. Word provides themes to enhance the appearance of a Web page.

To move to specific locations in a document you can use the Document Map, Bookmarks, and hyperlinks. The Document Map opens in a pane on the left of the screen, allowing you to click on headings located throughout the document. Bookmarks are placed anywhere in the document and given unique names. Hyperlinks allow you to click and link to another place in the document, another document, a Web page, or e-mail. They can be associated with text or graphics.

MICROSOFT OFFICE SPECIALIST OBJECTIVES SUMMARY

- Save documents in appropriate formats for different uses—MOS WW03S-2-2
- Insert and modify hyperlinks—MOS WW03S-2-3
- Create bulleted lists, and numbered lists and outlines—MOS WW03S-5-4
- Preview documents and Web pages—MOS WW03S-5-6
- Structure documents using XML—MOS WW03E-2-8
- Publish and edit Web documents in Word—MOS WW03E-4-2
- Use automated tools for document navigation—MOS WW03E-2-5

making the grade *answers*

SESSION 7.1

1. Heading levels, numbered lists, assigned outline levels

2. False

3. True

4. drag; Shift and Shift+Tab

5. False

SESSION 7.2

1. Web Page Wizard, Web page template, Save as Web Page . . .

2. theme, link bars, frames

3. True

4. Click Web Page Layout view

5. Format

SESSION 7.3

1. pane

2. Go To, Document Map, Bookmark, hyperlink

3. True; as long as they begin with a letter and contain no spaces

4. Existing file or Web page, place in the document, new document, or e-mail address

5. True

6. right-click

task reference *summary*

Task	Page #	Preferred Method
Organizing a new document using the Outline view	WD 7.4	• In a new document, switch to **Outline** view • Type each heading, and press **Enter** (Word formats the headings with the built-in style Heading 1) • To assign a heading to a lower level and apply the corresponding heading style, drag the heading's plus (1) or minus (2) or outline symbol to the right • To *promote* a heading to a higher level, drag the symbol to the left • To move a heading to a different location, drag the symbol up or down (the subordinate text under the heading moves with the heading) • After organizing the outline, switch to **Normal** view or **Print Layout** view to add detailed body text and graphics
Assigning outline levels to a paragraph	WD 7.7	• Switch to **Print Layout** view • Select a paragraph you want to assign an outline level to • On the Format menu, click **Paragraph**, and then click the **Indents and Spacing** tab • In the **Outline level** box, click the level you want
Creating an outline numbered list	WD 7.8	• On the Format menu, click **Bullets and Numbering**, and then click the **Outline Numbered** tab • Click a list format that does not contain the text Heading 1, and then click **OK** • Type the list, pressing **Enter** after each item • To *demote* the item to a lower numbering level, click anywhere in the item, and click **Increase Indent** on the Formatting toolbar • To promote the item to a higher numbering level, click anywhere in the item, and click **Decrease Indent** on the Formatting toolbar
Creating a PowerPoint slide show	WD 7.9	• Open the document with the outline that you want to use to create a PowerPoint presentation • On the File menu, point to **Send To**, and then click **Microsoft PowerPoint**
Using the Web page template	WD 7.12	• On the File menu, click **New** • In the New Document task pane, under templates, click **On My Computer** • Click the **Web Page** template • To create a blank Web page, on the File menu, click **New** • Under New in the New Document task pane, click **Web Page**
Saving a Web page from a Word document	WD 7.13	• On the File menu, click **Save as Web Page** • If you want to save the document in a different folder, locate and open the folder • In the File name box, type a name for the document • Click **Save**
Viewing a document as a Web page	WD 7.16	• Click on the View menu and select **Web Layout** or • Click **Web Layout view** on the buttons in the lower left of the document screen
Viewing the Document Map	WD 7.18	• On the menu bar, click **View, Document Map** to show the Document Map pane • To move through the document, click on any titles shown in the Document Map • Click **View, Document Map** again to turn off the Document Map
Adding a Bookmark	WD 7.20	• Select an item you want a Bookmark assigned to, or click where you want to insert a Bookmark • On the Insert menu, click **Bookmark** • Under Bookmark name, type or select a name • Click **Add** • To go to a Bookmark, click **Edit, Go To, Bookmark** and then select the name of the Bookmark

task reference *summary*

Task	Page #	Preferred Method
Creating a hyperlink within a document	WD 7.21	• Click **Insert** on the menu bar, and select **Hyperlink** or **Ctrl+K** • In the Insert Hyperlink dialog box, decide what you are linking • Select the correct **Link to**: Existing File or Web Page, Place in this Document, Create New Document, or E-mail Address • Choose or type the address text will link to • Click **OK**
Editing a hyperlink	WD 7.23	• Right-click on the hyperlink • Select **Hyperlink, Edit Hyperlink** • Make changes in the Edit Hyperlink dialog box • Click **OK** or • Click the **Remove Link** button

TRUE/FALSE

1. FTP transfers files between users.

2. HTML tags contain all the information you'd like to include in your Web page.

3. A hyperlink is colored and italicized text or a graphic that you click to go to a file, a location in a file, an HTML page on the World Wide Web, or an HTML page on an intranet.

4. XML stands for Extensible Markup Language.

5. A Web page is a text file with HTML code, pictures, and other components capable of being interpreted by a Web browser.

FILL-IN

1. Each _____ in Word becomes a new slide when an outline is sent to PowerPoint.

2. A _____ is a network within an organization that uses Internet technologies such as the HTTP or FTP protocol.

3. _____ Transfer Protocol (HTTP) is the protocol used by the World Wide Web.

4. Web _____ are text files with HTML code, pictures, and other components capable of being interpreted by a Web browser.

5. _____ Style Sheets (CSS) is a part of a Web page that defines styles controlling the way a Web page or a part of a Web page appears in a browser.

MULTIPLE CHOICE

1. Which of the following is an outline-type overview of the document's organization, showing the headings arranged hierarchically in a narrow, scrollable pane?
   a. Document Map
   b. Frame
   c. Hyperlink
   d. Bookmark

2. Which of the following is the named sub-window of a frames page?
   a. Document Map
   b. Frame
   c. Hyperlink
   d. Bookmark

3. Which of the following is a location or selection of text named for reference purposes?
   a. Document Map
   b. Frame
   c. Hyperlink
   d. Bookmark

4. Which of the following is a colored and underlined text or a graphic that you click to go to a file, a location in a file, an HTML page on the World Wide Web, or an HTML page on an intranet?
   a. Document Map
   b. Frame
   c. Hyperlink
   d. Bookmark

5. Which of the following is the protocol used by the World Wide Web?
   a. FTP
   b. HTTP
   c. Hyperlink
   d. All of the above

review of concepts

REVIEW QUESTIONS

1. Describe the design applied to slides in PowerPoint that results from a Word outline.

2. Discuss what can be done with the Web Page Wizard.

3. How are frames created in a Web page using Word?

4. List five features of Word not supported by Web browsers.

5. How can the appearance of a Word document as a Web page be checked before being saved as a Web page?

CREATE THE QUESTION

For each of the following answers, create an appropriate, short question.

ANSWER	QUESTION
1. Web browser	_____
2. Theme	_____
3. HTML	_____
4. Web Page Wizard	_____
5. Link bar	_____
6. CSS	_____

FACT OR FICTION

1. A Bookmark is a location or selection of text named for reference purposes. Word marks the location with the name you specify. Bookmarks are more than placeholders. For example, you can use them to create and number cross-references.

2. A CSS is a part of a Web page that defines styles controlling the way a Web page or a part of a Web page appears in a browser. Microsoft Office stores embedded style sheets at the top of each Web page.

3. HTML is the named sub-window of a frames page. The frame appears in a Web browser as one of a number of window regions in which pages can be displayed. The frame can be scrollable and resizable, and it can have a border.

4. A hyperlink is colored and underlined text or a graphic that you click to go to a file, a location in a file, an HTML page on the World Wide Web, or an HTML page on an intranet.

5. A Web page is software that interprets HTML files, formats them into Web pages, and displays them. A Web page, such as Microsoft Internet Explorer, can follow hyperlinks, transfer files, and play sound or video files that are embedded in Web pages.

1. Adding a Slide to the Applied Animal Nutrition Lecture

Dr. Schweitzer wants you to add a slide to the end of his lecture containing the following:

- Your name
- Your birthplace
- Your favorite food

Create the file and then send the outline to PowerPoint and create a presentation (see Figure 7.22).

1. Open the file **wd07Lecture2.doc**

2. Save the file as **Lecture2.doc**

3. View the document in the Outline view

4. At the bottom of the outline, type your first and last name

5. Apply the default style of **Heading 1**

6. Type your state of birth on the next line

7. Apply the default style of **Heading 2**

8. Type your favorite food on the next line

9. Apply the default style of **Heading 2**

10. Save your document

11. With this new outline still active in Word, click **File, Send To, Microsoft PowerPoint**

12. Add a **Slide Design** of your choice

13. Make sure that your name is the title on the last slide and your city of birth and favorite food are points under your name

14. Save your document

15. Print out the outline or slides as directed by your instructor

FIGURE 7.22

New PowerPoint slide for Dr. Schweitzer's lecture

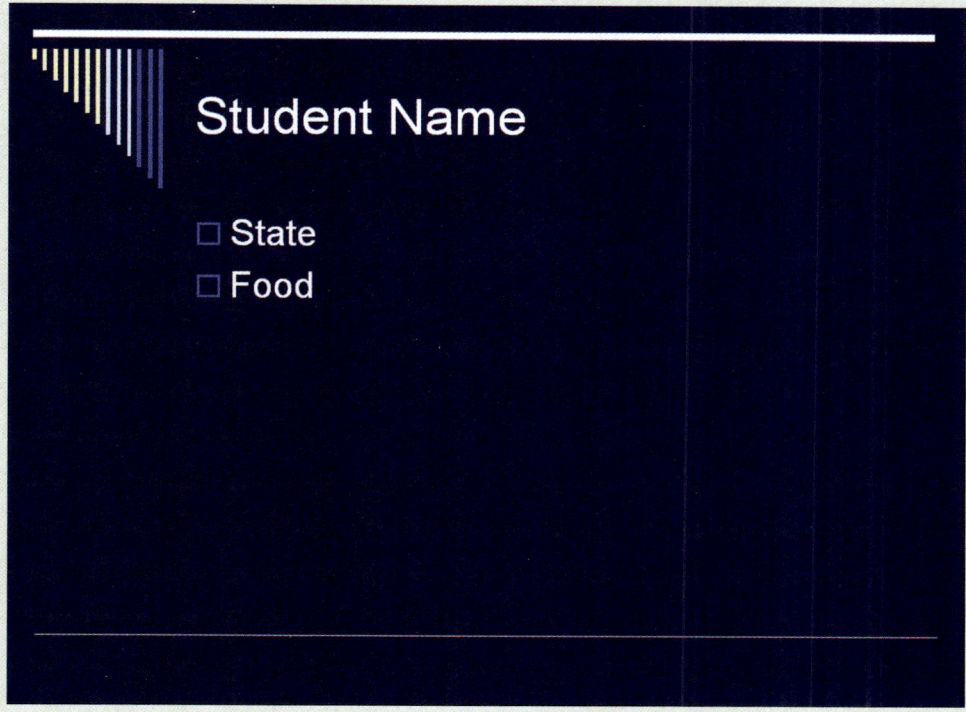

2. Create a Web Page for a Local Restaurant

You are the manager at The Egg Roll Chinese restaurant. The restaurant is located in downtown Chicago and specializes in outstanding traditional Chinese dishes. You are interested in creating a Web page for the restaurant. A Web page will help give your customers directions to the restaurant, information on the food at the restaurant, and a link to interesting food facts.

1. Retrieve the data file **wd07Menu.doc**

2. Save the file as **Menu1.doc**

3. Click **File, Save As**

4. Select Save As type as **Web Page**

5. Save as a Web page using the same filename

6. Click **Save**

7. Check your data files to verify that you have the file Menu1.htm

8. Insert a blank line after the title Menu

9. Add the following text in Arial 12: **Visit the International Food Information Council Foundation for more information on international foods**

10. Select the words **International Food Information Council Foundation**

11. Click **Insert, Hyperlink**

12. In the Address Field type **http://ific.org**

13. Click **OK**

14. Test your hyperlink

15. Using a Web browser, compare your Web page to Figure 7.23

16. Save your work

FIGURE 7.23

The Egg Roll Chinese Restaurant Web page

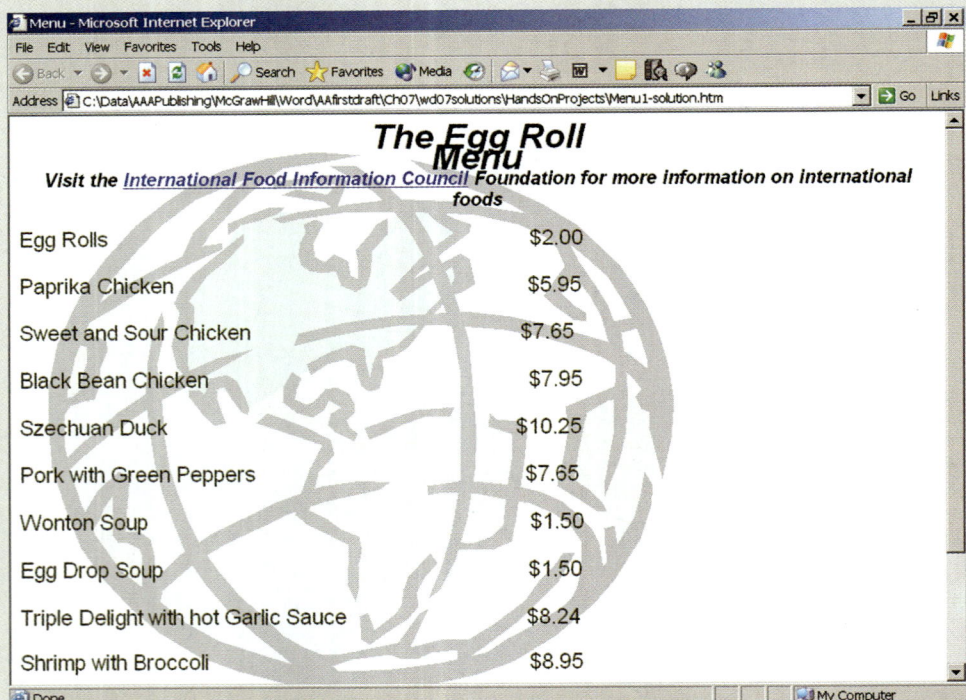

1. Using the Web Page Wizard or Template to Create a Web Page

Creating a personal Web page is a great way to introduce yourself to potential employers. You can paste the link to your personal Web page right in your resume. This will allow any potential employers who are interested in finding out more about you to easily connect directly to your Web page with a simple click.

Use the Web Page Wizard or a Web page template to create a Web page about yourself. Be sure to include all of the following:

- Personal mission
- Personal goals
- Career objectives
- Achievements
- Work experience
- Education

The Web Page Wizard will require you to supply quite a bit of information and would make a great class project. If you just want to create a simple Web page for yourself, use the template **wd07Webpage.dot** (see Figure 7.24).

FIGURE 7.24

Simple Web page template

Type other information or insert photo here	**Your Name Goes Here**	Type other information or insert photo here
	Paragraph About You Goes Here	
	Select text you would like to replace and type over it. Use styles such as Heading 1-3 and Normal in the Style control on the Formatting toolbar.	Insert photo here
	The quick brown fox jumps over the lazy dog. The quick brown fox jumps over the lazy dog. The quick brown fox jumps over the lazy dog. The quick brown fox jumps over the lazy dog. The quick brown fox jumps over the lazy dog.	
	List your Hobbies Here	
	The quick brown fox jumps over the lazy dog. The quick brown fox jumps over the lazy dog. The quick brown fox jumps over the lazy dog. The quick brown fox jumps over the lazy dog. The quick brown fox jumps over the lazy dog.	
	The quick brown fox jumps over the lazy dog. The quick brown fox jumps over the lazy dog. The quick brown fox jumps over the lazy dog. The quick brown fox jumps over the lazy dog. The quick brown fox jumps over the lazy dog.	
	List your Favorite Websites here	
	The quick brown fox jumps over the lazy dog. The quick brown fox jumps over the lazy dog. The quick brown fox jumps over the lazy dog. The quick brown fox jumps over the lazy dog. The quick brown fox	

2. Creating a PowerPoint Slide Show from an Outline

Let's create a document discussing how you can create PowerPoint slides from a Word document. Retrieve the file **wd07Howto.doc** and create the proper outline headings (level 1, level 2, and so on), style headings (Heading 1, Heading 2, and Heading 3), or use the Promote/Demote buttons for this outline. Save the outline as **Howto1.doc**. Send your Howto1.doc to PowerPoint and create a slide show. Select a design from the PowerPoint options; add some clip art (on blank pages where it says to add text); and save your PowerPoint presentation as **Howto1.ppt** (see Figures 7.25).

FIGURE 7.25

How to slides

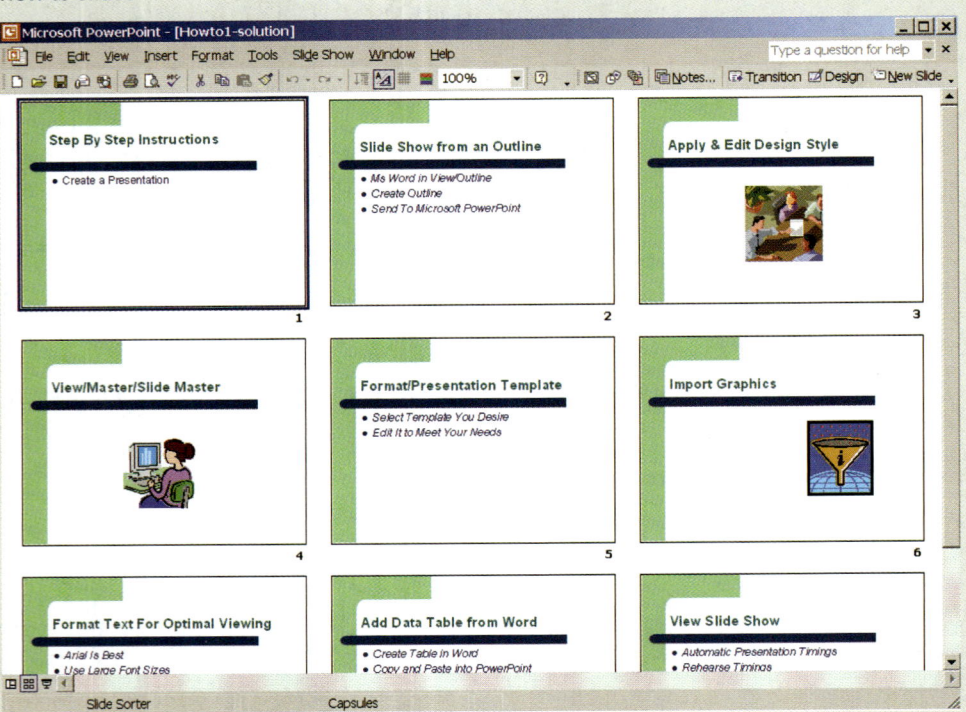

1. Outlining and Presenting E-Commerce Elements

You developed some information in Word for a presentation on e-commerce elements. Originally, you didn't know anything about outlining in Word or sending an outline to PowerPoint to begin a presentation, so your document just specifies Slide 1, Slide 2, and so on (see Figure 7.26). Now you wish to create an outline and send it to PowerPoint for your presentation. Use the text in the file **wd07Ecommerce.doc** and save the file as **ECommerce1.doc**. Create an outline and send this outline to PowerPoint. (*Note*: Delete the slide identifications of Slide 1, Slide 2, and so on.) Add your name and the date as the last outline item. After sending the outline to PowerPoint, save the outline and the PowerPoint slides as **Ecommerce1.ppt**. Before you save the PowerPoint slides, select a design for the slides that allows all your text to fit on the appropriate pages.

FIGURE 7.26

Text for e-commerce elements outline

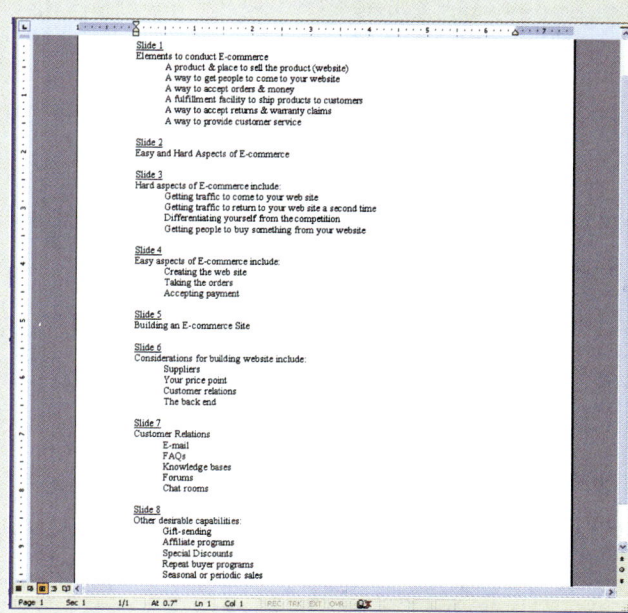

FIGURE 7.27

E-commerce slides

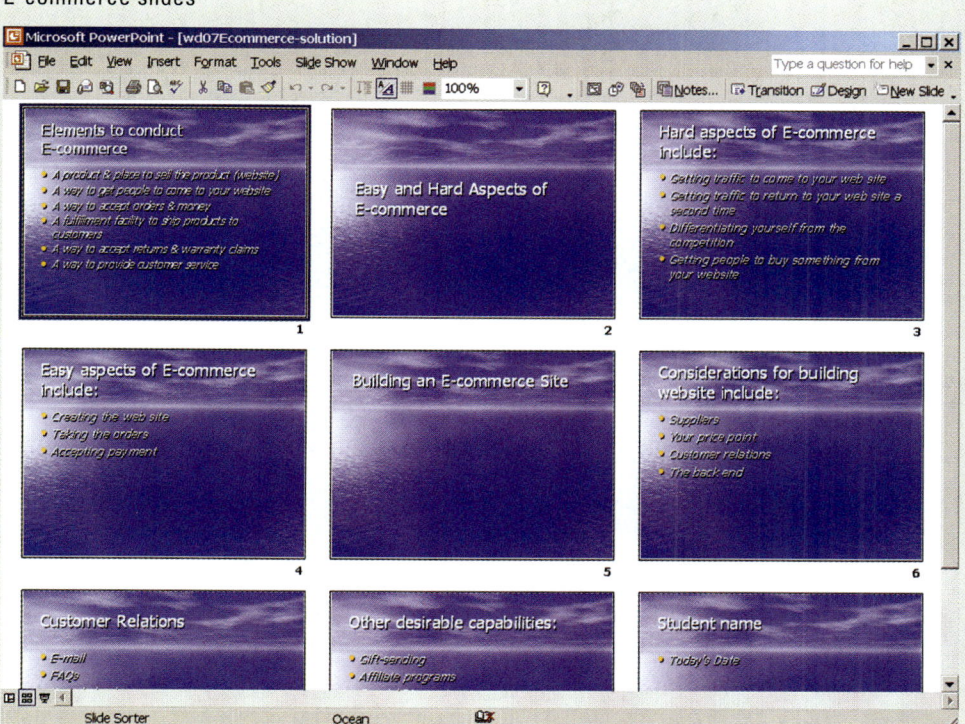

www.mhhe.com/i-series

2. Saving an E-Commerce Document as a Web Page

E-commerce is a fast-growing and exciting area. You are currently working for a company that specializes in consulting to e-commerce businesses. Your boss has asked you to put together a Web page discussing the current issues surrounding e-commerce businesses. The Web page will be accessed by all of the company employees whenever they need to research e-commerce issues.

You have already created a Word document containing information about the current e-commerce issues. This document is saved as **wd07EcommerceWeb.doc**. Retrieve this document and save it as **EcommerceWeb1.doc**. Apply a theme (Format, Theme) of your choice before saving it as a Web page. Also, try to incorporate a couple of hyperlinks to other interesting e-commerce Web sites such as:

- Ecommerce Times— http://www.ecommercetimes.com
- Ecommerce Guide— http://ecommerce.internet.com
- Ecommerce News for IT Managers— http://www.internetnews.com/ec-news

Compare your work to Figure 7.28

FIGURE 7.28

E-commerce document saved as a Web page with the rice paper theme applied

Electronic Commerce over the Internet Facilitated on a Global Basis

The Internet is emerging as a global marketplace. The legal framework supporting commercial transactions on the Internet should be governed by consistent principles across state, national, and international borders that lead to predictable results regardless of the jurisdiction in which a particular buyer or seller resides.

Issues

This paper covers nine areas where international agreements are needed to preserve the Internet as a non-regulatory medium, one in which competition and consumer choice will shape the marketplace. Although there are significant areas of overlap, these items can be divided into three main subgroups: financial issues, legal issues, and market access issues.

Financial Issues

- Customs and taxation
- Electronic payments

Legal Issues

1. Creating a Table with Internet Links to Your Favorite Web Sites

As everyone knows, the Internet provides a wealth of information. We all have favorite sites and our reasons for these sites being our favorites. Search the Web and find 10 of your favorite Web sites. Create a document called **MySites.doc** and list your 10 favorite Web sites and create a hyperlink for each site.

2. Outlining an Article from an Encyclopedia

Several online encyclopedias are available on the Web including (see Figure 7.29):

- Encyclopedia Britannica— http://www.britannica.com/
- Columbia Encyclopedia— http://www.bartleby.com/65/
- Encarta Online—http://encarta.msn.com/
- Facts Encyclopedia— http://www.refdesk.com/myency.html

Pick a topic to search for in one of these encyclopedias, or have your instructor assign a topic. Find an article on that subject. Outline the article using Word, by assigning outline levels. Then send your outline to PowerPoint to create slides. Your outline must produce at least five slides. The last slide (not counted as part of the five) includes your name and today's date. Save the file as **Encyclopedia1.doc**.

FIGURE   7.29

Encyclopedia Britannica Web site

around the world

1. Producing a Report on a Country

Sponsored by the Department of the Army, the Federal Research Division of the Library of Congress produces a continuing series of Country Studies/Area Handbooks. This online series presently contains studies of 100 countries and is available at the following Web site: rs6.loc.gov/frd/cs/cshome.html.

Information contained in the Country Studies On-Line is not copyrighted and thus is available for free and unrestricted use by researchers. As a courtesy, however, appropriate credit should be given to the series. Use this information to cut and paste a report on a country of your choice. Be sure to include graphics, headings, hyperlinks, and other interesting materials. Create a Web page from your report describing your country of choice.

2. Saving a Proposal for International Center as a Web Page

You have created a Word document that is a proposal to establish an international sustainable agriculture center. After creating this proposal you decide to post it to the Web as a Web page so others can read it. This document is saved as wd07Sustain.doc. Retrieve this document and save it as a Web page. Apply the Blends theme (Format, Theme) before saving it as a Web page. Compare your work to Figure 7.30.

FIGURE 7.30

Proposal for international sustainable agriculture center saved as a Web page with the Blends theme

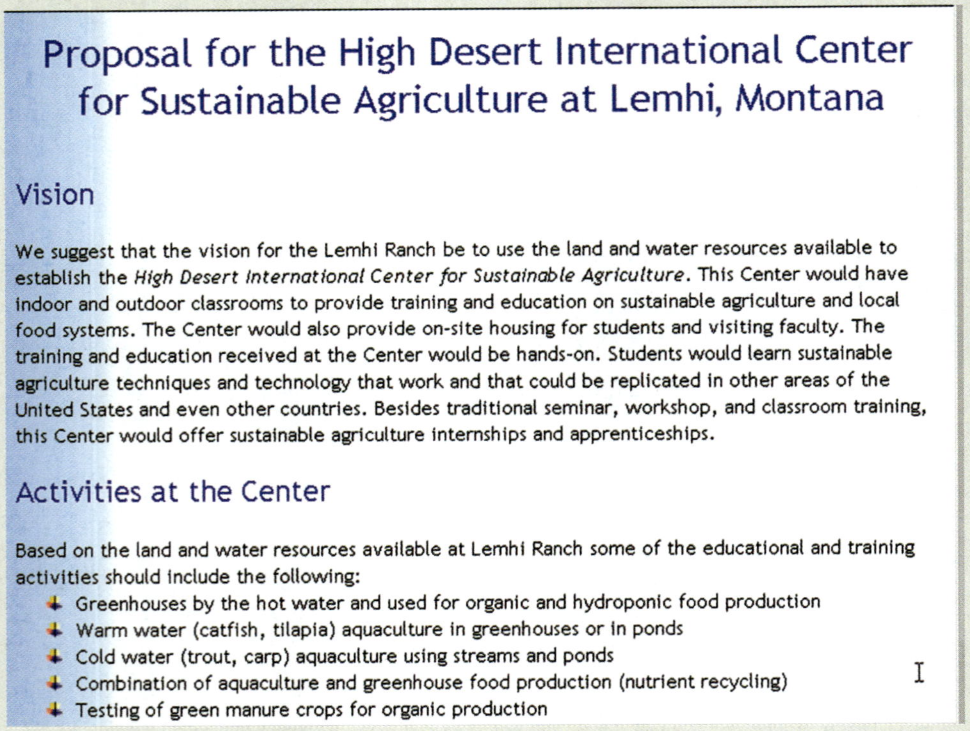

Proposal for the High Desert International Center for Sustainable Agriculture at Lemhi, Montana

Vision

We suggest that the vision for the Lemhi Ranch be to use the land and water resources available to establish the *High Desert International Center for Sustainable Agriculture*. This Center would have indoor and outdoor classrooms to provide training and education on sustainable agriculture and local food systems. The Center would also provide on-site housing for students and visiting faculty. The training and education received at the Center would be hands-on. Students would learn sustainable agriculture techniques and technology that work and that could be replicated in other areas of the United States and even other countries. Besides traditional seminar, workshop, and classroom training, this Center would offer sustainable agriculture internships and apprenticeships.

Activities at the Center

Based on the land and water resources available at Lemhi Ranch some of the educational and training activities should include the following:

- Greenhouses by the hot water and used for organic and hydroponic food production
- Warm water (catfish, tilapia) aquaculture in greenhouses or in ponds
- Cold water (trout, carp) aquaculture using streams and ponds
- Combination of aquaculture and greenhouse food production (nutrient recycling)
- Testing of green manure crops for organic production

running project

Creating Presentation Slides and Individual Web Pages for KUSD

In an effort to improve the overall image of the district, the superintendent, Helen McFee, made a commitment that the Kasota Unified School District will have a presence on the Internet with Web pages for school offices, programs, and faculty. Many of the classrooms in the school district are now equipped with computers and overhead projectors, so all members of a class can see computer presentations. Helen wants any presentations to be top-notch, so she plans to train faculty on the use of Word to develop PowerPoint presentations. She will do this using one of her presentations on how to develop a presentation. The outline for her presentation is saved as **wd07Presentation.doc**. She will retrieve this file and send it to PowerPoint to develop the slides for her presentation. After applying the Digital Dots design, save the PowerPoint presentation as **Presentation1.ppt** and compare it to Figure 7.31.

As a second part of Helen's effort to improve the electronic image of KUSD, she wants all faculty to produce a Web page. Using the template she will distribute, wd07Presenation.dot, Helen's Web page is shown in Figure 7.32. Create a Web page for Helen using the information in Figure 7.32.

FIGURE 7.31

Thumbnails of presentation tips slides

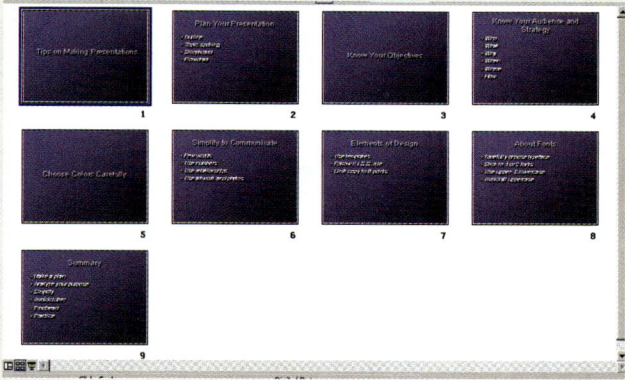

FIGURE 7.32

Helen McFee's Web page created from wd07Presentation.dot

Helen McFee

Contents
- Work Information
- Favorite Links
- Contact Information
- Biographical Information
- Personal Interests

Work Information

Superintendent of Kasota Unified School District (KUSD) since August 2000
Type some text.

Key responsibilities
Manage the instructional and budgetary affairs of KUSD; work to improve the image and working conditions of the faculty and staff in KUSD; provide leadership into the digital age.

Department or workgroup
Works with one assistant superintendent and four principals; also works as leader of district office staff.

Back to top

Favorite Links

1. Web Site Design Themes

A theme is a set of unified design elements that provide a look for your document using color, fonts, and graphics. Explain why you would use a theme and why themes are important to good Web site designs.

2. Finding Good Web Sites

Good Web site design is critical to the success of any Web site. Have you ever visited a Web site that was confusing and hard to navigate? Visit several different Web sites and create a document discussing what you liked and didn't like about the different Web sites you visited. Create a list of the top three elements that are necessary for a good Web site design.

Creating and Managing Long Documents

did you know?

water *in some of the deepest currents can move near the ocean bottom for thousands of years before returning to the surface, and water can be stored in ice caps or underground for millennia.*

in *1825 in San Luis Obispo, California, by the side of the highway that runs along the Pacific coast, the Milestone Motel was opened. It was the first motel: a type of hotel designed specifically for tourists to stop for the night in the course of a trip.*

at *the St. Louis World's Fair in 1904, tea seller Richard Blechynden was disappointed with the sales of the hot drink during the sweltering hot summer days, so he began serving it chilled with ice. The refreshing drink sold well, and now iced tea is a hot weather favorite around the world.*

Microsoft *Windows 2000 required 28 million lines of source code. A complete printout of its 28 million lines of source code would form a stack of pages 183 feet high (58 meters), about as tall as an 18-story building.*

Time *magazine has named a "Man of the Year" ever since 1927. In 1982, Time designated the computer as the "Man of the Year," calling it "the greatest influence for good or evil."*

how *do you subdivide a large document into segments that different groups can work on simultaneously and view the assembled and completed document? Read this chapter to find out.*

Chapter Objectives

- **Create and modify document indexes and tables— MOS WW03E-3-3**

- **Insert and modify endnotes, footnotes, captions, and cross-references—MOS WW03E-3-4**

- **Create and manage master documents and subdocuments— MOS WW03E-3-5**

Business Honor Society Bylaws Document

The Krannert Society is a new honor society for business students and has its national headquarters at Southern California College (SCC). The faculty advisor of the society, Faith Somerhill, has asked five students to help her rework the organization's bylaws. She has outlined the changes she wants made to the bylaws and has asked Robert Penrose to take charge of a group of five other students to modify the document. The bylaws are saved in three files to allow three groups of students to work independently on the three sections of the bylaws.

Robert created three groups, including the one in which he will participate, to make the required modifications to the Krannert Society bylaws. Now, almost three months later, the three groups have completed the first drafts of their documents. Robert wants to pull together the separate sections of the bylaws, make the formats consistent, check for correct page breaks, create a table of contents (TOC), and select words that will constitute the index that Robert will generate. Once the document is assembled from its constituent pieces, including the table of contents and index, Robert will print the final product. Robert wants you to assist him in creating a master document, which allows the teams to work with the document independently and yet view the entire work as one document whenever needed. Among the tasks you will complete include creating a master document and subdocuments, splitting and removing subdocuments, creating a table of contents, selecting index terms, and generating an index. Figure 8.1 shows a partial table of contents and the index for the completed document.

FIGURE 8.1

TOC and index of the Krannert Society Bylaws document

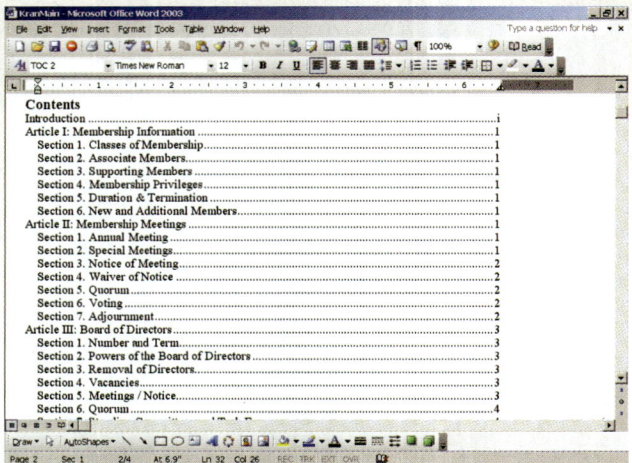

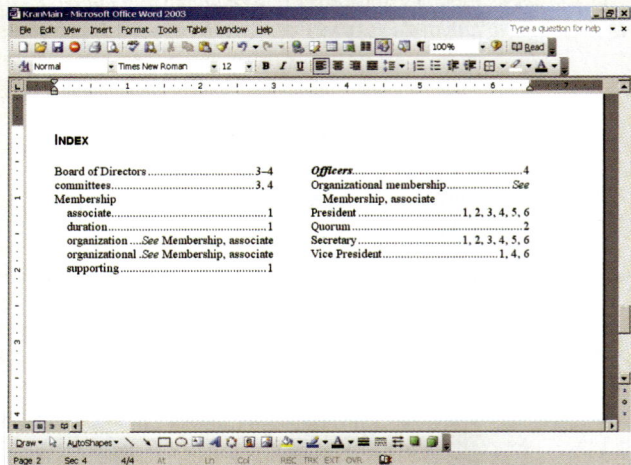

INTRODUCTION

Chapter 8 covers creating and managing master documents and subdocuments. You will learn how to create a master document that contains links to independently stored subdocuments. You will investigate how to insert subdocuments into a master document, expand and collapse subdocuments appearing in a master document, and split and remove subdocuments from a master document. You will learn how to customize page numbering across document sections, and how to manually and automatically generate a table of contents based on the headings in your consolidated document. Providing indexes is another key task you will learn in this chapter by selecting index terms and then generating the index containing the terms you have selected.

SESSION 8.1 CREATING A MASTER DOCUMENT AND SUBDOCUMENTS

In this session, you will learn how to create a master document and several subdocuments, allowing independent groups to work on separate document files that belong to the master document. You will learn how to create subdocuments, remove subdocuments, split a subdocument into two separate subdocuments, modify styles to ensure document sections print on a new page, and print the entire master document.

What Are a Master Document and Subdocuments?

Working with a long document such as the bylaws of the Krannert Society can be difficult due to the large number of pages. An attractive option to modifying a long document is to divide it into smaller documents with fewer pages. A *master document* is a file containing links to individual files that make up a larger document. Each file that is part of the master document is called a *subdocument*. You might create a master document to pull together the individual chapters of a book-length manuscript, allowing different authors to create or edit an individual chapter of the book. Similarly, a master document is a perfect way to subdivide a long technical manual into smaller, chapter-sized units stored as separate files. Each file is uniquely named and edited by one or two of the several team members assigned to create the manual. Figure 8.2 shows a graphic representation of a master document and its constituent subdocuments.

Whenever you have a large document to create or maintain, using the master document and subdocument approach has several advantages over maintaining a single, larger document. A master document approach allows you to do the following:

- Work with a long document as a single, complete document for activities such as printing, editing, search and replace, and formatting
- Display and collapse subdocuments to switch between details and overview of the document quickly
- Review and, if necessary, reorganize sections of a long document by moving subdocuments
- Organize and manage distinct document sections, opening and printing individual files when needed
- Coordinate editing individual, distinct parts of a longer document and distributing the individual subdocuments to different teams

You create and manage a master document and its subdocuments from the Outline view of the documents. Recall that you select Outline view by clicking the Outline View button on the scroll bar or by clicking the Outline command on the View menu. The Outline toolbar contains both outline buttons and master and subdocument buttons. Prior to preparing a master document and managing its subdocuments, you should become familiar with the Outline toolbar buttons dealing with master documents and

F I G U R E   8.2

Master document and its
subdocuments

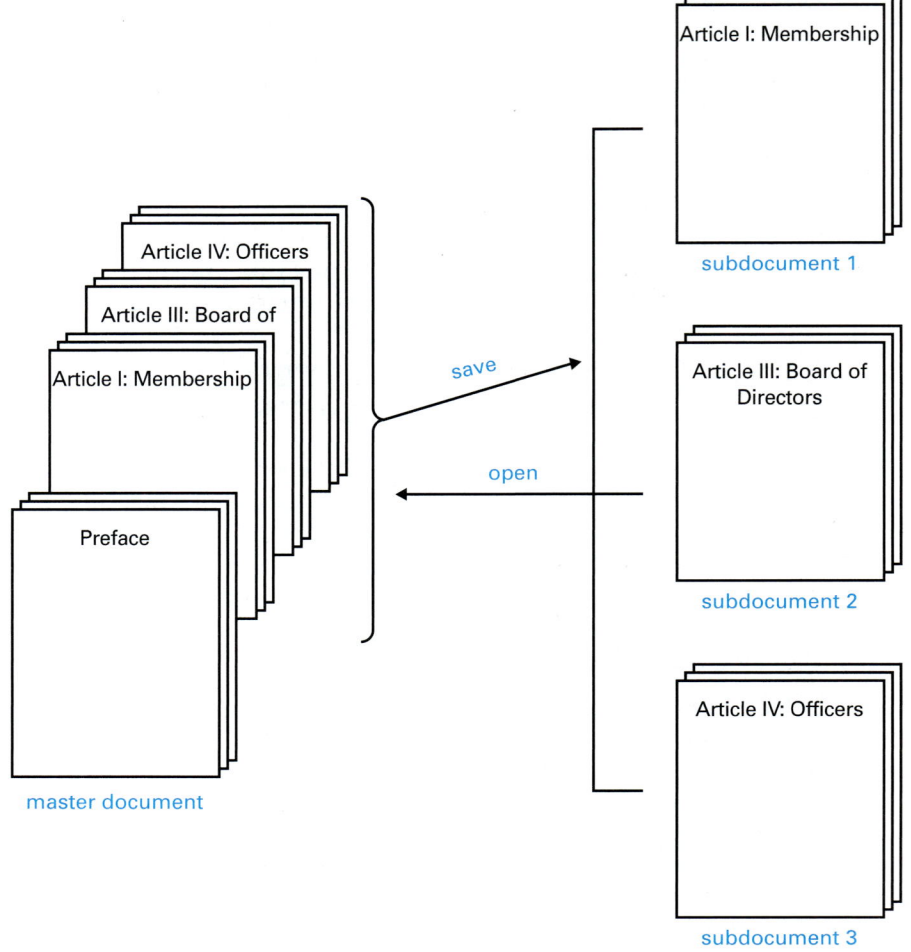

F I G U R E   8.3

Master Document buttons

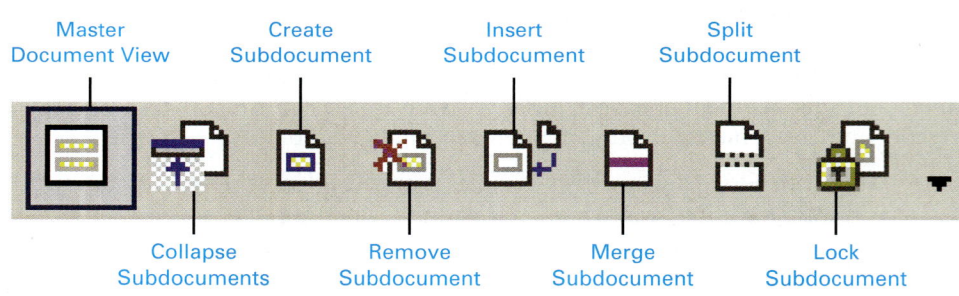

subdocuments. They are shown in Figure 8.3. As you read this chapter, you will learn
how you use each of the Master Document buttons.

Preparing to Create a Master Document and Subdocuments

If you are managing a project to produce a large document, you will quickly see the
benefit of working with master and subdocuments. Any large project requiring the organization and cooperation of several people also requires careful planning—right
down to assigning teams of people to produce each of the subdocuments and the master document. For any project consisting of teams of people, it is a good idea to create
a listing—perhaps a Word table—of the names of team members and the documents
for which they are responsible.

Besides organizing people into teams, it is important for the project leader to come up with a plan for storing the subdocuments and the master document—a plan that each team and its members understand. Such a document storage plan will help any team or the project leader keep track of files as they come and go. The best and simplest plan is to store all subdocuments and the master document in the same computer folder. Once everyone on the project knows the folder and disk on which the documents reside, Word will have no difficulties in locating the constituent parts. Then, whenever you want to integrate the subdocuments into a single master document to print a draft or the final version, Word will know exactly where to locate all required files. If you are using a networked system and choose to store the documents on a server, ensure that the network drive is accessible to all team members.

Creating a Master Document

You can create a master document and subdocuments two ways. You can start with an existing document and convert it into a master document by dividing it into subdocuments. Alternatively, you can create a master document from scratch and insert the headings and subheadings during the process and turn existing documents into subdocuments of the master document.

Using the first method, you could convert an existing document into a master document and then identify any number of subdocuments within it by selecting the Heading 1 style and then dividing the document at any Heading 1 style. Once you split an existing document into a master and a subdocument using the Outline view and the Heading 1 style, Word records the location of any subdocument you create.

With the second method, you create a master document from the beginning of your project. You create an outline in Outline view and then define your subdocuments as you see fit. Once you create a new document and display it in Outline view, enter the headings for the document title and subdocument titles. When you do so, Word automatically assigns the default style Heading 1. So ensure you assign each subdocument the Heading 1 style. Continue by creating subheadings (Heading 2, Heading 3, and so on). Once you are happy with the structure of the master document and its proposed Heading 1 subdocument divisions, save the file.

You will be using a combination of these two techniques in steps within this section. You will subdivide an existing document into a master and subdocument, and you will insert an existing document as a subdocument into the master document. Once you create the master document and its subdocuments, you can format, print, or edit the master or any of the subdocuments as you desire. For example, you can edit a subdocument file independently of any master document. Later, you can reopen the master document, and Word will automatically incorporate into the master document any changes anyone made to subdocuments. When you save the master document, Word automatically saves each of the subdocuments as well. Although the master document looks as though it actually contains its subdocuments, it does not. Instead, the master document contains the filename (a hyperlink) of its subdocuments, not the text of the subdocument.

help yourself *Click the* **Ask a Question** *combo box, type* **Master Document**, *and press* **Enter**. *Click the hyperlink* **About master documents** *to display information on understanding master and subdocument creation. Click the Help screen* **Close** *button when you are finished*

Opening the Master Document

Any document can become the master document. You will create a master document and then subdocuments by first opening the master document. Then, you will decide which other documents should be included as subdocuments to produce a completed master document.

WORD

task reference   Creating a Master Document

- Open in the usual way the document that is to be the master document
- Display nonprinting characters by clicking the **Show/Hide** ¶ button on the Standard toolbar
- Click **View** on the menu bar and then click **Outline**
- If necessary, click the **Master Document View** ▣ button on the Outlining toolbar to display the Outlining toolbar (see Figure 8.3)

You are ready to help Robert create a master document from an existing document.

Creating a master document from a file:

1. Start Word as usual, locate the folder containing your Chapter 8 data files, open **wd08KranMain.doc**, and save the file as **KranMain.doc**

2. Click the **Show/Hide** button on the Standard toolbar, if necessary, to display nonprintable characters such as paragraph marks and spaces

3. Click **View** on the menu bar and then click **Outline**. The document contents switch to Outline view, and the Outlining toolbar containing the Master Document buttons appears on the Outlining toolbar

4. Using the vertical scroll bar, scroll down the document until you see "Prepared by" at the top of the document window (see Figure 8.4)

FIGURE 8.4

Document in Master Document View

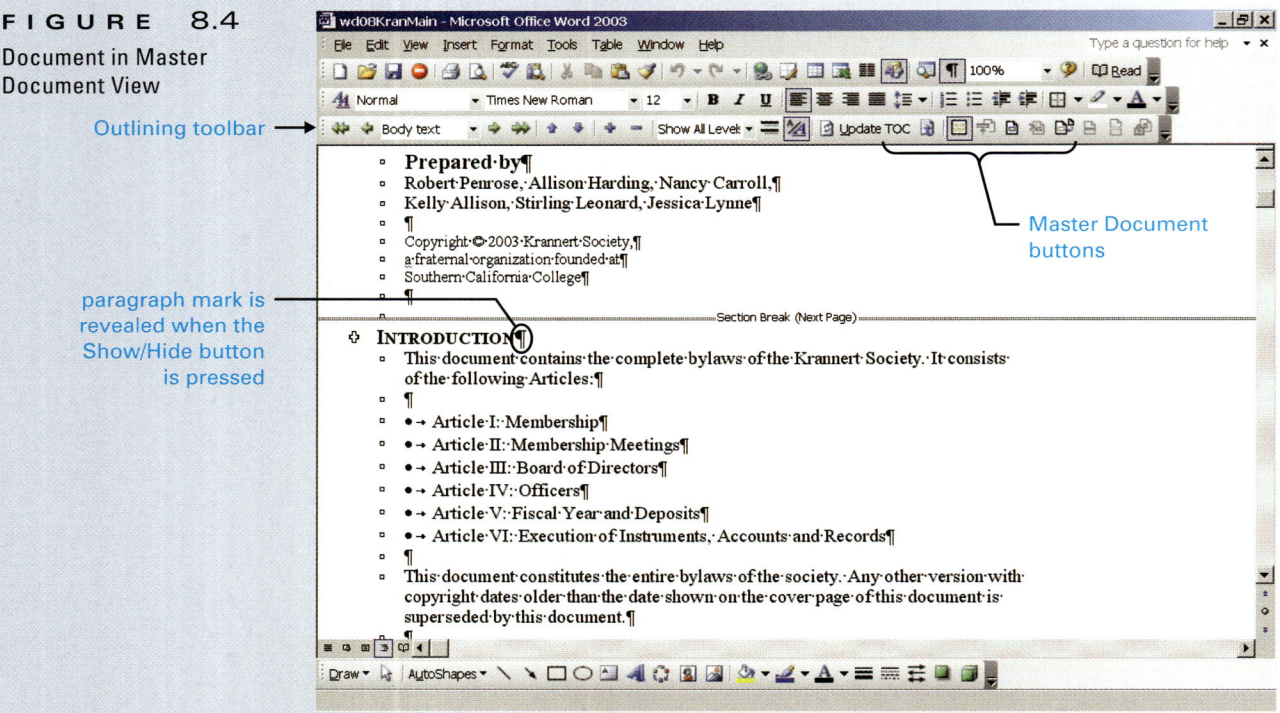

Outlining toolbar

Master Document buttons

paragraph mark is revealed when the Show/Hide button is pressed

> ### another**word** . . . on Creating Master Documents
>
> Merely opening a single document and displaying it in Outline view is not sufficient to make the document a master document. You must create subdocuments from the document before it becomes a master document

So that you keep the original subdocuments intact, you will open and save each one, in turn, under a new name. Then you will continue to make a master document and incorporate the newly named subdocuments.

Renaming subdocuments to preserve the original files:

1. Click **File** on the menu bar, click **Open**, and then double-click the file **wd08KranPart2.doc**

2. Click **File** on the menu bar, click **Save As**, type **KranPart2** in the File name text box, and then click the **Save** button. Word saves the file under its new name

3. Click **File** on the menu bar and then click **Close** to close the newly named file

4. Repeat steps 1 through 3, but open file **wd08KranPart3.doc** in step 1 and save it as **KranPart3** in step 2

With the three files renamed, you can always revert to the original files if needed to repeat the steps you have accomplished so far. From this point forward, you will be working with the renamed files. Now you are ready to make a full-fledged master document by incorporating other files as subdocuments in the master document.

Inserting Files as Subdocuments

You will help Robert create subdocuments by inserting files into the document currently open. Once you insert the first subdocument, then you have created a master document. Begin by inserting KranPart2.doc into KranMain as a subdocument.

Inserting a file as a subdocument of a master document:

1. With KranMain open in Word and the Outlining toolbar visible, press **Ctrl+End** to move the Word insertion point to the end of the document

2. Click the **Insert Subdocument** button on the Outlining toolbar. Word opens the Insert Subdocument dialog box. It resembles the Open dialog box

3. Double-click **KranPart2.doc** in the Insert Subdocument list of files. Scroll the display, if necessary, so you can see the top of the newly inserted subdocument (see Figure 8.5)

4. Click the **Show Level** list box arrow, located in the center of the Outlining toolbar, to display the outline levels

5. Click **Show Level 2** to display outline levels 1 and 2 but not the manual's text (see Figure 8.6)

another**way** . . . on Subdocument Locations

To view the path and folder in which a subdocument is stored, simply hover over the hyperlink. A Screen Tip reveals the link and reminds you to press Ctrl while clicking the link to move to the subdocument

F I G U R E   8.5
Inserted subdocument

section break

subdocument icon

outline markers

subdocument

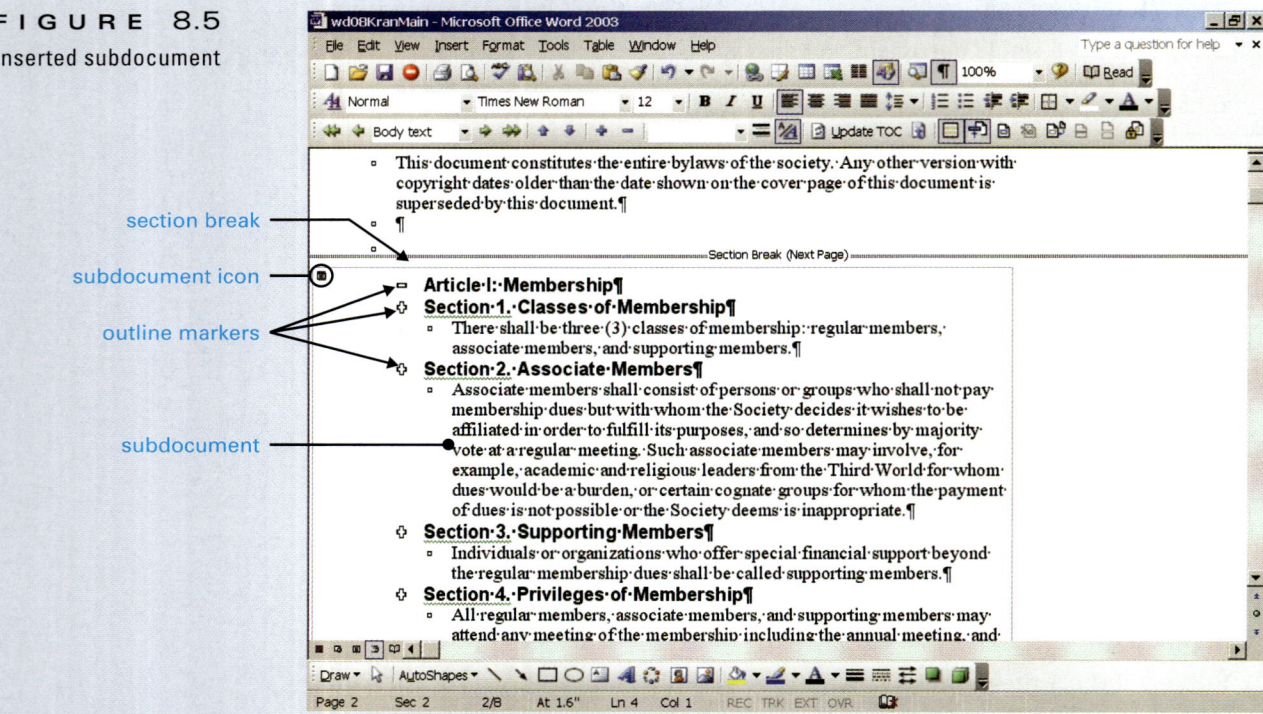

F I G U R E   8.6
Document displaying only headings

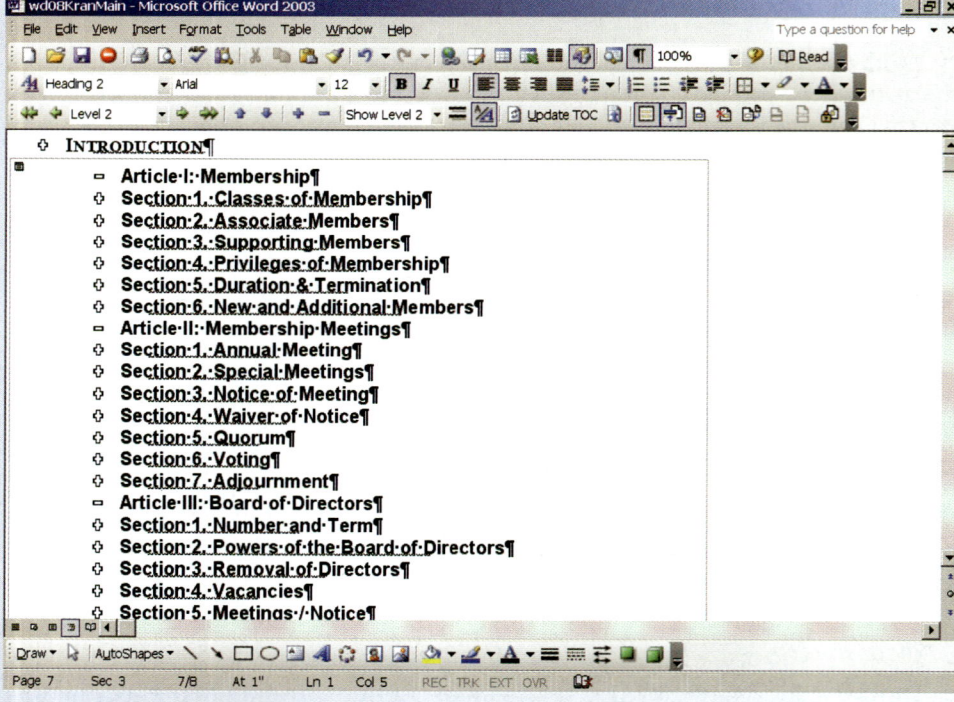

tip: *If the formatting doesn't appear to be the same as the document formatting shown in Figure 8.6, then click the Show Formatting* ¶ *button on the Outlining toolbar to view the formatting*

6. Click the **Show Level** list box arrow, and then click **Show All Levels** at the bottom of the list of choices. Word displays the document headings and all text in the main and subdocument

7. Press **Ctrl+End** to move the insertion point to the very bottom of the newly inserted subdocument in preparation to insert another subdocument

8. Repeat steps 2 through 5 to insert the subdocument **KranPart3.doc**

tip: *If a dialog box opens warning you that a style exists in a document but not in others, click **Yes** to proceed*

9. Scroll the document so you can see all of the headings in KranPart3, the subdocument you just added (see Figure 8.7)

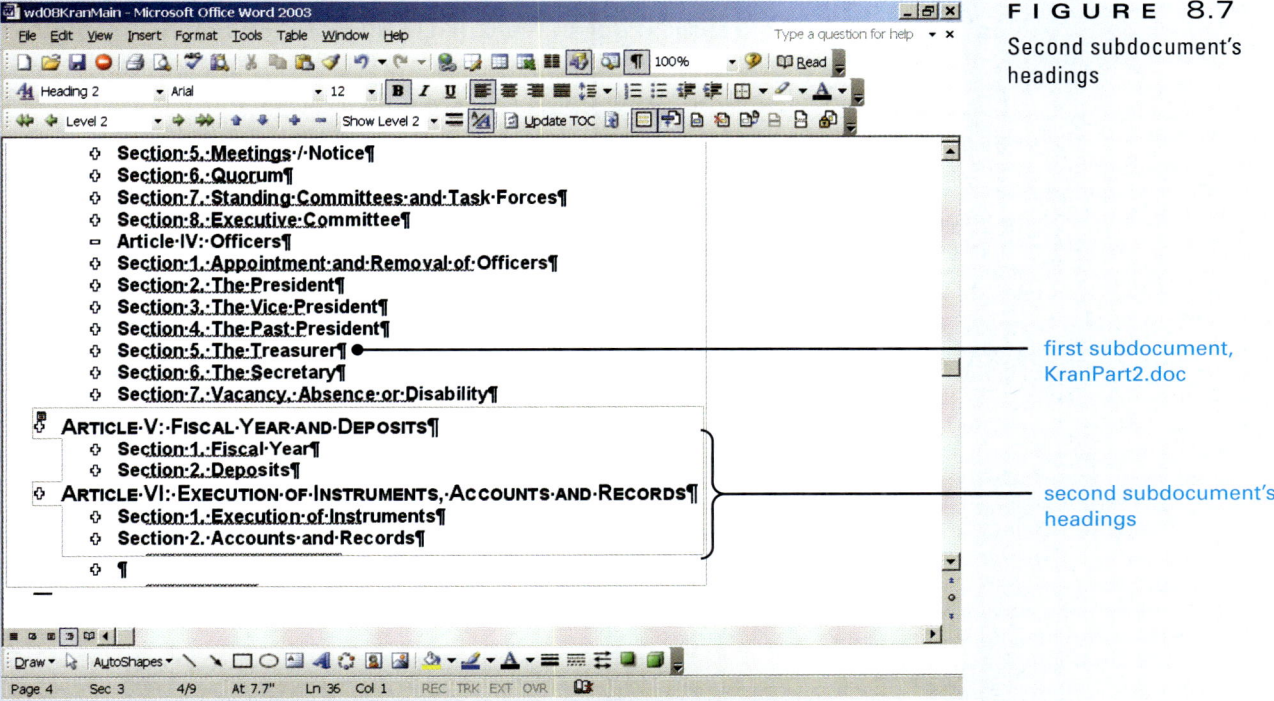

FIGURE 8.7
Second subdocument's headings

first subdocument, KranPart2.doc

second subdocument's headings

Now you have a master document because it contains the original document plus two inserted subdocuments. The next step is to save the document. When you save a master document, word automatically saves the subdocuments also.

Saving and closing a master document:

1. With the master document and two inserted subdocuments open, click **File** on the menu bar and then click **Save**. Word saves the master document and subdocuments

2. Click **File** on the menu bar and then click **Close** to close the master document

Word records the names and locations (folders and subfolders) where it stores the two subdocuments. When you reopen the master document, you will see the path name and the document names explicitly recorded in the location where the subdocuments are to be inserted. To understand this, you will reopen the master document to view it and the links to the subdocuments.

Opening a master document:

1. With Word open but not documents open, click **File** on the menu bar and then click **Open**

2. Using the *Look in* text box, navigate to the folder containing the master document and its two subdocuments—**KranMain.doc**, **KranPart2.doc**, and **KranPart3.doc**

3. Double-click **KranMain.doc** in the Open dialog box to open the master document

4. Scroll down the document past the title page and the introduction until you locate the section breaks and two links where the subdocuments used to appear (see Figure 8.8)

FIGURE 8.8

Master document with subdocument links

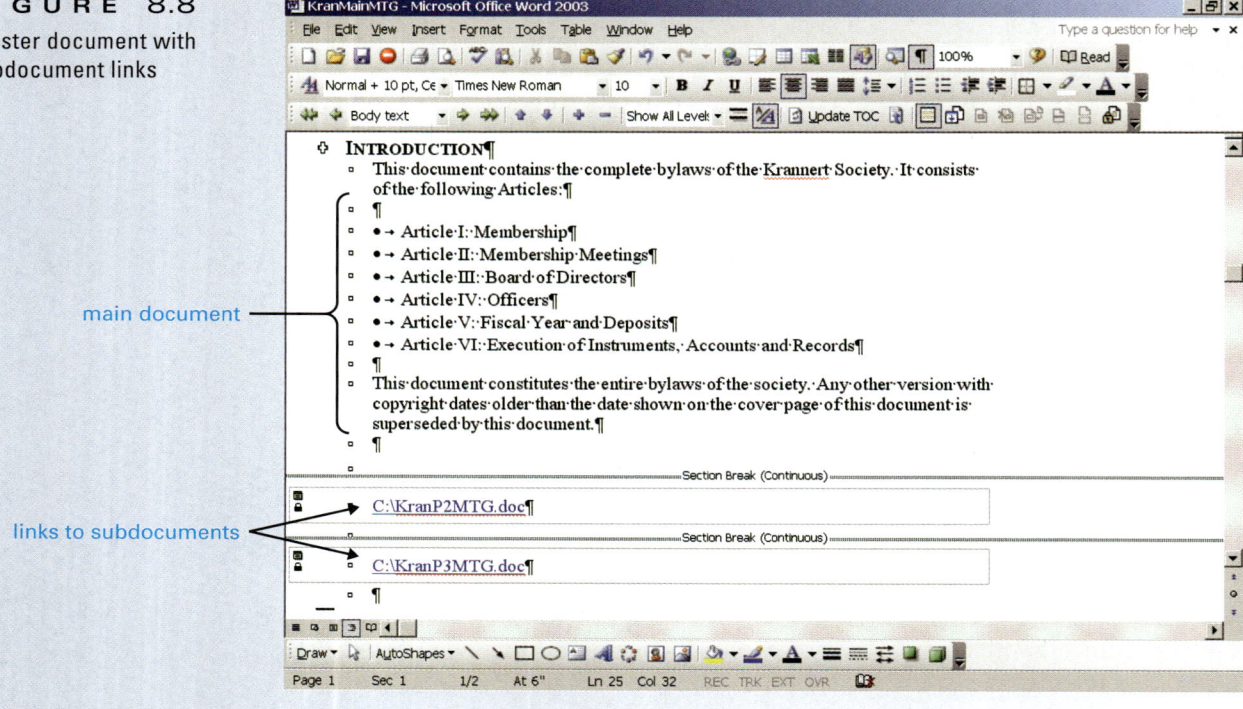

SESSION 8.1

making the grade

1. List three advantages to using a master document compared to a single, longer document.

2. Name two general ways to create a master document.

3. Name two general ways to create a subdocument.

4. A _____ document is a file containing links to individual files that make up a larger document.

5. A _____ is a file that is part of the master document.

SESSION 8.2 WORKING WITH A MASTER DOCUMENT AND SUBDOCUMENTS

---

anotherword ... on Subdocuments

If you reorganize your files and move subdocuments from one folder to another, Word will not be able to locate your files when you open the master document. You will get the error message "Error! Hyperlink reference not valid." If you must relocate the subdocuments, move them *with* the master document. Word will be able to find the subdocuments as long as they travel together with the master document to the same folder

---

Opening Subdocuments from the Master Document

You can modify a subdocument by opening it independently of the master document, or you can move to it directly from the master document, make any changes, and move back to the master document. This is the best choice, because you can operate on any subdocument without leaving the master document, and you can subsequently expand the subdocument within the master document to view it as it appears within the master document.

---

task reference | Moving to a Subdocument from a Master Document

- Press and hold the **Ctrl** key
- Click the subdocument hyperlink in the master document

Robert wants you to demonstrate to him how to move to a subdocument and then return to the master document. With the master document open, you demonstrate this to him in the following steps.

Moving to a subdocument from a master document:

1. Press and hold the **Ctrl** key

2. Click **KranPart2.doc**, the hyperlink to the first subdocument, and release the Ctrl key. Word opens the subdocument **KranPart2.doc** and displays the subdocument's name on the Taskbar (see Figure 8.9)

tip: *To move back to the master document, simply click the **KranMain.doc** button on the Taskbar. Alternatively, you can close the KranPart2 subdocument first by clicking **File** and then clicking **Close***

3. Click **File** and then click **Close** to close the **KranPart2.doc** document. Word redisplays the KranMain document with its two hyperlinks to its subdocuments

anotherway
... to Open a Subdocument from a Master Document

Double-click the subdocument icon, which is located near the left edge of the document—to the left of the subdocument hyperlink

FIGURE 8.9

Opening a subdocument from a master document

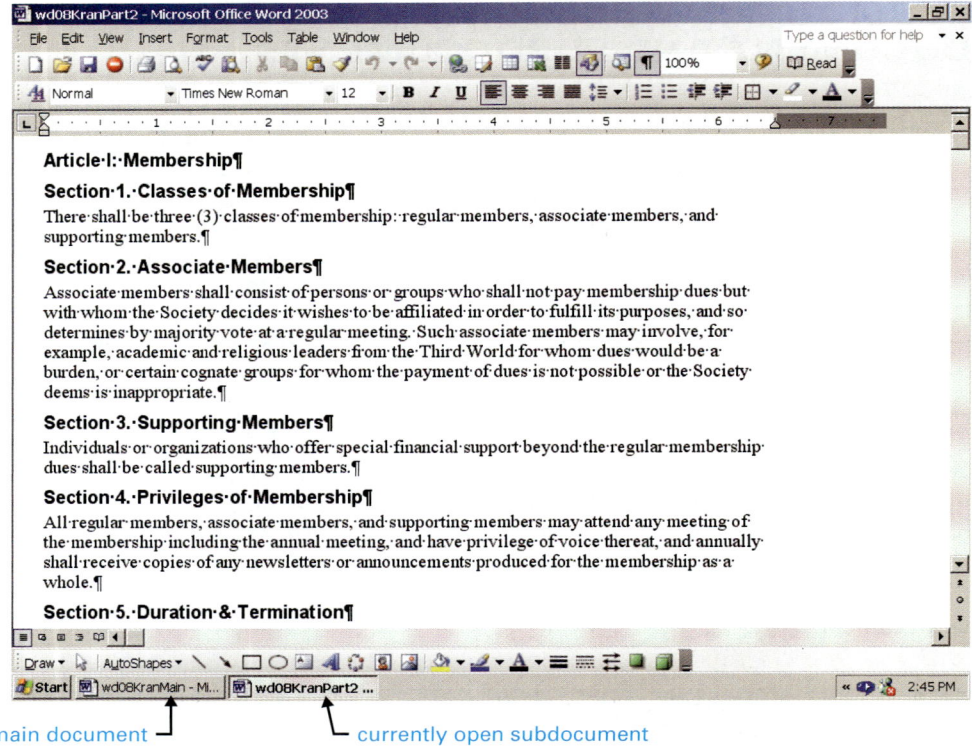

main document ⌐   └ currently open subdocument

Collapsing and Expanding Subdocuments

Robert reminds you that as you work on a master document and its subdocuments, it may be more convenient to view the entire document, the master document and the subdocuments displayed within the master document, to perform global search, modify formats consistently through the master document and its subdocuments, and check spelling. The Outlining toolbar provides several buttons to control the display of subdocuments *within* the master document. For example, when you want to check for consistent formatting simultaneously in the master document and its subdocuments, you will want to expand each subdocument. When you ***expand*** a subdocument, Word replaces its link in the master document with the text from the subdocument. When you collapse a subdocument, Word shows in the master document only the link to the subdocument.

Robert wants you to check the headings in both subdocuments to ensure they are consistent with the entire document. The best way to do that is to expand the subdocuments so they appear in place in the master document.

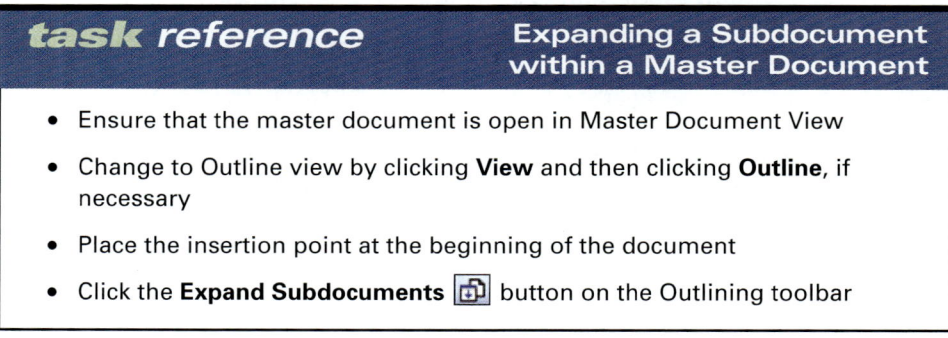

task reference   **Expanding a Subdocument within a Master Document**

- Ensure that the master document is open in Master Document View
- Change to Outline view by clicking **View** and then clicking **Outline**, if necessary
- Place the insertion point at the beginning of the document
- Click the **Expand Subdocuments** button on the Outlining toolbar

Expand the Krannert Bylaws subdocuments within the master document:

1. Ensure that the master document, KranMain.doc, is open in Master Document View, and ensure that the document appears in Outline view

2. Press **Ctrl+Home** to move the insertion point to the top of the master document and then click the **Expand Subdocuments** 🗗 button on the Outlining toolbar. Word expands both subdocuments within the master document.

3. Scroll down the document until you can see the first expanded subdocument (see Figure 8.10)

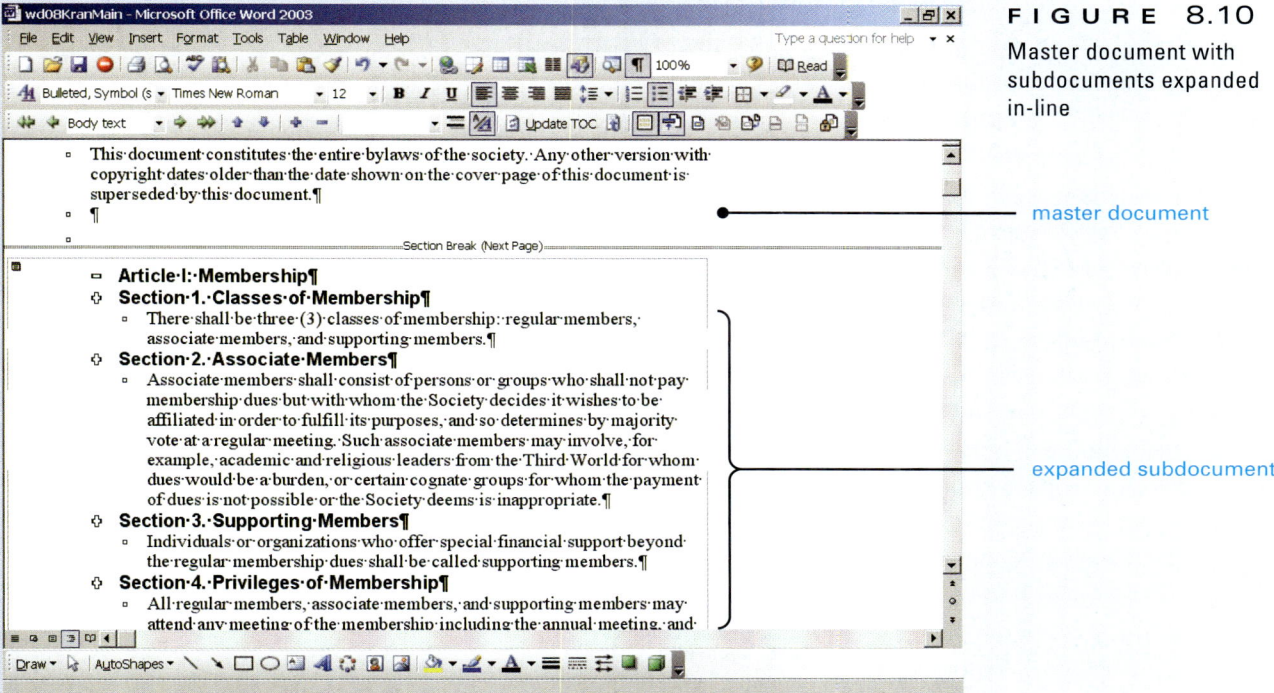

FIGURE 8.10

Master document with subdocuments expanded in-line

master document

expanded subdocument

Promoting Headings

Scrolling down the expanded document, you notice that the two subdocuments' headings are inconsistent. The first subdocument displays its "Article" headings at the same level as its "Section" headings, whereas the second subdocument's "Article" headings are one level higher. The latter are formatted with the Heading 1 style. Robert wants you to change the styles of the first subdocument's "Article" headings to the Heading 1 style—to match the second expanded subdocument. The easiest way is to promote the incorrectly formatted headings to Heading 1 style. When you **promote** a heading, you reformat the text to a higher level heading (lower number). You will alter the styles on all incorrect headings next.

Promoting document headings:

1. With the first expanded subdocument visible on your screen, click anywhere within the line "Article I: Membership"

2. Click the **Promote to Heading 1** button, the leftmost button on the Outlining toolbar. Word promotes the text by replacing its style with Heading 1

3. Repeat steps 1 and 2, promoting Article II, Article III, and Article IV to Heading 1

4. Save your changes by clicking **File** on the menu bar and then clicking **Save**. Word saves the altered subdocument and the master document (see Figure 8.11)

FIGURE 8.11

Master document with promoted headings

promoted headings

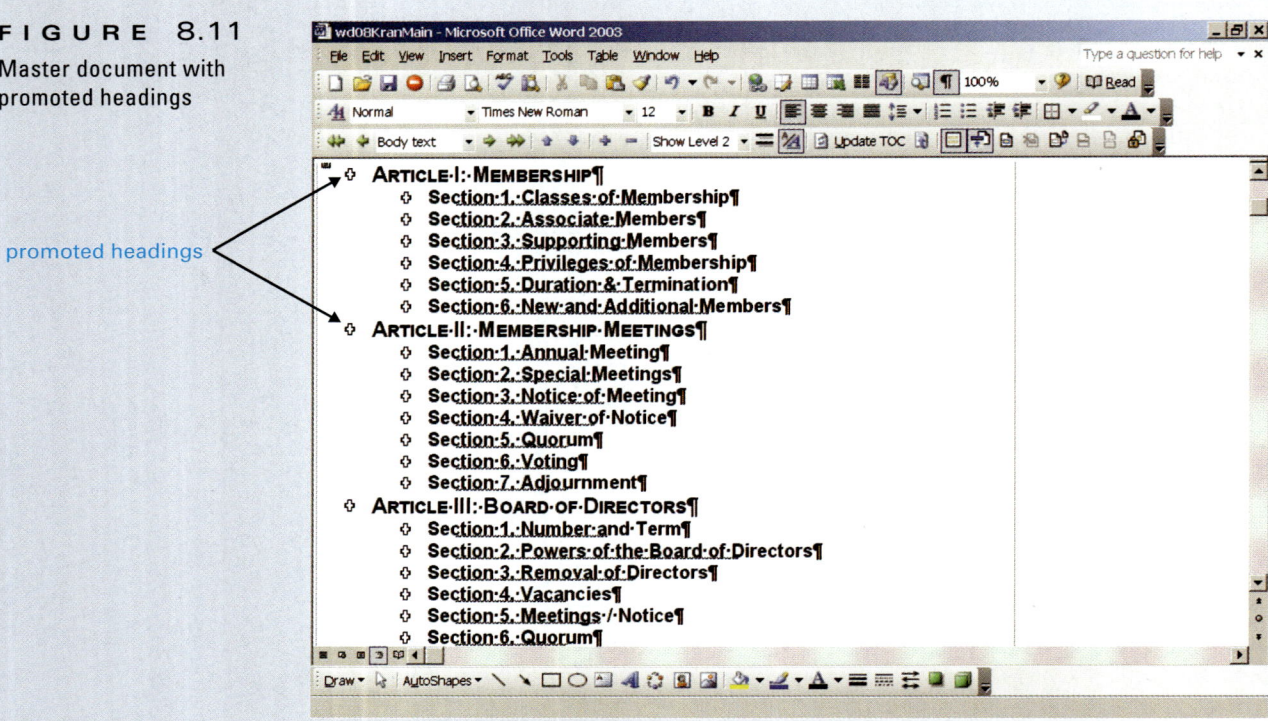

Creating Subdocuments

Robert wants to subdivide KranPart2 into two subdocuments, because he wants one team of students to be responsible for the first two articles of the bylaws (membership and membership meetings) and another team to work with the second two articles (board of directors and officers). By subdividing the KranPart2 document into two subdocuments, Robert divides the responsibilities so that one group works on member-related document modifications while the other group deals with the governing board and officers section of the bylaws. Subdividing a subdocument provides a smaller-sized document that is easier to work with. You *split* a document by dividing it into two subdocuments. Whenever a subdocument becomes too long or otherwise difficult to handle, you can always subdivide it into two or more subdocuments. When you save a newly split document, Word saves the subdocument using the newly created subdocument's first Heading 1 style as the header. This is one of the reasons you should create a different folder for each master document.

Splitting a Subdocument

Now you are ready to split the KranPart2 subdocument into two subdocuments, thereby creating a new subdocument.

---

task reference   **Splitting a Subdocument into Two Subdocuments**

- Ensure that the document you are about to split is in Master Document View

- Click **View** on the menu bar and then click **Outline** to display the subdocument in Outline view

- Click the **Show Level** list box arrow and click **Show All Levels** in the list to ensure that all headings and subheadings appear

- Create a new Heading 1 heading at the point where you want to make the split or raise an existing heading to a Heading 1 level

- Click the outline marker of the Heading 1 where you want to split the subdocument

- Click the **Split Subdocument** [icon] button on the Outlining toolbar

---

To split the KranPart2.doc into two separate files, you will create a new subdocument by splitting the existing subdocument at the Article III heading. After you split the subdocument, you will save it and the master document to preserve the new links.

Splitting a subdocument into two subdocuments:

1. Click the **Show Level** list box and then click **Show Level 2**

2. Click the **outline marker**, a plus sign, located to the left of the heading "Article III: Board of Directors" to ensure the entire heading and all sections beneath it are selected. Word selects the heading and all its subheadings (see Figure 8.12)

   tip: *If you see a link to the subdocument instead of the expanded subdocument within the master document, then click the **Expand Subdocuments** [icon] button on the Outlining toolbar*

3. Click the **Split Subdocument** [icon] button on the Outlining toolbar and then deselect the text by clicking elsewhere in the document. Word creates a subdocument outline around the new subdocument and inserts section breaks (see Figure 8.13)

4. Click the **Save** button on the Standard toolbar to save the new subdocument and the master document with its new subdocument link

   tip: *Word saves a new subdocument by using its first heading as the filename. In this example, Word saves the new subdocument, containing Article III and Article IV, in a new file called **Article III.doc***

5. To verify that Word has saved the new subdocument, click **File** and then click **Open**. Examine the filenames in the Open dialog box and verify that the file **Article III.doc** is among the filenames listed

6. Click the **Cancel** button in the Open dialog box to close it

FIGURE 8.12

Selecting a heading and its subheadings

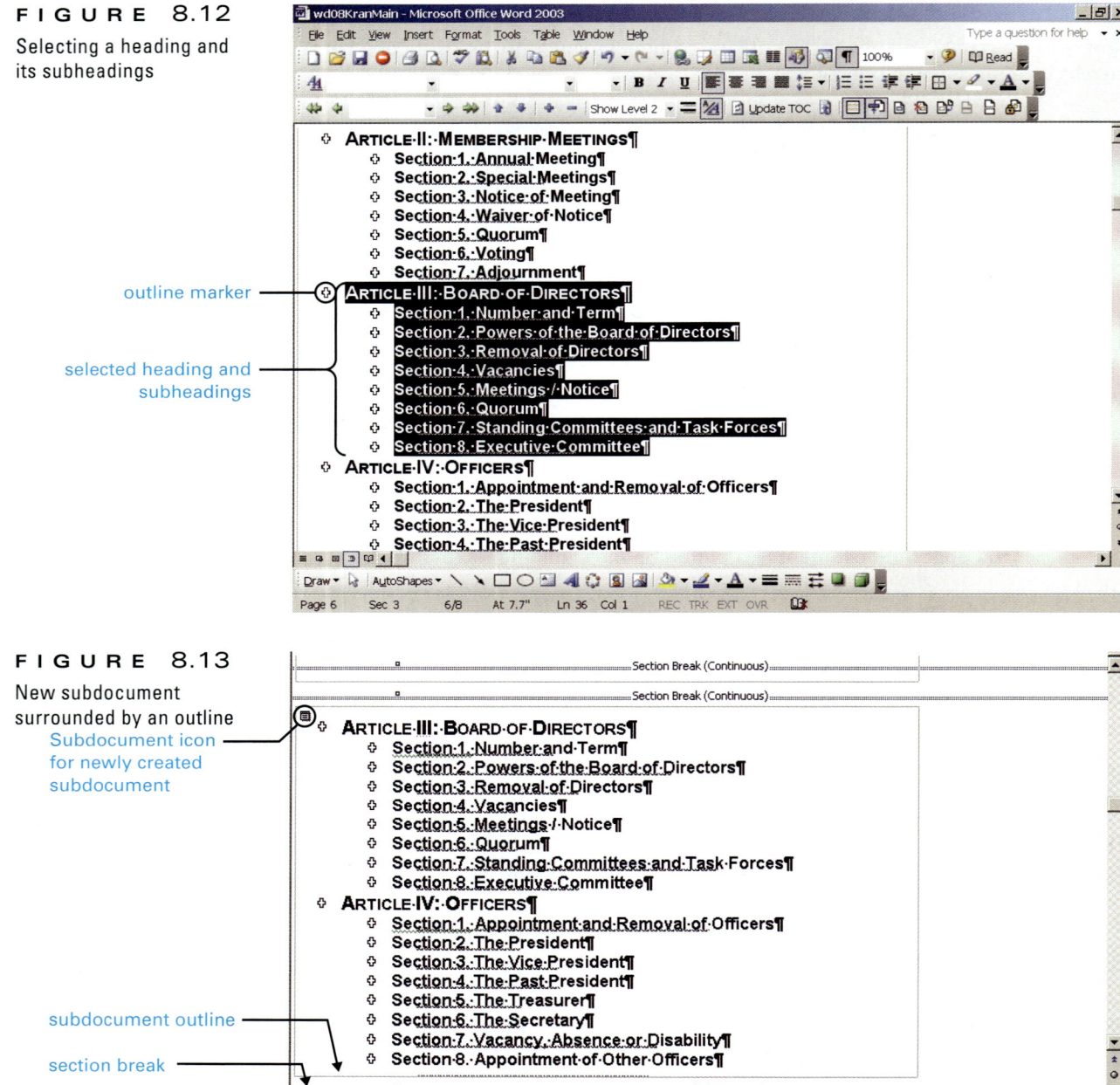

FIGURE 8.13

New subdocument surrounded by an outline

Subdocument icon for newly created subdocument

subdocument outline

section break

Merging Subdocuments

Although splitting documents into subdocuments facilitates editing and managing large documents, there are times when you will want to combine two subdocuments—either before working on them or after you have worked on them independently. You also may want to consolidate two subdocuments into a single subdocument whenever both of the subdocuments are small and, when combined, are easier to manage. To accomplish this, you merge two subdocuments. You *merge* subdocuments when you combine into one document two adjacent subdocuments. Merging two documents is analogous to pasting at the document level.

Robert examines the two subdocuments: **Article III.doc**, which you created above, and **KranPart3.doc**, which you inserted earlier in this session. Because both subdocuments are small and two team members have become busy with a secondary project, Robert decides it is best to combine the subdocuments **Article III.doc** and **KranPart3.doc** and assign the **KranPart3.doc** team to the combined subdocument. He requests that you merge the two subdocuments and then delete the **Article III.doc** so that no one mistakenly works on it when it is no longer part of the master document.

---

task reference   **Merging Subdocuments**

- Ensure that the document you are about to split is in Master Document View
- Click **Expand Subdocuments** button on the Outlining toolbar
- Ensure the subdocuments you want to merge are adjacent to one another
- Click the **Subdocument icon** of the first subdocument, press and hold down the **Shift** key, click the **Subdocument icon** of the second subdocument, and release the **Shift** key
- Click the **Merge Subdocument** button on the Outlining toolbar

---

Merging two subdocuments:

1. Ensure that the master document is open in Master Document View

2. Scroll down the master document until you locate the subdocument beginning with *Article III: Board of Directors,* and then click the **Subdocument icon** to the left and slightly above the Article III heading. Word selects the entire subdocument

3. Scroll down the document and locate the heading *Article V: Fiscal Year and Deposits*

4. Press and hold the **Shift** key, and then click the **Subdocument icon** to the left of the second subdocument that begins with the heading *Article V: Fiscal Year and Deposits* (see Figure 8.14)

tip: *You will notice the Merge Subdocument button light up with a bit of color when you select the second subdocument, indicating you can now merge the two subdocuments*

5. Release the **Shift** key and then click the **Merge Subdocument** button, which is on the Outlining toolbar (see Figure 8.14). Word merges the two documents into one subdocument

6. Save the altered master document and subdocuments by clicking the **Save** button on the Standard toolbar. Word saves the master document

When you merge two subdocuments into one, you can delete the file in which the second subdocument is stored because Word stores the merged subdocuments in the file formerly occupied by the first subdocument you select—nearest the top of the

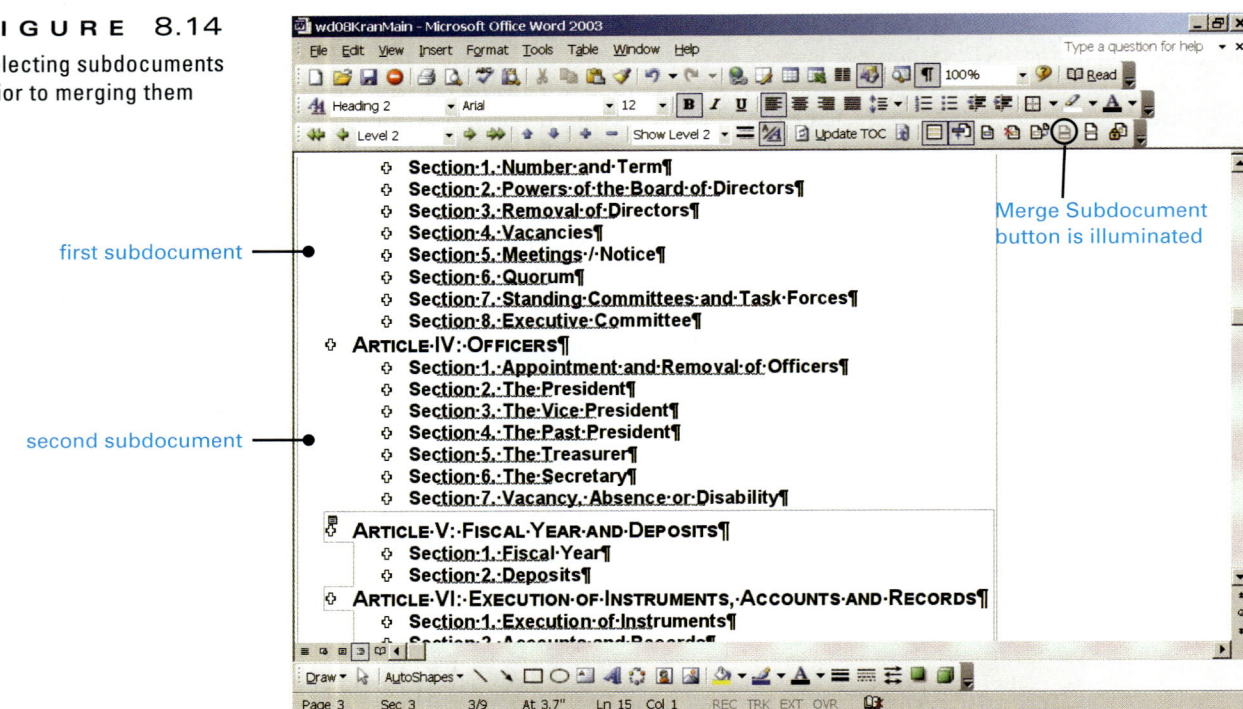

first subdocument

second subdocument

Merge Subdocument
button is illuminated

master document. In this case, you no longer need the subdocument file **KranPart3.doc**, because the merged document **Article III.doc** contains the combined subdocuments now. To ensure you delete the correct subdocument file, you will display the subdocument links by collapsing the subdocuments and examining their link names. In the steps that follow, you will delete the unneeded subdocument file.

Deleting an unneeded subdocument file:

1. To see all document links, click the **Show Level** list box and then click **Show All Levels** from the list of choices

2. Click the **Collapse Subdocuments** 🔁 button on the Outlining toolbar to reveal the subdocuments' filenames. Scroll to the bottom of the document to see the links (see Figure 8.15)

   Look carefully at the subdocument filenames in the master document. Notice that the subdocument files referenced by the master document are **KranPart2.doc** and **Article III.doc**. Because **KranPart3.doc** is not listed as a link in the master document, you no longer need it

3. Click **File** on the menu bar and then click **Open**. Word displays the Open dialog box

4. If necessary, use the Look in list box to navigate to the folder containing the file **KranPart3.doc**, right-click the filename **KranPart3.doc**, click **Delete** on the shortcut list, click **Yes** to delete the file, and click the **Cancel** button to close the Open dialog box

After merging two subdocuments, you may find section breaks appearing in the merged document that are unnecessary—section breaks inserted by Word when you

FIGURE 8.15

Examining the
subdocument filenames

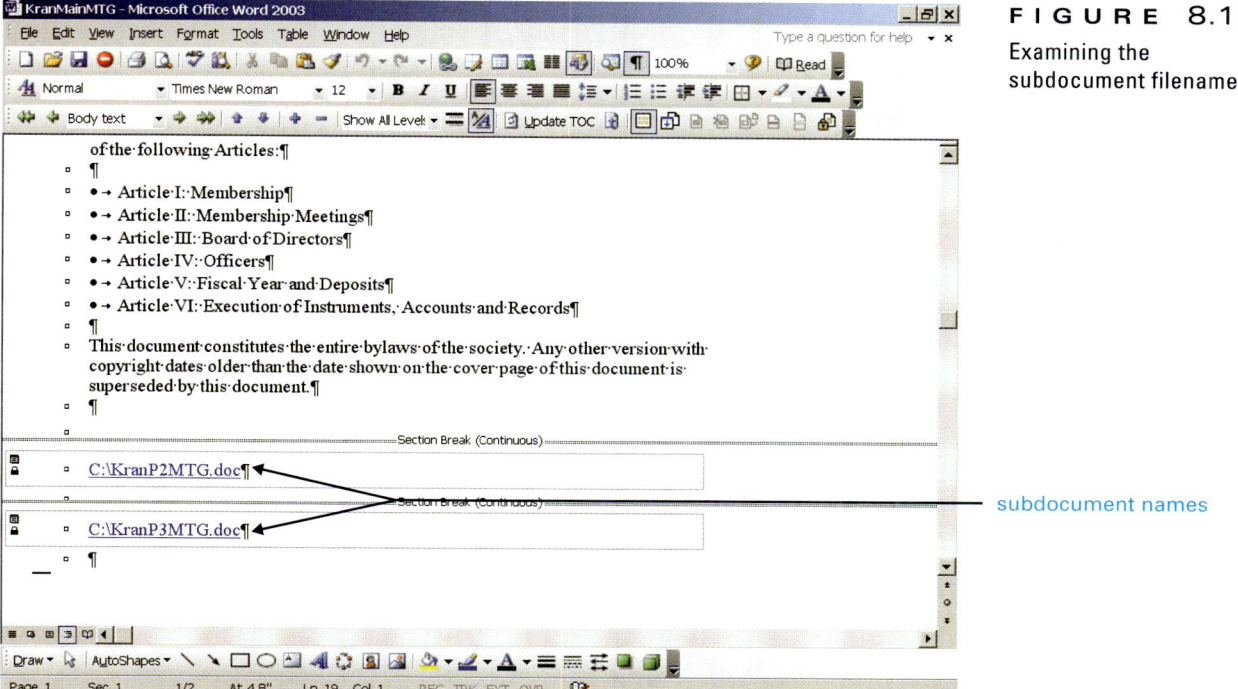

created or inserted the subdocuments. You can remove them by first collapsing the master document's subdocuments, opening the merged subdocument from the master document, removing the unwanted section break, saving the subdocument, and returning to the master document.

To clean up the new, merged subdocument, Article III.doc, follow these steps.

Removing a section break from a subdocument file:

1. If necessary, click the **Collapse Subdocuments** button on the Outlining toolbar to display the subdocuments' filenames

2. Scroll down to the end of the master document, locate the subdocument link for **Article III.doc**, press and hold the **Ctrl** key, move the mouse pointer over the subdocument link until it becomes a small hand, and click the subdocument link to open the subdocument

3. Release the **Ctrl** key, scroll the subdocument to locate the section break just above *Article V*

4. Click the section break line just above the *Article V* heading, and then press **Delete** to remove the section break

5. Click the **Save** button on the Standard toolbar to save the modified subdocument, click **File** on the menu bar, and then click **Close** to close the **Article III.doc** subdocument and redisplay the master document

6. Save the master document to preserve all the changes you have made by clicking the **Save** button on the Standard toolbar

Removing a Subdocument

You may encounter situations where you want to remove a subdocument from a master document. When you remove a subdocument, the subdocument is incorporated into the master document and no longer has a separate subdocument identity. Removing a subdocument can simplify a master document by decreasing the number of subdocuments linked to it. Although you will not remove any subdocuments from the bylaws master document, you should understand how to remove a subdocument.

---

task reference   Removing a Subdocument

- Ensure that the subdocument you are about to remove is expanded in the master document
- Click the subdocument's Subdocument icon to select the subdocument
- Click the **Remove Subdocument** 🔲 button on the Outlining toolbar, and then click anywhere in the master document text to deselect the highlighted text section

---

Reorganizing a Master Document

One of the biggest benefits of working with a master document and its subdocuments is that it is easy to rearrange the master document by moving around the subdocuments. Although Robert wants the bylaws subdocuments to remain in their present order and does not want to rearrange them, he asks you to outline the process for rearranging a master document's subdocuments. You tell Robert that the steps are as follows:

- Open the master document, click View on the menu bar, and then click Outline
- Click the Expand Subdocuments button on the Outlining toolbar
- Drag the Subdocument icon corresponding to the subdocument you want to move to the new location. As you drag the subdocument, a heavy line appears, indicating where the subdocument will be placed if you release the mouse button
- When the dark indicator line appears where you want to place your subdocument, release the mouse to drop the subdocument in place

You tell Robert to be careful when using this drag and drop method to move a subdocument: Be sure the indicator line is outside any subdocuments. Otherwise, you will create a nested subdocument, burying the subdocument within another subdocument and making it very difficult to find.

Renaming a Subdocument

You recall that when you create a subdocument and subsequently save it, Word chooses as the document name the first heading in the new subdocument. In this example, Word created a file called Article III.doc when you saved the master document, which automatically saved the newly created subdocument whose first heading began with "Article III." The automatic filename is not always the best choice, so Word allows you to rename a subdocument.

task *reference* Renaming a Subdocument

- Ensure that the master document is open in Master Document View
- Collapse all subdocuments by clicking the **Collapse Subdocuments** button on the Outlining toolbar
- Press and hold the **Ctrl** key, click the subdocument link for the document you want to rename, and release the **Ctrl** key
- When the subdocument opens in its own window, click **File** on the menu bar, click **Save As**, type the new subdocument name in the File name text box, and click the **Save** button
- Click **File** and then click **Close** to close the subdocument

Robert wants you to change the subdocument name Article III.doc to KranNewPart3.doc.

Renaming a subdocument file:

1. Ensure that the document appears in Master Document View and that the subdocuments are collapsed, showing the subdocuments' filenames (see Figure 8.16)

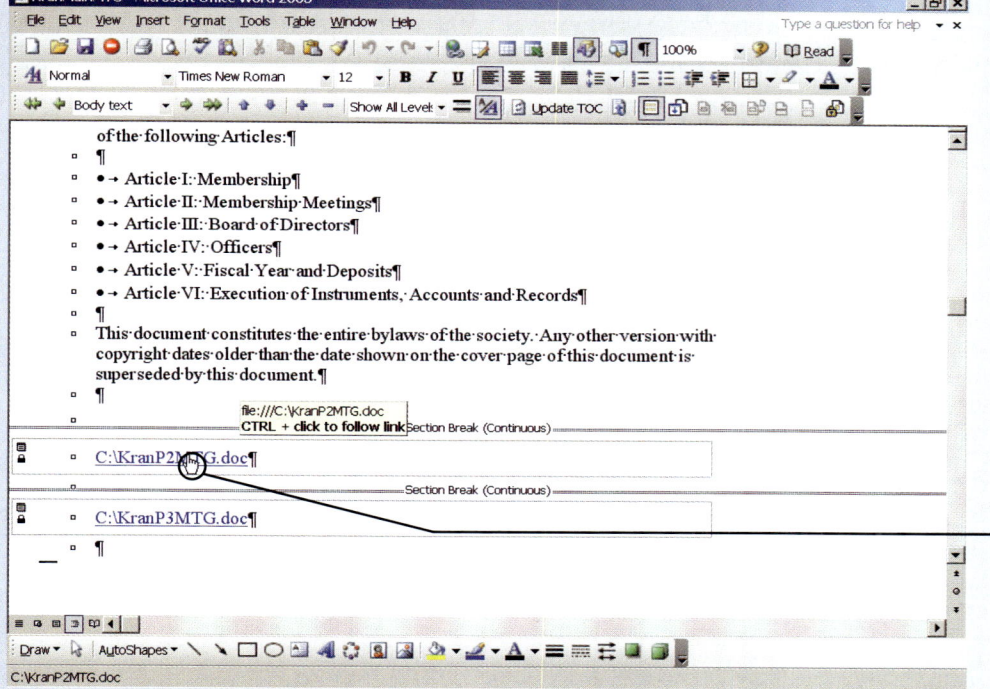

FIGURE 8.16

Preparing to open a subdocument

mouse pointer becomes a small hand when you press Ctrl and hover over a subdocument link

2. Press the **Ctrl** key, hover the mouse over the subdocument hyperlink for **Article III.doc**, click the **Article III.doc** hyperlink, and release the **Ctrl** key. Word opens **Article III.doc** in its own document window

3. Click **File** on the menu bar, click **Save As**, type **KranNewPart3.doc** in the *File name* list box, and click **Save** to save the subdocument under its new name

4. Click **File** on the menu bar and then click **Close** to close the **KranNewPart3.doc** subdocument window. Word redisplays the master document and shows the new document name, **KranNewPart3.doc**

5. To preserve the subdocument name changes in the master document, click the **Save** button on the Standard toolbar to save the master document

Notice that the new filename, **KranNewPart3.doc**, is the new hyperlink that appears in the master document (see Figure 8.17). (Your hyperlink may be different, depending on the folder in which you saved the document.) As long as you save a subdocument from *within* a master document, the master document can record the new name and later locate the file under its new name. However, if you rename a subdocument using, for example, Windows Explorer, outside the master document, then the next time you open the master document, Word will generate an error message similar to the one shown in Figure 8.18.

Printing a Master Document

Robert is pleased with the way you have organized the bylaws into a master document, called **KranMain.doc**, and two subdocuments, called **KranPart2.doc** and **KranNewPart3.doc**. He would like you to print out the entire bylaws so he can review and approve the final document.

task reference	Printing a Master Document

- Open the master document
- If necessary, expand the subdocuments by clicking the **Expand Subdocuments** button
- Click **View** on the menu bar and then click **Print Layout**
- Click **File** on the menu bar, click **Print**, and click **OK**

F I G U R E 8.17

New hyperlink in the master document

new document filename

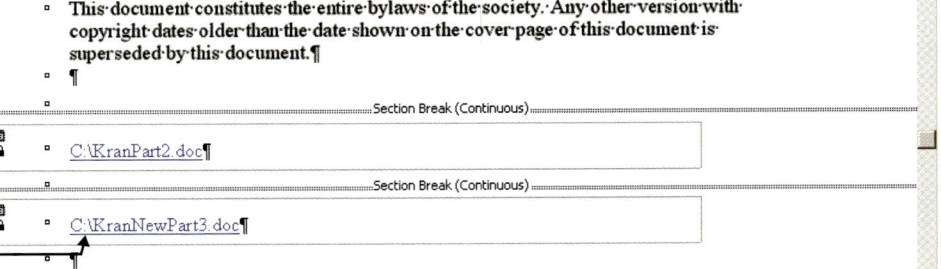

F I G U R E 8.18

Error message generated when Word cannot locate a subdocument

Printing a master document:

1. With the master document displayed in Master Document View, click the **Expand Subdocuments** [icon] button on the Outlining toolbar

2. Click **View** on the menu bar and then click **Print Layout**

3. Click **File** on the menu bar, click **Print**, make any adjustments you want in the Print dialog box, and then click **OK** to print the master document

4. Because you are done with the master document and its subdocuments for this session, close the document by clicking **File** on the menu bar and then click **Exit**. If Word prompts you to save changes, then click **Yes**

Robert is pleased with your work. You have created a master document and two subdocuments. Whenever you want to work on the bylaws, simply open the master document, KranMain.doc, and then make any changes to it or any of the subdocuments. When you have finished making changes to either the master documents or subdocuments, be sure to save the master document.

making the grade

SESSION 8.2

1. When you _____ a heading, you reformat the text to a higher level heading.

2. You _____ a document by dividing it into two subdocuments.

3. Click the Outlining toolbar _____ _____ button to display subdocuments within a master document.

4. When would you split a subdocument?

5. Modify the bylaws documents (the master document and its subdocuments) in the following way. Open the master document, **KranMain.doc**, and save it under the new name **KranMainMTG.doc**. Next, rename the **KranPart2.doc** to **KranP2MTG.doc**. Similarly, rename the **KranNewPart3.doc** to **KranP3MTG.doc**. Save the master document. Open **KranP2MTG.doc** from the master document and delete the heading Section 6, found in Article I: Membership, and all of the text up to the heading Article II. Save the subdocument. Open **KranP3MTG.doc** and delete Section 8, found in Article III, including all text describing the Executive Committee. Delete Articles IV and V from **KranP3MTG.doc** and all text beneath both of those headings. Renumber Article VI ("Article VI: Execution of Instruments, Accounts and Records") to Article IV. Add your name in the document header for the first section of the master document. Save the master document and subdocuments. Collapse the document, and click **Print** on the Standard toolbar. Click **No** when a dialog box appears asking if you want to open the subdocuments before continuing.

SESSION 8.3 MORE ON NUMBERING PAGES, CREATING AN INDEX, AND GENERATING A TABLE OF CONTENTS

In this section, you will learn how to number pages using two different numbering schemes. You will learn how to create an index for important terms by first marking candidate index terms and then generating an index from the marked terms. Finally, you will learn how to create a table of contents and keep it current.

Numbering Pages

Your master document has page numbering in place as do the subdocuments that are part of the main document. The page numbers run sequentially from 2 through 8 and appear on the bottom of each page except the first page. Longer documents, including books, term papers, and similar documents, typically consist of three parts: front matter, main matter, and back matter. *Front matter* includes the first several pages containing a title page, table of contents, preface, acknowledgments, and so on. These pages are usually numbered with lowercase Roman numerals such as i, ii, iii, iv, and so on. The first page of a document's main body and the remaining pages are numbered with Arabic numerals beginning with 1, although the first page of these pages usually does not contain a page number. *Back matter*, which typically contains appendices and an index, can extend the Arabic numbering scheme to the end of the document.

Numbering the Front Matter

Robert wants you to number the front matter with Roman numerals and to number the remaining document with Arabic numerals. Once you have implemented the page numbering changes, you will add a page footer to the document. You begin by modifying page numbering for the front matter.

Numbering front matter pages:

1. If you closed your bylaws document at the end of the previous session, then open the master document, **KranMain.doc**, display it in Outline view, click the **Expand Subdocuments** 🗗 button, click **View** on the menu bar, and then click **Print Layout**

2. Move the insertion point to the word *Introduction* on the second page of the document by clicking it, and then click **Insert** on the menu bar, and click **Page Numbers**. The Page Numbers dialog box opens

3. Click the **Format** button to display the Page Number Format dialog box, click the **Number format** list box, and then click **i, ii, iii, . . .** to change the page numbers to Roman numerals. Ensure that the Include chapter number check box is cleared

4. Click the **Start at** option button in the Page numbering panel. Ensure that i (Roman numeral one) appears in the Start at text box (see Figure 8.19)

5. Click **OK** to close the Page Number Format dialog box, and then click **OK** again to close the Page Numbers dialog box

6. Scroll to the bottom of the page to observe the page number in the footer

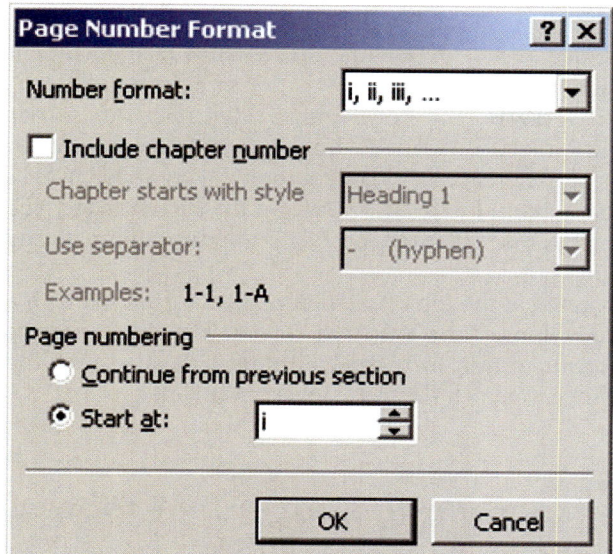

Numbering the Main Document Body

Now you need to reset the page numbering for the document's main matter to begin with page 1 and continue in ascending order to the end of the document.

Numbering the main matter pages:

1. Scroll to the next page and click anywhere in **Article I: Membership** located at the top of the page to move the insertion point

2. Click **Insert** on the menu bar, and click **Page Numbers**

tip: *If the Page Number command appears dim in the Insert menu, then your subdocument is locked. Unlock it by switching to Outline view, switching to Master Document View, and clicking the **Lock Document** button on the Outlining toolbar. Then, return to Print Layout view, and repeat step 2*

3. Click the **Format** button to display the Page Number Format dialog box; ensure that the Number format list box displays **1, 2, 3, . . .** so page numbers in the main matter display Arabic numbers

4. Click the **Start at** option button in the Page numbering panel. Ensure that 1 appears in the Start at list box one

5. Click **OK** to close the Page Number Format dialog box, and then click **OK** again to close the Page Numbers dialog box

6. Scroll to the bottom of the page to observe the page number in the footer

You have established page numbering so that the title page contains no number, the introduction page is numbered with a Roman numeral, and the remaining pages are numbered consecutively beginning at page 1 for the remainder of the document.

Inserting a Style Reference

Next, you will insert the title *Krannert Society Bylaws* into the footer of each document on the left side to help identify each page of the document, with the exception of the title page. Instead of typing the text in the footer, you will insert a style reference. A **style reference** is a field (named StyleRef) that is formatted with a style and then inserted in the document where a special style reference field code appears. The StyleRef field prints the first or last text formatted with the specified style on the current page. The advantage of using a style reference is that the text, wherever it appears, automatically changes if the style reference changes.

The title of the document, located at the top of the first page, is formatted with a special Title style. Therefore, you will insert the Title style reference in the document footer. If you ever change the document title, formatted with the Title style, then the footer contents automatically change to match the title. How convenient!

Inserting a style reference in the document footer:

1. Scroll to the second page containing the heading *Introduction* and click **Introduction** located at the top of the page

2. Click **View** on the menu bar and then click **Header and Footer**. Word displays the Header for Section 2

3. Click the **Switch Between Header and Footer** button on the Header and Footer toolbar to switch to the Section 2 footer

4. Click **Insert** on the menu bar and click **Field** to open the Field dialog box

5. Click the **Categories** list box and then click **Links and References**

6. Click **StyleRef** in the *Field names* list box. Scroll down and click **Title** in the *Style name* list box (see Figure 8.20)

FIGURE 8.20

Field dialog box

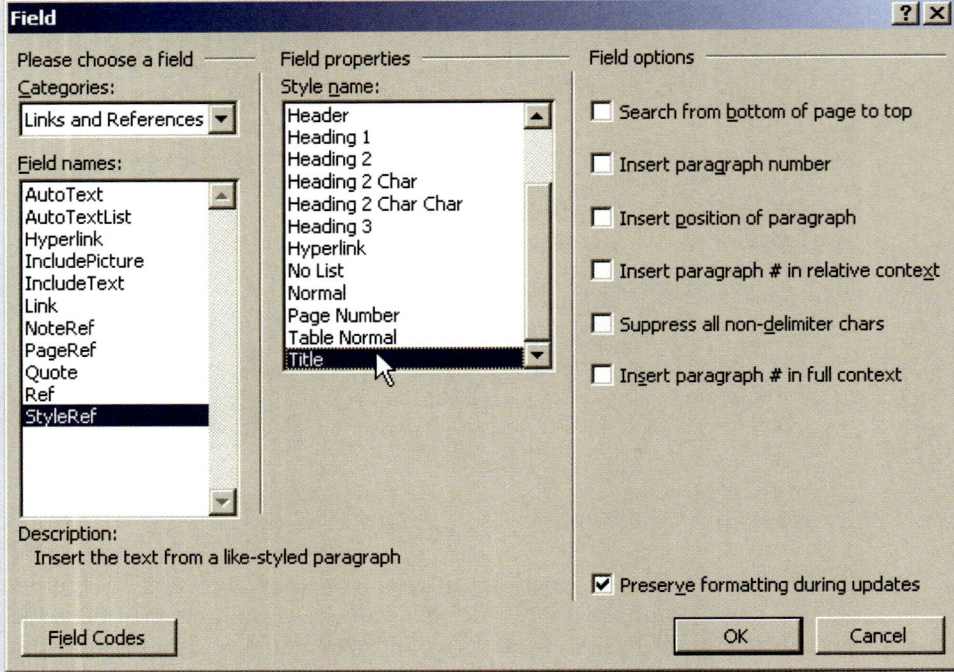

7. Click **OK** to close the Field dialog box. Observe the title Krannert Society Bylaws appearing in the footer on the left side. Each page in the document, except the title page, displays the text found in the document title and formatted with the Title style (see Figure 8.21)

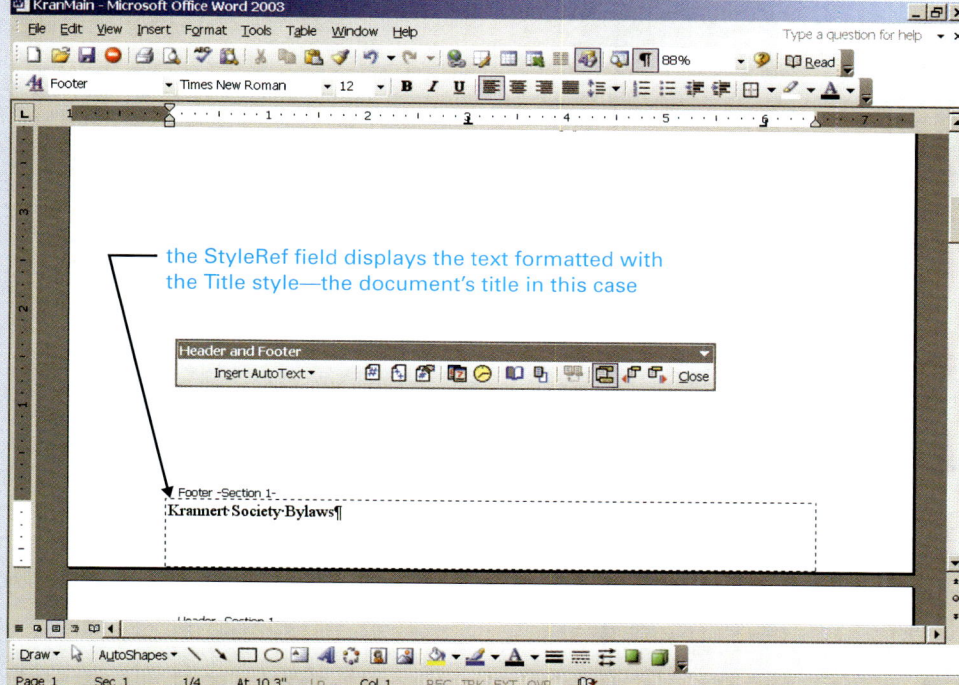

FIGURE 8.21

StyleRef field displays the document's title

8. Click the **Close** button on the Header and Footer toolbar to close the toolbar

9. Click the **Save** button on the Standard toolbar to save the changes you have made so far to the bylaws document

More on Creating Index Entries

Whenever you create a long document covering a lot of material, it is important for anyone reading the document to be able to locate the key items and topics that interest them. One way to aid readers who want to quickly locate topics that interest them is to create a good index. An *index* lists the words and phrases that occur in a document along with the page numbers on which they appear. Some people believe that the quality of an index can determine for a reader whether or not to read the document or book, or read or purchase another one.

Although the audience for your Krannert Society Bylaws is not large, Robert wants you to create an index so members can quickly locate key document paragraphs. The first step is to locate and mark words in the document that you want to include in the index. The second step is to generate the index and place it wherever you want—preferably at the end of the document. Word does all the difficult work including sorting all the index entries into alphabetical order, adding page numbers, deleting duplicate word/page number entries, and eliminating repeated entries.

Marking Index Entries

Robert tells you that there are two different ways to create an index entry. You can use text that is already in the document by selecting it. Additionally, you can add an index word that is not found in your document but is related to the material found in a sentence or a paragraph. An example of the second way to create an index entry is to add the index term *programming* and insert a pointer to a paragraph describing how to write Java statements. Even though *programming* might not appear in the paragraph, the paragraph certainly describes one programming language.

---

task reference   Marking Index Entries and Subentries

- Select the word or phrase you want to mark as an index entry, or place the insertion point where you want to add a new word or phrase, not found in the text, as an index entry
- Click **Insert** on the menu bar, point to **Reference**, click **Index and Tables**, click the **Index** tab, and then click the **Mark Entry** button
- Ensure the Current page option, in the Options panel, is selected
- If needed, type an index word or phrase in the Main entry text box, and then type an optional word or phrase in the Subentry text box
- Click the **Mark** button to mark the single occurrence

or

- Click the **Mark All** button to mark every occurrence of the selected word or phrase in the document
- Click the **Close** button to close the dialog box

You are ready to mark the first of several index words or phrases that Robert wants to appear in the document's index.

Marking a word or phrase as an index term:

1. Click **Outline view** on the status bar, and then ensure the subdocuments are expanded

2. Click the **Show Level** list box and then click **Show All Levels**, if necessary

3. Locate the text *Article III: Board of Directors* and double-click **Board** to select the word

4. Click **Insert** on the menu bar, point to **Reference**, click **Index and Tables**, click the **Index** tab (if necessary), and then click the **Mark Entry** button. Word displays the Mark Index Entry dialog box (see Figure 8.22)

5. Click the **Current page** option in the Options panel, if necessary, and then click the **Mark** button. Word inserts a hidden marker indicating the position of the index entry in the document (see Figure 8.23)

tip: *If you cannot see the index entry marker in the document, then click the **Show/Hide** ¶ button on the Standard toolbar to reveal hidden codes*

6. Click the **Close** button to close the Mark Index Entry dialog box

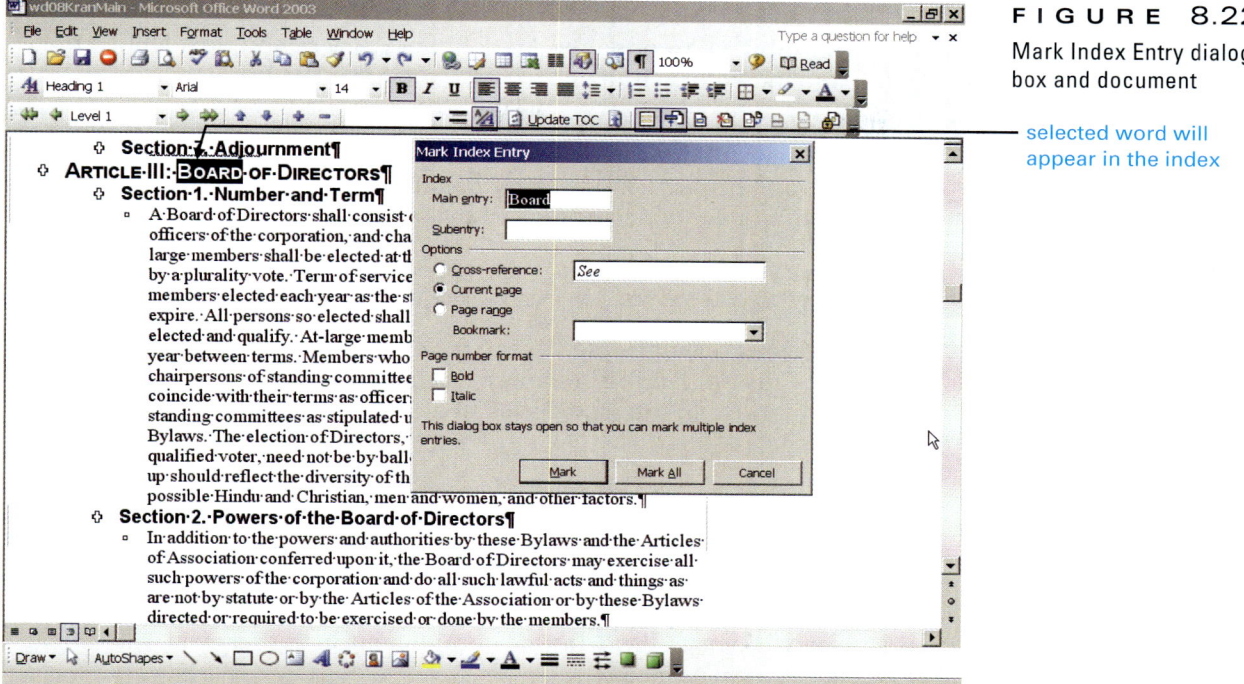

FIGURE 8.22
Mark Index Entry dialog box and document

selected word will appear in the index

FIGURE 8.23
Special code marking index entry's location

embedded code marking index word's location

After examining the document carefully for potential index words and phrases, Robert has decided that he wants you to mark only a few more words and phrases for the index. Later, after you generate a sample index from the marked index terms, Robert will examine the index. For now, however, he only wants a few words to test the usefulness of the index for such a short document. Robert wants you to mark all occurrences of the following words and phrases as index terms: *Vice President* and *President*. Later, you will add more index entries.

Marking every occurrence of a word or phrase as an index term:

1. Press **Ctrl+Home** to go to the top of the bylaws document

2. Press **Ctrl+F** to open the Find and Replace dialog box, replace any text that may appear in the Find what list box by typing **vice president** in the Find what list box, click the **Find Next** button, and click the **Cancel** button. Word locates and highlights the first occurrence of "Vice President" in the document

3. Press **Alt+Shift+X** to open the Mark Index Entry dialog box. Notice the candidate index term appears in the Mark entry list box

4. Click the **Current page** option in the Options panel, if necessary, then click the **Mark All** button, and then click anywhere within the document to deactivate the Mark Index Entry dialog box. Word inserts a hidden marker next to every occurrence of the index term in the document

tip: *The Mark Index Entry dialog box is one that you can leave open as you scroll through the document or execute the Find command to locate words to use as index terms*

5. Repeat steps 2 through 4 searching for and marking all occurrences of the word *President* in the document. Leave the Mark Index Entry dialog box open for use in the next series of steps

Word marks occurrences of the words *Vice President* and *President* as index entries, which you can see by the XE field code that appears immediately to the right of each index term. The code XE stands for index entry. Were you to create a complete index of all the important index terms in a document, you would continue to select a candidate index term and then mark them. Instead of continuing in this way, you will learn how to create subentries to an index.

Marking Subentries

Robert recognizes that any good index contains subentries as well as main entries. A *subentry* is a secondary topic you use to narrow the search of a specific topic. For example, the main entry *membership* in an index is more useful if it also lists subentries such as (in this case) the words *associate, supporting,* and *duration.* All three subentries describe the types of membership or the term length of a membership. If you were to list the three subentries as main entries, they would be too general to be useful. However, when listed under the main entry *membership,* the subentries serve to further refine the reader's search for a topic. After marking the subentries under *membership,* an index would display them this way:

    Membership
        associate, 2
        duration, 2
        supporting, 2

Marking subentries:

1. Scroll to *Article I: Membership* found on page 3 and then click to the right of *Section 2* and just to the left of the word *Associate* (you may have to move the Mark Index Entry dialog box to the side of the screen), click twice in the **Main entry** text box, type **Membership**, press **Tab**, type **associate** in the Subentry text box, and click the **Mark** button (see Figure 8.24)

2. Establish a new insertion point in the document by clicking to the right of *Section 3* and just to the left of the word *Supporting*

tip: *The first time you click the mouse outside the dialog box you deselect the dialog box. Click the mouse a second time to actually establish the new insertion point*

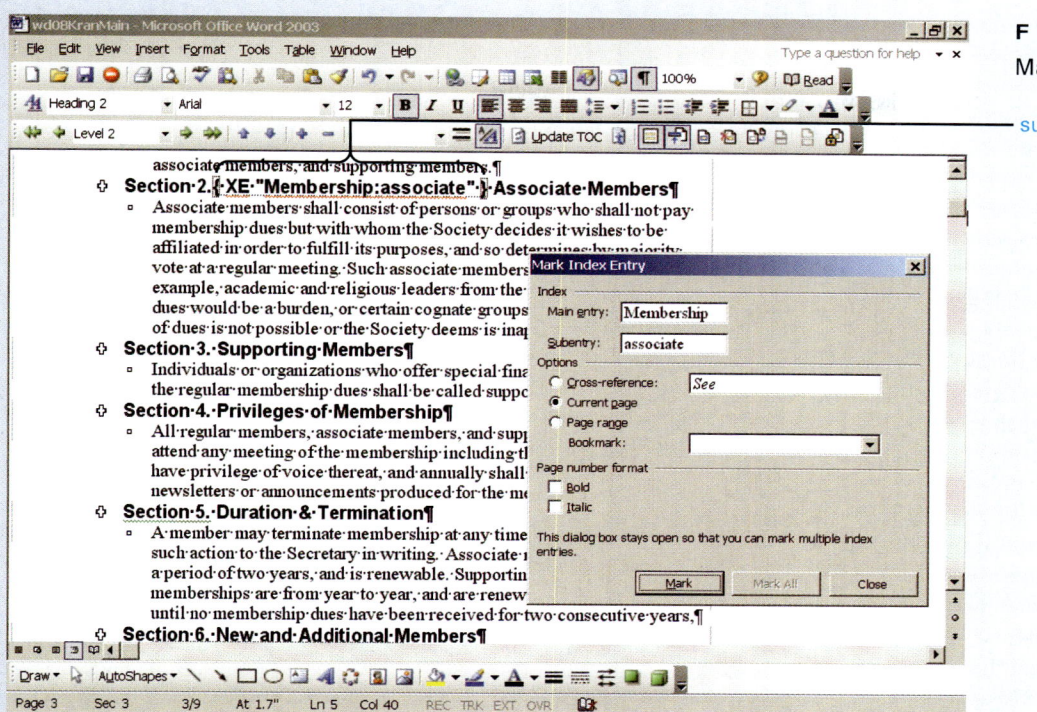

subentry field

3. Click twice in the **Main entry** text box, type **Membership**, press **Tab**, type **supporting** in the Subentry text box, and click the **Mark** button

4. Click to the right of *Section 5* and just to the left of the word *Duration*, click twice in the **Main entry** text box, type **Membership**, press **Tab**, type **duration** in the Subentry text box, and click the **Mark** button

Creating a Cross-Reference Index Entry

Robert wants you to create a cross-reference index entry. A cross-reference index entry points the reader to another word in the index rather than to a page number. For example, the Krannert Society Bylaws refers to organizations that are members as *associate members*. Therefore, you will create a cross-reference index entry that directs readers to "*See* Membership, associate" when they look up either "Membership, organization" or "Membership, organizational."

---

task reference　　　　Marking a Cross-Reference Index Entry

- Type the text for the index entry, or position the insertion point in the document

- Press **Alt+Shift+X** to display the Mark Index Entry dialog box

- Type the Main entry text

- Optionally, type a subentry index term in the Subentry text box

- Click the **Cross-reference** option

- Type the cross-reference entry you want to refer readers to following the word *See* in the cross-reference text box, and then click the **Mark** button

---

another way
. . . to Mark Subentries

Make subentries and reduce the number of mouse clicks by typing both the main entry and the subentry in the Main entry text box of the Mark Index Entries dialog box, separating the two entries with a colon. You can use this method to create up to seven levels of subentries. For example, type *Membership: associate* in the Main entry text box to create the subentry *associate* under the main entry *Membership*

Marking cross-reference index entries:

1. With the Mark Entry Index Entry dialog box open, click the document, scroll to *Article I: Membership* (page 3), and then click immediately to the left of *Section 2.* Next, double-click the **Main entry** text box, type **Membership**, press **Tab**, type **organization** in the Subentry text box, and click the **Cross-reference** button. The insertion point moves to the right of the word *See* in the Cross-reference text box

2. Type **Membership, associate** and then click the **Mark** button

3. Double-click the **Subentry** text box, type **organizational** in the Subentry text box, and then click the **Mark** button (see Figure 8.25). Word marks the second of two cross-reference index entries

FIGURE 8.25

Marking a cross-reference index entry

cross-reference index entry field

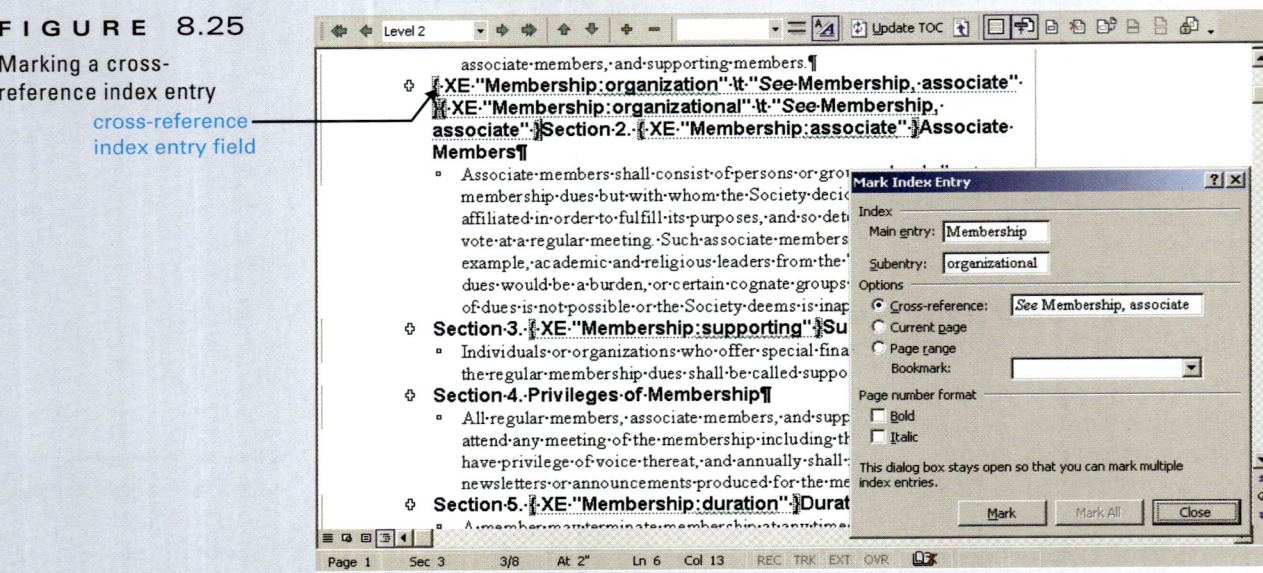

4. Double-click the **Main entry** text box, type **Organizational membership**, and then click the **Mark** button. This provides a main index entry that references an index subentry

5. Close the Mark Index Entry dialog box

Readers who look up *Organizational membership, membership, organization,* or *membership, organizational* are redirected to *Membership, associate* in the index. The first two index entries you created are cross-references consisting of a main entry and subentry, whereas the third index that you created in step 4 is an example of a main index entry cross-reference.

Creating a Page Range Index Entry

Besides main index entries and subentries, which list specific pages on which the entries fall, another type of index entry you may want to consider is one referring to a range of pages. For example, you may want to indicate that the topic Board of Directors spans two pages or that you can find a discussion of Officers (President, Vice President, etc.) on a page range.

By default, Word assigns to an index entry the page number corresponding to the current page. If you want to indicate that span of pages for a topic so your readers

browse all relevant pages, then do so by a slightly more complicated procedure: You select the pages that you want to mark for the index entry, create a Bookmark for the selected pages, and designate the Bookmark name as the page-range entry.

---

task reference Marking a Page Range Index Entry

- Select a range of pages, several paragraphs, a section, or a chapter for example
- Click **Insert** on the menu bar, click **Bookmark**
- Type the Bookmark name, and then click the **Add** button
- Press **Alt+Shift+X** to open the Mark Index Entry dialog box, if necessary
- Click the **Page range** option button, click the Bookmark list arrow, and click the Bookmark name you created above
- Click the **Mark** button

Robert would like you to mark all of the text of Article III: Board of Directors as an
index entry. Currently, it spans pages 5 and 6.

Creating a page range index entry:

1. Scroll the document until you see *Article III: Board of Directors,* and switch to Normal view
2. Click to the right of *Article III:* and immediately to the left of *Board of Directors.* Then, press and hold **Ctrl+Shift** and press the **down arrow** key repeatedly until you have selected the entire Article III, down to the last sentence just above the heading *Article IV: Officers*
3. Click **Insert** on the menu bar, and then click **Bookmark** to open the Bookmark dialog box
4. Type **BoardOfDirectors** (all one word with no spaces) in the Bookmark name list box, and then click the **Add** button to create the Bookmark
5. Press **Alt+Shift+X** to open the Mark Index Entry dialog box, and then click the **Page range** option button, click the **Bookmark** list arrow, and then click **BoardOfDirectors** (you may have to scroll to the top of the Bookmark list box to locate it, as shown in Figure 8.26)
6. Click the **Mark** button to insert the index entry field into the text, and then click the **Close** button to close the Mark Index Entry dialog box
7. Click anywhere to deselect the text, and click the **Save** button to save your document

Deleting an Index Entry

You may wish to remove index entries that are no longer useful either prior to generating an index or after. Deleting an index entry is as simple as deleting the index entry
field. Robert decides that it is unnecessary to have the index entry *Board,* because the
page range index entry *Board of Directors* also includes the term *Board.* He'd like you to
delete the Board index entry.

F I G U R E   8.26

Creating a page range
index entry

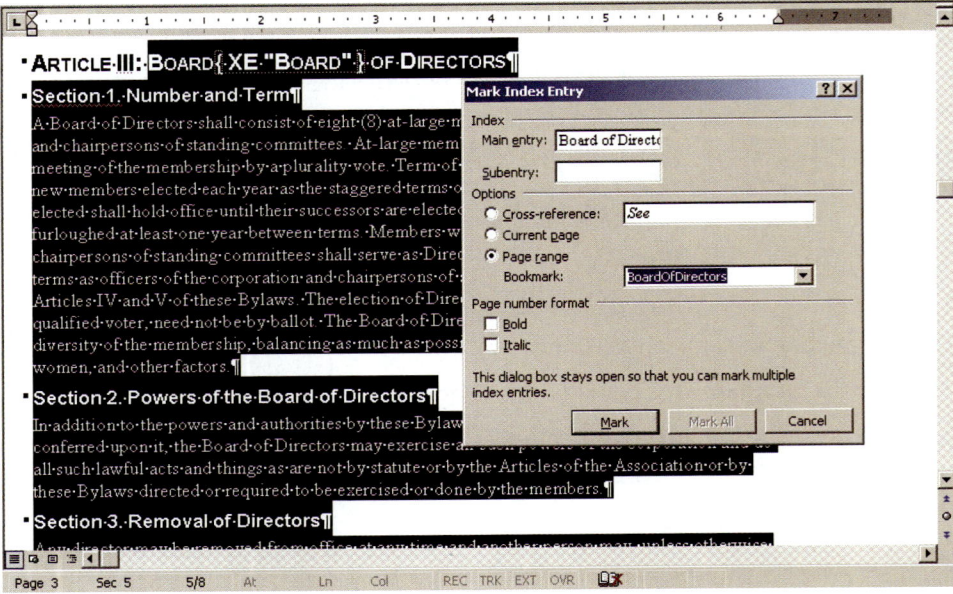

---

task reference   **Deleting an Index Entry**

- Display a document in Normal view, and click the **Show/Hide** ¶ button on
  the Standard toolbar to reveal the document's hidden codes

- Drag the mouse across the entire index entry field, including the curly
  braces, that you want to delete

- Press the **Delete** key

Deleting an index entry:

1. Scroll the document until you see *Article III: Board of Directors,* switch to
Normal view (if necessary), and press the **Show/Hide** button (if necessary) to reveal the hidden codes

2. Select the entire index entry field between the words *Board* and *of* in the
Article III heading. Be sure to include the curly braces in the selection
(see Figure 8.27)

F I G U R E   8.27

Selecting an index entry
field prior to deleting it

Section Break (Next Page)

ARTICLE·III:·BOARD{·XE·"BOARD"·}·OF·DIRECTORS¶

Section·1.·Number·and·Term¶

selected index entry field, —
including delimiting braces

A·Board·of·Directors·shall·consist·of·eight·(8)·at-large·members,·the·officers·of·the·corporation,·
and·chairpersons·of·standing·committees.·At-large·members·shall·be·elected·at·the·annual·
meeting·of·the·membership·by·a·plurality·vote.·Term·of·service·shall·be·four·(4)·years,·with·two·
new·members·elected·each·year·as·the·staggered·terms·of·board·members·expire.·All·persons·so·
elected·shall·hold·office·until·their·successors·are·elected·and·qualify.·At-large·members·must·be·
furloughed·at·least·one·year·between·terms.·Members·who·are·officers·of·the·corporation·and·
chairpersons·of·standing·committees·shall·serve·as·Directors·for·terms·that·coincide·with·their·

3. Press the **Delete** key. Word removes the index entry field

Formatting Entries

As you create index entries, you can specify formatting for both the characters of the index entry and the page numbers where the entries are located. Formatting index entries as you create them is an attractive alternative to formatting the entries after you generate the index. Just for practice, you will format one of the index entries—the index entry for Officers found in Article IV.

Formatting an index entry as you create it:

1. With the document in Normal view and the hidden codes revealed, double-click the word **Officers** in the heading *Article IV: Officers*

2. Click **Alt+Shift+X** to open the Mark Index Entry dialog box. Notice that *Officers* appears in the Main entry text box

3. If necessary, double-click **Officers** in the Main entry text box to select it

4. Press **Ctrl+B** to apply bold to the index entry, and then click **Ctrl+I** to apply Italic (see Figure 8.28)

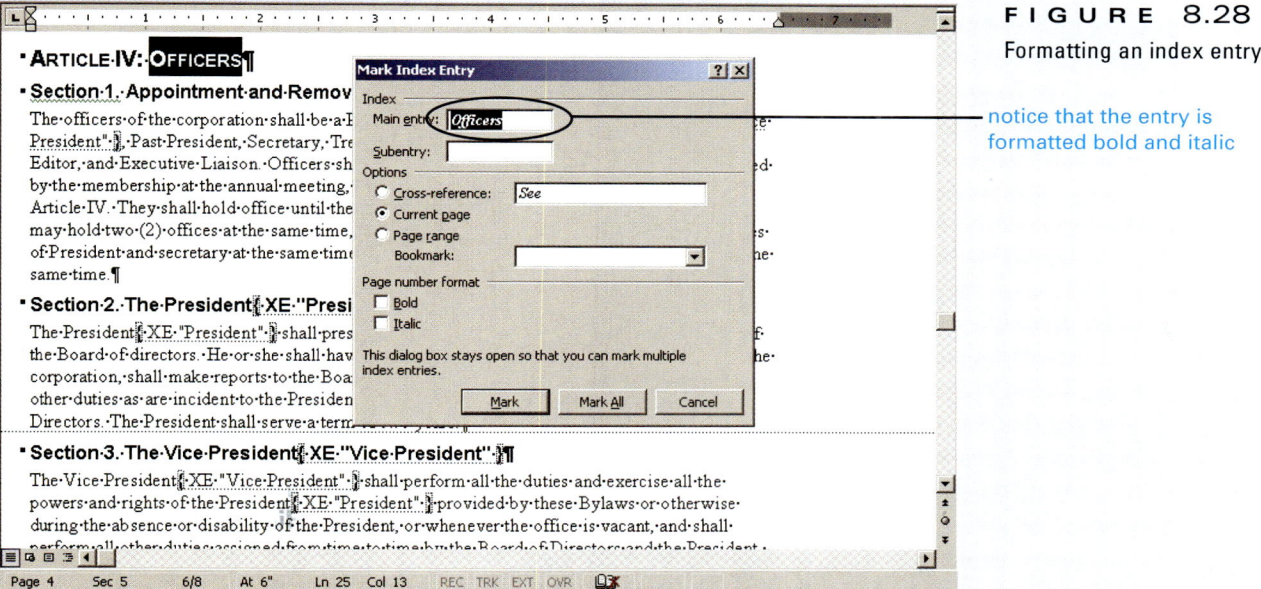

FIGURE 8.28
Formatting an index entry

notice that the entry is formatted bold and italic

tip: *The Bold and Italic check boxes appearing in the* Page number format *panel apply those character formats only to the page number, not to the index entry*

5. Click the **Mark** button and then click the **Close** button to close the dialog box

Of course, the formatting you applied to the index entry will not be evident until you generate an index, which you will do next.

With the small collection of index entries marked, you can execute the final step: generating the index.

More on Generating and Updating an Index

After you have marked the index entries you want to include in your index, you can proceed to generate the index. If you later decide to mark additional index entries, you can refresh your index to include the newly added terms.

Generating an Index

You are ready for Word to compile your list of index terms. When Word assembles the index, it collects all your marked index entries, assigns page numbers according to the pages on which they occur, alphabetizes the entries, and eliminates duplicate entries. Then, Word places the compiled index at the insertion point in your document.

Next, you will have Word compile your small index and place it at the end of your bylaws document, on a new page. However, before you do so, be sure to hide the non-printing characters, including the index codes, to ensure that Word assigns correct page numbers to index entries. Compiling an index with the nonprinting characters visible can cause Word to assign incorrect page numbers because the nonprinting characters can accumulate in a way that affects the location of page breaks.

---

task reference   Generating an Index

- Place the insertion point where you want to create the index
- Click **Insert** on the menu bar, point to **Reference**, and click **Index and Tables**
- Click **OK**

First, you will prepare to create the index by typing a heading, Index, and ensuring it will always print on a new page and stay with the index that follows it.

Entering the heading title "Index" at the end of the document:

1. Click the **Show/Hide** ¶ button on the Standard toolbar so nonprinting characters, including marked index entries, are not visible. Press **Ctrl+End** to move to the end of the document

   tip: If the index entry codes still appear in the text, then click **Tools** on the menu bar, click **Options**, click the **View** tab (if necessary), click the **Hidden text** check box, in the Formatting marks section of the dialog box, to clear the check box. Then click **OK** to close the dialog box

2. Type **Index** and press **Enter** to move to a new line

3. Double-click **Index** to select the entire word, click the **Style** list arrow on the left end of the Formatting toolbar, scroll the Style list to locate the Heading 1 style, and then click **Heading 1**. Word formats Index with the Heading 1 style

4. With *Index* still selected, click **Format** on the menu bar, click **Paragraph**, click the **Line and Page Breaks** tab, click the **Keep with next** check box to place a checkmark in it (if necessary), click the **Page break before** check box to place a checkmark in it (see Figure 8.29), and then click the **OK** button. Word inserts a page break above the *Index* and will keep it attached to the index you are about to generate—no matter how you reorganize the document

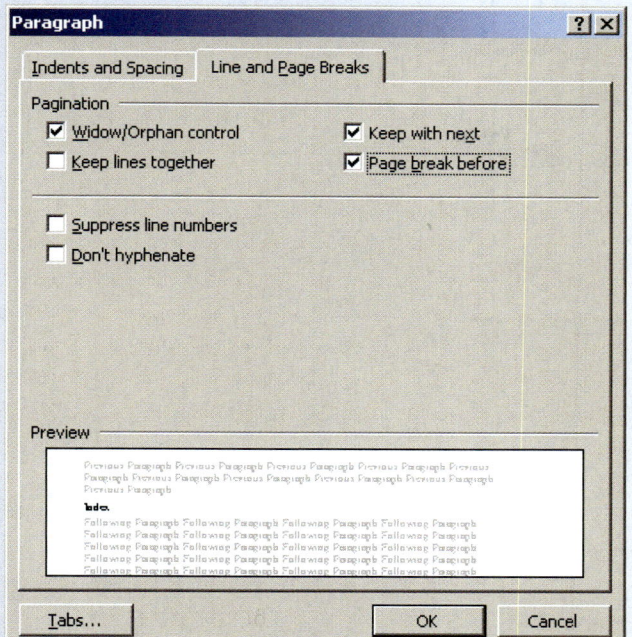

FIGURE 8.29

Forcing a page break
preceding a paragraph

5. Click below the word *Index* to deselect it, and then press the **Enter** key to add an extra blank line below the heading

Now you are ready for Word to build your index at the insertion point—at the end of the document.

Compiling an index:

1. Click **Insert** on the menu bar, point to **Reference**, click **Index and Tables**, and then click the **Index** tab, if necessary. Word opens the Index and Tables dialog box

2. Ensure that the Formats text list box displays *From template* so that the index entries contain formatting styles from your document's styles, not those of another document

3. Click the **Right align page numbers** check box to place a checkmark in it, and set the Columns spin control to **2** (see Figure 8.30) so that Word displays the index in two columns with right-aligned page numbers

4. Click **OK** to create the index. Word assembles and formats the index (see Figure 8.31)

5. Click the **Save** button on the Standard toolbar to save your work

You may wonder why the index appears to not be in two columns, even though you set the Columns control to 2 in step 3 above. The index appears different in Normal view than it does in Print Layout view—the way it appears on output. In Print Layout view, the index appears just as you requested—in two columns with right-aligned page numbers. Figure 8.32 shows the index in Print Layout view.

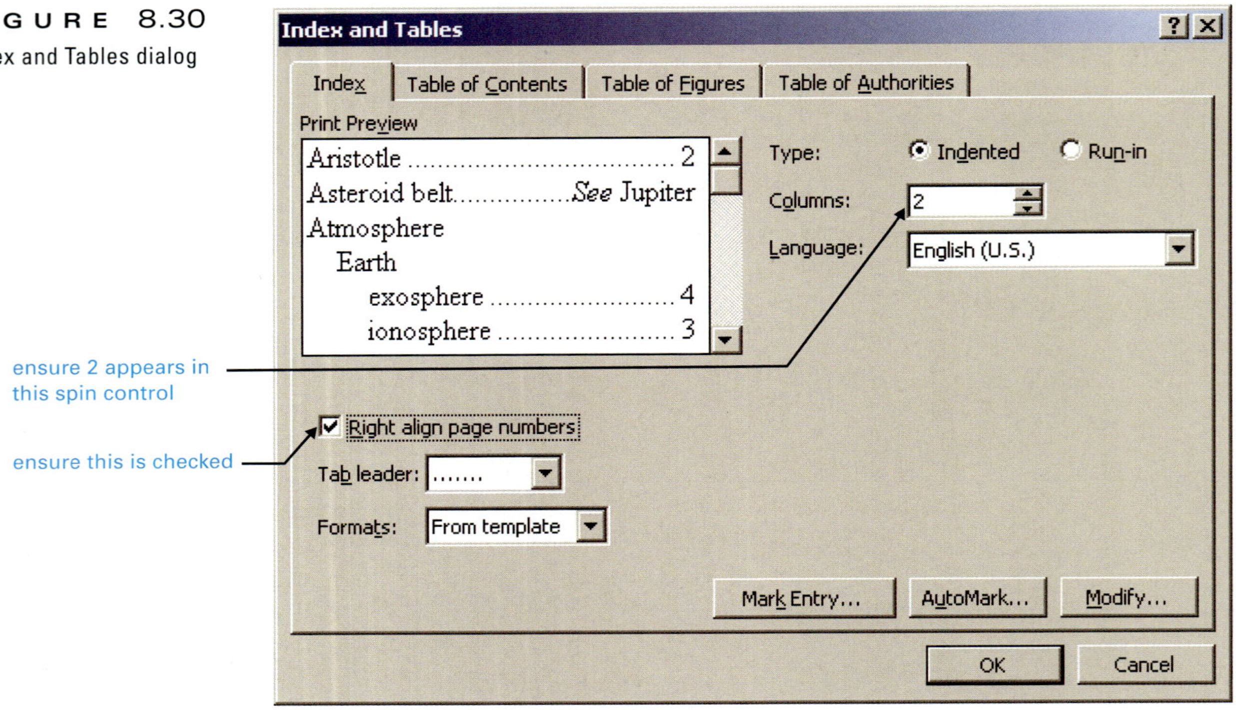

FIGURE 8.30

Index and Tables dialog box

FIGURE 8.31

Completed, short index

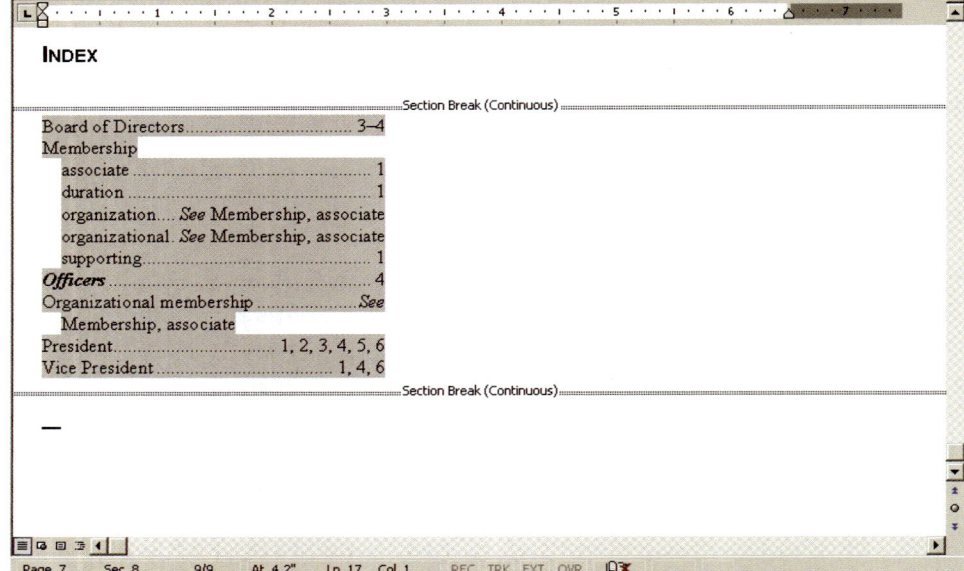

another word   . . . on Choosing the Index Format

Index formats available in the Formats list box of the Index and Tables dialog box include Classic, Fancy, Modern, Bulleted, Formal, and Simple. Each format has a different look, and choosing how you want your index to look is an important consideration. Classic, for example, centers the headings over the index column. Modern italicizes the heading and places a line above it. Experiment with different index formats and choose the one that is best suited for the document in which the index appears

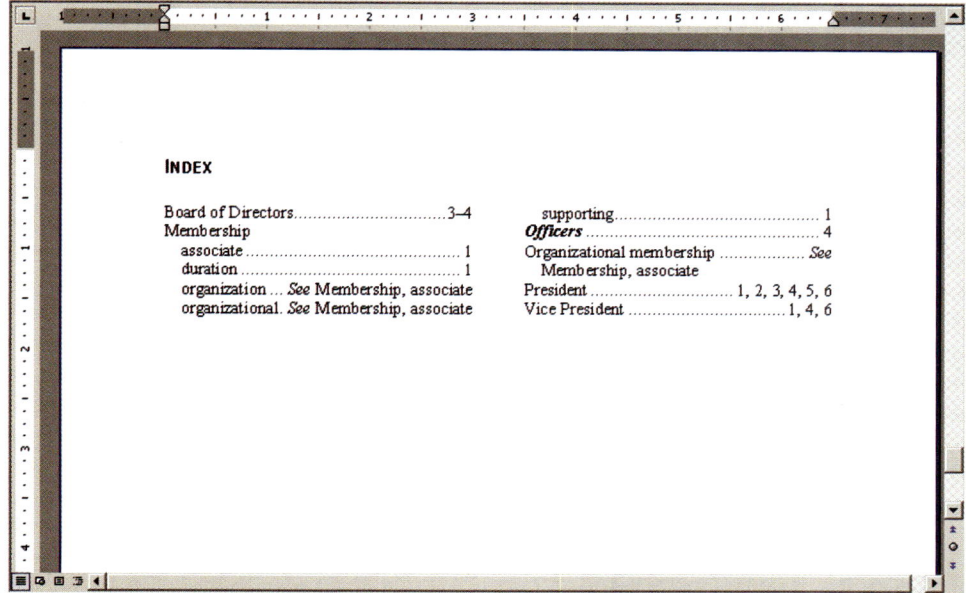

Updating an Index

Robert wants you to add another index term to the index. But you have already generated the index. Won't adding a new term be nearly impossible? You can always add a new index term by marking it in the document and then updating the index. Word places the new index term and its page references into the index in alphabetical order.

---

task reference   **Updating an Index**

- Mark any new index entries you want to add to an index
- Click anywhere within the index, and press **F9**

Robert wants you to add all occurrences of the word *committees* to the index. You begin by opening the Mark Index Entry dialog box and marking all occurrences of *committees* in the text. Then, you update the index.

Updating an index:

1. Double-click the word **committees** found in the first sentence of Section 1 under Article III: Board of Directors

2. Press **Alt+Shift+X** to open the Mark Index Entry dialog box, and then click the **Mark All** button

3. Click the **Close** button to close the Mark Index Entry dialog box

4. Press **Ctrl+End** to move to the bottom of the document below the index, and then click anywhere within the index entries to select the entire index

5. Ensure that the Show/Hide button is not pressed in and that the non-printing characters are not visible

WORD

6. Press the **F9** key to update the index. Word updates the index by adding *committees* to it

7. Click the **Save** button on the Standard toolbar to save your altered document

The final change you need to make to the Krannert Bylaws document is to add a table of contents. Adding a table of contents is very easy, and Robert is anxious to see the finished document with the table of contents and the index included.

help yourself *Click the **Ask a Question** combo box, type **table of contents**, click on **see more**, and press **Enter**. Click any of the hyperlinks to display additional information on creating, troubleshooting, and maintaining a table of contents. **Close** button when you are finished*

More on Creating an Effective Table of Contents

Just as an index helps a reader find important words or phrases in a long document, a *table of contents* lists the important headings that appear in your document and the pages on which they appear. Providing a good table of contents allows readers to find topics of interest to them and move quickly to the pages discussing those topics. Word makes the process of creating a table of contents (TOC) easy if you remember to follow a few simple suggestions.

One key to creating a helpful table of contents is careful use of Word's heading styles. A second key is to create understandable, clear headings that are unambiguous and helpful to your readers. If you format your important headings using Word's built-in Heading styles such as Heading 1, Heading 2, through Heading 9, you have done a major part of the work required to create a table of contents. Good headings are concise—from four to nine words usually—and they communicate the topic clearly. Avoid using cute or humorous headings, which frequently do not clearly impart the true topic of the section or paragraph to which they refer.

Robert wants you to finish up this first revision of the Krannert Society Bylaws by adding a table of contents that lists the major sections of the document. Because the Articles and Sections are already formatted with the styles Heading 1 and Heading 2, respectively, generating a table of contents is uncomplicated.

---

task reference   Creating a Table of Contents

- Place the insertion point where you want to add the table of contents

- Click **Insert** on the menu bar, point to **Reference**, and click **Index and Tables**

- Click the **Table of Contents** tab, select any options, and click **OK**

Creating a table of contents:

1. Scroll to the bottom of the first page of the document, and click on the blank line below the three-line copyright statement, which is just above the section break preceding the Introduction

2. Press **Enter** to create a new blank line, and then press the **Up Arrow** key to move up one line

3. Type **Contents**, double-click **Contents** to select it, click the **Font** list arrow on the Formatting toolbar, select **Times New Roman** (if necessary), click the **Font Size** list arrow, and click **14**

4. With *Contents* still selected, click **Format** on the menu bar, click **Paragraph**, click the **Line and Page Breaks** tab, click the **Keep with next** check box to place a checkmark in it (if necessary), click the **Page break before** check box to place a checkmark in it, and then click the **OK** button

5. Click the **Show/Hide** button, if necessary, to ensure that nonprinting characters are not visible in your document

6. Click the blank line below this new heading, click **Insert** on the menu bar, point to **Reference**, click **Index and Tables**, and then click the **Table of Contents** tab

7. Accept all the table of contents default values displayed on the Index and Tables dialog box, and then click the **OK** button. Word generates the table of contents (see Figure 8.33)

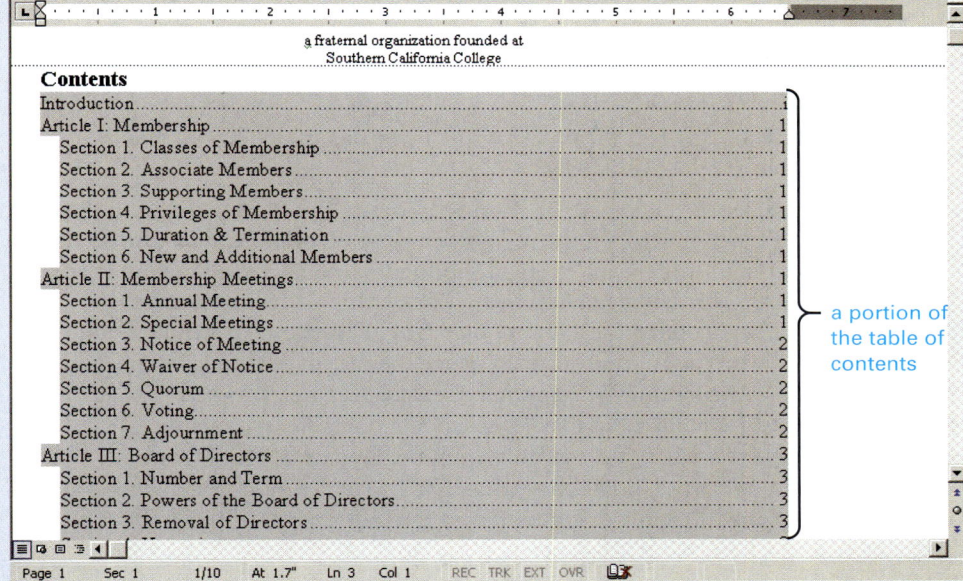

FIGURE 8.33

Table of contents

You have completed your work on the long document, Krannert Society Bylaws. Two tasks remain: save your document, and print it.

Saving and printing the entire document:

1. Place your name in the document header

2. Click **File** on the menu bar and then click **Save** to save your completed document

3. To ensure the latest values for the table of contents and index fields appear in their respective places, click **Tools** on the menu bar, click **Options**, click the **Print** tab, ensure that the **Update fields** check box is checked so that all fields are updated prior to printing them. Click the **OK** button to close the dialog box

4. Click **File**, click **Print**, and click **OK**. When Word prompts you to update your table of contents, be sure that the **Update page numbers only** option button is selected, and then click **OK**

5. Close the document and exit Word

Robert is pleased with the Krannert Society Bylaws document. Later, he will add more index terms and may expand the table of contents. For now, you can sit back and relax, because you have finished producing a long document complete with a table of contents and an index.

S E S S I O N   8 . 3

making *the grade*

1. Longer documents typically contain front matter, main matter, and _____ _____ .

2. Before you can create an index, you must select index terms. You locate a candidate index term and then _____ it, which is the formal term for placing an index entry code next to the word.

3. A _____ is a secondary topic used to narrow the search for a main topic or index entry.

4. Word includes any text formatted with any of the _____ styles to create table of contents entries.

5. Modify the latest version of the Krannert Society Bylaws document in the following ways. First, open the main document, **KranMain.doc**, display the document in Outline view, open all subdocuments, and display the entire document in Normal view. Add as an index entry all occurrences of the word *Secretary* (uppercase). Locate *Quorum* in Section 5 of Article II and mark that word as an index term. Change the title of Article I: Membership to *Article I: Membership Information*. Change the title of Section 4 of Article I to *Section 4. Membership Privileges*. Update the table of contents. Click the **Update entire table** option button when the Update Table of Contents dialog box appears. Update the index. Then, save the modified document and print only the table of contents and the index pages of the document.

SESSION 8.4 SUMMARY

Sometimes it is easier to manage long documents by creating one or more subdocuments that are linked to a master document. One or more people can work independently on subdocuments and the main document. The Outlining toolbar contains the tools to display a master document, expand subdocuments, split a subdocument into two subdocuments, merge a subdocument into a master document, and remove a subdocument. You can create a subdocument from part of an existing document, or you can insert a file as a subdocument of a containing, or master, document. If a subdocument becomes too large or cumbersome, splitting it into two subdocuments will reduce the size of the original subdocument. You can view the master document with subdocuments represented as hyperlinks, or you can expand the subdocuments within the master document so you can review the entire long document.

Page numbers for a document's front matter—the title page, preface, and table of contents, for example—are different from the page numbers displayed for the main matter and the document's back matter. You create and maintain distinct page numbering schemes by breaking a document into sections and applying different number types (Arabic or Roman) and starting values (1, ii, etc.) for each section.

Indexes help readers find key words and phrases in your document. Create an index by first marking index entries in the text or typing synonyms and marking their location in the text. Then, create an index at the insertion point's location point—usually the end of the document.

A table of contents provides topic names and corresponding page numbers to key areas of your long document. Because a table of contents uses Heading styles to select the topics it contains, plan ahead and format key headings in your document with the Heading 1, Heading 2, through Heading 9 styles. Generate a table of contents at the insertion point using the Insert, Reference, Index, and Tables command. When you print a document containing a table of contents, Word will ask you if you want to update the table of contents. Because the table of contents contains updatable fields whose values change as you modify a document, always indicate that Word is to update the page number values or the entire table of contents.

MICROSOFT OFFICE SPECIALIST OBJECTIVES SUMMARY

- Create and modify document indexes and tables—MOS WW03E-3-3
- Insert and modify endnotes, footnotes, captions, and cross-references—MOS WW03E-3-4
- Create and manage master documents and subdocuments—MOS WW03E-3-5

making the grade *answers*

SESSION 8.1

1. A master document allows you to do all of the following:
   - Work with a long document or work with individual subdocuments independently
   - Display and collapse subdocuments to switch between details and overview of a document easily and quickly
   - Review and reorganize complete sections of a long document by moving subdocuments as a unit
   - Organize and manage disparate document sections
   - Coordinate editing distinct parts of a longer document and distribute individual subdocuments to different teams of people

2. Create a master document by:
   - Subdividing an existing document into a master document
   - Creating a master document from scratch

3. Create a subdocument by:
   - Subdividing an existing document into one or more subdocuments
   - Creating subdocuments of the master document as needed

4. Master

5. Subdocument

SESSION 8.2

1. Promote

2. Split

3. Expand Subdocuments

4. When you want to subdivide a subdocument into two smaller subdocuments.

5. Solution file is **wd08KranMTG82.zip** (a zipped file containing three documents)

SESSION 8.3

1. back matter

2. mark

3. subentry

4. heading

5. Solution file is **wd08KranMTG83.zip** (a zipped file containing three documents)

task reference *summary*

Task	Page #	Preferred Method
Creating a master document	WD 8.6	• Open in the usual way the document that is to be the master document. Display nonprinting characters by clicking the **Show/Hide** button on the Standard toolbar, click **View** on the menu bar, and then click **Outline**. If necessary, click the **Master Document View** button on the Outlining toolbar to display the Outlining toolbar
Moving to a subdocument from a master document	WD 8.11	• Press and hold the **Ctrl** key, click the subdocument hyperlink in the master document
Expanding a subdocument within a master document	WD 8.12	• Ensure that the master document is open in Master Document View, change to Outline view by clicking **View** and then clicking **Outline**, if necessary. Place the insertion point at the beginning of the document. Click the **Expand Subdocuments** button on the Outlining toolbar
Splitting a subdocument into two subdocuments	WD 8.15	• Ensure that the document you are about to split is in Master Document View, click **View** on the menu bar and then click **Outline** to display the subdocument in Outline view • Click the **Show Level** list box arrow and click **Show All Levels** in the list to ensure that all headings and subheadings appear, create a new Heading 1 heading at the point where you want to make the split or raise an existing heading to a Heading 1 level, click the outline marker of the Heading 1 where you want to split the subdocument, and click the **Split Subdocument** button on the Outlining toolbar
Merging subdocuments	WD 8.17	• Ensure that the document you are about to split is in Master Document View, click **Expand Subdocuments** button on the Outlining toolbar, ensure the subdocuments you want to merge are adjacent to one another, click the **Subdocument icon** of the first subdocument, press and hold down the **Shift** key, click the **Subdocument icon** of the second subdocument, and release the **Shift** key, and click the **Merge Subdocument** button on the Outlining toolbar
Removing a subdocument	WD 8.20	• Ensure that the subdocument you are about to remove is expanded in the master document, click the subdocument's Subdocument icon to select the subdocument, click the Remove Subdocument button on the Outlining toolbar, and then click anywhere in the master document text to deselect the highlighted text section
Renaming a subdocument	WD 8.21	• Ensure that the master document is open in Master Document View, collapse all subdocuments by clicking the **Collapse Subdocuments** button on the Outlining toolbar, press and hold the **Ctrl** key, click the subdocument link for the document you want to rename, and release the **Ctrl** key. When the subdocument opens in its own window, click **File** on the menu bar, click **Save As**, type the new subdocument name in the File name text box, and click the **Save** button. Click **File** and then click **Close** to close the subdocument
Printing a master document	WD 8.22	• Open the master document. If necessary, expand the subdocuments by clicking the **Expand Subdocuments** button, click **View** on the menu bar and then click **Print Layout**, click **File** on the menu bar, click **Print**, and click **OK**
Marking index entries and subentries	WD 8.28	• Select the word or phrase you want to mark as an index entry, or place the insertion point where you want to add a new word or phrase, not found in the text, as an index entry, click **Insert**, on the menu bar, point to **Reference**, click **Index and Tables**, click the **Index** tab, and then click the **Mark Entry** button. Ensure the Current page option, in the Options panel, is selected. If needed, type an index word or phrase in the Main entry text box, and then type an optional word or phrase in the Subentry text box, click the **Mark** button to mark the single occurrence or click the **Mark All** button to mark every occurrence of the selected word or phrase in the document. Click the **Close** button to close the dialog box

task reference *summary*

Task	Page #	Preferred Method
Marking a cross-reference index entry	WD 8.31	• Type the text for the index entry, or position the insertion point in the document, press **Alt+Shift+X** to display the Mark Index Entry dialog box, type the Main entry text. Optionally, type a subentry index term in the Subentry text box, click the **Cross-reference** option, type the cross-reference entry you want to refer readers to following the word *See* in the cross-reference text box, and then click the **Mark** button
Marking a page range index entry	WD 8.33	• Select a range of pages, several paragraphs, a section, or a chapter, for example. Click **Insert** on the menu bar, click **Bookmark**, type the Bookmark name, and then click the **Add** button, press **Alt+Shift+X** to open the Mark Index Entry dialog box, if necessary, click the **Page range** option button, click the Bookmark list arrow, and click the Bookmark name you created above. Click the **Mark** button
Deleting an index entry	WD 8.34	• Display a document in Normal view, and click the **Show/Hide** button on the Standard toolbar to reveal the document's hidden codes, drag the mouse across the entire index entry field, including the curly braces, that you want to delete, press the **Delete** key
Generating an index	WD 8.36	• Place the insertion point where you want to create the index, click **Insert** on the menu bar, point to **Reference**, and click **Index and Tables**, and click **OK**
Updating an index	WD 8.39	• Mark any new index entries you want to add to an index, click anywhere within the index, and press **F9**
Creating a table of contents	WD 8.40	• Place the insertion point where you want to add the table of contents, click **Insert** on the menu bar, point to **Reference**, and click **Index and Tables**, click the **Table of Contents** tab, select any options, and click **OK**

TRUE/FALSE

1. Back matter is the last several pages containing a title page, table of contents, preface, acknowledgments, and so on.

2. Front matter typically contains appendices and an index.

3. A subdocument is a file that is part of the master document.

4. A subentry is a secondary topic you use to narrow the search of a specific topic.

5. A table of contents is a field that is formatted with a style and that is inserted in the document where a special style reference field code appears.

FILL-IN

1. A _____ document is a file containing links to individual files that make up a larger document.

2. Files that are part of a main document and appear as hyperlinks in it are called _____.

3. You can apply different page numbering schemes to each _____ of a Word document.

4. An _____ lists the words and phrases that occur in a document along with the page numbers on which they appear.

5. _____ matter is the first several pages containing a title page, table of contents, preface, acknowledgments, and so on.

MULTIPLE CHOICE

1. Which of the following is a file containing links to individual files that make up a larger document?
   a. Back matter
   b. Front matter
   c. Master document
   d. Subdocuments

2. Which of the following typically contains appendices and an index?
   a. Back matter
   b. Front matter
   c. Master document
   d. Subdocuments

3. Which of the following is the first several pages containing a title page, table of contents, preface, and acknowledgments?
   a. Back matter
   b. Front matter
   c. Master document
   d. Subdocuments

4. Which of the following is a secondary topic you use to narrow the search of a specific topic?
   a. Subentry
   b. Front matter
   c. Master document
   d. None of the above

5. What divides a subdocument into two subdocuments?
   a. Back matter
   b. Front matter
   c. Split
   d. Merge

REVIEW QUESTIONS

1. Which Word toolbar contains buttons such as Collapse Subdocuments and Remove Subdocument?

2. Before you can create an index, you must first do what?

3. Word creates a table of contents by including text formatted with what?

4. Explain one advantage of using a master document and subdocuments instead of using a single long document.

5. Suppose your master document displays subdocuments as hyperlinks. How do you display a subdocument without expanding it within a master document?

6. What is the shortcut for opening the Mark Index Entry dialog box?

CREATE THE QUESTION

For each of the following answers, create an appropriate, short question.

ANSWER	QUESTION
1. The general name for a document containing sub-documents.	_____
2. You can create this type of document by inserting a file into this main document.	_____
3. The action that occurs to combine into one document two adjacent subdocuments.	_____
4. A term for a field that is formatted with a style and that is inserted in the document where a special field code appears.	_____
5. Select the word or phrase and then press **Alt+Shift+X**	_____
6. This displays major topics in your document and the pages on which they occur.	_____

FACT OR FICTION

1. A style reference is a field (named StyleRef) that is formatted with a style and inserted in the document where a special style reference field code appears.

2. You might create a subdocument to pull together the individual chapters of a book-length manuscript, allowing different authors to create or edit an individual chapter of the book.

3. One of the advantages of using a master document and subdocument approach includes organizing and managing distinct document sections and opening and printing individual files when needed.

4. There are two ways to create a master document and subdocuments. First, you can start with an existing document and convert it into a master document by dividing it into subdocuments. Second, you can create a master document from scratch and insert the headings and subheadings during the process and turn existing documents into subdocuments of the master document.

5. Whenever a subdocument becomes too long or otherwise difficult to handle, you can always subdivide it into two or more subdocuments. When you save a newly split document, Word saves the subdocument using the newly created subdocument's third Heading 3 style as the header.

practice

1. Cranford College Excel Study Guide

Professor Nesbitt teaches an introduction to information systems class and is preparing a short document entitled Building Worksheets with Excel. He wants to hand out a brief introduction to Excel to his four information systems classes. To help him write the document, he has asked three groups of two students each to help him. The student groups have been given a brief outline of their individual topics, and the students have completed about one-half of the work. Each of the three groups has worked independently, and they have saved their work in three files. Professor Nesbitt wants to merge together the three documents into one master document, number the pages, create a table of contents, and print the document. Each group has used the same styles to format headings and paragraphs, so Professor Nesbitt anticipates using the Heading styles to create the table of contents. Help Professor Nesbitt create a master document and two subdocuments, number the pages, print the entire document, and save the resulting master/subdocument structure. You will begin by opening and saving the documents under new names to preserve the originals. One of the three document files will be the master document.

1. Launch Word, open **wd08Worksheet1.doc**, and save it as **NesbittMaster.doc**. Leave **NesbittMaster.doc** open

2. Open **wd08Worksheet2.doc**, save it as **NesbittPart2.doc**, and close NesbittPart2.doc; open **wd08Worksheet3.doc**, save it as **NesbittPart3.doc**, and close **NesbittPart3.doc**. Only NesbittMaster.doc is open

3. Press **Ctrl+End** to go to the bottom of the document, press **Enter** to add a blank line, click **View**, click **Outline**, click the **Insert Subdocument** button on the Outlining toolbar, click **NesbittPart2.doc** in Insert Subdocument list, and click **Open**

4. Click the **Insert Subdocument** button on the Outlining toolbar, click **NesbittPart3.doc** in Insert Subdocument list, and click **Open**

5. Click the **Save** button on the Standard toolbar to save the master document and subdocument structure

6. Click **View** on the menu bar, click **Normal**, and then click **Ctrl+Home** to position the insertion point at the top of the document

7. Press **Enter** and then press **Ctrl+Enter** to open a blank line on a new page at the top of the document. Move the insertion point to the first line above the page break, click the **Style** list box arrow on the left end of the Formatting toolbar, and click the **Normal** style

8. Click **Insert** on the menu bar, click **Page Numbers**, click the **Show number on first page** check box to clear it, click the **Format** button, click the **Start at** option button, and type **0** (zero) in the Start at text box

9. Click **OK** to close the Page Number Format text box, and click **OK** to close the Page Numbers text box

10. Switch back to Normal view, click the **Show/Hide ¶** button to turn it off (if necessary), click **Insert**, point to **Reference**, click **Index and Tables**, click the **Table of Contents** tab, and then click **OK**

11. Add your first and last names to the page header (for the TOC page), print the entire document (click **OK** when the Update Table of Contents dialog box appears), and save the document

2. Developing an Index for a Software Product Guide

You have written a short guide to using a valuable Internet tool called listproc (short for list processor), a generic term for a mailing list maintenance program. The mailing list program, which forwards any e-mail it receives to all members on the list, is sometimes difficult to understand and use. The paper is complete except it has no index. You will create an index of a few terms and then print the last page of the paper and the index.

1. Open the file **wd08Listproc.doc** and immediately save it as Listproc2.doc

2. Scroll to the heading COMMANDS, formatted with a Heading 1 style, and double-click the word HELP, found in the line below COMMANDS, press **Alt+Shift+X**, and click the Mark All button

3. Double-click the word **SET**, found a few lines below HELP on page 1, and then click the **Mark All** button

tip: *The Mark All button is dim when you double-click a word. However, you can click the Mark or Mark All buttons because the dialog box becomes active and the button clicks in one quick action*

4. Repeat step 3 with the word SUBSCRIBE, which is located a few lines below SET on page 2

5. Repeat step 3 with the word UNSUBSCRIBE, which is located two lines below SUBSCRIBE on page 2

6. Repeat step 3 with the word SIGNOFF, which is located below UNSUBSCRIBE on page 2

7. Click to the left of the word SIGNOFF to establish a new insertion point, click the Main entry text box, type **Quit**, click the Cross-reference option button, type **Signoff** in the Cross-reference text box, click the **Mark** button, and click the **Close** button on the Mark Index Entry dialog box to close it

8. Press **Ctrl+End** to move the insertion point to the last line in the document—below the word *Index*. Click the **Show/Hide** button to turn if off if necessary

9. Click **Insert** on the menu bar, point to Reference, click **Index and Tables**, click the Index tab (if necessary), and click **OK**

10. Type your **first and last names** in the header

11. Print the last page and the index page and compare it to Figure 8.34

FIGURE 8.34

Index page

<student name in header>

Index

help, 1, 4	signoff, 2
Quit. *See* Signoff	subscribe, 1
set, 1	unsubscribe, 2

challenge!

1. Creating a Master Document and Subdocuments for a Dissertation on Pakistan

As a professor at Southern University, you are advising Leonard Knolls, a political science Ph.D. candidate, on his dissertation about the political history of Bangladesh. Leonard has asked you to format the document according to the standards of the university. He has sent the document to you via e-mail, but owing to its large size, the document is divided among three files: **wd08Pakistan1.doc**, **wd08Pakistan2.doc**, and **wd08Pakistan3.doc**. Using wd08Pakistan1.doc as the master document, include wd02Pakistan2 and wd03Pakistan3 as subdocuments in their respective positions. Place your name in the document's header. Print the document and then save it. Compare your work to Figures 8.35 and 8.36.

FIGURE 8.35
Pakistan master document

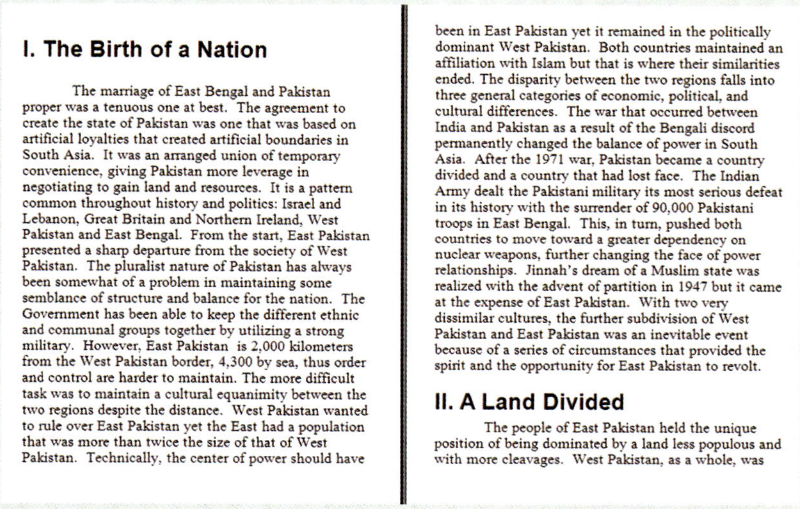

I. The Birth of a Nation

The marriage of East Bengal and Pakistan proper was a tenuous one at best. The agreement to create the state of Pakistan was one that was based on artificial loyalties that created artificial boundaries in South Asia. It was an arranged union of temporary convenience, giving Pakistan more leverage in negotiating to gain land and resources. It is a pattern common throughout history and politics: Israel and Lebanon, Great Britain and Northern Ireland, West Pakistan and East Bengal. From the start, East Pakistan presented a sharp departure from the society of West Pakistan. The pluralist nature of Pakistan has always been somewhat of a problem in maintaining some semblance of structure and balance for the nation. The Government has been able to keep the different ethnic and communal groups together by utilizing a strong military. However, East Pakistan is 2,000 kilometers from the West Pakistan border, 4,300 by sea, thus order and control are harder to maintain. The more difficult task was to maintain a cultural equanimity between the two regions despite the distance. West Pakistan wanted to rule over East Pakistan yet the East had a population that was more than twice the size of that of West Pakistan. Technically, the center of power should have been in East Pakistan yet it remained in the politically dominant West Pakistan. Both countries maintained an affiliation with Islam but that is where their similarities ended. The disparity between the two regions falls into three general categories of economic, political, and cultural differences. The war that occurred between India and Pakistan as a result of the Bengali discord permanently changed the balance of power in South Asia. After the 1971 war, Pakistan became a country divided and a country that had lost face. The Indian Army dealt the Pakistani military its most serious defeat in its history with the surrender of 90,000 Pakistani troops in East Bengal. This, in turn, pushed both countries to move toward a greater dependency on nuclear weapons, further changing the face of power relationships. Jinnah's dream of a Muslim state was realized with the advent of partition in 1947 but it came at the expense of East Pakistan. With two very dissimilar cultures, the further subdivision of West Pakistan and East Pakistan was an inevitable event because of a series of circumstances that provided the spirit and the opportunity for East Pakistan to revolt.

II. A Land Divided

The people of East Pakistan held the unique position of being dominated by a land less populous and with more cleavages. West Pakistan, as a whole, was

FIGURE 8.36
Pakistan subdocument

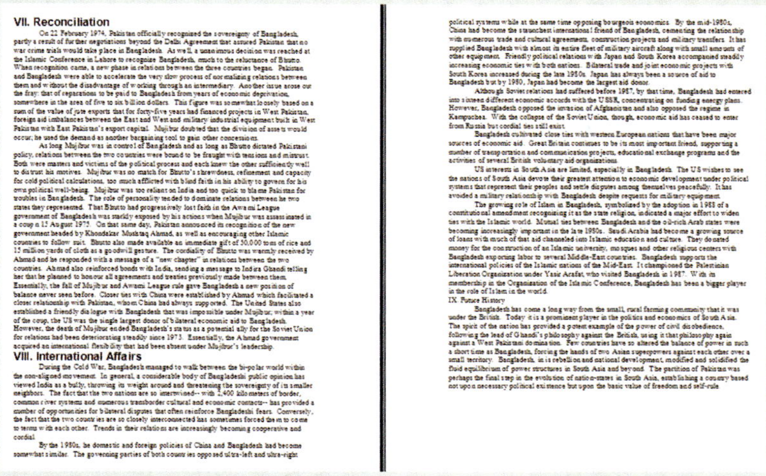

VII. Reconciliation

On 22 February 1974, Pakistan officially recognized the sovereignty of Bangladesh, partly a result of further negotiations beyond the Delhi Agreement that assured Pakistan that no war crime trials would take place in Bangladesh. As well, a unanimous decision was reached at the Islamic Conference in Lahore to recognize Bangladesh, much to the reluctance of Bhutto. When recognition came, a new phase in relations between the three countries began. Pakistan and Bangladesh were able to accelerate the very slow process of normalizing relations between them and without the disadvantage of working through an intermediary. Another issue arose out the fray: that of reparations to be paid to Bangladesh from years of economic deprivation, somewhere in the area of five to six billion dollars. This figure was somewhat loosely based on a sum of the value of jute exports that for forty-five years had financed projects in West Pakistan, foreign aid imbalances between the East and West and military industrial equipment built in West Pakistan with East Pakistan's export capital. Mujibur doubted that the division of assets would occur; he used the demand as another bargaining tool to gain other concessions.

As long Mujibur was in control of Bangladesh and as long as Bhutto dictated Pakistani policy, relations between the two countries were bound to be fraught with tensions and mistrust. Both were masters and victims of the political process and each knew the other sufficiently well to distrust his motives. Mujibur was no match for Bhutto's shrewdness, refinement and capacity for cold political calculations, too much afflicted with blind faith in his ability to govern for his own political well-being. Mujibur was too reliant on India and too quick to blame Pakistan for troubles in Bangladesh. The role of personality tended to dominate relations between he two states they represented. That Bhutto had progressively lost faith in the Awami League government of Bangladesh was starkly exposed by his actions when Mujibur was assassinated in a coup n 15 August 1975. On that same day, Pakistan announced its recognition of the new government headed by Khondakar Mushtaq Ahmad, as well as encouraging other Islamic countries to follow suit. Bhutto also made available an immediate gift of 50,000 tons of rice and 15 million yards of cloth as a goodwill gesture. The cordiality of Bhutto was warmly received by Ahmad and he responded with a message of a "new chapter" in relations between the two countries. Ahmad also reinforced bonds with India, sending a message to Indira Ghandi telling her that he planned to honour all agreements and treaties previously made between them. Essentially, the fall of Mujibur and Awami League rule gave Bangladesh a new position of balance never seen before. Closer ties with China were established by Ahmad which facilitated a closer relationship with Pakistan, whom China had always supported. The United States also established a friendly dialogue with Bangladesh that was impossible under Mujibur; within a year of the coup, the US was the single largest donor of bilateral economic aid to Bangladesh. However, the death of Mujibur ended Bangladesh's status as a potential ally for the Soviet Union for relations had been deteriorating steadily since 1973. Essentially, the Ahmad government acquired an international flexibility that had been absent under Mujibur's leadership.

VIII. International Affairs

During the Cold War, Bangladesh managed to walk between the bi-polar world within the non-aligned movement. In general, a considerable body of Bangladeshi public opinion has viewed India as a bully, throwing its weight around and threatening the sovereignty of its smaller neighbors. The fact that the two nations are so intertwined-- with 2,400 kilometers of border, common river systems and numerous transborder cultural and economic contacts-- has provided a number of opportunities for bilateral disputes that often reinforce Bangladeshi fears. Conversely, the fact that the two countries are so closely interconnected has sometimes forced them to come to terms with each other. Trends in their relations are increasingly becoming cooperative and cordial.

By the 1980s, he domestic and foreign policies of China and Bangladesh had become somewhat similar. The governing parties of both countries opposed ultra-left and ultra-right political systems while at the same time opposing bourgeois economics. By the mid-1980s, China had become the staunchest international friend of Bangladesh, cementing the relationship with numerous trade and cultural agreements, construction projects and military transfers. It has supplied Bangladesh with almost its entire fleet of military aircraft along with small amounts of other equipment. Friendly political relations with Japan and South Korea accompanied steadily increasing economic ties with both nations. Bilateral trade and joint economic projects with South Korea increased during the late 1980s. Japan has always been a source of aid to Bangladesh but by 1980, Japan had become the largest aid donor.

Although Soviet relations had suffered before 1987, by that time, Bangladesh had entered into sixteen different economic accords with the USSR, concentrating on funding energy plans. However, Bangladesh opposed the invasion of Afghanistan and also opposed the regime in Kampuchea. With the collapse of the Soviet Union, though, economic aid has ceased to enter from Russia but cordial ties still exist.

Bangladesh cultivated close ties with western European nations that have been major sources of economic aid. Great Britain continues to be its most important friend, supporting a number of transportation and communication projects, educational exchange programs and the activities of several British voluntary aid organizations.

US interests in South Asia are limited, especially in Bangladesh. The US wishes to see the nations of South Asia devote their greatest attention to economic development under political systems that represent their peoples and settle disputes among themselves peacefully. It has avoided a military relationship with Bangladesh despite requests for military equipment.

The growing role of Islam in Bangladesh, symbolized by the adoption in 1988 of a constitutional amendment recognizing it as the state religion, indicated a major effort to widen ties with the Islamic world. Mutual ties between Bangladesh and the oil-rich Arab states were becoming increasingly important in the late 1980s. Saudi Arabia had become a growing source of loans with much of that aid channeled into Islamic education and culture. They donated money for the construction of an Islamic university, mosques and other religious centers with Bangladesh exporting labor to several Middle-East countries. Bangladesh supports the international policies of the Islamic nations of the Mid-East. It championed the Palestinian Liberation Organization under Yasir Arafat, who visited Bangladesh in 1987. With its membership in the Organization of the Islamic Conference, Bangladesh has been a bigger player in the role of Islam in the world.

IX. Future History

Bangladesh has come a long way from the small, rural farming community that it was under the British. Today it is a prominent player in the politics and economics of South Asia. The spirit of the nation has provided a potent example of the power of civil disobedience, following the lead of Ghandi's philosophy against the British, using it that philosophy again against a West Pakistani domination. Few countries have so altered the balance of power in such a short time as Bangladesh, forcing the hands of two Asian superpowers against each other over a small territory. Bangladesh, in is rebellion and national development, modified and solidified the fluid equilibrium of power structures in South Asia and beyond. The partition of Pakistan was perhaps the final step in the evolution of nation-states in South Asia, establishing a country based not upon necessary political existence but upon the basic value of freedom and self-rule.

2. Scholarship Search

As an undergraduate majoring in finance at Filmore University, you are nearing graduation after four tumultuous, but enjoyable, years. In fact, you love the school so much that you decide to apply to Filmore Law School. While visiting the Graduate Admissions Office, you are advised to refer to their Web page for a document that provides information on scholarships that can fund your law school tuition. Unfortunately, in the chaos of a technical update, you discover to your dismay that the Web site has fractured the scholarship document into three separate documents:

wd08ScholarshipFunding.doc, wd08ScholarshipList.doc, and wd08ScholarshipErrata.doc. After you retrieve the documents, use wd08ScholarshipFunding.doc as your master document and attach wd08ScholarshipList.doc and wd08ScholarshipErrata.doc as subdocuments in that order. Include your name in the header, save the document as Scholarship2.doc, and print your expanded document. Compare your work to Figures 8.37 and 8.38.

FIGURE 8.37

Scholarship master document

I. Alternative Funding Sources

Scholarships and grants are considered the most preferable form of assistance in that they are "free" money to the student, with no expectation of repayment. Scholarships and grants are available from a variety of local, regional and national sources. Many private scholarships are promoted through law school financial aid offices. The organizations offering the educational scholarships send information and application material to these offices to announce to students. These are some examples of scholarships about which the Filmore Law School Financial Aid office has received information and maintains binders of information for students to apply:

FIGURE 8.38

Scholarship subdocument

II. Scholarships

- *The Food and Drug Law Institute:* awards H. Thomas Austern Writing Awards and Vincent A. Kleinfeld Scholarship Award Competition.
- *Black Women Lawyers Association of Los Angeles:* awarded to law students in good academic standing, financial need, and community service.
- *Justice Pauline Davis Hanson Scholarship established by Fresno County Women Lawyers:* to encourage and support outstanding academic achievement and commitment to service by women law students.
- *The Roscoe Pound Foundation; The Roscoe Hogan Environmental Law Essay Contest; Elaine Osborne Jacobson Award:* scholarships for women law students working in health care law.
- *Puerto Rican Legal Defense and Education Fund:* awarded to Latino law students who exhibit academic promise or commitment of service to the Latino community and financial need.
- *The Foundation of the State Bar of California:* awarded to students who have interest in community involvement and/or a commitment to practice public law. In addition, students must have demonstrated financial need and must maintain a GPA of 2.5 or better during their first year of law school.
- *Paralyzed Veterans of America, chartered by the Congress of the United States:* program to foster the study of war veterans.
- *State Bar of California:* labor and employment law section writing competition; worker's compensation writing competition.

e-business

1. Synthesizing a Privacy Statement for Globus Services

Globus Services provides best-of-breed Web hosting services for small- to medium-sized businesses. With over 5,000 clients in the United States and Canada, Globus provides a full gamut of e-commerce services ranging from domain name registration to a complete hosted electronic commerce storefront and support. Globus has recently revised their privacy statement. The privacy statement was developed by three groups. Therefore it is stored in three Word-format files. You are to create a master document from the three files, insert page numbers in the footer, and create a table of contents. Use Figures 8.39 and 8.40 as examples.

Begin by opening **wd08GlobusPartA.doc** as the main document. Then insert as subdocuments, in this order, the files **wd08GlobusPartB.doc** and then **wd08GlobusPartC.doc**. Place your name in the document's header. First, print the document with the two subdocuments collapsed—displaying their hyperlinks. Then, expand the document and print the first two pages. Save the master document as **GlobusMain.doc**.

FIGURE 8.39

GlobusPartA master document

Privacy Policy

Introduction

Globus Services is concerned about the privacy rights of its clients, visitors to its Web sites ("Site"), and the security of their data. Accordingly, we have adopted this Privacy Policy ("Privacy Policy") for this Site to ensure responsible use of the information you share with Globus Services and to make you aware of the terms and conditions of your use of this Site and our services. We may at any time revise this Privacy Policy by updating the Site.

You are bound by any such revisions and should therefore periodically visit this page to review the then current Privacy Policy. This Privacy Policy is incorporated by reference into Globus Services' client agreements. In the event any provisions contained in this Privacy Policy conflict with any terms, conditions, or clauses contained in an agreement between you and Globus Services, the provisions of the agreement shall govern. As used herein, the term "Globus Services" includes any and all divisions, affiliates, and subsidiary companies of Globus Services, if any.

Globus Services Contact Information

Contact us at the following address:
Globus Services, Inc.
P.O. Box 2134
Des Plaines, Il 45443
e-mail: contactus@globus.com

FIGURE 8.40

Globus table of contents

Use of the Site

The Site is owned and operated by Globus Services. No materials found on the Site or any other site owned, operated, or licensed by Globus Services may be copied, reproduced, republished, uploaded, posted, transmitted, or distributed in any way except as expressly provided by Globus Services. You may not distribute, modify, transmit, reuse, repost, or use the content of the Site without Globus Services' prior permission. Globus Services neither warrants nor represents that your use of materials displayed on the Site will not infringe rights of any third party. Because of the global nature of the Internet, you agree to comply with all local rules regarding online conduct and acceptable content, including all laws, rules, codes, and regulations of the country in which you reside.

Links to Third Party Web Sites

If you use any links provided in the Site to Web sites not owned, maintained, or hosted by Globus Services ("Off-Sites"), you will leave the Site. Globus Services is not responsible for any Off-Site's privacy policies or terms of use. No warranty is made with respect to the accuracy, timeliness, or suitability of the content of any Off-Sites, and Globus Services takes no responsibility for such sites. A link to an Off-Site is not an endorsement of the Off-Site, its content, or its sponsoring organization.

Limitation of Liability

Under no circumstances, including but not limited to negligence by act or omission, shall Globus Services or any party involved in creating, producing, or delivering the Site or its content, be liable for any direct, incidental, consequential, indirect, or punitive damages that

2. An E-Commerce Study Abroad Experience

Recently, as a student at Deacon College, you participated in a study abroad program with the University of Trinidad-Tobago. Upon returning to Deacon after a semester in the Caribbean, you are asked to assist some other students in creating a brochure about the island-nation, which will be placed on the college's Web site in order to inspire other students to take advantage of the study abroad program. Using the provided document **wd08Trinidad.doc**, first add page numbers so they appear at the bottom of each brochure page. Be sure to center the numbers. Next, insert a table of contents for the brochure: create the table using the *Formal* format, with a dashed tab leader. Finally, place your name in the document header, save the document as **Trinidad1.doc**, and print only the first page of the brochure, which contains the table of contents. Use Figure 8.41 as an example of the type of brochure you might want to create.

F I G U R E   8.41

Trinidad sample brochure

on the web

1. Indexing Temple University's Student Admission Statement

Donna Horn wants you to download the Temple University Admissions Requirements document from the Web, make some modifications to it, and print it. She cannot remember the Web address, but she tells you to use Google (www.google.com) to search for it. After the Google home page appears, click the **Advanced Search** link, type **Temple University Admissions** in the *with the exact phrase* list box, and choose Microsoft Word (.doc) in the *File Format* list box (see Figure 8.42). Click the **Google Search** button. Click the **Admissions Requirements** link in the search results, and click the Save button to save the document on your disk. Once you have saved the document, create an index consisting of these words: **ACT, CLEP, GED, SAT**, and **TOEFL**. Mark the phrase **American College Test** as a "see" reference (see . . .) for ACT. Add a new last page to the document, insert the word *Index* (format with a Heading 1 style), and generate the index below that word. Create a new first page, and insert a table of contents. (You will find one entry that is very long.) Enter your name in the document's header, insert page numbers in the footer (right aligned), and print the first and last pages of the document—the TOC and the index (see Figure 8.43).

FIGURE 8.42
Google search screen

FIGURE 8.43
Temple sample solution

Screen 2 of 11

Temple University Admissions Requirements

The application form for undergraduate admission to Temple University is available at Temple's Web Site (www.temple.edu), along with instructions for its completion. Application procedures for both freshman and transfer students are described here. For more information, please contact the Office of Undergraduate Admissions, (215) 204-7200.

Freshman Students
Temple requires that you hold a diploma from an accredited high school with specific required high school credits. If you are 18 years of age or older, you may submit a high school equivalency diploma earned through the General Education Development Test (GED).

No student shall be admitted to the University directly from high school who was graduated with a cumulative grade average of less than 2.0 (of 4.0) in all courses. A 2.0 average is the equivalent of a "C" average in most letter grading systems. We urge you to take additional high school courses in

Screen 3 of 11

mathematics, science, and foreign language, especially if you plan to major in mathematics, science, engineering, or language. If you lack some required high school credits, you may be offered admission on an exception basis.

College Entrance Examinations
Applicants to Temple University must take either the Scholastic Assessment Test (SAT) of the College Entrance Examination Board, or the American College Test (ACT) of the American College Testing Program. Both tests are offered several times each year. You may want to take the test in the spring of your junior year, then again in the fall of your senior year. To have your results reported directly to Temple, our SAT code is 2906, and our ACT code is 3724. It is best to talk with your high school guidance counselor about how and when to take these tests. If you are 22 years of age or older, these tests are usually not required.

Transfer Students
About half of all undergraduates who enter Temple annually transfer from two-year colleges or other four-year colleges and universities. If you have

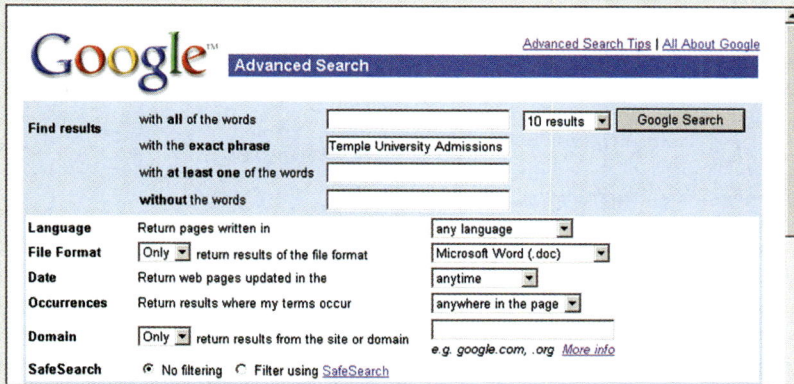

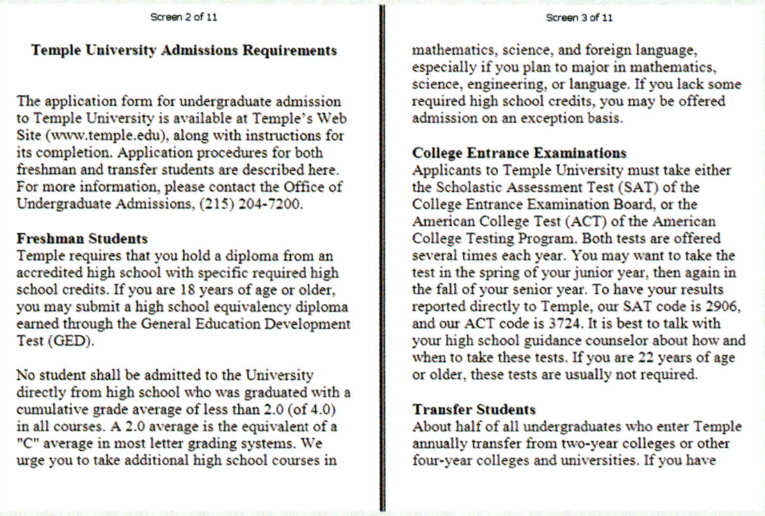

around the world

1. Submitting an Article to an International Journal

As an aspiring literary critic in London, you are preparing to submit an article to the monthly magazine of the Austen Society of London—a prominent group that discusses the various publications of Jane Austen. Before you submit your article, "A Satiric Analysis of Jane Austen's *Pride and Prejudice*," you decide that you want to include an index of names at the end of the document. Using **wd08Austen.doc**, create an index of at least 10 index entries, including the term "Austen." Be sure to utilize the *Fancy* index format. (*Fancy* is one of the Formats in the list box of the Index and Tables dialog box.) After you have created the index, remove the term "Austen" from your index—because it already appears on every page—and update the index. Insert your name into the header, save the document as **Austen1.doc**, and print it.

FIGURE 8.44

Sample of the Austen article

Screen 1 of 17

"A Satiric Analysis of Jane Austen's *Pride and Prejudice*"
Submitted for the approval of the Austen Society of London

      Though it is remarkable that a female author—in the early 19th century—was not only publishing, but attaining a certain degree of success, Jane Austen's disposition resided in an entirely different world than that of a number of her female contemporaries (albeit, very few existed in her day). Perhaps due to the relative degree of wealth that Austen was privy to, she didn't achieve the same aptitude for recognizing the inherent flaw in patriarchal society. By way of example, nearly simultaneous to the public release of *Pride and Prejudice*, Mary Wollstonecraft was advocating (in print) radical feminist values that even have yet to be fully embraced by modern society. When Austen was endorsing love as the mutual basis for marriage, Wollstonecraft was suggesting that a woman's greatest value as a wife was in her

Screen 2 of 17

criticized the endless superficiality of early Victorian society, Wollstonecraft demanded that women receive an equal education to that of men—stipulating further that women have an equal place in every level of economic, cultural, and political society. In other words, although it to her credit that she was raising a catalytic (and popular) voice in a time when few intellectuals wanted to rock England's mighty ship of state, Austen fell short of other existing female authors/theorists in her lackluster advancement of women's rights and values. In fact, *Pride and Prejudice* is an exercise in subtle misogyny: though a few of her female characters have admirable qualities (by today's standards), most of the novel's women possess a fatal flaw that ultimately defines each of them in a stereotypical form. In contrast, the men of Austen's fictional world are generally good-natured lads for whom their only culpability lies in their susceptibility to female seductiveness and deceptive wiles. Regardless, *Pride and*

running project

Kasota United School District

Dr. Trexell has drafted a comprehensive document outlining the requirements for graduation from the Kasota High School. Although the document contains a few misspellings and odd phrases here and there, Dr. Trexell wants you to create a table of contents and place it on the first page of the document. Before creating the TOC, insert a section above the first page of the existing document, set up page numbering so that the TOC is numbered with Roman numerals and the remainder of the document is numbered, beginning with page 1,

with Arabic (**1**, 2, 3, etc.) numbers. The first page should not contain a number. (Currently, the document has numbered pages, with the page number appearing in the footer.) When you have completed your work, place your name in the header on the table of contents page, and then print only the first three pages of the document—the TOC plus the first two pages of the document. The rough draft document is called **wd08Kasota.doc**. Compare your work with Figure 8.45.

FIGURE 8.45
Kasota table of contents

Screen i of 23

Guidance and Counseling Services
Graduation Requirements
   Elective Credits
   State Core 40
   Academic Honors Diploma Requirements
Grades and Grading Procedures
   Athletic Eligibility
   Audited Classes
   Class Rank
   Class Standing
   Final Examinations
   Grade Point Average
   Grade Weighted Classes
   Credits Granted for Classes Taken before High School
   Honor Roll
   Incomplete Grades
   Repeated Classes
   Semester Grades/Report Cards
   Valedictorian, Salutatorian
   Withdrawal from Class
Other Information and Requirements
   Advanced Placement Classes and Tests
   Arranged Programs
   Costs

Screen ii of 23

Minimum Load
Records
Requirements for Participation in Graduation Ceremonies
Schedule Changes
Procedure for Class Change
Class Drop

1. Master Documents and Subdocuments

Now that you are familiar with master documents and subdocuments, determine two additional advantages to using a master document and subdocuments over a larger single document that were not discussed in this chapter.

2. Document Naming Issues

When you split a master document, Word creates a new file for the subdocument whose name is the text of the first Heading 1 style in the new subdocument. If there is any chance that two or more master documents have subdocuments with the same name, one subdocument may overwrite the other. Discuss how you can solve this problem.

3. Using a TOC

Discuss the advantages and disadvantages of using a table of contents in a document and not an index. Discuss the advantages and disadvantages of using an index in a document and not a table of contents.

did you know?

Microsoft *reports that there are over 250 million users of Office worldwide.*

Japan *is one of the most competitive soft drink markets in the world; approximately 1,000 new soft drinks are launched in Japan every year, of which only a small number survive.*

Thomas *Jefferson drafted the Constitution of the United States on a portable desk that carried all of his favorite tools.*

team *members at Microsoft consumed approximately 115,000 slices of pizza while developing the Microsoft XP suite.*

the *word "stewardess" is the longest word in the English language that you type with one hand.*

a *pivot table is also known as a _____ . (Find the answer in this chapter.)*

Chapter Objectives

- **Create and maintain a list—MOS XL03E-1-14**
- **Freeze rows and columns—MOS XL03S-5-6**
- **Sort a list on multiple sort keys—MOS XL03S-2-2**
- **Enter, search for, modify, and delete records in a list with a data form—MOS XL03S-1-2**
- **Group and outline structured data—MOS XL03E-1-3**
- **Create outlines and subtotals—MOS XL03E-1-1**
- **Create and apply conditional formatting—MOS XL03E-2-2**
- **Create filters and advanced filters with AutoFilter—MOS XL03E-1-2**
- **Use worksheet labels and names in formulas—MOS XL03E-1-14**
- **Create a pivot table and pivot chart—MOS XL03E-1-8**
- **Create and use folders for workbook storage—MOS XL03S-5-9**

Computer Security, Inc.

Computer Security, Inc. (Comsec) is a small computer security contractor that provides computer security analysis, design, and software implementation for the U.S. government and commercial clients. Comsec competes for both private and U.S. government computer security contract work by submitting detailed bids outlining the work they will perform if awarded the contracts. Because all of their work involves computer security—a highly sensitive area—almost all of Comsec's work requires access to classified material or company confidential documents. Consequently, all of the security engineers (simply known as "engineers" within the company) have U.S. government clearances of either Secret or Top Secret. Some have even higher clearances for the 2 percent of Comsec's work that involves so-called black box security work. Most of the employees also hold clearances because they must handle classified documents.

Alice Rovik is Comsec's Human Resources (HR) manager. She maintains all employee records and is responsible for semiannual review reports, payroll processing, personnel records, recruiting data, employee training, and pension option information. At the heart of an HR system are personnel records. Personnel record maintenance includes activities such as maintaining employee records, tracking cost center data, recording and maintaining pension information, and absence and sick leave record keeping—to name a few. While most of this information resides in sophisticated database systems, Alice maintains a basic employee worksheet for quick calculations and ad hoc report generation. Because Comsec is a small company, Alice can take advantage of Excel's excellent list management facilities to satisfy many of her personnel information management needs. One of the worksheets Alice keeps close at hand lists employees' names, departments, titles, and other fundamental information. Figure 5.1 shows the worksheet, which she calls simply the "employee" worksheet. During the course of reading this chapter, you will be asked to manipulate the worksheet in various ways to produce summaries, filter the list, add and delete employee records, and produce pivot tables summarizing department data.

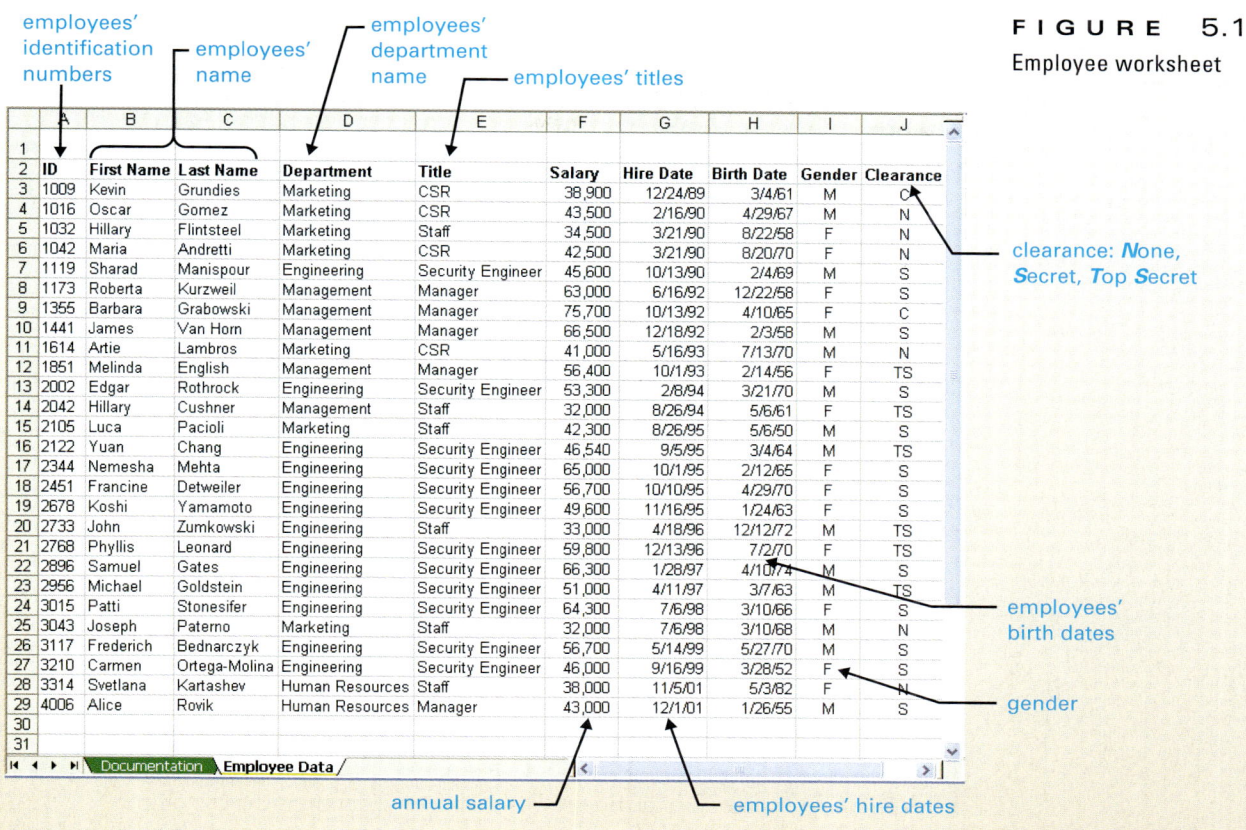

employees' identification numbers

employees' name

employees' department name

employees' titles

clearance: **N**one, **S**ecret, **T**op **S**ecret

employees' birth dates

gender

annual salary

employees' hire dates

	A	B	C	D	E	F	G	H	I	J
2	ID	First Name	Last Name	Department	Title	Salary	Hire Date	Birth Date	Gender	Clearance
3	1009	Kevin	Grundies	Marketing	CSR	38,900	12/24/89	3/4/61	M	C
4	1016	Oscar	Gomez	Marketing	CSR	43,500	2/16/90	4/29/67	M	N
5	1032	Hillary	Flintsteel	Marketing	Staff	34,500	3/21/90	8/22/58	F	N
6	1042	Maria	Andretti	Marketing	CSR	42,500	3/21/90	8/20/70	F	N
7	1119	Sharad	Manispour	Engineering	Security Engineer	45,600	10/13/90	2/4/69	M	S
8	1173	Roberta	Kurzweil	Management	Manager	63,000	6/16/92	12/22/58	F	S
9	1355	Barbara	Grabowski	Management	Manager	75,700	10/13/92	4/10/65	F	C
10	1441	James	Van Horn	Management	Manager	66,500	12/18/92	2/3/58	M	S
11	1614	Artie	Lambros	Marketing	CSR	41,000	5/16/93	7/13/70	M	N
12	1851	Melinda	English	Management	Manager	56,400	10/1/93	2/14/56	F	TS
13	2002	Edgar	Rothrock	Engineering	Security Engineer	53,300	2/8/94	3/21/70	M	S
14	2042	Hillary	Cushner	Management	Staff	32,000	8/26/94	5/6/61	F	TS
15	2105	Luca	Pacioli	Marketing	Staff	42,300	8/26/95	5/6/50	M	S
16	2122	Yuan	Chang	Engineering	Security Engineer	46,540	9/5/95	3/4/64	M	TS
17	2344	Nemesha	Mehta	Engineering	Security Engineer	65,000	10/1/95	2/12/65	F	S
18	2451	Francine	Detweiler	Engineering	Security Engineer	56,700	10/10/95	4/29/70	F	S
19	2678	Koshi	Yamamoto	Engineering	Security Engineer	49,600	11/16/95	1/24/63	F	S
20	2733	John	Zumkowski	Engineering	Staff	33,000	4/18/96	12/12/72	M	TS
21	2768	Phyllis	Leonard	Engineering	Security Engineer	59,800	12/13/96	7/2/70	F	TS
22	2896	Samuel	Gates	Engineering	Security Engineer	66,300	1/28/97	4/10/74	M	S
23	2956	Michael	Goldstein	Engineering	Security Engineer	51,000	4/11/97	3/7/63	M	TS
24	3015	Patti	Stonesifer	Engineering	Security Engineer	64,300	7/6/98	3/10/66	F	S
25	3043	Joseph	Paterno	Marketing	Staff	32,000	7/6/98	3/10/68	M	N
26	3117	Frederich	Bednarczyk	Engineering	Security Engineer	56,700	5/14/99	5/27/70	M	S
27	3210	Carmen	Ortega-Molina	Engineering	Security Engineer	46,000	9/16/99	3/28/52	F	S
28	3314	Svetlana	Kartashev	Human Resources	Staff	38,000	11/5/01	5/3/82	F	N
29	4006	Alice	Rovik	Human Resources	Manager	43,000	12/1/01	1/26/55	M	S

Documentation \ Employee Data /

Chapter 5 covers building and maintaining Office Excel 2003 lists, which are also called databases, and creating pivot tables. In this chapter you will use a personnel worksheet from Comsec, a computer security consulting and contracting company. You will sort the data various ways so that the list is in a more useful order. Using Excel's form feature, you will add, modify, and delete values in the list through a simple and intuitive form-based interface, which also facilitates searching for particular values.

Creating a data filter allows you to hide selected rows of the list to easily locate groups of records—worksheet rows—that contain the same value. You will learn how to sort a list into related groups and then create salary subtotals and other statistics for each identified group. Creating pivot tables, the capstone feature described in this chapter, illustrates how to create summaries by pairs of variables, or values. For example, you will learn how to use the PivotTable Wizard to quickly create a table displaying the average salary by department—all with a few simple keystrokes.

SESSION 5.1 CREATING AND USING LISTS

In this section, you will learn how to use Microsoft Office Excel 2003 to manage a list, or database. One of the most common uses of worksheets is to maintain lists of information: names and addresses of business contacts and students, and symbols and purchase prices of stocks, for example. You will learn how to sort the list into a meaningful order, modify the amount of the worksheet that displays on the page, find and replace information in a list, and use a data form to add, modify, and delete data.

Building a List

A *list* is a collection of data arranged in columns and rows in which each column displays one particular type of data. A list has the following characteristics:

- Each column contains the same category of information. In the personnel list highlighted in this chapter, for example, the ID column contains employee identification numbers and no other data

- The first row in the list contains labels identifying each column and its contents

- A list does not contain any blank rows

- A list is bordered on all four sides by empty rows and columns, or a list begins in row 1 or column A, each of which serves to delimit the list on the top or the left side, respectively

Figure 5.1 shows the employee worksheet containing a small amount of employee data. It contains fewer rows and columns than a typical employee worksheet to keep the example understandable without sacrificing elegance. Each column of a list is a *field* of related information describing some characteristic of the object, person, or place. Each row is called a *record*, which contains the fields that collectively describe a single object, person, or place. A collection of these records constitutes a list. Observe the Hire Date column. It contains only date values, and the dates recorded in the column—field—are the dates when each employee was hired—his or her first day to report to work. Observe one other important attribute about the list shown in Figure 5.1: The labels at the top of the list, or names that identify each column, are unique and formatted differently (boldface) from the information in rows below the label row. This is important, because it helps Excel determine that the first row is a label row identifying each column.

Begin your work on the employee workbook by opening it and saving it under its new name.

Opening the Employee worksheet and saving it under a new name:

1. Start Excel

2. Open the workbook **ex05Employee.xls** and immediately save it as **Employee1.xls** (see Figure 5.2)

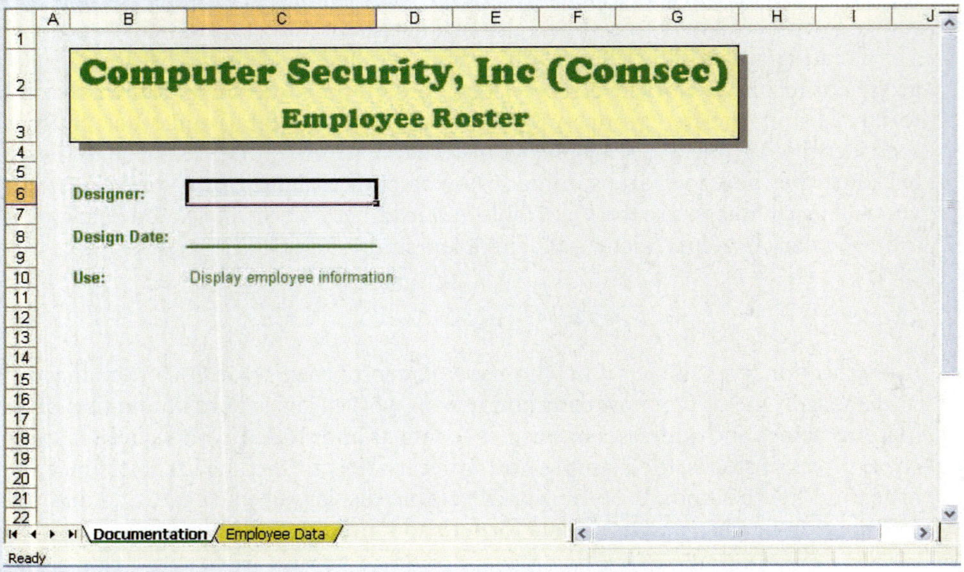

FIGURE 5.2

Documentation worksheet

3. Switch to the **Employee Data** worksheet (click the yellow **Employee Data** tab) to display the employee list. Row 2 contains labels that name each column. Scroll down the worksheet to reveal other rows in the employee list. Notice that the column headings go out of view as you scroll down the worksheet

A common problem occurring when you use a long list of data is that the labels identifying the columns soon scroll out of view as you go to the bottom of the list to enter new data. Without the labels at the top of the column, it is difficult to remember what to enter in each column—particularly when two columns contain similar data such as the Hire Date and Birth Date. There is more than one way to handle this problem.

Freezing Rows and Columns

Freezing rows and columns prevents certain columns, rows, or both from scrolling off the screen when you scroll an Excel window down or to the right. When you freeze one or more rows or columns, they form a two-sided frame that remains in place—almost like a two-sided picture frame in which the picture can move up or down while the frame remains in place.

---

task reference **Freezing Rows and Columns**

- Select the cell below and to the right of the row(s) and column(s) you want to freeze
- Click **Window** on the menu bar and then click **Freeze Panes**

You decide to freeze rows 1 and 2 containing the column headings and freeze columns A through C containing the employees' names.

Freezing label rows and employee name columns:

1. Click cell **D3**

2. Click **Window** on the menu bar and then click **Freeze Panes**. Notice dark lines appear at the boundaries of the frozen rows and columns

3. Click the vertical scroll bar down arrow to scroll down the worksheet. Notice that the labels remain fixed at the top of the worksheet

4. Click the horizontal scroll bar right arrow to scroll a few columns to the right. Notice that the first three columns (ID, First Name, and Last Name) remain fixed. Columns appear to scroll beneath the frozen columns (see Figure 5.3)

5. Press **Ctrl+Home**. When columns or rows are frozen, pressing Ctrl+Home makes active the cell directly below and to the right of frozen rows or columns

You can unfreeze rows or columns by clicking Unfreeze Panes in the Window menu. For now, leave the panes frozen.

FIGURE 5.3

Freezing rows and
columns in place

jump in row numbers

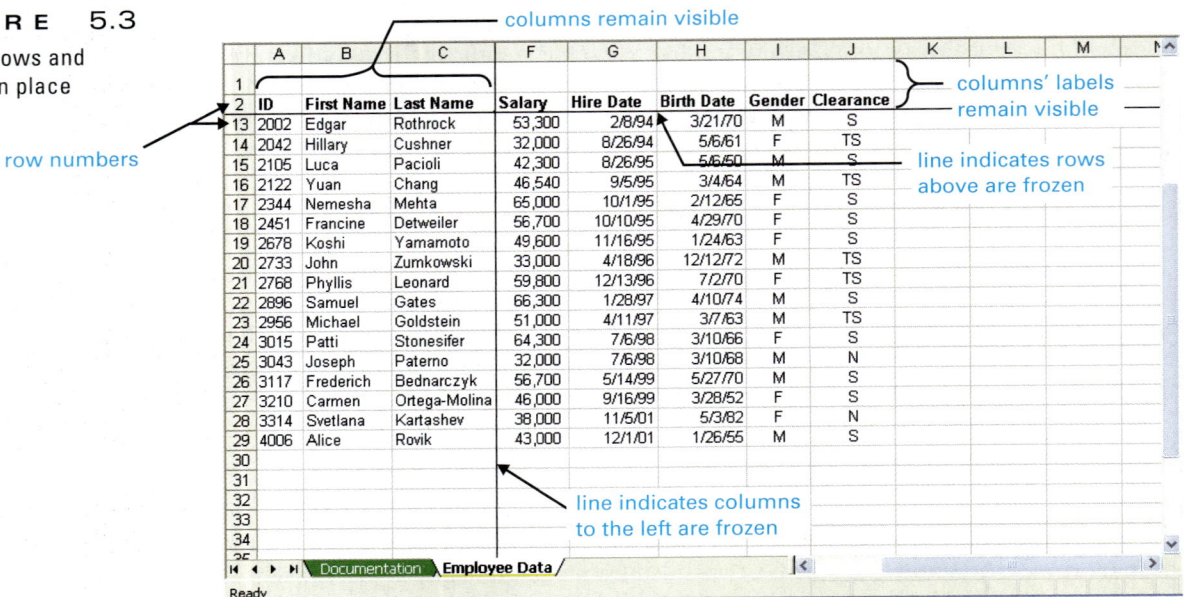

Using a Data Form to Maintain a List

Alice Rovik has several changes she wants to make to the Employee worksheet. You can make changes to lists using existing Excel commands to insert a row to add an employee record or delete a row to remove a record. However, you will find it easier to use Excel's Form command. A **data form** is a dialog box displaying one row of a list in text boxes in which you can add, locate, modify, or delete records. One advantage of using an Excel data form for record maintenance operations—updates, insertions, or deletions—is that it greatly reduces the chances of making data entry mistakes. Because a data form displays a single row at a time, your chance of transposing values from one row to another are smaller.

Adding a Record

task reference	Adding a Record to a List Using a Data Form

- Click any cell within the list
- Click **Data** and then click **Form**
- Click the **New** button
- Type the values for each field in the corresponding form text boxes, pressing the **Tab** key to move from one text box to another
- Press the **Enter** key
- Click the **Close** button after adding all records to the list

The first modification is to add a new employee to the list of employees on the Employee Data worksheet.

Adding a new record by using the data form:

1. Click any cell within the list (cell F4, for example)

2. Click **Data** on the menu bar and then click **Form** to display the Employee Data form (see Figure 5.4)

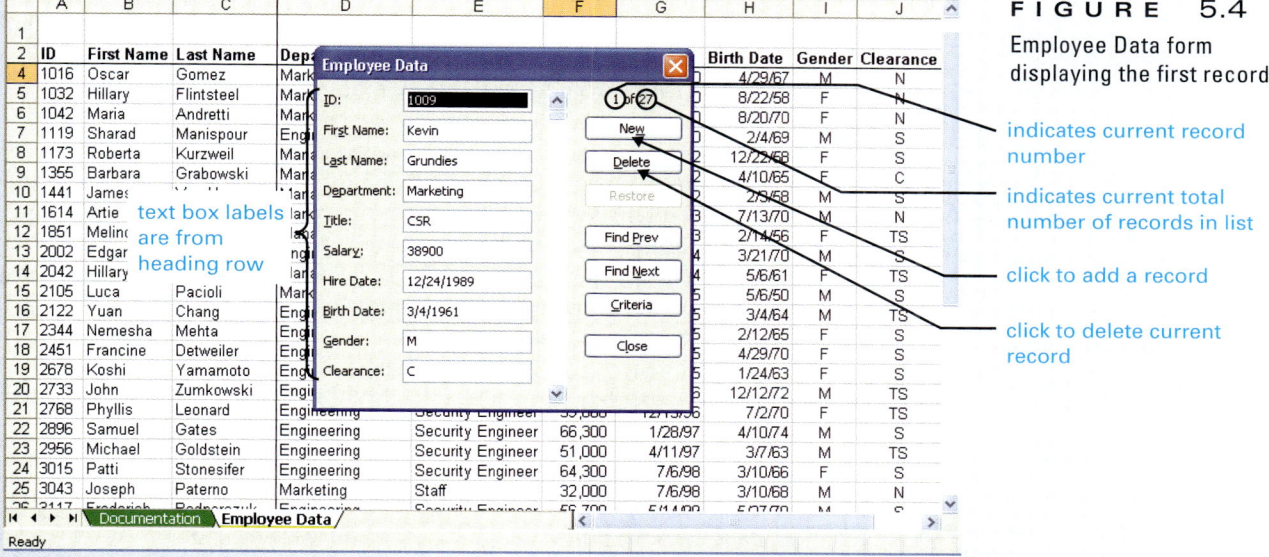

FIGURE 5.4

Employee Data form displaying the first record

indicates current record number

indicates current total number of records in list

click to add a record

click to delete current record

3. Click the data form's **New** button to clear the text boxes. Notice that "New Record" appears where the record number and total record count were previously

4. Type **4123** in the ID text box and then press **Tab** to move to the next text box

5. Type **Steve** in the First Name text box and then press **Tab**

6. Type **Ballmer** in the Last Name text box and then press **Tab**

7. Type **Engineering** in the Department text box and then press **Tab**

8. Type **Security Engineer** in the Title text box and then press **Tab**

9. Type **42900** in the Salary text box and then press **Tab**

10. Type **5/1/2002** in the Hire Date text box and then press **Tab**

11. Type **4/14/1970** in the Birth Date text box and then press **Tab**

12. Type **M** (uppercase, please) in the Gender text box and then press **Tab**

13. Type **N** (uppercase, please) in the Clearance text box

14. Press the **Enter** key to add the record to the list. Excel automatically adds the record to the end of the current data list and displays an empty data form

15. Click the **Close** button to close the data form and return to the worksheet

16. Press and hold the **End** key, then press the **down arrow** key, and release the **End** key to move to the last record in the list. Ensure that the last record in the list is Ballmer's record

After adding the new record to the list, you can proceed to make other alterations that Alice requested to the list. Recall that she wants one record deleted and another record edited.

Searching for a Record

The employee list is short and it is easy to locate any particular record by examining the list. In larger lists containing perhaps 500 rows or more, looking for a particular employee's record or a particular customer's invoice could be much more difficult. Fortunately, Excel's data form provides search capabilities. You will use the data form search method to locate a record just as you would for a very large list.

You can search for one or more records by specifying *search criteria*, which are values that the data form should match in specified data form fields. Beginning with the first record in the list, Excel inspects each record in turn until it either finds a record matching the search criteria or reaches the end of the list without finding a match. If more than one record matches the search criteria, Excel displays the first record it encounters in the data form. When you click the Find Next button, Excel continues the search by searching for the next matching record.

To modify or delete a record from a list, you have to locate it first. The fastest way to locate a record is to use the data form search facility. Once Excel finds the requested record, you can choose to change it, delete it, or do nothing at all to the record.

Searching for a record using a data form:

1. Click any cell within the employee list

2. Click **Data** on the menu bar and then click **Form**

3. Click the **Criteria** button. Excel blanks all the form's text boxes

4. Click the **Last Name** text box and type **manispour** to specify the search criteria

   tip: When typing character search criteria—names, street names, or other text labels—you need not worry about capitalization

   tip: You can type information in more than one text box to specify multiple search criteria. All specified criteria must be satisfied to match a record

5. Click the **Find Next** button. Sharad Manispour's record appears in the data form (see Figure 5.5)

FIGURE 5.5

Employee Data form displaying Sharad Manispour's record

Employee Data

ID:	1119
First Name:	Sharad
Last Name:	Manispour
Department:	Engineering
Title:	Security Engineer
Salary:	45600
Hire Date:	10/13/1990
Birth Date:	2/4/1969
Gender:	M
Clearance:	S

5 of 28

New
Delete
Restore
Find Prev
Find Next
Criteria
Close

Sharad's record is number 5 in the list of 28

Press the Find Next button to continue the search. If no record is found matching the criteria, the first record found appears in the data form

6. Drag the mouse across the **Title** text box to select its contents and then type **Manager** to correct Sharad's title

7. Double-click the **Salary** text box and then type **54500** (without a currency symbol or a comma)

8. Click the **Close** button. Excel replaces the record with its new contents

9. Examine row 7 to verify that Excel altered the Title and Salary fields for Sharad Manispour

Deleting a Record

The procedure you follow to delete a record from a list is similar to updating a record. You display the data form for the employee list, click the Criteria button, and type in suitable search criteria. When you locate the record, then you click the data form Delete button.

Unless you specify the exact spelling of text values, the search will fail to locate a matching record. One way to reduce the chance of this happening is to specify fewer characters in the search criteria field and use a wild card character on the end of the search criteria. A *wild card character* is a character that stands for one or more characters—a "don't care" symbol. Excel has two such characters: asterisk (*) and question mark (?). Use the question mark to substitute for a single character in a search criteria character string. Use the asterisk to match any number of characters. For example, the search text "pat?rno" matches paterno, patorno, or patirno. The more powerful wild character asterisk matches any characters that appear where it does in the search criteria. For example, the search criteria "G*" in the employee Last Name field matches Grundies, Gomez, Grabowski, Gates, and Goldstein. The more characters you specify preceding the asterisk, the more specific the search criteria are because all the characters preceding an asterisk wild card must match the corresponding field in those positions exactly.

---

task reference   Deleting a Record from a
                                              List with a Data Form

- Click any cell within the list
- Click **Data** and then click **Form**
- Click the **Criteria** button and enter the search criteria in one or more text boxes
- Click the **Find Next** button repeatedly until you locate the record to be deleted
- Press the **Delete** button and then click the **OK** button to confirm the deletion

---

Searching for a record using the asterisk wild card:

1. Click any cell within the employee list, click **Data** on the menu bar, and then click **Form** to display the first employee record in the data form

2. Click the **Criteria** button to prepare to enter the search criteria

3. Click the **Last Name** text box and type **pa*** (see Figure 5.6)

FIGURE 5.6

Using search criteria containing a wild card

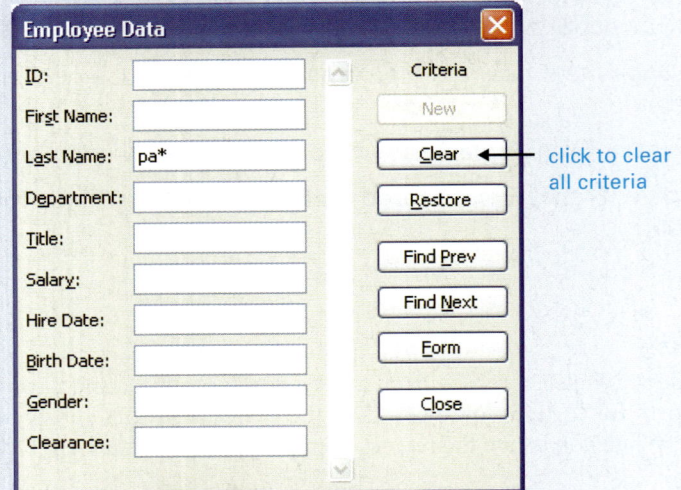

click to clear all criteria

4. Click the **Find Next** button to launch the search and display the first record satisfying the criteria. The data form displays Luca Pacioli's record. That is not the one you want to remove from the list

5. Click the **Find Next** button to continue searching down the list for a record whose last name field begins with "pa." Excel locates and displays Joseph Paterno's record—the record you want to delete

6. Click the **Delete** button. A warning dialog box appears

7. Click **OK** to confirm that you want to permanently delete the selected record

8. Click the **Close** button to close the data form and redisplay the worksheet

Scroll down so you can see rows 23 through 26. Prior to the deletion operation, Paterno's record occupied row 25. Notice that Frederich Bednarczyk's record now occupies that row. In other words, when you delete a record with a data form, Excel removes the entire row and moves up rows below it to fill the void.

Locating and Modifying Data with Find and Replace

When you must make a few modifications to various fields in an Excel list, the data form method illustrated above is the best way. However, when you have to make a change to one particular field in the list involving many records, then the Excel Find and Replace command is your best choice. For example, suppose you had to change the entries in the Gender column by replacing "M" with "Male" and "F" with "Female." Modifying each entry by hand would be tedious at best because each of the 27 employee rows would have to be modified individually. Using the Find and Replace command reduces the effort.

Alice observes the computer security industry trend that engineers working in security engineering and engineering departments typically hold the title "engineer" rather than "security engineer." She wants you to change that name wherever it occurs in the Title column.

Replacing a character string in many cells:

1. Select the cell range **E3:E29**

tip: *The fastest way to select the range of cells in a single column that contains no "holes"—each cell in the column has a value—is to click the topmost cell in the range, press and hold the **Shift** key, tap the **End** key, tap the **down arrow** key, and then release the **Shift** key. Excel highlights the entire range of filled cells between the first cell you select and the bottommost cell in the range*

2. Click **Edit** on the menu bar and then click **Replace** to display the Find and Replace dialog box

3. Click the **Find what** text box and type **security engineer**

4. Click the **Replace with** text box and type **Engineer** (be sure to capitalize the first letter of the title). Figure 5.7 shows the dialog box with both the search text and the replacement text in place

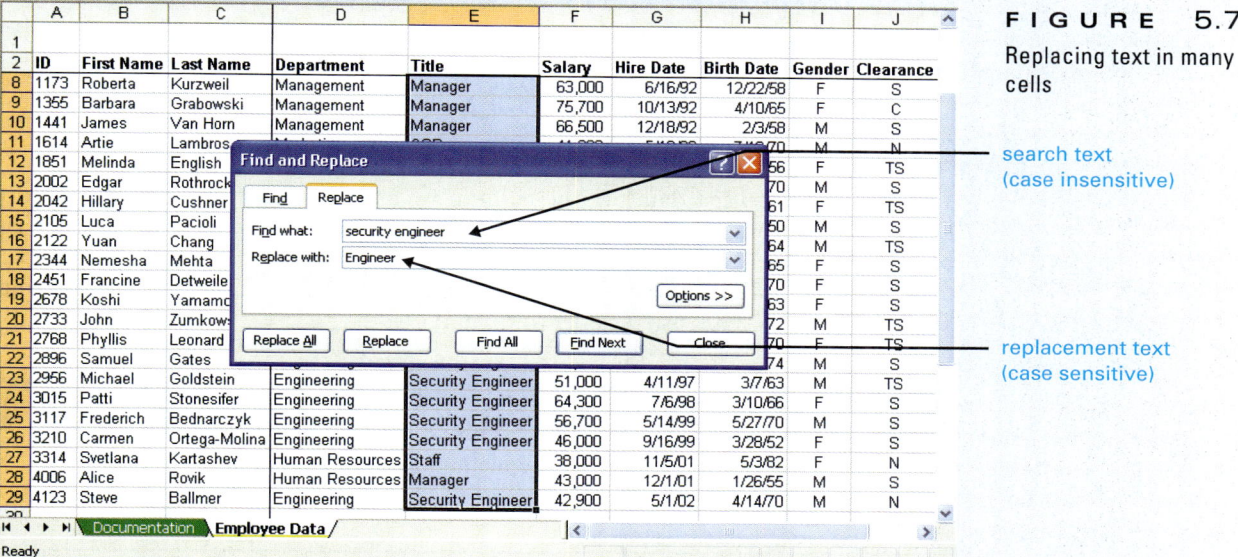

FIGURE 5.7

Replacing text in many cells

search text
(case insensitive)

replacement text
(case sensitive)

5. Click the **Replace All** button to replace all occurrences of *Security Engineer* in column E with *Engineer*. Excel displays in an information dialog box indicating it has made 12 replacements

6. Click **OK** to close the information dialog box, and then click **Close** to close the Find and Replace dialog box

Sorting Data

The employee list is kept in Hire Date order. When a new employee joins the company, his or her record is placed at the end of the list. Alice Rovik has a meeting next week with several top management people to discuss retirement benefits, and she wants to have the list in order by the Birth Date field for easy reference.

To sort rows of a list, you use one or more fields (columns) to determine the final position in the list that each row occupies. The field or fields you use to sort a list are called ***sort fields*** (or ***sort keys***). For instance, if you wanted to rearrange the rows of the Employee list so that they are in alphabetical order by last name, Last Name is the sort field. If more than one sort field is required to reorder a list, the first sort field is called the ***primary sort field***. Other sort fields used to reorder rows break any ties that occur in the primary sort field. This is common in telephone books, for example. Telephone book lists are sorted by last name, then first name, and then by middle initial. The primary sort field is last name, the secondary sort field is first name, and the third sort field (needed to break a tie between two or more with the name Joe Smith, for example) is middle initial.

Once you decide which fields are your list's sort fields, you decide whether to order the list in ascending or descending order for each sort field. *Ascending order* arranges text values alphabetically from A to Z, arranges numbers from smallest to largest, and arranges dates from earliest to most recent. *Descending order* does the opposite—it arranges text values alphabetically from Z to A, arranges numbers from largest to smallest, and arranges dates from most recent to earliest. Whether sorting in ascending order or descending order, blank fields are always placed at the bottom of the list.

While a list in employee ID order may be handy when adding employees, it is not a useful way to organize records when you want to know how many people work in the Engineering Department, for example. When you want to look up a particular employee's record, it is easier to do so if the list is in order by last name.

help yourself *Press **F1**, type **sort** in the Search text box of the Microsoft Excel Help task pane, and press **Enter**. Click the hyperlink **Sort a range** and then click the hyperlink **Sort by 4 columns** to reveal information about sorting on more than three fields. Click the Help screen **Close** button when you are finished, and then close the task pane*

Sorting a List by One Column

You can sort Excel list data on one column by using the Sort Ascending and Sort Descending buttons on the Excel Standard toolbar. Alternatively, you can use the Sort command of the Data menu. If you need to sort a list on only one field, the toolbar method is the fastest and simplest way. For more complex sort operations involving more than one column, use the Sort command.

task reference	Sorting a List on One Column

- Click any cell in the column in which you want to sort a list
- Click the **Sort Ascending** or the **Sort Descending** button

Sorting the employee list in ascending order by Birth Date:

1. Click cell **H3**, a birth date cell for the first employee row

tip: *You do not need to select the entire list or the entire column on which the list is sorted. Excel determines the list's boundaries by finding blank rows to the left and right of the list and blank columns above and below the list*

2. Click the **Sort Ascending** [↕] button on the Standard toolbar. Excel sorts the rows in order by the Birth Date column (see Figure 5.8)

Never select the entire column you want to designate as the sort field because Excel misinterprets your intentions and sorts the entries in the selected column only, rather than sorting the entire record along with the sort field. If you make this mistake, click Undo in the Edit menu to reverse the effects of the incorrect sort operation.

sort field →

	A	B	C	D	E	F	G	H	I	J
1										
2	ID	First Name	Last Name	Department	Title	Salary	Hire Date	Birth Date	Gender	Clearance
3	2105	Luca	Pacioli	Marketing	Staff	42,300	8/26/95	5/6/50	M	S
4	3210	Carmen	Ortega-Molina	Engineering	Engineer	46,000	9/16/99	3/28/52	F	S
5	4006	Alice	Rovik	Human Resources	Manager	43,000	12/1/01	1/26/55	M	S
6	1851	Melinda	English	Management	Manager	56,400	10/1/93	2/14/56	F	TS
7	1441	James	Van Horn	Management	Manager	66,500	12/18/92	2/3/58	M	S
8	1032	Hillary	Flintsteel	Marketing	Staff	34,500	3/21/90	8/22/58	F	N
9	1173	Roberta	Kurzweil	Management	Manager	63,000	6/16/92	12/22/58	F	S
10	1009	Kevin	Grundies	Marketing	CSR	38,900	12/24/89	3/4/61	M	C
11	2042	Hillary	Cushner	Management	Staff	32,000	8/26/94	5/6/61	F	TS
12	2678	Koshi	Yamamoto	Engineering	Engineer	49,600	11/16/95	1/24/63	F	S
13	2956	Michael	Goldstein	Engineering	Engineer	51,000	4/11/97	3/7/63	M	TS
14	2122	Yuan	Chang	Engineering	Engineer	46,540	9/5/95	3/4/64	M	TS
15	2344	Nemesha	Mehta	Engineering	Engineer	65,000	10/1/95	2/12/65	F	S
16	1355	Barbara	Grabowski	Management	Manager	75,700	10/13/92	4/10/65	F	C
17	3015	Patti	Stonesifer	Engineering	Engineer	64,300	7/6/98	3/10/66	F	S
18	1016	Oscar	Gomez	Marketing	CSR	43,500	2/16/90	4/29/67	M	N
19	1119	Sharad	Manispour	Engineering	Manager	54,500	10/13/90	2/4/69	M	S
20	2002	Edgar	Rothrock	Engineering	Engineer	53,300	2/8/94	3/21/70	M	S
21	4123	Steve	Ballmer	Engineering	Engineer	42,900	5/1/02	4/14/70	M	N
22	2451	Francine	Detweiler	Engineering	Engineer	56,700	10/10/95	4/29/70	F	S
23	3117	Frederich	Bednarczyk	Engineering	Engineer	56,700	5/14/99	5/27/70	M	S
24	2768	Phyllis	Leonard	Engineering	Engineer	59,800	12/13/96	7/2/70	F	TS
25	1614	Aris	Lambros	Marketing	CSR	41,000	5/16/93	7/13/70	M	N

Documentation **Employee Data**

Ready

F I G U R E   5.8

Employee list sorted by Birth Date

Sorting a List on Multiple Fields

Often, sorting a list on only one field is not adequate because larger lists frequently have groups of entries that are identical in a particular field. A *tie* exists when one or more records have the same value for a field. When ties occur, you must sort the groups of records that tie on a particular field by another field—the *secondary sort field*—to break the tie. For large lists, groups of records can match on both the primary sort field and the secondary sort field. In that case, sorting a list on three sort fields is necessary. Three sort fields are almost always sufficient to sort a list into order and eliminate all ties.

Alice Rovik wants the employee list sorted in order by department and then by employee last name and first name within each department. This type of sort operation goes beyond the capabilities of a single-key sort provided by the Sort Ascending or the Sort Descending buttons on the Standard toolbar. The Data menu Sort command provides the multiple-field sorting capability Alice requires.

---

task reference   Sorting a List on More Than One Field

- Click any cell within the list to be sorted

- Click **Data** on the menu bar and click **Sort**

- Click the **Sort by** list arrow to display the list's column headings. Click the column heading corresponding to the primary sort field, and click the **Ascending** or **Descending** option button

- Click the first **Then by** list arrow to display the list's column headings. Click the column heading of the secondary sort field, and then click the **Ascending** or **Descending** option button for the second sort field

- If necessary, click the second **Then by** list arrow to display the list's column headings. Click the column heading of the third sort field, and then click the **Ascending** or **Descending** option button for the third sort field

- Click the **OK** button to sort the list

EXCEL

Sorting the employee list in order by department and name within department:

1. Click any cell in the list

2. Click **Data** on the menu bar and then click **Sort**

3. Click the **Sort by** list box arrow to display a list of column headings, click **Department**, and, if necessary, click the **Ascending** option button

4. Click the first **Then by** list box arrow to display a list of column headings, click **Last Name**, and, if necessary, click the **Ascending** option button

5. Click the second **Then by** list box arrow to display a list of column headings, click **First Name**, and, if necessary, click the **Ascending** option button. Figure 5.9 shows the Sort dialog box after specifying three sort fields

FIGURE 5.9

Sort dialog box

primary sort field

second sort field

third sort field

click to select a custom sort order

choose *Ascending* or *Descending* for each field

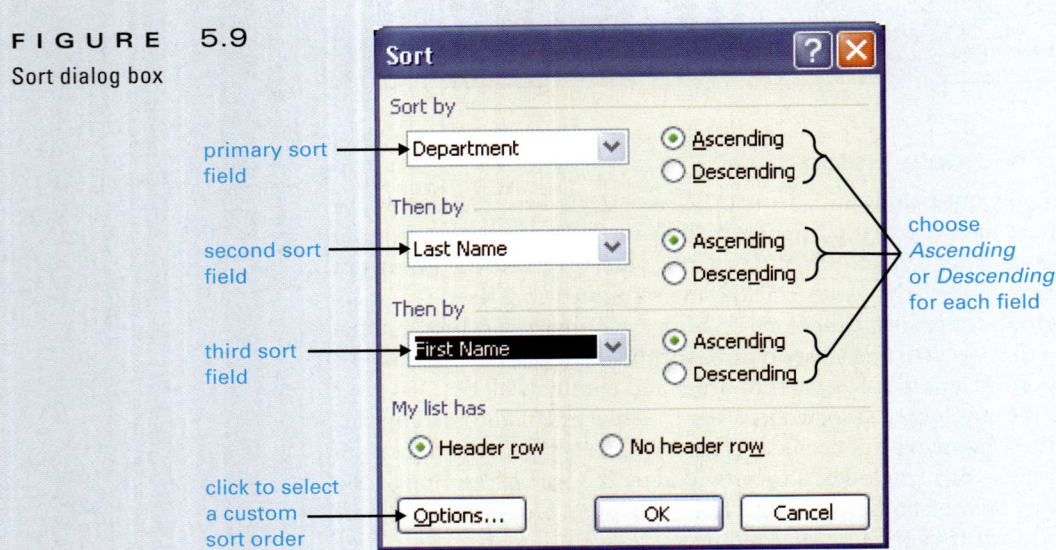

6. Click **OK** to sort the list into order on three sort fields. Excel sorts the list in order by department (first) and then last and first name within each department (see Figure 5.10)

Creating and Using Custom Sort Orders

Excel does not limit you to the standard sorting sequence. If you want to sort a series of labels in a particular order, you can define a custom sorting series. A ***custom sorting series*** or list is an ordered list you create to instruct Excel in what order to sort rows containing the list items. For example, imagine a list of student records containing a field called Year in School. The Year in School would contain "Freshman," "Sophomore," "Junior," and "Senior." Under normal circumstances, records sorted on the Year in School would rearrange rows so that they appear in this order: Freshman, Junior, Senior, and then Sophomore. However, most schools want the list sorted by year in school beginning with Freshman and ending with Senior. Creating a custom list containing Freshman, Sophomore, Junior, and then Senior—in that order—solves that particular sorting problem. (Excel already has the days of the week and the months of the year as custom sort orders, so you can sort time cards in Monday through Friday order or January through December.)

	A	B	C	D	E	F	G	H	I	J
1										
2	ID	First Name	Last Name	Department	Title	Salary	Hire Date	Birth Date	Gender	Clearance
3	4123	Steve	Ballmer	Engineering	Engineer	42,900	5/1/02	4/14/70	M	N
4	3117	Frederich	Bednarczyk	Engineering	Engineer	56,700	5/14/99	5/27/70	M	S
5	2122	Yuan	Chang	Engineering	Engineer	46,540	9/5/95	3/4/64	M	TS
6	2451	Francine	Detweiler	Engineering	Engineer	56,700	10/10/95	4/29/70	F	S
7	2896	Samuel	Gates	Engineering	Engineer	66,300	1/28/97	4/10/74	M	S
8	2956	Michael	Goldstein	Engineering	Engineer	51,000	4/11/97	3/7/63	M	TS
9	2768	Phyllis	Leonard	Engineering	Engineer	59,800	12/13/96	7/2/70	F	TS
10	1119	Sharad	Manispour	Engineering	Manager	54,500	10/13/90	2/4/69	M	S
11	2344	Nemesha	Mehta	Engineering	Engineer	65,000	10/1/95	2/12/65	F	S
12	3210	Carmen	Ortega-Molina	Engineering	Engineer	46,000	9/16/99	3/28/52	F	S
13	2002	Edgar	Rothrock	Engineering	Engineer	53,300	2/8/94	3/21/70	M	S
14	3015	Patti	Stonesifer	Engineering	Engineer	64,300	7/6/98	3/10/66	F	S
15	2678	Koshi	Yamamoto	Engineering	Engineer	49,600	11/16/95	1/24/63	F	S
16	2733	John	Zumkowski	Engineering	Staff	33,000	4/18/96	12/12/72	M	TS
17	3314	Svetlana	Kartashev	Human Resources	Staff	38,000	11/5/01	5/3/82	F	N
18	4006	Alice	Rovik	Human Resources	Manager	43,000	12/1/01	1/26/55	M	S
19	2042	Hillary	Cushner	Management	Staff	32,000	8/26/94	5/6/61	F	TS
20	1851	Melinda	English	Management	Manager	56,400	10/1/93	2/14/56	F	TS
21	1355	Barbara	Grabowski	Management	Manager	75,700	10/13/92	4/10/65	F	C
22	1173	Roberta	Kurzweil	Management	Manager	63,000	6/16/92	12/22/58	F	S
23	1441	James	Van Horn	Management	Manager	66,500	12/18/92	2/3/58	M	S
24	1042	Maria	Andretti	Marketing	CSR	42,500	3/21/90	8/20/70	F	N
25	1032	Hillary	Flintstool	Marketing	Staff	31,500	3/31/99	9/23/58	F	N

Documentation \ Employee Data

Ready

task reference   Creating a Custom Sort Order

- Click **Tools** on the menu bar, click **Options**, and then click the **Custom Lists** tab

- Click **NEW LIST** in the Custom lists list box

- In the List Entries section of the dialog box, type each item and press **Enter** to place it on the list

- When the list is complete, click the **Add** button to move the proposed list to the Custom lists panel

- Click the **OK** button to close the Options dialog box

Alice would like you to sort the list in a third way so that the departments appear in this order: Marketing, Human Resources, Management, and Engineering. You begin by defining a custom sort order. Once you have defined the list, you can sort the worksheet rows in order by the custom list.

Creating a custom sort order:

1. Click **Tools** on the menu bar and then click **Options**

2. Click the **Custom Lists** tab, and then click **NEW LIST** in the Custom lists box

3. In the List entries box, type **Marketing** and press **Enter**

4. Type **Human Resources** and press **Enter**

5. Type **Management** and press **Enter**

6. Type **Engineering** and click the **Add** button to add the list you typed to the Custom lists (see Figure 5.11)

7. Click **OK** to complete the custom sort list definition

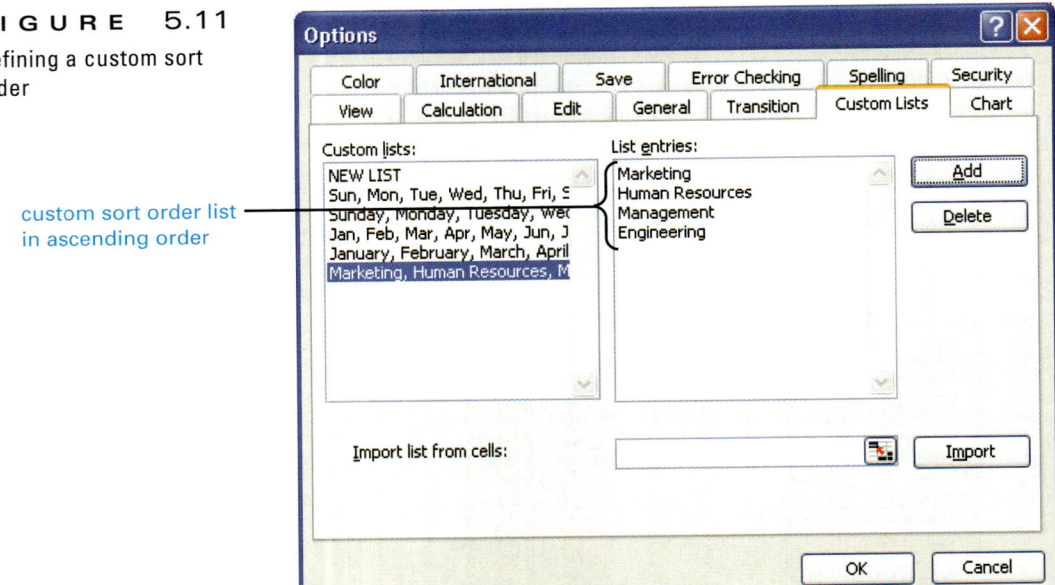

FIGURE 5.11

Defining a custom sort order

custom sort order list in ascending order

---

another**word**

. . . on Creating a Custom Sort Order

If the items in your custom list already appear in the correct order as text in your worksheet, you do not have to type them on the Custom Lists tab of the Tools, Options dialog box. Instead, select the list before choosing the Options command of the Tools menu. Your highlighted text list will appear automatically in the dialog box. Simply click the Import button to add the new custom sort order sequence to Excel's custom lists. The lists are remembered for all workbooks you load from Excel on that particular computer

Now you can sort the employee list by department names and then by employee names within the department using a procedure similar to the sort you performed above.

To delete a custom sort order list, select the list on the Custom Lists tab and click the Delete button. The list is eliminated. For now, leave the custom list in place to use in the next steps to sort your employee list by department names.

Sorting using a custom sort order:

1. Click any cell in the employee list

2. Click **Data** on the menu bar and then click **Sort**

3. Click the **Options** button to display the Sort Options dialog box

4. Click the **First key sort order** list box arrow, click the **Marketing, Human Resources** entry to notify Excel to use that custom sort order (see Figure 5.12), and then click **OK**

FIGURE 5.12

Selecting a custom sort order

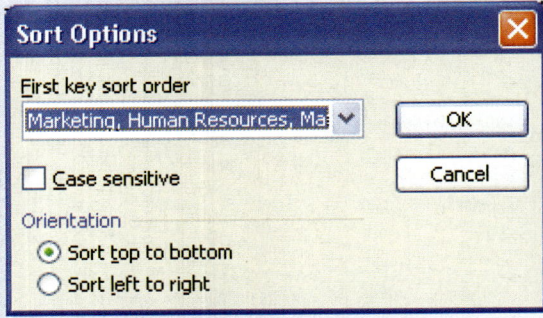

Because Excel remembers the field names and sort order for the Sort by and the two *Then by* sort fields, you do not need to reinstate them. Ensure that they say Department, Last Name, and First Name, respectively

5. Click **OK** to sort the list into order. Figure 5.13 shows the list sorted with the custom department sort order

a custom sort order based on *Department*

	A	B	C	D	E	F	G	H	I	J
1										
2	ID	First Name	Last Name	Department	Title	Salary	Hire Date	Birth Date	Gender	Clearance
3	1042	Maria	Andretti	Marketing	CSR	42,500	3/21/90	8/20/70	F	N
4	1032	Hillary	Flintsteel	Marketing	Staff	34,500	3/21/90	8/22/58	F	N
5	1016	Oscar	Gomez	Marketing	CSR	43,500	2/16/90	4/29/67	M	N
6	1009	Kevin	Grundies	Marketing	CSR	38,900	12/24/89	3/4/61	M	C
7	1614	Artie	Lambros	Marketing	CSR	41,000	5/16/93	7/13/70	M	N
8	2105	Luca	Pacioli	Marketing	Staff	42,300	8/26/95	5/6/50	M	S
9	3314	Svetlana	Kartashev	Human Resources	Staff	38,000	11/5/01	5/3/82	F	N
10	4006	Alice	Rovik	Human Resources	Manager	43,000	12/1/01	1/26/55	M	S
11	2042	Hillary	Cushner	Management	Staff	32,000	8/26/94	5/6/61	F	TS
12	1851	Melinda	English	Management	Manager	56,400	10/1/93	2/14/56	F	TS
13	1355	Barbara	Grabowski	Management	Manager	75,700	10/13/92	4/10/65	F	C
14	1173	Roberta	Kurzweil	Management	Manager	63,000	6/16/92	12/22/58	F	S
15	1441	James	Van Horn	Management	Manager	66,500	12/18/92	2/3/58	M	S
16	4123	Steve	Ballmer	Engineering	Engineer	42,900	5/1/02	4/14/70	M	N
17	3117	Frederick	Bednarczyk	Engineering	Engineer	56,700	5/14/99	5/27/70	M	S
18	2122	Yuan	Chang	Engineering	Engineer	46,540	9/5/95	3/4/64	M	TS
19	2451	Francine	Detweiler	Engineering	Engineer	56,700	10/10/95	4/29/70	F	S
20	2896	Samuel	Gates	Engineering	Engineer	66,300	1/28/97	4/10/74	M	S
21	2956	Michael	Goldstein	Engineering	Engineer	51,000	4/11/97	3/7/63	M	TS
22	2768	Phyllis	Leonard	Engineering	Engineer	59,800	12/13/96	7/2/70	F	TS
23	1119	Sharad	Manispour	Engineering	Manager	54,500	10/13/90	2/4/69	M	S
24	2344	Nemesha	Mehta	Engineering	Engineer	65,000	10/1/95	2/12/65	F	S

Ready

Documentation \ Employee Data /

FIGURE 5.13

Sorting with a custom sort order

anotherway

. . . to Increase or Decrease a Worksheet's Zoom Percentage

If you have a wheel button on your mouse, then you can use it in conjunction with the Ctrl key to quickly increase or decrease a worksheet's zoom percentage. Press and hold the **Ctrl** button and scroll the wheel button one direction to decrease the zoom percentage in small increments. Similarly, press and hold the **Ctrl** button and scroll the wheel button the opposite direction to increase the zoom percentage in small increments. Release the Ctrl button when you are done

Changing the Zoom Setting of a Worksheet

Sometimes it is handy to get a bird's eye view of a worksheet—to back up and view a larger portion of it on screen. Normally, Excel displays a worksheet at 100 percent magnification. The Zoom command of the View command (or the Zoom list box on the Standard toolbar) provides several preset viewing percentages, or you can specify an exact percentage of magnification. To view more of a worksheet—more columns and rows—you reduce the Zoom percentage. Similarly, you can zoom in and carefully examine a portion of a worksheet by increasing the Zoom percentage. Experiment with the Zoom percentage.

Decreasing the Zoom percentage:

1. Click **View** on the menu bar and then click **Zoom**

2. Click the **50%** option button to reduce the worksheet display to 50% of its normal size (see Figure 5.14)

3. Click **OK** to reduce the worksheet to 50% magnification

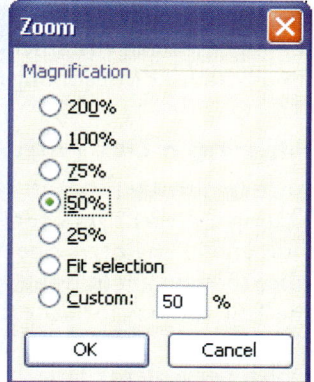

Zoom

Magnification

- ○ 200%
- ○ 100%
- ○ 75%
- ◉ 50%
- ○ 25%
- ○ Fit selection
- ○ Custom: 50 %

OK   Cancel

FIGURE 5.14

Zoom dialog box

EXCEL

When you want to zoom in for a close inspection of a few cells on the worksheet, you can do so by increasing the Zoom percentage to a value greater than 100 percent.

Increasing the Zoom percentage:

1. Click the **Zoom** control list arrow on the Standard toolbar

2. Click **200%**. Examine the worksheet

3. Return the worksheet to its normal display by clicking the **Zoom** control list arrow on the Standard toolbar and then clicking **100%**

4. Save the **Employee1.xls** workbook to preserve the work you completed in this session

SESSION 5.1

making *the grade*

1. A column of a data list is also called a _____.

2. A data list's row is also called what?

3. Execute the _____ _____ command of the Window menu to freeze rows and columns.

4. A _____ _____ is a dialog box displaying one row of a list in text boxes.

5. You can sort a list in order on a field containing department names by first creating a _____ list containing those names.

SESSION 5.2 CREATING FILTERS AND SUBTOTALS

In this section, you will learn how to create data filters to hide selected rows, how to apply conditional formats to draw attention to selected cells in the employee list, and how to insert subtotals beneath groups of related employee records.

Using Filters to Analyze a List

When viewing a long data list such as the employee list or lists with hundreds or thousands of rows, you may want to view just a portion of the list. For example, if you want to view records of customers who live in Michigan from your list of 3,000 customers, then you could sort the list on the State field and then scroll down to the section containing Michigan customers. Locating a group of records by sorting and scrolling is tedious and time-consuming. Filtering a list is easier.

Filtering a List with AutoFilter

Alice frequently needs to have a list of the engineers who work for Comsec. She is putting together a brochure that outlines the background and capabilities of the company and its engineers. She wants to list the names and clearance levels of the engineers. Alice thought about using a data form and specifying the search criteria "engineer" in the Title text box to locate the engineers, but that method displays only one record at a time. The best way to display the list of engineers is to ask Excel to list only records that match particular criteria, hiding the rows that do not. This method is called *filtering*.

Other Office products use filtering too. Microsoft Access uses filtering to retrieve rows that satisfy criteria through its query facility.

---

task reference   Filtering a List with AutoFilter

- Click any cell in the list

- Click **Data**, point to **Filter**, and click **AutoFilter** to turn each column into a list box with a list arrow beside each label

- Click the list arrow next to the label you want to use as a filter

- Click the criteria in the drop-down list by which you want to filter the list

---

AutoFilter is the filtering command that allows you to hide all rows in a list except those that match the criteria you specify. You will create a filter on the Title column to list the employees with the title "Engineer."

Filtering a list with the AutoFilter command:

1. Save the employee workbook as **Employee2.xls** to establish a new workbook name for this session

2. Click any cell within the employee list

3. Click **Data** on the menu bar, point to **Filter**, and click **AutoFilter**. Excel places list box arrows next to each label in the list's heading row

4. Click the **Title column** list arrow to display the filtering criteria available for that column. Excel analyzes each column, sorts it, and removes the duplicate values to form the filtering list for each column (see Figure 5.15)

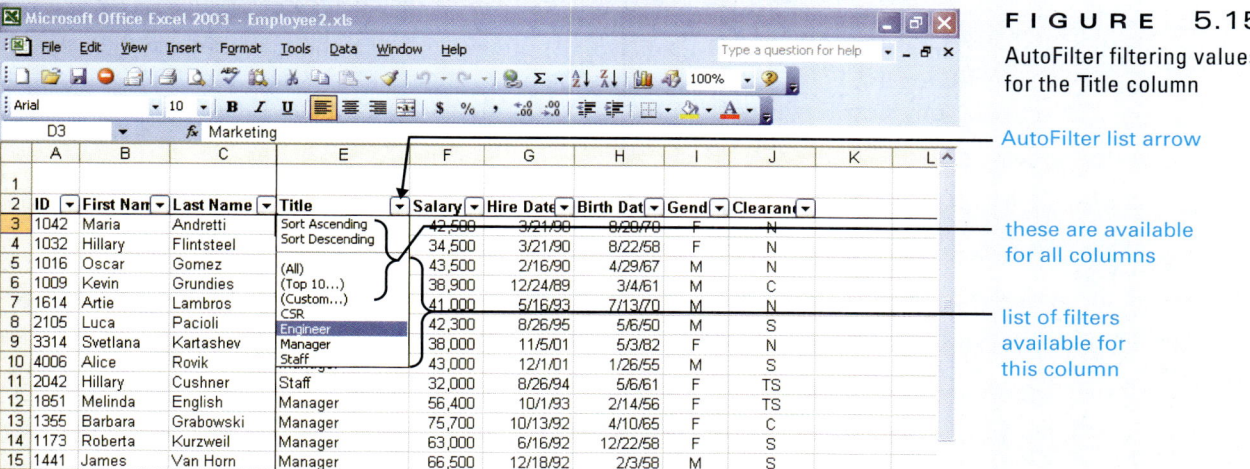

FIGURE 5.15

AutoFilter filtering values for the Title column

AutoFilter list arrow

these are available for all columns

list of filters available for this column

5. Click **Engineer** to hide all employees except those containing "Engineer" in the Title column

Excel counts the total number of records it filters and the total number of records and displays those numbers in the status bar ("12 of 27 records"). Missing rows are hidden, not deleted (see Figure 5.16).

FIGURE 5.16

Filtering records

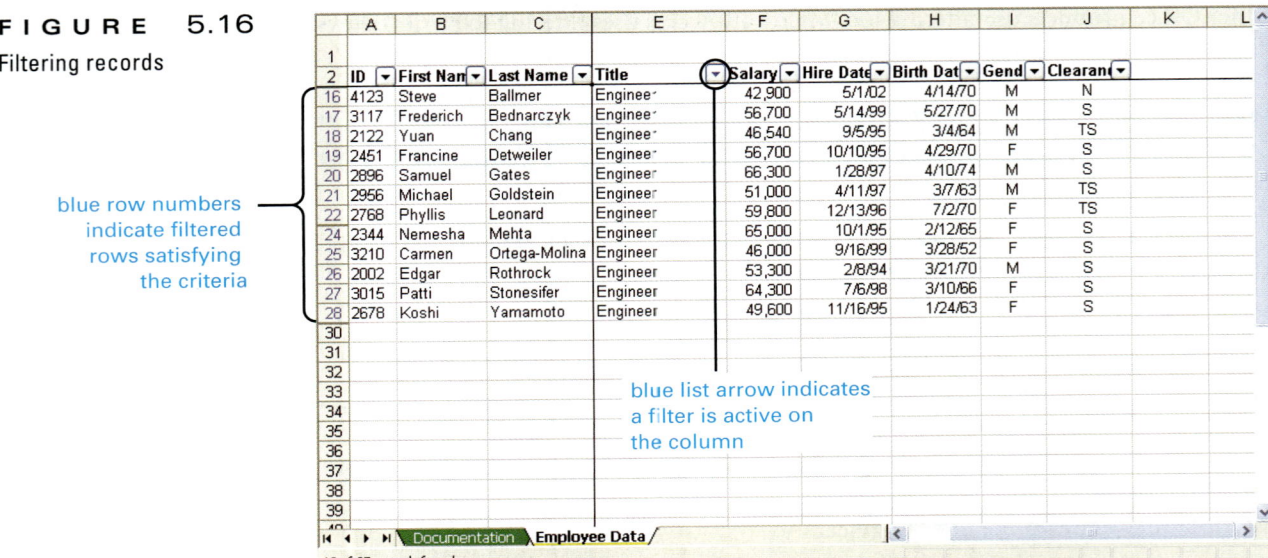

blue row numbers indicate filtered rows satisfying the criteria

blue list arrow indicates a filter is active on the column

12 of 27 records found

anotherword   . . . on Filtering a List

Because AutoFilter hides entire rows in the active sheet that do not match the AutoFilter criteria, avoid placing other worksheet information in the same rows as the list. Though outside the list, information in the same list as a hidden row is hidden also

Three filter choices appear in all list columns. They are *All*, *Top 10*, and *Custom*. *All* displays all items in the list and removes filtering from the column. *Top 10* displays the top or bottom *n* items, when sorted, in the list. You can click *Custom* to specify more complex filtering criteria.

The AutoFilter list also displays the choices *(Blanks)* and *(NonBlanks)* at the bottom of the AutoFilter list for any column that contains at least one blank entry. The (Blanks) and (NonBlanks) choices are handy because they allow you to display rows whose selected field contains blanks. Blank entries are often errors, and locating them can be difficult in long lists.

With any criteria in effect, you can refine your query by using several AutoFilter drop-down filters in tandem. Doing so further restricts the rows that appear in the filtered list. For example, if you want a list of engineers who have top secret clearances, you select Engineer from the Title drop-down filter list and then select TS from the Clearance drop-down list to combine filtering criteria.

Filtering a list with multiple criteria:

1. With the Title filter criteria ("Engineer") still in effect, click the **Clearance column** list arrow

2. Click **TS** in the Clearance filter list to limit rows to engineers with a top secret clearance (see Figure 5.17)

FIGURE 5.17

Using multiple criteria to filter a list

Filter criteria: "Engineer"   Filter criteria: "TS"

	A	B	C	E	F	G	H	I	J	K	L
1											
2	ID	First Nam	Last Name	Title	Salary	Hire Date	Birth Dat	Gender	Clearan		
18	2122	Yuan	Chang	Engineer	46,540	9/5/95	3/4/64	M	TS		
21	2956	Michael	Goldstein	Engineer	51,000	4/11/97	3/7/63	M	TS		
22	2768	Phyllis	Leonard	Engineer	59,800	12/13/96	7/2/70	F	TS		
30											

3. Remove the Clearance column filter by clicking the **Clearance column** list arrow and then by clicking **(All)** at the top of the list

- Click **Data**, point to **Filter**
- Click **Show All**

Removing all AutoFilter list filters:

1. Click **Data** on the menu bar

2. Point to **Filter** and then click **Show All**. All the records reappear, but the AutoFilter list arrows remain next to each column heading

Using Custom AutoFilters

The AutoFilters you applied in the preceding examples work for **exact match criteria**—criteria in which a row's field exactly matches a particular filter value. With custom criteria, you can specify the low and high values range that a field must satisfy instead of a single value.

Custom AutoFilters allow you to specify other relationships besides "is equal to." You specify criteria using any of the six relational operators: Less than, less than or equal to, greater than, greater than or equal to, or not equal to, or equal to. A **relational operator** compares two values, and the expression containing the values and the conditional operator result in either true or false. Relational operators in Excel expressions are written as the symbols $<, <=, =, >, >=, <>$. In Custom AutoFilters, relational operators appear in a list box as English phrases such as "is greater than or equal to" rather than their symbolic equivalent such as "$>=$".

Alice wants to send out mailers to all male employees who were born in the 1960s because a company policy change affects their health benefits. While she could sort the list and try to write down the affected employees' names born between 1960 and 1969 (inclusive), she knows that using a custom AutoFilter is a better solution.

Creating a more complex AutoFilter:

1. With all criteria cleared but the AutoFilter list arrows still visible, click the **Birth Date** column list arrow. The criteria filter list appears below the Birth Date column heading

2. Click **(Custom...)** to display the Custom AutoFilter dialog box (see Figure 5.18)

3. Click the top left list box and then click **is greater than or equal to**

4. Click the top right list box and then type **1/1/1960**

5. Click the **And** option button, if necessary

6. Click the bottom left list box and then click **is less than or equal to**

7. Click the bottom right list box and then type **12/31/1969** in the list box (see Figure 5.19)

8. Click **OK** to apply the custom filter and display the filtered employee list

FIGURE   5.18

Custom AutoFilter dialog box

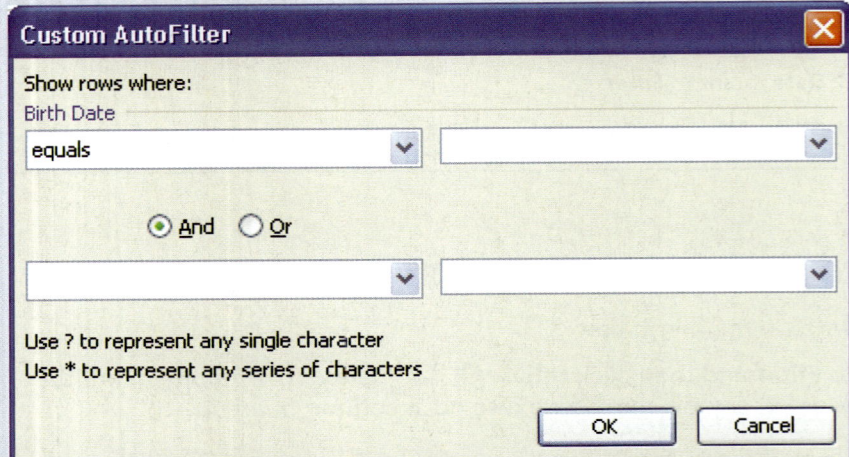

FIGURE   5.19

Custom AutoFilter dialog box with filters filled in

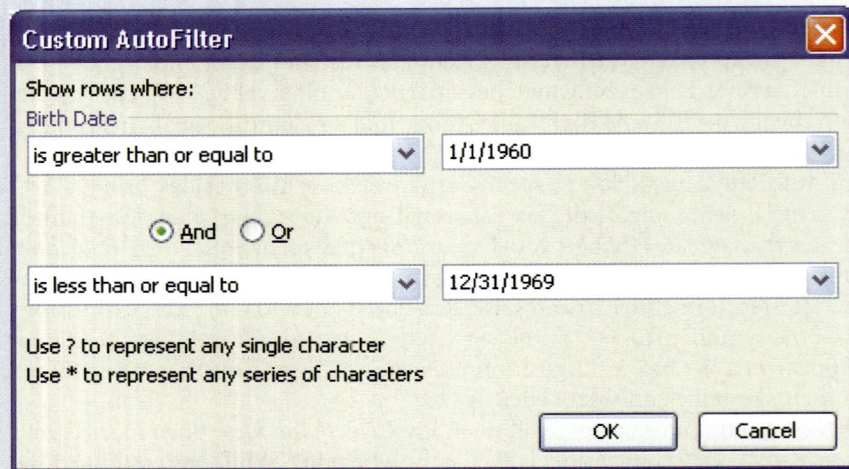

9. Click the **Gender** column list arrow. The criteria filter list appears below the Gender column heading

10. Click **M** in the Gender filter list to further restrict the list to males. Excel filters the list producing the required list of males born in the 1960s (see Figure 5.20)

FIGURE   5.20

Filtered list of males born in the 1960s

Criteria 1: born in the 1960s   Criteria 2: Male

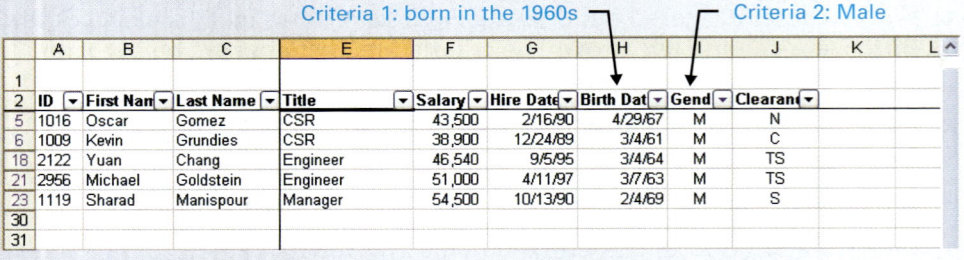

	ID	First Name	Last Name	Title	Salary	Hire Date	Birth Date	Gender	Clearance
2	ID	First Nam	Last Name	Title	Salary	Hire Date	Birth Dat	Gend	Clearan
5	1016	Oscar	Gomez	CSR	43,500	2/16/90	4/29/67	M	N
6	1009	Kevin	Grundies	CSR	38,900	12/24/89	3/4/61	M	C
18	2122	Yuan	Chang	Engineer	46,540	9/5/95	3/4/64	M	TS
21	2956	Michael	Goldstein	Engineer	51,000	4/11/97	3/7/63	M	TS
23	1119	Sharad	Manispour	Manager	54,500	10/13/90	2/4/69	M	S

Alice wants to interview the employees whose records are shown in Figure 5.20 in order of their birth data—oldest to youngest. She asks you to sort the list on the Birth Date field and then show her the resulting list (still filtered). After Alice reviews the list, she wants you to remove the AutoFilter so that all the employee rows reappear.

Sorting a filtered list and then restoring hidden rows:

1. Click any cell in the **Birth Date** column—inside the list, the column label, or outside the list

2. Click the **Sort Ascending** ▲↓ button on the Standard toolbar to sort the list in ascending birth date order. The filtered list appears in ascending birth date order

3. Click **Data** on the menu bar, point to **Filter**, and click **AutoFilter** to remove all filters. (You cannot undo the result of removing an AutoFilter)

Using Subtotals to Analyze a List

Whenever you have an Excel list with data whose columns each contain one type of data—a database or list such as the employee worksheet, for example—you can produce summary information about the numeric columns. The Employee worksheet is a typical example. With data arranged in order by department, it is convenient to insert SUM functions to compute the total salary of each department. Although you could write four SUM functions to total the salaries of all employees in each department, Excel provides a more convenient solution—the Subtotals command.

help yourself *Press **F1**, type **subtotal** in the Search text box of the Microsoft Excel Help task pane, and press **Enter**. Click the hyperlink **About subtotals** and then read the help information describing how the Subtotals command works. When you are done, click the Help screen **Close** button or click the **Print** icon in the toolbar to print the Help screen. Close the task pane*

Subtotals offers several list summary features including count, sum, average, minimum, and maximum—the same features provided by the stand-alone statistical functions of COUNTA, SUM, AVERAGE, MIN, and MAX. Unlike those functions, the Subtotals command automatically creates the appropriate formula when it senses a change in the value of a specified field. For the employee list, that field could be Department. Subtotals also provides the added convenience of outlining whereby you can display the rows that constitute a group or you can collapse the list, hiding all rows except the subtotal rows. Excel handles the details of hiding and revealing list rows as needed. The only requirement for the Subtotals command to do its work properly is that the list be sorted so that it is in order by the field you specify as the grouping field before you use the subtotals command.

How Subtotals Are Built

task reference	Subtotaling a List's Entries

- Sort the list by the column whose groups you want to subtotal
- Click any cell inside the list
- Click **Data** and then click **Subtotals**
- In the *At each change in* list box, click the name of the group on which you want a subtotal
- From the *Use function* list box, select the aggregate function you want to use
- In the *Add subtotal to* list box, select the column(s) containing the values you want to aggregate; in the *Add subtotal to* list box, clear the column(s) containing checkmarks for any values you *do not* want to aggregate
- Click **OK**

Alice wants to view the total salaries by department and the total of all departments' salaries. In preparation, first sort the list into order by Department, which is the field upon which subtotals are created. Remember, the last time you sorted the list, you used a custom sort list. You have to remove that list to sort the Department field in a "normal" way. First, you will remove the custom sort order.

Canceling a custom sort order:

1. Click cell **H3**, click **Data** on the menu bar, click **Sort**, and click the **Options** button to open the Sort Options dialog box (see Figure 5.12)
2. Click the **First key sort order** list box, and then click **Normal** at the top of the list
3. Click **OK** to close the Sort Options dialog box, and then click **OK** to close the Sort dialog box

Now you can sort the list in alphabetical order by department, because you canceled the custom Department sort order.

Sorting a list prior to creating subtotals:

1. Click cell **D3**, the first data cell under the Department column label
2. Click the **Sort Ascending** ![sort ascending icon] button on the Standard toolbar

Now that the list is sorted into department order, you can create summary information about departments. Because Alice wants a sum of salaries by department and the grand total salary value, you use the Subtotals command.

Summing salaries by departments:

1. Click **Data** on the menu bar and then click **Subtotals**. The Subtotal dialog box opens
2. Click the **At each change in** list box and then click **Department** in the drop-down list to tell Excel to create subtotals by department
3. Click the **Use function** list box and then click **Sum**. You want to sum the salary field, not count or average it
4. Scroll to the top of the *Add subtotal to* list box, then slowly scroll down the Add subtotal to list and remove any checkmarks in the column name check boxes
5. Scroll the list, if necessary, to locate and then click the **Salary** check box to place a checkmark in it. Salary is the column you want to sum (see Figure 5.21)
6. Ensure that the *Replace current subtotals* and the *Summary below data* check boxes are checked and that the *Page break between groups* check box is clear (see Figure 5.21)

tip: *By default, the* Replace current subtotals *check box is checked, meaning the subtotal you specify will replace the selected list's current subtotal. However, if you want to use more than one function, sum and average for example, you can execute the Data Subtotals a second time and specify the second subtotal function. The second time, however, deselect the* Replace current subtotals *check box to display both subtotal functions at once. You can repeat this for as many subtotal functions as you want for a group*

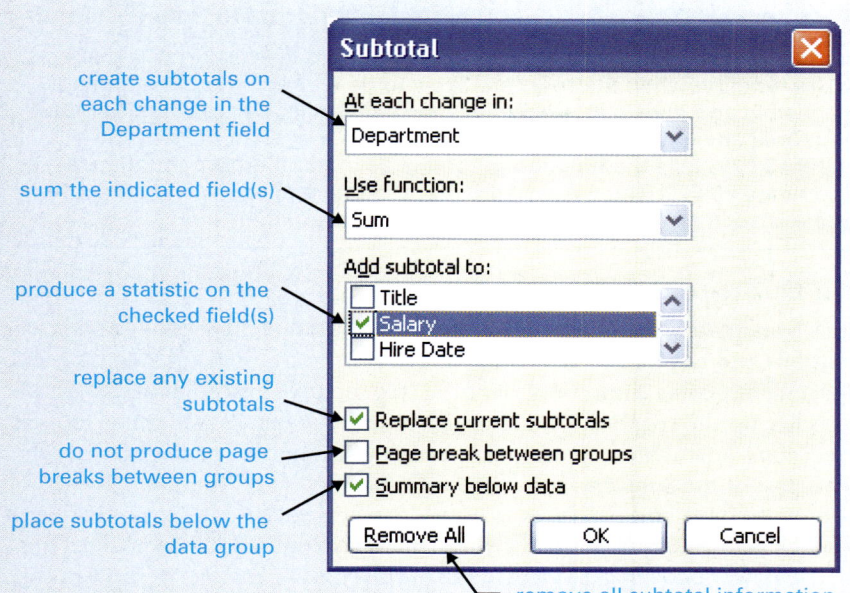

F I G U R E   5.21

Completed Subtotal
dialog box

create subtotals on each change in the Department field

sum the indicated field(s)

produce a statistic on the checked field(s)

replace any existing subtotals

do not produce page breaks between groups

place subtotals below the data group

remove all subtotal information

7. Click **OK** to insert the subtotals below each department group and the grand total below the last group's subtotal (see Figure 5.22)

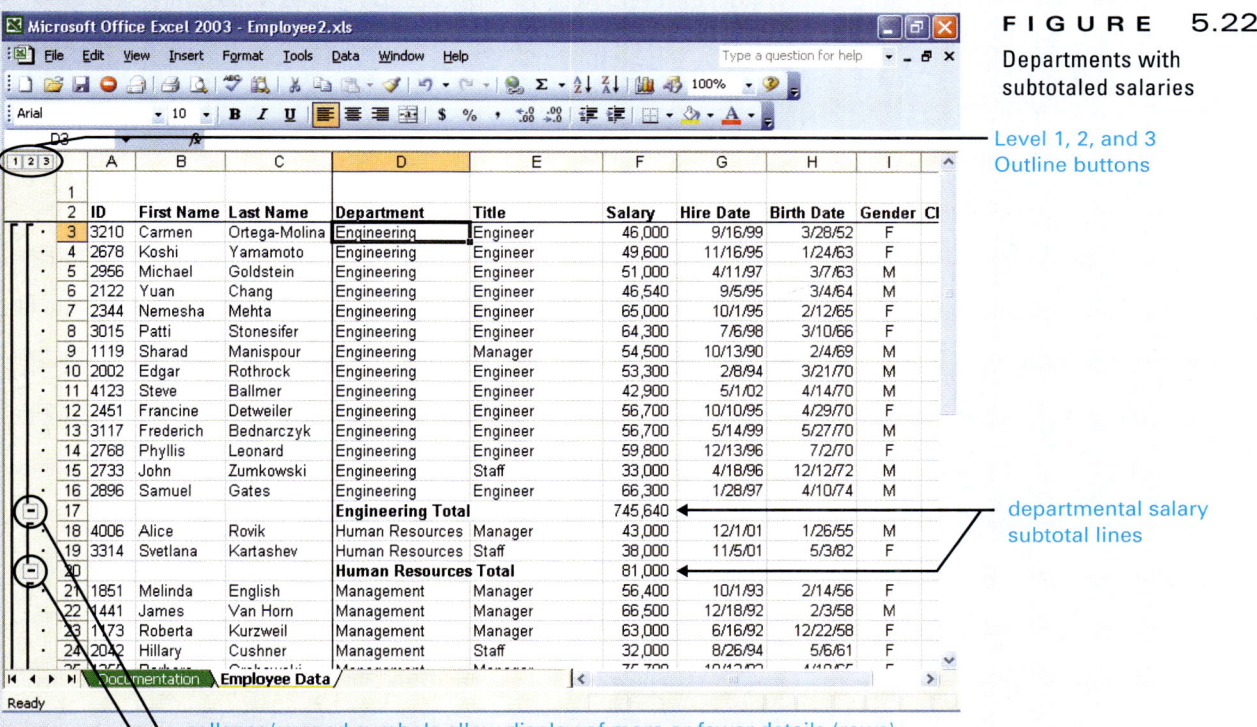

F I G U R E   5.22

Departments with subtotaled salaries

Level 1, 2, and 3 Outline buttons

departmental salary subtotal lines

collapse/expand symbols allow display of more or fewer details (rows)

8. Scroll through the list to view each department's subtotal and the total salary value for all departments (the value is 1,362,940, which is in cell F34)

9. If necessary, widen column F so that the total salary displays. Click cell **F34** containing the total salary for all departments, click **Format** on the menu bar, point to **Column**, and click **AutoFit Selection**. The column enlarges enough to display the total in cell F34

---

another*word*   . . . **on Using Subtotal to Sum a Column**

If you want to sum a column of numbers such as employees' salaries, avoid using the SUM function when the rows are likely to be filtered. The SUM function adds both visible and invisible cells in the specified range, whereas the Subtotal function ignores any hidden cells (rows) in the range. For example, writing **=Subtotal(9,F3:F29)** tells the function to total (9 as the first argument) the *visible* cells in the range F3:F29. The value of the first argument specifies the subtotal function to use such as average, min, count, and so on

---

Using the Subtotals Outline View

The subtotals by department are very handy and easy to create. Alice also wants to see just the subtotals and not all the details about the rows that are in each department. Upper management people commonly want the "big picture" instead of all the details. Often, the higher up the corporate ladder one is, the fewer details one needs to make sweeping decisions. Fortunately, Excel makes creating summaries a snap with another feature that is part of the Subtotals command—Outlines.

The Subtotals command produces two results when you use it. Not only does it produce subtotal statistics for identified groups, but it also outlines the worksheet's list. You can choose how much detail to view in the outline by clicking one of three outline buttons located at the top left side of the worksheet (see Figure 5.22). Commonly, the highest level, 3, is active. It displays all active list members, subtotals, and the grand total. Level 2 hides the individual list-member rows but displays subtotal information. The lowest level of detail, level 1, displays only the grand total information. Try the outline buttons to see how they work by doing the next exercise.

Using the outline feature of the subtotals:

1. Make D3—the upper leftmost cell in the frozen panels—the active cell by pressing **Ctrl+Home**

2. Click the **Level 2 Outline** [2] button (see Figure 5.23). Notice that the departmental salary subtotals and grand total appear, but Excel hides the detail rows

FIGURE   5.23

Level 2 outline

outline level buttons

outline expand buttons

grand total ——   —— group subtotals

3. Click the **Expand** [+] button to the left of row 26 to expand the Management department details

4. Click the **Level 1 Outline** [1] button to hide all information in the list except the grand total

5. Click the **Level 3 Outline** [3] button to expose all departments' detail rows

Although the employee list is relatively short, you can see how outlining a really long list can be useful. It allows anyone to see an overview of crucial statistics without having to see the details at the same time. Removing details helps a viewer focus on the "bottom line," much the same way a chart does.

Inserting Page Breaks into a List with Subtotals

Alice wants to distribute the employee information to four department heads for their use. Because she wants to keep each department's information confidential among the departments, she wants to print each department's employee information on a separate page so that she can distribute the four one-page reports to each department head. Though the worksheet prints on one page, you can create your own page breaks easily.

Inserting page breaks into a list containing subtotals:

1. Click **Data** on the menu bar and then click **Subtotals** to display the Subtotal dialog box

2. Click the **Page break between groups** check box (see Figure 5.21) to place a checkmark in it

3. Click **OK** to close the Subtotal dialog box. Dashed lines appear on the worksheet where Excel inserts page breaks

4. Click the **Print Preview** button on the Standard toolbar

5. Click the **Next** button on the Print Preview toolbar. Look at the top of the page (zoom in if necessary). Notice that the column labels do not appear at the top of the second page, but they do appear on the top of the first page

6. Click the **Close** button on the Print Preview toolbar to close the Print Preview window

Printing Row and Column Titles on Each Page

You noticed as you reviewed the worksheet in the previous exercise that the column headings appear only on the first page. Typically, you should display column headings on every page so that a reader does not have to leaf back to the first page to see the headings. Similarly, if you have a wide output in which every other page displays columns in the right half of a worksheet, you can tell Excel to print row headings in the first column of every page.

task reference — Displaying Row or Column Headings on Each Page

- Click **File** and then click **Page Setup**

- Click the **Sheet** tab

- Click the **Collapse dialog box** button on the **Rows to repeat at top** or **Columns to repeat at left** text boxes in the Print titles section

- Select the row(s) or column(s) you want to print on each page

- Click the **Expand dialog box** button again to reveal the Page Setup dialog box

- Click **OK**

Printing selected rows on each page:

1. Click **File** on the menu bar, click **Page Setup** to open the Page Setup dialog box, and then click the **Sheet** tab

2. Click the **Collapse dialog box** 🔳 button to the right of the **Rows to repeat at top**

3. Click the row 2 header to select the entire row, and then click the **Expand dialog box** 🔲 button to restore the Page Setup dialog box (see Figure 5.24)

FIGURE   5.24

Seleting a row to repeat on every page

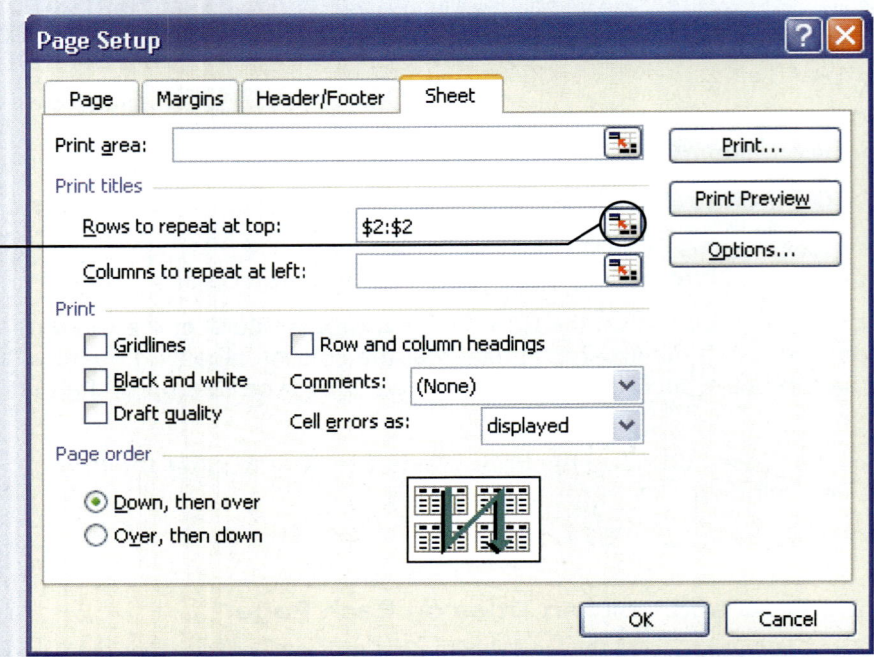

Collapse dialog box button

4. Click **OK**

5. Click the **Print Preview** button on the Standard toolbar and then click the **Next** button repeatedly to preview each output page and confirm that the first output line—the column labels—appears on every page

6. Click the **Close** button on the Print Preview toolbar

Clearing All Subtotal Information

You can remove subtotal information by executing the Data Subtotals command and then clicking a button that removes all totals.

Removing subtotals from a list:

1. Click any cell within the list, including a subtotal row, and then click **Data** on the menu bar

2. Click **Subtotals**. The Subtotal dialog box opens

3. Click the **Remove All** button. Excel removes all subtotal rows and closes the Subtotal dialog box

Manually Inserting and Removing Page Breaks

Excel removes all subtotal information from the employee worksheet and displays all employee rows. Excel allows you to insert manually your own page breaks without using the Subtotals command. Similar to the way you insert page breaks in Microsoft Word documents, Excel provides a Page Break command on the Insert menu.

Manually inserting page breaks into a worksheet:

1. Click the **row 17 header** button
2. Click **Insert** on the menu bar, and then click **Page Break**. Excel inserts a page break above the selected row and displays a dashed line to indicate the position of the page break
3. Repeat steps 1 and 2 two more times but substitute row headers **19** and then **24** in step 1. When you are done, Excel displays page breaks following rows 16, 18, and 23
4. Click any cell to deselect row 24
5. Click the **Print Preview** button on the Standard toolbar
6. Click repeatedly the **Next** button on the Print Preview toolbar to view each of the remaining three pages. Notice that the column heading row prints on each page because you set that option in an earlier series of steps
7. Click the **Close** button when you are finished previewing the page breaks

You can easily remove all manually inserted page breaks. Do that next.

Removing all page breaks from a worksheet:

1. Click the **Select All** button located at the intersection of the row heading and the column heading of the worksheet

tip: *You can press **Ctrl+A** to select all worksheet cells if you prefer*

2. Click **Insert** on the menu bar and then click **Reset All Page Breaks**. Excel removes all page breaks

Applying Conditional Formatting

Managers often want to highlight unusual values in a worksheet to draw attention to them. Perhaps you want to highlight exceptional sales volume, superior quality measures, or cars with unusually high repair costs. One way to highlight exceptional values is to locate a value you want to highlight, click Format on the menu bar, and then specify a series of format changes such as a background color or a change in the font color. While this is one solution, it is both laborious and error-prone.

Excel provides a better solution: *conditional formatting.* Conditional formatting automatically takes effect in a cell whenever the data in the cell satisfy criteria that you specify when you create the conditional format. Conditional formatting is an easy way to highlight significant values, because you can format a group of cells at once. Only the cells that meet the specified criteria display under the control of the conditional format. Cells containing the conditional format but not meeting the criteria display normally.

For example, suppose you are tracking accounts receivable and want to display groups of values in different font colors. To display accounts with a balance of more than $10,000 in blue, you can use conditional formatting. Balances less than or equal to $10,000 display in their usual black color.

---

task reference — Applying a Conditional Format to Cells

- Click the cell range to which you want to apply a conditional format
- Click **Format** on the menu bar and then click **Conditional Formatting**
- Enter the criteria for which Excel is to apply the special formatting
- Click the **Format** button on the Conditional Formatting dialog box, select the font color, style, underlining, borders, or other formatting to apply conditionally
- Click **OK** to close the Conditional Formatting dialog box
- Click **OK** to apply the conditional formatting to the selected cell(s)

Alice would like to highlight employee salaries that are at least $55,000. This will help her quickly identify the highest-paid employees. She asks you to apply a conditional format to the Salary column so that any value equal to or greater than $55,000 displays a background color of red and a font color of white.

Applying a conditional format to the Salary column:

1. Select cell range **F3:F29**

   tip: *You can select a filled partial column of cells by clicking the first cell (F3 in this case), holding the* **Shift** *key, tapping the* **End** *key, and then tapping the* **Down Arrow** *key*

2. Click **Format** on the menu bar and click **Conditional Formatting** to open the Conditional Formatting dialog box

3. Ensure that **Cell Value Is** appears in the first list box for Condition 1, because the Salary column contains values, not formulas that compute and display values

4. Click in the second list box for Condition 1 to display a list of choices and then click the **greater than or equal to** choice

5. Click in the third list box for Condition 1 and then type **55000**

6. Click the **Format** button in the Conditional Formatting dialog box. The Format Cells dialog box opens

7. Click the **Font** tab, if necessary, click the **Color** list box arrow, and then click the **white square** (fifth row from the top, eighth column) in the Font Color palette

8. Click the **Patterns** tab and then click the **red square** (third row from the top, first column)

9. Click **OK** to close the Format Cells dialog box (see Figure 5.25)

10. Click **OK** to apply the conditional formatting to the selected cell range

11. Click **Ctrl+Home** to make D3 the active cell. Excel displays 10 cells in the Salary column with the special conditional format (see Figure 5.26)

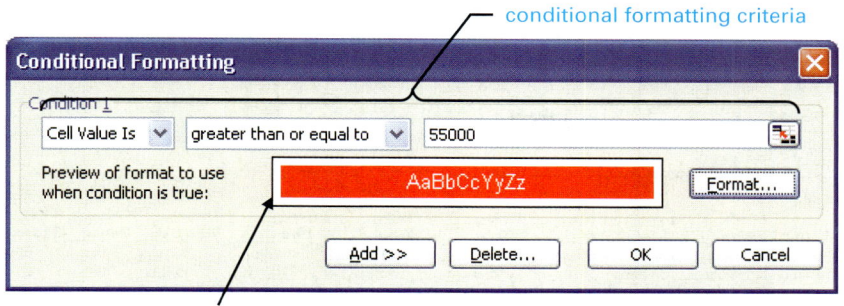

FIGURE 5.25

Setting conditional formatting criteria and format options

conditional formatting criteria

conditional formatting: red background and white characters

FIGURE 5.26

Selected cells displaying the conditional format

	ID	First Name	Last Name	Department	Title	Salary	Hire Date	Birth Date	Gender	Cleara
3	3210	Carmen	Ortega-Molina	Engineering	Engineer	46,000	9/16/99	3/28/52	F	S
4	2678	Koshi	Yamamoto	Engineering	Engineer	49,600	11/16/95	1/24/63	F	S
5	2956	Michael	Goldstein	Engineering	Engineer	51,000	4/11/97	3/7/63	M	TS
6	2122	Yuan	Chang	Engineering	Engineer	46,540	9/5/95	3/4/64	M	TS
7	2344	Nemesha	Mehta	Engineering	Engineer	65,000	10/1/95	2/12/65	F	S
8	3015	Patti	Stonesifer	Engineering	Engineer	64,300	7/6/98	3/10/66	F	S
9	1119	Sharad	Manispour	Engineering	Manager	54,500	10/13/90	2/4/69	M	S
10	2002	Edgar	Rothrock	Engineering	Engineer	53,300	2/8/94	3/21/70	M	S
11	4123	Steve	Ballmer	Engineering	Engineer	42,900	5/1/02	4/14/70	M	N
12	2451	Francine	Detweiler	Engineering	Engineer	56,700	10/10/95	4/29/70	F	S
13	3117	Frederich	Bednarczyk	Engineering	Engineer	56,700	5/14/99	5/27/70	M	S
14	2768	Phyllis	Leonard	Engineering	Engineer	59,800	12/13/96	7/2/70	F	TS
15	2733	John	Zumkowski	Engineering	Staff	33,000	4/18/96	12/12/72	M	TS
16	2896	Samuel	Gates	Engineering	Engineer	66,300	1/28/97	4/10/74	M	S
17	4006	Alice	Rovik	Human Resources	Manager	43,000	12/1/01	1/26/55	M	S
18	3314	Svetlana	Kartashev	Human Resources	Staff	38,000	11/5/01	5/3/82	F	N
19	1851	Melinda	English	Management	Manager	56,400	10/1/93	2/14/56	F	TS
20	1441	James	Van Horn	Management	Manager	66,500	12/18/92	2/3/58	M	S
21	1173	Roberta	Kurzweil	Management	Manager	63,000	6/16/92	12/22/58	F	S
22	2042	Hillary	Cushner	Management	Staff	32,000	8/26/94	5/6/61	F	TS
23	1355	Barbara	Grabowski	Management	Manager	75,700	10/13/92	4/10/65	F	C
24	2105	Luca	Pacioli	Marketing	Staff	42,300	8/26/95	5/6/50	M	S
25	1032	Hillary	Flintsteel	Marketing	Staff	34,500	3/21/90	8/22/58	F	N
26	1009	Kevin	Grundies	Marketing	CSR	38,900	12/24/89	3/4/61	M	C
27	1016	Oscar	Gomez	Marketing	CSR	43,500	2/16/90	4/29/67	M	N
28	1614	Artie	Lambros	Marketing	CSR	41,000	5/16/93	7/13/70	M	N
29	1042	Maria	Andretti	Marketing	CSR	42,500	3/21/90	8/20/70	F	N

Documentation Employee Data

If the value of any of the Salary cells changes and no longer meets the criteria for the conditional format, then Excel displays the cell in the usual way without the conditional format. The conditional format remains with the cells until you either reformat the cells or clear their formats.

Deleting a conditional format:

1. Select cell range **F3:F29**, the range of cells containing the conditional format

2. Click **Format** on the menu bar and click **Conditional Formatting** to open the Conditional Formatting dialog box

3. Click the **Delete** button on the Conditional Formatting dialog box. The Delete Conditional Format dialog box opens

4. Click the **Condition 1** check box to place a checkmark in it (see Figure 5.27), click **OK** to confirm your choice, and close the Delete Conditional Format dialog box

5. Click **OK** to close the Conditional Formatting dialog box and remove the conditional formatting from the selected cell range

FIGURE 5.27

Deleting a conditional format

cells with conditional format are highlighted

check *Condition 1* to delete that conditional format

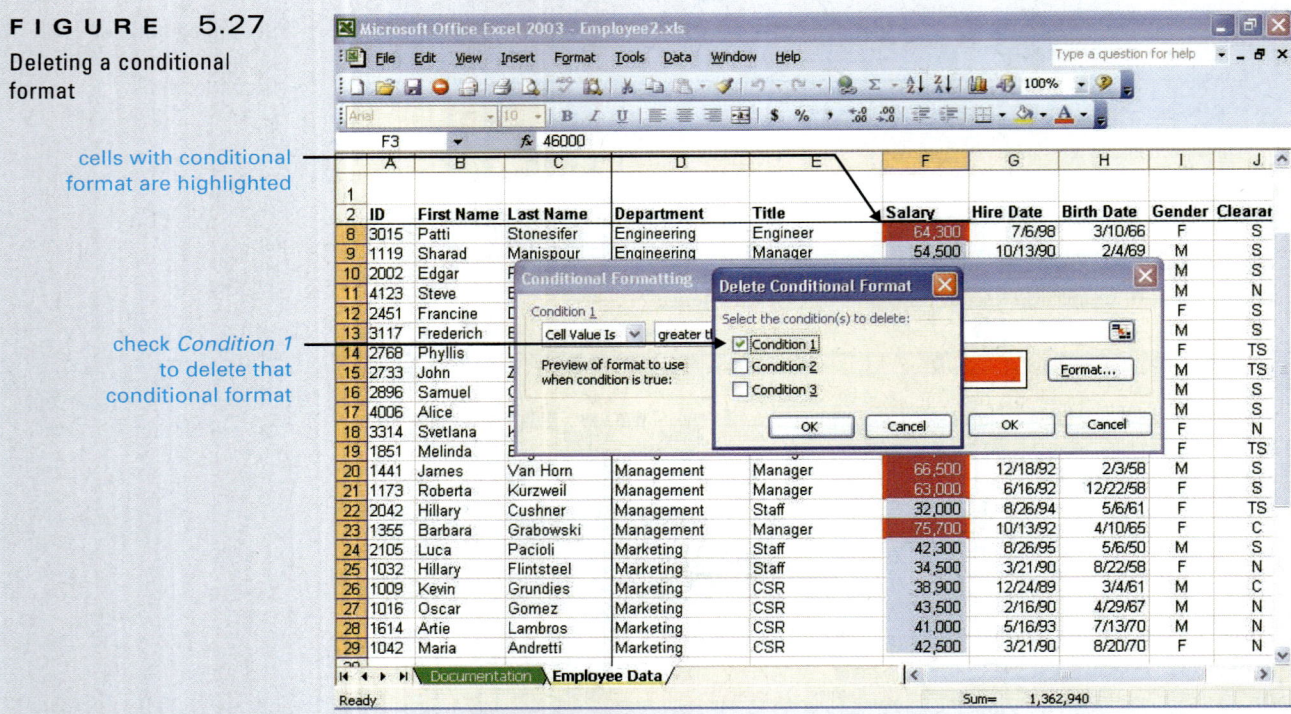

6. Press **Ctrl+Home** to make cell D3 active

7. Click the **Save** button on the Standard toolbar to save this version of the Employee worksheet **(Employee2.xls)**, close the worksheet, but leave Excel running. If you decide to take a break, close Excel. Remember to open Excel again before beginning Session 5.3

SESSION 5.2

making the grade

1. You have a list of 635 employees who work at the university and you want to print the list of employees who work in Warren Hall. You would use the _____ command from the menu bar to list the subset of employees who work in Warren Hall.

2. In order to print a list of banks in South Florida in order by City and then by bank name within each city, you would do what?

3. Suppose you want to display employees who earn $40,000 or less per year. How would you produce a list of those employees? Assume that the salary information is in a column called "Salary."

4. A list called Monthly Customer Sales contains sale dates, customer names, customer addresses, and total value of sales in three columns labeled "Sale Date," "Customer," "Address," and "Sales." Any customer may have several sales recorded in the list when he or she makes more than one purchase in the month. Describe in a sentence or two how you would produce a list, grouped by customer name, displaying each customer's list of sales followed by a total of all sales for each customer and a grand total for the month.

5. In a column containing dates, you could highlight selected dates—say dates that occur before June 14, 1980—by using the Cells command on the Format menu and applying font attributes to the selected cells directly. A better choice would be to execute a command that forces Excel to automatically highlight dates occurring before June 14, 1980. What is that command?

SESSION 5.3 CREATING AND USING PIVOT TABLES

In this section, you will learn how to summarize data in an Excel list to provide insights that are otherwise masked by the size and volume of data in a list.

Pivot Table Basics

Pivot tables provide a three-dimensional view of data that is often too complicated to understand in its raw list form. A **pivot table** is an interactive table enabling you quickly to group and summarize large amounts of data. The employee list is an example of a list that you could create a pivot table from in order to locate hidden information from the list. Pivot tables summarizing longer data lists are particularly valuable tools for revealing the information hidden in the details. A pivot table uses a two-dimensional list to create a three-dimensional table that summarizes large amounts of information in a small amount of space. Pivot tables are interactive because you can drag a field to another location and thus pivot the structure of the table. Pivot table data are linked to their underlying two-dimensional list. You can change the data in one or more parts of the list and then execute the Refresh pivot table command to recalculate the summary information.

In order to create a pivot table from data, the data must meet certain criteria. First, the data must be in tabular form. Each column must have a unique column label to identify each field. Each row must represent a unique fact or piece of data. Third, date values in the list should be formatted with a date format. Fourth, remove blank rows or columns from the list so Excel can easily identify the complete unbroken list.

Pivot tables can contain these elements: **row fields**, **column fields**, and **page fields**. Frequently, data such as year, gender, ID number, sales date, birth date, or hire date appear in pivot tables as row, column, or page fields. Numeric data appear in pivot tables' central position—**data fields**. The data fields contain the summary information such as average sales, average age, total sales, number of sales per month, or number of students in the sophomore class. The ability to move row fields to column fields and vice versa—to pivot the data—is the origin of the name for this analytical tool.

Pivot tables can help you simplify and understand the data in an Excel table or list. Consider the example of all the sales transactions for a large corporation, such as the worksheet shown in Figure 5.28 containing over 900 rows of transaction data. The Accounting Department creates financial statements from a series of internal financial reports that are based on the thousands of sales transactions, vendor payments, and other transactions. The highest levels of management rarely see transaction details. As you move down through levels of a company's organization, managers at successively lower rungs of the corporate ladder look at progressively more detail. In order to manage effectively, all managers depend on summary information. Pivot tables serve a function of creating summary information from a myriad of details contained in an Excel list of individual transactions. Figure 5.29 shows a pivot table that summarizes the data partially displayed in Figure 5.28 and provides a fact that the dollar volume of sales to New York customers by female sales representatives is greater than sales by male sales representatives. By clicking the list box displaying "NY," managers can compare performance of male versus female sales persons in other states.

While managers' financial and database reports are often static objects, pivot tables are dynamic and flexible, providing up-to-the-minute results and in a way that allows managers to alter their view of the summary. Instead of passively reading a report, anyone with an Excel pivot table can slice, dice, twist, and turn it until they change the summary into the information they are looking for. By altering a variable here and moving another variable there, you can make the sales per month by region suddenly jump out of the details of a list, much like viewing a hologram from a different angle.

F I G U R E   5.28

Sales list example

SaleID	Date	State	Sales Rep	Gender	Amount
12101	7/3/2004	CA	Watterson, Barbara	F	$ 5,470
12102	7/3/2004	NM	Goldman, Ted	M	$ 9,687
12103	7/3/2004	TX	Kole, David	M	$ 7,495
12104	7/3/2004	WI	Morrison, Alanis	F	$ 5,239
12105	7/3/2004	TX	Kole, David	M	$ 5,920
12106	7/3/2004	IL	Stonesifer, Patti	F	$ 3,349
12107	7/3/2004	CA	Pacioli, Luca	M	$ 4,061
12108	7/3/2004	IN	Kahn, Phillipe	M	$ 7,658
12109	7/3/2004	GA	Halstead, Whitney	F	$ 6,172
12110	7/3/2004	NH	English, Melinda	F	$ 9,253
12111	7/3/2004	CA	Minsky, Barbara	F	$ 8,586
12112	7/3/2004	TX	Bateman, Giles	M	$ 6,666
12113	7/3/2004	IL	Halstead, Whitney	F	$ 6,714
12114	7/3/2004	OH	Stonely, Sharon	F	$ 4,574
12115	7/3/2004	CA	English, Melinda	F	$ 11,150
12116	7/3/2004	ME	Watterson, Barbara	F	$ 7,299
12117	7/3/2004	CA	Pacioli, Luca	M	$ 4,740
12118	7/3/2004	OK	English, Melinda	F	$ 6,614
12119	7/3/2004	IL	Halstead, Whitney	F	$ 3,444
12120	7/3/2004	CA	Minsky, Barbara	F	$ 5,593
12121	7/3/2004	WI	Gates, William	M	$ 4,482
12122	7/3/2004	IA	Flintsteel, Hillary	F	$ 6,464
12123	7/4/2004	NV	Kole, David	M	$ 10,064
12124	7/4/2004	MI	Pacioli, Luca	M	$ 5,480
12125	7/4/2004	IN	Goldman, Ted	M	$ 2,458
12126	7/4/2004	CA	Stonely, Sharon	F	$ 5,210
12127	7/4/2004	FL	Kahn, Phillipe	M	$ 6,390
12128	7/4/2004	TX	Manispour, Sharad	M	$ 10,225
12129	7/4/2004	NY	Chang, Annie	F	$ 3,085
12130	7/4/2004	OH	Gates, William	M	$ 9,821

F I G U R E   5.29

Pivot table summarizing
sales data

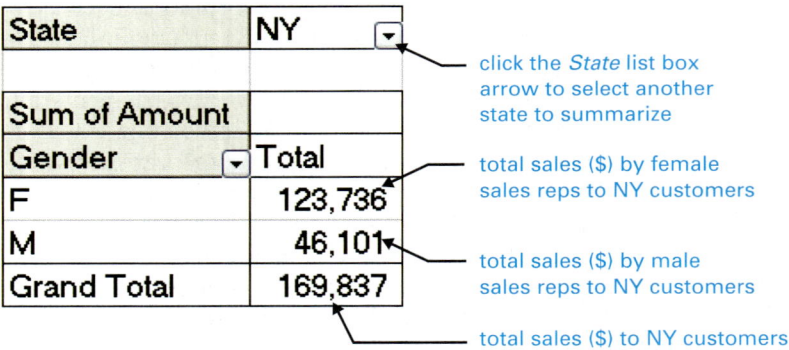

State	NY ▾
Sum of Amount	
Gender ▾	Total
F	123,736
M	46,101
Grand Total	169,837

click the *State* list box
arrow to select another
state to summarize

total sales ($) by female
sales reps to NY customers

total sales ($) by male
sales reps to NY customers

total sales ($) to NY customers

help yourself *Press **F1**, type **pivot table** in the Search text box of the Microsoft Excel Help task pane, and press **Enter**. Scroll the results panel, if necessary, and click the hyperlink **About PivotTable reports** to reveal information on creating pivot tables from data lists. You may want to click the **Print** icon on the Help toolbar to obtain a hard copy of the Help screen. Click the Help screen **Close** button when you are finished. Close the task pane*

When should you use a pivot table and when should you not? Pivot tables are useful to summarize data from a relatively long list of individual observations or transactions—hundreds or thousands of invoice lines for the year, a list of dates, times, and measurements of an experiment over time, or a long list of financial transactions. Extensive listings of observations logged into columns of characteristics provide the best material for creating revealing pivot tables. On the other hand, a pivot table is not useful to analyze data that are already in summary form. You can find many examples of already summarized data, data for which a pivot table makes little sense, maintained and available at the U.S. Census Bureau. They have collected thousands of statistical facts that summarize level of education by ethnicity, average income level by age, and so on.

Creating a Pivot Table

Alice wants you to create some pivot tables based on the raw data in the employee worksheet. Even though the list is short, there are several pieces of important information buried in the data list. For example, Alice would like a listing of the average salary by department. Then, she wants you to produce a breakdown of the employees by birth date so that she can get a better picture of the number of employees likely to retire in the next few years.

The best way to create a pivot table, especially if this is your first experience, is to use Excel's PivotTable Wizard. Like other Excel Wizards, the PivotTable Wizard guides you through a few steps to create a pivot table. You begin by opening the Employee workbook and then launching the PivotTable Wizard.

---

task reference   Creating a Pivot Table with
                             the PivotTable Wizard

- Click **Data** on the Standard toolbar and then click **PivotTable and PivotChart Report**

- Specify the data's location (Excel worksheet, external data source, and so on)

- Select the **PivotTable** option

- Click the **Layout** button (Wizard step 3)

- Design the layout by selecting the column fields, row fields, page fields, and data fields, and click **OK**

- Designate a location for the pivot table: on its own, separate page, or embedded on an existing worksheet page, and click the **Finish** button

---

Creating a pivot table:

1. If you took a break since the last session, be sure to launch Excel, if necessary, open **Employee2.xls**, and immediately save the workbook under the name **Employee3.xls**

2. Click **Window** on the menu bar and then click **Unfreeze Panes** to remove the panes you established earlier

3. Click any cell within the list, click **Data** on the menu bar, and then click **PivotTable and PivotChart Report** to launch the Pivot Table and PivotChart Wizard (Step 1) as shown in Figure 5.30

   Specify the source of the data that you want to summarize, including all rows and header columns

4. Click the **Microsoft Excel list or database** option button, if necessary, click the **PivotTable** option button in the lower panel of the first pivot table dialog box, and then click the **Next** button (see Figure 5.31)

F I G U R E   5.31

PivotTable Wizard, Step 2

cell range of list
to analyze

In the second PivotTable Wizard dialog box you specify the exact cell range containing the list (and column headers) to summarize. Because you clicked a member of the list *before* launching the Wizard, Excel correctly identifies the boundaries of your list

5. Click the **Next** button to open the third step dialog box (see Figure 5.32)

F I G U R E   5.32

PivotTable Wizard, Step 3

click to design the
layout of a pivot table

click to go to
the last step

click to back up one step
and make adjustments

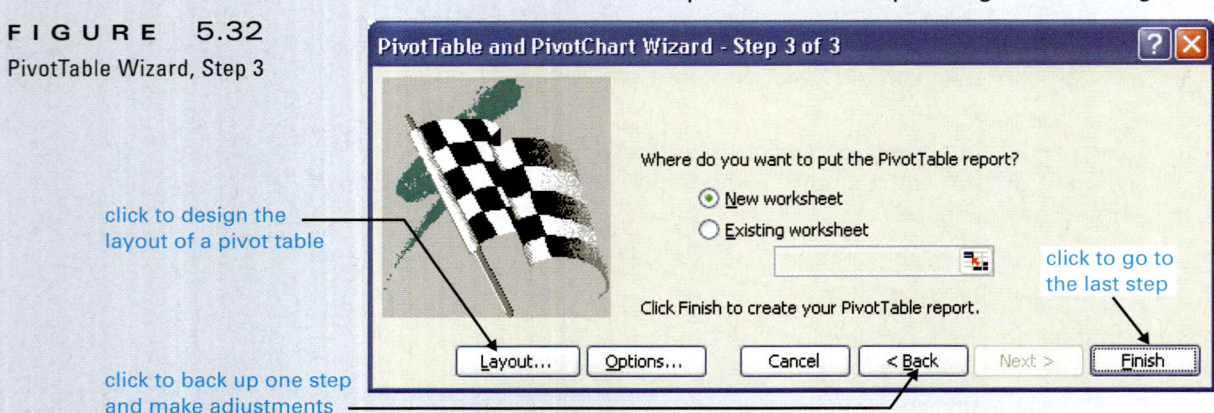

6. Ensure that the **New worksheet** option is selected to place the pivot table on its own page and then click **Finish**. Excel creates an empty pivot table on a new worksheet (see Figure 5.33)

Pivot table without data

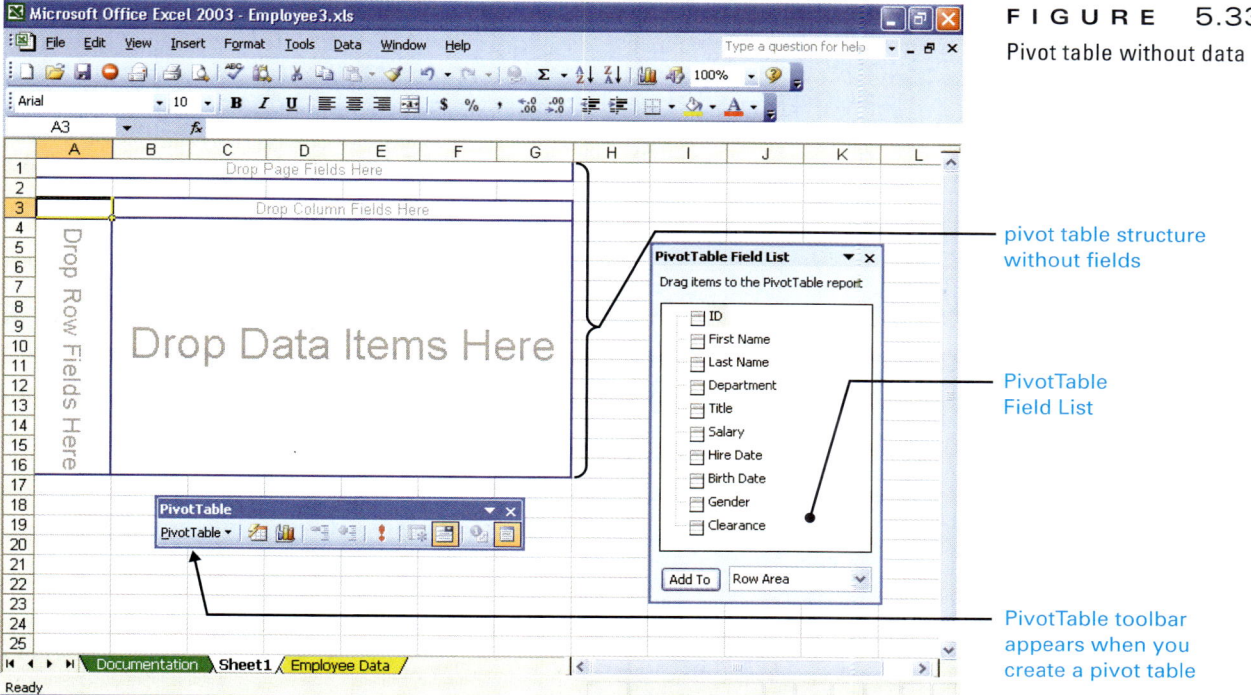

pivot table structure
without fields

PivotTable
Field List

PivotTable toolbar
appears when you
create a pivot table

Designing the Pivot Table Layout

You can define the initial layout of a pivot table within the framework of the PivotTable report. You select the fields you want to place in the row field, column field, page field, and data field whose design is outlined in the empty pivot table report framework. Into the data field of the pivot table frame, you drop the field name(s) from the data list that you want to summarize—to count, sum, average, and so forth. The PivotTable toolbar (see Figure 5.33 and Figure 5.34) contains field buttons that correspond to the list's

F I G U R E   5.34

PivotTable toolbar tools

Toolbar Icon	Button Name	Description
PivotTable ▾	PivotTable	Drop-down that displays shortcut menu of pivot table commands
	Format Report	Displays a list of pivot table report styles
	Chart Wizard	Creates a chart sheet from a pivot table
	Hide Detail	Hides detail lines of a pivot table field
	Show Detail	Reveals detail lines of a pivot table field
	Refresh External Data	Updates a pivot table after you have made changes to the underlying data
	Include Hidden Items in Totals	Items you have hidden are still counted in the PivotTable totals
	Always Display Items	Controls when Excel goes to an external data source to determine a pivot table value
	Field Settings	Opens the PivotTable Field dialog box containing options you can apply to the selected pivot table field
	Hide/Show Field List	Toggles between hiding and displaying the field list

field names. You can drag a field name button to any of the four areas of the pivot table framework—Drop Row Fields Here, Drop Column Fields Here, Drop Page Fields Here, or Drop Data Items Here—to design the layout of the pivot table.

The first pivot table you will create is average salary by department and gender. The values of the department will appear as row labels and the gender values will be column headings. In the Data Items area will be the expression that averages the Salary column in each of the several groups defined by department/gender value pairs. Create the pivot table layout next.

---

task reference   Selecting Pivot Table Fields

- Click and drag each field containing the data you want to summarize to the **Drop Data Items Here** area of the pivot table framework

- Click and drag each field you want to appear in columns to the **Drop Column Fields Here** area of the pivot table framework

- Click and drag each field you want to appear in rows to the **Drop Row Fields Here** area of the pivot table framework

- Click and drag each field you want to appear in pages to the **Drop Page Fields Here** area of the pivot table framework

---

Creating the pivot table layout:

1. Click and drag **Department** from the PivotTable Field List to the **Drop Row Fields Here** area of the pivot table framework. After you release the mouse, the Department field appears with a list arrow at the top of the Drop Row Fields Here area

tip: *If you click and drag the wrong field to the pivot table frame, remove the field by clicking the field button and dragging it anywhere off the pivot table frame*

2. Scroll the PivotTable Field List, if necessary, to reveal the Gender field, and then click and drag **Gender** from the PivotTable Field List to the **Drop Column Fields Here** area of the pivot table framework

3. Click and drag **Salary** from the PivotTable Field List to the **Drop Data Items Here** area of the pivot table framework. After you release the mouse, values immediately appear in rows and columns corresponding to the salary of each department by gender (see Figure 5.35)

tip: *The Sum of Salary button at the intersection of the row and column headings indicates the type of statistic displayed in the data area of the pivot table—salary sums*

SUM is the default function Excel uses for numeric fields placed in the Drop Data Items Here area of a pivot table. You can change the function to any of several other available statistical functions including COUNT, AVERAGE, MAX, MIN, PRODUCT, and others. The default function for nonnumeric data is COUNT. To change the summary value function displayed in the pivot table data field, simply click the Field Settings button on the PivotTable toolbar and select the summary function from the list Excel displays. Next, you will modify the numeric function summarizing the data from SUM to AVERAGE so that you can display average salaries by department and gender.

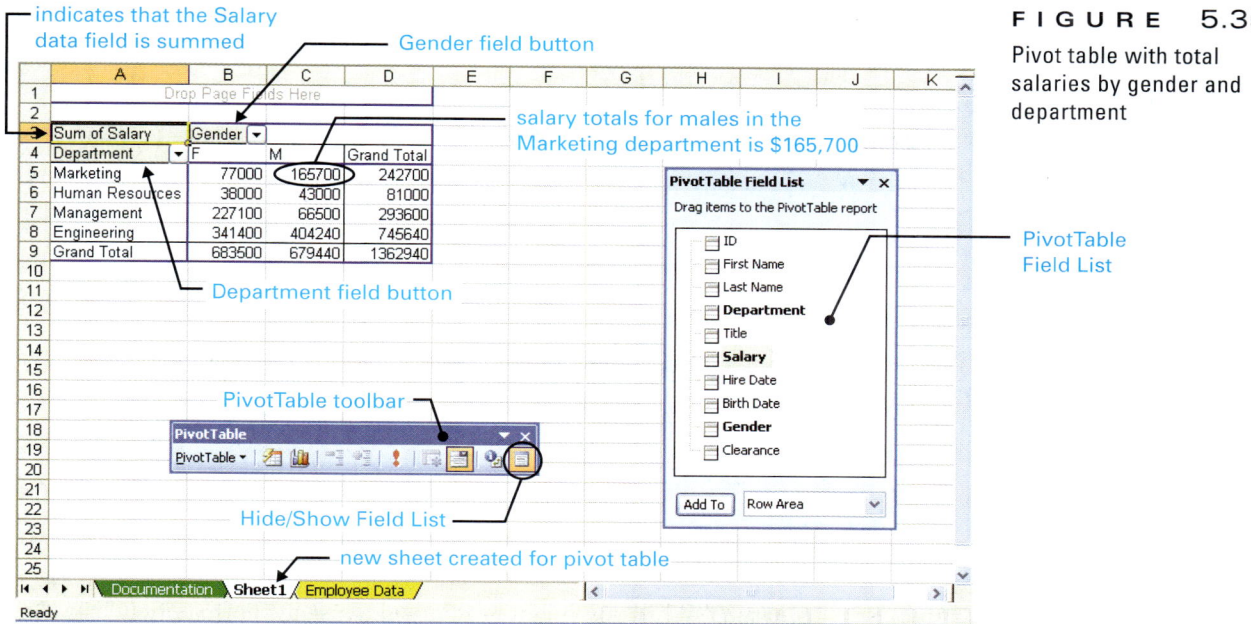

FIGURE   5.35

Pivot table with total salaries by gender and department

Selecting another pivot table summary function:

1. Click anywhere inside the pivot table framework and then click the **Field Settings** button on the PivotTable toolbar. The PivotTable Field dialog box opens

2. Click **Average** in the *Summarize by* list box (scroll the list box, if necessary) (see Figure 5.36)

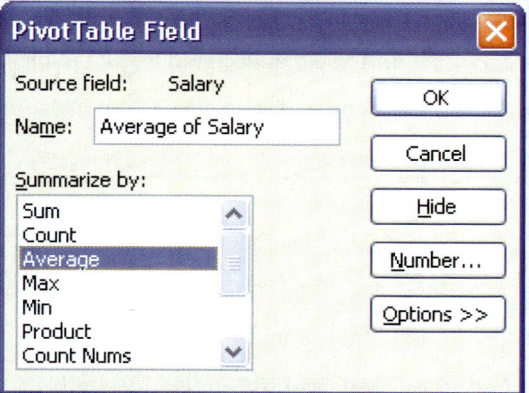

FIGURE   5.36
PivotTable Field dialog box

3. Click **OK** to return to the PivotTable report. The report displays the average salary by department and gender (see Figure 5.37)

4. Save the altered workbook under its current name, **Employee3.xls**

Changing the Formatting of a Pivot Table

The values in a pivot table are computed as part of the pivot table itself and cannot be changed manually. However, you can affect the formatting of the pivot table's contents. Additionally, you can change the calculations, field arrangement, and number of fields in a pivot table after it is created. One of the changes you may make to a pivot table's

F I G U R E 5.37

Pivot table showing
average salaries by
gender and department

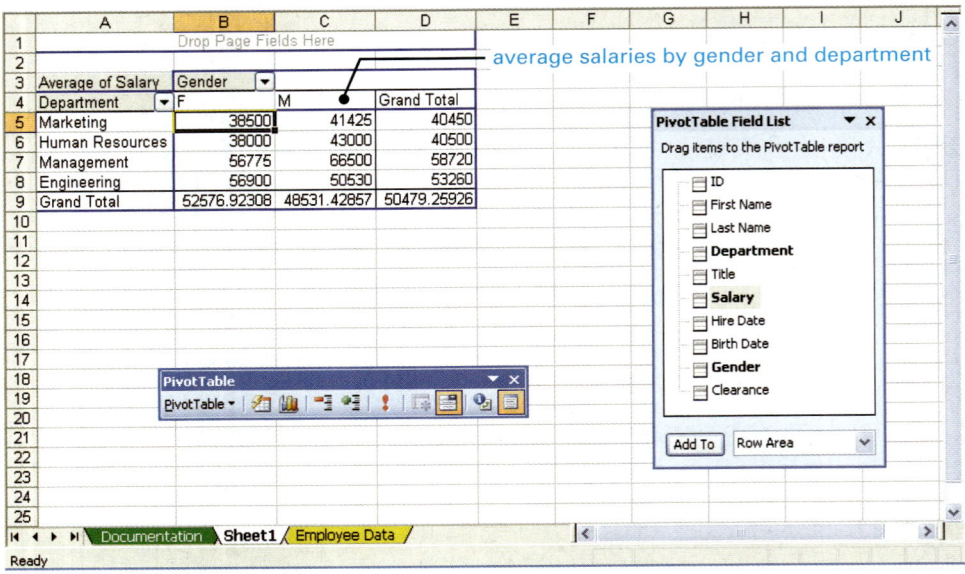

values is its formatting. While you might be tempted to use the Format menu bar command to modify the appearance of cells, be aware that Excel discards any formatting you apply through the Format menu whenever you rearrange a pivot table or refresh its contents. Instead, use the pivot table–supplied formatting commands. That way, Excel maintains the formatting even if you rearrange the table.

---

task reference   **Formatting Pivot Table Fields**

- Select any cell in the pivot table data item area

- Open the PivotTable toolbar, click **Field Settings**, and click the **Number** button

- Select a format from the Category list and make associated format choices

- Click **OK** to close the Format Cells dialog box and then click **OK** to close the PivotTable Field dialog box

---

Formatting pivot table values with a currency style:

1. Select cell range **B5:D9**

2. If necessary, display the PivotTable toolbar and then click the **Field Settings** button on the PivotTable toolbar. The PivotTable Field dialog box opens (see Figure 5.36)

3. Click the **Number** button on the PivotTable Field dialog box to open the Format Cells dialog box

4. Click **Accounting** in the Category list, double-click the **Decimal Places** spin box, type **0**, click the **Symbol** list box, and click **$**

5. Click **OK** to close the Format Cells dialog box, and then click **OK** to close the PivotTable Field dialog box

6. Click any cell within the pivot table to deselect the cell range. Excel formats the pivot table numeric entries (see Figure 5.38)

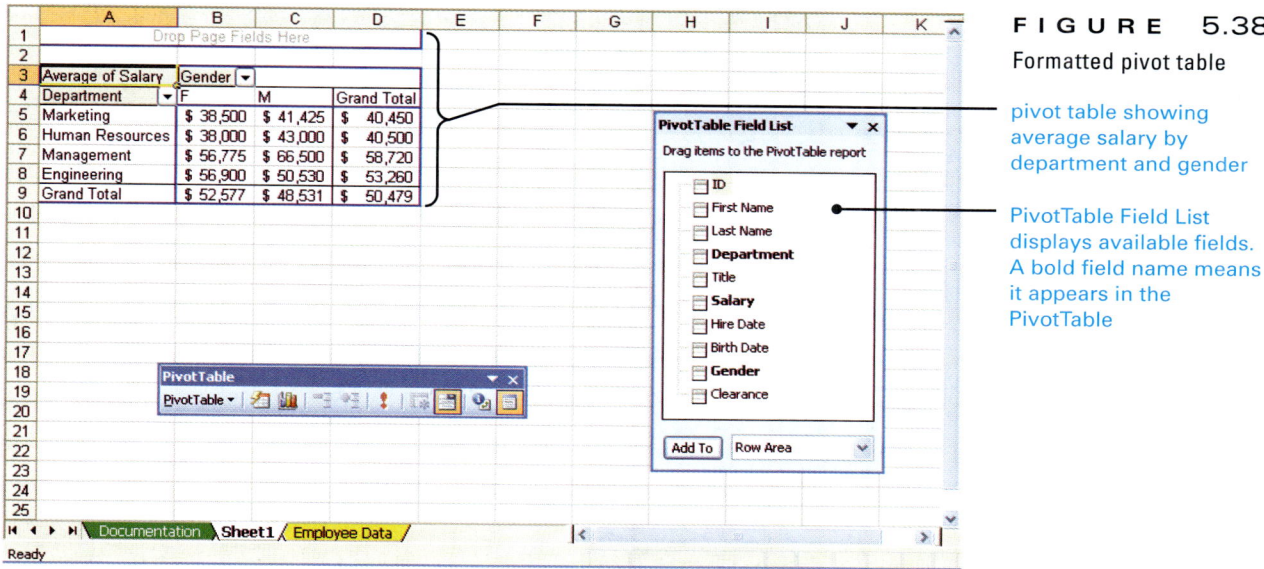

FIGURE 5.38
Formatted pivot table

pivot table showing
average salary by
department and gender

PivotTable Field List
displays available fields.
A bold field name means
it appears in the
PivotTable

The numbers in the pivot table look much better formatted, especially the Grand Total row (row 9), which contains averages rather than grand totals.

Rotating Pivot Table Fields

Perhaps the single most impressive feature of pivot tables is that you can rotate or pivot the values in pivot table column and row fields. By simply dragging a row or column button in a pivot table to a column or row position, you pivot the data to view it from a different perspective. For example, Alice wants to look at the departmental average salaries from a slightly different angle—with two rows for gender and the departments listed across four columns. She asks you to rotate the data so that she can see what new information the table reveals.

Rotating pivot table fields:

1. Move the mouse over the Gender field button appearing above cell B3 until the mouse changes to a four-headed arrow

2. Click the **Gender** field button and drag it below the Department field button—on top of the Marketing label in the PivotTable

3. Release the mouse button. The pivot table is reorganized so that the Gender is listed in the leftmost column and Department labels are listed in the column to the right

tip: *Click **Edit** and then click **Undo** and repeat steps 2 and 3 if you do not get the described result*

4. Hover the mouse over the Department field button in the PivotTable until the mouse changes to a four-headed arrow, click the **Department** field button, and then drag the field button up and just to the right of the Average of Salary label—over cell B3

5. Release the mouse button. Excel displays Gender in two rows and Departments in four columns. You may have to drag the PivotTable toolbar or the PivotTable Field List out of the way to see the entire PivotTable (see Figure 5.39)

FIGURE 5.39

Rearranged pivot table
fields

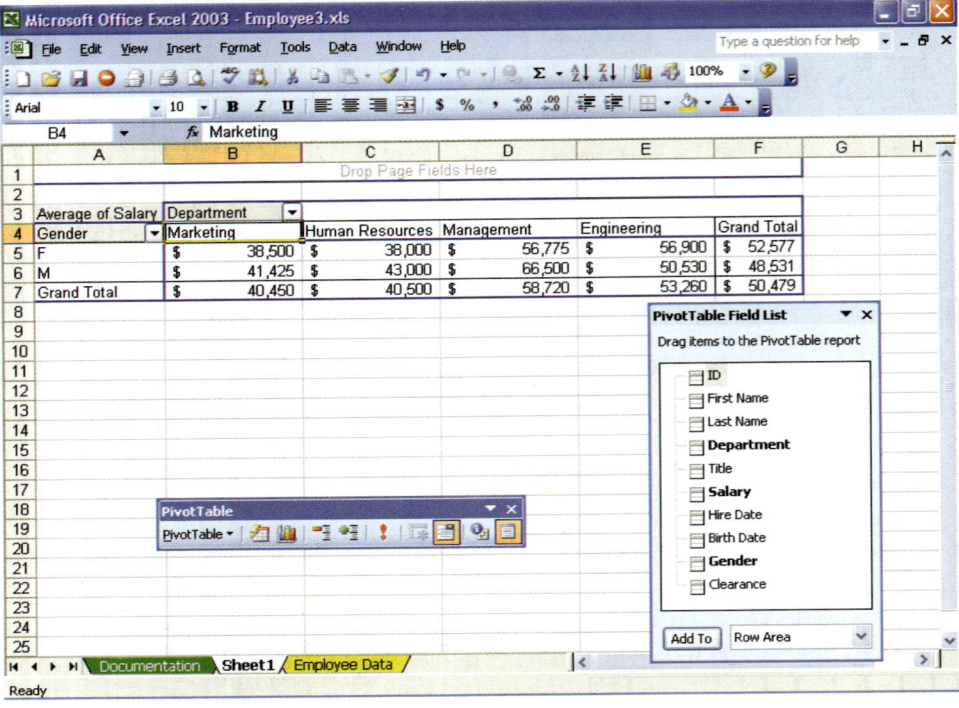

Removing and Adding Pivot Table Fields

You can change the composition of a pivot table anytime you want. If you decide that
you want to see average salaries of males versus females regardless of the departments
in which they work, you can remove the Department field from the pivot table. If you
want to see finer details about salaries, you might want to examine average salaries by
gender and clearance level among departments by adding the Clearance field to the
pivot table. And, you can even examine salaries by age groups.

Removing a Pivot Table Field

Alice realizes that comparing salaries by considering only gender is misleading. There are
a number of other factors that affect average salary of Comsec employees, such as se-
niority and clearance level. Nonetheless, she is interested in comparing the companywide
difference between the average salaries of females versus males. Creating the pivot table
to compute that value involves removing the Department data field from the pivot table.

Removing a field from a pivot table:

1. Click the **Department** field button and drag it to any cell *outside* the pivot
   table range. When the field button is no longer inside the pivot table, the
   mouse pointer changes to a small button displaying a red X below it—a
   symbol used throughout Microsoft Office to indicate *delete*

2. Release the mouse button. The pivot table is rearranged to display average salaries for males and females. When you remove a field, the original
   data remains unchanged—only the pivot table changes (see Figure 5.40)

Adding a Pivot Table Field

You can add any field to a pivot table that is identified as a column name and displays in the PivotTable toolbar. Simply click and drag one of the field buttons from the PivotTable toolbar to a row field, a column field, or a page field. Add the Clearance column to the column field in the pivot table and add the Department field to the row field to the left of the Gender button in the PivotTable.

	A	B	C
1	Drop Page Fields Here		
2			
3	Average of Salary		
4	Gender ▼	Total	
5	F	$52,577	
6	M	$48,531	
7	Grand Total	$50,479	
8			

Adding a field to a pivot table:

1. Click the **Clearance** field button found in the PivotTable Field List

tip: *If you do not have a PivotTable Field List visible, simply click the Hide/Show Field List button on the PivotTable toolbar (see Figure 5.35)*

2. Drag the **Clearance** field button to the column field in the pivot table (cell B3) and release the mouse button. Excel reorganizes the table to display average salaries with Gender in rows and Clearance across four columns

3. Click the **Department** field button, found in the PivotTable Field List, and drag it just to the right of the Gender button so that the mouse pointer hovers over the Gender list arrow and the large gray insertion I-beam appears to the right of the Gender field button (see Figure 5.41)

— field button while being dragged to the pivot table

	A	B	C	D	E	F	G
1			Drop Page Fields Here				
2							
3	Average of Salary	Clearance ▼					
4	Gender	C	N	S	TS	Grand Total	
5	F		75,700 $ 38,333	$ 57,433	$ 49,400	$ 52,577	
6	M	$ 38,900	$ 42,467	$ 54,657	$ 43,513	$ 48,531	
7	Grand Total	$ 57,300	$ 40,400	$ 55,938	$ 46,457	$ 50,479	
8							

gray I-beam indicates position of a proposed new field prior to releasing the mouse button

4. Release the mouse. Excel displays the newly rearranged format table, containing two row fields and one column field, to display average salaries broken out by Department, Gender, and Clearance level (see Figure 5.42). (You may want to drag the PivotTable Field list out of the way to see the pivot table)

You can sort a pivot table's row or column fields. Your pivot table Clearance fields may be listed in the same order as the custom sort order you created in Session 5.1: N, C, S, and TS. In any case, Alice wants the Clearance fields automatically sorted in ascending alphabetic order (C, N, S, and TS) each time the PivotTable report is updated. You do that next.

FIGURE   5.42

A three-field pivot table

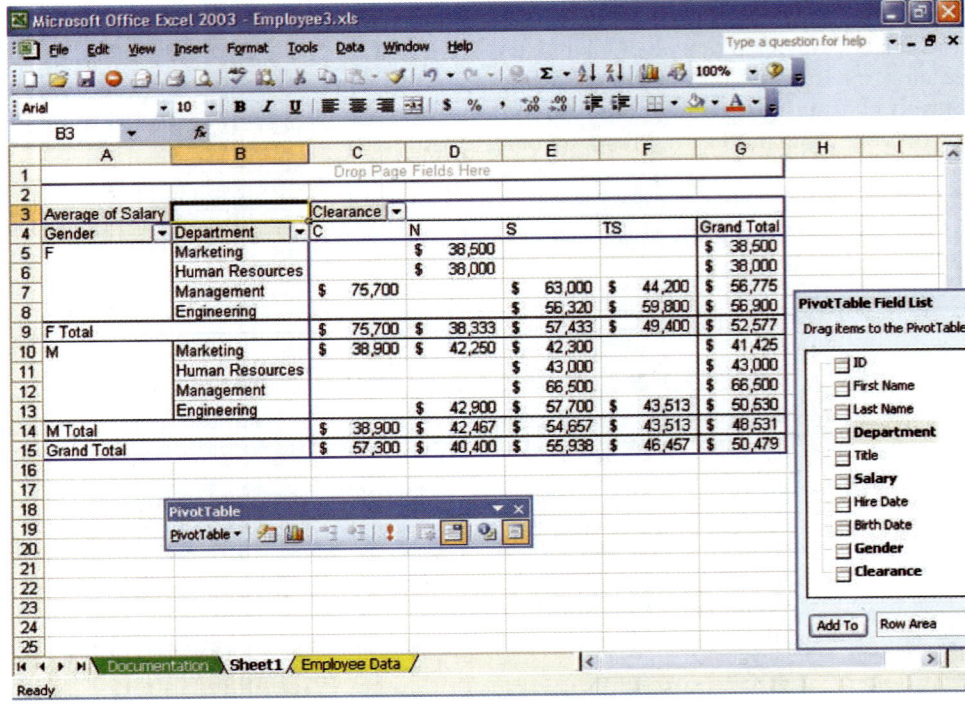

Sorting a pivot table by its column field:

1. Click any of the Clearance field column headers (N, C, S, or TS), and then click the **PivotTable** button located on the left end of the PivotTable toolbar. A menu of choices appears

2. Click **Sort and Top 10**. Excel displays the PivotTable Sort and Top 10 dialog box

3. Click the **Ascending** option button found in the AutoSort options panel, click the **Using field** list box, and click **Clearance** (if necessary). This designates the field that Excel will always keep in ascending order within a pivot table

4. Click **OK** to finalize your choices. Excel sorts the Clearance column labels and associated values into ascending order, left to right

Hiding Field Items

Perhaps the detail in a pivot table is too much, and you want to focus on one particular value. You can hide field items by clicking the list box arrow next to a field button and then select which items values you want to hide in a pivot table. Alice wants to produce two pivot table reports. The first one shows average salary by department and clearance level for males, hiding the information about females. The other report shows the same information for females, hiding the information about males. You produce the second report, female average salary information, next.

Hiding items in a pivot table:

1. Click the **Gender** list box arrow in the leftmost column of the pivot table to display a list of unique values constituting the Gender rank

2. Click the **M** check box to clear the checkmark and therefore hide the value of that item in the pivot table

3. Click **OK** to redisplay the pivot table with the male row information hidden

4. Print the report

5. Repeat steps 1 through 4, but in step 2 click the **M** check box to place a checkmark in it and click the **F** check box to clear that check box

After you complete the last step of the preceding series of steps, the pivot table displays average salaries for males only in each department at each of the four clearance levels.

Using Page Fields

You can use a pivot table's Page field to hide and unhide one or more data items. Page fields provide a slice, or cross section, of your data. You can look at the effect of one particular variable by placing the column in which it resides into a page field. While row or column fields allow you to select some or all items from a list of unique values by using check boxes, a page field allows you to select all values or one particular value, similar to option buttons. Page fields are a great choice when you want to view each unique field by itself.

Creating a pivot table containing a page field:

1. Click the **Employee Data** sheet tab to make that sheet active and click cell **D3** to make that cell active

2. Click **Data** on the menu bar and then click **PivotTable and PivotChart Report**. The first PivotTable Wizard dialog box opens

3. Click the **Microsoft Excel list or database** option, click the **PivotTable** option, and click the **Next** button

4. Click **Next** to accept the suggested cell range displayed in Step 2. An information dialog box opens explaining that a new report will use less memory if you base it on an existing report. Since this is unimportant for these two small pivot tables, click **No** to proceed

5. If necessary, click the **New worksheet** option to create the pivot table in a new worksheet, and then click the **Layout** button to specify the row, column, and page fields. The *PivotTable and PivotChart Wizard Layout* dialog box opens

6. Click the **Title** button and drag it to the **ROW** area of the layout in the dialog box, click the **Department** button and drag it to the **PAGE** area of the layout, and then click the **Salary** button and drag it to the **DATA** area of the layout. Excel labels it *Sum of Salary* (see Figure 5.43)

FIGURE 5.43

Selecting pivot table fields in the PivotTable Wizard

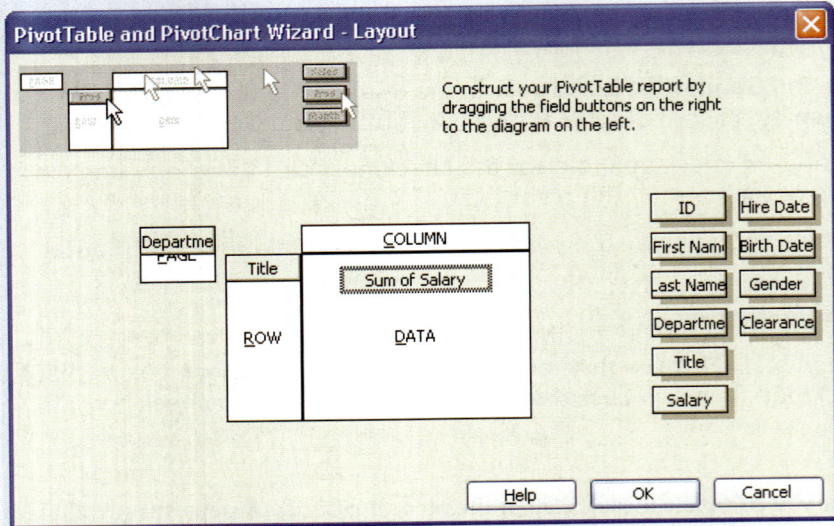

7. Double-click the **Sum of Salary** button in the DATA area of the pivot table layout to open the PivotTable Field dialog box, and click the **Average** function in the *Summarize by* list of functions

8. Format the entry by clicking the **Number** button, select **Accounting** in the Category list box, double-click the Decimal places text box, type **0**, select **$** in the Symbol list box, and click **OK** to close the Format Cells dialog box

9. Click **OK** to close the PivotTable Field dialog box, and then click **OK** to close the *PivotTable and PivotChart Wizard - Layout* dialog box

10. Click the **Finish** button. Excel creates a new worksheet containing the newly completed pivot table (see Figure 5.44)

FIGURE 5.44

Pivot table with a page field

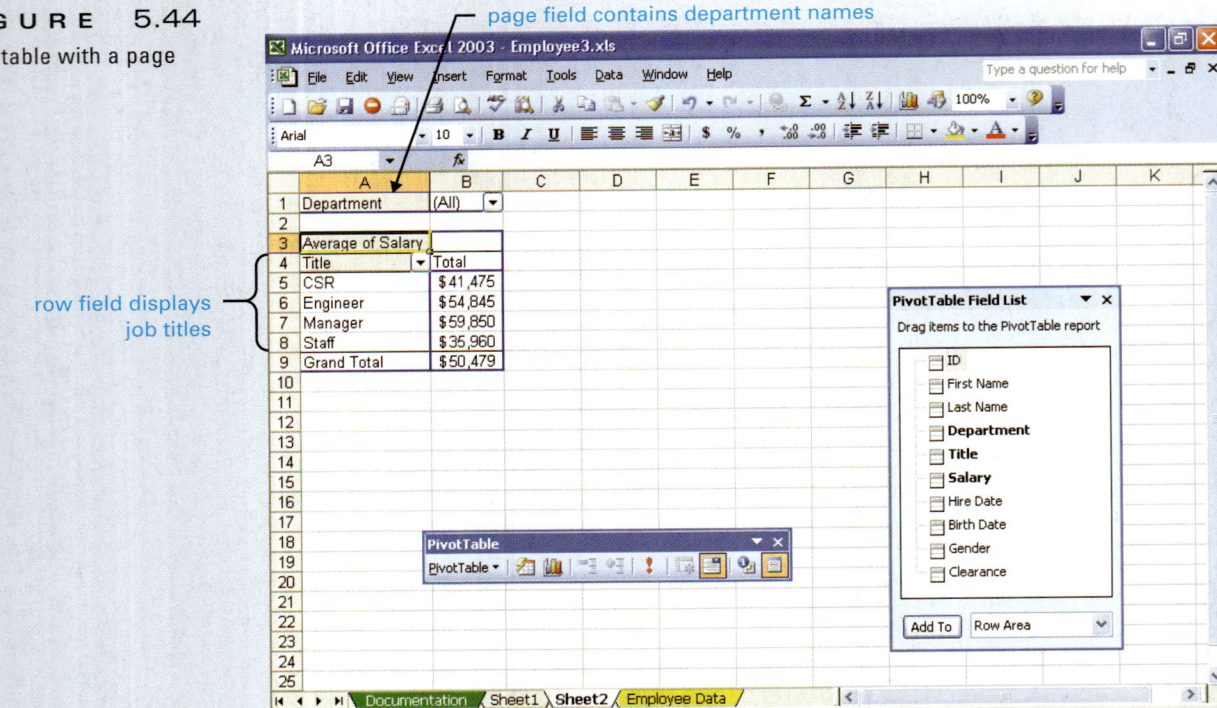

page field contains department names

row field displays job titles

11. Click the **arrow** to the right of the Department button, click **Engineering**, and click the **OK** button located near the bottom of the list. The pivot table displays average salaries by job title for members of the Engineering department

12. Click the **arrow** to the right of the Department button, click **(All)**, and click the **OK** button located near the bottom of the list to redisplay the average salary by job title for all departments

Experiment with the page field by clicking the arrow and selecting other department names. Notice that you have two choices with a page field: All or a particular value. Unlike Row or Column fields, you cannot select two or three departments to display a salary summary.

Refreshing a Pivot Table

Pivot tables represent summary information computed from a data list. Because pivot table values are calculated from underlying data, you should not alter the pivot table values directly. However, any data list that underlies a pivot table is likely to change over time. Employees come and go, they get salary raises, and they are promoted. Perhaps you find it odd, but changing data in a pivot table's data list does not alter the values in the pivot table summarizing the list. Whenever you make a change to a data list that is summarized by a pivot table, you must *refresh* the pivot table, that is, make Excel recalculate the values in the pivot table based on the data list's current values.

First, look at Figure 5.44, cell B7, and observe that the average salary of all managers is $59,850. Melinda English has received a 10 percent salary increase following her very favorable semiannual performance review. Her new salary is $62,040. Update her salary and then observe the effect on the pivot table.

> ### another**word**   . . . on Displaying Page Field Details
>
> If you are ever curious about which rows of a data list make up a summary cell value appearing in a pivot table, you can double-click the cell in question. Excel will quickly create a copy of the source data—the list of all items in the source list that Excel used to calculate the value in a cell—in a separate worksheet. For example, the pivot table shown in Figure 5.44 indicates the average salary for managers is $59,850. Double-click cell B7 and Excel will provide a listing of all the managers' rows contributing to that statistic in a separate worksheet

Modifying a data list entry through a data form:

1. Click the **Employee Data** sheet tab to activate it, and then click cell **A3** to ensure that a cell within the data is active

2. Click **Data** on the menu bar and click **Form** to open the Employee Data form

3. Click the **Criteria** button, click in the **Last Name** text box, type **English**, and press the **Find Next** button. Excel displays the record for Melinda English

4. Double-click the **Salary** field, type **62040** to replace the old salary with the new one, and click the **Close** button to close the Employee Data form

5. Click the **Sheet2** sheet tab containing the pivot table displaying the average salary by job title. Notice that the average salary for managers— Melinda English has that job title—is unchanged at $59,850

*another***way**
... to Refresh a
Pivot Table

Click any cell within
the pivot table

Click **Data** on the
menu bar and then
click **Refresh Data**

It is clear that Excel does not automatically refresh a pivot table when the data in its underlying data list changes. You will have to do that manually.

Refreshing a pivot table:

1. Click any cell within the pivot table. (The pivot table *does not* include row 2 separating the Page field from the rest of the pivot table)

2. Click the **Refresh Data** ![icon] button on the PivotTable toolbar. Excel recalculates the pivot table values. Cell B7 displays $60,790, which is the updated average salary for all managers (see Figure 5.45). Cell B9 also changes because it is an overall average (though it is labeled "Grand Total")

FIGURE   5.45

Refreshed pivot table

	A	B	C
1	Department	(All) ▼	
2			
3	Average of Salary		
4	Title ▼	Total	
5	CSR	$41,475	
6	Engineer	$54,845	
7	Manager	$60,790	← updated average salary value
8	Staff	$35,960	
9	Grand Total	$50,688	
10			

Creating a Chart from a Pivot Table

Recall that one of the benefits of using pivot tables is that they display summaries such as averages, sums, and subtotals based on the current grouping you have defined. You can add a pivot chart to the report. Like the pivot table, a pivot chart changes as you change the pivot table to which it is linked. You can examine the impact of one data grouping of a data list by using a page field and plotting the results in a pivot chart.

You can create a chart from a pivot table just as you would with any other type of worksheet data by using the Chart Wizard or selecting the Chart command from the Insert menu. For convenience, the PivotTable toolbar contains a copy of the Chart Wizard button.

Alice wants to create a chart, which will graphically illustrate the differences in average salary among the four job titles currently held by Comsec employees. She also wants to examine average salaries between males and females with the same job title. Alice asks you to create a Clustered bar chart, based on the pivot table, displaying average salaries among those with the same job title.

Producing a chart from a pivot table:

1. Click any cell within the pivot table (probably on worksheet Sheet2) that you just created

2. Click the **Hide Field List** button on the PivotTable toolbar to hide the PivotTable Field List

3. Click the **Chart Wizard** button on the PivotTable toolbar. A Stacked column chart and Chart toolbar appear on a new chart sheet, Chart1

4. To see the chart without all the toolbars, click **View** on the menu bar and then click **Full Screen** (see Figure 5.46)

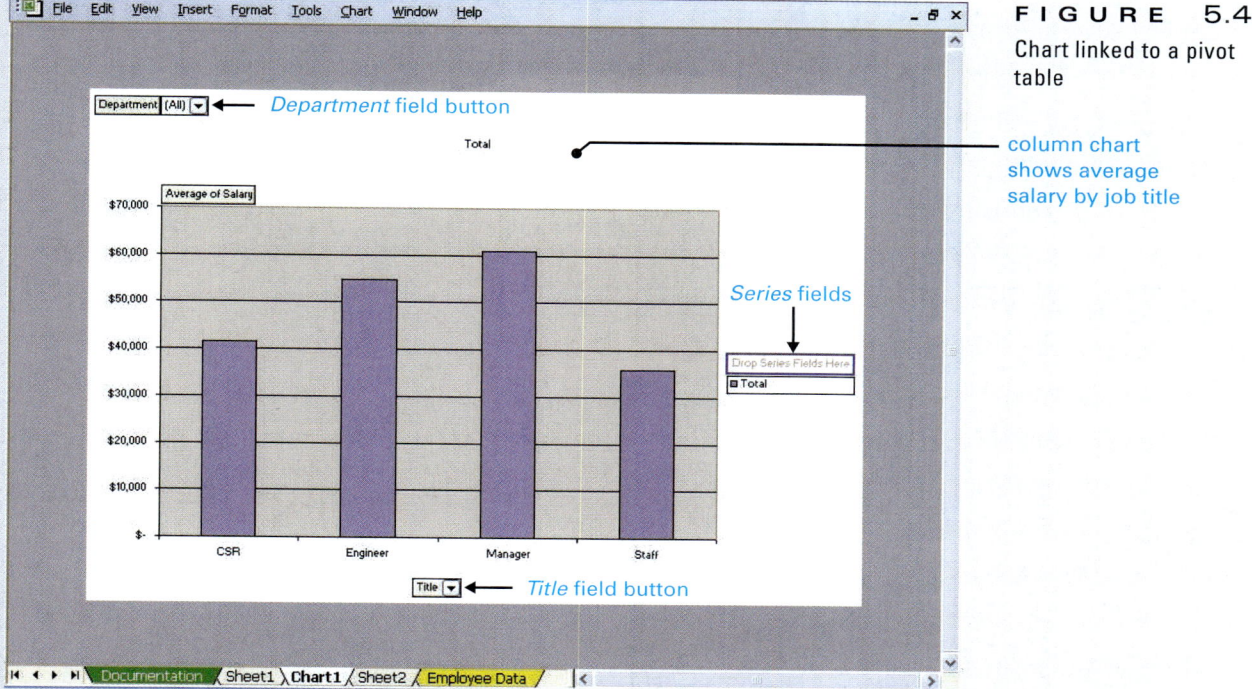

FIGURE 5.46

Chart linked to a pivot table

column chart shows average salary by job title

5. Restore the toolbars by clicking **View** on the menu bar and then clicking **Full Screen**

6. Click the **Chart Wizard** button on the PivotTable toolbar. The first of four Chart Wizard dialog boxes appears

7. Click **Bar** in the Chart type list box, click **Clustered Bar** (top row, first column) in the Chart subtype panel, and click the **Next** button. The *Chart Wizard - Step 3 of 4* dialog box appears

8. Double-click the **Chart title** text box to select all of its text, and then type **Average Salary by Department**

9. Click the **Category (X) axis** text box and type **Average Salary**, and then click the **Finish** button to complete the chart

10. Click the **Show Field List** button on the PivotTable toolbar to open the PivotTable Field List, and then click and drag the **Gender** field from the PivotTable Field List to the *Drop Series Fields Here* area on the right side of the chart

11. Click the **Hide Field List** button on the PivotTable toolbar to reveal more of the chart, right-click the PivotTable toolbar, and then click **PivotTable** in the list of toolbars to close it. Figure 5.47 shows the bar chart displaying average salaries by department

Pivot chart displaying
average salaries

click list arrow to display
data for all departments
or just one department

click list arrow to select
titles to hide or display

click arrow to
select *M, F,* or
(*Show All*)

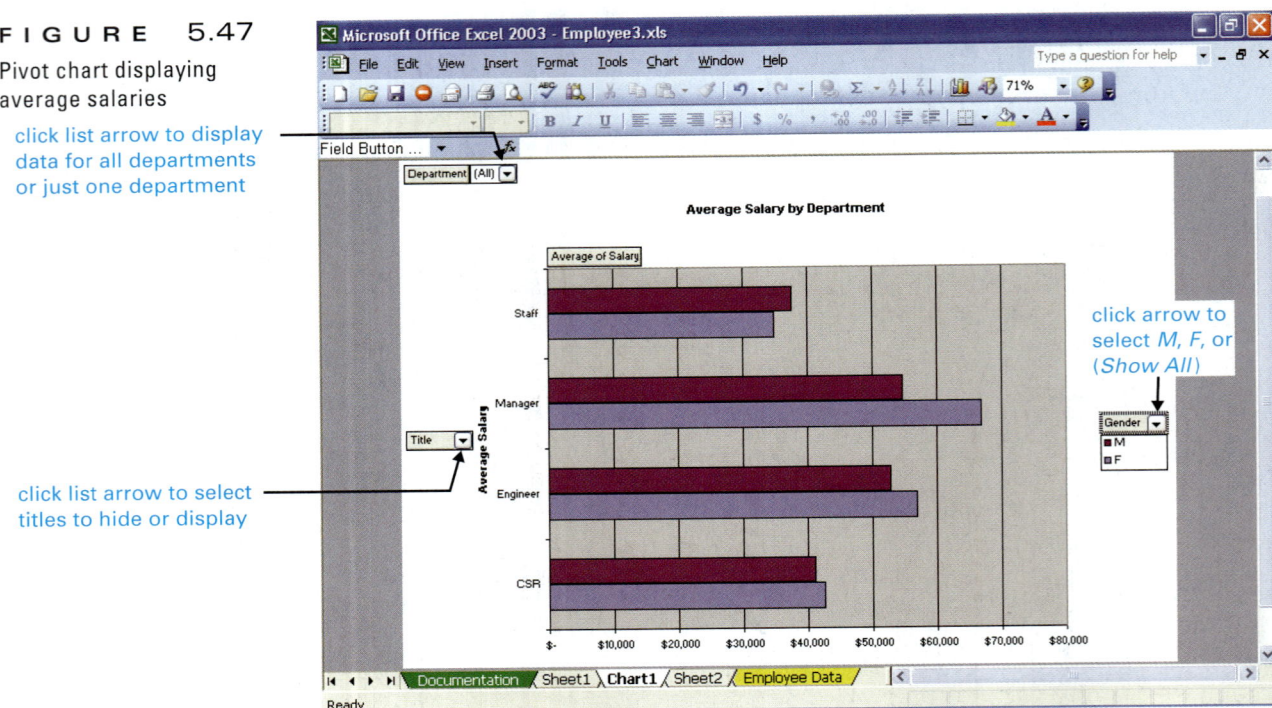

Finally, Alice wants you to print the entire workbook and save it.

Printing the Employee workbook and saving it in a new folder:

1. Click the **Documentation** sheet tab and type your name in cell C6 to the right of the label *Designer*

2. Click **File** on the menu bar, click **Print**, click the **Entire workbook** option button in the *Print what* panel, click the **Preview** button, adjust page margins, if necessary, and then click **Print** to print all worksheets in the Employee workbook

3. Click **File**, click **Save As**, and then click the **Create New Folder** button on the Save As toolbar to create a new folder

4. Type **Chapter5Complete** in the Name text box to create a folder name, click **OK**, click the **Save** button to save the workbook in the newly created folder

5. Click **File** and then click **Exit** to exit Excel

You show Alice your final workbook printouts. She is pleased with the results. Your pivot tables show the differences in average salaries by looking at different perspectives. The pivot table chart is an especially dramatic way to show the average salaries based on job titles and gender.

making *the grade*

1. Fields such as ID, LastName, Sex, and YearInSchool usually end up as _____ fields in a pivot table.

2. A field such as Salary, CommissionAmount, and Age usually ends up as _____ fields in a pivot table.

3. The default function that calculates pivot table summary information is what?

4. You can format a pivot table data field using the Format menu on the Standard toolbar or clicking the Number button on the PivotTable Field dialog box. Both format pivot table entries. Discuss the major advantage of using one method over the other.

5. You have created a pivot table from a list of products that you have sold during the week, but you discover a mistake in the sales price of two items. You make the change to the items in the list of sales. What else must you do to finalize your corrections?

SESSION 5.4 SUMMARY

An Excel list is a collection of data arranged in columns and rows in which each column displays one particular type of data. A label at the top of each column of the list identifies each column. To prevent the column-top labels from scrolling out of sight as you scroll down a long list, execute the Freeze Panes command on the Window menu. Using a data form facilitates adding, searching, and modifying a list. With the worksheet cursor inside the list, execute Form on the Data menu to create a form that uses the column labels for list box names.

Sort a data list on one column by making any cell in the column and in the list active and then clicking the Sort Ascending button or Sort Descending button on the Standard toolbar. More complicated sorts involving multiple columns require you to use the Sort command on the Data menu. You can sort data on up to three columns—a primary sort column and two tie-breaker columns. Blank fields always sort the corresponding row to the bottom of the list.

Apply an AutoFilter to a list to display rows satisfying criteria you select for one or more columns. Selecting match criteria on more than one column means multiple criteria must be true simultaneously for a row to remain in view. Excel hides other rows—those not matching the selection criteria. Criteria available through the AutoFilter list boxes are exact match criteria. More complex criteria such as selecting values greater than or equal to a particular value require the use of custom AutoFilters.

When you maintain data lists in order by one or more columns, you can use the Subtotal command to group and summarize the values in a group. Subtotal functions allow you to sum, average, and count values in numeric columns, and you can produce counts of character data. Using the outline buttons, you can expand or reduce the detail information visible in individual groups.

Pivot tables summarize lists by summarizing data based on one or more grouping criteria. You can choose from SUM, AVERAGE, COUNT, and several other aggregate functions in the data item area to summarize data based on row, column, and page fields consisting of columns. Pivot tables can reveal hidden information about groups of data in your lists. Pivot tables are also known as cross tabs or cross tab tables.

MICROSOFT OFFICE SPECIALIST OBJECTIVES SUMMARY

- Create and maintain a list—MOS XL03E-1-14
- Freeze rows and columns—MOS XL03S-5-6
- Create and use folders for workbook storage—MOS XL03S-5-9
- Sort a list on multiple sort keys—MOS XL03S-2-2
- Enter, search for, modify, and delete records in a list with a data form—MOS XL03S-1-2
- Group and outline structured data—MOS XL03E-1-3
- Create outlines and subtotals—MOS XL03E-1-1
- Create and apply conditional formatting—MOS XL03E-2-2
- Create filters and advanced filters with AutoFilter—MOS XL03E-1-2
- Use worksheet labels and names in formulas—MOS XL03E-1-14
- Create a pivot table and pivot chart—MOS XL03E-1-8

making the grade answers

SESSION 5.1

1. field

2. row

3. Freeze Panes

4. data form

5. custom

SESSION 5.2

1. Data, AutoFilter (and then filter the Location column with the address "Olin Hall").

2. Execute Data, Sort, select City in the Sort by list box, and select Bank Name in the Then by list box. The City (or whatever the column is labeled containing the city name) is the primary sort key, and Bank Name is the secondary sort key breaking ties in the City column.

3. Create an AutoFilter (Data, Filter, AutoFilter) and then create a custom filter (click Custom in the Salary list box) that reads "is less than or equal to" in the first Salary Custom AutoFilter text box and type "40000" in the second Salary Custom AutoFilter text box.

4. First, sort the customer list into order by customer name. Next, execute Data, Subtotals and specify "Customer" as the *At each change in* field on which subtotals are calculated. Click Sum in the *Use function* list box to produce a sum for each customer's sales. Check the Sales check box in the *Add subtotal to* list box to total the sales column.

5. The Conditional Formatting command found on the Format menu

SESSION 5.3

1. row, column, or page

2. data

3. SUM is the default function

4. Each time the pivot table refreshes data or changes, it "forgets' formatting applied through the Format menu. Formatting pivot table data cells within the PivotTable Wizard through the PivotTable Field dialog box applies formats that are not "forgotten" each time the pivot table is refreshed.

5. Refresh the pivot table

task reference summary

Task	Page #	Preferred Method
Freezing rows and columns	EX 5.5	• Select cell at upper-left corner • Click **Window**; click **Freeze Panes**
Adding a record to a list using a data form	EX 5.6	• Click list cell, click **Data**, click **Form** • Click **New**, type values in fields, press **Enter**, and click **Close**
Deleting a record from a list with a data form	EX 5.9	• Click list cell, click **Data**, click **Form** • Click **Criteria** button, Click **Find Next** as needed, click **Delete**, and click **OK**
Sorting a list on one column	EX 5.12	• Click cell in list • Click the **Sort Ascending** or **Sort Descending** button
Sorting a list on more than one field	EX 5.13	• Click list cell, click **Data**, click **Sort** • Specify Sort by and Ascending/Descending options • Repeat for up to two **Then by** fields • Click **OK**
Creating a custom sort order	EX 5.15	• Click **Tools**, click **Options**, click **Custom Lists** tab • Click **NEW LIST**, type each new member of the list in order • Click the **Add** button and click **OK**
Filtering a list with AutoFilter	EX 5.19	• Click list cell, click **Data** • Click **list arrow** on filtering column, click filter value from list
Clearing all AutoFilter filtering criteria	EX 5.21	• Click **Data**, point to **Filter** • Click **Show All** to remove all existing filters
Subtotaling a list's entries	EX 5.23	• Sort list by grouping column • Click a cell inside the list • Click **Data**, click **Subtotals** • Choose group column, choose aggregate function • Click **OK**
Displaying row or column headings on each page	EX 5.27	• Click **File**, click **Page Setup**, click the **Sheet** tab • Click **Collapse** dialog button on the **Specify Rows to repeat at top** or the **Specify Columns to repeat at left** • Specify row(s) or column(s) • Click **OK**
Applying a conditional format to cells	EX 5.30	• Click cell range to conditionally format • Click **Format**, Click **Conditional Formatting**, specify criteria • Click **Format** button on the Conditional Formatting dialog box and specify formatting options • Click **OK** • Click **OK**
Creating a pivot table with the PivotTable Wizard	EX 5.35	• Click **Data**, click the **PivotTable and PivotChart Report** • Specify the data's location • Select the **PivotTable** option and click the **Layout** button • Design pivot table layout by selecting row, column, data, and page fields and click **OK** • Designate location for pivot table as separate page or object on worksheet, click the **Finish** button
Selecting pivot table fields	EX 5.38	• Click and drag selected field(s) to summarize to Data Items area • Click and drag field buttons to Column, Row, and Page fields
Formatting pivot table fields	EX 5.40	• Select any cell in the pivot table data item area • Open the PivotTable toolbar, click **Field Settings**, and click the **Number** button • Select a format from the Category list and make associated format choices • Click **OK** to close the Format Cells dialog box and then click **OK** to close the PivotTable Field dialog box

TRUE OR FALSE

1. Never select the entire column you want to designate as the sort field.

2. The values of a pivot table can be changed manually.

3. Excel automatically refreshes a pivot table when the data in its underlying data list change.

4. You should resist the temptation to use the format menu bar command to alter a cell's appearance.

5. All, Top 10, and Custom are three filter choices that appear in all list columns.

FILL-IN

1. Pivot table fields correspond to _____ in a worksheet.

2. A(n) _____ sort key sorts the list on one column.

3. The easiest way to add a record to a long data list is to use a(n) _____ _____, which you access from the Data menu.

4. Use _____ (on the Data menu) to display only rows that match a particular value that you select from a list of values in the column's label list box.

5. You can display record groups on separate pages by inserting _____ _____(s) following each group in a list.

6. Use _____ _____ to format values in a special way for any values that match criteria for the cell range. For example, you can use this technique to display blue text for values less than $2,000.

MULTIPLE CHOICE

1. To which area would you not drag a field name button?
   a. Drop Row Fields Here
   b. Drop Column Fields Here
   c. Drop Page Fields Here
   d. Drop Data Items Here

2. A dialog box displaying one row of a list in text boxes is called a data
   a. label.
   b. marker.
   c. form.
   d. source.

3. The default Excel uses for numeric fields placed in the Drop Data Items Here area of a pivot table is
   a. AVERAGE.
   b. MAX.
   c. MIN.
   d. SUM.

4. What type of an operator compares two values?
   a. relational
   b. arithmetic
   c. mathematical
   d. comparison

5. The match criteria by which a field value matches a particular value are called
   a. primary.
   b. secondary.
   c. exact.
   d. object.

6. Sort form high to low order is called
   a. ascending.
   b. descending.
   c. primary.
   d. secondary.

REVIEW QUESTIONS

1. What is a list field and how is it related to record?

2. You have a long list of sales information including sales amount, salesperson, sale date, and customer city. What is a good way to create a worksheet showing total sales amount by city? Are there two different and equally good ways to approach this?

3. Explain why you must sort a list before using the Subtotals command. What would happen if you did not sort the list?

4. How is using a pivot table page field different from using a Row or Column field to select a particular value to summarize?

CREATE A QUESTION

For each of the following answers, create an appropriate, short question.

ANSWER	QUESTION
1. You have to sort the list first	_____
2. Click the Criteria button and type the field criteria	_____
3. Cells matching the criteria display with a special format	_____
4. Rows not matching the criteria are hidden	_____
5. Drag the field button to the Data Item area	_____
6. Drag the field button off the pivot table	_____

1. Filtering Fairmont Consulting's Charitable Contributions

Fairmont Consulting is a large computer consulting firm in northern California. Charles Fairmont, the CEO and founder of the firm, is well known for his philanthropic efforts. He believes that many of his employees also contribute to nonprofit organizations and wants to reward them for their efforts while encouraging others to contribute to charities. He started a program in which Fairmont Consulting matches 50 percent of each donation an employee makes to the charity of his or her choice. The only guidelines are that the charity must be a nonprofit organization and the firm's donation per employee may not exceed $500 a year.

Charles' assistant, Saundra, started an Excel file to record the firm's donations. Included are the day the request for a donation was submitted, the employee's name and ID number, the name of the charity, the dollar amount contributed by the firm, and the date the contribution was sent. Saundra wants you to give the completed record for December 2004 to the firm's accountants in order for the donations to be included in Fairmont's tax filings for the year.

1. Open the workbook **ex05Fairmont.xls** (see Figure 5.48) and save the workbook as **<yourname>Fairmont2.xls**

2. Add the following information:

Date Submitted:	**December 25, 2004**
Employee ID #:	**J24A**
Last Name:	**Greenburg**
First Name:	**Peter**
Organization:	**Leukemia Society**
Amount:	**$50**
Date Sent:	**December 29, 2004**
Date Submitted:	**December 27, 2004**
Employee ID #:	**1E5A**
Last Name:	**Taylor**
First Name:	**Steven**
Organization:	**Red Cross**
Amount:	**$200**
Date Sent:	**December 29, 2004**

3. Use the data form to determine how many organizations received single donations of over $100. Explain the steps you took

4. Sort the list alphabetically by organization and then by employee's last name. Include your name in the custom footer and then print the sorted list

5. Use the Subtotals command to total the contribution made per employee for the month of December. Print the sorted list

6. Use the AVERAGE function to determine the average donation made

7. Sort the list by donation value and compare these values to the average found in step 6. Include your name and print a list of all organizations that received a single donation above the average donation

F I G U R E 5.48

Fairmont Consulting worksheet

	A	B	C	D	E	F	G	H
1	Submitted	Employee ID	Last Name	First Name	Organization	Amount	Donation Sent	
2	11/29/2004	68B	Abbs	Don	Habitat for Humanity	$ 50	12/1/2004	
3	12/5/2004	08T	Adams	David	Red Cross	$ 100	12/6/2004	
4	12/9/2004	Y7CA	Ascott	Karen	Red Cross	$ 100	12/16/2004	
5	12/5/2004	M5NA	Bagby	Sharon	Rotary Club	$ 25	12/6/2004	
6	12/3/2004	39N	Butler	Barry	Rotary Club	$ 250	12/10/2004	
7	12/3/2004	0NNA	Clark	Jolene	Toastmasters	$ 20	12/5/2004	
8	12/2/2004	0NNA	Clark	Jolene	Make a Wish Foundation	$ 75	12/4/2004	
9	12/6/2004	0NNA	Clark	Jolene	Leukemia Society	$ 60	12/19/2004	
10	12/16/2004	CTBA	Donovan	Gary	Make a Wish Foundation	$ 130	12/21/2004	
11	12/12/2004	1XBA	Doster	Glenn	Amnesty International	$ 200	12/21/2004	
12	12/16/2004	L3H	Dunn	Elaine	Make a Wish Foundation	$ 225	12/29/2004	
13	12/4/2004	56NA	Foster	Scott	Rotary Club	$ 125	12/10/2004	
14	12/2/2004	56NA	Foster	Scott	Meals on Wheels	$ 125	12/26/2004	
15	12/17/2004	1F9A	Hughes	Gary	Red Cross	$ 50	12/22/2004	
16	12/27/2004	J5M	Johnson	Les	Foster Children's Fund	$ 25	12/30/2004	
17	12/10/2004	44JA	Kelleher	George	Romania Relief	$ 180	12/14/2004	
18	12/20/2004	57XA	Lomstein	Thomas	Meals on Wheels	$ 115	12/22/2004	
19	12/12/2004	FA5A	Peters	Roger	Toastmasters	$ 35	12/15/2004	
20	12/14/2004	FA5A	Peters	Roger	Foster Children's Fund	$ 80	12/19/2004	
21	12/6/2004	R9M	Simpson	Joseph	Red Cross	$ 50	12/19/2004	
22	12/13/2004	R9M	Simpson	Jospeh	Habitat for Humanity	$ 150	12/23/2004	
23	12/6/2004	08A	Thimsen	Timothy	Rotary Club	$ 50	12/14/2004	
24	12/3/2004	C3P	Warren	James	Lion's Club	$ 60	12/13/2004	
25	12/27/2004	R45A	Womak	Anthony	Habitat for Humanity	$ 100	12/29/2004	

Fairmont Data

Ready

2. Using Sorting and Filtering to Determine Top Students

Everingham Elementary School is preparing for the sixth-grade graduation ceremony. Part of the ceremony gives a special award for top students. One award is given to each male and female student with the highest scores in each of Math, English, and Science. Mrs. Moore is the only sixth-grade teacher, and she volunteered to compile a list of her students with grades above 95 percent in these subjects. She started the list, but fell ill and is unable to finish the list in time to prepare the awards.

You have been asked to finish the list and are given her work. Mrs. Moore has gathered the data in a spreadsheet called **ex05Grades.xls** (see Figure 5.49). Unfortunately, she also included all of her fifth-grade students with grades above 95 in these subjects.

1. Open the database **ex05Grades.xls**, save it as **<yourname>Grades2.xls** and begin by sorting by grades

2. Delete rows containing students in the fifth grade

3. Sort the list in descending order by Subject

4. Further sort the data within Subject by Grade in descending order. Include your name in a custom header and print the worksheet

5. Use the AutoFilter command to include only students whose Grade values are above 95. Print the worksheet

FIGURE 5.49

Everingham Elementary School Grades worksheet

	A	B	C	D	E	F	G	H	I	J
1	Name	M/F	Grade Level	Subject	Grade					
2	Brewer, Patty	F	6	Math	99					
3	Carter, Gretchen	F	6	English	97					
4	Cox, Catherine	F	6	Science	96					
5	Dutton, Jennifer	F	5	Science	100					
6	Lawrence, Melanie	F	6	English	95					
7	Nichols, Saundra	F	6	Science	98					
8	Peters, Stephanie	F	5	Math	99					
9	Sharp, Susan	F	5	English	97					
10	Trotter, Megan	F	6	Math	100					
11	Vogel, Betsy	F	5	English	98					
12	Allen, David	M	6	Science	99					
13	Armstrong, Robert	M	5	Science	98					
14	Duran, Tony	M	6	English	100					
15	Fong, Peter	M	5	Math	95					
16	Hammer, Bill	M	5	English	95					
17	Jordan, Brian	M	6	Math	95					
18	Meyers, Phillip	M	6	Science	100					
19	Newman, Bruce	M	5	Math	98					
20	Silva, Paul	M	6	English	95					
21	Zappala, Chris	M	6	Math	100					
22										
23										
24										
25										

Grades

Ready

1. Filtering Soda Sales

Shores, Incorporated, manufactures and bottles 10 different types of soda, three of which are citrus noncola sodas. Shores decided a few years ago to focus on its citrus drinks division instead of colas, since its competition has been neglecting this area. Shores was expecting to capture a large portion of this market, but sales have not been strong in this area, and the company wants to focus its marketing efforts to further promote these drinks. The president of Shores feels that a factor in poor sales is that the firm has been spreading its efforts over the three different brands of citrus beverages. He wants to drop one of the brands. He has asked you to look at the drinks sales figures to help determine which drink of the three they should stop producing and which regions consume the most of Shore's noncola sodas.

You are given data for the past three months. It is sorted by month, brand of soda, in which region sold, and number of cases sold in thousands. Open the workbook **ex05Shores.xls** (see Figure 5.50) and use the Save As command in the File menu to save the workbook under the name **<yourname>Shores2.xls**. Improve the formatting of the data and bold the headers for each column. Sort the soda lists by product, within product by month, and within product and month by region. Use the Subtotals command to display total cases sold by brand of soda per region. Include your name in the custom header and print this list of subtotals. Sort the data by month and within month by region. The months should appear in order of March, April, and May. Print the list. Determine the firm's worst-selling brand of soda. Is this the brand that should no longer be produced? Determine which soda and region have the highest sales. Prepare a pivot table to provide you with this information. Summarize each month's sales using a pivot table. Use the Chart Wizard button on the PivotTable toolbar to create a bar chart of total cases sold by month. Print the pivot table and bar chart.

FIGURE 5.50

Shores, Incorporated, worksheet

	A	B	C	D	E	F	G	H	I	J	K
1	Month	Soda	Region	Cases Sold (thousands)							
2	March	Quench	Western	100							
3	March	Quench	Central	20							
4	March	Quench	Mountain	40							
5	March	Quench	Eastern	30							
6	March	Source	Western	80							
7	March	Source	Central	90							
8	March	Source	Mountain	90							
9	March	Source	Eastern	70							
10	March	Lucid	Western	25							
11	March	Lucid	Central	70							
12	March	Lucid	Mountain	60							
13	March	Lucid	Eastern	50							
14											
15	April	Quench	Western	120							
16	April	Quench	Central	40							
17	April	Quench	Mountain	30							
18	April	Quench	Eastern	30							
19	April	Source	Western	90							
20	April	Source	Central	70							
21	April	Source	Mountain	100							
22	April	Source	Eastern	60							
23	April	Lucid	Western	30							
24	April	Lucid	Central	40							

Shores Data

Ready

2. Analyzing Doctor's Information with Subtotals and Pivot Tables

Before choosing a doctor, several patients call Montgomery Hospital's Client Services office to get more information on the various doctors' backgrounds and experience. Since the hospital staff is overworked, the office manager, Alice Honeycutt, wants to prepare a database of information for quick reference in order to quickly answer questions. The most common questions from callers are about each doctor's specialty and the number of years that each doctor has been practicing medicine. Alice has compiled the necessary information, but needs help in making some corrections and summarizing the data. Open the workbook **ex05Doctors.xls** (see Figure 5.51) and use the Save As command in the File menu to save the workbook under the name **<yourname>Doctors2.xls**. Freeze the column headings for last and first name row labels.

Use the data form to find Robert Gordon's information. Change his years of experience to **20**. Find the information for Charlie Maxwell and change his years of experience to **27**. Sort the data by Specialty and within Specialty by years of experience (most to least). Add your name to the custom header and print the list. Apply conditional formatting so that the Experience field for doctors with fewer than eight years of experience is boldface. Print all doctors with less than eight years of experience, sorted by specialty. (*Hint:* Use AutoFilter.) Prepare a pivot table to summarize the average years of experience by specialty. Print the pivot table report. Format the average year's experience values to display two decimal places. Create a clustered bar chart showing the average years of experience by specialty (based on the pivot table you created). Place your name in the header and print the chart.

FIGURE 5.51

Montgomery Hospital Physician Data worksheet

	A	B	C	D	E	F	G	H	I
1	Last Name	First Name	Specialty	Years of Experience					
2	Conner	John	Pediatrician	10					
3	Simpson	Brad	Obstetrician	6					
4	Lordio	Marcus	Internal Medicine	8					
5	Gruber	Elliott	Pulmonologist	13					
6	Maxwell	Charlie	Surgeon	17					
7	Gonzolaz	Emilio	Pediatrician	28					
8	Wright	James	Pediatrician	22					
9	Cooper	Steven	Optometrist	35					
10	Carey	Michael	Cardiologist	5					
11	Bower	Martin	Orthopedist	9					
12	Sandler	John	Dermatologist	7					
13	Richards	Sean	Surgeon	27					
14	Newman	Christopher	Orthopedist	28					
15	Forrester	David	Pulmonologist	14					
16	Kelley	Michael	Obstetrician	11					
17	Schwartz	Edward	Internal Medicine	31					
18	Eaton	Adam	Dermatologist	4					
19	Nichols	Timothy	Cardiologist	29					
20	Peters	Scott	Internal Medicine	25					
21	Hodge	Dennis	Internal Medicine	21					
22	Barks	Louis	Surgeon	4					
23	Gordon	Robert	Orthopedist	18					
24	Johnson	Larry	Optometrist	18					
25	Bakker	Grant	Cardiologist	9					

Physician Data

Ready

1. Haller Electronics Online Store Initiative

Haller Electronics is an electronics manufacturer specializing in televisions, DVDs, and CD players. Haller Electronics targets the market of customers who know what they want to purchase and don't like the sales atmosphere of large electronics stores. Management decided to launch an online store for customers to buy their products. Brief descriptions and prices of each product would be included for a quick-and-easy purchasing experience. In attempting to stay truly Web based, Haller Electronics' Customer Service Department doesn't have a toll-free telephone number. Instead, customers can reach them through the firm's Web site or by sending e-mail to the department. Most customer service contacts are general inquiries. The manager of the Customer Service Department, Todd Felks, wants to ensure that customers are receiving timely responses from his staff.

Todd has taken a sampling of the customer requests and is looking at those received Monday and Tuesday of last week. Included are the date received, type of product the customer is inquiring about, whether the customer used the e-mail address or the Web site, date a response was sent, number of days it took to send the response, and name of the customer service specialist who handled it. To encourage staff to quickly expedite responses, a bonus program was started that rewards staff based on how quickly they respond. These figures are also included in the worksheet. Begin by opening **ex05Service.xls**, which includes all of this information (see Figure 5.52). Immediately save the worksheet as **<yourname>Service2.xls** to preserve the original worksheet.

Todd needs you to help organize this data for a presentation he must make to the board of the firm. First, sort the list in ascending order by the *Sent By* column. Within *Sent By*, further sort the ties in descending order by *Days*, and then sort in ascending order by *Specialist*. Include your name in the header and print the list.

Re-sort the data, first in ascending order by *Days* and then in ascending order by *Specialist* for matching *Days* field values. Print the list. From this, which method of inquiries is getting faster responses?

FIGURE 5.52

Haller Electronics worksheet

	A	B	C	D	E	F	G
1	**Received**	**Product**	**Sent By**	**Responded**	**Days**	**Specialist**	**Bonus ($)**
2	Monday	CD	E-mail	Wednesday	2	Clark	10
3	Monday	CD	E-mail	Thursday	3	Clark	5
4	Monday	CD	E-mail	Tuesday	1	Gibbs	15
5	Monday	CD	E-mail	Thursday	3	Newman	5
6	Tuesday	CD	E-mail	Thursday	2	Newman	10
7	Monday	CD	Web Site	Monday	0	Matus	20
8	Tuesday	CD	Web Site	Wednesday	1	Clark	15
9	Monday	DVD	E-mail	Wednesday	2	Kuhn	10
10	Tuesday	DVD	E-mail	Thursday	2	Newman	10
11	Monday	DVD	Web Site	Monday	0	Kuhn	20
12	Monday	DVD	Web Site	Tuesday	1	Newman	15
13	Monday	DVD	Web Site	Thursday	3	Clark	5
14	Monday	DVD	Web Site	Monday	0	Gibbs	20
15	Tuesday	DVD	Web Site	Tuesday	0	Gibbs	20
16	Tuesday	DVD	Web Site	Wednesday	1	Kuhn	15
17	Tuesday	DVD	Web Site	Tuesday	0	Gibbs	20
18	Tuesday	DVD	Web Site	Wednesday	1	Gibbs	15
19	Tuesday	DVD	Web Site	Wednesday	1	Kuhn	15
20	Tuesday	DVD	Web Site	Tuesday	0	Matus	20
21	Monday	DVD	E-mail	Wednesday	2	Matus	10
22	Monday	TV	E-mail	Thursday	3	Gibbs	5
23	Monday	TV	Web Site	Tuesday	1	Matus	15
24	Monday	TV	Web Site	Monday	0	Newman	20
25	Tuesday	TV	Web Site	Tuesday	0	Kuhn	20

2. Martin's Futures Trading

Martin's Futures Trading is one of the hottest online futures trading companies in the market today. The company's target clients are day traders, and Martin's offers direct access trading for real-time ordering. There are a vast number of tools and services that Martin's offers to its clients including technical resources, intraday charting, end-of-day charting, and simulated trading (for people just learning how the markets work). This organization specializes in developing and maintaining new client relations. Whether a new client is trading one contract on pork bellies or 1,000 contracts, George Cushing, director of Martin's client management organization, believes that the client needs to have knowledge and access to the tools and experts in that area of trade. Client management maintains all individual trading records for each client. Included in a trading record is client name, type of contracts, dollar value, number of trades per day, and tools utilized for that trade. George would like to personally review the new futures traders' transactions each week. Doing so allows him to contact those whom he thinks may benefit from expert direction or exposure to a new tool. He needs your help to accomplish this.

Begin by opening **ex05FuturesTrading.xls** (see Figure 5.53), which includes the previous week's trading records, and immediately save the worksheet as **<yourname>FuturesTrading.xls**. Create a filter that hides any clients who did not actually execute a trade (the Total Dollar Value column contains a zero). Next, sort the list in descending order by *Number of Contracts* and then by *Total Dollar Value*. Highlight light green any cell containing a dollar value that exceeds $50,000. Type your name into the header, print the worksheet, and print the worksheet formulas.

FIGURE 5.53

Martin's Futures Trading worksheet

	A	B	C	D	E	F	G	H
1	Name	Security Type	Number of Contracts	Total Dollar Value	Tools Utilized			
2	White, George	Sugar	5	3570	Charts			
3	Lee, Christopher	Treasury Bonds	8	88160	Consultation			
4	Yang, Steve	Soybean Meal	2	3400	Literature			
5	Peterson, Lance	Wheat	6	2436	Literature			
6	Hogan, Barry	Hogs	10	43200	Charts			
7	Nelson, Cindy	S&Ps	4	0	Consultation			
8	Bonacci, Sam	British Pound	5	77100	Charts			
9	Passero, Phil	Swiss Franc	8	54480	Charts			
10	Stone, Julia	Copper	3	21090	Literature			
11	Glander, Irene	Lumber	6	10200	Charts			
12	Santoli, Timothy	Gold	7	2205	Literature			
13	Gorman, Dennis	S&Ps	23	20240	Literature			
14	White, George	Wheat	9	3654	Charts			
15	Lee, Christopher	Soybean Oil	6	9240	Consultation			
16	Yang, Steve	Swiss Franc	7	47670	Literature			
17	Peterson, Lance	Treasury Bonds	11	121220	Consultation			
18	Hogan, Barry	Lumber	10	17000	Consultation			
19	Nelson, Cindy	Copper	6	10380	Literature			
20	Bonacci, Sam	Soybean Meal	3	5100	Charts			
21	Passero, Phil	Wheat	7	2842	Charts			
22	Stone, Julia	Soybeans	2	1114	Consultation			
23	Glander, Irene	Wheat	7	2842	Literature			
24	Santoli, Timothy	Lumber	8	13600	Charts			
25	Gorman, Dennis	Gold	1	315	Consultation			

Ready | ◄ ► ►I \ **Futures** / Sheet2 / Sheet3 /

1. Analyzing California's Weather Patterns

Kevin Towers is the sales manager of the Kansas City office of a golfball manufacturing firm based in Michigan. For the past 18 months, his team has had record sales for its territory, and its sales were higher than any other offices. Management knows that Kevin's approach to teaching and motivating his staff has been greatly responsible for the phenomenal figures. To reward Kevin, and to hopefully spread his team's performance, he has been given the opportunity to spend four months in any of the firm's offices in California.

Kevin gladly accepts the offer and starts looking into where he wants to go. He decides he wants to be in a coastal city, and the firm has offices in San Diego, Los Angeles, and San Francisco. He will be in California from January 1 to April 30. Because he hasn't visited any of these three cities and wants to get in a lot of golf time, Kevin determines the main factor that will affect his decision is weather.

Begin by setting your browser to www.weather.com and locate the box in which you can enter the city or zip code for which you want information. Enter **San Diego, CA** and when the data appears, click the **Averages and Records** tab. Print this page and repeat this for Los Angeles and San Francisco. As Kevin is trying to predict the temperature and potential rainfall, focus on the Monthly Average and Records section on the top of the page. Do the following:

Create a spreadsheet to summarize the information you find. Record the temperature and rainfall in columns, and group the cities into four groups of rows labeled Average High, Average Low, Mean, and Average Precipitation. Fill in the appropriate data for each city and month. Because rain is Kevin's greatest concern, use conditional formatting to display the months with an average precipitation below 2.5 inches in blue and apply boldface. Place your name in a custom header and print the list. Prepare and format a pivot table summarizing total average precipitation by city. Print the pivot table. Print the new pivot table. Kevin also wants to be in the warmest weather possible while in California. Use conditional formatting to display the months with average high temperatures above 65 degrees in red and apply boldface. Print this worksheet. Looking at the average high temperatures above 65 degrees and average precipitation below 2 inches, to which city do you think Kevin should relocate? Explain your answer.

2. Analyzing Differences in Salaries

Howard Parker has just completed his MBA and has received several exciting job offers in the area of project management. He has lived in Austin, Texas, for most of his life and is looking to make a change. Since he received job offers from around the country, Howard has the opportunity to finally make a change and move to a new location. His problem is deciding which offer to take. All of his friends tell him to accept the job with the highest salary offer, but Howard knows it isn't that simple. Due to the great differences in cost of living, he knows he can't just look at the dollar figures; he must figure out which will give him the greatest standard of living. Howard decided that he must make the equivalent of a $65,000 salary in Austin—no matter where he moves.

Open **ex05Salaries.xls**, which contains information on the Howard's different job offers and save it as **<yourname>Salaries2.xls**. Go to www.homefair.com and click on the **moving** tab at the top of the page. Click the link **the salary calculator**™ found under the heading *Browse Categories*. This tool will enable you to help Howard figure out the equivalent of a $65,000 salary in each of the cities where he was offered a job. Follow the prompts on the Web site to enter Austin, Texas, as where moving from with a $65,000 salary. Run a calculation for each of the cities in which he was offered a job. Be sure to include that he wants to own a home, not rent. Input all of the salary equivalents in the Austin Eq. column. Type **Difference** in cell E1 and then create formulas in column E that calculate the difference between his offered salary and desired salary for each state. Include your name and print this spreadsheet.

Use the AutoFilter command to display only those offers that have a difference of $5,000 or more. Based on this, if Howard's main desire is having the greatest standard of living, which offer should he accept?

around the world

1. Analyzing Global Marketing Opportunities

Gretchen Kadletz had been a part-time tennis instructor for several years. As she had grown frustrated with the tennis equipment available in the market, she started her own company. With the aid of her attorneys and investors, she founded ProSwing to design tennis equipment and apparel.

Gretchen was able to develop a strong product line and was becoming successful in the United States. The area in which she was having trouble was the firm's international marketing strategy. One of her close friends, Susan Rawlings, suggested that Gretchen advertise the most effective way—by getting players to use and wear her products. While this was a good idea, Gretchen was not quite satisfied. She wanted to be sure that the players using her line were the players followed by the fans (her target market). She knew that this would bring ProSwing attention from tennis players around the world. She decided to concentrate on the tennis players with the highest current winnings, since they were likely to be very popular and visible to the fans. She would approach the top 25 international men and women players about using ProSwing products. She would then additionally advertise during tennis matches in the four countries most represented by the top 50 players in order to represent both the men and women top players.

Gretchen's assistant prepared a spreadsheet after finding recent sport statistics on the Web and compiled data on the top players. Included in the spreadsheet are the player's name, country of residence, most recent winnings, and gender. Currently, this database isn't very helpful to Gretchen and she needs your help to organize the data to plan her international strategy.

Begin by opening **ex05Tennis.xls** and then saving it as **<yourname>Tennis2.xls**. Sort the data in descending order by Winnings. Select and bold the data for the 25 players with the highest winnings. These are the players Gretchen will approach to use and wear ProSwing products. Include your name and print the data. Include your name in the worksheet header and print the worksheet. Remove bold from the 25 highest winners.

Next, sort the data in ascending order by Country and then in descending order by Winnings within each Country. Change the order of the columns so that Country is the first column, followed by Winnings, and then Player. Print the worksheet.

Use the Subtotals command to compute the total winnings for country. Collapse the subtotals so that only the country names and their totals appear, not the individual players or their genders. Ensure that all columns are wide enough. Print the Subtotaled worksheet.

2. Varoom Automotive Components

Julie Brown is Varoom's director of quality for worldwide motor manufacturing. Warranty issues are a major contributor to customer quality performance. Julie needs to track warranty claims for each manufacturing site. The customer quality engineers gather warranty information from the car manufacturers' database systems each month and then enter the data into a shared spreadsheet on the company's secure Web site. From the warranty information, Julie can decide which sites need her help in developing action plans to reduce warranty claims. Her sites' performance and action plans will then be presented at the quarterly director's meeting with Varoom's president.

Julie needs your help in organizing the data for her next meeting. Begin by opening **ex05Varoom.xls** and immediately save as **<yourname>Varoom.xls**. Begin by sorting the data in ascending order by these sort keys (simultaneously): Plant Location, Application, and Motor Description. Using the PivotTable Wizard, create a pivot table for Julie to show her an alternative approach to presenting the data. Within the PivotTable Wizard, drop *Motor Description* into the row field and drop *Plant Location* into the column field. Drop *% Defective* into the data items area. Finally, drop *Application* into the page field. Be sure to select **all** in the page field. Change the default SUM function to MAX for the numeric field using *Field Settings* in the *PivotTable* toolbar. Format the cells to display only two decimals. Before printing the document, format the data in the columns: Open the PivotTable toolbar, select **Table Options**, and click **Preserve formatting**. Next, right-align the column fields and data items. Select all worksheet tabs (press **Ctrl** and click each worksheet tab, in turn), type your name in all the worksheet headers, and print the entire workbook. Demonstrate to Julie the pivot table's flexibility by selecting *GM* as the only application's result to be displayed. Print this page also.

running project

Pro Golf Academy

Betty Carroll has obtained data from the cash registers showing sales for October of men's and women's golf shirts. She wants you to produce and print four reports described below. Each pivot table should be placed on a separate worksheet. Open **ex05ProGolf.xls** and save it as **<yourname>ProGolf5.xls**. Then do the following:

The first report is a pivot table listing total sales of all products broken out by *Item Name* and *Collection*. Figure 5.54 shows an example of this pivot table. The data item is the sum of the *Extended* column. The Row field is *Item Name*, and the Column field is either *women's* or *men's*. Format the sums to display the currency symbol and two decimal places. Produce column totals for men's and women's, but do not produce row totals. Rename the worksheet tab *Report 1*. Place your name in the worksheet header and print the worksheet containing this pivot table in landscape orientation.

The second report, also a pivot table, displays the sum of the *Total Sale* field for each Item Name and each Size. Place the *Item Name* in the Row field, the *Size* in the pivot table Column field, and

Collection in the Page field. Do not produce row totals in the pivot table, but allow column totals. Format the sums with currency symbols and two decimal places. Rename the worksheet tab *Report 2*. Place your name in the worksheet header and print this second pivot table worksheet in landscape orientation.

For the third report, Betty wants a list of all products in ascending order by Collection (1st), Item Name (2nd), and Date (3rd). Produce a subtotal of the Extended values for each unique Item Name, and ensure that each printed page prints the header row, which contains the column names. Place your name in the worksheet header, and print the third pivot table worksheet in landscape orientation. (*Hint:* Widen the column containing the grand total extended price.)

For the fourth report, use the Outline buttons to display only the subtotals by Item Name. Ensure that column A is wide enough to display the entire label for each product name—including the word *Total*. Print the summary report in landscape orientation. Based on this last report, which item has the largest dollar sales volume?

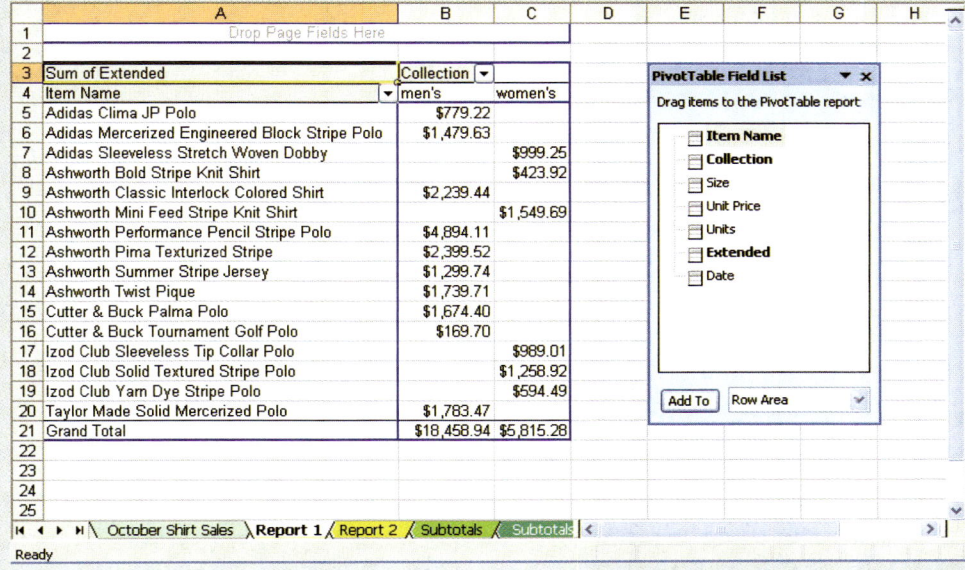

FIGURE 5.54

Pro Golf Academy example pivot table

1. Format? Format!

You have the choice of formatting a column of cells using the Conditional Formatting command or using the Cells command—both on the Format menu. Explain the difference between the two. For example, suppose you want to display all values in column A that are less than 40,000 in blue text. You could select the existing values meeting those requirements, select Format, Cells, and then apply a Font color. Or you could use conditional formatting to do the same thing. What is the advantage of conditional formatting over "conventional" formatting?

2. Pivot Table Revelations

What's the big deal about pivot tables? You have a long list of college alums and their donations. The list contains alums' names, addresses, cities, states, year of graduation, and last year's donation amount. There are over 25,000 alums in the list. What on earth does a pivot table provide that standard AVERAGE, SUM, and MAX functions do not? Describe a useful bit of information a pivot table could reveal from such a list that a fund-raiser might find helpful.

6

Employing Functions

did you
know?

the *Ross Ice Shelf, a very small portion of Antarctica, is hundreds of feet thick and about the same size in land area as France.*

in *the United States before 1933, the dime was legal as payment only in transactions of $10 or less. In that year, Congress made the dime legal tender for all transactions.*

since *the Lego Group began manufacturing blocks in 1949, more than 189 billion pieces in 2,000 different shapes have been produced. This is enough for about 30 Lego pieces for every living person on Earth.*

you *can replace absolute cell references in expressions with what? Find out how in this chapter.*

Chapter Objectives

- **Develop separate assumptions and output sections of a worksheet**
- **Use Insert Function to help write worksheet functions— MOS XL03S-2-3**
- **Provide data validation for selected worksheet cells— MOS XL03E-1-4**
- **Define and use names in functions in place of cell references— MOS XL03E-1-14**
- **Apply and modify cell styles—MOS XL03S-3-2**
- **Investigate the logical function IF—MOS XL03S-2-4**
- **Write the index function VLOOKUP—MOS XL03E-1-9**
- **Write financial functions including PV, PMT, PPMT, and IPMT— MOS XL03S-2-4**
- **Write and apply the NOW date function—MOS XL03S-2-4**

Cal Whittington Automobiles

Cal Whittington, owner of Cal Whittington Automobiles, or "Cal's Cars," has a medium-sized automobile dealership in Muncie, Indiana. Cal's reputation for honesty and integrity is known throughout Indiana, and his funny (some say, silly) television advertising has helped spread the word about his automobiles. Cal has a trained staff of salespersons and sells both new and used automobiles. Each salesperson's desk contains a personal computer that the salespersons can use to request credit histories of customers, do worksheet calculations using Excel, and search a car database listing cars both on their lot and in neighboring cities. Having an Internet connection is handy for the salespersons, because they can locate a requested make and model of just about any car or truck from a network of dealerships that work together to provide cars to each other.

In addition to selling automobiles, Cal's dealership also provides financing for both the new and used vehicles they sell. By having their own financing within the dealership, Cal's makes a small profit through its increased interest rates and provides convenient, no-hassle financing for customers who might have difficulty obtaining a consumer loan elsewhere. Whenever a customer requests Cal's dealership to provide financing, the salesperson asks the customer to fill out a form and then the salesperson obtains the customer's credit history and rating from credit reporting agencies such as Equifax (www.Equifax.com),

TransUnion (www.transunion.com), or Experian (www.experian.com). Then, the salesperson fills out an online form with the finance details including the customer's down payment, car purchase price, and loan information and electronically transmits the information to another location for processing. It takes as much as 20 minutes to receive the loan information results back from the processing center.

The report shows loan details such as the customer's name, loan amount, and interest rate. In addition, it contains a loan payment and amortization schedule showing details about each loan payment throughout the life of the loan. Cal's salespersons want to provide the loan information more quickly and have asked Cal to look into eliminating the step of submitting information to the processing center and instead using an Excel template on each salesperson's computer to speed report production. Cal agrees that doing so would be a great time-saver.

Jessica Allison, Cal's financial manager, has asked you to produce a simple loan information and amortization worksheet that salespersons can use to show customers details about their loans whenever Cal's company provides the financing for a sale. Jessica has dubbed it the Loan Analysis worksheet. Figure 6.1 shows an example of a completed Loan Analysis worksheet. Use that as a guideline as you create the report and enhance it by following the steps in this chapter.

FIGURE   6.1

Completed Loan Analysis worksheet

	A	B	C	D	E	F	G	H	I
1	**Assumptions**				**External Data**				
2	Customer Name	Francis Parker			Credit Rating	Interest Rate			
3	FICO Credit Rating	755			500	10.75%			
4	Purchase Price	$ 21,000			600	8.50%			
5	Down Payment	$ 3,000			700	7.50%			
6	Loan Term	3	(years)		800	6.50%			
7	Application Date	6/14/2004							
8									
9				**Outputs**					
10	Payment:	$ 559.91	per month			Today's Date:	6/23/04		
11	Interest Rate:	7.50%	per year						
12	Loan Term:	3	years						
13	Loan Amount:	$ 18,000.00							
14	Assessment:	$ 300.00							
15	**Payment**	**Beginning Balance**	**Principal Paid**	**Interest Paid**	**Total Principal**	**Total Interest**	**Ending Balance**		
16	1	$ 18,000.00	$ 447.41	$ 112.50	$ 447.41	$ 112.50	$ 17,552.59		
17	2	17,552.59	450.21	109.70	897.62	222.20	17,102.38		
18	3	17,102.38	453.02	106.89	1,350.64	329.09	16,649.36		
19	4	16,649.36	455.85	104.06	1,806.50	433.15	16,193.50		
20	5	16,193.50	458.70	101.21	2,265.20	534.36	15,734.80		
21	6	15,734.80	461.57	98.34	2,726.77	632.70	15,273.23		
22	7	15,273.23	464.45	95.46	3,191.22	728.16	14,808.78		
23	8	14,808.78	467.36	92.55	3,658.58	820.72	14,341.42		
24	9	14,341.42	470.28	89.63	4,128.86	910.35	13,871.14		
25	10	13,871.14	473.22	86.69	4,602.07	997.05	13,397.93		
26	11	13,397.93	476.17	83.74	5,078.25	1,080.78	12,921.75		
27	12	12,921.75	479.15	80.76	5,557.40	1,161.54	12,442.60		
28	13	12,442.60	482.15	77.77	6,039.55	1,239.31	11,960.45		
29	14	11,960.45	485.16	74.75	6,524.70	1,314.06	11,475.30		

Documentation \ **Loan Analysis** /

Chapter 6 covers more Excel functions. Earlier chapters described a few mathematical functions such as SUM, AVERAGE, MIN, and MAX. Excel has several hundred functions, and it would be boring and difficult to cover all of them in this textbook. In this chapter, you will use several of the most common and important Excel functions including the financial functions, lookup functions, the NOW date function, and logical functions. In addition, you will learn how to create and use names and labels in formulas in place of cell references.

SESSION 6.1 USING DATA VALIDATION, NAMES, AND IF AND INDEX FUNCTIONS

In this section, you will learn how to create a data entry area of your worksheet separate from the output area—the area containing the formulas and calculations that depend on the assumptions portion of a worksheet. In addition, you will write functions to validate data entries to ensure that they are reasonable, use names to write formulas that reference names rather than cell addresses, and use an index function called VLOOKUP to search a table. This session emphasizes both the use and understanding of selected functions and how to validate data before you enter the data into a worksheet.

Introduction to Functions

Worksheet functions are special Excel built-in tools that perform complex calculations quickly and easily. Similar to special keys such as SQRT on a calculator, Excel functions compute square roots, loan amortizations, and a wide variety of statistical calculations. Excel has more than 240 built-in functions that perform calculations ranging from computing the absolute value (ABS) of a number to returning the two-tailed P-value of a z-test (ZTEST) and everything in between. Each Excel function is a member of one of

Function Group	Description
Database	Analyze data stored in lists or databases
Date and Time	Manipulate dates and times
Financial	Present value, amortization, and interest-related functions
Information	Determines the type of data in a cell (blank, numeric, empty)
Logical	AND, OR, NOT functions to calculate yes/no answers
Lookup and Reference	Search tables and return answers, determine row or column number of a cell
Math and Trigonometry	LOG, MOD, PI, COS, and other common math and trig functions
Statistical	Standard statistical functions including average, max, and standard deviation
Text	Character extraction, manipulation, and counting functions for text (labels)

several function groups. Figure 6.2 lists the function categories and briefly describes them. You are not going to learn about the 200-plus functions in this chapter. Instead, you will learn about some very important and often-used functions.

When you want to use a function with which you are not familiar, you can use Insert Function to select the function you need and simultaneously learn about the function and its arguments in the Wizard's steps. Alternatively, you can search for an appropriate function by typing a brief description of what you want to do. Excel then returns a list of function names and descriptions that you can browse.

Working with Functions

Recall that worksheet functions have two parts. The first part is the name of the function. The second part is a list of zero or more function ***arguments*** enclosed in parentheses, which are sometimes called ***argument lists***. Of course, if a function is the first thing you write in an expression, it is preceded by an equals sign. Function names such as PMT describe, very briefly, what the function does (PayMenT, for example). Arguments specify the values, cells, or expressions that the function uses as input to compute its final value. All Office Excel 2003 functions return a single answer—the value of the function's evaluation. While most Excel functions have arguments, a few do not. Normally, a function without any arguments would be doomed to return the same value over and over because there are no input values (arguments) from which the function can compute a different answer. However, the few functions that have no arguments return different values each time they are used because they rely on outside values such as an ever-changing clock value or a random pattern to create a unique answer each time. Functions have the general form

```
function-name (argument list)
```

where "function name" is the function's name and "argument list" is zero or more arguments separated by commas forming the list placed inside of parentheses. Functions that have no arguments still must have opening and closing parentheses. The NOW() and RAND() functions are two examples. NOW returns the current date and time, but it has no argument list. Similarly, the RAND function returns a random number in the range of zero to one. If you were to accidentally omit the parentheses from any function that has no arguments, Excel would misinterpret your entry as a special user-defined name (discussed in this chapter) rather than a function name and would display an error message. Therefore it is important to always use parentheses following a function's name—either with or without arguments as required by the function.

Most functions have a particular number of arguments arranged in a particular order. An example is the date-category function DATE, which returns a number that represents, within Excel, a date and time. The function has the general form

```
DATE(year, month, day)
```

If you were to enter month information as the first argument, then the DATE function would return a spurious answer. Arguments like these are called **positional arguments** because their position in the argument list is important and inflexible. Other functions such as SUM, a function with which you are already familiar, have a maximum of 30 arguments. The arguments in the SUM function list are not positional. That is, the first argument has no particular significance different from any other arguments in the list. While 30 arguments may seem rather restrictive, one or more arguments can be a cell range and thus extend the total number of cells involved in the function. With the SUM function, for example, it is just as easy to sum 300,000 cells as it is to sum 30 in a single function. The trick is to use large cell ranges as individual arguments.

Organizing a Worksheet into Sections

For uncomplicated worksheets, it is common to divide them into at least two sections. More complex worksheets often consist of multiple worksheet pages woven together. For Cal's worksheet, it is helpful to divide the worksheet into sections. Doing so reduces or eliminates confusion about where a worksheet user is to enter values unique to each new customer. Cal's financial manager, Jessica Allison, has divided the **prototype** (a proposed model) worksheet into three sections called Assumptions, External Data, and Outputs. The Assumptions section contains input information unique to each customer and used by all the other formulas in the worksheet. They are called assumptions because the results of the worksheet in the output section depend upon the values of the assumptions. The external data section contains interest rate information, also used by formulas in the worksheet, whose values fluctuate based on the prime lending rate and other external factors. The outputs section performs calculations using the assumptions values and displays the results.

Providing an Assumptions Framework

Begin constructing the loan worksheet by opening the prototype worksheet that Jessica has constructed. Jessica has preformatted several worksheet cells to allow you to concentrate on the constants, formulas, and functions in the Loan Analysis worksheet that constitutes what you are learning.

Opening and saving the Loan Analysis workbook:

1. Start Excel

2. Open the workbook **ex06CalsCars.xls** and immediately save it as **CalsCars1.xls**

3. Click the **Loan Analysis** worksheet tab to display the loan details (see Figure 6.3)

FIGURE 6.3

Main Loan Analysis
worksheet

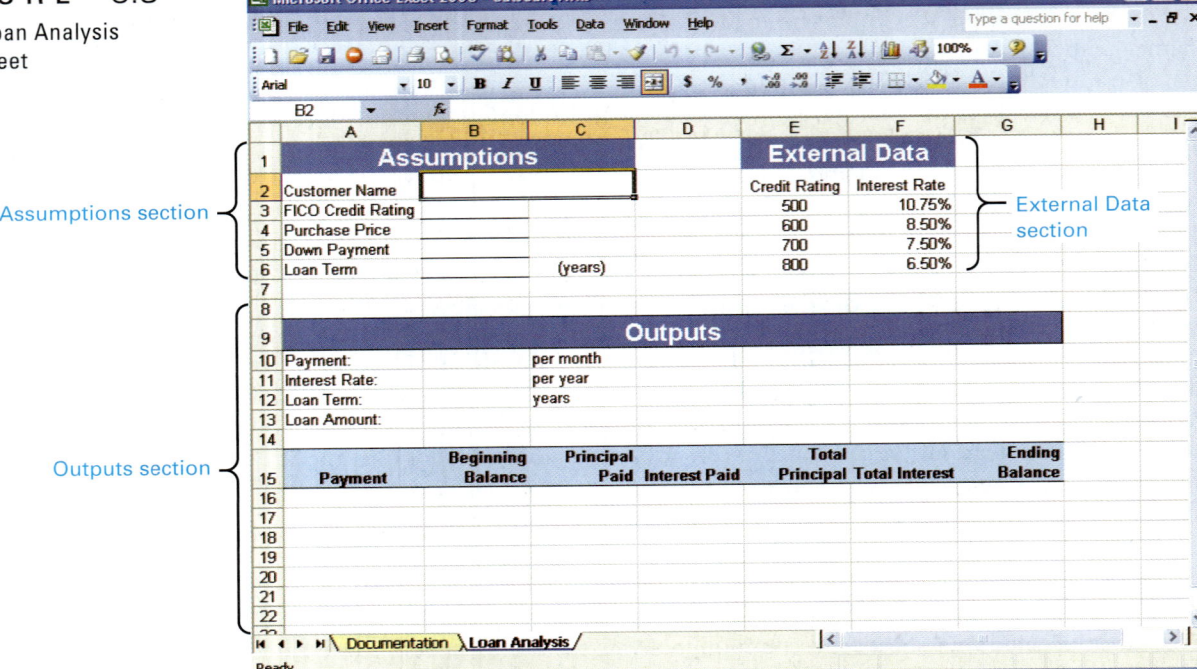

FIGURE 6.4

Initial Assumptions values
and their meanings

Assumptions Cell	Description/Use	Value
B2	Customer's name	Francis Parker
B3	Credit rating number (obtained from credit report)	755
B4	Vehicle purchase price (negotiated)	21000
B5	Customer's down payment	3000
B6	Loan duration in years	3

Assumptions Data

With the general structure of the Loan Analysis worksheet in mind, you can enter the assumptions information—example data—that you will use to test the worksheet. In Session 6.2, you will add formulas to the Outputs section of the worksheet that depend on the assumptions values you are entering next. Later, when you are convinced that the worksheet works properly, you can erase the entries in the Assumptions section and save the workbook so that others can use it without erasing the data you have entered. Figure 6.4 lists the first set of values you will enter and briefly describes them.

Entering input values in the Assumptions area:

1. Click cell **B2** and type **Francis Parker**

2. Click cell **B3** and type **755**

3. Click cell **B4** and type **21000**

4. Click cell **B5** and type **3000**

5. Click cell **B6**, type **3**, and press **Enter** to complete the entry. Notice that the values in cells B4 and B5 display currency symbols (see Figure 6.5)

assumptions filled in

	A	B	C	D	E	F	G	H	I
1		**Assumptions**				**External Data**			
2	Customer Name	Francis Parker			Credit Rating	Interest Rate			
3	FICO Credit Rating	755			500	10.75%			
4	Purchase Price	$ 21,000			600	8.50%			
5	Down Payment	$ 3,000			700	7.50%			
6	Loan Term	3	(years)		800	6.50%			
7									
8									

FIGURE   6.5

Completed Assumptions section

External Data

The External Data section contains two completed columns of data. What do those represent? They are data that have been generated from external sources and entered here. The first column contains four values that the credit industry uses to report consumers' creditworthiness. The four values represent arbitrary groups of values. The first value, 500, is the lower limit of values ranging from 500 to 599. Second in the list, the value 600 is the lower limit of a range of values from 600 to 699. The third value, 700, is the smallest value in the range of values from 700 to 799. Finally, the value 800 represents any values from 800 up to infinity. While these credit ratings are similar to those used throughout the United States, they may not correspond to the lowest or highest possible credit rating scales or match current interest rates for the given credit rating range.

The second column in the External Data section represents interest rates that correspond to different credit rating groups. A person whose credit report shows a creditworthiness rating of 654 can qualify for a loan interest rate of 8.50 percent, because 654 falls in the category 600 to 699. Because a higher credit rating represents a lower risk that the consumer will default on the loan, higher credit ratings receive lower interest rates. You will later use the table to locate and assign a consumer a particular interest rate. The rate will be based on the consumer's reported credit rating obtained from one of the credit reporting agencies mentioned previously.

Supplying Data Validation

As a worksheet designer, you should always be aware that anyone using your worksheet could accidentally type the wrong data into one of the several input cells in the Assumptions area of your worksheet. Invalid entries include mistakes like entering text instead of a value or a value that is incorrect because it is too large or too small. Called *range errors*, values that are either too large or too small (negative or too close to zero, for example) do not make sense in the context of the application. For example, typing 50 in cell B6, the loan term duration in years, would be incorrect. Similarly, a negative value in cell B6 is incorrect. A credit rating value that is negative or larger than 800 is also incorrect. How can you detect or prevent range errors?

Excel can apply rules about the range of values and type of data that are allowed for one cell or a range of cells. Specifying data validation for individual cells allows you to restrict the type and value of information users enter into a worksheet. For example, you can specify that users must enter values in the range of 1 to 5 (years) in cell B6, the loan length in years. Similarly, you can restrict the values in cell B3 to values from 500 to 899.

Specifying Valid Data Value Ranges

Jessica wants you to restrict the value that a user can type into loan term cell B6 to values in the range of 1 to 5. Cal's does not offer loans for less than one year or more than five.

Restricting data values to a specific range and data type:

1. Click cell **B6** to select the cell to which you will apply data validation

2. Click **Data** and then click **Validation** to open the Data Validation dialog box

3. Click the **Settings** tab, if necessary, click the **Allow** list box to reveal the list of values, and click **Whole number**. The dialog box reveals several new text boxes, which depend on the value you select in the Allow list box (see Figure 6.6)

FIGURE   6.6

Partially completed Data Validation dialog box

select data type restriction from this list

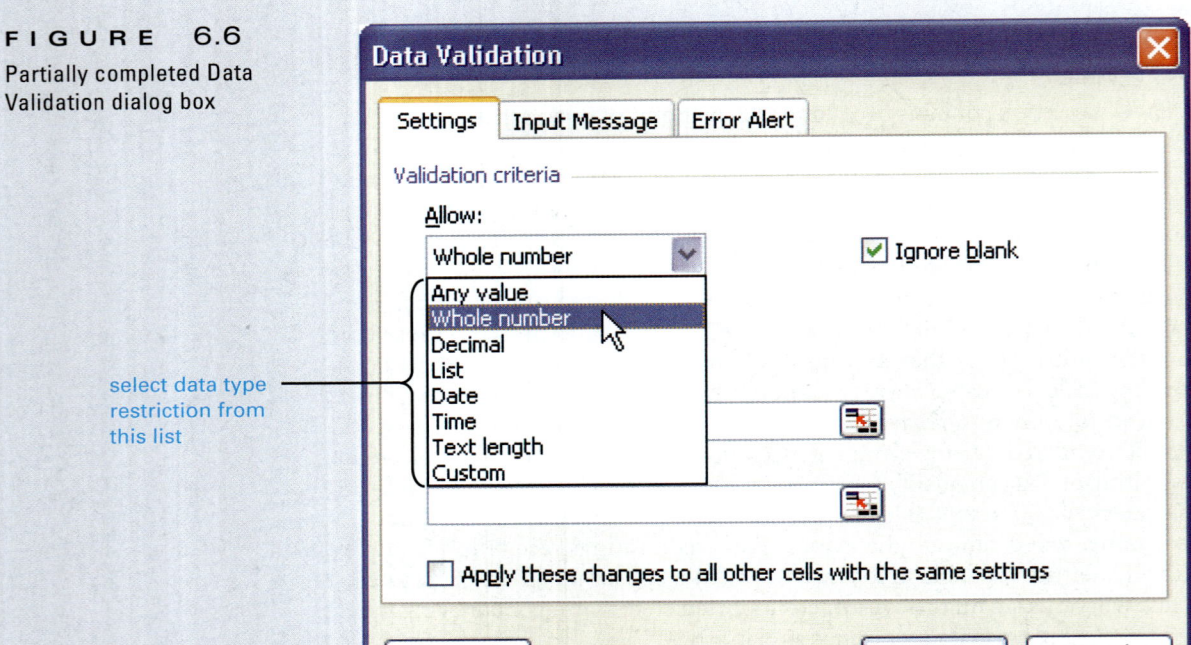

4. Click the **Data** list box to reveal a list of choices and click **Between** in the Data list box

5. Click the **Minimum** text box and type **1**

6. Click the **Maximum** text box and type **5**

tip: *If you clicked OK or pressed Enter by mistake and closed the Data Validation dialog box, don't worry. Simply reexecute steps 1 through 3 above and continue*

Providing a Data Entry Message

You can specify the message to display as someone begins to enter information into cell B6. The Data Validation dialog box should still be open as you do the following steps.

Entering an informative Data Validation input message:

1. Click the **Input Message** tab in the Data Validation dialog box, and ensure that the *Show input message when cell is selected* check box is checked

2. Click the **Title** text box and type **Valid Loan Term Value**

3. Click the **Input message** text box and type **Loan term must be from 1 to 5**

From now on, whenever anyone clicks cell B6, the Data Validation input message appears automatically. It will help reduce the risk that a user will enter an invalid value for the loan term.

Giving Data Entry Error Feedback

The Data Validation dialog box provides a third tab in which you can optionally specify an error message that Excel displays if the data in the cell does not meet the criteria specified on the Settings tab. This is the best way to bring data entry errors to a user's attention.

Entering an error alert message:

1. Click the **Error Alert** tab in the Data Validation dialog box, and ensure that the *Show error after invalid data is entered* check box is checked

2. Click the **Style** list box and click **Stop** (if necessary). Three levels of alert are available: Information, Warning, and Stop. The action each of the three alert levels causes appears in Figure 6.7

Type	Button Label	Action If Button Is Clicked
Information	OK	Value entered into the cell; processing continues normally
	Cancel	Value is not entered into the cell
Warning	Yes	Value entered in cell; processing continues normally
	No	Value placed in cell; Excel stops, waiting for you to enter another value
	Cancel	Value is not entered into the cell
Stop	Retry	Value remains; Excel stops and waits for you to enter another value
	Cancel	Value is not entered into the cell

FIGURE 6.7

Error Alert Style messages and actions

3. Click the **Title** text box and type **Error!** What you type in the Title text box appears at the top of the error message when Excel detects a data input error

EXCEL

4. Click the **Error message** text box and type **Loan term must be between 1 and 5. Your entry is incorrect. Please enter a correct value.** The message appears when Excel detects an invalid value in the cell

5. Click the **OK** button to close the Data Validation dialog box and finalize your settings

Testing Data Validation

After the Data Validation dialog box closes, you notice that the input message appears. That is because cell B6 is active. With the data validation rule intact, you can test it to ensure that invalid entries do not escape Excel's attention.

Testing data validation rules for cell B6:

1. Click cell **B5** to make it active momentarily, then click cell **B6**. The Data Validation input message appears indicating the range of valid data for the loan term (see Figure 6.8)

FIGURE 6.8

Input message display

input message appears whenever the cell selected is active

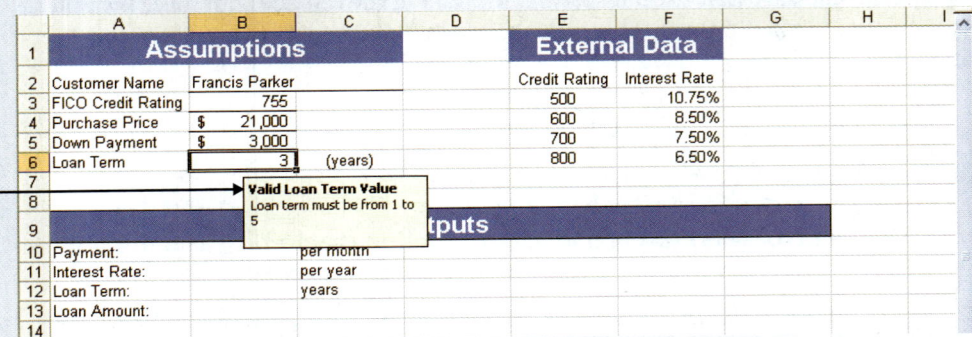

2. Type **17** and then press **Enter** to attempt to finalize the value and move to another worksheet cell. The error alert message you specified earlier in the Data Validation dialog box appears (see Figure 6.9)

   You can click **Retry** to correct the mistake or you can click **Cancel** to erase your incorrect entry. Clicking Cancel restores cell B6 to the value it had prior to your incorrect entry

3. Click the **Retry** button

4. Type **3** and press **Enter**. Because this value is within the specified range of 1 to 5, Excel permits the entry and then makes cell B7 active

Defining Names

Until now, you have referenced cells using their addresses. In larger worksheets, it is easy to forget which cells contain particular values. When you are enhancing a worksheet someone else developed, you will likely examine the formulas to determine what calculations various parts of the worksheet are performing to better understand its flow and structure. Formulas such as =B4*C5−A7−C42 provide little information about the purpose of the expression. An alternative expression such as hoursworked*hourlyrate−statetax−federaltax is much easier to understand because the

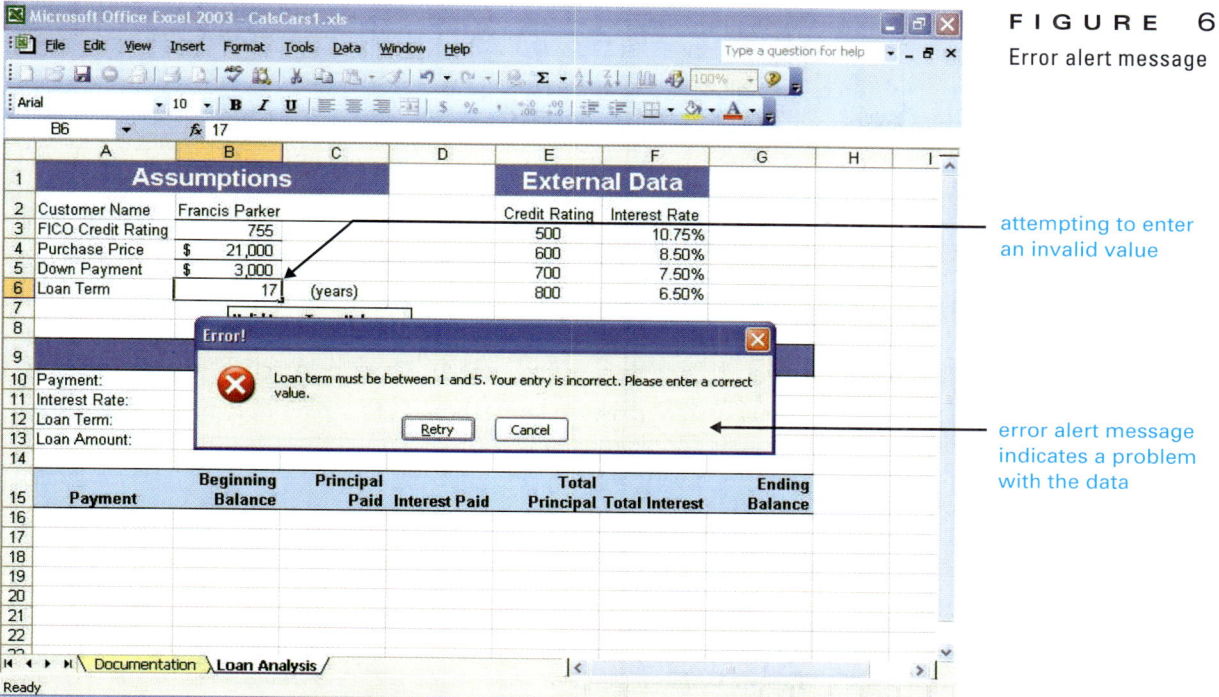

FIGURE 6.9

Error alert message

formula is built with names that infer their purpose. Excel provides an extremely helpful feature that allows you to assign a name to a cell or cell range and then use the name anywhere you would use the cell address. A **name** (also known as a **range name**) is a name that you assign to a cell or cell range that can replace a cell address or cell range in expressions or functions. Names provide several benefits over using cell addresses.

- Names are easier to remember than cell addresses as you create formulas referencing cells
- Names provide documentation because the name reveals the purpose of the cell and clarifies formulas that contain names
- Excel treats names in copied formulas as though they are absolute cell references, which is an advantage when you clone a formula that you want to refer to a fixed location or cell

Names must be spelled in a particular way. Rules for names are the following:

- Names must begin with a letter or an underscore character
- The remaining characters in the name can be letters, numbers, periods, and underscore characters
- The maximum length of a name is 255 characters, although short and meaningful names are better
- Capitalization is ignored in names. (Excel considers the names "Payment" and "payment" as identical)
- Names can be words, but spaces are not allowed. Instead, use the underscore character in place of a space for multi-word names. (Gross_Pay is a legitimate name)
- Names can be single letters, with the exception of the letters R and C, but this is a bad idea
- Names that resemble cell references cannot be used. (For example, IR42 is not allowed)
- Simply stated, define names using six or more characters that contain letters and numbers and that are meaningful words

task reference	Naming a Cell or Cell Range

- Select the cell or cell range you want to name
- Click the **Name box** in the formula bar
- Type the name and press **Enter**

An alternative way to assign a name to a cell or cell range is to execute Insert, Name, Define, and type the name. You can use either method.

Defining a Name with a Menu Bar Command

Jessica wants you to assign names to key cells and cell ranges to make creating formulas easier. She suggests you define names for cells containing the purchase price, down payment, loan term, and the table containing the FICO (Fair, Isaac and Company) credit ratings and interest rates. (See www.fairisaac.com.) Defining names to key assumptions will make it easier to write formulas in the Outputs area that reference the cells in the Assumptions section of the worksheet.

help yourself *Press **F1**, type **name a cell** in the Search text box of the Microsoft Excel Help task pane, and press **Enter**. Click the hyperlink **Name cells in a workbook** and then click the **Name a cell or a range of cells** hyperlink to reveal information on naming cells. Maximize the Help screen if necessary. Click the Help screen **Close** button when you are finished, and close the task pane*

Defining a name:

1. Click cell **B3**

2. Click **Insert**, point to **Name**, and click **Define** to open the Define Name dialog box in which you define and delete names. Excel suggests the name FICO_Credit_Rating, which appears in the *Names in workbook* text box, because the label appears to the left of the selected cell

3. Type **CreditRating** (no spaces) in the *Names in workbook* text box to name cell B3 (see Figure 6.10), and then press **Enter**

4. Repeat steps 2 and 3 to name the following cells with the following names (Remember: Do not use spaces anywhere):

B4	**PurchasePrice**	B10	**PeriodicPayment**
B5	**DownPayment**	B11	**InterestRate**
B6	**LoanTerm**	B13	**LoanAmount**

With cell B13 still selected, look at the Name box located at the left end of the Formula bar. Notice that it displays the name you assigned cell B13—*LoanAmount*. Whenever you select a cell or cell range that has a defined name, the name appears in the Name box.

Note that when you define a name, the worksheet name is part of the definition and the cell reference is absolute. The name defined for cell B13, for example, is assigned to cell 'Loan Analysis'!$B$13. Loan Analysis is part of the name because it identifies the sheet on which the name is found—a true three-dimensional name.

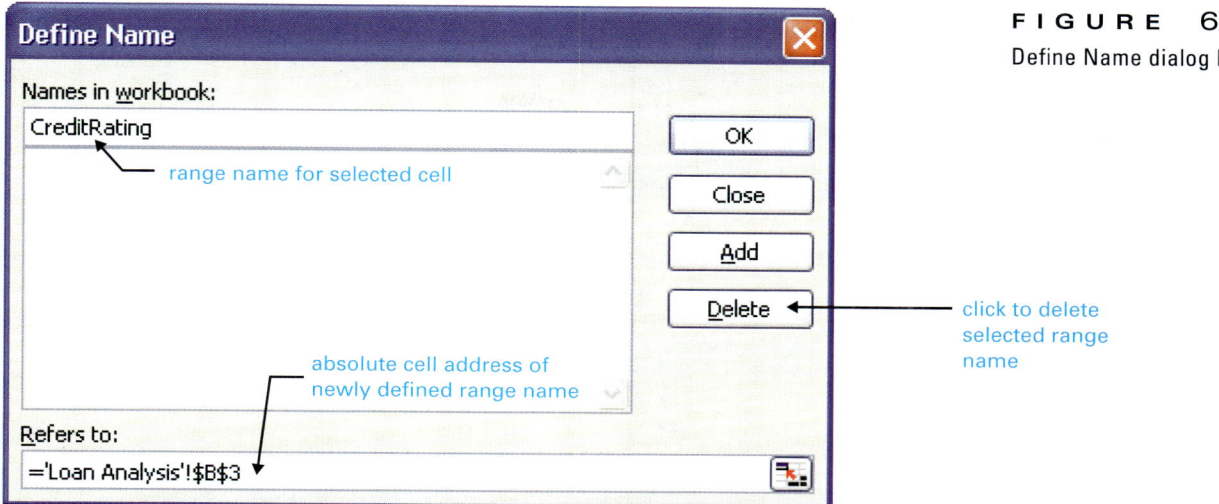

FIGURE   6.10
Define Name dialog box

Defining a Name Using the Name Box

The most convenient way to assign a name is to use the Name box located on the left end of the formula bar. You can use the Name box either to define a name or to go to a named cell or cell range. A name defined in one worksheet is available to all worksheets in the workbook. If you have a large worksheet, clicking a name in the Name box list of names is a convenient way to move directly to a cell. For example, you could name the entire Assumptions area of the worksheet with the name Assumptions. Then, when you click the name Assumptions in the Name box, Excel goes to that section of the worksheet and highlights the name. In fact, whenever you want to know which cell or cell range is assigned a particular name, simply select the name from the Name box list.

---

*another*word   . . . on Names

Normally, names you define are workbook-level names. A ***workbook-level name*** (range name) is a name you define that is available for use in formulas from *any* worksheet in a workbook. You can create a ***worksheet-level name***, which is a name that is available only on the worksheet in which it is defined. To define a worksheet-level name, precede the name with the name of the worksheet followed by an exclamation point. For example, you could define a worksheet-level name SalePrice on the worksheet Sheet12 by typing Sheet12!SalePrice as you define the name

---

Using the Name box to define a name:

1. Select cell range **E3:F6**, the cell range to which you want to assign a name

2. Click inside the Name box, type **CreditTable** (see Figure 6.11), and press **Enter**

tip: *If you accidentally enter the name in cell E3, then press the **Esc** key to nullify your action. Select cell range **E3:F6** again and be sure to click inside the Name box, which is on the left end of the formula bar. If you pressed **Enter** before discovering the mistake, click **Edit**, Undo, and repeat steps 1 and 2*

FIGURE 6.11

Defining a name with the Name box

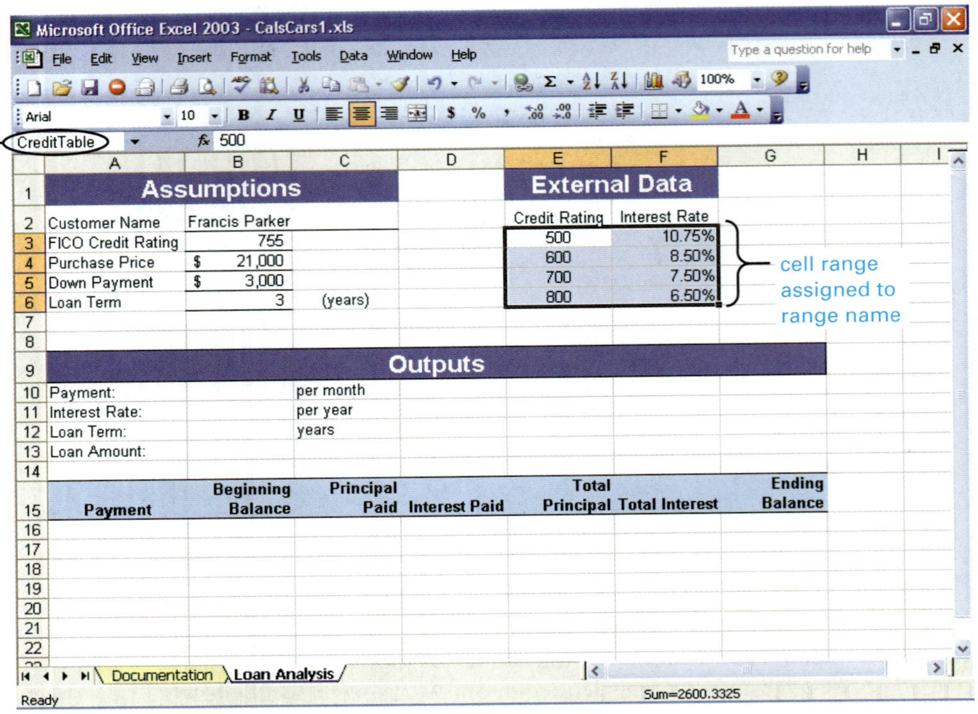

Name box ─

tip: After you define a name for a range of cells, the name does not appear in the Name box unless you select the entire area

Using Names in Formulas

The purpose of worksheet and workbook names is so that you can use them instead of cell addresses in formulas that you create to complete the loan analysis worksheet. When you use a name, Excel treats it like an absolute cell reference. You begin by writing the formula for cell B13 to compute the loan amount.

Creating a formula containing names:

1. Select cell **B13**, the cell that will contain the loan amount

2. Type **=PurchasePrice−DownPayment** and press **Enter**. The loan amount appears in cell B13

3. Click cell **B13** to make it active again and press the **F2** function key to edit the formula. Notice the names appearing in the formula (see Figure 6.12). They are color-coded to match the outlines around the independent cells that the formula references

4. Press the **Esc** key to cancel the edit cell request

---

task reference   Deleting a Name

- Click **Insert**, point to **Name**, and then click the **Define** button
- Click the name in the *Names in workbook* list that you want to delete
- Click the **Delete** button and then click the **OK** button

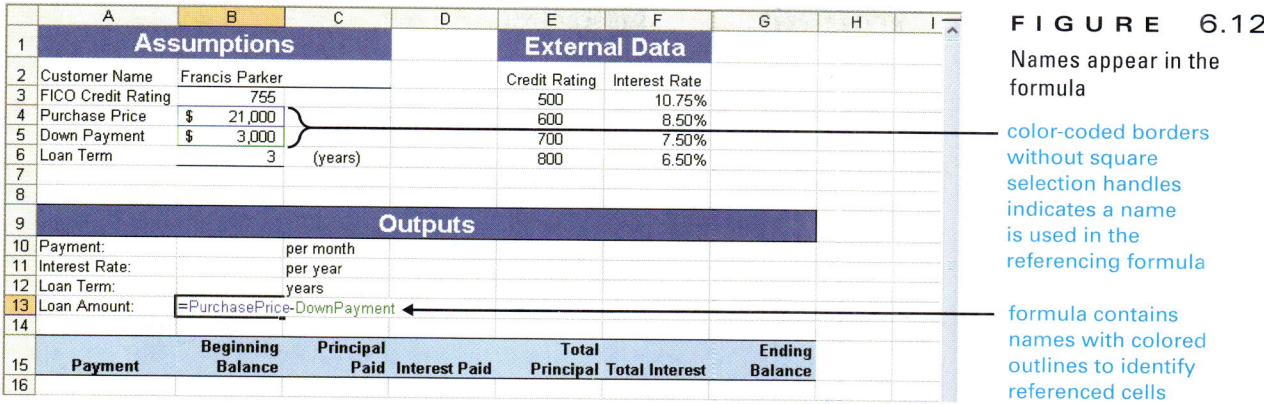

FIGURE   6.12
Names appear in the formula

color-coded borders without square selection handles indicates a name is used in the referencing formula

formula contains names with colored outlines to identify referenced cells

Using IF and Index Functions

Making Alternative Choices with the IF Function

Last month, Cal's Cars began charging a special fee to any customer whose loan is over 80 percent of the purchase price of a car. Cal's management created the special assessment to cover the cost of insuring loans. The special assessment is $300. History has shown Cal and his managers that there is a much higher loan default rate among customers who finance more than 80 percent of a vehicle's purchase price than among those who do not. The special assessment, which Cal calls a "processing fee," will reduce Cal's risk with insurance to cover the balance of a loan should a customer simply quit making loan payments (default) on the loan. There is no special assessment for customers who finance 80 percent or less of their vehicle's purchase price.

Writing a formula to capture the preceding business rule requires a new statement —one in which there is one outcome from two possible choices. The two possible outcomes are a $300 fee for loans in which the ratio of loan amount to purchase price is greater than 0.8 or no fee for ratios less than or equal to 0.8. You will encounter many situations in which the formula you write in a cell can have two or more possible outcomes from which to choose depending on another cell or cells' value(s). Excel anticipates this and provides the function IF, belonging to the logical function category. The IF function has the following form:

```
IF(conditional test, expression if true, expression if false)
```

A **conditional test** is an equation that compares two values, functions, formula labels, or logical values. Every conditional test equation must include a **relational operator**, which compares two parts of a formula. The result of the comparison is either true or false. For example, in the conditional test A1>B2, the greater than symbol (>) relational operator compares the values in cells A1 and B2. IF A1 is greater than B2, then the result of the conditional test is true. Otherwise, it is false. Figure 6.13 shows a complete list of Excel's relational operators.

The second and third arguments of the IF function can be constants or arbitrarily complex expressions. The IF function displays the computed value of only one of the two argument expressions, depending on the evaluation of the conditional test. If the conditional test is true, Excel calculates and displays the value of the second argument. Otherwise (if the test is false), Excel calculates and displays the value of the third argument. Thus, you can create a formula whose output depends on a condition—a value in another cell.

In the Loan Analysis worksheet, the conditional expression you will write examines the ratio of the loan amount to the purchase price. You create a ratio simply by dividing one value by

FIGURE   6.13
Excel's relational operators

Relational Operator	Meaning
<	Less than
>	Greater than
=	Equal to
<=	Less than or equal to
>=	Greater than or equal to
<>	Not equal to

EXCEL

FIGURE 6.14

Logic of the IF function

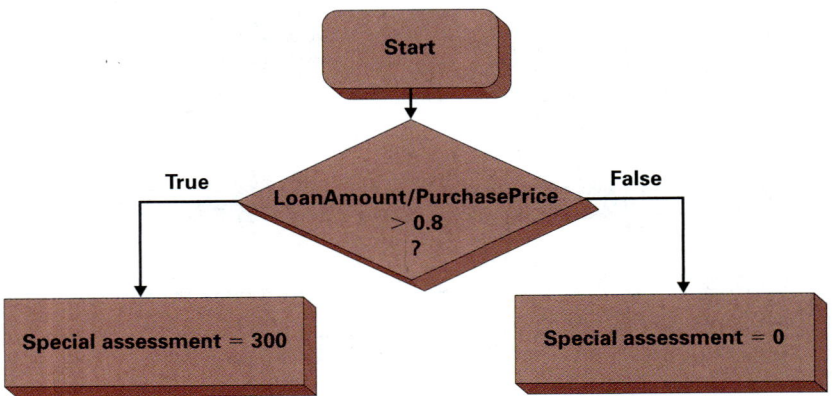

IF(LoanAmount/PurchasePrice > 0.8, 300, 0)

another. If the ratio is greater than 0.8, then the special assessment is $300. Otherwise, the special assessment is $0. Figure 6.14 shows the IF function and the logic of the expression.

Now you are ready to enter the IF function to determine whether the customer must pay the special assessment of $300 or not. In addition to the special assessment, you should conditionally display the label "Assessment" in cell A14 when processing fee appears in cell B14.

Writing an IF function:

1. Click cell **A14**, the cell that will display *Assessment* if the ratio of loan amount to purchase price is greater than 0.8—the same criteria for displaying (or not) an assessment fee of $300

2. Type **=IF(LoanAmount/PurchasePrice > 0.8, "Assessment:", "")** and press **Enter**

tip: *Notice that the second argument contains two quotation marks in a row without a blank between them. The IF function can display character string expressions such as "Assessment" as well as numeric expressions*

When you are unsure of a function and want help writing it, use the Insert Function button to the left of the formula bar or the Insert Function command. Executing Insert Function opens a dialog box that lists functions by categories and helps you build the function.

Using Insert Function to write an IF function:

1. Click cell **B14** to make it active

2. Click the **Insert Function** button next to the formula bar to open the Insert Function dialog box

3. Click the **Or select a category** list box to display its list of function categories

4. Click **Logical** in the list of function category choices, click **IF** in the *Select a function* list box, and then click **OK**. The Function Arguments dialog box opens

5. Click the **Logical_Test** text box and type
   LoanAmount/PurchasePrice > 0.8 (no spaces in this line). Notice that the moment you type 0.8, the label TRUE appears to the right of the box

6. Click the **Value_if_true** text box and type **300**, which is the value to return if the condition is true

7. Click the **Value_if_false** text box and type **0**, which is the value to return if the condition is false (see Figure 6.15)

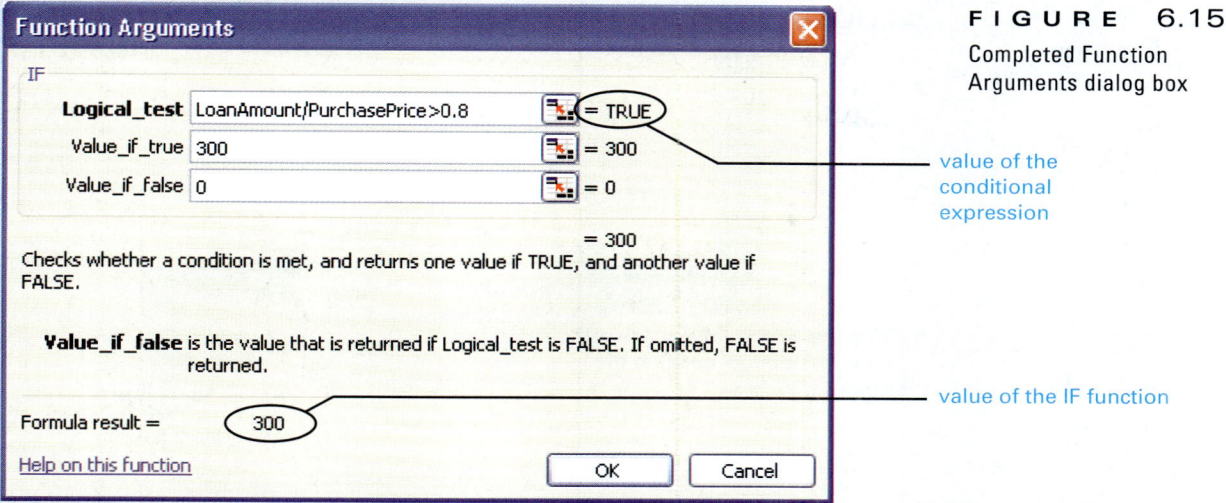

FIGURE 6.15

Completed Function Arguments dialog box

value of the conditional expression

value of the IF function

8. Click **OK** to complete the function

Excel places the completed IF function into cell B14, calculates the value of the function, and displays $300.00 because the ratio of the down payment to the purchase price is greater than 0.8

Using the VLOOKUP Function

You will encounter many situations in which you need to look up an answer from a table of possible answers. For example, an instructor needs a convenient way to look up letter grades that correspond to students' percentage values, or an express shipping company determines shipping prices by a package's weight and the location to which it will be shipped. Or a tax consultant finds it convenient to look up the state or federal tax rate for a client using the client's gross income and number of dependents.

Situations like the preceding ones call for a special class of functions called lookup functions, also known as table lookup functions. Excel provides several *lookup functions*, which use a search value to search a table—a range of cells—for a match or close match and then return a value from the table as a result. The table that a lookup function searches is called the *lookup table*, and the value being used to search the lookup table is called the *lookup value*. With Excel lookup functions, you specify the value or cell address of the lookup value, the cell range of the lookup table, and the column or row that contains the values you want to return as an answer.

Excel provides two lookup functions: HLOOKUP and VLOOKUP. You use the HLOOKUP function, which stands for horizontal lookup, for lookup tables in which the lookup column is in the first row of a multi-row table. You use the VLOOKUP function, which stands for vertical lookup, for a vertical lookup table—one in which the search values are in the first column of the table. For either lookup function to work

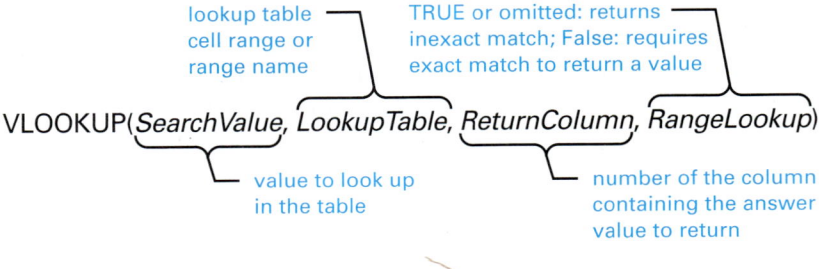

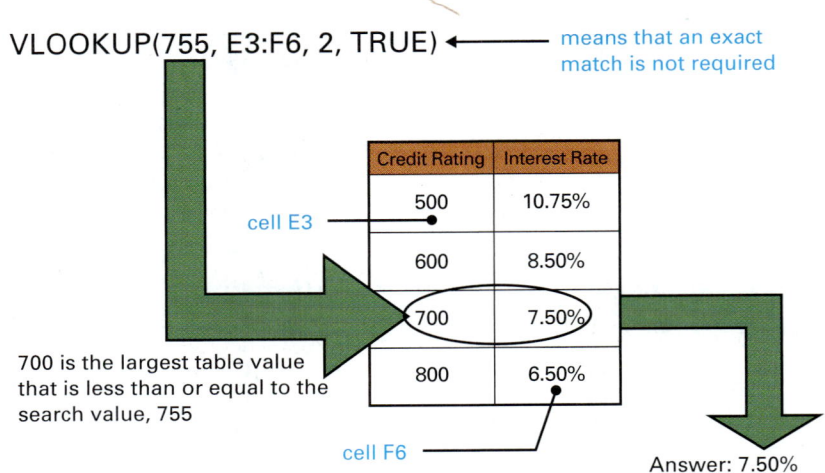

properly, the horizontal or vertical table must be sorted from low to high on the values in the first row (HLOOKUP) or first column (VLOOKUP). Otherwise, either function returns spurious results.

The VLOOKUP function has the general form shown in Figure 6.16. Before you apply the VLOOKUP function to the Loan Analysis worksheet, examine its parts for a better understanding of how it works.

The first argument of the function is the lookup value. The VLOOKUP function uses that value to search the lookup table. The second argument is the lookup table, which is the cell range or name specifying the lookup table's location. The third argument is the column containing the data you want VLOOKUP to retrieve. Finally, the fourth argument can be FALSE, TRUE, or omitted. If it is FALSE, VLOOKUP will look for an exact match in the lookup table. If it does not find a value in the first column exactly matching the lookup value, VLOOKUP returns #N/A error value. If the argument is TRUE or omitted (most people omit the argument), then VLOOKUP searches the first column looking for the largest value in the first column that is less than or equal to the search value. You can better understand this function by applying it to the Loan Analysis worksheet.

Cal's Loan Analysis worksheet can use a lookup function in cell B11 to retrieve the interest rate from a table by searching the table you named CreditTable (cells E3 through F6) using the FICO Credit Rating value in cell B3 as the lookup value. The CreditTable is arranged in columns, and it is sorted in ascending order on the first column—Credit Rating. With the lookup table arranged in this way, you will use the VLOOKUP function because the search values are in the first column. Figure 6.17 shows a graphical example of the VLOOKUP function and how it searches the lookup table and returns an applicable interest rate based on a customer's credit rating number.

task reference   Using the VLOOKUP Function

- Create a lookup table and sort the table in ascending order by the leftmost column
- Place in columns to the right of the search columns values you want to return as answers
- Write a VLOOKUP function referencing a cell containing the lookup value, the lookup table, and the column containing the answer

Jessica asks you to write a function in cell B11 that will use the customer's credit rating in the Assumptions section, cell B3, and look up and return the applicable interest rate from the lookup table.

Writing a VLOOKUP function:

1. Click cell **B11**
2. Click **Insert**, and then click **Function**
3. Click the **Or select a category**
4. Click **Lookup & Reference** in list of choices, scroll to the bottom of the *Select a function* list, click **VLOOKUP**, and click **OK**
5. Type **CreditRating** in the *Lookup_value* text box and press the **Tab** key
6. Type **CreditTable**, which is the name of the lookup table, and press the **Tab** key
7. Type **2** in the Col_index_num box because you want VLOOKUP to return an answer from the second column of the lookup table (see Figure 6.18)

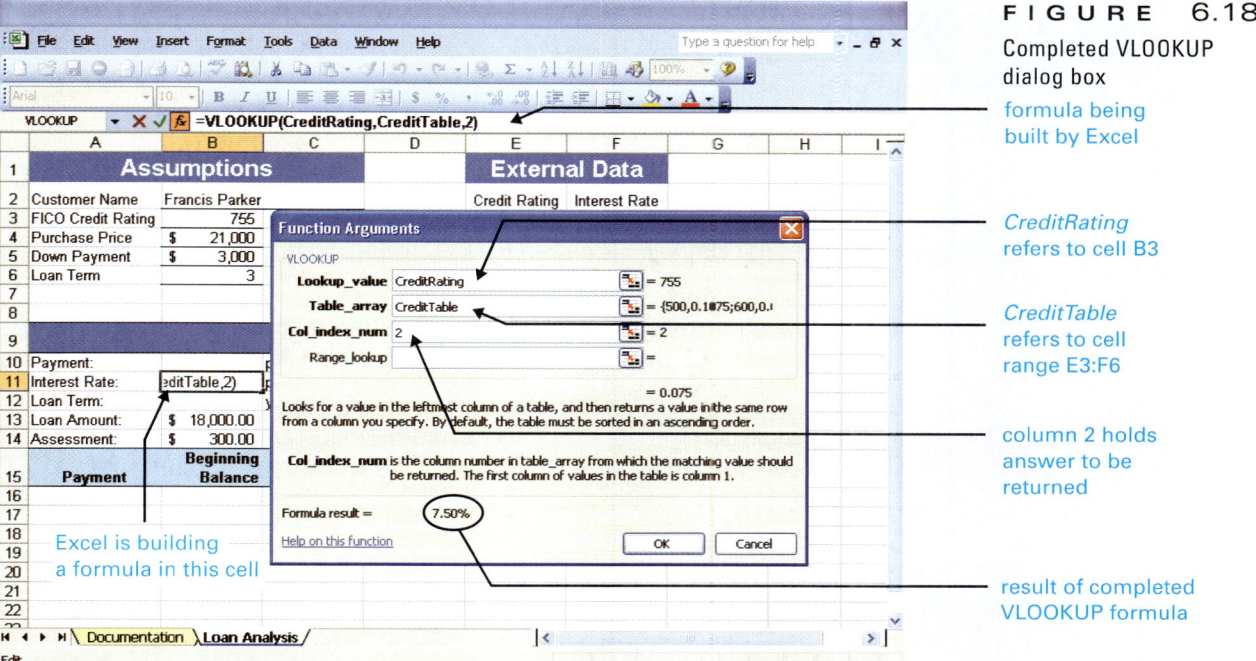

FIGURE 6.18

Completed VLOOKUP dialog box

formula being built by Excel

CreditRating refers to cell B3

CreditTable refers to cell range E3:F6

column 2 holds answer to be returned

result of completed VLOOKUP formula

8. Click **OK** to complete the function definition and close the VLOOKUP function dialog box. The function returns and displays the value 7.50%, which is the interest rate corresponding to the credit rating of 755

The last activity before ending this session is to write a simple formula in cell B12 that displays the loan term. While the loan term used in calculations is found in the Assumptions area, a second copy of it is handy to place in the Outputs section.

Writing the loan term formula:

1. Click cell **B12**
2. Type **=LoanTerm**

You have done a lot of work on the Loan Analysis worksheet in this session. Always save a worksheet before going on to the next session.

Saving the loan analysis worksheet:

1. Click **Save** button on the Standard toolbar to save the work you completed in this session
2. Click **File** on the menu bar and click **Exit**

Congratulations. You have learned a great deal about several important functions. In the next section, you will write several financial functions to produce a schedule of loan repayments that indicate how much you pay each month and how much of the payment reduces the loan balance and how much pays each month's interest.

SESSION 6.1

making the grade

1. Enclosed in parentheses following a function's name are one or more _____.

2. The _____ section of a worksheet contains input values used by other formulas in the worksheet.

3. You can use data _____ to restrict the information being entered into a worksheet cell.

4. You provide error messages with data validation techniques by specifying an error _____ message in the Data Validation dialog box.

5. When a cell can take on one of two possible values based on whether or not some condition is true—the value in another cell is 15 percent or greater, for instance—you should use the _____ function.

SESSION 6.2 USING FINANCIAL AND DATE FUNCTIONS

In this section, you will learn how to write several financial functions including PMT, PPMT, IPMT, and PV. You will also write dates and date functions. You will use AutoFill to copy an ascending series of values in a column and, later, to create several families of related formulas throughout your worksheet.

Using Financial Analysis Functions

Excel's financial functions allow you to extend your proficiency beyond the simpler functions of SUM, MIN, and MAX. You can use the financial and date functions to perform quite sophisticated financial and date calculations without the need to know the theory behind the functions. This session provides you with both the understanding of financial and date functions and experience using them in worksheets to see how they work. Excel's financial functions allow you to take control of many important monetary calculations such as the amount of a monthly payment of a mortgage, the present value of a future steady flow of revenue, or the amount of a loan payment that goes to pay off the principal and the amount that pays the periodic interest.

The financial functions you will encounter in this session all have a common basis. Each is in a family of functions that calculates basic rates of return and payment amounts. A fundamental concept in finance is the *time value of money*. In its simplest form, the **time value of money** means that receiving $100 today is more valuable than receiving it next year. Why? Because you could put the $100 in a bank and earn interest for a year and end up with more than $100 next year—perhaps $105 or $110. Financial functions answer questions such as this one: "How much money do I have to place in an investment that pays 5 percent per year in order to accumulate $10,000 in 10 years?" Other Excel financial functions answer the question "How much is my monthly payment for a $6,000 loan at 8 percent per year for three years?"

help yourself *Press **F1**, type **payment** in the Search text box of the Microsoft Excel Help task pane, and press **Enter**. Scroll down the list to locate and then click the hyperlink **PMT** and then read and scroll down the Help screen to read about the function Maximize the Help screen if necessary. Click the Help screen **Close** button when you are finished, and then close the task pane*

Using the Payment Function, PMT

PMT is one of the Excel functions that calculates payments for a loan or investment that pays a fixed amount at a periodic rate. PMT, which stands for *payment*, is the most commonly used payment function. The PMT function calculates the periodic payment given three values: the periodic interest rate, the number of payments, and the loan amount (called the *present value*). Loan payments are amortized. **Amortization** is the process of distributing periodic payments over the life of a loan. The amount borrowed is the **principal**. The interest percentage is called the **rate**, and the time period over which you make periodic payments is the **term**.

A periodic payment is a fixed payment that you make on a regular basis—once every year, every month, every day, and so on. Part of the payment covers the interest on the loan and part of the payment repays a portion of the loan (principal). After the final loan payment, the loan's balance is zero—it is paid off. Over the life of a loan repayment, more of each monthly payment goes toward reducing the loan amount and less goes toward paying interest on the loan. The general form of the payment function, PMT, is shown in Figure 6.19.

Jessica wants you to work on the periodic payment function that will compute the monthly payment amounts for each customer and display that value in cell B10.

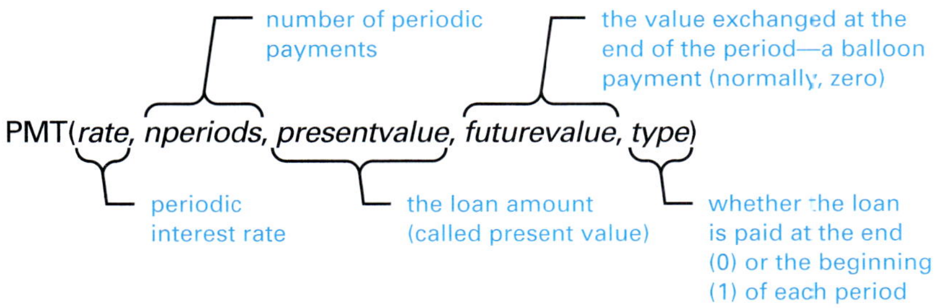

PMT(*rate, nperiods, presentvalue, futurevalue, type*)

number of periodic payments

the value exchanged at the end of the period—a balloon payment (normally, zero)

periodic interest rate

the loan amount (called present value)

whether the loan is paid at the end (0) or the beginning (1) of each period

FIGURE 6.19

PMT function syntax

The PMT function references the InterestRate (cell B11), LoanTerm (cell B6), and LoanAmount (cell B13). All of Cal's customers make monthly payments. For example, in a three-year loan, a customer will make 36 payments—one per month. The frequency of the payment affects the interest rate. When you are dealing with *monthly* payments, remember to divide the annual interest rate by 12 (months) to yield a monthly interest rate.

Opening the loan workbook:

1. Start Excel and open the loan analysis workbook **CalsCars1.xls**

2. Immediately save workbook as **CalsCars2.xls** to preserve the original workbook in case you want to revert to the final version you saved in Session 6.1

Now you can write the formula for the monthly payment.

Writing the PMT function:

1. Click cell **B10**

2. Click **Insert**, click **Function**, type **periodic payment** in the *Search for a function* text box, click the **Go** button, ensure that **PMT** is highlighted in the *Select a function* list box, and click **OK**. The PMT function dialog box opens

3. If necessary, click the **Rate** text box and then type **InterestRate/12**. (You can write an arithmetic expression as a function argument)

4. Click the **Nper** text box and type **LoanTerm*12**. Making monthly payments means that you must multiply the number of years (in the cell named LoanTerm) by the number of payments per year (12)

5. Click the **Pv** text box and type **-LoanAmount**. The minus sign preceding LoanAmount reverses the sign of the function's result. Excel calculates the periodic (monthly) payment and displays it in the dialog box (see Figure 6.20)

6. Click **OK** to complete the function. The PMT function dialog box closes

The LoanAmount cell displays $559.91, which is the monthly payment on a loan of $18,000 for three years at 7.5 percent annual interest. The calculated result is not precise to the penny. Examine Figure 6.20 and you will see that the answer is actually 559.9119269 to seven decimal places. Formatting visually rounds that number to $559.91. Such a small difference will not affect what you do here, but you will learn to use the ROUND function in this session to counteract any cumulative effects such a number would have on a long-term loan or other investment.

Building a Loan Amortization Schedule

Jessica thinks that customers will want to know exactly how much of their loan payment is going toward repaying the loan and how much is going toward interest. She wants you to build a complete month-by-month amortization schedule. An *amortiza-*

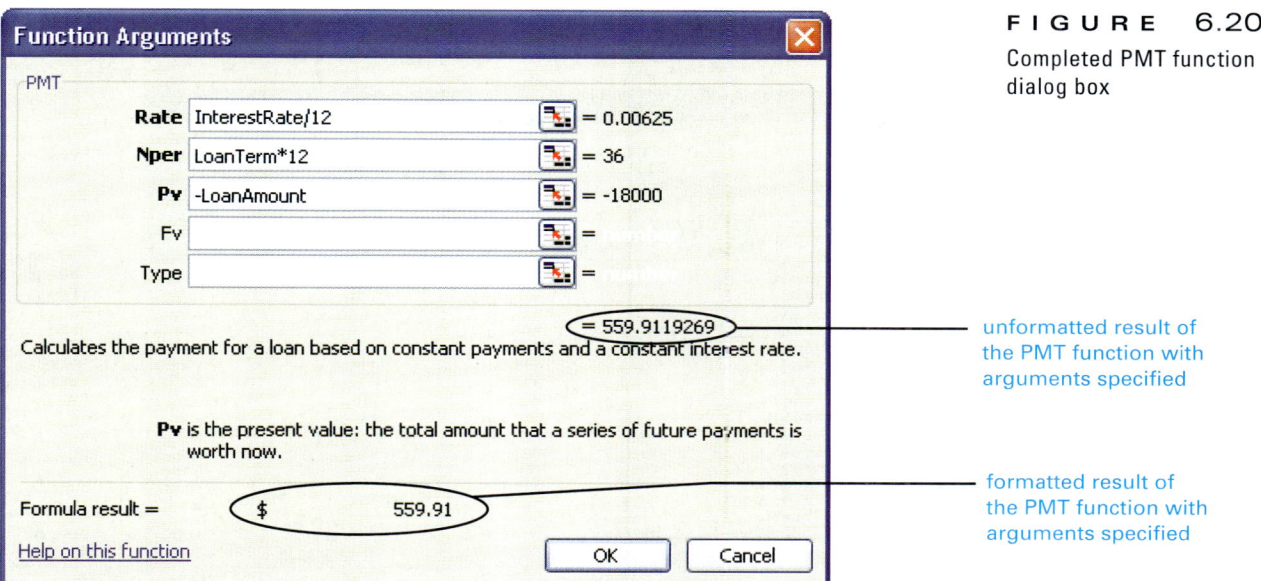

unformatted result of
the PMT function with
arguments specified

formatted result of
the PMT function with
arguments specified

tion schedule lists the monthly payment, the amount of the payment applied toward reducing the principal (loan amount), and the amount of the payment that pays the interest due each month. In addition, she wants you to display, each month, the beginning balance of the loan amount, the total paid so far toward the principal, and the total paid so far in interest charges. The column labels that appear in row 15 are the beginning of the amortization schedule.

There will be 36 rows of information in the amortization schedule for this example because it will take 36 payments to pay off the loan. Each row represents a month in the 36-month payout schedule. It would be nice if you could automatically allocate 12, 24, 36, or 48 rows in the amortization schedule based on the value in the LoanTerm cell.

Creating a Series of Constants with the Fill Handle

The Payment column is designed to hold the payment number beginning at 1 and ending, in this case, at 36. Although you could enter the values in cells A16 through A51 one at a time, it is much faster to enter the initial two values and then clone the remaining 34 values using the fill handle.

Creating and formatting an ascending number series:

1. Click cell **A16** and type **1**

2. Click cell **A17**, type **2**, and press **Enter**

3. Select the cell range **A16:A17**

4. Hover the mouse over the fill handle in the lower-right corner of cell **A17**, click and drag the fill handle down through cell **A51**, and release the mouse. The values 1 through 36 fill cells A16 through A51, and Excel displays the AutoFill Options Smart Tag

5. With cell range A16:A51 still selected, click the **Center** alignment button on the Formatting toolbar (see Figure 6.21) and click cell **B16**

EXCEL

FIGURE 6.21

Payment column completed

	A	B	C	D	E	F	G	H	I
6	Loan Term	3	(years)		800	6.50%			
7									
8									
9				**Outputs**					
10	Payment:	$559.91	per month						
11	Interest Rate:	7.50%	per year						
12	Loan Term:	3	years						
13	Loan Amount:	$ 18,000.00							
14	Assessment:	$ 300.00							
15	Payment	Beginning Balance	Principal Paid	Interest Paid	Total Principal	Total Interest	Ending Balance		
16	1								
17	2								
18	3								
19	4								
20	5								
21	6								
22	7								
23	8								
24	9								
25	10								
26	11								
27	12								
28	13								

Payment column displaying some of the ascending numbers

Documentation \ Loan Analysis /

Ready   Sum=666

Writing a PV Function

The next formula you will write will appear in cell B16, the first of 36 that will display the beginning balance each month. The beginning balance is the amount of the loan left to pay after making the previous month's payment. The first month, the beginning balance is equal to the full loan amount. The beginning balance the second month is the original loan amount minus the amount of the payment applied in month one to pay off the loan. Although you could simply write the formula =LoanAmount (or the equivalent formula, =B13) in cell B16, you will use the present value function, PV, instead. Using the PMT value, interest rate, and loan term as arguments, the PV function returns the original loan amount as its computed result. If it does, that proves the periodic payment in cell B10 is correct. Otherwise, something is wrong.

Writing a PV function to compute the Beginning Balance:

1. If necessary, click cell **B16** to make it the active cell

2. Type **=PV(InterestRate/12,LoanTerm*12,-PeriodicPayment)** and press **Enter**. Remember to not include any spaces in the formula. Excel displays $18,000.00

tip: *One of the tricky things about financial functions, something mentioned earlier, is the sign of the resulting number. A negative sign means the money is flowing out of your pocket, and a positive sign means the money is flowing into your pocket. Because you want a positive value for the loan balance, be sure to type a minus sign preceding PeriodicPayment.*

The present value of a series of mortgage payments should equal the loan amount, because it represents the current value of a loan—far less than its value in the future as it collects interest.

Writing a PPMT Function

The amount of each loan payment that is applied to reduce the principal—eventually making it zero—varies throughout the term of the loan. For example, the amount of the $559.91 monthly payment that goes toward paying off the loan (the principal) is

F I G U R E   6.22

PPMT function syntax

payment period number   value of the loan today

PPMT(*rate*, period #, *nperiod*, *presentvalue*, *futurevalue*)

periodic interest rate   number of periodic payments   residual value of the loan at the end of the term (optional argument)

$447.41 the first month. The remainder of the payment, $112.50, is the interest on $18,000 for one month. When the last payment is due, the amount of the loan payment going toward paying off the loan is $556.43, whereas only $3.48 is due in interest. Thus, over the term of a loan, the payment toward reducing the loan increases, and the payment toward interest decreases.

Excel provides the PPMT function to compute the amount of a fixed periodic payment that goes to reduce the principal. Another function, IPMT, computes the interest portion of a payment, and you will learn about it after you investigate the PPMT function.

The PPMT function requires four arguments: the periodic interest rate, the particular period this payment is for, the total number of payments, and the present value of the loan. The fourth required argument, present value of the loan, is the total amount that a series of future payments is worth now—the loan principal. When creating a series of these formulas in a loan amortization schedule, the only argument of the four that changes is the second one. For the first period payment, it is 1; for the second period payment, it is 2 (or references a cell containing 2); and so on. The general form of the PPMT function appears in Figure 6.22.

Jessica wants each row of the amortization schedule to display the portion of the $559.91 payment that goes to pay off the loan. You code the function next.

Writing a PPMT function to compute the principal reduction amount:

1. Click cell **C16** to make it the active cell

2. Type **=PPMT(InterestRate/12,A16,LoanTerm*12,–LoanAmount)** and press **Enter**. Excel displays $447.41, which is the portion of the payment that reduces the principal this month

Be careful to place a minus sign just before typing LoanAmount in the fourth argument so Excel computes and displays a positive value.

Recall that using a name is the same as using the absolute reference of the cell address. This is particularly important because you will copy this formula and others down through the 35 other rows of the loan amortization schedule. You want all cell references to point to the original interest rate, loan term, and loan amount values throughout the amortization schedule. Using names instead of cell addresses guarantees that Excel will not change the references or adjust them in any way. The only cell reference that Excel will adjust when the formula is copied is the second argument, A16. Because you want the second argument to reference each of the individual payment numbers in column A, allowing the reference to remain a relative reference is perfect. Excel will adjust that reference as it copies the formula down through the amortization schedule rows.

Writing an IPMT Function

Cell D16 will contain a formula that computes the amount of the payment that is applied to pay the current month's interest. You will use the IPMT (Interest Payment) function to compute the interest payment. With this first formula as a guide, you will copy it down through all 36 months in the schedule in later steps. The general form of the IPMT function is similar to PPMT. Simply use the same form as PPMT but substitute IPMT for the function name preceding the opening parenthesis starting the function list.

Writing an IPMT function to compute the period's interest:

1. Click cell **D16** to make it the active cell

2. Type **=IPMT(InterestRate/12,A16,LoanTerm*12,–LoanAmount)** and click the **Enter** button on the left end of the formula bar to complete the formula and keep cell D16 the active cell (see Figure 6.23)

FIGURE 6.23

Worksheet with PPMT and IPMT functions

IPMT function and arguments

PPMT function result

IPMT function result

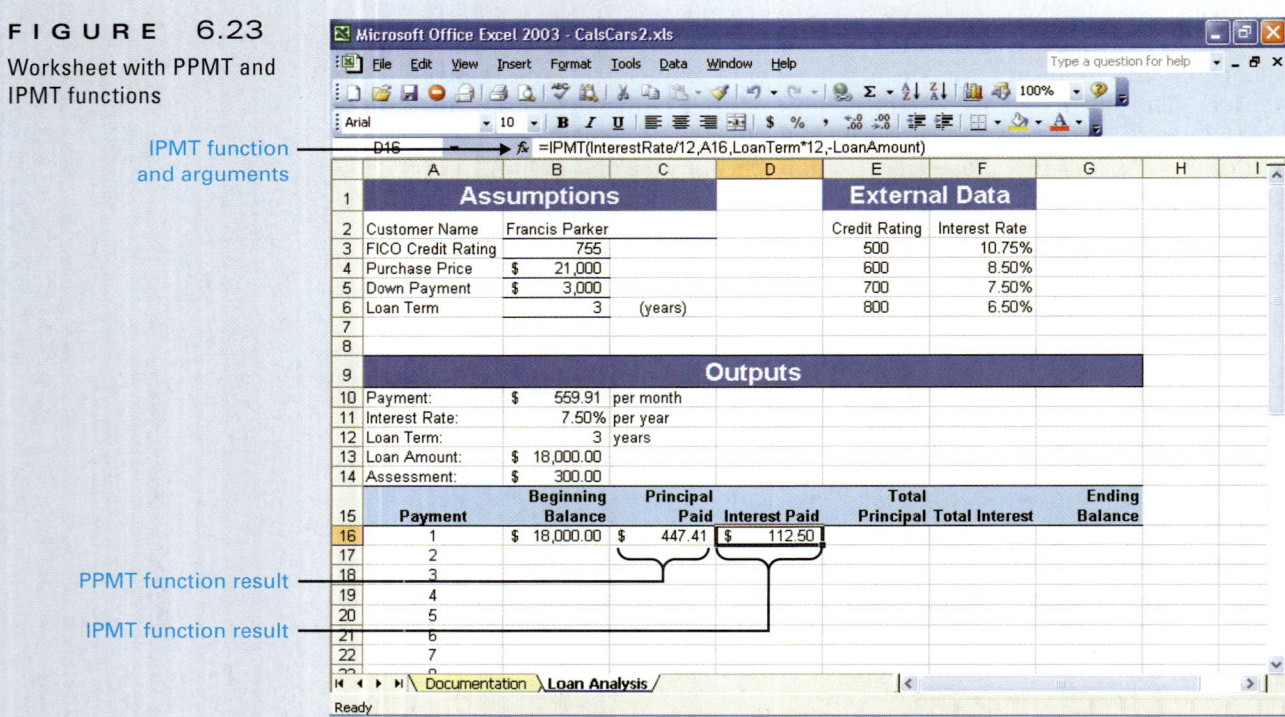

Building Principal, Interest, and Ending Balance Formulas

You have three formulas to build before the first row of the loan amortization schedule is complete. Once that line is done, the remaining 35 lines of the schedule will be simple to create. The Total Principal column holds a running sum of the payments to reduce the loan. The Total Interest column holds the sum of all the interest payments up to and including the current payment. In the last column is the Ending Balance. It is the amount of the principal left to pay. It is equal to the beginning balance for the month minus the Principal Paid amount. You will create these simple formulas in the next steps.

Writing Total Principal, Total Interest, and Ending Balance formulas:

1. Click cell **E16** and type =**C16**

2. Click cell **F16** and type =**D16**

3. Click cell **G16**, type =**B16-C16**, and press **Enter**. The value $17,552.59 appears and is the unpaid loan balance after the first payment is made

Cell E16 shows that of the $559.91 monthly payment, $112.50 is this month's interest payment and $447.41 reduces the loan balance. Each month, the sum of these two numbers is always the same—the monthly payment amount.

If creating formulas required you to write 36 rows of six formulas each, you'd be in for a lot of work. Thankfully, that is not the way worksheet products are designed. You can create a series of formulas that are unique and, often, clone them down or across worksheet cells to create an entire family of related but slightly different formulas.

Jessica tells you that you can create a unique formula for the beginning balance for the second payment and then clone the remainder of the first payment's formulas to the second payment row. With a few adjusting tweaks to selected second payment row formulas, you will have a model row that you can then copy to payment rows 3 through 36.

Writing a general-purpose Beginning Balance formula:

1. Click cell **B17**

2. Type =**G16**, and press **Enter**. The value $17552.59 appears in cell B17

The quickest way to create the formulas for the remainder of the second payment's row is to copy the corresponding formulas from the first payment's row and then make a couple of minor formula adjustments.

Using the fill handle to clone and then adjust selected formulas for the second payment row:

1. Select the cell range **C16:G16**

2. Click the **fill handle**, drag the mouse down one row until the AutoFill outline highlights the cell range C17:G17, and then release the mouse

3. Click cell **E17**, the Total Principal cell for the second payment, type =**C17+E16**, and press **Enter**. Excel displays $897.62

4. Click cell **F17**, the Total Interest cell for the second payment whose formula you are going to replace with a new one, type =**D17+F16**, and press **Enter**. Excel displays $222.20 (see Figure 6.24)

EXCEL

FIGURE 6.24

Amortization schedule
with second payment's
row completed

	A	B	C	D	E	F	G	H	I
1	**Assumptions**				**External Data**				
2	Customer Name	Francis Parker			Credit Rating	Interest Rate			
3	FICO Credit Rating	755			500	10.75%			
4	Purchase Price	$ 21,000			600	8.50%			
5	Down Payment	$ 3,000			700	7.50%			
6	Loan Term	3	(years)		800	6.50%			
7									
8									
9	**Outputs**								
10	Payment:	$559.91	per month						
11	Interest Rate:	7.50%	per year						
12	Loan Term:	3	years						
13	Loan Amount:	$ 18,000.00							
14	Assessment:	$ 300.00							
15	Payment	Beginning Balance	Principal Paid	Interest Paid	Total Principal	Total Interest	Ending Balance		
16	1	$18,000.00	$447.41	$112.50	$447.41	$112.50	$17,552.59		
17	2	$17,552.59	$450.21	$109.70	$897.62	$222.20	$17,102.38		
18	3								
19	4								
20	5								
21	6								
22	7								

H ◄ ► H \ Documentation \ Loan Analysis /

Ready

Format the first row so that it displays accounting-style currency symbols and then format the second payment row so that it does not display currency symbols at all. You will also format cell B10 containing the periodic payment to match formatting in other cells.

Adding a formatting style to the Style list:

1. Click cell **Format** and then click **Style**. The Style dialog box appears

2. Type **AcctSpecial** in the *Style name* list box to name the new formatting style you are creating, click the **Modify** button, click the **Number** tab (if necessary), and click **Accounting** in the Category list

3. Ensure that the Decimal places list box contains 2, click the **Symbol** list box, click **None** in the list of format choices, click **OK** to close the Format Cells dialog box, click **Add** to save the newly created style, and click **Close** to close the Style dialog box without applying the style

Once you have created a customized and named formatting style, you can apply it to any cells in any worksheet you open on the computer on which you created the style.

Formatting cells with the Format Painter and the Style list:

1. Click cell **B13** containing the loan amount. Cell B13 has the format you want to duplicate in other cells

2. Double-click the **Format Painter** button on the Standard toolbar to copy the format of cell B13. Double-clicking the Format Painter button turns it on until you click it again to turn it off. This allows you to paint a cell's format onto more than one cell or cell range

3. Click cell **B10**

4. Click and drag the cell range **B16:G16** and release the mouse. The first row takes on the same currency format as cell B13

5. Click the **Format Painter** button to deactivate it

6. Click and drag the cell range **B17:G17**, click **Format** on the menu bar, click **Style**, click the Style name list arrow, click AcctSpecial, and click OK. Excel applies the custom style you created in earlier steps to the selected cells (see Figure 6.25)

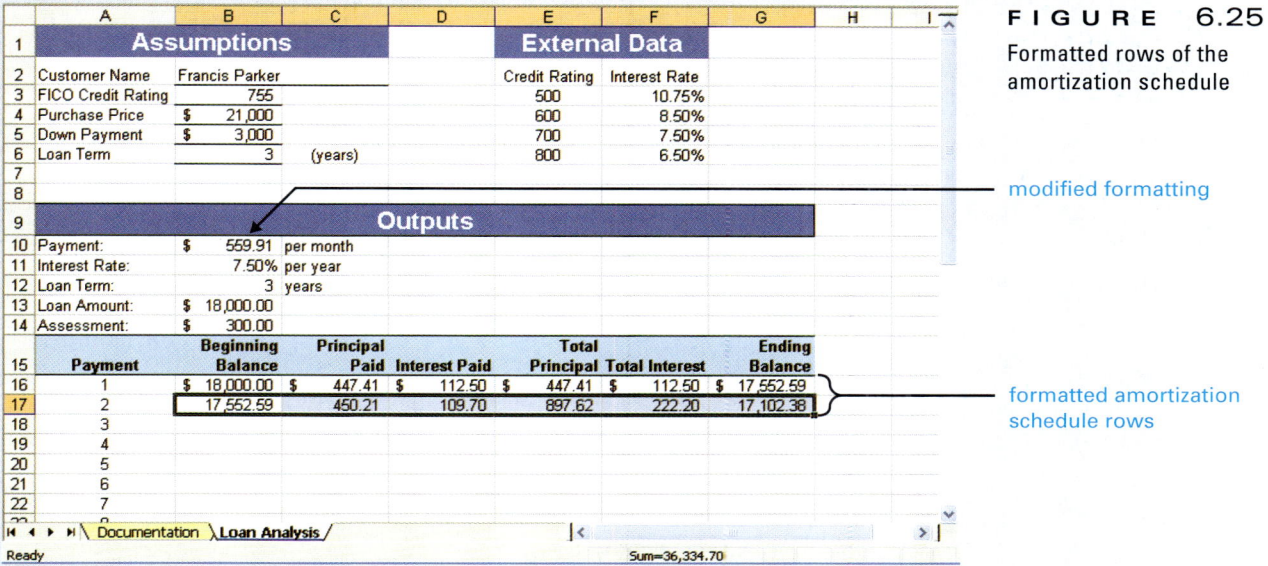

FIGURE   6.25

Formatted rows of the amortization schedule

modified formatting

formatted amortization schedule rows

Using AutoFill to Complete a Series of Related Formulas

Completing the amortization schedule will be surprisingly simple. Because you have created a model row—row 17—whose formulas contain cell references that use both absolute references (names) and relative references in the appropriate way, the row is a model row for the remaining rows. A *model row* contains distinct formulas that you can copy to other rows and not have to modify any copied cell formulas afterward.

You are ready to copy row 17 to rows 18 through 51.

Using the fill handle to copy formulas and complete the loan amortization schedule:

1. If necessary, select the cell range **B17:G17**

2. Move the mouse to the fill handle near the lower-right corner of cell **G17**. The mouse pointer changes to a small plus symbol

3. Click the mouse and slowly drag the fill handle down through row 51 so that Excel highlights the range **B17:G51** and then release the mouse (see Figure 6.26)

tip: *If you fill up too few rows, click and drag the fill handle to fill the remaining rows of the amortization schedule. If you fill up too many rows, delete the extra rows*

4. Scroll down the worksheet until you reach row 51. Notice that the final loan payment reduces the ending balance to zero. In other words, the last payment is just enough to pay off the remaining balance of $556.43 and pay the last month's interest of $3.48.

FIGURE   6.26

Completed amortization
schedule

	A	B	C	D	E	F	G	H	I
28	13	12,442.60	482.15	77.77	6,039.55	1,239.31	11,960.45		
29	14	11,960.45	485.16	74.75	6,524.70	1,314.06	11,475.30		
30	15	11,475.30	488.19	71.72	7,012.90	1,385.78	10,987.10		
31	16	10,987.10	491.24	68.67	7,504.14	1,454.45	10,495.86		
32	17	10,495.86	494.31	65.60	7,998.45	1,520.05	10,001.55		
33	18	10,001.55	497.40	62.51	8,495.85	1,582.56	9,504.15		
34	19	9,504.15	500.51	59.40	8,996.36	1,641.96	9,003.64		
35	20	9,003.64	503.64	56.27	9,500.00	1,698.23	8,500.00		
36	21	8,500.00	506.79	53.12	10,006.79	1,751.36	7,993.21		
37	22	7,993.21	509.95	49.96	10,516.75	1,801.32	7,483.25		
38	23	7,483.25	513.14	46.77	11,029.89	1,848.09	6,970.11		
39	24	6,970.11	516.35	43.56	11,546.24	1,891.65	6,453.76		
40	25	6,453.76	519.58	40.34	12,065.81	1,931.99	5,934.19		
41	26	5,934.19	522.82	37.09	12,588.63	1,969.08	5,411.37		
42	27	5,411.37	526.09	33.82	13,114.73	2,002.90	4,885.27		
43	28	4,885.27	529.38	30.53	13,644.10	2,033.43	4,355.90		
44	29	4,355.90	532.69	27.22	14,176.79	2,060.65	3,823.21		
45	30	3,823.21	536.02	23.90	14,712.81	2,084.55	3,287.19		
46	31	3,287.19	539.37	20.54	15,252.18	2,105.09	2,747.82		
47	32	2,747.82	542.74	17.17	15,794.91	2,122.27	2,205.09		
48	33	2,205.09	546.13	13.78	16,341.04	2,136.05	1,658.96		
49	34	1,658.96	549.54	10.37	16,890.59	2,146.42	1,109.41		
50	35	1,109.41	552.98	6.93	17,443.57	2,153.35	556.43		
51	36	556.43	556.43	3.48	18,000.00	2,156.83	0.00		
52									

K ◀ ▶ H \ Documentation \ **Loan Analysis** /

Ready   Sum=1,028,571.16

ending loan balance is zero ———

AutoFill Smart Tag appears after a copy operation ———

5. Click **Ctrl+Home** to deselect the cell range and make cell A1 active

6. Save the workbook

Working with Date Functions

Excel has 14 date and time functions available. When you enter a date manually, you simply type it in one of several acceptable forms. Excel recognizes that the information is a date and stores it in a special form. For example, if you type into a cell *10/17/2003* without an equal sign preceding it, Excel assumes you are entering the date October 17, 2003, and stores the date in a special date-valued form. The preceding form is called a *date constant*. Similarly, you can type *October 17, 2003* and Excel will recognize the entry as a date and store it in the same, date-valued form. However, Excel recognizes = *10/17/2003* as an expression whose value is 0.000294, rounded to six decimal places.

There are occasions when you cannot or do not want to enter a fixed date because either it is unknown at the time or it varies with time. For instance, you might want to label a worksheet with the current date. If you type 6/14/2003 into a worksheet cell, the date is static—it never changes. If you want a date that is always current, you can use the Excel function NOW.

Jessica wants you to document the worksheet by adding two dates to the Outputs section of the worksheet: the date that the customer applied for the loan (the application date) and the current date each time the worksheet is printed. The former date is simply a date-valued expression such as 10/17/2003 whereas the latter date uses the NOW function to pick up the current date from the computer's internal clock/calendar. The loan application date requires a label as well as the date constant. Because the application date is an input value, you will place it in the Assumptions section.

Entering a date constant into a worksheet cell:

1. Click cell **A7**, type **Application Date**, and press **Enter**. Because you want to place an underline in cell B7 displaying the application date, you can copy the format from an existing cell, B6

2. Click cell **B6**, click the **Format Painter** button on the Standard toolbar, and click cell **B7**. Excel copies the format from cell B6 to cell B7. An underline displays in cell B7

tip: *If you accidentally paint the format on the wrong cell, simply click Undo Paste Special in the Edit menu to reverse the last action*

3. With B7 active, type **6/14/2004** and press **Enter**. Excel displays the date in cell B7. The underline in cell B7 emphasizes that it contains an input value—something an employee must type

4. If cell B7 displays a two-digit year, then execute step 5. If cell B7 displays a four-digit date, then skip step 5

tip: *If the date in cell B7 displays only two digits for the year, then the default date set for your machine may be set to show two years. You can change the date format by executing step 5*

5. Click cell **B7**, click **Format** on the menu bar, click **Cells**, click the **Number** tab, click **Date** in the Category list, scroll the Type list box until you locate the example date format 3/14/2001, click **3/14/2001**, and click **OK** to format cell B7 so it displays a four-digit year (see Figure 6.27)

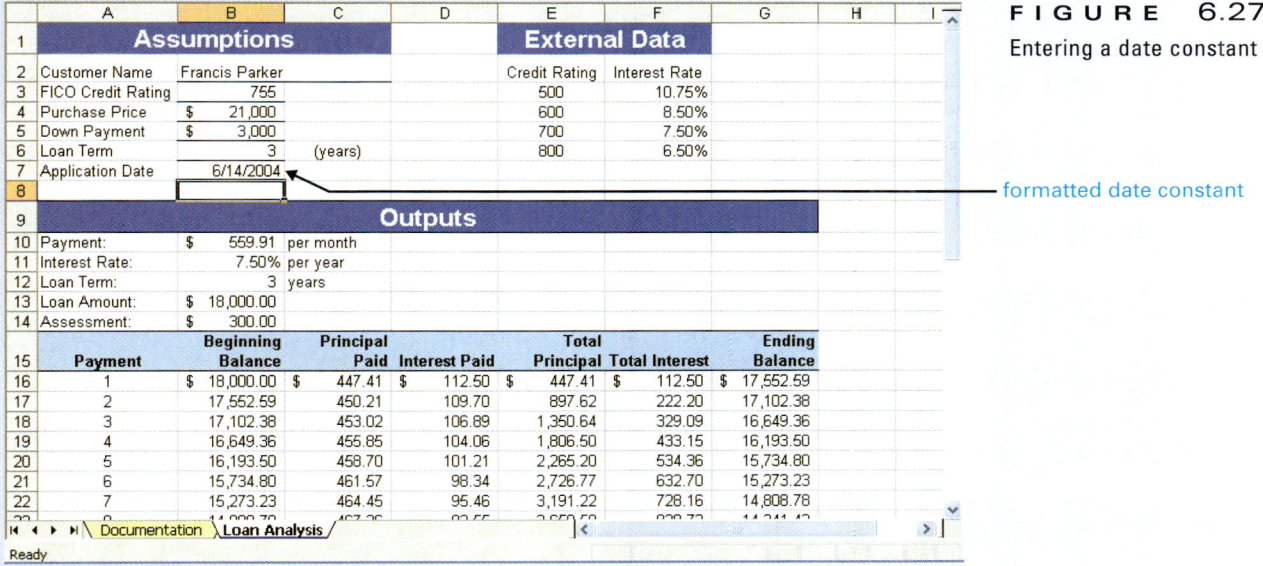

FIGURE 6.27

Entering a date constant

formatted date constant

Using the NOW Function

Several date functions use your computer's clock to determine the current date and time. The NOW function is the most commonly used of these functions. It is one of the Excel functions that has no arguments, but you must be sure to write it with both the opening and closing parentheses immediately following its name. Its form is simply

NOW ( )

If you forget the parentheses and type, instead, =*NOW* in a cell, Excel will generate and display the error message "#NAME?" The error message occurs because Excel thinks you are using a name called NOW, but you have not created that name. If you omit the pair of parentheses when you type the NOW function, simply edit the cell and include the opening and closing parentheses side by side.

Writing the NOW function:

1. Click cell **F10**, type **Today's Date:** and then press the **Tab** key
2. In cell G10, type **=NOW()** and press **Enter**. Depending on the exact width of column G, cell G10 displays either pound signs (#) or the date and time side by side in the cell

Regardless of which form displays in your worksheet (pound signs or the date and time), you will format the cell so that it displays the date but not the time in the next set of steps.

Formatting Date-Valued Cells

By default, the NOW function determines and displays both the current date and the current time. Jessica tells you that the time is unnecessary and distracting. She asks you to format the cell so that it displays the current date and omits the current time. To display the date only, you simply use one of the available date formats to exclude the time of day.

Formatting a date-valued cell to display only the date:

1. Right-click cell **G10**. A shortcut menu appears
2. Click **Format Cells** on the shortcut menu
3. If necessary, click the **Number** tab
4. Click **Date** in the Category list box,
5. Scroll the Type list to locate the example format 3/14/01, and click **3/14/01** in the Type list box (see Figure 6.28)

FIGURE 6.28

Formatting a date-valued cell

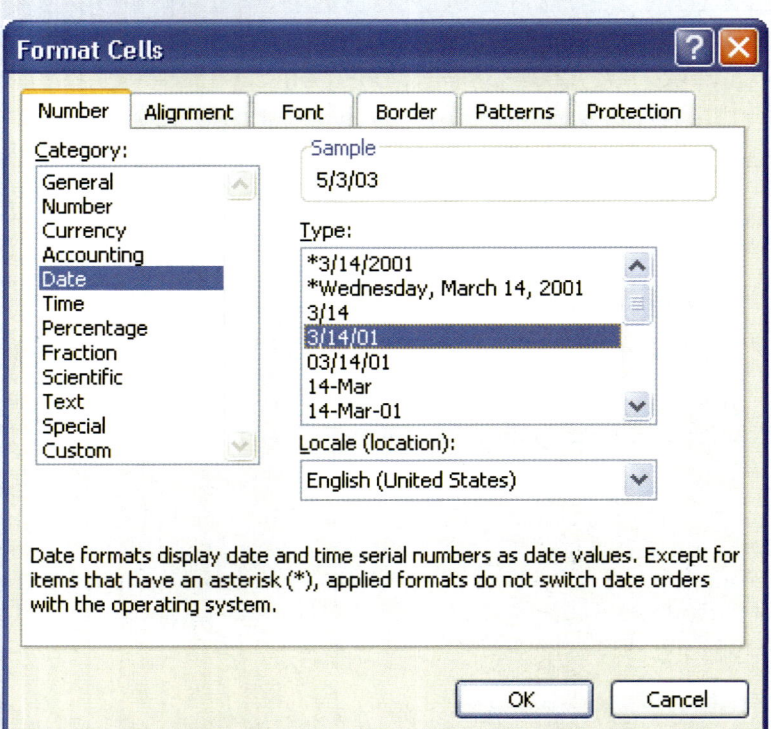

6. Click **OK** to finalize your choices and close the Format Cells dialog box (see Figure 6.29)

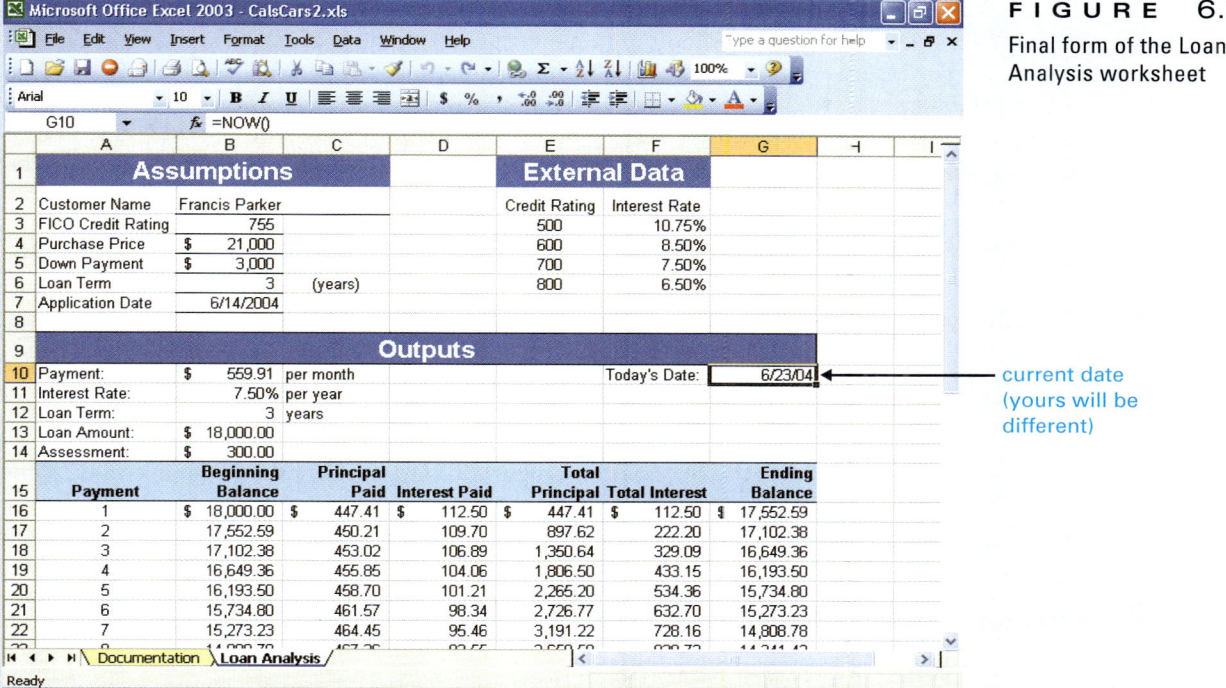

current date (yours will be different)

Your worksheet's current date will be different from the date displayed in Figure 6.29

7. Save your workbook and exit Excel

You have completed a lot of work on the loan amortization workbook and learned about several important financial and date functions.

---

making the grade

S E S S I O N   6 . 2

1. The process of distributing periodic payments over the life of a loan is called _____.

2. The Excel built-in function that computes the periodic payment is called _____.

3. A periodic payment includes money to repay the loan and money for _____ on the outstanding loan amount.

4. The _____ function computes today's value of a future series of cash flows. Today's value of the cash flow is called its _____ value.

5. The _____ function has no arguments, and you use it to retrieve the date and time from your computer's clock and display it.

SESSION 6.3 SUMMARY

Excel functions are built-in tools that perform calculations quickly and easily. Excel's functions are grouped by type. Most Excel functions have one or more arguments enclosed in parentheses following the function name. A function operates on the input values and expressions in its argument list enclosed in parentheses and it returns a single value. Most functions have positional arguments that must be arranged in a particular order.

Creating worksheets used by others often requires that you provide built-in tests for input data to ensure that they are reasonable and within range. Excel's data validation provides automatic input data checking and allows you to specify the range of allowed values in an input value, an input (help) message, and an error message.

Names allow you to assign a name to a cell or range of cells. They have an advantage over cell references because you can assign a meaningful and memorable name; you can remember names as you write expressions referencing the named cells. Secondly, names function as absolute cell references, making it simpler to copy formulas that reference named ranges.

The IF function allows you to create alternative expressions based on a condition. IF evaluates a condition, which is its first argument, and calculates and displays one expression's value if the condition is true or displays the other expression's value if the condition is false.

VLOOKUP is one of several index functions that does a table search with a search value and returns an answer from the table lookup operation. The two most popular lookup functions are VLOOKUP and HLOOKUP. Both are identical in function except for the arrangement of the lookup table—one uses a vertical lookup table and the other uses a horizontal lookup table.

Financial functions including PMT, PPMT, IPMT, and PV are all related. Each function operates on the theory of the time value of money: Money today is worth more than the same amount of money tomorrow. PMT computes a periodic payment given the interest rate, principal amount, and period. PPMT and IPMT compute the amount of the periodic payment for a particular period that pays off the principal (PPMT) and the amount that pays the interest due on the principal (IPMT). PV, or present value, computes today's value of a future steady stream of cash flows.

Worksheet date functions work with date-valued cells. The NOW function displays the current date and time. Special formats are available for formatting the NOW cell to display various forms of the date or to display various forms of the time. NOW obtains its information from the system clock, which also contains a calendar.

MICROSOFT OFFICE SPECIALIST OBJECTIVES SUMMARY

- Use Insert Function to help write worksheet functions—MOS XL03S-2-3
- Investigate the logical function IF—MOS XL03S-2-4
- Write financial functions including PV, PMT, PPMT, and IPMT—MOS XL03S-2-4
- Write and apply the NOW date function—MOS XL03S-2-4
- Apply and modify cell styles—MOS XL03S-3-2
- Provide data validation for selected worksheet cells—MOS XL03E-1-4
- Write the index function VLOOKUP—MOS XL03E-1-9
- Define and use names in functions in place of cell references—MOS XL03E-1-14

making the grade *answers*

SESSION 6.1

1. arguments
2. assumption(s) or input(s)
3. validation
4. alert
5. IF

SESSION 6.2

1. amortization
2. PMT
3. interest
4. PV; present value
5. NOW

task reference *summary*

Task	Page #	Preferred Method
Naming a cell or cell range	EX 6.12	• Select the cell or cell range you want to name • Click the **Name box** in the formula bar • Type the name and press **Enter**
Deleting a name	EX 6.14	• Click **Insert**, point to **Name**, and then click the **Define** button • Click the name in the *Names in workbook* list that you want to delete • Click the **Delete** button and then click the **OK** button
Using the VLOOKUP function	EX 6.19	• Create a lookup table and sort the table in ascending order by the leftmost column • Place in columns to the right of the search columns values you want to return as answers • Write a VLOOKUP function referencing a cell containing the lookup value, the lookup table, and the column containing the answer

EXCEL

TRUE OR FALSE

1. A range error indicates that a value is either too large or too small.

2. The time value of money states that $10 tomorrow is worth more than $10 today.

3. Excel functions operate on the input values and expressions in its argument list enclosed in parentheses.

4. The NOW function only returns and displays the current time.

5. By default all worksheet cells are locked.

FILL-IN

1. It is convenient to divide a worksheet into a(n) _____ section and an output section.

2. Use data _____ to ensure that a worksheet user enters an appropriate value into a cell or cell range.

3. A(n) _____ name acts like an absolute cell reference when you copy a formula containing it to other cells.

4. The _____ function has three arguments: a conditional expression and two alternative expressions. One expression displays if the condition is true, and the other displays otherwise.

5. Some functions have no arguments. An example is the _____ function, which returns the date and time.

6. To compute a periodic payment, use the PMT function. Its arguments are the _____, the number of periods, and the present value or loan amount.

MULTIPLE CHOICE

1. Which is not an argument of the VLOOKUP function?
   a. the match value
   b. the lookup table
   c. the return data
   d. the range lookup

2. Cells that you do not want Excel to protect when you apply worksheet protection are
   a. assumption cells.
   b. changing cells.
   c. unlocked cells.
   d. target cells.

3. Which of the following is not a financial function?
   a. PMT
   b. PVMT
   c. IPMT
   d. PV

4. The IF function has which of the following forms?
   a. IF(conditional test, expression if false, expression if true)
   b. IF(expression if false, expression if true, conditional test)
   c. IF(expression true, expression false, conditional test)
   d. IF(conditional test, expression true, expression false)

5. Cell references have an advantage over names. This is due to which of the following?
   a. A cell reference is more meaningful.
   b. A cell reference is more memorable.
   c. It is simpler to copy formulas that reference cell ranges.
   d. Cell names are easier to remember than cell references.

REVIEW QUESTIONS

1. Discuss how cell protection differs from data validation.

2. Suppose you want to write an expression in cell B7 that guarantees that a value a user enters into cell A1 is positive. Discuss how you would use an expression involving the IF function in cell B7 to return the positive value of any value entered in cell A1.

3. Describe the meaning of "the time value of money" and provide a concrete example using a savings account.

4. Explain the difference between these two expressions: **=7/21/2004** and **7/21/2004**.

5. Describe what happens if you type **=NOW** into a worksheet cell and press Enter. Assume that today's date is January 14, 2004.

6. Explain why locking or unlocking worksheet cells is not sufficient to protect or unprotect them.

CREATE THE QUESTION

For each of the following answers, create an appropriate short question.

ANSWER

1. It displays an error alert message

2. The first argument of an IF function

3. The greatest value that is less than or equal to the search value

4. The Name box is the fastest way

5. The IPMT function calculates and displays that value

6. Double-click the tab, type a new name, and press Enter

QUESTION

_____

_____

_____

_____

_____

_____

1. Determining Savings Match with Data Validation

Shelly Mueller has been studying German since her freshman year in high school. This summer, she has decided to participate in a study-abroad program sponsored by the German Club at her school. Her parents feel this will be a good learning experience for her and have agreed to pay for the cost of the program.

Shelly has a part-time job at a nearby stationery store where she earns $125 a week. She has two full months to save money for the trip before she leaves on the first of June. To encourage and help her with her savings, her grandfather has agreed to contribute to her savings. Shelly has kept track of her savings for each week and needs to send the summary to her grandfather. Since her grandfather is matching her savings, Shelly has decided to put in equal amounts for the "Match" row as she entered in the Savings row.

1. Open the workbook **ex06Savings.xls** (see Figure 6.30) and save it as **<yourname>Savings2.xls**

2. Click cell **A5** and type **Match**. Click cell **B5** and enter the formula **=B4**. Using the fill handle, copy this formula into the cell range **C5:I5**. Include your name in a custom header and print this sheet

3. Delete the formulas in the cell range **B5:I5**. Click cell **B5**, click **Data**, and then click **Validation** to activate the Data Validation dialog box. Use the data validation tool to ensure that no amount greater than $50 or less than $1 will be entered for the Match value

4. Type the title **Valid Amount** and type the input message **Valid amounts are less than or equal to $50**

5. Type an error alert message titled **Invalid Amount** and type the message **The amount you entered is greater than $50**. Use the stop style for this alert

6. Test the data validation by entering **$75** for the match value of cell B5. What happens?

7. Using the fill handle, copy these validation terms in cells **C5:I5**

8. Enter the correct match values, using the values in the Savings row and the $50 match limit as your guide

9. After the values for the fourth week of May, create a column titled **Totals**. (Type **Totals** in cell J2.) Write a SUM function in cell J4 to total the Savings row for both months

10. Using the fill handle, copy the formula into cell J5 so that it includes the total matching contribution for her grandfather

11. Click cell J6, and then write a formula that displays the grand total amount Shelley will have for her trip. Label it **Grand Total** and adjust the cell widths, heights, and colors so that the worksheet is attractive

12. Include your name in the custom header, save the workbook, and print the worksheet

FIGURE   6.30

Savings match workbook

	A	B	C	D	E	F	G	H	I	J	K	L
1												
2	Month	April				May						
3	Week		1	2	3	4	1	2	3	4		
4	Savings	$75	$75	$50	$40	$40	$80	$75	$50			
5												

2. Deciding between Loan Options by Total Payment

James Thomas has been out of college for three years. Now that he has had the chance to put aside some of his income, he would like to look for a new car. He has been able to save $4,000 and has decided that he would like a car that is two years old with no more than 20,000 miles on it. He found a car that meets his criteria. The current owner wants $10,500 for the car. James will apply his savings to the purchase, but needs a loan for the remaining $6,500. He went to several local banks to find the best loan offer.

ABC Bank has a loan available at 9.5 percent interest for two years. The interest compounds monthly and James' payments would be due at the end of each month. XYZ Bank has a loan available at 9 percent interest for 2½ years. This loan also compounds monthly with payments due at the end of each month.

James needs your help to determine which loan alternative is best. He wants to determine which loan has the lowest monthly payment. He has entered each bank's offer in the worksheet called **ex06CarLoan.xls**.

1. Open **ex06CarLoan.xls** (see Figure 6.31) and save it as **<yourname>CarLoan2.xls** to preserve the original worksheet

2. Click cell **A6** and type **Periodic Payment**

3. Click cell **B6**, click **Insert** on the menu bar, and then click **Function**

4. Click **Financial** in the *Or select a category* list box, click **PMT** in the *Select a function* list box, and click **OK**

5. Based on the information given for ABC Bank, in the **Rate** text box write a formula referencing the interest rate cell, cell **B4**. Remember to divide the interest rate by the number of payments per year

6. Click the **Nper** text box and type the formula for the total number of payments you will make for the entire life of the loan. Remember to multiply the loan duration in years (a reference to the cell containing it) by the number of payments per year

7. Click the **Pv** text box, type − (minus) followed by the cell address containing the principal amount, **B3**, and then click **OK**

8. Copy the formula in cell **B6** to cell **C6** to also create the PMT function for the loan from XYZ Bank

9. Based on the monthly payment figures alone for each bank, which appears to be the better loan for James? Highlight this bank's information with a Light Green fill color. (Click the **Fill Color** list arrow on the Formatting toolbar and click the color **Light Green**)

10. Place your name in your worksheet's header, save the workbook, and print the worksheet

11. After examining your results, you decide to determine the total payments that James will make to each bank for their loan to make sure he chooses the right loan for his car. Title the row below Periodic Payment **Total Payments**. In cell **B7**, create a formula to multiply the monthly payment in B6 by the number of months in ABC Bank's loan term

12. Create a similar formula in cell **C7** using the monthly payment and months in the loan for XYZ Bank. Be sure the Total Payments display positive values

13. Based on the total payments, which loan should James take? Highlight the information for this bank and print the worksheet

14. Save the workbook

FIGURE 6.31

Loan options workbook

	A	B	C	D	E
1					
2		ABC Bank	XYZ Bank		
3	Loan Amount	$6,500	$6,500		
4	Interest Rate	9.50%	9%		
5	Term (years)	2	2.5		

1. Forecasting Interest Expense Using Amortization Schedules

Sharon Crowley has always wanted to blend her business savvy with her love of cooking. After college, she attended culinary school for two years specializing in pastries and desserts, and she decided to fulfill her lifelong dream to open her own dessert shop.

Sharon was able to qualify for a small business loan through her local credit union that would cover the costs of needed machinery and supplies and the first few payments of her lease for a total of $25,000. The loan rate is 8.75 percent and is to be paid monthly over a four-year period. Sharon wants to be able to forecast what her interest expenses will be for tax purposes. She has asked you to create an amortization schedule to detail the loan over its term.

Do the following. Open **ex06Desserts.xls** (see Figure 6.32) and save the workbook as **<yourname>Desserts2.xls**. Sharon has already figured out what her monthly payment would be using the PMT function, but she input the wrong rate for the loan. Change the interest rate in cell B4 to 8.75 percent. What happens to her monthly payment after the rate is adjusted? Enter the dates that each payment is due under the Date heading (cell A14), with the first payment due on March 31, 2004, in cell A15. Use the AutoFill feature to complete the sequential series April 30, 2004, through February 29, 2008. To represent the payment numbers, type **1** in cell B15 and **2** in cell B16. Use the AutoFill feature to complete the sequential series 3 through 48 in the Payment Number column. In cell

C15, type the formula **=B3** to display the initial unpaid loan balance.

Click cell **D15**, click **Insert** on the menu bar, click **Function**, type **payment** in the *Search for a function* text box, click the **Go** button, and then click **PPMT** in the Function name. Enter the necessary information by typing cell references in each list box for the function. *Important:* Be sure to make cell references in the Rate, Nper, and Pv text boxes absolute references. The cell reference in the Per text box must be relative. Fill in the remaining information for Per (relative cell reference), Nper (absolute cell reference), and Pv (absolute cell reference), and then click **OK**. Change the formula, if necessary, so that the result is a positive number. Click cell **E15**, and write the formula

```
=-IPMT($3$4/12,B15,$B$5*12,$B$3)
```

To complete the information for the first payment due on March 31, 2004, the ending balance must be determined. Create a formula for cell **F15** that subtracts the Repayment of Principal from the Beginning Balance (cell **C15**). Create a formula for the Beginning Balance for cell **C16** (payment 2) by referencing the Ending Balance of the previous month (using all relative references). Copy the remaining formulas from payment 1 (cells **D15:F15**) to the cells for payment 2 (to cells **D16:F16**). Now copy the formulas in cell range **C16:F16** to the cell range **C17:F62** to complete the schedule. What is the Ending Balance for payment 48? Include your name in the worksheet header and print the worksheet. Save the workbook.

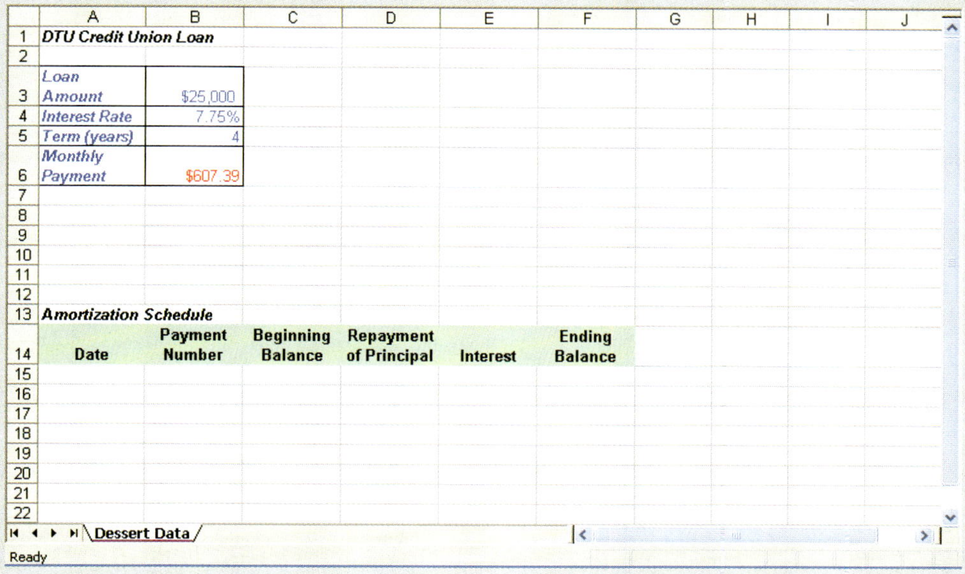

FIGURE 6.32

Sharon Crowley interest expense workbook

2. Computing Shipping Costs for West Coast Imports

West Coast Imports sells fine, imported gifts through the mail. The shipping manager tracks the shipping costs and total costs on a daily basis in a worksheet she maintains. At the end of each day, she erases the input data in preparation for the next day's orders. You will help the shipping manager by writing formulas that help her calculate the shipping cost for each package. You will employ data validation to ensure that the package weight and shipping zone are valid, thus providing a check on those values as the shipping manager enters them.

Shipping costs depend upon the weight of a package and the zone to which it is being shipped. For this problem, there are six shipping zones. Begin by opening the workbook **ex06Shipping.xls** (see Figure 6.33), save the workbook as **<yourname>Shipping2.xls**, and then make the changes specified in the following paragraphs.

Enter into cell C1 the function to display today's date. Format the cell to display the date (mm/dd/yy format) only. Select the cell range A4:A22 and use the Data Validation to ensure that a user can enter only whole numbers between 1 and 6. Type **Enter a value between 1 and 6.** for both the Input Message and Error Alert. Select the cell range D4:D22 and use the Data Validation to ensure that a user can enter only whole numbers between 1 and 100. Type **Enter a value between 1 and 100.** for both the Input Message and Error Alert. Select the cell range A34:G68 (the shipping cost table) and assign it the name *Shipping*. Across the top of the table are the six zones and along the left edge are package weights. At the intersection of a zone and a weight is the shipping cost. For example, a 9-pound package shipped to zone 4 costs $10.60. Write in cell E4 the VLOOKUP expression that looks up the weight in the Shipping table and returns the cost. (*Hint:* Look up the weight in cell D4, write **Shipping** as the second argument, and reference the zone in cell A4 in a simple expression as the third argument to determine the lookup column returned—the zone number plus 1.) Clone the formula down through the rest of the column. Write the formula in F4 for the total cost—charge plus shipping cost—and copy it down the column. Form totals for the Charge, Weight, Shipping Expense, and Total columns in cells C24 through F24. Place the label *Total* in cell B24. Place a page break in cell A30 so the shipping table prints on a new page. Place your name in the worksheet header, print the worksheet, and print the formulas for cells E4 through F24 only. Sort the Orders by zone and use the Data Subtotal command to display subtotals of the Charge, Weight, Shipping Expense, and Total columns by zone. Ensure that column A is wide enough to display the newly inserted subtotal labels (particularly, "Grand Total"), then print the subtotal list of orders. (You do not need to print the second page containing the shipping table.)

FIGURE 6.33

Split screen showing order data and Shipping Costs table

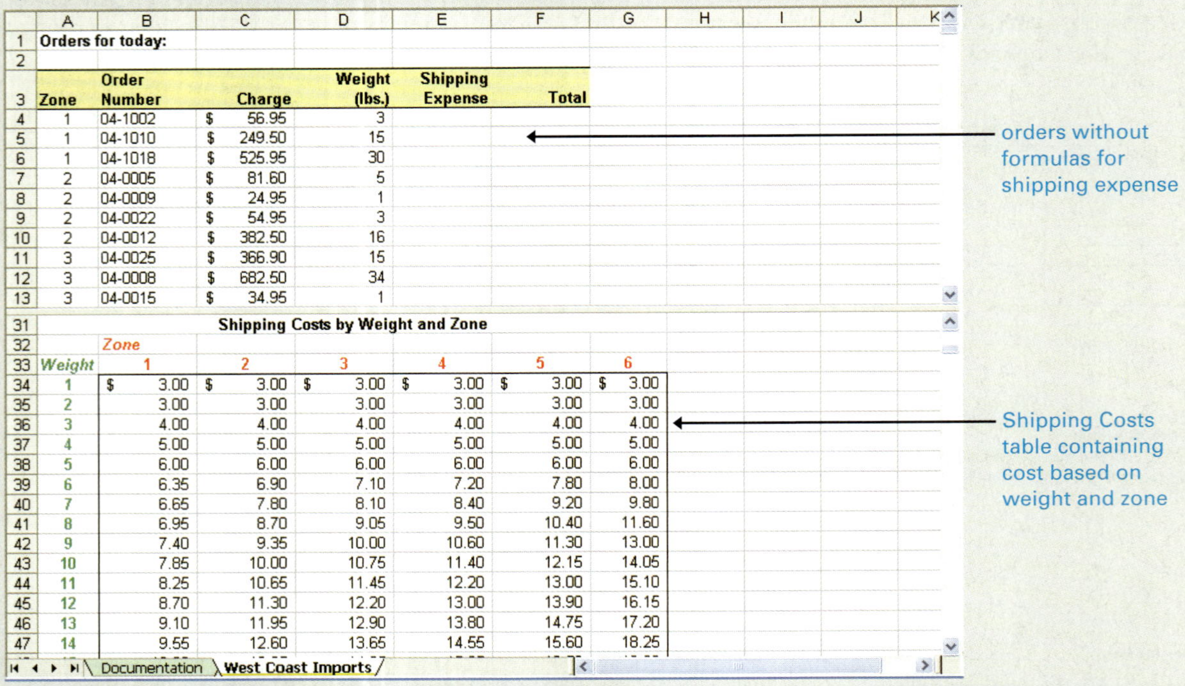

	A	B	C	D	E	F	G
1	**Orders for today:**						
2							
3	**Zone**	**Order Number**	**Charge**	**Weight (lbs.)**	**Shipping Expense**	**Total**	
4	1	04-1002	$ 56.95	3			
5	1	04-1010	$ 249.50	15			
6	1	04-1018	$ 525.95	30			
7	2	04-0005	$ 81.60	5			
8	2	04-0009	$ 24.95	1			
9	2	04-0022	$ 54.95	3			
10	2	04-0012	$ 382.50	16			
11	3	04-0025	$ 366.90	15			
12	3	04-0008	$ 682.50	34			
13	3	04-0015	$ 34.95	1			
31			**Shipping Costs by Weight and Zone**				
32		*Zone*					
33	*Weight*	1	2	3	4	5	6
34	1	$ 3.00	$ 3.00	$ 3.00	$ 3.00	$ 3.00	$ 3.00
35	2	3.00	3.00	3.00	3.00	3.00	3.00
36	3	4.00	4.00	4.00	4.00	4.00	4.00
37	4	5.00	5.00	5.00	5.00	5.00	5.00
38	5	6.00	6.00	6.00	6.00	6.00	6.00
39	6	6.35	6.90	7.10	7.20	7.80	8.00
40	7	6.65	7.80	8.10	8.40	9.20	9.80
41	8	6.95	8.70	9.05	9.50	10.40	11.60
42	9	7.40	9.35	10.00	10.60	11.30	13.00
43	10	7.85	10.00	10.75	11.40	12.15	14.05
44	11	8.25	10.65	11.45	12.20	13.00	15.10
45	12	8.70	11.30	12.20	13.00	13.90	16.15
46	13	9.10	11.95	12.90	13.80	14.75	17.20
47	14	9.55	12.60	13.65	14.55	15.60	18.25

1. Deciding between Investment Opportunities Using Payment

Jonathan Leitman owns a small, yet successful, custom furniture company. For the past few years, he has done little marketing since current customers refer most of his new customers to him. This past year, his business has greatly increased and he has decided to grow the business. He has already looked into opening a larger production facility, purchasing new machines and tools, and hiring a few carpenters to assist him. The initial cost of expanding the business will be $225,000, and Jonathan knows he will be able to raise this initial capital. Jonathan's problem is that he doesn't know how he should market his company.

A business consultant has recommended two options to him. The first option is that Jonathan hires a Web designer to create a Web site for the firm. The consultant feels this would be the best marketing opportunity since he could include pictures, dimensions, costs, and anything else a potential customer would want to know. The greatest advantage of the Web site is that orders could be placed directly through the Web site. The second option is to hire an advertising agency to design and implement a marketing campaign for the company. The main advantage of the advertising campaign option is that it would give the company exposure to a lot of potential customers who would not otherwise hear about the company's products.

Jonathan's consultant has estimated the additional initial cost for each of the options. The Web site will incur an additional initial cost of $250,000. Hiring an advertising agency will require an initial cost of $325,000. After meeting with his loan officer, Jonathan was approved for an additional $325,000 for his loan at a rate of 9.5 percent for three years with payments due monthly. In addition, the advertising agency has a relationship with the bank that would result in a reduction of the annual interest rate to 4.5 percent if Jonathan hires the agency.

Jonathan has asked you to help him decide which he should invest in—a Web site or an advertising campaign. He can choose only one of the options due to capital restraints. Open workbook **ex06Leitman.xls** and save it as **<yourname>Leitman6.xls**. Create a worksheet, titled **Payments**, that summarizes the initial cost and loan terms for each option. Remember to include in the initial cost the total of the initial costs of each investment and the initial cost of the facility, tools, and new carpenters. Using the Payment Function, determine the monthly payment and total payments for each investment option. Jonathan wants to compare interest and principal payments for each option since both the interest rates and principal amounts are different. He does not want to look at all 36 months, but has asked you to include in your worksheet a breakdown of the interest, principal, and total payments for the first and second month. If Jonathan's goal is to pay as little interest as possible, which option should he choose based on these results?

Improve the worksheet's appearance and make all payment amounts appear in red. Open the worksheet titled **Documentation** and, in row 4, enter Investment and Loan Options. In cell **B7**, enter **Prepared by: Jonathan Leitman**. In cell **B9**, enter **Analyzed by:** followed by your name. Click in cell **B11** and enter **Date:** followed by the current date. Make the appearance of the documentation sheet similar to the payments worksheet in font and color. Save the workbook again to preserve your work and print it.

2. Avante's Avocados

George Avante has been an avocado grower all his life. His great-grandfather started the family grove in Temecula, California. It has since been passed from generation to generation. Currently all his crops are sold to local grocery chains where Avante's gets approximately $0.25 each. The local grocery chains in turn sell the avocados for up to $1.00 each. George has decided that through the Internet, he can provide avocados, potentially nationwide, at a much better price to the consumer and achieve a higher profit for Avante's. His idea is based on the fact that so many other growers of oranges, grapefruits, apples, and exotic fruits have done the same by filling orders over the Internet and shipping directly to the private homes and businesses. With the romantic history behind the Avante grove, the beautiful location in the mountains of Temecula, the organic growth process, and the family involvement in actually personally picking avocados, an enticing Web site has been created and the market tested.

All the initial results look promising. However, George first must evaluate the financial implications of the costs associated with the new business. He will need to invest money in packaging equipment, new computers, and software, and remodel part of his current facilities to handle his own packaging operation. That will require a small business loan. Plus, there are many other new costs that Avante's will incur such as the actual packaging and shipping material, additional labor, Web site maintenance, and so on. George has already estimated these values and has added them to his current fixed and variable costs. George is uncertain where his breakeven point is, how the new loan payment impacts that point, and if he has the capacity to produce enough avocados to break even. If Avante's breakeven quantity exceeds the capacity, George still has options. He can adjust the sales price or change the terms of the loan. For now, though, he needs to base his decision on the established loan numbers and pricing.

Create a workbook that allows George to determine Avante's breakeven quantity. Open the workbook titled **ex06Avocado.xls**. Immediately save it as **<yourname>Avocado6.xls**. The Avante's Avocados worksheet has been broken into two sections: *Assumptions* and *Outputs*. In the Assumptions section you will see that George has already entered his estimates for costs, loan amount, capacity, etc. However, the Outputs section does not yet have any formulas. You need to create the formulas to perform the calculations so that George can make an informed decision. Start by naming each of the cells in the Assumptions section that contain values. Use the labels that appear to the left of the cells. (*Hint:* select the cell range **A2:B8**, click **Insert**, point to **Name**, click **Create**, ensure the **Left column** check box contains a checkmark, and click **OK**.) Next, write a payment function using PMT to calculate the *Loan Payment* per month in cell B11. Then write a formula to calculate the monthly *New Fixed Costs* (Current Fixed Costs + Loan Payment) in cell B12. Your formulas must use the cell names and not the actual values or cell address. Name both cells after the formulas are completed, as you did for the Assumptions section.

The last item that needs to be calculated is the *Breakeven Quantity*. For your worksheet, this is defined as the quantity of avocados that Avante's must sell each month to cover costs. Selling more avocados will result in a profit and selling less will result in a loss. The method for calculating the Breakeven Quantity is in the worksheet. You will have to rearrange the formula and solve for Quantity. (Breakeven Quantity equals the fixed cost divided by the result of the price less the variable cost per piece.) Finally, use an IF function to compare the *Breakeven Quantity* to the *Capacity* in cell B14. If the Breakeven Quantity is greater than the Capacity, display the phrase "Quantity Required Exceeds Capacity." If it is not greater than the Capacity, display the phrase "OK to Implement Project." Type your name in the header, save your workbook, and print it. Next print the worksheet formulas. Make sure you adjust the column widths so that the entire formula is displayed.

1. Using Future Values to Choose a Savings Vehicle

The Tallaricos' oldest son will be starting college in a little over a year. Since the tuition will be due at that time, they have decided to pull some of their money out of the stock market and invest in very conservative savings vehicles. They feel that they don't want to take any risks with this money. It must be available to pay for college. The first year's tuition will be approximately $24,000 and this is the amount for which the Tallaricoses want an alternative investment.

Open **ex06Conservative.xls** and save the workbook as **<yourname>Conservative2.xls**. First define the appropriate cells with the names **Rate**, **Years**, **Payment**, and **FutureValue**, as the columns are labeled. You have decided to go to www.bankrate.com to get the latest rates for each of these investments. When the Web page opens, click the **Rates** tab. In the box labeled **Overnight Averages**, click **Today's averages**. Once that page appears, scroll down until you see the Rates for Savings investments. Input these rates into the worksheet and input the information for Years and Payment. Remember that each investment will be for one year. For the money market account and checking account, Mr. Tallarico will make monthly contributions of $2,000 for the year period.

For the Future Value column, click cell **E5** and then click **Insert**, click **Function**, and locate the **Future Value** function. Use the given information to input the Future Value formula. Remember that the money market and checking accounts pay interest monthly. Once this is computed, use the fill handle to drag the formula into the needed cells in the Future Value column. Which savings vehicle should Mr. Tallarico use to invest $20,000? Include your name in the header, print the worksheet, and save the workbook.

2. Selling or Holding Stocks Using Lookup Tables

Professor Pasquale is a finance professor at the Stockdale City University. He started trading his own stocks a few years ago to illustrate how the stock market works for his class lectures. What started out as an experiment has become a hobby for the professor and he has his own online account in which he can place all of his trades and get any data on the stock market that he may need. He would like you to create a worksheet illustrating how each stock has performed for him, which he will use as an illustration in his finance class.

Open **ex06Stocks.xls** and save the workbook as **<yourname>Stocks2.xls**. Professor Pasquale wants you to look up the price of each stock on the day it was purchased three months ago from today's date and its price today. He then wants you to write formulas to calculate each stock's net change in price.

First, enter today's date in cell **C4**, and then copy it down through the cell range **C5:C10**. Next, ensure that the Date of Purchase and Current Date columns display dates with four-digit years by formatting them, if needed. Use your favorite browser and go to finance.yahoo.com (do not type www before finance). Click the **Stock Research** hyperlink, click the **Historical Quotes** link. For each stock, enter the ticker symbol, date of purchase, and today's date. The Web site will give you the price of the stock for each day during this period. Retrieve the closing price on the date of purchase and today's date and input these data into the worksheet for each stock. Write formulas in the Net Change column to subtract the purchase price from the current price.

Include your name in the worksheet header. Change the worksheet printing orientation to Landscape so that it prints on one page, print the worksheet, and save the workbook.

around the world

1. Comparing Semester Abroad Costs

Karen's university has a strong study abroad program. The university has developed relationships with many well-respected schools around the world and offers semester-length programs with course work completed at these schools. Karen is graduating next year and wants to spend the next semester in Europe.

You work in the office for study abroad programs and are friends with Karen. She has asked you to help her summarize the costs associated with each program so that she can make a decision. You need to design a worksheet for her and it needs to be clear and accurate. The program in Spain has the following costs: tuition $8,500, room and board $3,000, and airfare of $750. The France program has the following costs: tuition $7,200, room and board $4,500, and airfare of $975. The England program has the following costs: tuition $11,000, room and board $2,800 and airfare of $895. Karen also wants to take $2,000 with her for spending money, no matter which program she chooses. Open **ex06AbroadCosts.xls** and save it as **<yourname>AbroadCosts6.xls**. Input these costs into a worksheet and label the worksheet Abroad Costs. Create a column titled Total Costs and create the appropriate formula so the total cost of each program is included on the worksheet.

Based on your results, Karen has decided she must choose between Spain and France. A local French Club will loan Karen the full amount needed at an interest rate of 8.75 percent. She will need to make monthly payments on the loan for 10 years. For the Spanish program, she would take out a loan from the university at an interest rate of 9 percent. She would also have to make monthly payments on this loan, but for a total of seven years. Summarize this information on the Loan Costs worksheet. Create a column titled Monthly Payment and use the Payment function to calculate the monthly payment for each loan. Karen decides that she will choose the program with the lowest monthly payment because she feels it will cost her less overall. You think this way of thinking is incorrect and illustrate by showing her the Future Value of each loan, which is how much she really pays for each. Create a column for this information and input the appropriate financial formula to give the future value of each loan. Include your name in the header of both worksheets and print them both. Save your workbook.

2. Patrice Williams' Marathon Tours

Patrice Williams has been working as a group leader in an adventure racing company coordinating and escorting a group of 150 to 300 athletes from the United States to various race locations around the world. Patrice has developed what she thinks would be the ideal tour package for many great racing destinations. Typically, a package goes on sale one year in advance, and within six months the majority of the participants have signed up for the tour. Next year she will organize and implement a tour to London for the Flora London Marathon. Global Marathons offers a payment plan to attract enough customers to keep the event profitable. To avoid a loss associated with a dramatic change in the destination currency, she could borrow the final tour package amount and use that money to pay all the major costs up front.

Open the workbook titled **ex06Marathon.xls**. Immediately save the file as **<yourname>Marathon6.xls**. The worksheet has been broken into three sections: *Assumptions, External Data,* and *Outputs.* In the *Assumptions* section Patrice has supplied all the current information for you to perform the calculations.

Patrice gives a discount to all nonrunner participants traveling in the group. That discount is just the cost of the entry fee to the marathon. Patrice's margin for each participant is $250. She also requires a $200 deposit at the time the participant signs up for the tour. The hotels have provided their room rates based on occupancy level, which she has already converted to U.S. dollars (in the *External Data* section). You need to create the appropriate formulas for each variable in the *Outputs* section as well as an amortization schedule.

Start by naming each of the cells in the *Assumptions* section that contain values. Use the labels that appear to the left of the cells. It isn't necessary to label the hotel information. Complete the Hotel Calculations table, which is designed to figure the cost per hotel for the number of double rooms and single rooms and then total these values. Use the VLOOKUP function to calculate these costs. Total the results. In the *Totals* and *Deductions* section of *Outputs* create the appropriate functions to realize the *Total Package Costs,* as well as *Total Deposits* and *Total Margins.* Note the costs are total, not per person. Since Patrice doesn't need to take a loan out for the total amount, you need to reduce the *Total Package Costs* by those items under *Deductions.* This will give you the *Loan Amount.* Then, write a PMT function to calculate the *Monthly Payment.* Finally, complete the amortization schedule at the bottom of the worksheet. Compare the total interest paid with Patrice's *Total Margin.* Type your name in the header, save your workbook, and print it. Print the worksheet formulas. Adjust the column widths so that each formula is fully visible.

running project

Pro Golf Academy

Betty Carroll is worried about her cash flow this month. Each month she places her order for golf shirts by the 5th of the month to ensure delivery for the next month. January and February have been lean months this year, and she will need to order over $10,000 worth of golf shirts to carry her through next month. She has put together a worksheet containing her estimate of the number of each type of golf shirt she will need to purchase from her wholesale distributor and their individual unit (wholesale) costs. The total cost is over $10,000. She has calculated that she will be able to pay $2,000 cash, but she wants to obtain a loan for the balance to help her cash flow. She reasons that financing this next purchase over a one-year period will allow her enough cash and sales to pay off the loan and maintain a good cash flow. She asks you to put together a loan amortization schedule for the proposed loan's 12 payment periods beginning on March 1.

Begin by loading **ex06ProGolf.xls** and save it as **<yourname>ProGolf6.xls**. Type some documentation information on the Documentation worksheet such as the creation date, the author's name, the modification date, and the store's name.

Create the loan amortization information on this sheet. Model the worksheet after the loan analysis worksheet you created for this chapter, except omit the External Data section and use labels in the Assumptions area that are appropriate for her business (see Figure 6.34). (Use "Inventory Total Price" instead of "Purchase Price.") Omit the FICO® Credit Rating information. For the Application Date, write a function to display the current date and format the cell to display the date only. Assume the annual interest rate is 9.75 percent (inventory financing is more risky than automobile financing). Create the same columns in the amortization section as there are in the chapter case problem: Payment, Beginning Balance, Principal Paid, Interest Paid, Total Principal, Total Interest, and Ending Balance. The value in the Inventory Finance Amount should be the total order value (see the sum on the Purchases worksheet). The loan amount value is the Inventory Total Price minus $2,000 (Betty's down payment on the shirt purchase). Create names for the cells containing Inventory Total Price, Down Payment, Loan Term, Periodic Payment, Interest Rate, and Loan Amount. Move the Interest Rate label and the interest rate up into the Assumptions section, since it is now a user-input value. Unlike the chapter example, there is no special assessment fee. Use data validation for the cell containing the value of the Inventory Total Price so that a user can enter a value only in the range of $0 through $25,000. Format all the worksheet cells in an attractive way (see Figure 6.34).

Color the Documentation worksheet tab green, color the Purchases worksheet tab yellow, and color the Loan Amortization worksheet tab blue. Ensure that the Loan Amortization worksheet prints in landscape orientation. Write your name in each worksheet's header and print all three worksheets when you are done. Print the formulas for the Loan Amortization worksheet to demonstrate your use of names. Remember to save your finished workbook.

FIGURE 6.34

Example format for the Loan Amortization worksheet

	A	B	C	D	E	F	G	H
1	Assumptions							
2	Customer Name	Pro Golf Academy						
3	Inventory Finance Amount	$ 10,552.10						
4	Down Payment	$ 2,000.00						
5	Loan Term	1	year(s)					
6	Interest Rate	9.75%	per year					
7	Application Date	1/4/04						
8								
9	Outputs							
10	Periodic Payment:	$ xxxxxx.xx	per month					
11	Loan Term:	1	year(s)					
12	Loan Amt.	$ 8,552.10						
13								
14	Payment	Beginning Balance	Principal Paid	Interest Paid	Total Principal	Total Interest	Ending Balance	
15	1	$ xxxxxx.xx	$ xxxxxx.xx	$ xxxxxx.xx	$ xxxxxx.xx	$ xxxxxx.xx	$ xxxxxx.xx	
16	2	xxxxxx.xx	xxxxxx.xx	xxxxxx.xx	xxxxxx.xx	xxxxxx.xx	xxxxxx.xx	
17	3	xxxxxx.xx	xxxxxx.xx	xxxxxx.xx	xxxxxx.xx	xxxxxx.xx	xxxxxx.xx	
18	4	xxxxxx.xx	xxxxxx.xx	xxxxxx.xx	xxxxxx.xx	xxxxxx.xx	xxxxxx.xx	
19	5	xxxxxx.xx	xxxxxx.xx	xxxxxx.xx	xxxxxx.xx	xxxxxx.xx	xxxxxx.xx	
20	6	xxxxxx.xx	xxxxxx.xx	xxxxxx.xx	xxxxxx.xx	xxxxxx.xx	xxxxxx.xx	
21	7	xxxxxx.xx	xxxxxx.xx	xxxxxx.xx	xxxxxx.xx	xxxxxx.xx	xxxxxx.xx	
22	8	xxxxxx.xx	xxxxxx.xx	xxxxxx.xx	xxxxxx.xx	xxxxxx.xx	xxxxxx.xx	
23	9	xxxxxx.xx	xxxxxx.xx	xxxxxx.xx	xxxxxx.xx	xxxxxx.xx	xxxxxx.xx	
24	10	xxxxxx.xx	xxxxxx.xx	xxxxxx.xx	xxxxxx.xx	xxxxxx.xx	xxxxxx.xx	
25	11	xxxxxx.xx	xxxxxx.xx	xxxxxx.xx	xxxxxx.xx	xxxxxx.xx	xxxxxx.xx	
26	12	xxxxxx.xx	xxxxxx.xx	xxxxxx.xx	xxxxxx.xx	xxxxxx.xx	(0.00)	
27								
28								
29								

Documentation / Purchases / Loan Amortization

1. What's in a Name?

Explain the advantages and disadvantages of using a name in place of a cell or cell range in formulas. Begin by considering a VLOOKUP function similar to the one used in the chapter case. What advantage does using a table name instead of a cell range have?

2. Present Value

Suppose you won a cash prize for the most valuable cost-saving suggestion of the year, and your award is 10% of the probable savings, or $60,000. However, you do not get a lump sum payment of $60,000. Instead, the company will pay you the prize money in equal monthly installments of $1,000 per month for five years. You would like to have the money now to use as a down payment on a condominium. Your company agrees to pay you a lump sum next week. How do you figure out what is an equitable, reasonable amount? Describe how to arrive at a fair market value and what variables you must consider in determining the lump sum payment.

CHAPTER

seven

7

Developing Multiple Worksheet and Workbook Applications

did you know?

the *game of a cat's cradle—two players alternately stretch a looped string over their fingers to produce different designs—has been around since about 1760.*

there *are 110 calories per hour consumed during an hour of typing—only 30 more than those used while sleeping.*

Cleveland *spelled backwards is "DNA level C."*

as *of January 1998, American Express had not issued a single credit card with an expiration date past December 1999. The company hoped to protect cardholders from Y2K problems.*

ostriches *are the second fastest animal in the world. They can run at 40 miles per hour for at least 30 minutes.*

you *can reference worksheet cells that are stored on disk but not currently open. Learn more about this in the chapter.*

Chapter Objectives

- Design a multiple-sheet workbook and understand when it is useful
- Modify the onscreen window layout—MOS XL03S-5-6
- Set the default number of worksheets—MOS XL03E-5-3
- Insert, delete, and reposition worksheets in a workbook—MOS XL03S-5-4
- Creating a workbook template—MOS XL03E-4-4
- Rename a worksheet tab and color it—MOS XL03S-3-4
- Establish worksheet page settings—MOS XL03S-5-7
- Group worksheets in a workbook and enter data in multiple sheets at once
- Consolidate and summarize data using three-dimensional formulas
- Use cell Watch—MOS XL03E-1-13
- Reference cells in other workbooks using link formulas
- Maintain and update linked workbooks

Bridgewater Engineering Company (BECO)

Bridgewater Engineering Company (BECO) builds industrial tools and machines for heavy industry. Jack Leonard established the firm in 1951 in Somerville, New Jersey. After Jack retired, Stirling Leonard, Jack's son, took over as CEO. In addition to the plant in Somerville, BECO has plants in two other locations: Van Buren, Arkansas, and West Lafayette, Indiana.

The three plants collectively employ 175 people and 9 administrators. The workforce consists of trained, versatile mechanics led by professional engineers. BECO is experienced and equipped to build special machinery and equipment of all kinds including the installation of electrical, hydraulic, and pneumatic power components and their controls. Each spacious plant has over 10,000 square feet of workspace with 28 feet of headroom in all manufacturing areas. BECO's own facilities include lathes, vertical and horizontal boring mills, planers, and assorted machinery for milling, drilling, welding, and control assembly. BECO builds all machinery from scratch, using steel rods, sheet steel, and other sheet metals to fashion the custom-built machinery that customers order. Examples of machinery that BECO builds include lathes, surface grinders, drill presses, boring mills, band saws, and Turret mills—all products used in heavy manufacturing.

Stirling was slow to embrace computing, but two years ago he finally converted many of BECO's financial and job-bidding systems over to computer professionals who designed automated systems for him. He has maintained control and interest in tracking sales of machine tools and machines that BECO manufactures to give him a good overview of sales by machine type. He wants a summary of sales of machinery by all three plants in a handy, simple, easy-to-read format. Your job is to first study the three manufacturing plants' workbooks and then devise a workbook or workbooks that merge the data from the three plants together into a single overview worksheet. Figure 7.1 shows an example of the summary worksheet displaying total sales of the three BECO plants.

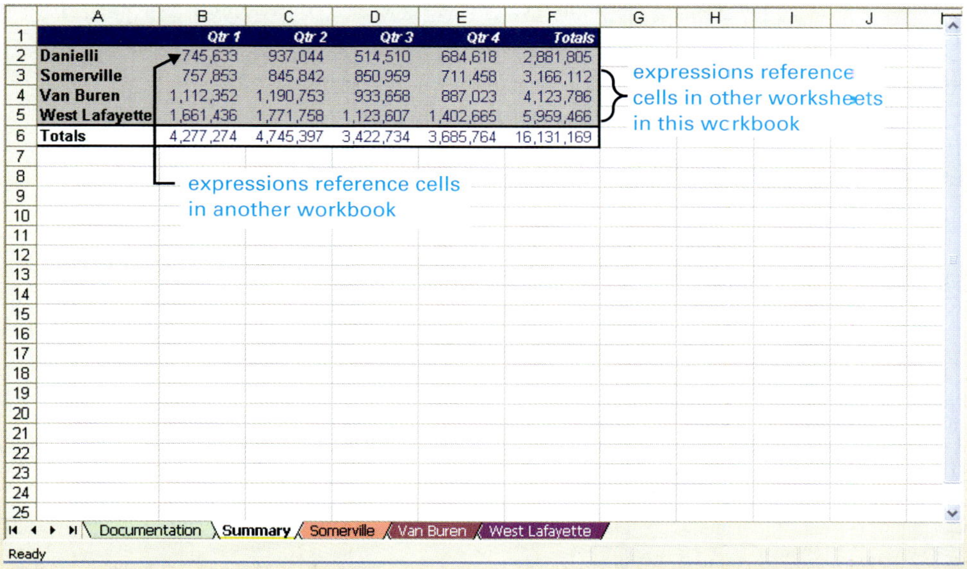

FIGURE 7.1

Summary of BECO machine sales

Figure 7.1 Summary of BECO machine sales

	A	B	C	D	E	F
1		Qtr 1	Qtr 2	Qtr 3	Qtr 4	Totals
2	Danielli	745,633	937,044	514,510	684,618	2,881,805
3	Somerville	757,853	845,842	850,959	711,458	3,166,112
4	Van Buren	1,112,352	1,190,753	933,658	887,023	4,123,786
5	West Lafayette	1,661,436	1,771,758	1,123,607	1,402,665	5,959,466
6	Totals	4,277,274	4,745,397	3,422,734	3,685,764	16,131,169

expressions reference cells in other worksheets in this workbook

expressions reference cells in another workbook

Documentation | Summary | Somerville | Van Buren | West Lafayette

Ready

Chapter 7 covers writing formulas that reference other worksheets in the workbook and other workbooks stored on your computer. In particular, you will learn about the benefits of using multiple worksheets to organize related data and how to create ***three-dimensional formulas (3-D)***—formulas that reference other worksheets in the current workbook. When you create formulas that reference cells in other worksheets, you link the referenced workbooks to the worksheet containing the reference to other workbooks. When you have completed this chapter, you will understand three-dimensional formulas and link formulas thoroughly.

SESSION 7.1 WORKING WITH MULTIPLE WORKSHEETS

In this section, you will learn why it is advantageous to keep related data in separate worksheets of a workbook, and you will write formulas that reference information on other worksheets in the same workbook. You will learn the benefits of grouping worksheets before formatting them or typing text and values common to all grouped worksheets.

Using Multiple Worksheets

Using more than one worksheet in a workbook is one of the best ways to organize your data. Almost all of the Excel applications you have examined in the first six chapters of this textbook consisted of one worksheet with a few small exceptions. There are several advantages to storing data on separate worksheets of a workbook.

Why Multiple Worksheets Are Useful

Using multiple worksheets to store distinct, related information on separate worksheets makes sense for several reasons. Consider, for example, the Pro Golf Academy case that appears in each chapter. Suppose that Betty Carroll wanted to keep the sales of golf

FIGURE 7.2

Somerville sales
information

sales for each machine
type by quarter

machines manufactured
in Somerville

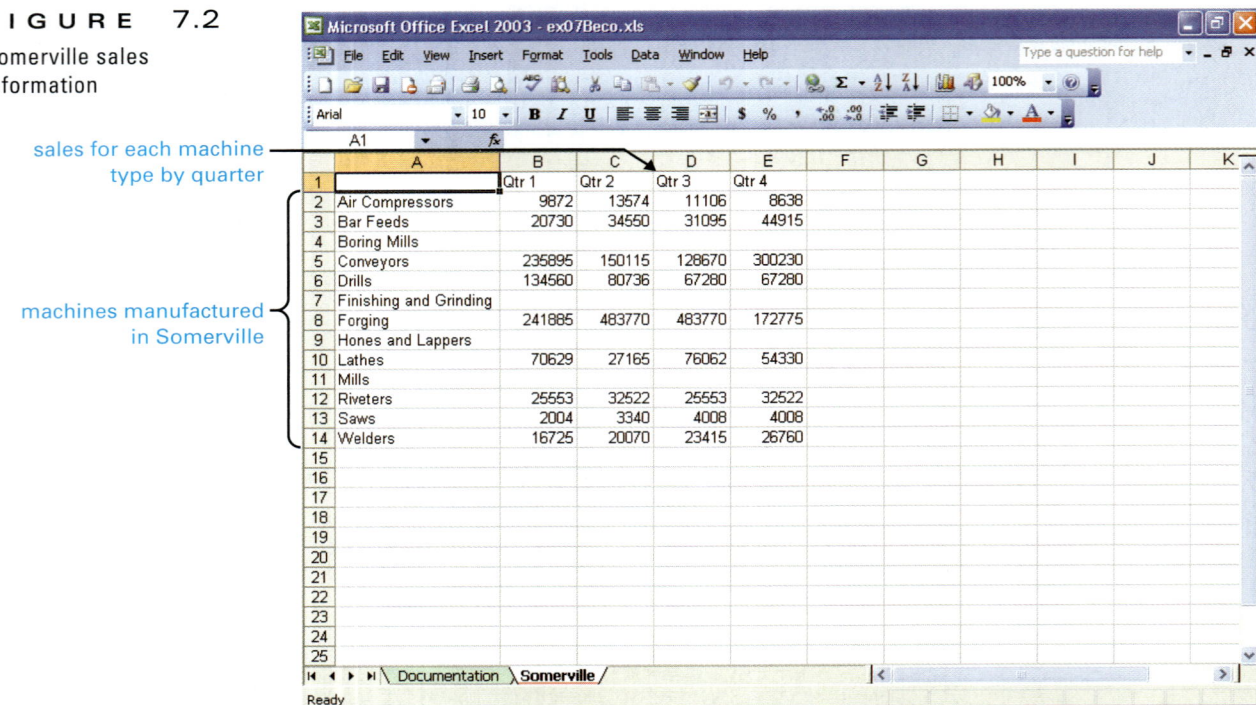

clubs separate from the sales of golf shirts. The simplest way to maintain a logical separation between product categories is by placing each on its own worksheet. Because each worksheet can have its own margin settings, unique page header and footer, print area, and other worksheet-specific settings, you can tailor print characteristics of each worksheet independently of other worksheets. Another advantage multiple worksheets provide is that you can protect individual worksheets in a workbook independently from others.

Designing a Multiple-Sheet Workbook

The BECO workbook, **ex07Beco.xls**, contains a documentation worksheet, which is the first worksheet in a workbook. Following the documentation worksheet is a worksheet containing sales data for BECO's Somerville plant. The worksheet lists the most recent four quarters of sales broken down by machine type (see Figure 7.2).

Sales information for BECO's other two plants is kept in separate workbooks. Sales data for the Van Buren plant are stored in the Excel workbook **ex07VanBuren.xls**, and sales data for the West Lafayette plant are in **ex07WestLafayette.xls**. When complete, the BECO workbook will contain worksheets from all three plants in one workbook. In addition to the detail worksheets, the workbook will contain a summary worksheet. A *summary worksheet*, sometimes called a *consolidation worksheet*, contains a digest or synopsis of the information contained in the individual worksheets. Frequently, the summary worksheet appears at the front of the workbook, either before the documentation worksheet or immediately after it. Figure 7.3 depicts the overall structure of the BECO workbook containing three plants' worksheets, a summary sheet, and a documentation sheet—all in one workbook.

Managing Worksheets

Stirling wants you to become familiar with creating, moving, deleting, and renaming worksheets in a workbook. He knows you will be called on to manipulate worksheets within a workbook. You will learn how to create, move, and rename a worksheet a few pages later. First, Stirling wants you to change the default number of worksheets in a workbook.

FIGURE 7.3

Structure of the BECO workbook

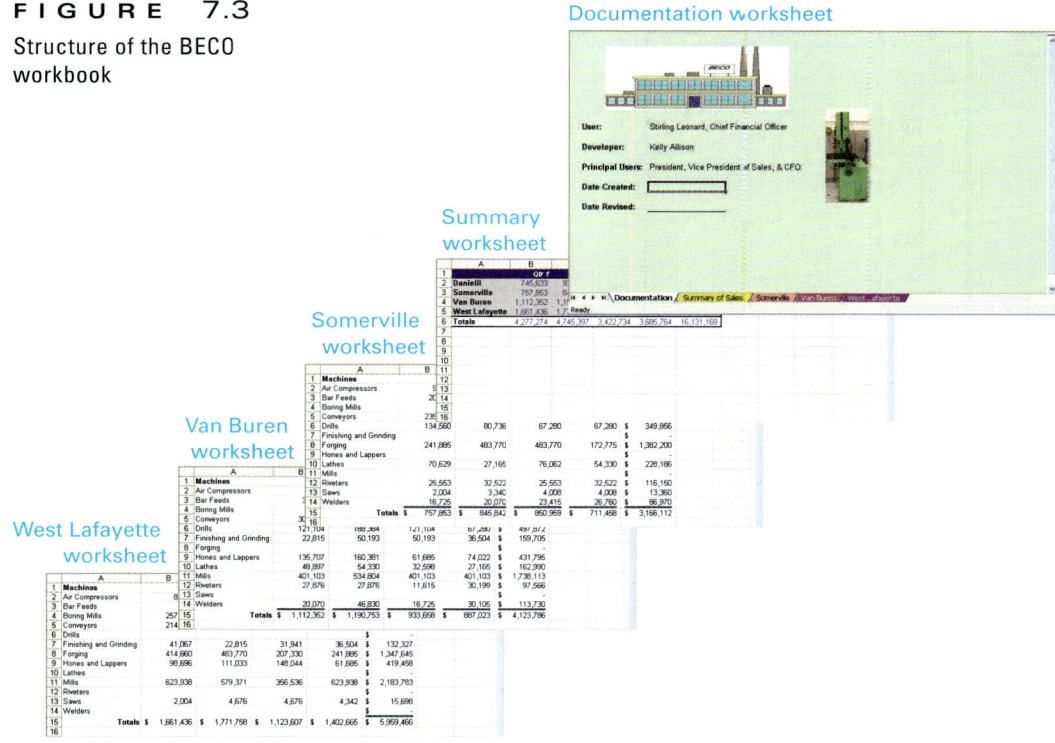

Setting the Number of Worksheets Created for a New Workbook

When you create a new workbook, an Excel Tools menu setting determines the number of worksheets in the workbook. Stirling asks you to set the default number of worksheets to two so that each *new* workbook you create on your computer will contain just two worksheets. You explain to Stirling that changing the number of worksheets does not alter any existing workbooks—either currently open or not.

Setting the number of worksheets in a new workbook:

1. Start Excel as usual, close the task pane, click **Tools**, click **Options**, and then click the **General** tab to display the general Excel settings

2. Drag the mouse across the value currently in the *Sheets in new workbook* spin control, type **2** (see Figure 7.4), and click **OK** to complete the selection and close the Options dialog box

Test the new setting by creating a new workbook. When you create a new workbook, Excel will create only two worksheets.

Testing the new worksheet number setting:

1. Click the **New** button on the Standard toolbar to create a new workbook. Notice that the new workbook has two worksheets, Sheet1 and Sheet2

EXCEL

FIGURE 7.4

Setting the initial number
of worksheets in a new
workbook

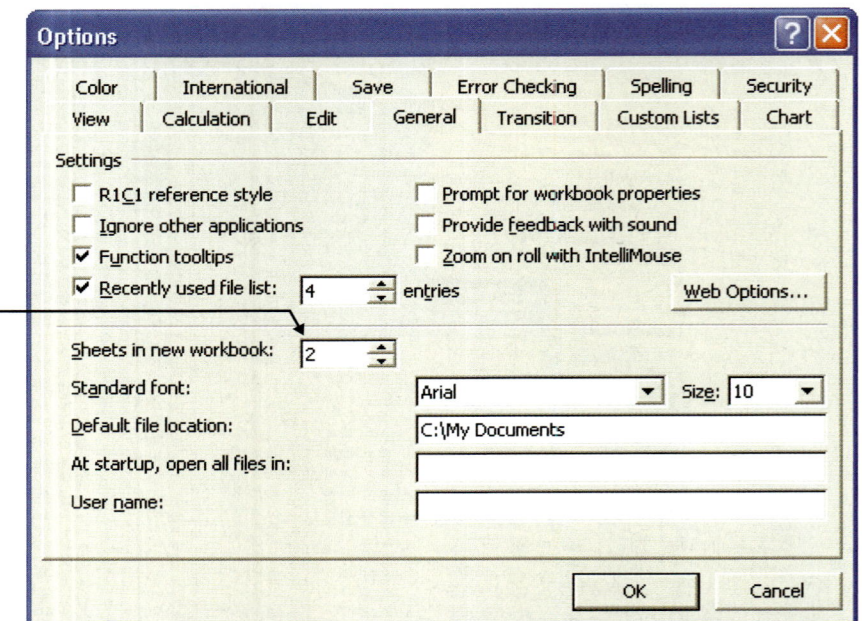

Initial number of
sheets created in a
new workbook

Deleting a Worksheet

You may wish to delete one or more worksheets in a workbook—especially "extra" worksheets that are empty. Steps that follow show you how.

---

task Reference   **Deleting a Worksheet**

- Right-click the worksheet tab of the worksheet you want to delete

- Click **Delete** on the shortcut menu

Deleting a worksheet from a workbook:

FIGURE 7.5

Sheet tab shortcut menu

1. Right-click the **Sheet2** worksheet tab. A shortcut menu appears (see Figure 7.5)

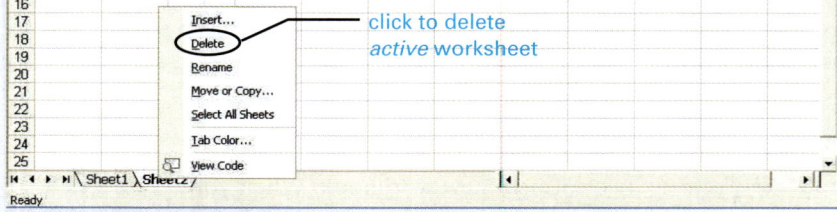

click to delete
active worksheet

2. Click **Delete** to remove the worksheet from the workbook. Excel deletes Sheet2 and displays Sheet1

tip: *If Excel displays the warning message "Data may exist in the sheet(s) selected for deletion. To permanently delete the data, press Delete," that means you typed a value on the empty worksheet Sheet3 at some point. Click* **Delete** *to delete the worksheet*

Because you are done with the current workbooks, you can close them. You can close all workbooks using one command.

Closing all open workbooks at once:

1. Close all workbooks but leave Excel running: Press and hold the **Shift** key, click **File**, and then release the **Shift** key

2. Click **Close all** on the File menu to close all workbooks

tip: *If a prompt appears asking if you want to save changes you made, click **No***

Creating a Template from a Workbook

Whenever several worksheets or workbooks will have the same structure and appearance, it is handy to create a general workbook that has the content and formatting that is common to worksheets you will be manipulating. Such a file is called a template. You can open a template whenever you want to create workbooks that are identical in structure and content.

---

task reference   Saving a Workbook as a Template

- Activate the workbook you want to save as a template, click **File** and then click **Save As**

- Type the template name (but not its extension) in the File name list box

- Click the **Save as type** list box, scroll the list box to locate and then click **Template (*.xlt)**

- Click the **Save** button

Stirling has a worksheet that has the contents and formatting he'd like you to use whenever you create a BECO style workbook. It is called **ex07BecoTemplate.xls** and he wants you to save it as an Excel template.

Opening a workbook and saving it as a template:

1. Open the workbook **ex07BecoTemplate.xls**

2. Click **File**, click **Save As**, and type **BecoTemplate** (no spaces) in the File name list box

3. Click the **Save as type** list box, locate and then click the entry **Template (*.xlt)** from the list, and click the **Save** button. Excel saves the workbook as a template in its Templates folder and displays its new name, **BecoTemplate.xlt**, on the title bar

4. Click **File**, and then **Close** to close the template

Combining Multiple Worksheets into One Workbook

One of BECO's administrators created the two-worksheet workbook containing the Documentation worksheet and sales information about the Somerville plant for four quarters and several machine types (see Figure 7.2). Data for the other two plants are in separate workbooks. Your first task is to open all three workbooks and then combine the three workbooks into one workbook.

Because Stirling wants you to combine all three workbooks into one workbook, you will open the Van Buren workbook and then copy the worksheet into the main BECO workbook by dragging the worksheet's tab.

---

task reference   Copying Worksheets from Other Workbooks

- Open the master workbook—the workbook into which you want to copy worksheets from other workbooks

- Open all other workbooks containing worksheets you want to copy to the master workbook

- In any of the open Excel workbooks, click **Window**, click **Arrange**, click the **Tiled** option button, and click **OK**

- Press and hold the **Ctrl** key, and then click and drag to the master workbook the tab of the worksheet you want to copy

- Release the mouse when the down-pointing arrow is in the correct tab location in the master workbook, and then release the **Ctrl** key

---

Copying the Van Buren worksheet to the BECO master workbook:

1. Open the workbook **ex07Beco.xls** and immediately save it as **Beco2.xls** to preserve the original workbook

2. Review the Documentation worksheet. Because all Documentation worksheet cells except C18 are locked, worksheet protection prevents you from selecting any cell except C18

3. Click the **Somerville** worksheet tab to make that worksheet active

4. Open the workbook **ex07VanBuren.xls**

5. Click **Window**, click **Arrange**, click (if necessary) the **Tiled** option button in the Arrange Windows dialog box, and click the **OK** button. The active worksheets of both workbooks appear side by side

6. Click the **ex07VanBuren.xls** title bar, if necessary, to ensure that the Van Buren workbook is active

7. Press and hold the **Ctrl** key, click and drag the **Van Buren** worksheet tab to the **Beco2.xls** workbook, and release the mouse when the worksheet position indicator, a down-pointing arrow, appears to the right of the Somerville tab (see Figure 7.6)

8. Release the **Ctrl** key. Excel copies the Van Buren worksheet to the Beco2 workbook and makes Van Buren the active worksheet

FIGURE 7.6

Copying the Van Buren
worksheet

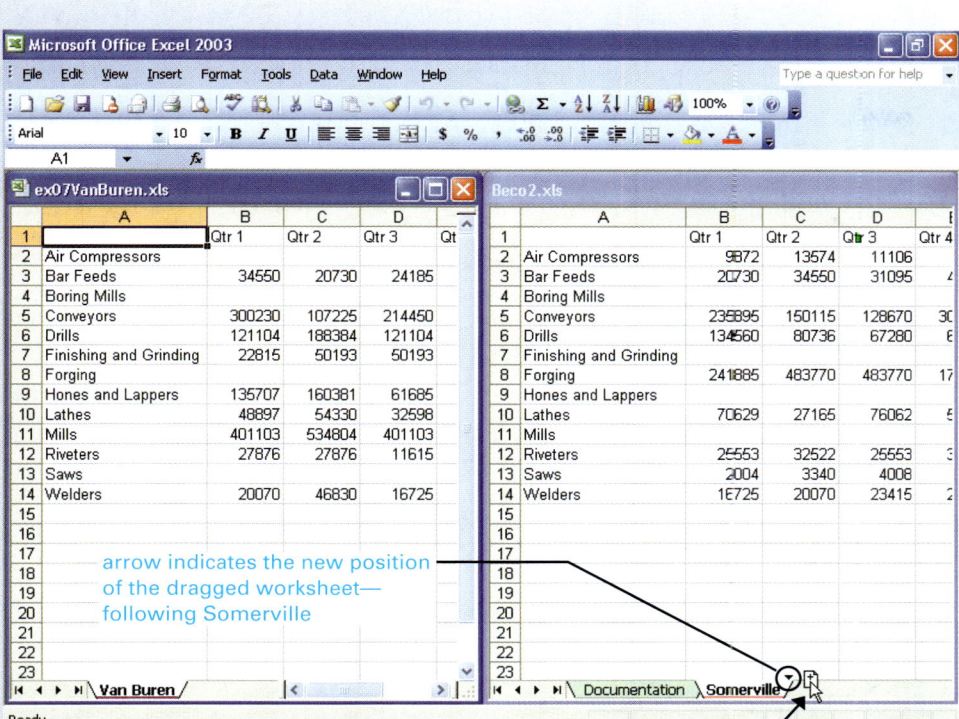

9. Click the Title bar of the **ex07VanBuren.xls** workbook, click **File** on the
   menu bar, and click **Close** to close the workbook

tip: *If you attempt to close* **Beco2.xls** *by mistake, Excel will ask you if you want to save
your changes. Click the* **Cancel** *button to leave* **Beco2.xls** *open. Then repeat step 9*

10. Click the **Maximize** button on the **Beco2.xls** Title bar to maximize it

---

another**word**

. . . on Dragging a Worksheet Tab to Another Workbook

When you press and hold the Ctrl key before you drag a worksheet tab to
another workbook, you are copying it. If you simply drag a worksheet tab
to another open workbook, the worksheet is cut from the original workbook
and pasted into the destination workbook. If the worksheet you cut from a
workbook is its only worksheet, Excel closes that workbook

Next, you copy the West Lafayette worksheet into the **Beco2.xls** workbook to complete the two-worksheet copy operation. This time, you will use a different method to
copy the worksheet.

Copying the West Lafayette worksheet to the
BECO master workbook:

1. Open the workbook **ex07WestLafayette.xls**

2. Click **Edit** and click **Move or Copy Sheet**. The Move or Copy dialog box opens

3. Click the **To book** list box to display the list of workbooks and click **Beco2.xls** from the list of workbook choices

4. Click the **(move to end)** choice in the *Before sheet* list box and click the **Create a copy** check box to *copy* the worksheet, making it the last worksheet in the destination workbook **Beco2.xls** (see Figure 7.7)

F I G U R E   7.7
Move or Copy dialog box

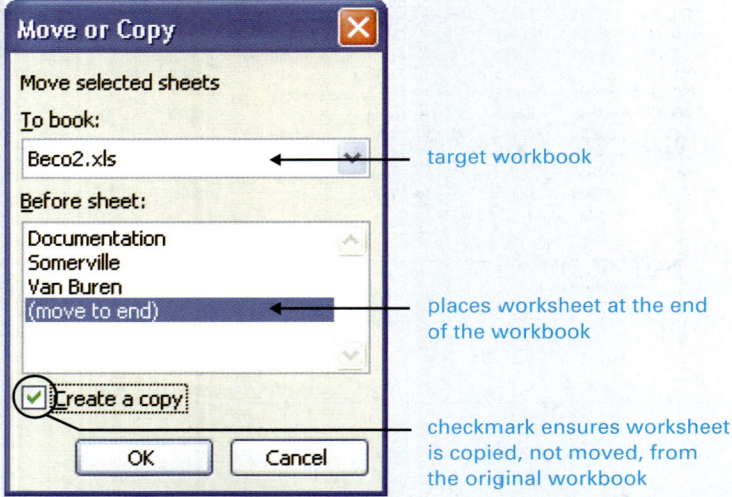

5. Click **OK**. Excel copies the worksheet to **Beco2.xls** and makes it the active worksheet

6. Right-click the **ex07WestLafayette** button on the Taskbar and then click **Close** in the shortcut menu to close the workbook **ex07WestLafayette.xls**

7. Maximize the workbook and then save it

Now the BECO workbook contains four worksheets: Documentation, Somerville, Van Buren, and West Lafayette. The latter three worksheets contain sales information about all three BECO plants in one workbook.

Adding a Worksheet to a Workbook

Remembering that Stirling wants to summarize BECO's sales in a single worksheet that displays sales by machine across all three plants, you realize you will have to add a new worksheet to the BECO workbook. You will do that next.

Adding a new worksheet to a workbook:

1. With the West Lafayette worksheet of the **Beco2.xls** workbook active, click **Insert**

2. Click **Worksheet**. Excel adds a worksheet called Sheet1 in front of the West Lafayette worksheet. It makes the newly added worksheet active

tip: *If you practiced inserting a new worksheet more than once with an open workbook, the inserted worksheet name may be a different name such as Sheet2 or Sheet3, for example*

Moving a Worksheet

Because the worksheet will summarize the values in the three sales worksheets, you ask Stirling where he would like you to place a summary worksheet. Stirling tells you he prefers having a summary worksheet precede all the detail worksheets, but he wants the Documentation worksheet to remain the first worksheet in the workbook.

Move the new worksheet between the Documentation and Somerville worksheets:

1. Click **Edit**, and then click **Move or Copy Sheet**. The Move or Copy dialog box appears

2. Click **Somerville** in the *Before sheet* list box, and ensure that the Create a copy check box is cleared. (You do not want to create a copy of the worksheet.)

3. Click **OK** in the Move or Copy dialog box. Excel moves the worksheet to its new position between the Documentation and Somerville worksheets

anotherway
. . . to Insert a New Worksheet

Right-click the worksheet in front of which you want to insert a new worksheet

Click **Insert** on the pop-up menu

Ensure that the Worksheet icon is selected in the General tab and click the **OK** button

Stirling wants you to become familiar with inserting a worksheet from a template. Because you created a template called BecoTemplate earlier, you will use that as the model for a new worksheet to insert into the BECO workbook.

Inserting a Worksheet Using a Template

When you create a template, you can create a workbook from the template by clicking File, clicking New, and then choosing the appropriate template from templates on your computer (the On my computer hyperlink) whose hyperlinks appear in the New Workbook task pane.

Inserting a worksheet from a template:

1. Right-click the **Somerville** worksheet tab. A shortcut menu appears

2. Click **Insert**, click the **BecoTemplate** icon in the Insert dialog box, and click **OK**. Excel inserts a worksheet from the template, complete with labels in column A and row 1

Because you will build a slightly different worksheet than what the template supplies, you will delete the newly added worksheet using a simple method not used before.

Deleting a worksheet using the shortcut menu:

1. Right-click the **Sheet1(2)** worksheet tab. A shortcut menu appears

2. Click **Delete**. Excel displays a delete confirmation dialog box

3. Click the **Delete** button in the confirmation dialog box to delete the worksheet

4. Click the **Sheet1** worksheet tab to activate that worksheet

Renaming a Worksheet and Coloring a Worksheet Tab

The summary worksheet is an important one, and Stirling wants it to stand out. He asks you to rename the worksheet to Summary and to change the color of the tab to bright yellow.

Renaming a worksheet and coloring its tab:

1. Double-click the worksheet tab of the newly added worksheet (the tab name darkens), type **Summary**, and press **Enter**. Excel renames the worksheet

2. Right-click the **Summary** worksheet tab. A shortcut menu appears (see Figure 7.8)

F I G U R E   7.8

Worksheet tab shortcut menu

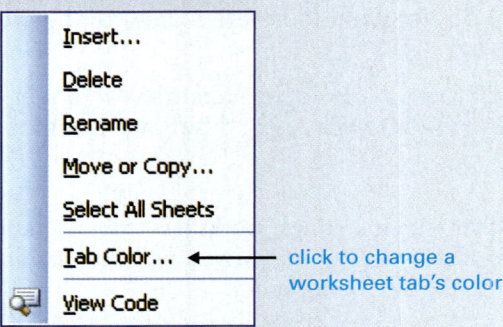

click to change a
worksheet tab's color

3. Click **Tab Color**. The Format Tab Color dialog box appears

4. Click the **Yellow** color well (fourth row from the top, third column) (see Figure 7.9)

F I G U R E   7.9

Selecting a worksheet tab color

Yellow color well

5. Click **OK**. The dialog box closes and a fringe of yellow appears at the bottom of the Summary tab

6. Click the **Somerville** worksheet tab to make that worksheet active and notice the Summary tab—it is bright yellow (see Figure 7.10)

F I G U R E   7.10

Brightly colored worksheet tab

yellow color adds emphasis to the worksheet tab

With all the worksheets in place, including the empty Summary worksheet, you are ready to create formulas that reference cells and cell ranges in other worksheets and to work with multiple worksheets as a group.

Grouping Worksheets

When you need to enter the same labels or formulas in several worksheets within a workbook, you can save a lot of time by grouping worksheets and then entering information common to multiple sheets in one operation. For instance, neither the summary worksheet nor any of the three other sales information worksheets have a column label identifying the contents of column A—machines. While you could type "Machines" in cell A1 in each worksheet separately, it saves time to group the worksheets and then type the label once. Grouping worksheets is also beneficial when you want to insert or delete rows common to all grouped worksheets or format cells, rows, or columns of all grouped worksheets in the same way.

help yourself *Press **F1**, type **group worksheets** in the Search text box of the Microsoft Excel Help task pane, and press **Enter**. Click the hyperlink **About viewing workbooks and worksheets**. Maximize the Help screen if necessary. Click the Help screen **Close** button when you are finished, and close the task pane*

Entering Text into Worksheet Groups

Although the three sales worksheets contain the labels Qtr 1, Qtr 2, Qtr 3, and Qtr 4 to indicate sales in each of the four calendar quarters, the Summary worksheet does not. Whenever you want to modify several worksheets simultaneously, you must first group them.

---

task reference   **Grouping Contiguous Worksheets**

- Click the worksheet tab of the first worksheet in the group

- Use the tab scrolling buttons, if necessary, to bring the last worksheet tab of the proposed group into view

- Hold down the **Shift** key and click the last worksheet tab in the group

Grouping Noncontiguous Worksheets

- Click the worksheet tab of the first worksheet you want in the group

- Press and hold the **Ctrl** key and then click each worksheet you want to include in the group

- When you are done, release the **Ctrl** key

Stirling wants you to type "Machines" in cell A1 of each of the three manufacturing plants' worksheets. If you first group the worksheets into which you want to enter the label and then type it in one of them, Excel places the label in all worksheets in the group. Worksheet users sometimes call this **drilling down**, because it changes several layers—grouped worksheets—in a workbook.

*Grouping worksheets and entering a label
in all of them at once:*

1. With the **Somerville** worksheet active, press and hold down **Shift**,
   click the **West Lafayette** worksheet tab, and release the **Shift** key. Excel
   indicates the grouped worksheets by coloring their tabs (temporarily)
   white (see Figure 7.11)

FIGURE 7.11

Grouped worksheets

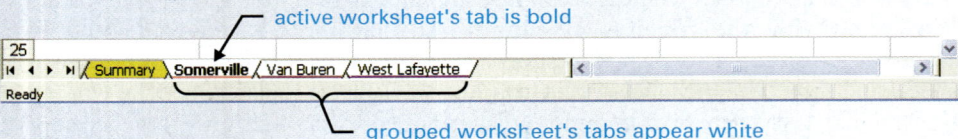

active worksheet's tab is bold

grouped worksheet's tabs appear white

2. Click cell **A1**, type **Machines**, and press **Enter**

3. Click the **Van Buren** worksheet tab and verify that cell A1 contains
   "Machines"

4. Click the **West Lafayette** worksheet tab and verify that cell A1 contains
   "Machines" Grouping worksheets and then entering data into one cell
   places data into the same cells in all grouped worksheets

Notice that the name of the active worksheet of a grouped set is bold. Clicking any
of the worksheet tabs in the grouped set makes the worksheet active, but it does not ungroup them. This happens because there is at least one worksheet in the workbook that
is *not* part of the worksheet group.

---

task reference   **Ungrouping Worksheets**

- Right-click any worksheet tab and click **Ungroup Sheets** from the shortcut
  menu

Ungroup the worksheets so that you can work independently on each worksheet.

Ungrouping worksheets:

1. Right-click the **Somerville** worksheet tab

2. Click **Ungroup Sheets** in the shortcut menu

Copying Formulas and Data into Worksheet Groups

Stirling tells you there are several ways to copy formulas from one worksheet to other
worksheets. If you want to copy one or more formulas to more than one worksheet, the
most efficient way is to copy the formulas to grouped worksheets rather than copying to
individual sheets, one sheet at a time. In the next series of steps, you will create the sum
of the columns for each quarter's sales and place the sums at the bottom of each column.
You begin by creating a summation for sales at the Somerville plant. Then you will copy
those formulas to the same cells in the Van Buren and West Lafayette worksheets.

Writing summation formulas in the Somerville worksheet:

1. Click the **Somerville** worksheet tab and then select the cell range **B2:E15**

2. Click the **AutoSum** button on the Standard toolbar. Excel places four SUM functions in the cell range B15:E15

3. Click cell **B15** to deselect the selected range and display the newly created SUM function in the formula bar (see Figure 7.12)

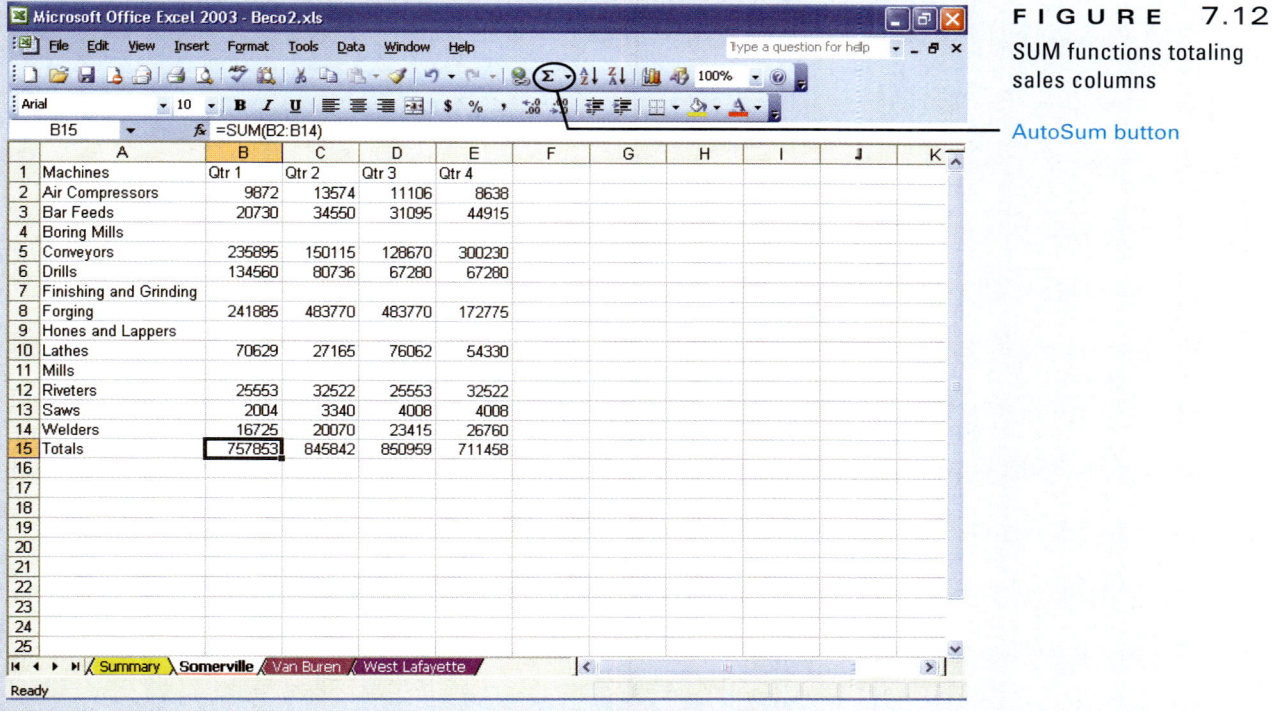

FIGURE 7.12

SUM functions totaling sales columns

AutoSum button

Copying formulas to other worksheets in a workbook:

1. Select the cell range **B15:E15**, which contains four SUM functions

2. Press and hold the **Shift** key and click the **West Lafayette** worksheet tab, and then release the **Shift** key. Excel groups the three sales worksheets

3. Click **Edit**, point to **Fill**, and click **Across Worksheets**. The Fill Across Worksheets dialog box appears (see Figure 7.13)

4. Click the **All** option button (if necessary) and then click **OK**

5. Click cell **A15** to deselect the cell range

6. Right-click any worksheet in the group and then click **Ungroup Sheets** in the shortcut menu. Excel ungroups the worksheets

FIGURE 7.13

The Fill Across Workbooks
dialog box

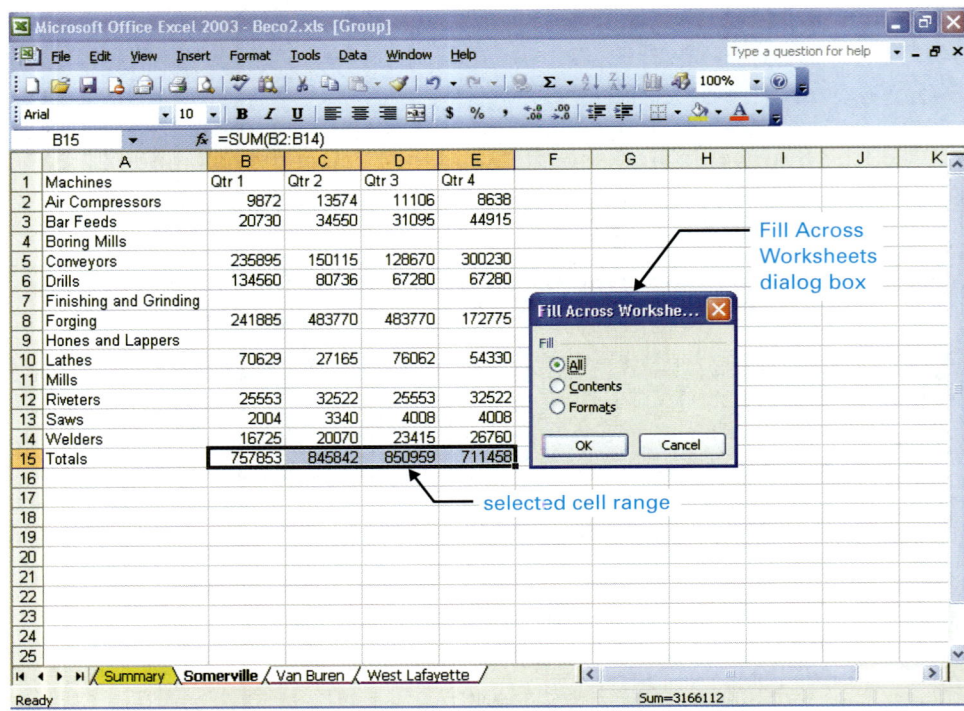

The Fill Across Worksheets command copies the selected cells to all other worksheets in the group to exactly the same cell range as the source cells. The All option copies both cells' contents and their formatting. Alternatively, you can choose to copy only contents or only formatting by selecting either Contents or Formats, respectively.

Writing Formulas and Data into Worksheet Groups

An alternative way to enter formulas and data into grouped worksheets is to group the worksheets first and then write the formulas and data. When you press Enter to complete a formula or execute a copy operation on one worksheet, Excel automatically copies formulas and data to other members of the worksheet group.

Writing formulas and labels to grouped worksheets:

1. Click the **Somerville** worksheet tab, hold down the **Shift** key, click the **West Lafayette** worksheet tab, and release the **Shift** key to group the three worksheets

2. Click cell **A15** and type **Totals**

3. Click cell **F1** and type **Totals**

4. Click cell **F2**, type **=SUM(B2:E2)**, and click the **Enter** checkmark (see Figure 7.14) on the formula bar to enter the formula and keep cell F2 active

5. Move the mouse to the fill handle in the lower-right corner of cell **F2**, click and drag it down through cell **F15**, and release the mouse. Excel fills in cells F3 through F15 with row totals. Cell F15 is a grand total because it sums cells B15 through E15, which are column totals

6. Click cell **F2** to deselect the cell range (see Figure 7.15) and make that cell active so that you can inspect its formula

	A	B	C	D	E	F	G	H	I	J	K
1	Machines	Qtr 1	Qtr 2	Qtr 3	Qtr 4	Totals					
2	Air Compressors	9872	13574	11106	8638	=SUM(B2:E2)					
3	Bar Feeds	20730	34550	31095	44915						
4	Boring Mills										
5	Conveyors	235895	150115	128670	300230						
6	Drills	134560	80736	67280	67280						
7	Finishing and Grinding										
8	Forging	241885	483770	483770	172775						
9	Hones and Lappers										
10	Lathes	70629	27165	76062	54330						
11	Mills										
12	Riveters	25553	32522	25553	32522						
13	Saws	2004	3340	4008	4008						
14	Welders	16725	20070	23415	26760						
15	Totals	757853	845842	850959	711458						
16											

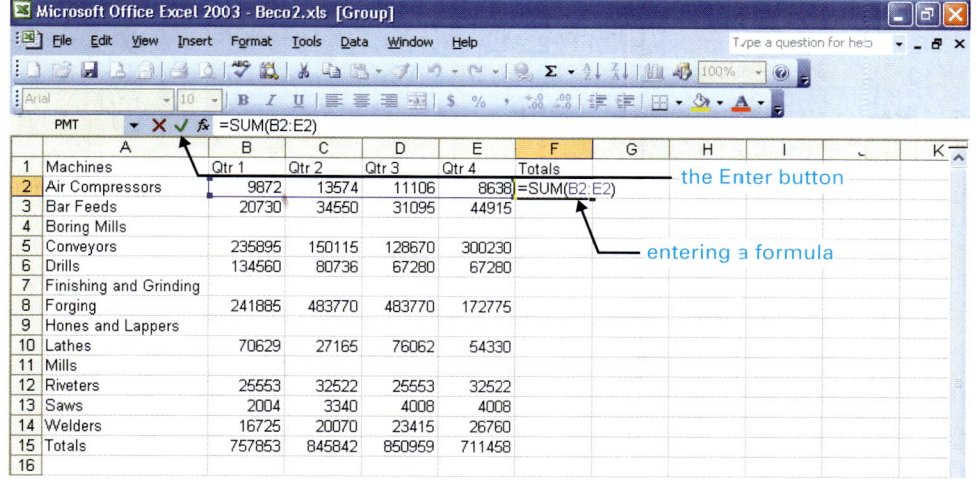

FIGURE 7.14
Entering a formula in three worksheets simultaneously

	A	B	C	D	E	F	G	H	I	J	K
1	Machines	Qtr 1	Qtr 2	Qtr 3	Qtr 4	Totals					
2	Air Compressors	9872	13574	11106	8638	43190					
3	Bar Feeds	20730	34550	31095	44915	131290					
4	Boring Mills					0					
5	Conveyors	235895	150115	128670	300230	814910					
6	Drills	134560	80736	67280	67280	349856					
7	Finishing and Grinding					0					
8	Forging	241885	483770	483770	172775	1382200					
9	Hones and Lappers					0					
10	Lathes	70629	27165	76062	54330	228186					
11	Mills					0					
12	Riveters	25553	32522	25553	32522	116150					
13	Saws	2004	3340	4008	4008	13360					
14	Welders	16725	20070	23415	26760	86970					
15	Totals	757853	845842	850959	711458	3166112					
16											

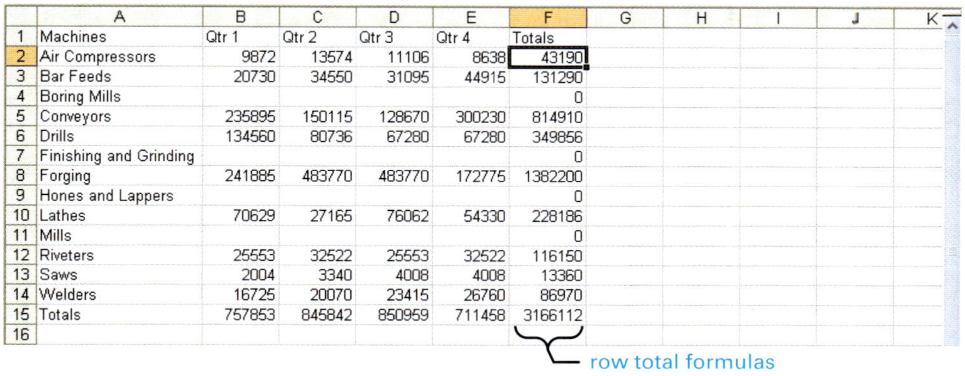

FIGURE 7.15
Drill-down formulas completed

Formatting Worksheet Groups

Formatting a cell or cell range in the active worksheet of a group of worksheets also formats the same cell or cell range in *all* group members. That is particularly handy when you want several worksheets to have the same appearance, helping to convey the message that similarly formatted worksheets are related to one another.

Stirling wants you to make several format changes to the three sales worksheets—Somerville, Van Buren, and West Lafayette. Because each of the three worksheets will be formatted in the same way, you will format the grouped worksheets and save time. By carefully selecting cell ranges, you can combine some of the preceding formatting steps to include more cells.

Formatting sales values with the accounting format:

1. With the three worksheets still grouped, click the **Somerville** worksheet tab, and then click and drag cell range **B2:F15**
2. Right-click anywhere inside the selected cells, click **Format Cells** on the shortcut menu, and click the **Number** tab
3. Click **Accounting** in the Category list, type **0** in the Decimal places spinner control, click the **Symbol** list box, click **None**, and click **OK**

4. Click and drag the cell range **F2:F15**

5. Press and hold the **Ctrl** key, click and drag the cell range **B15:E15**, and re-lease the **Ctrl** key. Excel highlights the two cell ranges F2:F15 and B15:E15, the Totals column and row

6. Right-click any cell within the selected ranges, click **Format Cells** on the shortcut menu, and click the **Number** tab (if necessary)

tip: *If you right-click outside the range of selected cells, press **Esc**, reselect the two cell ranges, and repeat step 6*

7. Click the **Symbol** list box, click **$**, and click **OK**

8. Click cell **B1** to deselect the cell ranges and to prepare for the next steps (see Figure 7.16)

FIGURE 7.16

Applying the accounting format to grouped worksheets

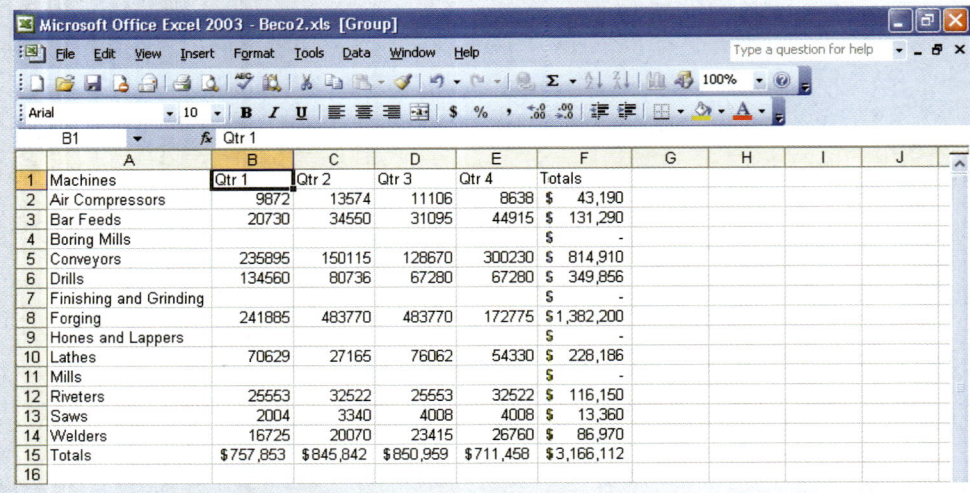

Next, you will right-align and boldface labels in cells B1 through F1 and the "Totals" label in cell A15, and you will boldface the label "Machines" in cell A1.

Right-aligning and bolding labels in grouped worksheets:

1. With the three worksheets still grouped and the Somerville worksheet active, select cell range **B1:F1**

2. Press and hold the **Ctrl** key, select cell **A15**, and release the **Ctrl** key

3. Click the **Align Right** button on the Formatting toolbar

4. Press and hold the **Ctrl** key, select cell **A1**, and release the **Ctrl** key. Cell A1 is added to the group of selected cells

5. Click the **Bold** button on the Formatting toolbar. Excel applies boldface to the 21 selected cells (seven cells in each of three worksheets comprising the grouped worksheets)

The last few formatting changes Stirling wants you to make are to place a double underline under the cell range B14:F14 to mark the bottom of the sales columns and then to widen columns B through F to 13 characters to accommodate the row totals and make the columns easier to distinguish from one another.

Applying underlining and increasing column widths:

1. Select the cell range **B14:F14**

2. Click **Format** and click **Cells**. The Format Cells dialog box opens

3. Click the **Font** tab, click the **Underline** list box (see Figure 7.17), and click **Double Accounting**. The Preview text box displays a facsimile of the double underline

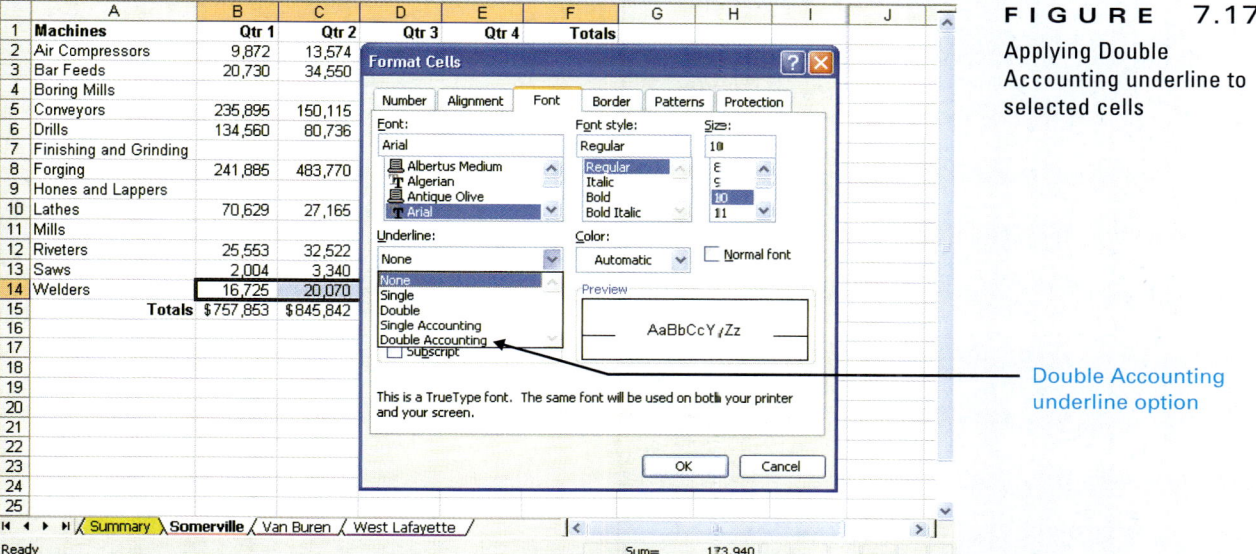

FIGURE 7.17

Applying Double Accounting underline to selected cells

Double Accounting underline option

4. Click **OK** to apply the formatting changes and close the Format Cells dialog box

5. Select columns **B** through **F** by dragging the mouse through their column heading buttons, right-click anywhere within the selected columns, click **Column Width**, type **13** in the Column Width text box, and click **OK**. Excel expands columns B through F on the three worksheets in the group to 13 characters in width

6. Click cell **A1** to deselect the column range (see Figure 7.18)

Satisfy yourself that the three worksheets all contain the same format changes by clicking the Van Buren and West Lafayette worksheet tabs and viewing their formats.

Establishing Worksheet Page Settings

After you format the worksheet, you give Stirling a copy of it on disk. He opens it and examines the worksheets over the weekend. Monday morning, he stops by your office and comments that some of the sales worksheets print on multiple pages and that the three plants' worksheets all have different print margins. He asks you to make all the sales worksheets page layouts uniform, including the print margins and page layout. In

FIGURE 7.18

Worksheet after modifying
column widths

	A	B	C	D	E	F	G	H
1	**Machines**	**Qtr 1**	**Qtr 2**	**Qtr 3**	**Qtr 4**	**Totals**		
2	Air Compressors	9,872	13,574	11,106	8,638	$ 43,190		
3	Bar Feeds	20,730	34,550	31,095	44,915	$ 131,290		
4	Boring Mills					$ -		
5	Conveyors	235,895	150,115	128,670	300,230	$ 814,910		
6	Drills	134,560	80,736	67,280	67,280	$ 349,856		
7	Finishing and Grinding					$ -		
8	Forging	241,885	483,770	483,770	172,775	$ 1,382,200		
9	Hones and Lappers					$ -		
10	Lathes	70,629	27,165	76,062	54,330	$ 228,186		
11	Mills					$ -		
12	Riveters	25,553	32,522	25,553	32,522	$ 116,150		
13	Saws	2,004	3,340	4,008	4,008	$ 13,360		
14	Welders	16,725	20,070	23,415	26,760	$ 86,970		
15	Totals $	757,853	$ 845,842	$ 850,959	$ 711,458	$ 3,166,112		
16								
17								

First Worksheet tab scroll button

Previous Worksheet tab scroll button

Next Worksheet tab scroll button

Last Worksheet tab scroll button

Summary \ **Somerville** / Van Buren / West Lafayette

worksheet tab scrolling buttons

Ready

addition, he would like you to place each worksheet's name (Somerville, Van Buren, or West Lafayette) in the left section of the footer so that each worksheet is identified by its tab name. Looking ahead, you decide to include the Summary worksheet in the worksheet grouping so that it will have the same page setup as the sales worksheets that it summarizes.

The best way to take care of the page setup and footer details Stirling requests is to work with grouped worksheets.

Adding a worksheet to an existing worksheet group:

1. With the three plants' worksheets grouped, press and hold the **Ctrl** key

2. Click the **Summary** worksheet tab to include it in the worksheet group and release the **Ctrl** key

Establishing page setup settings for grouped worksheets:

1. Click **File** and click **Page Setup**. The Page Setup dialog box opens

2. Click the **Margins** tab, double-click the **Left** margin spin control to select its current value, and type **0.75**

3. Double-click the **Right** margin spin control, and type **0.75**

4. Click the **Header/Footer** tab and click the **Custom Footer** button. The Footer dialog box appears

5. Click the **Center section** text box, type **Worksheet:**, press the **Spacebar**, and click the **Tab Name** button. The Tab Name button displays "&[Tab]" because it is a variable—Excel fills in each unique worksheet tab name depending on which worksheet is printed (see Figure 7.19)

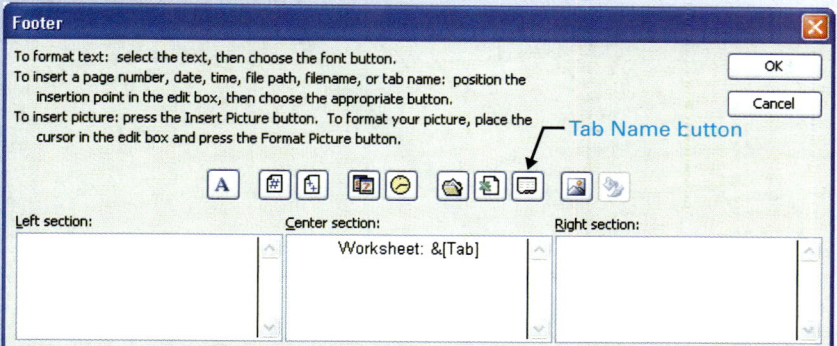

FIGURE 7.19

Setting the page footer for each worksheet in the group

6. Click **OK** to apply your page setting choices and close the Footer dialog box, and then click **OK** to close the Page Setup dialog box.

You probably notice that a dashed line appears to the right of column F on the active worksheet. The line is a page break indicator. It appears when you modify any of the page setup values such as the left or right margins. You can remove the page breaks by clicking Tools, clicking Options, clicking the View tab, and clearing the Page breaks check box in the Window options pane. Then click OK to apply your worksheet options.

Because you have completed your work with the worksheet group, you can ungroup them.

Ungrouping worksheets:

1. Right-click any of the worksheet tabs in the grouped worksheets

2. Click **Ungroup Sheets** in the shortcut menu. Excel ungroups the four-worksheet group

Consolidating and Summarizing Data with 3-D Formulas

Until now, you have written *two-dimensional formulas*, which are formulas that reference cells that are on the same worksheet. Now that you have information about the three BECO plants in multiple worksheets of a single workbook, you can create formulas on one worksheet that summarize the information found on three other worksheets. Formulas that reference cells in other worksheet cells are called three-dimensional (or 3-D) formulas. Each worksheet of a workbook is analogous to the board of a tic-tac-toe game.

Three-dimensional formulas can consolidate data from multiple worksheets. When you *consolidate* information, you are summarizing data from multiple worksheets. For example, you could write a formula in the Summary worksheet that totals sales by division. Or, you could write a function to average sales for the first quarter (Qtr 1) for all machines manufactured by all three plants. Consolidating information presents a simplified picture to someone who does not necessarily want to know all the details—a division manager or the president of a company, for example.

FIGURE 7.20

Consolidating sales information

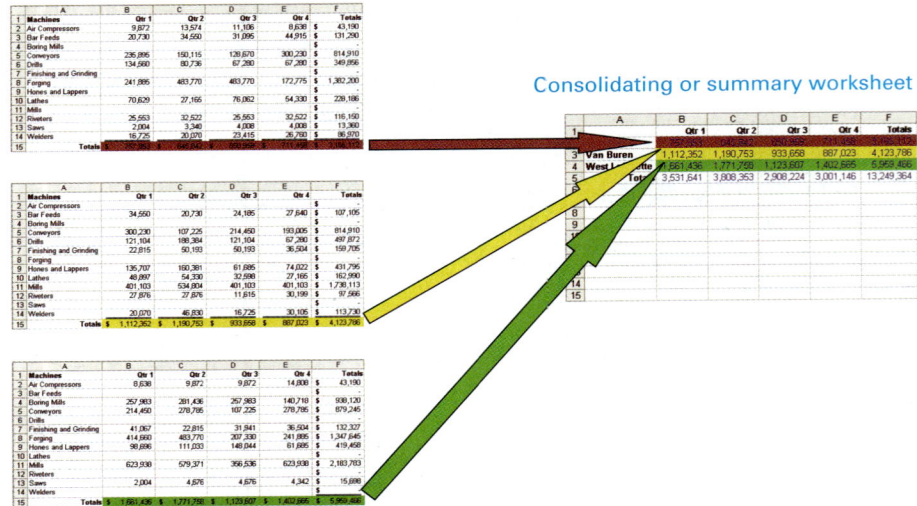

Figure 7.20 shows a graphical example of how you might summarize the sales worksheets for Bridgewater Engineering Company. The summary provides Stirling with a clear picture of sales by each of the plants without confusing details.

Before you write formulas that reference other worksheets' cells, look at the general form of a three-dimensional reference. It is

```
'sheetname'!cell-range
```

Sheetname is the name of the worksheet, and *cell-range* is the cell or cell range in the referenced worksheet. The exclamation point (called "bang" by programmers) separates the worksheet name from the cell range. When a worksheet name contains a space, such as *Van Buren* and *West Lafayette*, then the sheet name must be enclosed in apostrophes. For example, suppose you want cell B4 on the Summary worksheet to reference the sum of all first quarter sales at the Van Buren plant—cell B15 in the Van Buren worksheet. That 3-D formula is:

```
='Van Buren'!B15
```

To refer to cell B5 in the Somerville worksheet from another worksheet, you can omit the apostrophes because the sheet name does not contain spaces:

```
=Somerville!B5
```

How would you write a formula in the Summary worksheet to total the sales of all machines manufactured and sold by the West Lafayette plant? The West Lafayette plant's sales values are stored in the cell range B2:E14 on the West Lafayette worksheet. The Summary worksheet would refer to that cell range as an argument of the SUM function this way:

```
=SUM('West Lafayette'!B2:E14)
```

Naturally, whether you refer to a single cell or a cell range in a three-dimensional reference, that reference must make sense in the formula in which it is used. Otherwise, Excel will display an error in the cell. However, that would be illegal in an expression that does not allow a cell range—an expression such as

```
='West Lafayette'!B2:E14/52
```

You can specify a range of *worksheets* in a three-dimensional reference just as you can specify a range of cells in a two-dimensional reference. A reference to a range of sheets must include the first and last names of the worksheets in the range, and no other, separated by a colon, followed by an exclamation point, and then followed by a cell or cell range. For example, the 3-D reference 'Somerville:West Lafayette'!B10 refers to cell B10 found in each of three worksheets from Somerville through West Lafayette.

When would you ever use a sheet range in an expression? There are several cases where that type of 3-D reference is handy. The first quarter sales for each plant, conveniently, are found in the cell range B2:B14 on three worksheets (Somerville, Van Buren, and West Lafayette). You refer to the "silo" of cells in that 3-D range with the notation within the SUM function this way:

```
=SUM('Somerville:West Lafayette'!B2:B14)
```

When you include several worksheets in a sheet range, you do not enclose each worksheet name in its own apostrophes, even if some worksheet names contain spaces. Instead, enclose the entire range—the first worksheet name, the colon, and the final worksheet name—in apostrophes and follow the worksheet range with an exclamation point to mark the end of the worksheet range.

Writing 3-D Formulas

Happily, you have two choices when writing 3-D cell references. You can manually type the references, or you can use Excel's point mode to create a cell range expression automatically. If you use point mode, you must first select the *worksheet* range before you select the *cell* range, not the other way around.

---

task *reference*   Writing a Formula Containing
                              a 3-D Reference

- After clicking the cell where you want the formula to appear, type =, type a function name, and type (. However, if you are not writing a function, then simply type =

- Click the sheet tab of the worksheet containing the cell or cell range you want to reference

- If a worksheet range is needed, then press and hold the **Shift** key and click the last worksheet tab in the range

- Click the cell or cell range you want to reference

- Complete the formula (type a concluding right parentheses for a function, for instance), and then press **Enter**

Placing formulas and labels in the Summary worksheet:

1. Right-click any of the worksheet tab scroll buttons (to the left of the leftmost worksheet tab) and then click **Summary**. The Summary worksheet becomes active

2. Click cell **B1**, type ='Somerville'!B1, and press **Enter** to reference the Qtr 1 label on the Somerville worksheet. Naturally, you could type the label Qtr 1 too. Using a reference is better. If the label on the Somerville worksheet changes, then the label on the Summary worksheet automatically changes too

3. Click cell **B1**, drag its fill handle, and drag through the cell range **C1:F1**

4. Select the cell range **A2:A5**

5. Type **Somerville**, press **Enter**, type **Van Buren**, press **Enter**, type **West Lafayette**, press **Enter**, type **Totals**, and press **Enter**

6. Click the column A heading button, click **Format**, point to **Column**, and click **AutoFit Selection**. Excel resizes the column to fit the widest entry

7. Drag column heading buttons **B** through **F** to select the columns, right-click anywhere *within* the selected columns, click **Column Width**, type **13** in the Column width text box, and click **OK** to resize columns B through F

8. Click cell **B1** to deselect the column range and display the 3-D formula in the formula bar (see Figure 7.21)

FIGURE 7.21

Summary worksheet with 3-D formulas

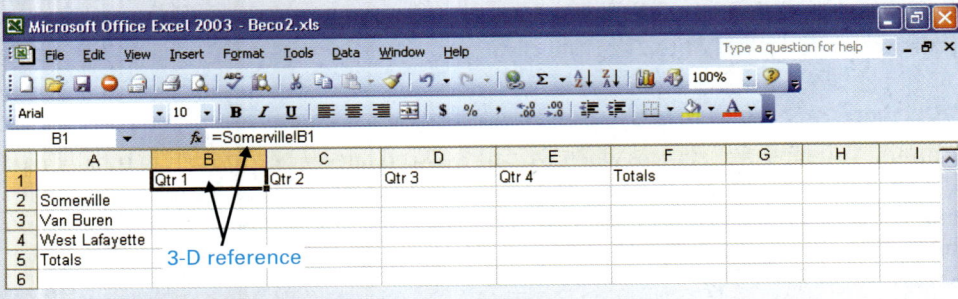

help yourself *Press **F1**, type **cell link** in the Search text box of the Microsoft Excel Help task pane, and press **Enter**. Click the hyperlink **Create a link to another cell, workbook, or program**. Finally, click **Create a link between cells in different workbooks**. Click the Help screen **Close** button when you are finished*

Now you are ready to write consolidating formulas. First, you will write a formula to sum the first quarter sales for the Somerville plant. Although the sum of Qtr 1 sales is in cell B15 on the Somerville worksheet, you prefer to write your own formula using a cell range in a 3-D reference as a double-check.

Writing formulas referencing other worksheets:

1. Click cell **B2** and type **=SUM(**

2. Click the **Somerville** worksheet tab

3. Click and drag the cell range **B2:B14**, and press **Enter**. Excel returns to the active worksheet, Summary, and displays the value 757,853 in cell B2

4. Click cell **B2**, drag the fill handle to cell **E2**, and release the mouse. Excel fills in the remainder of the Somerville total sales for each quarter, and it automatically adjusts the cell references (even for 3-D references) to reflect their location (see Figure 7.22)

Filling in the remaining SUM formulas is the same process as above. This time, however, you will create the first-quarter SUM formulas for the Van Buren and West Lafayette plants. Then you will copy that pair of formulas across their rows to save time.

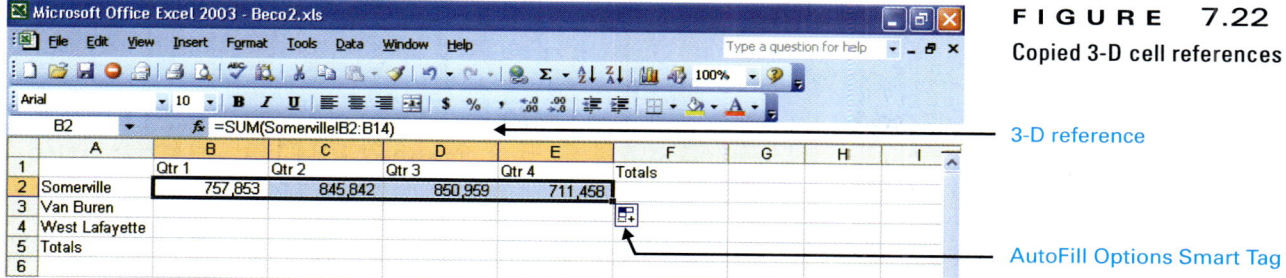

3-D reference

AutoFill Options Smart Tag

Writing and copying the remaining 3-D SUM formulas:

1. Click cell **B3** and type **=SUM(**

2. Click the **Van Buren** worksheet tab. (You may have to scroll through the worksheet tabs to locate it)

3. Drag the mouse through the cell range **B2:B14**, and press **Enter**. Excel returns to the active worksheet and displays the value 1,112,352 in cell B3

4. In cell **B4** type **=SUM(**

5. Click the **West Lafayette** worksheet tab. (You may have to scroll through the worksheet tabs to locate it)

6. Drag the mouse through the cell range **B2:B14**, and press **Enter**. Excel returns to the active worksheet, Summary, and displays the value 1,661,436 in cell B4

7. Select the cell range **B3:B4**, drag the cell pair's fill handle from cell **B4** to cell **E4**, and release the mouse. Excel copies the formulas and adjusts all cell references

Setting up a Watch Window

You can see the effect on any Qtr 1 sums on the Summary worksheet when you change a value on a dependent worksheet such as Somerville. Establishing a cell watch is a handy way to keep tabs on a formula in one worksheet while changing values in another worksheet. Displayed in a separate window, a cell Watch Window shows the current value of formula-containing cells that you identify.

Watching a cell and its formula in the Watch Window:

1. Click cell **B2**, which summarizes Somerville's first quarter

2. Click **Tools**, point to **Formula Auditing**, and click **Show Watch Window** to open the Watch Window

3. Click **Add Watch**, and then click **Add**. The Watch Window displays 757,853 in the Value column which is the current value of Summary worksheet cell B2

4. Click the **Somerville** worksheet tab, click cell **B9** (Hones and Lappers for Qtr 1), type **98765**, and press **Enter**. The value of the Watch Window cell B2 changes to 865,618

EXCEL

5. Click the **Undo** button on the Standard toolbar to reverse the change. Watch Window value reverts to its original value

6. Click the first row in the Watch Window, click the **Delete Watch** button on the Watch Window toolbar, and click the **Close** button on the Watch Window title bar to close the window

7. Click the **Summary** worksheet tab to reactivate that worksheet

Totaling Formulas Containing 3-D References

You can sum cells containing references to other worksheets just as you can any other cells. Now that you have summarized the sales from three other worksheets by calendar quarter and company, you can form row and column totals and compute a grand total. The row totals will appear in cells F2 through F4 of the Summary worksheet, and column totals will appear in cells B5 through E5. The grand total will appear at the intersection of the row totals and the column totals, in cell F5.

Using Excel's AutoSum button to write SUM functions:

1. On the Summary worksheet, click and drag the cell range **B2:F5**

2. Click the **AutoSum** button on the Standard toolbar. Row totals, column totals, and a grand total appear

3. Click any cell to deselect the range (see Figure 7.23)

FIGURE 7.23

AutoSum creates totals and a grand total

	A	B	C	D	E	F	G	H	I
1		Qtr 1	Qtr 2	Qtr 3	Qtr 4	Totals			
2	Somerville	757,853	845,842	850,959	711,458	3,166,112			
3	Van Buren	1,112,352	1,190,753	933,658	887,023	4,123,786			
4	West Lafayette	1,661,436	1,771,758	1,123,607	1,402,665	5,959,466			
5	Totals	3,531,641	3,808,353	2,908,224	3,001,146	13,249,364			
6									

Formatting the Summary Worksheet

With the summary formulas complete, you are ready to format the Summary worksheet for Stirling and the managers. You have already formatted the supporting worksheets. (*Supporting* worksheets are worksheets that are referenced by other worksheets and thus support those worksheets.) You can use Excel's AutoFormat command to format a range of cells.

Formatting the summary worksheet cells with AutoFormat:

1. Click and drag the cell range **A1:F5**

2. Click **Format** and then click **AutoFormat**. The AutoFormat dialog box appears

3. Drag the scroll button down until you see Classic 3 (see Figure 7.24)

4. Click **Classic 3** to select it, click **OK** to apply that format, and then click any cell to deselect the cell range

FIGURE 7.24
Selecting an AutoFormat

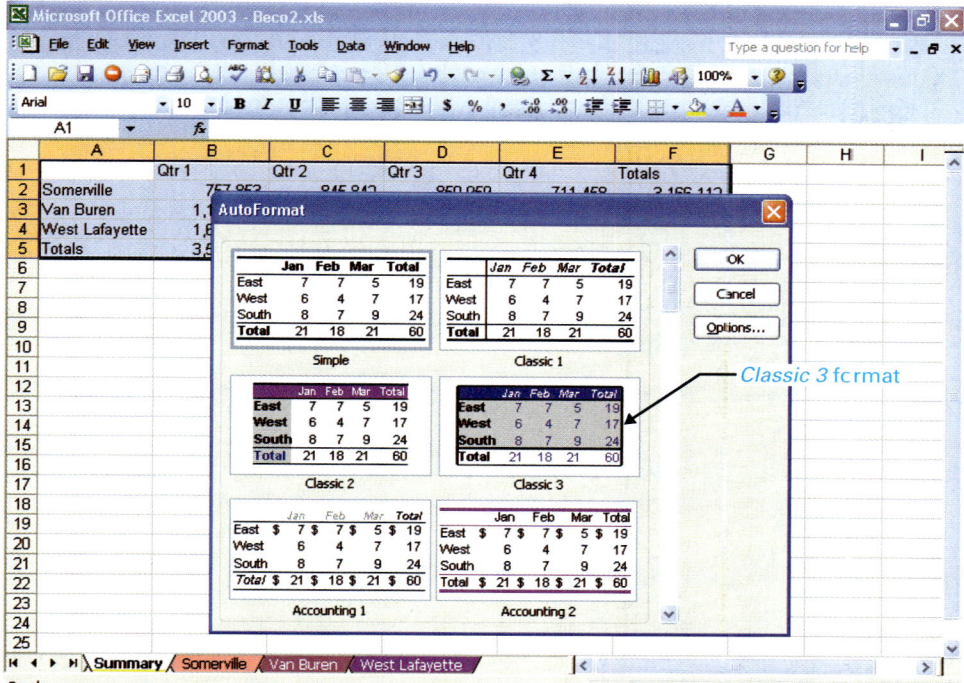

Printing Multiple Worksheets

Previously, when you printed out a worksheet that was part of a workbook of several worksheets, you simply clicked File, Print, and OK to print the worksheet. Printing more than one worksheet is just as easy. The only additional step is that you must first select (group) the worksheets and then print them.

---

task reference   Printing Multiple Worksheets

- Group the worksheets you want to print by pressing **Ctrl** and then clicking the worksheet tabs or by pressing **Shift** and clicking the first and last worksheets in a contiguous group

- Click **File**, click **Print**, ensure that the **Active sheet(s)** option button is selected, and click **OK**

You print the worksheets for Stirling—all sheets except the Documentation worksheet, as per Stirling's request.

Printing multiple worksheets:

1. Click the **Summary** worksheet tab, press and hold the **Shift** key, click the **West Lafayette** worksheet tab, and release the **Shift** key

2. Click **File**, click **Print**, ensure that the **Active sheet(s)** option button in the *Print what* panel is selected, click the **Preview** button, click the **Next** button repeatedly to examine each of the four pages, and then click the **Print** button

3. Right-click the **Summary** worksheet tab and then click **Ungroup Sheets** in the shortcut menu

Whenever you want to print *all* the worksheets in a workbook, you do not need to group the worksheets. Instead, click the *Entire workbook* option in the *Print what* panel. That option directs Excel to print all of a workbook's worksheets.

You have made a lot of changes to your workbook. Save it in case you want to take a break or return to work on the workbook another time.

Saving the BECO workbook:

1. Click the **Documentation** worksheet tab, and edit the Date Revised value (cell C18) to today's date

2. Click the **Save** button on the Standard toolbar to save the completed workbook

3. Click **File**, click **Save As** and type **Beco3.xls**, and then click the **Save** button to save an identical copy under a new name in preparation for Session 7.2

4. Click **File**, and then click **Close** to close the workbook

Deleting an Excel Template

Earlier in this session, you created a template called **BecoTemplate.xlt**, and Excel saved it in the Templates folder on the computer on which you are working. Now it is time to do a little housecleaning. You are going to remove the **BecoTemplate.xlt** template so that readers who might use this computer in the future will not encounter an error when they try to save the BecoTemplate template while reading the textbook.

---

task reference   Deleting an Excel Template

- Click **File** on the menu bar, click **New**, and click **On my computer** in the Templates panel of the task pane

- Right-click the template that you want to delete, and click **Delete**

- Click **OK** when asked if you want to send the template to the Recycle Bin

---

Deleting the BecoTemplate Template and closing Excel:

1. Click **File** on the menu bar and click **New** to open the task pane

2. Click **On my computer** in the Templates panel of the task pane

3. Right click the **BecoTemplate** template in the list of templates, click **Delete** in the pop-up menu, and click **Yes**. Excel deletes the BecoTemplate

4. Click the **Cancel** button to close the Templates dialog box

5. Click **File** and then click **Exit** to exit Excel

making *the grade*

1. You can view multiple workbooks on screen by clicking Window and then clicking the _____ command.

2. Group contiguous worksheets together by clicking the first worksheet tab, pressing the _____ key, and clicking the last worksheet tab in the series of tabs.

3. By default, a worksheet you add to a workbook appears where in the workbook?

4. Enter the same value in grouped worksheets by typing the expression and pressing Enter. That is also known as _____ down.

5. Perhaps the easiest way to select a particular tab in a workbook with many worksheets is to right-click any _____ scroll button and then click the worksheet tab name from the shortcut that appears.

SESSION 7.2 WORKING WITH MULTIPLE WORKBOOKS

In this section, you will learn how to write formulas that reference another *workbook*. You will learn how to instruct Excel to locate and retrieve information from another workbook stored on your computer, even when the referenced workbook is not open. You will create an Excel Workspace to preserve the onscreen relationship between open workbooks and worksheets.

Retrieving Data from Other Workbooks

In the previous session, you created 3-D formulas that referenced cells from other worksheets within the same workbook. Excel allows you to extend the concept of three-dimensional references to include other workbooks on your computer. For example, you could write a formula in the Summary worksheet in the BECO workbook that averages or totals a cell group in any workbook you worked on in Chapter 6.

Linking Workbooks

A three-dimensional reference to a cell in another workbook resembles a three-dimensional reference to another worksheet in the same workbook. The only difference is that any 3-D reference to another workbook must contain the workbook's location and name in addition to the worksheet name and cell address or cell range. The general form of a 3-D reference to another workbook—also called a **link**, a **dynamic link**, or an **external reference**—is this:

```
'Location[workbook-name]worksheet-name'!cell-range
```

Location is the disk drive and folder name that contains the workbook. The folder may be within other folders, and the disk drive and folders that lead to the workbook are known as the **path**. Enclose a workbook name in brackets to distinguish it from both the path preceding it and the worksheet name that follows it. The location, workbook name, and worksheet name or name range are enclosed in apostrophes. Following the worksheet name is an exclamation point and the cell reference, cell range, or cell name.

You notice that each part of the link becomes more specific from left to right. For example, suppose you are working on the Summary worksheet in the BECO workbook and you want to display the value of a cell in another workbook. The workbook you

FIGURE 7.25

Link workbook reference

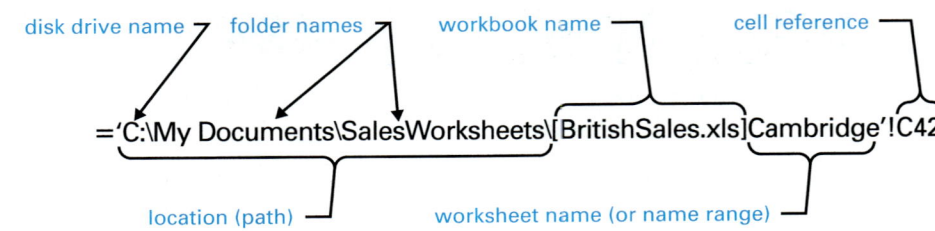

want to link to is on the drive and path C:\My Documents\SalesWorksheets\, the workbook name is **BritishSales.xls**, the worksheet name is Cambridge, and the cell containing the value you want to reference is C42. You would write the link reference to the cell as shown in Figure 7.25

You notice that apostrophes enclose the Location[workbook-name]worksheet-name part of the 3-D cell reference. This is required when the location, workbook name, or worksheet name contain spaces. If there are no spaces in the location, workbook name, or worksheet name, you can omit the apostrophes. You can drop the location portion of the 3-D reference if the workbook to which you are linking is in the same folder as the active workbook in which you are typing the link expression.

Advantages of Linked Workbooks

Workbook links are also called dynamic links because a change in a cell linked to another workbook automatically propagates to any expression that references the changed cell. This happens for links in open workbooks as well as workbooks that are not currently open or loaded. When you open a workbook containing a link to another workbook, Excel informs you that the worksheet contains dynamic links. If you approve, Excel opens referenced workbooks, inspects referenced cells, updates formulas containing the references to other worksheets' cells when necessary, and then closes the referenced workbooks. A workbook containing a worksheet to which a link formula refers is called a *supporting workbook*. A workbook containing a link to a supporting worksheet is called a *dependent workbook,* because one or more of its cells' value depend on the value stored in another workbook.

---

task *reference*　　　　Building Link References
　　　　　　　　　　　　　　　　by Pointing

- Open the supporting workbook containing the cell or cells you will reference in another worksheet and workbook

- Make the workbook containing the link reference active and click the cell to contain the link reference

- Type the formula up to the point in which you reference the cell or cell range in another workbook

- Click the taskbar button corresponding to the supporting workbook to make it active

- Click the worksheet tab containing the cell or cell range to reference

- Click the cell or drag the cell range of the cell(s) you want to reference and press **Enter**

Creating a series of linked workbooks is often a better alternative than creating and using one larger workbook containing worksheets from all the referenced workbooks for several reasons. One of the most important advantages is that linked workbooks require less memory than a single multisheet workbook. Smaller workbooks containing dynamic links to other workbooks load and open faster than equivalent larger workbooks containing all the referenced worksheets.

Creating and Maintaining Linked Workbooks

Over the weekend, Stirling Leonard and members of BECO's board completed the paperwork to acquire a company called Danielli, Incorporated. Danielli is a small company that was a BECO competitor and manufactures some of the same types of machinery as BECO. While Stirling is busy with details of the merger, he wants you to incorporate some of the gross sales information Danielli keeps in its Excel workbook with the sales information in the BECO workbook. Danielli management wants to maintain physically separate workbooks for at least six months. To provide that separation, Stirling asks you to link to the Danielli workbook in order to summarize its sales in the BECO workbook. Both Stirling and Danielli's former CEO, Larry Sweet, agree that this is the best way to maintain a logical separation and yet have a consolidated sales statement.

Opening the Danielli workbook:

1. If you closed Excel at the end of the previous session, then start Excel

2. Open the workbook **ex07Danielli.xls** (see Figure 7.26)

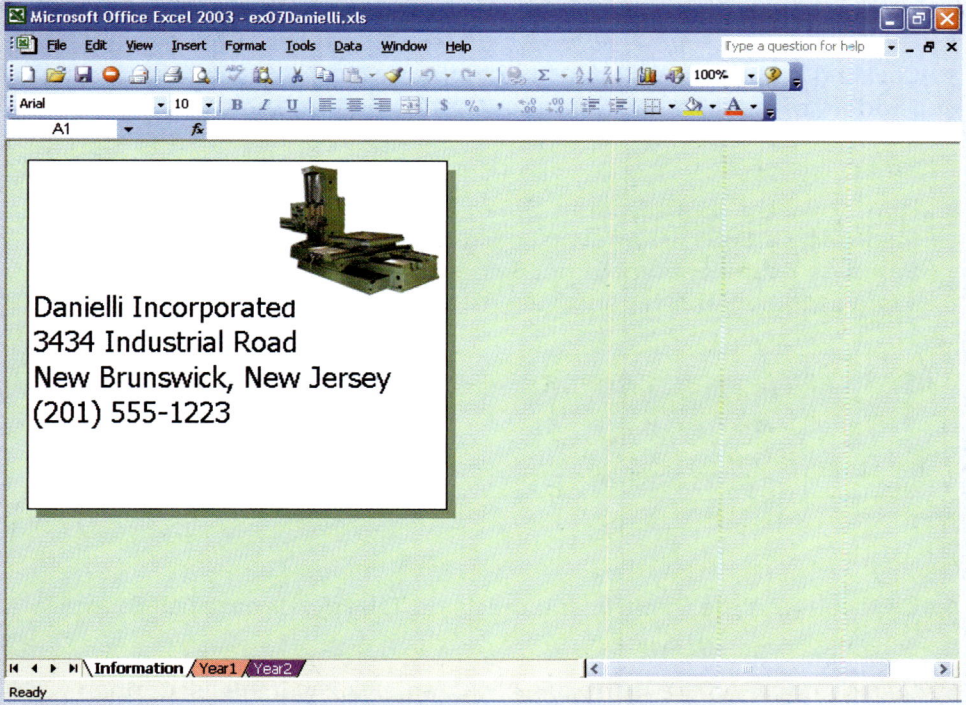

FIGURE 7.26

Danielli Information worksheet

3. Save the worksheet as **Danielli3.xls**. (There is no **Danielli2.xls** worksheet, but the digit *3* in the name will keep the worksheet synchronized with the BECO worksheet version 3)

4. Click the **Year1** worksheet tab and briefly review the worksheet's contents

5. Click the **Year2** worksheet tab and briefly review the worksheet's contents

6. Click the **Name** box list arrow and then click the name **Qtr2** from the list. Notice the name refers to the cell range C5:F5

7. Click the **Name** box list arrow and then click the name **Qtr4** from the list. Notice the name refers to the cell range C7:F7

You notice that the Danielli worksheet arranges sales in a manner different from BECO. Danielli's quarters are arranged in rows and products run across columns. BECO's quarter sales are in columns and products are stored in rows. This is a problem if you want to copy a link formula either down or across in the BECO worksheet. However, Danielli's workbook creator assigned names to each quarter to facilitate referencing the product sales values by a name rather than by a cell range.

With the Danielli supporting worksheet open, you are ready to write your first external or link formula. Stirling wants you to summarize sales of Danielli for the four quarters and include the summary in the Summary worksheet of the **Beco3.xls** workbook. The plant's names are listed in alphabetical order in the Summary worksheet, so Stirling wants Danielli listed at the top of the list—just above the Somerville summary row.

Opening the BECO workbook and entering a link formula:

1. Open the **Beco3.xls** workbook

2. Click the **Summary** worksheet tab, right-click cell **A2**, click **Insert** on the shortcut menu, click the **Entire row** option button, and click **OK** to insert a new row 2. Excel adds a new row and displays the Insert Options Smart Tag icon

3. Hover over the Insert Options Smart Tag until a list arrow appears, click the **Insert Options** list arrow (see Figure 7.27) and then click the **Format Same As Below** option button. Excel formats the newly added row the same as the other sales summary rows, not the header row

FIGURE 7.27

Formatting the new sales summary row

click to format row 2 to match row 3

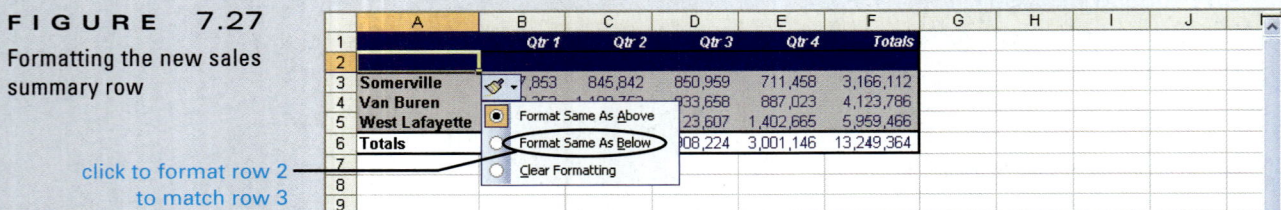

4. Click cell **A2**, type **Danielli**, and press the **Tab** key to make cell B2 active

5. In cell B2, type **=SUM(**

6. Click **Window** on the menu bar, click **Danielli3.xls** in the list of open workbooks, click the **Year2** worksheet tab, drag the mouse through the cell range **C4:F4** (see Figure 7.28), and press **Enter** to complete the formula

7. Click the **Danielli3.xls** button on the Taskbar to make that worksheet active, click **File** on the menu bar, and click **Close** to close **Danielli3.xls**. Excel makes BECO the active workbook again

FIGURE 7.28

Selecting a cell range in an external workbook

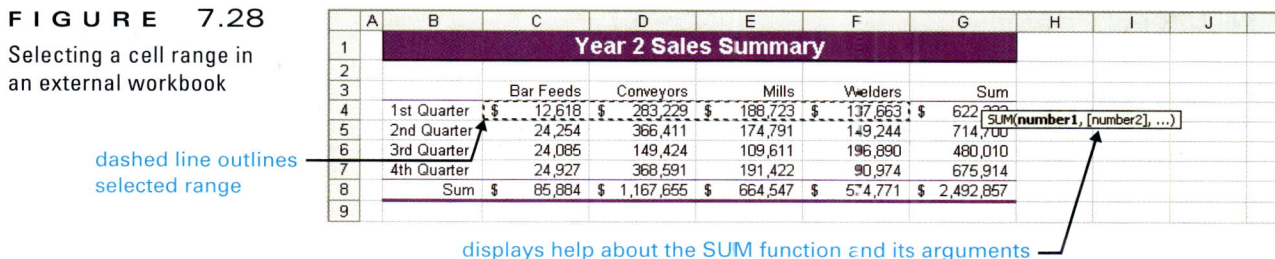

dashed line outlines selected range

displays help about the SUM function and its arguments

You may be tempted to create the remaining Danielli formulas to be placed in cells C2 through E2 by copying the formula in cell B2. Unfortunately, the cells in the Danielli workbook are not arranged to accommodate a left-to-right copy as you did for the other BECO worksheets. Instead, you will have to build the remaining three link formulas by hand. In addition, you want a row total in cell F2, which you can copy from cell F3. Use the names Qtr2, Qtr3, and Qtr4 in the link formulas. The previous names are defined in the **Danielli3.xls** workbook for the three remaining cell ranges. Using names greatly simplifies your work because you do not need to worry about how the Danielli worksheet designer may have redesigned the worksheet—just as long as the names remain intact. That's why some worksheet designers call worksheets that use names "smart worksheets."

Creating the remaining link formulas by typing them:

1. Click cell **C2** in the Summary worksheet, type **=SUM('** (be sure to type the apostrophe following the left parenthesis)

2. Type the path to *your* Danielli worksheet, then type **[Danielli3.xls]Year2'!Qtr2)**, and press **Enter**. Excel displays the sum of Danielli's second quarter sales, 714,700

tip: *If you make a mistake in typing the link reference, Excel will display an error message such as "That name is not valid." If so, press the **Esc** key to go into edit mode, check the link formula very carefully, use your arrow keys to move to the mistake, correct it, and press **Enter***

3. Click cell **C2**, press **Ctrl+C** to place the formula on the Clipboard, click and drag the cell range **D2:E2**, and press **Ctrl+V** to paste in the two formulas

4. Click cell **D2**, press the **F2** function key to edit the cell, press the **Backspace** key twice to erase the last two characters in the formula, type **3)**, and press **Enter**

5. Click cell **E2**, press the **F2** function key to edit the cell, press the **Backspace** key twice to erase the last two characters in the formula, type **4)**, and press **Enter**

6. Click cell **F2** and then click the **AutoSum** button on the Standard toolbar, and press **Enter** to approve the AutoSum-suggested cell range and complete the formula (see Figure 7.29)

At first glance, all the values seem to be fine. However, you probably noticed that the totals in row 6 are unchanged. That is because Excel did not adjust the SUM functions in those rows after you added the Danielli row. Because the newly added row is out of range of the SUM functions in row 6, Excel does not know to automatically adjust the cell references to include the new row. Therefore, you need to fix those formulas before going on.

EXCEL

FIGURE 7.29
Worksheet after entering
four link formulas

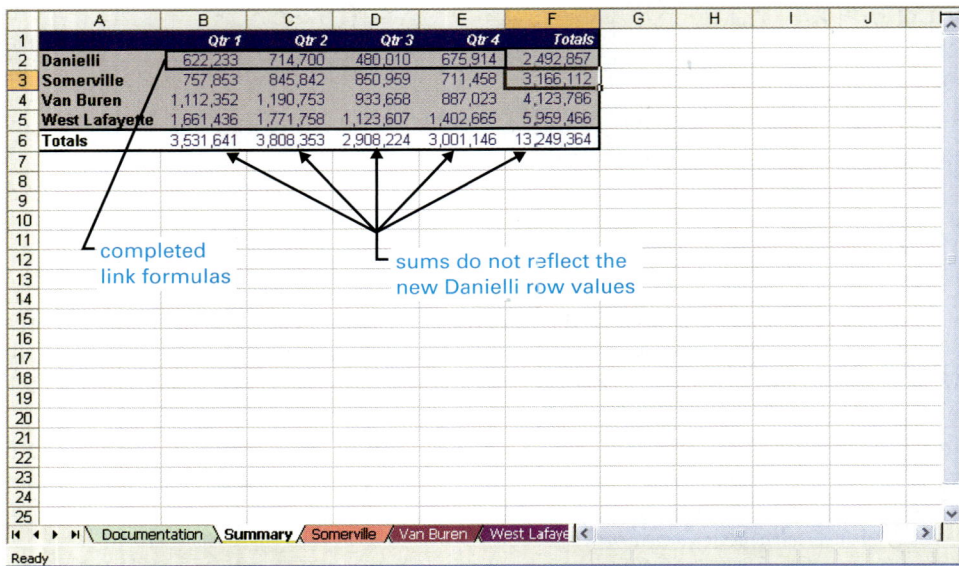

Modifying quarter summation formulas:

1. Select the cell range **B2:F6**, which includes the incorrect SUM function values in row 6 and the totals in column F

2. Click the **AutoSum** button on the Standard toolbar. Excel places updated SUM functions in cells B6 through F6

tip: *If any of the cells displays ######, widen the column in which the pound signs appear. Simply double-click the right border of the column heading button to widen it to an optimal width*

3. Click cell **A1** to deselect the range

Updating Linked Workbooks

When you save a workbook containing links to other workbooks, Excel stores the most recent calculation of those results. If you later open a supporting workbook after closing the dependent workbook and make changes to various cells, the values of the dependent workbook are not updated until you open the dependent workbook. Excel recognizes that the workbook contains formulas that are dependent on workbooks that are closed and asks if you want to update the links. If you click the Update button, Excel locates the supporting workbook, reads the link cell values from it, and updates the dependent workbook. If you click the Don't Update button, the workbook opens without updating the linked cells. In that case, dependent formulas retain their values from the last time the workbook was saved.

Erik Gepetti, Danielli's manager, just discovered an error in the **Danielli3.xls** workbook. The value in cell F7 (total sales of welders in the fourth quarter) is incorrect. Instead of $90,974, the value should be zero. You agree to make the change and ensure that Excel automatically updates the link value in the dependent workbook **Beco3.xls**.

Modifying values in a supporting workbook:

1. Click **Edit** and click **Links**. The Edit Links dialog box appears (see Figure 7.30)

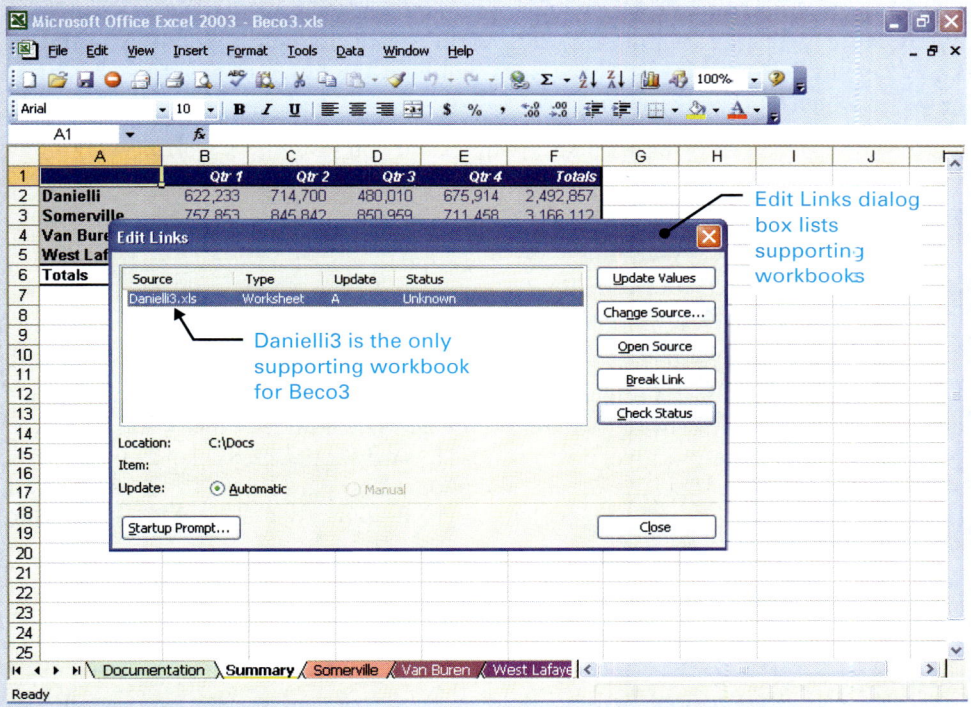

FIGURE 7.30
Edit Links dialog box

2. With the **Danielli3.xls** workbook name in the Edit Links list selected, click the **Open Source** button to open the selected workbook. Excel opens **Danielli3.xls** and makes it active

3. Click the **Year2** worksheet tab (if necessary), click cell **F7** and type **0** (zero), and press **Enter** to indicate no sales of welders in the fourth quarter

tip: *You can also press the **Delete** key to empty the cell. In this case, either way is fine. If you were to compute averages or minimums on these sales figures, you should press Delete instead of typing zero*

4. Click the **Save** button on the Standard toolbar to save the changed **Danielli3.xls** workbook, click **File** on the menu bar, and click **Close** to close the **Danielli3.xls** workbook. Excel makes **Beco3.xls** the active workbook. Notice that the value in cell E2 is now 584,940 (see Figure 7.31)

EXCEL

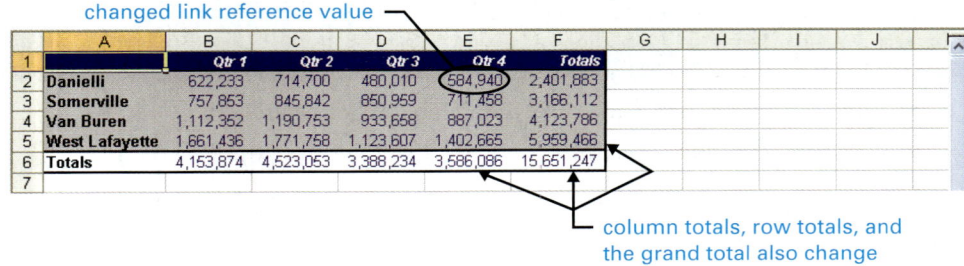

changed link reference value

	A	B	C	D	E	F	G	H	I	J
1		Qtr 1	Qtr 2	Qtr 3	Qtr 4	Totals				
2	Danielli	622,233	714,700	480,010	584,940	2,401,883				
3	Somerville	757,853	845,842	850,959	711,458	3,166,112				
4	Van Buren	1,112,352	1,190,753	933,658	887,023	4,123,786				
5	West Lafayette	1,861,436	1,771,758	1,123,607	1,402,665	5,959,466				
6	Totals	4,153,874	4,523,053	3,388,234	3,586,086	15,651,247				
7										

column totals, row totals, and
the grand total also change

Saving Linked Workbooks

You can save the dependent workbook, **Beco3.xls**, and the supporting workbook, **Danielli3.xls**, under names different from their original names by executing the Save As command in the File menu. For example, Stirling may want to save the supporting workbook **Danielli3.xls** under a name such as **DanielliPlant.xls**. Nothing prevents you or someone else from saving either workbook under a new name, but you must be careful when saving a supporting workbook under a new name.

Because these are common scenarios, Stirling wants to make sure both you and he know how to deal with them. Three cases highlight the different scenarios that arise based on which workbooks are open or closed:

1. Both **Bec03.xls** and **Danielli3.xls** are open and you save the *supporting* workbook, **Danielli3.xls**, under a different filename

2. Both **Bec03.xls** and **Danielli3.xls** are open and you save the *dependent* workbook, **Beco3.xls**, under a different filename

3. **Bec03.xls** is closed and **Danielli3.xls** is open and you save the *supporting* workbook, **Danielli3.xls**, under a different filename

What happens to all the links in the dependent workbook when you save (and optionally close) **Danielli3.xls** under a different name? Excel automatically and without notification alters all link formulas to reflect the new name under which you save a supporting workbook. For example, if you choose to save **Danielli3.xls** as **Acquisition.xls** after you execute File, Save As to save the supporting workbook, Excel changes all the links in cells B2:E2 to reflect that change. The link formula in cell B2, for example, becomes:

```
=SUM([Acquisition.xls]Year2!Qtr1)
```

Excel makes the change because the dependent workbook is open and available for change.

In case 2, nothing happens to the links in the dependent workbook. After all, you are changing the name of a workbook that is not a supporting workbook. All formulas remain the same.

Case 3 is the most interesting one. If you change the name of a supporting workbook when the dependent workbook to which it is linked is closed, then Excel cannot make changes to the links in the closed dependent workbook. When you later open **Beco3.xls**, the dependent workbook, Excel searches for **Danielli3.xls**. If you saved **Danielli3.xls** under the new name, **Acquisition.xls**, Excel will update **Beco3.xls** based on the old worksheet values stored in **Danielli3.xls**, not the new workbook **Acquisition.xls**. Worse yet, if you deleted **Danielli3.xls** after saving it under its new name, Excel will not be able to locate the workbook and thus will not be able to update link reference values in the dependent workbook. In this case, Excel issues an error message. Because you need to know how to handle this case—someone changes the names of one or more supporting workbooks—you will experience it firsthand.

In the steps that follow, you will experience just such a situation. It shows you that if you rename a supporting workbook or move it to another drive or directory, you must tell Excel the new name of the supporting workbook or where you moved it so that Excel can modify the link references, which is not the same as updating the *values* in a link reference.

Redirecting link references to a renamed supporting workbook:

1. Click **File** on the menu bar, click **Close**, and click **Yes** when asked if you want to save your changes to **Beco3.xls**. **Beco3.xls** closes, but Excel remains running

2. Click the **Open** button on the Standard toolbar. The Open dialog box opens

3. Navigate to the disk drive and folder containing the supporting workbook **Danielli3.xls**, right-click the filename in the Open dialog box, click **Rename** in the shortcut menu. Excel highlights the name **Danielli3.xls** in edit mode in the Open dialog box

4. Type the new name **Acquisition.xls**, press **Enter** to complete the file renaming process, but do not open the renamed dependent workbook

5. Navigate to the disk and folder containing **Beco3.xls** workbook and then double-click **Beco3.xls** to open the workbook. Excel opens the workbook and displays a dialog box asking if you want to update links

6. Click the **Update** button. Excel displays an alert box indicating it cannot update links (see Figure 7.32)

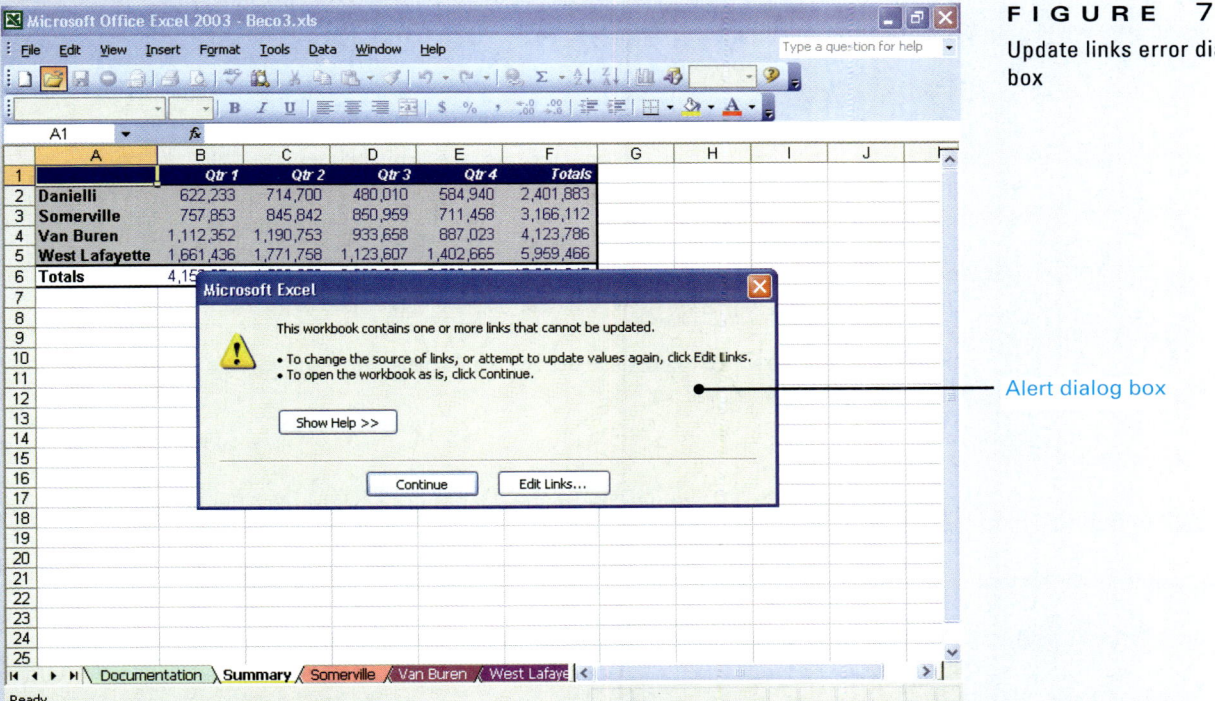

FIGURE 7.32
Update links error dialog box

Alert dialog box

7. Click the **Edit Links** button so that you can help Excel find the renamed supporting workbook. The Edit Links dialog box appears (see Figure 7.33)

FIGURE 7.33

Edit Links dialog box

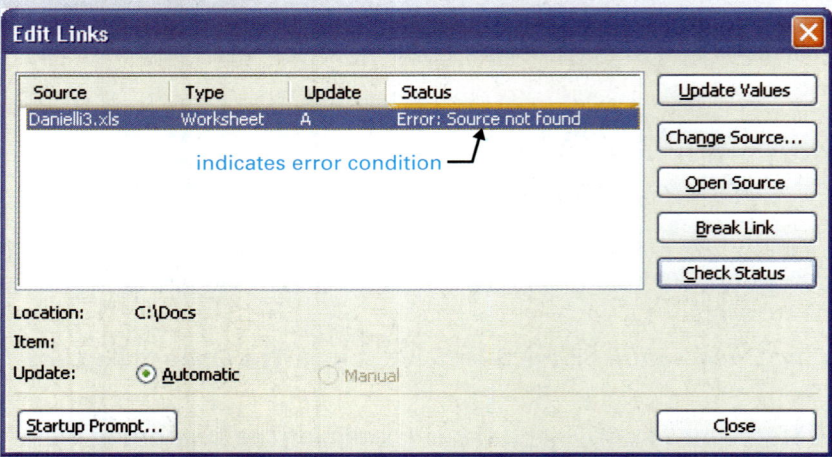

8. Click the **Change Source** button in the Edit Links dialog box. The Change Source dialog box opens

9. Go to the folder containing the **Acquisition.xls** workbook, click the **Acquisition.xls** filename in the Change Source list of files and folders, and click the **OK** button. The Edit Links dialog box reappears and displays OK in the Status list (see Figure 7.34)

FIGURE 7.34

Edit Links dialog box with updated link locations

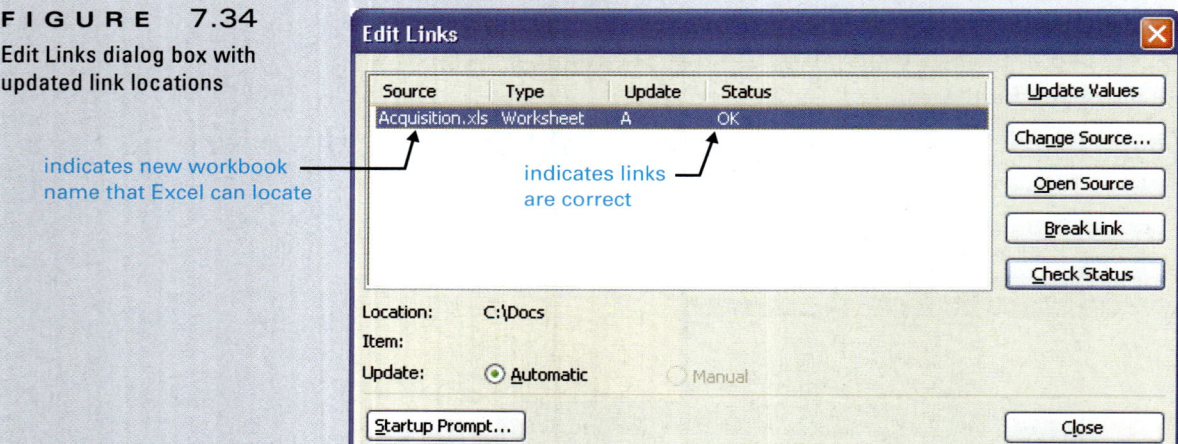

10. Click the **Update Values** button, and then click the **Close** button to close the Edit Links dialog box

You have done a lot of work and completed the workbook. Stirling is pleased. Save the workbook and exit Excel.

Saving your final BECO workbook and closing Excel:

1. Click the **Save** button on the Standard toolbar to save your changed **Beco3.xls** workbook

2. Click **File** on the menu bar and then click **Exit** to close Excel

making *the grade*

1. A reference to a cell in another workbook is called a _____, a dynamic _____, or a(n) _____ reference.

2. The disk drive and folders that lead to a workbook are known as the _____.

3. In an external reference, the workbook name is always enclosed in _____, even if it does not contain spaces.

4. The path, workbook name, and worksheet name of an external reference in which the path or the worksheet name contains a blank must be enclosed in what?

5. It is better to _____ worksheets when you want to type the same entry in the same location across multiple worksheets.

SESSION 7.3 SUMMARY

Three-dimensional formulas reference cells in other worksheets of a workbook. The cell references include the worksheet name enclosed in square brackets, an exclamation point, and a cell or cell range. A 3-D or link reference acts like any other cell reference.

You can combine worksheets from other workbooks into one workbook by opening all workbooks, clicking Window and then Arrange to display all workbooks on one screen. Then click and drag a worksheet tab from one window to a workbook in another window to cut and paste a worksheet. To copy a worksheet, press and hold Ctrl and then click and drag a worksheet tab to a workbook in another window.

You can group worksheets in a workbook by clicking the first worksheet tab and then shift-clicking (hold Shift and then click the mouse) the last worksheet of a contiguous set of worksheet tabs. Group noncontiguous worksheet tabs by Ctrl-clicking individual worksheet tabs. With worksheets grouped you can type text in one worksheet cell and the text is placed in all grouped worksheets in the same cell location. Similarly, you can format entries in the same cell(s) on grouped worksheets at the same time. Grouping allows you to establish the same page-level settings, such as page numbers and margins, for all worksheets in a group.

You can forge links between one workbook and a cell or cells of another workbook. Such cell references are called links, dynamic links, or external links. Workbooks containing external links are called dependent workbooks, and the workbooks to which they refer are called supporting workbooks. External links contain three parts: a path, a workbook name, and a cell or cell range. The combination of a path and a workbook name are enclosed in apostrophes if either the path or the workbook name contains spaces. If you rename a supporting workbook file, you have to reestablish the dependent program's link references to the renamed workbook. When one or more values in a supporting workbook change, the dependent workbook is updated with the new values the next time it is loaded.

MICROSOFT OFFICE SPECIALIST OBJECTIVES SUMMARY

- Insert and modify formulas—MOS XL03S-2-3
- Rename a worksheet tab and color it—MOS XL03S-3-4
- Insert, delete, and reposition worksheets in a workbook—MOS XL03S-5-4
- Modify the onscreen window layout—MOS XL03S-5-6

- Establish worksheet page settings—MOS XL03S-5-7
- Use cell Watch—MOS XL03E-1-13
- Define, modify, and use named ranges—MOS XL03E-1-14
- Create a workbook template—MOS XL03E-4-4
- Set the default number of worksheets—MOS XL03E-5-3

making the grade *answers*

SESSION 7.1

1. Arrange
2. Shift
3. Before the current, active worksheet
4. drilling
5. tab

SESSION 7.2

1. link, link, external
2. path
3. brackets, or square brackets
4. apostrophes
5. group

task reference summary

Task	Page #	Preferred Method
Deleting a worksheet	EX 7.6	• Right-click the tab of the worksheet to delete • Click **Delete** on the shortcut menu
Saving a Workbook as a Template	EX 7.7	• Activate the workbook you want to save as a template, click **File** and then click **Save As** • Type the template name in the File name list box, click the **Save as type** list box, scroll the list box to locate and then click **Template (*.xlt)**, and click **Save** button
Copying worksheets from other workbooks	EX 7.8	• Open the master workbook—the workbook into which you want to copy worksheets from other workbooks • Open all other workbooks containing worksheets you want to copy to the master workbook • In any of the open Excel workbooks, click **Window**, click **Arrange**, click the **Tiled** option button, and click **OK** • Press and hold the **Ctrl** key, and then click and drag to the master workbook the tab of the worksheet you want to copy • Release the mouse when the down-pointing arrow is in the correct tab location in the master workbook, and then release the **Ctrl** key
Grouping contiguous worksheets	EX 7.13	• Click the worksheet tab of the first worksheet in the group • Use the tab scrolling buttons if necessary to bring the last worksheet tab of the proposed group into view • Hold down the **Shift** key and click the last worksheet tab in the group
Grouping noncontiguous worksheets	EX 7.13	• Click the worksheet tab of the first worksheet you want in the group • Press and hold the **Ctrl** key and then click each worksheet you want to include in the group • When you are done, release the **Ctrl** key
Ungrouping worksheets	EX 7.14	• Click the worksheet tab of any worksheet not in the worksheet group • If all worksheets in the workbook are grouped, right-click any worksheet tab and click **Ungroup Sheets** from the shortcut menu

task reference *summary*

Task	Page #	Preferred Method
Writing a formula containing a 3-D reference	EX 7.23	• After clicking the cell where you want the formula to appear, type =, type a function name, and type the left parenthesis. If no function is needed, then type = • Click the sheet tab of the worksheet containing the cell or cell range you want to reference • If a worksheet range is needed, then press and hold the **Shift** key and click the last worksheet tab in the range • Click the cell or cell range you want to reference • Complete the formula (type a concluding right parenthesis for a function, for instance) and then press **Enter**
Printing multiple worksheets	EX 7.27	• Group the worksheets you want to print by pressing **Ctrl** and then clicking the worksheet tabs or pressing **Shift** and clicking the first and last worksheets in a contiguous group • Click **File**, click **Print**, ensure the **Active sheet(s)** option button is selected, and click **OK**
Deleting an Excel Template	EX 7.28	• Click **File** on the menu bar, click **New**, and click **On my computer** in the Templates panel of the task pane • Right-click the template which you want to delete, and click **Delete**, and click **OK** when asked if you want to send the template to the Recycle Bin
Building link references by pointing	EX 7.30	• Open the supporting workbook • Make active the workbook to contain the link reference and the cell to contain the link reference • Type the formula up to the point in which you reference the cell or cell range in another workbook • Click the Taskbar button corresponding to the supporting workbook to make it active • Click the worksheet tab containing the cell or cell range to reference • Click the cell or drag the cell range of the cell(s) you want to reference and press **Enter**
Opening a supporting workbook from a dependent workbook	EX 7.35	• Open the dependent workbook containing the link reference • Click **Edit** and then click **Links** • Click the name of the supporting workbook you want to open from the Links list • Click the **Open Source** button

EXCEL

TRUE OR FALSE

1. Linked workbooks require less memory than an equivalent multisheet workbook.

2. Formatting a cell in the active worksheet of a group of worksheets will format the same cell in all group members.

3. When you include several worksheets in a sheet range, enclose each worksheet name in its own apostrophes.

4. Workbooks containing external links are called dependent workbooks.

5. To print all the worksheets in a workbook, you must first group the worksheets.

FILL-IN

1. A(n) _____ worksheet is sometimes called a consolidation worksheet.

2. One way to copy a worksheet from one workbook to another is to display the source and target workbooks, press and hold the _____ key, and drag the worksheet from the source workbook to the target workbook.

3. Add a blank worksheet to a workbook by clicking Insert on the menu bar and then clicking _____.

4. When you press and hold the Ctrl key and then click two or more worksheet tabs in a workbook, you are _____ the worksheets.

5. In a workbook with many worksheets, you can speed up accessing worksheets by assigning a unique range _____ to cell A1 of each worksheet. Then you can access the _____ Box left of the formula bar to switch from one worksheet to another.

6. Worksheets that contain cells referenced by expressions in another workbook are called _____ worksheets.

MULTIPLE CHOICE

1. Which is not considered part of the general form of an external link?
   a. a workbook name
   b. a cell or cell range
   c. a path
   d. a cell value

2. A workbook containing a link to a supporting worksheet is called a
   a. supporting workbook.
   b. dependent workbook.
   c. summary workbook.
   d. consolidation workbook.

3. Entering data in the same cell of several workbooks simultaneously is called
   a. filling down.
   b. driving down.
   c. auto filling.
   d. drilling down.

4. When will dependent formulas retain their values from the last time the worksheet was saved?
   a. if the dependent workbook is opened without updating the links
   b. each time the dependent workbook is opened, regardless of the update status you chose
   c. if the supporting workbook's cells are changed and the dependent workbook is open
   d. if the dependent workbook is opened with an update to the links

5. What will Excel do if you save the dependent workbook under a different filename while the supporting and dependent workbooks are open?
   a. Nothing happens to the links in the dependent workbook. All formulas remain the same.
   b. Excel will issue an error message because it won't be able to locate the workbook.
   c. Excel automatically and without notification alters all link formulas to reflect the new name.
   d. Excel doesn't allow you to save a dependent workbook under a different filename without saving the supporting workbook under a different filename as well.

review of concepts

REVIEW QUESTIONS

1. Discuss the fastest way to enter the text **Acme Consolidated** in cell A12 of seven worksheets of the same workbook.

2. What is the advantage of a summary or consolidating worksheet?

3. Discuss what, if anything, is wrong with the following expression (assuming that the workbook exists and contains the referenced worksheet):

```
=SUM(C:\My Worksheets for Beco\[Danielli.xls]Sales!B4:B12)
```

4. What happens if you change the name of a supporting workbook when the dependent workbook is closed?

CREATE A QUESTION

For each of the following answers, create an appropriate short question.

ANSWER	QUESTION
1. Click Edit, click Links, and then click the Change Source button	_____
2. =[SalesDetail]Sales!C12	_____
3. Click the Qtr1 worksheet tab, press the Ctrl key, click the Qtr2 worksheet tab, click cell A1, and type Sales Information	_____
4. Click File on the menu bar and then click Save Workspace	_____
5. Click and drag the worksheet tab from where it is to another location	_____

practice

1. Summarizing Sales Data Using Reference Tools

Reed Lanterns makes specialty and custom lanterns and lamps. Its clients range from amusement parks to business buildings to private home builders. Reed currently has 11 sales representatives across the country to promote the firm and service its clients. Scott Reed, the owner of Reed Lanterns, has decided to promote one of the representatives to sales manager. Scott has asked you to help him determine which sales representative should be promoted to the management position. He would like you to summarize the sales reps' sales per quarter for the past two years in order to see which sales rep has sold the most.

Scott has reviewed the worksheets you have created and has given you some suggestions. He would like you to add a worksheet to summarize the sales representatives' figures for the past two years. There are also some formatting changes he would like you to complete to improve the appearance of the worksheet.

1. Open **ex07ReedReps.xls** and save it as **<yourname>ReedReps2.xls** (see Figure 7.35). These two worksheets are what you have created for Scott

2. Insert a Documentation sheet so that it is the first worksheet in the workbook. Enter the workbook name, **Reed Sales Representative Report**, your name, and the date

3. Insert a worksheet at the end of the workbook titled **Sales Summary**. Create the following column titles and place them in the cell range A1:D1: **Sales Rep**, **2003 Total Sales**, **2004 Total Sales**, and **Total Sales**

4. Use 3-D references to place the reps' names in the Sales Summary worksheet, cells **A2** through **A12**, by referring to their cell addresses in the 2004 Totals worksheet

5. In the Sales Summary worksheet, type a 3-D cell reference in cells **B2** and **C2** referring to cell **F3** in the 2003 Totals and 2004 Totals worksheets, respectively. Select cells **B2:C2** and drag the fill handle down through the cell range **B12:C12** to complete columns B and C

6. For the Total Sales column, select cell range **B2:D12** and then use the AutoSum button to create SUM functions in column D. Be sure that all currency figures display two decimal places and the Accounting format with the currency symbol

7. To improve the appearance of the worksheets, do the following. In the 2003 and 2004 Totals worksheets, make the font of the top row 14 point, bold, and blue. In these worksheets and the Sales Summary worksheet, make the column headings' font bold and blue, and fill the cells in light yellow

8. Format the column headings in the Sales Summary worksheet so that the cells are bordered as in the 2003 and 2004 Totals worksheets

9. In the Sales Summary worksheet, determine which rep had the greatest sales and should be promoted to manager. Display this rep by filling his information with a light green background. Remove the onscreen gridlines from the Documentation worksheet. Place your name in the worksheet header of each worksheet, save the workbook, and print all sheets in the workbook

FIGURE   7.35

Reed Lanterns workbook

	A	B	C	D	E	F	G	J	K
1			2003 Sales Representative Report						
2	Sales Reps	1st Qtr	2nd Qtr	3rd Qtr	4th Qtr	Rep Total	Rep Average		
3	Steve	$ 6,767.00	$ 5,656.00	$ 3,434.00	$ 3,432.00	$ 19,289.00	$ 4,822.25		
4	Darin	$ 7,878.00	$ 2,323.00	$ 3,433.00	$ 3,432.00	$ 17,066.00	$ 4,266.50		
5	Trevor	$ 4,323.00	$ 6,245.00	$ 6,256.00	$ 6,283.00	$ 23,107.00	$ 5,776.75		
6	Cindie	$ 7,878.00	$ 6,767.00	$ 7,667.00	$ 2,312.00	$ 24,624.00	$ 6,156.00		
7	Jason	$ 4,567.00	$ 7,876.00	$ 7,878.00	$ 2,123.00	$ 22,444.00	$ 5,611.00		
8	Kim	$ 4,238.00	$ 4,445.00	$ 4,876.00	$ 3,213.00	$ 16,772.00	$ 4,193.00		
9	Jessica	$ 6,218.00	$ 6,219.00	$ 6,072.00	$ 6,074.00	$ 24,583.00	$ 6,145.75		
10	Madison	$ 3,432.00	$ 5,550.00	$ 4,545.00	$ 6,245.00	$ 19,772.00	$ 4,943.00		
11	Brian	$ 7,878.00	$ 4,532.00	$ 3,434.00	$ 8,989.00	$ 24,833.00	$ 6,208.25		
12	Jon	$ 5,678.00	$ 9,997.00	$ 8,878.00	$ 7,778.00	$ 32,331.00	$ 8,082.75		
13	Dave	$ 7,878.00	$ 3,434.00	$ 7,899.00	$ 7,878.00	$ 27,089.00	$ 6,772.25		
14									
15									
16									
17									
18									
19									
20									
21									
22									
23									
24									

\ 2003 Totals / 2004 Totals /

Edit

2. Producing a Consolidated Income Statement for Delzura Machinery

Delzura Machinery firm builds glass-beveling machinery for both professional and hobbyist customers. It produces and sells a small lathe-style glass-beveling machine with four stations for $1,350 up through a large industrial-model beveling machine for $14,000.

Phyllis Dobkin, the executive vice president, wants you to create a one-page summary workbook that summarizes the key figures from each workbook. Each workbook contains a similar format because the same person created both of them. Key figures Phyllis wants you to place on a summary workbook are Net Sales, Cost of Goods Sold, Gross Profit, Total Operating Expenses, and Net Income.

1. Open the supporting workbooks **ex07DelzuraHawthorne.xls**, **ex07DelzuraPortland.xls**, and the main workbook you will alter and save called **ex07DelzuraMain.xls**

2. Make **ex07DelzuraMain.xls** active, save the workbook as **<yourname>DelzuraMain2.xls**, click the **Summary** worksheet tab, and type the following labels in the indicated cells: A1: **Consolidated Income Statement**; A4: **Net Sales**; A6: **Cost of Goods Sold**; A8: **Gross Profit**; A10: **Total Operating Expenses**; A12: **Net Income**; B3: **Hawthorne**; and C3: **Portland**

3. Bold cells **B3** and **C3**, select cell **A1** and drag the mouse across the cell range **A1:C1**, click the **Merge and Center** button, and format the merged cells to **Bold** and 12 pt

4. Display portions of all three worksheets by clicking **Window** on the menu bar, click **Arrange**, click the **Tiled** option button, and click **OK**

5. In preparation for writing link formulas, click the **ex07DelzuraHawthorne.xls** Title bar to make it active and then click the **Hawthorne** worksheet tab

6. Click the **ex07DelzuraPortland.xls** Title bar to make it active, then click the **Portland** worksheet tab, and then click the **DelzuraMain2.xls** title bar to make it active

7. In the DelzuraMain2.xls worksheet, click cell **B4**, type **=SUM(**, click the **ex07DelzuraHawthorne.xls** Title bar, drag cell range **B4:E4** in the Hawthorne workbook, type **)**, and press **Enter**. (Excel displays the value $ 462,735 and formats the entry)

8. Click cell **C4**, type **=SUM(**, (don't type the comma) click the **ex07DelzuraPortland.xls** Title bar, drag cell range **B4:E4** in the Portland workbook, type **)**, and press **Enter**. (Excel displays the value $529,286 and formats the entry)

9. Click cell **B6**, type **=**, (don't type the comma) click the **ex07DelzuraHawthorne.xls** Title bar, click cell **F5** in the Hawthorne workbook, and press **Enter**

10. Click cell **C6**, type **=**, (don't type the comma) click the **ex07DelzuraPortland.xls** Title bar, click cell **F5** in the Portland workbook, and press **Enter**

11. Click cell **B8**, type **=B4–B6**, press **Enter**, and copy cell **B8** to cell **C8**

12. Click cell **B10**, type **=**, click the **ex07DelzuraHawthorne.xls** Title bar, click cell **F14** in the Hawthorne workbook, and press **Enter**

13. Click cell **C10**, type **=**, click the **ex07DelzuraPortland.xls** Title bar, click cell **F14** in the Portland workbook, and press **Enter**

14. Click cell **B12**, type **=B8–B10**, press **Enter**, and copy cell **B12** to cell **C12**

15. Format the eight cells displaying values to accounting format, zero decimal places, and currency symbols

16. Close the **ex07DelzuraHawthorne.xls** and **ex07DelzuraPortland.xls** workbooks, and click **No** if you are asked if you want to save changes

17. Click the **Maximize** button on the Title bar of **DelzuraMain2.xls**, click the **Comments** worksheet tab, fill in your name in the Developer text box, type in yesterday's date in the Date Created text box, and type in today's date in the Date Revised text box

18. Click the **Summary** worksheet tab of **DelzuraMain2.xls**, click **File**, click **Page Setup**, click **Header/Footer**, fill in your name in the header section, click **OK** to close the Page Setup dialog box, save the workbook, and print both worksheets of the workbook

challenge

1. Summarizing Contract Billing and Bonuses with Excel

Kelleher & MacCollum is an accounting firm that services large corporations in the northeastern United States. The main role of the firm's consultants, however, is not examining financial statements during audits or tax season; instead, the consultants at Kelleher & MacCollum are highly regarded as accounting experts. They are hired by corporations to come into their accounting offices, analyze current policies and procedures, recommend changes and improvements, and consult management on the best way to implement the needed changes.

The last three firms that hired Kelleher & MacCollum to recommend changes to their Accounting Departments specifically asked for the team led by Aaron Cole. These were the most successful contracts in the firm's history. The gross billing for each company was over $100,000, far exceeding any past contracts. The CEO of Kelleher & MacCollum, Dennis Kelleher, wants to reward Aaron and his team members for their excellent work. He has decided to give each team member a bonus of 5 percent of their gross billing for these three contracts. In addition to this 5 percent, Aaron Cole will also receive an additional 5 percent bonus on the total amount billed to all three contracts.

Currently, the amount billed per contract is by consultant name, hours billed, and charge per hour. The total charge for each consultant and the total charge for the contract are also included. Each consultant's charge per hour is based on his or her levels of education, experience, and knowledge. Dennis Kelleher needs a summary of all three contracts' figures in order to determine the appropriate bonus amounts. He has asked you to create a Summary worksheet of this information.

Open the workbook **ex07Kelleher.xls** and save as **<yourname>Kelleher2.xls**. (See Figure 7.36.) Insert a documentation worksheet, called *Documentation*, and enter the workbook name, your name, and the date in the first column. At the end of the workbook, insert a new sheet called **Total Billing**. Use the Fill Across Worksheets command in the Edit menu to copy the column titles from the Front & Leaf worksheet to the Total Billing worksheet and the consultants' names from the Front & Leaf worksheet. In the Hours Billed column of the Total Billing worksheet, insert the sum for each consultant's hours from the corresponding cells of the three contract worksheets. From the Front & Leaf worksheet, use the Edit, Fill Across Worksheets command to copy the dollar amounts from the Charge per Hour column to fill in the same column in the Total Billing worksheet.

In the Total Billing worksheet, title column D **Total Billed**. For each cell corresponding to each person's row, create a formula that multiplies the Hours Billed by the Charge per Hour. At the bottom of the Total Billed column, sum the consultant Total Billed values. Title column E **Bonus**. In this column, create formulas that multiply the Total Billed per consultant by 5 percent to determine their bonus amount. Remember that Aaron Cole receives a 5 percent bonus of his total hours billed and 5 percent of all hours billed. Total this column and bold the total value at the bottom of the column. Save your changes. Include your name in the header of each worksheet and print the Total Billing worksheet.

FIGURE 7.36

Kelleher & MacCollum initial workbook

	A	B	C	D	E	F	G	H
1	**Front & Leaf Publishing**							
2								
3	**Consultant**	**Hours Billed**	**Charge per Hour**					
4	Aaron Cole	40	$150	$6,000				
5	Cliff Sellers	40	$80	$3,200				
6	Brian Campbell	60	$95	$5,700				
7	Joseph Hackett	80	$100	$8,000				
8	Laurie Baker	120	$80	$9,600				
9	Joanna Sellis	80	$120	$9,600				
10	Karen Watson	65	$110	$7,150				
11	Susan Moore	95	$100	$9,500				
12	Angela Hall	55	$85	$4,675				
13	Tina Hunter	75	$75	$5,625				
14	Derek Yen	110	$120	$13,200				
15	Hector Martin	120	$110	$13,200				
16	Kelly Rosen	65	$85	$5,525				
17				$100,975				
18								
19								
20								
21								
22								
23								
24								

2. Consolidating Information for a Toy Robot Seller

Elizabeth Brodkin is the chief financial officer for Robotic Creations, a company that sells four categories of robot toys: educational robots, tin robots, transformers, and robot pets. She maintains two very simple workbooks. The main workbook contains four worksheets in which she keeps a summary of sales by quarter of three of the four categories of robot toys. Called **ex07Robot**, the workbook also contains a documentation worksheet on the front. The second workbook, called **ex07RobotPets**, tracks sales of the robot pet category of robots. She would like you to help her in two major ways. First, she wants you to copy the single worksheet in ex07RobotPets into the ex07Robot workbook and place it between the Tin Robots worksheet and the Transformers worksheet. Secondly, she wants you to insert a new worksheet after all the worksheets in the ex07Robot workbook. That worksheet should summarize the sales of each of the robot categories. You should apply an attractive format to the summary worksheet and color the worksheet tabs of any worksheets you added to the workbook. The summary worksheet contains text with the four quarters listed in column A and labels in cells B1 through E1 containing the labels for the four categories of robots. Be sure to label each worksheet with your name in the header and the sheet name in the footer, and print all worksheets.

Begin by opening **ex07Robot.xls** and save the workbook as **<yourname>Robot2.xls**. Then open **ex07RobotPets.xls**. Copy the Robot Pets worksheet to the **<yourname>Robot2.xls** (see Figure 7.37) workbook. Add a new worksheet to the **<yourname>Robot2.xls** workbook and rename it *Sales Summary*. Create link formulas to the other worksheets to summarize sales. Save your finished work and print all worksheets in the **<yourname>Robot2.xls** workbook.

FIGURE 7.37

Robotic Creations workbook

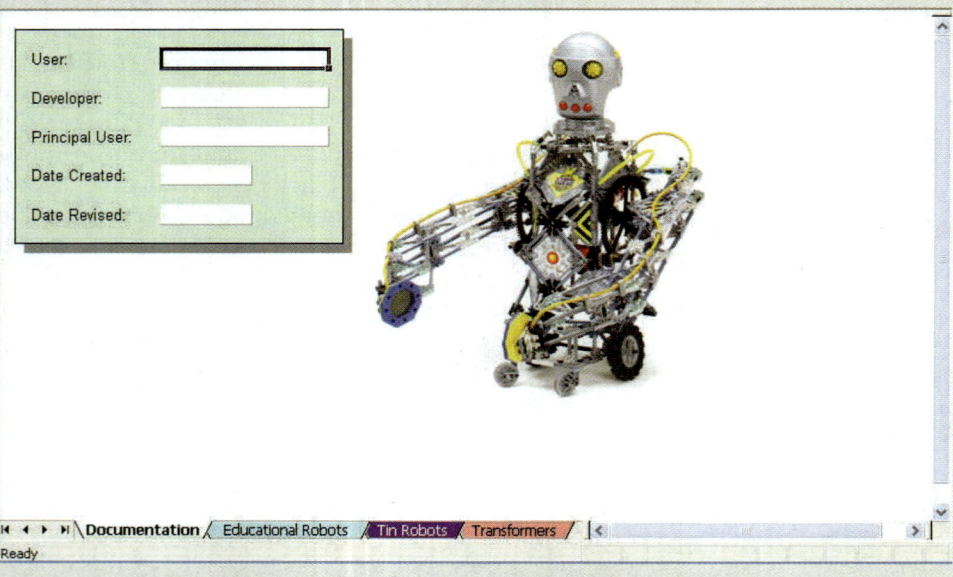

1. Summarizing Multiple Worksheets and Workbooks

Assist Insurance is a Web-based insurance company. Assist Insurance (AI) has advertised throughout the southern states as their office is in Tennessee. AI is a site that the public uses to find the best health care insurance plans for their individual needs. They pride themselves on their excellent customer service and low prices. The CFO of AI feels that there is a market segment that AI could dominate—students. Since AI's prices are so low, their services are attractive to the typical student. After several meetings, the board decided that in order to get more student clients, they plan to open a few test locations in selected cities. Recent studies have shown that Web-based businesses that are also in front of students and easily accessible are more successful than those with Web-only services. The board has approved the opening of six test locations.

As an intern at AI, you have been assigned to the project of determining the areas where AI should open an office. AI wants these offices to be in the six cities with the greatest amount of student awareness. In other words, AI needs to determine in which cities they are currently best known. Your manager has already narrowed it down to three states: Florida, Georgia, and Louisiana. Each state's figures for the past four quarters have been recorded in an individual notebook. Open **ex07AIFlorida.xls** and save as **AIFlorida2.xls**. Do the same for the worksheets **ex07AIGeorgia.xls** and **ex07AILouisiana.xls**—save the workbooks as **AIGeorgia2.xls** and **AILouisiana2.xls**, respectively. For each state, the following statistics are available for each quarter: the number of hits the Web site received from that city, the number of hits that resulted in purchases, the average age of site visitor, and the number of hits received from students. For each state, you will need to create a summary sheet to summarize the past four quarters' figures. Once each workbook is summarized, the information will need to be incorporated into a single summary workbook.

The board is only concerned with the number of hits and the number of hits received from students. Create a summary sheet for each state so that column A contains the same information on each worksheet for each individual state. Title Column B **Hits** and column C **Student Hits**. For column D, create the title **Percent from Students**. Create formulas for columns B and C, using 3-D cell references, so that they total the corresponding figures for each city from each quarter. For column D, create a formula that will divide the number of student hits by total hits. This will give the percentage of hits that were received from students. Fill the formulas for each city. Format this column in percentages with one decimal point.

Create a new workbook and name it **AISummaryReport**. Create a documentation worksheet and place on it the title of the workbook, the names of three states summarized, your name, and the date. Create a summary worksheet, called AI Summary Report, grouped into distinct rows by state. Use a light green color to highlight the three state names, below which are the cities within the state. Include within each state's group of cities the information from each state's summary sheet. Create columns to include the total number of hits, number of hits received from students, and total percentage of hits from students. Improve the appearance of the worksheet (bold column headings, use *Wrap text* alignment, etc.) and use a light yellow background color to highlight the rows of the four cities with the greatest response from students. (*Hint:* Sort all cities on percent, note the highest values, and click Edit, Undo to restore the rows to their original order.) Type your name in the AISummaryReport header. Print the AISummaryReport workbook and follow the summary worksheet with the summary worksheet for each state.

2. Pampered Paws

Pampered Paws is a pet store that sells pet products and provides a pet-sitting service for clients who do not want to board their animals in a kennel. Pampered Paws pet-sitting clients prefer to leave their pets at home—in surroundings that are familiar to their pets and comforting to them. For a reasonable daily fee, a Pampered Paws employee will visit a client's pet in its home twice daily. During each 15-minute visit, the employee plays with the client's pet and checks the pet's food and water. The employees walk dogs and, on occasion, cats as part of the service. (They draw the line at turtles, however.)

Pampered Paws has a thriving retail store selling a complete line of pet food and other products. Grace Jackson, Pampered Paws's owner, has hired a Web developer to create a Web store in which Pampered Paws will sell most of their products online. She wants you to help her analyze the profitability of the company's product offerings to estimate the profitability of a comparable online business.

Pampered Paws has captured the sales of the cat and dog food portion of their business and in an Excel workbook. Figure 7.38 shows one of the sales accumulation worksheets. The sales workbook contains six worksheets, one for each month, listing sales in date order for the first six months of the year. Grace wants you to add three worksheets to the workbook to summarize the two quarter and one half-year sales. Label the quarterly summary worksheets *Quarter 1* and *Quarter 2*, and label the half-year worksheet *Summary*.

Start by loading **ex07PamperedPaws.xls** and immediately saving it as **<yourname>Paws.xls**. Insert the three new worksheets. Place the Quarter 1 worksheet before the January worksheet, place the Quarter 2 worksheet between the March and April worksheets, and place the Summary worksheet between the Documentation and Quarter 1 worksheets. Color both the Quarter 1 and Quarter 2 worksheet tabs green. Quarter 1 should summarize both the total number of bags sold and the total sales amount for January through March. Quarter 2 should be similar to Quarter 1, except it summarizes sales for April through June. Follow this model for both Quarter 1 and Quarter 2: Place the text **Total Bags** in B1, the text **Total Sales** in C1, the text **January** in A2, **February** in A3, and **March** in A4. Write link formulas in B2 to sum January's total bags sold and in C2 to sum January's total sales. Repeat these two formulas for February and March. Follow the same pattern for Quarter 2, but write the link formulas and month names for April through June.

Color the Summary worksheet's tab red. Its structure is as follows: Place the label **Quarter 1** in cell A2, the label **Quarter 2** in cell A3, the label **Total Bags** in B1, and the label **Total Sales** in C1. Write four link formulas that total bags sold and dollar sales from the Quarter 1 worksheet. Similarly, sum the bags and total the sales from the Quarter 2 worksheet. Format the three worksheets you added in an attractive manner. Place your name in the *Left section* of the three worksheets' headers, place the worksheet name in the *Center section* of the worksheets' headers, and save the workbook. Print only the three summary worksheets, Summary, Quarter 1, and Quarter 2. (*Hint:* group the three worksheets prior to printing.)

FIGURE 7.38

Example Pampered Paws pet food sales worksheet

	A	B	C	D	E	F	G	H
1	**Item Name**	**Animal**	**Size (lb)**	**Unit Price**	**Bags**	**Total Sale**	**Date**	
2	Eukanuba Kitten	cat	6.5	$ 15.99	3	$ 47.97	01/01/02	
3	Iams Chunks	dog	8	$ 8.99	8	$ 71.92	01/01/02	
4	Nutro Max Weight Control Formula	dog	5	$ 5.99	8	$ 47.92	01/02/02	
5	Nature's Recipe Puppy Lamb Meal & Rice Canine	dog	5	$ 5.99	10	$ 59.90	01/02/02	
6	Science Diet Canine Large Breed Growth	dog	5	$ 7.99	7	$ 55.93	01/02/02	
7	Natural Life Feline Adult Formula	cat	4	$ 5.99	9	$ 53.91	01/02/02	
8	Natural Life Kitten Formula	cat	4	$ 5.99	8	$ 47.92	01/03/02	
9	Eukanuba Premium Performance	dog	8	$ 11.49	5	$ 57.45	01/03/02	
10	Iams Chunks	dog	8	$ 8.99	6	$ 53.94	01/03/02	
11	Bil-Jac Cat Food	cat	7	$ 9.99	1	$ 9.99	01/03/02	
12	Iams Hairball Care Formula	cat	4	$ 7.99	6	$ 47.94	01/03/02	
13	Pro-Plan Senior Formula	dog	8	$ 8.49	9	$ 76.41	01/03/02	
14	Natural Life Feline Adult Formula	cat	4	$ 5.99	2	$ 11.98	01/03/02	
15	Nature's Recipe Puppy Lamb Meal & Rice Canine	dog	5	$ 5.99	5	$ 29.95	01/04/02	
16	Authority Puppy with Real Lamb	dog	5	$ 4.99	1	$ 4.99	01/04/02	
17	Natural Life Kitten Formula	cat	4	$ 5.99	3	$ 17.97	01/04/02	
18	Eukanuba Premium Performance	dog	8	$ 11.49	10	$ 114.90	01/04/02	
19	Authority Adult with Real Chicken	dog	5	$ 4.99	4	$ 19.96	01/05/02	
20	Bil-Jac Senior Dog Food	dog	7	$ 9.99	4	$ 39.96	01/05/02	
21	Iams Hairball Care Formula	cat	4	$ 7.99	10	$ 79.90	01/05/02	
22	Eukanuba Premium Performance	dog	8	$ 11.49	6	$ 68.94	01/06/02	
23	Natural Life Feline Adult Formula	cat	4	$ 5.99	4	$ 23.96	01/07/02	
24	Bil-Jac Puppy Food	dog	7	$ 9.99	9	$ 89.91	01/07/02	
25	Eukanuba Premium Performance	dog	8	$ 11.49	7	$ 80.43	01/08/02	

Documentation \ **January** \ February \ March \ April \ May \ June

Ready

1. Analyzing and Selecting the Best Law Schools Using the Web

Roger Thornburg graduated from college three years ago. He has been working for his father's law firm and has decided to pursue his law degree. Since Roger plans on returning home after he graduates to continue working with his father, he wants to spend his law school career far away from home. For the three years he will be in school, Roger has picked two states on opposite ends of the country where he wants to go to school—California and New York. Fortunately, both states are home to several of the top-tier law schools. Since Roger is working six days a week, he has asked you to help him in his application process by finding information online regarding law schools in these two states.

Because Roger is only interested in schools among the top 25, he suggests you go to a Web site that lists schools in order of ranking: www.usnews.com. (You may want to use Google or another search engine and search with the terms "law school rank".) When on the home page, select **Best Grad Schools** under **Rankings and Ratings**. Under Best Graduate Schools, look at the section titled **Law**. You will be using Top Law Schools for your information. Open **ex07LawSchools.xls** and save as **<yourname>LawSchools2.xls**. This is the workbook Roger has started in which you will record the information you find on the Web. He has created a worksheet for each state and created column headings to organize the criteria most important to him in choosing schools to apply to—each university's name, rank, overall score, average undergraduate GPA of in-

coming students, and the average LSAT score of those students. For each worksheet, use the information from the Web to fill in the appropriate data for the schools in each state that appear in the top 25.

After glancing at the results, Roger asks you to add a column titled Diversity. He knows that he will best benefit from going away to school if he is part of a diverse student body. Go back to the Best Graduate Schools page, look under the Law heading, and select Diversity Rankings. Use these figures to fill in the needed data. To further narrow down Roger's choice of schools, he wants you to highlight the information for the top two schools in each state. To do this, under each column heading (rank/score/etc.) highlight the two cells with the highest score or ranking. Determine which two schools from each state have the greatest number of highlighted cells.

Create a worksheet titled Summary. In the summary worksheet, include the same column headings as in the state worksheets. Consolidate the information for the top two universities from each state in this worksheet so that it reflects the data for the top four schools. Again highlight the two cells under each column with the highest score or ranking. Conclude which two universities have the greatest scores for Roger's criteria. Highlight the names of those two universities. Create a documentation worksheet and on it include your name, the date, and the title **Law School Rankings**. Group all the worksheets and then place your name in the worksheet headers and place the worksheet name in the worksheet footers. Print the entire workbook.

hands-on projects

around the world

1. Wilton Industries International Sales Consolidation Workbook

Wilton Industries International has sales offices in North America, Europe, the Pacific Basin, Latin America, and Asia. Jerry Parr keeps track of the sales in each region for each month. Currently he has collected sales, in millions of U.S. dollars, in a workbook named **ex07Wilton.xls**. Your task is to use link formulas to summarize data from the individual month's sales in both the summary worksheet and two quarterly worksheets you will add to the workbook.

Open **ex07Wilton.xls** and save it immediately as **<yourname>Wilton2.xls**. Next, add two new worksheets and rename them **Qtr1** and **Qtr2**. Rename the sheet called Sheet1 to **Summary**. Reorder the sequence of worksheets so that Summary is followed by these: Qtr1, Jan, Feb, Mar, Qtr2, Apr, May, and Jun. Place the label **Quarter 1 Sales** in cell **A1** on the **Qtr1** worksheet. Place the label **Quarter2 Sales** in cell **A1** on the **Qtr2** worksheet. Merge and Center format the Quarter 1 and Quarter 2 labels across cells A1 and B1 in each worksheet and then apply boldface to both labels. Write link formulas in cells A2 through A6 that will display the region labels on the Jan worksheet in cells A2 through A6. Do the same thing for the Qtr2 worksheet. On the Qtr1 worksheet in cells B2 through B7, write line formulas that sum the sales for each region in the first three months. Do the same thing for the Qtr2 worksheet: Write link formulas to sum sales for April through June by region. Group Qtr1 and Qtr2 and then format cell B2 with the Accounting format, display two decimal places, and display the currency symbol. Format cells B3 through B6 the same way, but omit the currency symbol. Click cell A1 and then ungroup the worksheets. Color the Qtr1 and Qtr2 worksheet tabs green. Color the Summary worksheet tab red.

The summary worksheet should summarize sales for the five regions for each quarter. Write link formulas that reference the total sales on the Qtr1 and Qtr2 summary worksheets for each region (e.g., =Qtr1!B3 for cell B4 on the summary worksheet). Remove the gridlines from the onscreen display of the Summary worksheet. Italicize the five region names on the Summary worksheet. Place your name in the header and place the worksheet names in the footer. Remember to use the code for the worksheet names. Save the workbook and print it.

2. Jump Start

Jump Start is a small family owned "functional food products" company. They have been producing, selling, and distributing sports drinks, energy bars, and energy gels for 15 years. Jump Start operates sales and distribution offices in Paris, Vancouver, Toronto, Minneapolis, Beijing, and Tokyo. Each site is responsible for managing product promotions, sales, ordering, and distribution for their region. As assistant to the vice president of Global Sales, you need to consolidate all the pertinent information from each region.

Begin by opening **ex07JumpStart.xls**. Save this file as **<yourname>JumpStart2.xls**. The workbook contains worksheets for four regions. (The Beijing and Tokyo offices send their information directly to you in separate files. You will open those files later.) First, insert a new worksheet and name it *Summary* and color the worksheet tab bright yellow. Next, group the original worksheets so that they can be formatted exactly the same. Begin by formatting all the original worksheets to have Boldface column titles and column widths of 12 Characters. Cells A7 and A14 should be Boldface as well. Right Align the column titles for each month and for the column *Totals*. In the Sales (Units) and Sales Revenue sections create the appropriate formulas for each Totals (column and row) cell. In the Sales Revenue section, format the cells to have an Accounting format with only the Totals cells containing a currency symbol and zero decimals. Add a Double Accounting underline to cells B13 through N13.

On the *Summary* worksheet, create two tables—one titled *Sales (Units)* and the other titled *Sales Revenue*. Merge the cells such that each section title is legible. In cells A3 and A13 type in the column title *Site*. Directly below Site add the name of each sales office (Tokyo, Vancouver, and so on). Make sure the site names are in Ascending order and the column title (Site) is in Boldface. In cells B3 through F3 add the column titles of *Q1* through *Q4* and *Totals*. Right Align these cells and Boldface them. Format cells B13 through F13 the same way. In cells A10 and A20 type in the row titles *Totals* and boldface them. Format the column widths to be 10 Characters. Now open the information files for Beijing and Tokyo, **ex07Beijing.xls** and **ex07Tokyo.xls**. Write link formulas to sum all the quarterly data. This will require links such as =SUM(Vancouver!B7:D7) and =[ex07Beijing.xls] Beijing!$B$7. Also sum each Totals cell and format the Sales Revenue section with the same Accounting format as the original worksheets. Place your name in the header and the worksheet names in the footer for all worksheets. Format the Page Setup to be Landscape and to fit on one page. Save your file, and print it. Next print the worksheet formulas.

Pro Golf Academy

Pro Golf Academy has tracked their sales of the men's and women's golf apparel and captured the sales data in a workbook called **ex07ProGolf.xls** (see Figure 7.39). It contains six worksheets, one for each month, listing sales in date order for the first six months of the year. Betty wants you to add three worksheets to the workbook, write link expressions to summarize the sales information, and print only the three worksheets you are about to add (*Summary, Quarter 1,* and *Quarter 2*). Two of the new worksheets are the quarterly summaries. Label the first of these worksheets **Quarter 1** and the second one **Quarter 2**. Place the worksheet Quarter 1 just before the January worksheet and place the worksheet Quarter 2 between the March and April worksheets. Quarter 1 should summarize both the total number of units sold and the total sales amount for the months of January, February, and March. Quarter 2 should be similar to Quarter 1, except it summarizes sales for April through June.

Start by loading **ex07ProGolf.xls** and save it as **<yourname>ProGolf7.xls**. Insert the three new worksheets and move them into their locations among the worksheets. The **Summary** worksheet should be the first worksheet in the workbook.

Color its worksheet tab red. It displays four numbers and four labels. The numbers are the total quarter 1 units sold, total quarter 1 sales, total quarter 2 units sold, and total quarter 2 sales. Color the two quarter worksheet tabs bright yellow. Next, follow this model for both Quarter 1 and Quarter 2: Place the text **Total Units** in **B1**, the text **Total Sales** in **C1**, the text **January** in **A2**, **February** in **A3**, and **March** in **A4**. Write link formulas in B2 to sum January's total units sold and in C2 to sum January's total sales. Repeat these two formulas for February and March. Follow the same pattern for Quarter 2, but write the link formulas and month names for April through June. The Summary worksheet is simple: Place the label **Quarter 1** in cell **A2**, the label **Quarter 2** in cell **A3**, the label **Total Units** in **B1**, and **Total Sales** in **C1**. Write four link formulas that sum quarter 1 total units and total sales from the Quarter 1 worksheet and sum quarter 2 total units and total sales from the Quarter 2 worksheet. Format the three newly added worksheets in an attractive manner, place your name in all nine worksheet headers, save the workbook, but print only the three summary worksheets—Summary, Quarter 1, and Quarter 2.

FIGURE 7.39

Pro Golf Academy apparel sales data workbook

	A	B	C	D	E	F	G	H
1	Item Name	Collection	Size	Unit Price	Units	Extended	Date	
2	Adidas Clima JP Polo	men's	M	$ 29.97	1	$ 29.97	1/1/2004	
3	Adidas Clima JP Polo	men's	M	$ 29.97	6	$ 179.82	1/1/2004	
4	Taylor Made Solid Mercerized Polo	men's	M	$ 34.97	6	$ 209.82	1/1/2004	
5	Adidas Mercerized Engineered Block Stripe Polo	men's	XL	$ 39.99	7	$ 279.93	1/2/2004	
6	Ashworth Performance Pencil Stripe Polo	men's	M	$ 54.99	8	$ 439.92	1/2/2004	
7	Izod Club Solid Textured Stripe Polo	women's	S	$ 34.97	8	$ 279.76	1/2/2004	
8	Taylor Made Solid Mercerized Polo	men's	M	$ 34.97	10	$ 349.70	1/4/2004	
9	Ashworth Summer Stripe Jersey	men's	XL	$ 49.99	1	$ 49.99	1/5/2004	
10	Ashworth Twist Pique	men's	XL	$ 59.99	7	$ 419.93	1/5/2004	
11	Cutter & Buck Palma Polo	men's	M	$ 29.90	7	$ 209.30	1/5/2004	
12	Cutter & Buck Palma Polo	men's	M	$ 29.90	8	$ 239.20	1/5/2004	
13	Izod Club Sleeveless Tip Collar Polo	women's	M	$ 29.97	5	$ 149.85	1/5/2004	
14	Ashworth Classic Interlock Colored Shirt	men's	M	$ 39.99	5	$ 199.95	1/5/2004	
15	Ashworth Pima Texturized Stripe	men's	L	$ 49.99	10	$ 499.90	1/5/2004	
16	Ashworth Summer Stripe Jersey	men's	XL	$ 49.99	3	$ 149.97	1/5/2004	
17	Ashworth Twist Pique	men's	XL	$ 59.99	5	$ 299.95	1/5/2004	
18	Ashworth Performance Pencil Stripe Polo	men's	M	$ 54.99	10	$ 549.90	1/7/2004	
19	Izod Club Solid Textured Stripe Polo	women's	S	$ 34.97	10	$ 349.70	1/7/2004	
20	Izod Club Yarn Dye Stripe Polo	women's	L	$ 34.97	5	$ 174.85	1/7/2004	
21	Ashworth Performance Pencil Stripe Polo	men's	M	$ 54.99	5	$ 274.95	1/8/2004	
22	Cutter & Buck Palma Polo	men's	M	$ 29.90	1	$ 29.90	1/8/2004	
23	Izod Club Sleeveless Tip Collar Polo	women's	M	$ 29.97	3	$ 89.91	1/8/2004	
24	Taylor Made Solid Mercerized Polo	men's	M	$ 34.97	4	$ 139.88	1/8/2004	
25	Adidas Mercerized Engineered Block Stripe Polo	men's	XL	$ 39.99	4	$ 159.96	1/9/2004	

January / February / March / April / May / June

Ready

1. Moving from One Worksheet to Another Quickly

Suppose a workbook contains 13 worksheets—one for each month and a summary worksheet. Each worksheet tab contains an appropriate label. If you write a lot of link formulas in the summary worksheet, you have to move to various worksheet tabs to "point" to the referenced cells on other pages. Come up with another method, besides right-clicking the worksheet tab scroll buttons, to select a worksheet name and move to it directly. Does the alternative way have any advantages such as the number of sheets or the ease with which you can jump to other worksheets?

2. Worksheet Groups and Link Formulas to External Workbooks

Provide insights describing why you might want to consolidate information from multiple workbooks on one worksheet of a separate workbook. In your discussion, provide reasons why a company would maintain information on distinct workbooks. In other words, why not simply place all the information on separate worksheets of a single workbook. Consider workgroups, team members, and so on, in your analysis.

CHAPTER

eight

8

Auditing, Sharing, Protecting, and Publishing Workbooks

did you know?

Cary Grant's real name was Archibald Leach, for whom John Cleese's character in A Fish Called Wanda was named.

a fly can react to a perceived danger by changing direction in 30 milliseconds.

one-third of the solar energy hitting Earth evaporates water—about 95,000 cubic miles each year.

in the tenth century, the Grand Vizier of Persia, Abdul Kassem Ismael, ported his entire library with him wherever he went. Four hundred camels, trained to walk in alphabetical order, carried the entire 117,000-volume library.

Excel provides a rich variety of auditing and worksheet protection features. Read this chapter to learn more about those features.

Chapter Objectives

- Use the Audit toolbar
- Locate a cell's precedent cells and dependent cells— MOS XL03E-1-11
- Display and clear tracer arrows—MOS XL03E-1-11
- Locate and correct errors using audit tools—MOS XL03E-1-12
- Share a workbook with other users—MOS XL03E-3-3
- Insert comments and review others' comments—MOS XL03S-4-1
- Track, accept, and reject changes made to a workbook— MOS XL03E-3-5
- Merge multiple versions of the same workbook— MOS XL03E-3-4
- Protect workbooks and worksheets—MOS XL03E-3-1
- Password protect a worksheet—MOS XL03E-3-2
- Hide worksheets—MOS XL03S-3-4
- Publish workbooks to the Web—MOS XL03E-4-3
- Insert hyperlinks—MOS XL03S-5-3

Nivaca International Art Treasures

Nivaca International Art Treasures ("Nivaca") is a pure play e-commerce company—it has no storefront besides its Web site. Nivaca specializes in discovering, marketing, and making available to the public art that is produced by artists located in difficult-to-reach corners of the world. Nivaca agents and buyers trek to remote locations from the Andes Mountains to the rain forests of Africa seeking isolated villages—especially in communities where artists produce high quality objects that have very narrow distribution. Nivaca's noble mission is to encourage economic development in Third World countries, to promote artists located in particularly impoverished regions, and to provide customers with wonderful art at bargain prices.

While artists in isolated communities have always been able to sell their goods in small quantities to local residents, they have never been able to gain wider exposure for their goods. Shipping goods to other countries has been a problem for most artists in difficult to reach locations because they are not close to mass transportation. Some villages have had to rely on horses or mules to deliver their few goods to larger villages often hundreds of miles away. Occasionally an adventurous tourist would stumble onto a village producing a particular type of art, purchase and transport the artwork out of the country, and tell friends about the wonderful art he or she found. Typically, such art cannot be shipped to others without personally contacting the artists, so visiting the village in person has been the only way to purchase locally made art objects—until recently.

Nivaca is filling the void between local producers and world consumers. Their guiding rule is that the artists must earn more than the going local rates and the customer must pay less than market rate for the art. Nivaca arranges to pick up and ship objects to consumers who view and order art from their Web site.

Through **disintermediation**—eliminating the often-expensive "middleman" who traditionally charges up to 15 times the actual value—everyone benefits. Recently, for example, a large, upscale New York department store sold vases produced by artists in San Pedro, Peru, for $350 and more. Unlike large department stores, Nivaca is able to offer the same type of vase for $11 (plus shipping). What's more, the San Pedro producers make more profit from the $11 sale than they do from the $350 sale. That's exactly where Nivaca flourishes.

Naturally, Nivaca uses Excel in many capacities: to track sales, to provide managers with summary and detailed customer billing and retention information, and to provide a variety of other management reports. Lately, they have had some anomalies in their reports, where they suspect there are some errant formulas. John Lounsbury, Nivaca's chief financial officer (CFO), wants you to examine some of their Excel reports and locate any mistakes they contain. In addition, John wants you to provide worksheet protection on a field submission report so that their field representatives cannot accidentally overwrite critical formulas in the reporting worksheets they use. Finally, John wants to publish the workbook on the company's intranet so others can review it. Figure 8.1 shows one of those Excel worksheets that Nivaca managers use.

Example worksheet used by Nivaca managers

	A	B	C	D	E	F	G	H	I	
1	**Monthly Sales**									
2		Retail								
3	Month / Region	January	February	March	April	May	June	July	August	Sep
4	Andes	122,911.42	157,762.52	46,866.36	45,665.37	49,405.82	50,461.99	58,624.02	165,627.33	167
5	Brazil	99,219.15	132,017.60	65,522.02	168,450.79	36,711.45	149,269.82	57,660.49	167,146.20	68
6	India	43,567.88	39,211.09	34,854.30	31,368.87	27,883.44	25,095.10	22,306.75	20,076.08	17
7	Indonesia	71,027.53	76,090.02	80,041.43	123,693.87	115,185.85	111,543.85	48,402.21	45,678.90	123
8	Mexico	93,151.71	57,914.09	125,387.37	72,551.89	54,858.28	94,175.32	63,076.07	134,811.55	95
9	Thailand	68,045.29	113,992.57	42,669.25	69,079.62	83,479.12	71,080.25	90,540.51	39,703.56	167
10	West Africa	152,135.72	46296.72	101,255.14	140,369.58	78,857.96	143,980.72	63,477.77	162,471.45	158
11	Subtotal	650,058.70	576,987.89	496,595.87	651,179.99	446,381.92	645,607.05	404,087.82	735,515.07	798
12										
13		Wholesale								
14	Month / Region	January	February	March	April	May	June	July	August	Sep
15	Andes	22,712.36	9,300.51	5,550.61	641.24	9,382.64	5,948.35	371.92	8,074.69	15
16	Brazil	3,665.10	39,383.83	17,456.22	27,677.58	3,311.74	18,562.27	2,142.46	10,026.49	4
17	India	3,981.74	6,117.35	4,498.82	6,966.94	3,179.90	179.64	1,758.23	551.66	2
18	Indonesia	9,364.86	5,376.28	14,459.45	562.60	31,793.61	2,022.40	10,371.94	3,328.37	23
19	Mexico	15,888.38	6,836.70	26,894.34	17,978.80	1,439.67	22,248.00	4,767.63	11,534.19	8
20	Thailand	15,927.15	22,834.76	12,386.68	108.88	7,968.73	11,386.04	6,815.19	2,418.21	30
21	West Africa	11,233.19	13,135.53	3,310.28	19,702.93	14,663.75	21,638.52	3,657.93	45,215.18	2
22	Subtotal	82,772.78	102,984.96	84,556.40	73,638.97	71,740.04	31,985.22	29,885.30	81,148.79	87
23										
24	Total	#REF!	679,972.85	581,152.27	724,818.96	518,121.96	727,592.27	433,973.12	816,663.86	886
25										
26										
27										
28										

⊩ ◂ ▸ ⊩ \ Logo ∕ Quarterly Summary ∖ **Monthly Sales** ∕ Commissions ∕

INTRODUCTION

Chapter 8 covers the Excel auditing tools that allow you to locate precedent and dependent cells with tracer arrows, locate and correct errors, and erase cell-to-cell tracer arrows. You will learn how to share a workbook on a network with colleagues, review their comments and suggested changes, and insert your own comments. Using Excel's publishing tools, you will convert a workbook into HTML-based Web pages that you can place on the Web, allowing anyone with access to the pages the ability to review and modify the Web version of a workbook.

SESSION 8.1 AUDITING A WORKBOOK

In this session, you will learn how to use the rich set of Excel auditing tools to locate and correct errors in cells. You will use the Auditing toolbar to locate cells referenced by a particular cell and to locate cells that depend on a particular cell. Using the Trace Error tool, you will locate and examine several errant formulas that can cause other cells depending on the errant cells to be incorrect also.

CHAPTER OUTLINE

EX 8.3

EXCEL

Using Audit Tools

Excel has several powerful features that can help you locate potential trouble spots in your workbook including locating cells whose value depends on a particular cell and finding errors. Worksheets can contain errors that are not obvious because the results appear to be reasonable. Close examination and spot testing can reveal errors. Excel recognizes potential trouble spots and displays symbols such as #VALUE! in cells that contain one or more references to cells whose value cannot be determined or calculated correctly Excel goes further by marking more subtle potential mistakes such as numbers entered as strings or formulas that don't match similar ones nearby. In the latter case, Excel notes these with a warning flag in the corner of the suspect cell.

John senses that there are mistakes in the workbook containing Nivaca's summary of sales for the last year. He asks you to perform a quality check on the workbook to ensure the results are accurate. He's sensitive to stockholder criticism of other corporations' financial statements, and he wants no inaccuracies while he is at Nivaca's helm. You will use Excel's Formula Auditing toolbar to uncover the source of any errant formulas.

Excel's Formula Auditing toolbar provides tools to check worksheet formulas by using a graphical representation of the relationships between selected cells containing the formulas. You open the Formula Auditing toolbar to examine its contents. An *error indicator,* a small triangle, appears in the upper-left corner of a cell whenever Excel finds a formula that breaks one of its internal rules for valid formulas.

Opening the Nivaca workbook and displaying the Formula Auditing toolbar:

1. Start Excel as usual

2. Open the workbook **ex08Nivaca.xls** and immediately save it as **<yourname>Nivaca2.xls** to preserve the original workbook. Review the Cover Sheet worksheet

3. Click the **Quarterly Summary** worksheet tab. It summarizes the sales for the current year by quarter and region. Notice the seven regions containing art and artists whom Nivaca represents (see Figure 8.2). Several cells display error indicators

FIGURE 8.2

Nivaca's Quarterly Summary worksheet

	A	B	C	D	E	F	G	H
1	Quarterly Summary							
2								
3	Quarter / Region	Qtr 1	Qtr 2	Qtr 3	Qtr 4			
4	Andes	365,103.78	161,505.41	415,373.24	372,834.03			
5	Brazil	357,263.92	403,983.65	309,704.15	205,761.26			
6	India	132,231.19	94,673.90	65,389.86	50,702.25			
7	Indonesia	256,359.57	384,802.18	255,331.42	424,576.55			
8	Mexico	326,072.59	263,251.96	317,822.12	451,081.07			
9	Thailand	275,855.70	243,102.64	337,314.18	337,789.33			
10	West Africa	281,069.86	419,213.46	436,273.34	349,269.30			
11								
12	Subtotal	$ 1,993,956.61	$ 1,551,319.74	$ 2,137,208.31	$ 2,192,013.79			
13								
14		Retail	Wholesale					
15	Total	$ 7,315,772.32	#REF!					
16								
17								
18								
19								
20								
21								
22								
23								

Logo \ **Quarterly Summary** / Monthly Sales \ Commissions /

Ready

4. Click **Tools**, point to **Formula Auditing**, and then click **Show Formula Auditing Toolbar.** Excel displays the Formula Auditing toolbar (see Figure 8.3)

F I G U R E   8.3

The Formula Auditing toolbar

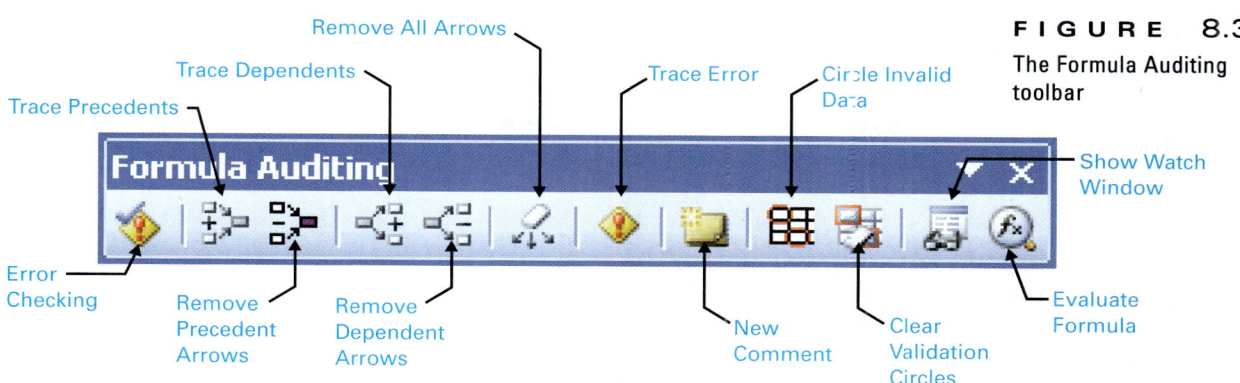

Several of the Formula Auditing tools draw graphical arrows on your worksheet called tracer arrows. A **tracer arrow** displays the relationship between the active cell and another cell related to it. Excel has two types of tracer arrows. One type of tracer arrow points to dependent cells. The other type of tracer arrow points to precedent cells. A **dependent cell** uses the value of the active cell in its formula. A **precedent cell** is one whose value is used (referenced) by the active cell. One way to visualize the relationship between a particular cell (the active cell) and other worksheet cells is to trace either its precedent cells or its dependent cells with the corresponding tools found in the Formula Auditing toolbar. For example, if the formula =Max(A1:A5) is in cell A10, then cell A10 has precedent cells (A1:A5) and no obvious dependent cells. Cell A1 has a dependent cell, A10, but no apparent precedent cells. Any particular cell may have both precedent cells and dependent cells, however.

Tracing Precedent Cells

Cell C12 contains one clue John saw that might indicate the Quarterly Summary worksheet contains errors. Its value is 20 to 25 percent smaller than the subtotals for the first, third, and fourth quarters (see Figure 8.2). In addition, cell C12 and several other cells display error Smart Tag indicators in the upper-left corner of their cells. You begin your audit activities by auditing cell C12.

---

task reference   Tracing Precedent or Dependent Cells

- Select the cell whose formula you want to trace

- Click the **Trace Precedents** button on the Formula Auditing toolbar to display tracer arrows pointing to the formula's precedent cells

or

- Click the **Trace Dependents** button on the Formula Auditing toolbar to display tracer arrows pointing to cells that are dependent on the formula's value

---

Tracing the precedent cells for a formula:

1. Click cell **C12**, and then click the **Trace Precedents** button on the Formula Auditing toolbar. Excel displays tracer arrows that point to a block of cells above it surrounded by a color border called a **range finder**. An error alert Smart Tag also appears

2. Hover the mouse over the error alert Smart Tag. A screen tip indicates the perceived anomaly (see Figure 8.4)

FIGURE 8.4

Precedent cell tracer arrows and the error alert Smart Tag

tracer arrow and box surrounding dependent cell range

error alert

screen tip indicating possible error cause

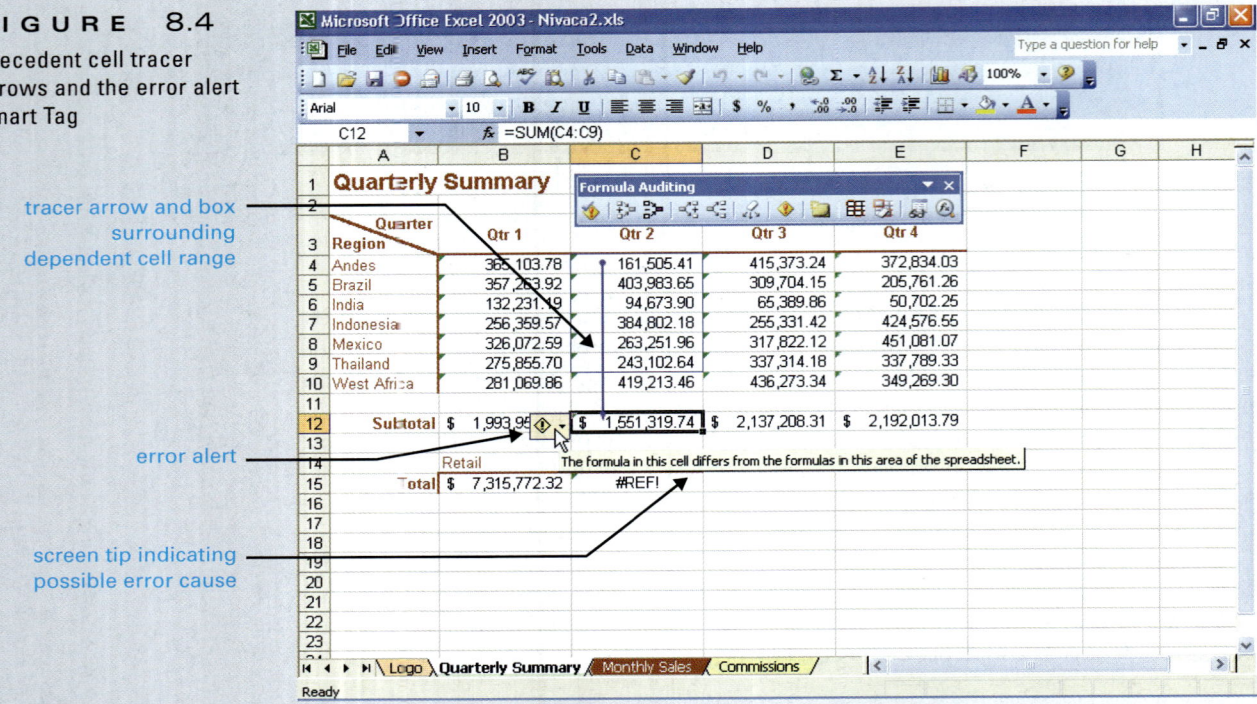

The tracer arrow indicates the group of precedent cells. A rectangle appears whenever the precedent cells are written as a cell range in the audited cell. The screen tip and the tracer arrow and rectangle indicate that the cell range in the formula stored in cell C12 omits cell C10 (West Africa). You correct that error next.

Correcting an incorrect SUM formula:

1. With cell **C12** still selected, click the formula bar

2. Change the formula to =**SUM(C4:C10)**, and press **Enter**. The tracer arrow disappears and the value of the second quarter sales has changed to $1,970,533.20. This is in line with other quarters' values

Another value that appears to be significantly different from other quarters' values is cell B10, which contains the first quarter sales from the region of West Africa. Notice that it is approximately 30 percent smaller than West Africa's other quarterly sales summary values. You audit that cell next.

Auditing West Africa's first quarter sales formula:

1. Click cell **B10**

2. Click the **Trace Precedents** button on the Formula Auditing toolbar. A tracer arrow appears pointing to a worksheet icon (see Figure 8.5)

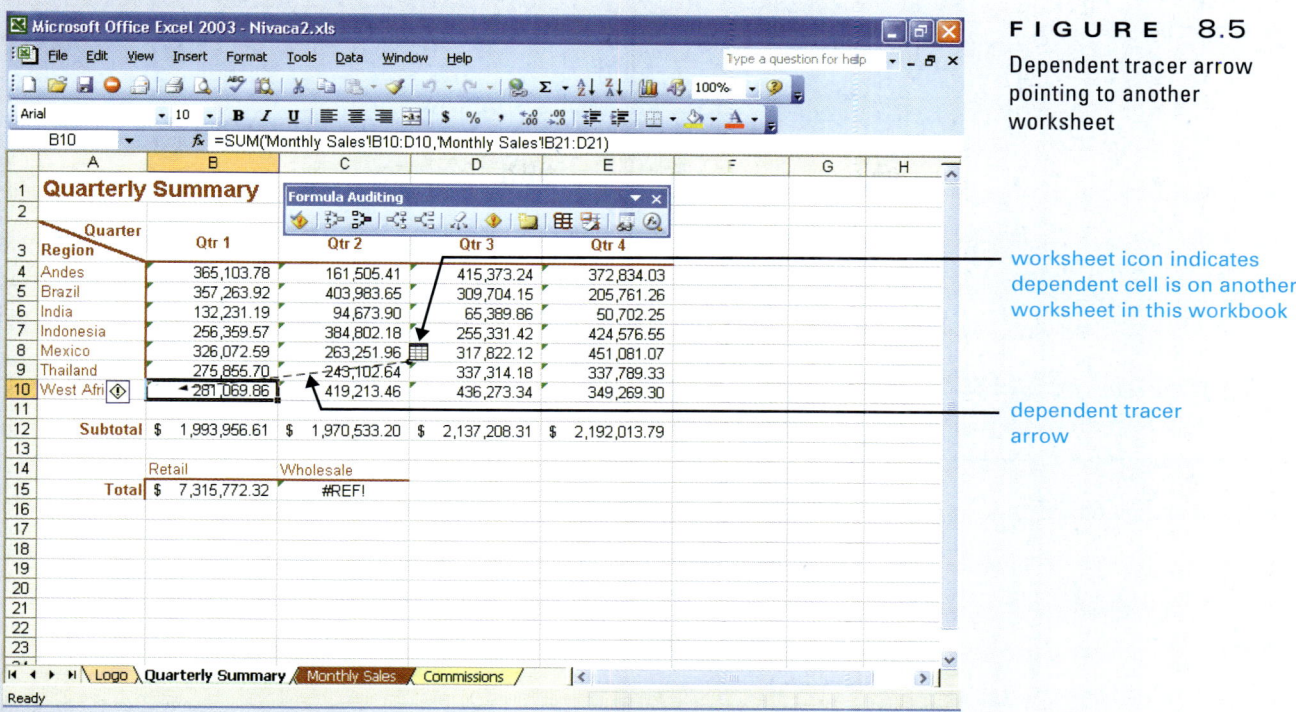

FIGURE 8.5
Dependent tracer arrow
pointing to another
worksheet

worksheet icon indicates
dependent cell is on another
worksheet in this workbook

dependent tracer
arrow

3. Move the mouse pointer over the tracer arrow until it becomes an arrow-head, then double-click the **tracer arrow**. The Go To dialog box appears

4. Click **'[Nivaca2.xls]Monthly Sales'!B10$D$10** (Figure 8.6), and then click **OK** to open the Monthly Sales worksheet (Figure 8.6). Excel selects one of the cell ranges upon which cell B10 depends. Cell C10 looks suspicious, but you will investigate that one later

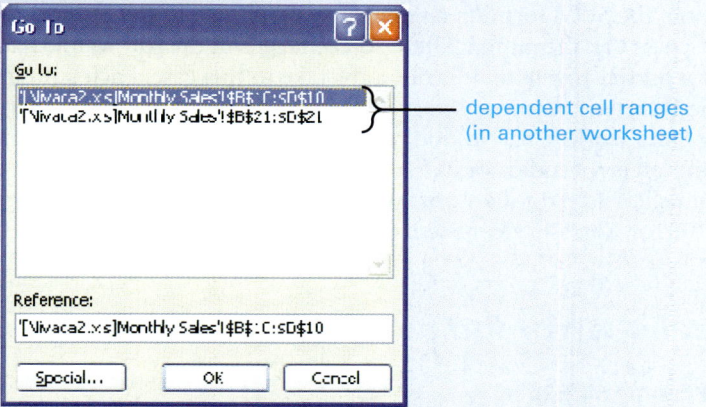

FIGURE 8.6
Go To dialog box

dependent cell ranges
(in another worksheet)

tip: *Your filename will be slightly different. It will contain your name in addition to "Nivaca2.xls"*

5. Click the **Quarterly Summary** worksheet tab, hover over cell B10's error alert box, and then click the **error alert box** ◇ to reveal different options for revealing and dealing with the cell's error (see Figure 8.7)

F I G U R E   8.7

Error alert box option list

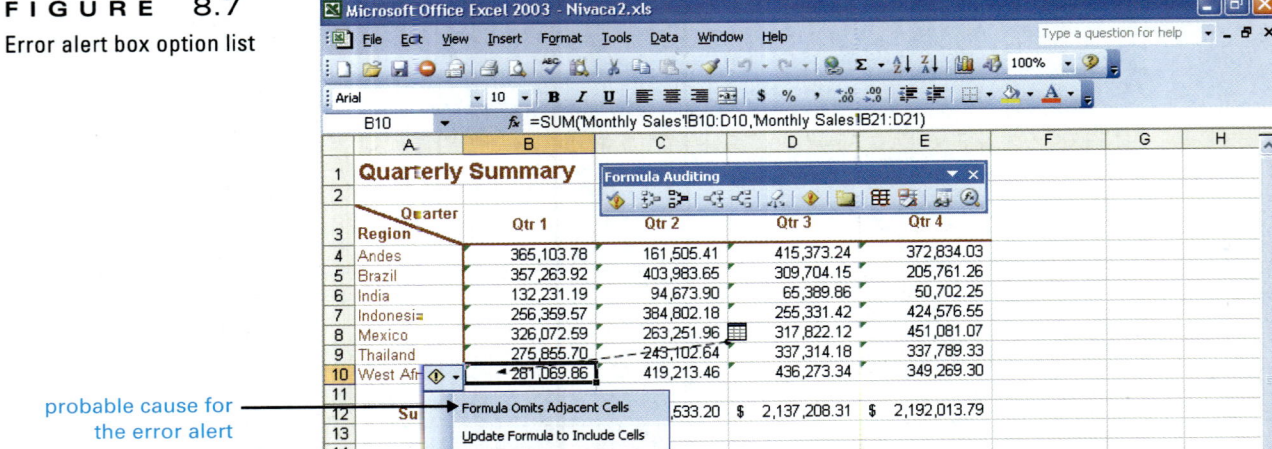

probable cause for
the error alert

error alert option list

---

anotherword   **. . . on Double-Clicking a Tracer Arrow**

Double-clicking a tracer arrow is handy for locating a dependent or precedent cell on another worksheet. It works equally well for locating dependent or precedent cells on the *same* worksheet. Double-clicking a tracer arrow makes the cell at the other end of the arrow active

---

The suspect error is at the top of the list "Formula Omits Adjacent Cells," and you understand the reason: the SUM formula references a partial row in the Monthly Sales worksheet. Excel suspects you meant to include adjacent cells in the row. While Excel is often correct about a partial-row sum, it is not a mistake in this case. Each sum in the range B4:D10 on the Quarterly Summary worksheet totals only 3 of the 12 months' values in the Monthly Sales worksheet. No doubt you have noticed that each cell in cell range B4:E10 contains an error indicator in the upper-left corner. If you click any other cell in that range and click its error alert box, you will see that Excel displays the same "Formula Omits…" error. You will clear these error indicators next.

Removing cells' error indicators:

1. Select the cell range **B4:E10**

2. Click the **error alert box** that appears to the left of cell B4

3. Click **Ignore Error** in the error alert box list. Excel removes all of the error indicators from the cells in the selection

4. Click any cell to deselect the cell range

help yourself *Press **F1**, type **formula auditing** in the Search text box of the Microsoft Excel Help task pane, and press **Enter**. Click the hyperlink **Display the relationships between formulas and cells** and then click the **Show All** hyperlink to helpful information on tracing precedent and dependent cells. Maximize the Help dialog box, if necessary. Click the help screen **Close** button when you are finished, and close the task pane*

Tracing Dependent Cells

John notices two other apparent mistakes on the Monthly Sales worksheet and asks you to investigate it. Cell C10 contains an error indicator (unlike its neighboring cells), and cell B24 displays an obvious error, the text "#REF!." You begin by investigating cell C10.

Correcting an errant formula:

1. Click the **Monthly Sales** worksheet tab, and then click cell **C10**

2. Click the **error alert box**. The error message at the top of the error alert list, "Number Stored as Text," means that cell C10 contains text (whose value is zero) rather than a value. Look at the formula bar. The value begins with an apostrophe that someone apparently typed by mistake (see Figure 8.8)

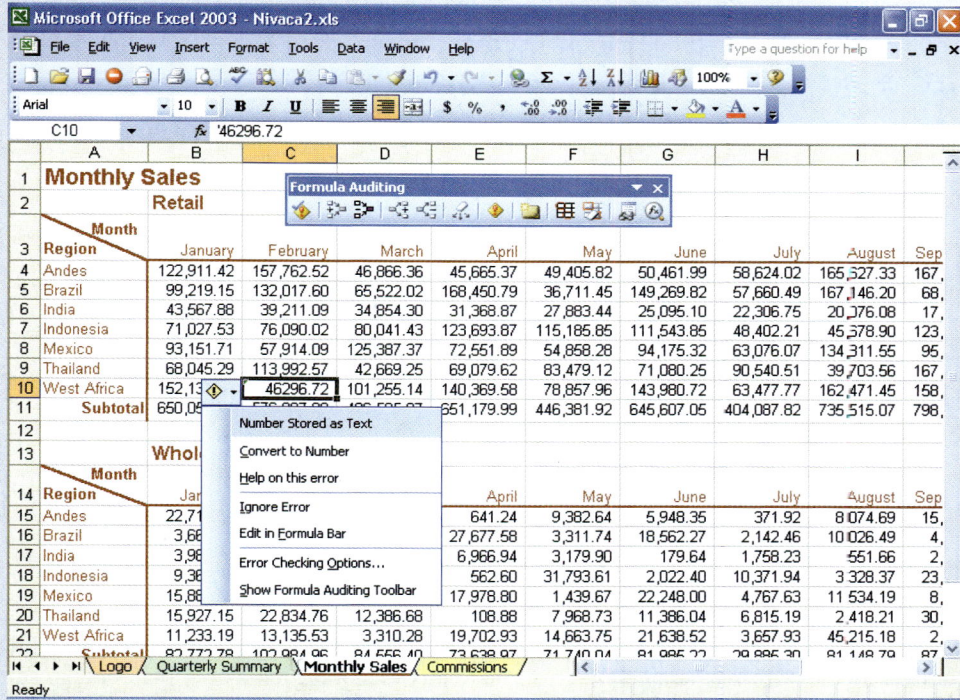

FIGURE 8.8

A "Number Stored as Text" error

Before correcting the error, you want to see what other cells are affected by the incorrect value in this formula. To see what cells reference a formula in error, you trace the cell's dependents.

Tracing a cell's dependents:

1. With cell C10 still selected, click the **Trace Dependents** button on the Formula Auditing toolbar. Excel creates tracer arrows pointing to cell C11, a subtotal, and to another worksheet

2. Hover over and double-click the **tracer arrow** pointing to another worksheet, click **'[Nivaca2.xls]Quarterly Summary'!$B$10** in the Go To list box, and click **OK** to jump to the referenced worksheet. Cell B10, the selected cell, is dependent on the value in the errant cell, C10 on the Monthly Sales worksheet

tip: *Your filename will be slightly different. It will contain your name in addition to "Nivaca2.xls"*

3. With cell B10 on the Quarterly Summary worksheet still selected, click the **Trace Dependents** button. Excel draws a tracer arrow from cell B10 to cell B12 (see Figure 8.9). Notice that the subtotal for West Africa's first quarter is currently 281,069.86

FIGURE   8.9

Tracing dependent cells

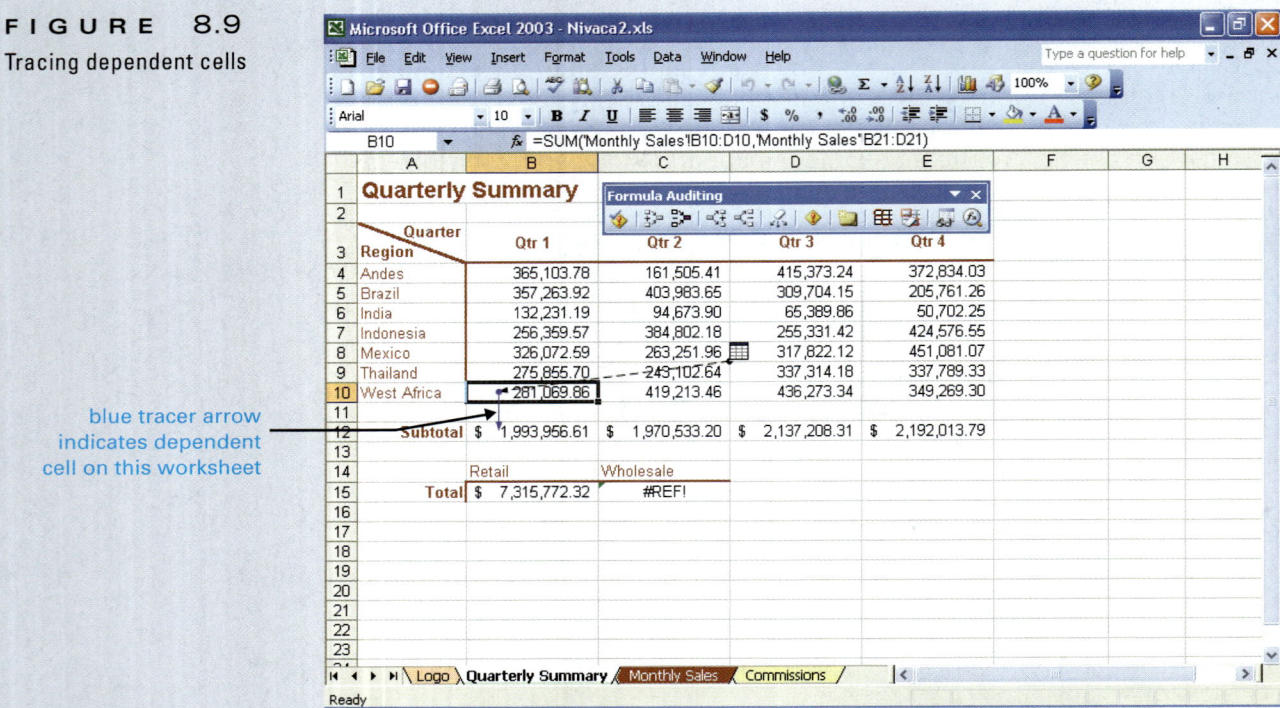

blue tracer arrow indicates dependent cell on this worksheet

Clearing Tracer Arrows

Each time you trace another cell's precedents or dependents, another set of tracer arrows appears. When the screen becomes cluttered with tracer arrows, it can be difficult to trace the flow from a particular active cell to all of its precedents or dependents. If so, then it is a good time to clear out all tracer arrows and trace a cell's precedents or dependents (or both) with a clean slate.

Removing tracer arrows from a display:

1. Click the **Remove All Arrows** 🔣 button on the Formula Auditing toolbar. Excel removes the tracer arrow

2. Click the **Monthly Sales** worksheet tab, and then click the **Remove All Arrows** button on the Formula Auditing toolbar to remove the tracer arrows from that worksheet

Correcting Errors

The error in cell C10 persists, so you will correct it now that you have traced the affected cells on other worksheets.

Correcting an error using the error alert list:

1. Click cell **C10**, if necessary

2. Click the **error alert box**. An error alert list appears (see Figure 8.8)

3. Click **Convert to Number** in the list. Excel changes the text string into a numeric value

4. Clean up the formatting: click cell **C8**, click the **Format Painter** on the Standard toolbar, and click cell **C10**. Excel formats cell C10 to match the rest of the column

5. Click the **Quarterly Summary** worksheet tab, and examine cell B10. Notice its value is now 327,366.58—increased from its previous value of 281,069.86. Correcting the error modifies any dependent cells too, of course

For some less subtle errors, Excel displays an error value. An *error value* is the result of a formula that Excel cannot resolve and provides a clear warning that there is a problem. Figure 8.10 lists several of the error values and their descriptions. In addition to listing an error value in a cell, Excel attempts to discern the cause of the error, indicating, when possible, that a formula is dividing by zero or that a referenced cell has been deleted. One of these error values appears on the Monthly Sales worksheet, and you will fix it next.

Locating Other Errors

You can use the Error Checking button on the Formula Auditing toolbar to provide information about possible causes and remedies for error values.

Error Value	Description and Possible Error Source
#DIV/0!	A formula contains a division by a value or expression that is zero. Ensure the divisor is not a reference to an empty cell or does not evaluate to zero
#NAME?	The text in a formula is not a defined name. Check for typing mistakes
#N/A	No information is available for the calculation in your formula. Any cells that reference cells containing the #N/A value also return #N/A
#NULL!	Using two cell ranges in a formula that do not intersect
#NUM!	An argument in a function that requires a number but is, instead, text. It can also indicate that the result of a formula is too large or too small to be represented in a worksheet
#REF!	A formula referring to a cell that was deleted when the row containing it was deleted
#VALUE!	You have entered a formula that refers to a text entry. This can occur when you specify a range of cells for a function argument that requires a single value or cell reference

FIGURE 8.10

Excel error values and their meanings

EXCEL

Viewing error information:

1. With the Quarterly Summary worksheet still active, click cell **C15**
2. Click the **Error Checking** 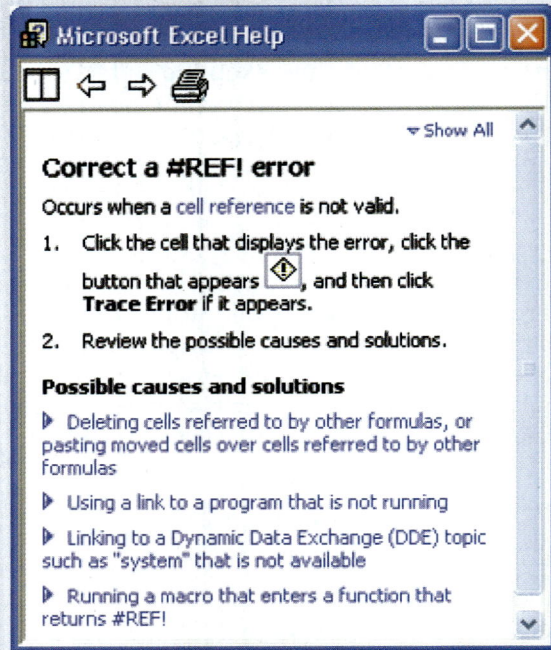 button on the Formula Auditing toolbar. Excel opens the Error Checking dialog box
3. Click the **Help on this error** button in the Error Checking dialog box. Excel displays help and suggests some possible solutions (see Figure 8.11)

FIGURE 8.11

Error alert help

4. After reviewing the Help window, close it by clicking the **Close** button
5. Click the **Resume** button on the Error Checking dialog box to restore its dimmed buttons (see Figure 8.12)

FIGURE 8.12

Error Checking dialog box

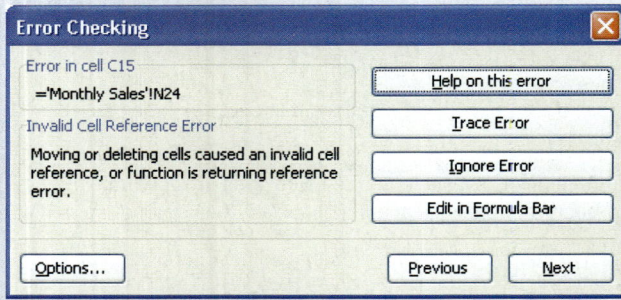

---

task reference   **Tracing Errors**

- Click the cell displaying an error value
- Click the **Trace Error** button on the Formula Auditing toolbar
- Follow any tracer arrows back to the error source

A possible cause of the #REF! error value is that the formula in cell C15 references a cell that subsequently was deleted—perhaps when the entire row containing it was deleted. Any other cells dependent on a cell displaying #REF! also display that error value. The Trace Error button on the Error Checking dialog box can help you locate the source of the error. It performs the same action as the Formula Auditing toolbar's Trace Error button.

Locating the error source:

1. Click the **Trace Error** button on the Error Checking dialog box, and then close the Error Checking dialog box. A tracer arrow appears pointing to a worksheet icon. This means the error source is on another worksheet

2. Move the mouse pointer over the tracer arrow until it becomes an arrowhead, then double-click the **tracer arrow**. The Go To dialog box appears

3. Click '**[Nivaca2.xls]Monthly Sales**'!**$N$24**, and click **OK** to activate the Monthly Sales worksheet. Cell N24 on the Monthly Sales worksheet becomes active

4. Click the **Trace Error** button on the Formula Auditing toolbar. A red tracer arrow appears leading from cell B24 to cell N24 along with a blue tracer arrow leading from cell B22 to B24 (see Figure 8.13)

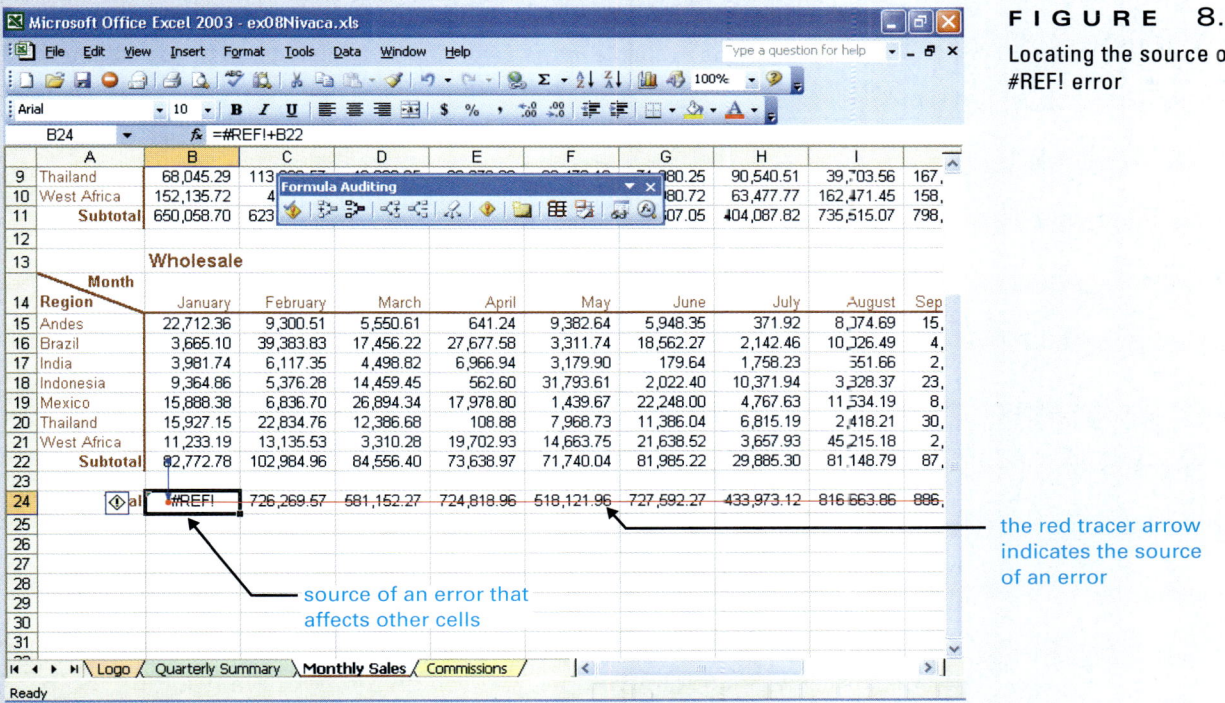

source of an error that affects other cells

the red tracer arrow indicates the source of an error

FIGURE 8.13

Locating the source of the #REF! error

The red tracer arrow, indicating an error source, clearly points to cell B24. If you look at the formula bar, you will see the errant formula =#REF!+B22. This indicates that the formula is referencing a cell that was subsequently deleted—perhaps when the row or column containing it was deleted. Because cell B24 should total January Retail and Wholesale sales (cells B11 and B22), the correction is simple. Replace the #REF! indicator in the formula with a reference to cell B11.

Correcting an errant formula:

1. Click cell **B24**, if necessary, type **=B11+B22**, and press **Enter** to correct the formula

2. Click the **Remove All Arrows** button on the Formula Auditing toolbar to clear the display of all tracer arrows. Notice that the #REF! error value has disappeared from both cell B24 and (if you scroll to the right) cell N24

As you have seen earlier, not all formula errors display error values. They are more subtle, such as the numeric value that is stored as a string. Excel has a great tool for sniffing out more subtle errors—the Error Checking button on the Formula Auditing toolbar. The Error Checking button surveys the active worksheet looking for suspected mistakes, and it tags any suspect cells with green triangles in their upper-left corners. You can examine each tagged cell to determine if it needs to be corrected.

---

task reference   Finding Subtle Errors

- Click the worksheet tab of the worksheet whose integrity you want to check

- Click the **Error Checking** button on the Formula Auditing toolbar

- Use the options available in the Error Checking dialog box to correct the errant formula, or click the Next button to go to the next suspicious formula

---

Certifying that the worksheet is error-free means you should use the Error Checking tool to seek out any errors you may have overlooked. After completing the error-checking procedures, you can be confident that the worksheet is in good shape. You perform this final error check next.

Seeking out subtle errors in the workbook:

1. Click the **Error Checking** button on the Formula Auditing toolbar. Excel displays a message box indicating that no errors have been found on the Monthly Sales worksheet

2. Click **OK**

3. Click the **Quarterly Summary** worksheet tab, click the **Error Checking** button, and then click the **OK** button when the message box appears suggesting that Excel found no errors in the worksheet

4. Click the **Remove All Arrows** button on the Formula Auditing toolbar to clear the display of all tracer arrows

5. Click the **Commissions** worksheet tab, click the **Error Checking** button, and then click the **OK** button when the message box appears suggesting that Excel found no errors in the worksheet

Excel's tracer arrows and its rich set of error checking features allow you to quickly locate and correct errors in formulas.

Examining Worksheet Formulas

Sometimes the best way to get the larger view of a worksheet's formulas is to review them on screen simultaneously. Excel's *Formula Auditing Mode* displays all of a worksheet's formulas on screen rather than the values they represent. In selected exercises at the end of some previous chapters you have revealed worksheet formulas in order to print them. Printing worksheet formulas is an excellent way to document a workbook, and it provides an overall visual check for formula integrity. Review formulas by executing the steps that follow.

Displaying worksheet formulas:

1. Click the **Quarterly Summary** worksheet tab

2. Click **Tools**, point to **Formula Auditing**, and click **Formula Auditing Mode**. Excel displays each of the formulas of the Quarterly Summary worksheet

3. Click cell **B12** to display its precedent cells (see Figure 8.14)

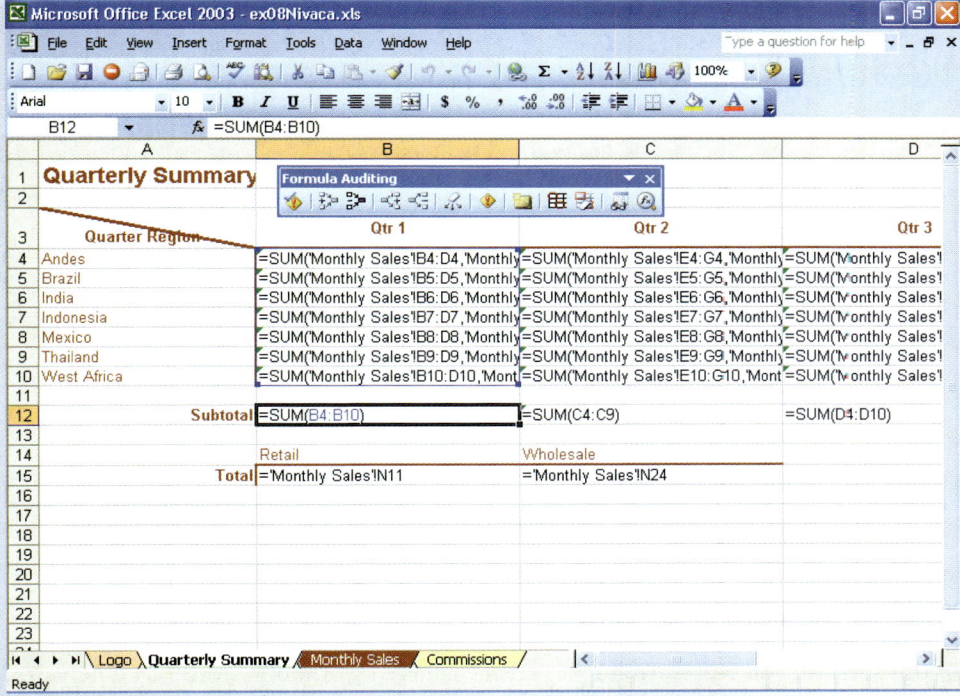

FIGURE   8.14

Displaying a worksheet's formulas

4. Click **Ctrl+`** (grave accent key) to switch back to Normal Mode. Clicking Ctrl+` toggles back and forth between Formula Auditing Mode and Normal Mode

tip: *The grave accent key is normally located above the Tab key. It is not the apostrophe key, which is next to the Enter key*

5. Close the Formula Auditing toolbar

Your error search-and-correct activities are complete. Therefore, you can save and close the workbook and close Excel.

Saving and closing the Nivaca workbook:

1. Press and hold the **Shift** key, click the **Commissions** worksheet tab, release the **Shift** key to group the worksheets, and click cell **A1** (this makes cell A1 the active cell on each selected worksheet)

2. Click the **Logo** worksheet tab to ungroup the worksheets and make Logo the active worksheet

3. Click the **Close Window** button, and then click **Yes** when asked if you want to save your changes

4. Exit Excel

John is pleased with the corrections you have made to the Nivaca workbook. He wants you to pass the shared workbook around to colleagues so they can review the workbook and make suggestions about its design and content. In the next sessions, you will learn how to use several collaboration tools and review the suggestions of others.

SESSION 8.1

making *the grade*

1. Excel displays the error value _____ when a cell contains a formula that references a cell whose value cannot be determined or calculated correctly.

2. A(n) _____ _____ appears in the left corner of a cell whenever Excel finds a formula that breaks one of its internal rules for formation of valid formulas.

3. A _____ cell is one whose value is referenced by the active cell.

4. A _____ _____ graphically displays the relationship between the active cell and another cell.

5. The _____ _____ toolbar contains buttons to aid you in locating errors in a workbook.

SESSION 8.2 SHARING A WORKBOOK AND TRACKING CHANGES

In this section, you will learn how to create a shared workbook stored on a network, how to insert hyperlinks, and how to locate and review team members' comments they make on a shared workbook. You will see how to accept or reject suggested changes, and how to resolve potential conflicts when more than one shared workbook user makes a change to the same cell.

Sharing a Workbook

Not so many years ago, if you wanted to share a workbook with a colleague, you had to copy it onto a floppy disk, carry it down the hall, and have the person with whom you want to share the workbook copy it to his or her computer. This "sneakernet" approach was used more than anyone wanted to admit. Today, infrastructure changes have all but done away with the sneakernet approach. Now, most organizations provide their employees or students with computers connected to a network. Usually, the network is also connected to the Internet. Sharing Excel workbooks is a lot easier due to networks. Microsoft Excel provides terrific tools that allow you to take advantage of network technology to share workbooks with other users in your organization.

A *shared workbook* is an Excel workbook that more than one person can open, modify, and save. Excel allows simultaneous modification of a workbook, which is not uncommon for workbooks stored on networks. Users sharing a workbook can also access it serially—one user after another. In this case, the work of one user who saves the shared workbook appears in the workbook loaded by a subsequent workbook user.

When you try to open a shared Excel workbook stored on a network drive while another user has it open for modifications, Excel permits you to do so. However, there are some restrictions on what you can do when you share a workbook. When you open a workbook for sharing, you can enter text, numbers, and cell formatting; modify formulas; and copy, paste, and move data by dragging the mouse. You can insert columns and rows. However, you *cannot* insert blocks of cells, merge cells, insert charts, create hyperlinks, create outlines, insert automatic subtotals, insert worksheets, or create data tables or pivot tables. In addition, the following are disabled in shared workbooks: Conditional Formatting, Data Validation commands, and Scenarios. Still, sharing a workbook has the obvious advantage that multiple people can access and modify a single, shared copy of a workbook. Sharing a workbook avoids a lot of hassles with determining how to consolidate multiple, independently modified versions of a workbook.

help yourself *Press **F1**, type **sharing a workbook** in the Search text box of the Microsoft Excel Help task pane, and press **Enter**. Click the hyperlink **Edit a shared workbook**. (You may have to scroll the Search Results list box.) Click the Help screen **Close** button when you are finished, and close the task pane*

Creating a Shared Workbook

Since you last saved the Nivaca workbook, John Lounsbury wants to circulate it to two other people for their review and comments: Carol Lloyd and Nick Kildahl. The first step is to open the workbook to be shared, establish a couple of sharing parameters, and save it on the network with a folder that all team members can access.

Establishing a shared Nivaca workbook:

1. If you took a break at the end of the previous session, ensure Excel is running and then open **\<yourname\>Nivaca2.xls**

2. Click **Tools**, click **Share Workbook**. Excel opens the Share Workbook dialog box

3. Click the **Allow changes by more than one user at the same time** check box so that multiple users can make simultaneous modifications to the workbook (see Figure 8.15)

4. Click **OK**. Excel displays a message indicating that the workbook will be saved and requesting your permission to continue

5. Click **OK** to save the shared workbook. Note that the text "[Shared]" appears on the Title bar following the workbook filename

FIGURE 8.15
Share Workbook dialog box

John notifies Carol and Nick that the workbook is available for their review, and he tells them the folder and network address where he saved the workbook. He checks the shared workbook periodically to track changes that may occur to it.

Dealing with Conflicting Changes

Naturally, when more than one person work on a shared workbook, conflicts can arise. For example, one person could make a change to cell B7 and another person could later make a different change to the same cell. Whenever someone saves a workbook containing conflicting changes, Excel displays the Resolve Conflicts dialog box. The conflicting changes appear and allow the person saving the workbook to decide which changes to preserve and which not to preserve. Anyone sharing a workbook can choose to save or discard changes when there are conflicts. Excel stores rejected changes in a tracking log. The tracking log allows shared-workbook users to rescind rejected changes. In this case, the final authority on incorporating changes is John Lounsbury. John closes the workbook and waits for further comments and changes from Carol and Nick.

Saving your workbook:

1. Click the **Logo** worksheet tab, and then click cell **A1**

2. Click the **Close Window** button on the right end of the menu bar to close the worksheet

3. Click **Yes** when asked if you want to save your changes

Tracking Changes

Both Carol and Nick have had a chance to go over the workbook and make changes to it. They have inserted comments and edited formulas, and now it is time for you to review the comments and suggested changes. The last person to save the workbook, Nick Kildahl, has renamed it **ex08NivacaShared.xls**. You will open the latest version of the workbook and save it under a new name.

Opening the shared and modified Nivaca workbook:

1. Open the workbook **ex08NivacaShared.xls**

2. Save the workbook as **<yourname>Nivaca3.xls**

Locating, Reviewing, and Deleting Comments

Nick sent John an e-mail indicating that he has inserted some comments that he wants to make sure that John reviews. He's also made a couple of changes to cell formulas. John asks you to review the comments and then delete them when you are done.

Reviewing others' comments:

1. Click **View**, point to **Toolbars**, and then click **Reviewing** to open the Reviewing toolbar

2. Dock the Reviewing toolbar at the top of the screen and just below the Standard and Formatting toolbars

3. Click the **Next Comment** 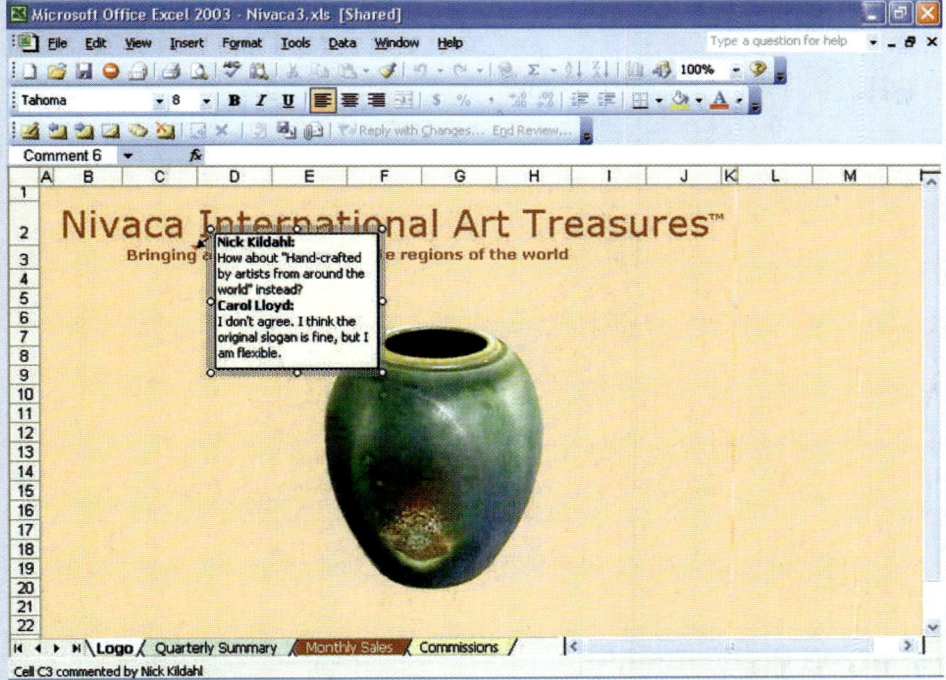 button on the Reviewing toolbar. Excel displays the first comment on the Logo worksheet (Figure 8.16)

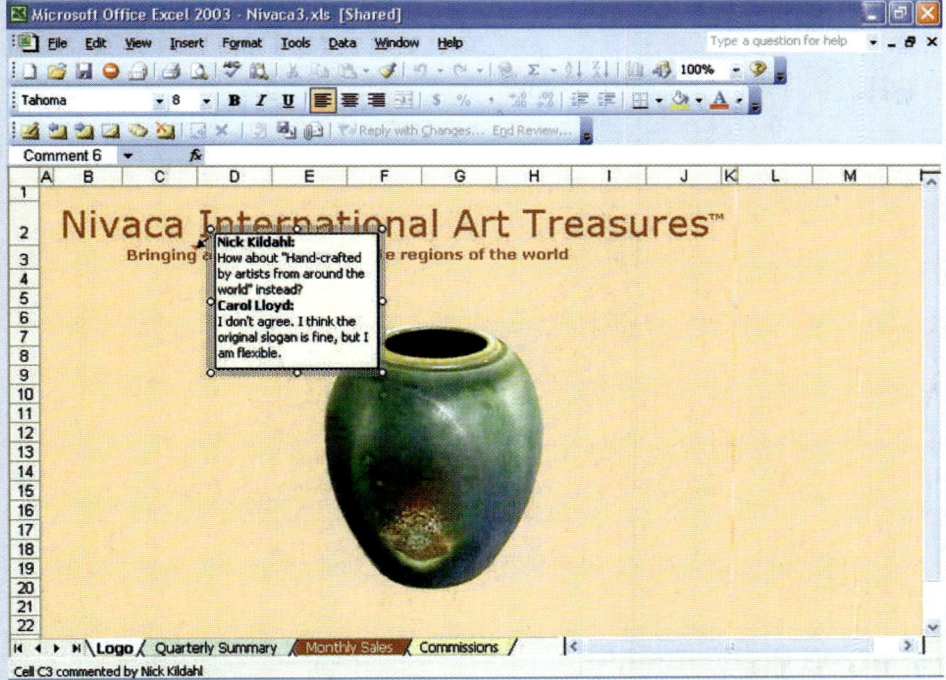

F I G U R E   8.16
Reviewing a comment

4. Click the **Next Comment** button again to go to the next comment, which is located in cell B19. It indicates that Nivaca did not do wholesale business in Mexico for January or February

5. Click the **Next Comment** button once more to read the final comment, which is on the Commissions worksheet

6. Click the **Next Comment** button. Excel informs you that you have reached the end of the workbook

7. Click **OK** to redisplay the first comment on the Logo worksheet

You report back to John about the comments' contents. He asks you to delete all of them before continuing your review process.

Deleting comments in a shared workbook:

1. With the first comment on the Logo worksheet displayed, click the **Delete Comment** button on the Reviewing toolbar

2. Click the **Next Comment** button to move to the second comment, and then click the **Delete Comment** button to remove it

3. Click the **Next Comment** button to move to the third comment, and then click the **Delete Comment** button to remove it

4. Right-click the empty area to the right of the menu bar (or any toolbar). Excel displays a list of toolbars (see Figure 8.17)

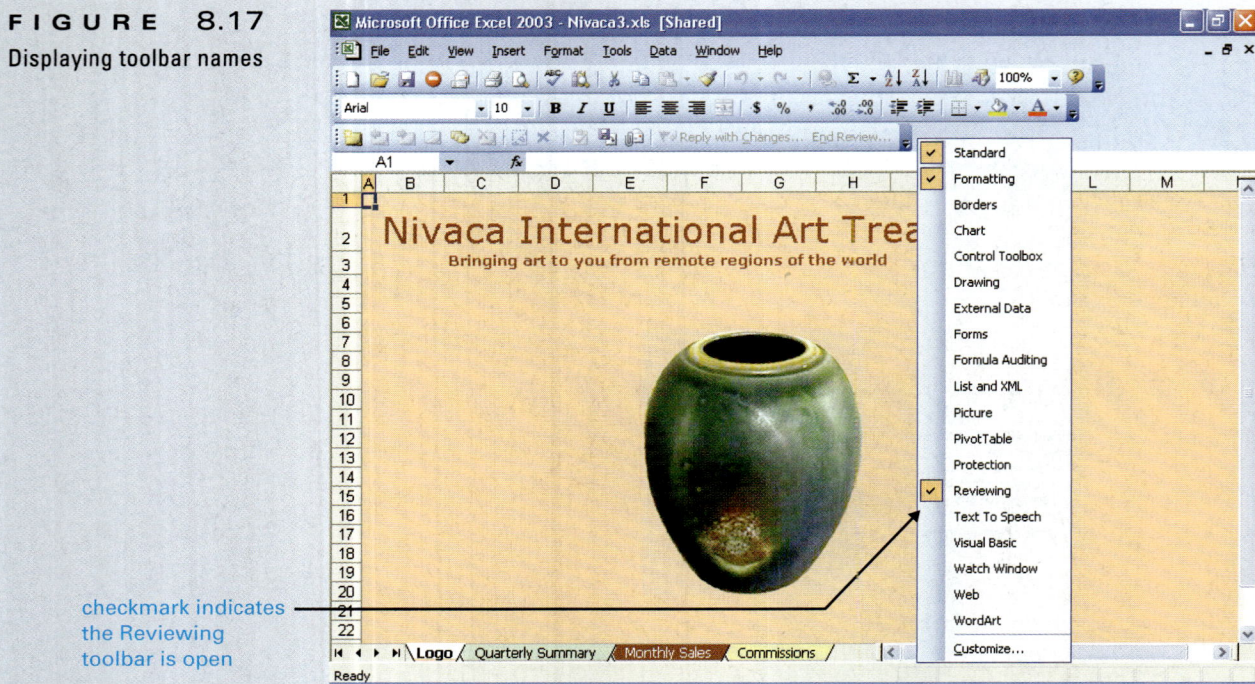

checkmark indicates
the Reviewing
toolbar is open

5. Click Reviewing to close the Reviewing toolbar

Evaluating Suggested Changes

You can decide at any time to go through a shared workbook and review the changes others have made to it. However, changes made by others to the worksheet are tracked (recorded) only if you select the Track Changes While Editing check box in the Highlight Changes dialog box prior to first saving the workbook for sharing. John took care of that, so all changes made since then have been recorded.

Excel stores any changes to a shared workbook in a tracking log file. The normal default for keeping the log file is 30 days, but you can change that value. Excel does not record some types of changes, such as format modifications, in the log file—a change that Carol made to the monthly retail and wholesale sales values, for instance. Excel facilitates tracking changes by displaying a change in a text box next to the changed cell and indicates who made the change and when it was made.

---

task reference   **Tracking Worksheet Changes**

- Click **Tools**, point to **Track Changes**, and click **Highlight Changes**
- Click the list arrow next to the When check box, and click one of the available time periods
- Click the list arrow next to the Who list box, and then click one of the available names whose changes you want to track
- Click the **Where** reference box and indicate which part of the workbook you want to review changes
- Click the **List changes on a new sheet** check box to collect and display the changes on a separate worksheet
- Click **OK** to finalize your choices

Display all changes anyone (except you) made to the Nivaca workbook next.

Highlighting shared workbook changes:

1. Click **Tools**, point to **Track Changes**, and click **Highlight Changes**. Excel displays the Highlight Changes dialog box

2. Click the list arrow next to the When check box, and then click **All**

3. Click the list arrow next to the Who check box, and then click **Everyone but Me**. Excel automatically checks the Who check box after you make a selection (see Figure 8.18)

4. Ensure your selections match Figure 8.18, and then click **OK**. If a dialog box appears indicating "No changes were found . . . ," then click the **OK** button to close the dialog box

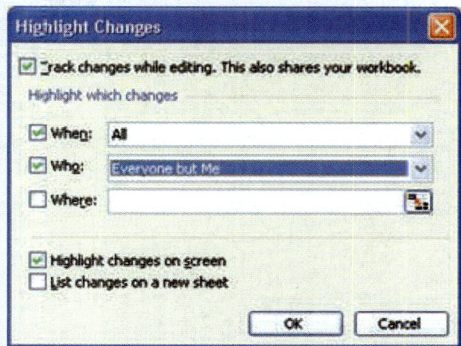

FIGURE   8.18

Highlight Changes dialog box

Now you are ready to review the substantive changes others made to the workbook, one change at a time.

Reviewing changes made by others:

1. Click the **Quarterly Summary** worksheet tab

2. A comment indicator appears in cell C1. Hover the mouse pointer over cell C1. A comment appears indicating that Nick Kildahl moved cells A13:C14 to this current location on the date and time indicated in the comment (see Figure 8.19). Reviewing each change in this manner can be error-prone. Instead, have Excel place all changes on a separate worksheet in the following steps

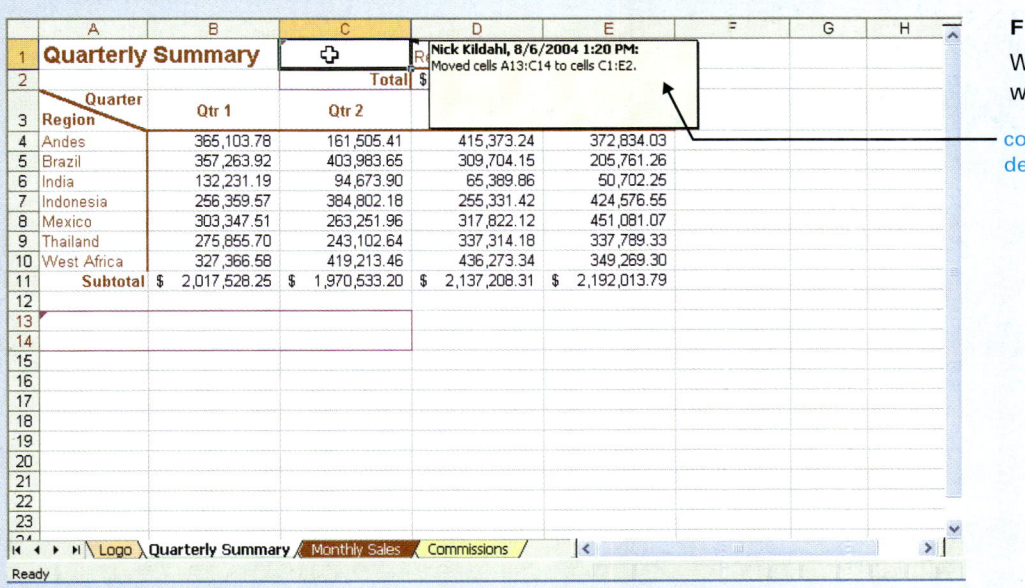

FIGURE   8.19

Who made a change and when it occurred

comment indicates details of a change

3. Click **Tools**, point to **Track Changes**, and click **Highlight Changes**. Excel opens the Highlight Changes dialog box

4. Click the **List changes on a new sheet** check box, and then click **OK**. Excel writes the tracking log to a separate worksheet, and then makes that worksheet active (see Figure 8.20)

EXCEL

FIGURE 8.20

Track Changes History worksheet

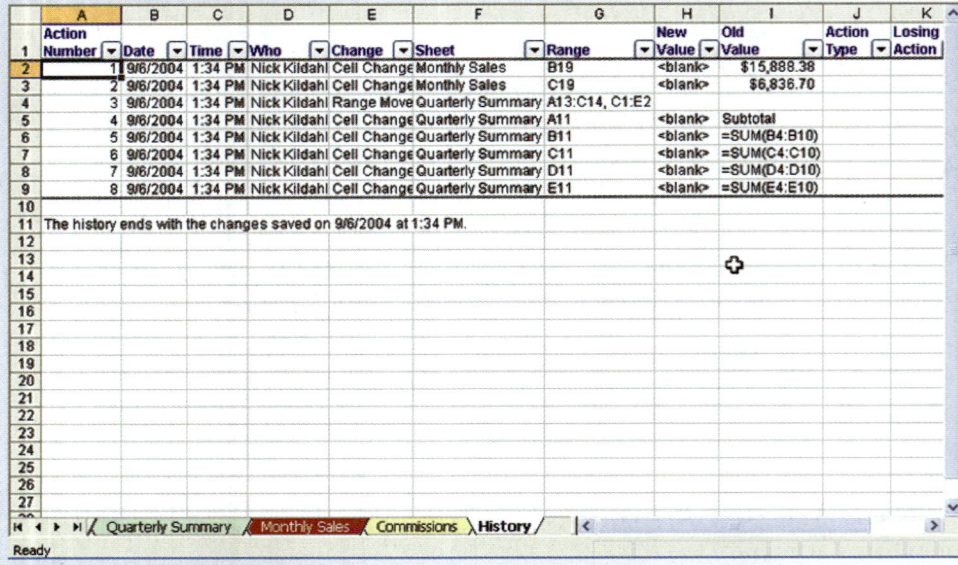

Action Number	Date	Time	Who	Change	Sheet	Range	New Value	Old Value	Action Type	Losing Action
1	9/6/2004	1:34 PM	Nick Kildahl	Cell Change	Monthly Sales	B19	<blank>	$15,888.38		
2	9/6/2004	1:34 PM	Nick Kildahl	Cell Change	Monthly Sales	C19	<blank>	$6,836.70		
3	9/6/2004	1:34 PM	Nick Kildahl	Range Move	Quarterly Summary	A13:C14, C1:E2				
4	9/6/2004	1:34 PM	Nick Kildahl	Cell Change	Quarterly Summary	A11	<blank>	Subtotal		
5	9/6/2004	1:34 PM	Nick Kildahl	Cell Change	Quarterly Summary	B11	<blank>	=SUM(B4:B10)		
6	9/6/2004	1:34 PM	Nick Kildahl	Cell Change	Quarterly Summary	C11	<blank>	=SUM(C4:C10)		
7	9/6/2004	1:34 PM	Nick Kildahl	Cell Change	Quarterly Summary	D11	<blank>	=SUM(D4:D10)		
8	9/6/2004	1:34 PM	Nick Kildahl	Cell Change	Quarterly Summary	E11	<blank>	=SUM(E4:E10)		

The history ends with the changes saved on 9/6/2004 at 1:34 PM.

Quarterly Summary / Monthly Sales / Commissions \ History /

Ready

5. Examine the worksheet's contents. It details who made a change, when it was made, and old and new values

The track changes worksheet, labeled *History*, persists only until you close or save the workbook. When you reopen the workbook, the History worksheet and the log it contains disappear—even if you saved the workbook after Excel inserted the History worksheet.

Accepting or Rejecting Changes to a Shared Workbook

John reviews the change history, and asks you to reject some changes and accept others. He outlined the details in a note. You proceed to make the requested changes next.

---

task reference   Accepting and Rejecting Suggested Changes to Cells

- With a shared workbook open, click **Tools**, point to **Track Changes**, and click **Accept or Reject Changes**
- Click the list arrow next to the When check box, and click one of the available time periods
- Click the list arrow next to the Who list box, and then click one of the available names whose changes you want to accept or reject
- Click the **Where** reference box and indicate which part of the workbook you want to review changes
- Click **OK** to finalize your choices

Accepting and rejecting selected changes to a shared workbook:

1. Click **Tools**, point to **Track Changes**, and click **Accept or Reject Changes**. Excel opens the *Select Changes to Accept or Reject* dialog box
2. Click the **When** check box to clear its checkmark

3. If necessary, click the list arrow next to the Who list box, and then click **Everyone but Me**

4. Click **OK**. Excel displays the Accept or Reject Changes dialog box and highlights cell B19 (see Figure 8.21). You will accept that change

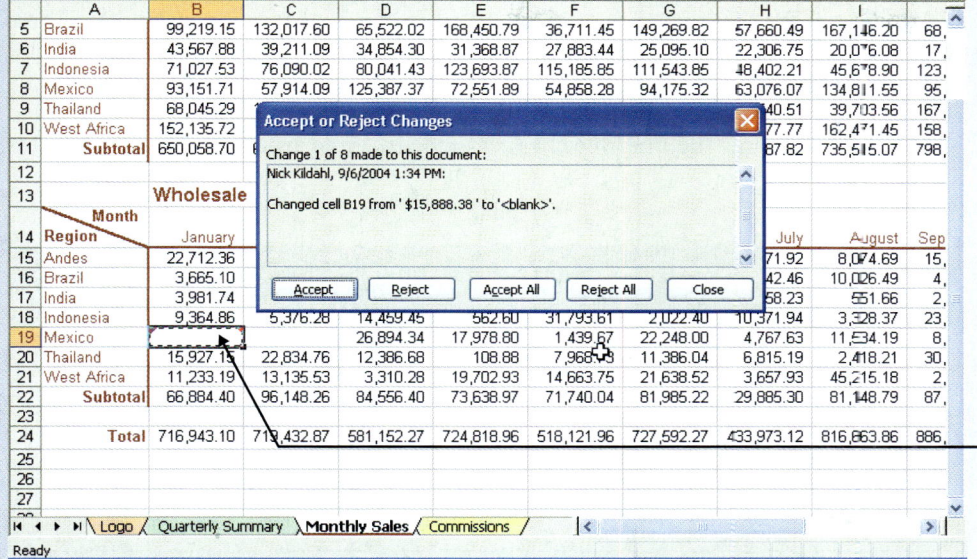

FIGURE 8.21

Highlighted change ready for review

cell containing the change that Nick suggested

5. Click the **Accept** button. Excel displays the next change

6. Click the **Accept** button to accept the suggested change to cell C19. Excel displays the change in which cells were moved from A13:C14 to C1:E2

7. Click the **Reject** button to revoke the change of moving the retail and wholesale summary values. Excel highlights the cell range A11:E11, indicating Nick deleted it

8. Click the **Accept** button five times in sequence to affirm the suggested deletion of the five cells in the cell range A11:E11. Excel closes the Accept or Reject Changes dialog box

You have reviewed changes and made your final decisions. You no longer need to share the workbook with Carol or Nick. Therefore, you will instruct Excel to stop Track Changes as you edit the workbook and then you will turn off workbook sharing.

Halting Track Changes and canceling the shared workbook session:

1. Click **Tools**, point to **Track Changes**, and click **Highlight Changes**. Excel opens the Highlight Changes dialog box

2. Click the **Track changes while editing** check box to clear its checkmark, and then click **OK**. If Excel displays a message indicating it will remove the workbook for shared use, then click **Yes**. Excel saves the workbook, clearing it for exclusive, nonshared use. Notice that the Title bar no longer displays "[Shared]" following the worksheet name

Merging Changes to Multiple Copies of a Workbook

An alternative method of consolidating changes made by multiple persons to the same workbook is to merge workbooks. In order to merge workbooks, several conditions must be met. First, you must distribute copies of the same workbook to anyone who wants to provide changes. Second, each copy of the workbook must have a name different from the other copies. Third, you cannot password protect the workbooks. Finally, the change history must be turned on. Suppose you have distributed three copies of the same workbook to three different people in your group (for comments) and you have named them Nivaca1.xls, Nivaca2.xls, and Nivaca3.xls. Assuming the original workbook, prior to saving copies, conforms to the conditions mentioned above, you can merge the multiple changes made by three groups as described in this Task Reference.

---

task reference   **Merging Multiple Versions of the Same Workbook**

- Open the workbook into which you want to merge changes

- Click **Tools** on the menu bar and click **Compare and Merge Workbooks**

- Press and hold the **Ctrl** key and click each workbook listed in the *Select Files to Merge Into Current Workbook* dialog box that you want to merge, and click **OK**

After you complete the Workbook Merge operation, be sure to Save the master copy to which you merged the changes.

Saving and closing the Nivaca workbook:

1. Click the **Close Window** button, and then click **Yes** when asked if you want to save your changes

2. Exit Excel

You, Carol, and Nick have completed editing the shared workbook. Next, you will take Nick's suggestion and hide the Commissions worksheet and protect the workbook.

SESSION 8.2

making the grade

1. More than one person can simultaneously open and modify a _____ workbook.

2. A _____ change occurs when two or more users make a change to the same worksheet cell. Excel recognizes this condition and displays a dialog box asking you to decide which change takes precedence.

3. Display the _____ toolbar to easily locate comments, one after another, in a workbook.

4. Excel tracks changes in a shared workbook only if you first check the *Track Changes While Editing* check box in the _____ Changes dialog box.

5. Excel stores any changes made to a shared workbook in a _____ _____ file.

SESSION 8.3 PROTECTING AND PUBLISHING WORKBOOKS

In this section, you will learn how to hide cell formulas, hide entire worksheets, and unlock selected worksheet cells. In addition, you will learn how to enforce worksheet and workbook protection, and publish a complete workbook to the Web.

Protecting Workbooks and Worksheets

In a protected worksheet, you can apply the Hidden protection format to any cell whose formula you want to hide. Subsequently, when a user selects a hidden cell, its formula does not appear in the formula bar. One reason you might want to hide a cell's formula is that it is proprietary. That is, you don't want the actual calculation accidentally revealed to someone who might obtain a copy of the worksheet. When a cell's formula is hidden, the formula's results are still visible. For example, if you hide the formula $=Sum(A1:A42)*.42+.28*SalesTotals$, then the result of that formula (say, $42567.89) appears in the cell. Only the formula, itself, is invisible.

When you *protect a worksheet*, Excel disallows any changes to any cells that are locked. A user cannot delete columns or rows, change format, or change the contents of protected cells. Normally, a worksheet designer applies worksheet protection as the last step before releasing the workbook to the users or customers. Typically, worksheet formulas—cells displaying calculations that depend on other cells—receive protection. Cells that contain input values, which users must be able to change, must remain unprotected. Therefore, you will want to explicitly unlock those cells.

Excel offers many features allowing you to protect your work. You can protect a worksheet, an entire workbook, individual cells, graphics, charts, scenarios, and more. You can allow specific types of editing on protected worksheets and other objects.

Protection is a two-step process. First, you unlock cells for which you want users to be able to type new data. Second, you enforce Excel protection rules by explicitly turning on worksheet protection through a menu. When a cell is *unlocked*, it is not protected. Only locked cells are protected. By default, Excel locks *all* cells in a workbook.

After you enable protection, you cannot change a locked cell. If you attempt to do so, Excel issues an error message. Protection is available independently to each worksheet in a workbook, so you can choose to protect some worksheets and not protect others in the same workbook.

help yourself *Press **F1**, type **protect a workbook** in the Search text box of the Microsoft Excel Help task pane, and press **Enter**. Click the hyperlink **About worksheet and workbook protection**. Maximize the Help screen, and then click the hyperlink **Protecting worksheet elements**. Click the Help screen **Close** button when you are finished, and close the task pane*

Hiding Cells and Worksheets

John wants you to hide the formulas located in the range B4:E10 on the Quarterly Summary worksheet. Recall that those formulas summarize sales by region and quarter. John simply does not want a casual viewer to see the formulas. You begin by opening the workbook you saved in the last session and saving it under a new name.

Opening the Nivaca workbook and saving it under a new name:

1. If you took a break at the end of the previous session, then ensure Excel is running and then open **<yourname>Nivaca3.xls**

2. Save the workbook as **<yourname>Nivaca4.xls**

EXCEL

Next, you can hide the formulas for the cell range B4:E10.

Hiding select cells' formulas:

1. Click the **Quarterly Summary** worksheet tab

2. Select the cell range **B4:E10**

3. Click **Format**, click **Cells**, and then click the **Protection** tab of the Format Cells dialog box

4. Click the **Hidden** check box to place a checkmark in it (see Figure 8.22), and then click **OK**

FIGURE 8.22

Hiding selected cell formulas

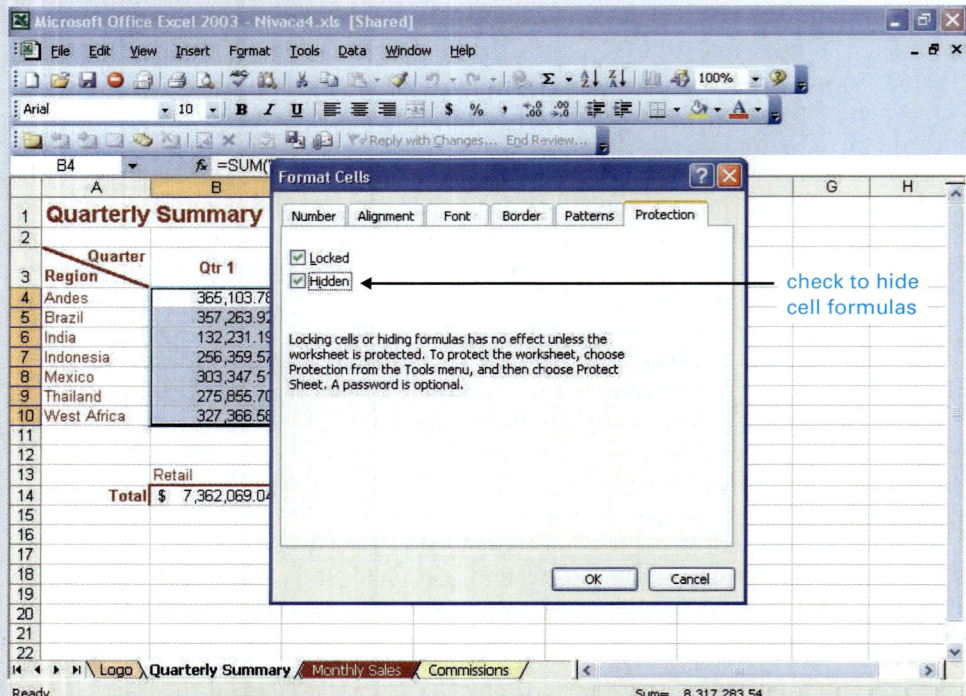

5. Click cell **B4** to make it active

Notice that the formula bar still displays the worksheet formula for cell B4. Excel does not actually hide the formulas until you enable worksheet protection. You will do that later in this session.

You can also hide entire worksheets of a workbook. All data and any calculations in a hidden workbook are still available to any other worksheets via references. Unlike hiding cell formulas, hiding a worksheet occurs immediately. Once a worksheet is hidden, the Unhide command is available in the Format Sheet command sequence.

---

task reference   **Hiding a Worksheet**

- Click the worksheet tab of the worksheet you want to hide
- Click **Format**, point to **Sheet**, and click **Hide**

task reference — Unhiding a Worksheet

- Click **Format**, point to **Sheet**, and click **Unhide**
- In the Unhide dialog box, click the name of the worksheet you want to unhide from the list, and click **OK**

Next, you will hide the Commissions worksheet.

Hiding the Commissions worksheet:

1. Click the **Commissions** worksheet tab to make the worksheet active

2. Click **Format** on the menu bar, point to **Sheet**, and click **Hide**. Excel immediately removes the Commissions worksheet tab, effectively rendering the worksheet invisible, and makes the Monthly Sales worksheet active

Before moving on, ensure you know how to unhide a worksheet by locating the Unhide command. Because John wants the Commissions worksheet to remain hidden, you will stop short of actually unhiding the worksheet in the steps below.

Locating the Unhide command:

1. Click **Format**, point to **Sheet**, and click **Unhide**. Excel displays the Unhide dialog box and lists the only currently hidden worksheet (see Figure 8.23)

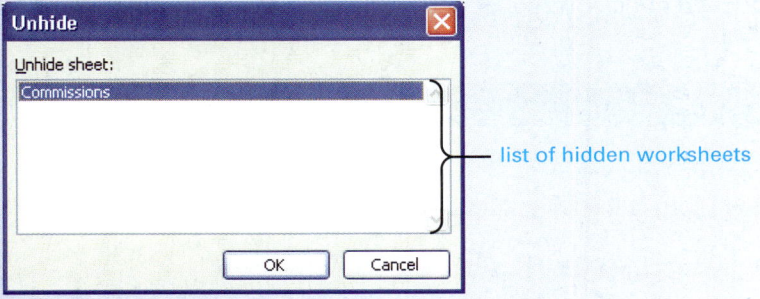

FIGURE 8.23
Unhide dialog box used to reveal hidden worksheets

2. Click the **Cancel** button to close the dialog box because you don't want to unhide the Commissions worksheet for the moment

Unlocking Worksheet Cells

You have learned from John that managers enter data into the Monthly Sales worksheet for each month's sales by region. Sometimes, the managers accidentally overwrite formulas in the worksheet that subtotal and total columns or rows. To prevent that from occurring in the future, John wants you to protect all worksheet formulas on the Monthly Sales worksheet, allowing managers to access only the cells holding both retail and wholesale sales values—cell ranges B4:M10 and B15:M21, respectively.

Excel has several features that allow you to protect individual cells. By default, Excel locks all cells in a workbook but disables protection. When enabled, protection prevents users from entering data into locked cells. If you try to alter a locked cell, Excel displays an error message. Therefore, you protect cells of a worksheet by *unlocking* any cells into which users can enter data or alter existing information. In most applications, a vast majority of a worksheet's cells remain locked.

---

task reference   **Unlocking Cells**

- Select the cell or cell range you want to be unlocked

- Click **Format**, click **Cells**, and then click the **Protection** tab

- Click the **Locked** check box to clear its checkmark and click **OK**

Preventing inadvertent modifications to formulas means that you unlock selected data entry cells in the Monthly Sales worksheet. Then, you enable worksheet protection.

Unlocking selected worksheet cells:

1. With the Monthly Sales worksheet active, click and drag the cell range **B4:M10**

2. Press and hold the **Ctrl** key, click and drag the cell range **B15:M21**, and release the **Ctrl** key

3. Click **Format** and then click **Cells**. The Format Cells dialog box opens

4. Click the **Protection** tab, if necessary. Notice that the Locked check box contains a checkmark, reinforcing the fact that cells are locked by default

5. Click the **Locked** check box to clear its checkmark (see Figure 8.24) and then click **OK**

FIGURE 8.24
Unlocking selected cells

clear the Locked check box
to unlock selected cells

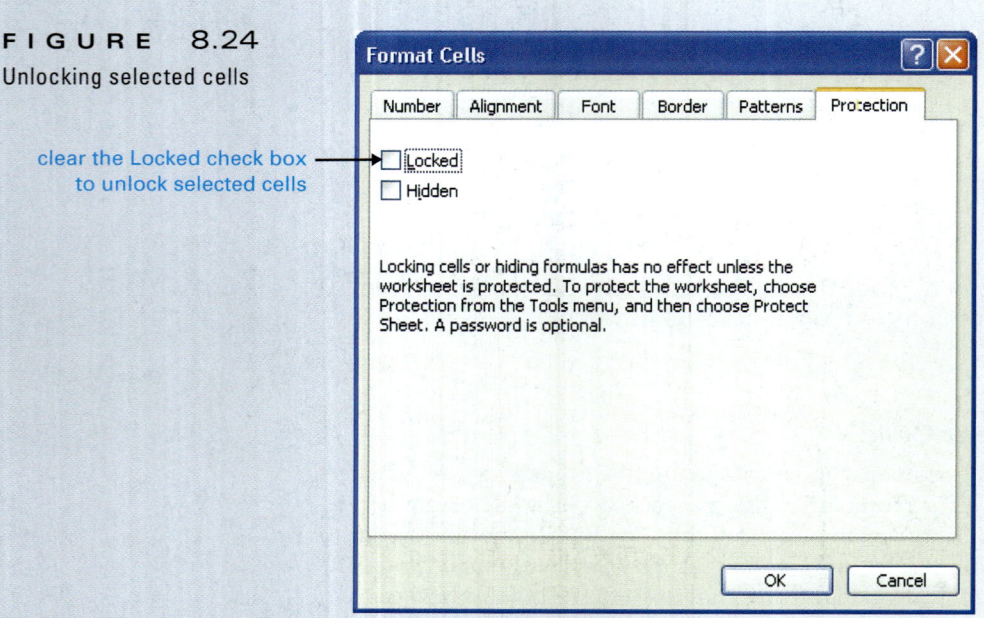

1. Sharing a Workbook

Discuss why someone would share a workbook. Include in the discussion at least three advantages and discuss when changes are selected or deleted and who does it. What settings, if any, must you turn on to locate changes and determine who made them?

2. Web Accessible Workbooks

Why would you publish an Excel workbook to the Web? Discuss why you would choose to publish an interactive versus a noninteractive workbook. How can you keep the Web version of a workbook synchronized with a stored copy on someone's PC?

CHAPTER five

5

Customizing Forms and Reports

know?
did you

a *goldfish is the only animal that can see both infrared and ultraviolet light.*

there *are more than 50,000 earthquakes throughout the world each year.*

the *highest place people have settled in the United States is Climax, Colorado, at 11,360 feet above sea level.*

in *reality, electric lightbulbs existed 50 years prior to Thomas Edison's 1879 U.S. patent date.*

it *really can be too cold to snow! During very cold weather, the capacity of the air to contain moisture is reduced and most of the vapor is deposited as frost, resulting in extremely low humidity. In these conditions snow cannot form.*

to *find out what year mechanical engineering professor M. W. Thring said, "Within ten to twenty years' time we could have a robot that will completely eliminate all routine operations around the house and remove the drudgery from human life," visit* www.mhhe.com/i-series.

Chapter Objectives

- **Build and modify a form in Design View—MOS AC03S-1-9 and MOS AC03S-3-2**

- **Understand the Form toolbox**

- **Create a report in Design View—MOS AC03S-3-3**

- **Summarize report data**

- **Preview and print reports**

- **Add and modify report control properties—MOS AC03S-1-11**

- **Sort records in forms—MOS AC03S-3-5**

- **Preview reports for print—MOS AC03S-4-2**

KoryoKicks: Customizing Database Input and Output

Missy and Micah Hampton are in the midst of building a database to support their entrepreneurial business. The twins began the business to earn some extra spending money for college and have been very successful teaching self-defense classes and selling martial arts supplies on campus. As most small businesses do, they initially kept records manually but found that method ineffective as the data needed to efficiently make business decisions became increasingly complex.

Most entrepreneurs have a business idea and give little thought to data that must be stored, maintained, and analyzed for the business to thrive. The volume and complexity of these data increase with the success of the business as does the need to make more complex business decisions and appear professional to customers and suppliers. Finding effective ways to store and analyze business data is a critical factor in business success.

Since Missy and Micah were not familiar with database technology, they have had to learn a new technology while they were learning to run a successful business and going to school. They have worked with you for the past several months learning Microsoft Access 2003 and evaluating the data storage and reporting needs of KoryoKicks. The current database contains tables to track customers, products, orders, and vendors. There are a number of select queries to analyze sales, unpaid invoices, and product demand. A Crosstab Query to calculate total sales by month and state has let the twins know how their products sell in each state over time. Simple reports have been developed to document the status of sales and product orders.

While all of this is helpful, the twins need more complex analytical information, friendlier forms, and more professional reports. Since they will be hiring part-time help to load and maintain data, the database interface must be improved by adding custom forms developed using Form Design View. In addition, more powerful reporting features will improve data analysis, and the use of Report Design View to customize printed output will help the business project a more professional image (see Figure 5.1).

The twins know that no amount of information can guarantee the result of a decision, but timely and effective information can significantly improve the likelihood of a positive outcome. They expect to improve their decision-making ability by learning more ways to use Microsoft Access form and report facilities.

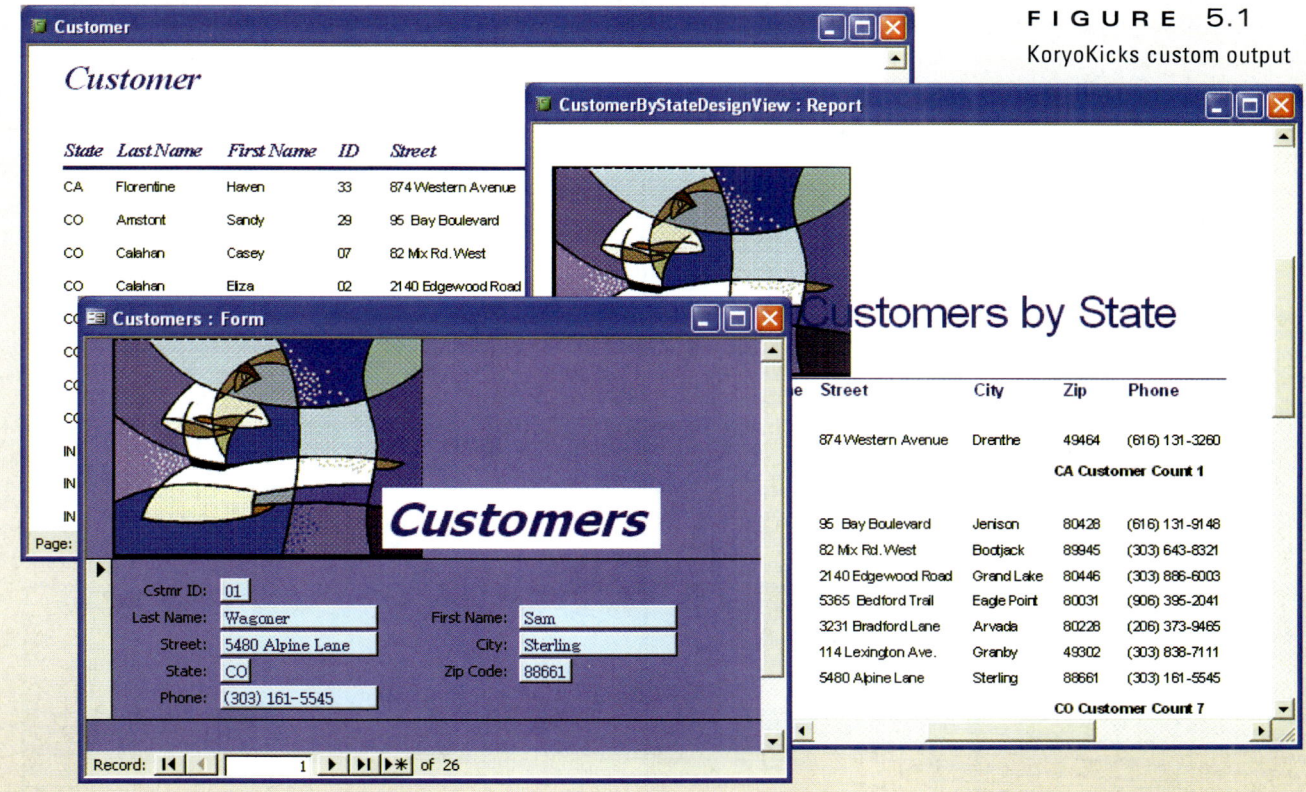

FIGURE 5.1

KoryoKicks custom output

SESSION 5.1 MAINTAINING DATA WITH FORMS

The form object is used to create a custom screen interface used to enter and display database data. Forms also create user interfaces called *switchboards* that open other forms and reports in the database, and custom dialog boxes to accept user input and carry out an action based on the input.

Most forms are bound to one or more tables or queries referred to as the form's *record source*. All of the fields from the underlying tables and queries do not need to be included in the form.

Defining a Form in Form Design View

You already have created forms using form Wizards and modified the result by adding images. It's time to take a look at how forms work from the ground up. The design of a form stores all of the specifications for the appearance and function of the form including information about its underlying record source. Calculations are stored in the form's design and executed just before data are displayed to the user. The data displayed in the form (except calculations) are stored and/or retrieved from its underlying record source.

Form Design View

Forms are built using graphical objects called controls. Each control has a special purpose. A *Label* control is used to display descriptive text to the user. A ***Text Box*** control is used to enter and display data from the record source or execute and display a calculated value. These underlying controls were introduced in the previous chapter when Form Design View was used to add a graphic to the AutoForm Wizard form. Customizing an AutoForm is often the fastest way to develop a usable product.

When a new form is created in Design View (see Figure 5.2), you begin with an empty form and a toolbox containing the tools (controls) needed to create the form elements. Controls are added to the form to build the desired functionality. Since the developer is in complete control of the format, it is always best to have an idea of the operation and design of the end product before beginning.

To design a form, decide what fields need to be included. If the fields are from different tables, it is often better to create a query that joins the tables and selects the appropriate records. After documenting the fields to be included, organize a layout for those fields and any other necessary elements that are to be included such as a logo. Figure 5.3 shows a sample form design for KoryoKicks Customers input.

FIGURE 5.2

A new form in Design View

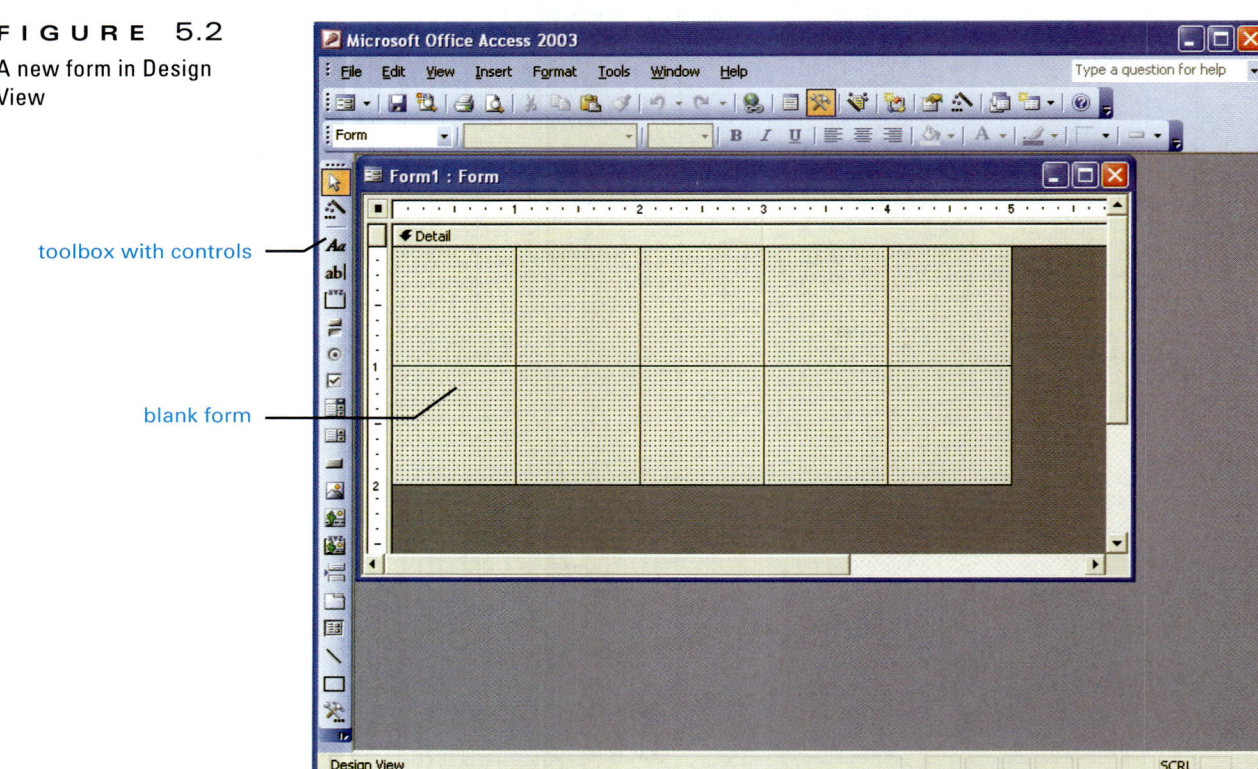

toolbox with controls

blank form

FIGURE 5.3

Customers Form Design

KoryoKicksLogo

Customers

Cstmr ID:	XXX		
Last Name:	XXXXXXXXXXXXXXXXXXX	First Name:	XXXXXXXXXXXXXXXXX
Street:	XXXXXXXXXXXXXXXXXX	City:	XXXXXXXXXXXXXXXXX
State:	XXX	Zip Code:	XXXXXX
Phone:	XXXXXXXXXXX		

The design reflects the complete layout of the form including titles, graphics, captions, and field length. In the design shown, the field captions appear as the twins want to see them on the form. Xs are used to indicate the placement and the length of the data display area. When the form is built, the captions will be in Label controls and the data values will be displayed in Text Box controls. The KoryoKicks logo will reside in an Image control and the form title will be entered in a Label control. Since you have a good idea of the data and its layout for the Customers form, it is time to start building it.

The Form Toolbox and Field List

The Form toolbox is a special toolbar with all of the controls that can be added to a form. If you forget what a Toolbox button is, display a Screen Tip by pausing the mouse pointer over it. Like all toolbars, the toolbox can be displayed or removed from display using the View menu. It also can be anchored or unanchored by dragging its Title bar.

When a control is placed on the form, its *properties* are set, to direct what it will display and how it will appear on the form. A few of the properties that can be set will alter a control's background color, foreground color, and font. Controls and their uses are outlined in Figure 5.4.

Form controls are classified as bound, unbound, or calculated. **Bound** controls display data from a record source and are said to be bound to a field in the underlying table or query. Bound controls are typically added using the Field List dialog box rather than the toolbox. **Unbound** controls are not linked to a record source and so display fixed data such as the title of a form, instructions, or labels for other form elements. A **calculated** control stores the instructions on how to complete the calculation using one or more fields of the record source and displays the calculated value.

The simplest way to create a bound control is to open the Field List dialog box for the record source using the Field List button of the Form Design toolbar. With the Field List dialog box open, select a field and drag it to the form surface. Repeat this process for each field that is to display on the form. Bound controls can be rearranged on the form by dragging until they are positioned where you would like.

Bound controls created in this fashion will consist of a text box to display the field value and a label to hold a caption. The Caption property of a Label displays the

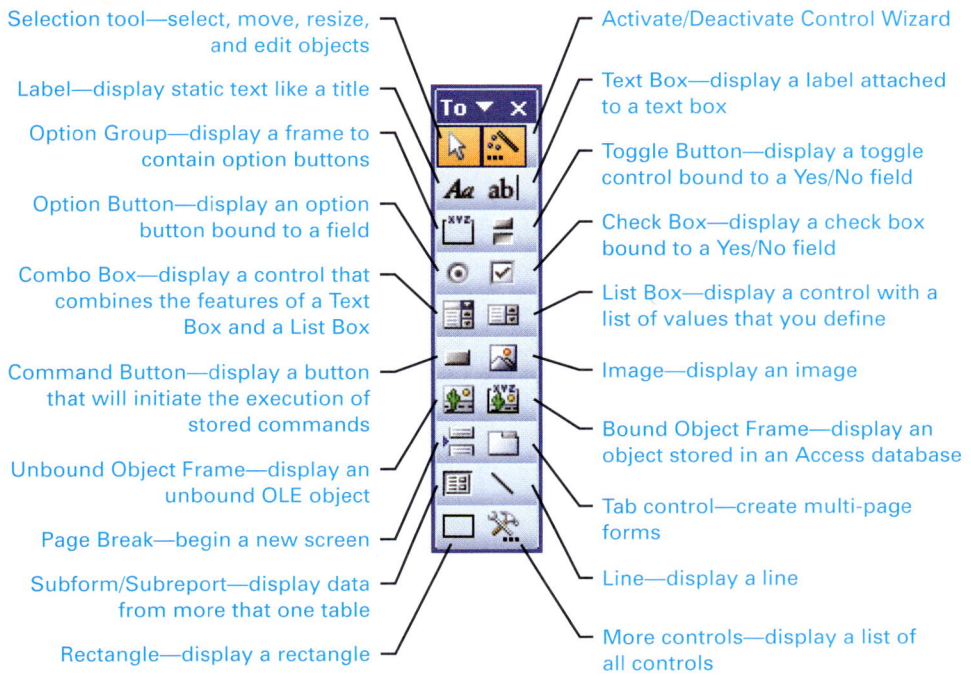

Selection tool—select, move, resize, and edit objects

Label—display static text like a title

Option Group—display a frame to contain option buttons

Option Button—display an option button bound to a field

Combo Box—display a control that combines the features of a Text Box and a List Box

Command Button—display a button that will initiate the execution of stored commands

Unbound Object Frame—display an unbound OLE object

Page Break—begin a new screen

Subform/Subreport—display data from more that one table

Rectangle—display a rectangle

Activate/Deactivate Control Wizard

Text Box—display a label attached to a text box

Toggle Button—display a toggle control bound to a Yes/No field

Check Box—display a check box bound to a Yes/No field

List Box—display a control with a list of values that you define

Image—display an image

Bound Object Frame—display an object stored in an Access database

Tab control—create multi-page forms

Line—display a line

More controls—display a list of all controls

FIGURE 5.4

The Form toolbox

ACCESS

Caption value set for the field in the table design. The Field Name is the default Caption property value and will display in the label when no custom value is set.

Building a Form in Design View

Missy and Micah like using the Customer form to enter new customers, but they believe that the format could be improved. Rather than customize the existing form, you decide to rebuild it in Design View to get some practice with building forms from scratch.

---

task reference   Open a New Form in Design View

- In the Database Window of an open database, click the **Forms** object
- Click the **New** button on the Database Window toolbar
- In the New Form dialog box, click **Design View**
- Select the table or query that will be the record source for the form and click **OK**

Creating the Customer form in Design View:

1. Open the **ac05KoryoKicks.mdb** database
2. Select the **Forms** object from the Database Window
3. Click the **New** button on the Database Window toolbar
4. Verify that **Design View** is selected from the list of ways to create forms
5. Select **Customer** as the source of data for this form and click **OK**

FIGURE 5.5

Customer form Design View

Form Design toolbox anchored to left window border

Customer table field list

ruler

blank form with grid

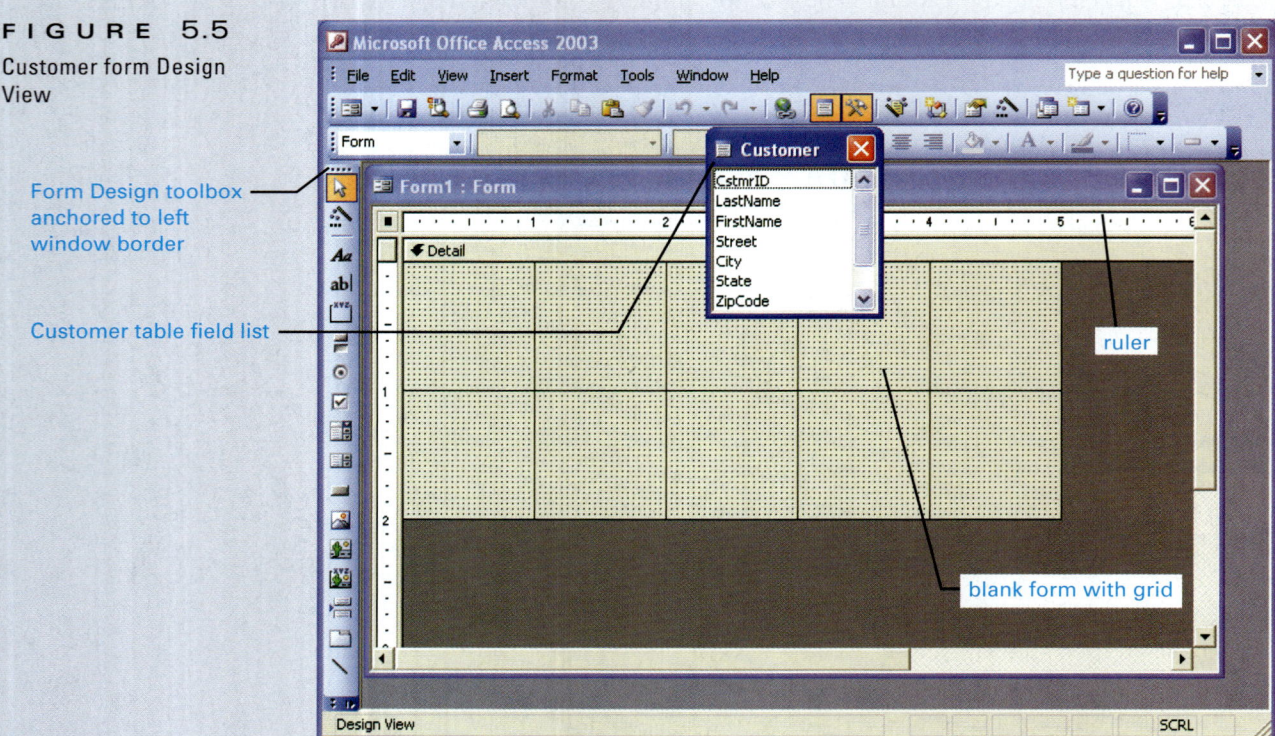

tip: *If your screen is missing the ruler, grid, or toolbox, use the View menu to add them. The toolbox may be floating or anchored without impacting functionality. Drag the toolbox Title bar to anchor or unanchor it*

6. Select all of the fields in the Field List dialog box by double-clicking its Title bar (see Figure 5.6)

tip: *If the field list is not displaying, click the Field List button on the Form Design toolbar*

7. Drag the selected fields to the form

tip: *Your form should generally match the appearance shown, but fields do not need to be positioned exactly since they will be moved to their final locations later*

CstmrID Label control —

CstmrID Text Box control

double-click to select all

rulers to aid in control alignment

text box move handle

sizing handle

label move handle

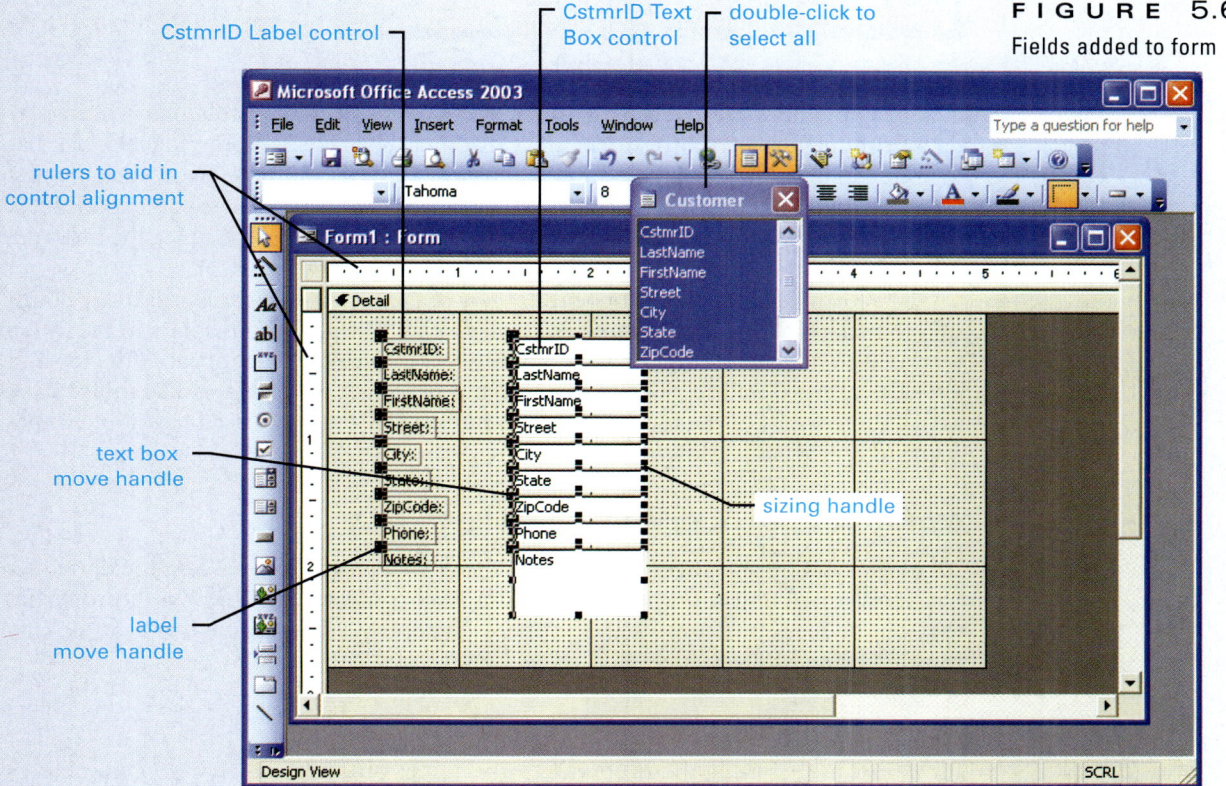

FIGURE 5.6

Fields added to form

8. The simplest edit in Design View is to delete a field. Click the form background to deselect all fields and then click the **Notes** field and press the **Del** key to remove it from the form (we will place it on a new form page later)

tip: *When you click on the Notes field, both the Label control and the Text Box control are selected*

9. Close the field list, since you won't need it for some time, by clicking the X in its Title bar

tip: *The field list has Customer in the Title bar*

10. Click the **Save** 💾 button and name the form **Customers**

FIGURE 5.7

Form Properties pages

Properties pages for
the Detail form section

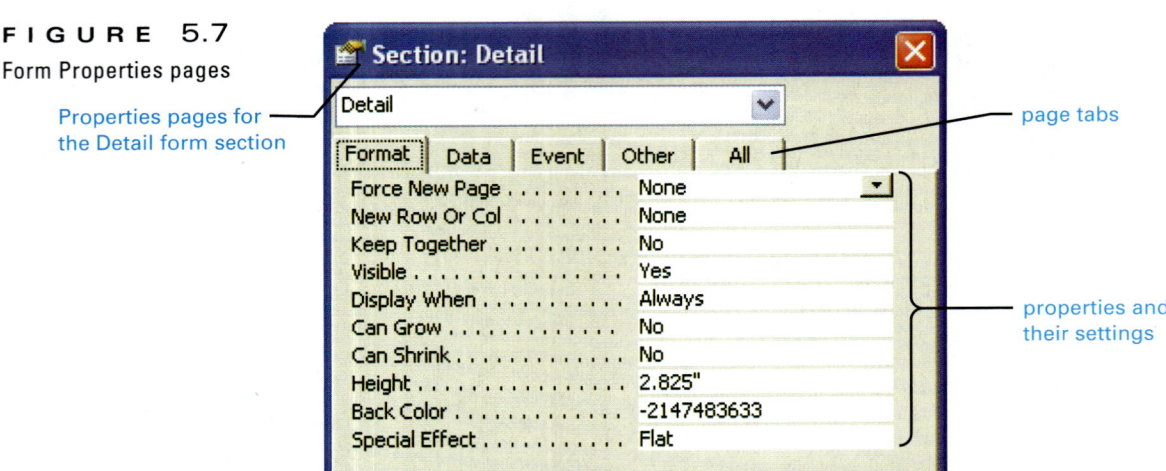

FIGURE 5.7

Form Properties pages

Properties pages for the Detail form section · page tabs · properties and their settings

You now have created a blank form and added bound controls that will display data from the form's record source, the Customer table. Fields from the Field List dialog box can be added one at a time or in groups. To select multiple fields, click the first field and then hold down the Ctrl key as you click the other fields. As you experienced, double-clicking the Field List Title bar will select all fields in the list. Once the fields are selected, drag and drop them on the form Detail section.

The form Detail section can be resized by dragging its borders. This is often necessary to make the form fit the controls it will display. The grid that displays in the Detail section is to help position the controls effectively. The rulers that appear at the top and left sides of the Detail section are to assist in positioning controls and also indicate the actual dimensions of the form. The Undo button can always be used to undo changes made to the Detail section or a control.

Modifying Properties

All objects have ***properties*** that control behavior. In Form Design View, the developer has access to all object properties, providing full control. One object with properties that can be set is the form itself. In turn, each control added to the form can be customized using its properties.

Form Properties

Properties are set using the ***Properties pages*** for an object (see Figure 5.7). An object's Properties pages can be opened either by selecting the object and clicking the Properties button on the Form Design toolbar or by right-clicking the object and selecting Properties from the pop-up menu.

The properties that can be set are specific to each type of object, but the general layout of the Properties page is always the same. The object that owns the Properties pages is listed in the Title bar; the properties are divided by type on tabbed pages. The first Properties page to present is the Format page, which contains properties about how the object will display.

Changing form properties:

1. Verify that the **ac05KoryoKicks.mdb** database is open and that the **Customers** form created in the previous steps is in Design View

2. Right-click on a blank area of the form and select **Properties** from the pop-up menu

3. Click in the Back Color property in either the Format or All tab

4. Select the ellipse to the right of the current Back Color property

5. Click the sixth square on the third row (light blue) square and click **OK**

6. Close the Properties pages

The form is now light blue because the Back Color property was set in the Properties pages. Changing the size of the form by dragging its borders also sets the form properties related to size. This could be done manually in the Properties pages, but it is easier to drag the borders. You can change the properties of the controls on a form by moving them, changing their size, or setting other properties on the Properties pages.

Adjusting Controls on a Form

Both a Label and a Text Box control represent each field from the table. Since developers typically want to manipulate both at the same time, both are selected when either one is clicked. The square *handles* that appear on a selected control can be used to resize it. A selected control can be moved to a new position on the form using drag and drop. The Text Box and Label controls for a field move in concert unless a move handle is used. The largest square (top left) on a label or text box is called the *move handle* and will allow each component of the bound control to be moved independently.

Multiple controls on a form can be selected and operated on simultaneously. To select multiple controls, click and drag a selection box around the controls or click the first control and then hold down the Shift key while selecting subsequent controls. Once the controls are selected, resize, move, or set properties such as the background color.

---

task reference   Select and Move Form Controls

- Select the control to be operated on by clicking it. The Shift key can be used to select multiple controls

- Drag the control(s) to the new location. Use the large move handle to independently move components of a bound control

---

Repositioning Customers form controls:

1. Verify that the **ac05KoryoKicks.mdb** database is open and that the **Customers** form created in the previous steps is in Design View

2. First let's organize the work area. Click in the CstmrID text box to select the field and then drag it to the position shown in Figure 5.8

3. Click and drag a selection box around the remaining fields and position them as shown in Figure 5.8

4. Now let's put the fields where the twins want them. Select **FirstName** and drag it until it is on the same line and to the right of LastName

FIGURE 5.8
Repositioned Customers
controls

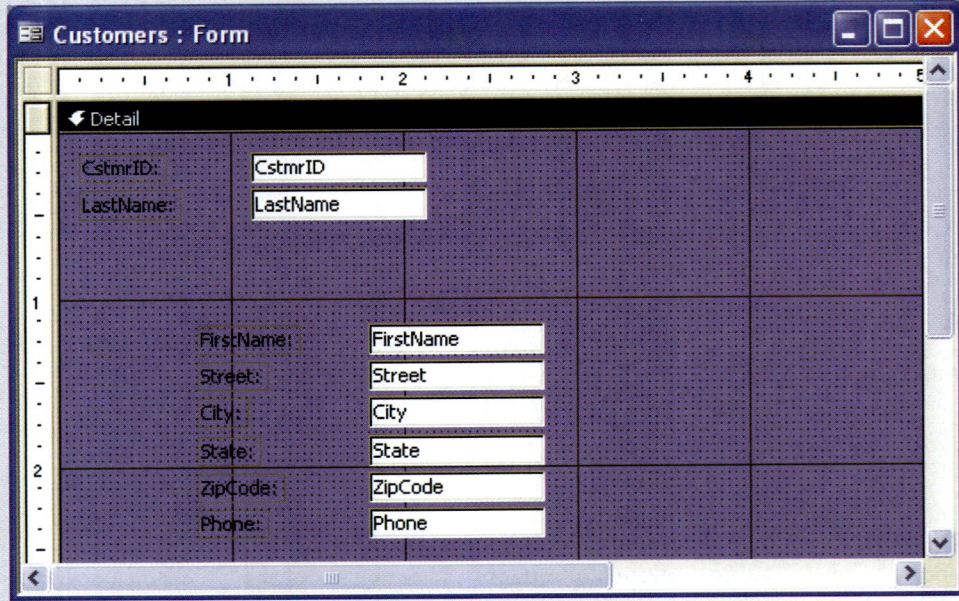

FIGURE 5.8
Repositioned Customers
controls

tip: *If something is selected that you don't want, deselect it by clicking on the form surface away from any control. The mouse pointer changes to a hand when you can drag the selection*

5. Select **Street** and move it up until it is under LastName

6. Select **City** and move it to the right of Street, aligned with FirstName

7. Select **State** and move it up until it is under Street

8. Select **ZipCode** and move it to the right of State, aligned with City

9. Select **Phone** and move it up until it is under State

10. Drag the borders of the Detail pane to reduce its size, as shown in Figure 5.9

FIGURE 5.9
Customers Design View

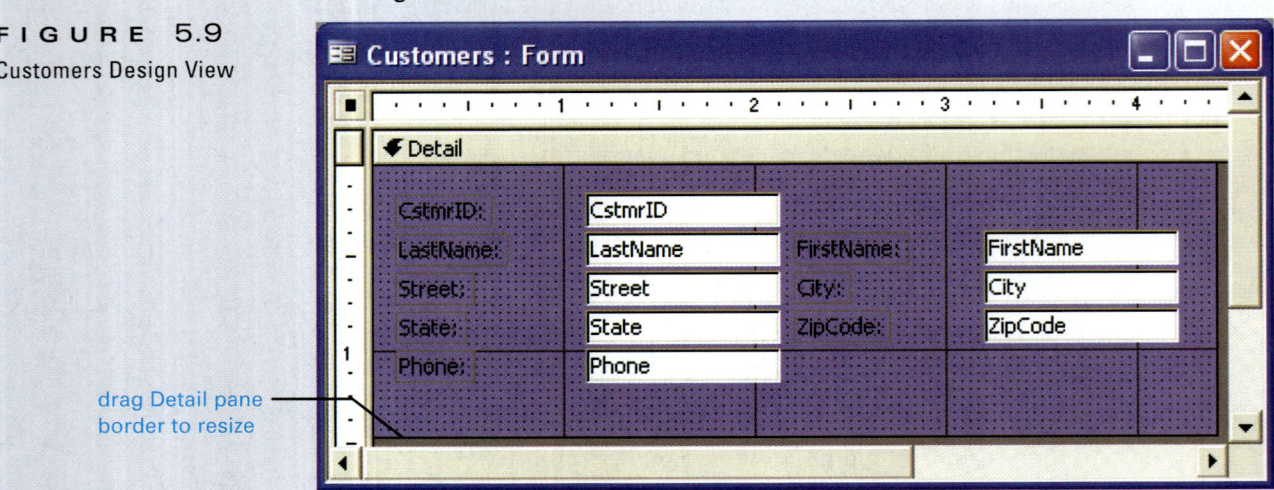

drag Detail pane
border to resize

11. Click the **Form View** ⊞ ▾ button to preview the results

Click the **Design View** ⊞ ▾ button and click the **Save** 🖫 button to save the form

When moving fields it is important to notice the mouse pointer's shape. A hand with all of the fingers extended indicates that the selection can be moved to a new location. This will drag both the label and text box of a bound control. A pointing hand indicates that a move handle has been accessed to move the parts of a bound control independently. A two-headed arrow indicates that a *sizing handle* is being used to resize the control.

The field names from the table are usually picked for technical reasons and are often not what the user wants to see. To change the content of any label, set the Caption property of the field in Table Design. The benefit of setting this property is that its value is the default for any form or report created. A label can be directly edited, but this is effective for the current object only and will not be reflected in other forms or reports.

After previewing the form, the twins have decided they want spaces in the field labels. The fields need to be adjusted to match the size of the data that they will display. For example, the CstmrID, State, and ZipCode fields are much too large for their data. They would also like the labels to be right-justified and closer to the text boxes to make the relationship easier to view. These changes will require setting the properties of the Label controls.

---

task reference · Set Control Properties

- Right-click the control to open the pop-up menu

- Select **Properties** from the pop-up menu

- Select the appropriate Properties tab (usually Format)

- Navigate to the property and change its setting

---

help yourself *Use the Type a Question combo box to improve your understanding of setting control properties by typing* **control properties**. *Review the contents of* About customizing a control *and* About property sheets. *Close the Help window when you are finished*

Changing labels:

1. Verify that the **ac05KoryoKicks.mdb** database is open with the **Customers** form created in the previous steps in Design View

2. Click an insertion point in the CstmrID label and add a space between Cstmr and ID (see Figure 5.10)

tip: *With the label selected, use the I-beam to click an insertion point between the r and I. When this is successful, the label background becomes white and a blinking insertion point appears. This text edit area behaves like a little word processor*

3. Repeat this process for LastName, FirstName, and ZipCode

4. Now let's put the fields where the twins want them. Click and drag a selection box around the CstmrID, Last Name, Street, State, and Phone Labels (not text boxes)

   a. Right-click on a selected label and choose **Properties** from the pop-up menu

   b. Scroll down to Text Align on the All tab and choose **Right**

   c. Close the Multiple Selection dialog box

   d. From the **Format** menu choose **Align** and then **Right**

F I G U R E   5.10

Updated labels for the
Customers form

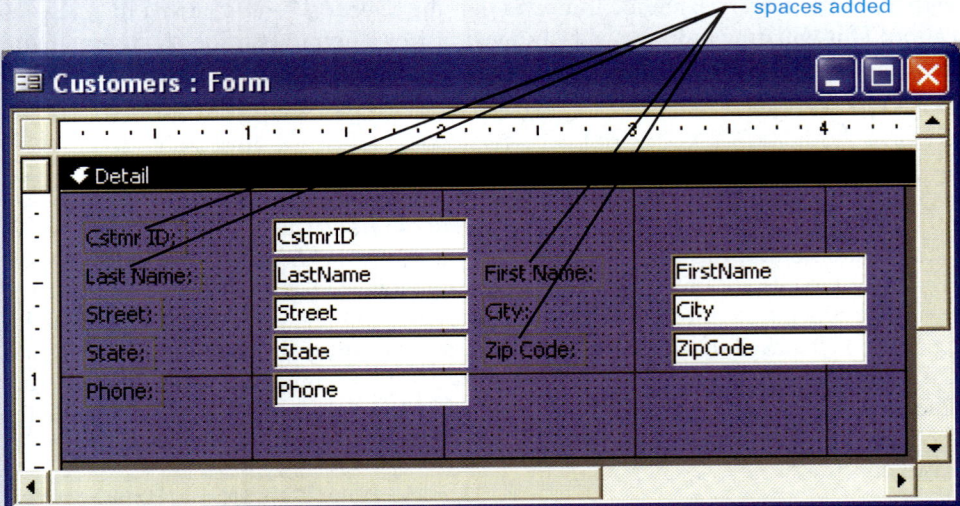

tip: *All labels should be right-justified. If they are not, check your selection and try step 4b again*

5. Repeat step 4 for the right-column labels

6. Since the labels are in the correct position, you will move the text boxes to be closer to the labels. Select the CstmrID text box and use the move handle to reposition it until only one grid line shows between the label and the text box

F I G U R E   5.11

Repositioned labels for the
Customers form

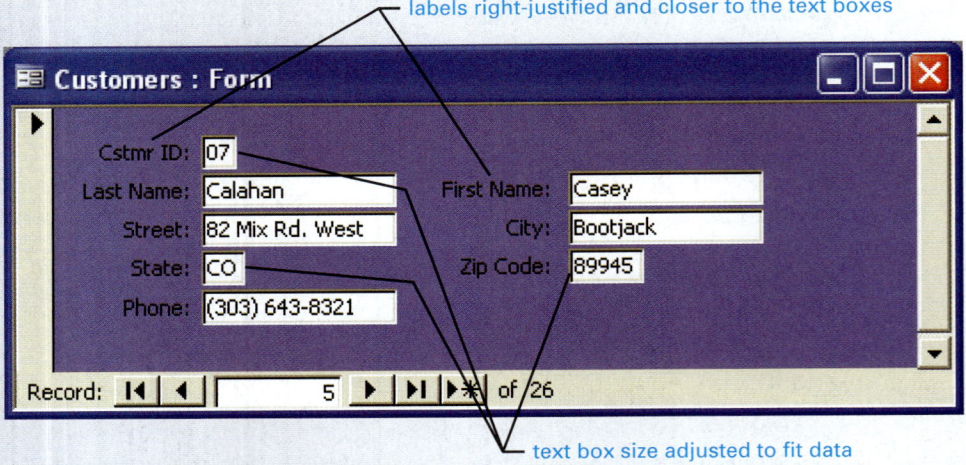

*another***way**
. . . to Change
Label Text

The text displayed in a Label control is a property of that control. All properties, including the displayed text, can be changed from the Properties pages. Right-click on the label to activate the shortcut menu and select Properties to open the Properties pages. Set the Caption property to control the displayed text

7. Repeat this process for all of the other labels

8. Select the text box for CstmrID and use the sizing handles to reduce its size to display about three characters

9. Check your results in Form View and adjust the field width as needed to properly display the data (see Figure 5.11)

tip: *You will need to move through the records and view the field with various data values to ensure that you have correctly modified the width*

10. Repeat this process for State and ZipCode

11. Move the right column controls close to the left column with four grid lines between them

12. Save your changes

The properties of multiple selected objects can be set simultaneously. When working on multiple objects, the selected objects must be of the same type (e.g., changing the alignment of all the labels in earlier steps). In the next steps you will simultaneously modify the properties of all the text boxes on the form, by changing their Back Color and Font.

Changing text boxes:

1. Verify that the **ac05KoryoKicks.mdb** database is open and that the **Customers** form created in the previous steps is in Design View

2. Select *all* of the text boxes on the form by holding down the Shift key as you click

3. Open the Properties pages by clicking the **Properties** button from the toolbar (the shortcut menu also can be used)

4. Click in the **Font Name** property and select **Batang**

tip: *You will need to scroll down to find the Font property in the Format tab. If you do not have Batang, select another font. All available properties are in alphabetical order on the All tab. Move the Properties pages by dragging the Title bar to see the results of your changes*

5. Click in the **Fore Color** property and then click the ellipse

6. In the Color dialog box select the **Define Custom Colors** button to create a custom color for the text box backgrounds

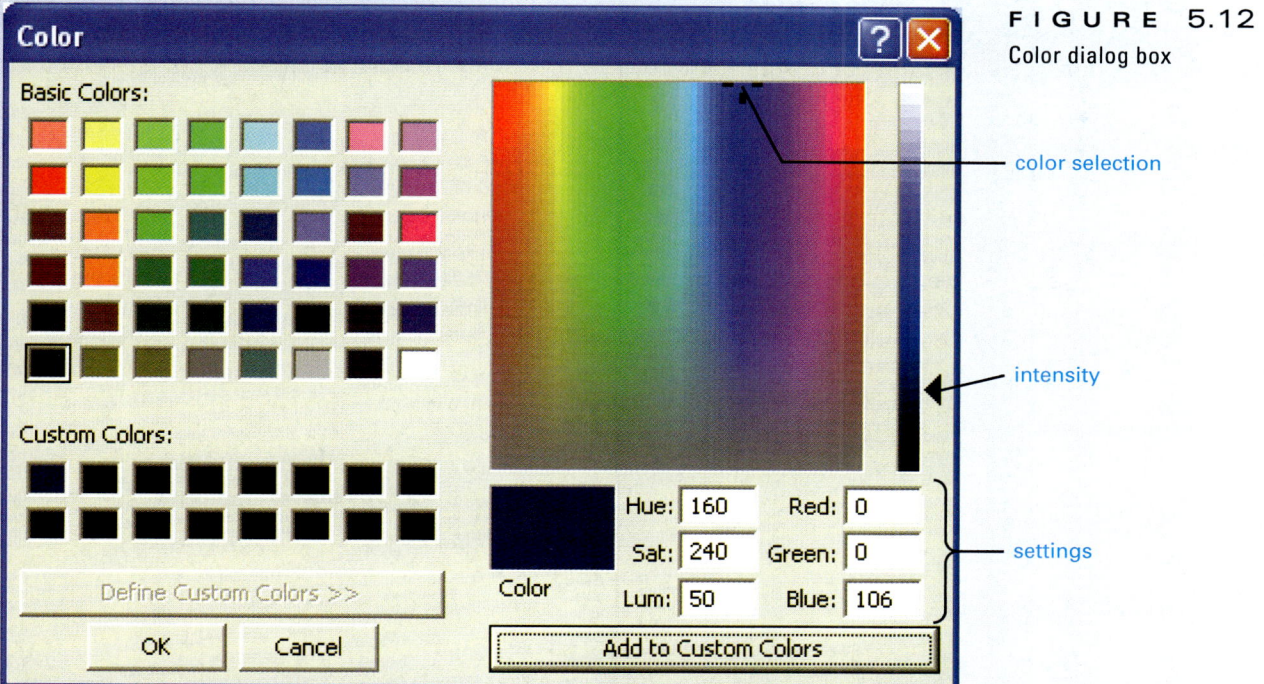

FIGURE 5.12
Color dialog box

color selection

intensity

settings

7. You can click to choose color and intensity or enter the settings manually. Set Hue, Sat, Lum, Red, Green, and Blue to match Figure 5.12; click **Add to Custom Colors**; and click **OK**

8. Set the **Special Effect** property to **Raised**

9. Set the Back Color property to Hue **120**, Sat **240**, Lum **216**, Red **204**, Green **255**, Blue **255**.

FIGURE 5.13

Modified text boxes

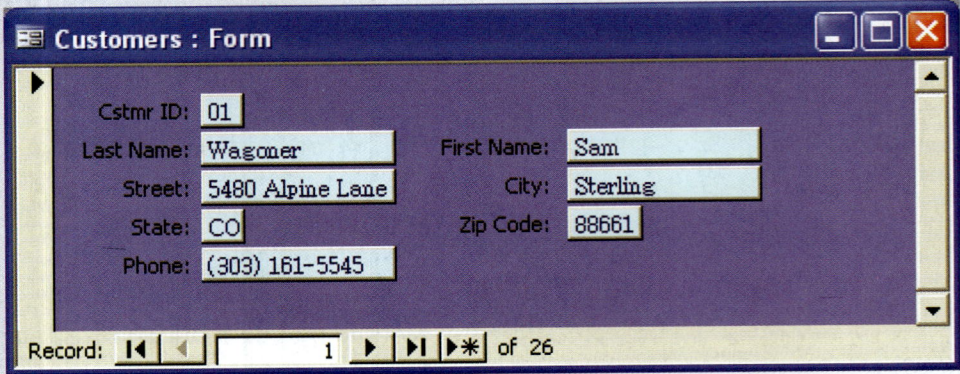

10. Close the Multiple Selection dialog box and use the Form View to preview your changes

11. Save the form

Although color adds interest and draws the eye, use color sparingly when creating forms that will be used frequently. Default colors are used throughout the Microsoft Office System Applications, and users understand how the various colors are normally applied. Using these defaults can make your application easier to learn. In addition, color viewed over time can increase eye fatigue, making the screen harder to read.

If you do use color, be consistent in its application. The same color should always mean the same thing. Make sure that the contrast between the background color and the text color is sufficient for easy readability. In general, pale backgrounds with dark text are the most effective.

Inserting Form Headers and Footers

So far in this chapter, form modifications have been made to the Detail section of the form. Recall that in an earlier chapter a graphic was inserted into the Header section of a form created using a Wizard. Each form section has a specific function and behavior. The *Form Detail section* of a form is typically used to display data from a record source. The *Form Header section* will appear at the top of the form when it is displayed in Form View and at the beginning of a printed selection of forms. The *Form Footer section* will appear at the bottom of a form when it is displayed in Form View and at the end of a printed selection of forms.

Form Header and Footer sections are characteristically used to add titles, instructions, and buttons to the top or bottom of a form. The header and footer contents are static—they do not change as the data displayed in the Detail section change.

task *reference*   Show Form Headers and Footers

- Open a form in Design View
- Select **Form Header/Footer** from the **View** menu

Adding Form Header/Footer:

1. Verify that the **ac05KoryoKicks.mdb** database is open and that the **Customers** form created in the previous steps is in Design View

2. On the **View** menu select **Form Header/Footer**

tip: *If both the Header and Footer sections do not display, drag the border of the Form Design Window and expand it until all three form sections display*

Section selectors   Section bars

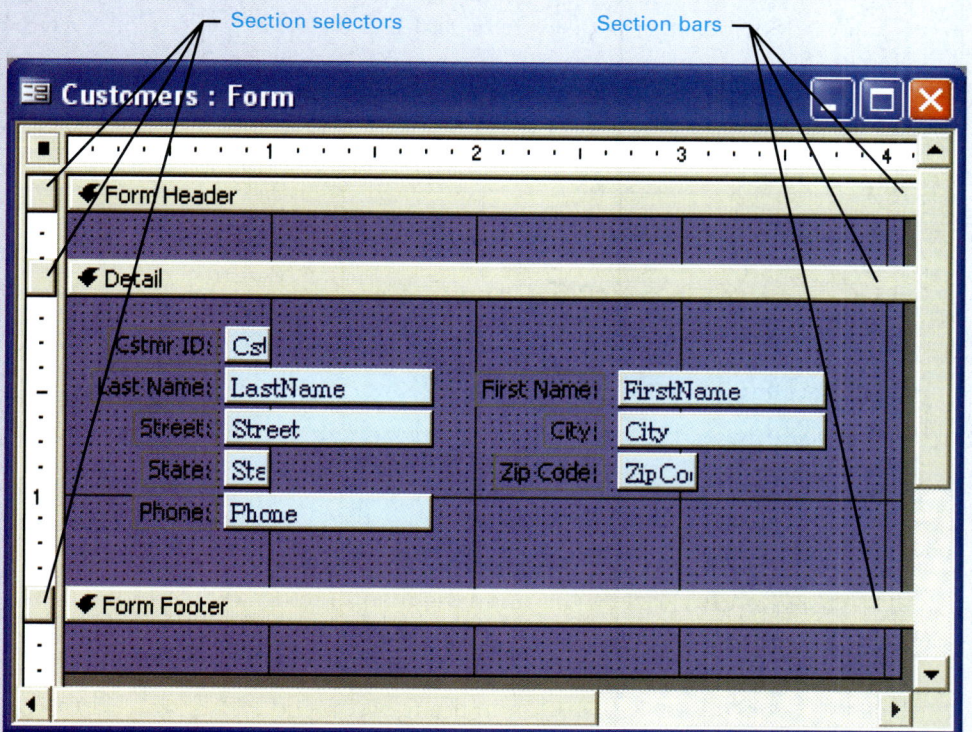

F I G U R E 5.14

Customers form with Header and Footer sections

3. Use Form View to preview the changes

*another***word**   **. . . on Form Headers and Footers**

Headers and footers can only be added and removed together. If you don't want both a header and a footer, you can set the Visible property of the section that you don't want to No, or set its Height property to 0

ACCESS

Deselecting Form Header/Footer on the View menu will remove both sections from the form along with any controls they contain. Either the Section selectors or Section bars (see Figure 5.14) can be used to select a form section. Once a section is selected, it can be operated on by adding controls or setting its properties.

To complete the design of the Customers form, you need to add the logo and form title. These are unbound controls that will be placed in the form header. The logo will be placed in an Image control and the form title will be in a Label control. These controls are available from the toolbox.

---

task reference   Add Toolbox Controls to a Form

- Open a form in Design View
- If necessary, activate the toolbox using the **Toolbox** button on the Form Design toolbar
- Verify that the Toolbox **Control Wizards** button is depressed (a blue outline will show around it)
- Click the Toolbox control that is to be added to the form
- Click in the form section that will contain the control
- Set the control's properties by entering its contents, sizing, moving, and using the Properties pages

---

Adding content to the Form Header:

1. Verify that the **ac05KoryoKicks.mdb** database is open and that the **Customers** form created in the previous steps is in Design View

2. Select the **Image control** button from the toolbox and then click in the Form Header to activate the Control Wizard

tip: *If the Wizard does not activate, delete the Image control, click the Control Wizard button in the toolbox to activate Wizards, and repeat step 2*

3. The Image Control Wizard will open the Insert Picture dialog box. Navigate to the data files for this chapter and select **ac05KoryoKicks.gif**. The logo shown in Figure 5.15 should display in the Image control

4. Click the **Label control** button in the toolbox and click in the Form Header next to the image

5. Type **Customers** (there is no Label Control Wizard)

6. Right-click on the Customers Label control and select **Properties** from the pop-up menu

7. Set the following properties

Back Style	**Normal**
Font Name	**Tahoma**
Font Size	**26**
Font Weight	**Extra bold**
Font Italic	**Yes**

anotherway
... to Change Label Text

The Formatting toolbar can be used to set the Font Name, Font Size, Italic, and Color properties of a control when you are using standard values. The Font Weight and custom color used in the Customers form are not available using this method

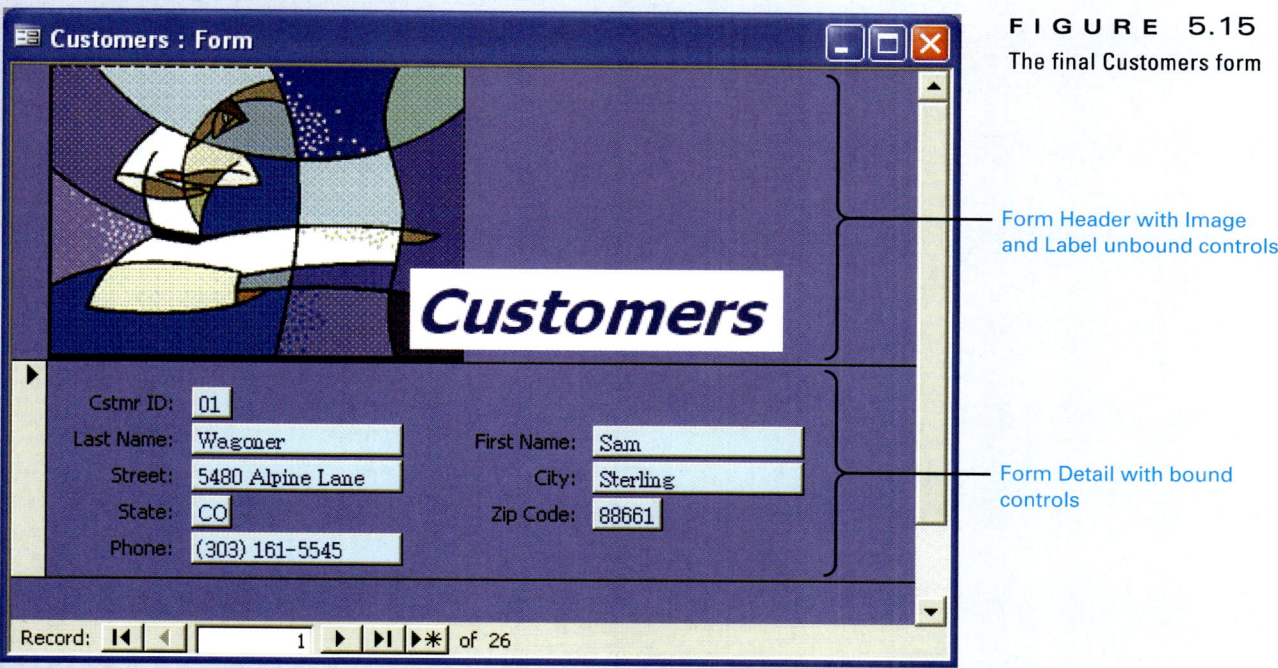

The final Customers form

Form Header with Image and Label unbound controls

Form Detail with bound controls

8. Click in the **Fore Color** property (to set the text color) and then click the **ellipse** to the right of the property

9. Click the **Define Custom Colors** button. Set Hue to **174**, Sat to **240**, Lum to **60**, Red to **44**, Green to **0**, and Blue to **128**; click **Add to Custom Colors**; and click **OK**

10. Close the Properties pages

11. Drag the Customer label until it is in the position shown. Resize as needed

12. Use Form View to preview the changes

13. Save the form

In the previous steps, adding an Image control to the form initiated the Image Control Wizard. The complex controls in the toolbox have **Control Wizards** designed to walk users through the process of building the control's content. The Control Wizards button on the toolbox will enable and disable these Wizards. Figure 5.16 indicates which controls have Wizards available.

As controls are added to a form, they are actually layered so that the most recently added control is on the top layer. This layering is called **z-order**. You may notice as you adjust the position and size of controls that one may be on top of another. For example, in the Customers Form Header, the label is in front of the image because it was added last. To change the z-order of a control, use cut and paste to remove this control from its current layer and paste it to the top layer.

Navigating Data with Forms

Besides using forms to page through data in the underlying record source (table or query), users need to be able to navigate directly to a specific record or records to perform maintenance. Forms already have been used to view data and print the current

F I G U R E 5.16

Toolbox Control Wizards availability

Button Name	Control Wizard?	Button Name	Control Wizard?
Bound Object Frame	Yes	Option Button	No
Check Box	No	Option Group	Yes
Combo Box	Yes	Page Break	No
Command Button	Yes	Rectangle	No
Control Wizards	No	Select Objects	No
Image	Yes	Subform/Subreport	Yes
Label	No	Tab Control	No
Line	No	Text Box	No
List Box	Yes	Toggle Button	Yes
More Controls	No	Unbound Object Frame	Yes

record, but it is also possible to use Find to navigate to a specific record and filters to create a subset of data to work on. Find and filters in Form View work in the same fashion as was covered in Datasheet View.

Finding Data with Forms

By default, a form displays all of the data in the underlying record source (table or query). When there are hundreds or even thousands of records, it can be an arduous task to find the ones that you want to work on without some helpful database tools.

Access provides a Find tool for locating and updating specific records. It can be used in many of the views of a database including the Form View. Click in the field containing the values to be searched, and then click the Find button on the toolbar. The Find and Replace dialog box is used to set the criteria for a search. Valid criteria are outlined in Figure 5.17.

When entering the Find What criteria, wildcards play an important role. A question mark (?) can be used to match any single character, and the asterisk (*) wildcard will replace any number of characters. The Find and Replace dialog box also can be used to replace values that have been found. It is best to test the Find and then add the Replace value so that data are not accidentally destroyed.

Finding form records:

1. Verify that the **ac05KoryoKicks.mdb** database is open and that the **Customers** form created in the previous steps is in Form View

2. Select the **LastName** field and click the **Find** 🔍 button on the toolbar

3. Enter *g* in the Find What criteria to find all last names containing the letter g, and click **Find Next**

4. Repeat clicking **Find Next** until no more matches are found

tip: *Wagoner, Gray, and Guo should all be found*

5. Close the Find dialog box

F I G U R E 5.17

Find and Replace dialog box components

Critieria	Action		
Find What	Sets the value that will be matched in the search		
Look In	Determines what will be searched. The default is the active column, but you also can choose to search the entire table.		
Match	Any Part of Field	Matches if the *Find What* value is anywhere in the field	
	Whole Field	Matches if the Find What value is all that is in the field	
	Start of Field	Matches if the Find What value is at the start of the field	
Search	All	Searches for a match in the entire *Look In* area	
	Up	Searches for a match above the cursor in the *Look In* area	
	Down	Searches for a match below the cursor in the *Look In* area	
Match Case	Matches the case of *Find What* when clicked on		

Filtering Form Records

Recall from the datasheet filtering discussion that there are four ways to apply filters. The first, Filter by Selection, returns records that match the value selected in the form. The second, Filter by Form, presents an empty version of the current form where match values can be typed. Filter for Input accepts a value or expression used to restrict the records, and the Advanced Filter/Sort window presents a design grid used to create criteria from scratch. Regardless of the type of filter being applied, the goal is to select only records that meet the stated criteria. Creating the criteria is slightly different for each type of filter.

Filtering form records:

1. Verify that the **ac05KoryoKicks.mdb** database is open and that the **Customers** form created in the previous steps is in Form View

2. Navigate to a record containing Wagoner and select the **g** (this is the same as *g*) and click **Filter By Selection** in the toolbar

3. Use the navigation buttons to explore the filtered records

4. Use the **Remove Filter** button to return to the entire record set

5. Click the **Filter By Form** button. Like "*g*" should display as the current criteria (see Figure 5.18)

6. Click the **OR** tab and add the condition **s*** (Access will convert this to Like "s*") as a Last Name criterion

7. Click the **Apply Filter** button (see Figure 5.19)

tip: *Gray, Guo, Smith, and Wagoner should all be found*

8. Click in Last Name and click the **Sort Ascending** button

FIGURE 5.18
Filtered records by **g**

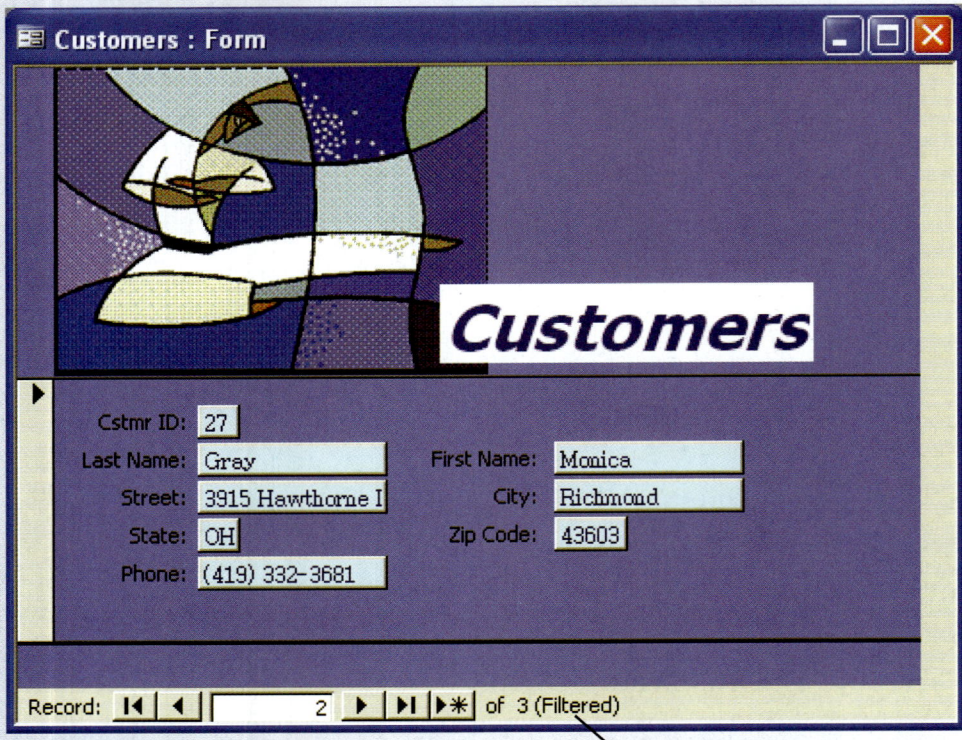

3 records met the filter criteria

FIGURE 5.19
Filtered records by ***g*
and s*** and then sorted by
Last Name

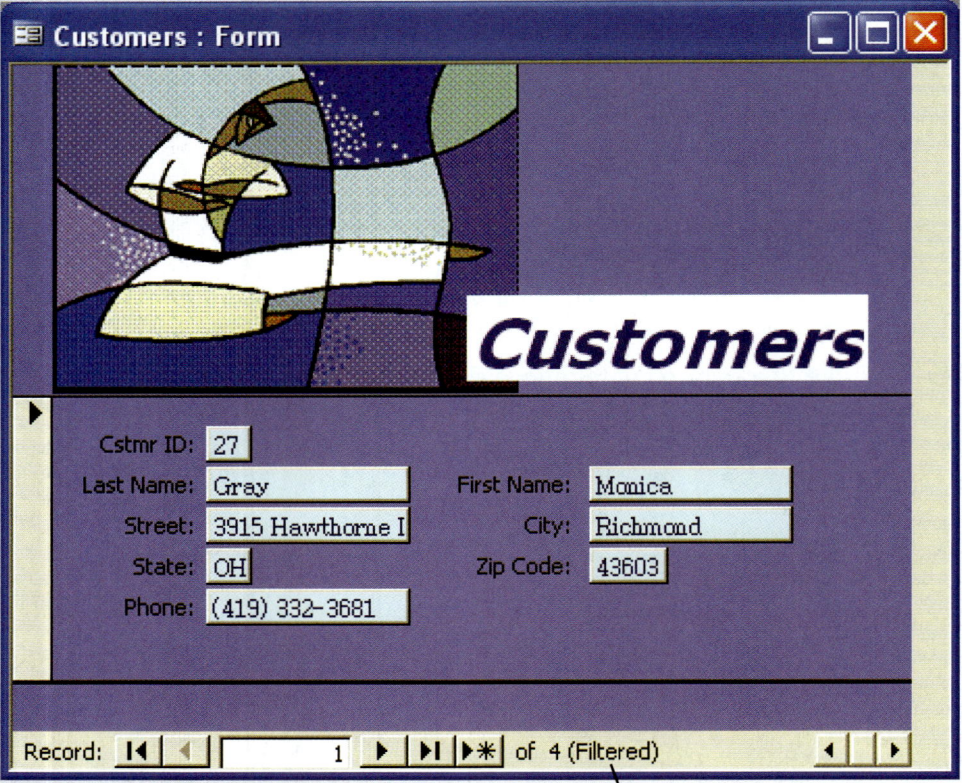

4 records of filtered data
sorted by Last Name

9. Use the record navigation buttons to explore the filtered records

10. Return to Filter by Form and use the **Save As Query** button and name the query **LastNameFilter**

11. Use the **Remove Filter** 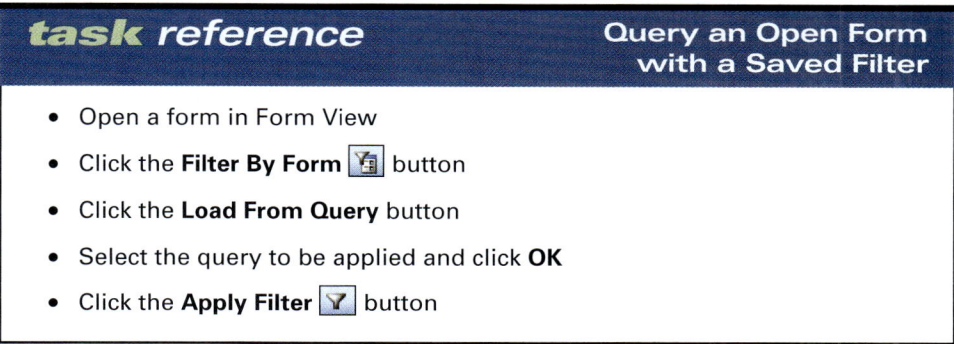 button to return to the entire record set

A filter can be saved as a query for reuse by clicking the Save As Query button on the Filter/Sort toolbar. Filter by Form and Filter for Input both can be used to filter by multiple criteria. Only Filter by Selection and Filter by Form were demonstrated, but Filter for Input and Advanced Filter/Sort can be accessed using the Filter option of the Records menu or the pop-up menu. Filters saved as queries also can be applied to an open form using the Filter by Form facility.

task reference — Query an Open Form with a Saved Filter

- Open a form in Form View
- Click the **Filter By Form** button
- Click the **Load From Query** button
- Select the query to be applied and click **OK**
- Click the **Apply Filter** button

Querying an open form:

1. Verify that the **ac05KoryoKicks.mdb** database is open and that the **Customers** form created in the previous steps is in Form View

2. Click the **Filter By Form** button

3. Click the **Load From Query** button

4. Choose **LastNameFilter** from the Applicable Filter dialog box and click **OK**

5. Click the **Apply Filter** button

6. Close the form

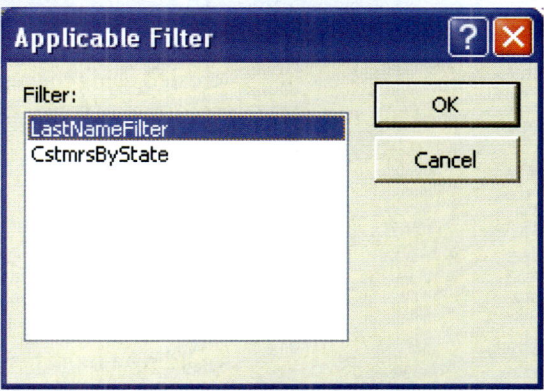

FIGURE 5.20
Applicable Filter dialog box

Using Forms to Maintain Data and Print Selected Records

Forms are built to display and maintain data. Besides creating a custom interface, forms allow control over the subset of data being operated on. Recall that the form itself is based on a record source, which is a table or query. If the record source is a table, all records from that table can initially be viewed, maintained, or printed in the form. If the record source is a query, only the records selected by the query are available to the form.

When a filter or query is applied to the record source, a subset of the data matching the criteria is returned. Until the query or filter is removed, all operations are processed against the subset of data, which impacts the data that are available for maintenance, printing, and other operations.

One of the simplest mistakes to make is to forget to remove a query or filter and then apply another criterion. For example, if a filter to select Ohio customers is applied and then a filter for orders over $100, the result will be Ohio customers who ordered over $100 of goods. If the intent was to give a discount to all orders over $100, customers who are not from Ohio would be missed.

Printing all of the records in the record source is accomplished using the Print button on the toolbar. When forms were first introduced, you learned to use the Print dialog box activated from the File menu to print the current record using the Selected Records option. To print a specific subset of the data such as customers who ordered replacement parts, filter for that subset and then use the Print button to print the selected records.

SESSION 5.1

making the grade

1. What would you do to change the alignment of all the labels on a form?

2. Describe the difference between bound and unbound controls.

3. What are object properties and why do you set them?

4. Why would you use Form Design View rather than a Wizard to create a form?

SESSION 5.2 CREATING COMPLEX REPORTS

The report object allows the creation of a custom hard copy output based on the data in one or more database tables. Printed output can be created using each of the database objects (forms, tables, and queries) that have already been explored, but the report object provides the greatest power and flexibility for creating printed output. Printed output from the other database objects is often used for internal analytical reporting, but when a report goes outside a department or organization, a formal report is usually created using the report object. Public reports, billing statements, and mailing labels are common organizational reports that could use the improved visual impact provided by custom reports.

Defining a Report in Report Design View

Creating a report in Design View provides complete control of all the report elements and their properties, making Design View much more powerful than using a Wizard. While the Report Design View is very similar to Form Design View, the process of building a report is more complex.

Report Sections

Reports can have up to seven types of sections (see Figure 5.21). The exact number of sections is determined by the report layout. The controls placed in the *Report Detail section* will appear once for each record in the underlying record source. The *Group Header/Footer sections* appear before and after each group of records. Group Header/Footer sections can be added individually or in pairs for each level of grouping in the report. The *Page Header/Footer sections* appear at the top and bottom of each report page. The *Report Header/Footer sections* are added in pairs and appear at the beginning and end of the report.

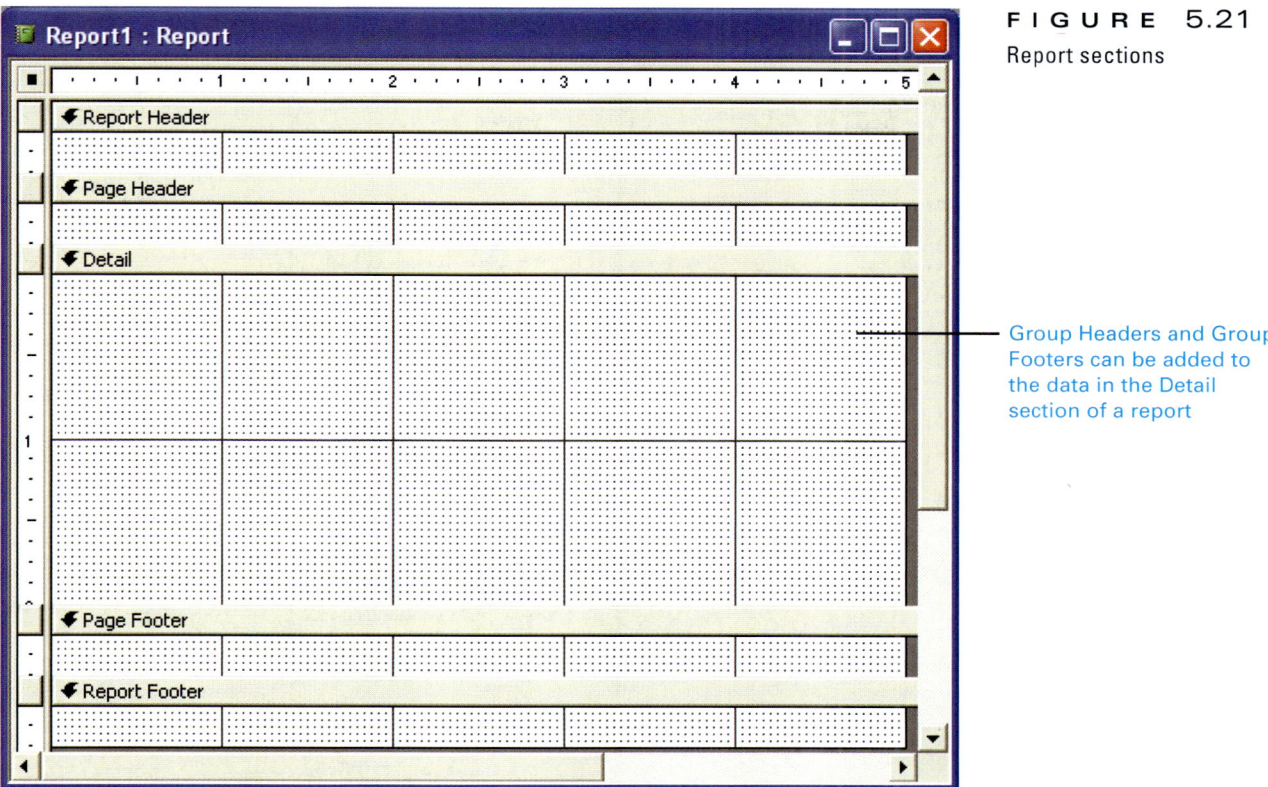

Group Headers and Group Footers can be added to the data in the Detail section of a report

Each section has a **Selection bar** that can be adjusted to resize the section. Empty sections can have their size set to 0 or their Visible property set to No so that they do not display in the final report. If, for example, your report needs a Report Header but not a Report Footer, you could set the Report Footer size to 0.

The Report Header section normally contains the title of the report with the date and any other information that will print once at the beginning of the report. The Page Header contains information that should appear at the top of each page such as a page number, column headings for the report fields, and a reduced report title. The Group Header indicates the field or fields that will control data summaries.

The Group Footer section holds the summary that will be printed at the end of each detail group. For example, the order total would be printed each time the OrderNumber (group field) changes. The Page Footer section is used for page numbers and other information that needs to print at the bottom of every report page. If a report has both a Page Footer and a Report Footer, the print order of the last page is Report Footer and then Page Footer. The Report Footer section normally holds information that will be printed only once at the end of the report such as grand totals and report footnotes.

Since the Report Design View is complex, it is important to design a report before attempting to build it. One significant difference between designing forms and reports is that forms generally display one record per page in columns, while reports generally display several records of data per printed page in rows.

Start the report design with the Detail section by outlining where the rows of data will display. Decide what fields need to be included for each record. After documenting what fields are to be included, choose a layout for those fields and any other elements that are to be included such as a calculation or a graphic. The Detail section repeats for each record, so only one line of output needs to be specified. Figure 5.22 shows a sample form design for KoryoKicks Customers input.

F I G U R E 5.22

Customers report design

Report Header prints at beginning of report

State	Last Name	First Name	Street	City	Zip	Phone

KoryoKicks logo   Customers by State

XX

	XXXXXXXXX	XXXXXXXXXX	XXXXXXXXXXXXXXXXXXX	XXXXXXXXXX	XXXXX	XXXXXXXXXXXXX
	XXXXXXXXX	XXXXXXXXXX	XXXXXXXXXXXXXXXXXXX	XXXXXXXXXX	XXXXX	XXXXXXXXXXXXX
	XXXXXXXXX	XXXXXXXXXX	XXXXXXXXXXXXXXXXXXX	XXXXXXXXXX	XXXXX	XXXXXXXXXXXXX

XX Customer Count XX

XX

	XXXXXXXXX	XXXXXXXXXX	XXXXXXXXXXXXXXXXXXX	XXXXXXXXXX	XXXXX	XXXXXXXXXXXXX
	XXXXXXXXX	XXXXXXXXXX	XXXXXXXXXXXXXXXXXXX	XXXXXXXXXX	XXXXX	XXXXXXXXXXXXX
	XXXXXXXXX	XXXXXXXXXX	XXXXXXXXXXXXXXXXXXX	XXXXXXXXXX	XXXXX	XXXXXXXXXXXXX

XX Customer Count XX

XX

	XXXXXXXXX	XXXXXXXXXX	XXXXXXXXXXXXXXXXXXX	XXXXXXXXXX	XXXXX	XXXXXXXXXXXXX
	XXXXXXXXX	XXXXXXXXXX	XXXXXXXXXXXXXXXXXXX	XXXXXXXXXX	XXXXX	XXXXXXXXXXXXX
	XXXXXXXXX	XXXXXXXXXX	XXXXXXXXXXXXXXXXXXX	XXXXXXXXXX	XXXXX	XXXXXXXXXXXXX

XX Customer Count XX

Grand Total Customer Count XX

Report date   Report time   Page XX of XX

Page Header prints on every page

Group Footer prints when State changes

Report Footer prints at end of report

Page Footer prints on every page

Group Header prints before each group

Headers are generally easier to design than footers, so let's look at those next. Most reports have a title. If your title is to appear only once at the beginning of the report, place it in the Report Header. If your title is to appear on every page, place it in the Page Header. Some reports place a large-font title in the Report Header and a small-font title in the Page Header so that the report is identified on every page without wasting page space.

Report and Page Headers can contain any other static data that your report requires. Candidates for these sections include page numbers, the report date, prepared by information, a report overview, and the company logo. The Page Header should contain the column labels that identify the data in the Detail section. Group Headers and Footers will be discussed in the Calculating and Summarizing Data topic. Place the remaining information in the header that prints with the desired frequency. When a report contains both a Report Header and a Page Header, the Report Header prints first on the initial report page.

Footers are pretty straightforward when there are no calculations involved. Place page numbers, explanatory text, legend of symbols, and preparation and use notes in the footer that prints with the frequency needed.

The design reflects the complete layout of the report including titles, graphics, captions, and field lengths. In the design shown, the field captions appear as the twins want to see them on the report and Xs are used to indicate where the data will display and the length of the data display area. The fields placed in the Detail section will print for each record in the record source and are depicted on the design as the repeated lines within each state group. The notations with the figure indicate the contents of the other report sections.

In Report Design View, field captions will be in Label controls and the field data will be displayed in Text Box controls. The data are grouped by state, and a count of customers in each state is displayed. The KoryoKicks logo will display in an Image control, and the form title will be entered in a Label.

Since a common development technique is to build a report using the AutoReport Wizard and then to customize it in Design View, it is important to understand how the

Wizard behaves. The Wizard places the title provided in the Report Header section. The date and page numbers are placed in the Page Footer. The field names are used as column headings and are placed in the Page Header when there is no grouping.

Whether the report is developed completely in Report Design View or was customized after the Wizard created the first cut, it is called a **custom report**. Custom reports are more time consuming to create and maintain and should be used only when the Wizard cannot create the output that is needed.

The Report Toolbox and Field List

The toolbox used in Report Design View is the same as that used in Form Design View. Recall that the toolbox can be positioned anywhere on the screen and has Screen Tips that can be activated and deactivated using the View menu. The toolbar buttons are presented in Figure 5.4 if you need to review them.

When a control is placed in a report section, its properties direct what it will display and how it will appear. The Data properties of a bound control (those linked to a record source) are set to direct what field it will display. Data properties are set automatically when the record source field list is used to add the control to your report or when the first cut of the report is created with the Wizard. Control Wizards with step-by-step instructions are available for the more complex toolbox options. Figure 5.16 outlines the availability of Control Wizards.

Customizing an AutoReport Wizard Form

To become familiar with the Report Design View, we'll start with a simple report on the KoryoKicks Customer table that has been built for you. The Wizard was used to create a report that will display all of the Customer fields except Notes in order by customer name within state. The report was saved as AutoReportCustomer.

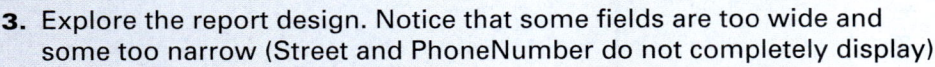

Customizing the Customer AutoReport:

1. Verify that the **ac05KoryoKicks.mdb** database is open

2. In the Database Window, select the **Reports** object and the **AutoReportCustomer** report, and click the **Design View** button

3. Explore the report design. Notice that some fields are too wide and some too narrow (Street and PhoneNumber do not completely display)

FIGURE 5.23

Updated
AutoReportCustomer

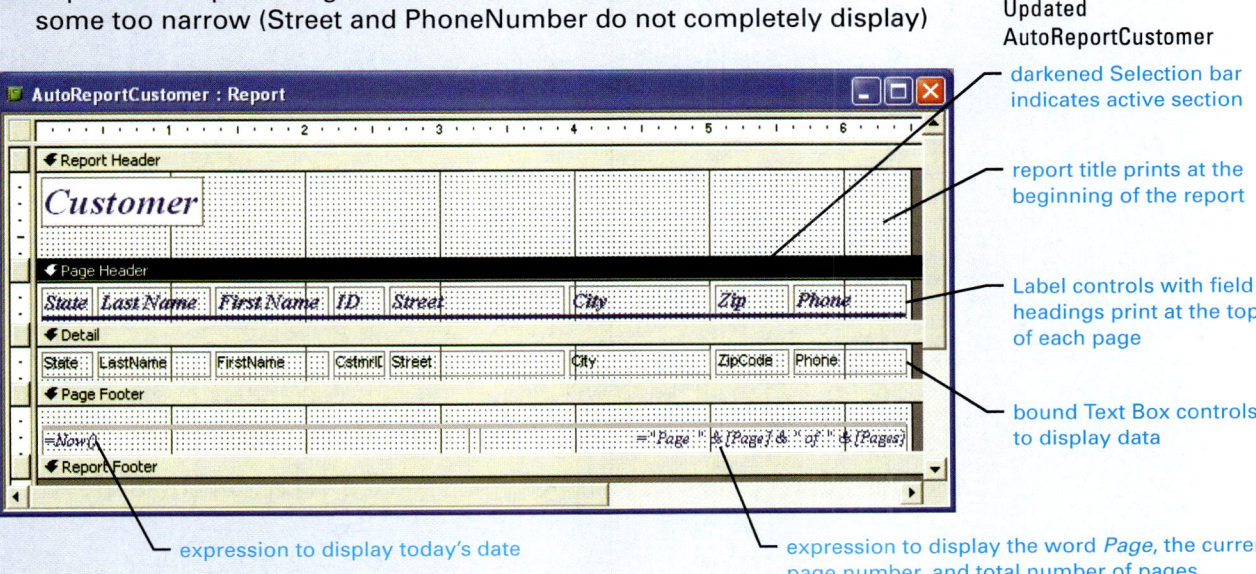

darkened Selection bar indicates active section

report title prints at the beginning of the report

Label controls with field headings print at the top of each page

bound Text Box controls to display data

expression to display today's date

expression to display the word *Page*, the current page number, and total number of pages

4. Use the **Print Preview View** 🔍▾ button to preview the report and then return to Design View

5. Modify the field labels as follows

LastName	**Last Name**
FirstName	**First Name**
CstmrID	**ID**
ZipCode	**Zip**

   tip: *Click an insertion point in the label and then make corrections*

6. Use the sizing handles to reduce the size of the Label and Text Box controls associated with State, Last Name, First Name, ID, City, and Zip

   tip: *Use the View and Design buttons to move between Report views and verify the validity of your results. Each field should display all of the heading and data without too much space left over*

7. Use the move handle to adjust the positions of Last Name, First Name, ID, and Street, removing the extra space between them caused by reducing field sizes

8. Use the sizing handles to increase the size of Street until all of its data display on every detail row of the report

9. Move City, Zip, and Phone to adjust for the resizing, as shown in Figure 5.24

FIGURE 5.24

Edited AutoReportCustomer

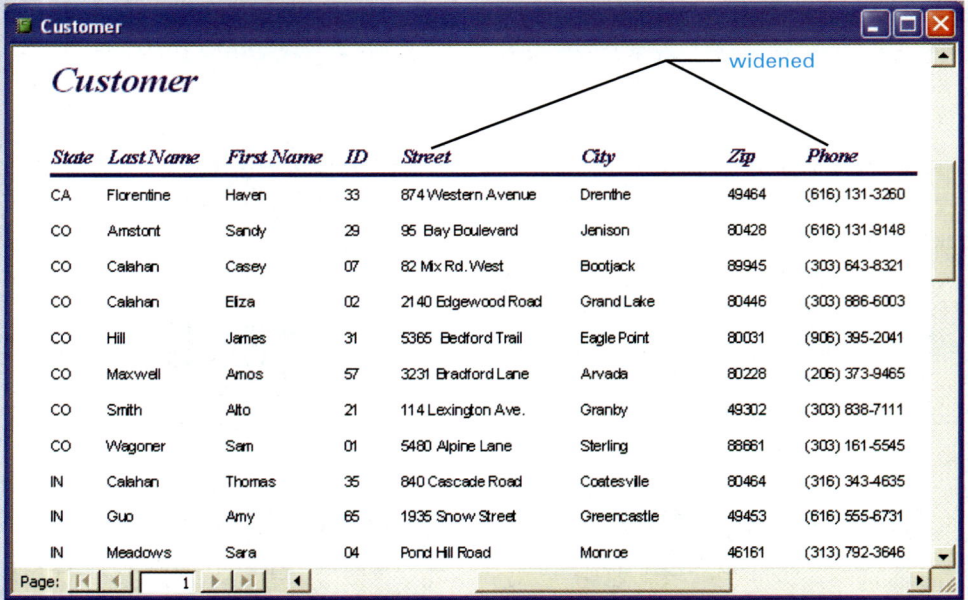

10. Resize Phone so that it will display the complete phone number

11. Edit the title to read **Customers by State**

12. Preview your results and save your changes as **CustomerByState** when you are satisfied

In this process the contents of the Report Header, Page Header, and Detail sections of this simple report were edited. The Page Footer contains expressions that will be discussed later. The Report Footer has been set to a Height of 0 so that it will not display.

Building a Form in Design View

Let's build a Customers by State Report in Design View. The CstmrsByState query has already been prepared as the record source to simplify the process.

---

task reference   **Create a Report in Design View**

- In the Database Window click the **Reports** object and click the **New** button

- Click **Design View** as the way to develop the report, select the record source from the drop-down list, and click **OK**

Building the Customer report in Design View:

1. Verify that the **ac05KoryoKicks.mdb** database is open

2. In the Database Window, select the **Reports** object and click the **New** button

3. In the New Report dialog box, select **Design View**, select **CstmrsByState** as the record source, and click **OK**

4. Double-click on the Title bar of the field list to select all of the fields from the record source table, drag the fields to the Detail section of the report, and drop them

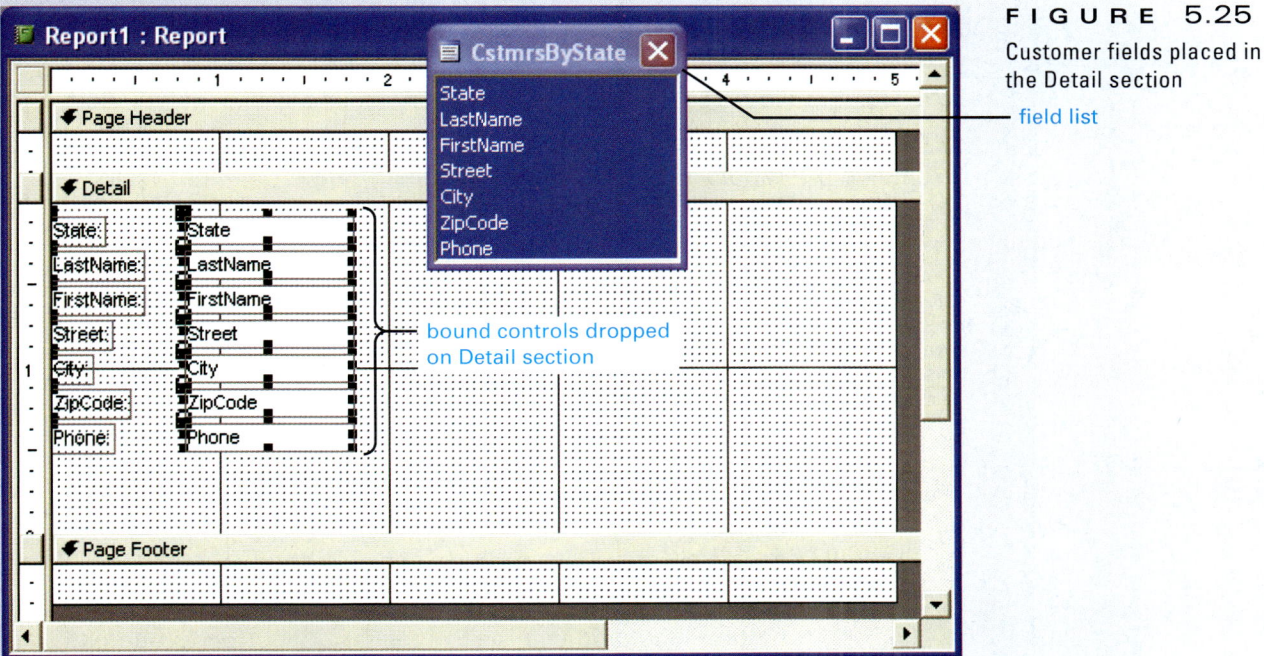

FIGURE 5.25

Customer fields placed in the Detail section

field list

bound controls dropped on Detail section

5. Click on the background to deselect the fields and then close the field list since it won't be used again

6. Use Shift to select all of the labels with field headings and use Cut to remove them from the Detail section

7. Click the **Page Header bar** and paste the labels there

8. With all of the labels selected, activate the Properties pages and change the Font Size to **10** points, Font Weight to **bold**, and Fore Color to the darkest custom blue previously developed

9. Organize and edit the labels in the Page Header and the text boxes in the Detail section as shown in Figure 5.26

FIGURE 5.26

Redesigned Page Header and Detail section

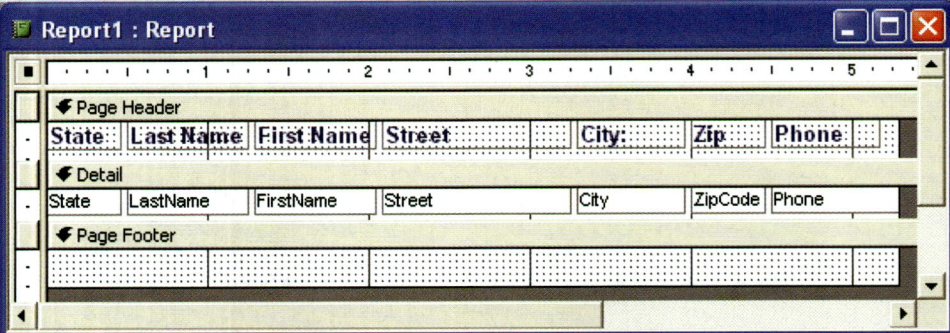

10. Reduce the size of the Page Header section by dragging the Detail bar up until there is just enough room for the labels

tip: *Remember to preview your results. Use move handles and size handles to adjust the position and size of controls. Get the labels and text boxes as close as you can to the positions shown. We'll work on exact alignment in the next set of steps*

11. Organize the text boxes in the Detail section to match Figure 5.26

12. Reduce the size of the Detail section by dragging the Page Footer Selection bar up until there is just enough room for the text boxes

13. Use the **View** button to preview the results. Make any needed adjustments to column widths

14. Save the report as **CustomerByStateDesignView**

In Figure 5.26 the text displaying in the column headings has been changed to match the labels from the form design. You still need to apply those changes to your report. By default, a colon (:) is included after each field name. You will need to remove the colons, add spaces, and abbreviate headings that are too long.

Editing label Captions:

1. Verify that the **ac05KoryoKicks.mdb** database is open and that **CustomerByStateDesignView** is open in Design View

2. Click on the **State** label and use the **Properties** button to open its Properties pages

3. Remove the colon from the **Caption** property

4. Use the drop-down list at the top of the Properties pages to move to the next label (LastName)

tip: *The text box controls are represented by the field name of the data they will contain. Labels are numbered beginning with Label01*

5. Edit this label to remove the colon (:); add spaces between words

6. Repeat this process for FirstName, Street, City, State, and Phone

7. Use the drop-down list at the top of the Properties pages to select the **ZipCode**

8. Remove the colon from the **Caption** and edit it to read **Zip**

9. Preview and save your changes

You also could have clicked in each label and edited the Captions directly. Use whichever method you prefer. Working in the Properties pages can be easier when you are setting multiple properties or working on multiple controls. Editing in the report design is simpler when you are changing the Caption of a label or two.

The foundation of the final report is complete, but the controls need to be aligned exactly before moving on to the other report sections. Access provides an *Align* command that allows multiple controls to be selected and aligned to each other or to the grid. A row of objects can be aligned by their top edges (Align Top) or their bottom edges (Align Bottom). A column of objects can be aligned by their left edges (Align Left) or right edges (Align Right). Once the controls are aligned to each other, drag them as a unit to their exact report position.

For the Customer by State report to look professional, the rows need to be straight and the headings need to align exactly over the data. The Align command is the way to make that happen.

Aligning Customer report controls:

1. Verify that the **ac05KoryoKicks.mdb** database is open and that **CustomerByStateDesignView**, created in the previous steps, is open in Design View

2. Select all of the Label controls in the Page Header section by clicking the first control and then holding down the Shift key to select the remaining controls

3. Activate the **Format** menu, choose **Align**, and then click **Top** to align the tops of the selected controls (see Figure 5.27)

4. Now that the labels are aligned to each other, move them (they are already selected) to the top of the Header section

5. Repeat this process to align the Text Box controls and place them at the top of the Details section

6. Select the State label and hold down the Shift key and select the State text box

7. Activate the **Format** menu, choose **Align**, and then click **Left** to align the left sides of the controls

FIGURE 5.27

Aligning control tops

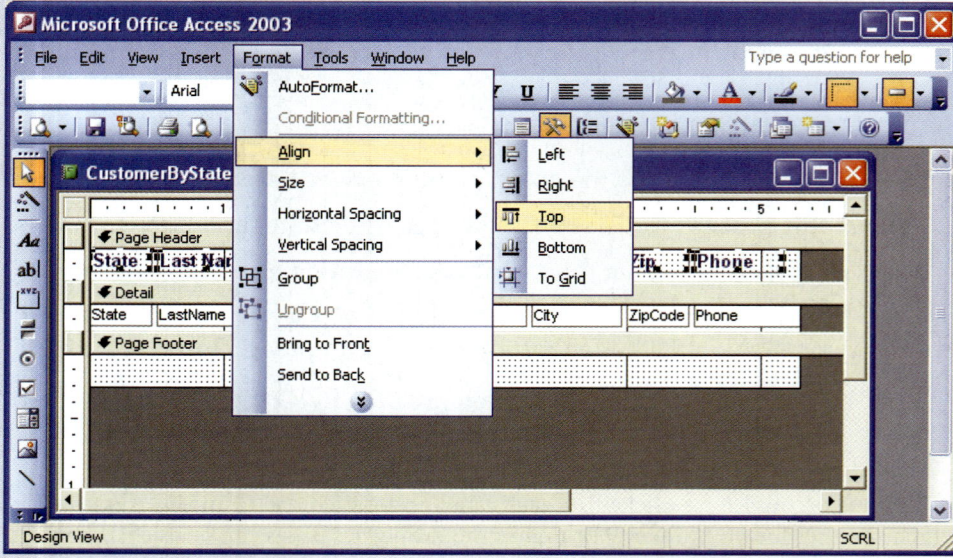

8. Adjust the position of both controls if necessary

9. Repeat steps 6 through 8 for the remaining Header/Detail pairs as needed to make your report look like Figure 5.28

FIGURE 5.28

Aligned report

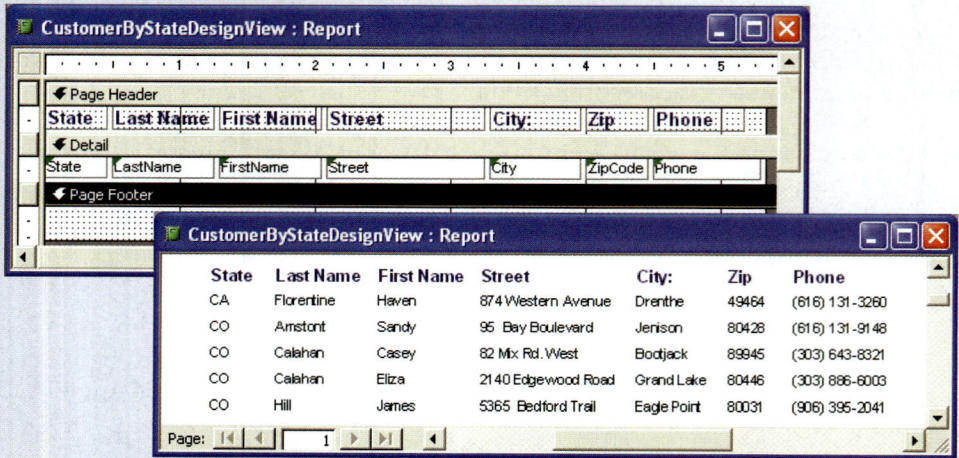

10. Preview and save the report

Now that the detail portion of the report is complete, it is time to add the contents of the Page Footer and the Report Header.

Adding and Modifying Unbound Controls

The remaining elements of the report are composed of unbound controls. Recall that unbound controls are not dependent on the values in the underlying record source. The Page Footer section is already on the form, so we will begin building it. The date and time are added using the *=**Now()*** function, a predefined calculation that returns the current date and time. All calculations begin with an equals sign (=). The format applied to the text box containing the =Now() controls how it will display.

Building the Page Footer

The Page Header was added to the form to contain the field labels. When the header was added, the Page Footer also was added since they are paired. The report displays the report date, time, and page number at the bottom of each page or in the Page Footer.

Adding the Customer report date and time:

1. Verify that the **ac05KoryoKicks.mdb** database is open and that **CustomerByStateDesignView**, created in the previous steps, is open in Design View

2. If the toolbox is not displaying, select the **Toolbox** button to activate it

3. Select the **Text Box** abl tool from the toolbox and click in the Page Footer

tip: *The label displays the word Text with a number. Your number may be different since it reflects what you have been doing in your session*

4. Select the label and press **Del** since the report doesn't need it

5. Select the text box (it says unbound) and use the move handle to move it to the left side of the report

6. Click in the text box and type **=Now()** and use the View button to preview your changes

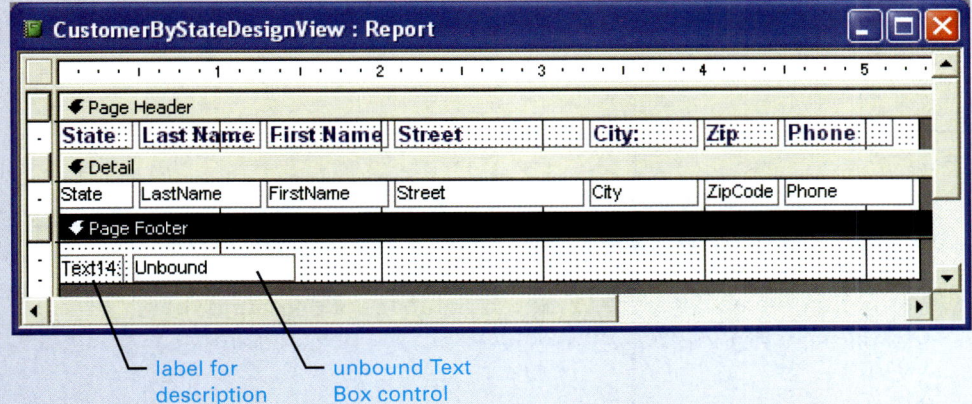

label for description   unbound Text Box control

FIGURE 5.29
Text box with label added to Page Footer

tip: *You will need to scroll to the bottom of the report. Both the date and time should display in one text box until the format is changed*

7. Select the text box and use **Ctrl+C** to place it on the Clipboard

8. Select the Page Footer and use **Ctrl+V** to paste a second copy of the text box in the footer

9. Position the second copy to the right of the first

10. Click the leftmost text box, use the **Properties** button to activate the Properties pages, and set the Format property to **Long Date**

11. Set the Format property of the second text box to **Medium Time** and the Text Align property to **Left**

12. Use the View button to preview your changes and make any needed adjustments to the position and size of the text boxes (see Figure 5.30)

13. Save the report

FIGURE 5.30

Date and time in Page Footer

Two text boxes with the =Now() calculation were used to display the date and time so that they could be formatted the way the twins wanted them. Whenever this report is printed, the =Now() function will retrieve the current system date and time. The Text Box format will cause the first text box to display a long date and the second to display a medium date.

Page numbers are added to a report in a similar fashion with an unbound control and a function. The text box and function can be entered manually or from the Insert menu. Regardless of how the page function is added, it automatically places the correct page number on each page of the report.

---

task reference Add Page Numbers to a Report in Design View

- Display the report in Design View
- Choose **Page Numbers** from the **Insert** menu
- Select the formatting, position, and alignment options that you want and click **OK**

Adding page numbers to the Customer report:

1. Verify that the **ac05KoryoKicks.mdb** database is open and that **CustomerByStateDesignView**, created in the previous steps, is open in Design View

2. Choose **Page Numbers** from the **Insert** menu

3. Choose the following options:

   Page N of M

   Bottom of Page [Footer]

   Alignment—Right

   Show Number on First Page—Checked

4. Click **OK**

5. Use the View button to preview the results (see Figure 5.31)

6. Save the report

Any other information that is to print at the bottom of each report page can be added using the methods demonstrated.

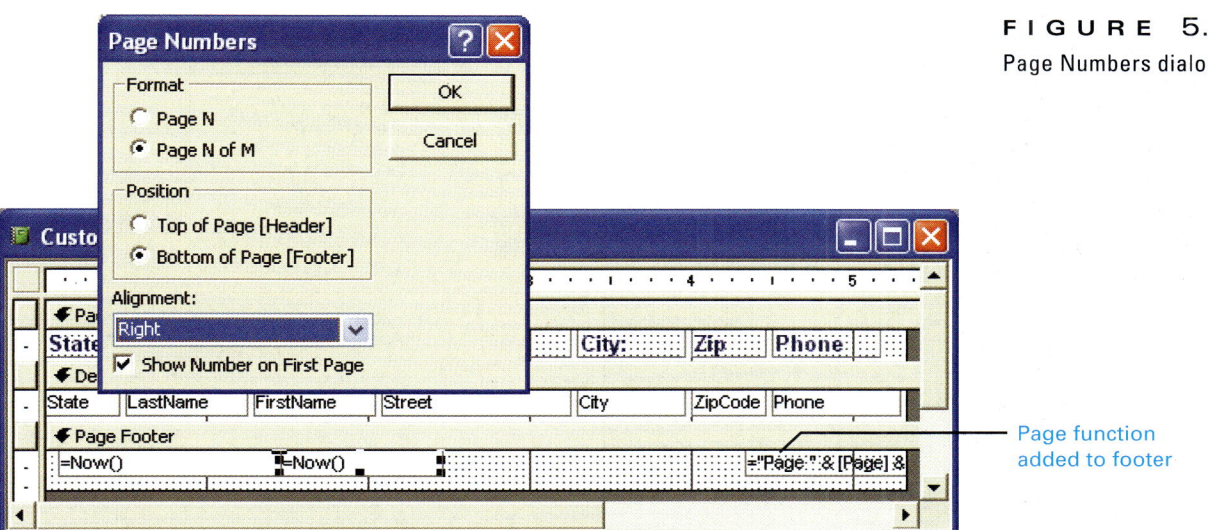

Page function
added to footer

Building the Report Header

To complete the basic report, the Report Header section will need to be added to hold the report title. Recall that a Report Header appears only once at the beginning of a report. The title will be entered in a Label and formatted with an increased font size and color.

Adding the Report Header to the Customer report:

1. Verify that the **ac05KoryoKicks.mdb** database is open and that **CustomerByStateDesignView**, created in the previous steps, is open in Design View

2. Click the **View** menu option and select **Report Header/Footer** to add the sections to the report

3. If the toolbox is not displaying, select the **Toolbox** button to activate it

4. Select the **Image** tool from the toolbox and click the Report Header

tip: If the Image Control Wizard does not initiate, click the Control Wizards button in the toolbox

5. Navigate to the files for this chapter and chose **ac05KoryoKicksLogo.gif** as the graphic to display

6. Select the **Label** tool from the toolbox and click in the Report Header to the right of the logo

7. Type **Customers by State**

8. Select the title label and open the Properties pages, set the Font Size to **26**, and the Fore Color to the custom dark blue (hue **174**, sat **240**, lum **60**, red **4**, green **0**, blue **128**) previously added to the palette

9. Choose **To Fit** from the **Size** option of the **Format** menu to expand the label. Position the label as shown in Figure 5.32

10. Use the View button to preview the results

11. Save the report

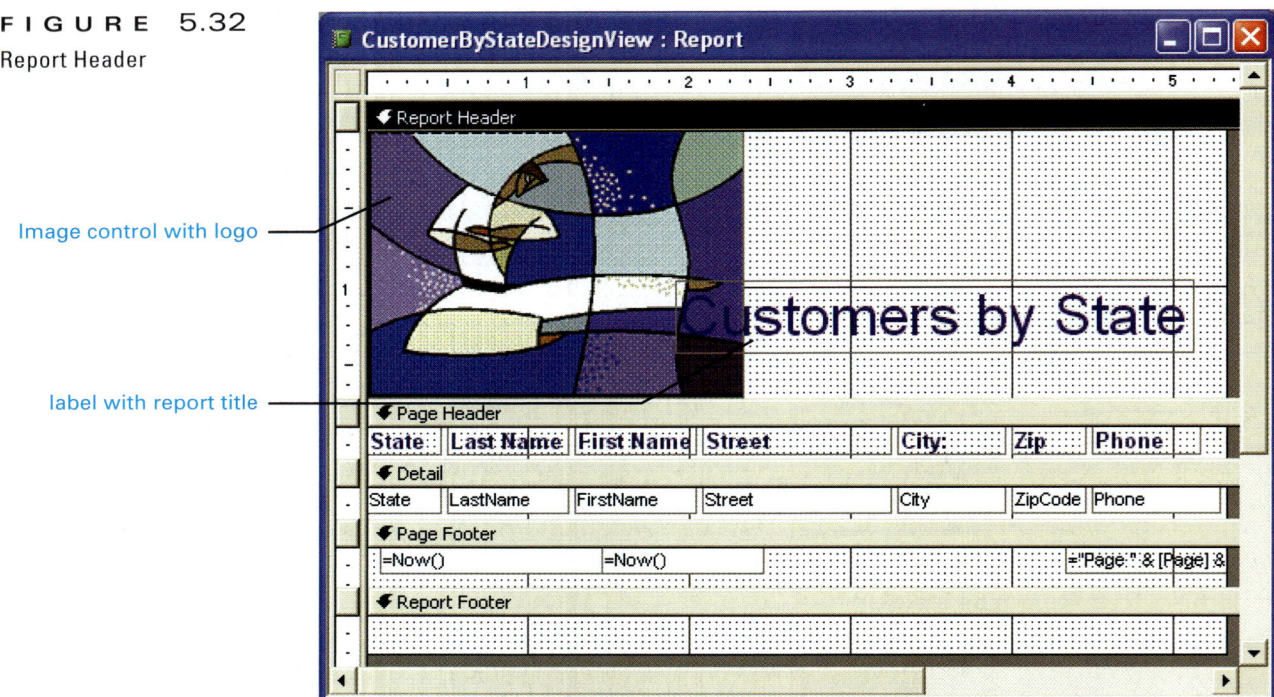

Image control with logo

label with report title

It should now be apparent that creating and using custom colors is easy when they are added to the palette. Custom colors can greatly enhance the professional look of any report.

Adding Separators

The AutoReport Wizard places lines to separate the data from the column headings and Page Footer. The Line control is used to add such separators to your report. Like other report objects, the properties of the line determine how it displays.

Adding separators to the Customer report:

1. Verify that the **ac05KoryoKicks.mdb** database is open and that **CustomerByStateDesignView**, created in the previous steps, is open in Design View

2. Use the Detail section border to expand the height of the Page Header section to make space for the line

3. Click the **Line** ◥ tool on the Drawing toolbar

4. Click in the Page Header section above the column headers, hold down the Shift key, and drag the line the full width of the report

tip: *Holding down the Shift key while dragging a line keeps the line straight. You can use this technique when resizing the line too*

5. Activate the Line's Properties ☞ pages
   a. Set the Border Color to the custom dark blue that you have developed
   b. Set the Border Width to 1 pt
   c. Close the Properties dialog box

6. Use the Report Footer border to expand the height of the Page Footer section making room for the line

7. Select the Line tool and hold down the Shift key while dragging a line above the Page Footer controls

8. Activate the Line's Properties 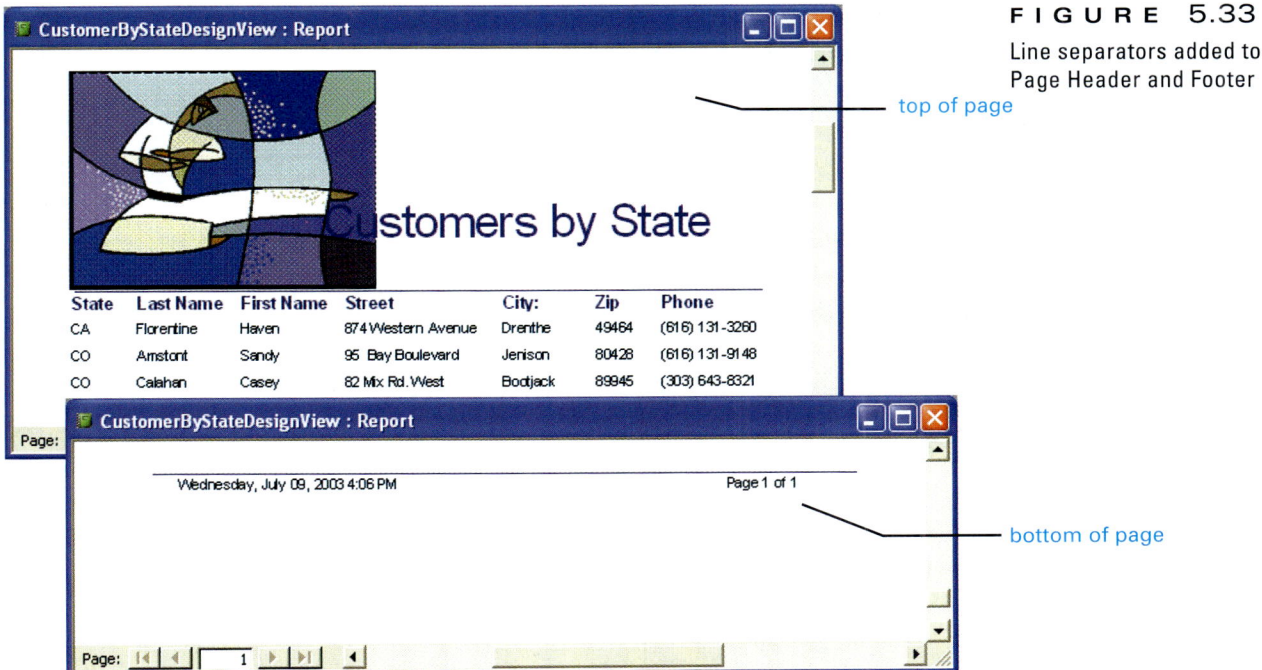 pages and set the Border Color to the custom dark blue that you have developed and the Border Width to 1 pt

9. Use the View button to preview the results and adjust the lines to match the left and right margins of the data (see Figure 5.33)

10. Save the report

Missy and Micah would like the report to present the data in order by state and customer name. They also want the number of customers in each state counted.

Calculating and Summarizing Data

The Design View of Access reports can be used to sort, group, and calculate. The Sorting and Grouping button on the toolbar activates the Sorting and Grouping dialog box where field(s) can be selected or expressions built that will control the order of data presentation. These fields also can be used to group data, to keep records with the same value together, or to calculate subtotals.

Calculating Totals

The simplest calculations involve totaling or counting all of the values of a field. The =**Sum**() function is used to calculate the total of numeric fields. The =**Max**() and =**Min**() functions will return the maximum or minimum value of a numeric or date field. The =**Count**() function can be used to count the number of entries in either numeric or text fields. The Report Footer section is the most likely place for grand totals, since it prints once at the end of the report.

FIGURE 5.33

Line separators added to Page Header and Footer

For the KoryoKicks report, the twins want a total count of their customers so the =Count() function will be used. The equals (=) sign indicates that the text box will display a calculated value. Count is the name of the function that controls the calculation. A field name is included in the parenthesis to tell Access what to count. In this case, it is not terribly important which of the fields is counted, but we'll use =Count(LastName) to count the number of LastName entries in the table. The basic syntax for applying a function is =functionname(field) where field indicates what is to be operated on, like =Count(LastName).

Adding a report total (Count) to the Customer report:

1. Verify that the **ac05KoryoKicks.mdb** database is open and that **CustomerByStateDesignView**, created in the previous steps, is open in Design View

2. Click the **Text Box** abl tool

3. Click in the right half of the Report Footer to add a text box and its associated label

4. Click in the label and type **Grand Total Customer Count**

5. Click in the text box and type **=Count(LastName)**

FIGURE 5.34

Total count of customers

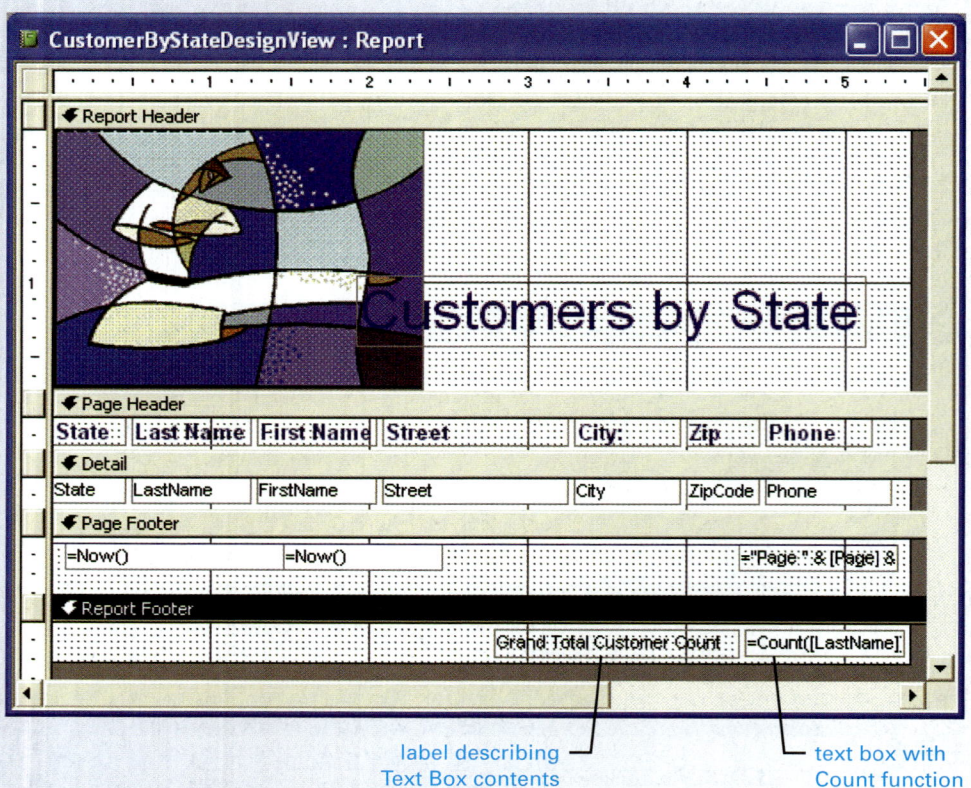

label describing Text Box contents

text box with Count function

6. Use the View button to preview the results

tip: *The Report Footer will appear after the last record but before the Page Footer on the last page of the report*

7. Save the report

One text box is added to the Report Footer for each Grand Total calculation being specified. In a report calculating customer charges, possible calculations include the grand total charge (=Sum), the minimum charge (=Min), and the maximum charge (=Max). Including all three calculations would require adding three text boxes with the appropriate expression in each.

Sorting and Grouping Data

The ability to sort and group data was introduced with the Report Wizard. As expected, sorting controls the order that data are presented in the report. Grouping controls what groups of data are used for page breaks or subtotals. For example, to create a count of customers in each state, the records will be grouped by state. When grouping is applied to a field or fields, the records also must be sorted by those field(s) so that the data to be grouped always present together in the report.

The Sorting and Grouping dialog box allows the selection of a field or fields that will control the presentation order of the report. Each field selected can be further specified to control its sort order and grouping properties. If Grouping Properties are not specified for a selected field, a sort on that field is created. If Grouping Properties are set, either a Group Header, a Group Footer, or both are added to the report design. The contents of the Group Header and Footer must be specified using the techniques covered for other components of the report design.

task reference — Control Sorting and Grouping in a Report

- Display the report in Design View
- Click the **Sorting and Grouping** button on the toolbar
- Use the Field/Expression drop-down list box to select each field that you want to use to sort or group data. Each selected Field/Expression will be on a different line of the grid
- Select the Sort order for each Field/Expression listed. The order of multiple fields determines their priority in the sort
- Select the grouping option(s) for each field
- Close the Sorting and Grouping dialog box
- Add the necessary controls and content to any Group Headers and Footers created

help yourself Use the Type a Question combo box to improve your understanding of grouping data by typing **grouping records**. Review the contents of About grouping records and Change sorting and grouping levels. Close the Help window when you are finished

Adding Sorting and Grouping to the Customer report:

1. Verify that the **ac05KoryoKicks.mdb** database is open and that **CustomerByStateDesignView**, created in the previous steps, is open in Design View

2. Click the **Sorting and Grouping** [≣] button on the toolbar

3. Use the drop-down list box to select **State** as the first sort field, **LastName** as the second, and **FirstName** as the third

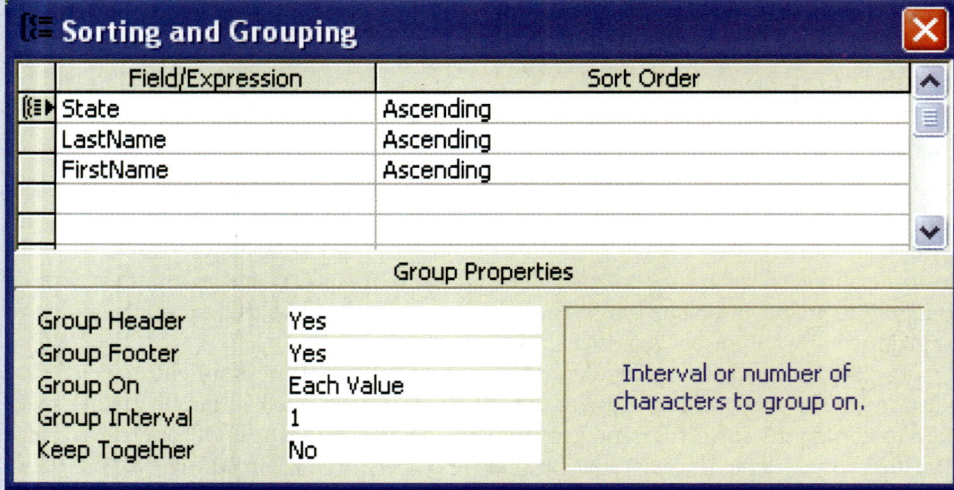

4. Set both the Group Header and Group Footer properties of *State* to **Yes**

tip: *State Header and Footer sections should be added to the report. If you set other fields for grouping, they will add the additional headers and/or footers you specify to the report*

5. Close the Sorting and Grouping dialog box

6. Save the report

Now both the Group Header and Group Footer sections for State need to have their contents defined. A Group Header usually contains the field that identifies the group, in this case State. Since the header prints at the beginning of each new group, placing State in the Group Header section will cause it to print once at the beginning of each new state, rather than repeating the state on every detail line.

The Group Footer usually contains the calculations for the group and any group-specific text. For the KoryoKicks report, the Group Footer will contain the count of customers in a state. This is the same calculation as was entered in the Report Footer section, but in the Group Footer it will be printed at the end of each state and zeroed to begin counting the next state.

Adding State Header and Footer content:

1. Verify that the **ac05KoryoKicks.mdb** database is open and that **CustomerByStateDesignView**, created in the previous steps, is open in Design View

2. Click the **State** field in the Detail section and use the **Cut** button to place it on the Clipboard

3. Click the **State Header** bar and use the **Paste** button to place the State field in this section

4. Click the **Text Box** [abl] tool and then click in the **State Footer** to the right of center

5. Delete the label, leaving only the text box (it contains the text "unbound")

6. Type **=State & " Customer Count " & Count(LastName)**

tip: *Be sure to type the space before and after Customer Count. You can expand the text box using the sizing handles so that you can see the entire expression. Access will convert the statement to =[State]&"CustomerCount"&Count([LastName])*

7. Using the Formatting toolbar, set the State Footer text box properties to **Bold** and **Align Right**

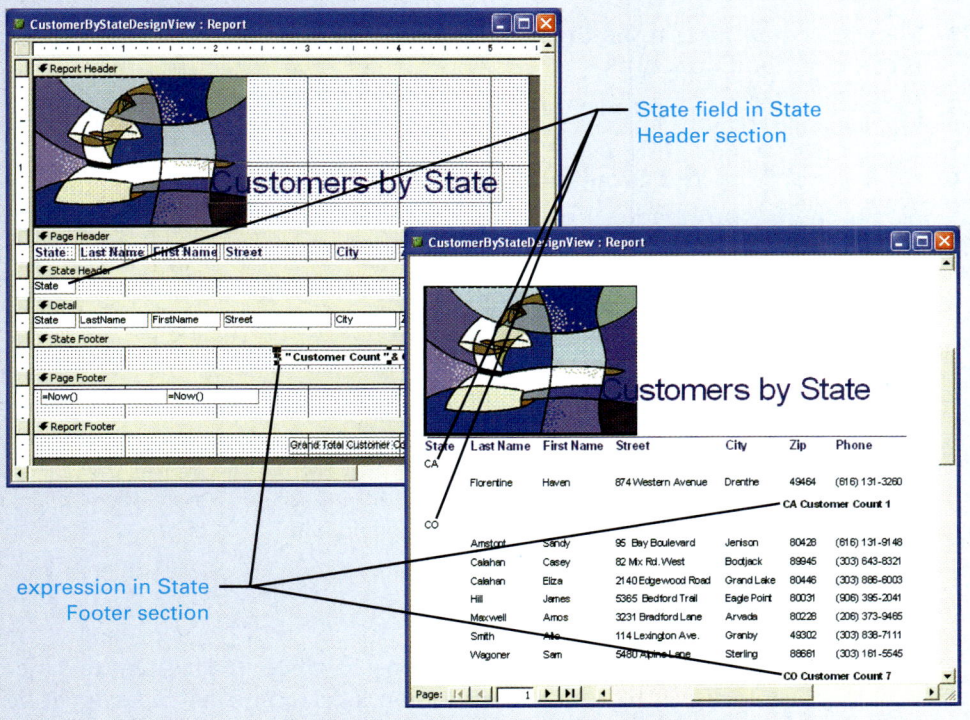

State field in State Header section

expression in State Footer section

FIGURE 5.36

Completed Customer by State report

8. Use the View button to preview the report and return to Design View

9. Save the report

Add one text box to the Group Footer for each group calculation that is being specified. The ampersand (&) operator is used to ***concatenate*** different parts of an expression. When double quotes (") are included in an expression, the values between the double quotes will display exactly as entered, including spaces. There are no double quotes around field names because they will be replaced with the current field value. For example, =LastName&" , "&FirstName would cause the value of LastName, a comma and a space, and the value of FirstName to display in a text box.

The expression used in the report created in the previous steps was `=State&"Customer Count" &Count(LastName)`. This expression causes the current value of State to print, followed by a space, the text Customer Count, another space, and the result of the expression Count(LastName).

Hiding Duplicate Report Values

After previewing the report, the twins decide they don't want State in the Group Header section taking up a whole line of the report. They would like State displayed on the first line of each group. To accomplish this, you will need to put State back in the Detail section of the report, remove the State Header, and format State so that duplicate values do not display.

Hiding duplicate State values:

1. Verify that the **ac05KoryoKicks.mdb** database is open and that **CustomerByStateDesignView**, created in the previous steps, is open in Design View

2. Click the **State** field in the State Header section and use the **Cut** button to place it on the Clipboard

3. Click the **Detail** bar and use the **Paste** button to place the State field in this section

4. Click the **Sorting and Grouping** button
   a. Set the Group Header property of State to **No**
   b. Close the Sorting and Grouping dialog box

5. Click **State** and use the **Properties** [icon] button to activate its Properties pages
   a. Set the Hide Duplicates property to **Yes**
   b. Close the Properties dialog box

6. Using the Formatting toolbar, set the State Footer text box property to the custom dark blue Fore Color

7. Use the View button to preview the report and return to Design View (see Figure 5.37)

8. Save the report

Two final versions of the CustomersByState report have been created. One that uses the Group Header to display the group identification and a second that hides duplicate values in the group field (State). The advantage of hiding duplicates is that more data display on a report page. The advantage of using the Group Header is that it can make the beginning of a group easier to identify.

Lines, boxes, and other formatting can be added to make the groups on your report more clear. Formatting is a matter of preference, but in general keep it simple. Don't use too many colors, lines, or unnecessary indents that can detract from the purpose of the report.

Previewing and Printing Reports

The Print Preview View button on the toolbar has been used throughout the steps to evaluate design changes in a WYSIWYG (what you see is what you get) environment. Print Preview is also used to set up the printer before printing. The Setup button opens

FIGURE 5.37
Updated Customer by
State report

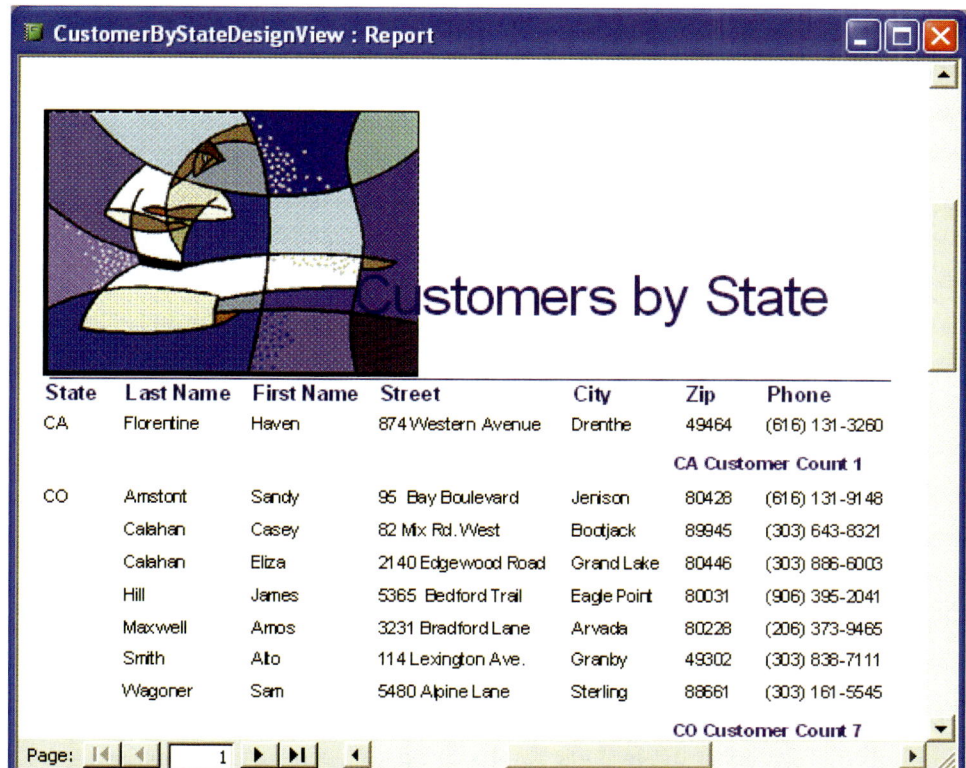

a dialog box with settings for page margins, page orientation, alternate printers, paper source, and other printer-specific options. The settings available from Setup are specific to your software configuration and printer installation, so the options beyond setting margins and page orientation will vary from computer to computer.

Both the magnifier glass and the percent drop-down list box control the zoom of your preview. The three buttons between the zoom controls set the view to one page, two pages, or multiple pages of the report. When uncertain about the function of a button, pause the cursor over it to view Screen Tips. The OfficeLinks button is used to send the report design to other Office products such as Word and Excel. The Print button will send the report directly to the printer without any further options.

Reports have a third view, Layout Preview, that also can be used to view the impact of design changes. A Layout Preview shows only a few sample records to evaluate the overall impact of design updates without reviewing multiple pages of output.

making the grade

SESSION 5.2

1. Describe the function of the Detail section of a report.

2. How do you decide whether to place a calculation in the Report Footer or a Group Footer?

3. What is the difference between a control's sizing handle and its move handles?

4. How do you determine what control to use when building a report?

SESSION 5.3 SUMMARY

Access form and report objects are designed to support different output needs. The form object is used to create screen output used to view and update data. The report object is used to create formal printed output. The output from all Access objects can be printed, but the report object is specifically designed to format printed output. Both forms and reports are bound to a record source such as a table or query.

Controls are the building blocks used to build both forms and reports. The toolbox is a special toolbar that contains controls. The Field List dialog box displays all of the fields from the record source. Bound controls are those that display data from the record source fields. Unbound controls are those that display data not bound to the record source such as report titles, logos, and lines.

The Design Views used to develop both custom forms and reports are very similar. The main design area is called the Detail section. Controls added to the Detail section most commonly display data from the underlying record source. Text Box controls are used to display fields and calculations. Label controls are used to display text that doesn't change such as the report title or field headings. A Line control is used to draw lines on a form or report. The Image control will display a variety of image formats.

The easiest way to add a bound control is to drag fields from the field list. The bulk of bound controls are placed in the Detail section of a form or report. Unbound controls are added to a form or report by clicking the tool in the toolbox and then clicking the surface where the control is to display. For simple controls such as a Label, use the Properties button to activate the Properties pages. The properties of an object control what and how it displays. More complex controls such as the Image control have Control Wizards for step-by-step instructions on setting control properties.

Visit www.mhhe.com/i-series/ to explore related topics.

MICROSOFT OFFICE SPECIALIST OBJECTIVES SUMMARY

- Modifying form properties—MOS AC03S-1-9
- Adding calculated controls to a report section—MOS AC03S-1-11
- Showing and hiding headers and footers—MOS AC03S-3-2
- Aligning, resizing, and spacing controls—MOS AC03S-3-3
- Changing margins and page orientation—MOS AC03S-3-3
- Previewing for print—MOS AC03S-4-2

making the grade *answers*

SESSION 5.1

1. Open the form in Design View. Select all of the labels to be adjusted by holding down the Shift key while you click. Use either the justification buttons on the toolbar or the Properties pages to change the alignment.

2. Bound controls display data from a table or query and are bound to the field that the control will display. The contents of a bound control change as the user moves through records. An unbound control is not attached to a record source and displays static data.

3. Object properties are set using Properties pages, by resizing the object, by moving the object, or by formatting the object. Properties are settings that control how an object appears or behaves. They are set to change such things as the background color, font, or format of an object.

4. Form Design View allows the developer to have full control over the alignment, layout, and properties of form elements. Often forms developed using a Wizard are customized in Design View.

SESSION 5.2

1. The Detail section of a report is used to define the fields that will be displayed for each row of data in the record source.

2. The frequency of the calculation determines where you place the calculation. If the calculation is to print summary information about the groups on the report, the calculation needs to be in the Group Footer. If the calculation is to summarize all of the records in the record source, place it in the Report Footer.

3. Sizing handles are smaller and used to resize the control. The large handle at the top left of a control will move joined controls independently.

4. Controls are chosen by what they are to display. Labels hold text that doesn't change such as the title of a report. Text boxes hold calculations and display values from record source fields. Images hold graphics such as a logo.

task reference *summary*

Task	Page #	Preferred Method
Open a new form in Design View	AC 5.6	• In the Database Window of an open database, click the **Forms** object • Click the **New** button on the Database Window toolbar • In the New Form dialog box, click **Design View** • Select the table or query that will be the record source for the form and click **OK**
Select and move form controls	AC 5.9	• Select the control to be operated on by clicking it. The Shift key can be used to select multiple controls • Drag the control(s) to the new location. Use the large move handle to independently move components of a bound control
Set control properties	AC 5.11	• Right-click the control to open the pop-up menu • Select **Properties** from the pop-up menu • Select the appropriate Properties tab (usually Format) • Navigate to the property and change its setting
Show Form Headers and Footers	AC 5.15	• Open a form in Design View • Select **Form Header/Footer** from the **View** menu

task reference *summary*

Task	Page #	Preferred Method
Add Toolbox controls to a design	AC 5.16	• Open a form or report in Design View • If necessary, activate the toolbox using the **Toolbox** button on the Form Design toolbar • Verify that the Toolbox **Control Wizards** button is depressed (a blue outline will show around it) • Click the Toolbox control that is to be added to the form • Click in the Form section that will contain the control • Set the control's properties using the Properties pages activated with the Properties button
Query an open form with a saved filter	AC 5.21	• Open a form in Form View • Click the **Filter By Form** button • Click the **Load From Query** button • Select the query to be applied and click **OK** • Click the **Apply Filter** button
Create a report in Design View	AC 5.27	• In the Database Window click the **Reports** object and click the **New** button • Click **Design View** as the way to develop the report, select the record source from the drop-down list, and click **OK**
Add page numbers to a report in Design View	AC 5.32	• Display the report in Design View • Choose **Page Numbers** from the **Insert** menu • Select the formatting, position, and alignment options that you want and click **OK**
Control Sorting and Grouping in a report	AC 5.37	• Display the report in Design View • Click the **Sorting and Grouping** button on the toolbar • Use the Field/Expression drop-down list box to select each field that you want to use to sort or group data. Each selected Field/Expression will be on a different line of the grid • Select the Sort order for each Field/Expression listed. The order of multiple fields determines their priority in the sort • Select the grouping option(s) for each field • Close the Sorting and Grouping dialog box • Add the necessary controls and content to any Group Headers and Footers created

TRUE/FALSE

1. A Label control must always be added to a form with an associated Text Box control.

2. You must be in Form Design View to adjust the properties of a Form control.

3. The Align option of the Format menu operates to align selected controls to each other.

4. The largest handle of a selected control can be used to resize it.

5. Control properties can only be updated from the Properties pages.

6. In Report Design View, the field list contains all database fields in the record source that can be added to the design.

FILL-IN

1. Use the _____ key to select multiple controls on a form or report.

2. The _____ property controls the font color of text.

3. The squares that allow you to resize and move controls are called _____.

4. Sections are added to report or form design using the _____ menu.

5. Use _____ to remove controls from a section so that they can be pasted into a new section.

6. An _____ control is not linked to the data in a record source.

7. Use the _____ key when dragging a line to keep it straight.

MULTIPLE CHOICE

1. The _____ control is used to create separators in a report.
   a. Text
   b. Line
   c. Bound Object
   d. all of the above

2. Report page numbers are inserted in Report Design View from the _____ menu.
   a. Tools
   b. Format
   c. Insert
   d. View

3. Calculated report values _____.
   a. are added using an unbound control
   b. must begin with =
   c. are recalculated each time the report is run
   d. all of the above

4. Report content to appear once at the end of the report should be placed in the _____ section.
   a. Report Footer
   b. Report Header
   c. Detail
   d. Page Footer

5. Objects added to a form are layered in what is called _____.
   a. z-order
   b. stack order
   c. control order
   d. none of the above

review of concepts

REVIEW QUESTIONS

Each of the following topics should be addressed in one to three paragraphs.

1. When setting properties for multiple controls, what governs the controls that you can choose?

2. Why should you add a custom color to the palette?

3. Explain the use of grouping in reports.

4. Discuss all of the ways that you can control what records print from a form.

5. Explain why both the form and report objects are needed in Access.

CREATE THE QUESTION

For each of the following answers, create the question.

ANSWER	QUESTION
1. Click the Wizard button on the toolbar	_____
2. Controls	_____
3. Sections, controls, toolbox, grid, and ruler, to name a few	_____
4. Caption, Fore Color, Font Name, Font Weight, and Font Size, to name a few	_____
5. The most efficient way is to use the field list	_____
6. Sorting and Grouping	_____
7. Label control	_____

FACT OR FICTION

For each of the following, determine whether the statement is fact, fiction, or both and present your arguments for that conclusion.

1. You must set properties for every control added to a report or form.

2. Only calculations can be included in the expression for a calculated control.

3. A calculated control stores the instructions on how to calculate a value, not a precise value.

4. The toolbox must always appear anchored to the left of the Design Window.

5. The only way to align controls on a form or report is to use the ruler and grid.

6. A Text Box control added to a form or report in Design View is always accompanied by a Label control.

7. When modifying a form or report in Design View, a pointing hand indicates that a control or controls are being resized.

1. Forms and Reports for Cyberia Coffee Shop

Cyberia Coffee Shop is a Barona, California, neighborhood coffee shop. Besides serving gourmet coffee, Cyberia dishes up sandwiches and desserts. Local bands, Internet connections, and floor-to-ceiling books on every wall provide entertainment. Li Houng, the proprietor, has decided that a database would be helpful in the acquisition of new books. Although customers rarely buy books, they do disappear or fall apart from use. Li needs a way to keep track of what books he has so that he doesn't pick up duplicates. You will use the Wizards and then Design View to create a custom form and report.

1. Start Access and open **ac05Cyberia.mdb**

2. Select the **Form** object and double-click on **Create form by using wizard**

3. Select the **Books** table, move all fields to the Selected fields list, and click **Next**

4. Select **Columnar** and click **Next**

5. Select **Sumi Painting** and click **Next**

6. Click **Finish** and then use the **View** button to change to Design View

7. Use the Detail Selector bar to expand the height of the form header

FIGURE 5.38

Books form and report

8. Click the **Image** control and then click in the Form Header

9. Navigate to the files for this chapter and select **ac05Cyberia.tif**

10. Position the logo in the top left corner and adjust the size of the Form Header to the logo size

11. Add a Label Control to the Form Header section. Place the text **Books** in it, set it to **26** point **Franklin Gothic Heavy** (or another heavy font), and position it as shown in Figure 5.38

12. Save the form as **Books**

13. Create a report that groups the records by author

   a. Select the **Report** object and double-click on **Create report by using wizard**

   b. Move all of the fields to the Selected fields list Group by Author and click **Finish**

   c. Click the **View** button to switch to Design View

   d. Select the Books label and move it to the right

   e. Click the **Image** tool, click in the Report Header, navigate to the files for this chapter, and select **ac05Cyberia.tif**

   f. Move the label Books until it is positioned overlapping the logo. Format it to match step 11. Set Back Style to **Transparent**

   g. Use **Cut** and **Paste** to move the label to the foreground

   h. Adjust columns to match data and add spaces to labels

   i. Save the report as **BooksByAuthor**

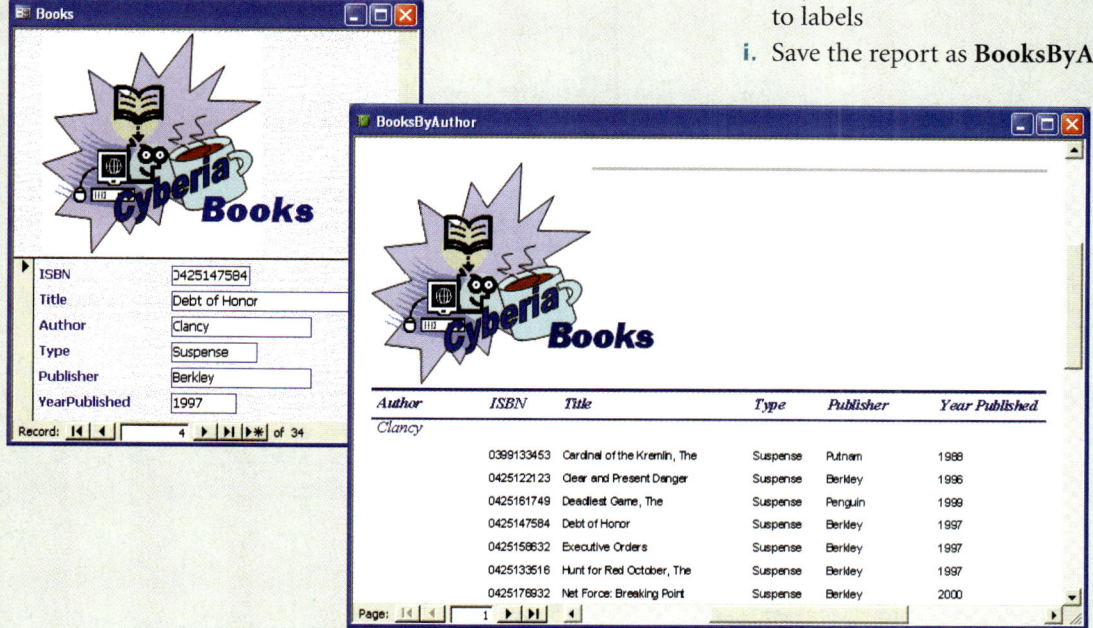

2. Using a Database to Store Student Grades

Prairie Valley College is implementing a centralized gradebook for all faculty members. Currently each faculty member maintains a paper or Microsoft Excel gradebook. The goal of a centralized repository for grades is to improve the record keeping of individual faculty members, allow students to review their own course grades throughout the semester in an automated format, and provide management with necessary grade reports. Test data have been added to the table, and you will be creating a custom form and report for teachers to use.

1. Start Access and open **ac05Gradebook.mdb**

2. Open the **Gradebook** table and review the data. There is one record for each student assignment in each course

3. Use the Form Wizard to create the default columnar form with all fields for the Gradebook table. Use the SumiPainting style and name the form **GradebookUpdate**

4. Use Form Design View to customize the form. Refer to Figure 5.39
   a. Reorganize the fields to match the figure

b. Adjust the field labels so that all text displays and contains spaces. Delete unnecessary labels

c. Adjust the size of text boxes to better fit the data

d. Add a line to separate course data from student data

e. Add the graphic **ac05GradebookLogo.gif** to the heading section of the form

f. Add a Label control to the Heading section of the form and place the text **Gradebook Pilot** in it. Make the text 28 point

g. Preview your results and make any necessary adjustments before saving and closing the form

5. Use the Report Wizard to build and customize the **GradebookReport** with the following features
   a. Create the basic report with the Report Wizard using all the fields from the GradebookQuery. Set the report to Group By Course ID and StudentName. Use the Summary Options to Sum Score. Sort by Assignment. Use the **Align Left 2** layout and the **Formal** style. Use the default name

   b. In Form Design View add a space to the Gradebook Report title

   c. Add the graphic **ac05GradebookLogo.gif** to the heading section of the form

   d. Adjust the position of the Header contents to match the figure

6. If your work is complete, exit Access; otherwise, continue to the next assignment

FIGURE 5.39

GradebookUpdate form and GradebookReport

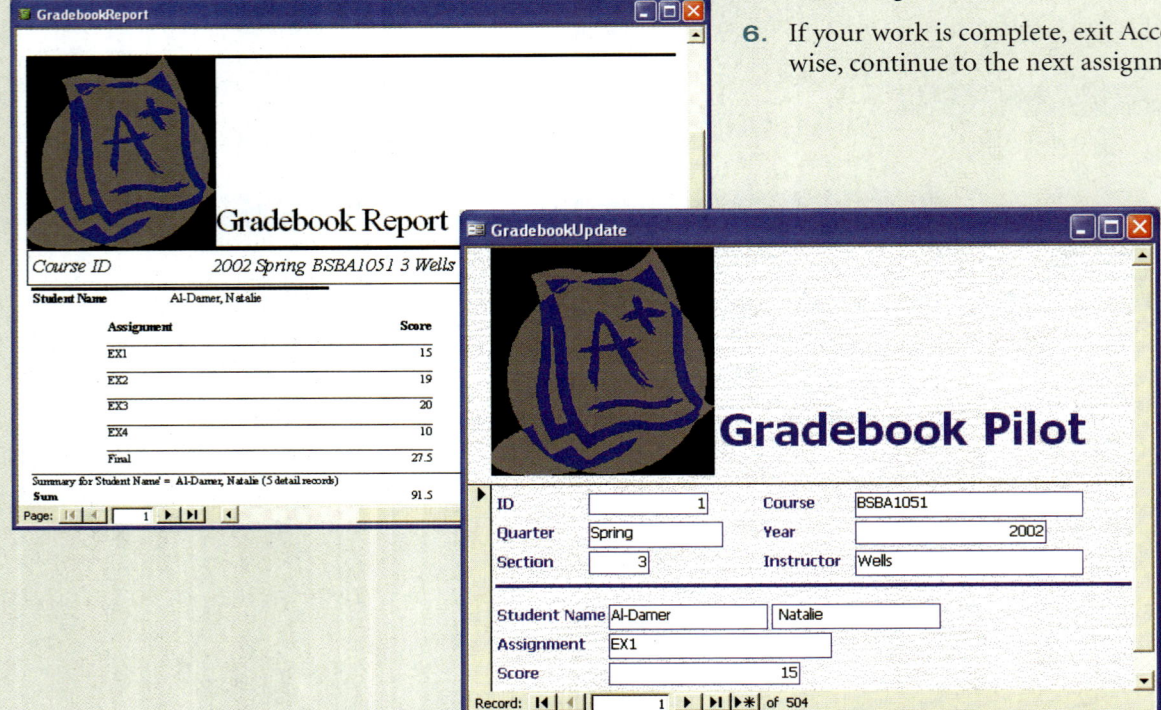

challenge!

1. Sorting and Grouping for Cyberia Coffee Shop

Cyberia Coffee Shop was introduced in the Practice exercise for this chapter. You have developed a form and simple report to help Li Houng track his book purchases. Now he would like reports that his customers can use to find books by a specific author or in a particular category.

1. Start Access and open **ac05CyberiaChallenge.mdb**

2. Open a new blank report on the books table in Design View

3. Use the field list to place all of the Books fields into the Detail section of the report and close the field list

4. Select all of the labels and cut them out of the Detail section; select the Page Header section and paste them there

5. Edit the labels to remove the colons (:) and make them all dark blue

6. Order the labels Author, Title, Type, Publisher, YearPublished, ISBN, and make the Page Header just tall enough for the labels

7. Align the text boxes in the detail section to match the Page Header. Use Report View to make sure

field sizes are appropriate. Make the Detail section just tall enough for the text boxes

8. Add the Report Header/Footer sections and use the Image control to place **ac05Cyberia.tif** in the top left corner of the Report Header

9. Add a label with the properties that cause the text Report Title to display in Times New Roman, 28 point, italic, and dark blue

10. Size the label appropriately

11. Save the report as **BooksByAuthor** and make the following adjustments to the design
    a. Change the title to Books By Author and adjust the size of the label
    b. Use the Sorting and Grouping dialog box to sort by Author and then Title. Display a Group Footer for Author
    c. Use the Properties of the Author control to hide duplicate values
    d. Add a calculated control to the Author Footer that displays an appropriate message and the count of books by each author
    e. Save the report

12. Return to the GroupByTemplate and make the following changes
    a. Save the report as **BooksByCategory**
    b. Change the report title and field order (Type, Title, Author, YearPublished, Publisher, ISBN)
    c. Count the number of reports in each category
    d. Use the Properties of the Type control to hide duplicate values

F I G U R E 5.40

Books GroupByTemplate and BooksByAuthor report

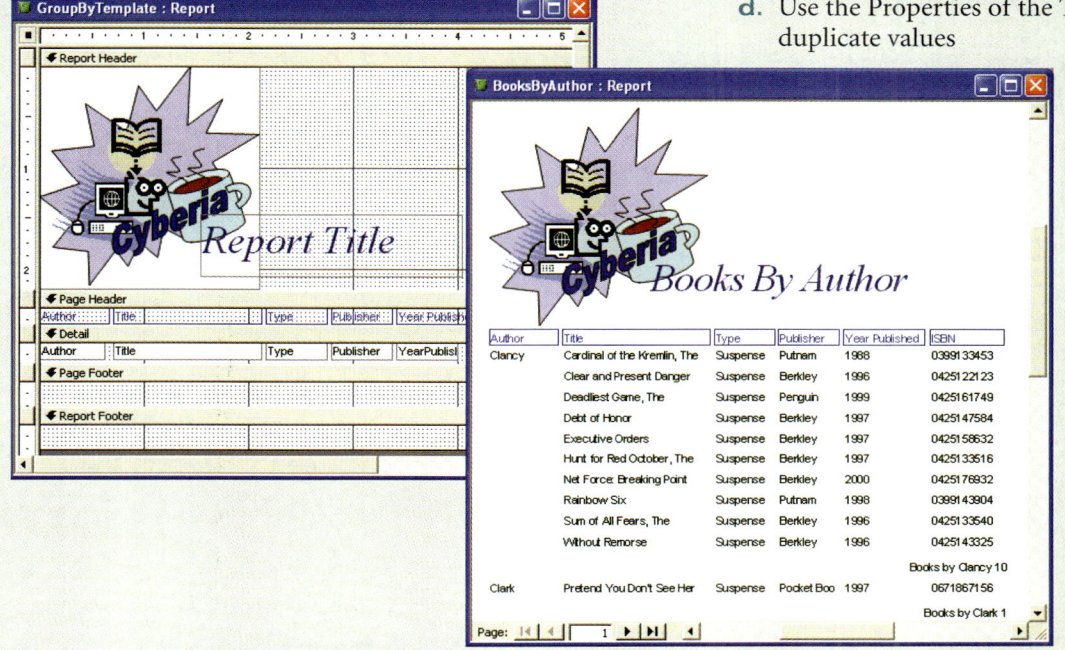

2. Sorting and Grouping Gradebook Data

Prairie Valley College is implementing a centralized gradebook for all faculty members. Testing of the prototype began in a Practice exercise for this chapter. You will continue testing the prototype by building a custom report to list the courses that each student has taken.

1. Start Access and open **ac05GradebookChallenge.mdb**. Review the existing table

2. Open a new blank report on the **SelectDistinct** query in Design View. Add all fields to the report

3. Use the AutoFormat button to add the Corporate style to the report

4. Add a Report Header section and refer to Figure 5.41 as you complete the following

   a. Use a label to add the text **Student Courses Report**. Make the text 22-point extra bold and be sure that all characters display in Report View

   b. Add the graphic **ac05GradebookLogo.gif**

   c. Use the Insert menu to add report run Date and Time. Use the format 6/6/2004 9:36AM. The text boxes will load over the graphic. Arrange the header contents to match Figure 5.41

5. Add page numbers with the format Page N as a centered Page Footer. Show the number on the first page

6. Use the Sorting and Grouping dialog box to sort by an expression that combines student last and first names (=[StudentLast] & "," & [StudentFirst])

   a. Set the Group Header to **Yes**

   b. Set Keep Together to **Whole Group**

   c. Move StudentLast and StudentFirst text boxes into the left side of the Group Header. Set them to 11-point font

   d. Delete the StudentFirst label in the Page Header and make the StudentLast label read **Student**

   e. Place the controls for Course, Quarter, Year, and Instructor in the Detail section. Cut the labels and paste them into the Group Header. Arrange the labels above the corresponding Text Box controls. Refer to Figure 5.41

7. Edit the Label controls so that they do not contain a colon(:). Draw a line under the labels

8. In the Detail section

   a. Adjust the height to fit the controls

   b. Draw a line under the Text Box controls in the Detail section. Make it the same length as the one drawn in step 7

9. Compare your results to Figure 5.41 and make any necessary adjustments

10. Save the report as **StudentCoursesReport**

11. If your work is complete, exit Access; otherwise, continue to the next assignment

FIGURE 5.41
Student Courses Report

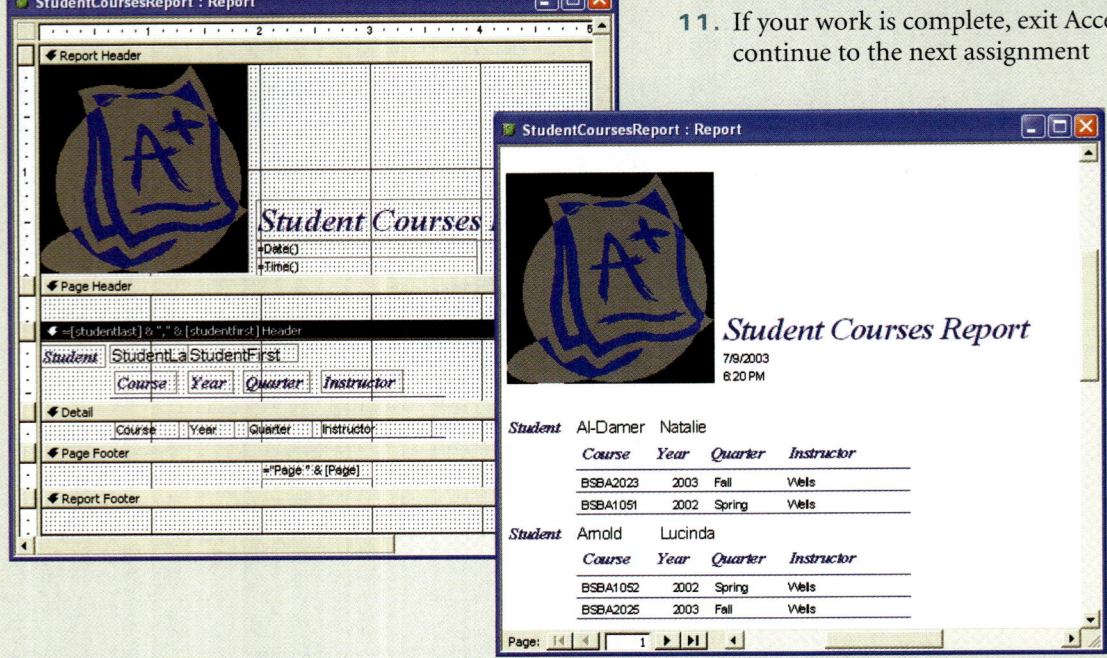

e-business

1. Previewing SportsPix Photographs on the Web

SportsPix is a digital photography operation that specializes in taking pictures of youth sports teams. Ray Damask and Grace Bishop began photographing sports teams when their nephew was playing soccer at the local YMCA. They shoot individual and team pictures for baseball, softball, soccer, football, volleyball, tennis, and martial arts. You have developed a prototype of a Photographs table that you believe will help Ray and Grace. You have selected some test data from the information that they provided and entered it into the table. Create the form and report outlined to ensure the effectiveness of this solution.

1. Start Access and open the **ac05SportsPix.mdb** database

2. Use Design View to create the form depicted in Figure 5.42 for the **Photographs** table

   a. The logo is **ac05Sportspix.tif**. Do not use a Header section

   b. Set the form properties to make the background light blue

   c. Set the Border Style property of all the text boxes to Solid and the Border Color to a complementary darker blue

   d. Align all controls

   e. Adjust the size of all controls and form sections to fit the data

   f. Remove the colons (:) from Labels

   g. Save the form as **PhotoInput**

3. Open the **Photographs** form and add records for yourself and two of your friends. You should all be on the same team and have had your pictures taken at the same time and at the same location. Use Film Id 5443

4. Create the report shown in Figure 5.42 for the **Photographs** table. This report will become a Web page that will allow photographs to be previewed and purchased

   a. Add the logo (**ac05Sportspix.tif**), lines, and colors shown

   b. Add a Group Header for Location and a Group Footer for Team

      i. Set the properties of both Location and Team to suppress duplicate values

      ii. Count the Subjects for each team in the Group Footer

   c. Format Time to ShortTime and ensure that the text box is large enough to display all of the date

   d. Place the report date and Page XX of XX in the Page Footer

   e. Save the report as **PhotosByLocationAndTeam**

5. If your work is complete, exit Access; otherwise, continue to the next assignment

FIGURE 5.42

Photographs form and report

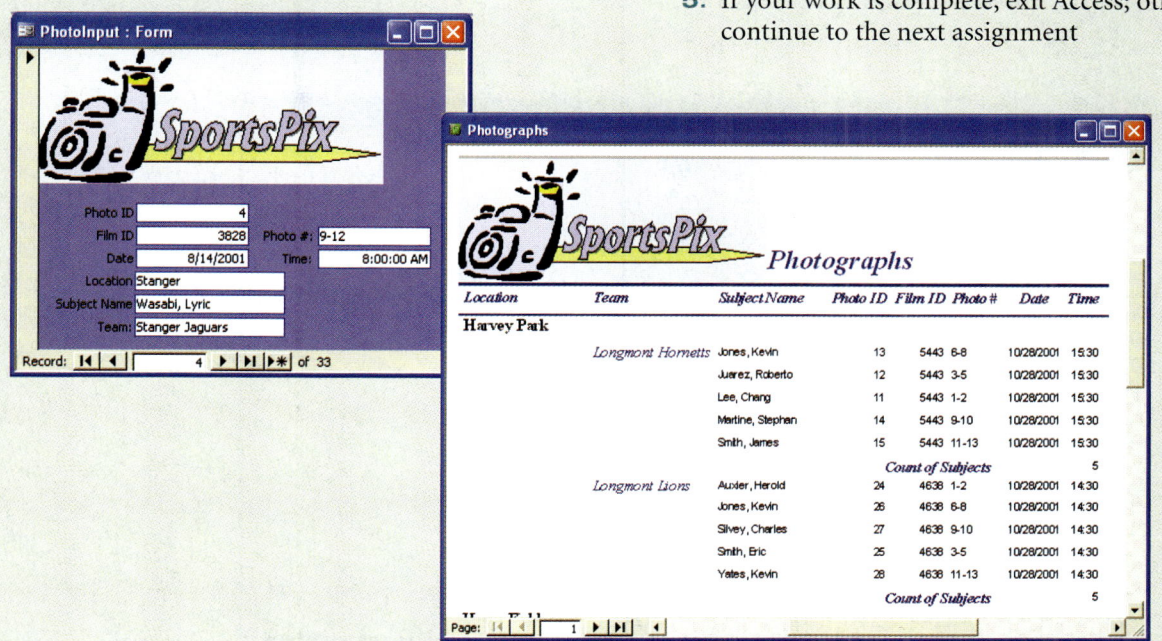

2. Custom Output for NMO Energy

NMO Energy supplies products to consumer energy companies across the United States. NMO maintains a list of current customers for potential clients to review. Some of these companies have agreed to provide references and referrals. This reference list is maintained in Microsoft Access and placed on the company's Web site. You will create a custom form that will be used to update this list and the custom report that will be posted to the Web.

1. Open Access and open **ac05NMOEnergy.mdb**

2. Open the **References** table and review the contents. Close the table

3. Use the Wizard to create the default columnar form for the References table. Name the form **ReferencesUpdate**. Customize the form as follows

   a. Add spaces to separate the words in each field name

   b. Change the color of the text box text to dark blue. Set the Back Style to **Transparent** and Special Effect to **Raised**

   c. Add the logo **ac05NMOLogo.gif** to the Header section

   d. Add a label to the Header with the text **NMO Customer References**. Change the text color to black, the back color to dark blue, and set the font size to 14

4. Test the form by adding a new record for **Excel Energy** with an internal ID of **EXEN**

5. Use the Wizard to create the report that will be available from NMO's Web site. Name the report **CustomerReferences**. The completed report should have the following attributes

   a. Include only the CompanyName field sorted in ascending order

   b. Use the Tabular layout and Corporate style

   c. Add spaces between the words in the title and field name

   d. Add the logo **ac05NMOLogo.gif** to the Header section. Set the title text box back color to dark blue and the fore color to black. Arrange the header objects as shown in Figure 5.43

   e. Add the bullet **aco5DiamondBullett.emf** to the left of the customer name in the Detail section

   f. Extend the line in the Page Header section to match the width of the page

   g. Format the Date to Medium Date. Adjust the size to fit the data

   h. Add a Label control to the right of the date and cause it to display the current time in the Medium Time format. Delete the label. Adjust the size and position of these two controls so that they appear side-by-side on the left of the Page Footer

   i. Add a label to the center of the Page Footer section and place your name in it

6. Close the database and exit Access if your work is complete

FIGURE 5.43

NMO Custom form and report

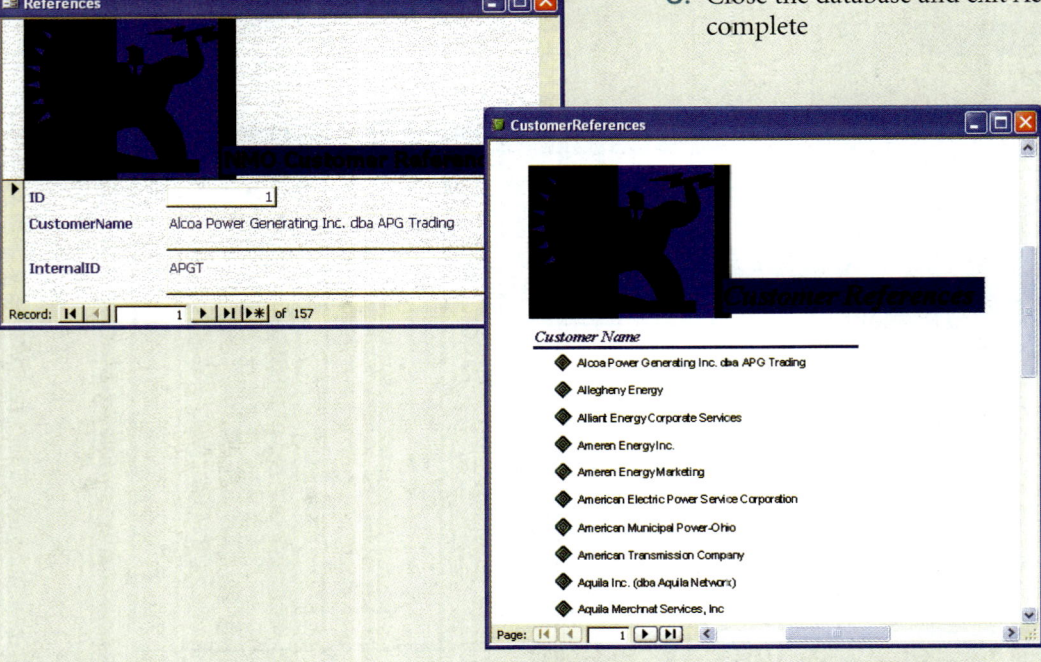

1. Terra Patrimonium Agricultural Chemicals Customer Analysis

Terra Patrimonium (Latin for "land of our fathers") is a company that provides agricultural chemicals, supplies, and services to farmers. Vaughn Michaels, the president and founder, is experienced at using Excel and accounting software but has asked you to help create the database forms and reports needed to support the organization.

1. To prepare for this exercise, use a search engine to find three farm pictures that are representative of healthy corn, barley, soy bean, or sorghum crops

2. Start Access and open **ac05TerraPatrimonium.mdb**

3. Create a new form in Design View to display healthy crops using Terra Patrimonium chemicals. The form will be placed on the Web later

   a. Use an Image control to display the image **ac05TerraPatrimonium.tif** at the top left of the form

   b. Use a Label control to insert **Bountiful Terra Patrimonium Crops** as a title below the logo. Set the font color to brown and the font size to 18 points

   c. Use the Expedition Auto Format

   d. Use Image controls to insert and arrange your pictures

   e. Save the form as **Bounty**

4. Create the form shown in Figure 5.44, save it as **CstmrInput**, and use the form to add the following data starting with CstmrNmbr **150**

Greg Mendenhall	2481 W. State Rd 1000, Monrovia, IA 55738
Kerry Preston	68888 S State Rd 115, Red Oak, IA 51828
Lonnie McCammack	14486 E IA265, Creston, IA 51828
George McCammack	20281 E IA265, Creston, IA 51828
Gordon Foss	74589 South IA 71, Morton Mills, IA 51826
Randy Knetzer	RR 12, Box 217, Osceola, IA 53871
Michael Knudson	2829 Hwy 2 East, Mount Ayr, IA 51627
Bob Kalahari	RR 2 Box 105, Knoxville, IA 51726
Joseph Kabassa	RR 2 Box 162, Knoxville, IA 51726
Jason Van Horne	RR 12 Box 189, Osceola, IA 53871
Dominic Black	RR 1, Box 98, Osceola, IA 53871

5. Make up a phone number for each customer added in 4 and set First Contact to today's date

6. Use Design View to create the report shown in Figure 5.44 and save it as **PhoneList**

7. Use the Sorting and Grouping dialog box to Group by State. Put the State text box in the State Header and suppress duplicates. Add Last Name and First Name sorts

8. Set Last Name to hide duplicates

9. Close the TerraPatrimonium database and exit Access if your work is complete

FIGURE 5.44

CstmrInput form and PhoneListByState report

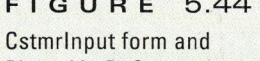

Last Name not repeated

hands-on projects

around the world

1. TechRocks Seminars Forms and Reports

TechRocks Seminars is an organization of independent seminar facilitators who provide onsite technical training to large businesses around the world. The facilitators build curriculum that is marketed by TechRocks. TechRocks books the seminars, arranges facilities, enrolls participants, and collects the money. While the facilitators are not employees of TechRocks, they provide the service that is marketed and their skills and schedules need to be available to all TechRocks offices.

Aisha Jackson has been charged with tracking facilitators and their classification. She has asked you to help develop the reports that will be placed on the company's Web site for use by all of the organization's offices in scheduling seminars.

1. Start Access and open the **ac05Seminars.mdb** database

2. Create a data entry form for the Facilitators table in Design View

   a. Add the **ac05TechRocks.tif** logo to the Form Header

   b. Set the form background color to a blue that complements the logo

   c. Organize and align all controls for effective use and full data display

   d. Save the form as **FacilitatorsInput**

3. Use the Enrollment table to create a report listing the students currently enrolled in each seminar

   a. The field order is Seminar ID, Last Name, First Name, Phone Number, and Student Number

   b. Adjust all controls to display all of their contents

   c. Adjust the color and content of the column headings as shown in Figure 5.45

   d. Align all controls

   e. Add a blue line below the column headings. Create two copies of the line. Place one above the image and one above the heading

   f. Use Sorting and Grouping to sort by Seminar ID, Last Name, and First Name. Add a Group Footer for Seminar ID

   g. Suppress the display of duplicate Seminar ID values

   h. Add a text box with the expression **=[Seminar ID] & " students " & Count([Last Name])** to the Seminar ID Footer

   tip: *Make sure to include the spaces. In this table the field names have spaces and so must be enclosed in square brackets []. The spaces before and after students in " students " prints the spaces after the Seminar ID and before the student count*

   i. Place the report date, time, and Page XX of XX in the Page Footer. Format the date and time to long format

   j. Set the Visible property of the Report Footer to **No**

   k. Place **ac05TechRocks.tif** in the Report Header and add the three labels (one for each word)

   l. Set the position and color of the title labels as shown

   m. Save the report as **StudentsBySeminar**

4. If your work is complete, exit Access; otherwise, continue to the next assignment

FIGURE 5.45

Students by Seminar report

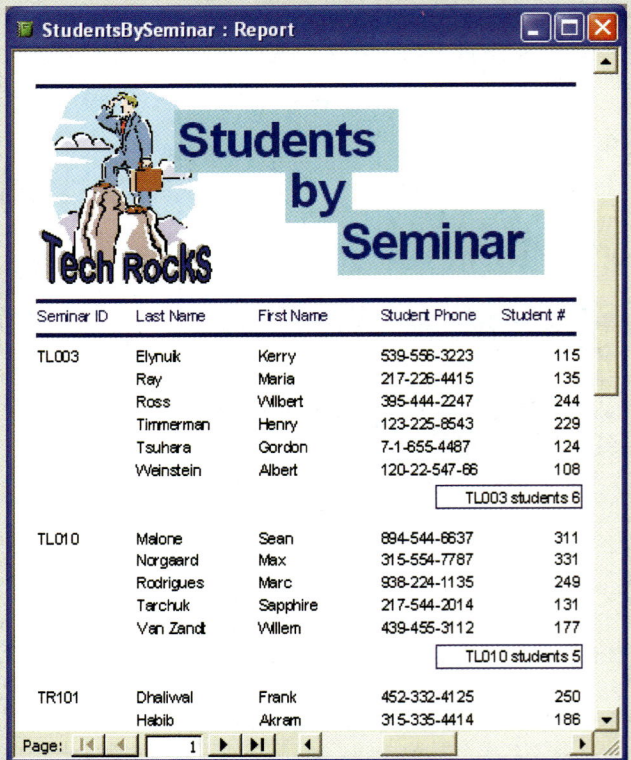

running project: tnt web design

Custom Forms and Reports for TnT

As TnT grows, so does the complexity of its database. Tori and Tonya now have over 65 employees and several hundred customers, so it is becoming critical to have simple data entry and reporting.

1. Start Access and open the **ac05TnT.mdb** database. Familiarize yourself with each table
2. Create a custom form for the Employees table
   a. Use the format shown in Figure 5.46

   tip: *You will need to add Label controls for the Name and Address headers in the Detail section*

   b. Use the **Rectangle** tool to group the data as shown. The Border Width is **Hairline** and the Border Color is a medium blue
   c. Set the Visible property of the Form Footer to **No**
   d. Add the TnT logo from **ac05TnT.tif**
   e. Use two separate labels to add the form title. Make each label 28 point, bold, italic, and dark blue
   f. Save the form as **EmployeeUpdate**
3. Create a custom report for the Employees table
   a. The Detail line contains Job Class, Last Name, First Name, State, and Phone
   b. Adjust the headings, align and size all controls, and set the headings to dark blue
   c. Use Sorting and Grouping to sort the data by JobClass, LastName, and FirstName

   d. Set the Properties of JobClass to Hide Duplicates
   e. Create a Report Header containing the TnT logo and three labels (one for each word) with the report title **Employees** is 28 point, bold, italic, and dark blue. By is 24 point, italic, and dark blue. **Job Classification** is 18 point, italic, and dark blue
   f. Create a Page Footer with the report date (mm/dd/yyyy), military time at the left margin, Page XX of XX at the right margin, and a blue line above it
   g. Set the Visible property of the Report Footer to **No**
   h. Save the report as **EmployeesByJobClass**

FIGURE 5.47

Employees by Job Classification report

FIGURE 5.46

Employee Update form

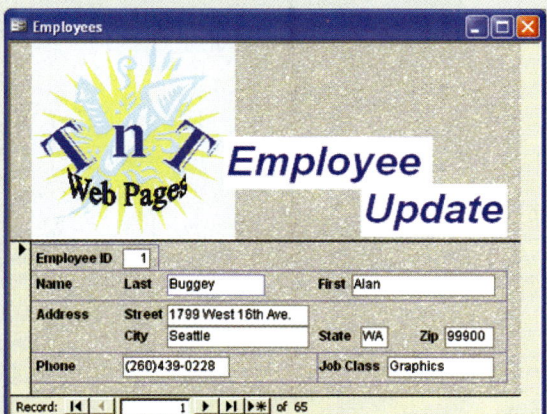

1. Create a Personal Database

A previous Analysis problem in Chapter 1 asked you to evaluate your personal needs and select an area such as classes, grades, or belongings that could benefit from a database. The instructions asked that a new blank database named ac01<yourname>.mdb be created and Wizards used to create table(s) in the database. At least one table should be populated with 10 or more records and then use the Wizards to create an update form and simple report for the populated table.

If you did not compete this assignment earlier, complete it now naming the file **ac05PersonalDatabase.mdb**. If you have already completed this assignment, use Microsoft Windows to rename your file as indicated. Use the skills from this chapter to customize the form and report. Add a graphic to each. Align the controls. Create more effective labels. Add calculations. If necessary, create a new report that uses Sorting and Grouping.

2. Start a Personal Business

The second Analysis problem in Chapter 1 asked you to assume that you were starting a personal services business such as mowing lawns or tutoring and then to create a new blank database named ac01<yourname>Business.mdb. Wizards were used to create table(s) in the database and at least one table was populated with 10 or more records. Wizards were also used to create an update form and simple report for the populated table.

If you did not complete this assignment earlier, complete it now naming the file **ac05PersonalBusiness.mdb**. If you have already completed this assignment, use Microsoft Windows to rename your file as indicated. Use the skills from this chapter to customize the form and report. Add a graphic to each. Align the controls. Create more effective labels. Add calculations. If necessary, create a new report that uses Sorting and Grouping.

CHAPTER six

Defining Table Relationships

did you know?

the *average person takes seven minutes to fall asleep.*

the *dial tone of a normal telephone is in the key of F.*

"live *so that you wouldn't mind selling your pet parrot to the town gossip."—Will Rogers*

cutting *an onion releases a passive sulfur compound created by propanethiol S-oxide gas and enzymes contained in the onion. When this upwardly mobile gas encounters the water produced by the tear ducts in our eyelids, it produces sulfuric acid.*

quicksand *is buoyant. Anything or anyone who steps into it can float much higher than is possible in water alone.*

to *find out who predicted that "No flying machine will ever fly from New York to Paris," in 1908, visit www.mhhe.com/i-series.*

Chapter Objectives

- **Review the types of table relationships**
- **Build table relationships in the Relationships window—MOS AC03S-1-5**
- **Change the properties of table relationships including join type and referential integrity—MOS AC03S-1-6**
- **Query multiple tables**
- **Create and use multitable custom forms including subdatasheets and subforms**
- **Create multitable custom reports**
- **Identify object dependencies—MOS AC03S-4-1**

KoryoKicks: Relating and Indexing Tables

The data, forms, and reports for KoryoKicks are shaping up nicely. Missy and Micah are very comfortable entering data, running queries, and printing reports. They have enjoyed learning about the Design View of reports and forms and even like manipulating the controls and properties to get exactly the look and performance they want. Missy and Micah are accomplished users of the database that you have set up, but they want to be able to develop their own databases so that they are no longer dependent on outside expertise.

Although the twins were very involved in every stage of developing the current database and even built some of the components with your help, they do not understand how to set up tables, relationships, queries, forms, and reports without assistance. They still have lots of questions about how database objects really work such as:

- What records are retrieved when multiple tables are involved in a Select Query?
- How can the data from all KoryoKicks tables be maintained from one form?
- Why can't an order be added before Customer data is placed in the Customer table?
- What is the point of indexing a field or group of fields? How can you tell if indexing has done any good?
- Why use a query to build a form or report instead of just going directly to the tables involved?
- What is stopping us from modifying and deleting records for customers that have been entered with errors?
- We keep hearing that SQL is the language of relational databases. We haven't see any SQL yet, so where is it?

You and the twins sit down and develop a plan to address their questions and improve their comfort level with the inner workings of Microsoft Access. Since the twins are very comfortable with the use of single tables to create queries, forms, and reports, you will start with table relationships and how they impact output. Figure 6.1 displays some of the components that will be used in this process.

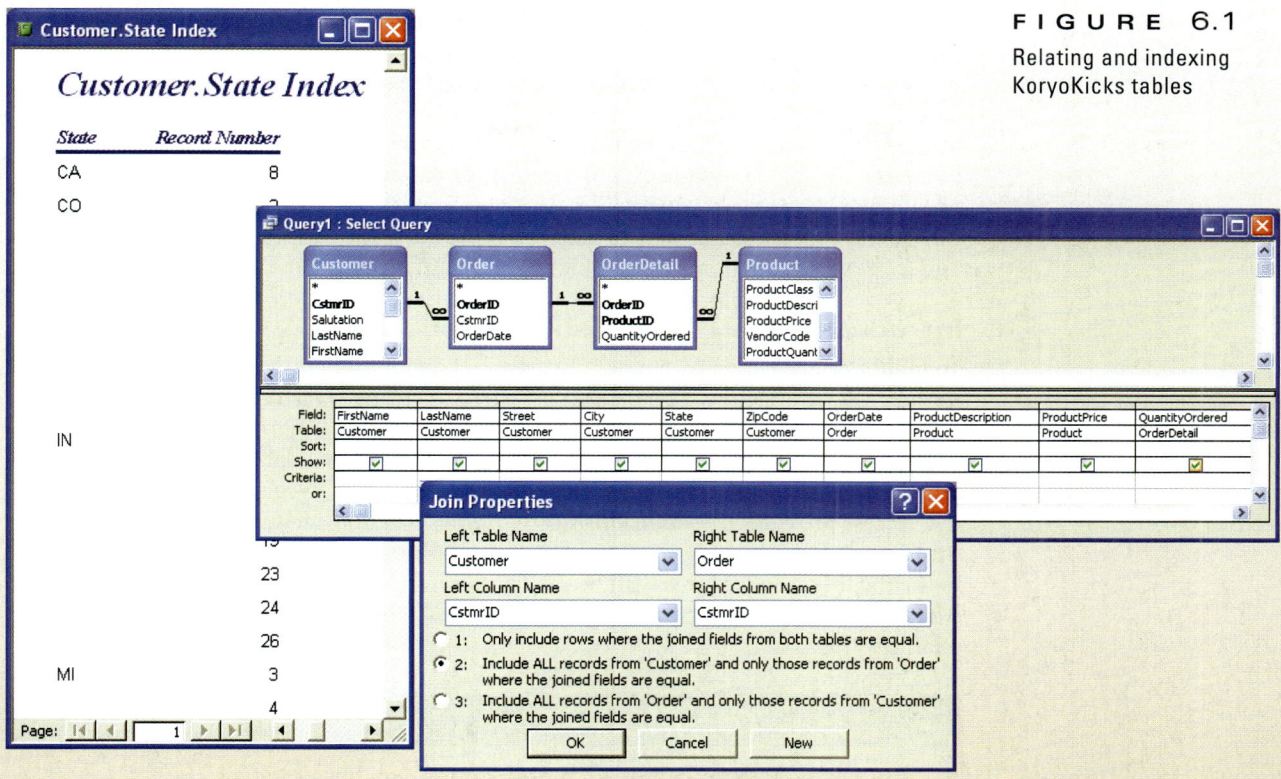

FIGURE 6.1

Relating and indexing
KoryoKicks tables

SESSION 6.1 RELATING TABLES

Chapter 1 introduced the concepts and terminology of relational database management systems. Subsequent chapters presented methods of using these database objects (tables, queries, forms, and reports) to view and manipulate the data held in a single table.

Chapter 2 discussed how to properly design relational databases using a common-sense version of the more formal normalization rules. Data are placed in multiple tables to reduce redundancy and increase integrity. Defining common table fields (foreign keys) so that data from multiple tables could be joined using queries was presented as an integral component of effective design.

The focus of this chapter is learning to build and use table relationships. It is not enough to create table designs with common fields in related tables. Like all other database objects, relationships have properties. The properties of each relationship must be correctly defined for the relationship to behave as expected.

Understanding Types of Relationships

Table relationships fall into one of three general categories: one-to-one (1:1), one-to-many (1:∞), or many-to-many (∞:∞). This notation identifies how many records in the first table are related to how many records in the second table. Thus, the one-to-many notation means that one record from the ***primary table*** is related to many records in the ***related table***. In the KoryoKicks database, one customer can place many orders, so the relationship between the Customer and Orders tables is one-to-many.

Many-to-many relationships must be broken into multiple one-to-many relationships in the design phase of relational database development. Many-to-many relationships between tables are accommodated in databases by adding a junction table. A junction table contains the primary key columns of the two tables to be related. A one-to-many relationship from the primary key columns of each of those two tables is then created to the matching columns in the junction table. In KoryoKicks the relationship between the Order and Product tables would be a many-to-many relationship. One order can involve multiple products and one product can appear on multiple orders. OrderDetail is a junction table containing the primary key from both Order and Product.

Introducing the Relationships Window

To build a relationship, two tables must share a common field, but the fields do not have to carry the same name. The fields must carry the same Data Type and Field Size. Since all many-to-many relationships are broken down at design time, only one-to-one or one-to-many relationships will be defined in an active relational database. One-to-one relationships are less common, so we will concentrate on one-to-many relationships.

Access provides the *Relationships window* to define, view, and edit table relationships. In a properly designed database, every table is related to at least one other table in the database. Some tables can be related to multiple tables. It is also possible to relate a table to itself. It is important to know which table is the primary table when building relationships.

> **task reference**   View Table Relationships
>
> - Click the **Relationships** button on the Database toolbar
> - If relationships exist, they will be displayed. If there are no current relationships, you can add tables and build relationships between them

Viewing KoryoKicks relationships:

1. Verify that the **ac06KoryoKicks.mdb** database is open (see Figure 6.2)
2. Click the **Relationships** button on the Database toolbar

tip: It does not matter what database object is active during this process

3. Leave the Relationships window open so that you can refer to it as it is being discussed

The Relationships window for KoryoKicks (see Figure 6.2) shows a field list for each table with relationship lines depicting how the tables are related to each other. The notation on the relationship line indicates the type of relationship and which table is primary in the relationship. For example, the Customer.CstmrID (CstmrID field of the Customer table) field defines a one-to-many relationship with the Order.CstmrID (CstmrID field of the Order table). The Customer table is primary in this relationship since it is on the one side, meaning that each Customer.CstmrID record can link to multiple Order.CstmrID records.

The Customer table is related to one other database table, Order. The Order table, however, is related to both the Customer and the OrderDetail tables. Order is the related table in the Customer/Order relationship and the primary table in the Order/OrderDetail relationship. When speaking of related table pairs, it is customary to list the primary table first.

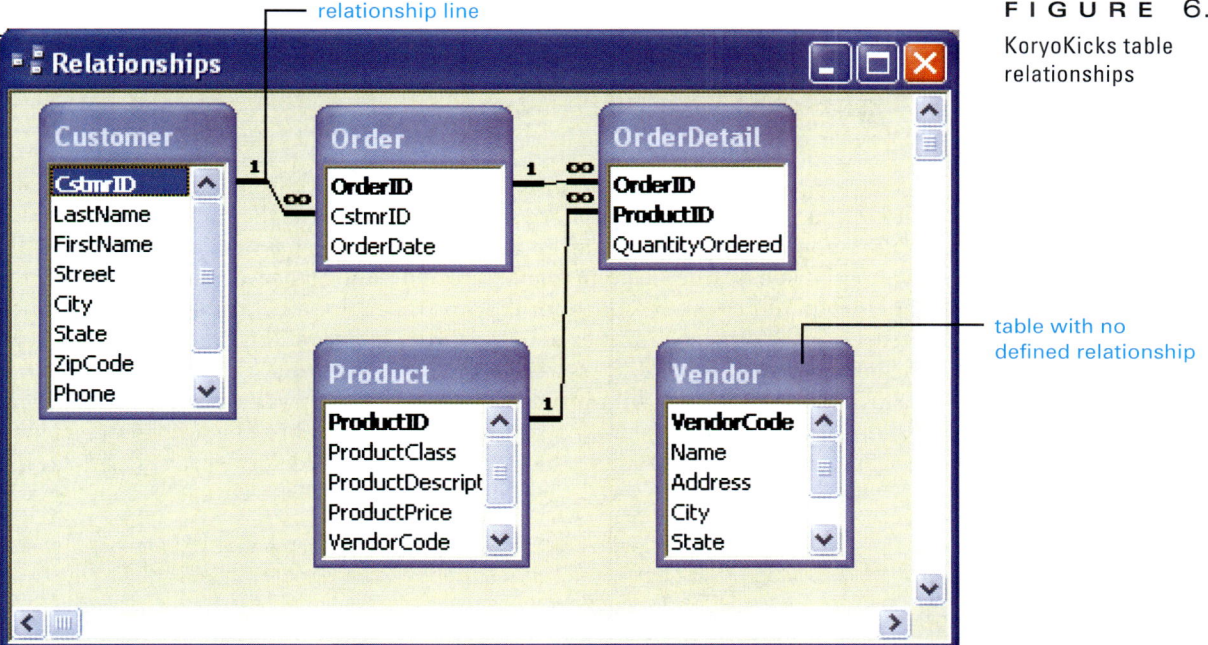

Think about invoices or bills that you have received. They contain your name, address, an order or invoice number, and each product that you ordered with a description and a quantity. Take a look at the KoryoKicks relationships and find all of the components needed for an invoice. It should be clear by now that without the ability to join tables, users would be restricted to working with the data from each table independently. In such an environment, KoryoKicks would not be able to combine data from the Customer, Order, and Product tables to create an invoice since the Customer table holds the customer's name and address, the Order table contains the order date, the Order Detail table holds the quantity ordered, and the Product table holds descriptions of each product.

The KoryoKicks invoice needs fields from each of the tables. Let's look at the relationships from a business perspective to understand what they mean in practice. Here are the KoryoKicks relationships from left to right in the Relationships window:

- One customer can place multiple orders
- One order can have multiple details (products and quantities)
- One product can appear on multiple order details

Ideally relationships are defined before any data are placed in the related table, but there is nothing in Access to prevent adding or editing relationships in an active database. Adding or changing the properties of relationships is governed by the rules of referential integrity. Your efforts to add or edit relationships also will be governed by these rules.

Referential Integrity

The rules of referential integrity govern table relationships and are sometimes referred to as parent/child rules. These rules prevent "orphans" such as an OrderDetail for a product that is not in the Products table or an order for a CstmrID that is not in the Customer table. For a relationship to be valid,

- The primary record must exist before a secondary record of that foreign key can be added to the related table (parent key must exist before the child can use that key)

- Changing the value of the primary table field that governs the relationship is not allowed if there are related records (the parent cannot be removed while it still has children)
- Deleting the record in the primary table is not allowed if there are related records (the parent cannot be deleted while it still has children)

Take another look at the KoryoKicks Relationships window. What referential integrity means in practice is that the record on the one side of the relationship must exist before any related records can be added on the many side. For example, in the KoryoKicks database, the Customer table record defining a new customer must be created before an Order can be added for that customer. For an OrderDetail record to be created, both the OrderID must exist in the Order table and the ProductID must exist in the Product table.

Further, the parent record cannot be deleted or its key value changed while there are still related child records. In KoryoKicks, a customer cannot be deleted or assigned a new CstmrID in the Customer table while there are orders for that CstmrID in the Order table.

help yourself *Use the Type a Question combo box to improve your understanding of table relationships by typing* **referential integrity**. *Review the contents of* About table relationships. *Close the Help window when you are finished*

Cascade Update and Delete

Double-clicking on a relationship line will open the Edit Relationships dialog box, which displays the properties of that relationship. When table relationships are defined, an option is provided to not enforce referential integrity (a very bad idea for data integrity). When referential integrity is enforced, there are options on how it is enforced.

The referential integrity options are check boxes shown in Figure 6.3 that are labeled:

- Enforce Referential Integrity, which should always be checked
- Cascade Update Related Fields
- Cascade Delete Related Records

When *Cascade Update Related Fields* is checked, any changes made to the key value of the primary table also will be applied to records in the related table. With this option, if you need to change a CstmrID for some reason, making the change in the Customer table would also update the CstmrID of related child records in the Order table.

Selecting the *Cascade Delete Related Records* check box will cause related records to be deleted when the primary record is deleted. In KoryoKicks, deleting a customer from the Customer table will also delete all orders for that customer. Cascade deletes are not always a good idea since it would allow a customer and all of the customer's orders to be deleted without verifying each delete.

---

task *reference*   **View Relationship Properties**

- Click the **Relationships** 🔳 button on the Database toolbar
- If relationships exist, they will be displayed. If there are no current relationships, you can add tables and build relationships between them
- Double-click the relationship line that you would like to view
- The Edit Relationships dialog box displays the properties of that relationship

primary table and field(s)
defining the relationship

related table and field(s)
defining the relationship

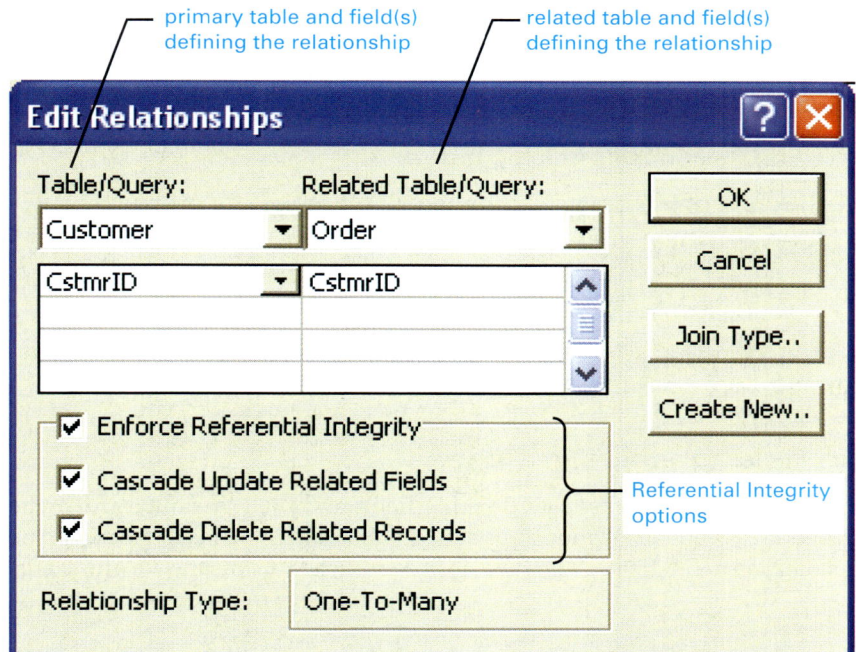

FIGURE 6.3

Edit Relationships dialog box

Referential Integrity options

Viewing KoryoKicks relationship properties:

1. Verify that the **ac06KoryoKicks.mdb** database is open

2. If you are not currently viewing the Relationships window, click the **Relationships** button on the Database toolbar

3. Double-click the one-to-many relationship line between Customer and Order

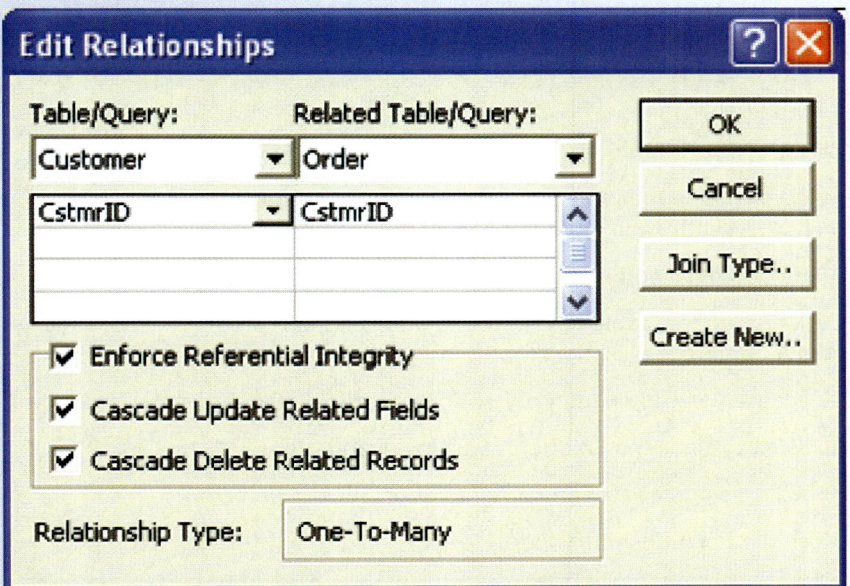

FIGURE 6.4

Customer/Order Edit Relationships dialog box

ACCESS

4. Notice that the common field is named CstmrID in both tables, the refer-ential integrity is enforced, and both cascade updates and deletes are activated

5. Close the Edit Relationships dialog box

6. Double-click one of the other relationships and review its properties

7. Close **ac06KoryoKicks.mdb**

Now that existing relationships have been explored, let's take a look at how to build new relationships.

Creating Relationships in Access

Building a new database table involves defining fields and their attributes. After the table definitions are complete, relationships between tables in the same database can be built using common table fields. This task is accomplished using the Relationships window.

One-to-One

One-to-one relationships exist when one record in the primary table is related to no more than one record in the related table. Normally the data in the related table would be part of the primary table, so these relationships are not common. They are created when the data in the related tables are used infrequently or when the primary table size exceeds the Access limit, causing the table to be split.

Both tables in a one-to-one relationship have the same primary key. When a rela-tionship is created from the primary key of one table to the primary key of another table, a one-to-one relationship is defined. We'll demonstrate this by creating a rela-tionship between the KoryoKicks Customer table and a dummy table created for this purpose, CustomerPart2.

---

task reference   Create a Relationship

- Click the **Relationships** [icon] button on the Database toolbar

- If relationships exist, they will be displayed

- Click the **Show Table** [icon] button on the toolbar

- Select the table that you want to relate and click the **Add** button. Repeat this process for each table to be related

- When you have added all of the necessary tables, click **Close**

- Click the primary table field of the relationship and drag to the secondary field to initiate the relationship

- Select the Referential Integrity options in the Edit Relationships dialog box

- Click **OK** to close the Edit Relationships dialog box

- Repeat this process for any other relationships to be built

- Close the Relationships window

Building a one-to-one relationship:

1. Verify that the **ac06KoryoKicks.mdb** database is open

2. Use the **Relationships** button from the toolbar to activate the Relationships window (see Figure 6.5)

3. Click the **Show Tables** button from the toolbar to display the list of tables that can be related

4. Select the **CustomerPart2** table and click the **Add** button to add the second table of customer data

5. **Close** the Show Table dialog box

6. Click **Customer.CstmrID** and drag to **CustomerPart2.CstmrID** to open the Edit Relationships dialog box for this relationship

tip: *Recall that the notation Customer.CstmrID identifies the table.field*

7. Click on all of the referential integrity options to enforce referential integrity and activate cascade updates and deletes

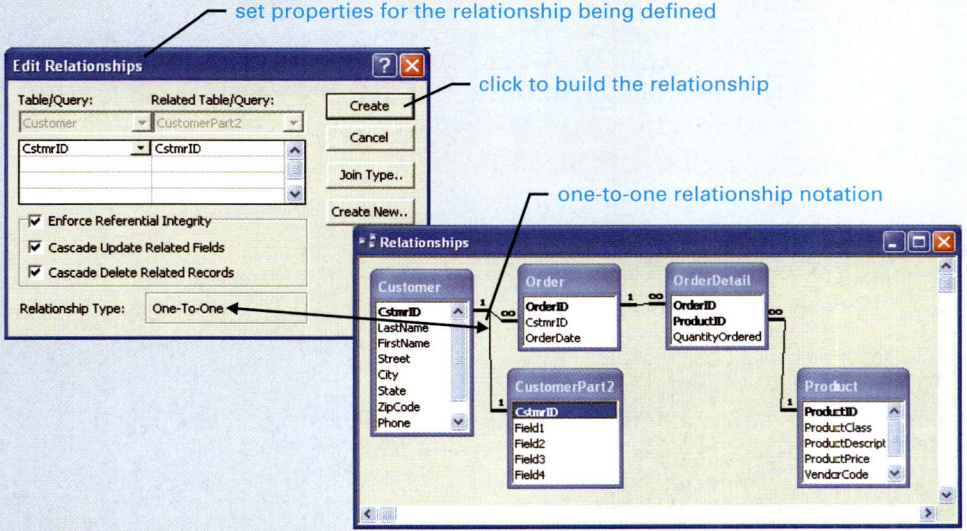

FIGURE 6.5

One-to-one relationship

8. Click **Create**

9. Close the Relationships window and click **Yes** to save your changes

This relationship was created for demonstration purposes and is not functional for KoryoKicks. A relationship sometimes needs to be deleted from a production database because it was created in error, or is no longer needed. Delete a relationship in the Relationships window by clicking the relationship line and then pressing the Del key.

Since the CustomerPart2 table is not needed, both the table and the relationship just built will be deleted. Deleting either table in the relationship also deletes the relationship. A table can be deleted from the Tables object list in the Database Window or from the Relationships window. Deleting the table from the Database Window permanently removes it from the database.

Deleting a table and its associated relationships:

1. Verify that the **ac06KoryoKicks.mdb** database is open

2. In the Database Window, click on the **Tables** object

3. Select the **CustomerPart2** table and click **Del**; respond **Yes** to both delete prompts

FIGURE 6.6

Deleting a table and its relationships

4. Use the **Relationships** button to open the Relationships window and verify that update

5. Leave the Relationships window open for the next steps

Table deletes cannot be undone, so execute them with caution. Using Windows Backup utilities to create a backup copy of a database before deleting tables is advisable.

One-to-Many

One-to-many relationships, when one record in the primary table can be related to multiple records in the related table, are the most common relationship type. Creating a one-to-many relationship is very similar to the technique just reviewed to create one-to-one relationships.

Both tables in a one-to-many relationship have the same field or foreign key. This shared field *cannot* be the primary key of the related (second) table although it may be one field in a composite primary key. Clicking the field in the primary table and dragging it to the related field in the second table opens the Edit Relationships window. Set the relationship properties, most importantly referential integrity, and click Create to build the relationship.

Building a one-to-many relationship:

1. Verify that the **ac06KoryoKicks.mdb** database is open

2. Click the **Show Tables** button on the toolbar to display the list of tables that can be related

3. Add the table **Vendor** to the Relationships window. Close the Show Tables dialog box

tip: *You can drag the Title bar of a table to move it in the Relationships window*

4. Click and drag a relationship from **Vendor.VendorCode** to **Product.VendorCode**

tip: *If you miss and build the relationship between the wrong fields, select the relationship line and press **Del***

5. Check only Enforce Referential Integrity and click **Create**

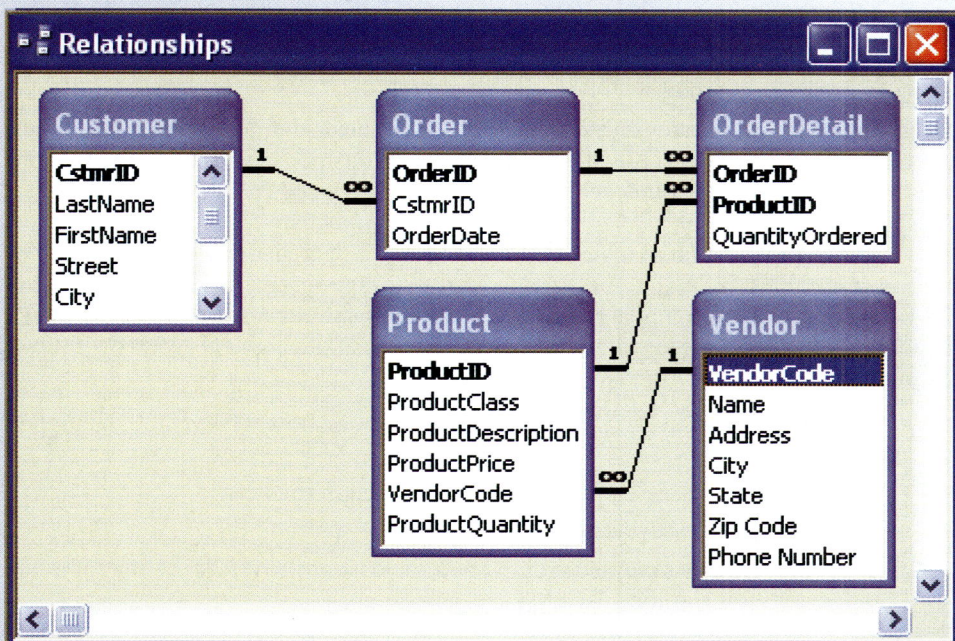

FIGURE 6.7
KoryoKicks table relationships

6. Compare your results with Figure 6.7 and make any necessary changes

7. Close the Relationships window

Although the type of relationship is not directly specified, the fields used and the direction of the drag-and-drop operation control how the relationship is built. The field at the starting point of the drag operation should always be the primary (one side) of the relationship even though the relationships often will be built correctly if the direction is reversed.

Dragging from the primary key field of one table to the primary key field of another table will create a one-to-one relationship, reflecting the fact that key fields can contain only one occurrence of each value. Dragging from the primary key field of one table to a nonkey field in another table builds a one-to-many relationship with the key field's table as primary since it can contain only one occurrence of each key value. When dragging from a nonkey field to a nonkey field, the direction of the drag operation determines which table is primary in the relationship.

The KoryoKicks OrderDetail table has a compound key using both OrderID and ProductID. Since the relationships built with the Order and Product tables only use part of the compound key, they are one-to-many.

Any attempt to create a relationship between tables that already contain data will fail if the existing data violate the referential integrity rules selected. For example, trying to relate the Customer and Order tables would fail if there were orders in the Order table for a customer that was not in the Customer table. When all violations are repaired in the existing data, the relationships can be edited to enforce referential integrity rules for all new data entry.

Building and Using Indexes

Microsoft Access uses indexes to find and sort records faster. Access uses indexes in a table as you use an index in a book: to find data, it looks up the location of the data in the index. Indexes can be based on a single field or on multiple fields. Multiple-field indexes are used to distinguish between records in which the first field may have the same value such as LastName and FirstName.

Single-Field Indexes

Access automatically creates indexes on primary key fields defined in the Design View of a table. Foreign key fields used to define table relationships in the Relationships window are also automatically indexed. Additional indexes can be created to improve database performance.

Consider indexing large tables with fields that are searched frequently, sorted, or used to join tables. Indexing does require extra storage space and does not improve the performance of all database operations, so they should not be overused. When database performance needs to be improved, consider indexing fields with the following qualities:

- The field's data type is Text, Number, Currency, or Date/Time (OLE data types can't be indexed)
- Frequent searches are executed for values stored in the field
- The field is frequently used to sort
- The field contains many different values (if most of the values are the same, an index does not significantly improve performance)

When two or more fields are used frequently in combination such as LastName and FirstName, it makes sense to create a multiple-field index containing both fields. Such an index can provide dramatic performance improvements for large tables. Up to 10 fields can be included in a multiple-field index.

In the KoryoKicks database, the most frequent searches will involve the Customer table. Several Customer table forms, queries, and reports use the State field to order the results, so State is a prime candidate for indexing. Normally, database performance would be tracked before creating an index to determine whether or not indexing produced the desired results. An index should improve the search, sort, and query performance or be removed and other ways to improve performance evaluated.

One way to track performance is to ask users to document response times and their satisfaction with specific operations such as a query or report. This is a subjective measure, but can be effective. Microsoft Access provides a tool to analyze database performance that will be covered in a later session. The Performance Analyzer suggests updates that could improve database performance with no indication of the degree of improvement likely. Third-party vendors provide the most comprehensive performance tools that can be used to verify execution and response times before and after indexing.

Creating an index actually creates an index table, similar to Figure 6.8, telling Access which records in the table belong to each index value. When an operation is performed using the index, Access is able to look up values in the index and then move directly to the associated table records. Figure 6.8 shows a portion of the index for the State field of the Customer table. In a query that retrieves CA records, Access will use the index to retrieve only record 14 of the Customer table. This is much faster than searching every record in the Customer table for a match.

FIGURE 6.8

A portion of the
Customer.State Index

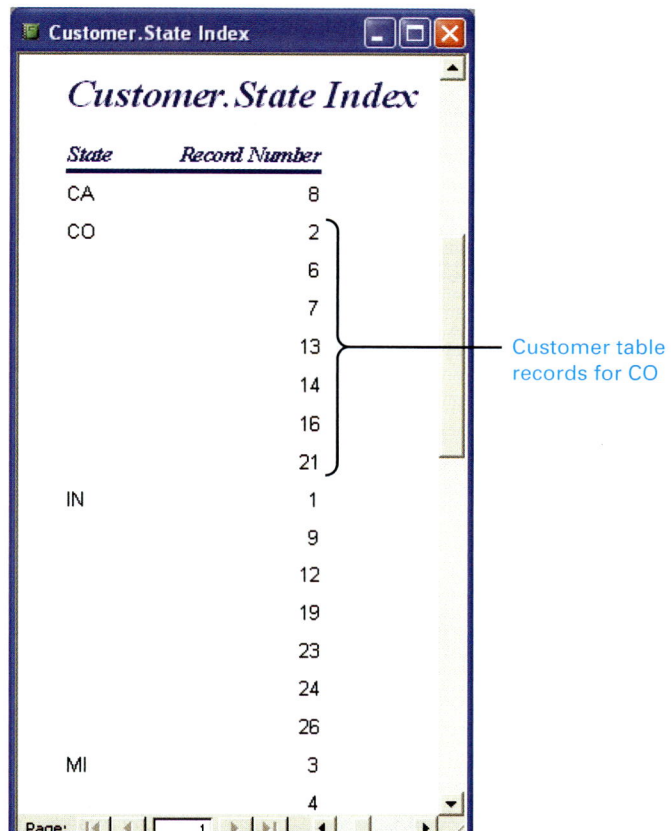

task reference — Index a Table Field

- Open the table in Design View
- Select the field to be indexed from the Field Name column
- Set the Indexed field property to **Yes (Duplicates OK)** or **Yes (No Duplicates)**
- Close the table design and save the changes

Indexing Customer.State:

1. Verify that the **ac06KoryoKicks.mdb** database is open
2. Open the Design View of the Customer table
3. Select CstmrID and notice the Indexed property setting
4. Select the **State** field
5. Set the Indexed property of State to **Yes (Duplicates OK)** as shown in Figure 6.9

tip: *Yes (No Duplicates) would be used if there were no records in the table with the same index value. The primary key of a table would have an Indexed value of Yes (No Duplicates)*

6. Close the Design View and save your changes

active field

Indexed property
of active field

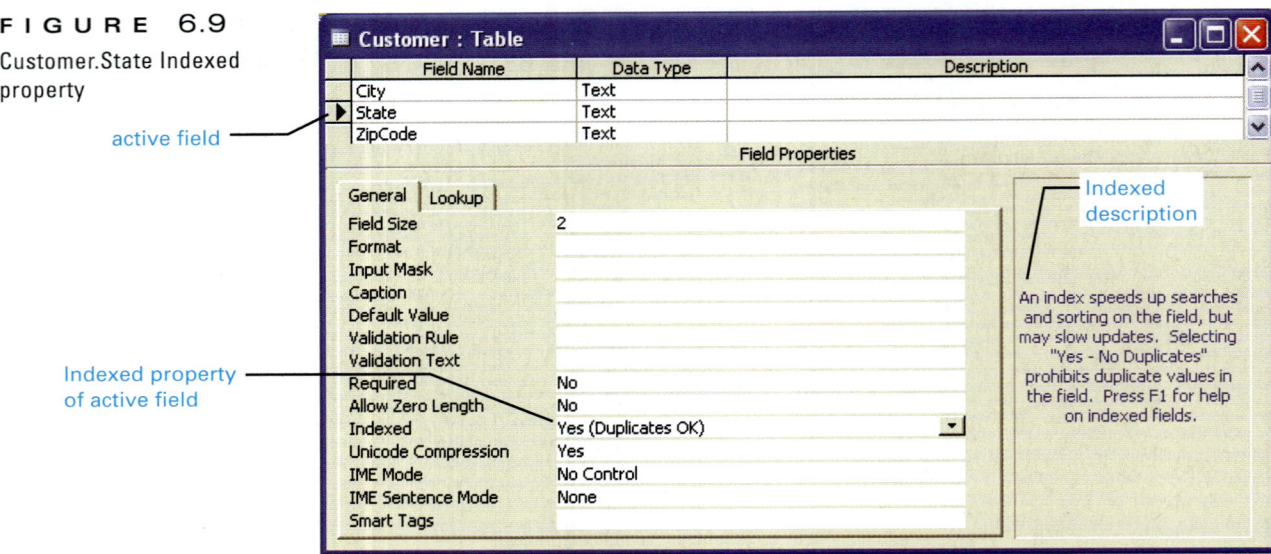

Indexes created automatically, such as the primary key index, cannot be deleted. Deleting other indexes simply requires setting the Indexed property of the field to No. Since the data held in each database are unique, there is no standard increase in performance gained from indexing. Additionally, an index that does not improve performance with the current data may be beneficial as more data are stored.

another**way**
. . . to Set and
Delete Indexes

Indexes also can be created, updated, and deleted using the Indexes 📝 button from the Design View of a table. Since this is the only way to set multifield indexes, it is covered in that topic

task reference   Delete an Index

- Open the table in **Design View**
- Select the field whose index is to be removed from the Field Name column
- Set the Indexed field property to **No** (this does not impact the field or its data)
- Close the table design and save the changes

There are two disadvantages to adding indexes. Since creating an index actually adds a new table to a database, it enlarges the size of the database. Second, when values are added or changed in an indexed field, the index also must be updated, slowing the overall update process. Indexes should be monitored and retained only if they improve sort, select, and query performance.

Multiple-Field Indexes

As was mentioned, *multiple-field indexes* are created when fields are used in combination to sort or search a table. The most common example of LastName and FirstName exists in the KoryoKicks Customer table. Multifield indexes cannot be set in the table design, but are set in the Indexes dialog box that can only be accessed from the Design View of a table.

task reference   View the Indexes of a Table

- Open the table in **Design View**
- Click the **Indexes** 📝 button of the toolbar
- Click an index to review its properties

Viewing Customer table indexes:

1. Verify that the **ac06KoryoKicks.mdb** database is open
2. Open the Design View of the Customer table
3. Click the **Indexes** 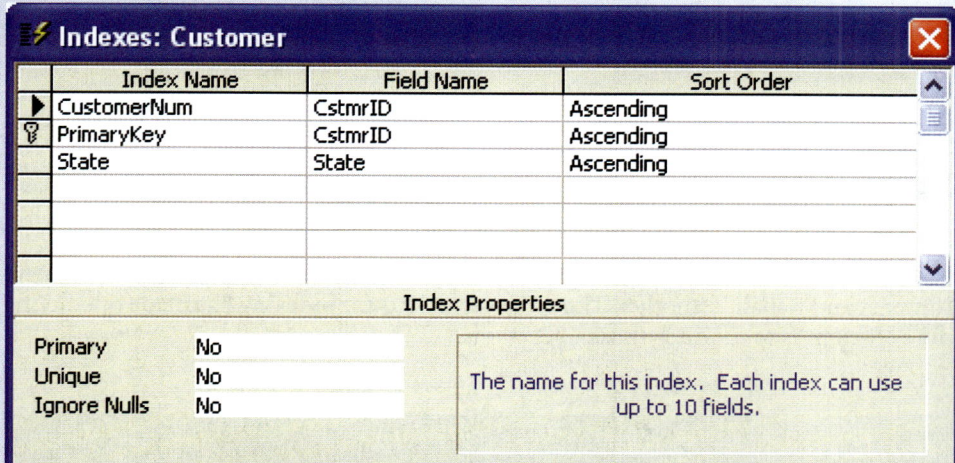 button on the toolbar
4. Click on each index to review its properties

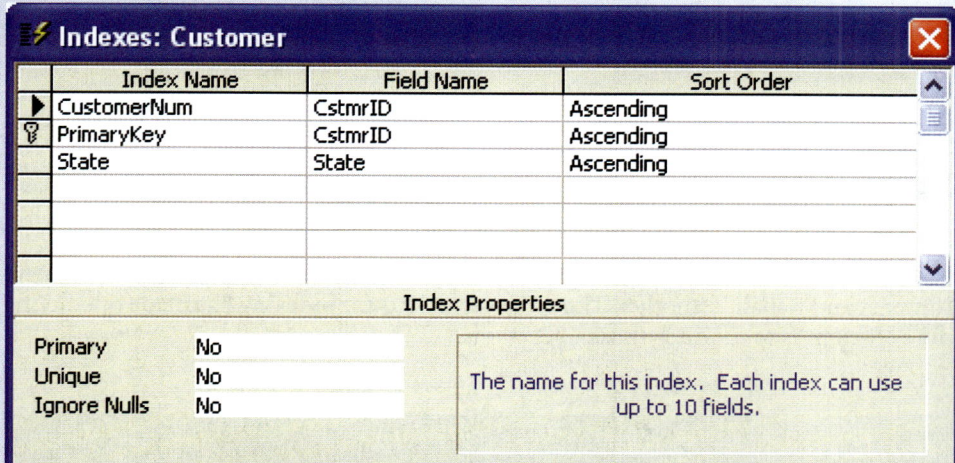

FIGURE 6.10
Customer table indexes

The Customer table should have three indexes. The PrimaryKey index was created by Access when CstmrID was set as the primary key field. The CustomerNum index also was created by Access to be used as a foreign key when linking to other tables. The State index was built in the previous steps. Selecting an index in the Indexes dialog box and pressing the Del key will delete that index from the database.

Setting a multifield Customer table index:

1. Verify that the **ac06KoryoKicks.mdb** database is open
2. If necessary, open the Design View of the Customer table and then click the **Indexes** 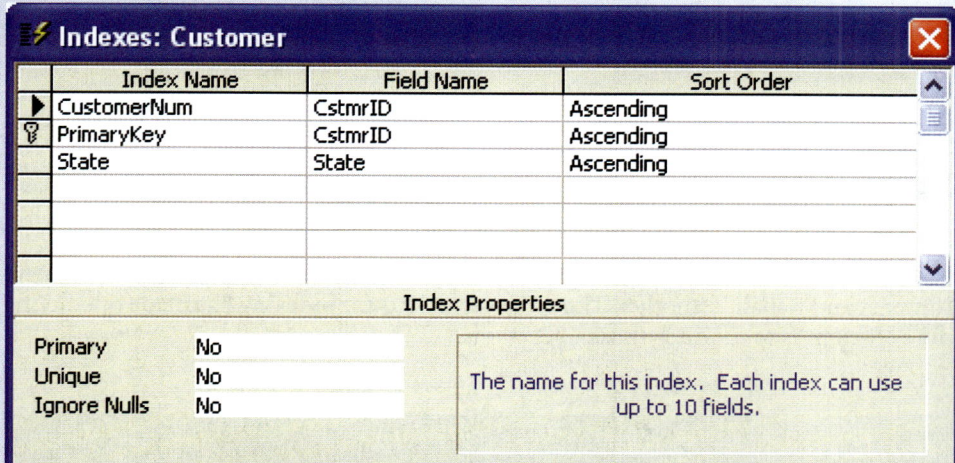 button on the toolbar
3. In the first empty Index Name type **WholeName**

tip: *Index names can be anything that you want, but something reflecting the field(s) involved usually works best*

4. In the Field Name column, click the arrow and select **LastName**, the first field for the index
5. In the Field Name column of the next row, click the arrow and select **FirstName**, the second field for the index

tip: *This step can be repeated to add up to 10 fields to the index*

6. Select the sort order for each index field. Ascending, the default, is correct for this index (see Figure 6.11)
7. Close the Indexes window
8. Close the Customer table Design View, saving your changes

FIGURE 6.11

WholeName Customer
table index

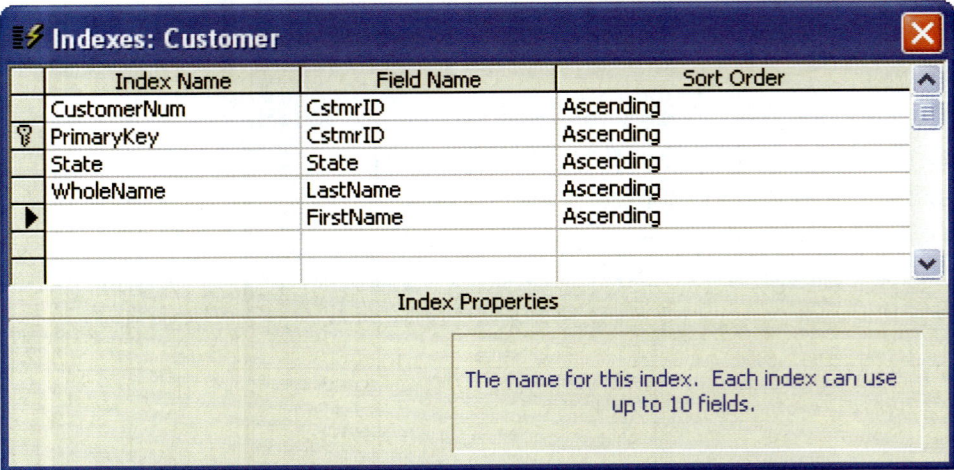

Remember that indexing is only one way to improve database performance; Compact and Repair is another. The only way to know if indexing has made operations more efficient is to monitor those operations.

SESSION 6.1

making the grade

1. How would you view existing table relationships?

2. What is the relevance of the direction of the drag operation that creates a new relationship?

3. Why is referential integrity important?

4. Why are indexes important?

SESSION 6.2 CREATING OUTPUT WITH RELATED TABLES

You have been using data in related tables without an understanding of how these operations are really accomplished. When table relationships are properly defined, creating a query, form, or report using data from multiple tables is simply a matter of selecting the fields and arranging them as you would like.

Constructing Multitable Queries

Combining the data from two or more tables is usually accomplished using a query and is called joining the tables. Access supports three types of joins. The most common join is called an inner join and is the default join operation.

Inner Join

Joining the data from multiple tables can be accomplished by matching records with a common value. Typically the values being matched are in fields with defined relationships. For example, matching OrderDetail. ProductID to Product.ProductID would allow retrieval of the Product. ProductDescription using a defined relationship. Existing relationships are displayed as join lines in the query grid and display the one-to-many notation when referential integrity is enforced. Even if no relationships have been defined between the tables selected for a query, Microsoft Access will infer a relationship if they contain fields with the same name.

Sometimes data from unrelated tables are needed. In this case, there is no field that will connect the data in one table to another table, so one or more extra tables must be added to the query as a bridge between the two unrelated tables. Data from the bridge tables need not be displayed in the query result. For example, to retrieve fields from the KoryoKicks Customer and OrderDetail tables, the Order table would be included as a bridge because it is related to each of the tables containing the desired data.

Records that don't have matching join field values can be either included or excluded from the query result. An ***inner join*** specifies that a row is created in the query result only when the join values of both tables match. For example, joining the KoryoKicks Customer and Order table using the default inner join will return rows only for customers who have placed orders. If any customers have not placed orders, they will not be included in the inner join query results.

As an example, you will create the query that will join all of the tables in the KoryoKicks database using the relationships built in the previous session. The result will contain only customers who have placed orders and will be used to create invoices in the Multitable Report topic.

Creating a multitable query, InvoiceJoin:

1. Verify that the **ac06KoryoKicks.mdb** database is open

2. Select the **Queries** object and click **New**

3. Select Design View from the New Query dialog box and click **OK**

4. Add **Customer**, **Order**, **OrderDetail**, and **Product** tables to the query design

tip: *Although the position of the tables in the Design Window is not important, the order shown is the most effective way to view the relationships. If needed, drag the tables to the positions shown*

5. Close the Show Table dialog box

6. From the Customer table add **FirstName**, **LastName**, **Street**, **City**, **State**, and **ZipCode** to the QBE grid

7. From the Order table, add **OrderDate**

8. From the Product table add **ProductDescription** and **ProductPrice**

9. From the OrderDetail table add **QuantityOrdered**

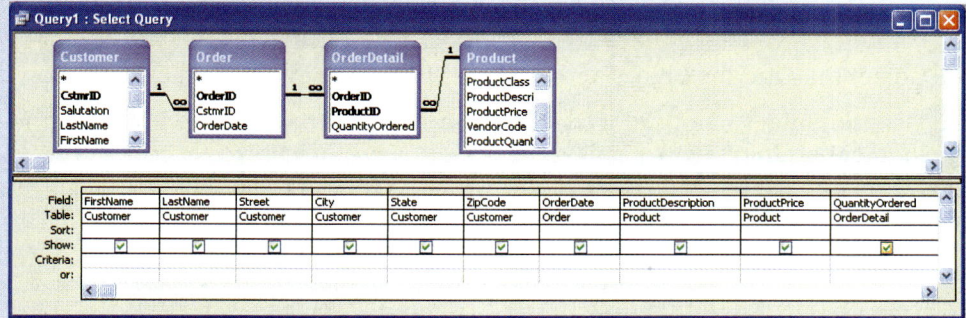

FIGURE 6.12

Select Query joining most of the KoryoKicks tables

10. Click the **Run** ! button to view the query results

FIGURE 6.13

Inner join results

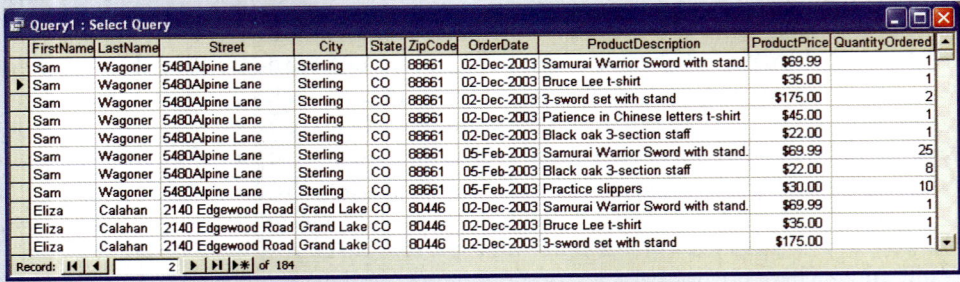

11. Save the Query as **InvoiceJoin**

Inner joins are also called equi-joins because the values of the join fields must match for a row to be created in the query result. Remember that when there is a Customer table record with no orders, there will be no entry in the query result. To verify this, Judy Johnson is CstmrID 105 in the Customer table. Since there is no order for this customer in OrderDetail, her record does not appear in the result of InvoiceJoin.

Outer Join

There are two types of outer joins. The *left outer join* selects all of the records from the first (left) table and joins them to values that match the other table. A left outer join would display all of the records from the previous inner join example, plus Judy Johnson's record since it is in the left table.

help yourself *Use the Type a Question combo box to improve your understanding of joining tables by typing* **join types**. *Review the contents of* About joining tables or queries in a query *and* Modify a join in a query. *Close the Help window when you are finished*

The *right outer join* selects all of the records from the right (second) table and only those with matching values from the left table. For example, in the Customer/Order join, a right outer join would show all orders whether or not they are associated with a customer. This relationship can't be demonstrated with KoryoKicks because the referential integrity rules selected when the table relationships were built preclude this type of entry.

Creating a KoryoKicks left outer join query:

1. Verify that the **ac06KoryoKicks.mdb** database is open

2. Select the **Queries** object and open the **InvoiceJoin** query in Design View

3. Use the **Save As** option of the **File** menu to save the query with the name **InvoiceLeftJoin**

4. Delete the OrderDetail and Product tables from the top of the query design

tip: *This action automatically removes the fields from the design grid previously selected from these tables*

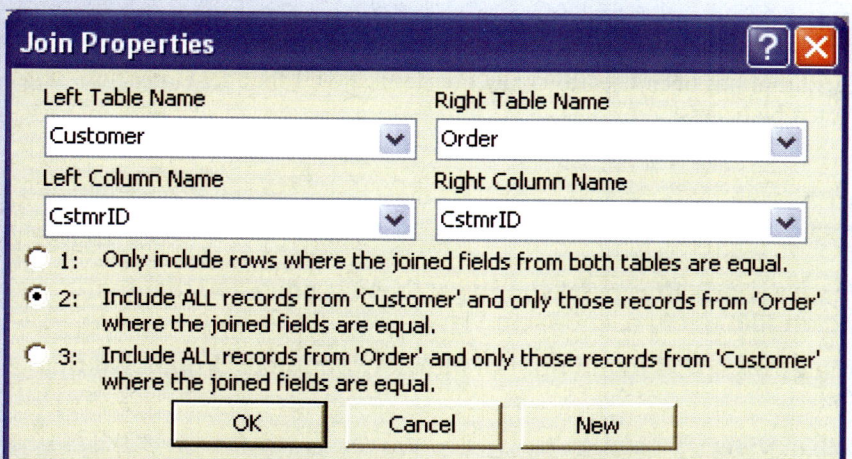

FIGURE 6.14
Setting join properties

5. Double-click the relationship line between the Customer and Order tables to open the Join Properties dialog box (see Figure 6.14)

6. Select option button **2: Include ALL records from 'Customer' and only those records from 'Order' where the joined fields are equal** and click **OK**

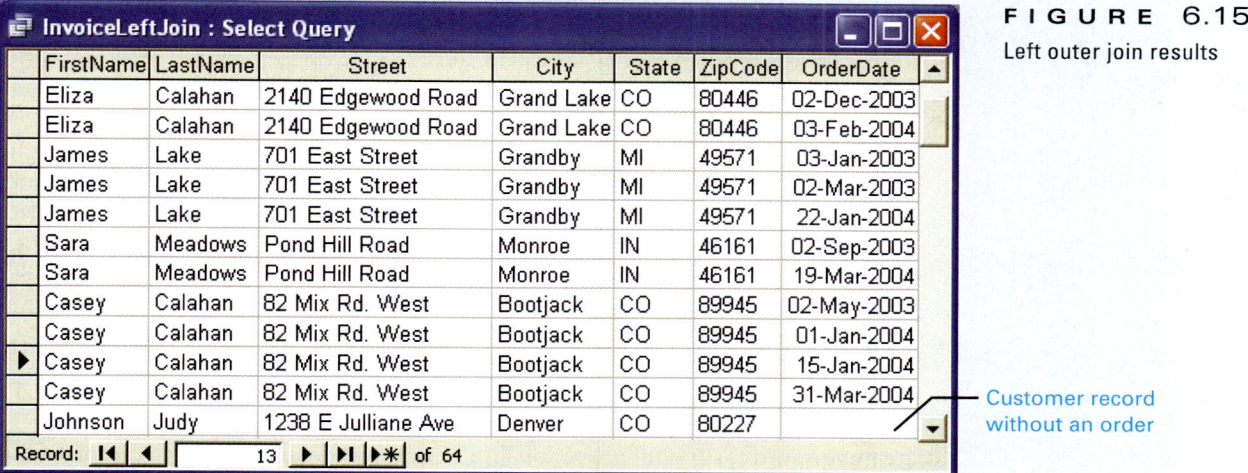

FIGURE 6.15
Left outer join results

7. Run the query to view the results (see Figure 6.15)

tip: *If your results do not show the record for Judy Johnson, return to Design View and repeat steps 5–7*

8. Leave the query open in Design View for the next series of steps

Left and right outer joins can involve only two tables, so the OrderDetail and Product tables were removed from the previous example. If other tables need to be included in the final result, a second query joining the InvoiceLeftJoin query results to other tables would be built. As was demonstrated, the results of the query can differ depending on the type of join and the order in which the joins are performed.

To fully understand how Access determines which is the left or right table, we need to take a look at the underlying SQL. Recall that SQL (Structured Query Language) is the standard language used to query relational databases. The QBE (Query by Example) grid that has been used to create queries is a GUI that generates SQL statements executed by Access.

Viewing the SQL for the InvoiceLeftJoin query:

1. Verify that the **ac06KoryoKicks.mdb** database is open and that the **InvoiceLeftJoin** query is in Design View

2. Click the down arrow to the right of the View button to drop down the view list

3. Select **SQL View**

FIGURE 6.16

SQL View of
InvoiceLeftJoin

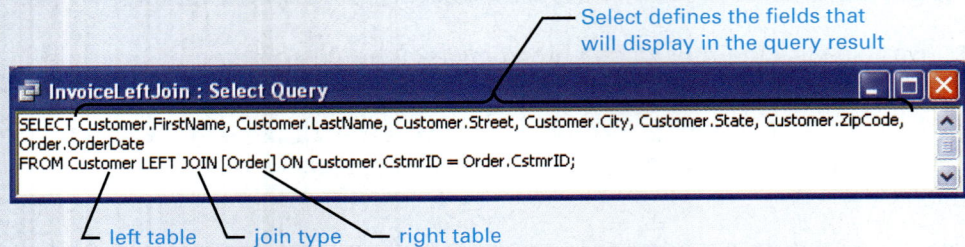

Select defines the fields that
will display in the query result

InvoiceLeftJoin : Select Query

SELECT Customer.FirstName, Customer.LastName, Customer.Street, Customer.City, Customer.State, Customer.ZipCode, Order.OrderDate
FROM Customer LEFT JOIN [Order] ON Customer.CstmrID = Order.CstmrID;

left table   join type   right table

4. Close the SQL View saving your updates

The order in which tables are added to the design pane of the QBE grid determines their order in the resulting SQL statement. Since tables can be moved in the design grid, the order in which they appear is not always indicative of which was added first. When a left or right outer join is specified, it will be based on the order in which the tables were added to the query and to the order in which they appear in the SQL statement in the SQL pane. It is always best to check the SQL to be sure of the query results.

Developing Multitable Forms

To create a multitable form, a relationship between the tables must be defined first. Since the relationships in the KoryoKicks database have already been set, it is ready for multitable operations.

Creating a Lookup Field

The Lookup Wizard data type has already been used to create a Lookup field in the Order table. When table relationships are set, a Lookup field provides a list of valid values used when entering data. This makes data entry easier and ensures the consistency of the data in that field.

The relationship defined between the Customer and the Order tables forces the user to enter the CstmrID for a customer that is already in the primary (Customer) table. In Chapter 4, a Lookup field was created to retrieve the customer's last and first name from the Customer table and display it in a drop-down list for the user. A Lookup field can get its list of values from a table or query, or from a fixed set of values provided when it is created.

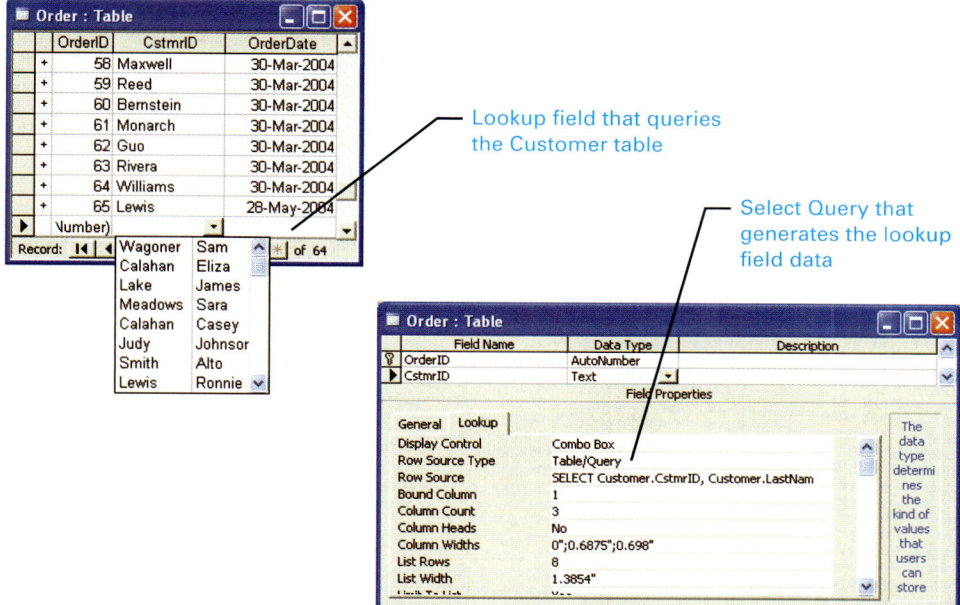

Figure 6.17 shows the Order table in both Datasheet and Design Views. In Datasheet View, the user sees the result of the Lookup field. In Design View, the query developed by the Wizard to look up the CstmrID is visible.

Lookup fields also can display a fixed list of possible values. This is effective when there is a limited set of valid values for a field. A good example would be the salutation used for customers in correspondence. A Salutation field with values of Ms., Mrs., and Mr. would be an effective way to add these data to a table. Other uses for such a Lookup field would be the departments of an organization, sales regions, or book classifications. In other words, any field with limited values should use a Lookup field to improve data integrity.

Creating a fixed-list Customer Lookup field:

1. Verify that the **ac06KoryoKicks.mdb** database is open

2. Open the Customer table in Design View

3. Insert a row in the field design after CstmrID and before LastName

4. Name the new field **Salutation** and make its data type **Lookup Wizard**

5. Select **I will type in the values that I want** from the Lookup Wizard dialog box and click **Next**

tip: *The other option, I want the Lookup column to look up the values in a table or query, was used to create the list of customers from the Customer table when you click in the CstmrID field of the Order table*

6. Type **Mr.** as a value in the cell of the Lookup column

7. Type **Ms.** in the next cell, **Mrs.** in the third cell, and click **Next**

8. Click **Finish** and set the Field Size to **5**

9. Select **Salutation** and then click the **Lookup** tab in the bottom portion of the screen to view the Lookup criteria created by the Wizard (see Figure 6.18)

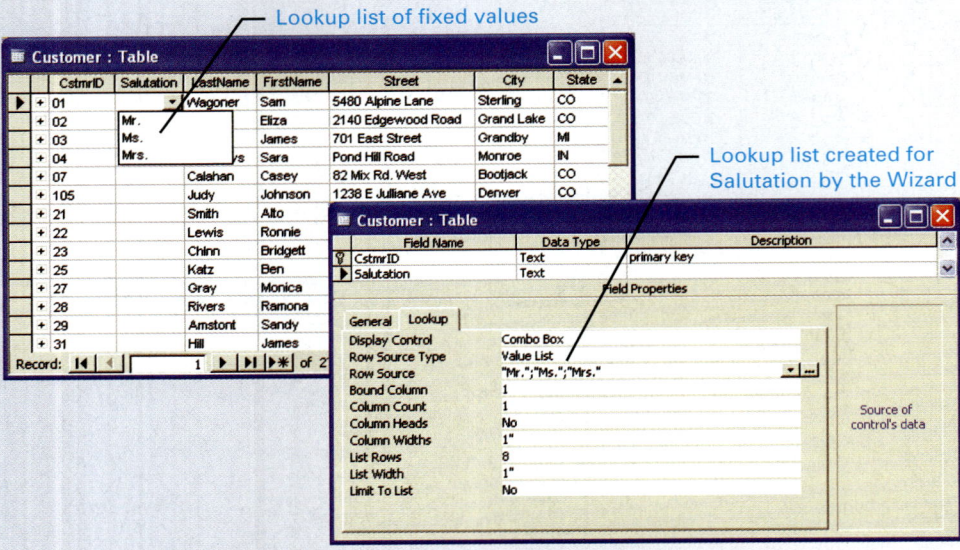

10. Click the **Datasheet** View button and save your changes

11. Click in the **Salutation** field to drop down the Lookup list. Assign an appropriate value to each record

12. Close the Customer table

Of course, a Lookup list can be created by typing the values in the Row Source property of the Lookup tab using the format shown. Alternatively SQL can be used to compose queries that will pull data from related tables such as the Customer table previously demonstrated. The Lookup Wizard simply ensures the validity of the syntax.

Lookup fields can be very powerful in improving data integrity and increasing data entry efficiency. Consider the time that is saved by the phone number Lookup employed by pizza delivery organizations. The customer provides a phone number, which is used to look up an address and in some cases an order history. All the person taking the order has to enter are a phone number and any changes to the current order. This saves typing and greatly reduces errors. Another example is entering a zip code in an Internet form that is used to look up the correct city and state. The rule of thumb is, if the data exist or can be derived, don't have the user reenter them.

Displaying Related Data in a Subdatasheet

When the relationships between tables are set in a database, the related table data can be viewed from the primary table. Again the KoryoKicks Customer table provides a good example. The Customer table is the primary table in the relationship between the Customer and the Order tables. Clicking the plus (+) sign in a Customer record will display the related Order records (see Figure 6.19). Further, the Order table is primary in the relationship between the Order and the OrderDetail tables, so the associated OrderDetail can be viewed by clicking the plus (+) sign in the Order record. The final relationship in the chain, the Product table, cannot be viewed because OrderDetail is the related (not the primary) table in this relationship.

To view related records in this fashion, nothing beyond setting up the table relationships was required. The KoryoKicks database has had this ability since relationships between the tables were built.

FIGURE 6.19

Customer table
subdatasheets

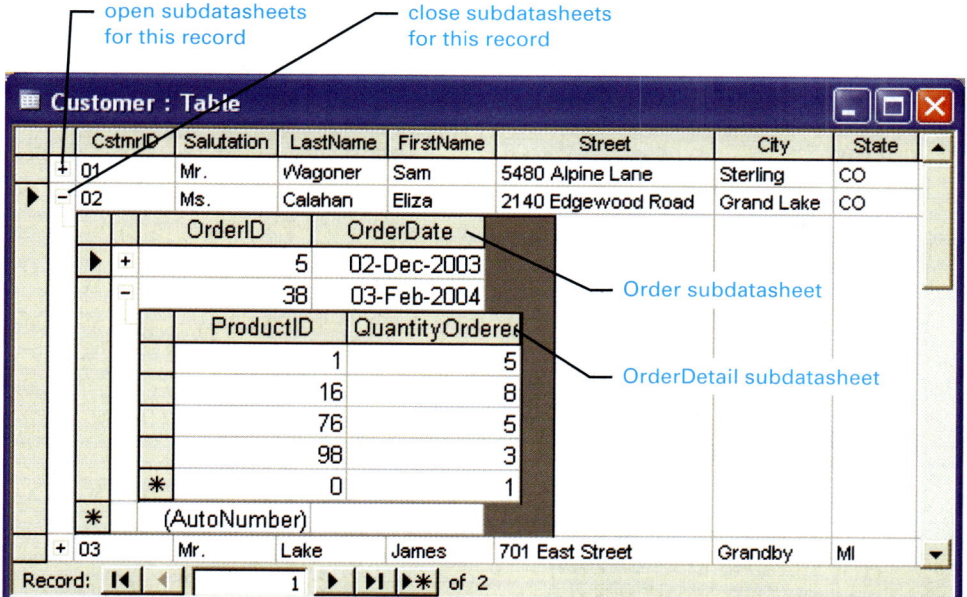

Creating a Main Form and SubForm

While subdatasheets are a fast and effective way to view related data, they are busy and sometimes confusing. Forms that show only a single record from the primary table and all of the related records provide better clarity. One way to accomplish this is to use a *main form* to display the primary table data with a synchronized *subform* to display the related data from the second table. The subform is inserted into the main form to display data from a related table (see Figure 6.19). Form/subform combinations also can be referred to as hierarchical forms, master/detail forms, or parent/child forms.

The Form Wizard is a fast way to create main form/subform combinations. As you know, forms and reports created using Wizards can be customized in Design View to improve their appearance and effectiveness. When using the Wizard to select data for the form, the primary table fields are selected first and then the related table fields. If the form is to be used to maintain table data, each table should appear in its own form or subform.

Creating a KoryoKicks main form/subform:

1. Verify that the **ac06KoryoKicks.mdb** database is open

2. Select the **Forms** object and click **New**

3. Select **Form Wizard**, choose **Customer** as the record source for the form, and click **OK**

4. Select **all fields** from the Customer table

5. Select the **Order** table from the drop-down list

6. Select **all fields** from the Order table and click **Next**

7. Select **by Customer** as the way to view data and click **Next**

8. Select **Tabular** as the layout for your subform and click **Next**

9. Choose **Ricepaper** as the style and click **Next**

10. Title the form **Customer Order** and click **Finish**

FIGURE 6.20

Customer form with a
subform

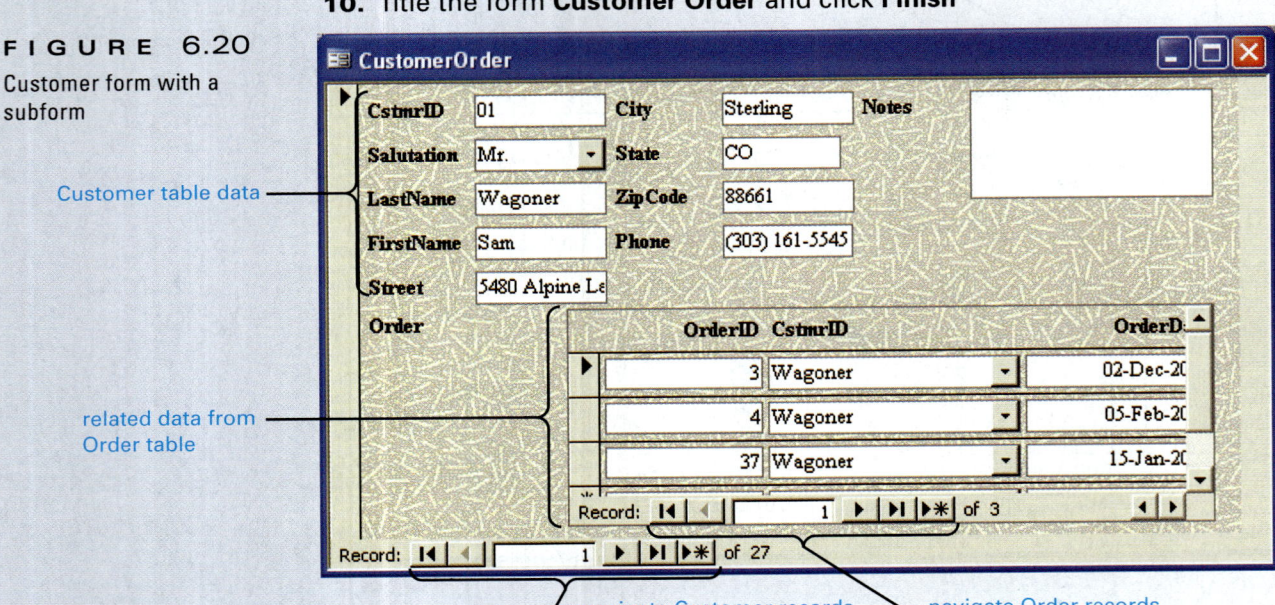

11. Practice navigating the main form and the subform

This form could obviously benefit from customization. At a minimum, the size and alignment of existing fields should be adjusted to fit the data.

Customizing the KoryoKicks main form/subform:

1. Verify that the **ac06KoryoKicks.mdb** database is open with the **Customer Order** form in Design View

2. Use the **Size** option of the **Format** menu to adjust the size of each Label to fit its contents. Add spaces between words

tip: *You can select all of the Label controls by holding down the Shift button*

3. Delete Notes. Move each text box closer to its associated label and arrange them as shown in Figure 6.21.

4. Adjust the position of the subform. Add spaces to the labels

tip: *When you click the subform Label, the label and subform each displays a move handle since they are linked (like a bound text box and its label)*

5. Use the Line tool to draw a line that separates the areas of the form

6. Adjust the headings and compress the field width for the three subform columns as shown in Figure 6.21

7. Use the **Form View** button to preview your changes

tip: *You will be prompted to save both the form and the subform*

8. Close the form and save your changes (see Figure 6.22)

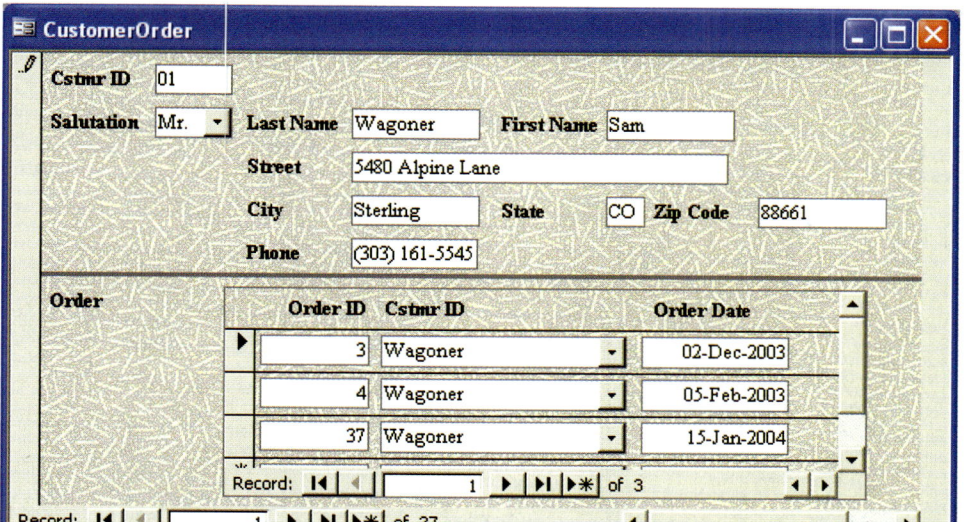

FIGURE 6.21
Customized
CustomerOrder form

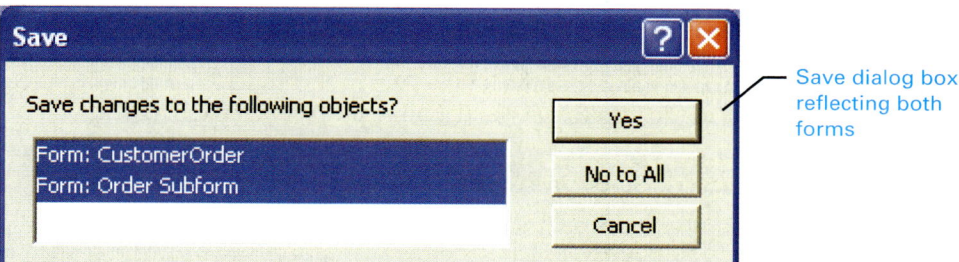

FIGURE 6.22
Main form/subform save

Save dialog box
reflecting both
forms

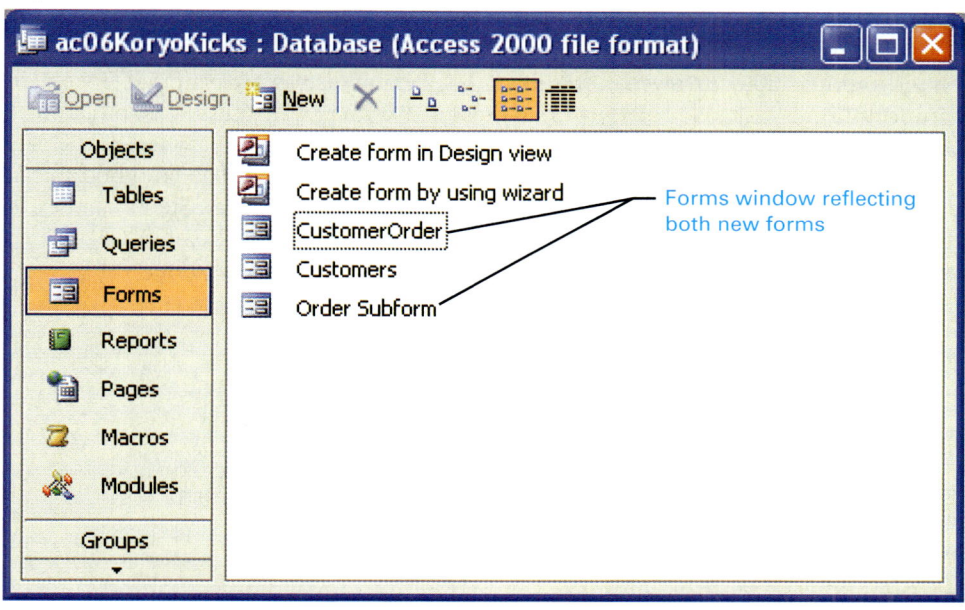

Forms window reflecting
both new forms

When a main form/subform pair is built, it is actually creating two forms, both of which are listed in the Forms object window. Figure 6.22 shows the save prompt reflecting the two forms and the Forms object window after the save is complete. The Order Subform is in reality a form that has been embedded into the Customer form. Double-click Order Subform, and it will open independently. The subform also can be viewed and edited in Design View without the Customer form being open.

FIGURE   6.23

Customer filtered by Grand

select filter value and click Filter By Selection button

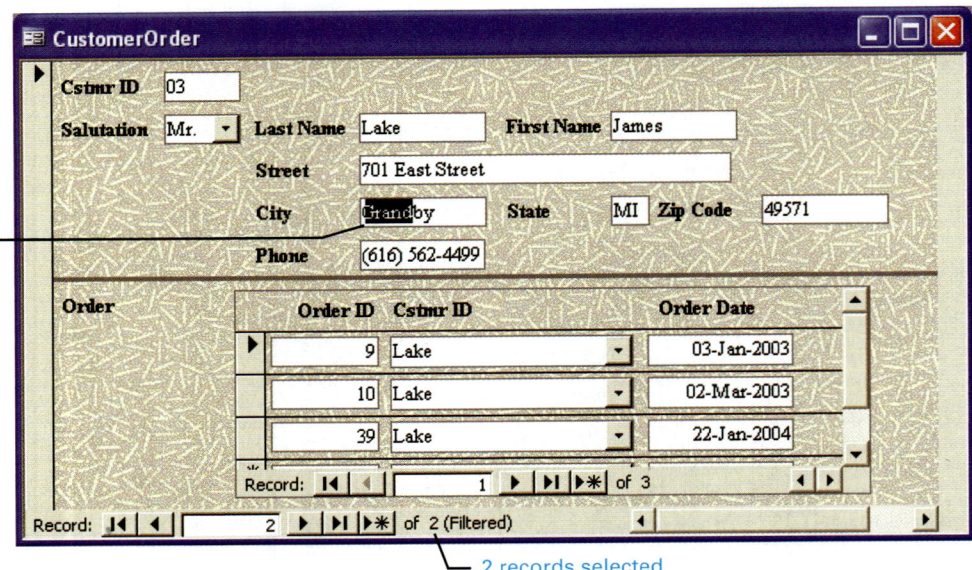

2 records selected

When the Customer form is opened, both this form and the embedded subform display. Forms are used to view and update the data in the underlying record source. Since this form involves four tables, we will demonstrate its update capabilities.

Using a Main Form/Subform

Users typically don't care about the technical details of how their applications work; they just want them to be effective. The Customer main form/subform just created is very efficient for the user to view all of the orders a particular customer has placed and is visually more appealing than the default subdatasheet.

All of the techniques used to order and find data on a single table form can be used on the multiple tables involved in this form. The default display order for data in a main form/subform is controlled by the primary table, Customer in this case. If no other order is specified, data will display ordered by the primary key of the primary table. The user can select a field and use the sort buttons to sort by that selection. The Find button can be used to search for a particular value, such as a LastName of Rivera. Filters can be applied to retrieve and manipulate a subset of the data (see Figure 6.23) and new records can be created. Remember to remove any applied filters before proceeding.

Using the KoryoKicks main form/subform:

1. Verify that the **ac06KoryoKicks.mdb** database is open

2. Select the **Forms** object and double-click the **Order Subform**

3. Navigate through the orders

4. Add a new order for **Thomas Calahan** with today's date

tip: *OrderID is an AutoNumber field and will be generated. The date format is dd-mmm-yyyy, for example, 10-Oct-2003*

5. **Close** the Orders Subform

6. Open the **CustomerOrder** form

7. Navigate through the customers using the lower navigation buttons

8. Add yourself as a customer with CstmrID **328**

9. Add two orders for yourself

10. Close the form

Multitable forms can be used to update data only when they represent one-to-many relationships. The main form is the primary side of the relationship and the subform is the related table. When forms are nested, each subform must be nested in its primary table's form (see Figure 6.24).

It is usually most effective to have one subform for each table involved. The main form can have as many subforms as are needed to represent the data. Subforms also can contain subforms—up to seven layers deep. Figure 6.24 shows three levels of nested subforms. The outer form is the Customer table data, which contains the Order table subform, which in turn contains the OrderDetail table subform.

Specifying Multitable Reports

Unlike forms, which are built to interact with the data, multitable reports retrieve data and report on them without further interaction. Because of this, reports are typically based on queries that retrieve the required data so that the report is only responsible for formatting.

Selecting Data from Multiple Tables

Although queries are commonly the foundation for reports, the Report Wizard can help create a report without first creating a query. As with other "automatic" things that we have looked at, a SQL query is being built and submitted behind the scenes.

To demonstrate the use of queries, an invoice report will be created without using a query as its data source and then the same report will be created with a query. The restriction of not using a query is that the report will display all of the data returned by

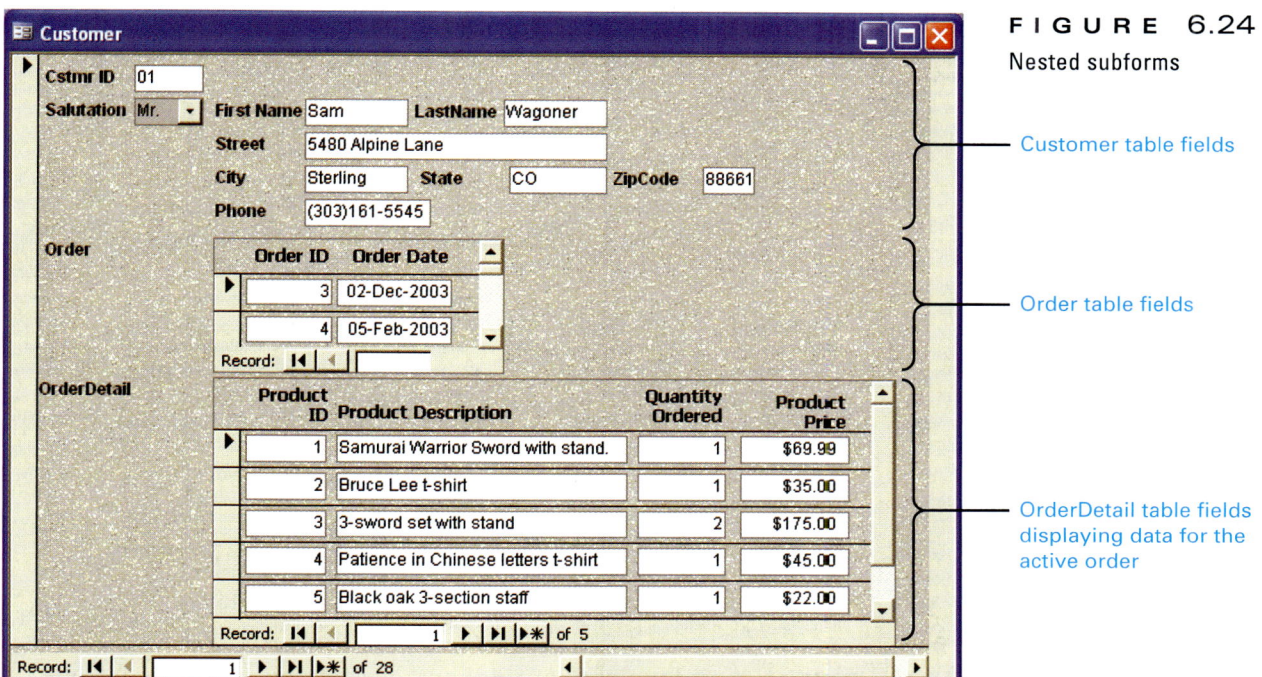

FIGURE 6.24

Nested subforms

Customer table fields

Order table fields

OrderDetail table fields displaying data for the active order

joining the tables—a subset cannot be specified. When a query is used, a subset of the data can be retrieved for the report. For example, only invoices for customers who have made purchases in the last month could be printed. The invoices query would select those records and make them available to the invoice report for formatting.

Building the KoryoKicks Invoice report without a user-defined query:

1. Verify that the **ac06KoryoKicks.mdb** database is open

2. Click the **Reports** object and select **New**

3. Choose **Report Wizard** and click **OK**

4. Add all of the fields from the **Customer, Order, OrderDetail**, and **Product** tables to the Selected Fields list and click **Next**

5. The default by Customer is appropriate for this report, but explore the other options and then return the selection to **by Customer**

6. Add two levels of grouping, **Customer.CstmrID** and **Order.OrderID**, and click **Next**

FIGURE 6.25

Invoice report grouping

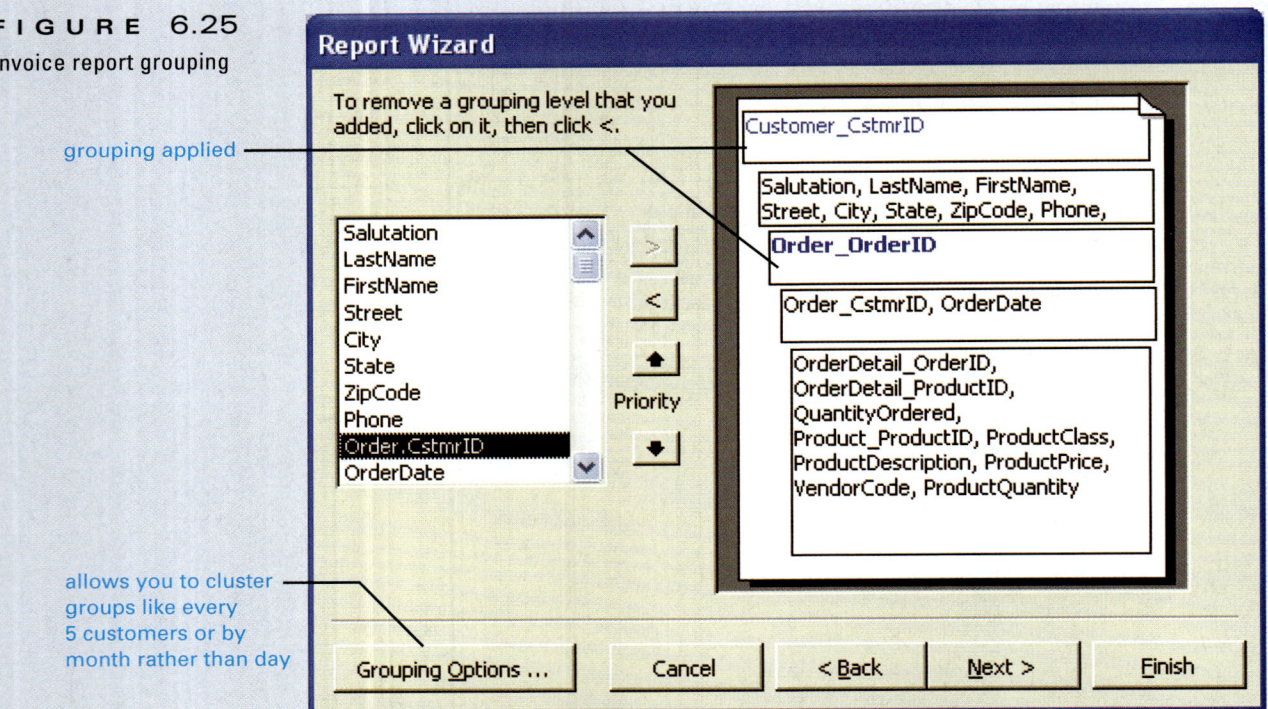

grouping applied

allows you to cluster groups like every 5 customers or by month rather than day

7. Select **OrderDetail_ProductID** as the only sort field and click **Next**

tip: *No summary options are applied, because there is no detail line item total to sum since we did not use a query as the record source*

8. Choose **Align Left 1** as the Layout style, **Landscape** as the page Orientation, and click **Next**

9. Select **Formal** as the Style and click **Next**

10. Name the Report **InvoicesNoQuery** and click **Finish**

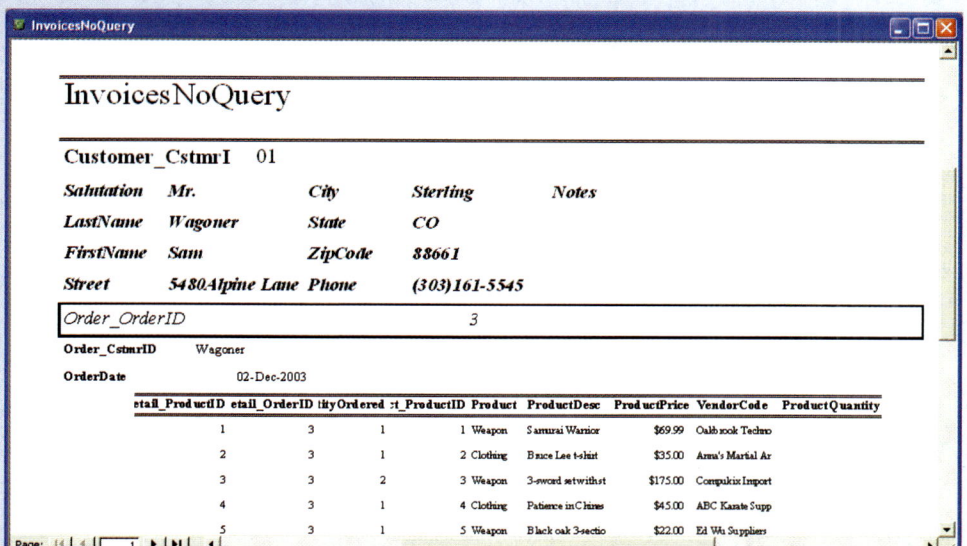

FIGURE 6.26
InvoicesNoQuery report

11. Close the report

The report created in the previous steps is a very effective first cut at invoices, but it needs considerable customization. The company logo needs to be added, the alignment of the labels and text boxes adjusted, and page breaks added between each invoice. Additionally, the calculations to total each detail line item and provide an invoice total and a grand total would need to be added manually.

Sorting, Grouping, and Calculating Report Data

Obviously the Report Wizard provides the ability to sort, group, and calculate data in the record source. Queries also provide the ability to sort, group, and calculate. The question then is "How do I know where to sort, group, and calculate when using a query as the record source for a report?"

There are probably as many answers to this question as there are people working with databases. There are no absolutes, and many approaches are effective. For many the best approach is the one that will minimize the customization needs of the report. With that in mind, a good rule of thumb is to sort and place calculations that display with each row of data, such as a detail line total, in the query. That leaves grouping and summary calculations, such as invoice total and report total, to be added in the report.

To try this reporting approach, the InvoiceJoin query created earlier will be modified to include sorting and the detail line calculation. This updated query will be used as the data source for the Report Wizard.

Modifying the InvoiceJoin query:

1. Verify that the **ac06KoryoKicks.mdb** database is open

2. Click the **Queries** object

3. Choose **InvoiceJoin** and click the **Design** View button

4. Double-click on **Customer.CstmrID** and **Order.OrderID** to add them to the query since they will be needed on the invoice

5. Drag the fields to the order that will be used in the invoice by clicking the bar above each Field Name to select a column. Then drag the selected column to the correct position. The final field order should be OrderID, OrderDate, CstmrID, FirstName, LastName, Street, City, State, ZipCode, QuantityOrdered, ProductDescription, and ProductPrice

6. Use the **Save As** option of the **File** menu to save your changes with the name **InvoiceJoinWithCalc**

7. In the first empty column add the expression **ItemTotal:QuantityOrdered*ProductPrice**

FIGURE 6.27
InvoiceJoinWithCalc expression

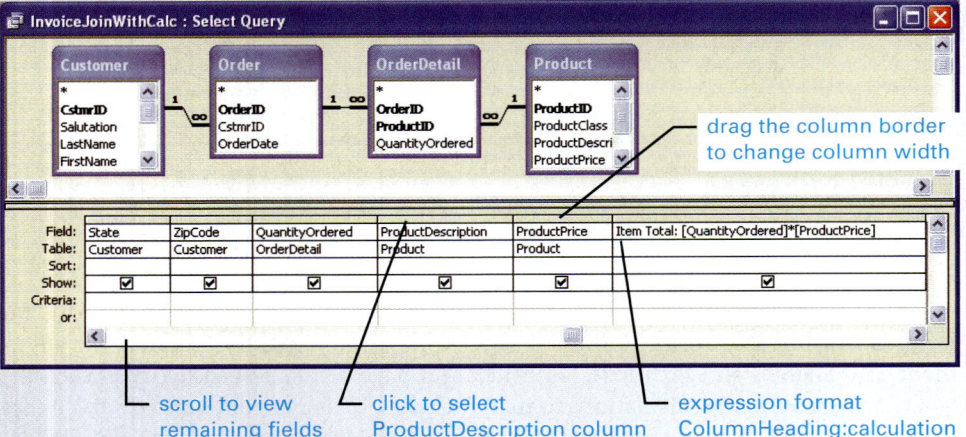

anotherway
... to Create InvoiceJoinWithCalc

If you prefer working with lists of table fields rather than the QBE grid, it might be easier to create a new query rather than extensively editing the InvoiceJoin query. You could use the Query Wizard to select and order the fields from the related tables and then use the QBE grid to add the calculation

8. Add the **Between #7/1/2003# And #7/31/2003#** selection criteria to OrderDate so that only orders for July of 2003 will be invoiced

tip: *Access will add the # signs if you do not type them*

9. Use the **Run** ! button to view the query results. Verify the column order, the calculation, and the selection

10. Close the query saving your updates

Besides simplifying the customization that will need to be done on the invoice report, creating the InvoiceJoinWithCalc query also allows the organization, calculation, and selection of data to be verified prior to report generation. It is helpful to know that the correct data are going into your report since that directly impacts the validity of the report result.

InvoiceJoinWithCalc report:

1. Verify that the **ac06KoryoKicks.mdb** database is open

2. Select the **Reports** object and Click **New**

3. Select **Report Wizard**, and **InvoiceJoinWithCalc** as the data source, and click **OK**

tip: *If an empty report opens in Design View, close it and repeat steps 2 and 3, being sure to select the Report Wizard*

4. Move all of the fields of InvoiceJoinWithCalc to the Selected Fields box and click **Next**

5. Add grouping for **OrderID** and **CustmrID** and click **Next**

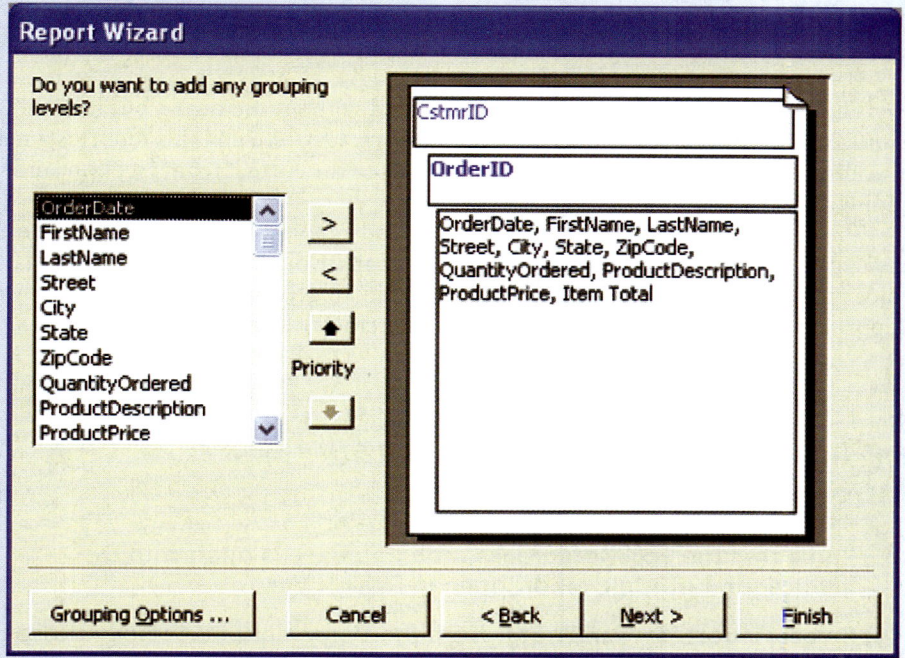

FIGURE 6.28

Grouping added to InvoiceJoinWithCalc report

6. Sort by **ProductDescription** and click **Summary Options**

7. Check the **Sum** calculation for QuantityOrdered and ItemTotal to calculate group totals on these fields

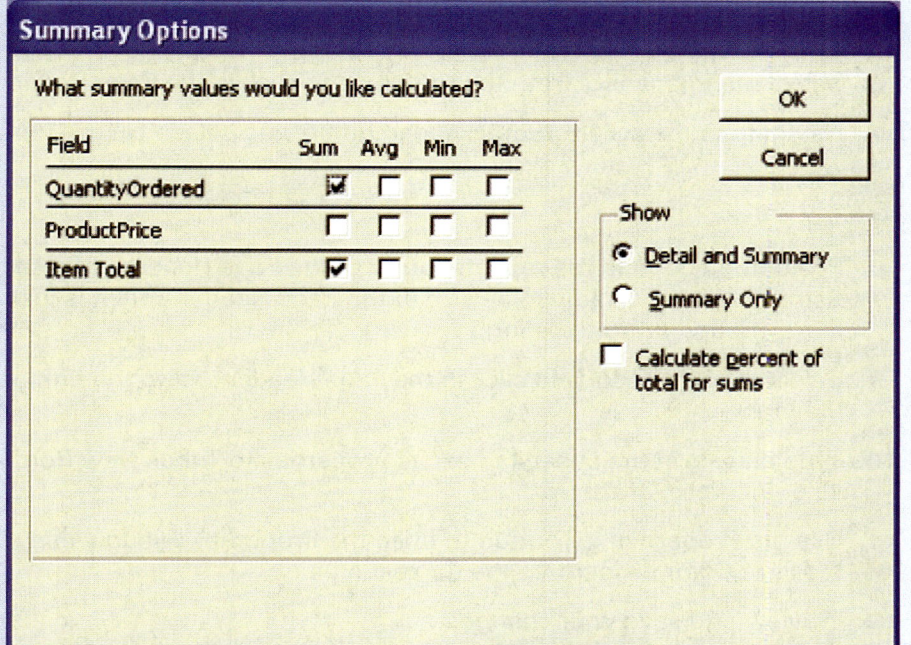

FIGURE 6.29

Adding group calculations to InvoiceJoinWithCalc report

8. Click **OK** and then **Next**

9. Select **Align Left 1** as the layout and **Landscape** as the page orientation, and click **Next**

10. Choose **Formal** as the report style and click **Next**

11. Click **Finish** to preview the report

This report is very similar to the one created without the query, but it has the advantage of already having the calculations in place. Customizing this report is a matter of adding a logo and title, reorganizing the fields to the correct report section, and then adding the page break.

To print on each invoice page, the logo and report title need to be in the Page Header section of the report. The GrandTotal of all invoices would print on the last invoice page, so it will be deleted. The simplest way to accomplish this is to remove the Report Header/Footer sections, which also will remove all controls they contain.

Creating a logo and title for the InvoiceJoinWithCalc report:

1. Verify that the **ac06KoryoKicks.mdb** database is open with the **InvoiceJoinWithCalc** report open in Design View

2. Select **Report Header/Footer** from the **View** menu to remove those sections of the report

3. Answer **Yes** to the prompt informing you that this operation is not reversible

4. If the Field List is open, close it since it won't be needed

5. Use the CstmrID Header bar to expand the space in the Page Header

6. Select the **Image** tool from the toolbox and click in the Page Header

7. Navigate to the **ac06KoryoKicksLogo.gif** file and select it

tip: *You may need to change the Type of File in the Open dialog box to Tag Image File Format or All Files*

8. Position the logo in the top left corner of the Page Header and use the CstmrID Header to adjust the size of the Page Header until it is just large enough to hold the logo

9. Select the **Label** tool and click in the Page Header just to the right of the logo

10. Type **Invoice** in the Label and set its properties to Times New Roman, 48 point, italic, and bold

11. Use the **Properties** button to open the Properties window and set the Fore Color property to the darkest blue

12. Preview and save your changes

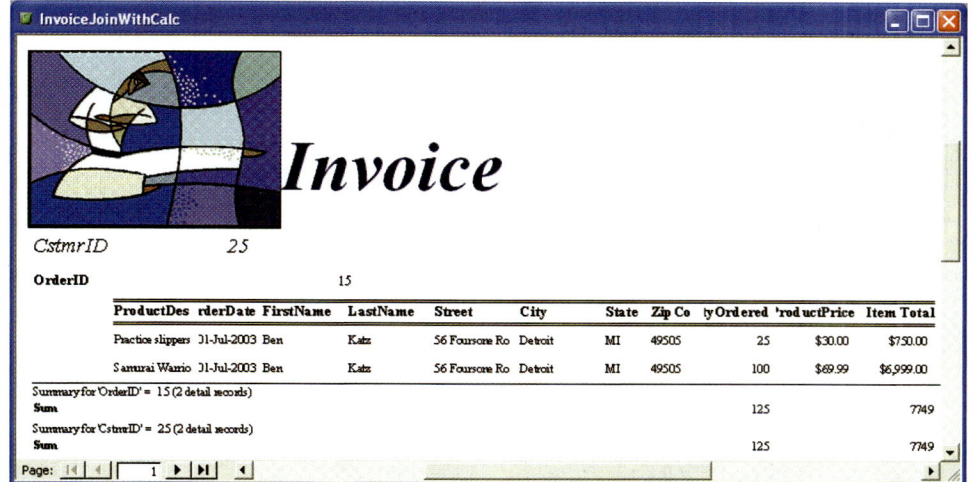

FIGURE 6.30

KoryoKicks logo and
report title

The most arduous reorganization tasks involve moving fields the Wizard placed in the Detail portion of the report. The first field that we'll address is OrderDate. The OrderDate only needs to appear once per order and most reasonably should be in the OrderID Group Header.

Modify the OrderID Header of the InvoiceJoinWithCalc report:

1. Verify that the **ac06KoryoKicks.mdb** database is open with the **InvoiceJoinWithCalc** report open in Design View

2. Adjust the size of the OrderID label and text box to match the data. Add a space between the words in the label

3. Select the **OrderDate** label and drag it to the right of the OrderID text box

4. Select the **OrderDate** text box in the Detail section, click the **Cut** button on the toolbar, click the **OrderID Header**, and click the **Paste** button on the toolbar

5. Click the **OrderID** label, click the **Format Painter** 🖌 button on the toolbar, and click the **OrderDate** text box to transfer the format to it

tip: *Double-clicking the Format Painter allows you to paint the format of the current object to multiple other objects. Clicking the Format Painter again turns it off*

6. Resize the OrderDate controls and position them as shown in Figure 6.31

7. Hold down the **Shift** key while using the **Line** tool to draw a line above the fields of the OrderID Header

8. Preview and save your updates

FIGURE 6.31

KoryoKicks headers

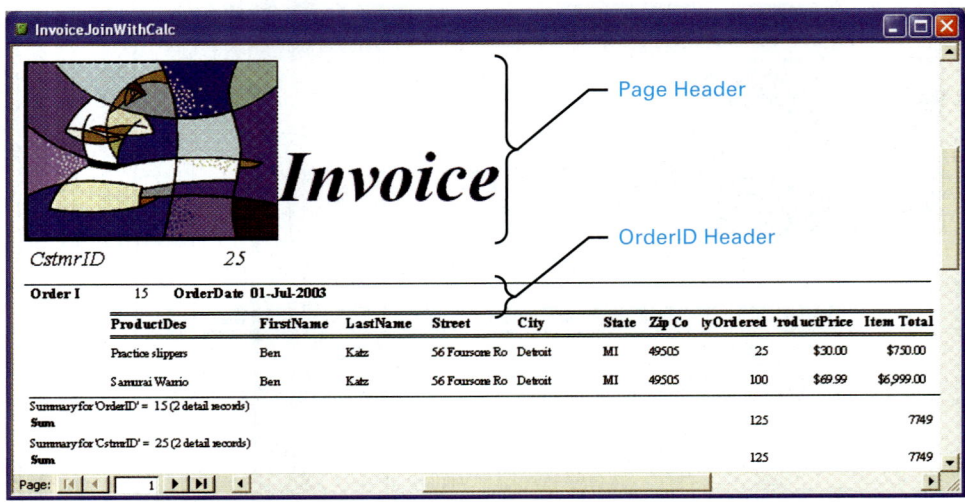

The customer name and address needs to appear only once per invoice and belongs in the CstmrID Group Header. The process of moving and formatting them is very similar to that just performed to modify the OrderID; however, both the text boxes and labels need to be moved since neither are currently in the CstmrID Group Header.

Modify the CstmrID Header of the InvoiceJoinWithCalc report:

1. Verify that the **ac06KoryoKicks.mdb** database is open with the **InvoiceJoinWithCalc** report open in Design View

2. Drag the OrderID Header section border to increase the height of the CstmrID Header section

3. Select the labels for FirstName, LastName, Street, City, State, and Zip by holding down the Shift key as you click

4. Cut the selection and paste it into the CstmrID Header section

5. Repeat the Cut and Paste process for the text boxes

6. Arrange the FirstName, LastName, Street, City, State, and ZipCode labels as shown in Figure 6.32. Arrange the text boxes below the labels

7. Edit the ZipCode caption to read Zip and add spaces to the Captions of the other labels

8. Adjust the size and position the CstmrID label and text box. Add a space to the label

9. Set all of the Text Box controls to display 10 point

10. Preview the report and adjust the size of the controls to display all of the data

11. Use the Format menu to finalize control alignment in the CstmrID Header section

12. Preview and save your updates

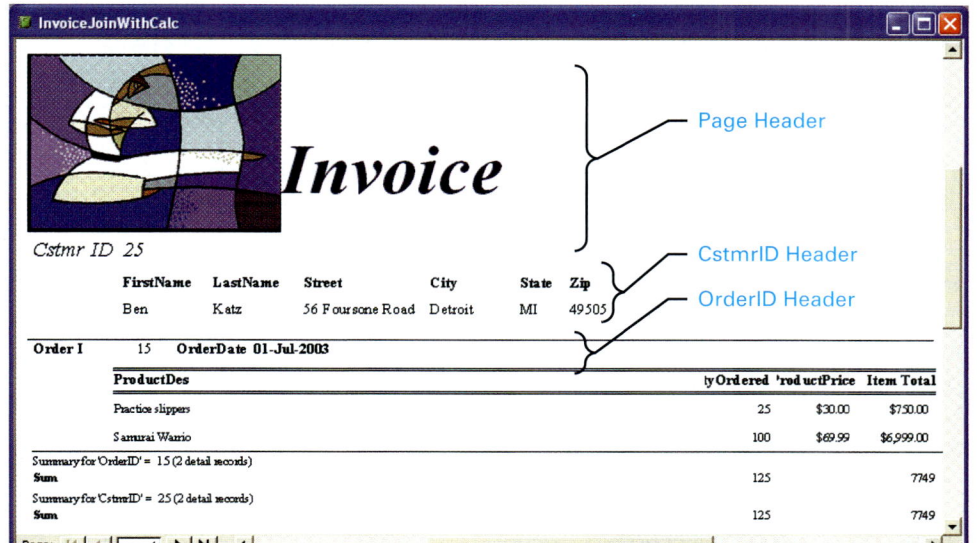

FIGURE 6.32
KoryoKicks headers

The Wizard added a Group Footer section for both OrderID and CstmrID. Both footers contain the same information unless a customer has placed multiple orders in the time period selected, so the CstmrID Footer needs to be eliminated. After this footer is removed and the Detail section sized and aligned, the Page Break tool will be used to print one invoice per page.

Modify the Detail and Footer sections of the InvoiceJoinWithCalc report:

1. Verify that the **ac06KoryoKicks.mdb** database is open with the **InvoiceJoinWithCalc** report open in Design View

2. Select the Text Box controls in the Detail section and set them to 10 point. Adjust the text box width to match its data

3. Select Quantity, ProductPrice, and ItemTotal text boxes and select Right Alignment so that the numbers will line up. Add spaces to labels and adjust label width

4. Align the Text Box controls in the Detail section with their corresponding Label controls in the CstmrID Header section

tip: *The numeric fields need to right-align and the text fields need to left-align*

5. Click the Sorting and Grouping button, select the CstmrID row, and set the Group Footer value to **No**

6. Respond **Yes** to the prompt and close the Sorting and Grouping dialog box

7. Delete the text box in the OrderID footer containing = "Summary for " & . . .

8. In the OrderID Footer, select the the two labels and set them to 10-point bold. Set the two text boxes to 10-point

ACCESS

9. Edit the Sum label to read **Count of items sold** and add a Label control for the other text box containing **Order Total**

10. Set the Format for the sum of ItemTotal to **currency**

11. Add a line above the Footer contents and organize them as shown in Figure 6.33

FIGURE 6.33

KoryoKicks invoice

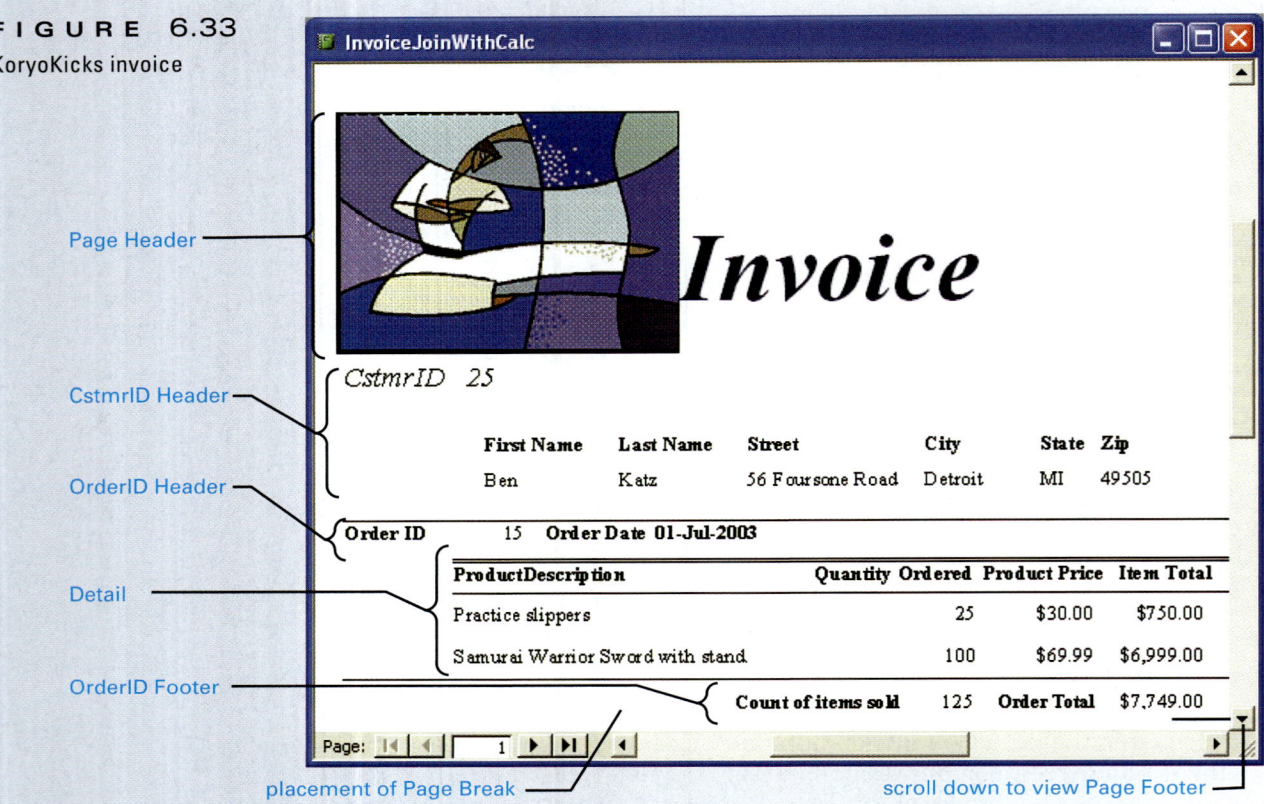

12. Click the Page Break tool and click below the contents of the OrderID Footer

tip: *The page break appears as six dots (. . . . . .) on the report*

13. Preview the report and adjust as needed

14. Save and close the report

---

another**word**   . . . on Modifying Database Objects

In this chapter you have modified queries, forms, and reports. Sometimes the modification was to improve the functionality. Sometimes it was to improve the visual impact. Regardless of why you are modifying an object, it is always wise to keep the original object as a backup. When making large numbers of changes, you should create intermediate backups also. A copy of the original design can be made using copy and paste in the Objects list before opening the object. You can use the Save As option of the File menu to save intermediate work under different names. Attaching sequential letters or numbers to the file-name works well (InvoicesNoQuery1, InvoicesNoQuery2, and so on). Rename the final file and delete all unneeded files when you are done

The KoryoKicks Invoice is a complex report involving four tables, two levels of grouping, detail line calculations, and summary calculations. No matter how this report is approached, it will be time consuming to develop, but once it is completed it can be used over and over again. The way this report is implemented, the twins will need to edit the selection criteria of the query before each report run. A more efficient methodology using Parameter queries will be introduced in later chapters.

Viewing Object Dependencies

Databases are storehouses of related data and objects. For example, each form or report is tied to a record source and each query is based on a table or tables. One common way to introduce errors into a database is to delete an object such as a table that removes the record source of another object that is still useful. In this situation, the useful object will generate a missing data source error because the data on which it is based are no longer available.

It is almost impossible to remember all interdependencies in a production database. Before deleting or maintaining a database object, it is valuable to know how it interacts with other database objects so you can make effective maintenance choices. Fortunately, Access 2003 provides a simple way to view table, query, form, and report dependencies, thereby reducing the likelihood of introducing errors through maintenance on these objects. Dependency data are not available for Data Access Pages, macros, or modules.

---

task reference   Viewing Object Dependencies

- Open the task pane and use the drop-down arrow to select **Object Dependencies**

- In the dependency pane

  - Review the list of objects that use the selected object

  - To view the list of objects that are being used by the selected object, click **Objects that I depend on** at the top of the pane

  - To view dependency information for an object listed in the pane, simply click on the expand icon (+) next to it

---

Viewing KoryoKicks object dependencies:

1. Verify that the **ac06KoryoKicks.mdb** database is open with no open objects

2. Select the **Tables** object and the **Customer** table

3. Open the task pane and use the drop-down arrow to select **Object Dependencies**

tip: Click the New button on the toolbar to open the task pane

4. Review the *Things that cause dependencies* link

5. Review the list of tables, queries, forms, and reports that could be impacted by changing or deleting the Customer table

FIGURE 6.34

The Customer table object dependencies

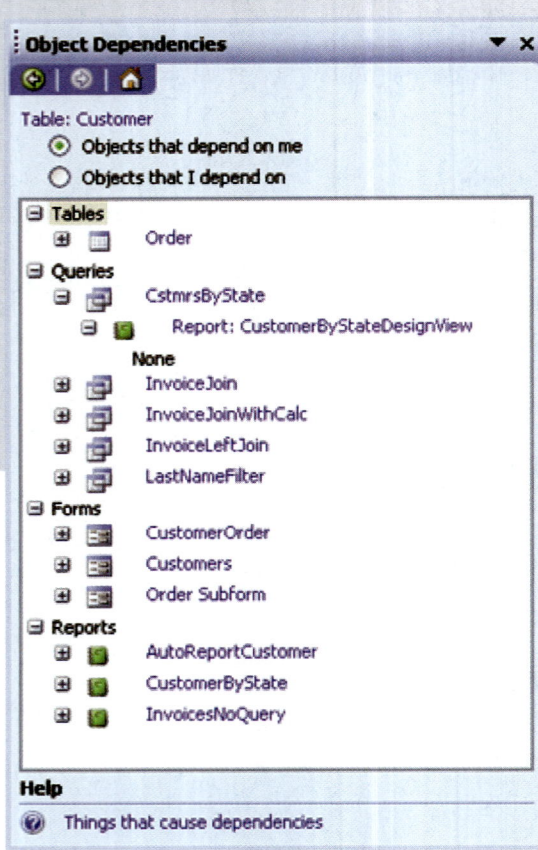

6. Click the + to the left of the CstmrsByState query to see the second-level dependencies for the Customer table (objects that are dependent on CstmrsByState and so could be impacted by changes to the Customer table)

7. Click the + to the left of the Report: CustomerByStateDesignView to view the third-level dependencies for the Customer table (objects that are dependent on the CstmrsByState query and so could be impacted by changes to the Customer table)

8. Click the **Objects that I depend on** option button and review the objects that could impact the Customer table

Database objects are dependent on each other anytime they share a defined relationship, a Lookup field, or use a data source. It is a good idea to review object dependencies before deleting or changing the design of any database object to avoid causing database errors through maintenance.

SESSION 6.2

making *the grade*

1. How would you decide whether to use an inner join or one of the outer join queries?

2. Why would you want to see the SQL generated by a query that you create in the QBE grid?

3. How do you know which table to open when you want to view related data in a subdatasheet?

4. Why would you consider adding indexes to your database tables?

5. Why would you use a query as the record source for a form?

SESSION 6.3 SUMMARY

To reduce data redundancy and increase data validity, database data are stored in multiple tables. Multiple tables reduce data redundancy because data that are common to multiple records are stored only once and then joined to each related row using a query. Data validity is improved because there is only one place to add or update each piece of data.

Only one-to-one and one-to-many relationships can be defined in a relational database. Many-to-many relationships use a junction table containing the key fields of both original tables, so that a one-to-many relationship is built from each of the original tables to the junction table.

While properly designed multiple-table databases greatly enhance the reliability of the data, it is necessary to understand and define appropriate relationships between the tables to control updates, deletions, and joins for output. Each defined relationship has properties that control its behavior. Referential integrity rules control how data in related tables can be entered and updated. Referential integrity rules can be turned off, enforced, or partially enforced. Double-click a relationship line in the Relationships window to set these options. In general, database data are more reliable when all referential rules are enforced.

When creating a multitable query, the relationship lines can be double-clicked to set the join properties. The default, inner join, returns records when the join field values of both tables match. A left outer join returns all of the rows from the left table and rows from the right table with a matching foreign key value. A right outer join returns all of the rows from the right table and rows from the left table with a matching foreign key value.

Data from multiple tables can be updated using the default primary datasheet and related subdatasheets. To open a subdatasheet, click the plus sign in the primary datasheet row. Related table data also can be displayed in a main form/subform combination. Data from the primary table are displayed in the main form and those from the related table are displayed in the subform.

Visit www.mhhe.com/i-series/ to explore related topics.

MICROSOFT OFFICE SPECIALIST OBJECTIVES SUMMARY

- Create and modify one-to-many relationships—MOS AC03S-1-5
- Enforce referential integrity—MOS AC03S-1-6
- Identify object dependencies—MOS AC03S-4-1

ACCESS

making the grade *answers*

SESSION 6.1

1. With the database open, click the Relationships button to activate the Relationships window. The properties of each relationship can be viewed by double-clicking the relationship line.

2. The drag operation is from the primary field to the related field.

3. Referential integrity rules govern how data are entered and deleted in related tables. They prevent orphans by requiring that the parent record exist before child records can be added to the related table, and that the parent can't be removed while it still has active children.

4. Access uses indexes to speed sort and search operations. An index is a table that can be used to look up index values and then move directly to the fields containing that value.

SESSION 6.2

1. Inner join queries are used when you want only rows of data where both tables have the same join field value. Use one of the outer joins when you want all of the data in one or the other table, regardless of whether there is a matching value in the other table.

2. You might want to see the SQL to verify which table is the left and which is the right table in the defined relationship. It could also help you learn SQL so that you could type your own queries for operations like Lookup fields.

3. Open the primary table. A plus sign displays in front of each record that will allow you to open the related table records.

4. Indexes improve search and sort operations. Candidates for indexing include fields that are frequently used in these operations, are not automatically indexed (like primary and foreign key values), and contain a wide range of values.

5. Queries allow you to verify the validity of data selection and calculations before applying formatting in the form.

task reference *summary*

Task	Page #	Preferred Method
View table relationships	AC 6.4	• Click the **Relationships** button on the Database toolbar • If relationships exist, they will be displayed. If there are no current relationships, you can add tables and build relationships between them
View relationship properties	AC 6.6	• Click the **Relationships** button on the Database toolbar • If relationships exist, they will be displayed. If there are no current relationships, you can add tables and build relationships between them • Double-click the relationship line that you would like to view • The Edit Relationships dialog box displays the properties of that relationship
Create a relationship	AC 6.8	• Click the **Relationships** button on the Database toolbar • If relationships exist, they will be displayed • Click the **Show Table** button on the toolbar • Select the table that you want to relate and click the **Add** button. Repeat this process for each table to be related • When you have added all of the necessary tables, click **Close** • Click the primary table field of the relationship and drag to the secondary field to initiate the relationship • Select the Referential Integrity options in the Edit Relationships dialog box • Click **OK** to close the Edit Relationships dialog box • Repeat this process for any other relationships to be built • Close the Relationships window

task reference *summary*

Task	Page #	Preferred Method
Index a table field	AC 6.13	• Open the table in **Design View** • Select the field to be indexed from the Field Name column • Set the Indexed field property to **Yes (Duplicates OK)** or **Yes (No Duplicates)** • Close the table design and save the changes
Delete an index	AC 6.14	• Open the table in **Design View** • Select the field whose index is to be removed from the Field Name column • Set the Indexed field property to **No** (this does not impact the field or its data) • Close the table design and save the changes
View the indexes of a table	AC 6.14	• Open the table in **Design View** • Click the **Indexes** button of the toolbar • Click an index to review its properties
Viewing object dependencies	AC 6.37	• Open the task pane and use the drop-down arrow to select **Object Dependencies** • In the dependency pane • Review the list of objects that use the selected object • To view the list of objects that are being used by the selected object, click **Objects that I depend on** at the top of the pane • To view dependency information for an object listed in the pane, simply click on the expand icon (+) next to it

TRUE/FALSE

1. A many-to-many relationship must be broken up into two one-to-many relationships before it can be implemented in Microsoft Access.

2. A left outer join query retrieves all records from the right table and only matching records from the left table.

3. The only way to tell whether or not indexing works is to monitor performance before and after an index is applied.

4. A key value in the primary table cannot be changed while there are records with that key value in the related table unless Cascade Update Related Fields is checked for that relationship.

5. When ∞ appears next to a table on a relationship line, data must be added to that table before related (same key value) records can be added to the table on the one side of the relationship.

6. The table on the one side of a relationship is also called the parent or primary table.

FILL-IN

1. Indexing is accomplished in _____ View.

2. A _____ retrieves all of the records in the second table, but only rows of the second table with matching foreign key values.

3. The _____ menu option is used to align multiple selected controls.

4. The _____ menu option causes a Label control Caption text to right-justify.

5. The _____ table is on the many side of a one-to-many relationship.

6. When a primary record is deleted, all related secondary records (those with the same key value) will automatically delete when _____ is set.

7. To build a one-to-one relationship, both tables must have the same _____.

MULTIPLE CHOICE

1. In a one-to-many relationship the primary key of the primary table _____ match exactly the primary key of the related table.
   a. must
   b. should
   c. cannot
   d. all of the above

2. The Referential Integrity setting that automatically updates the key field of related records when the primary key of the primary table is altered is _____.
   a. Cascade Update Related Fields
   b. Enforce Referential Integrity
   c. Cascade Delete Related Records
   d. AutoUpdate Related Records

3. An index created on more than one field is referred to as a _____.
   a. compound index
   b. complex index
   c. multiple-field index
   d. none of the above

4. When relationships have been set, related data can be viewed in Datasheet View by _____.
   a. running a query
   b. clicking the plus (+) sign
   c. clicking the Subdatasheet button
   d. all of the above

5. When a query selects all records in the first (left) table and only matching records from the second (right) table, the join is a _____.
   a. left inner join
   b. right inner join
   c. right outer join
   d. left outer join

REVIEW QUESTIONS

Each of the following topics should be addressed in one to three paragraphs.

1. Give an example of a one-to-many relationship between tables and explain how it might be used.

2. Describe the relationship line notations in the Relationships window and how they can impact the construction of a main form/subform.

3. How are many-to-many relationships handled?

4. How would you delete a relationship that was built in error or is no longer needed?

5. What is the importance of cascade updates and deletes?

CREATE THE QUESTION

For each of the following answers, create the question.

ANSWER	QUESTION
1. Yes (No Duplicates)	
2. SQL View button	
3. Lookup fields	
4. The report or form section and all of the controls it contains are permanently deleted	
5. The Sorting and Grouping dialog box	
6. Double-click the relationship line in the Relationships window	
7. Drag the large box in the upper left-hand corner of a control selected in Form Design View	

FACT OR FICTION

For each of the following, determine whether the statement is fact, fiction, or both and present your arguments for that conclusion.

1. Calculations must always be completed in a query before creating a report.

2. Both a Group Header and a Group Footer must exist on a report for each defined group.

3. For the best database performance, index every field in a table.

4. To create a new relationship, you must drag from the primary table to the related table.

5. You can drag and drop controls from one form section to another.

6. Often the same report can be built using either table(s) or a query as the data source.

7. A logo placed in the Report Header section of a report will print on each page.

practice

1. Altamonte High School Booster Club Donation Tracking—Part I: Setting Table Relationships

Altamonte High School Booster Club is an organization of students, teachers, parents, and community members who sponsor high school activities. The Boosters are using an Access database to track donations.

1. Start Access and open **ac06AltamonteBoosters.mdb**

2. Use Figure 6.35 to create and populate the **DonationClass** table depicted in the figure

3. Close the DonationClass table and use the **Relationships** button to open the Relationships window

4. Add the **Boosters** and **DonationClass** tables to the Relationships window

5. Drag a relationship from **DonationClass.Class** (Class in the DonationClass table) to **Boosters.DonationClass** (DonationClass in the Boosters table)

6. Close the Relationships window, saving your updates

7. Open the Donations table in Design View

8. Use the Lookup Wizard to create a Lookup field for Booster that retrieves the Name field from the Boosters table. Sort the Lookup by Name and do not display ID

tip: *To test the Lookup field, open the Donations table in Datasheet View. A drop-down list of names should be available in the Booster column*

9. Open the Relationships window and add the Donations table

tip: *You may need to use the **Show Table** button to display the Show Tables dialog box*

10. Adding the Lookup field created a relationship between the Donations table and the Boosters table without any attributes (no notation on the lines)

11. Double-click the Donations/Boosters relationship line

12. Click on all of the Referential Integrity options and click **OK**

13. Open the Boosters/DonationClass relationship, click on Enforce Referential Integrity, and then click **OK**. Do not check any other Referential Integrity options

14. Verify your table relationships using Figure 6.36

15. Close the Edit Relationships dialog box saving your changes

16. Open the Boosters table in Datasheet View

17. Add yourself as a booster in Class 1

18. Use the subdatasheets to add two donations for yourself dated last month and this month for $15 and $25, respectively

19. Close the AltamonteBoosters database and exit Access if your work is complete

FIGURE 6.35

DonationClass table

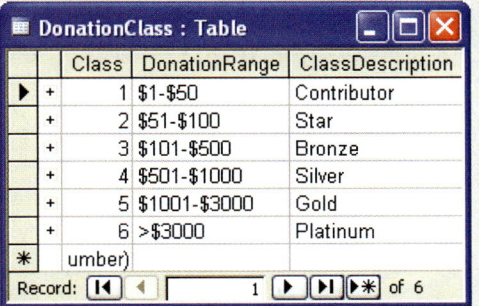

FIGURE 6.36

AltamonteBoosters table relationships

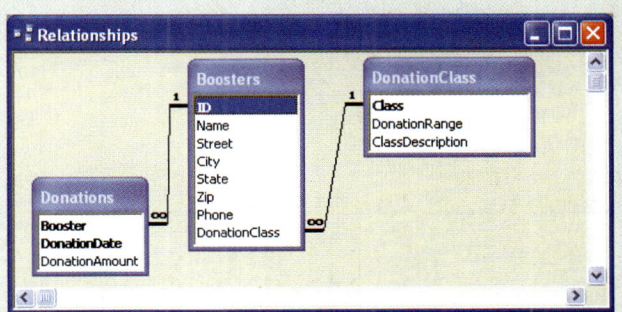

AC 6.45

2. Building Table Relationships for NMO Energy

NMO Energy supplies products to consumer energy companies across the United States. NMO has a large sales force with offices in various locations. Each company that does business with NMO has an assigned salesperson. Each salesperson supports multiple companies. Two tables are in the Microsoft Access database for NMO, Salesforce and Customer. You will build a Lookup field from Customer to Salesforce to simplify updates.

1. Start Access and open **ac06NMOEnergy.mdb**

2. Open the Customer table in Design View

    a. Use the Lookup Wizard to create a Lookup field for SalesID that retrieves the LastName and FirstName of the Salesperson from the Salesforce table

    b. Do not display the SalesID in the Lookup

3. Use the Relationships button on the toolbar to open the Relationships window

    a. Double-click the relationship between the Salesforce and Customer table to open the relationship created by the Lookup field

    b. Verify that the relationship between Salesforce.SalesID and Customer.SalesID is one-to-many

    c. Enforce Referential Integrity

    d. Do not Cascade Update or Cascade Delete Related Records

    e. Close the Relationships window saving your changes

4. Test the Lookup field

    a. Open the Salesforce table and add yourself as a salesperson

    b. Close the Salesforce table

    c. Open the Customer table

    d. Use the Lookup field to make yourself the salesperson for customers 71, 81, and 93

    e. Close the Customer table

5. Test the relationship

    a. Open the Salesforce table

    b. Use the subdatasheet to add **Mississippi Power and Light** as a new company for Ramona Amstont. Use MPLI as the InternalCode

    c. Use the subdatasheet to add the local power company to your customer list. Select an appropriate InternalCode

6. If your work is complete, exit Access; otherwise, continue to the next assignment

FIGURE 6.37

Salesforce Lookup field

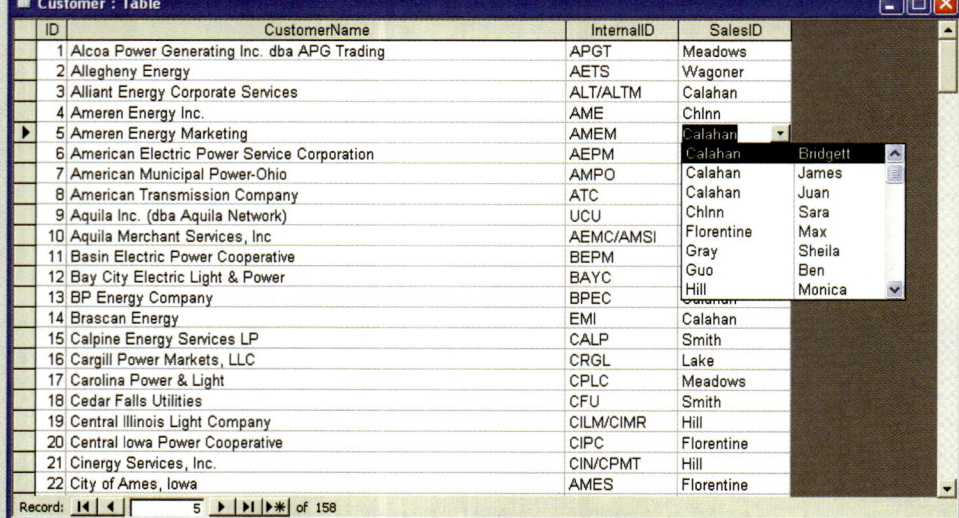

challenge!

1. Altamonte High School Booster Club—Part II: Using Related Tables

1. Start Access and the **ac06AltamonteBoosters.mdb** database

tip: *If you did not complete the Practice assignment, you will need to do so now*

2. Use the Form Wizard to create a main form/ subform
   a. The main form should display all of the Boosters table fields
   b. The subform should display all of the Donations table fields
   c. Set the data to be viewed **by Boosters**
   d. Use the **Tabular** layout for the subform
   e. Use the **Blueprint** style
   f. Name the form **BoostersDonations**
   g. Refer to Figure 6.38 and customize the main form and subform so that all the labels display and the field sizes are appropriate

3. Use the form to add another donation for Matthew Hoff for the current date and **$700**. Change his DonationClass to **6**

4. Close the form, saving your changes

5. Create a query that
   a. Selects **Boosters.DonationClass**, **Boosters.Name**, **Donations.DonationDate**, and **Donations.DonationAmount**
   b. Selects all of the donations for October 2003

6. Save the query as **Oct03Donations**

7. Use the Report Wizard to create a report using **Oct03Donations** as the record source
   a. List data by Donation
   b. Group the data by DonationClass
   c. Sort the data by **Name** and **DonationDate**
   d. Total **DonationAmount**
   e. Use **Block** format and **Casual** style, and name it **BoostersOct03Donations**

8. Customize the report using Figure 6.39 as a guide
   a. Change title to **Altamonte HS Boosters**
   b. Add a Label control under the report title with a Caption property of **October 2003 Donations Report**, teal color, bold, and a point size of 14
   c. Adjust the labels and text boxes so that all of the data display
   d. Adjust the first group Summary label so that it is indented
   e. Delete the Group Footer Sum label
   f. Align the = Sum text box in the Amount column to the right of the Summary label
   g. Align the Grand Total = Sum text box in the Amount column

9. Close the AltamonteBoosters database and exit Access if your work is complete

F I G U R E   6.39

Customized October 2003 Donations Report

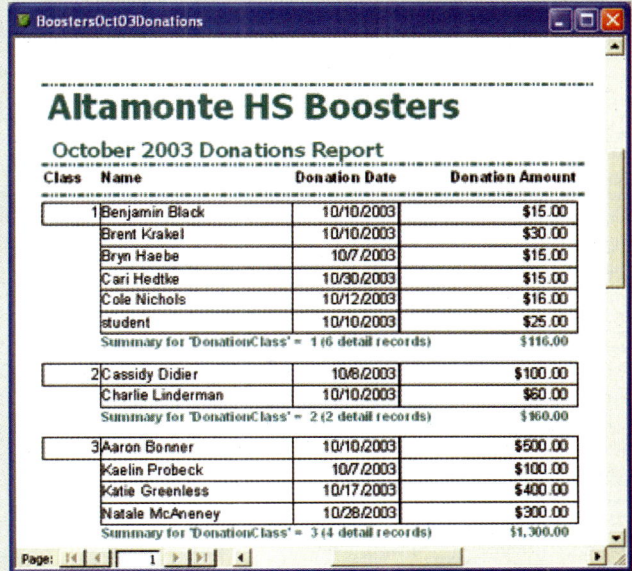

F I G U R E   6.38

BoostersDonations form

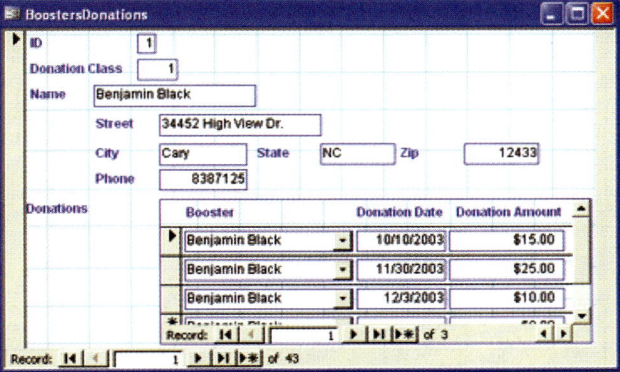

2. Multitable Operations for NMO Energy

NMO Energy supplies products to consumer energy companies across the United States. NMO has a large sales force with offices in various locations. Two tables are in the Microsoft Access database for NMO, Salesforce and Customer. In the Practice exercise for this chapter, a Lookup field was built and properties for the relationship assigned.

1. Start Access and open **ac06NMOEnergy.mdb**

2. If you have not already completed steps 1 through 3 from the second Practice exercise in this chapter, do so now

3. Use the Form Wizard to create a main form/subform pair

   a. The Salesforce form should be the main form

   b. The Customer form should be the subform

   c. All fields of both tables should display

   d. Use the **Tabular** layout for the subform

   e. Use the **SumiPainting** style

   f. Name the form **SalesforceCustomers**

   g. Customize the form to match Figure 6.40. You will need to adjust both the height and width of text boxes

4. Use the Report Wizard to create a report showing customers grouped by employee

   a. Include **SalesID**, **LastName**, **FirstName**, and **Phone** from the Salesforce table

   b. Include all fields from the Customer table

   c. View the data by Salesforce

   d. Group by SalesID

   e. Sort by CustomerName

   f. Use the **Align Left 1** layout and the **Soft Gray** style

   g. Name the report **SalesforceCustomers**

   h. Customize the report so that all labels have spaces and table names are not included

   i. Make the report title **Customers by Salesperson**

   j. Adjust the size of the LastName and FirstName control and place them on the same row. Move PhoneNumber up directly under FirstName. Move the row labels up until it is just under PhoneNumber and adjust the height of the Salesforce_SalesID Header to be just tall enough for the revised design

5. If your work is complete, exit Access; otherwise, continue to the next assignment

FIGURE   6.40

NMOEnergy SalesforceCustomers form

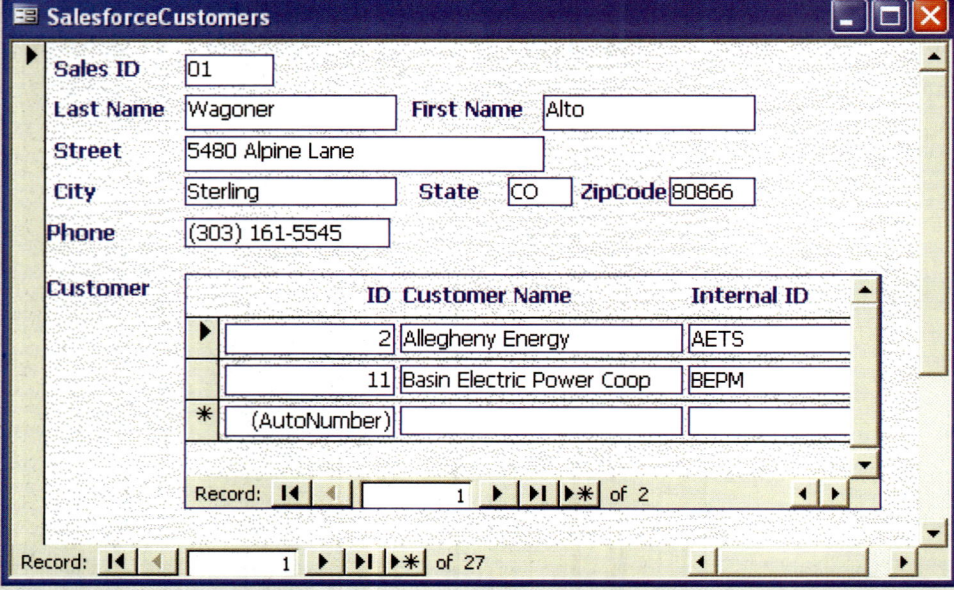

1. Curbside Recycling

Curbside Recycling is enhancing its Web presence so customers can view their current account status and the profit position of the organization.

1. Open the **ac06CurbsideRecycling.mdb** database

2. Open the Relationships window and review the relationship between the Customer and the CustomerRecords tables

3. Open the Edit Relationships dialog box and click on all of the referential integrity options

4. Close the Edit Relationships dialog box and the Relationships window, saving your changes

5. Users have reported significant delays when searching by LastName and FirstName. Create a multicolumn index called **Name** to try to address this issue

6. Use the Form Wizard to create a main form/subform for maintaining table data
   a. Include all fields from both tables
   b. View the data **by Customer**
   c. Use the Datasheet View for the subform
   d. Select the **Standard** style
   e. Name the form **CustomerRecordsUpdate**

FIGURE 6.41

Updating table relationships

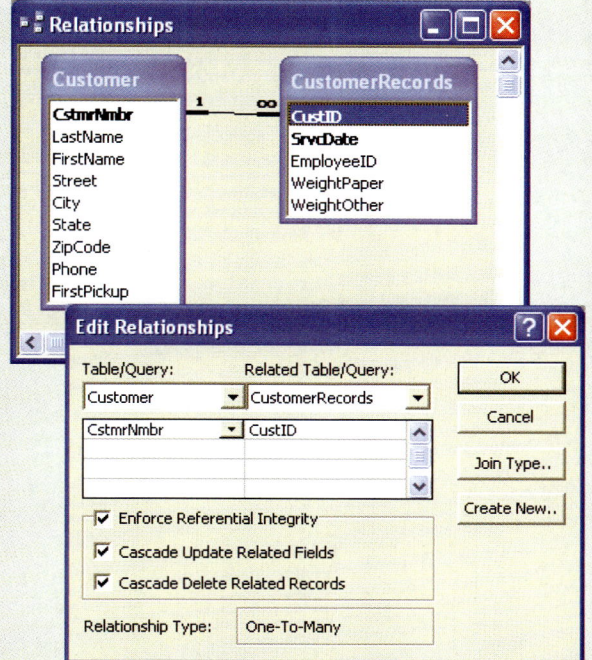

7. Customize the form to improve its functionality
   a. Narrow the subform to about 4 inches
   b. Add spaces to the form and subform labels
   c. Change to Form View and drag the subform column widths to display the column headings and data

tip: You cannot change the width in Design View because you have chosen a Datasheet for the subform

8. Use the Report Wizard to create a report
   a. Select **CstmrNmbr**, **LastName**, and **FirstName** from the Customer table
   b. Select **SrvcDate**, **WeightPaper**, and **WeightOther** from the CustomerRecords table
   c. View the data by **Customer**
   d. Sort the data by **SrvcDate**
   e. Sum both weight fields
   f. Use **Block** format
   g. Use **Compact** style
   h. Name the report **CustomerPickups**

9. Customize the report
   a. Add spaces to the labels
   b. Adjust the field widths to fit the size of the column headings and labels
   c. Change the label for the sum to **Total Weight** and put the totals under the correct column
   d. Preview and save your changes

10. If your work is complete, exit Access; otherwise, continue to the next assignment

FIGURE 6.42

Customized CustomerRecordsUpdate form

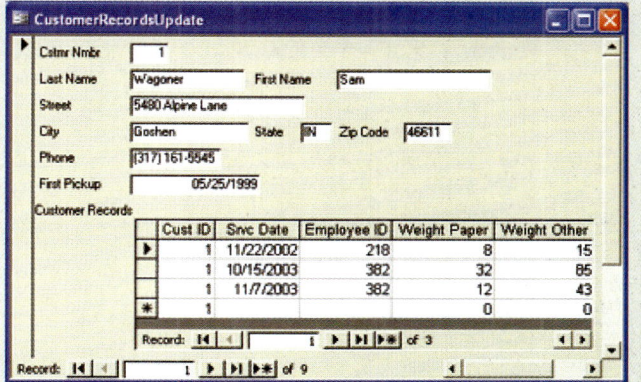

2. Using Multiple Tables to Track Employee Skills

Community Hospital, like most hospitals nationwide, is feeling the crunch of insufficient medical staff. To effectively treat patients, it has had to change the way it does business. One of these changes is to try to match staff to patients' needs rather than try to staff to cover any possible need. In order to schedule staff, the Scheduling Department needed a way to track and report each employee's current set of skills. You will create a custom report that will be posted to the Web to allow the nurses in charge of a unit to assign patients to nurses based on the patient's needs and the nurse's skills.

There are a number of tables in the **ac06Community Hospital.mdb** database, and this report requires an understanding of three of them. The Employee table holds general data about each employee being tracked. The Competency table holds data about each measurable competency needed by the hospital. The Competency Assignment table uses EmployeeID and CompetencyID to assign competencies to individual employees who have met those requirements. You will create a list of employees and their skills organized by Unit. This report will be posted to the hospital intranet so that all charge nurses have access to it for patient assignment.

FIGURE 6.43

NursingSkills report

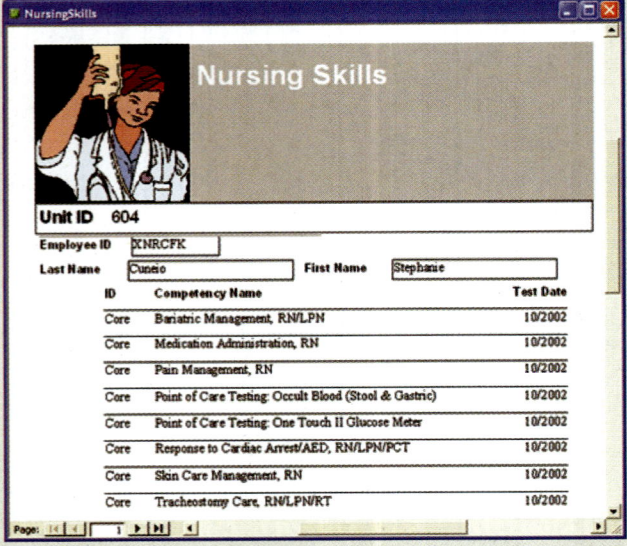

1. Open Access and open **ac06CommunityHospital.mdb**

2. Review the data in the tables that will be used for this report. Close the tables when done

3. Open the Relationships window. Build relationships from Employee to Competency Assignment and Employee to Unit. Enforce referential integrity

4. Use the Report Wizard to create the report shown in Figure 6.43 that will be available from the hospital's Web site. Name the report **NursingSkills**. The completed report should have the following attributes

   a. Include only **EmployeeID**, **LastName**, **FirstName**, and **UnitID** from the Employee table

   b. Include **CompetencyID** and **TestDate** from the CompetencyAssignment table

   c. Include **CompetencyName** from the Competency table

   d. List the Data by Employee grouped by Unit

   e. Order the Data by CompetencyID and CompetencyName

   f. Use the **Align Left 2** layout and the **Soft Gray** style

   g. Add the image **ac06Nurse.gif** to the Header section

   h. Change the CompetencyId heading to ID. Edit the remaining report controls so that the title and headings have spaces. Change the widths of the ID and CompetencyName columns to match the size of the data. Move LastName and FirstName to the same row and move the competency headings to the row where FirstName was

5. Close the database and exit Access if your work is complete

on the web

1. Academic Software Multitable Relationships and Reports

Academic Software, as the name implies, is a clearing-house for educational software. You are improving its existing Access database.

1. Use a search engine to find at least three academic software titles and prices for the K–12 environment. Find at least three free download titles

2. Open the **ac06Software.mdb** database

3. Open the Relationships window and review the relationship between tblVendor and tblSoftware

4. Open the Edit Relationships dialog box and click on Cascade Updates and Deletes

5. Close the Edit Relationships dialog box and the Relationships window

6. Users have reported significant delays when searching by tblSoftware.Category. Index this field to try to address these issues

7. Open tblVendor and use the subdatasheet to add the three software titles that you found to the Edusoft Inc. vendor with Software Numbers 7000–7002. Add a new vendor named **Web Downloads** with a VendorCode of **WD**

8. Open a new query in Design View and put both tables on the QBE grid
   a. From tblSoftware add **Category**, **Name**, **Quantity**, **Price**, and **VendorCode**
   b. From tblVendor add **Name**, **Address**, **City**, **State**, **ZipCode**, and **Phone Number** (see Figure 6.44)
   c. Run the query (see Figure 6.45)
   d. Save the query as **SoftwareByCategory**

9. With the Report Wizard, create a report using the SoftwareByCategory query
   a. Use the **by tblSoftware** option
   b. Group by **Category**
   c. Sort by **tblSoftware.Name**
   d. Select the **Landscape** page orientation and **Stepped** layout
   e. Choose the **Soft Gray** style
   f. Name the report **SoftwareByCategory**

10. Customize the report using Figure 6.46 as a guide

FIGURE 6.44

SoftwareByCategory query

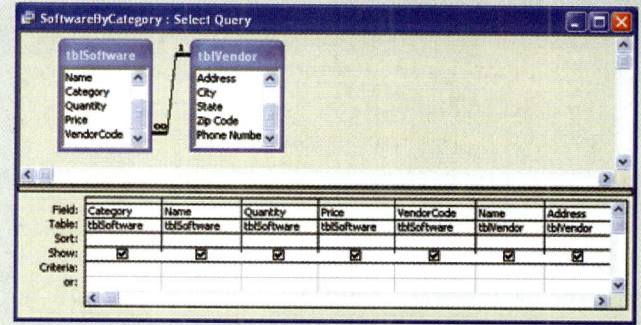

FIGURE 6.45

SoftwareByCategory report

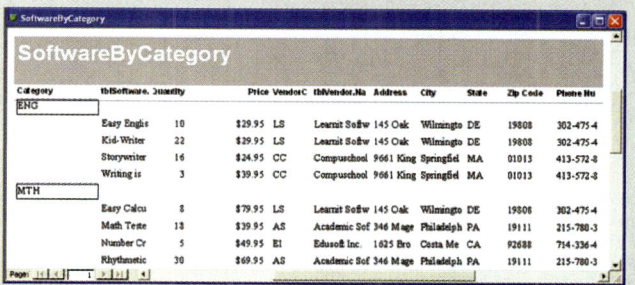

FIGURE 6.46

Customized SoftwareByCategory report

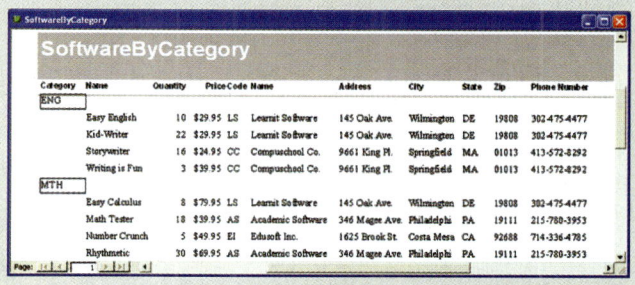

hands-on projects

around the world

1. TechRocks Seminars Forms and Reports

TechRocks Seminars provides onsite technical training to large businesses around the world. You will build the Table relationships and test the multitable abilities.

1. Start Access and open the **ac06Seminars.mdb** database

2. Open the Relationships window

   a. Use the **Show Tables** button to add the Facilitators table to the Relationships window

   b. Open the Facilitators/Seminars relationship and enforce all referential integrity rules

   c. Open the Seminars/Enrollment relationship and enforce all referential integrity rules

   d. Use Figure 6.47 to verify your relationships and then close the Relationships window

3. Create a multitable query in Design View

   a. From the Seminars table select **Seminar ID**, **Description**, **Date**, **Time**, **Hours**, and **Place**

   b. From the Facilitators table select **LastName**, **FirstName**, and **Phone**

   c. From the Enrollment table select **Student Number**, **Last Name**, **First Name**, and **Student Phone**

   d. Save the query as **StudentListing**

4. Use the StudentListing query to create a report listing the students currently enrolled in each seminar

   a. Initiate the Report Wizard

   b. Select the **StudentListing** query as the data source

   c. Select all of the fields from the query

   d. Select **by Seminars** as the way to view the report

   e. No additional grouping is necessary

   f. Select **Align Left1** as the layout

   g. Select the **Bold** style

   h. Name the report **StudentListingBySeminar**

5. Customize the StudentsBySeminar report. Refer to Figure 6.48

   a. Change the title and column headings as shown

   b. Adjust the size of labels and text boxes

   c. Rearrange the Seminar ID Header fields as shown. Be careful to adjust the *Facilitator* name fields not the enrollment name fields

   d. Adjust the length of the lines above and below the header (there are two above and two below even though it looks like one line each)

   e. Activate the Sorting and Grouping dialog box and add a Group Footer for Seminar ID

   f. Insert a Page Break in the Seminar ID Footer section

   g. Preview and save your work

FIGURE 6.47

Seminars table relationships

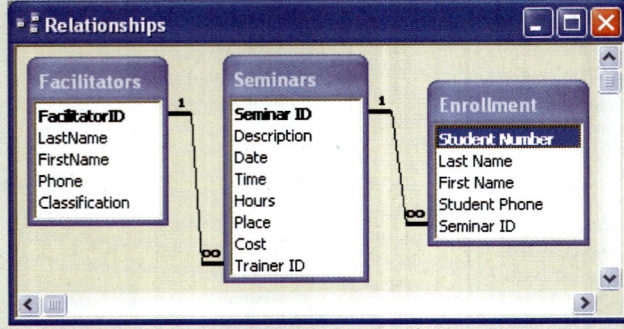

FIGURE 6.48

Customized StudentListingBySeminar report

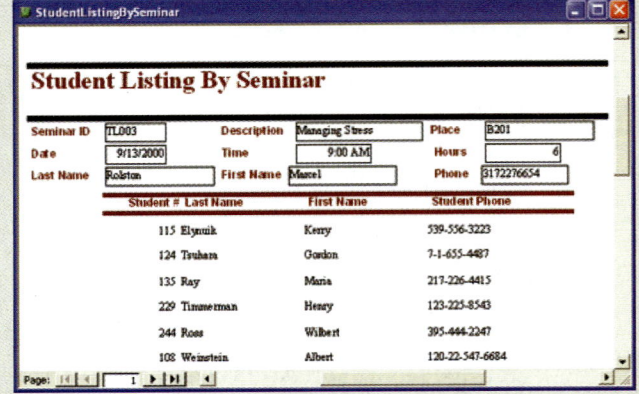

running project: tnt web design

Custom Forms and Reports for TnT

As TnT grows, so does the complexity of its database. Tori and Tonya now have over 65 employees and several hundred customers. Employees and projects are spread across the United States, so it is becoming critical to have simple data entry and reporting.

1. Start Access and open the **ac06TnT.mdb** database. Familiarize yourself with each table if necessary
2. Open the Relationships window
    a. Edit the tblCustomers/CustomerSites relationship
    b. Enforce all referential integrity rules
    c. Close the Relationships window and save your changes
3. Use the Query Wizard to create a query listing fields from each table
    a. From the tblCustomers select **cusName** and **cusAddress**
    b. From CustomerSites select **URL**
    c. From Employees select **LastName** and **FirstName**
    d. Save the query as **CustomerWebSites**

4. Use the Report Wizard to create a report with all of the fields of the CustomerWebSites query
    a. No additional sorting or grouping is needed
    b. Choose **Stepped** layout
    c. Select **Soft Gray** style
    d. Save the report as **CustomerWebSite**
5. Customize the CustomerWebSite report
    a. Put spaces in the report title
    b. Remove the "cus" prefix from the Customer table fields
    c. Change the LastName label to **Development Manager**
    d. Delete the FirstName label
    e. Expand the URL label and text box
    f. Adjust the position of controls to match Figure 6.49
6. If your work is complete, exit Access; otherwise continue to the next assignment

F I G U R E 6.49

TnT Relationships

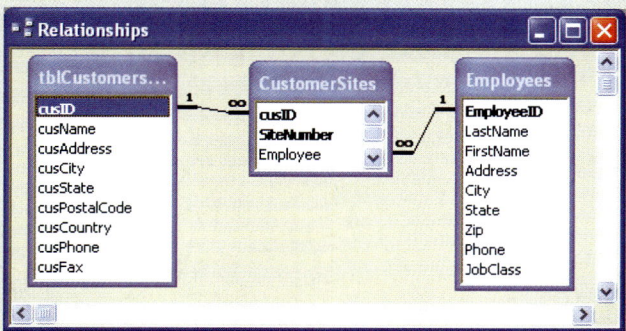

F I G U R E 6.50

CustomerWebSites report

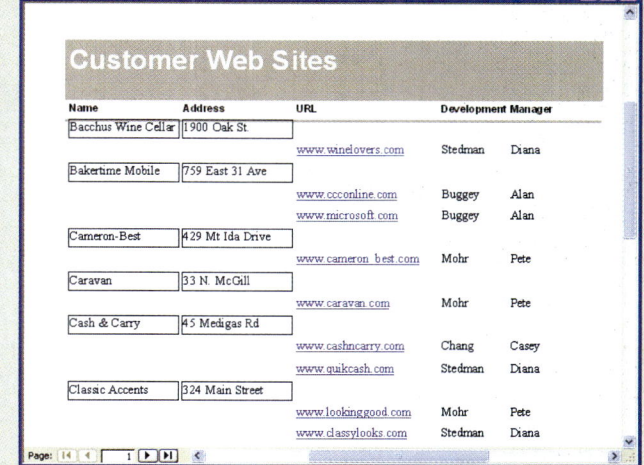

1. Create a Multitable Database to Invoice Customers

Create a new database named **ac06CustomersMultiTableDatabase.mdb**. Select a small business that is of interest to you such as selling skateboard products, a clothing boutique, or a bakery and create a database to support billing customers. The database must store data about customers, products, prices, and orders. Build all necessary table relationships. Include data for at least 10 customers and 10 orders. Create an invoice report using a query to join the table data. Name the query **InvoiceQuery** and the report **InvoiceWithQuery**. Create a second invoice without using a query. Name this report **InvoiceNoQuery**. Customize both reports to align report headings, include a line item calculation, and include an invoice total calculation.

2. Create a Multitable Database to Track Employees

Create a new database named **ac06Employees MultiTableDatabase.mdb**. Select a local or Internet business that you frequent and create a database that can be used to track their employees. The database must contain tables for employees, benefits, and departments. The Department table should have a DepartmentID, DepartmentDescription, and DepartmentManager at a minimum. All employees must belong to a department and have benefits. Build all necessary table relationships. Include data for at least 10 employees and 3 departments. Create a query named **EmployeesByDepartmentQuery** that will list the department, manager, and all employees for that department. Use the query to create an **EmployeesByDepartmentReport**. Group the data by department and manager. List all employees. Add a calculated field with an appropriate label that will count the number of employees in each department.

Maintaining Databases

did you know?

playing *cards were originally invented by the Chinese.*

the *average human has over 1,500 dreams every year.*

"for *every complex problem, there is a solution that is simple, neat, and wrong."—Henry L. Mencken*

Victoria *Woodhall became the first woman to run for president of the United States in 1872.*

the *largest nerve in the human body is the sciatic nerve, which is about 2 cm wide and runs from the spinal cord down the back of each leg.*

corporations *and government agencies report that the average cost to investigate, repair, and secure computer systems that have been hacked is $1 million per intrusion.*

to *find out how many times a day the average person laughs, visit* www.mhhe.com/i-series.

Chapter Objectives

- **Use data validation criteria to ensure data accuracy**
- **Create and modify custom input masks—MOS AC03S-1-4**
- **Add user permissions to a database**
- **Set database passwords**
- **Use database replication to synchronize multiple copies of a database**
- **Apply database encryption to secure data**
- **Use the Database Splitter to protect databases from modification and to create a front and back end**

KoryoKicks: Database Design Review

Missy and Micah have been using the KoryoKicks database for several months and believe that it is time to reevaluate its design. When the database was built, KoryoKicks was a simple organization. Missy and Micah, the only employees, taught a few martial arts and self-defense classes and sold martial arts supplies to their students. The twins handled all of the deliveries, kept track of the money, and taught all classes.

Because their products were successful, the twins recruited two additional instructors allowing them to offer four times as many classes. They also began to use the Internet and a local mall kiosk to market martial arts supplies. The mall kiosk is managed by a friend and most deliveries are handled by still another. A bookkeeper has been hired to manage Internet product orders, bill customers, and book money received. In short, KoryoKicks is a more complex business handling more than four times the initial product volume and supporting seven employees (including Missy and Micah) operating from multiple locations.

Because employees are now responsible for a specialized group of tasks, the current single database with a single set of reports is not effective. The twins have built additional queries, forms, and reports to try to address these evolving needs, but the database has become cumbersome. There are too many database objects, which slows overall

performance. Since multiple people are using the database, more data entry errors are cropping up caused by individual style differences and varying user skill levels. There is a real need to share the database using a network, the Internet, or specialized data subsets.

A design review is the process used to evaluate the effectiveness of an operational database, evaluate necessary changes, and develop a plan to implement changes. The first step of a design review is to gather known issues and problems with each database object. Missy and Micah documented their own concerns and then talked to each of the other users. These issues can be as minor as "I don't like the date format on this screen" or more critical such as "I have to adjust the tax on every invoice because the tax rate changed and the database has not been updated." Some of the current issues include

- Data entry errors need to be reduced
- The Phone input mask is confusing users and therefore does not provide the expected result of simplifying data entry
- Consistency in the capitalization of data would improve the data's value
- Sharing the database on one computer in one location is cumbersome and results in data not being entered for an extended period of time, and sometimes completely lost

- Many fields could benefit from default quantities
- Some of the fields that are now blank should not allow blank values
- Security has become an issue since there are so many database users and the database is physically on a computer in a shared area

Since issues with the current performance of the database have been identified, the next logical step is to evaluate the various ways that Access can be used to address each issue. Missy and Micah have asked you to help in this process because they are unfamiliar with these features.

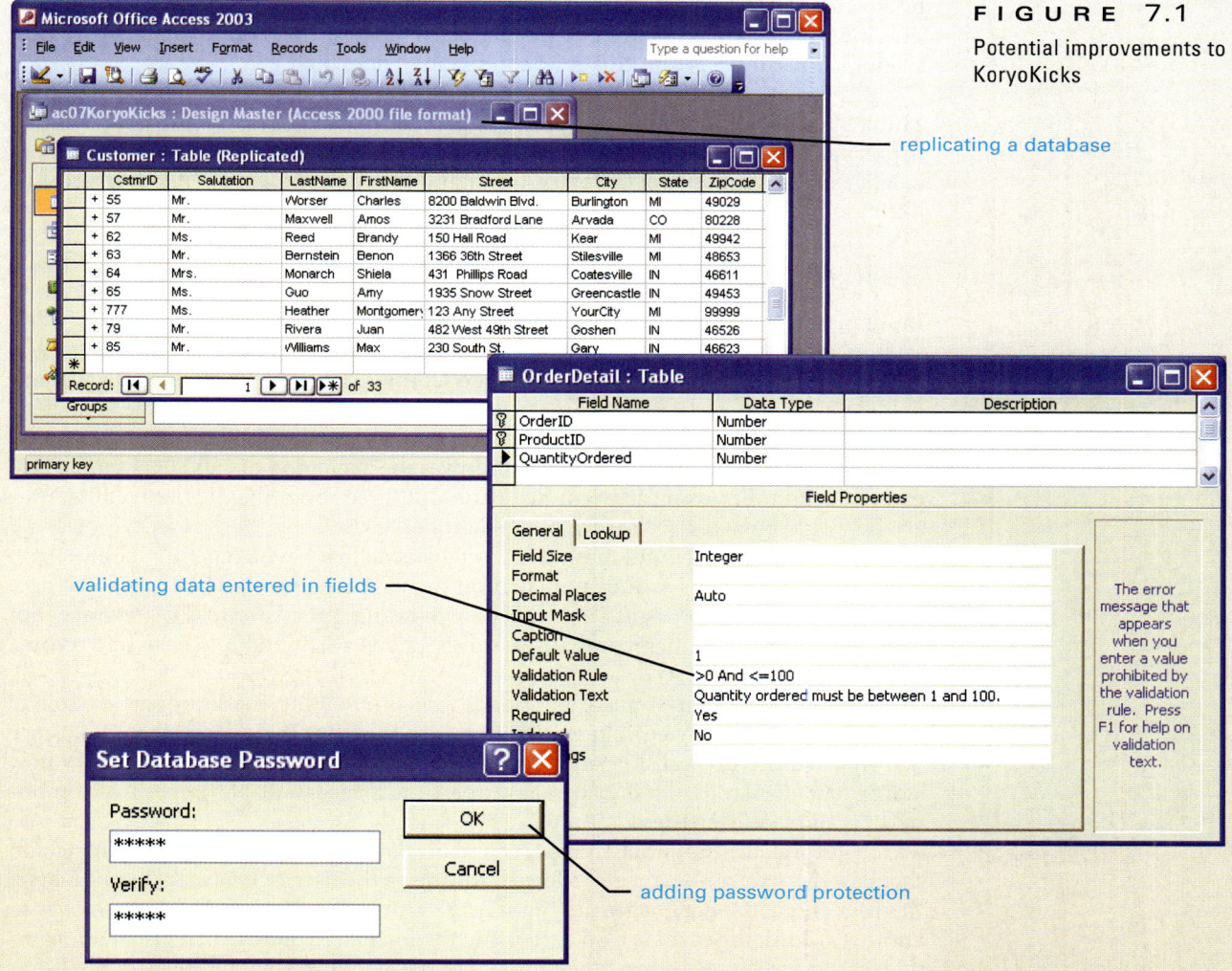

FIGURE 7.1

Potential improvements to KoryoKicks

replicating a database

validating data entered in fields

adding password protection

SESSION 7.1 REFINING TABLE DESIGN

The design of any database needs to be reviewed periodically to ensure that the user's needs are being appropriately met and that it is optimized for performance. Databases are designed to fit the needs of their users at a given point in time. Over time these needs change for a number of reasons. Change is fundamental to the growth and success of any organization or business, so over time data and data analysis needs can change dramatically. It is also true that the more people use a database, the more they want from the database. Users become more familiar with their data over time and recognize additional touches that would improve the usability of the database.

Add to the mix that you get better at designing, developing, and supporting databases, and it is easy to see that leaving a database alone is dooming it to failure. On the system optimization side, databases that are not optimized become slow and hog system resources. Disk space and seek time are wasted by storing records that could be archived because they are never accessed in the active database. Besides impacting other applications on the system by not sharing resources, these issues also can impact user satisfaction.

Don't panic. If the original database design was sound, most of these concerns can be addressed by adding tables to hold the new data, adding fields to existing tables, refining indexes, archiving unused records, and building new queries, forms, and reports. The more heavily a database is used, the more critical this review is. This is where spending the time up front to design sound tables pays off.

It is sometimes difficult to see the need for maintenance on a functioning system. Think about what it would cost the organization if this database failed. How much happier and more efficient could the users be with an optimized database? Maintaining a database is like changing the oil or tuning up your car. It significantly decreases the likelihood of a major disaster.

Building Custom Input Masks

Input masks were introduced in Chapter 2 as a way to improve data entry by providing a template like (_____)_____–_____ for the user to follow when entering data. Input masks are field properties and can be set for Text, Date, Number, and Currency field types. Input masks make what needs to be entered clear to users and reduces their keystrokes.

Reducing input keystrokes always improves the likelihood of valid data. In the case of a phone number, using an input mask cuts out three keystrokes ((,), and -) that otherwise would be necessary for the phone number to display in the desired format.

Consider building input masks for any table data that have a repetitive component. Repetitive components include punctuation such as parentheses, dashes, periods (decimal places), slashes, at signs (@), and so on. Cutting out a keystroke or two may not seem like much, but remember that keystrokes add up when multiple fields and records are considered.

When using an input mask with repetitive components, mask properties control whether or not those fixed values are stored with the data. Typically they are not, since it would require extra disk space, and the Format property allows control over how stored data display. Using the Format property, it is easy to display repetitive components without storing them.

In general, the Input Mask property and display Format property should match on the data entry forms because it is less confusing to the user. When they do not match, the user enters the data using the Input Mask template and when he or she moves to another record, the entry is displayed using the format. Avoiding such visual ambiguities will lead to happier users. Remember that setting the Format property of the field's text box on a form or report can control the display format for that output. Output formats are covered in the next topic.

To create an input mask, provide Access with a string outlining what is to be presented to the user, what will be accepted as valid input, and what will be stored. Figure 7.2 lists the valid mask characters. Any character not listed in Figure 7.2 becomes a literal when included in an input mask. Characters in the list must be preceded by a backslash to literally appear in the mask.

The Input Mask Wizard is great for creating default masks, but like most Wizards it lacks the flexibility to effectively create complex or uncommon masks. Figure 7.3 depicts some of the masks that could be applied to a 15-character field with an explanation of their results.

In the KoryoKicks Customer table, the Input Mask property of the Phone field was set in Chapter 2 with the Wizard for a standard phone number. Users often do not like this mask because it makes it difficult to *not* enter the area code. Even though the area code does not have to be entered, the user must space by the first three characters of the input mask. If your data always include the area code, this setup is satisfactory. If, however, your data do not include the area code a significant amount of the time, the area code should be split into another field that the user could tab past.

Missy and Micah are not happy with the Phone input mask for KoryoKicks data so it has been removed. They have noticed that they are inconsistent in capitalizing customer's names and decide that a mask for the Name fields is in order. State and Zip Code also need input masks to reduce entry errors.

Character	Description
0	Required digit (0–9), no plus (+) or minus (−) sign
9	Optional digit, no plus (+) or minus (−) sign
#	Optional digit, plus (+) or minus (−) sign allowed
L	Required letter (A–Z)
?	Optional letter (A–Z)
A	Required letter or digit
a	Optional letter or digit
&	Required character or space
C	Optional character or space
.,:;-/	Placeholders and separators
<	Causes all characters that follow to be converted to lowercase
>	Causes all characters that follow to be converted to uppercase
!	Causes input mask to display from right to left
\	Used to display any of the characters in this table as a literal
Password	Creates a password entry text box with all entries displayed as *

FIGURE 7.2

Input mask definition characters

FIGURE 7.3

Input mask examples

Input Mask	Sample Display	Explanation
00000-999;;_	_____-____	Zip Code mask created by the Wizard. 0s are required positions, 9s are optional positions. Both require digits for valid data. The dash is a literal that will not be stored due to the;; notation. The _ notation sets that as the character that displays to the user.
000-00-0000;;_	___-__-____	SSN mask created by the Wizard. All 0s represent required digits. The dashes display as literals and ;;_ causes the literal characters (-) not to be stored. The _ notation sets that as the character that displays to the user.
!(999) 000-0000;;_	(___) ___-____	Phone Number mask created by the Wizard. 0s are required digits, 9s are optional digits, the dashes and parentheses are literals that will not be stored due to the ;;_ notation. The ! causes the field to display from right to left. The _ notation sets that as the character that displays to the user.
>L<?????????		The first letter entered will be converted to uppercase before it is stored. The remaining nine characters are optional but, if entered, will be converted to lowercase before being stored.

Customizing the Customer table input masks:

1. Start Access and open **ac07KoryoKicks.mdb**

2. Open the **Customer** table in Design View

3. Select the **LastName** field. This is a 30-character text field that should always begin with a capital letter, followed by up to 29 lowercase letters

4. Click the **Input Mask** property of LastName and type
>L<?????????????????????????????

tip: > L< followed by 29 question marks

5. Click the **FirstName** field. This is a 30-character text field that should always begin with a capital letter, followed by up to 29 lowercase letters

6. Click the **Input Mask** property of FirstName and type
>L<?????????????????????????????

tip: > L< followed by 29 question marks

7. Click the State field. This is a 2-character text field that should always contain two uppercase letters

8. Click the **Input Mask** property of State and type **>LL** to force the entry of two uppercase letters

9. Click in the ZipCode field. This is a 5-digit required field

10. Click the **Input Mask** property of ZipCode and type **00000**

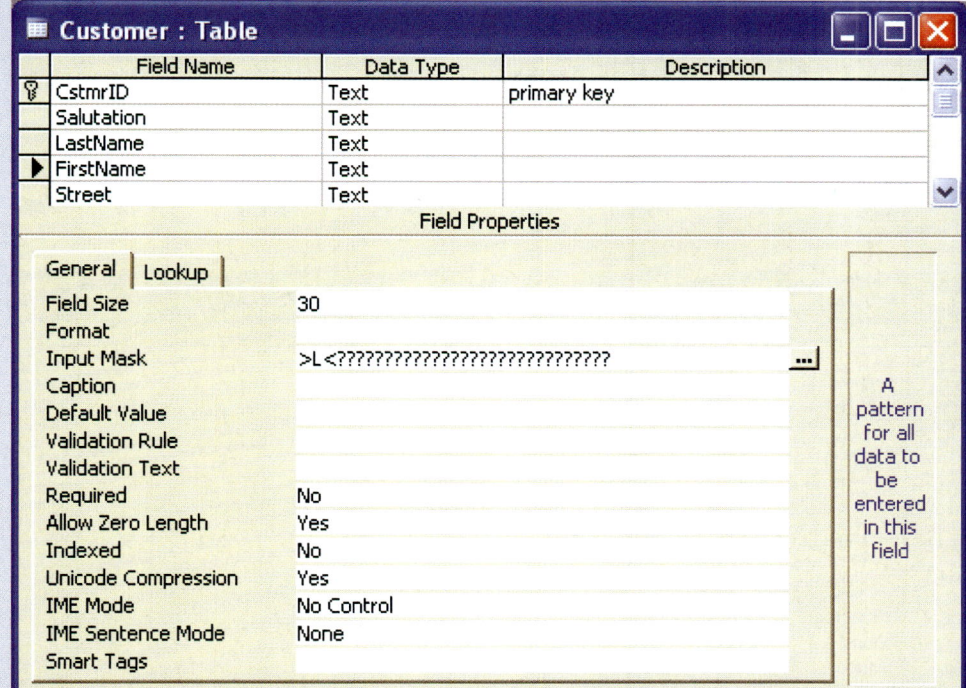

FIGURE 7.4
FirstName input mask

11. Switch to Datasheet View, saving your changes

12. Make up the data for two new customers. Use CstmrID 100 and 101. Enter the first record in all lowercase and observe the result. Enter the second record in all uppercase and observe the result

Input masks are a simple way to improve data validity and user satisfaction without negatively impacting performance. It is important to be sure that the masks don't get in the user's way (like the phone number example). Adding, editing, or deleting an input mask has no impact on existing table data, since the template is only activated on input. Input masks do impact editing existing data because newly entered data must meet the mask criteria.

Defining Custom Output Formats

Output formats were introduced in Chapter 2 as the way to control how a value displays. Output formatting is controlled by the Format property of a field. The Format property set in table design becomes the default format of that field in queries, forms, and reports. As was mentioned in the input mask discussion, the Format property set in table design should match the Input Mask property.

The twins are not satisfied with the Order.OrderDate (OrderDate field of the Order table) input mask/format combination. It works great for data entry when the input mask ____ /____ /____ is displayed. The problem arises when editing an existing date. The Format property is set as dd-mmm-yyyy, so when a portion of a date (such as the dd component) is selected and a new value entered, the input mask generates an error because it doesn't know what to do with the dashes generated by the Format property. Since the twins will be satisfied with a dd/mm/yyyy format, you will update the table.

Customizing the Order.OrderDate field format:

1. Verify that Access is running with **ac07KoryoKicks.mdb** as the open database

2. Open the **Order** table in Design View

3. Select the **OrderDate** field and review the current Input Mask and Format properties

FIGURE 7.5

Order.OrderDate properties

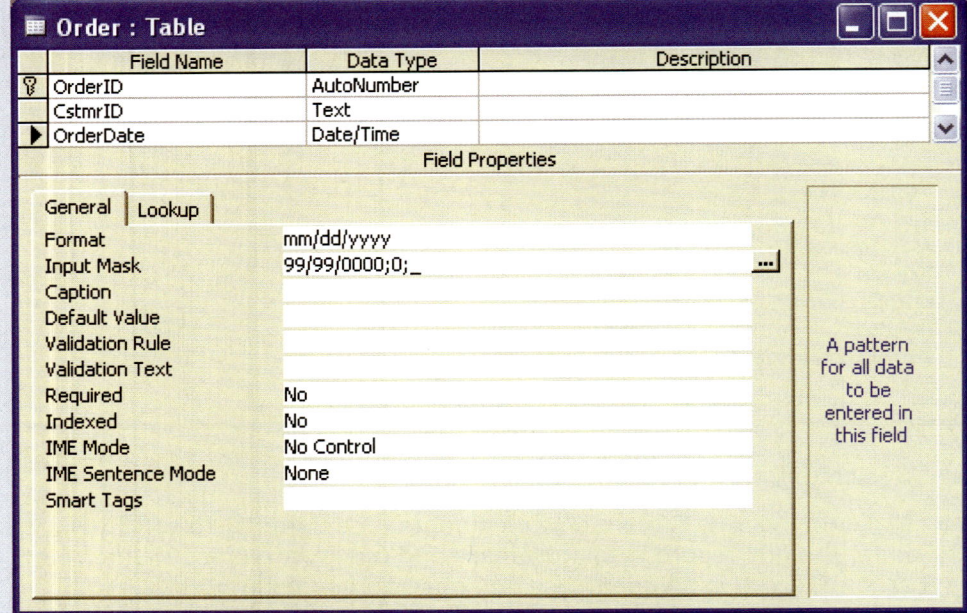

4. Click the **Format** property of OrderDate and type **mm/dd/yyyy** and change the input mask to match the figure (see Figure 7.5)

5. Move to Datasheet View, saving your changes

6. Add orders for Sara Meadows and Juan Rivera with today's date (OrderID is an AutoNumber field and will be generated) to observe the effectiveness of your changes

7. Edit the day on each of these new records to yesterday's date

tip: *If the change has been correctly applied, you should be able to select and change the day portion of the date successfully*

When custom forms and reports are created, Design View is used to set the Format property of the Text Box control displaying the field. This action does not impact the field and what it stores, or change the Format set in table design, but simply applies a template altering how a field is displayed on that particular form or report. The Text Box Format property overrides the Format property set in table design and is applied only to that text box. In both form and report design, the *Format Painter* is available to copy formats from one control to another.

When setting a Format property, selections can be made from a list of predefined formats for AutoNumber, Number, Currency, Date/Time, and Yes/No data types or a custom format can be defined. Text data types do not have any predefined formatting. Formats cannot be applied to OLE Object data types.

Number and date data types have predefined formats displayed in a drop-down list. To improve consistency among applications, the regional settings from Microsoft Windows Control Panel are used for the predefined Number and Date/Time formats. Changing the Windows format does change the display but does not perform conversions. This can cause problems when moving between computers with different regional settings. For example, the value 5.47 displayed with currency format would result in $5.47 in the United States and 5,47kr on a computer set for Denmark. One or both of the displayed currency values would be inaccurate since no conversion was performed. In such cases, a custom format should be entered representing the true currency of the data. Custom formats override the Windows settings.

Using Data Validation

Data validation is another area that can often improve the usability and validity of database data. Validation settings are used to check the accuracy of data entered by the user. Several of the field properties that can be set in table design to validate data are covered in the following topics.

Default Value Field Property

Each field in a Microsoft Access table has a Default Value property that can be set to the most common value for that field. This value will display in that field for new records. The user can accept this entry by tabbing past it or can stop and type a new entry to override the default. Default values are beneficial because they reduce typing and improve data integrity.

The twins have determined that most of their remote customers are in Michigan and they would like MI to be the default state value. Since most orders are for the current date, they would also like that default added to the Order table. The default order quantity was set to 1 when the table was developed and is working well.

Adding default values to the KoryoKicks database:

1. Verify that **ac07KoryoKicks.mdb** database is open

2. Open the **Customer** table in Design View

3. Select the **State** field

4. Click the **Default Value** property of State and type **MI**

tip: *Access will add double quotes around this string value, resulting in "MI"*

help yourself *Use the Type a Question combo box to improve your understanding of how to validate data by typing* **data validation**. *Review the contents of About restricting or validating data and Validate or restrict data entry in a table. Close the Help window when you are finished*

5. Change to Datasheet View and test the default value by adding records for two classmates. Use CstmrIDs 106 and 107. For the first record accept the default value. For the second record set the State to NM

6. Close the Customer table

7. Open the **Order** table in Design View

8. Click in the **OrderDate** field and type **=Now** in the Default Value property (see Figure 7.6)

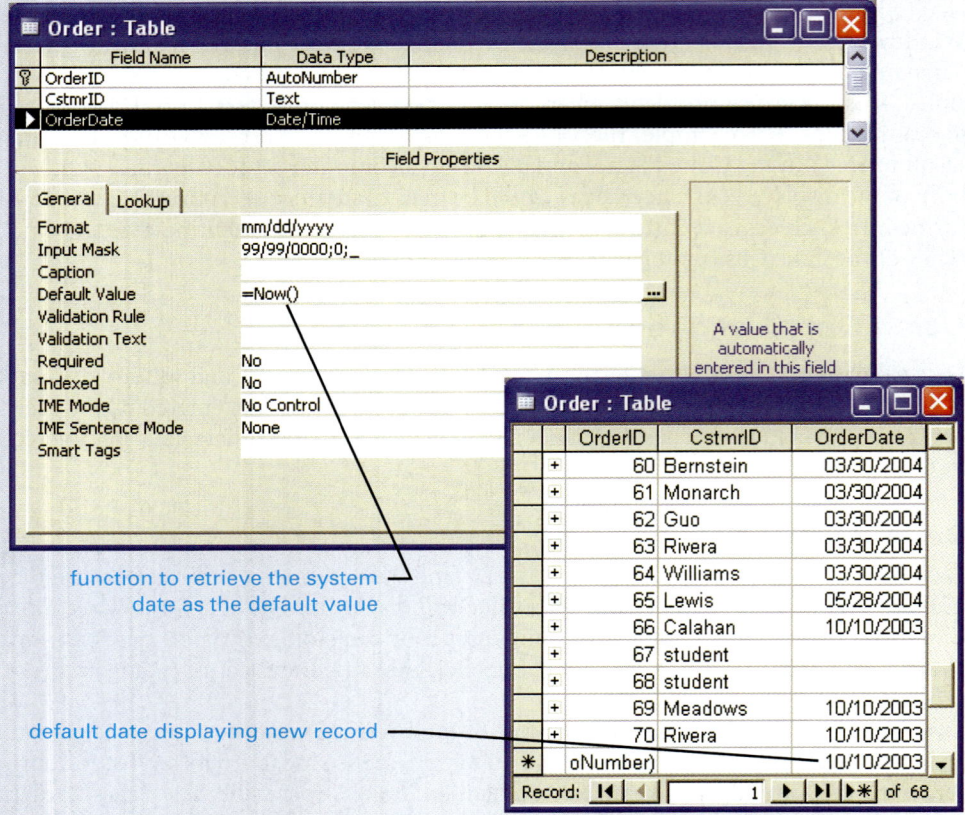

tip: *Access will convert it to =Now() since the parentheses are required for correct function syntax*

9. **Switch to Datasheet View and add an order for each of the two class-mates added earlier. Accept the default of today's date for your order. Set the date from your friend's order to tomorrow**

Default values are not limited to fixed quantities such as 1 or "MI" but can also use expressions like =Now(). An expression can be either typed, as was done in the steps, or built using the Expression Builder. An ellipsis (. . .) will appear to the right of the Default Value property after it is clicked. Clicking the ellipsis will activate the Expression Builder.

Required and Allow Zero Length Field Properties

The Required and Allow Zero Length field properties work together to control the types of blank values allowed in a field. Microsoft Access differentiates between *null* values and *zero-length strings*. A null value indicates missing or unknown data. A field is null when nothing has been entered. A zero-length string can be used to indicate that no data are supposed to be in a field. The user creates a zero-length string by typing two double quotes with nothing between them (""").

Sometimes it is important to differentiate between when a data value is not known and when it does not exist. For example, if a fax number field was added to the customer table, a null value could indicate that the fax number is not currently known, while a zero-length string would indicate that the customer does not have a fax. While there is nothing visual to differentiate these values, queries searching for nulls will not return zero-length strings and vice versa.

FIGURE 7.7

Combinations of Required and Allow Zero Length values

Required	Allow Zero Length	Result
No	No	Allows blank values when you don't need to distinguish blank values that indicate unknown data from blank values that indicate you know there's no value
Yes	No	Prevents users from leaving a field blank
Yes	Yes	Allows blank values in a field only when you know that there are no data. In this case, the only way to leave a field blank is to type double quotation marks with no space between them, or press the Spacebar to enter a zero-length string
No	Yes	Allows both types of blank values so that you can distinguish blank values that indicate unknown data from blank values that indicate you know there are no data

The Required property of a field determines whether it can be left blank during data entry, resulting in a null value. The Allow Zero Length property determines whether a zero-length string ("") can be entered in a field. Allow Zero Length property is only valid for Text, Memo, or Hyperlink fields. (See Figure 7.7.)

In the KoryoKicks tables, the OrderDetail table needs to require the user to enter a product and a quantity. In the Order table, the OrderDate needs to be required. In the Customer table, everything but notes and phone should be required. There is no need to differentiate between types of blank values, so the Allow Zero Length value will remain No.

---

task reference **Controlling Blank Data Values**

- Open the table in Design View

- Click the field whose blank values you would like to control

- Set Required to **Yes** to disallow blank values (Allow Zero Length should be set to No)

Requiring fields in the KoryoKicks database:

1. Verify that **ac07KoryoKicks.mdb** database is open

2. Open the **Customer** table in Design View

3. Click in **LastName** and double-click the **Required** property to change it to **Yes**

4. Repeat this process for **FirstName**, **Street**, **City**, **State**, and **ZipCode**

5. Close the Design View of Customer, saving your changes and validating existing data (see Figure 7.8)

FIGURE 7.8

Checking existing data for
missing values

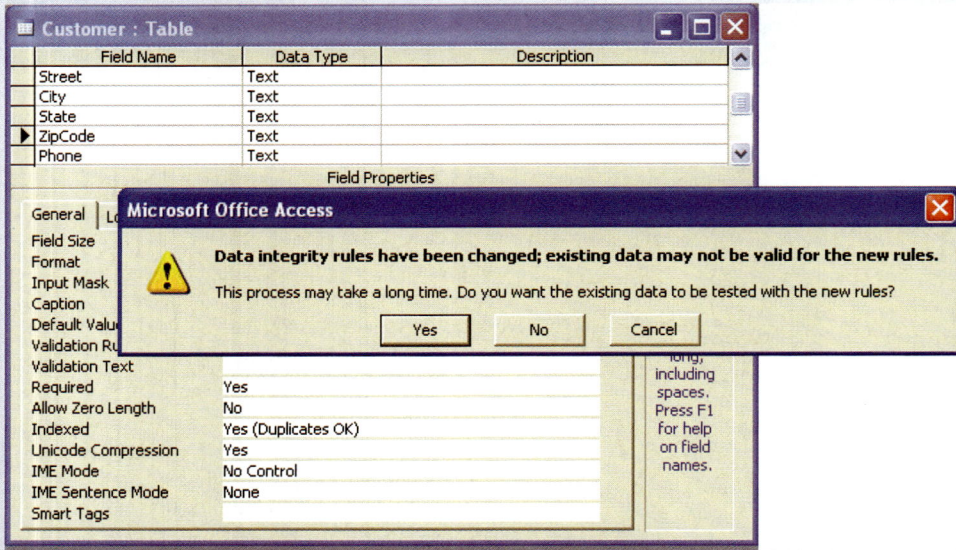

6. Open **OrderDetail** in Design View and set the Required property of **QuantityOrdered** to **Yes**

tip: *ProductID does not have to be set to Required because as a key field it is already required*

7. Close the Design View of OrderDetail

8. Open **Order** in Design View and set the CstmrID and OrderDate fields to Required

9. Close the Design View of Order

The Required property of a field can only be set in Design View, but it is applied throughout all database objects (datasheets, forms, and reports). When the table design is saved after updating a Required property, Access presents the option of checking existing records for compliance. Entry can be required in future records whether or not there are currently blank fields.

Validation Rules and Validation Text Field Properties

The Validation Rule and Validation Text properties work together to help verify the data values entered by users. Validation rules are based on expected data values. For example, when accepting credit card payments, expired cards are not valid. In such a case, the validation rule would be $>=(=now())$. Recall that $=now()$ is a function that will return the current system date and time. The function is enclosed in parentheses to separate it from the relational operator, $>=$. The expression $>=(=now())$ says that the date entered must be greater than or equal to today's date.

Validation text contains the message that will display to the user when the data entered do not meet the validation rule. Continuing with the credit card expiration date example, the Validation text might be *Expired Credit Card. Check the expiration date or choose another card* (see Figure 7.9). If, for example, an expiration date of 1/03 is entered, the Validation text would be displayed and the user must either enter data that pass the validation or abandon his or her changes. Validation rules cannot be overridden, so be very sure of the rules created.

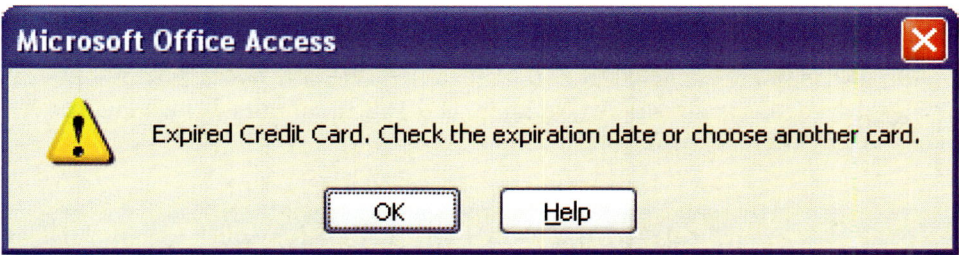

Validation rules and their associated Validation text are most effectively added to the field properties of table design. Like other field properties, validation rules can be set in a form or report, but it is ineffective to validate data entry only on specific forms. Validation rules and text can be added to table field properties at any time, and then the rules will be enforced by all controls for that field (even those created before the rule).

Validation rules follow the syntax rules of expressions. String data are enclosed in double quotes (""), Date data are enclosed in pound signs (##), and numeric data are not enclosed in any character. All relational operators can be used ($>$, $<$, $>=$, $<=$, $<>$). Compound conditions can be connected with *And* or *Or*. Use *And* when both conditions must be true for the data entered to be valid. Use *Or* when only one condition must be true for the data to be valid. For example, $>=\#1/1/2003\#$ And $<\#1/1/2004\#$ would accept any date in the year 2003, but the Validation Text dialog box would be issued for any date outside this range.

Figure 7.10 contains validation expressions for text, number, and date data types with the appropriate delimiters. The use of And and Or to create compound conditions for validation is demonstrated, as is the use of wildcards. The wildcards ?, ∗, and # can be used to create match values for data validation in the same fashion that they were used to create filter and query criteria.

FIGURE 7.10

Sample validation rules

Sample Validation Rule	Sample Validation Text	Result
<>0	Please enter a non-zero value	Validation text will display when a non-zero value is entered
0 Or >25	Please enter zero or a number greater than 25	Validation text will display when values 1 through 24 or a negative number is entered
<=Now()	Date must be earlier than today	Validation text will display when dates equal to or later than the current system date are entered
>100 And <1,000	Please enter a number between 100 and 1,000	Validation text will display when a value of 100 or less is entered or a value of 1,000 or greater is entered
Like "X???"	Please enter a 4-character string beginning with X	Validation text will display when X is not the first character or the text entered is not 4 characters
"M" Or "F"	Please enter M for male or F for female	Validation text will display for any value not equal to M or F. This text is case sensitive
>#10/1/01# And <#10/31/01#	Please enter an October date	Validation text will display for values not between the dates in the condition

Missy and Micah have determined that their KoryoKicks customers always need to order 100 or fewer units of each invoice item. KoryoKicks can't deliver larger volumes and current distributors can't handle them either. OrderDates also need to be the current date or later (backdating is not allowed). Adding these validation rules will help reduce errors in orders and improve customer satisfaction.

---

task reference — Defining Field Validation Rules

- Open the table in Design View

- Click the field that will be monitored by the validation rule

- Select the **Validation Rule** property for that field

- Type the validation expression or use the Expression Builder by clicking the ellipsis to the right of the Validation Rule text box

- Click the Validation Text property box for the same field and enter the text that is to display when the validation rule is broken

- Save the table update

  - If the validation rule has been set for a field that already contains data, Access will ask if you want to apply the new rule to existing data

  - If there are no existing data in the field, there will be no prompt

---

Adding field validation to the KoryoKicks database:

1. Verify that **ac07KoryoKicks.mdb** is open

2. Open the **OrderDetail** table in Design View

3. Click the **QuantityOrdered** field

   a. Click the **Validation Rule** property and type **>0 And <=100**
   b. Click the **Validation Text** property and type **Quantity ordered must be between 1 and 100.** (see Figure 7.11)

4. Switch to Datasheet View, saving your changes and answering **Yes** to the data integrity prompt

5. Enter an order detail that violates the rule

tip: *Closing the OrderDetail in the next step will allow you to abandon this record*

6. Close OrderDetail

7. Open the **Order** table in Design View

8. Click the **OrderDate** field

   a. Set the **Validation Rule** property and type **>=Now()**
   b. Set the **Validation Text** property and type **The date must be greater than or equal to today.**

9. Switch to Datasheet View, saving your changes and answering **Yes** to the data integrity prompt. Read and close the data violations notification

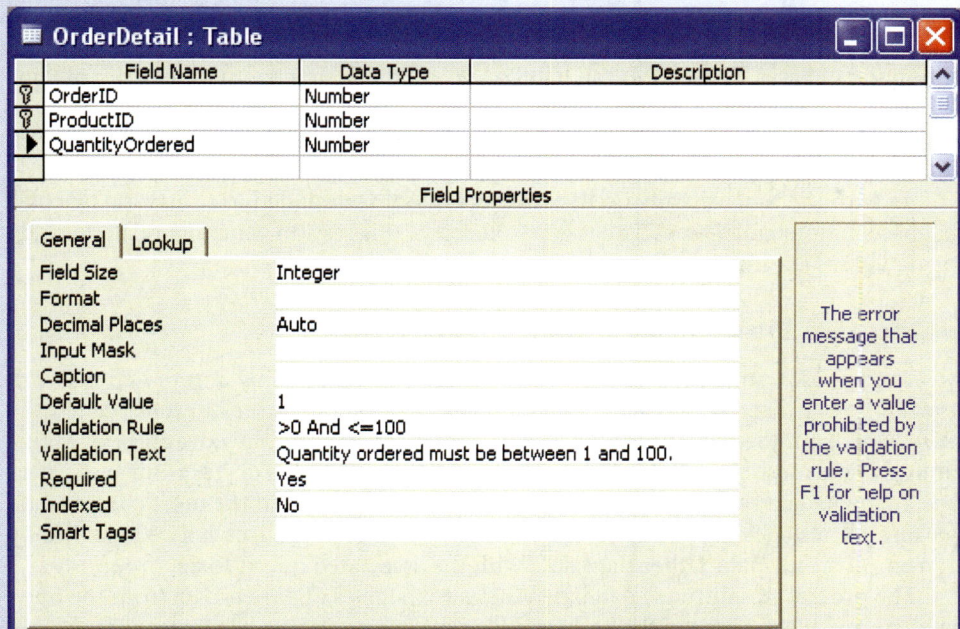

FIGURE 7.11
OrderDetails validation
rule and validation text

10. Enter a record that violates the rule, move to another record to view the validation text, and then respond **OK**

11. Close the Order table to abandon the erroneous record

Although validation rules and text can be added to tables at any time, difficulty can arise when testing these rules. The only way to check the rules that have been added is to add both valid and invalid data.

When testing validation rules, it is best to use a trait to mark the records so that they can be deleted when testing is complete. For example, customers named Dummy1, Dummy2, and so on could be added to the Customer table, along with Order and OrderDetail records added for those records. When testing is complete, deleting the Dummy records would remove all of the test data.

Validation rules and text are the simplest tools for validating data, but they lack flexibility and cannot compare data from field to field or across records. Users cannot override the rule and there is no check to ensure that values are internally consistent. For example, a man's medical records should not include pregnancy data, but validation rules cannot check for that condition. Record validation, macros, and Visual Basic code provide the power to perform more extensive validation.

making the grade

1. How can you determine whether or not a field should have an input mask?

2. How are Input Mask and Format properties of a field different?

3. How would you determine the default value of a field?

4. Why use validation rules for table fields?

SESSION 7.2 ACCESS DATABASE TOOLS

The Tools menu in Microsoft Access contains a variety of facilities to help maintain and optimize databases. These tools can help to analyze the design and performance of your database, convert to other versions of Access, secure data, and so on. Some of these tools already have been introduced. Convert Database and Compact and Repair Database are examples of tools that already have been explored.

As with the tools already used, each Access tool is designed to satisfy a particular database maintenance need. The tools explored in this session generally relate to sharing databases among several users and securing data.

Using the Database Splitter Wizard

Access databases can be stored on a network drive and shared by authorized network users. One approach to sharing a database is to separate the user interface, called the *front-end*, from the data, or the ***back-end***. This approach has the advantage of maintaining one data source while allowing each user to control his or her front-end interface. A single data source means that users always have access to the most current data because all updates are made to the same tables. It also reduces network traffic by transmitting only data rather than data with the associated query, form, or report.

The process of splitting a database removes the tables and their data from the open database and places them in the back-end file. The open database becomes the front-end file, with arrow icons in front of the table names to indicate the link to the back-end.

---

task reference   **Splitting a Database**

- Back up the database

- On the **Tools** menu, point to **Database Utilities**, and then click **Database Splitter**

- Follow the Database Splitter Wizard instructions

Splitting the KoryoKicks database:

1. Verify that **ac07KoryoKicks.mdb** is open

2. Select **File** and then **Backup Database** and place a copy of ac07KoryoKicks.mdb in your homework folder

3. Open the copy of **ac07KoryoKicks.mdb**

4. On the **Tools** menu, point to **Database Utilities**, and then click **Database Splitter**

5. Click **Split Database**

6. Select your homework folder as the location, accept the default name for the back-end, and click **Split**

tip: *By default _be is included in the back-end filename and the front-end name is not changed. The back-end holding the tables would normally be on a shared network drive*

7. Notice the icons in front of each table name indicating that you are now working in a front-end file

8. Save the front-end

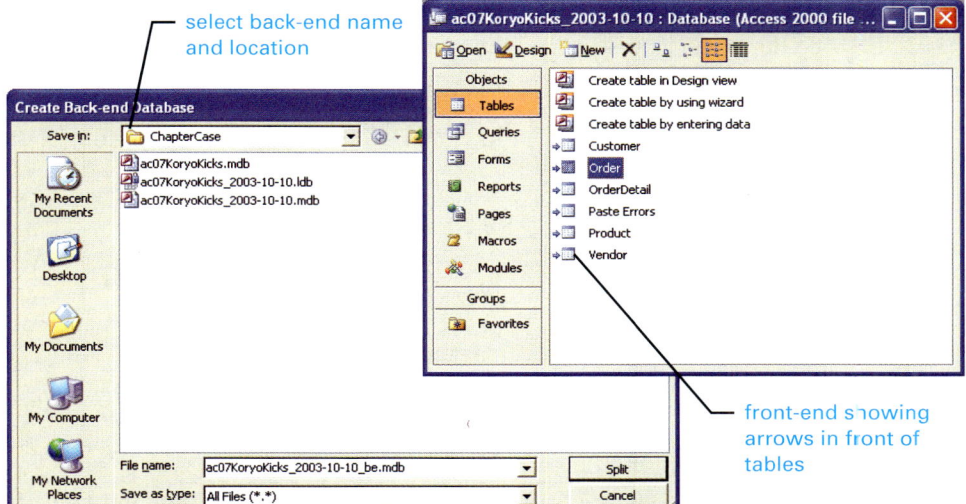

FIGURE 7.12

Creating the back-end

The front-end file contains all of the queries, forms, and reports. Each user can store a copy of this file on his or her computer and customize it for his or her needs. One copy of the back-end file containing the data is stored on a shared network drive.

Commercial software developers split databases so that they can implement interface changes without impacting the data stored by clients. Each copy of the front-end has access to the data stored in the back-end, but cannot change table design. Opening the back-end database will allow table design changes to be specified.

Exploring the split KoryoKicks database:

1. Open the front-end copy of **ac07KoryoKicks.mdb** if it is not open from the previous steps

2. Select the **Customer** table and then click **Design**

tip: *Click the Tables object in the Database Window, then click Customer, and then Design. A dialog box notice that this is a linked file will display*

3. Click **Yes** to open the table in Design View. You can review table design but not modify it

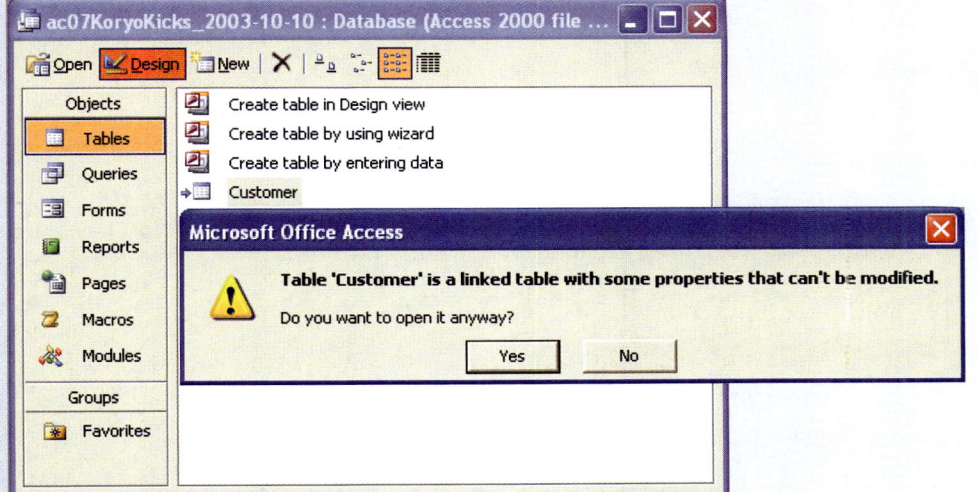

FIGURE 7.13

Viewing the design of a linked table

ACCESS

4. Close the Customer table Design View. Close the database

5. Open the back-end file

6. Select the **Customer** table and then click **Design**. You have complete access to modify table design in the back-end database

7. Close

Once a database has been split, there is no facility for rejoining it. If the back-end file moves to a new drive or folder, the links in all of the front-ends must be adjusted using the Linked Table Manager (Tools/Database Utilities, Linked Table Manager).

Using the Database performance Analyzer

The Database Performance Analyzer is a tool that reviews database objects and suggests improvements. The goal is to optimize database performance, but the performance of Access itself or the computer running Access cannot be evaluated in this manner. When the Performance Analyzer starts, a dialog box used to select database objects for evaluation is displayed. The Analyzer will review the specified objects and recommend changes that could benefit performance.

The proposed changes are classified by their potential benefit (Recommendation, Suggestion, Idea, and Fixed). Items classified as Fixed have already been repaired. Recommendations have the most potential benefit, while Ideas have the least. It is important to carefully review each proposed change in light of the database design and utilization.

---

task reference   Optimizing Database Objects

- Open the database to be optimized

- Click the **Tools** menu, then **Analyze**, and then **Performance**

- Select the tab for the database object (table, query, report, form, etc.) that you would like to analyze

- Click the check box of each object to be evaluated or click Select All to select all objects in the list

- Select objects from other tabs if desired

- Click **OK**

- Review and apply results as needed

Optimizing KoryoKicks database objects:

1. Open the original copy of **ac07KoryoKicks.mdb**

2. Click the **Tools** menu, then **Analyze**, and then **Performance**

3. Select the **Tables** tab and check each table (see Figure 7.14)

tip: *The check box in front of each table must be checked—selecting a table does not check the check box*

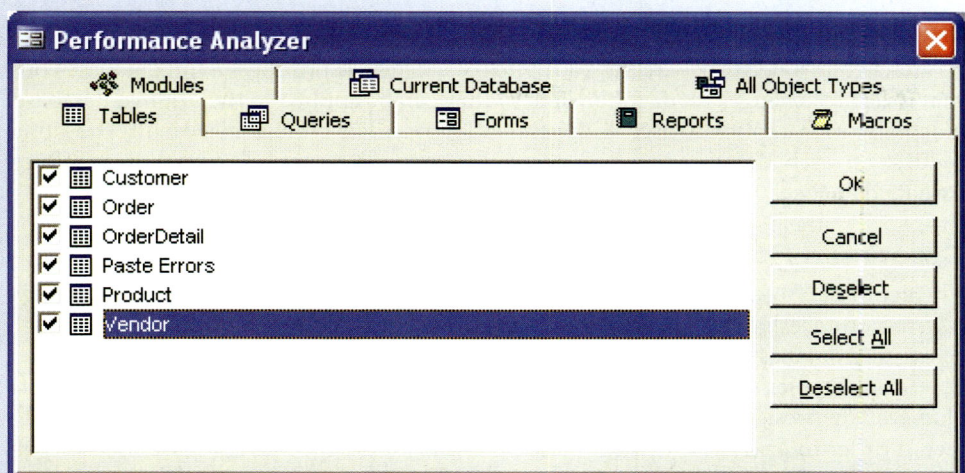

4. Click **OK**

5. Review the suggestions by clicking each and reading the Analysis Notes. None of the suggestions are consistent with the design in this case, so don't apply them

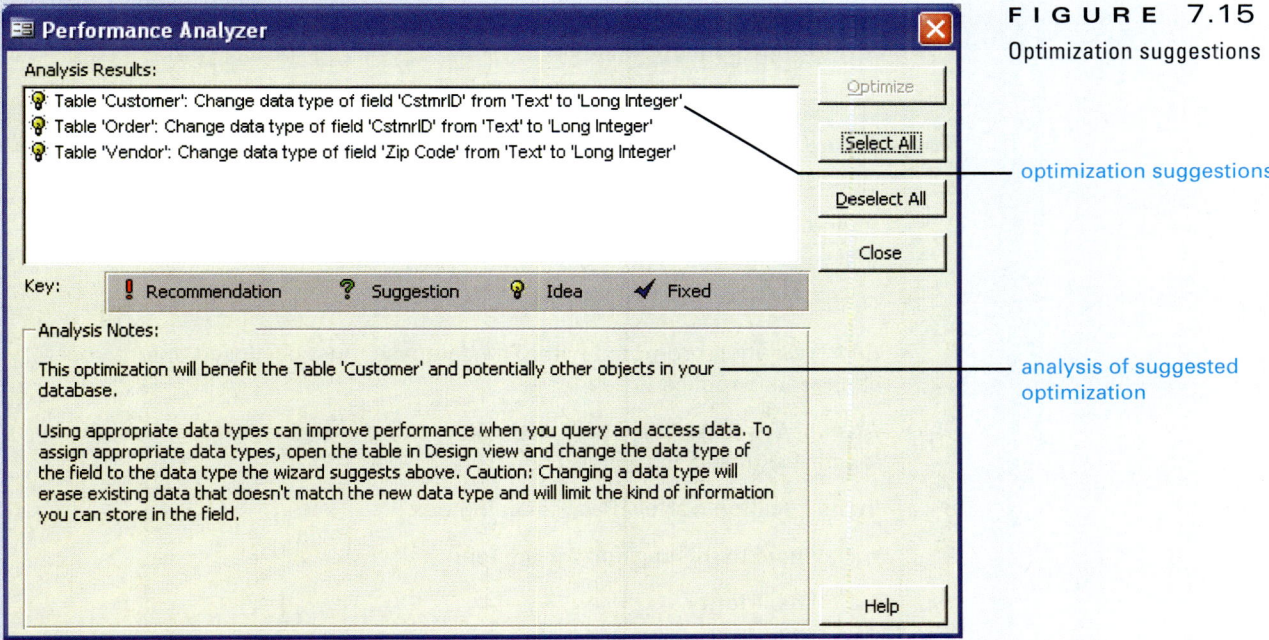

optimization suggestions

analysis of suggested optimization

6. Click **Close**

After reviewing the Analysis Notes, you can elect to have Access perform Recommendation and Suggestions optimizations for you. Click the Recommendation or Suggestion optimizations to be performed and then click the Optimize button. Idea optimizations must be completed manually by following the instructions in the Analysis Notes.

Replicating a Database

Replication is a way of sharing database data between computers that may or may not be attached to a network. Creating a *replica* of a database produces a full database copy that will track changes made to the data so they can be applied to the original database. Normally each replica is used independently and then synchronized with the other replicas on a scheduled basis. Users of replicas are not guaranteed to have the most up-to-date data, because data can be modified in each replica.

Creating a Replica

The act of creating a replica causes the original database to be marked as the *Design Master*. The Design Master and all of its replicas are called the *replica set*. The design of existing database objects can be updated in the Design Master, but not in a replica.

Special tables in both the Design Master and replica databases keep track of data changes. The Design Master also tracks changes made to the design of any database object in order to pass these updates to the replicas. These special tables are used in *synchronization*, the process of updating the Design Master and its replicas so that all copies reflect the same status.

Each replica created has a priority assigned to using a number between 0 (lowest) and 100 (highest). When conflicting updates are made to different replicas of the database, the priority is used to resolve them. The Design Master has a priority of 100. The default priority of a replica is 90, but any valid priority can be assigned. Changes made to the Design Master always have precedence over those made to a replica. During synchronization, the priority setting of each replica is evaluated and the record with the highest priority wins in any conflicts.

---

task reference   Replicating a Database

- Open the database to be replicated

- Remove any password protection (covered later in this session) and ensure that the database is not open by any other users

- On the **Tools** menu, point to **Replication**, and then click **Create Replica**

- Click **Yes** when prompted with: The database must be closed before you can create a replica

- Answer **Yes** when prompted with: Converting a database into a Design Master results in changes . . .

- In the Location of New Replica dialog box

  - Navigate to the location for the replica

  - Set the **Priority**

  - Check the **Prevent deletes** check box to prevent record deletions in the replica

  - In the Save as type box, select the replica Visibility

  - Click **OK**

Replicating KoryoKicks:

1. Verify that the original copy of **ac07KoryoKicks.mdb** is open

2. On the **Tools** menu, point to **Replication**, and then click **Create Replica**

tip: *You will not have enough space on the A: drive to create a replica set, so you will need to use another drive like C:*

3. Click **Yes** to close the database

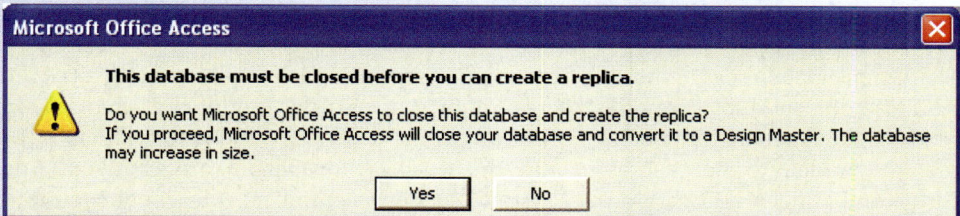

FIGURE 7.16

Create a replica

4. Click **Yes** when prompted with: Converting a database into a Design Master results in changes . . .

5. Click **OK** in the Location of New Replica dialog box to accept the default location, name, priority, and deletion settings

6. Click **OK** to complete the replication process in the dialog box reading Microsoft Access has converted . . .

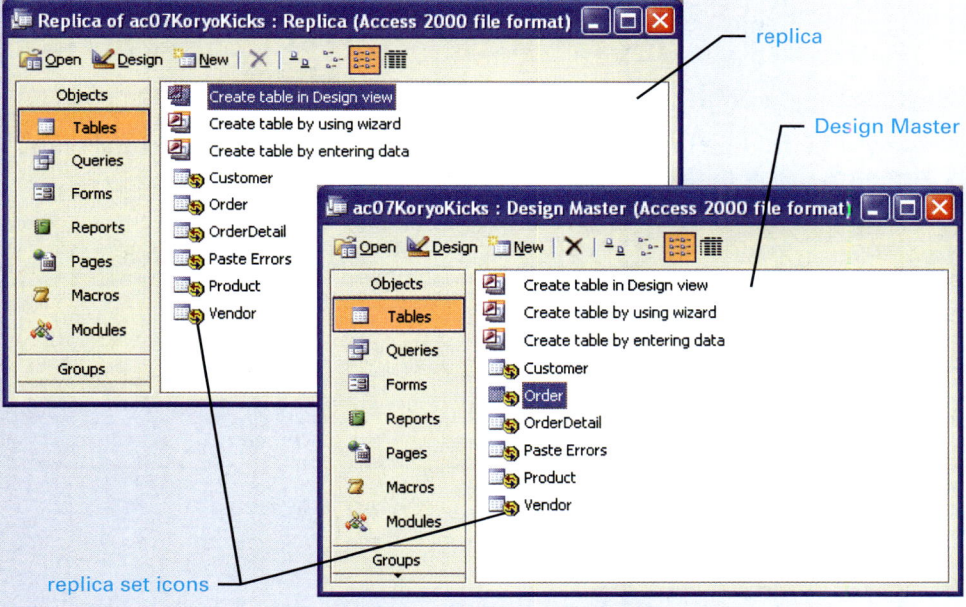

FIGURE 7.17

Design Master and replica

7. Notice that the Title bar now says Design Master and the icons to the left of each database object (table, query, form, and report) indicate that this database belongs to a replica set

8. Close the Design Master

9. Open the Replica

10. Notice the word *Replica* in the Title bar and the icons to the left of each database object (table, query, form, and report) indicate that this database belongs to a replica set

ACCESS

When a database is replicated, the Design Master and each replica contain all of the database objects (tables, queries, forms, reports, and so on). Significant changes are made to the database during the replication process. Fields are added to each table, tables are added to the database, and the database properties are changed. Any AutoNumber fields that previously generated sequential numbers will generate random numbers to reduce synchronization conflicts caused by users adding two different records using the same AutoNumber. The overall result is a larger database.

The backup created in the replication process has a .bak file extension. It can be used to create an emergency replica set. It will not be possible to synchronize replicas made from the backup with replicas made from the original.

Updating KoryoKicks replica data:

1. Open the **Replica of ac07KoryoKicks.mdb** if it is not still open from the previous steps

2. Open the **Customer** table

3. Add a record for **Heather Montgomery** with a CstmrID of 777 (make up the remaining data)

FIGURE 7.18

Adding a new customer to the replica

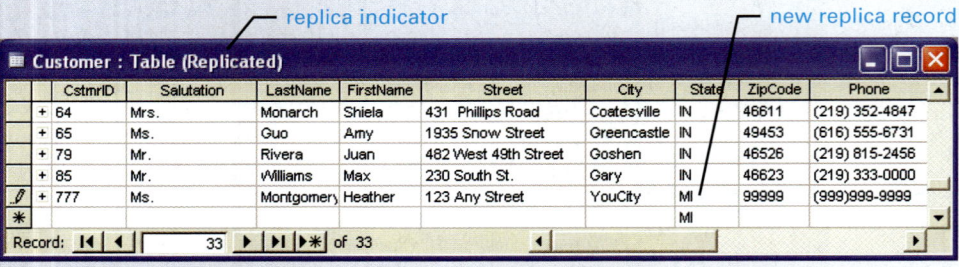

replica indicator — new replica record

	CstmrID	Salutation	LastName	FirstName	Street	City	State	ZipCode	Phone
+	64	Mrs.	Monarch	Shiela	431 Phillips Road	Coatesville	IN	46611	(219) 352-4847
+	65	Ms.	Guo	Amy	1935 Snow Street	Greencastle	IN	49453	(616) 555-6731
+	79	Mr.	Rivera	Juan	482 West 49th Street	Goshen	IN	46526	(219) 815-2456
+	85	Mr.	Williams	Max	230 South St.	Gary	IN	46623	(219) 333-0000
+	777	Ms.	Montgomery	Heather	123 Any Street	YouCity	MI	99999	(999)999-9999
*							MI		

Record: 33 of 33

4. Close the Customer table

The new record has been added to the replica but does not exist in the Design Master. As you can imagine, multiple users with replicas can make a significant number of updates to each copy of the database. Changes also can be made in the Design Master that need to be synchronized with the replicas. When multiple copies of a database have high-volume updates, replication may not be the most successful method of sharing data for users who need current information. It can be very effective, however, if synchronization is performed frequently, or if the various users typically update and use different data.

Synchronization

Once replicas have been generated, each database can be updated independently of the others. Exchanging updated records between two or more members of a replica set is called *synchronization*. Two replica set members are synchronized, or in sync, when the changes made individually in each have been applied to the other.

---

task reference — Synchronizing Replicated Databases

- Open the replica to be synchronized
- On the **Tools** menu, point to **Replication**, and then click **Synchronize Now**
- Select the other replica set member to be synchronized from the Directly with Replica drop-down list box
- Click **OK**
- Respond **Yes** when prompted to close the database for synchronization
- Respond **OK** when notified that the process has been completed

---

The previous steps created one replica and a Design Master for the KoryoKicks database. The new record added to the replica needs to be applied to the Design Master so that the databases are synchronized again.

Synchronizing KoryoKicks:

1. Open the **Replica of ac07KoryoKicks.mdb** if it is not still open from the previous steps

2. On the **Tools** menu, point to **Replication**, and then click **Synchronize Now**

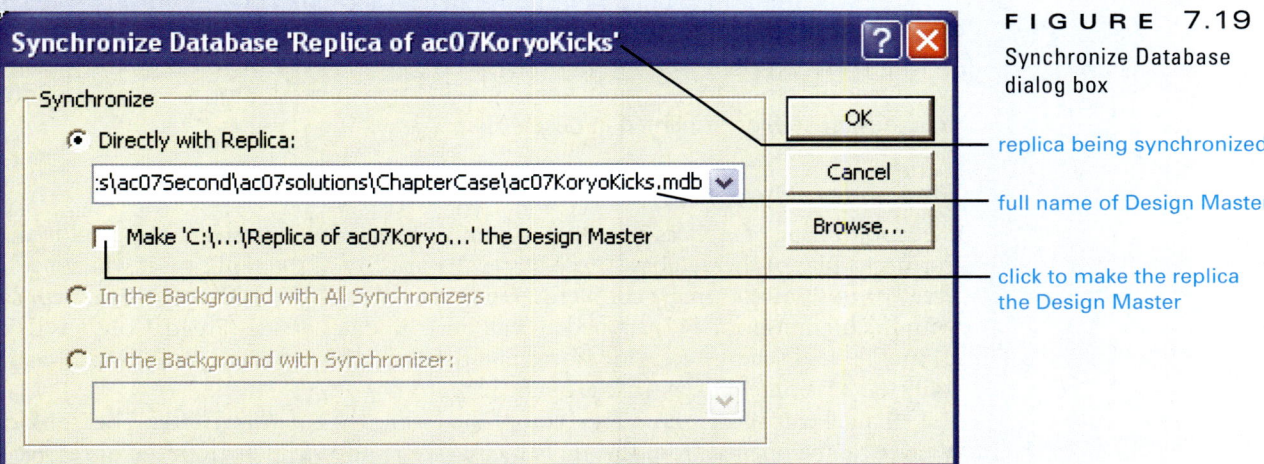

FIGURE 7.19
Synchronize Database dialog box

replica being synchronized

full name of Design Master

click to make the replica the Design Master

3. Select the Design Master name from the drop-down list

tip: *If the Design Master name does not display, use the Browse button to locate it*

4. Click **OK**

5. Respond **Yes** when prompted to close the database for synchronization

6. Respond **OK** when notified that the process has been completed

7. Close the replica and open **ac07KoryoKicks.mdb**—the Design Master

8. Open the Customer table and locate record 777

FIGURE 7.20

Replica record added to the Design Master by synchronization

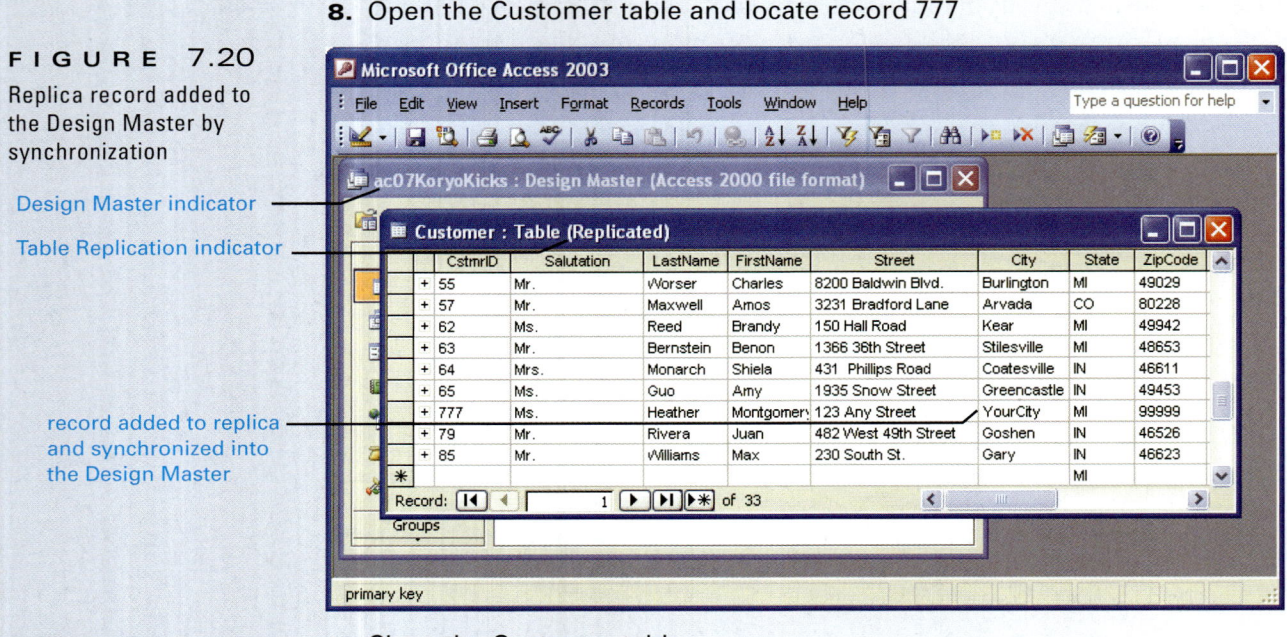

Design Master indicator

Table Replication indicator

record added to replica and synchronized into the Design Master

9. Close the Customer table

This was a very simple example of adding one record to the replica and then using synchronization to update the Design Master with the same record. Normally synchronization is completed at regular intervals, like the close of business each day or Friday at 4:00 P.M.

The synchronization method demonstrated is called *direct synchronization* and is effective for replica sets that are stored on the same computer or in shared folders of a network. The alternate Indirect and Internet synchronization methods can be applied when it is necessary to synchronize using a dial-up connection or the Internet. Both methods are well documented in Access Help.

Resolving Synchronization Conflicts

Synchronization of replicas can result in conflicts created by unrestricted updates to the various copies of the database. Access uses the priority of the replica (set when it was created) to resolve as many conflicting updates as it can. The update from the replica with the highest priority is applied and all other updates are discarded. Conflicts that cannot be resolved by Access are stored and the user is prompted to resolve them manually the next time the database is opened.

Manual conflict resolution is accomplished using the *Conflict Viewer*. The Conflict Viewer can be opened from the Tools menu (see Figure 7.21) or from the unresolved conflicts prompt that displays when a database containing conflicts is opened. When using the Tools menu, you will be notified when there are no conflicts and the Conflict Viewer will not open. If there are conflicts, possible resolutions will be presented in a selection list.

The most common conflict is a simultaneous update conflict that occurs if changes have been made to the same record in more than one replica set member. Conflicts also can be caused by two or more replicas adding a new record with the same key or applying updates that impact referential integrity. Remember that referential integrity stops parent records from being deleted when there are still child records. If one database deletes a parent and all of its children while another adds a new child, a referential

F I G U R E 7.21

Initiating the Conflict
Viewer

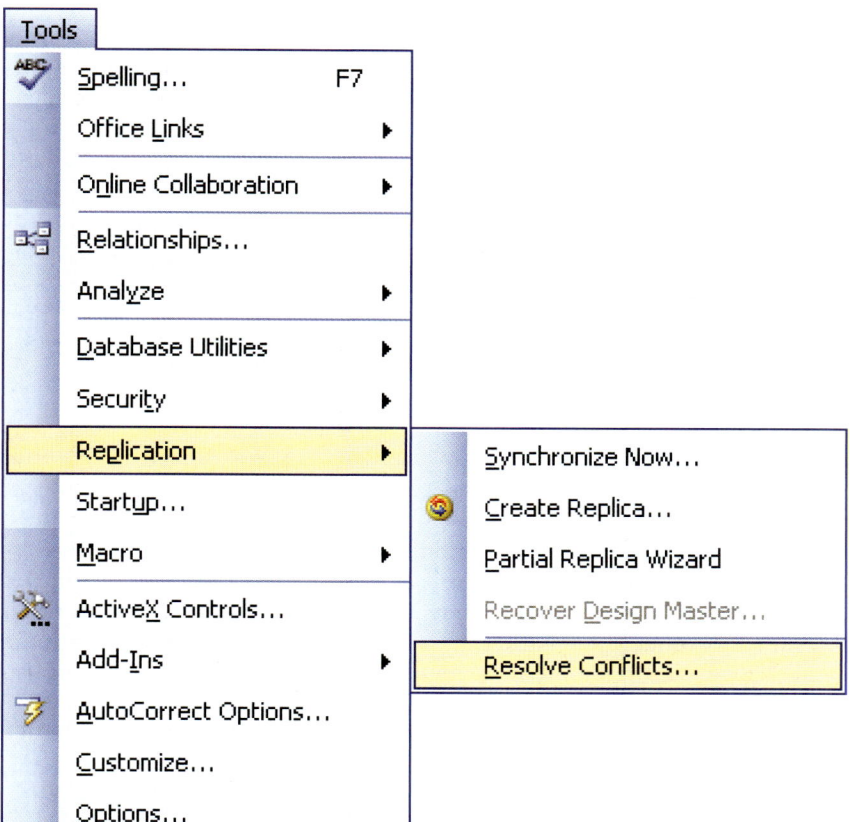

integrity conflict would result. Regardless of the source of synchronization conflicts, it is important to review and resolve them each time synchronization is performed.

Retaining and Deleting Replicas

Each replica that is created has a retention period that controls the number of days non-synchronized records are kept. The default retention period is 60 days, but any period between 5 and 32,000 days is valid. Set a long retention period if the replicas do not synchronize frequently and a short retention period for frequently synchronized replicas. Shorter retention periods keep replica sizes smaller and improve database performance.

The Design Master and replica must be synchronized within the retention period. If synchronization is not accomplished before the replica expires, the replica will be removed from the replica set when synchronization is attempted. Synchronization must occur whether or not any updates have been made.

Mechanically deleting a replica is the same as deleting any other file in the Microsoft Windows environment. Use Windows Explorer, select the file, and press the Delete key. A Yes response will place the replica in the Recycle Bin until it is emptied. A word of caution, however: deleting a replica without synchronizing will lose any changes that it contains. Deleting the Design Master removes the controlling database of the replica set. The other members of the set cannot be synchronized until a new Design Master is assigned.

It is best not to delete a Design Master, but replicas can be deleted with no impact when they are no longer needed. The Design Master retains all of its attributes and continues to track updates for synchronization whether or not there are any current replicas. New replicas can be created as the need arises.

Securing an Access Database

All data stored for business or operational purposes are valuable and need to be protected from theft, loss, misuse, and unwanted updates. Whether the breech is accidental, mischievous, or malicious, the result of unauthorized database access is usually damaged or destroyed data. Protecting data from unauthorized access requires careful planning. The level of security should match the importance of the data.

Microsoft Access data files can be read by a number of utility and word-processor programs, meaning that data can be viewed outside the environment in which they were created. Access supports several methods of controlling access to a database and its objects. These methods range from simple to complex. The simpler methods are less costly and less secure, but are adequate for restricting access to nonessential data. More time and care should be taken with critical data.

Hiding Files

One of the simplest protections is to hide your sensitive files from the casual observer. Microsoft Windows assigns properties to each file that is saved including the Hidden property. A hidden file does not display in a standard file listing like that provided by Windows Explorer. Setting the Hidden property is accomplished by right-clicking on the file, selecting Properties, and clicking Hidden. Even though the file is not visible, it can be manipulated using its name. For example, a hidden file can be opened with the standard Open dialog box by typing its name rather than clicking a name in the file list. Viewing hidden files is also easy; set the folder's properties to Show Hidden Files.

---

task reference   **Hiding a Database**

- Open Windows Explorer

- Navigate to the file to be hidden

- Right-click on the file to be hidden

- Click the **Properties** option

- Click the **Hidden** attribute

- Click **OK**

Hiding the KoryoKicks backup:

1. Close the open Access database

2. Use the Start menu to open Windows Explorer

tip: *Usually Start/AllPrograms/Accessories/Windows Explorer*

3. Navigate to the backup of KoryoKicks created during replication, **ac07KoryoKicks.bak**

4. Right-click on ac07KoryoKicks.bak

5. Choose **Properties**

6. Select the **Hidden** check box and click **OK** (see Figure 7.22)

7. Click **OK**

8. Press **F5** to refresh Windows Explorer

tip: *ac07KoryoKicks.bak should be grayed out or not listed because it is hidden. If the file does display, the folder options on your computer (steps 9–11) have already been set and you will need to reverse them to see how a hidden file behaves*

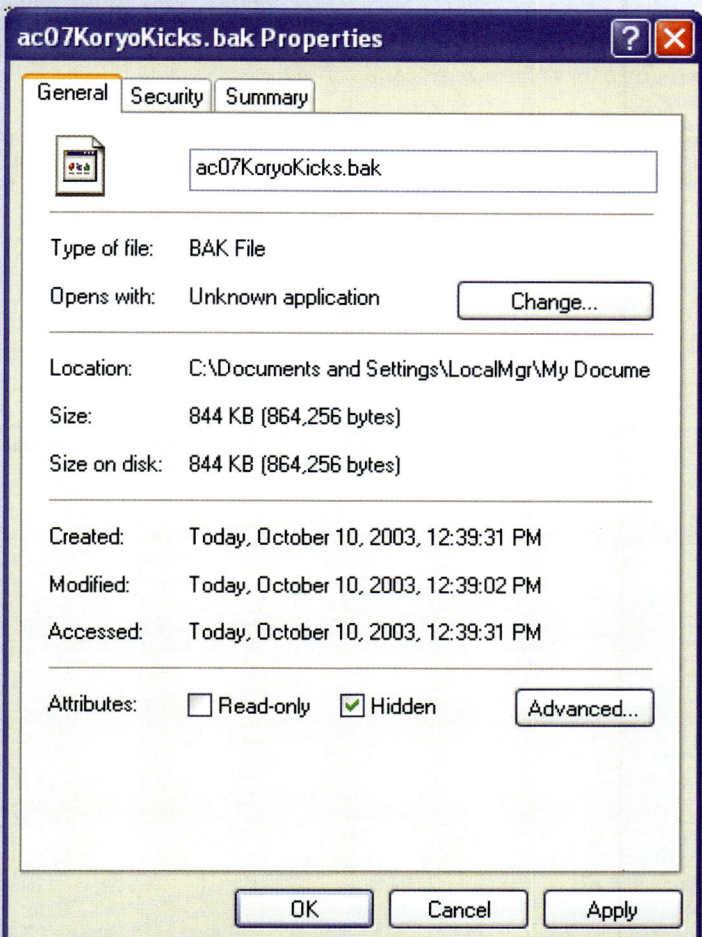

FIGURE 7.22
File Properties dialog box

9. Click **Tools** and select **Folder Options**

10. Click the **View** tab

11. Click **Show Hidden Files and Folders** and click **OK**

tip: *If ac07KoryoKicks.bak is not visible, press F5*

Setting a folder's Show Hidden Files and Folders properties causes all hidden files and folders to display in the current folder. Selecting the Like Current Folder button, rather than OK, will cause all folders to display hidden files. Since hidden files can be so readily displayed, hiding the file only keeps it out of the hands of people who don't really know how to look.

Encoding Data

Encoding is a simple method of securing a database. Encoding a database ensures that it is indecipherable to utility and word-processor programs. This method is most effective for a database that is being transported on a storage medium or digitally transmitted. Since the process of opening an encoded database in Access decodes it, this is not an effective way to stop Access users from viewing and updating the database.

An important component of security is that only specific users can apply and remove database security measures. The person who created a database is its *owner* and has full security rights to it. When multiple users or user groups have been defined for a database, the users who have full rights are members of the administrator group called Admins. Only the owner or a member of the Admins group can open the database exclusively so that no other users have access and can set security.

---

task reference   Encoding a Database

- Open Access with no open database

- Open the **Tools** menu, pause over **Security**, and click **Encode/Decode Database** . . .

- Enter a folder and a name for the database to be encoded and click **OK**

- Enter a folder and name for the encoded database and click **Save**

Encoding KoryoKicks:

1. Open Access and close any open database

2. On the **Tools** menu, point to **Security**, and then click **Encode/Decode Database** . . .

FIGURE 7.23

Encoding menu selections

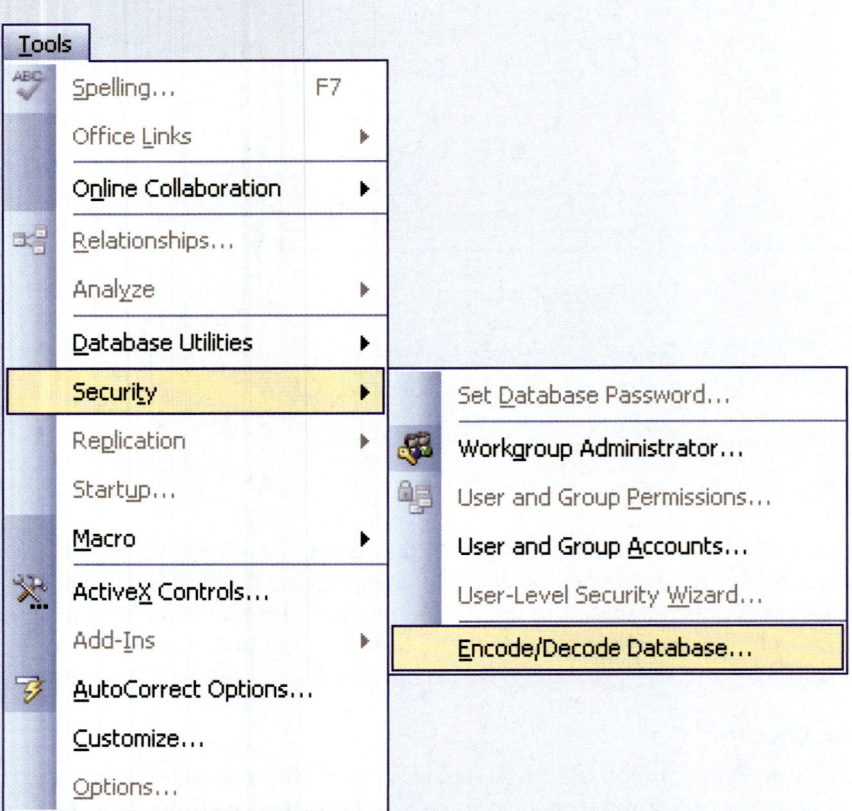

3. Navigate to the folder containing your files and select **ac07KoryoKicks.mdb** as the database to encode

4. Click **OK**

5. Name the encoded database **Encodedac07KoryoKicks.mdb**

6. Click **Save**

When naming the encoded file, one option is to use the same name as the original file. If the encoding operation is successful, the database is replaced with the encoded version. If the encoding operation fails, the original file is retained. Data added to an encoded file are encoded before they are stored. Data are decoded by Access before they are displayed to the user. Decoding a database is the reverse of encoding.

Continually encoding and decoding the data as the database is used can slow database performance. It is best to encode the database for transport and decode it for use.

help yourself *Use the Type a Question combo box to improve your understanding of the options available for securing an Access database by typing* **security**. *Review the contents of* Overview of Access security. *Close the Help window when you are finished*

Setting Password Protection

Missy and Micah would like to add a password to the KoryoKicks database to control who has access to the data. Adding a *password* or passwords to a database is the simplest way to prevent unauthorized access to the data and other objects it contains. Users will have to provide the password before they are able to open the file. The Password dialog box displays asterisks as the user enters the password to keep others from viewing it.

Opening an Access database in the usual fashion allows *shared* access. Shared access means that two or more users can open the same database simultaneously. *Exclusive* access is required while setting a password to prevent other users from entering the database.

task reference   Password Protecting a Database

- Open Access with no open database
- Click the **Open** button on the Database toolbar
- Navigate to the folder and select the file to be password protected
- Click the Open button's list arrow and select **Open Exclusive**
- Open the **Tools** menu, pause over **Security**, and then click **Set Database Password**
- Type the password in the Password text box, repeat the same password in the Verify text box, and then press **Enter**

Adding a password to KoryoKicks:

1. Use Windows Explorer to create a copy of **ac07KoryoKicks.bak** and rename the copy **ac07KoryoKicksPassword.mdb**

ACCESS

  2. Open Access and close any open databases

  3. Click the **Open** button

  4. Locate **ac07KoryoKicksPassword.mdb** and click it

  5. Click the list arrow on the Open button

F I G U R E   7.24

Open button options

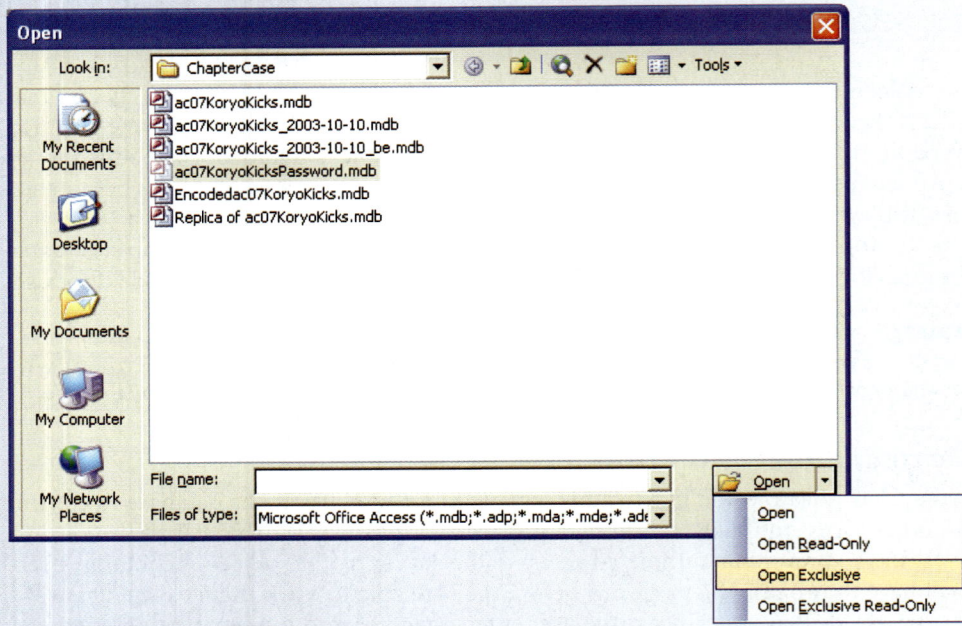

  6. Select **Open Exclusive**

  7. Select **Tools**, pause over **Security**, and then click **Set Database Password**

tip: *If Set Database Password is grayed out, the database is not exclusively opened. Close it and repeat steps 2 through 5*

F I G U R E   7.25

Set Database Password
dialog box

  8. Type **gizmo** in the Password text box

  9. Type **gizmo** in the Verify text box

 10. Click **OK**

 11. Close ac07KoryoKicks.mdb leaving Access open

Figure 7.24 displays all of the available open modes. As previously discussed, choosing Open results in shared access and choosing Open Exclusive locks the database so that no other users have access. The *Open Read-Only* option allows shared access for reading database objects. Read access allows all actions that do not update any database objects. Examples of allowable read-only operations include printing reports and running queries. The *Open Exclusive Read-Only* option locks out other users and allows you read access.

A new password must be entered twice to prevent typing errors in the password. Access passwords are case sensitive, so be very careful when entering them. Pick a password that is easy to remember since opening the database is not possible without the password. Replicated databases should not be password protected, since the password halts the synchronization process. Testing the password is accomplished by trying to open the database.

Testing the KoryoKicks password:

FIGURE 7.26

Password dialog box

1. Click the Open button

2. Locate **ac07KoryoKicksPassword.mdb** and click it

3. Click the **Open** button

4. Type **GIZMO** and click **OK**

tip: *Passwords are case sensitive, so GIZMO will not work*

5. Respond OK to the prompt that you have entered an invalid password

6. Type **gizmo** and click **OK**

Passwords are unencrypted so that they can be viewed by other users from the password file. This can be handy for forgotten passwords, but does not provide the most effective password protection. Encrypted passwords can be set with user-level security.

Removing the KoryoKicks password:

1. Verify that Access is running and that **ac07KoryoKicks.mdb** is open

2. Click the **Tools menu**, then **Security**, and then **Unset Database Password** (see Figure 7.27)

3. Type **gizmo** and click **OK**

Removing a password from a file is accomplished with the file open. With the Security option of the Tools menu displaying, select Unset Database Password and enter the correct password when prompted. Successfully entering the password will remove it from the file.

User-Level Security

In a multiuser database **user-level security** settings can allow some users to have full access to the database while others have restricted access. Restricted access might keep certain users from replicating the database, changing the database design, creating new tables, changing the database password, or almost any other operation.

F I G U R E   7.27

Removing a password

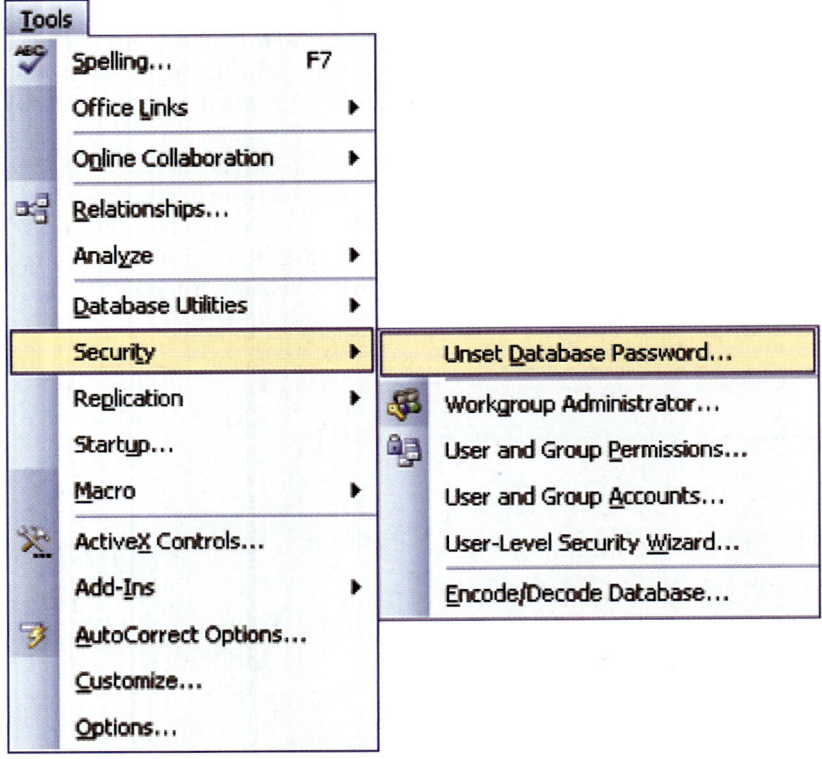

User-level security provides the most comprehensive security available for an Access database. When user-level security is applied, the user must type a password to enter the database. The password used is matched against a list of users to establish a level of access to each database object called **permissions**.

Each user has a set of permissions that determine what operations they can perform on each table, query, form, report, and macro. Permissions are either explicit or implicit. **Explicit permissions** are granted directly to each user by setting a user account. **Implicit permissions** are granted to a user group and inherited by the users belonging to that group.

Permissions can be changed for a database object by

- Members of the Admins group
- The owner of the object
- Any user who has Administer permission for the object

The user who creates a table, query, form, report, or macro is the owner of that object. Additionally, the group of users that can change permissions in the database also can change the ownership of these objects, or they can re-create these objects, which is another way to change ownership of the objects. Access provides the User-Level Security Wizard to aid in implementing common security schemes.

task reference   Setting User-Level Security

- Open the Access database to be secured
- On the **Tools** menu, pause over **Security** and then click **User-Level Security Wizard**
- Follow the Wizard instructions

Setting KoryoKicks user-level security:

1. Verify that Access is running and that **ac07KoryoKicksPassword.mdb** is open

2. Open the **Tools** menu and pause over **Security** and then click **User-Level Security Wizard**

3. Click **Next** to create a new workgroup information file

4. Read and accept the defaults on this Wizard page by clicking **Next**

5. Accept the default of securing all database objects by clicking **Next**

6. Create user groups
   a. Check **Full Permissions** and read the Group Permissions description
   b. Check **Full Data Users** and read the Group Permissions description

tip: *You are creating two unique and encrypted user groups with different permissions. The Administrator group is created by default*

7. Click **Next**

8. Accept the default of not assigning Users group permissions by clicking **Next**

9. Add users and passwords
   a. Add **user1** with a password of **user1** and then click **Add This User to the List**
   b. Add **user2** with a password of **user2** and then click **Add This User to the List**
   c. Click **Next**

10. Add users to the groups (see Figure 7.28)
    a. Select **user1** from the drop-down list and click **Full Permissions**
    b. Select user2 from the drop-down list and click **Full Data Users**

11. Click **Next**

12. Name the backup **KoryoKicksUserSecurityBak** and click **Finish**

13. Print the Security report and save it

The KoryoKicks database now has three users with unique passwords. The username and password used to open the database determine the operations that can be performed.

Testing KoryoKicks user-level security:

1. Close Access and reopen it using the ac07KoryoKicksPassword.mdb icon placed on your desktop by the previous steps

2. Log on as user2 and try to change the database design

The Administrator user name and password will allow full access to the database including altering security settings. Logging on as user1 will allow full access to the database except assigning permissions to other users while user2 will allow data editing, but no updates to database objects.

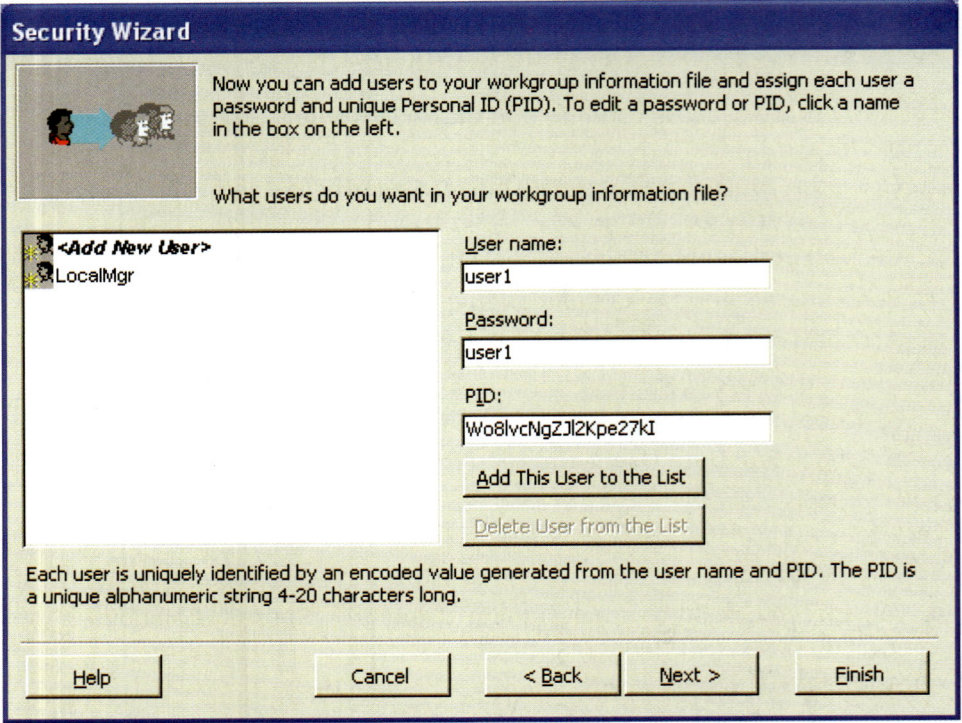

SESSION 7.2

making the grade

1. What is the purpose of splitting a database?
2. What tool will suggest changes to improve database performance?
3. How is replicating a database different from splitting a database?
4. When should you consider securing an Access database?

SESSION 7.3 SUMMARY

Every database requires periodic maintenance to repair known problems regardless of how well it was designed. Preventive maintenance or design reviews are performed to reduce the likelihood of a serious system failure. The frequency of preventive maintenance is determined by how critical the data are to the operation of the organization.

Periodic maintenance starts with the users evaluating the system and suggesting modifications that would improve usability and performance. User issues typically involve ease of data entry, validity of data, and reporting. Input masks, formats, default values, data validation, and other field properties are usually the way to address such issues. Access also provides the Database Performance Analyzer for monitoring database performance and suggesting areas for object design improvement.

Often design changes are necessary because the organization using the data or the business operations supported by the data have changed. New tables, fields, and reports can be created to support business changes, but organizational changes are more complex. When multiple users need access to the same data, effective methods of sharing must be employed. One alternative for sharing is to create replicas of a database that must be synchronized so that all replicas reflect the same data.

The method chosen for sharing data is determined by whether or not the organization is networked and the level of access needed by each user. Another sharing method splits the database into a front-end and back-end. Each user maintains unique front-end (queries, forms, and reports) with access to the data held in the back-end.

When a database is exposed to risk of violation, it is wise to implement security measures. Security is also needed when there are multiple users with differing levels of responsibility. Encoding can be used to secure a database being transported. A simple password can ensure that only authorized users access the data. End-user security uses permissions to determine exactly what operations a user can perform on each database object.

MICROSOFT OFFICE SPECIALIST OBJECTIVES SUMMARY

- Modify field properties for tables in Design View—AC03S-1-4

making the grade *answers*

SESSION 7.1

1. Input masks speed data entry by reducing keystrokes. They also improve reliability by not requiring users to enter repetitive data. Any field containing data with a repetitive component such as punctuation should be considered for an input mask.

2. Both the Input Mask and Format properties are similar since they use the same definition characters. The input mask displays a pattern for the user to enter data, such as (___)___-___. You can choose whether or not the punctuation is stored with the data. If the punctuation is not stored with the data, it will need to be added before displaying data from the field to the user. The Format property is used to add repeating characters to data retrieved from a table.

3. The default value assigned to a field should be the most common data value for the field.

4. Validation rules are designed to improve data validity by ensuring that data entered into a field are appropriate for that field.

SESSION 7.2

1. Splitting a database separates the data from the queries, forms, and reports that use it. This is normally done in a networked environment to share the data while allowing users to have their own custom queries, forms, and reports.

2. Database Performance Analyzer

3. When a database is replicated, there are multiple full copies of the database that have to be synchronized with each other. A split database maintains only one copy of the data in a central location that is shared by all users. With a split database, each user has his or her own front-end (queries, forms, and reports) based on the centralized data.

4. Databases should be secured whenever there is risk of theft, inappropriate use, or unwanted data altering.

ACCESS

task reference summary

Task	Page #	Preferred Method
Controlling blank data values	AC 7.11	• Open the table in Design View • Click the field whose blank values you would like to control • Set Required to **Yes** to disallow blank values (Allow Zero Length should be set to No)

Defining field validation rules	AC 7.14	• Open the table in Design View
		• Click the field that will be monitored by the validation rule
		• Select the **Validation Rule** property for that field
		• Type the validation expression or use the Expression Builder by clicking the ellipsis to the right of the Validation Rule text box
		• Click the Validation Text property box for the same field and enter the text that is to display when the validation rule is broken
		• Save the table update
		  • If the validation rule has been set for a field that already contains data, Access will ask if you want to apply the new rule to existing data
		  • If there are no existing data in the field, there will be no prompt

Splitting a database	AC 7.16	• Back up the database • On the **Tools** menu, point to **Database Utilities**, and then click **Database Splitter** • Follow the Database Splitter Wizard instructions
Optimizing database objects	AC 7.18	• Open the database to be optimized • Click the **Tools** menu, then **Analyze**, and then **Performance** • Select the tab for the database object (table, query, report, form, etc.) that you would like to analyze • Click the check box of each object to be evaluated or click Select All to select all objects in the list • Select objects from other tabs if desired • Click **OK** • Review and apply results as needed

Replicating a database	AC 7.20	• Open the database to be replicated
		• Remove any password protection and ensure that the database is not open by any other users
		• On the **Tools** menu, point to **Replication**, and then click **Create Replica**
		• Click **Yes** when prompted with: The database must be closed before you can create a replica
		• Answer **Yes** when prompted with: Converting a database into a Design Master results in changes . . .
		• In the Location of New Replica dialog box
		  • Navigate to the location for the replica
		  • Set the **Priority**
		  • Check the **Prevent deletes** check box to prevent record deletions in the replica
		  • In the Save as type box, select the replica visibility
		  • Click **OK**

Synchronizing replicated databases	AC 7.23	• Open the replica to be synchronized • On the **Tools** menu, point to **Replication**, and then click **Synchronize Now** • Select the other replica set member to be synchronized from the Directly with Replica drop-down list box • Click **OK** • Respond **Yes** when prompted to close the database for synchronization • Respond **OK** when notified that the process has been completed

task reference *summary*

Task	Page #	Preferred Method
Hiding a database	AC 7.26	• Open Windows Explorer • Navigate to the file to be hidden • Right-click on the file to be hidden • Click the **Properties** option • Click the **Hidden** attribute • Click **OK**
Encoding a database	AC 7.28	• Open Access with no open database • Open the **Tools** menu, pause over **Security**, and click **Encode/Decode Database** ... • Enter a folder and a name for the database to be encoded and click **OK** • Enter a folder and name for the encoded database and click **Save**
Password protecting a database	AC 7.29	• Open Access with no open database • Click the **Open** button on the Database toolbar • Navigate to the folder and select the file to be password protected • Click the Open button's list arrow and select **Open Exclusive** • Open the **Tools** menu, pause over **Security**, and then click **Set Database Password** • Type the password in the Password text box, repeat the same password in the Verify text box, and then press **Enter**
Setting user-level security	AC 7.32	• Open the Access database to be secured • On the **Tools** menu, pause over **Security** and then click **User-Level Security Wizard** • Follow the Wizard instructions

TRUE/FALSE

1. Microsoft Access will *not* allow an output format to be selected that does not match the input mask display.

2. The Input Mask property **0L** indicates that data entered in this field must consist of a required number followed by a required letter.

3. The Validation Text property of a field contains the validation rule that data being entered in this field must follow.

4. A field with a validation rule of *"Mr" Or "Ms" Or "Mrs"* will only accept one of the three listed values.

5. When both the Required and Allow Zero Length properties of a field are set to No, the field will accept blank values.

6. A front-end and back-end version of a database are created through database replication.

FILL-IN

1. Passwords protect a database from _____ access.

2. The least effective method of securing a database discussed is _____.

3. Administrators and owners can grant _____ to database objects.

4. Encoding is not effective in protecting against people who own _____ software.

5. One of the easiest ways to improve the validity of database data is to reduce _____.

6. The _____ input mask character causes all text that follows to be converted to lowercase.

7. The _____ can be used to copy formatting from one control to another control in both Form and Report Design Views.

MULTIPLE CHOICE

1. A security permission granted to a specific user is called a(n) _____ permission.
   a. implied
   b. explicit
   c. implicit
   d. personal

2. To set passwords the database must be opened using the _____ option of the Open button.
   a. Open
   b. Open Single User
   c. Open Read-Only
   d. Open Exclusive

3. _____ causes the data in an Access database to be indecipherable to utility and word-processing programs.
   a. Hiding
   b. Scanning
   c. Encoding
   d. None of the above

4. The act of updating the Design Master of a replicate set with data from a replica is called _____.
   a. synchronization
   b. master update
   c. harmonizing
   d. all of the above

5. The Database Performance Analyzer automatically repairs items classified as _____.
   a. Critical
   b. Fixed
   c. Auto
   d. Idea

review of concepts

REVIEW QUESTIONS

Each of the following topics should be addressed in one to three paragraphs.

1. Consider the data that your college or university stores about you and suggest some validation rules that would be effective for improving data validity with that type of data.

2. Explain the relationship between validation rules and validation text.

3. Assume that you have created a database that will track service calls for billing purposes. The minimum service call is 30 minutes. How would you set up and verify the performance of data entry restrictions on the ServiceTime field?

4. Why is it important for split databases to be on a network?

5. If your database resides on a desktop computer and you are taking a business trip with a laptop, what is the most effective way to take your database with you?

CREATE THE QUESTION

For each of the following answers, create the question.

ANSWER	QUESTION
1. _____ – _____ – _____	_____
2. The Text Box format overrides the format set in the table definition	_____
3. When you can identify a value that is most often entered in a field	_____
4. Please enter a value between 1 and 100	_____
5. The back-end	_____
6. The front-end	_____
7. It indicates missing or unknown data	_____

FACT OR FICTION

For each of the following, determine whether the statement is fact, fiction, or both and present your arguments for that conclusion.

1. The queries, forms, and reports contained in the front-end file of a split database cannot be updated.

2. You should always follow the suggestions of the Database Performance Analyzer.

3. When you add a record to a replica, the other members of the replica set are automatically updated.

4. Synchronization conflicts that cannot be resolved with the priority must be handled manually with the Conflict Viewer.

5. Deleting a replica does not impact the Design Master or the remaining replicas.

6. The Format property set in table design can be overridden for the Text Box control displaying the field in Form Design View.

7. Well-designed Microsoft Access databases will not require periodic design reviews.

practice

1. Altamonte High School Booster Club Donation Tracking—Part III: Database Design Review

The Altamonte Boosters have been using their database for several months and are encountering some problems. Since there are no input masks or validation rules, and multiple users, the data are not at all consistent. The capitalization of names is an issue and incomplete data entry occurs too frequently. A database design review has been completed uncovering the need for the updates outlined below.

1. Start Access and open **ac07AltamonteBoosters.mdb**

tip: *You cannot use your copy of the database from the previous chapter, since there have been modifications for this chapter*

2. Open the **Boosters** table

   a. Make each field required by setting the Required property to **Yes**

   b. Correct the Field Size property of Name to **25**

   c. Change the Data Type of Phone to **Text**. Set Size to 13 and use the ellipsis (. . .) to set the input mask to **Phone Number**. Do not store the symbols

   d. Edit the Phone Input Mask property to be **!(000)000-0000** since the area code in Altamonte is required

   e. Change the Data Type of Zip to **Text** with a size of 5 and set an input mask of **00000**

   f. Since all of the boosters are in-state, the zip code should begin with 27. Enter the validation rule **Like "27???"**

   g. Enter the validation text **Booster's Zip Code must begin with 27**

   h. Since most of the boosters are in the **27234** zip code, set that as the default value of Zip

   i. Set the Default property of the State field to **NC**

3. Save your changes to the Boosters table and respond yes to the prompt informing you that validation rules have changed

4. To test your updates, change to Datasheet View

   a. Create a new booster record for **Mark Funk** and try to move to another record

   tip: *You should receive a validation message for the missing street address*

   b. Add a Street address for Mark Funk in **Cary, NC**

   c. Leave the Zip blank and try to move to another record

   d. Enter a Zip of **33228** and try to move to another record (see Figure 7.29)

   e. Change the Zip to **27228** and try to move to another record

   f. Enter a Phone of **3174382851** and try to move to another record

   g. Set DonationClass to **1** and move to another record

   tip: *Now you have tested and corrected each modification to the database and the record should be accepted for update*

5. Close the Boosters table

6. Exit Access if your work is complete

FIGURE 7.29

Testing Boosters design changes

		ID	Name	Street	City	State	Zip	Phone	DonationClass
+		27	Brendan Linehan	10428 S. Christopher Dr.	Cary	NC	27433	(336)670-3854	5
+		28	Connie Long	10089 S. Pinedale Dr.	Cary	NC	27433	(336)838-7870	1
+		29	Johnny Long	10995 Hwy 285	Cary	NC	27433	(336)816-9329	4
+		30	Drew Lund	7350 Brook Forest Dr.	Cary	NC	27433	(336)838-8144	1
+		31	Brett Mahns	11559 Broken Arrow Dr.	Apex	NC	27439	(336)670-8519	3
+		32	Evan Manning	26467 DeBerry St.	Apex	NC	27439	(336)674-4971	5
+		33	Ricky Maus	33971 Nova Rd.	Cary	NC	27433	(336)816-0411	3
+		34	Natale McAneney	20448 Cypress Dr.	Apex	NC	27439	(336)674-2764	3
+		35	Ryan Mills	13282 Omaha St.	Pine	NC	27470	(336)838-2967	2
+		36	Cole Nichols	10153 Buena Vista Dr.	Cary	NC	27433	(336)838-0638	1
+		37	Jeffrey Peterson	28486 Cragmont Dr.					1
+		38	Kaelin Probeck	8791 S. Rudd Rd.					3
+		39	Timmy Thomas	9780 S. Warhawk Rd.					5
+		40	Rachel Van Bibber	11744 Little Turtle Lan					2
+		41	Katherine Watters	20464 Cypress Dr.					3
+		42	Matthew Wilson	19393 Silver Ranch R					1
⚲	+	44	Mark Funk	123 Any Street	Cary	NC	33228	(317)438-2851	1
*		(Number)				NC	27234		0

Microsoft Office Access

⚠ Booster's Zip code must begin with 27.

OK   Help

Boosters : Table

Record: 43 of 43

2. BBs Shoes Database Design Review

BBs is a family-owned shoe store specializing in athletic shoes. The store is owned by Roberto (Berto) and Benita Lopez, who developed their own Microsoft Access database to track the shoe inventory. Since Berto and Benita are new to Access databases, they have asked you to help them complete a design review.

1. Start Access and open **ac07BBsShoes.mdb**

2. Familiarize yourself with the database
   a. Open the Inventory table in Design View and review the current table design
   b. Switch to Datasheet View and review the sample data Berto and Benita have provided
   c. Take a look at the existing form and report

3. The biggest problems that Berto and Benita have identified are data entry errors. They would like you to add some validation rules to improve the integrity of their data
   a. Create a validation rule that will accept ShoePrice values between 50 and 250. Make the validation text **Valid shoe prices are between 50 and 250 inclusive.**
   b. Create a validation rule that will accept QtyOnHand values between 0 and 100. Make the validation text **Valid quantities are between 0 and 100 inclusive.**

4. Create an input mask for the Location field that will require the user to enter an uppercase letter followed by at least one digit. Refer to Figures 7.2 and 7.3

5. Set the default QtyOnHand value to **12**, since that is the most common order quantity and therefore the most common quantity on hand value

6. Another problem area for BBs Shoes is missing data. None of the Inventory table's fields should be blank. Set the Required property to **Yes** and the Allow Zero Length property to **No** for each nonkey field in the table

7. Switch to Datasheet View, save your changes, and answer **Yes** to the data integrity prompt

8. Verify your design changes using data for your favorite athletic shoes using a StockNbr value of **TX99999**
   a. Enter a price that violates the validation rule and document the result
   b. Enter a QtyOnHand that violates the validation rule and document the result (see Figure 7.30)
   c. Enter a Location of 7A and document the result
   d. Try to leave each nonkey field blank and document the result

9. After making any needed adjustments to the table design, enter the shoes with a valid ShoeDescription and Price. Make the QtyOnHand **15** and the Location **B4**

10. If your work is complete, exit Access; otherwise, continue to the next assignment

FIGURE 7.30

Testing BBs Shoes design changes

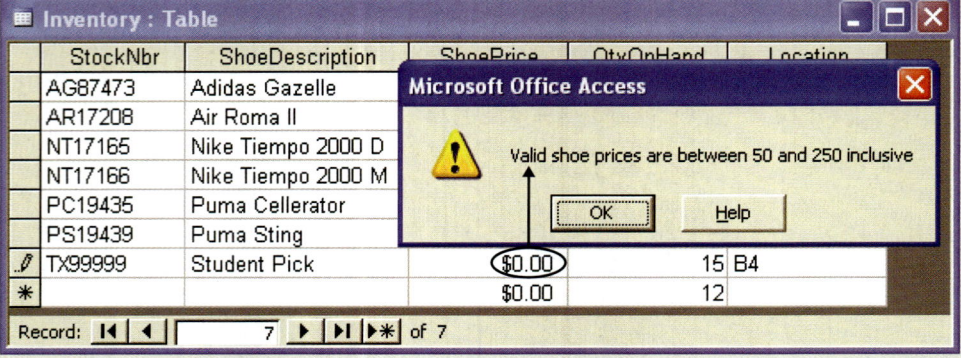

challenge!

1. Altamonte High School Booster Club Donation Tracking—Part IV: Exploring Alternatives for Sharing the Database

The Altamonte Boosters are preparing for a fund-raising drive and believe that it would be more effective to have a way for multiple members to update the database. Since the computers holding the databases will not be networked, replication will provide the most effective way to share database access. At this point they think that there should be three users: the club president, vice president, and fund-raising chair.

1. If you did not complete the Altamonte Practice project in this chapter, do so now

2. Open **ac07AltamonteBoosters.mdb**

tip: *You can use your copy of the database from the Practice project in this chapter. You cannot use your copy of the database from the previous chapter since there have been modifications for this chapter*

3. Use the Performance Analyzer to evaluate the performance of all tables in the AlatamonteBoosters database. Document the Analysis Results and outline whether or not the results should be acted on

4. Create a replica set for the three users. The Design Master will be retained by the club president and each of the other users will need a replica (see Figure 7.31)

a. Use the Tools menu to create the first replica with the following attributes:

   i. Create a backup and close the open database when prompted

   ii. Name the replica **ReplicaAltamonte1** and save it in a folder named **ReplicaAltamonte**

   iii. Click on the **Prevent Deletes** check box so that this replica can't delete existing records

b. Use the Tools menu to create the second replica, named **ReplicaAltamonte2**, with the same attributes as ReplicaAltamonte1

tip: *You will not be prompted to create a backup in subsequent replications*

5. Passwords cannot be applied to replicated databases, so each user will have to be responsible for securing his or her computer and folders to protect the database. For added security, use Windows Explorer to

a. Create a folder in ReplicaAtlamonte database for each user named **VPres** and **Chair**

b. Move ReplicaAltamonte1 to Vpres, and ReplicaAltamonte2 to Chair

c. Hide the VPres and Chair folders

6. Open the Design Master and initiate synchronization on Altamonte1. Since it has been moved, you will need to browse to the hidden folder

7. Exit Access if your work is complete

FIGURE 7.31

AltamonteBoosters Design Master and replicas

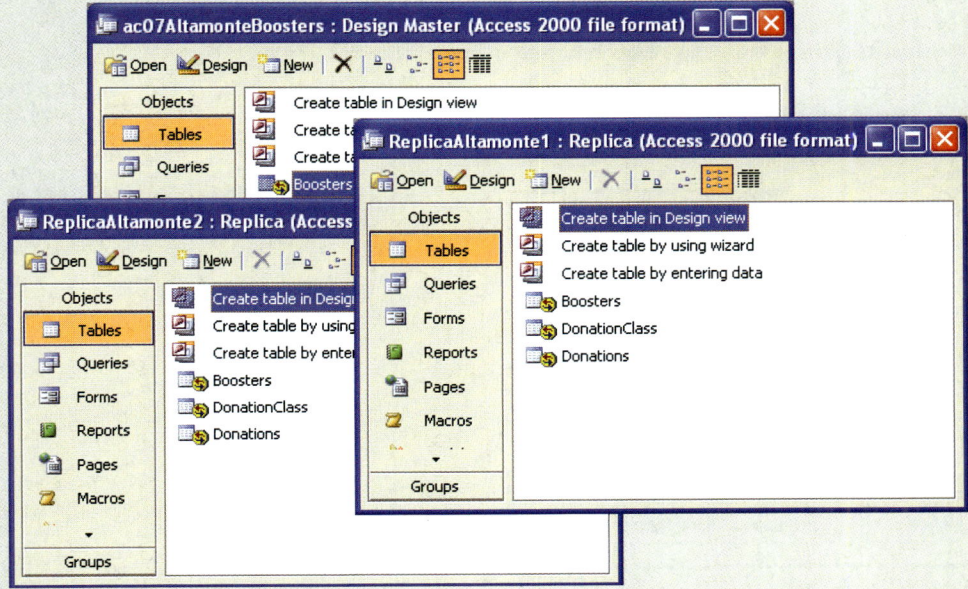

AC 7.43

2. HealthCare2Go Design Review

HealthCare2Go is a temporary services agency providing short-term employees to the medical community. Riki Lee has built a database that is functioning fairly well, but she believes the design can be improved to increase data reliability. Additionally, new users are being added to the system and security needs to be developed to protect against unauthorized updates to the data.

1. Start Access and open **ac07HealthCare2Go.mdb**

2. Open the TempEmployees table in Datasheet View and review the existing data

3. Switch to Design View and review the table's field definitions

4. Set the Required and Allow Zero Length properties so that LastName, FirstName, Phone, and JobClass must have values entered and will not accept ""

5. Set Formats to obtain the following results
   a. Always display the State value in uppercase
   b. Ensure that the first letter of both LastName and FirstName is always uppercase
   c. Display Phone as (___)___-_____
   d. Display the SocialSecNmbr with dashes

6. Set input masks to obtain the following results
   a. Ensure that 9 numbers are entered in the SocialSecNmbr field
   b. Ensure that 5 numbers are entered in the Zip field

7. Set a default value of WA for the State field

8. Add a new record testing each required field, format, and input mask

9. Use the User-Level Security Wizard to create a new workgroup for this database
   a. Check both **Full Data Users** and **Full Permissions**
   b. Do not assign the additional User group permissions
   c. Create three users and their associated passwords (see Figure 7.32)
      i. testuser1/test1as a Full Data Users group member
      ii. testuser2/test2 as a Full Permissions group member
      iii. <yourlastname>/<yourlastname> as an Admins group member
   d. Name the backup **ac07HealthCare2GoBak.mdb**
   e. Print the security report and save it
   f. Repeatedly close the database using the icon on your desktop and test each password
   g. Place a copy of your desktop icon in your homework folder

10. If your work is complete, exit Access; otherwise, continue to the next assignment

FIGURE 7.32

HealthCare2Go group assignments

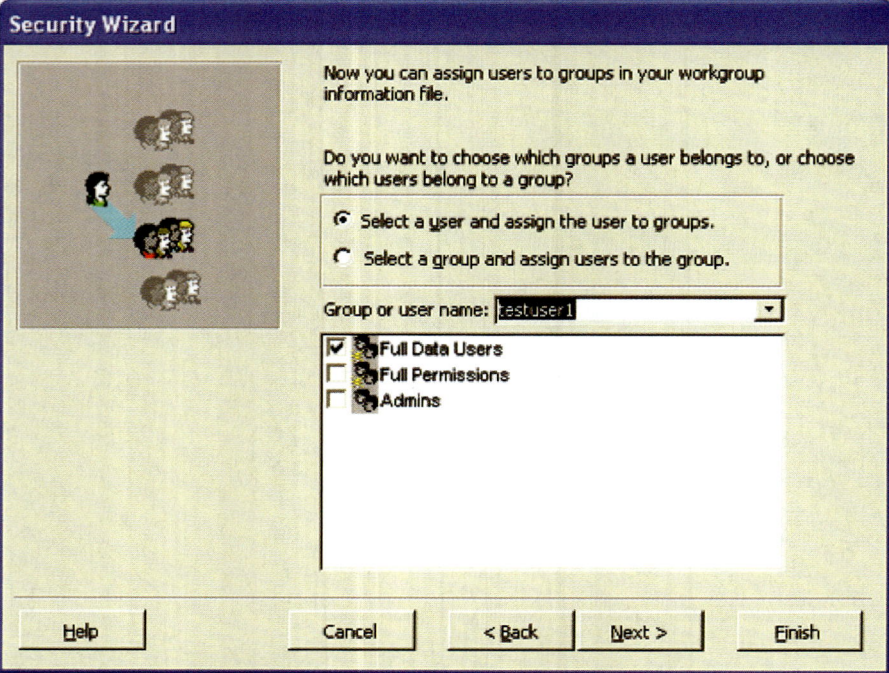

e-business

1. Curbside Recycling

A design review for the Curbside Recycling Access database has been completed and a list of updates compiled. The updates include adding input masks and default values and replicating the database.

1. Start Access and open **ac07CurbsideRecycling.mdb**

tip: *You cannot use your copy of the database from the previous chapter since there have been modifications for this chapter*

2. Open the Customer table

   a. Make each field required by setting the Required property to **Yes**

tip: *CstmrNmbr is the key field and so is already required*

   b. Create a Phone input mask that requires the area code to be entered

   c. Create an input mask for ZipCode that requires all five digits to be entered

   d. Create an input mask for State that requires both characters to be entered

   e. Apply a Short Date input mask to FirstPickup

   f. Based on the current data, set appropriate default values for City, State, and Zip

   g. Test these updates with **Connor McKinsey, 838 E. Jay St., Indianapolis, IN, 46121, 7518300848.** Use the current date for FirstPickup

   h. Close the Customer table

3. Use the **Replication** option of the **Tools** menu to create replicas (see Figure 7.33)

   a. Create a new folder for the replicas named **CurbsideReplicas**

   b. Set the appropriate properties to stop the replica from deleting records and name the replica **Curbside1**

   c. Create a second replica that cannot delete records, **Curbside2**, in the same folder

4. You are in the Design Master where changes to database design should be made

   a. Open the Customer table in Design View

   b. Set an input mask for First Name that causes the first letter to be capitalized

   c. Set an input mask for Last Name that causes the first letter to be capitalized

5. Open Curbside1

   a. Open the Customer table in Design View

   b. Verify that the input masks for First and Last Names do not exist yet in the replica

   c. On the **Tools** menu, point to **Replication** and select **Synchronize Now**

     i. Respond **Yes** to closing open objects

     ii. Select the **Design Master** for synchronization and click **OK**

   d. Open the Customer table in Design View and verify that the input masks for First and Last Names now exist

6. Exit Access if your work is complete

FIGURE 7.33

Curbside replicas

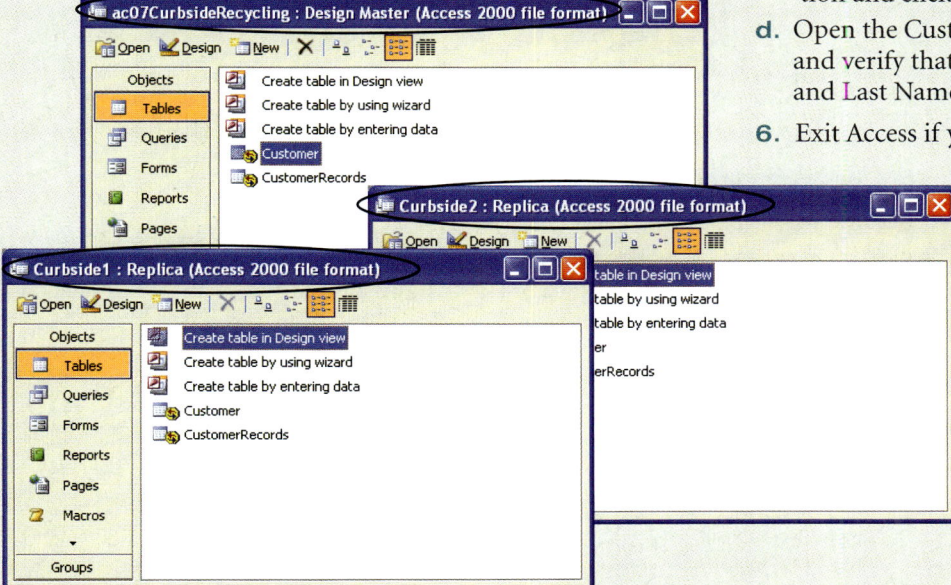

2. SportBabies.com Design Review

SportBabies.com is an online storefront selling replica sports uniforms for babies and toddlers. A Microsoft Access database to support this Web site was developed by an employee who has moved on to another position. The database has not been implemented and currently contains a small number of test records. You have inherited the database development project and need to evaluate its design before updating it to meet current business needs.

1. Open Access and open **ac07SportBabies.mdb**

2. Open the ProductList table in Datasheet View and review the existing data

3. Switch to Design View and review the table's field definitions

4. Run the Database Performance Analyzer and document the results. Be sure to include the form and report in your evaluation

5. You have determined that knowing that a product is in stock would benefit potential customers and improve sales. Add a new field, **QtyOnHand** before the Price column. Make this field an **Integer** data type

6. Set the following default values
   a. MatchingCap, HomeJersey, and AwayJersey should each default to Yes (checked)
   b. Price should default to 42.38

7. Create a validation rule to ensure that the price entered is between 25 and 200 inclusive. Be sure to include appropriate validation text

8. Make League, Team, Player, and Price required fields that will not allow a zero-length value

9. Use a new product to test each of your design updates. Print the table design

10. Use the User-Level Security Wizard to create a new user group for this database
    a. Check both **Full Data Users** and **Full Permissions**
    b. Do not assign the additional User group permissions (see Figure 7.34)
    c. Create three users and their associated passwords
       i. testuser1/test1 as a member of Full Data Users
       ii. testuser2/test2 as a member of Full Permissions
       iii. <yourlastname>/<yourlastname> as a member of Admins
    d. Print the security report and save it
    e. Repeatedly close and open the database using the icon on your desktop to test each password
    f. Place a copy of your desktop icon in your homework folder

11. Close the database and exit Access if your work is complete

FIGURE 7.34

SportBabies.com passwords

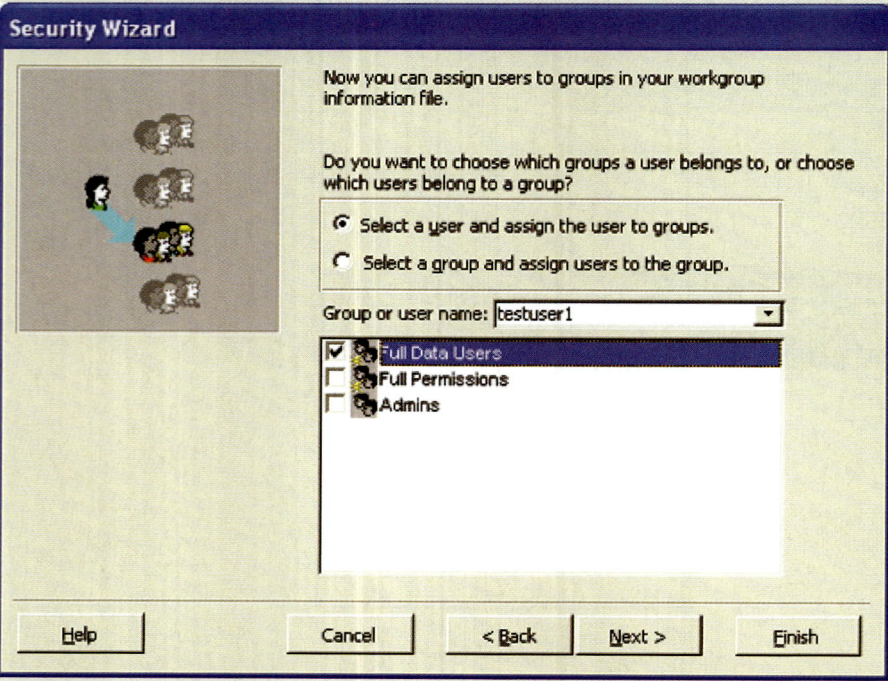

1. Academic Software

The design review for the Access database used by Academic Software has been completed and a list of updates compiled. Additionally, Academic has installed a network and plans to split the database so that the various users can customize their front-end components.

1. Use your favorite search engine to find an Academic software title for the study of chemistry

2. Start Access and open **ac07Software.mdb**

tip: *You cannot use your copy of the database from the previous chapter since there have been modifications for this chapter*

3. Open tblVendor

   a. Make each field required by setting the Required property to **Yes**

   b. Use Find and Replace to remove the dashes from the current phone numbers

   c. Use the ellipsis (. . .) to set the input mask to **Phone Number**. Do not store the symbols

   d. Edit the Phone input mask to require the area code to be entered

   e. Create an input mask for Zip that requires all five digits to be entered

   f. Create an input mask for State that requires both characters to be entered

   g. Test these updates with **RS, Ricks Software, 838 E. Jay St., Indianapolis, IN, 46121, 7518300848**

   h. Close ac07Software.mdb

4. Use the File menu to create a backup of the database named **ac07SoftwareBak.mdb** before splitting it

5. Use the **Database Utilities** option of the **Tools** menu to activate the Database Splitter Wizard

   a. Name the back-end file **ac07Software_be.mdb**

tip: *This file would normally be placed on a shared network disk so that all of the front-ends would have access to it. The front-end can be copied to any number of computers*

   b. Select **tblSoftware** and click **Design** (see Figure 7.35)

tip: *A message will warn you that this is a linked table, which means that the data are stored in the back-end and you are in the front-end*

   c. Use the Query Wizard to create a query, **tblSoftwareQuery**, displaying Name, Category, and Vendor Code

6. Open **ac07Software_be.mdb**

   a. Open **tblSoftware** and add the validation rule "MTH" Or "ENG" Or "SCI" to the Category field

   b. Add appropriate validation text for the Category field

7. Open **ac07Software.mdb** and add a record to the Software for **NewsNow** with a SoftwareNumber of **6060**, Category of **Che**, and VendorCode of **LS**

tip: *You should receive the message from the validation rule added to the back-end*

8. Change Che to **SCI** and move to another record to save the change

9. Add a record for the software title that you located on the Internet with a VendorCode of **CC**

10. Exit Access if your work is complete

FIGURE 7.35

Front-end of Software.mdb

message generated after clicking Design for tblSoftware

tables are maintained from back-end of a split database

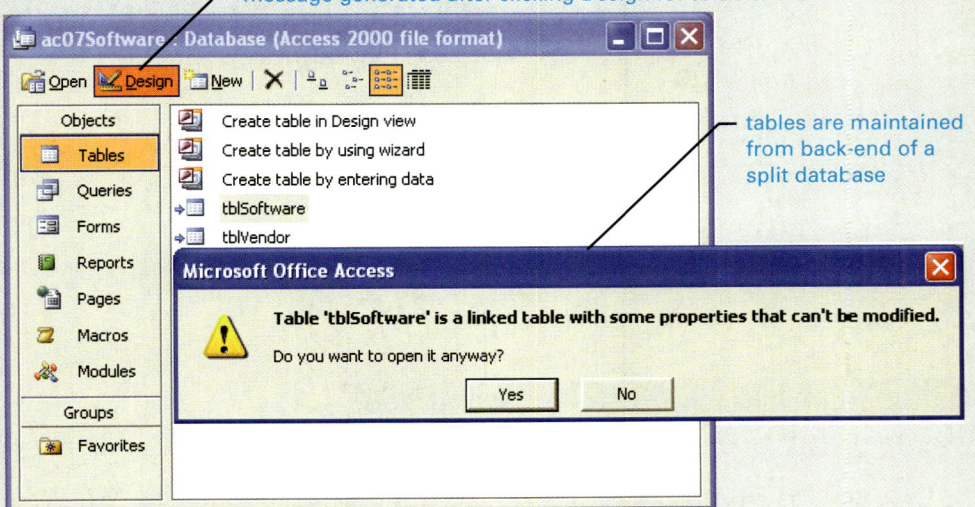

AC 7.47

ACCESS

hands-on projects

around the world

1. TechRocks Seminars

The design review for the TechRocks Access database used to track seminars, facilitators, and enrollment has been completed. Several design updates to improve usability have been approved. Additionally, TechRocks enrollment will now be handled from multiple locations around the world, so users in various offices must have access to the data. Since the offices are not networked, replicated databases using Internet synchronization is the planned approach.

1. Start Access and open **ac07SSeminars.mdb**

tip: *You cannot use your copy of the database from the previous chapter since there have been modifications for this chapter*

2. Open the **Seminars** table in Design View

   a. Make SeminarID, Date, Time, and Hours required by setting the Required property to **Yes**

   b. Set an input mask for SeminarID that requires the entry of 5 characters (letters or digits)

   c. Set an input mask for SeminarTime of **Medium Time**

   d. Set the default seminar cost to 250

   e. Set a data validation rule to ensure that the Cost entered is between $50 and $2,500. Do not set validation text; the default message is sufficient

tip: *Use the Between comparison operator*

   f. Set a data validation rule to ensure that Hours is between 16 and 80 (see Figure 7.36)

g. Use the Datasheet View to test these updates with a new seminar **XX134** and Trainer **5**. Be sure to enter invalid values for each field before settling on valid values

h. Close Seminars

3. Activate the **Tools** menu, pause over **Replication**, and select **Create Replica**

   a. Create a folder **ReplicaSeminars**

   b. Name this replica **ParisSeminars.mdb**

   c. Create a second replica called **LondonSeminars.mdb** with a priority of **70**. Store this replica in the same folder

4. Open **ParisSeminars.mdb**

   a. Open the **Enrollment** table

   b. Locate record one for student 114 and change the student's name to **Edna**

5. Open **LondonSeminars.mdb**

   a. Open the **Enrollment** table

   b. Locate record 114 and change the student's name to **Evan**

   c. Open the **Tools** menu, point to **Replication**, select **Synchronize Now**, and select **ParisSeminars.mdb** as the database to synchronize with

tip: *You may need to manually resolve the conflict in favor of the Paris changes, but they should resolve themselves if the priorities were set correctly*

   d. Open the Enrollment table to verify that the Paris change (Edna) was used to resolve the conflict

6. Open the Enrollment table of ac07ParisSeminars.mdb to verify that it still holds the value Edna for student 114

7. Exit Access if your work is complete

FIGURE 7.36

Validation rule violation message

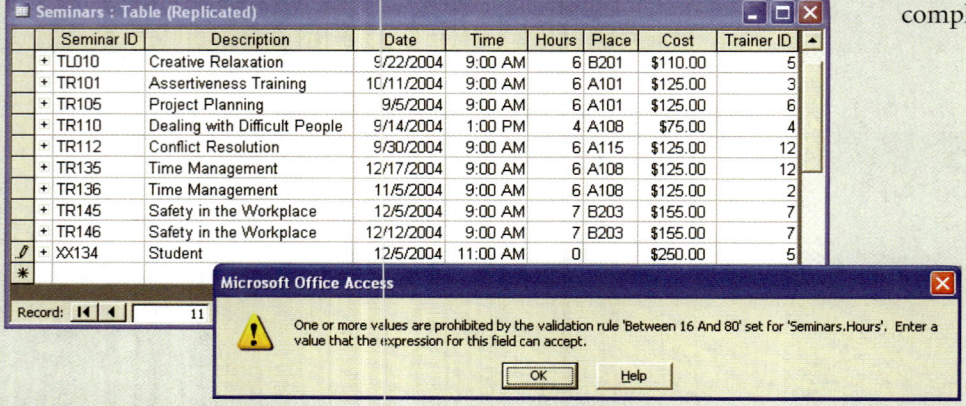

running project: tnt web design

Database Maintenance and Security

TnT has continued to grow and the database is out of control. In a recent design review, inactive records were archived and a plan for refining table design outlined. Since there are a large number of users who need to be able to view and report on data, but only a few users who need to be able to update data, two user groups will be created.

1. Start Access and open **ac07TnT.mdb**

tip: *You cannot use your copy of the database from the previous chapter since there have been modifications for this chapter*

2. Open the **Employees** table in Design View
   a. Make each field required by setting the Required property to **Yes**
   b. Create an input mask for First Name that will cause the first letter to always be up-percase and subsequent letters lowercase
   c. Create an input mask for Last Name that will cause the first letter to always be up-percase and subsequent letters lowercase
   d. Create an input mask for State that re-quires both characters to be entered
   e. Use the ellipsis (. . .) to set the input mask to **Phone**. Do not store the symbols.
   f. Edit the Phone input mask to require the area code to be entered

FIGURE 7.37

Creating a Read-Only Users Group

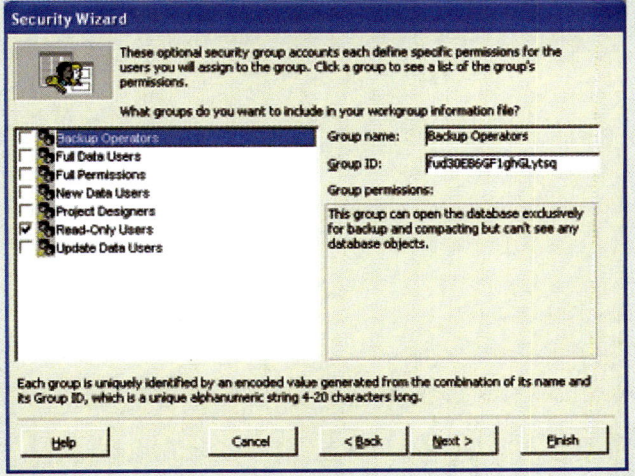

g. Create an input mask for Zip that requires all five digits to be entered
h. Test these updates with a record for **Bob Willson** with a JobClass of **QA**
i. Close Employees

3. Activate the **Tools** menu, point to **Security**, and select **User-Level Security Wizard**
   a. Click **Next** on the first panel
   b. Click **Next** again to accept the default names
   c. Click **Next** again to secure all database objects
   d. Check **Read-Only Users** to create a group for the users who can't update the database

tip: *The Administrators group has full rights to the database and is created automatically*

   e. Click **Next**
   f. Click **Next** to bypass setting permissions for users
   g. Create users
      i. **Tori**, with password **purple**
      ii. **Tonya**, with password **yellow**
      iii. **Readers**, with password of **seeit**
   h. Click **Next**

4. Assign permissions to the users you added
   a. Select **Tori** from the drop-down list and click **Admins**
   b. Repeat this process for **Tonya**
   c. Select **Readers** from the drop-down list and click **Read-Only Users**
   d. Click **Finish**
   e. Print the report and save it

5. Use the icon on your desktop to test each password

6. Exit Access if your work is complete

AC 7.49

1. Design Review of a Multitable Database to Invoice Customers

Locate your copy of the database named **ac06CustomersMultiTableDatabase.mdb** created in the Analysis assignment from Chapter 6. Use Microsoft Windows Explorer to create a copy of the file named **ac07CustomersMultiTableDatabase.mdb** and then open the copy in Microsoft Access. Take a look at the data and forecast issues that would most likely be uncovered by questioning users in a design review. Be sure to evaluate

- Default values
- Fields that are required but might be left blank
- Fields that need input masks and formats
- Fields that could benefit from default values
- Fields that need validation rules

Update your database design with at least five items from your list. Use the Database Splitter Wizard to create a front-end and back-end from your updated database.

2. Design Review of a Multitable Database to Track Employees

Locate your copy of the database named **ac06EmployeesMultiTableDatabase.mdb** created in the Analysis assignment from Chapter 6. Use Microsoft Windows Explorer to create a copy of the file named **ac07EmployeesMultiTableDatabase.mdb** and then open the copy in Microsoft Access. Take a look at the data and forecast issues that would most likely be uncovered by questioning users in a design review. Be sure to evaluate

- Default values
- Fields that are required but might be left blank
- Fields that need input masks and formats
- Fields that could benefit from default values
- Fields that need validation rules

Update your database design with at least five items from your list. Use the Database Splitter Wizard to create a front-end and back-end from your updated database.

Integrating with Other Applications

did you know?

most *landfilled trash retains its original weight, volume, and form for 40 years.*

a *"jiffy" is an actual unit of time for 1/100th of a second.*

there *are more insects in one square mile of rural land than there are human beings on the entire earth.*

a *chameleon's tongue is twice the length of its body.*

the *Neanderthal's brain was bigger than yours is.*

any *month that starts on a Sunday will have a Friday the 13th in it.*

to *find out what the most popular first name in the world is, visit* *www.mhhe.com/i-series.*

Chapter Objectives

- **Use Microsoft Graph to chart data in tables or queries**
- **Import data to Access—MOS AC03S-2-3**
- **Export data from Access—MOS AC03S-4-4**
- **Create a Data Access Page using the Page Wizard— MOS AC03S-1-12**
- **Use Design View to modify a Data Access Page**

KoryoKicks: Interactive Web Reporting

KoryoKicks, like most successful businesses, has outgrown its current physical environment, distribution channels, and organization structure. Products are being back-ordered because the existing production facilities can't meet the demand. Orders are not being processed in a timely manner because the volume is more than the current staff can handle. Adding employees and products is a reasonable step, but that will mean an added need for space and money.

Missy and Micah have enlisted the help of a marketing research firm to determine the real potential of their market and to create a diversification plan to help protect against business losses. Until now the business has been low-risk because the only real investment was the cost to secure and ship products that had already been paid for. Employees have also been paid using money already collected. To support growth, the twins must consider hiring full-time employees, acquiring facilities, and securing a business loan. The overall business risk is increasing making the need for planning and reporting more critical.

The twins are attending college in Colorado and don't plan to leave until they graduate. Current research indicates that most of their products are shipped to Indiana, Ohio, and Michigan. Placing facilities close to the largest demand can reduce overhead, so they are considering facilities in Indiana. Their aunt is a CPA who lives in Indianapolis and is willing to champion KoryoKicks in that area.

Accepting orders, shipping products, and billing customers from two sites will require new data sharing and communication methods. The twins believe that the Web will provide the necessary communication channels. The KoryoKicks database can be replicated and the Internet used for synchronization. In addition, Data Access Pages can be used for shared reporting.

Before finalizing a plan, the twins need to create a sales forecast that will be used to determine how many employees and how much space are needed at each location. They will need to learn about the charting utility, Microsoft Graph, in order to analyze the history of sales trends and then forecast them into the future. Existing documents from Word and Excel will need to be incorporated to appropriately present their business. The resulting forecast will be the foundation of the business plan they will present to lenders in order to secure the loan necessary to accomplish the goals outlined.

The twins do not want to build the data storage, reporting, and sharing infrastructure until they are further along in their business plan. However, they do want to see exactly how the necessary components work before they commit to a design that will support their expanding business.

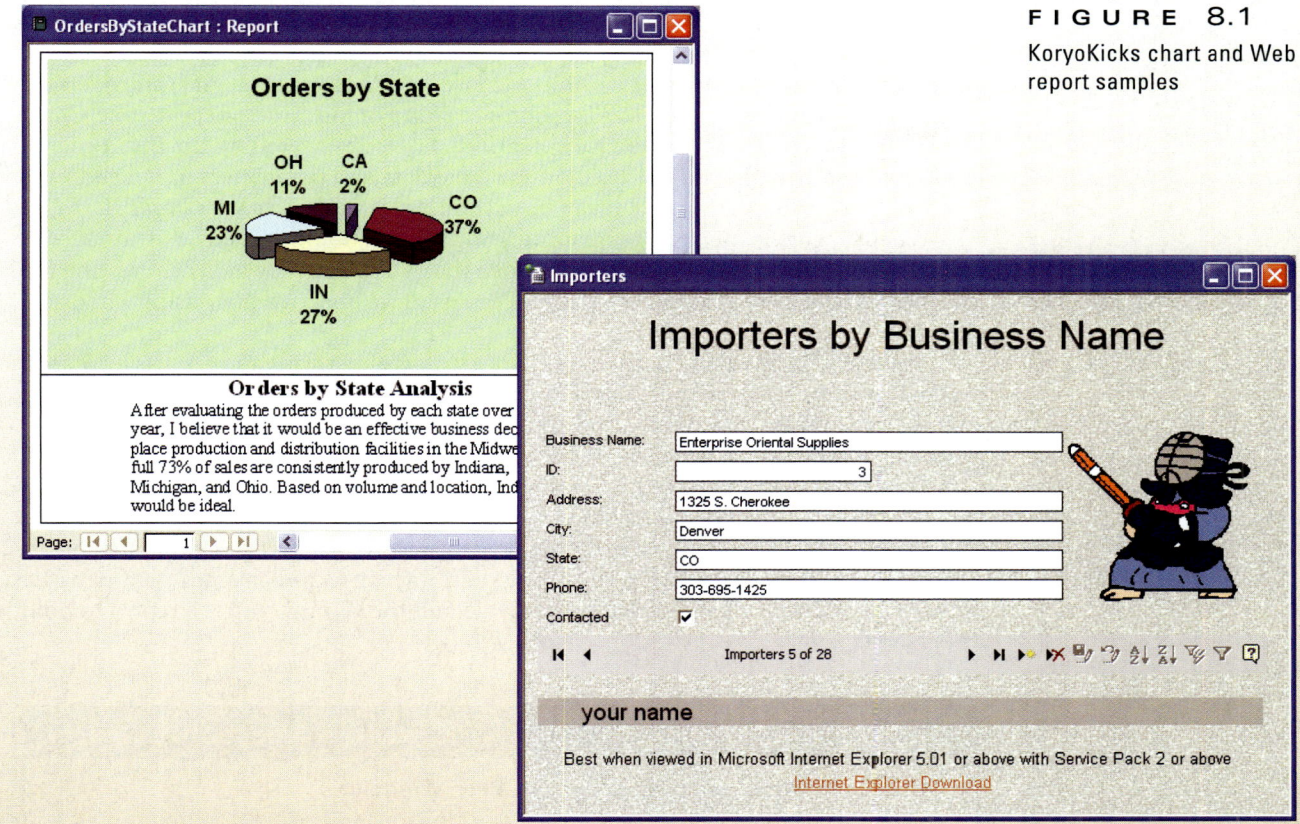

FIGURE 8.1
KoryoKicks chart and Web report samples

SESSION 8.1 OFFICE INTEGRATION

A basic tenet of computing is not to re-create anything that already exists. Office System products are designed to integrate with each other to avoid re-creating documents, data, and formatting when another form of output is needed. Microsoft Office System applications are able to import and export multiple Office file formats to facilitate sharing documents across software platforms. The formats of other common documents such as Paradox, DBase, and Lotus 1-2-3 also can be accessed.

Importing and exporting are made possible through the features of **OLE (object linking and embedding)**. Most programs designed for the Microsoft operating system support some level of OLE. Programs designed for other operating systems typically don't support OLE.

Adding a Chart to a Form or Report

Sometimes it is not necessary to import or export data to obtain alternative formatting. Office products include an array of applets that provide commonly needed features. WordArt is an example of a small application that is available in all office applications that use the Drawing toolbar. Similarly, the Microsoft Graph is a small application available in Access, Excel, and PowerPoint to create charts and graphs based on table data.

AC 8.3

ACCESS

Embedding a Chart in a Report

Charts are used to represent numeric data graphically. Graphs can be added to a form or report using the Chart Wizard or imported from Microsoft Excel. The **Chart Wizard** steps users through the process of defining a **chart** on an Access report. The Chart Wizard can be accessed from the New Report dialog box or by using the Insert menu. An embedded chart is created based on the table data and parameters provided to the Wizard. Once a chart is created, it can be customized using **Microsoft Graph.**

When a chart involves large quantities of data that do not already exist in Access, when there are complex calculations, or when the data are already in Excel, creating the chart in Excel and then importing it to Access is more effective than using Microsoft Graph.

The twins believe that charts can enhance the existing forms and reports by graphically displaying data relationships. For example, the Customers by State report could use a chart to show the number of customers from each state, or the Orders report could display a chart of orders by state.

Using the Chart Wizard, the fields to be plotted can be selected from any existing table or query. The chart can be based on all of the data in the table using sums or the chart can depict only the data from the current record. A chart based on a record is called a **record-bound chart** and will change as the active record changes. A chart based on all of the data is called a **global chart.** By default the Wizard creates a report to hold the chart.

---

task reference   Create a Microsoft Graph

- Click the **Reports** object in the Database Window

- Click **New** to activate the New Report dialog box

- Select **Chart Wizard**, use the drop-down list to select the query or table containing the data to be charted, and then click **OK** to initiate the Chart Wizard

- Follow the instructions to select the field(s) with the data to be charted, select the chart type, specify the layout, and add a chart title

---

Creating a report with a chart:

1. Verify that Access is running with **ac08KoryoKicks.mdb** open

2. Click the **Reports** object in the Database Window

3. Click **New** to open the New Report dialog box

4. Click **Chart Wizard**, select **CustomerStateJoin** from the drop-down list, and choose **OK** (see Figure 8.2)

5. Move the **State** and **QuantityOrdered** fields to the Fields for Chart list box and click **Next**

6. Review the available chart types, then select **3-D Pie Chart**, and click **Next** (see Figure 8.3)

7. Use the **Preview Chart** button to see a sample of the chart that you are building

tip: *Microsoft Graph displays dummy data for the design process*

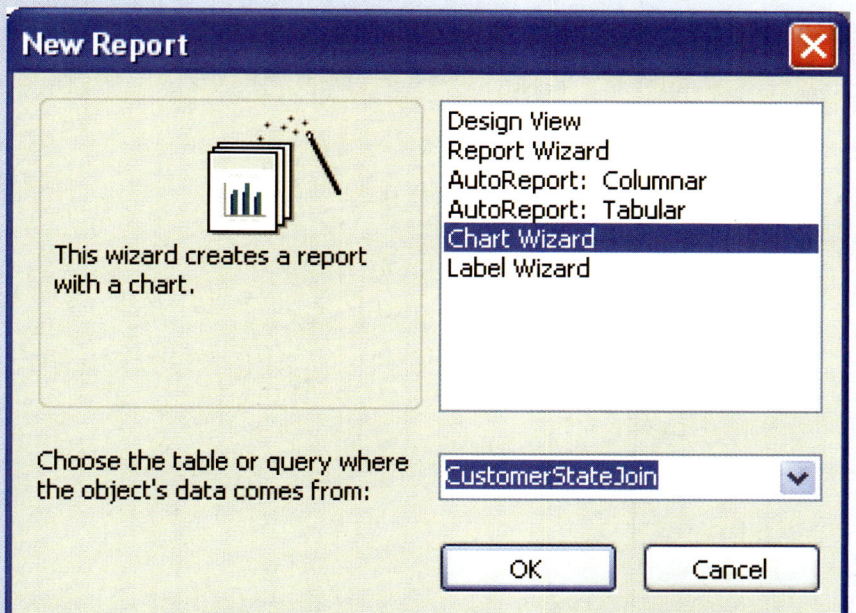

FIGURE 8.2
Initiating the Chart Wizard

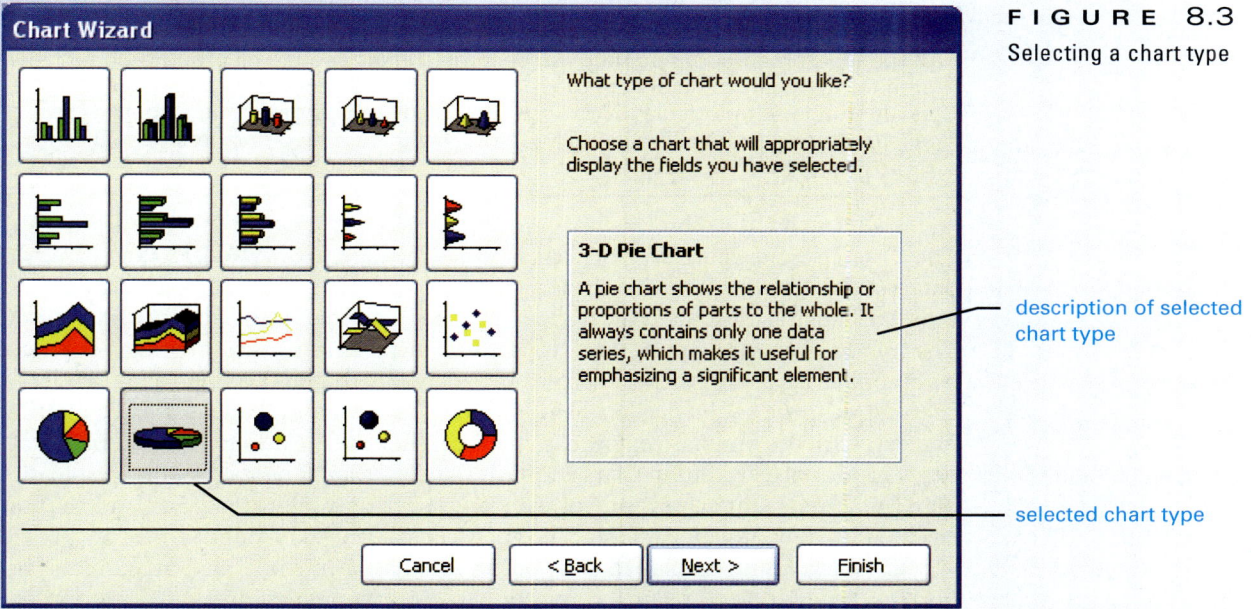

FIGURE 8.3
Selecting a chart type

description of selected chart type

selected chart type

8. Double-click on the value being plotted, **SumOfQuantityOrdered**, to see the other summary options available. Click **Cancel** when you have completed your review

9. Click **Next**

10. Enter **Orders by State** as the Chart Title and click **Finish** (see Figure 8.4)

11. Use the toolbar Zoom button to preview the chart

12. Change to Design View

13. Click **Save** and name the report **OrdersByStateChart**

FIGURE 8.4
The OrdersByStateChart
report

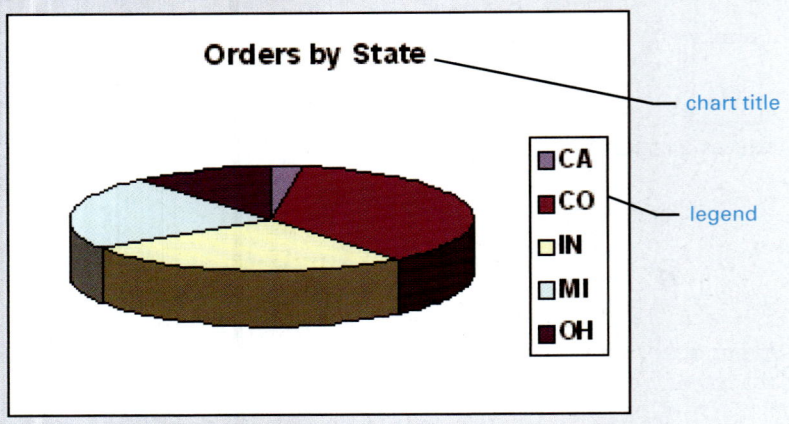

---

another*word*   . . . on Embedding Charts

Sometimes you will want to add a chart to an existing report or form. This is accomplished by opening the report in Design View and selecting the Chart option of the Insert menu. The pointer will become a chart used to click and drag an area for the chart to display in the report. The Chart Wizard will initiate as soon as an area for chart display is indicated. The advantage of adding a chart to an existing report or form is the ability to display the detailed data beside a graphic representation of the data

---

The OrdersByStateChart is a global chart created using the Chart Wizard and based on data from an Access query. The chart is placed in the Detail section of a standard Access report. Changing the data in the underlying tables will change the display of this chart. The Chart Wizard presented 20 chart types for your selection. These represent the most commonly used chart types available from Microsoft Graph. It is important to select a chart type that best suits the data being plotted and the report audience. When plotting one data series to emphasize how each value in the series relates to the total of all values, a pie or stacked column chart is appropriate. Area and line charts work best to display data movement across time or categories such as a sales trend. Bar and column charts effectively show the relationships between categories of values.

The chart being developed is an object that has been embedded in an Access report. ***Embedded*** objects retain a connection to the program that developed them, called the *source* program. The application holding the object, in this case Microsoft Graph, is called the *destination*. Double-clicking an embedded object will open the source program in edit mode.

Editing a Chart

Editing a chart involves either altering the look of the chart or changing the data used to create it. Changes to the data need to be made in the table(s) on which a chart is based. The simplest visual change is to adjust the size of the chart on the form or report, which is accomplished by dragging the object borders. Other changes are accomplished by double-clicking the chart to activate Microsoft Graph.

Because Graph is the source program, it has greater functionality than that provided by the Wizard. For example, the Wizard presented 20 chart types while Graph organizes the charts into 14 chart types with at least 2 subtypes each, providing many more options. Chart types include pie, line, column, and bar. Subtypes define formatting within a type. For example, a pie chart has flat and 3-D subtypes.

When Microsoft Graph is active, its menus and toolbars display. The Graph menu and toolbar are designed for manipulating and formatting the chart. For example, the Chart menu contains options for changing the chart type, setting chart options that control how the data are charted, and controlling the 3-D view.

Editing a chart also involves moving and formatting the various components of the chart. For example, a legend can be moved, a wedge of a pie exploded, the color of a data series changed, and chart titles adjusted. Those familiar with Microsoft Graph from other Office applications will recognize the datasheet and data that display when editing. In other applications, the datasheet is used to enter the data to be plotted. Since Access holds data in tables, the datasheet is not used and any changes that are made there will not be reflected in the chart. That being the case, closing the datasheet frees screen space and avoids confusion about the chart data source.

Missy and Micah would like the OrdersByStateChart to have a background consistent with the KoryoKicks color scheme. They also want each wedge of the pie labeled with the state and the legend eliminated.

Modifying the OrdersByStateChart:

1. Verify that Access is running with **ac08KoryoKicks.mdb** open with the OrdersByStateChart report open in Design View

tip: *The Orders By State chart should be in the Detail section of the report*

2. Click the chart object to select it and then use the bottom-right sizing handle to expand its height and width until it is the width of the report page

3. Double-click on the chart to open Microsoft Graph (see Figure 8.5)

4. Close the Datasheet Window since it is not useful in Access

5. Right-click on the chart background and click **Format Chart Area**

6. Choose the light blue color square and click **OK**

7. Right-click on the chart background, click **Chart Options**, click the **Legend** tab, and uncheck **Show legend**

tip: *The Office Assistant provides information about these options if it is active*

8. Click the **Data Labels** tab, click **Category name** and **Percentage,** and then click **OK**

9. Click off the chart area to leave **Microsoft Graph**

10. Click the **Print Preview** button on the toolbar (see Figure 8.6)

tip: *Your chart (rather than the default chart) will display as it will print*

11. Close and save

The twins believe that the pie chart is probably the most effective way to present these data but would like to see some alternatives. It is usually helpful to review charting alternatives before settling on the chart type that best presents the data.

FIGURE 8.5
Microsoft Graph window

Microsoft Graph menus and toolbar

chart based on default data—used for formatting

datasheet with default data

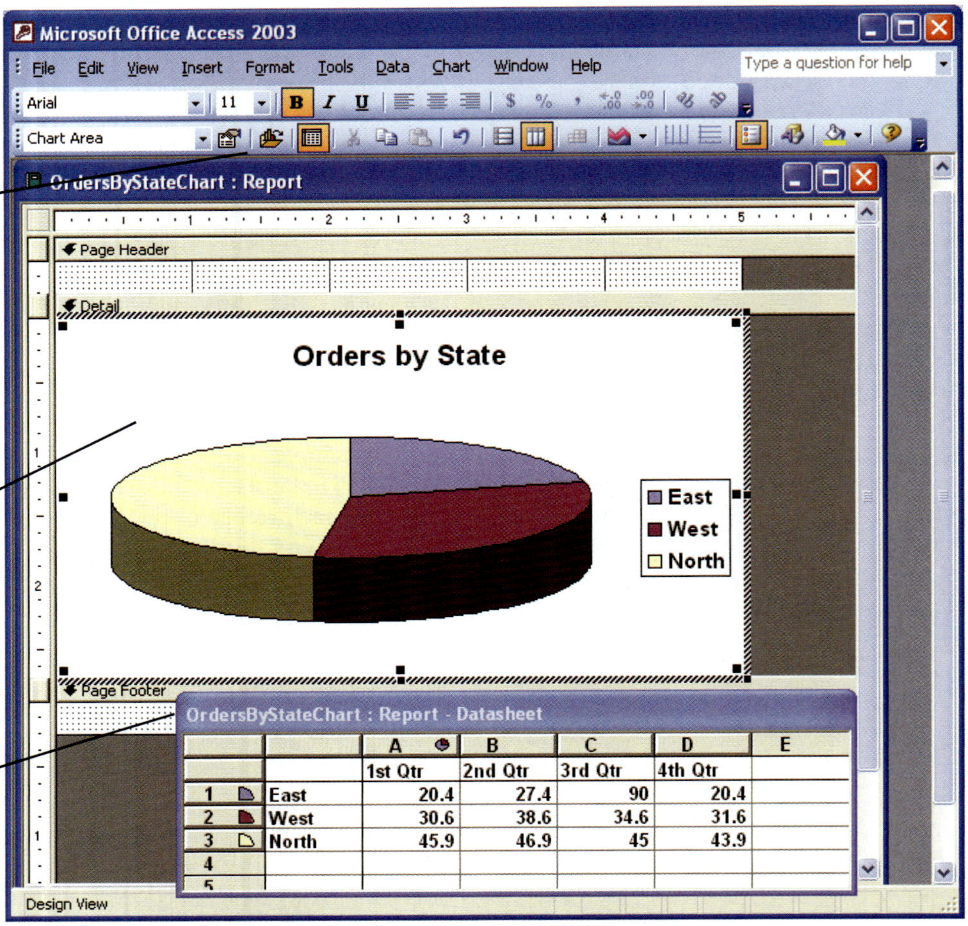

FIGURE 8.6
OrdersByStateChart with formatting

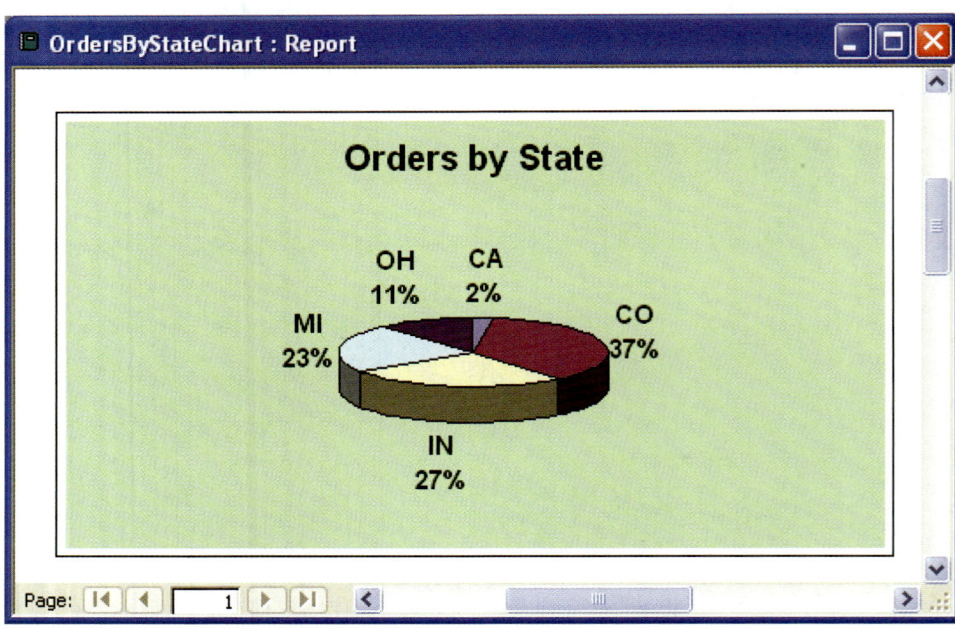

Exploring chart types and subtypes for OrderByStateChart:

1. Verify that Access is running with **ac08KoryoKicks.mdb** open w th the OrdersByStateChart report in Design View

2. Double-click on the chart to open Microsoft Graph and close the datasheet

3. Select **Chart Type** from the **Chart** menu

4. Review the current chart type and subtype

5. Select the first subtype for a Column chart and press and hold the button to view the sample

6. Select the **Line** chart type and preview the result

7. Experiment with other chart types and subtypes

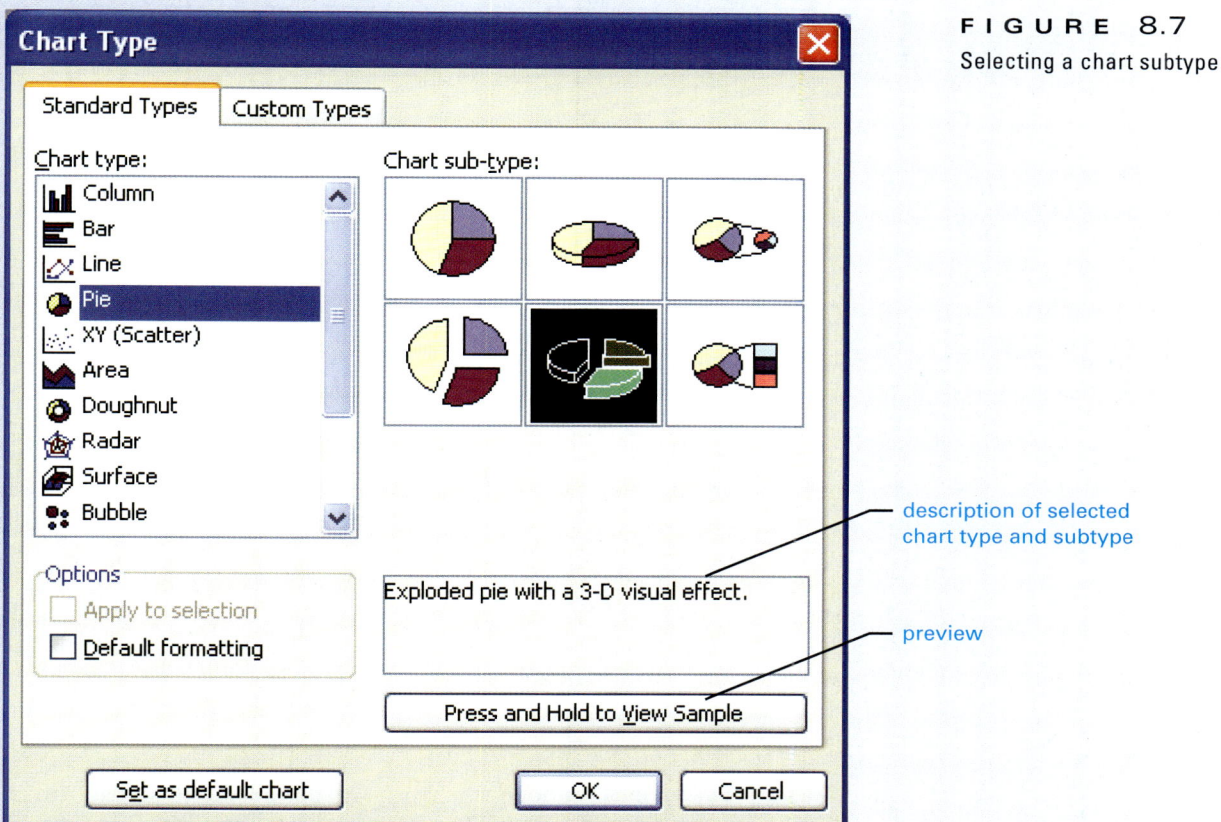

8. Select **Pie** chart type, **Exploded 3-D** subtype, and click **OK**

9. Click off the chart to close Microsoft Graph

10. Use Print Preview to review the changes (see Figure 8.8)

11. Save the OrdersByStateChart

F I G U R E 8.8
Exploded Pie chart

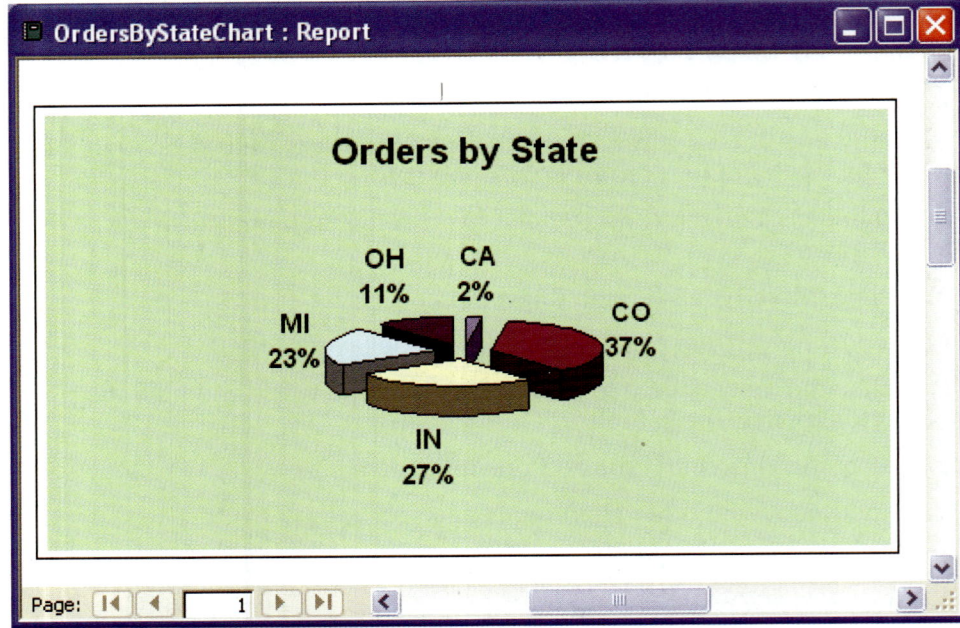

Because a pie chart is being used, there is no need for X- or Y-axis labels. Bar, column, and line charts all use axes that typically need to be labeled using the Chart Options selection of the Chart menu. This option also can be used to modify the chart title.

Chart options allow control of the titles, axes, gridlines, legend, data labels, and data table display. The gridlines behind the chart can be turned off or made finer using the Gridlines tab. The chart legend can be turned off or placed in a new location with the Legend tab. Data labels can be added to the chart displaying the value plotted and the datasheet can be displayed in the slide with the chart.

Each chart object can be selected and modified. Font, size, and orientation can be set for text objects. Shape objects can have fill colors, border colors, and shapes options set. The chart consists of a plot area that holds the graph and a chart area that holds everything else. Both the plot area and chart area can be set to a custom color, fill, or pattern. By default, both are transparent.

In addition to all of the standard chart components that have been covered, Microsoft Graph allows text to be added to a chart by typing. Additional text may be needed to draw out information or emphasize a point. Typing opens a text box that can be moved, modified, or formatted like any other object.

Importing and Linking Objects

Oftentimes the data in one or more Access tables will need to be combined with objects stored in an external format such as HTML, Excel, Word, or another Access database. When this occurs, the external objects can be brought into Access using the import facilities. Besides graphics and text, other database file formats such as Fox Pro and dBase can be imported.

An *imported* object displays in an Access container such as a table or unbound object on a form or report. For example, an Excel spreadsheet can be converted to an Access table or text from Word can be placed in an unbound object on a report through importing.

During the import process, settings determine how the Access object is related to the original file. When an imported object is just a picture of the contents of a file, it is said to be *linked*. Linked files cannot be updated from Access. Double-clicking a linked object will open the source application where edits can be applied. Link the object if it is important to retain one copy of the file with a connection to the source application.

The other option for importing an object is to embed it. Embedding an object places a complete copy of the object in the Access container. An embedded object is a full copy completely separate from the original file and can be updated without impacting the source file.

Adding Objects to a Form or Report

The simplest imports are used to place objects on an Access form or report. You already have used this method to add graphics to both forms and reports.

---

task reference — Importing with an Unbound Object Frame on a Form or Report

- Open the Design View of the form or report to contain the imported object
- Click the **Unbound Object Frame** tool in the toolbox
- Click and drag the area on the form or report that will contain the object
- In the Microsoft Access dialog box
  - Click **Create From File**
  - Browse to the file for import
  - Click the Link check box to create a linked object or leave it unchecked to create an embedded object
  - Click **OK**

Linking a Word document to the OrdersByStateChart report:

1. Verify that Access is running with **ac08KoryoKicks.mdb** open with the OrdersByStateChart report in Design View

2. Expand the report Detail section by dragging the Detail border up and the Page Footer border down

3. Click the **Unbound Object Frame** tool in the toolbox and then click and drag the area in the Detail section of the report that will hold the Word object (see Figure 8.9)

4. Click **Create from File**, use the Browse button to navigate to **ac08OrdersAnalysis.doc**, check the **Link** check box, and click **OK**

5. Size and reposition the object to resemble if needed

6. Double-click the object to open Word

7. In Word
   a. Select all of the text
   b. Use the ruler to adjust the margins for the Access object as shown in Figure 8.10
   c. Save the changes and close Word

FIGURE 8.9

Linking a Word document

path and filename of your import file

description of Link—unclick Link to see embedded description

area for object

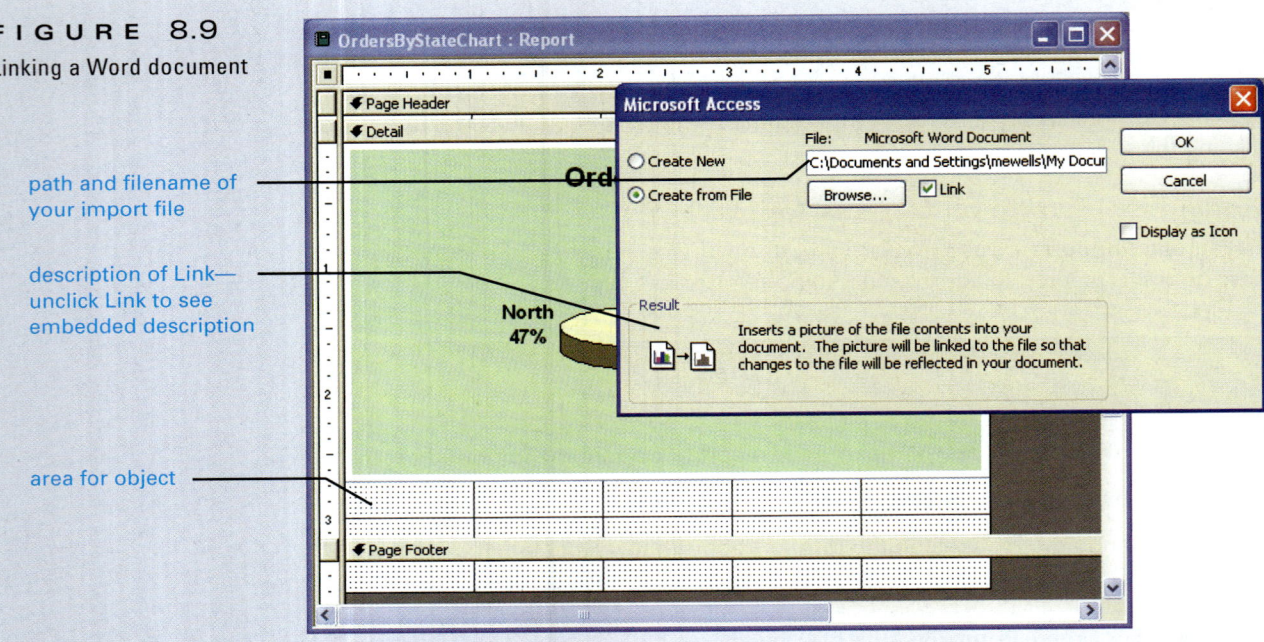

8. If your report does not reflect the margin changes, close and reopen Design View to update the link

9. Activate Print Preview to review your changes (see Figure 8.11)

10. Save

FIGURE 8.10

Adjusting margins with the Word ruler

drag box to adjust left margin of selection

drag to adjust right margin of selection

anotherway
. . . to Update Linked Objects

Linked objects do not maintain continual contact with the source document. Once a report or form is open and displaying a linked object, the object won't change until the link is updated. You can manually update the link using the OLE/DDE Links option of the Edit menu. The dialog box allows you to select a link or links to update and then click the Update Now button

Because the Linked check box was used in the import process, the Access report holds only a picture of the Word document. Updates to the document are made using Word and are reflected in the Access copy each time the link is updated. By default, the Update option of a linked object is set to Automatic, which will refresh the object each time it is opened.

Of course, if the Linked check box had been left unchecked, the Word document would have been embedded in the Access report. Embedding is the best option when the Access copy of the document needs to be manipulated independently of the Word version of the document. To experience the difference between manipulating a linked and an embedded object, the linked Word document will be deleted and reimported as an embedded object.

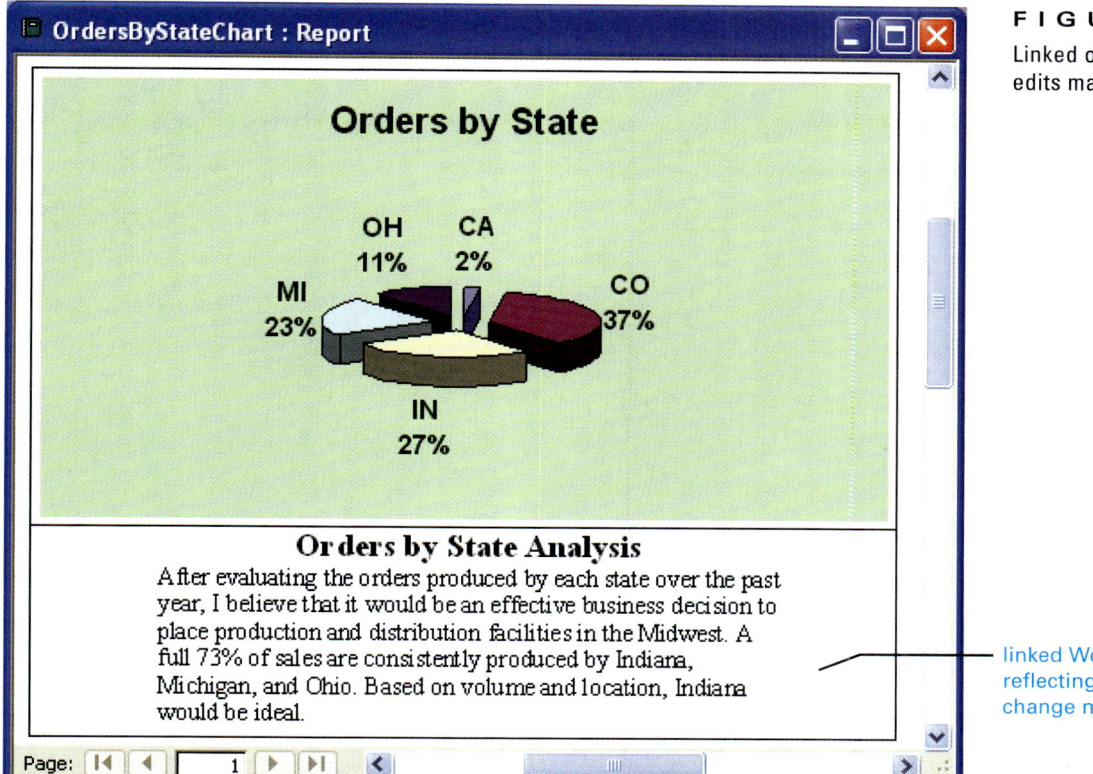

F I G U R E   8.11
Linked object reflecting
edits made in Word

linked Word object
reflecting margin
change made in Word

Embedding a Word document in the OrdersByStateChart report:

1. Verify that Access is running with **ac08KoryoKicks.mdb** open with the OrdersByStateChart report in Design View

2. Click the Unbound Object Frame containing the Word document and press the Delete key

3. Select the **Unbound Object Frame** tool from the toolbox and then click and drag the area to contain the Word document

4. Click **Create from File**, navigate to **ac08OrdersAnalysis.doc**, uncheck the **Link** check box, and click **OK** (see Figure 8.12)

5. Size and reposition the object to resemble Figure 8.13 if needed

6. Double-click the object to initiate editing

7. Click the cursor after the period in the last line of text and press **Enter**

8. Type your full name and then use the toolbar to center the text

9. Click outside of the Unbound Object Frame object to end editing and save your changes

10. Save the report changes

FIGURE 8.12
Embedding a Word document

file type to be embedded

Link unchecked to embed

description of embed operation

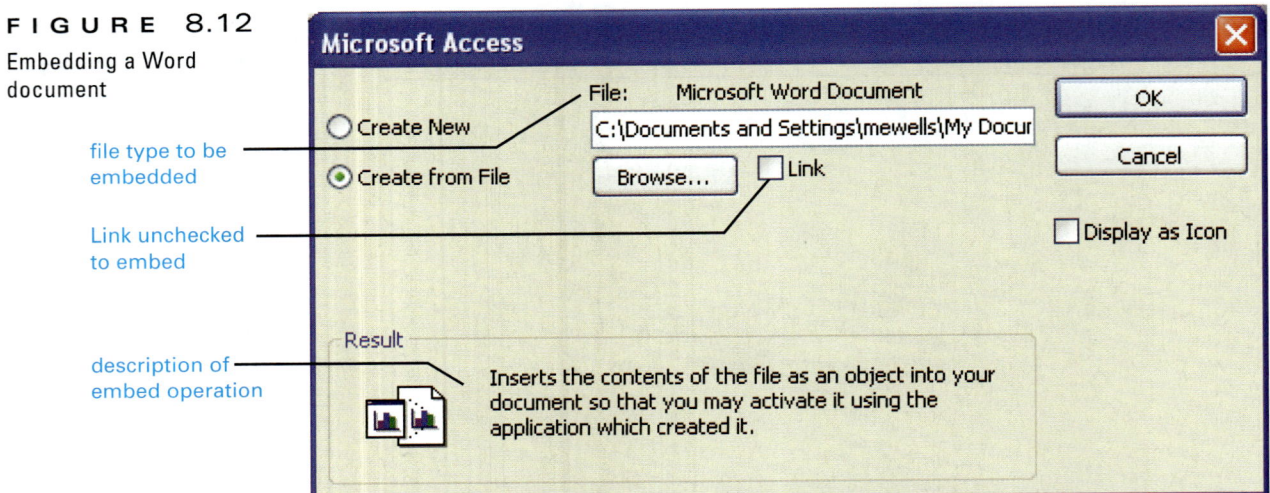

FIGURE 8.13
Editing an embedded Word document

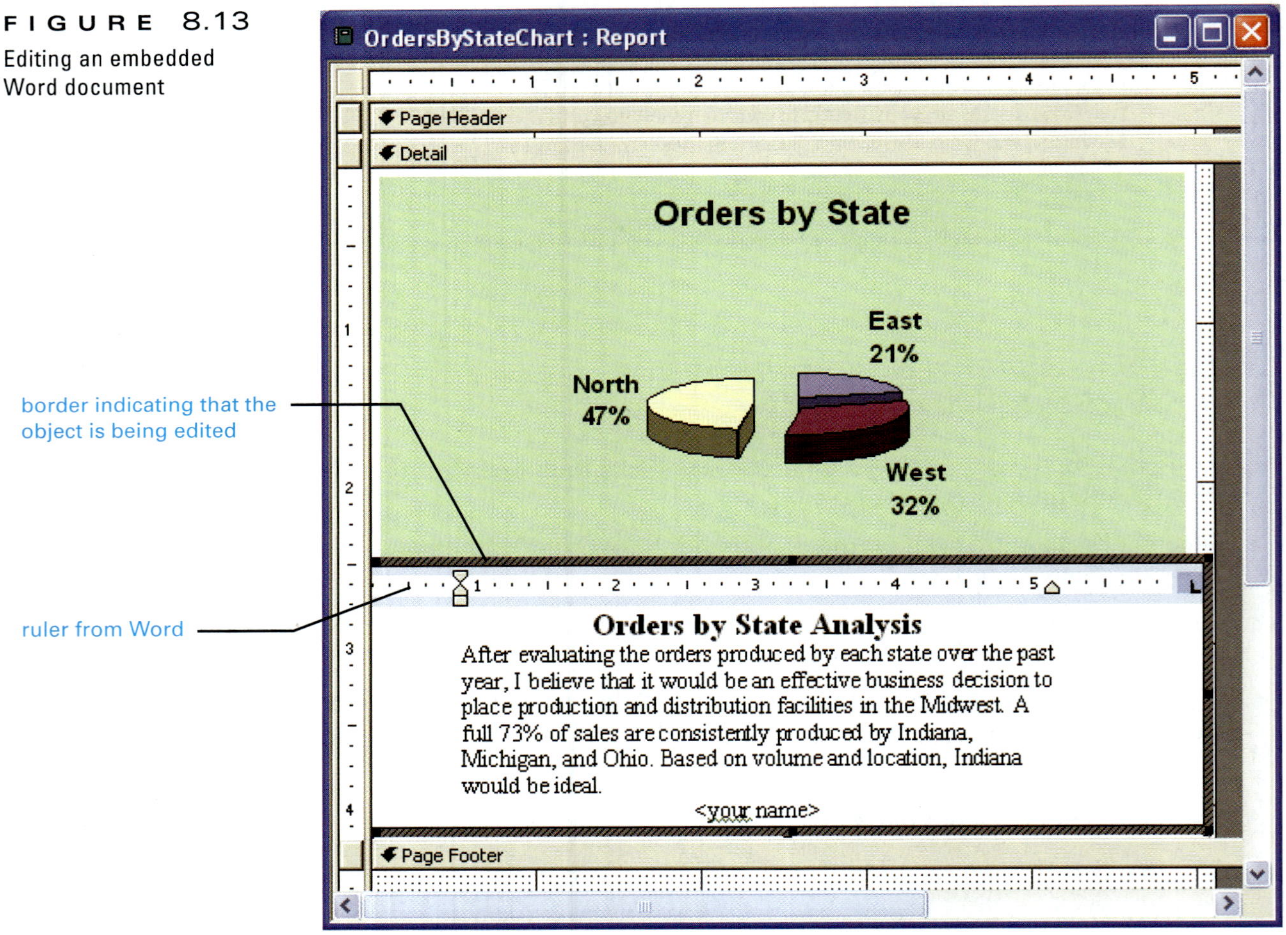

border indicating that the object is being edited

ruler from Word

In the previous steps a *linked* Word document was edited using a full version of Word, indicating that there is only one copy of the document controlled by Word. In this set of steps, edits were performed on the same Word document that had been *embedded*. An Edit Window provided the same features as Word but indicated that this copy of the document is independently updated by Access. Let's take a look at the Word document to verify that the changes made to the embedded document did not impact it.

Verifying the status of the source Word document:

1. Click the **Start** button on the Taskbar, point to **Programs**, and select **Microsoft Word**

2. Use the Open button on the toolbar to open **ac08OrdersAnalysis.doc**

3. Notice that the margin changes applied to the linked document are saved. Your name, which was added to the embedded version of the document, is not part of the source but is retained in the OrdersByStateChart report

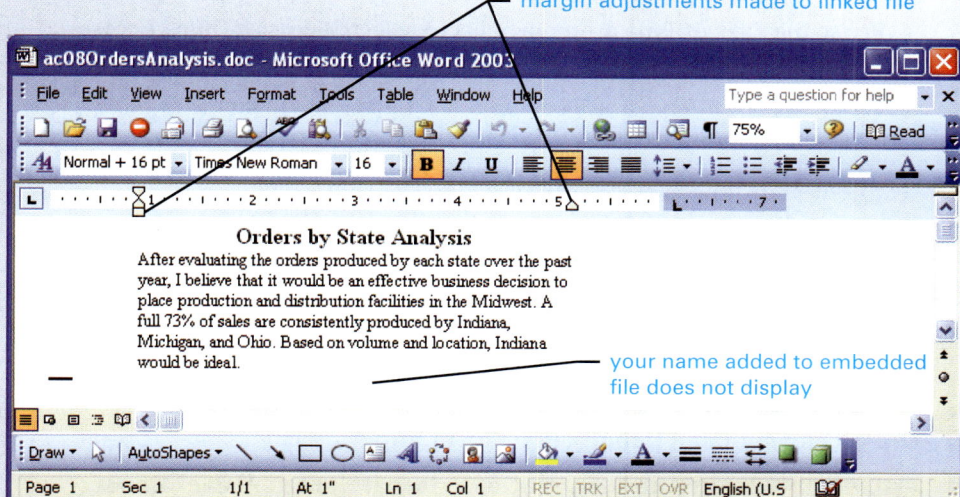

margin adjustments made to linked file

your name added to embedded file does not display

FIGURE 8.14
ac08OrdersAnalysis.doc

4. Close Word

The same linking and embedding procedures demonstrated can be used to place objects on Access forms. Any OLE-compliant application can be imported. All of the Microsoft Office products support OLE, as do most applications developed by other vendors for the Windows environment.

Using Data from Another Access Database

Sometimes due to a design flaw or change in business practice, it is desirable to use data that are stored in multiple Access database files or in files maintained by another database program. In such cases the data tables can be imported into Access and treated like any other Access table, or linked so that they retain the properties of the original database and can be maintained in the source. The process is very similar to importing application objects, but the result is data that can be used like any native Access table.

Missy and Micah have created a NewCustomerContacts database used to create form letters in Microsoft Word. These letters introduced KoryoKicks products and services to new audiences with the goal of signing up new customers. The twins would like the table to be incorporated in the KoryoKicks database so they only have to worry about sharing one database file.

<table>
<tr><td colspan="2">

task reference

Import or Link to Another Access Database
</td></tr>
</table>

- Open the Access database that is to contain the imported data
- Open the **File** menu, point to **Get External Data**, and then do one of the following:
  - Click **Import** to create Access tables from the external data
  - Click **Link Tables** to create links to tables that remain in the source location
- In the Import or Link dialog box
  - Use the Files of Type drop-down list to select **Microsoft Office Access (*.mdb, *.mda, *.mde)** as the type of file to be linked or imported
  - Use the Look in box to select the drive, folder, and filename of the file to be imported or linked
  - Select the import tables and click **Import**

Importing ac08NewCustomerContacts.mdb:

1. Verify that Access is open with the **ac08KoryoKicks.mdb** database open and no active object (table, query, form, report, etc.)

2. Activate the **File** menu, point to **Get External Data**, and click **Import**

3. From the Import dialog box select **ac08NewCustomerContacts.mdb** and click **Import**

tip: *Verify that the Files of type box will display Microsoft Access files for you to select from*

4. On the Tables tab of the Import Objects dialog box, select **Contacts** and click **OK**

FIGURE 8.15

Import Objects options

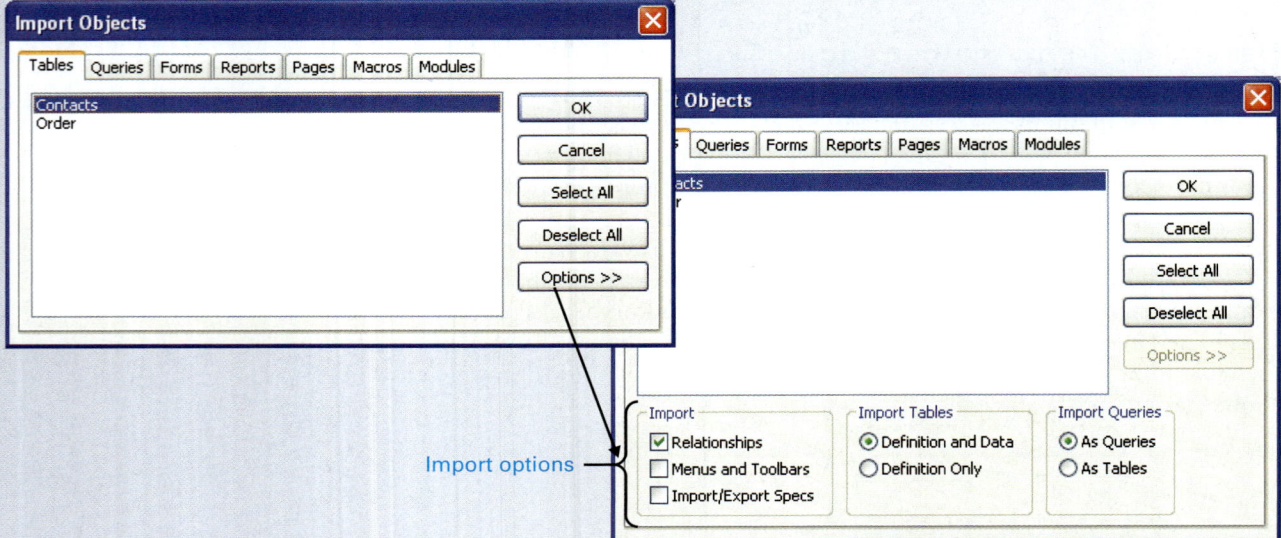

tip: *Notice that Queries, Forms, Reports, and other database objects also can be imported*

5. Open the **Contacts** table in Datasheet View to preview the data

6. Switch to Design View

7. Close the view

When importing data from another Access database, either both the table and its contents or just the definition can be imported, using the options shown in Figure 8.15. The Contacts table now belongs to the KoryoKicks database and you have full control over its design and contents. The original ac08NewCustomerContacts.mdb is not impacted by changes made in KoryoKicks.

The procedure for linking data is very similar to that used to import data. The twins want to evaluate the difference between embedding and linking the Contacts table so a linked copy needs to be created.

Linking ac08NewCustomerContacts.mdb:

1. Verify that Access is open with the **ac08KoryoKicks.mdb** database active with no open objects (tables, queries, forms, reports, etc.)

2. Activate the **File** menu, point to **Get External Data**, and click **Link Tables**

3. From the Link dialog box select **ac08NewCustomerContacts.mdb** and click **Link**

4. On the Tables tab of the Link Tables dialog box, select **Contacts** and click **OK**

5. Right-click on the linked copy and rename it **ContactsLinked**

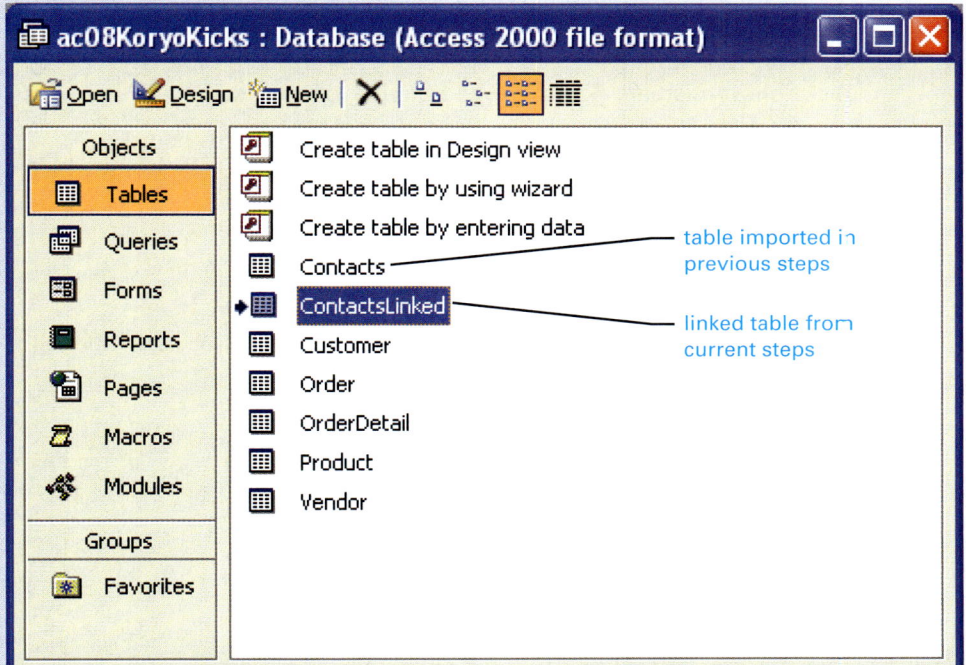

FIGURE 8.16

Imported and Linked Contacts tables

6. Open the ContactsLinked table in Datasheet View to preview the data

7. Switch to Design View

tip: *You will be notified that this is a linked table*

8. Close the view

For the most part, linked tables behave the same as any other Microsoft Access table. The icon to the left of the table name indicates that the table is linked and a dialog box is a reminder that much of the table design can't be modified outside the original database. Linked tables can be used to create queries, forms, and reports. No changes can be made to the design, but properties can be set to control local behavior.

Importing Data from Excel

Since Microsoft Excel is designed to store and analyze data, many users already have a great deal of valuable data stored in spreadsheet format before learning to use an Access database. The data stored in Excel do not need to be reentered because they can be imported and stored in a table for use in Access.

Imported Excel data can be either linked or embedded. Before beginning the process, it is important to make sure that the data in the spreadsheet are arranged appropriately into fields (columns) and records (rows). The twins have been trying to recruit new businesses to distribute for KoryoKicks products. They have been tracking these contacts in an Excel spreadsheet that should be incorporated in the KoryoKicks database.

---

task reference   **Import or Link to an**
                                       Excel Spreadsheet

- Open the Access database that is to contain the imported data

- Open the **File** menu, point to **Get External Data**, and then click **Import**

  - Click **Import** to create Access tables from the external data

  - Click **Link Tables** to create links to tables that remain in the source location

- In the Import or Link dialog box

  - Use the Files of Type drop-down list to select **Microsoft Excel (*.xls)** as the type of file to be linked or imported

  - Use the Look in box to select the drive, folder, and filename of the file to be imported or linked

  - Follow the Import Spreadsheet Wizard instructions

Importing ac08Importers.xls:

1. Verify that Access is open with the **ac08KoryoKicks.mdb** database active

2. Activate the **File** menu, point to **Get External Data**, and click **Import**

3. In the Import dialog box

   a. Use the Look in drop-down list to navigate to the folder containing your files

   b. Set Files of type to **Microsoft Excel (*.xls)**

   c. Select **ac08Importers.xls** and click **Import**

4. Verify that the Import Spreadsheet Wizard selections match those shown in Figure 8.17 and click **Next**

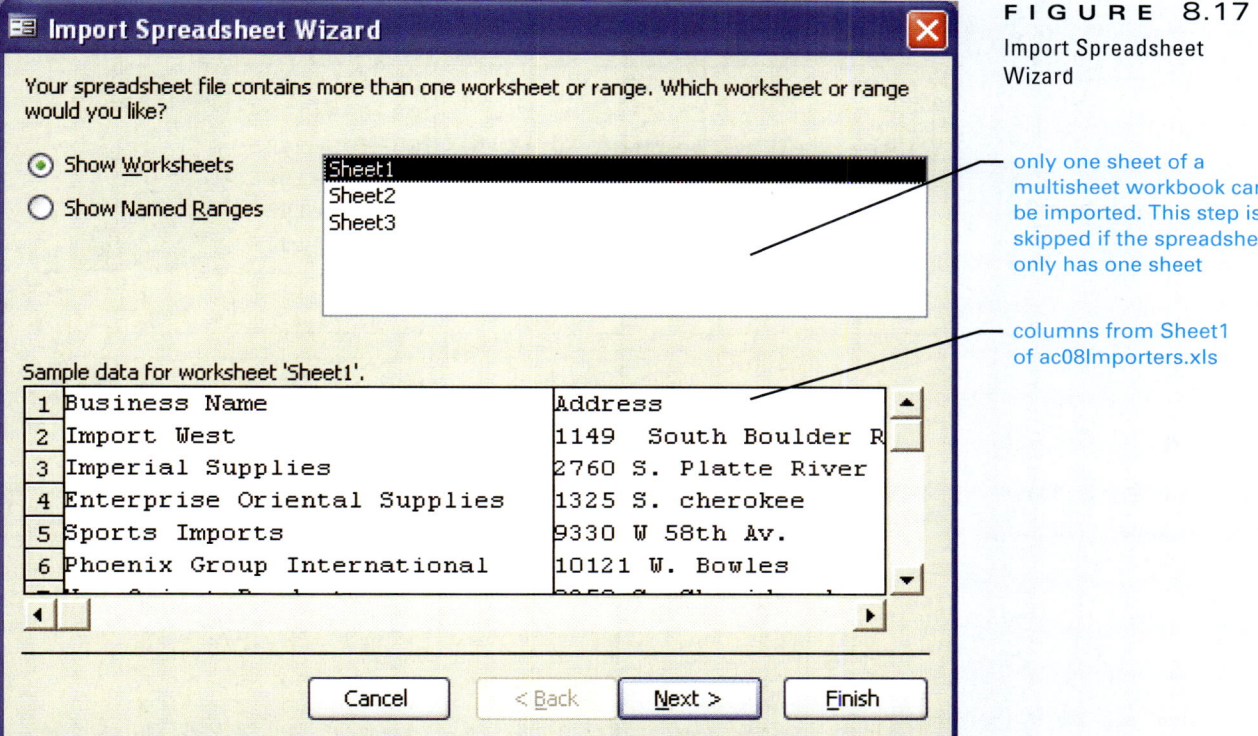

FIGURE 8.17

Import Spreadsheet Wizard

— only one sheet of a multisheet workbook can be imported. This step is skipped if the spreadsheet only has one sheet

— columns from Sheet1 of ac08Importers.xls

5. Check the **First Row Contains Column Headings** check box so that the Excel column headings will be used as Access field names and click **Next**

6. Verify that **In a New Table** is selected and click **Next**

7. Explore selecting fields to set their properties. Do not set any properties and click **Next** (see Figure 8.18)

8. Verify that **Let Access Add Primary Key** is selected so that Access will add an AutoNumber field to the table for a key and click **Next**

9. Name the table **Importers** and click **Finish**

10. Click **OK** in the Finished Importing message dialog box

11. Open Importers in Design View and change the data type of Contacted to **Yes/No** (see Figure 8.19)

12. Switch to Datasheet View, saving your changes. Close the datasheet when your review is complete

FIGURE 8.18

Setting Import Field Options

Options for selected field

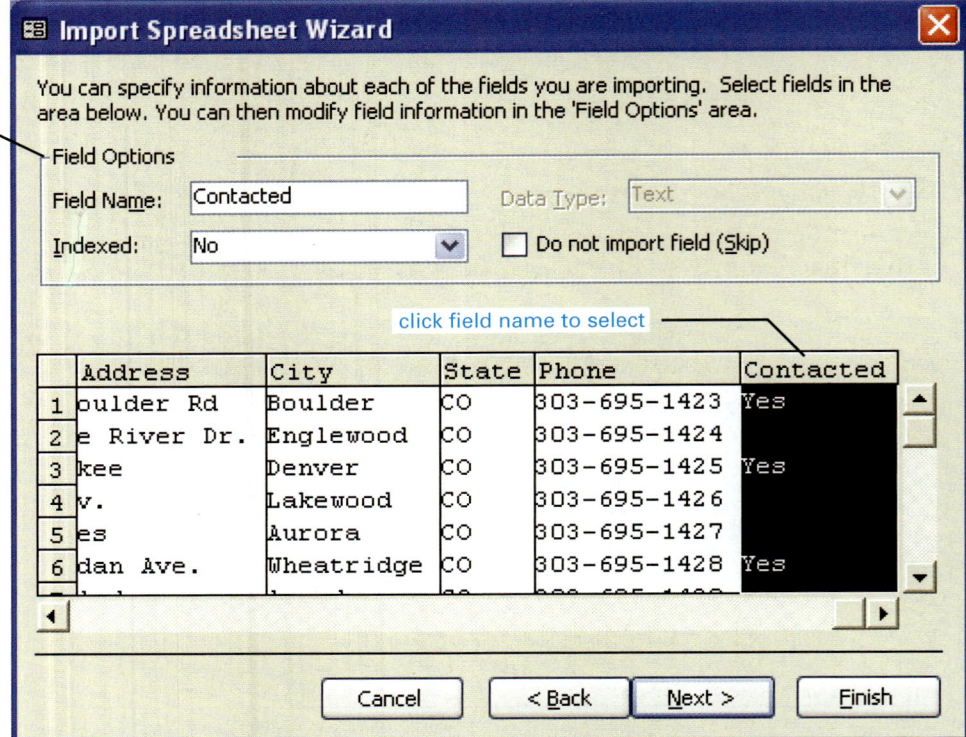

FIGURE 8.19

Importers table

The import options control whether all of the data from a spreadsheet are retrieved or only data in a named range of cells. Spreadsheet data can be used to create a new table or append to the data already in an existing table. To successfully append the data to an existing table, the spreadsheet column headings must match the Access field names exactly.

Access assigns data types to the import fields based on their content. It is important to review data types and other field properties before using the imported table.

Retrieving Data from Other Applications

Besides being able to import data from most other Office System products, Microsoft Access can accept a variety of other file formats including Lotus 1-2-3, Text files, HTML, Paradox, XML, and dBase. The process to import or link these file types is the same as that used for Excel since each file type can be selected from the Look in box of the Import or Link dialog box. Each file format has a Wizard to provide instruction on the conversion process. Paradox and dBase require special drivers that are provided by Microsoft Technical Support if the native software is not locally installed.

If data to be imported are not in one of the supported file formats, try to use the source application to save it in a supported file format. Almost every database and spreadsheet has the ability to save comma delimited text files that can then be imported by Access. For example, a Microsoft Works database cannot be directly imported into Microsoft Access. Works can save the database as a comma delimited text file that can be imported.

Regardless of the file type being imported, the data must be stored in a format that can be recognized as fields and records. For example, HTML tables can be effectively imported, but lists are less successful. Access Help has extensive information on importing from supported file types that will be helpful if you ever need to perform these tasks.

Exporting Data

Access also has the ability to export database objects to other file formats. While Access has powerful data storage and retrieval capabilities, other applications provide better analytical and formatting capabilities. For example, Access is the ideal tool for gathering sales data, but Excel would be a better choice for using those data to create a model used to forecast future sales.

help yourself *Use the Type a Question combo box to improve your understanding of how to export data by typing* **export**. *Review the contents of* About exporting data and database objects *and* Export data or database objects. *Close the Help window when you are finished*

Organizations often use different database programs that may need to share data. The different programs can be the result of varying needs across the organization or simply a matter of preference. Regardless of why data for the same organization are stored in multiple formats, Access's import and export capabilities usually can facilitate sharing data. Most other database software packages support similar import and export features.

Sharing Access Data with Word-Processing Applications

Although Microsoft Access data can be shared with virtually any word-processing application, this discussion will focus on Microsoft Word since it provides the simplest and cleanest integration.

Data from a Microsoft Access table can be used in conjunction with Word Mail Merge to create form letters based on data stored in a table or query. This process can use an existing Word document, or create a new merge document if it does not exist.

The second sharing method uses the formatting and publishing capabilities of Word to enhance Access output. The output of any Access datasheet, form, or report can be exported in Rich Text Format (.rtf) that can then be opened and manipulated with Word or any word processor supporting the format. The Rich Text Format preserves fonts, styles, and other formatting.

The twins would like to use the ProductByState Crosstab Query results as a table in a Word document that they are preparing. You will export it for them.

---

task reference   **Export an Access Object**
to Microsoft Word

- Open the Access database with the object to be exported
- Select the object to be exported in the Database Window (it is best to preview the object before exporting)
- Open the **Tools** menu, point to **Office Links**, and then either
  - Select **Merge It with Microsoft Word** to use an Access table or query as the data source for a Word merge document
  or
  - Select **Publish It with Microsoft Word** to create an .rtf file in the default database folder (usually C:\My Documents or the folder containing the database) with the same name as the exported object

---

Exporting ProductByStateCrosstab.rtf:

1. Verify that Access is open with the **ac08KoryoKicks.mdb** database active

2. In the Database Window select the **Queries** object and open **ProductByStateCrosstab**

3. Activate the **Tools** menu, point to **Office Links**, and click **Publish It with Microsoft Word**

FIGURE 8.20

ProductByStateCrosstab.rtf

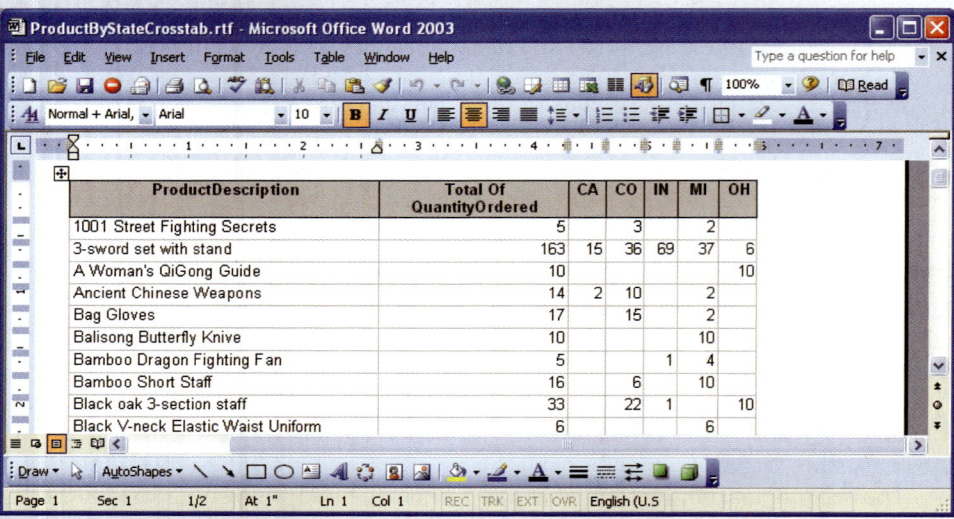

4. Add your name to the Word document as a centered header and save it to your homework folder.

tip: *Use the Header and Footer selection from the View menu*

5. Close Word

When the Office Tools option of the Tools menu is used to export an Access object, Word automatically opens with the exported file displaying. With the document open,

Word has full access to it with formatting capabilities that are far superior to those provided by Access. Word supports multicolumn reporting, drop cap text formatting, borders, graphics, and sectioning to apply differing formats to various report components. Word also can be used to create a report based on multiple Access outputs by combining exported data into one document.

Finally, to output a .txt file or control the folder and name of the file, use the Export option of the File menu. The Export To dialog box contains options used to select a folder, filename, and output format for the object being exported. Both .rtf and .txt files can be opened by most word-processing applications. An .rtf file retains formatting while a .txt file does not.

Exporting Access Data to Spreadsheet Applications

Microsoft Access database objects also can be exported to a number of spreadsheet file formats. Spreadsheets enhance datasheet formatting options and provide greater analytical capabilities than Access. Microsoft Excel or any of the other supported spreadsheet file formats can provide modeling, forecasting, what-if analysis, and charting capabilities that greatly exceed those available in Access.

The simplest way to apply Excel features to an Access object is to use the Office Links option of the Tools menu just demonstrated to export a word-processing file. Missy and Micah would like to perform what-if analysis on the orders data generated by the OrderData query.

---

task reference   **Export an Access Object to an Excel Spreadsheet**

- Open the Access database that contains the data to be exported

- Select the object to be exported in the Database Window (it is best to preview the object before exporting)

- Open the **Tools** menu, point to **Office Links**, and then click **Analyze It with Microsoft Excel**

Exporting OrderData.xls:

1. Verify that Access is open with the **ac08KoryoKicks.mdb** database active

2. In the Database Window select the **Queries** object and open **OrderData**

3. Activate the **Tools** menu, point to **Office Links**, and click **Analyze It with Microsoft Excel** (see Figure 8.21)

4. Add your name to the Excel worksheet in cell F1 and save it in your homework folder

---

When the Office Tools option of the Tools menu is used to export an Access object to Excel, Excel automatically opens with the exported file displaying. The exported file will normally be saved in either C:\My Documents or the folder containing the database. The name of the exported object is used as the filename. The OrderData.xls file can now be modified like any native Excel file. The .xls file is not linked to Access and will not reflect database updates.

FIGURE 8.21

OrderData.xls

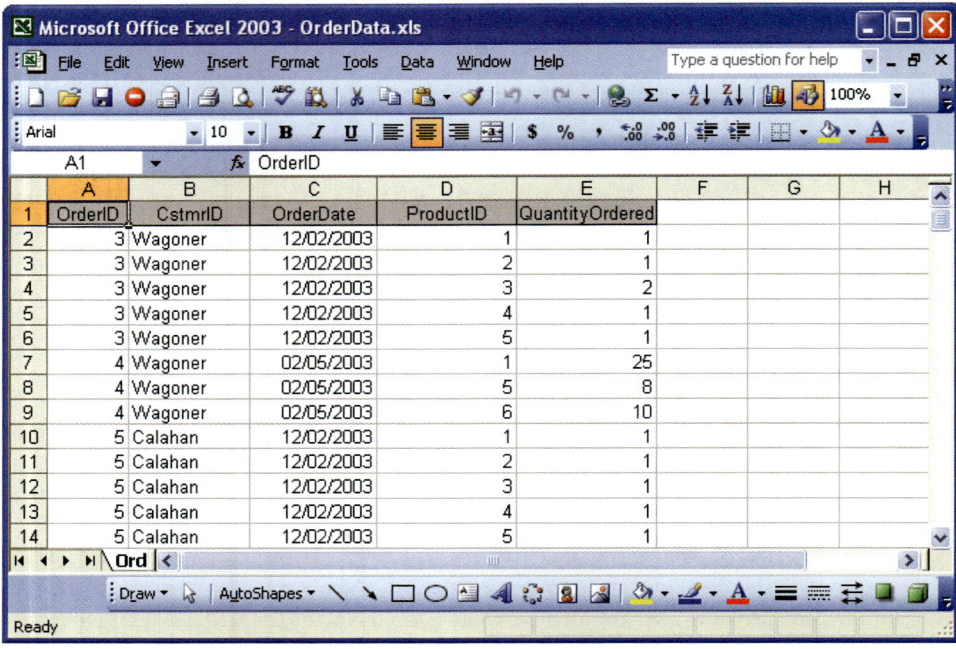

To output a spreadsheet format other than Excel or control the folder and name of the file, use the Export option of the File menu. The Export To dialog box provides options to select a folder, filename, and output format for the object being exported. Older versions of Excel, Lotus 1-2-3, dBase, and Paradox selections are available from the Save As type drop-down list. The non-Excel options require conversion software that is not included in the typical Access install.

SESSION 8.1

making *the grade*

1. How are the Chart Wizard and Microsoft Graph related?

2. What is a source application?

3. How do you determine whether to link or embed an object?

4. Why is a chart type important?

SESSION 8.2 WEB PUBLICATION

Access Web technology tools are designed for sharing data, queries, forms, and reports generated from Access using an intranet or the Internet. Access provides an array of Web publication methodologies to meet the differing needs of organizations.

Reviewing Web Technologies

The *World Wide Web (WWW)*, or simply the Web, is an international network of linked documents that share a common computer network called the *Internet*. Each computer on the network can be located by a unique address called a *Uniform Resource Locator (URL)*. These computers are called *Web Servers* because they run server software that allows a web of linked documents to be viewed using a *Web browser*. Web pages also can be delivered over private networks called *intranets* to share documents within an organization or using both Internet and intranet technology called an *extranet*.

FIGURE 8.22

An HTML example

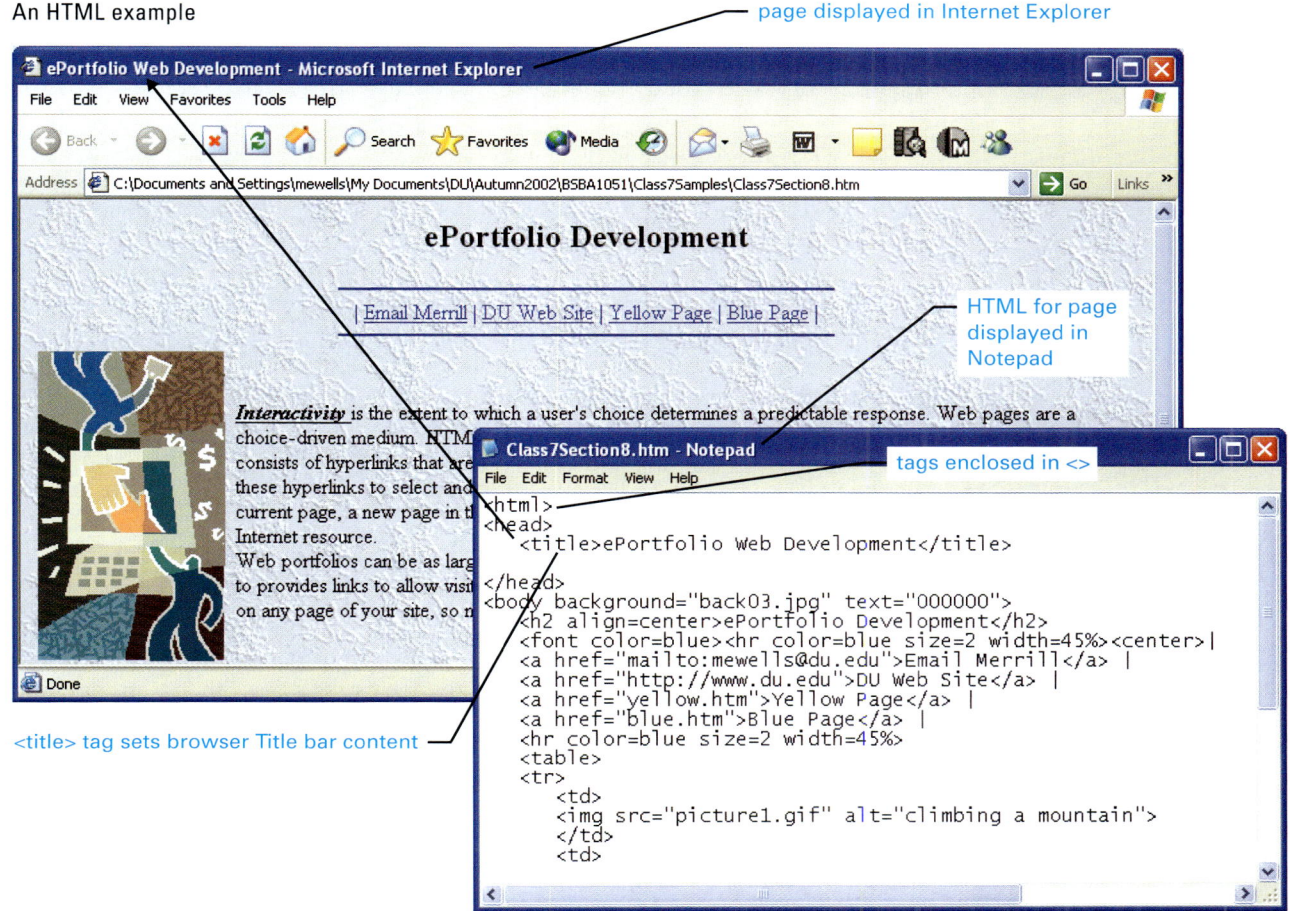

People who use the Web from work are typically provided continual access through a local server. Most home users who use the Web are not continuously connected to the Internet but, typically, a phone or other type of cable is used to connect to an **Internet Service Provider**, a company that sells the use of its Internet Servers to individuals and businesses.

Regardless of whether the documents are on the Internet, an intranet, or an extranet, they can be viewed using a Web browser such as Microsoft Internet Explorer or Netscape Navigator. **Hypertext Markup Language (HTML)** is used to provide instructions to the Web browser outlining how to deliver the page content. HTML instructions are enclosed in <> and are called **tags**. As its name implies, HTML was developed to deliver text but it has been expanded to deliver graphics and multimedia content as well. HTML tags set fonts, colors, position, and other formatting characteristics of text. Tags also control what graphic file displays and what other document is opened when a **hyperlink** is clicked. Hyperlinks define the paths between Web documents and typically display in a different color than nonlinked text. (See Figure 8.22.)

Figure 8.22 shows an example of a Web page documenting a physics lab assignment created with Office products. The table of data and chart were created in Excel and exported to Word, where the explanatory text was added, and then the page was saved as Filtered HTML (filtering removes Office-specific tags added by the generator). The document was submitted for grading by placing it on the school's intranet. Notice the tags enclosed in <> brackets and the relationship between the <title> tag and the Internet Explorer Title bar. While this type of conversion is fast and relatively painless, it may not provide the most efficient HTML code or fastest Web page load times.

Building HTML Pages

The preferred method of creating HTML pages with new content is to type the tags and text of a page into a basic text editor like Notepad and save the file with an .htm (or .html) extension. When the content for a page already exists, it can be converted by any Office application and many other applications.

Most Web pages are static; that is, their content does not change. Dynamic Web pages contain data that are updated to reflect the current status of something such as the price of a stock. Microsoft Access has the ability to create both *static Web pages* and *dynamic Web pages* based on database objects.

Static Web pages created from an Access object cannot be updated from a browser, and changes made to the data after the static page was generated are not reflected. The content of a dynamic Web page is updated each time that page is viewed so that it reflects the current status of the object. Certain types of dynamic Web pages will allow users to update the Access database object using a Web browser.

KoryoKicks will need both static and dynamic Web pages to support sharing information between geographically dispersed locations. Objects from the KoryoKicks database will be converted to HTML and stored on a Web server where they can be viewed and sometimes updated using a Web browser.

Creating a Static HTML Document

The simplest Web pages to generate are static—those that do not update as the data change and cannot be modified by Web users. Static Web pages can be generated from tables, queries, forms, or reports in an existing Access database. Tables, queries, and forms will display as datasheets on the Web page. Reports will appear with HTML versions of the page formatting, which does not always provide ideal conversions. Static Web pages can be viewed using any current Web browser and are best for data that change infrequently.

---

task reference   Export an Access Object
                                        to a Static HTML Page

- Open the Access database that contains the data to be exported

- Select the object to be exported in the Database Window (it is best to preview the object before exporting)

- Open the **File** menu and click **Export**

- In the Export To dialog box

  - Use the Save In box to select the drive and folder for the Web page

  - Set the Save As Type to **HTML Documents (*.html; *.htm)**

  - In the File Name box, enter the name for the Web page (it is best not to use spaces in these names)

  - **Save Formatted** should be clicked to retain the formatting applied to the datasheet in Access and activate the next two options

  - Check **AutoStart** to display the page in your default browser

  - In the HTML Output Options dialog box

  - Apply an HTML template to standardize formatting (Optional)

  - Click **OK**

Exporting Importers.html:

1. Verify that Access is open with the **ac08KoryoKicks.mdb** database active

2. In the Database Window select the **Tables** object and open **Importers**

3. Activate the **File** menu and click **Export**

4. In the Export Table Importers To dialog box

   a. Set the Save In drive and folder
   b. Set the Save As box to **HTML Documents (*.html; *.htm)**
   c. Check **Save Formatted, AutoStart**, and then click **Export All**

5. In the HTML Output Options dialog box click **OK** (see Figure 8.23)

— the display of Netscape and
other browsers will vary slightly

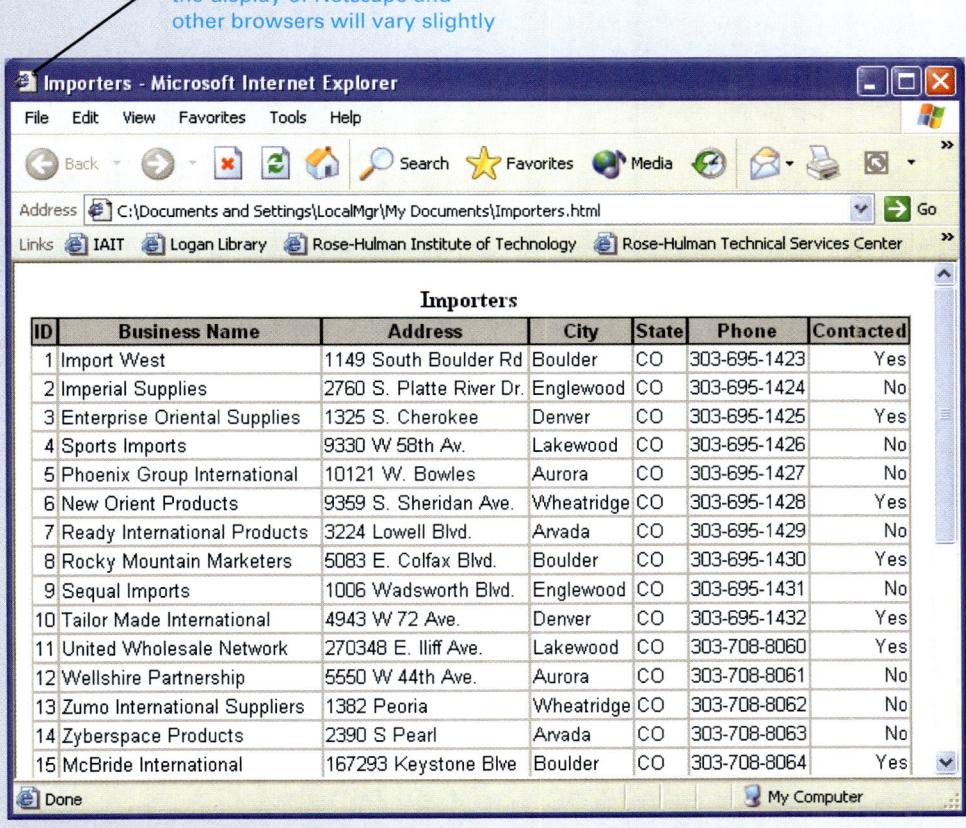

FIGURE 8.23

Importers.html displayed
in Internet Explorer

6. If your browser is Internet Explorer, click **View** and **Source** to review the HTML code for the generated page

7. Close Notepad

8. Close the browser window

Once a static Web page is built, it can be edited outside of Access using Notepad or any other text editor to add links, create additional content, or modify the design. Most browsers have an option on the File menu that will allow a local drive file to be opened so changes can be reviewed.

To make manual changes, update the HTML code in the editor software, save the file, and then refresh the browser screen to see the impact. When the page is complete, it can be loaded into a folder on a Web server where it can be accessed via the Internet. The URL used to retrieve a Web page that has been placed on a Web server is the WebServerAddress+ path+filename.

The process for creating static HTML pages from queries, forms, and reports is the same, but the result is slightly different. An Access report creates one HTML file for each printed page of the report numbered sequentially. The CustomersByState-Chart report would create CustomersByState-Chart.html, CustomersByState-ChartPage2.html, CustomersByState-ChartPage3.html, and so on. OLE objects stored in a database, including most graphics, do not display on the HTML page but they can be added manually or using a template file.

Using Access to View and Update an HTML Page

Microsoft Access Web tools integrate well with those of other Microsoft products. The Access Web toolbar is very similar to the Microsoft Internet Explorer toolbar and allows users to modify and view Access-based Web pages without leaving the Access interface. If Microsoft Internet Explorer is not the default browser, you will not be able to complete these steps.

---

task reference   Use Internet Explorer to View
a Static HTML Page

- Open Access
- From the **View** menu, pause over **Toolbars** and then click **Web**
- On the Web toolbar, drop down the **Go** list and select **Open Hyperlink**
- Click the **Browse** button in the Open Internet Address dialog box
- Use the Browse dialog box to navigate to the file to be viewed
- Select the file and click **Open**
- Click **OK**

Using the Access Web toolbar to view Importers.html:

1. Verify that Access is open
2. Open the **View** menu, point to **Toolbars**, and select **Web**
3. Drop down the **Go** list on the Web toolbar and click **Open Hyperlink**
4. Click the **Browse** button in the Open Internet Address dialog box (see Figure 8.24)
5. Use the Browse dialog box to select the drive and folder containing Importers.html and double-click **Importers.html**
6. Click **OK**

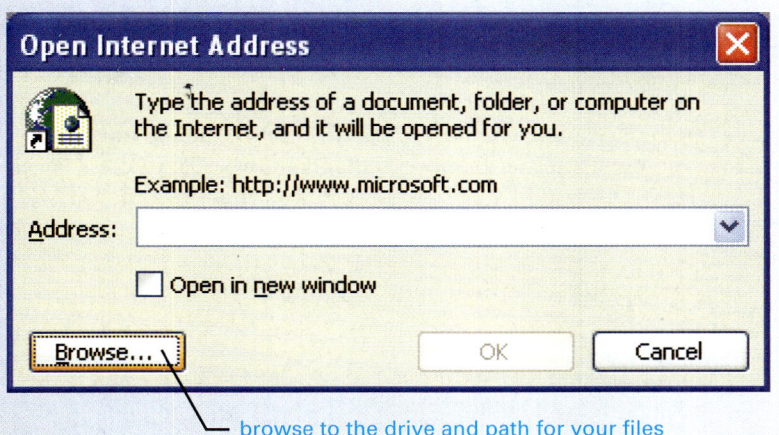

browse to the drive and path for your files

7. The page opens in its own browser window. Click **View** and **Source** to review the HTML code for the generated page

8. In the first few lines find the <CAPTION><B>Importers</B></CAPTION> and edit it to be **Importers - your name** (see Figure 8.25)

tip: *Be sure to edit only text between <CAPTION><B> and <\B></CAPTION>*

9. Use the File menu to Save and then close Notepad

10. Use the Refresh button of Internet Explorer to update the browser view

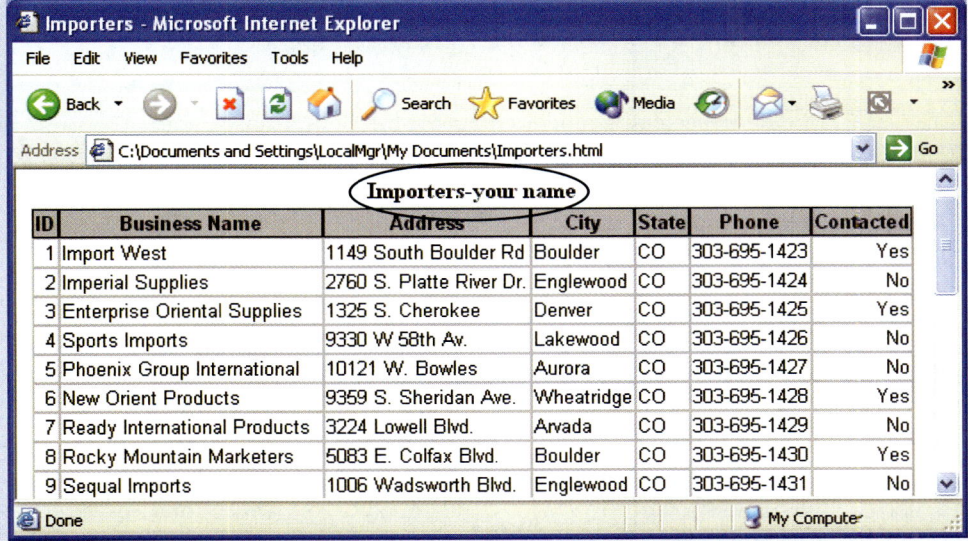

11. Close the browser window and the Importers table

Static HTML pages must be reexported to display updated data. Each time a page is regenerated, any customizations such as added text, graphics, or navigation will need to be reapplied. Because recustomizing is tedious and prone to error, it is a good idea to create HTML templates. An HTML template is a file that contains HTML instructions for creating a Web page and can include text, graphics, and navigation. When a template is applied, Access will place its content based on the instructions, and the remainder of the page is not impacted. In the Export process the HTML Output Options dialog box has an option to specify a template.

Creating Data Access Pages

Data Access Pages are built using Dynamic HTML and can be viewed only in browsers supporting that technology (Internet Explorer 5.0 and above). Data Access Pages consist of an exported HTML page and a new database object that links the HTML file to a database object. Because this connection is maintained, Data Access Pages can be used to view, edit, update, delete, filter, group, and sort live data in the database using a Web browser. Data Access Pages also can contain components from spreadsheets, Pivot tables, or charts.

help yourself *Use the Type a Question combo box to improve your understanding of the Web page options available from Access database by typing **about web pages**. Review the contents of About data access pages. Close the Help window when you are finished*

Displaying Data and Reports

To make Data Access Pages available from the Internet, publish the HTML pages to a Web server. The Access database supporting the pages also must be made available to page users. The best security is provided by placing the HTML pages and the database on the same server. It is a good idea to place the database on a shared server before you create Data Access Pages. Moving the database after pages are created will cause the connection between the database and the HTML page to be interrupted.

task *reference*	Use the Page Wizard to Create a Data Access Page

- Open the database containing the data for the Data Access Page
- Click the **Pages** object in the Database Window
- Double-click **Create data access page by using wizard**
- Follow the Wizard instructions

Using the Page Wizard to create ImportersDataAccess.htm:

1. Verify that Access is running with **ac08KoryoKicks.mdb** open
2. Click the **Pages** object in the Database Window
3. Double-click **Create data access page by using wizard**
4. Select the **Importers** table and move all of the fields to the Selected Fields list and click **Next** (see Figure 8.26)
5. Click **Next** without setting any grouping
6. Choose **BusinessName** for the ascending sort and click **Next**
7. Click **Finish** (see Figure 8.27)
8. Click in the Title placeholder and type **Importers by Business Name**

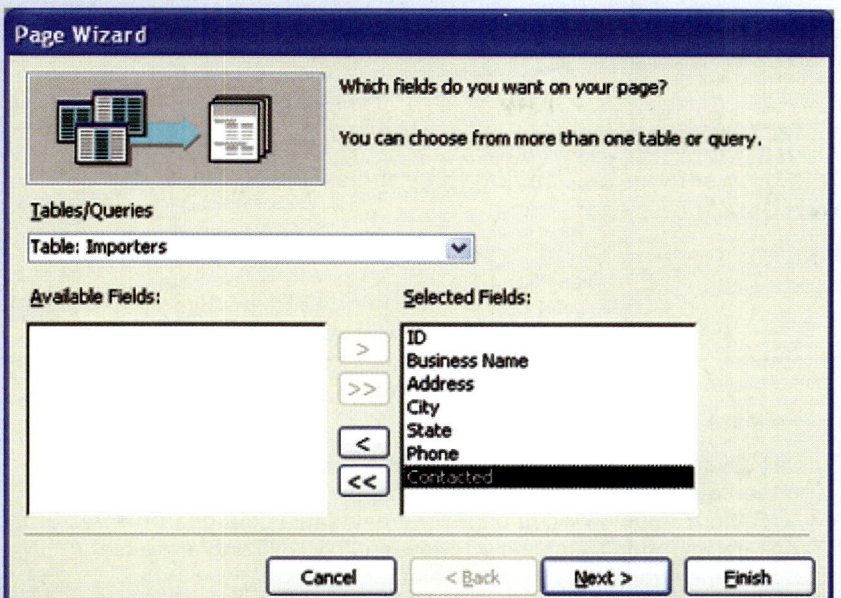

FIGURE 8.26
The Page Wizard

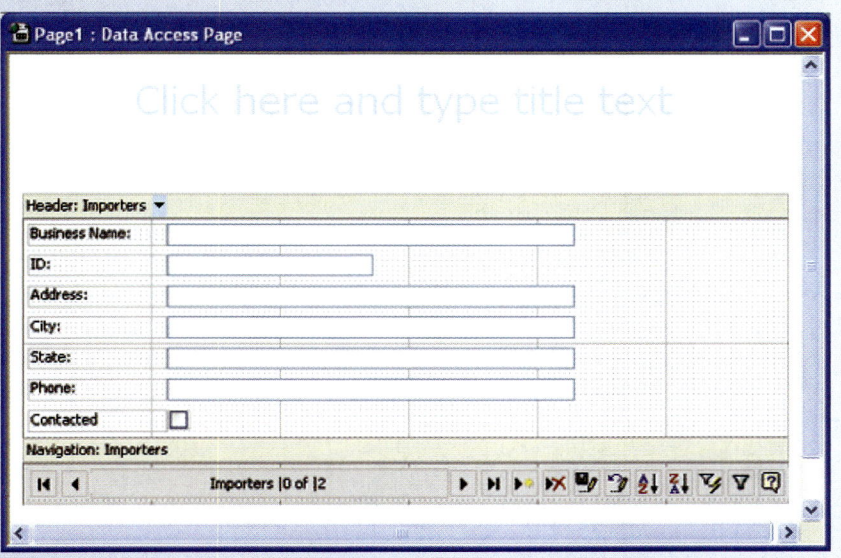

FIGURE 8.27
Data Access Page Design
View

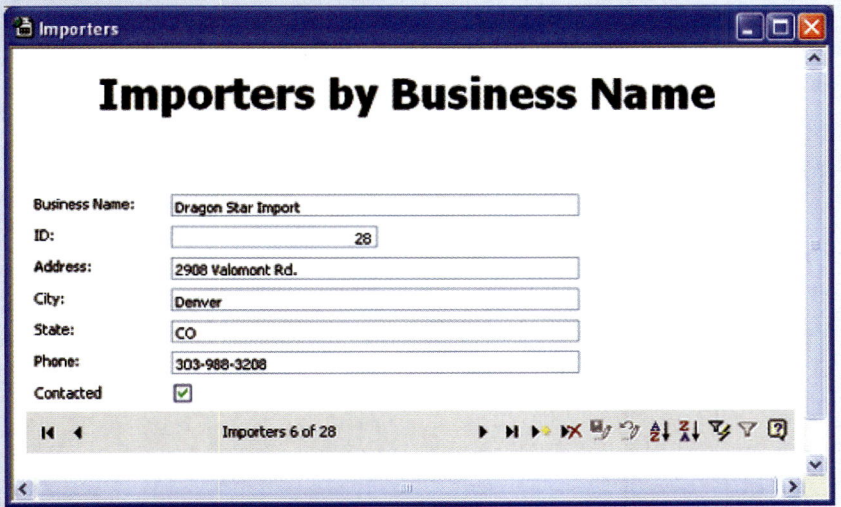

FIGURE 8.28
Data Access Page in the
browser

tip: *If the Title placeholder is not visible, click in the header area*

9. Click the View ▣▾ button

10. Use the navigation bar to move through the records (see Figure 8.28)

11. Close the browser window, saving the page as **ImportersDataAccess.htm**

12. Click **OK**

---

another**way**

. . . to Create a Data Access Page

Access provides several options for creating a Data Access Page. The steps have covered using the Page Wizard, but a page also can be created from scratch in Design View, created from an existing page, or created in a columnar format. Select the Pages object in the Database Window and click New to activate the New Access Data Page with all of the page creation options.

- Design View—Create a new page without using a Wizard

- Existing Web Page—Use an existing Web page to create a Data Access Page

- Page Wizard—Automatically generate a page based on your field selections. You also can specify grouping and sorting options

- AutoPage—Columnar—Creates a default page based on your table or query selection.

You cannot specify fields, grouping, or sorting

The Importers Data Access Page has an appearance similar to a form displaying one record at a time. In the browser, the ***Record Navigation toolbar*** is used to move from record to record, add new records, delete records, edit records, and sort and filter data. Most of the buttons should be familiar because they appear on other Access toolbars. Screen tips will display for each button when the cursor pauses over it.

Adding scrolling text to ImportersDataAccess.html:

1. Verify that Access is running with **ac08KoryoKicks.mdb** open

2. Select the **Pages** object from the Database Window

3. Select the **ImportedDataAccess** Page and click the **Design** button

4. Click the **Scrolling Text** ▣ tool in the toolbox and drag the area below the Record Navigation toolbar on the Data Access Page (see Figure 8.29)

5. Select the default Marquee text and type your name

6. Right-click on the Scrolling Text object and select Element Properties
   a. Set Background Color to silver
   b. Close the Properties dialog box

7. Click the **View** button (see Figure 8.30)

8. Close the window and save the changes

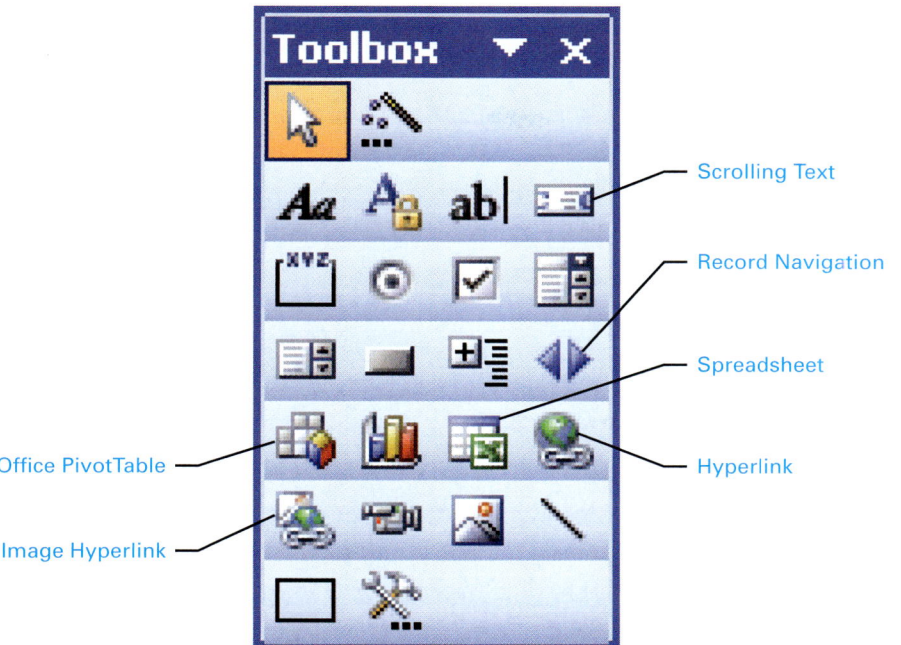

F I G U R E 8.29
Data Access Page Design
View toolbox

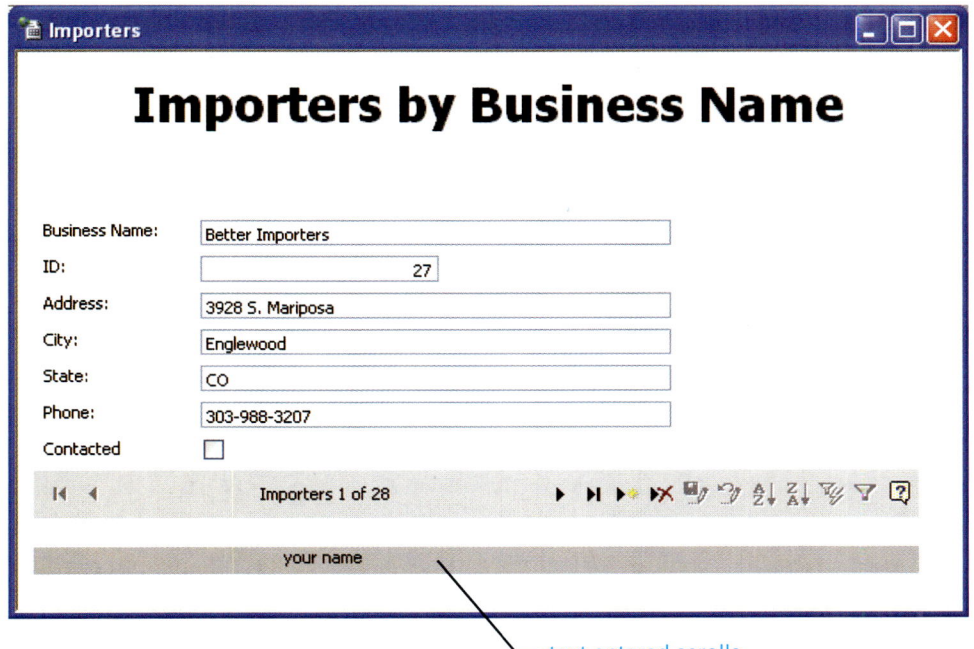

F I G U R E 8.30
Scrolling text

Making edits in the Design View of a Data Access Page is very similar to updating a form or report. Notice that some of the toolbox buttons are specific to Data Access Pages. The most important differences are noted in Figure 8.29.

Adding an Image to ImportersDataAccess.htm:

1. Verify that Access is running with **ac08KoryoKicks.mdb** open

2. Select the **Pages** object from the Database Window

3. Select the **ImportersDataAccess** Page and click the **Design** button

4. Click the **Image** tool in the toolbox and drag the area shown in Figure 8.31

5. Navigate to the files for this chapter and select **ac08Warrior.gif**

6. Click the **View** button

7. Close the window and save the changes

8. Use Windows Explorer to view the files in the ImportersDataAccess_Files folder

9. Close Windows Explorer

Access provides artistic themes that can be applied to pages for visual impact. Themes are available from the Format menu and can be changed at any time without impacting the presentation.

Applying a Theme to ImportersDataAccess.htm:

1. Verify that Access is running with **ac08KoryoKicks.mdb** open

2. Select the **Pages** object from the Database Window

3. Select the **ImportersDataAccess** Page and click the **Design** button

4. Open the **Format** menu and select **Theme**

5. Click through the available themes to preview them

6. Select **Sandstone** and click **OK** (see Figure 8.32)

7. Click the **View** button to see the page results

8. Click the Save button and then close the window

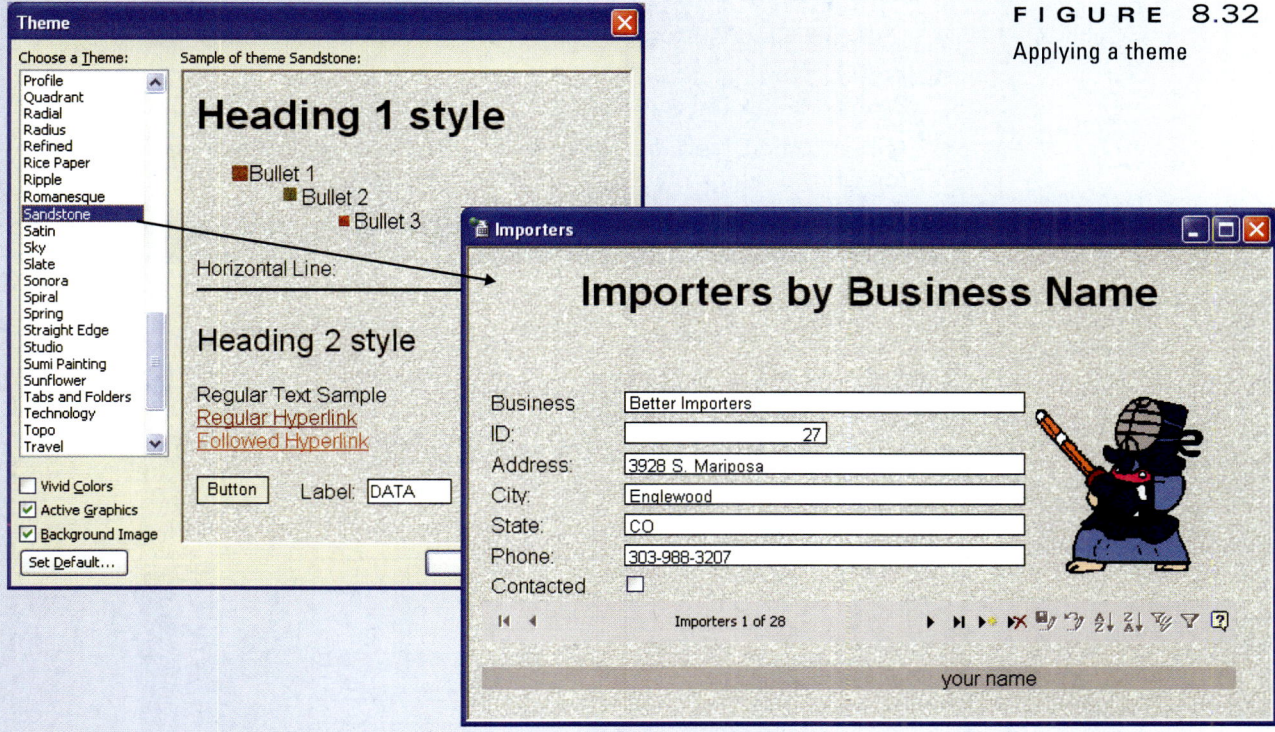

F I G U R E   8.32

Applying a theme

Any bullets, backgrounds, or graphics displayed in a Data Access Page are stored in a folder that must be moved with the Data Access Page. The folder will carry the name of your page with an underscore and the word Files. So the supporting files for ImportersDataAccess are stored in a folder named ImportersDataAccess_Files. The folder should contain an .xml file with references to the other objects on the page and the .gif file containing the image. The remaining files were generated by the theme applied.

Allowing Database Access

When Data Access Pages, the supporting files, and the database have been properly loaded on a shared server, live database data can be updated. The process is similar to using a form to update data in an open Access database, but is accomplished from a browser.

Updating the database using ImportersDataAccess.htm:

1. Close Access if it is open

2. Use Windows Explorer to navigate to the **ImportersDataAccess.htm** file and double-click to open it

tip: *The icon for this file incorporates both the Web page and Access icons. If Internet Explorer is not your default browser, you will need to open IE and use the File menu to open ImportersDataAccess.htm. You cannot accomplish these steps with a browser that doesn't support Data Access technology*

3. Move to record 2 and edit the business name to read **Tao Asian Supplies**

4. Click the **Save** button on the Record Navigation toolbar

5. Move to the Golden Orient Products record, check the **Contacted** check box, and click the **Save** button on the Record Navigation toolbar

6. Move to the Diversified Women's Center record and use the **Delete** button on the Record Navigation toolbar to delete it

F I G U R E   8.33
Saving edits

7. Answer **Yes** when notified that the delete cannot be undone

8. Use the New button on the Record Navigation toolbar to add a new importer to the list named **<yourname>Imports**. Make up the remaining data. Do not leave any fields blank

9. Use the Save button or move to the previous record to save the change

10. Close Internet Explorer

11. Open **ac08KoryoKicks.mdb** and review the updates that have been applied to the Importers table

For demonstration purposes, the steps in this topic are using local files that are not stored on a shared server. Using a Web browser to update a database through a Data Access Page will work the same way from an intranet or the Internet as it did with these local files.

Because Data Access Pages are based on live data, sorts and filters can be used to control the order of records and what records display. These features work from the Record Navigation toolbar when viewing a page in the browser.

Sorting and filtering ImportersDataAccess.htm:

1. Close Access if it is open

2. Use Windows Explorer to navigate to the **ImportersDataAccess.htm** file and double-click to open it

tip: *If your default browser is not Internet Explorer, you will need to open IE and use the File menu to open this file*

3. Click in the **City** field and then click the **Sort Descending** button on the Record Navigation toolbar

4. Move through the records to verify the sort

5. Click in the **Business Name** field and then click **Sort Ascending** button on the Record Navigation toolbar to return those data to their original order

6. Select the city **Englewood** and then click the **Filter By Selection** button on the Record Navigation toolbar

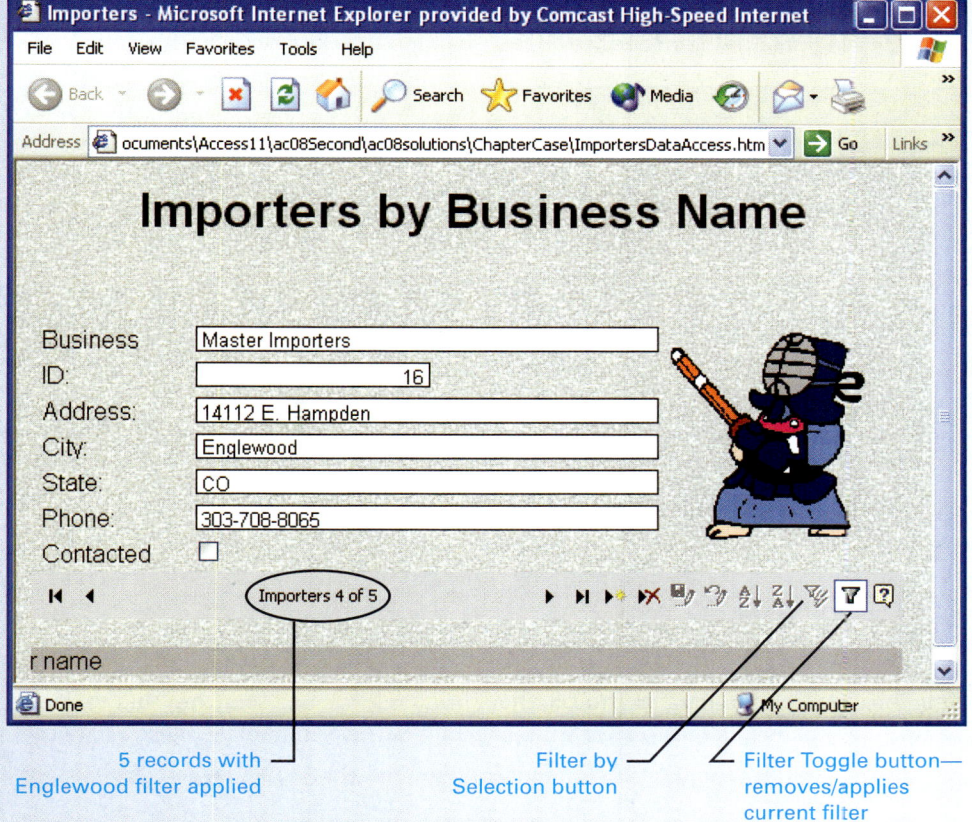

FIGURE 8.34
Filter by Selection

5 records with Englewood filter applied

Filter by Selection button

Filter Toggle button— removes/applies current filter

7. Use the **Filter Toggle button** on the Record Navigation toolbar to remove and then reapply the filter

8. Close the Internet Explorer Window

Filter by Selection is the only filtering methodology available from a browser. Remember that Filter by Selection supports partial-field filtering but not multiple-field filtering. Selecting the first character of a field retrieves all records starting with that character. Selecting any other character in a field will return all records containing that character.

Repairing Links to Data Access Pages

Data Access Pages allow access to the live database data by maintaining a link between the Data Access Web page and the database. Moving or renaming either the database or the Data Access Web page can cause this link to be invalid. Moving the Data Access Web page without its associated data folder (pagename-field) can also damage this link.

To avoid Data Access Pages that are no longer connected to an active database, place the database on the shared intranet or Internet server before creating the pages. For the most consistent results, the Data Access Pages should be placed on the same server as the database. When the link between a database and its Data Access Pages is destroyed, follow the instructions in the next Task Reference to repair it.

---

task reference   Repair Broken Data
                                       Access Page Links

- Open the Data Access Page with a broken database link in Design View
- Click **Update Link** in the informational dialog box
  - Navigate to the network folder containing the Data Access Page
  - Select the page and click **OK**
  - Click **OK** in the dialog box explaining that the connection needs to be repaired
- On the right-hand side of the Data Access Page Design View, click the **Page connection properties** option in the Field List Window
  - On the Connection tab, click the ellipsis (…) and update the database name
  - Click **Open**
  - Click the **Test Connection** button
  - When the test works, click **OK**
  - Click **OK** again to end the update

Importing an HTML Document as an Access Table

A fundamental concept of database storage is that data should be entered and validated only once. After valid data are stored, they should always be used from that validated source. This principle reduces errors and is more efficient than reentering data each time a new data storage or evaluation technology is needed.

Building an Access Table from a Web Page

To support this concept, Access can use and incorporate data from sources outside itself. Since the World Wide Web is a great informational resource, one of the formats that Access can interpret is HTML. When Web page data are compiled as a table or list, they can be directly converted to an Access table.

Missy and Micah have used Web search utilities to locate Web merchants selling martial arts supplies. Their goal is to research and contact these companies as potential distributors of KoryoKicks products. After the page resulting from the search was saved, it was edited in Notepad to remove the unneeded page components such as the search engine and logo. Now the data retrieved can be loaded directly into an Access table.

---

task reference — Importing an HTML Document as an Access Table

- Open the database to hold the imported table
- Verify that the layout of the data to be imported is either a list or a table
- On the **File** menu, point to **Get External Data**, and then click **Import**
- Select the HTML file for import and click **Import** (be sure to set the Files of Type to HTML documents)
- Complete the Wizard dialog boxes

Importing WebImporters.htm as an Access table:

1. Verify that Access is running with **ac08KoryoKicks.mdb** open

2. Use Internet Explorer to preview ac08WebImporters.htm

   tip: *On the Web toolbar in Access click* **Go**, *then* **Open Hyperlink**, *and then* **Browse**

3. Close the Internet Explorer window

4. On the Access **File** menu, point to **Get External Data**, and then click **Import**

5. In the Import dialog box
   a. Set Files of Type to **HTML Documents (*.html; .htm)**
   b. Navigate to the drive and folder containing files for this chapter, select **ac08WebImporters.htm**, and click **Import**

6. In the Import Wizard (see Figure 8.35)
   a. Click **First Row Contains Column Headings** and then click **Next**
   b. Click **Next** to save the HTML import in a new table
   c. Change the Merchants data type to **Hyperlink** and the Description data type to **Memo**, and click **Next**

   tip: *You may need to scroll to find these fields*

   d. Click **Next** to let Access assign a primary key
   e. Type **WebImporters** in the Import to Table box and click **Finish**

7. Click **OK** to the Import Complete message

The WebImporters table has successfully been created from the modified HTML document. You should also see an _ImportError table. This table contains a record for each improperly imported row that Access detected. The most common import problem occurs when the data are longer than the field can hold and are truncated in the import process.

F I G U R E   8.35

The Import HTML Wizard

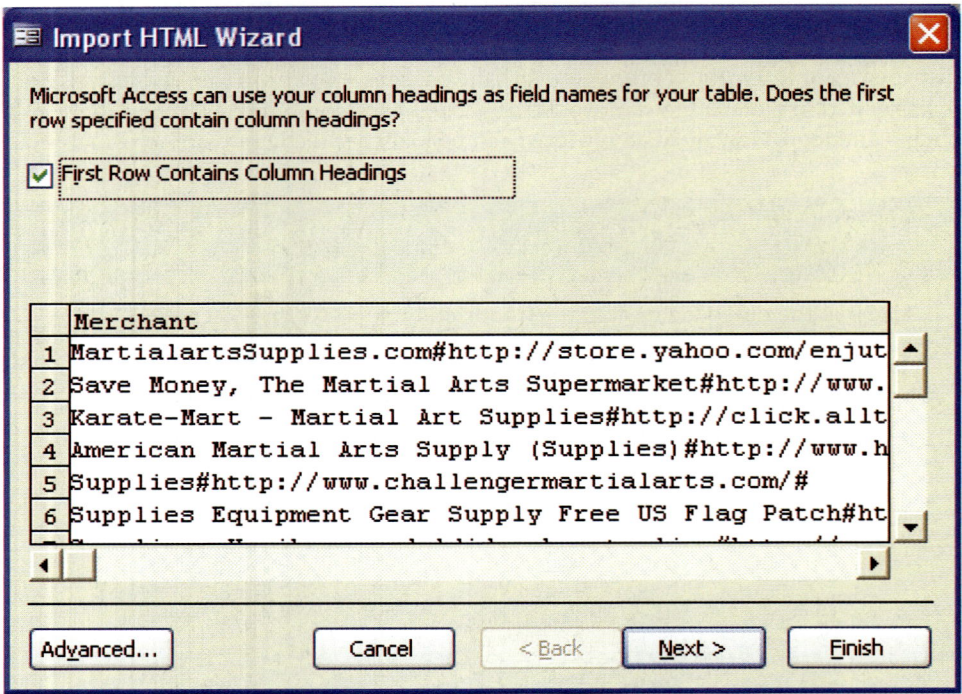

Confirming the import:

1. Verify that Access is running with **ac08KoryoKicks.mdb** open

2. Click the **Tables** object in the Database Window

3. Double-click the **WebImporters** table to open it and confirm the import

4. Double-click the column button border for each field to adjust its width

F I G U R E   8.36

WebImporters table

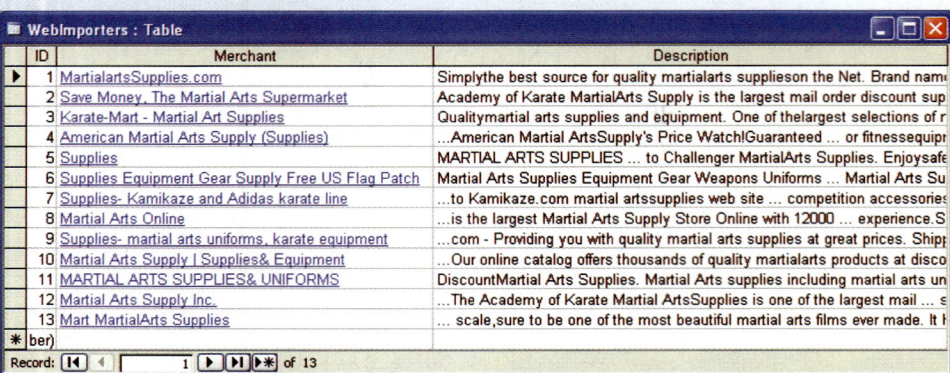

5. Close the window and save your changes

6. Double-click **Martial Arts Supplies ImportError** to evaluate any import issues (see Figure 8.37)

7. Review the errors and close the window

The import errors encountered in this case are in the second field, the hyperlink to the importers. The links that were truncated will need to be repaired. Additionally, the text in the memo field has some spacing problems, but overall the conversion is good.

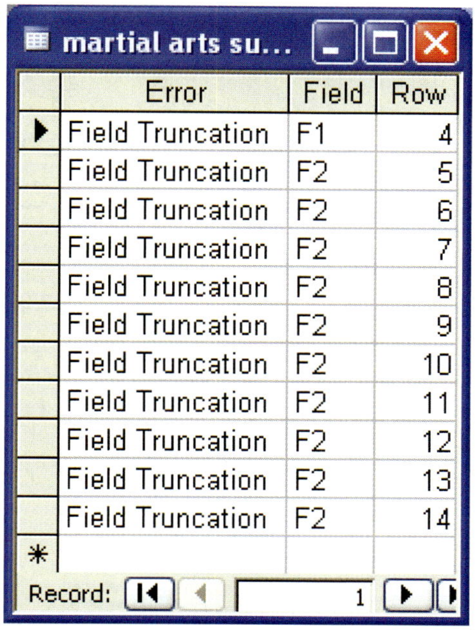

martial arts su...

	Error	Field	Row
▶	Field Truncation	F1	4
	Field Truncation	F2	5
	Field Truncation	F2	6
	Field Truncation	F2	7
	Field Truncation	F2	8
	Field Truncation	F2	9
	Field Truncation	F2	10
	Field Truncation	F2	11
	Field Truncation	F2	12
	Field Truncation	F2	13
	Field Truncation	F2	14
*			

Record: 1

FIGURE 8.37
Martial arts supplies __ImportErrors table

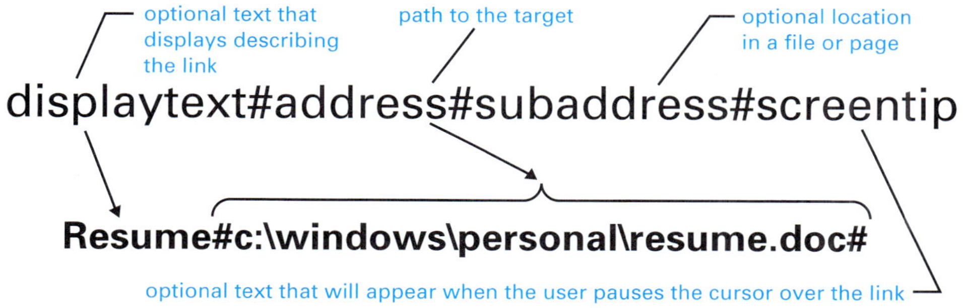

FIGURE 8.38
Hyperlink address

Constructing World Wide Web Hyperlinks

Most people associate hyperlinks with Web pages, but since they are really pointers from one object to another object, they can be used to link to pictures, e-mail addresses, or files. The hyperlink itself can display as text or a clickable image.

Hyperlinks can be used to navigate to another file, open another Web page, send an e-mail message, or start a file transfer (FTP). When pointing to text or a picture that contains a hyperlink, the pointer becomes a hand, indicating that it is something that can be clicked. When a hyperlink is clicked, the destination is displayed, opened, or run, depending on the type of destination. For example, a hyperlink to a sound file opens the file in a media player, and a hyperlink to a Web page displays the page in the Web browser.

Access provides a dialog box with the component parts of a hyperlink address (see Figure 8.38). Each address can have up to four parts separated by the number sign (#), but only the address is required.

In an Access table setting the data type of a field to hyperlink allows users to enter any type of a link into the field. When the user enters more than the required address component of a hyperlink, only the display text is visible. This is also true of a text box that is formatted to display hyperlinks. In either case, to see the rest of the entry, click in a cell and press F2.

The error table for WebImporters indicates that there are potential problems with the hyperlink for record and several Description field truncations. We will ignore Description truncations but test and repair each hyperlink. To review and repair these links, the correct URL for the pages must be known. The twins have returned to the Internet and retrieved the correct addresses so that this import can be completed.

Entering and repairing a hyperlink in WebImporters:

1. Verify that Access is running with **ac08KoryoKicks.mdb** open

2. Click the **Tables** object in the Database Window and open **WebImporters** in Design View

3. Confirm that the Merchant field has a Data Type property of Hyperlink

4. Use the View button to switch to Datasheet View and pause the cursor over each hyperlink to preview its URL

5. For records 2, 3, and 6
   a. Right-click on the hyperlink, point to **Hyperlink**, and click **Edit Hyperlink**
   b. Review and edit the links
      i. Record 2 does not need to be changed
      ii. Record 3 needs to have the address changed to www.Karate-mart.com (Access will add the protocol http://)
      iii. Record 6 needs an address of www.allblackbelt.com

FIGURE 8.39

Editing Hyperlinks

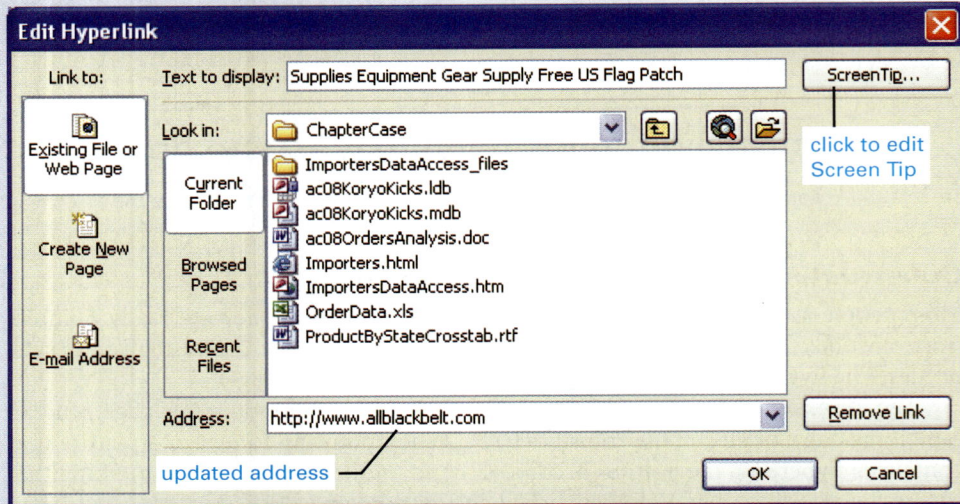

6. Click in the Merchant column of the new record row and click the **Insert Hyperlink** button on the Standard toolbar

7. In the Insert Hyperlink dialog box: (see Figure 8.40)
   a. Enter **KoryoKicks** as the Display text
   b. Click the ScreenTip button, enter **KoryoKicks**, and click **OK**
   c. Navigate to **ac08KoryoKicksHome.html**, select it, and click **OK**

tip: *This file is with the other files for this chapter, not on the Internet*

8. Click the KoryoKicks link—it should open the skeleton of a new home page

9. Add text describing KoryoKicks to the Description field and close the view

The address to a destination object can be either absolute or relative. An *absolute address* is said to be fully qualified because it includes all of the information needed to find an object including the protocol (http, ftp, …), the server address, the path, and the filename. A *relative address* omits some of the address components. When components are omitted, they default to the values of the source object (the object containing the hyperlink). For example if the source document http://www.microsoft.com/index/htm contains a link samples.htm, the source protocol (http) and address (www.microsoft.com) are used to determine the full address of the destination, http://www.microsoft.com/samples.htm.

Absolute addresses do not function when files are moved to a new location. Relative addresses will function after files are moved, as long as they are still in the same relative locations (the folders and filenames remain the same).

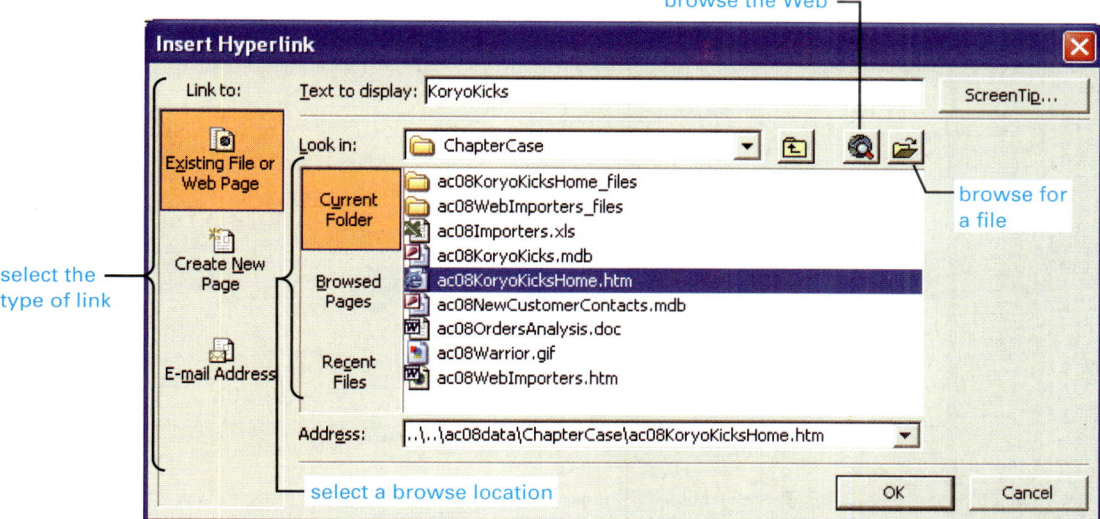

FIGURE 8.40

Adding the KoryoKicks hyperlink

---

task reference — Construct a Web Page or File Hyperlink

- Open the form, report, or Data Access Page in Design View

- Click the Insert Hyperlink 🔗 button in the toolbox and drag the display area on the form, report, or Data Access Page

- In the Insert Hyperlink dialog box

  - Select the type of object to **Link to** (Existing File or Web Page, Object in This Database, Create New Page, or E-Mail Address)

  - Enter the **Text to display** for the hyperlink (if this is blank, the URL will display)

  - Enter the **Screen Tip text** (if this is blank, the URL displays when the user pauses the cursor over the link)

  - In the Address box, type or browse to the path of a file or a URL

  - Click **OK**

ACCESS

Adding a hyperlink to ImportersDataAccess:

1. Verify that Access is running with **ac08KoryoKicks.mdb** open

2. Click the **Pages** object in the Database Window and Open **ImportersDataAccess** in Design View

3. Click the **Label** [Aa] tool in the toolbox

   a. Click and drag the area shown in Figure 8.41 below the name marquee

FIGURE 8.41

Hyperlink added to ImportersDataAccess

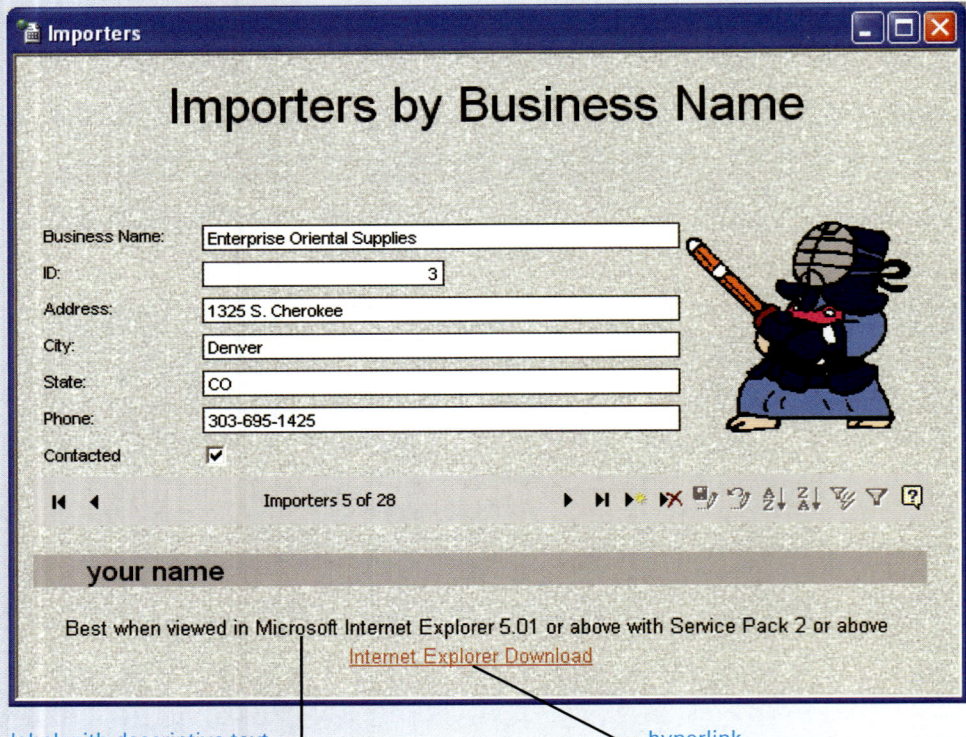

4. Click the **Hyperlink** [🖳] tool in the toolbox

   b. Click in the label and type **Best when viewed in Microsoft Internet Explorer 5.01 with Service Pack 2 or above**

   a. Click and drag the area shown in Figure 8.41 below the label just created, making it the width of the page
   b. In the Text to display box type **Internet Explorer Download**
   c. Click the ScreenTip button, type **Newest IE Version!**, and click **OK**
   d. In the address type www.microsoft.com
   e. Click **OK**

5. Change the label and Hyperlink text to 10-point and center align both

6. Click the View button to preview the page

7. Close the window, saving the changes

When adding a hyperlink to a Data Access Page, a special Hyperlink control is used. Forms and reports do not have a Hyperlink control, but use labels with the hyperlink information entered into the properties of the label. To test the hyperlink on the ImportersDataAccess Page, you switched to Page View and clicked the link. When testing a hyperlink stored in a label on a form or report, right-click the label, point to Hyperlink, and then click Open.

Take another look at the Insert Hyperlink dialog box (Figure 8.40) and note the similarities to a standard Open dialog box. Notice also that it contains items specific to locating a file for a hyperlink. The Link to options are used to define the type of link Access should create. We have created links using Existing File or Web Page, but there are also options to link to a Page in This Database, Create New Page, and E-mail Address. The HTML syntax for each of these options is unique, but the process to create them in Access is the same.

The Look In options are used to search the Current Folder, which works like a standard Open File dialog box. Browsed Pages, which will list Internet Explorer's browsing history, also can be used to select a Web address, or Recent Files can be used to easily link to a file that was recently opened.

The twins are now satisfied that they understand the import, export, and Web capabilities of Access. They believe that they will help immensely in managing and sharing data in a distributed organization. They will evaluate and begin implementing these features when their business plan is complete.

making the grade

1. What is the difference between a static HTML page and a Data Access Page?

2. Why are relative and absolute addresses important?

3. How is the data content of a static Web page updated?

4. What is the Record Navigation toolbar?

SESSION 8.3 SUMMARY

Sharing data is important in reducing data entry and saving time. Allowing multiple applications to have access to the same data allows users to apply the best formatting and analytical tools available in every situation. Access can import data from external sources such as Word, Excel, or another database. Embedded objects belong to the Access database while linked objects remain under the control of their source program.

The Chart Wizard uses Microsoft Graph to create graphs based on numeric data stored in a table. There are a number of chart types that can be created including bar, pie, column, and line. A global chart reflects summaries from all of the table data, while a record-bound chart is based on a single record. Once created, charts can be modified to display other chart types, contain explanatory text, and customize each chart component.

The Access Tools menu contains an Office Links option that automates data sharing with Microsoft Word and Excel. The Export option of the File menu can be used to export other file types such as .txt, HTML, or Paradox. HTML pages created from using the Export menu are static.

Dynamic Web pages called Data Access Pages are created using the Pages object in the Database Window. An HTML page that can be used to interact with live data is created along with a database object that maintains the connection between the database and the HTML page. Creating and editing a Data Access Page is very similar to the Design View of an Access form or report. The Data Access Design toolbar contains controls specifically designed for creating Web pages such as the Scrolling Text control and the Hyperlink control. Data Access Pages work best with Microsoft Internet Explorer 5.01 with Service Pack 2 or above.

MICROSOFT OFFICE SPECIALIST OBJECTIVES SUMMARY

- Create a Data Access Page—AC03S-1-12
- Import data to Access—AC03S-2-3
- Export data from Access—AC03S-4-4

making the grade *answers*

SESSION 8.1

1. The Chart Wizard walks you through creating a chart using Microsoft Graph. Microsoft Graph is used to edit an existing chart.

2. The source application is the software that originated a linked or embedded object.

3. Embedded objects are a copy of the original that can be edited independently. Linked objects are just a picture and should be used when you want only one copy of a file.

4. The chart type controls how the data are plotted. Chart types include bar, pie, column, and radial.

SESSION 8.2

1. Static HTML pages cannot be used to update a database and so are not browser specific. Data Access Pages allow database updates and require specific browser technology.

2. Hyperlinks use addresses to point to another object. Absolute addresses contain all of the components while relative addresses omit some components. The missing components are assigned the values of the current page.

3. Static Web pages do not maintain any connection to the original data and so must be reexported to display updated data.

4. The Record Navigation toolbar displays on a Data Access Page and is used to edit, filter, and move through displayed records.

task reference *summary*

Task	Page #	Preferred Method
Create a Microsoft Graph	AC 8.4	• Click the **Reports** object in the Database Window • Click **New** to activate the New Report dialog box • Select **Chart Wizard**, use the drop-down list to select the query or table containing the data to be charted, and then click **OK** to initiate the Chart Wizard • Follow the instructions to select the field(s) with the data to be charted, select the chart type, specify the layout, and add a chart title
Importing with an unbound object frame on a form or report	AC 8.11	• Open the Design View of the form or report to contain the imported object • Click the **Unbound Object Frame** tool in the toolbox • Click and drag the area on the form or report that will contain the object • In the Microsoft Access dialog box • Click **Create From File** • Browse to the file for import • Click the Link check box to create a linked object or leave it unclicked to create an embedded object • Click **OK**

task reference summary

Task	Page #	Preferred Method

Import or link to another Access database	AC 8.16	• Open the Access database that is to contain the imported data
		• Open the **File** menu, point to **Get External Data**, and then do one of the following:
		  • Click **Import** to create Access tables from the external data
		  • Click **Link Tables** to create links to tables that remain in the source location
		• In the Import or Link dialog box
		  • Use the Files of Type drop-down list to select **Microsoft Office Access (*.mdb, *.mda, *.mde)** as the type of file to be linked or imported
		  • Use the Look in box to select the drive, folder, and filename of the file to be imported or linked
		  • Select the import tables and click **Import**

Import or link to an Excel spreadsheet	AC 8.18	• Open the Access database that is to contain the imported data
		• Open the **File** menu, point to **Get External Data**, and then click **Import**
		  • Click **Import** to create Access tables from the external data
		  • Click **Link Tables** to create links to tables that remain in the source location
		• In the Import or Link dialog box
		  • Use the Files of Type drop-down list to select **Microsoft Excel (*.xls)** as the type of file to be linked or imported
		  • Use the Look in box to select the drive, folder, and filename of the file to be imported or linked
		  • Follow the Import Spreadsheet Wizard instructions

Export an Access object to Microsoft Word	AC 8.22	• Open the Access database with the object to be exported
		• Select the object to be exported in the Database Window (it is best to preview the object before exporting)
		• Open the **Tools** menu, point to **Office Links**, and then either
		  • Select **Merge It with Microsoft Word** to use an Access table or query as the data source for a Word merge document
		  or
		  • Select **Publish It with Microsoft Word** to create an .rtf file in the default database folder (usually C:\ My Documents or the folder containing the database) with the same name as the exported object

Export an Access object to an Excel spreadsheet	AC 8.23	• Open the Access database that contains the data to be exported • Select the object to be exported in the Database Window (it is best to preview the object before exporting) • Open the **Tools** menu, point to **Office Links**, and then click **Analyze It with Microsoft Excel**

Export an Access object to a static HTML page	AC 8.26	• Open the Access database that contains the data to be exported
		• Select the object to be exported in the Database Window (it is best to preview the object before exporting)
		• Open the **File** menu and click **Export**
		• In the Export To dialog box
		  • Use the Save In box to select the drive and folder for the Web page
		  • Set the Save As Type to **HTML Documents (*.html; *.htm)**
		  • In the File Name box, enter the name for the Web page (it is best not to use spaces in these names)
		  • **Save Formatted** should be clicked to retain the formatting applied to the datasheet in Access and activate the next two options
		  • Check **AutoStart** to display the page in your default browser
		  • In the HTML Output Options dialog box
		    • Apply an HTML template to standardize formatting (Optional)
		    • Click **OK**

Use Internet Explorer to view a static HTML page	AC 8.28	• Open Access • From the **View** menu, pause over **Toolbars** and then click **Web** • On the Web toolbar, drop down the **Go** list and select **Open Hyperlink**

task reference *summary*

Task	Page #	Preferred Method
		• Click the **Browse** button in the Open Internet Address dialog box • Use the Browse dialog box to navigate to the file to be viewed • Select the file and click **Open** • Click **OK**
Use the Page Wizard to create a Data Access Page	AC 8.30	• Open the database containing the data for the Data Access Page • Click the **Pages** object in the Database Window • Double-click **Create data access page by using wizard** • Follow the Wizard instructions
Repair broken Data Access Page links	AC 8.38	• Open the Data Access Page with a broken database link in Design View • Click **Update Link** in the informational dialog box • Navigate to the network folder containing the Data Access Page • Select the page and click **OK** • Click **OK** in the dialog box explaining that the connection needs to be repaired • On the right-hand side of the Data Access Page Design View, click the **Page connection properties** option in the Field List Window • On the Connection tab, click the ellipsis (…) and update the database name • Click **Open** • Click the **Test Connection** button • When the test works, click **OK** • Click **OK** again to end the update
Importing an HTML document as an Access table	AC 8.39	• Open the database to hold the imported table • Verify that the layout of the data to be imported is either a list or a table • On the **File** menu, point to **Get External Data**, and then click **Import** • Select the HTML file for import and click **Import** (be sure to set the Files of Type to HTML documents) • Complete the Wizard dialog boxes
Construct a Web page or file hyperlink	AC 8.43	• Open the form, report, or Data Access Page in Design View • Click the Insert Hyperlink 🔗 button in the toolbox and drag the display area on the form, report, or Data Access Page • In the Insert Hyperlink dialog box • Select the type of object to **Link to** (Existing File or Web Page, Object in This Database, Create New Page, or E-Mail Address) • Enter the **Text to display** for the hyperlink (if this is blank, the URL will display) • Enter the **Screen Tip text** (if this is blank, the URL displays when the user pauses the cursor over the link) • In the Address box, type or browse to the path of a file or a URL • Click **OK**

TRUE/FALSE

1. A chart based on all the data in a table is called a record-bound chart.

2. A pie chart is best suited for showing how several series of data change over time.

3. Linked data must be edited in the application that created it.

4. Data imported from Microsoft Excel cannot contain column headings in the first row of the worksheet.

5. HTML tags instruct the Web browser on how to format page content and are enclosed in {}.

6. A URL is a pointer to an object such as a Web page, e-mail address, or other file.

FILL-IN

1. An _____ combines the technologies of an intranet and the Internet.

2. A company that sells the use of its Internet connection is a(n) _____.

3. _____ allow a database table to be updated from a Web browser.

4. HTML instructions are called _____.

5. An HTML _____ can be imported into Access as a table.

6. A Web page with content that doesn't change or link to the database is a(n) _____ Web page.

7. Saving Microsoft Access data to a format that can be used by another application such as Microsoft Word is called _____.

MULTIPLE CHOICE

1. When a Data Access Page is moved or renamed, the _____ to its Microsoft Access database must be updated.
   a. implied connection
   b. explicit connection
   c. relation
   d. link

2. Which of the following can be specified when creating a hyperlink in Microsoft Access?
   a. display text
   b. Screen Tip
   c. Web page address
   d. all of the above

3. Built-in artistic templates that can be applied to Data Access Pages are called _____.
   a. Themes
   b. Formats
   c. Encrypting
   d. none of the above

4. Data Access Pages allow database data to be viewed and updated using a(n) _____.
   a. plug in
   b. Microsoft Access player
   c. Web browser
   d. all of the above

5. A(n) _____ Web page does not change to reflect updates to the data stored in the associated Microsoft Access database.
   a. fixed
   b. static
   c. auto
   d. printed

review of concepts

REVIEW QUESTIONS

Each of the following topics should be addressed in one to three paragraphs.

1. Why would you use a template when creating Web pages from Access objects?

2. Why is the Access Web toolbar important?

3. Discuss the components of a hyperlink.

4. The address provided in a hyperlink specifies a protocol. What is this?

5. Why are the toolbox tools different for Data Access Pages and Reports?

CREATE THE QUESTION

For each of the following answers, create the question.

ANSWER	QUESTION
1. Import Wizard	_____
2. A column chart	_____
3. The legend	_____
4. Unbound Object Frame	_____
5. The linked check box	_____
6. OLE	_____
7. Destination application	_____

FACT OR FICTION

For each of the following, determine whether the statement is fact, fiction, or both and present your arguments for that conclusion.

1. Embedding an object is always the best option when you want to maintain only one copy of the object.

2. Object linking and embedding can be used to import and export all file formats.

3. Imported Excel data can be placed in an Access table or an Unbound Object Frame.

4. The Office Links feature is a simple way to share features of other Office products.

5. The Internet is the only way to share Access forms, reports, and data.

6. Once created and placed on a Data Access Page, the formatting of a chart cannot be updated.

7. A Record Navigation toolbar is used to allow users to move from record to record in a Data Access Page.

practice

1. Altamonte High School Booster Club Donation Tracking—Part V: Sharing Database Data

The Altamonte Boosters database has been successfully secured and data validation added to ensure data integrity. Now it is time to look at options for sharing data that do not impact security and integrity. The leadership believes that importing and exporting appropriate file formats will allow them to share data using e-mail attachments. The organization has a secured area on the school's Web server that can be used to share Web documents with authorized members.

1. Start Access and open **ac08AltamonteBoosters.mdb**

tip: *You cannot use your copy of the database from the previous chapter since there have been modifications for this chapter*

2. Use the Query Wizard to create a query that totals the donations made for each class of donor. These data will be charted
   a. From the **Boosters** table move the **DonationClass** field to the Selected Fields list
   b. From the **Donations** table move the **DonationAmount** field to the Selected Fields list
   c. From the **DonationClass** table move the **ClassDescription** field to the Selected Fields list
   d. Click **Next**

FIGURE 8.42
DonationsByClassChart

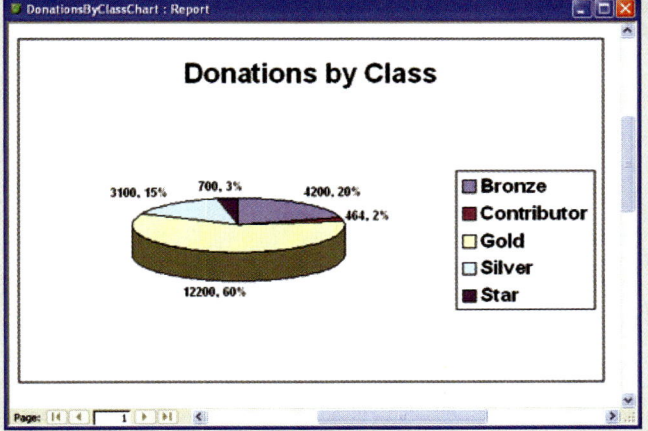

   e. Select the **Summary** Option button and then use the Summary Options button to **Sum** DonationAmount
   f. Click **Next**
   g. Name the query **DonationsByClass** and click **Finish**
   h. Close the Query window after verifying the result

3. Select the Reports object from the Database Window
   a. Click the **New** button
   b. Select the **Chart Wizard**, select **DonationsByClass** as the data source, and click **OK**

4. In the Chart Wizard
   a. Select **ClassDescription** and **Sum of DonationAmount** as the fields for the chart and click **Next**
   b. Select **3-D Pie** as the chart type and then click **Next**
   c. Preview the chart and then click **Next**
   d. Title the chart **Donations by Class** and click **Finish** (see Figure 8.42)
   e. Double-click on the chart in Design View to open Microsoft Graph
      i. Right-click in the chart area (not on the pie itself) and select **Chart Options**
      ii. On the Data Labels tab check **Values** and **Percentage**
      iii. Click **OK**
   f. Enlarge the chart area by dragging a sizing handle to be 5 inches wide by 4 inches tall

5. Close and save the form, naming it **DonationsByClassChart**

6. Open the DonationsByClassChart in Report View to preview your work and then close it

7. Save the DonationsByClassChart as a static HTML page

8. Exit Access if your work is complete

2. ScaleModels.com—Part I: Charting Database Data

ScaleModels.com uses the Internet to sell scale models of classic cars. The storefront deals largely with American classics scaled to 1/18, 1/24, 1/42, or 1/64 actual size. Currently the Web site is being manually maintained, but since a product list is being developed in Microsoft Access, you have been asked to create prototype Data Access Pages that could be used instead. Owner Rico Juarez believes that Data Access Pages will improve customer service by allowing them to see what is actually in inventory and reduce the current overhead required to continually update static Web pages.

1. Start Access and open **ac08ScaleModels.mdb**

2. Use the Query Wizard to create a query that totals QtyOnHand by Make. These data will be charted

   a. Select **Make** and **QtyOnHand** from the Catalog table

   b. Click Next

   c. Select the **Summary** Option button and then use the Summary Options button to sum QtyOnHand and click **OK**

   d. Click **Next**

   e. Name the query **QtyOnHandByMake**

3. Select the Reports object from the Database Window

   a. Click the **New** button

   b. Select the Chart Wizard, select **QtyOnHandByMake** as the data source, and click **OK**

4. In the Chart Wizard

   a. Select all QtyOnHandByMake fields to be in the chart and click **Next**

   b. Select **3-D Pie** as the chart type and click **Next**

   c. Preview the chart and click **Next**

   d. Accept the default chart name by clicking Finish

5. Change to Report Design View and double-click on the chart to open Microsoft Graph

   a. Right-click in the chart area (not on the pie itself) and select **Chart Options**

   b. Edit the Chart Title to **Quantity on hand by Make**

   c. Use the Legend tab to turn off the legend display

   d. Use the Data Labels tab to display both the category name and value on each pie wedge

   e. Click **OK**

   f. Use the sizing handles to make the chart 5 inches wide by 3 inches tall

6. Click outside of the chart area to close Microsoft Graph and change to Report View to evaluate the results obtained

7. Return to Report Design View and double-click the chart to edit it

   a. Enlarge the chart area to 6.5 inches wide by 4 inches tall

   b. Double-click one of the data labels to open the Format Data Labels dialog box, and change the font size to 10-point

   c. Verify your updates in Report View (see Figure 8.43)

   d. Close the report saving it as **QtyOnHandByMake**

8. If your work is complete, exit Access; otherwise, continue to the next assignment

FIGURE 8.43

Quantity on Hand by Make chart

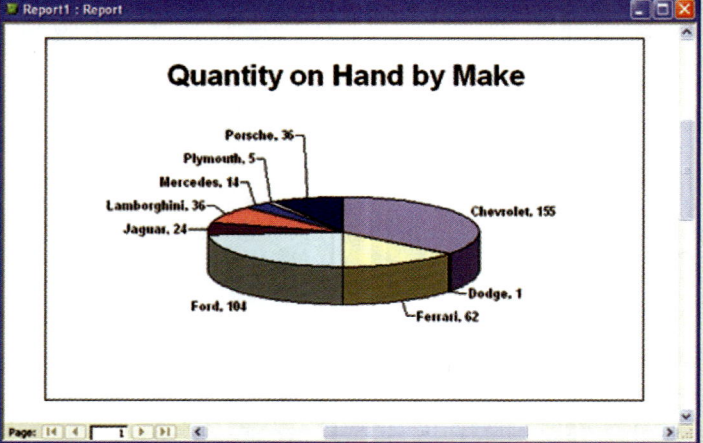

challenge!

1. Altamonte High School Booster Club Donation Tracking—Part VI: Exploring Alternatives for Sharing the Database

The Altamonte Boosters' fund-raising drive is complete and it is time to publish the results for the next meeting.

1. If you did not complete the Practice project for this chapter, start Access and open **ac08AltamonteBoosters.mdb** and complete it

tip: *You can use your copy of the database from the Practice project in this chapter. You cannot use your copy of the database from the previous chapter since there have been modifications for this chapter*

2. Review the chart created in the Practice steps and then open Microsoft Word and write a brief (3–4 line) summary of what the chart presents. Save the document as **ac08AltamonteSummary.doc**

3. Open the DonationsByClassChart report in Design View

   a. Enlarge the report by dragging the Detail and Page Footer borders

   b. Use an Unbound Object control to import (embed) ac08AltamonteSummary.doc and position it below the chart

   c. Double-click on the unbound object to enter edit mode and adjust the margins to the size of your form (see Figure 8.44)

tip: *You may need to enlarge the form to adjust the right margin and then reduce the size again*

   d. Preview your work, update as needed, and save

4. From the Pages object of the Database Window

   a. Use the Page Wizard to create a Data Access Page based on the Boosters table named **AltamonteBoosters**

   b. Include all fields from the Boosters table

   c. Sort by Name

   d. Make the title **Altamonte H. S. Boosters**

   e. Use the View button to preview the page (see Figure 8.45)

tip: *Select a DonationClass, then click the + to the left to view the boosters for that DonationClass*

   f. Use the AltamonteBoosters Data Access Page to add a record for **Pierre Verrizen** in DonationClass **3**. Supply the remaining data

5. Exit Access if your work is complete

FIGURE 8.44

Fund-raising chart and description from Word

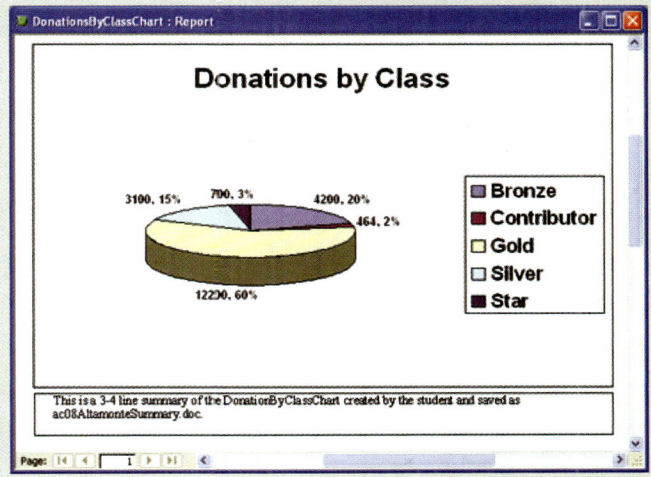

FIGURE 8.45

AltamonteBoosters Data Access Page

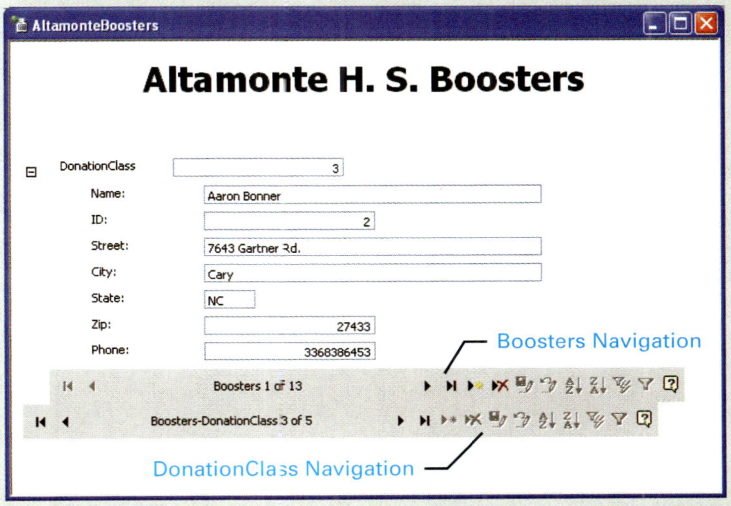

2. ScaleModels.com—Part II: Data Access Pages

Design of the ScaleModels.com database is complete, and it is time to evaluate the use of Data Access Pages to create interactive Web pages based on live data.

1. Start Access and open your copy of **ac08ScaleModels.mdb.** If you did not complete the ScaleModels.com Practice exercise for this chapter, do so now

2. Review the chart created in the Practice steps and then open Microsoft Word
   a. In Microsoft Word, write a brief description (3–4 lines) of what the chart represents
   b. Close Microsoft Word and save the document as **ac08ScaleModelSummary.doc**

3. In Microsoft Access, open the QtyOnHandByMake report in Design View
   a. Use an Unbound Object control to import (embed) ac08ScaleModelSummary.doc
   b. Double-click on the unbound object to enter edit mode and adjust the margins to the size of the form
   c. Preview your work, update as needed, and save

4. From the Pages object of the Database Window
   a. Use the Page Wizard to create a Data Access Page based on the Catalog table

   b. Include all fields for the Catalog table
   c. Group by Make and sort by Model
   d. Name the page **Catalog**

5. From the Design View of the Catalog Data Access Page
   a. Add a page title of **Scale Model Catalog**
   b. Use an Image control to insert **ac08ScaleModel.gif** to the left of the title
   c. Adjust the image size so that the title fits on one line
   d. Switch to Page View and test the Data Access Page by adding your favorite car to the table (see Figure 8.46)

6. From the Pages object of the Database Window
   a. Use the Page Wizard to create a Data Access Page based on the QtyOnHandByMake query
   b. Include all fields
   c. Group by Make
   d. Accept the default page name
   e. Add a title and the ac08ScaleModel.GIF image
   f. Switch between Page View and Design View making any necessary adjustments
   g. Close and save

7. If your work is complete, exit Access; otherwise, continue to the next assignment

FIGURE 8.46
Scale Model Catalog Data Access Page

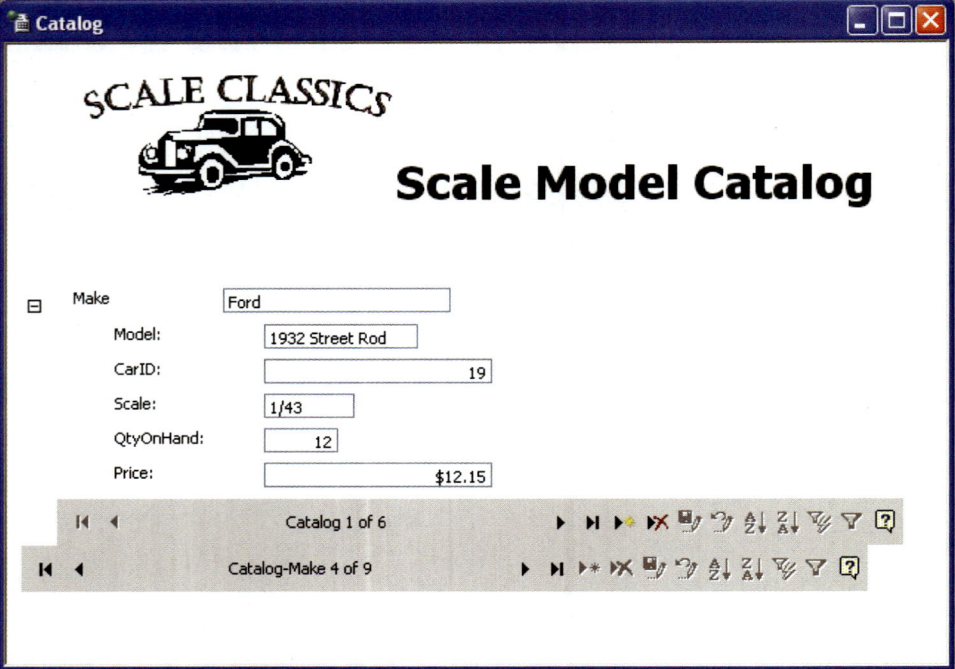

1. Curbside Recycling

Earth First, the parent company of Curbside Recycling, is sponsoring a recycling competition between the cities that it serves. The status of the competition will be posted on the Web site and the city that recycles the most will receive a donation earmarked for park renovation.

1. Start Access and open **ac08CurbsideRecycling.mdb**

tip: *You cannot use your copy of the database from the previous chapter since there have been modifications for this chapter*

2. Use the **Get External Data** option of the **File** menu to import **ac08Competition.xls**

tip: *Use Excel to preview this file before import*

  a. There are no headings in the file

  b. Import to a new table

  c. Name Field1 **City** and Field2 **TonsRecycled**

  d. Let Access set the key

  e. Name the table **Competition**

  f. Open Competition to verify the import and then close it

3. Create a Data Access Page with a chart based on the Competition table

  a. Click the **Pages** object in the database Window and open a new page in Design View

  b. Set the title to **Earth First Recycling Competition**

  c. Click the Office Chart tool in the toolbox and then click an area on the page surface that covers the width of the page

  d. Click the Office Chart to open the Commands and Options dialog box if necessary

  e. In the Commands and Options dialog box

    i. Click **Data from the following Web page item** and then click **DataSource Details** button

    ii. Select **Competition** from the Data member table, view, or cube name drop-down list

tip: *If you lose the Commands and Options dialog box, right-click on the chart*

    iii. Click the **Type** tab and select **Bar** and **3-D clustered**

    iv. Close the Commands and Options dialog box

  f. Use the Field List button on the Standard toolbar if you do not have a field list displaying

    i. Open the Competition field list using the +

    ii. Drag **City** to the Drop Category Field area of the chart

    iii. Drag **TonsRecycled** to the Drop Data Fields Here area of the chart

    iv. Save the Data Access page as **Competition**

  g. Adjust the chart height and width for readability

4. Open Competition in Internet Explorer

  a. Drop down the City list and uncheck one to see the chart result (see Figure 8.47)

  b. You can change the data in the Drop areas too

5. Exit Access if your work is complete

FIGURE 8.47

Internet Explorer with Competition Data Access Page

2. Sharing xXtreMeSportz.com Data

Casey Lewis, Evan Roach, and Wei Wong are extreme sports enthusiasts. They play hockey, skateboard, and snowboard. After discussing it with many of their friends the three decided to create a cooperative organization for extreme sports aficionados. The main goal of the co-op would be to act as a clearinghouse for equipment and events so that members would be able to purchase supplies, clothing, and event tickets at a bulk reduced rate.

After enlisting over 300 local members, the partners launched the www.xXtreMeSportz.com Web site to communicate their services and recruit additional members. Keeping the Web site updated with new services has become too time-consuming, so the partners have agreed to use Data Access Pages from a Microsoft Access database.

1. Open Access and then open **ac08xXtreMeSportz.mdb**

2. Current services are maintained in a Microsoft Excel spreadsheet named ac08xXtreMeSportzLinks.xls
    a. Use Excel to view the contents of this file
    b. Use the **Get External Data** option of the **File** menu to import the contents of this file into the **Links** table. The first row of the spreadsheet contains the Column Headings
    c. Verify the validity of the import

3. Use the Report Wizard to create a report based on the Links table
    a. Include all fields from the table except LinkID and Group by LinkCategory
    b. Customize the report to ensure that all Link data display. Set the Can Grow property of the Description text box to **Yes**
    c. Make the title **xXtreMeSportz.com Links**
    d. When you are satisfied, export the report as a static HTML page named **xXtreMeSportzLinks**

4. Use the Page Wizard to create a Data Access Page based on the Links table
    a. Include all table fields
    b. Group the data by LinkCategory
    c. Name the page **LinkUpdatePage**

5. Customize the LinkUpdatePage in Design View
    a. Set the title to **xXtreMeSportz Links Update**
    b. Use an Image control to insert a **ac08xXtreMeSportz.gif** to the left of the title
    c. Adjust the title and image so they display on one line
    d. Add the **Blends** theme
    e. Review your changes in Page View and make any needed updates (see Figure 8.48)

6. Close the database and exit Access if your work is complete

FIGURE 8.48

xXtreMeSportz.com Web pages

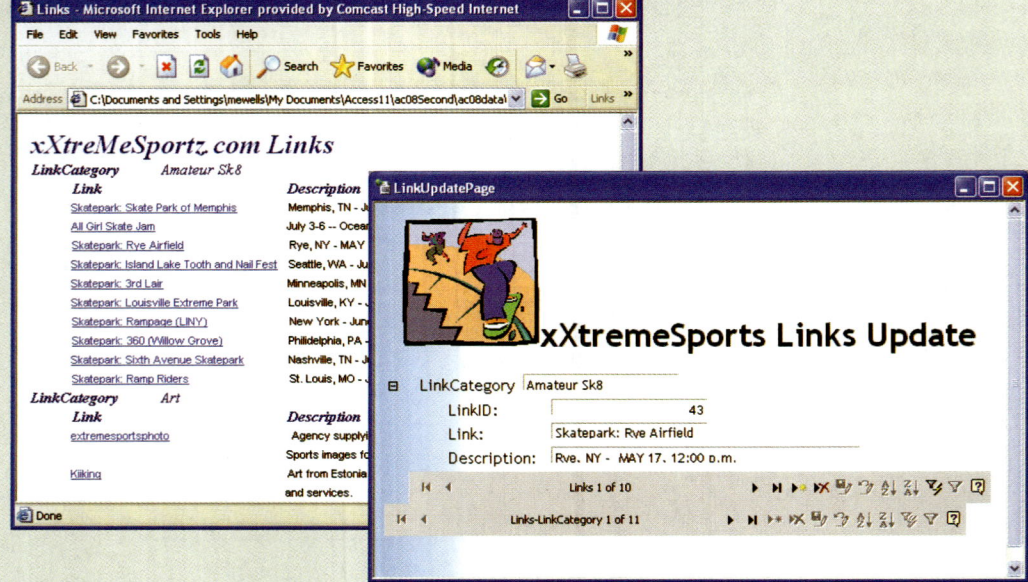

1. Academic Software

Academic Software is a fairly large organization with diverse data needs. In the past users have created the data that they needed to complete each job. Now that a functioning database is available, the goal is to use import, export, and Web capabilities to avoid re-creating data.

1. Use your favorite search engine to locate two foreign language software titles suitable for academic language study. Be sure to note the prices too

2. Start Access and open **ac08Software.mdb**

tip: *You cannot use your copy of the database from the previous chapter since there have been modifications for this chapter*

3. Several users have been tracking new software titles in an Excel spreadsheet. Use the import capabilities of Access to add these data to tblSoftware

   a. Open tblSoftware to view the existing 12 records

   b. Close tblSoftware

   c. Import **ac08SoftwareTitles.xls**

tip: *Open it in Excel first to review the content*

   i. The file does have column headings in the first row

   ii. Proceed with the import even if there are warnings

FIGURE 8.49

Software Data Access Page

   d. Open tblSoftware to verify the addition of 12 records

tip: *Only 10 of the 12 records from Excel were imported because the other 2 records violate the validation rule set for Category (="MTH" Or ="ENG" Or ="SCI")*

   e. Add "LNG" to the validation rule and repeat the import

tip: *Duplicate key violations will keep the 10 records that imported the first time from being duplicated*

   f. Open tblSoftware, verify that the two LNG software titles have been added, and close the table

4. From the Pages object of the Database Window

   a. Use the Page Wizard to create a Data Access Page based on the tblSoftware table named **Software TitlesbyVendor**

   b. Include all fields from the tblSoftware table

   c. Sort by Name

   d. Make the title **Software Titles by Vendor**

   e. Apply the Technology theme

   f. Use the View button to preview the page (see Figure 8.49)

tip: *Select a VendorCode, then click the + to the left to view the titles for that vendor*

   g. Use the Software Data Access Page to add a record for the software titles located on the Internet. Add them to VendorCode **EI** with a Category of **LNG**

5. Exit Access if your work is complete

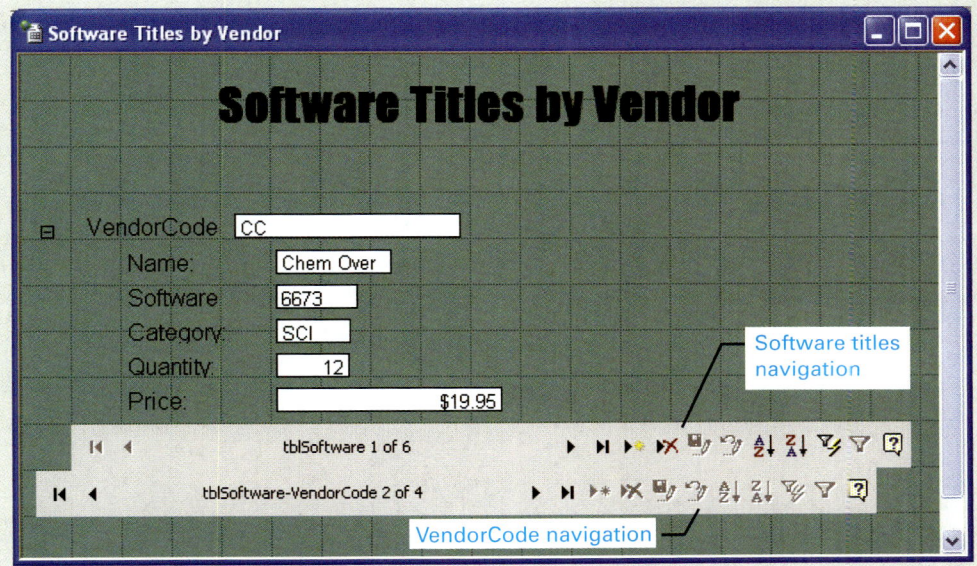

around the world

1. TechRocks Seminars

TechRocks Seminars is a worldwide organization with requirements to share data, analysis, and update capabilities. Management has decided to try using Data Access Pages to allow all of the sites to enter students into a class.

1. Start Access and open **ac08Seminars.mdb**

tip: *You cannot use your copy of the database from the previous chapter since there have been modifications for this chapter*

2. Activate the **Pages** object in the Database Window
   a. Activate the Page Wizard
   b. Set the **Enrollment** table as the data source and move all of its fields to the field list
   c. Group the data by **SeminarID**
   d. Sort by LastName and FirstName
   e. Name the page **Enrollment**

3. In the Design View of the Enrollment Data Access Page
   a. Make the page title **Seminar Enrollment**
   b. Use an Image control to add **ac08Seminars.gif** positioned as shown in Figure 8.50
   c. Add a scrolling text box the width of the page and below the data area with the text **New Class! Data Access Pages. Limited Enrollment**, and set the Font size to **Medium**

tip: *Right-click on the marquee and select **Element Properties***

   d. Add the **Corporate** theme
   e. Adjust the height, width, and position of the contents to match Figure 8.50 and fully display the data

4. Open **Enrollment**
   a. Move to seminar TR105
   b. Move through the records and then add two new records for **Kate Whittey** and **Thomas Elliott**. Make up the remaining data

5. Create a Data Access Page from the StudentListing query
   a. Activate the Page Wizard and select **StudentListing** as the data source
   b. Use all of the StudentListing fields
   c. Group by **SeminarID**
   d. Sort by LastName and FirstName

6. Use Design View to customize the page
   a. Apply the **Corporate** theme
   b. Add spaces between words in labels
   c. Add the title **StudentListing** with **ac08Seminars.gif**
   d. Move Description, LastName, FirstName, Place, Phone, Date, Time, and Hours to the Student Listing-SeminarID header

7. Exit Access if your work is complete

FIGURE 8.50

Enrollment Data Access Page

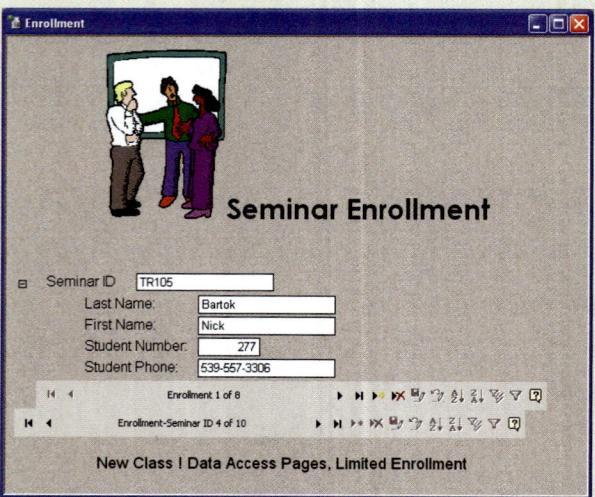

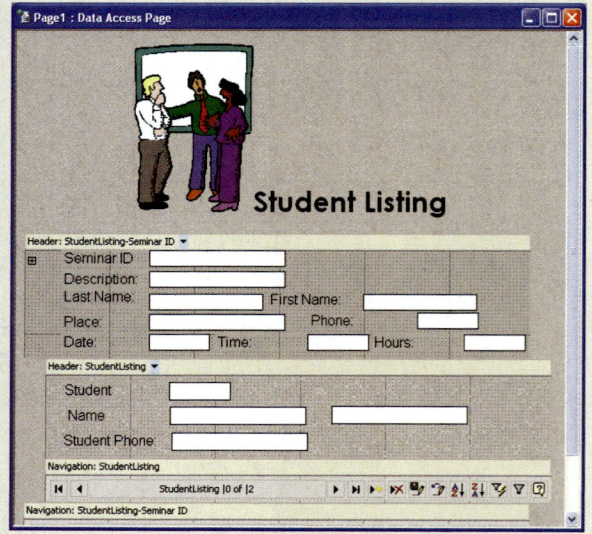

running project: tnt web design

Web Publishing from Access

TnT is continuing in its use of Access to gather and analyze data. It is time to develop the interfaces from the database to the Web site to provide current and accurate data and improve data sharing.

1. Start Access and open **ac08TnT.mdb**

tip: *You cannot use your copy of the database from the previous chapter since there have been modifications for this chapter*

2. Open the CustomerSites table and use the Hyperlink button on the Standard toolbar to update the following hyperlinks:
    a. MMB Holdings Site 1—Set the display text and Screen Tip to **MMB Holdings, Inc**. Remove the comma from the display text, and add the Address
    b. MMB Holdings Site 2—Set the display text and Screen Tip to **Your Holdings!** and add the address
    c. Omega Distributions—Set the display text and Screen Tip to **Omega Distributions** and add the address

tip: *While this process should be repeated for all of the links, for brevity we will just pretend that they are all displaying descriptive text and have addresses*

3. Export the CustomerSites table as a static Web page and then use Internet Explorer to review it. You should notice that the improperly entered hyperlinks display as text not links. The properly entered hyperlinks would work if the Web pages actually existed. This export has other problems we will not address (see Figure 8.51)

4. Export the EmployeesByJobClass report as a static Web page and then use Internet Explorer to review it. Notice that two HTML pages are created and that the navigation is automatically added to the bottom of each page. This is the public version of the report that cannot be updated

5. Create a Data Access Page based on the Employees table that will reside in a secure area of the intranet to update the Employees table
    a. Use all fields from the table
    b. Group by **JobClass** and sort by **LastName** and **FirstName**
    c. Check the **Apply theme** check box and then apply **Edge**
    d. Set the title to **Employees by Job Classification**
    e. Preview the result
6. Close Access if your work is complete

FIGURE 8.51
CustomerSites.html

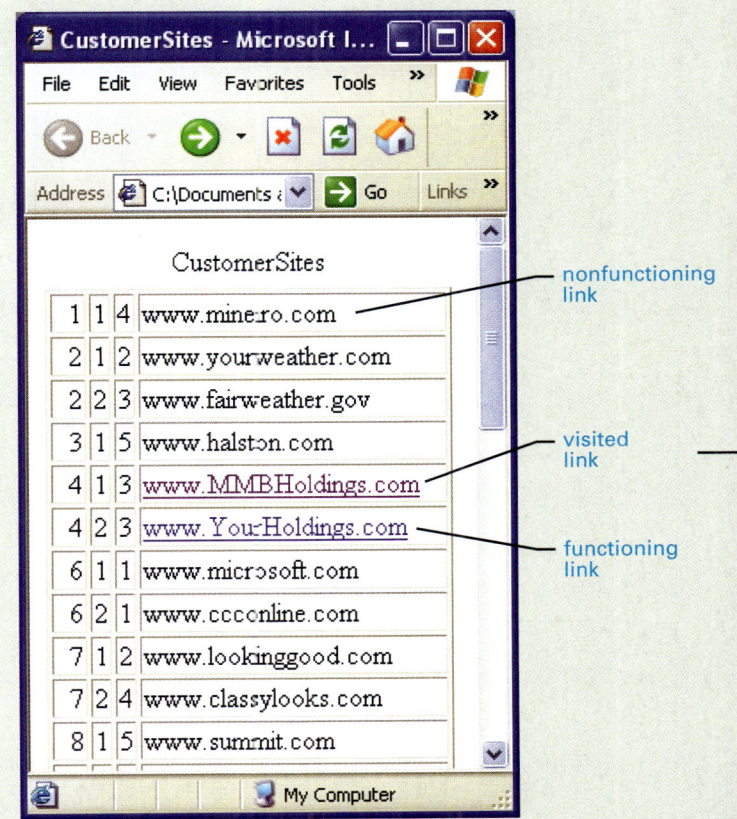

nonfunctioning link

visited link

functioning link

1. Sharing a Multitable Database to Invoice Customers

Locate your copy of the database named **ac07CustomersMultiTableDatabase.mdb** created in the Chapter 7 Analysis assignment. Use Microsoft Windows Explorer to create a copy of the file named **ac08CustomersMultiTableDatabase.mdb** and open the copy in Microsoft Access. Take a look at your current database objects and determine how to implement each of the following:

- Create a graph on a report page. Customize the graph to include a title and appropriate labels
- Embed data from either Microsoft Excel or Microsoft Word in the report
- Create a static HTML document from the report
- Create a Data Access Page with a title and image for at least one of your tables
- Include a hyperlink on your Data Access Page and apply a theme

2. Sharing a Multitable Database to Track Employees

Locate your copy of the database named **ac07EmployeesMultiTableDatabase.mdb** created in the Chapter 7 Analysis assignment. Use Microsoft Windows Explorer to create a copy of the file named **ac08EmployeesMultiTableDatabase.mdb** and open the copy in Microsoft Access. Take a look at your current database objects and determine how to implement each of the following:

- Create a graph on a report page. Customize the graph to include a title and appropriate labels
- Embed data from either Microsoft Excel or Microsoft Word in the report
- Create a static HTML document from the report
- Create a Data Access Page with a title and image for at least one of your tables
- Include a hyperlink on your Data Access Page and apply a theme

Creating a Multimedia Presentation

did you know?

ants *don't sleep.*

over *80 percent of professional boxers have suffered brain damage.*

the *first Oreo cookie was sold in 1912.*

dragonflies *are one of the fastest insects, flying 50 to 60 mph.*

a *pineapple is a berry.*

there *are 31,557,600 seconds in a year.*

frogs *live on every continent except _____.*

Chapter Objectives

- **Apply and customize Slide Transitions—MOS PP035-2-5**
- **Animate slide objects**
- **Insert and configure sound, movie, and animated GIF clips— MOS PP035-1-5**
- **Create a self-running presentation**
- **Use presentation rehearsal features—MOS PP035-4-3**

Teaching Vital Statistics with PowerPoint

Connor Mackenzie and his partner Margarita Gonzalez are medical trainers who work with families in crisis at the Center for Family Provided Medical Treatment. A wide range of medical events can cause a family member to require medical supervision and care on an ongoing basis. The level of care families need to learn to provide can be as simple as monitoring vital statistics or as complex as ongoing physical therapy or the administration of special medications.

Initially the center provided only individual planning and instruction to each family, but they came to realize that family members giving medical care needed a support group and a way to refresh and update their care skills. While providing individual care plans with training on how to furnish that treatment is critical, contact with other families is an effective way to relieve the stresses of constant care and provide ongoing training.

FIGURE 5.1
Vital statistics kiosk

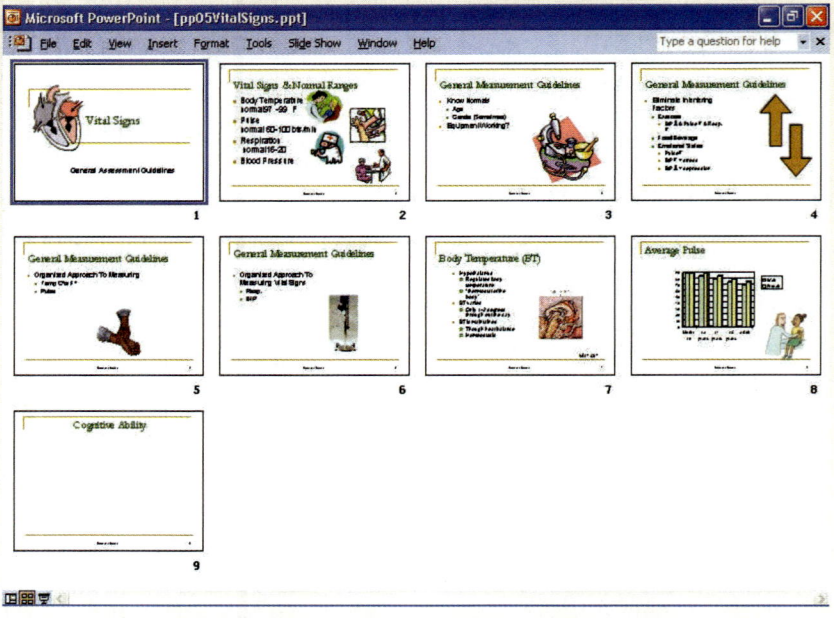

In addition to having gatherings for families, Connor and Margarita have developed short family seminars that encompass the basic skills needed by all family members. Each presentation is 30 minutes or less and covers appropriate skills and statistics for all patient groups.

Since the tradition of family care training has been one-on-one, Connor and Margarita will develop new presentations based on materials they have gathered. The most frequently used presentation describes common vital statistics and their norms. Caregivers must understand this foundational material before moving on to more specific instructions of how to assess a patient. This presentation has been ported to PowerPoint from a Word document and some relevant graphics added. Connor and Margarita want to add animations and sounds to create a self-running kiosk. With a self-running kiosk, family members will be able to review the material at their own convenience.

SESSION 5.1 USING ANIMATIONS

Animation is an important component of a compelling PowerPoint presentation. Motion of slide objects helps draw the audience's attention to important presentation points. During a slide show, animations control the way a slide enters and leaves the screen, how text moves on and off the screen, and how other slide objects behave. These behaviors were introduced in Chapter 3 with preset animations called Animation Schemes. While Animation Schemes are easy to apply and add interest to a presentation, they offer no variety and only text is animated. This session will address customized animation of any slide object.

Animating Slide Objects

Animation can be used to add motion to any slide object including text, graphics, and charts. Slide objects can be animated individually or in groups. For example, a line of text can be animated as a unit or each character can have motion.

Slide Transitions

The largest PowerPoint object that you can animate is a slide. *Slide Transitions* control the visual effect that displays between slides in a slide show. The available transitions range from mild to dramatic in their impact. All slides can use the same transition, or different transitions can be assigned to each slide.

It is often tempting to use a different transition between each slide, but this can be distracting if dramatic effects are being used. You should choose transitions that are appropriate for your audience and presentation content. More importantly you need to strike a balance between using unique transitions to make the presentation interesting and keeping the focus on the content.

---

task reference   **Apply a Slide Transition**

- Select the slide(s) the transition will be applied to. If no slide(s) is selected, the transition will be applied to all slides

- From the **Slide Show** menu select **Slide Transition**

- Select a transition effect

FIGURE 5.2

Slide Transition task pane

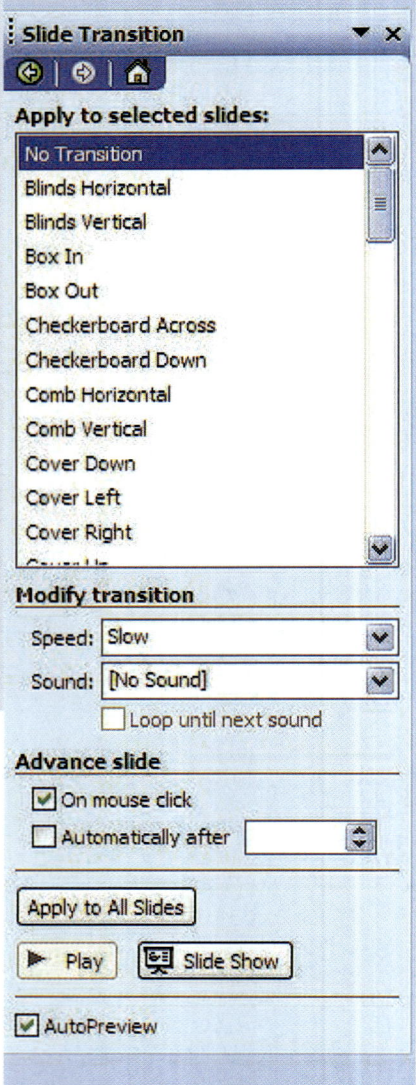

Adding transitions to VitalSigns.ppt:

1. Start PowerPoint and open **pp05VitalSigns.ppt**

2. Select slide 1

3. From the **Slide Show** menu select **Slide Transition** (Figure 5.2)

4. In the Slide Transition task pane, click **Shape Circle**

tip: *If AutoPreview is checked, the selected transition will be demonstrated on the current slide automatically*

5. Click the **Play** button to see the result

6. Press **F5** to start the slide show and view a full screen version of the transition

7. Press **Esc** to end the presentation

8. Set the transition for slide 2 to **Newsflash**

9. Set the transition for slide 3 to **Wheel Clockwise, 4 Spokes**

10. Set the transition for slide 4 to **Wheel Clockwise, 3 Spokes**

11. Set transitions that you find appealing for slides 5 through 9

12. Save the presentation as **<yourname>VitalSigns.ppt**

---

anotherword   . . . **on Setting Slide Transitions**

You can create the same transition settings for multiple slides by selecting the slides in the Outline pane and then setting the transition. Multiple contiguous slides can be selected by clicking the first slide and then holding the Shift key while clicking the last slide. Noncontiguous slides can be selected by clicking the first slide and then holding down the Ctrl key while clicking subsequent slides

---

For most presentations it is best to use the same or similar transitions for each slide. Similar transitions help the presentation to be more cohesive. You can use more dramatic transitions to indicate a topic change or the importance of a particular slide. To improve the effect of a transition, its speed and other *properties* can be customized.

Setting VitalSigns.ppt transition properties:

1. Move to slide 1 and make the following settings to the Slide Transitions panel on the task pane

   a. Set the Speed to **Fast**

   b. Set the sound to **Click**

   c. Check both Advance Slide options and set the time to 2 seconds (see Figure 5.3)

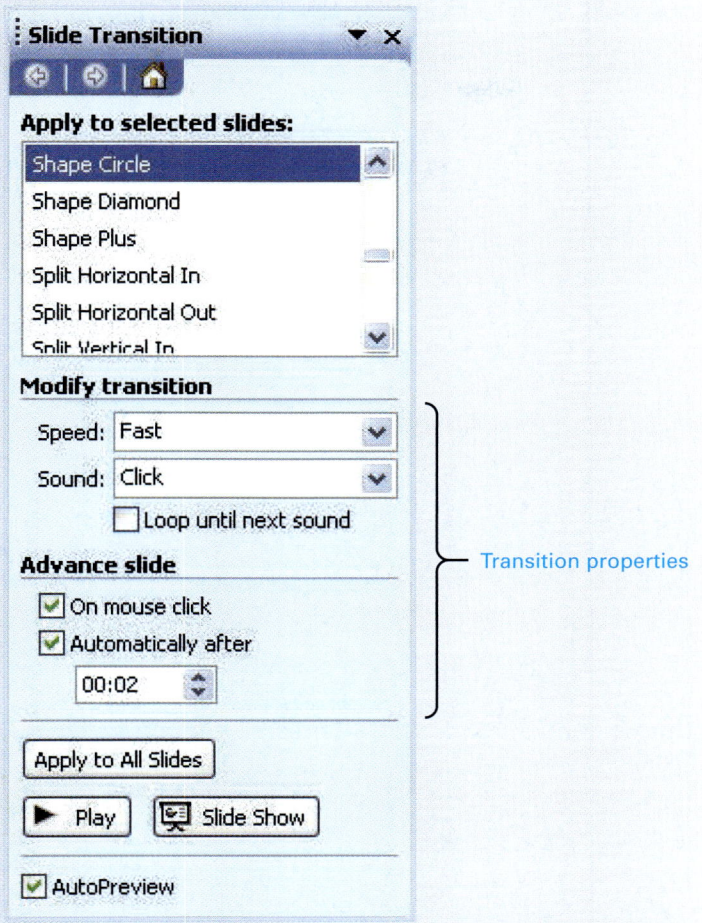

Transition properties

2. Move to slide 2

   a. Set the Speed to **Medium**

   b. Set the sound to **Chime**

   c. Do not set a time option for advancing the slide

3. Press **F5** to see the impact of these changes

4. Press the **Spacebar** to move to slide 2

5. Press **Esc** to end the presentation

    To improve their impact, transitions can be modified to control the pace and add a sound. The pace can be matched to a sound so that all of the elements of the transition begin and end together. *Slide timings* can be recorded while practicing the presentation or set in the Slide Transition pane. The timing options cause the presentation to advance to the next slide using a mouse click, a preset time period, or both.

---

task reference   Set Slide Timing While Rehearsing

- Activate the timing feature
  - On the **Slide Show** menu, click **Set Up Show**
  - Under **Advance slides**, click **Use timings, if present**
- Set the time for each slide
  - On the **Slide Show** menu click **Rehearse Timings**
  - Rehearse the show to set timings automatically as you advance
  - At the end of the show, click **Yes** to accept automatic timings or **No** to start again

---

anotherway
. . . to Set Timings for a Slide Show

When you know the speed that is appropriate for a presentation, you can set the times manually by repeating the following steps for each timed slide.

- Select the slide to be timed
- On the **Slide Show** menu, click **Slide Transition**
- In the task pane under Advance slide, scroll to the desired amount of time

Adding automatic timings to VitalSigns.ppt:

1. Click **Slide Show** menu, click **Set Up Show**

2. Under Advance slides, click **Use timings, if present**

3. Move to slide 1

4. Click the **Slide Show** menu and then click **Rehearse Timings**

5. Move through the presentation practicing your narration at the desired speed

6. When you reach the end of the slide show, answer **Yes** to save your times

tip: *Answering **No** will not save the times. To set new times return to step 2*

7. Review the times displayed in Slide Sorter view (see Figure 5.4)

8. Run the presentation without clicking to review the automatic timing

9. Press **Esc** to end the presentation

Automatic timings can be used to keep a speaker-led presentation on task, or to create a self-running kiosk. When the presentation is self-running, it can be initiated by a user or looped to continuously run. Self-running presentations often include sound files with slide narration that can be used to control slide timings as well.

Animating and Dimming Text

You can add motion to any object on a PowerPoint slide using the *Custom Animation* settings from the Custom Animation panel of the task pane. The preset Animation Schemes previously introduced use default settings to animate slide text. Using Custom Animations, each character of text on a slide can be controlled independently, grouped by word, or animated by paragraph.

Text can be animated on Entrance, Exit, or both using a wide range of standard motion paths or a custom path developed to exactly match slide layout. Emphasis like a font change, color change, spinning, and desaturation can be added. The effects chosen are determined by how dramatic you need your presentation to be.

FIGURE 5.4
Timings in Slide Sorter view

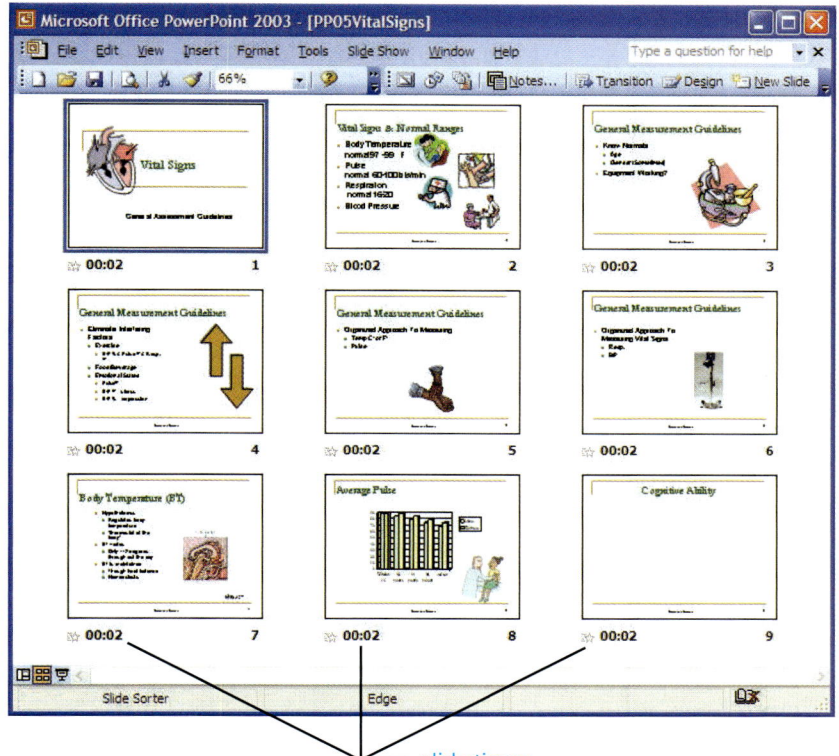

slide times

---

task reference Adding Custom Animations to Text

- In Normal view, select the text object to be animated

- From the task pane drop-down list select **Custom Animation**

- In the Custom Animation task pane click **Add Effects** and select the desired effect(s)

Adding Entrance animations to VitalSigns text:

1. Click **View**, click **Normal**, move to slide 1 and select the title placeholder containing the text *Vital Signs*

2. Click **Slide Show,** click **Set Up Show**, set the Advance Slides option to **Manually** to turn off the previously set timings, and then click **OK**

3. Click **Slide Show** and then click **Custom Animation**

4. In the Custom Animation pane, click **Add Effect**, pause over **Entrance**, and click **More Effects** to view the full list of available entrance effects (see Figure 5.5)

5. Preview several available options

tip: *Check Preview Effect and move the Add Entrance Effect dialog box to preview your selections*

FIGURE 5.5

Animating the title
placeholder

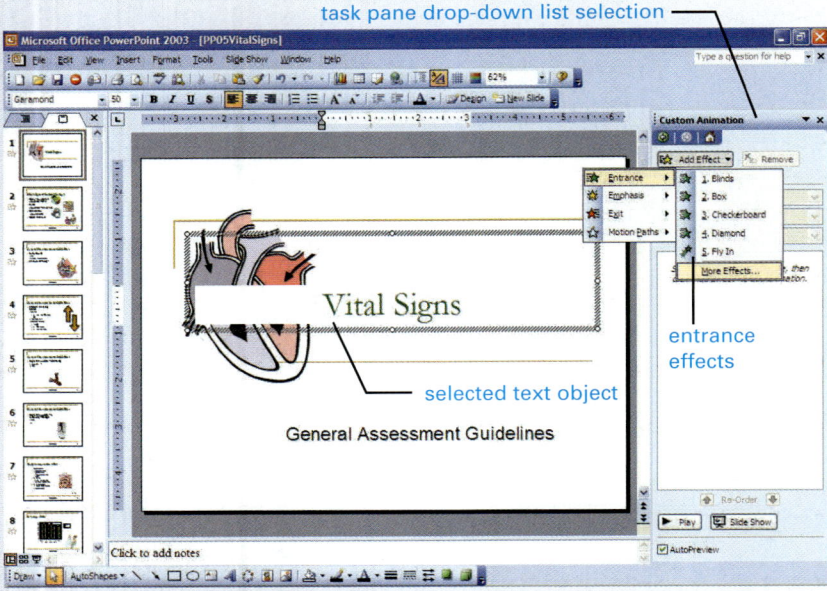

6. Click **Crawl In** and click **OK**

7. On the Custom Animation panel of the task pane

  a. Set the Direction to **From Left**

  b. Set the Speed to **Medium**

  c. Drop down the complete list of modifications, click **Effect Options**,
     and set the Animate text option to **By letter**

  d. Click **OK** (see Figure 5.6)

FIGURE 5.6

Modifying effect
properties

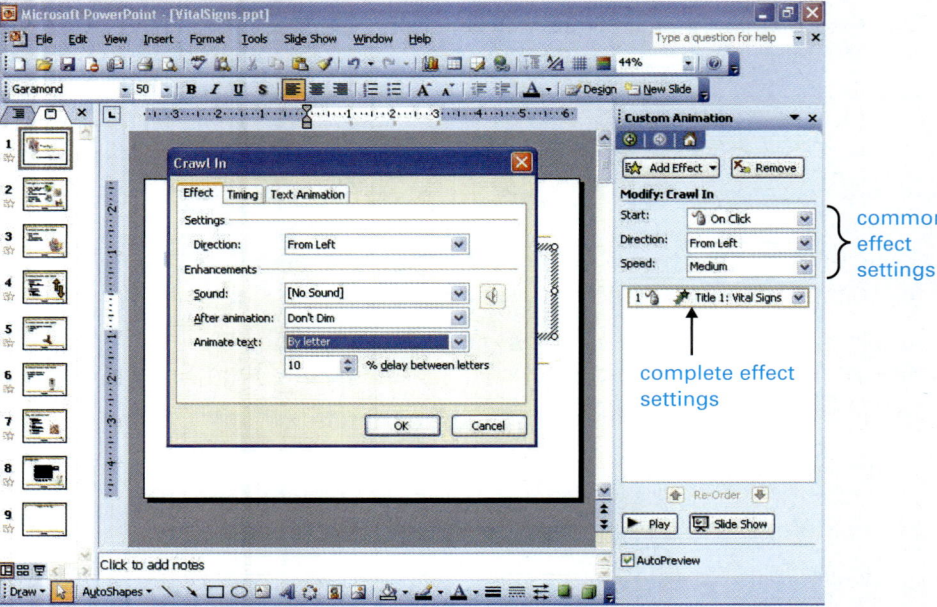

8. Click **Play** to preview the settings

tip: *You will not need to click to initiate each animation when the Play button is used. To click through the animations, use the Slide Show view*

9. Click the subtitle placeholder (General Assessment Guidelines)

   a. Set the Entrance effect to **Appear**

   b. Drop down the complete list of modifications for this effect, click **Effect Options**, and set the Animate text option to **By word** and click **OK**

10. Click **Play** to preview the settings, then press **Esc** to end the presentation

11. Save the presentation

Effects are placed in the Custom Animation list in the order that they are specified. A nonprinting number tag appears that identifies each animation on the slide. The number tag does not display during the slide show, but serves to uniquely identify each animation. Additional effects like a brush-on underline, change in text color, or spinning text can be applied to the text already displayed on a slide to add further emphasis.

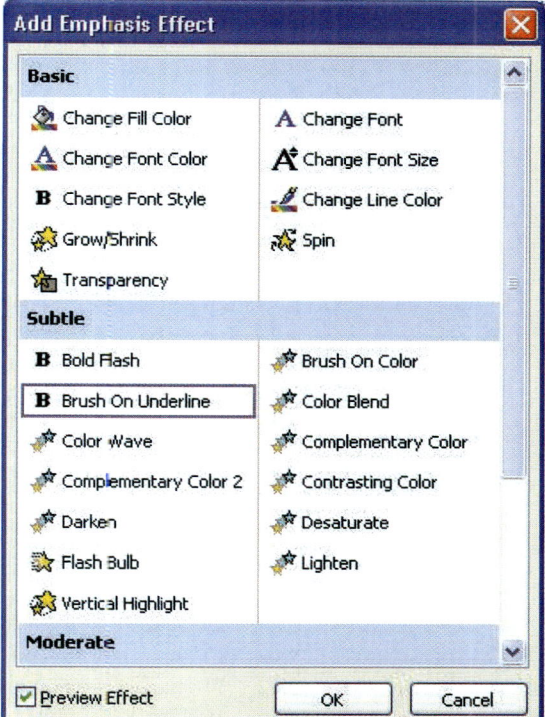

F I G U R E 5.7

Emphasis effects

Adding Emphasis animations to VitalSigns text:

1. Move to slide 1

2. Select the title placeholder

3. If necessary, select **Custom Animation** from the task pane drop-down list

4. Click the **Add Effect** button in the task pane, pause over **Emphasis**, and choose **More Effects** to view the full list of available Entrance effects

5. Select **Brush On Underline** (see Figure 5.7) and click **OK**

6. Click **Play** to preview the animations

The same basic effects that control how text enters a slide can be applied to their exit.

Adding Exit animations to VitalSigns text:

1. Make sure slide 1 is the active slide and that the title placeholder is selected

2. If necessary, select **Custom Animation** from the task pane drop-down list

3. Click the **Add Effect** button in the task pane, pause over **Exit**, and choose **More Effects** to view the full list of available Entrance effects (see Figure 5.8)

4. Select **Whip** (in the "Exciting" group) and click **OK**

5. Click **Play** to preview the animations

FIGURE 5.8

Exit effects

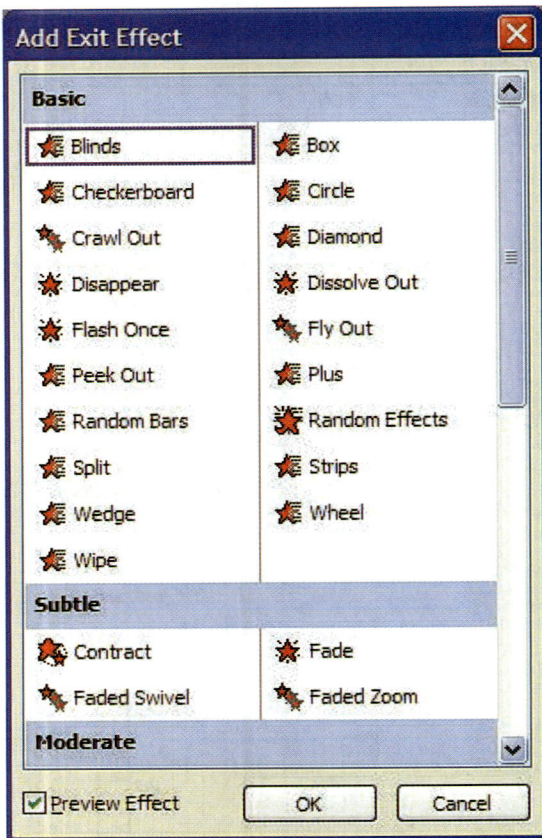

Animated text can have a ***dimming effect*** applied to it by changing its color. This feature is particularly useful in presenter-led or narrated presentations to help keep the audience on topic by dimming text that has already been discussed. Normally dimming is applied to the bulleted text contained in a body text placeholder. When there are multiple bullets, the animation of a bulleted list can be set to load all bullets as a unit, each bullet, or by word or each bullet letter.

Adding dimming effects to VitalSigns text:

1. Move to slide 2 and click in the body placeholder

2. If necessary, click **Custom Animation** from the task pane drop-down list

3. Click the **Add Effect** button in the task pane, pause over **Entrance**, and choose **Crawl In**. You may have to click **More Effects** if this is not available

4. Click the double carat to expand the Custom Animation list to display all of the components of this animation (see Figure 5.9)

5. Drop down the complete list of modifications for this effect and click **Effect Options** to open the dialog box

   a. Click the **Text Animation** tab, drop down the Group text list and review the options (Keep the *By 1st level paragraphs* selection)

tip: *The* As One Object *selection will move all bullets simultaneously*

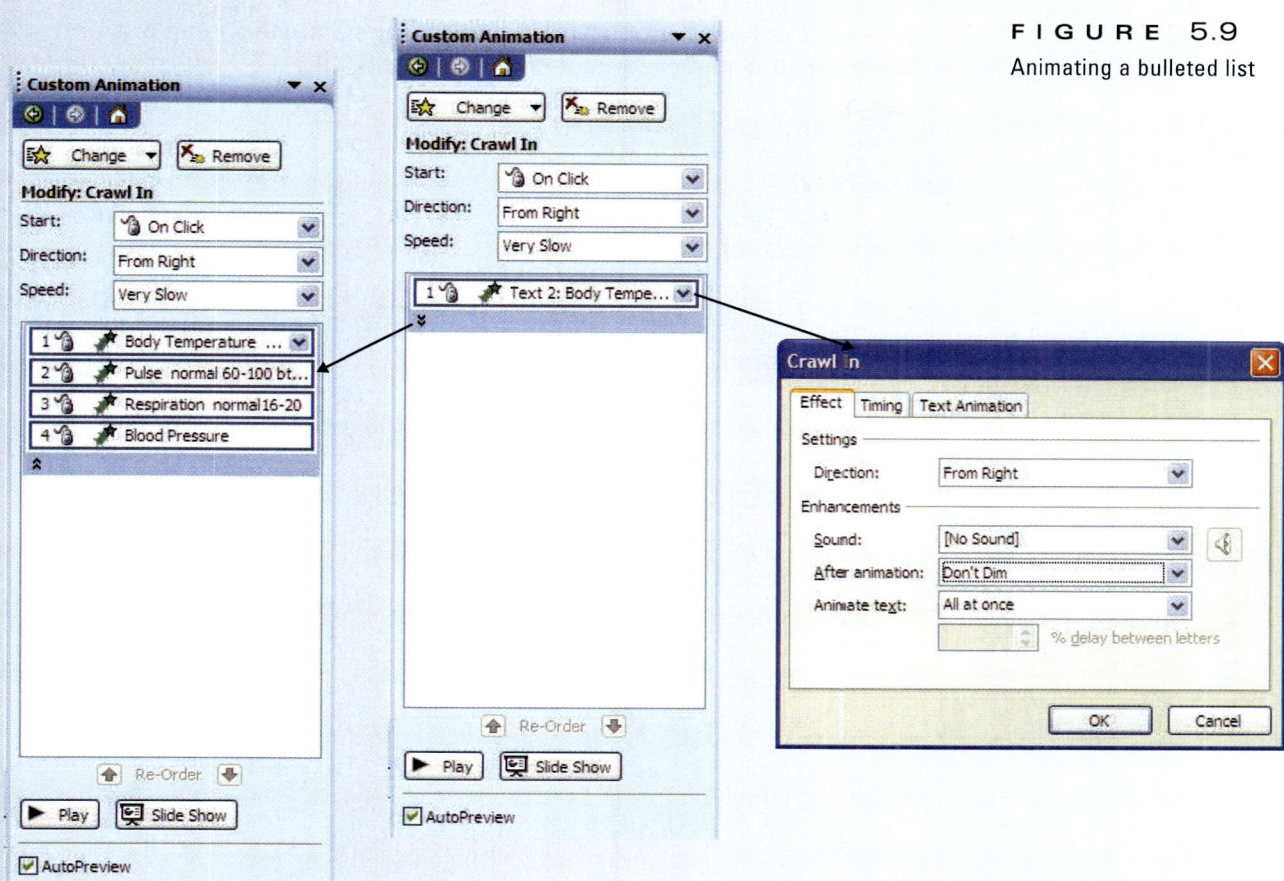

F I G U R E 5.9

Animating a bulleted list

b. Click the **Effect** tab, set the Direction option to **From Right**, the After Animation color to **gray**, and click **OK**

6. Click **Play** to preview the animations

The options of the Text Animation tab control how the text is grouped for animation. Set the animation level to correspond with the spoken component of the presentation. As you click through the bullets, the animation for the current bullet plays and any previous bullet will have the After Animation color applied.

Animating Graphic Objects

In addition to animating text, PowerPoint has the ability to animate graphics, charts, and drawn objects. The options for these objects are very similar to those for animating text.

Animating VitalSigns graphics:

1. Click in the body temperature image on slide 2

2. Click the **Add Effect** button in the task pane, pause over **Entrance**, and click **Crawl In**

3. Click the **Reorder** buttons to move this image animation to a position just under the associated bullet (see Figure 5.10)

FIGURE 5.10
Reordering animations

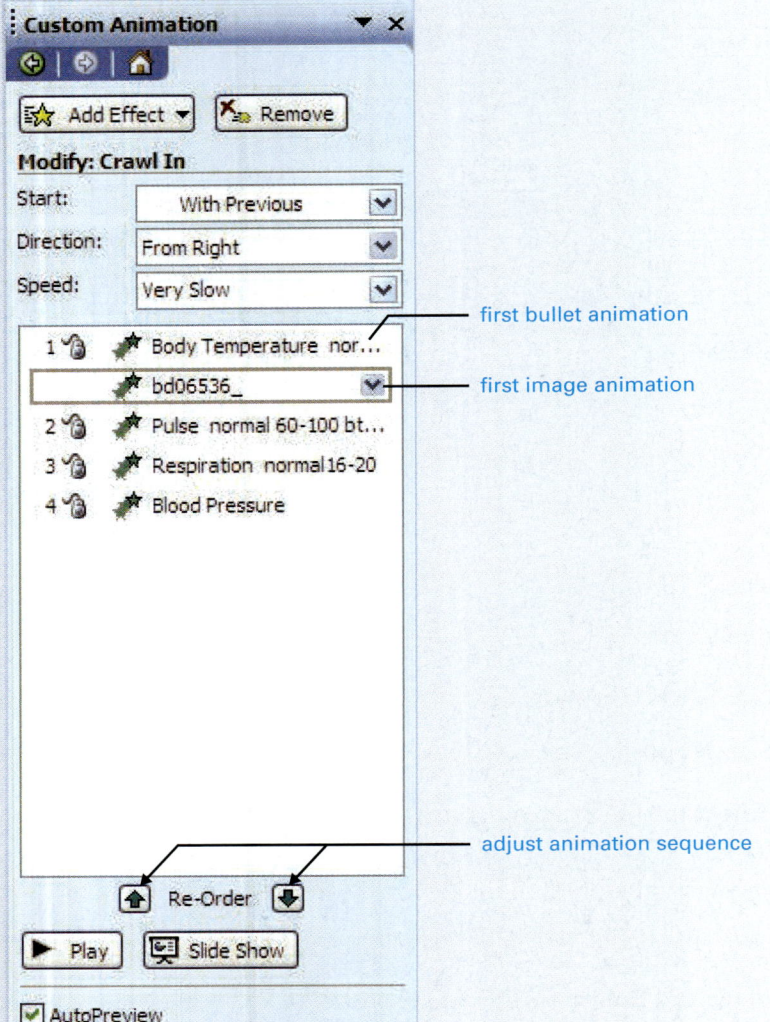

FIGURE 5.10
Reordering animations

anotherway

. . . to Change the Animation Order

The steps demonstrated the use of the Reorder buttons to change animation order. Selecting an animation and dragging it to a new location will also work

4. Set the Start option to **With Previous** to cause the bullet content and image to enter simultaneously

5. Repeat steps 2 to 4 to animate the remaining images with the appropriate bullet (see Figure 5.11)

6. Click **Play** to preview the animations

The Start options of an animation are set to control when it begins to play. Using *With Previous* causes two or more objects to play their animations simultaneously. The After Previous option causes two or more animations to play sequentially. These options reduce the number of mouse clicks required to play all of the animations on a slide.

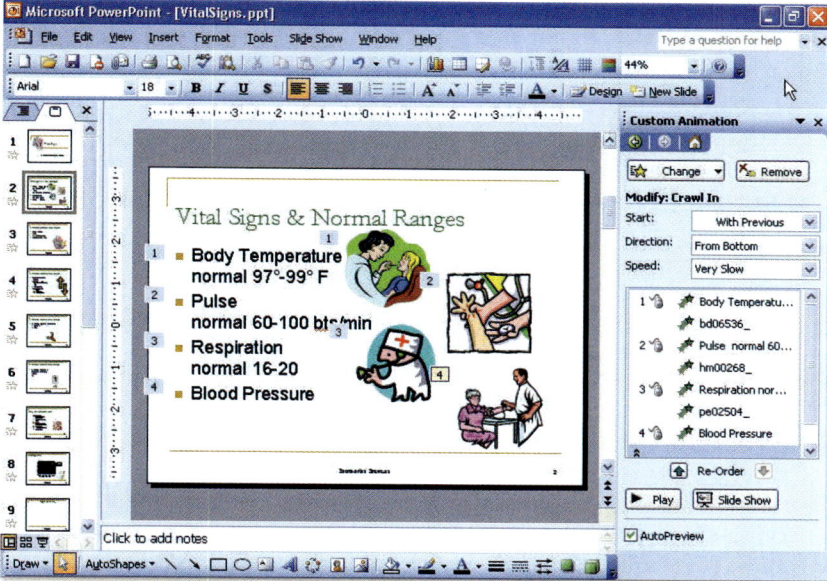

FIGURE 5.11
Final slide 2 animations

---

anotherword
. . . on the Advanced Timeline

When you preview animations, the timeline at the bottom of the Custom Animation list displays the exact timing of each animation. The drop-down list for an animation contains a Show Advanced Timeline option. The Advanced Timeline allows you to control how animations relate to each other by dragging the borders of the timeline marker

---

Other animations options are available from the Timing tab of the Effect Options selection. These options will allow more complete control of start times, delays between animations, the speed of the action, the duration of an animation, how each animation is repeated, and the trigger that initiates the animation.

Animating Chart Objects

Organization charts, numeric charts, and other diagram types are objects on a slide and can be animated in part or as a whole. Animating the component parts of a diagram allows a presenter or narration to address a specific element of the chart, while drawing the audience's attention to that element.

---

task reference   Animating a Chart or Diagram

- In Normal view, select the object to be animated

- From the task pane drop-down list select **Custom Animation**

- To animate the whole object, in the Custom Animation task pane click **Add Effects** and select the desired effect(s)

- To animate individual chart elements

  - In the Custom Animation task pane, select the animation applied to the chart

  - Click the down arrow and select **Effect Options**

  - On the Chart Animation or Diagram Animation tab, select an option from the Group Diagram list

Animating the VitalSigns chart:

1. Move to slide 8 and click in the chart

2. On the Custom Animation pane of the task panel, click the **Add Effect** button, pause over **Entrance**, and click **Appear**

3. Click the drop-down arrow of the chart animation and then click **Effect Options**

4. Click the **Chart Animation** tab, click the Group chart list box arrow, click **By series**, and click **OK**

5. Click the **Slide Show** button to preview the animation

The Chart Animation tab of the Effect Options dialog box controls how each component of a chart is animated. Choosing *By series* caused the Male data series to present and then the Female data series. Choosing *By category* would cause the Under 10 data to display, then the 12 years, the 14 years, and so on. Choose the group option that corresponds to the narration about the chart.

When you are animating charts and diagrams, it is most effective to preview the animations in Slide Show view where you will have to click through them. The Play button does not require you to click through and usually presents the information too rapidly to see the impact of any changes that you have made. The custom effects discussed when animating text and images can also be applied to charts and diagrams. Developers have full control over the Start, Time, Speed, Dimming, and other options.

help yourself: *Click the Type a Question for help combo box, type* **media clips**, *and press* **Enter**. *Click the hyperlink* **Add a movie or animated GIF to a slide** *and then click the hyperlink* **Add a movie or animated GIF file** *in the dialog box to display Help on how you can insert movies and sounds from an external file. Click the Help screen dialog box* **Close** *button when you are finished*

Media Clips

Another simple way you can add motion to a slide is to use a *media clip* instead of a static image. Use caution however, because media clips that repeat the same action for a long time can annoy and distract the audience.

Media clips include movies and animated GIF files. An animated GIF file carries a .gif extension like a static gif image, but includes multiple images that stream to create an animation effect. Animated GIFs are common on the Web. Movies are video files (.avi, .mov, .qt, .mpg, and .mpeg) created on a computer. Typical movies can include audio and video.

The Clip Organizer can contain both animated GIF and movie clips. Media can be inserted from any compatible file type. Sources for media clips include the Internet, media CDs that can be purchased anywhere computer software is sold, and custom media created specifically for a presentation. Movie files are linked to your presentation rather than embedded inside it (like images). If a presentation with a movie is ported to another computer, any linked files must also be moved for it to function properly.

All of the clips in the Clip Organizer are short and simple. The media clips available from your computer are determined by the software installed and the options that were selected during the install process. Custom movies can be added using the Movies and Sounds option of the Insert menu.

FIGURE 5.12
Animated chart

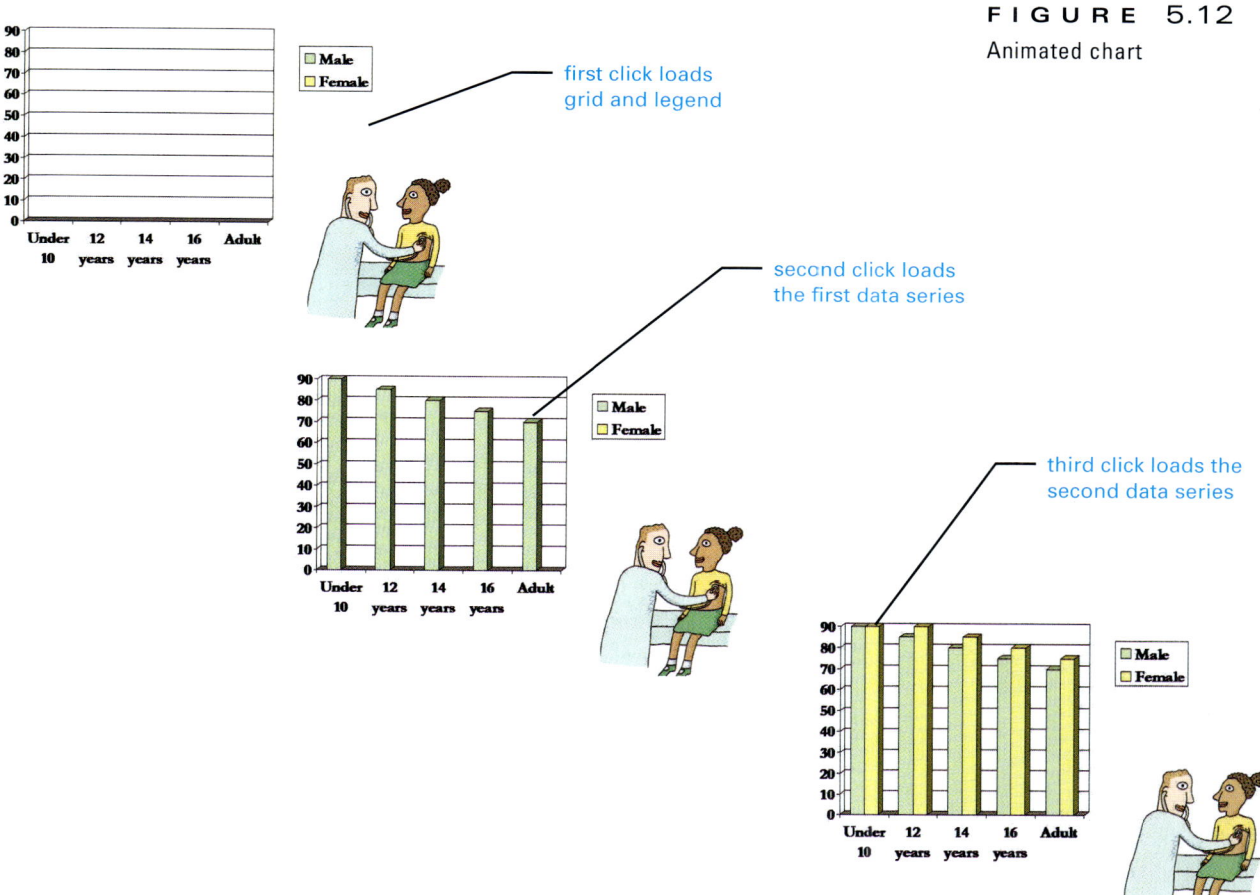

first click loads
grid and legend

second click loads
the first data series

third click loads the
second data series

---

task reference   Inserting a Media Clip

- In Normal view, move to the slide that will contain the clip

- Use the Slide Layout panel of the task pane to select a layout with a media placeholder

- Click the **Insert Media Clip** icon

- Browse through the available selections until you find a clip that you want, click the clip, and click **OK**

- Use Slide Show view to preview the media clip

Adding animated GIFs to VitalSigns:

1. Click slide 9 in the Outline pane to move to that slide

2. Click **Insert**, point to **Movies and Sounds**, and click **Movie from File** to open the Insert Movie dialog box

3. Click the **Files of type** list box arrow, click **All Files (*.*)**, use the Look in list box to locate and then click the file **pp05ekg.avi**, and then click **OK**

4. Click the **Automatically** button when the dialog box appears asking if you want the movie to start in the slide show

5. Move the icon representing the movie so that its upper edge is close to the camel-colored border. Drag the lower-right sizing handle so the icon's bottom almost touches the lower, camel-colored border

6. Repeat steps 2 and 3, substituting **pp05Gears.gif** in step 3. Position and size the icon so it resembles the one shown in Figure 5.13.

FIGURE 5.13

Motion clips

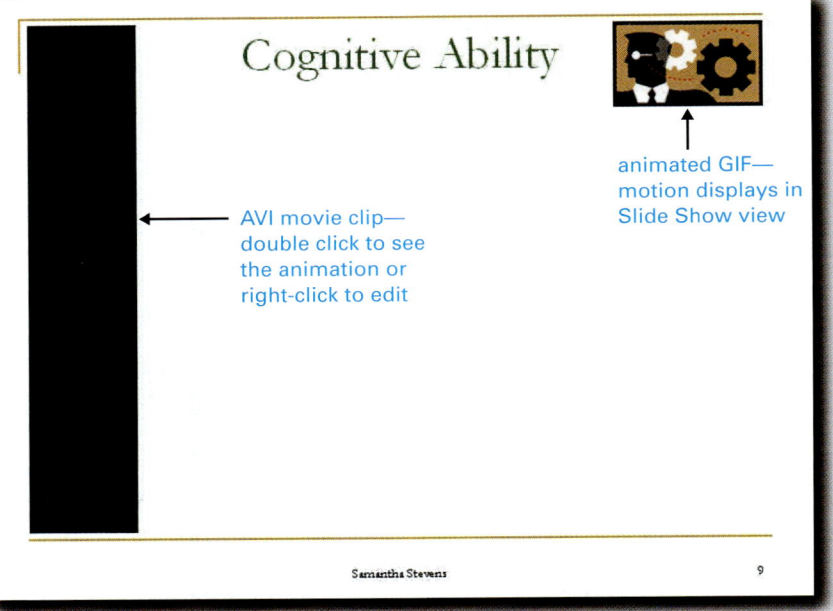

7. Right-click the **ekg** icon in slide 9, click **Edit Movie Object**, click the **Loop until stopped** check box to place a checkmark in it, and click **OK**

8. Press **Shift+F5** to preview your movies. Press **Esc** when you are done to stop the presentation

These steps demonstrated the insertion of a standard movie clip using an avi format and an animated GIF. Both motion clips are simple, but the avi format provides more control. An animated GIF cannot be started and stopped: it plays from the time the slide opens until it closes. The AVI file can be started automatically, by a mouse click or by using some other trigger. AVI files can also be caused to loop or play a specified number of times. Generally AVI files can support all video components and are longer than animated GIFs.

If you try to insert a movie and PowerPoint issues a message or won't play it, you may still be able to use the clip through Windows Media Player. Open Windows Media Player (usually in the Accessories menu) and try running the movie. If the movie doesn't play, Windows Media Player will provide diagnostics that can help address the problem.

If the movie will play in Windows Media Player, use the Insert menu to add a Media Clip object to your presentation. A movie played through the Media Player is not controlled through PowerPoint settings but uses the Media Player buttons to start, stop, rewind, and control volume.

Hiding a Slide during a Slide Show

Sometimes a single presentation can be customized to meet the needs of multiple audiences or presentation forums. For example, the same presentation could be used for a 30-minute and a 20-minute presentation. The simplest way to accomplish this is to create the 30-minute presentation and then hide some of the slides for the shorter version.

*another***word** . . . on Controlling Movies

Custom Animation sequences can be applied to media clips to control their play. The Start With Previous option will play the movie automatically after another animation completes, while Timing can be used to start on a mouse click, and Triggers can be used to set a custom event to initiate play

task reference

Hide a Slide

- Select the slide to hide on the Slides tab in Normal view

- Click **Slide Show** and then click **Hide Slide**

Hiding a slide in VitalSigns:

1. Move to slide 4 and insert a new slide with the title *More on Exercise*

2. Select slide 5 (the new slide), click **Slide Show**, and click **Hide Slide**

3. Move to slide 4 and press **F5** to preview your presentation (it should skip the new slide 5)

4. While the slide show is running, press **5** and then press **Enter** to display slide 5

5. Press **Esc** to end the show

6. Change to Slide Sorter view and locate the hidden slide indicator (see Figure 5.14)

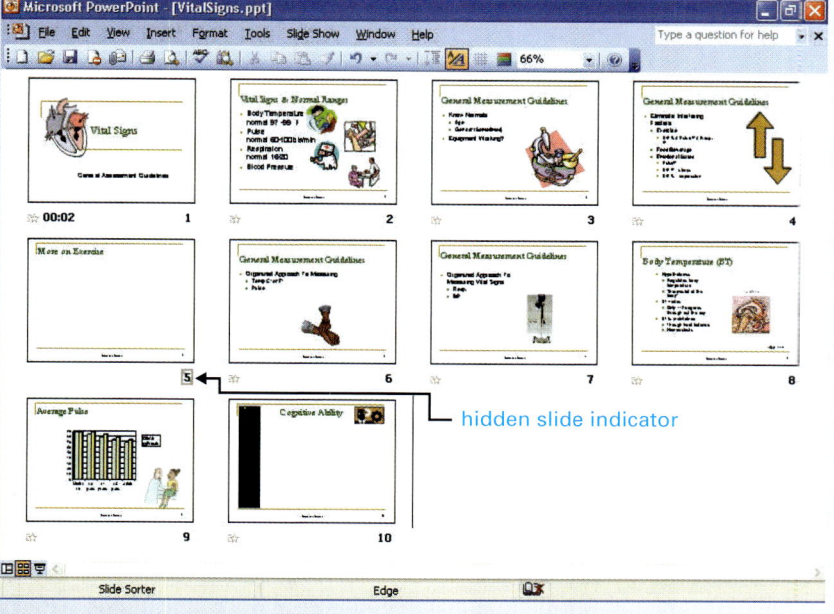

FIGURE 5.14
Hidden slide

hidden slide indicator

tip: *The Slides tab of Normal view also indicates which slides are hidden*

A hidden slide still resides in the presentation, but will not display in Slide Show view unless you activate the Slide Navigator and select the hidden slide. The only indication that a slide is hidden is the slash through the slide number in Slide Sorter view. Unhiding a slide uses the same process as hiding a slide since the Hide Slide menu option is a toggle.

Creating a Self-Running Slide Show

Self-running slide shows are often called *kiosks.* Kiosks can be used to present product information at a trade show or other high-traffic location. If you have any presentation that needs to run without human intervention, it should be treated as a kiosk. Typically such a show is completely self-contained with automatic slide timings, narration, and security to control how the show is stopped.

---

task *reference* Create a Self-Running Presentation

- Click **Slide Show** and then click **Set Up Show**

- Click **Loop continuously until 'Esc'**

Making VitalSigns a self-running presentation:

1. Click **Slide Show** and then click **Set Up Show**

    a. In the Show Options area, click **Loop continuously until 'Esc'**

    b. In the Advance slides area, click **Using timings, if present**

    c. Click **OK** (see Figure 5.15)

FIGURE 5.15

Set Up Show dialog box

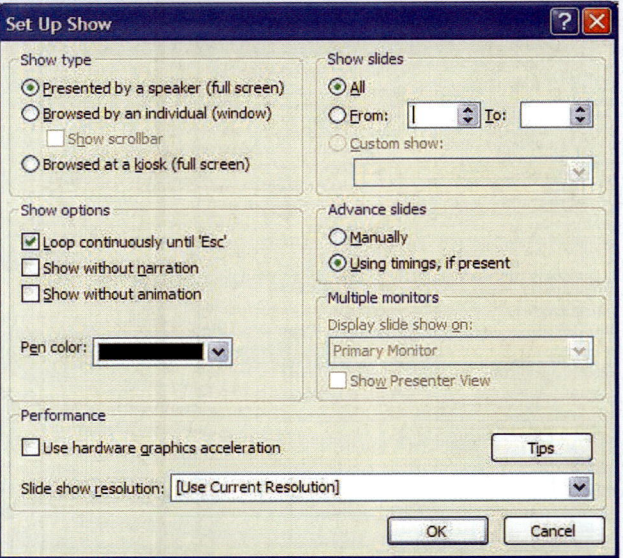

2. Press **F5** to run the presentation

tip: *The timings that have been set by rehearsing the slide show and setting animations will be used to move through the show automatically*

3. Use the **Esc** key to stop the presentation at any point

4. Click the **Save** button on the Standard toolbar, and close PowerPoint

Timings must be set for all slides and animations for a presentation to run without intervention. Another way to cause a show to loop is to select the Browsed at a kiosk (full screen) from the Set Up Show dialog box. This setting will loop the presentation and restrict users from changing it.

making the grade

1. Differentiate between applying an Animation Scheme and a Custom Animation.

2. What are the benefits of using the rehearsal features of PowerPoint?

3. How is a kiosk different from a speaker-led presentation?

4. Differentiate between animating slide objects and adding media clips to a presentation.

SESSION 5.2 USING OTHER AUDIO MULTIMEDIA COMPONENTS

PowerPoint includes intrinsic audio clips that can be applied to transitions, animations, or inserted into a slide and controlled by the presenter. Because audio is a key component in any presentation, PowerPoint supports a variety of ways to create and insert sounds. Audio multimedia components can be inserted from existing sound files, played from a CD, or recorded within PowerPoint.

To preview audio components added to a presentation, you will need speakers and a sound card. If you would like to record sounds, you will also need a microphone. To find out what hardware is installed on your computer, use the Windows Control Panel to check the multimedia and sounds settings.

task reference   Insert a Sound Clip

- Click **Insert**, pause over **Movies and Sounds** and click

  - **Sound from Media Gallery** to insert a sound stored in the Microsoft Media Gallery

  - **Sound from File** to insert a sound that you have stored in a file on your computer

  - **Play CD Audio Track** to play a specific track from the CD loaded in your CD tray

  - **Record Sound** to record your own sound or narration

- Right-click on the sound icon and use the Edit Sound Object options to customize the sound settings

- Use the Reorder buttons on the Custom Animation panel of the task pane to control the play order of the sound

Adding Audio Components

Sounds added to PowerPoint slides can originate in the Microsoft Clip Organizer or be stored in a file on your computer, an available network, the Internet, or a CD. Custom sounds and narrations can be recorded using the features of PowerPoint or any audio recording software. Regardless of how they are created, sound clips are inserted like the other media that you have learned.

Adding a sound clip to VitalSigns:

1. Open PowerPoint and then open **<yourname>VitalSigns.ppt**. Display the presentation in Normal view.

2. Move to slide 1

3. Click **Insert**, point to **Movies and Sounds**, and click **Sound from File**

    a. Navigate to the files for this chapter and click **pp05HeartMonitor.wav**

    b. Click **OK**

    c. Click **Automatically** to the prompt (see Figure 5.16)

FIGURE 5.16

Sound icon

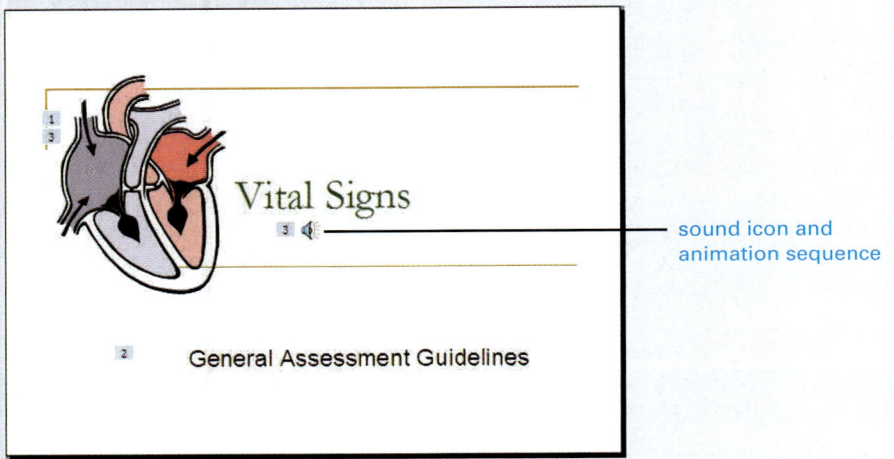

4. Right-click on the sound icon and select **Edit Sound Object**

5. Check **Loop until stopped** in the Sound Options dialog box and click **OK**

6. Use the Custom Animation panel of the task pane to move the sound to the first position on the play list

tip: *You can use the Reorder buttons or drag and drop the sound to relocate it*

7. Press **Shift+F5** to preview your changes on this slide

A sound icon is automatically placed on a slide containing an inserted audio component. If the sound is not set to play automatically, clicking the sound icon will initiate play. If the sound is set to play automatically, the icon can be dragged off the slide so that it does not display during a slide show. Use the Custom Animation Start options to control when an automatic sound starts.

Because sound files can be large, they are usually linked rather than embedded in a presentation. The default is to link all files larger than 100 KB, but the size can be customized using the Options dialog box of the Tools menu. Unless the file size is dramatically increased, most added sound files will need to be moved with your presentation for them to work on another computer.

Intrinsic Sounds

Intrinsic sounds are those that are native to the Microsoft PowerPoint. You can add intrinsic sounds to a transition, a Custom Animation, or insert them on a slide. Unless larger sounds have been added to the Microsoft Clip Organizer, the available sounds are very short (small file size) and are usually designed to be looped. As previously discussed, the clips available from the Microsoft Clip Organizer are dependent on the options chosen when Microsoft Office was installed.

---

task reference   Add Sound to a Transition or Animation

The transitions and animations must be set before sounds can be added to them

- Move to the slide where sounds will be added to transitions and/or animations

- Activate the task panel pane for Slide Transitions to add a sound to a transition or the pane for Custom Animations to add a sound to an animated object

- Use the sound drop-down list to select the sound

Adding transition and animation sounds:

1. Move to slide 2

2. Use the task pane drop-down button to open the Slide Transition panel

3. Experiment with the available sounds in the Sounds drop-down list before settling on **Whoosh** (see Figure 5.17)

tip: *Loop until next slide will cause the sound to loop until the next slide enters the screen*

4. Click **Play** to preview the change

5. Use the task pane drop-down button to open the Custom Animation panel

6. Double-click on the first animation to open the Effect Options (Crawl In) dialog box

tip: *You could also select the Effect Options item from the animation's drop-down list*

7. Experiment with the available audio in the Sounds drop-down list, select **Arrow** and click **OK**

8. Press **Shift+F5** to preview your changes

9. Repeat steps 6 through 8 to add sounds to the other text animations on this slide

10. Save the presentation

F I G U R E   5.17

Adding sound to a Slide
Transition

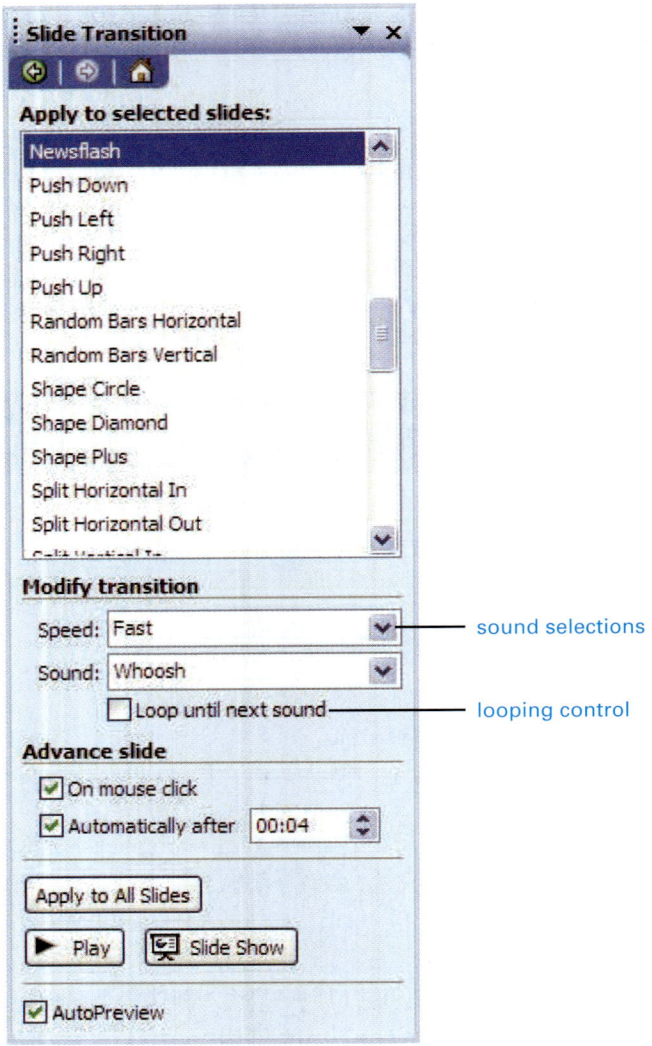

For sounds to be added in this fashion, animations and transitions must already be set. The last option on the list of available sounds is *Other* sound. This option can be used to add a sound from a file to a transition or animation. This option will allow you to add narration to each animated object.

Sound Files

Using audio content from a CD allows alternate sounds to be played during a slide show without updating the presentation. CD sounds are not embedded in your presentation, but played from their external location. If you specify a track to play from a CD, the presentation will play that track from whatever CD is currently in the tray. If you don't have a CD handy, then simply skip the next set of steps called "Adding a CD track to Vital Signs."

Adding a CD track to VitalSigns:

1. Place an audio CD in your CD tray

2. Move to slide 3

3. Click the **Insert** menu, pause over **Movies and Sounds**, and click **Play CD Audio Track**

   a. In the *Insert CD Audio* dialog box, select the first and last track(s) to be played and then click **OK**

tip: *Selecting the same Start and End track will cause only that track to play*

   b. Answer **Automatically** to have the track(s) play automatically. No would require you to click the icon to play the track(s)

4. Drag the CD icon to the footer portion of the slide to remove it from the main body

5. Press **Shift+F5** to preview the audio

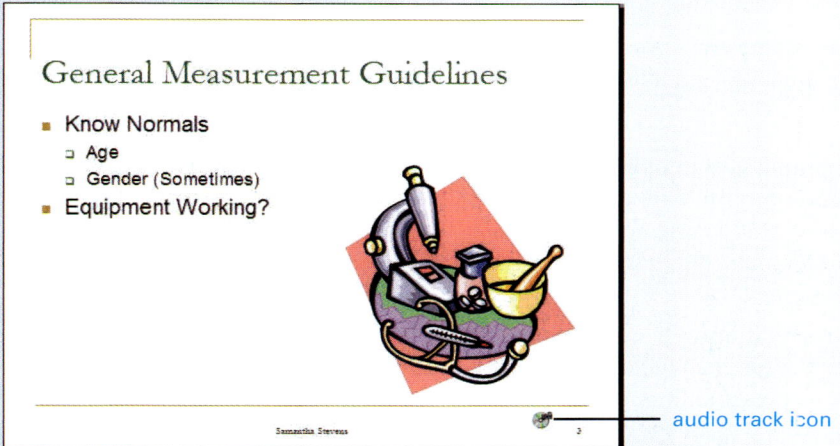

audio track icon

FIGURE 5.18

CD audio track icon

A music CD must be in the CD-ROM drive during the presentation for a CD audio track to play. This music is always played from the CD, not embedded into your PowerPoint document. Once a CD audio track has been specified, the Custom Animation settings can be used to control how play begins and ends. The default action is to end play on a mouse-click, but other options can cause the clip to play until the current slide is exited or for several slides. To change the CD track that plays or the duration of play, use the Edit Sound Object from the pop-up menu option activated by right-clicking on the CD icon.

Stop or Delete Sound Objects

All sounds inserted from a CD or file display an icon on the slide. Deleting this icon also deletes the sound from the slide. Remember you can drag the icon off the edge of the slide so that it is not visible during the presentation (see Figure 5.19).

To remove a sound added to a transition or animation, open the task pane panel for the animation containing the sound (either the Slide Transition or Custom Animation panel) and update the Sound selection. The [Stop Previous Sound] option of the Sound drop-down list stops a sound still playing from a previous transition or animation. The [No Sound] option removes any sound currently associated with this animation.

The Edit Sound Object dialog box can be used to stop a sound from playing without removing it from the presentation using the Edit Sound Object settings. Right-click

FIGURE 5.19
CD audio track icon off the edge of the slide

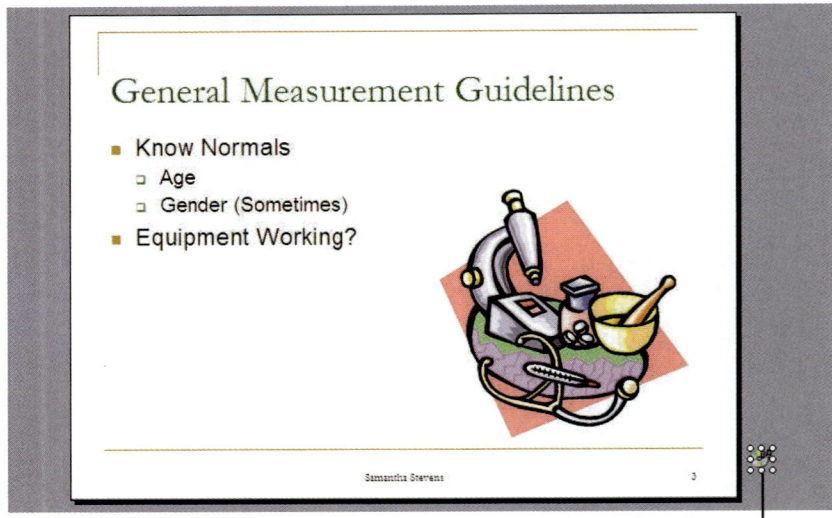

CD icon positioned not to display during show ┐

on the sound icon to open the pop-up menu with the Edit Sound Object option. Set the sound object to play on a specific triggering event so that you can decide whether or not to play it during a show.

Narration

Most presentations rely on narration to deliver the bulk of their content. When there is a live presenter, the narration is spoken during the slide show. Self-running presentations, Web presentations, and kiosks need to contain recorded narration so that the audience receives all of the available information without adding more text to the slides than can be easily read.

help yourself: Click the Type a Question for help *combo box, type* **narration**, *and press* **Enter**. *Click the hyperlink* **Record a voice narration** *and review the steps presented in order to either link or embed the voice narration. Click the Help screen* **Close** *button when you are finished*

Voice narration can be created in a sound studio, using a PC-based recording software like Sound Recorder that ships with Windows, or from within the presentation itself. The sound quality desired determines the recording method. A sound studio costs the most and provides the best quality sound. Recording from within PowerPoint is easy, but produces the lowest sound quality and least control. The biggest advantage of recording narration from within PowerPoint is that it can be accomplished during a live presentation and can include audience comments as well as the basic narrative.

When you record a narration from within PowerPoint, a sound icon on the slide(s) is placed with the associated sound. Like other types of sound files, narration can be set to play automatically or when triggered by a mouse click or other event. Narration can be created for each slide, or for the entire presentation. When multiple sounds are set for a slide, narration takes precedence.

When you only need a portion of the slide show to be narrated, it is useful to record your voice comment or narration on individual slides in a slide show. This is a simple way to ensure that the voice directly relates to the slide content being displayed. (If you do not have a microphone available, then simply read but not do the steps that follow.)

Adding a narration to a VitalSigns slide:

1. Move to slide 4

2. Click **Insert**, point to **Movies and Sounds**, and then click **Record Sound**

 a. Name the sound **Exercise**

 b. Click the **Record** button and speak the following narration into your microphone **Exercise causes blood pressure to decrease while increasing pulse and respiration. Vital signs should not be taken within 30 minutes of vigorous exercise if it can be at all avoided**

 c. Click the **Stop** button (see Figure 5.20)

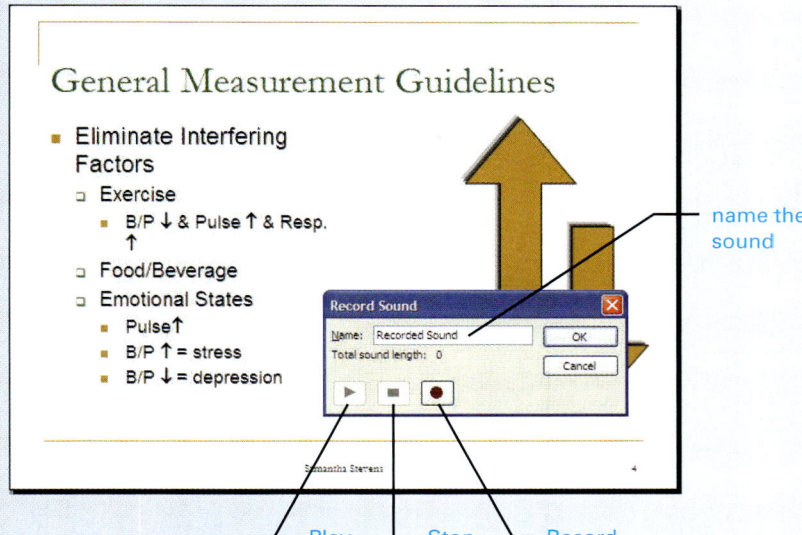

F I G U R E 5.20
Recording narration

 d. Click **OK**

tip: *To complete this step, you must have a sound card and microphone on your computer*

3. Preview the audio by pressing **Shift+F5**

tip: *You will need to click the sound icon*

4. Open the *Custom Animation* panel of the task pane

5. Drop down the list for the sound object and click **Timing**

6. On the Timing tab, set the Start option to **With Previous** and click **OK**

tip: *This will start the sound when the slide opens*

7. Press **Shift+F5** to preview the audio

The Timing options set in the previous steps control the narration. The Start settings control when the narration begins, while the Repeat settings control when it ends. Since this narration is associated with this slide, its timings relate to the slide also. Repeat settings include playing the narration a specific number of times, until the user clicks again, or until the slide is exited.

If you would like the narration to continue throughout a self-running presentation, the Slide Show menu has an option that will record your narration and save the timings of each mouse click so that your presentation is perfectly synchronized.

Adding a timed narration to the VitalSigns presentation:

1. Move to slide 1

2. Click **Slide Show** and click **Record Narration**

    a. Click the **Set Microphone Level** button (see Figure 5.21), read the text as instructed, and click **OK**

    b. Click the **Change Quality** button, select **CD Quality** from the Name drop-down list, and click **OK**

tip: *The CD setting will produce the best sound file possible with your recording situation. The resulting file size is large and may cause a problem if you do not have much disk space*

    c. Click **OK** to close the Record Narration dialog box and begin recording

    d. Read the content of each slide as you click through the show

tip: *You can pause and reinitiate the recording process by right-clicking and selecting either Pause Narration or Resume Narration. The Esc key will stop the recording process*

    e. When you come to the end of the show, click **Save** to store the timings as well as the narration (see Figure 2.21)

tip: *Normally the narration would contain much more information than just reading the slides. This was done for demonstration purposes only*

F I G U R E 5.21

Recording narration for an entire presentation

set recording properties

check to link the narration file

save or discard narration timings

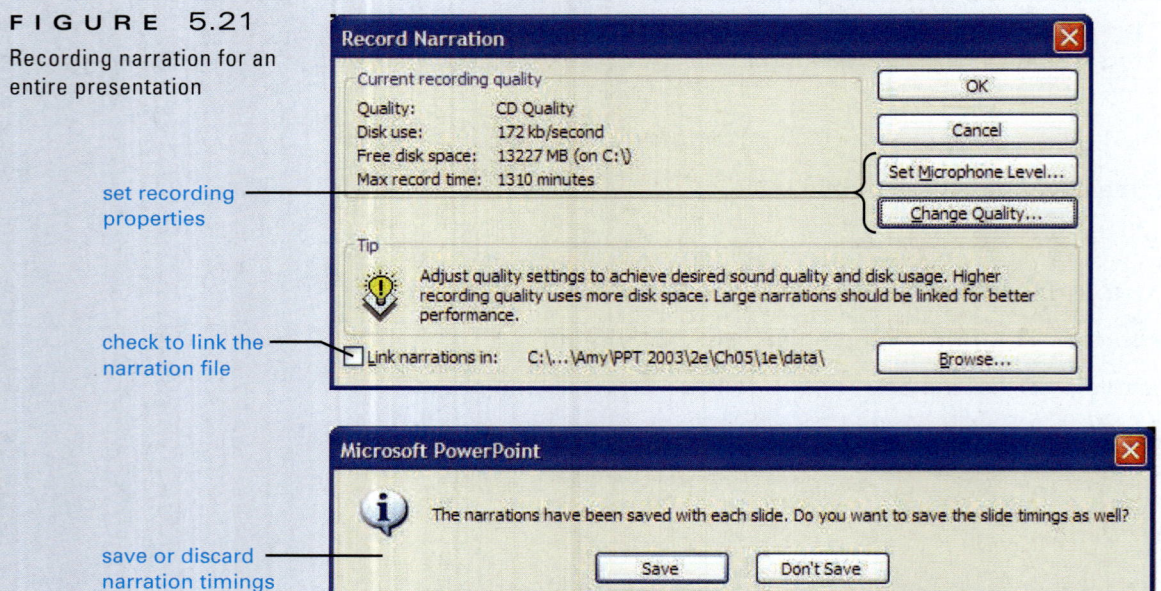

3. Move to slide 1 and press **F5** to preview the narration and timing

tip: *Esc will stop a self-running slide show*

The timings created as the narration is recorded are usually the most appropriate for a self-running slide show. If the initial timings or narration are not effective for you, you can repeat the process to record a new narration. There is no mechanism to update only a portion of the narration. The narration sound icon appears on the first slide only. Deleting that icon will remove the narration from the entire presentation. Only one sound can play at a time when running a slide show. If there are multiple sounds on a slide, the narration will take precedence.

A presentation narration can be **embedded** or stored in a **linked** file. Embedded narrations are the default, but result in large PowerPoint file sizes. Linked sound files yield smaller PowerPoint file sizes, but the sound file must be ported with the presentation.

To create a linked narration, click Link narrations in the check box of the Record Narration dialog box (see Figure 5.21) before beginning to record. You will be prompted for a location to store the linked sound file and a filename. A further advantage of linked sound is that it will play faster.

A narrated presentation can be run with or without the narration. The Set Up Show option of the Slide Show menu contains the options that control whether or not a narration is played. Click Show without narration. Recall that this dialog box can also be used to advance slides manually or using the timings.

Identifying Sources for Media

The Microsoft Clip Organizer is a starting point for locating high-impact media for your presentation. Other sources will be needed for presentations about unique topics or to obtain the most professional look.

Improving Presentation Performance

As more and more media are added to a presentation, the size of the PowerPoint file will increase and the presentation can become sluggish. Compressing the media can significantly decrease file size and improve performance. This is especially true if media have been added and deleted to obtain the desired look and feel.

Compressing VitalSigns graphics:

1. Move to slide 1

2. Right-click on the heart image and click **Show Picture Toolbar**

3. On the picture toolbar, click the **Compress Pictures** [🖾] button (see Figure 5.22)

4. Click **OK**

5. Click the **Apply** button when prompted about the possibility of reduced image quality

The settings chosen have optimized the presentation for delivery using a screen or via the Web. This provides the greatest compression available. If a presentation is to be printed, use the settings that will best support printing. The performance improvement and file size reduction experienced will depend on how much media are in your presentation and the settings that you select.

FIGURE 5.22

Compressing pictures

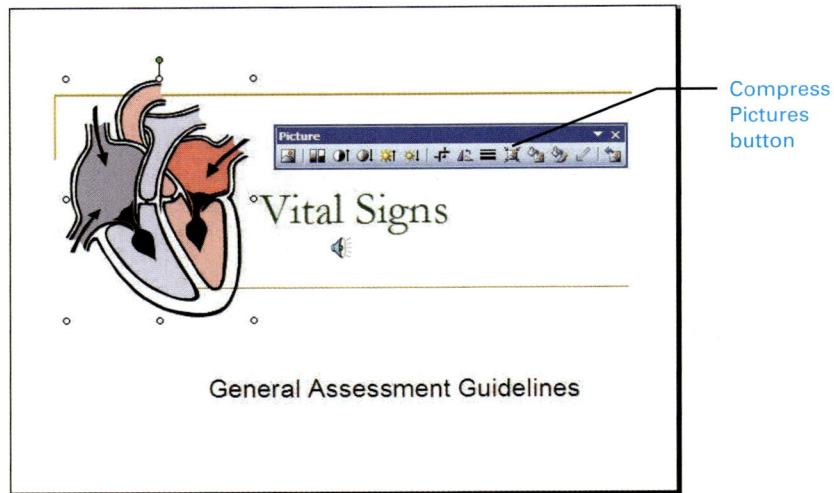

Other Sources for Media

The Microsoft Design Gallery Live is a Web-based collection of media available to licensed Microsoft Office users. This collection contains the same types of media as the Microsoft Clip Organizer installed with Office, but is continually updated. This is a good place to locate seasonal art and clips that follow the style and color schemes available from the Clip Organizer. The simplest way to reach online clips is to use the link from the Insert Clip Art pane of the task panel.

Using the Office Online clip art collection:

1. If the task panel is not open, open it from the View menu (or press **Ctrl+F1**) and then use the task pane drop-down list to open the **Clip Art** pane

2. Click the **Clip art on Office Online** link near the bottom of the task pane

tip: *You must have an active Internet connection for this link to work. Because this is a frequently updated Web site, the layout may vary significantly from that depicted*

3. In the Office Online browser page, (see Figure 5.23), enter the search criteria

    Search for: **computers**
    Search: **All media types**

4. Click the **Search** button (a green arrow) found to the right of the Search Criteria text box

5. Select a piece of clip art by checking its check box (select any one). Then, click the **Download 1 item** hyperlink (on the lower left side of the browser window), click the **Download Now** button

6. When the File Download dialog box opens, click the **Open** button. Click **Later** if the *Add Clips to Organizer* dialog box appears. Close the Microsoft Clip Organizer dialog box

7. Close the Web browser

8. Move to slide 5, type **computer** in the *Search for* text box in the Clip Art panel, scroll the results list until you find the new clip art you downloaded from the Web, and click it to insert it into your presentation

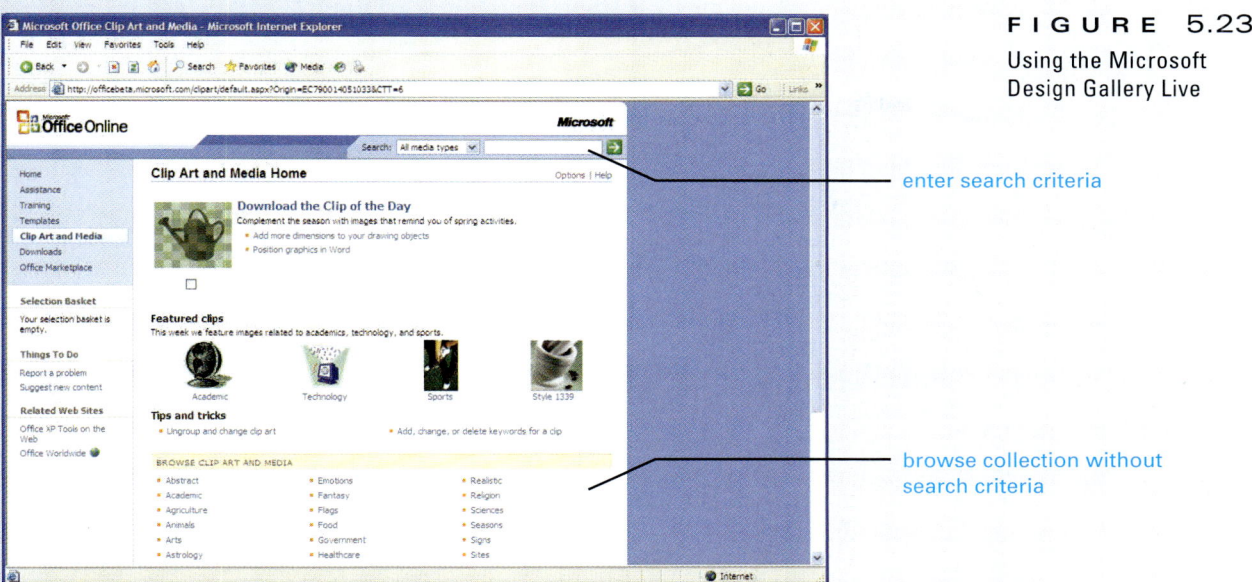

FIGURE 5.23
Using the Microsoft
Design Gallery Live

enter search criteria

browse collection without
search criteria

9. Click **File** on the menu bar, click **Exit**, and click **Yes** when asked if you want to save your changes. PowerPoint saves your changes and then closes

The World Wide Web interface of Design Gallery Live allows online media searches using an interface similar to the Clip Organizer. When media of interest are located, clicking them will provide a larger preview. Each clip has a check box that can be used to select multiple clips for simultaneous download, or a clip's download button can be used to store a single clip locally. Once a clip has been downloaded, it can be added to the Clip Organizer or inserted as a file.

There are many other sources of free and low-cost media on the Internet. Any **Internet search engine** (Yahoo!, WebCrawler, Google, etc.) can be used to locate artwork. The search criteria are determined by the presentation content. Searches for wide-open topics like *free art* will return many possible matches, while specific searches like *free Christmas gif* are more likely to retrieve appropriate art.

Most software stores carry a selection of CDs that contain sounds, graphics, pictures, movies, and animations that are suitable for use in presentations. CDs traditionally contain media that are similar in some fashion, such as style, topic, or artist. The **royalty** for using these media can be covered by the cost of the CD, or additional payment can be required based on how the media are used.

Custom images can also be created using a digital still camera, a digital video camera, or a scanner. Using these methods to create your own custom media is more difficult than it would initially appear. The digital media that result from these methods are rarely usable without using specialty software to edit, retouch, crop, and restore the images and sounds. Each media type requires access to and knowledge of specialty software used to create professional media.

Remember to allow a significant portion of development time for research when planning to locate media on CDs or the Web. Previewing vast quantities of artwork is very time consuming.

All media, regardless of how they are displayed, are covered by **copyright law.** Copyright laws give the owner of the art all rights to control its distribution and use. A **license agreement** is used to legally outline the rights and responsibilities of anyone who uses copyrighted materials. Most artwork available for download can be used in

another*way*
**. . . to Use
Microsoft Design
Gallery Live**

If you have a live Internet connection, online clips are available from the Microsoft Clip Organizer. Online clips have an online logo, but are listed with the rest of the media clips as long as the Search in criteria is set to Everywhere

private presentations without charge, but carefully read the license agreements before you download. Commercial use of most works requires acknowledgment of the creator and a payment. Some media licenses have a time limit or quantity restriction that determines when payment needs to be made. Most licenses also preclude using any part of the work as the foundation of another work for profit.

There are also many Web sites that provide media for hire. Media prices vary widely, but typically increase with the quality and uniqueness of the work. Web-based graphic art studios are similar to online shopping sites that allow shoppers to browse merchandise and add art for purchase to a shopping cart. If you cannot find exactly the right clip, the work can be commissioned. These sites protect the media from download until payment is received and often embed digital signatures to protect media copyrights.

SESSION 5.2

making the grade

1. Differentiate between animation/transition sounds and sound clips.

2. When a CD track is set to play on a slide, what happens if the wrong CD is in the CD tray?

3. How can you remove a sound icon from the slide without removing the sound?

4. How do you determine what method to use when recording a PowerPoint narration?

SESSION 5.3 SUMMARY

Animation Schemes were introduced in Chapter 3 as a simple way to apply preset movements to slide text. This chapter covers Custom Animations that can be applied to any slide object. Slide objects include the slide itself and any text, chart, image, or drawing object. Animations can be applied to control the way the object enters, exits, or displays on the slide. The properties of each animation are set in the task panel and control the speed, order, sound, and other effects that control animation behavior.

When multiple slide objects are animated, the Animation pane of the task panel is used to control the order of play. Animations can play simultaneously, sequentially, or the Advanced Timeline can be used for more complete control. Animated GIF files and movies can also be inserted to add motion to a presentation.

Voice narration can be recorded for a slide, a group of slides, or the entire presentation. When the narration is for a slide, the sound icon is stored on the slide and animation settings control when the narration is played. Narration for the entire presentation displays an icon on the beginning slide. The simplest way to record a complete voice narration with slide timings is to record the presentation while clicking through it. This feature is activated using the Record Narration from the Slide Show menu.

A presentation can be customized to meet the needs of a new audience or presentation time reduced by hiding slides. Hidden slides can still be edited, but will not play during a normal presentation. Right-clicking will allow you to navigate to a hidden slide. Slide Sorter view and the slide panel of Normal view display a slash through the slide number, but there is no visible difference in other views.

The Slide Show menu contains a number of options for setting up a presentation. One option is to create a self-running presentation or a kiosk. When this is done, the presentation can run without intervention or as the user clicks through it. Typically options are selected to keep the viewer from interrupting the presentation or making changes to it.

MICROSOFT OFFICE SPECIALIST
OBJECTIVES SUMMARY

- Apply and customize Slide Transitions—MOS PP035-2-5
- Insert and configure sound, movie, and animated GIF clips—MOS PP035-1-5
- Use presentation rehearsal features—MOS PP035-4-3

making the grade *answers*

SESSION 5.1

1. Animation Schemes are preset animations for slide text that can be applied from the Animation Schemes panel of the task pane. Custom Animations are applied from the Custom Animation panel of the task pane and will allow you to animate any slide object.

2. The rehearsal features will allow you to practice a presentation, but more significantly it will record timings that can be used during the presentation to automatically advance slides.

3. Kiosks are typically standalone presentations that are used to present information when support people are not present. Self-running kiosks can use the timings set while rehearsing so that users do not have to click through the presentation.

4. Slide objects such as images, text, and charts can be animated to add motion as they enter or leave the slide. Media clips are complete animations that can be added to a presentation from the Microsoft Media Gallery.

SESSION 5.2

1. Sound clips are inserted into a presentation and are represented by a sound icon. Inserted sounds can play automatically or based on a triggering event like a mouse click. Animation and transition sounds can only be added to animations and transitions. These sounds are very short like a chime. Sounds from external files can also be added to transitions and animations using the Other Sound selection.

2. If the tract set to play exists on the CD, it will play. If the track does not exist, nothing will play.

3. Dragging the icon off the edge of a slide will leave the sound intact without displaying an icon.

4. Self-running presentations with narration on each slide are best recorded using the Slide Show menu to record the narration and set automatic slide timings. Narration for a single slide can be recorded from the Insert menu.

task reference *summary*

Task	Page #	Preferred Method
Apply a slide transition	PP 5.3	• Select the slide(s) the transition will be applied to. If no slide(s) is selected, the transition will be applied to all slides. • From the **Slide Show** menu select **Slide Transition** • Select a transition effect

Set slide timing while rehearsing	PP 5.6	• Activate the timing feature
		  • On the **Slide Show** menu, click **Set Up Show**
		  • Under **Advance slides**, click **Use timings, if present**
		• Set the time for each slide
		  • On the **Slide Show** menu click **Rehearse Timings**
		  • Rehearse the show to set timings automatically as you advance
		  • At the end of the show, click **Yes** to accept automatic timings or **No** to start again

POWERPOINT

task reference summary

Task	Page #	Preferred Method
Adding custom animations to text	PP 5.7	• In Normal view, select the text object to be animated • From the task pane drop-down list select **Custom Animation** • In the Custom Animation task pane click **Add Effects** and select the desired effect(s)
Animating a chart or diagram	PP 5.13	• In Normal view, select the object to be animated • From the task pane drop-down list select **Custom Animation** • To animate the whole object, in the Custom Animation task pane click **Add Effects** and select the desired effect(s) • To animate individual chart elements • In the Custom Animation task pane, select the animation applied to the chart • Click the down arrow and select **Effect Options** • On the Chart Animation or Diagram Animation tab, select an option from the Group Diagram list
Inserting a media clip	PP 5.15	• In Normal view, move to the slide that will contain the clip • Use the Slide Layout panel of the task pane to select a layout with a media placeholder • Click the **Insert Media Clip** icon • Browse through the available selections until you find a clip that you want, click the clip, and click **OK** • Use Slide Show view to preview the media clip
Hide a slide	PP 5.17	• Select the slide to hide on the Slides tab in Normal view • Click **Slide Show** and then click **Hide Slide**
Create a self-running presentation	PP 5.18	• Click **Slide Show** and then click **Set Up Show** • Click **Loop continuously until 'Esc'**
Insert a sound clip	PP 5.19	• Click **Insert**, pause over **Movies and Sounds** and click • **Sound from Media Gallery** to insert a sound stored in the Microsoft Media Gallery • **Sound from File** to insert a sound that you have stored in a file on your computer • **Play CD Audio Track** to play a specific track from the CD loaded in your CD tray • **Record Sound** to record your own sound or narration • Right-click on the sound icon and use the Edit Sound Object options to customize the sound settings • Use the Reorder buttons on the Custom Animation panel of the task pane to control the play order of the sound
Add sound to a transition or animation	PP 5.21	The transitions and animations must be set before sounds can be added to them • Move to the slide where sounds will be added to transitions and/or animations • Activate the task panel pane for Slide Transitions to add a sound to a transition or Custom Animations to add a sound to an animated object • Use the sound drop-down list to select the sound

TRUE OR FALSE

1. Slide Transitions control the sound effects that play between slides in a slide show.

2. Slide timings can only be incremented according to the preset time periods set in PowerPoint.

3. PowerPoint is unable to use animation features with charts or diagrams.

4. Self-running slide shows are often called kiosks.

5. Intrinsic sounds are those that are native to PowerPoint.

6. An embedded file and a linked file basically have the same results.

FILL-IN

1. The _____ animation timing option is used to play multiple animations at the same time.

2. _____ images will reduce the overall size of a PowerPoint presentation.

3. _____ is a Web site of media provided for licensed Microsoft Office users.

4. The agreements that govern legal use of copyrighted media are called _____.

5. The _____ menu contains the option to set a Slide Transition.

MULTIPLE CHOICE

1. A slide timing can cause the slide presentation to advance to the next slide using:
   a. a mouse click
   b. a preset time period
   c. both a and b
   d. none of the above

2. Text can be animated on:
   a. entrance
   b. exit
   c. custom path
   d. all of the above

3. The Clip Organizer can contain:
   a. GIF files
   b. movie clips
   c. customized media
   d. all of the above

4. Because sound files can be large, they are usually _____ rather than _____.
   a. linked, embedded
   b. embedded, linked
   c. a or b
   d. none of the above

5. CD sounds are not embedded in your presentation, but played from their _____.
   a. external location
   b. native media player
   c. a or b
   d. none of the above

6. Copyright laws give the owner of any artwork all rights to:
   a. sell
   b. distribute
   c. use
   d. all of the above

review of concepts

REVIEW QUESTIONS

Each of the following topics should be addressed in one to three paragraphs.

1. Discuss how you would find appropriate graphics for a presentation used to recruit high school girls for sports teams.

2. How would you apply the same transition to slides 2, 4, 7, and 9 of a presentation?

3. How effective is it to add an intrinsic sound like camera to each animation and transition in a presentation?

4. Why use multimedia in a slide show?

5. How would you select and add a range of CD tracks to a slide?

CREATE THE QUESTION

For each of the following answers, create the question.

ANSWER	QUESTION
1. Custom Animation panel	_____
2. Speed property	_____
3. Rehearse timings and recording a narration	_____
4. Font, color, spinning, and desaturation, for example	_____
5. Reorder button	_____

FACT OR FICTION

1. Slide Transitions control the visual effect that displays between slides in a slide show. The available transitions range from mild to dramatic in their impact.

2. Slide timings can be recorded while practicing the presentation or set in the Slide Transition pane. The timing options cause the presentation to advance to the next slide using a mouse click, a preset time period, or both.

3. PowerPoint has the ability to animate graphics, charts, and drawn objects. However, the options for these objects are different from those for animating text.

4. The Media Gallery can contain both animated GIF and movie clips. Media can be inserted from any compatible file type.

5. Sounds added to PowerPoint slides must originate in the Microsoft Clip Gallery or be stored in a file on your computer. Custom sounds and narrations can be recorded using the features of PowerPoint or any audio recording software.

1. Heap Collectors

Heap Collectors is a company that collects donated vehicles and delivers them to their final resting place. The recipient business organizations will typically pay the towing fee. However, nonprofit organizations usually do not. In that case, Heap Collectors is able to collect most of its fee from grants, a small portion of which comes as a pass-through when donors contribute to charities. You have been asked to create a PowerPoint presentation to be viewed at community centers.

1. Start PowerPoint and open **pp05HeapCollectors.ppt**

2. On slide 1 add a car graphic retrieved from a CD or an online gallery and then add a **Fly In** from Left Entrance animation with an appropriate sound. Make the sound occur first and then the title **Fly In** from Left (After previous), followed by the subtitle and graphic with the same format

3. On slide 2 arrange several graphics of vehicles to look "junky" and then group them into a single object. Set the animation for the grouped car graphic to **Dissolve In**, Very Fast, then have the title **Dissolve In**, Very Fast, and finally set the text to **Dissolve In** line by line on mouse click

4. On slide 3, add a graphic of a motorcycle, an older car, and the sound of a motorcycle starting up (insert **pp05MotorCycleSound.wav**). Set the following in the order presented

    a. Set a **Newsflash** Slide Transition

    b. Set the title to **Fly In** with **driveby.wav** as the simultaneous sound on mouse click

    c. The remaining text should **Fly In** Very Fast after the mouse is clicked

    d. Add an Exit effect for the motorcycle graphic causing it to **Fly Out** playing the motorcycle sound simultaneously on mouse click

5. On slide 4, add the graphic of a horse with a car (Clips Online), and insert sounds of a horse snorting and galloping (Clip Organizer). Set the following in the order presented

    a. Play the horse snort first on click

    b. Set the title to **Dissolve In**, Very Fast on click

    c. Set the text to **Wipe, From Top**, Very Fast after previous

    d. Set the graphic to move off the screen with the galloping sound after previous

6. On slide 5 insert a graphic of coins and the sounds of coins dropping (Clip Organizer). Set the following in the order presented

    a. Add a **Flash Bulb Emphasis** effect to the title

    b. Have the text enter line-by-line by clicking the mouse as the coins dropping sound plays

7. On slide 6 insert a graphic of hands with keys (Clips Online). Set the following in the order presented

    a. Set the title to **Dissolve In** on click

    b. Make the text display as a group using **Wipe, From Left**, all at once, with previous

8. Drag the sound icons off each slide so that they do not display during the presentation

9. Save the presentation as **<yourname>HeapCollectors.ppt**

FIGURE 5.24

Heap Collectors opening slide

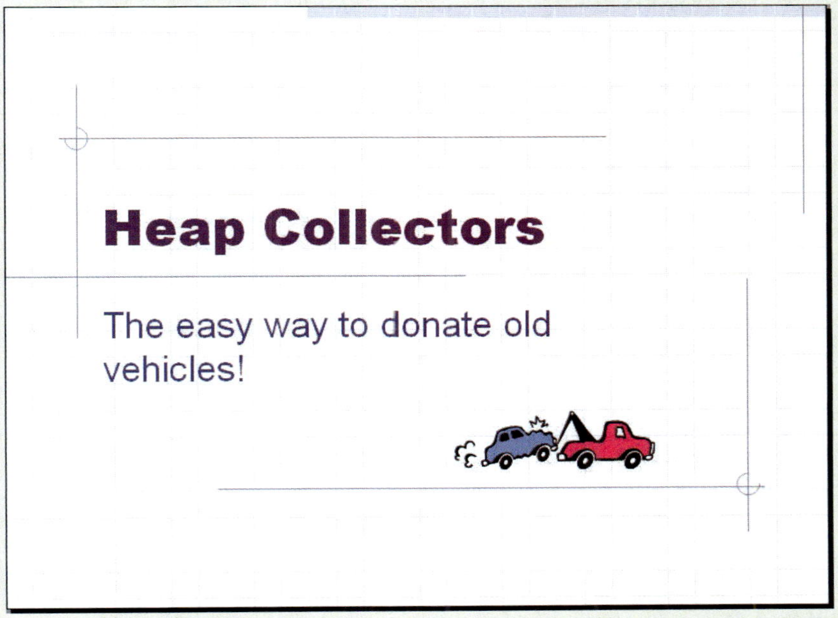

2. Air Traffic

During peak air travel times in the United States, there are about 5,000 airplanes in the sky every hour. This translates to approximately 50,000 aircraft operating in the sky each day. The task of ensuring safe operations of commercial and private aircraft falls on air traffic controllers. They must coordinate the movements of thousands of aircraft, keep them at safe distances from each other, direct them during takeoff and landing from airports, direct them around bad weather, and ensure that traffic flows smoothly with minimal delays. You have been asked to create a PowerPoint presentation to be viewed at various airports as an information kiosk.

1. Start PowerPoint and open **pp05AirTraffic.ppt**

2. On slide 1 add an airplane graphic retrieved from a CD or an online gallery and then add a **Fly In** From Right Entrance animation with an appropriate sound. Make the sound occur first and then the title **Fly In** From Right (After previous)

3. On slide 2 arrange a graphic of an airplane and a tower and then group them into a single object. Set the animation for the grouped graphic to **Dissolve In**, Very Fast On Click, then have the title **Dissolve In**, Very Fast After Previous and finally set the text to **Dissolve In** line-by-line on mouse click

4. On slide 3, add a graphic of airplane traffic and the sound of an airplane flying overhead. Set the following in the order presented

   a. Set a **Newsflash** Slide Transition, advance on mouse click

   b. Set the title to **Fly In** with **jetpass.wav** as the simultaneous sound, both On Click

   c. The remaining text should **Fly In** Very Fast after the mouse is clicked

   d. Add an exit effect for the traffic graphic causing it to **Fly Out** Very Slow After Previous, playing the airplane flying overhead sound simultaneously

5. On slide 4, add the graphic of a pilot (Clips Organizer), and insert sounds of a plane engine (Clips Online). Set the following in the order presented

   a. Play the airplane engine first On Click

   b. Set the title to **Wipe**, From Left, Very Fast, After Previous

   c. Set the text to **Dissolve In**, Very Fast, After Previous as a group

   d. Set the graphic to move off the screen with the airplane engine After Previous

6. On slide 5 insert a graphic of a pilot that you did not use in the previous slide. Set the following in the order presented

   a. Add a **Brush On Underline** emphasis effect to the title On Click

   b. Have the text enter line-by-line by clicking the mouse

7. On slide 6 insert a graphic associated with the airlines and the clip **Airport Ambiance** sound clip (Clips Online). Set the following in the order presented

   a. Set the title to **Dissolve In** On Click

   b. Play the music clip After Previous

   c. Make the text display as a group using **Wipe**, From Right, With Previous

8. Drag the sound icons off each slide so that they do not display during the presentation

9. Save the presentation as **<yourname>AirTraffic.ppt**

FIGURE 5.25

Air Traffic opening slide

1. Plaza at the Mall

The covered mall has replaced stand-alone shopping areas. These cities-within-a-city favor block-long shops punctuated with a corner or intersection. Intersections are an opportunity to entertain the public, and frequently there will be performers, trade shows, and other displays to draw people. By keeping the public within the mall, there is a greater likelihood they will continue to shop. Hence the vitality of the mall is ensured. Plaza at the Mall is a consulting company that designs activities for those intersections at malls across the United States. Their focus is multifold, including decorations for all occasions, exhibits, and entertainment of all kinds. When mall retailers subscribe to Plaza's services, they are guaranteed events for every month of the year. You have been asked to prepare a PowerPoint presentation to illustrate what Plaza at the Mall can provide.

1. Start PowerPoint and open **pp05PlazaMall.ppt**

2. Open the Slide Master, add a **Zoom** Entrance effect to the Firework graphic, and click **Close Master View** on the Slide Master View toolbar

3. On slide 1 add a **Pinwheel** Entrance effect to the title that spins each letter individually After Previous

4. Move to slide 2
   a. Add the **Faded Swivel** Entrance effect to the title and set it to play without a mouse click
   b. Add the **Fly In** Entrance effect to the bulleted text. Adjust the settings so that each bullet enters after a mouse click and becomes a medium gray after the next mouse click

5. Move to slide 3
   a. Add the **Compress** Entrance effect to the title and set it to play without a mouse click
   b. Add the **Checkerboard** Entrance effect to the bullets and set the options to load each major bullet (1st level paragraph) on a mouse click

6. Move to slide 4
   a. Add the **Box** Entrance effect to the title and set it to play automatically
   b. Set the bulleted text to **Fly In**, From Bottom by 1st level paragraph

7. Move to slide 5
   a. Add the **Pinwheel** Entrance effect to the title and set it to play automatically
   b. Cause the bulleted text to **Dissolve In** by 1st level paragraph

8. Add a **Bounce** Entrance effect to the title of slide 6. Add graphic(s) and sound(s) to convey the idea of a festival or fun atmosphere

9. Add transitions and animations of your own choosing to slides 7 and 8

10. Test the presentation and save it as **<yourname>PlazaMall.ppt**

FIGURE 5.26

Plaza at the Mall opening slide

2. Brew HA-HA!

Founded in 2000, the Foothills Brewing Company is nestled in the foothills of Denver, Colorado. In its first year, the brewery produced 1,500 barrels of beer. Their lagers and ales are still brewed in small batches, hand-crafted by a team of dedicated workers with only the highest ideals of quality. This pride, along with their brewing process, is what creates the great brews. Foothills Brewing Company uses only the finest ingredients—British and American barley, German yeast, European and Washington State hops, and the pure artesian water from the Rockies.

Foothills beer has no preservatives, additives, or stabilizers and is cold filtered. The result is beer that is the finest and freshest tasting as proven by our loyal customers and great chefs of the West who use Foothills beer in their recipes.

You have been asked to create an informational presentation on the brewing process.

1. Start PowerPoint and open **pp05BrewHAHA.ppt** (see Figure 5.27)

2. Open the Slide Master, add a **Spiral In** Entrance effect to the beer buddies graphic, play On Click, and **Close Master View** on the Slide Master View toolbar

3. On slide 1 add a **Spiral In** Entrance effect to the subtitle and play the **Whoosh** sound at the same time

4. Move to slide 2
   a. Add the **Wipe** From Left Entrance effect to the title to play On Click
   b. Add the **Fly In** Entrance effect to the bulleted text. Adjust the settings so that each bullet enters after a mouse click, and the first bullet turns a medium gray after the next mouse click

5. Move to slide 3
   a. Add the **Dissolve In** Entrance effect to the title and set it to play without a mouse click
   b. Add the **Appear** Entrance effect to the bullets and set the options to load each major bullet (2nd level paragraph) on a mouse click

6. Move to slide 4
   a. Add the **Checker Board** Entrance effect to the title and set it to play automatically
   b. Set the bulleted text to **Peek In**, From Bottom by 1st level paragraph, On Click
   c. Set the 2nd level bullets to enter **Light Speed** fast With Previous

7. Move to slide 5
   a. Add the **Glide** Entrance effect to the title and set it to play automatically
   b. Cause the bulleted text to **Thread** in by 1st level paragraph
   c. Cause the bulleted text to **Boomerang** in by 2nd level paragraph with the beer mug image

8. Add transitions and animations of your own choosing to slides 6 and 7

9. Move to slide 8
   a. Add the **Fly In**, From Bottom, Entrance effect to the title and set it to play automatically
   b. Cause the bulleted text to **Fly In** From Right at the same time with the title

10. Test the presentation and save it as **<yourname>BrewHAHA.ppt**

FIGURE 5.27
Brew HA-HA! opening slide

1. Exotic Flora

Exotic Flora is an international association of florists that was introduced in Chapter 1. The basic presentation was created to introduce the organization's services, but no graphics or animations were added. The goal is to place self-running kiosks on the Web site and in malls around the world. The purpose of the kiosk is to present the floral arrangements that can be purchased through the network. Now you will add photographs to go with the text, develop transitions, and set the presentation to run automatically.

1. Start PowerPoint and open **pp05ExoticFlora.ppt**

2. Search for photographs of exotic flower arrangements to be used on two of the slides. Try to find some of the flowers listed on the slides

3. Move to slide 3

   a. Refer to Figure 5.28 as you add a 3-D rectangle to frame the picture. To add a 3-D rectangle, click the **Rectangle** ☐ on the Drawing toolbar, click and drag the rectangle on a slide, click the **3-D Style** ▣ button on the Drawing toolbar, and click the **3-D Style 1** icon (first row, first column) from the pop-up list of icons. Insert **pp05Splash.jpg** from the files for this chapter

   b. Size and arrange the image and frame and then group them

   c. Copy both the image and frame and paste them on slide 1

4. Move to slide 4. Using the techniques from the previous step, insert and frame **pp05HA2.jpg**. Copy and paste the image and frame to slide 1

5. Move to slide 6. Using the same techniques, insert and frame **pp05KeaMix.jpg**

6. Move to slide 7. Using the same techniques, insert and frame **pp05OhanuMix.jpg**

7. On slides 2 and 5 add a rectangle with 3-D effect to frame the picture. Insert one of the images that you located. Adjust the frame and image and then group them. Copy one of the groups to slide 1

8. Arrange the three frames and images on slide 1 to create a display similar to that shown in Figure 5.29. Be sure to control the stacking order

9. Set transitions and animations for each slide. Set the slide show to automatically advance after 4 seconds on each slide

10. Save the presentation as **<yourname>ExoticFlora.ppt**

FIGURE 5.28

3-D rectangle framing splash.jpg

FIGURE 5.29

Grouping framed images

2. e-Business . . . What Is All the Hype?

Unless you have been living under a rock for the last few years, you have heard about e-business! And you have heard about it from several different angles. For example:

- You have heard about the companies that offer e-commerce because you have been bombarded by their TV and radio ads

- You have read the news stories about the shift to e-business and the hype that has developed around e-business companies

- You have seen the huge valuations that Web companies get in the stock market, even when they don't make a profit

- And you may have purchased something on the Web, so you have direct personal experience with e-business

You have been asked to create a brief overview of what e-business is, to be used as a kiosk.

1. Start PowerPoint and open **pp05e-Business.ppt** (see Figure 5.30)

2. On slide 1 add a graphical image (Clips Online) that represents e-business (you should search for e-commerce as well) and then add a **Fly In** From Right Entrance animation

3. Move to slide 2. Insert a graphical image that represents a transaction or money exchange

   a. Add a 3-D rectangle to frame the picture

   b. Size and arrange the image and frame, and then group as one

4. Move to slide 4. Using the techniques from the previous step, insert and frame a graphical image that represents purchasing

5. Move to slide 5. Using the same techniques, insert and frame a graphical image that represents a Web site

6. On slides 6 and 7 add whatever images you feel would complement the slides

7. Set transitions and animations for each slide. Set the slide show to automatically advance after 5 seconds on each slide

8. Save the presentation as **<yourname>e-Business.ppt**

FIGURE 5.30
e-Business opening slide

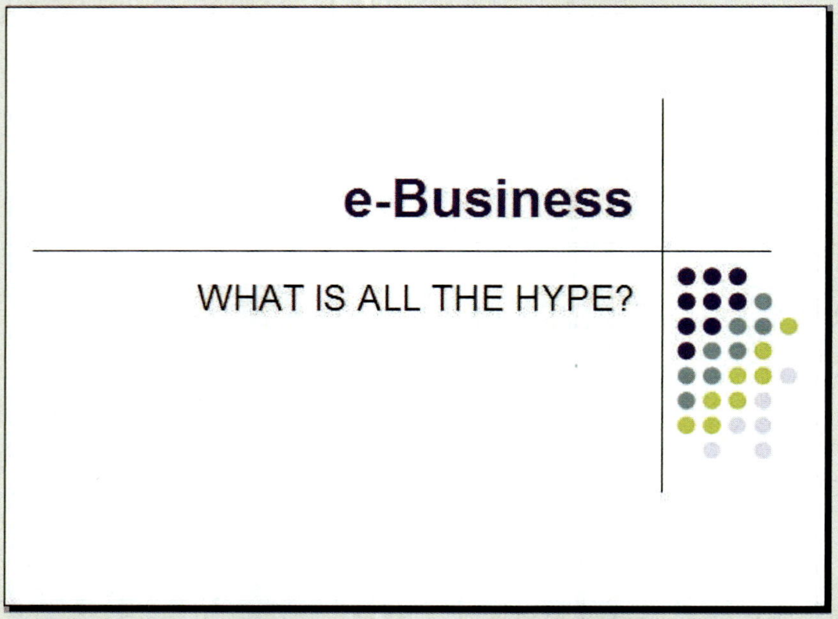

1. European Union Currency

Twelve European countries are in the process of changing or have changed their currency to European Union (EU) notes and coins. The coins have one side that is standard among all countries. On the obverse, each country will decorate the coins with their own designs. The notes will be uniform. Making this change is a tremendous undertaking, and one that has not been entirely well received. For most, a change can be frightening. To ease the transition, the Web site www.EUnotesandcoins.com has been designated. You have been asked to prepare a presentation that will help American travelers understand and use the new currency.

1. Visit http://money.msn.co.uk/euro or use a search engine of your choice to find a Web site containing data and graphics for this presentation

2. Open PowerPoint presentation **pp05EUCurrency.ppt**

3. Save the presentation as **<yourname>EuroCurrency.ppt**

4. Add a currency-related graphic to slide 1
   a. Set a **Diamond** Entrance for both the title and graphic. Cause the animations to play simultaneously after the slide loads
   b. Set a **Fly In** Entrance for the subtitle that plays automatically after the title animation is completed

5. Move to the slide 2 and add graphics (at least two) representing the euro countries
   a. Add a **Diamond** Entrance to the slide title that plays automatically
   b. Add a **Shimmer** Emphasis to the country names. No mouse click should be required
   c. Use a **Spin** Emphasis to animate the graphics. Do not require a mouse click

6. Move to slide 3 and add graphics depicting the use of coins
   a. Add a **Dissolve In** Entrance to the title that plays automatically
   b. Use a **Checkerboard** Entrance to have the bullets enter one at a time by mouse click

7. Move to slide 4 and add graphics of paper notes and coins. Set the following animations to occur without mouse clicks
   a. Animate the coins to drop into position with an appropriate sound
   b. Set the title animation to **Fly In** From Bottom Right
   c. Set the bulleted text to have a **Grow/Shrink** Emphasis

8. Move to slide 14
   a. Insert appropriate graphics
   b. Animate all slide elements

9. Using images from your research, add graphics to at least three of the remaining slides to complete the information being presented. Resize the graphic, if necessary

10. Review the presentation and make any needed adjustments. Save it once again

FIGURE 5.31
Euro Currency opening slide

Euro Currency

Recognizing the New Currency

2. Hummergear.com

Hummergear.com is a leading-edge e-commerce provider of accessories and parts for Hummers. They have over 15 years of automotive experience, and have spent countless hours combining knowledge of the industry with a state-of-the-art e-commerce application to bring you the most sought after accessories available for the Hummer. Their Web site was designed with the consumer in mind, to make online accessory shopping easy, fast, and simple. Hummergear.com has also carefully selected the brands to carry in order to provide consumers with only the best available products at reasonable prices. No other automotive accessory Web site offers an equivalent level of selection and service.

1. Use a search engine to locate graphics for this presentation

2. Start PowerPoint and open **pp05HummerGear.ppt**

3. Save the presentation as **<yourname>HummerGear.ppt**

4. On slide 1
   a. Set a **Fly In** Entrance for both the title and graphic. Cause the animations to play simultaneously after the slide loads
   b. Set a **Diamond** Entrance for the subtitle that plays automatically after the title animation is completed

5. Move to slide 2 and add graphics (at least two) representing two of the accessories listed
   a. Add a **Spinner** In Entrance effect to the slide title that plays automatically
   b. Add a **Shimmer** Emphasis effect to the accessory names. No mouse click should be required
   c. Use a **Diamond** Entrance effect to animate the graphics. Do not require a mouse click

6. Move to slide 3 and add graphics that complement one of the bulleted items
   a. Add a **Dissolve In** Entrance effect to the title that plays automatically
   b. Use a **Checkerboard** Entrance effect to have the bullets enter one at a time by mouse click

7. Move to slide 4 and add graphics that represent money. Set the following animations to occur without mouse clicks
   a. Animate the money graphic to drop into position with an appropriate sound
   b. Set the title animation to **Fly In** From Bottom Right
   c. Set the bulleted text to have a **Grow/Shrink** Emphasis effect

8. Move to slide 5
   a. Insert an appropriate graphic
   b. Animate all slide elements

9. Review the presentation and make any needed adjustments

10. Save the presentation again

FIGURE 5.32
Hummergear opening slide

around the world

1. Golden Globe, Inc.

Golden Globe is a successful exploration company that contracts with development companies across the world to locate gold ore. Gold ores are frequently found in association with various copper minerals such as malachite, copper sulfate, copper carbonate, chalcopyrite (copper iron sulfide), or silver. Golden Globe's business strategy has been to identify areas through geologic maps that correspond to known gold ore locations in association with copper or silver veins. Once an area has been identified, Golden Globe sends its geologists into the field to explore more fully. If substantial veins of gold are found, Golden Globe is given a bonus of 15 percent of the profits from the tonnage collected during the first year. With this in mind, Golden Globe has become a top-ranking gold exploration company in the world. Golden Globe has been hired to complete a preliminary assessment of the feasibility of marketable gold ore in the northwest sector of Australia. You have been asked to prepare a PowerPoint presentation for the Queensland Development Company on Golden Globe's preliminary report.

1. Start PowerPoint and open **pp05GoldenGlobe.ppt**

2. Set all slides to have a **Box Out** slide transition, and Advance on mouse click

3. Move to slide 1
   a. Add an intrinsic sound that will play without clicking. Move the sound icon off the slide
   b. Add an **Unfold** Entrance effect to the title that plays automatically
   c. Add the **Rise Up** Entrance effect to the subtitle that plays automatically after the title

4. Move to slide 2 and add a graphic
   a. Set the Box Out slide transition to have a Chime
   b. Add the **Box** Entrance animation to both the title and the graphic. Make the animations play simultaneously

5. Move to slide 3. Add the **Fold** Entrance effect to the bulleted text to play With Previous

6. Move to slide 4. Animate the chart to appear **By series** on mouse click

7. Move to slide 5. Add an appropriate graphic. Animate the graphic and title to **Spiral In** simultaneously

8. Repeat step 7 for slides 6 through 8

9. Move to slide 9
   a. Add and organize several relevant graphics
   b. Animate the bullets with a **Fly In** From Bottom Right Entrance effect
   c. Dim the text to light blue

10. Review the presentation and make any adjustments

11. Save your presentation as **<yourname>GoldenGlobe.ppt**

FIGURE 5.33

Golden Globe opening slide

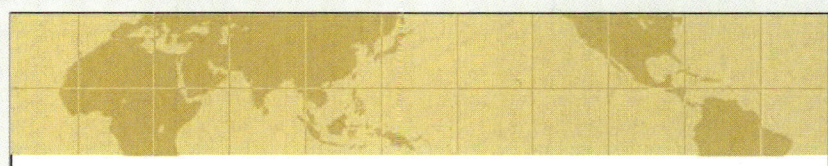

Golden Globe, Inc.

Australian Shelf Exploration
Preliminary Report for
Queensland Development Company

2. USGTF

Founded in 1989, the United States Golf Teachers Federation began making history by training and certifying golf teaching professionals for the golfing public. By opening the door to those who previously were never given the opportunity to teach golf, the USGTF started a trend that has led the game through a decade of growth and popularity never seen before.

Today, the USGTF is the largest organization of strictly golf teaching professionals in the world with over 13,000 members. The USGTF is a founding member of the World Golf Teachers Federation® and is one of 35 member nations that make up this entity. Both federations help to establish the world's standard for golf teaching professionals.

The USGTF educational theme is that of progressive learning. They incorporate four levels of certification for the golf teaching professional. It is not required to attend Level I or Level II prior to attending the Level III full certification. This approach allows the golfer the opportunity to progress comfortably at his or her own pace in the golf teaching industry.

1. Start PowerPoint and open **pp05USGTF.ppt**

2. Set all slides to have a **Box In** Slide Transition

3. Move to slide 1 and play the **Whoosh** sound with the title
   a. Add an **Unfold** Entrance effect to the title that plays automatically
   b. Add the **Rise Up** Entrance effect to the subtitle that plays automatically after the title

4. Move to slide 2 and add a graphic
   a. Set the **Box In** Slide Transition to have a **Drum Roll**
   b. Add the **Peek In** animation to both the title and the graphic. Make the animations play simultaneously

5. Move to slide 3. Add the **Fly In** Entrance effect to the bulleted text

6. Move to slide 4. Add the **Diamond** Entrance effect on the bulleted text

7. Move to slide 5. Animate the graphic and title to **Spiral In** simultaneously

8. Repeat step 7 for slides 6 through 8

9. Test the presentation and make any adjustments

10. Save your presentation as **<yourname>USGTF.ppt**

FIGURE 5.34
USGTF opening slide

running project

Montgomery-Wellish Foods, Inc.: Preparing MWF FoodsPresentation to Be Self-Running

In the last chapter, you created a presentation designed to instruct new trainees on effective presentation skills. It was shown at one of the training meetings. Daniel Wellish would now like that presentation to be adapted so that it can run automatically at future training seminars or for trainees to review. You will need to make some adaptations to fit these new circumstances.

1. Open **pp05MWFoodsPresentation.ppt** in PowerPoint
2. Locate an appropriate animated GIF for the first slide, insert it, and configure it to play automatically
3. Use the techniques from this chapter to improve the graphics on each remaining slide of your presentation (try 3-D framing)

4. Set animations on each slide
   a. Set each title to **Fly In** From Right without a mouse click
   b. Set bulleted text to **Box** by 1st level paragraph when triggered by a mouse click
   c. Animate the graphics and set the animation to play at the same time as the title animation
   d. Dim text from previous bullets
5. Record a narration for the presentation using **PP05MWFscript.doc** as your guide. Print the script for the best results. Use the options from the Slide Show menu. Remember to speak slowly and distinctly and pause between points. If necessary, rerecord
6. Save the presentation as **<yourname>MWFoods.ppt**

FIGURE 5.35
Montgomery-Wellish opening slide

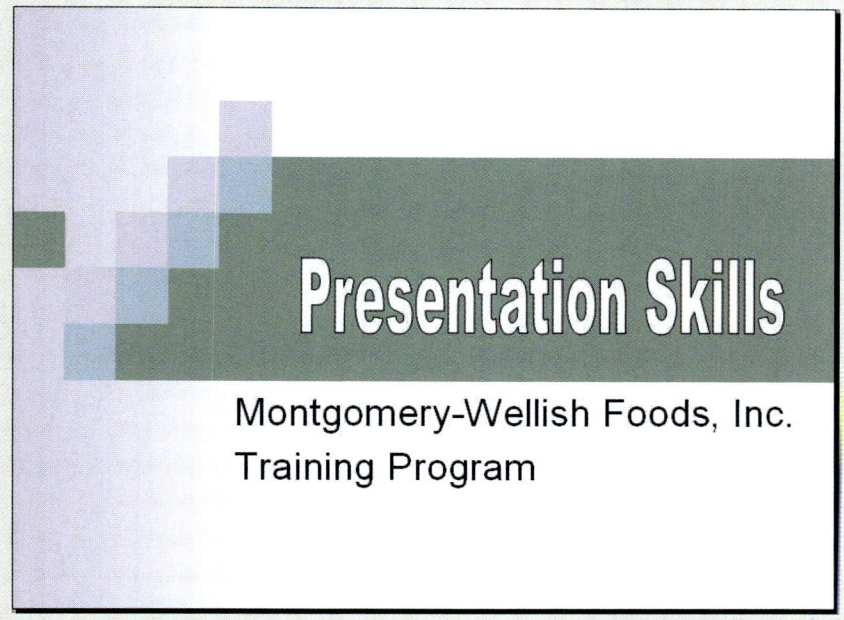

analysis

1. Timing a Presentation

You can specify the amount of time allotted to each slide during a presentation and test yourself during rehearsal using the slide meter. Create an outline of the steps that are needed in order to create the timing effects.

2. Using Specialized Animations

Using specialized animations, you can apply animations to particular objects. You can introduce text, bullets, or images all at once or one at a time. Create an outline of the steps that are needed in order to animate text, bullets, and graphical images.

did you
know?

the *most abundant metal in the Earth's crust is aluminum.*

seventy-five *percent of the hacking victims—most often corporations and government agencies—have found that it costs an average of $1 million per intrusion to investigate, repair, and secure their systems once they've been hacked.*

the *Wright brothers' historic flight covered a distance less than the length of today's Space Shuttle.*

"any *sufficiently advanced technology is indistinguishable from a rigged demo," James Klass*

nearly *60 percent of women say they receive at least 11 e-mails a day, whereas only _____ percent of men say they do.*

Chapter Objectives

- **Create and add Office Art elements to slides using the Drawing toolbar—MOS PP035-1-4**

- **Modify PowerPoint Design templates using color schemes**

- **Create and apply custom color schemes**

- **Customize slide backgrounds using bitmaps—MOS PP035-2-3**

- **Add graphic elements to presentation notes**

Using PowerPoint to Report Progress

For the past year Ian Matubo has been the vice president of Human Resources for Aggregate Petroleum, a large oil and gas company with holdings in the United States, Canada, and Mexico. Aggregate has offices, filling stations, refineries, and oil wells throughout the North American continent with over 10,000 employees.

The organization is divided into 12 regions for management, distribution, and reporting purposes. Each region has a director of Human Resources who reports to Ian. Each director manages a staff responsible for all personnel issues in their region. Responsibilities include advertising for new employees, interviewing potential employees, screening résumés, managing employee benefits, documenting employee performance, resolving work-related conflicts, sponsoring employee recreational activities, monitoring disciplinary actions, and supervising terminations.

Large businesses like Aggregate use operations and procedures manuals to ensure common practice and equitable treatment of employees across the entire organization. Such manuals outline exactly what steps must be taken to hire, interview, fire, or discipline an employee. Actions that an employee must take to resolve conflict with another employee, a manager, or with the organization as a whole are also documented. Aggregate's current manual is over three years old and no longer reflects up-to-date practice or law.

For the past month Ian and the Human Resource directors have been evaluating the updates that need to be applied to the operations and procedures manual. They have estimated that the update process will require four to six months, and they believe that it is important to involve the rest of Aggregate's employees in the process. Toward this end, Ian will begin presenting the status of this project at each region's monthly managers' meeting. For the first report, Ian will travel to each region and update the managers using a projected PowerPoint presentation. The remaining status updates will use PowerPoint's Web and broadcast capabilities so that Ian can present without traveling.

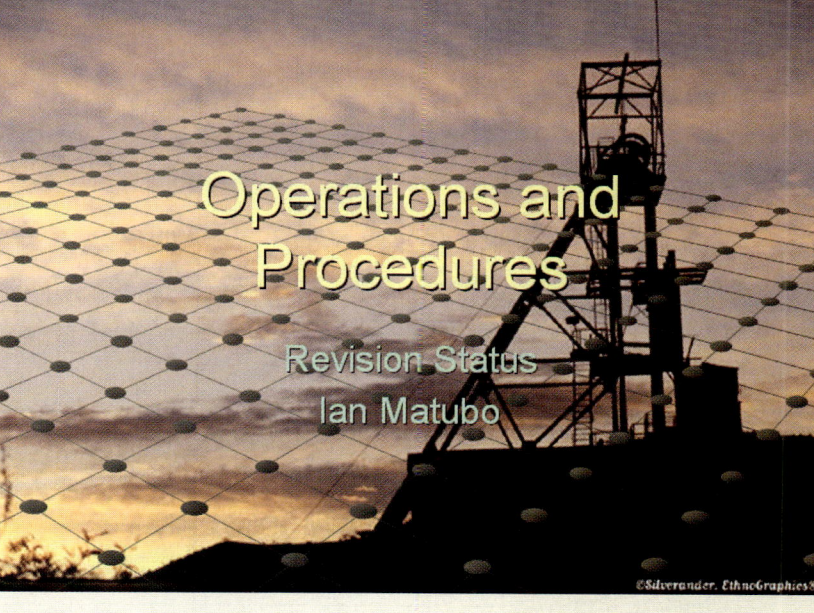

FIGURE 6.1

Artwork for Ian's presentation

Ian has begun to develop his initial presentation using the AutoContent Wizard's template for reporting on the progress or status of a project. He believes that this template will be very effective in guiding him in the creation of slide content. Since he will be presenting to a large professional audience, he would like a customized business look for the slide show and has asked you to work on colors and graphics that would be effective.

SESSION 6.1 CHOOSING A COLOR SCHEME

Making a presentation aesthetically pleasing is an important component in maintaining audience attention and producing a professional-looking slide show. PowerPoint templates use a **color scheme** to control the colors for the slide background, body text, lines, shadows, title text, fills, hyperlinks, and accents. PowerPoint's features make it easy to evaluate various color schemes until you find the one that will best suit current needs.

Using Color Schemes

Selecting an effective color scheme or **palette** involves evaluating the audience and the presentation forum. Color sets the tone of a presentation and must be appealing to viewers. The method of delivery (projected, printed, or computer monitor) impacts the value of selected colors.

A great deal of research has been compiled on the most effective use of color. Consider the audience, tone, speaker's personality, and what is being communicated when selecting colors. A complete discussion of color theory is beyond the scope of this chapter; you should refer to art and color theory materials for guidance in these matters.

Intrinsic Color Schemes

The slide template of a presentation determines the initial color scheme applied to a slide show. Each Design template, including the blank template, has a default color scheme and several alternate color schemes referred to as *intrinsic color schemes*. Alternate schemes display in the Slide Design—Color Schemes panel of the task pane. Each scheme has been developed by artists with color theory, audience appeal, and effective content delivery in mind. Additionally, custom colors can be used with any palette or a completely custom palette can be developed. Ian would like to use the colors of Aggregate's logo for his presentation, if they will work effectively.

---

task reference   **Select a Color Scheme**

- Select a Design template
- Select the slide(s) the color scheme will be applied to
- Use the drop-down menu of the task pane to activate the Slide Design—Color Scheme panel
- Click a color scheme

Changing the pp06StatusReport.ppt color scheme:

1. Start PowerPoint and open **pp06StatusReport.ppt**

tip: *The Digital Dots Design template has already been applied to all slides in the presentation*

2. Open the Online pane, if necessary, click the **Slides** tab, and then click slide 1 to move to it

3. Press **Ctrl+F1**, if necessary, to open the task pane and use the drop-down menu of the task pane to activate the Slide Design—Color Scheme panel

4. Click the **Color Schemes** hyperlink at the top of the task pane, move the mouse near the left edge of the task pane until it turns to a double-headed arrow. Then, click and drag the left edge of the task pane until the color schemes appear in two columns. Release the mouse

5. Click on each available color scheme to evaluate its impact on the presentation (see Figure 6.2)

6. Click the color scheme with a dark gray slide background (see Figure 6.3)

7. Save your presentation as **<yourname>StatusReport.ppt**

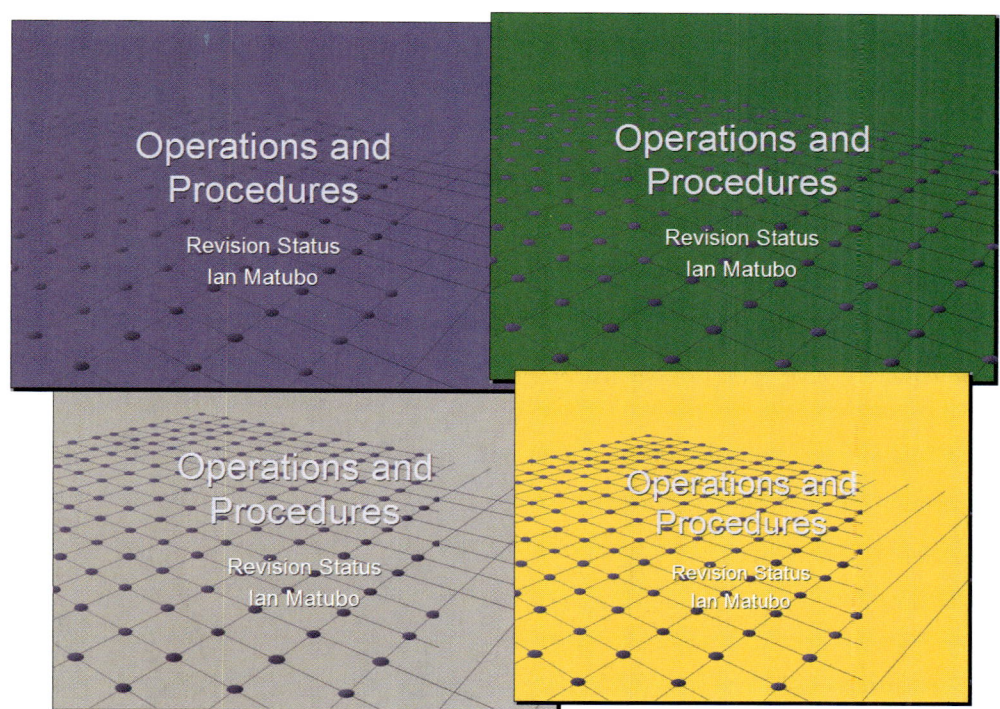

FIGURE 6.2

Title page with various color schemes

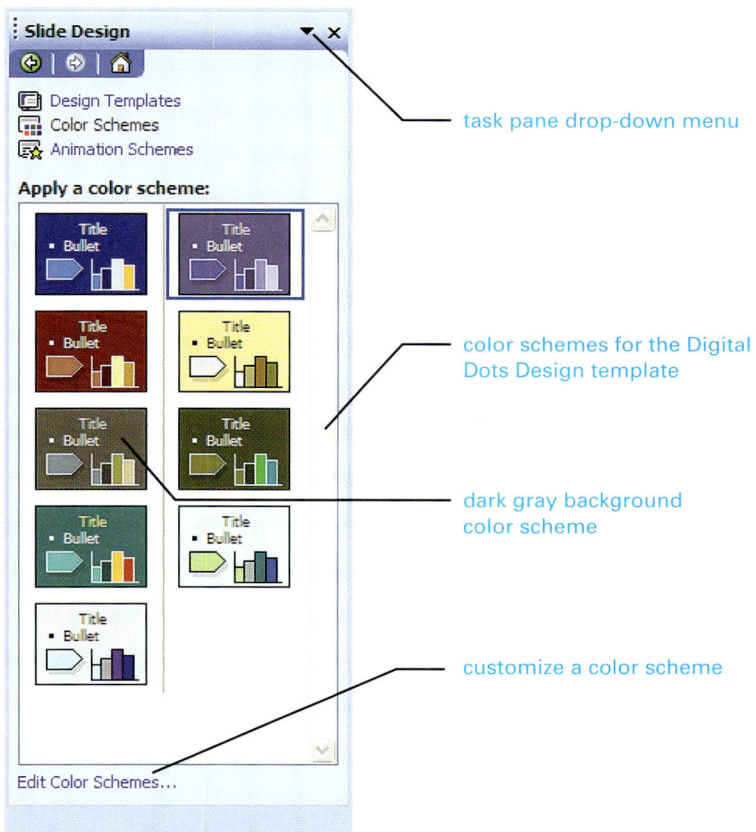

task pane drop-down menu

color schemes for the Digital Dots Design template

dark gray background color scheme

customize a color scheme

FIGURE 6.3

Digital Dots color schemes

The color scheme selected impacts the personality and readability of the presentation. In general, you should remember that light backgrounds are best for printed presentations and dark backgrounds work best for on-screen or projected presentations. Regardless of how your presentation will be delivered, legible text always requires high contrast between the text and background.

Projected presentations should be previewed with the projector that you will use whenever possible. Projection can introduce unpredictable color distortions such as brown tones appearing orange in the projected image. These distortions vary from projector to projector and can cause the audience to be unable to read slide text and decipher images. Colors that work well for projection can look very unappealing on the presenter's monitor but still provide the most effective viewing environment for the audience.

Sometimes it is essential to draw attention to an important topic or to visually let the audience know that a new subject is being introduced. One way to accomplish this is by using different color schemes within the same presentation.

Using multiple color schemes in pp06StatusReport.ppt:

1. Move to slide 3

2. Hover the mouse over the Color Scheme with a teal background (fourth row, first column), and click the arrow (see Figure 6.4)

FIGURE 6.4

Color Scheme drop-down button

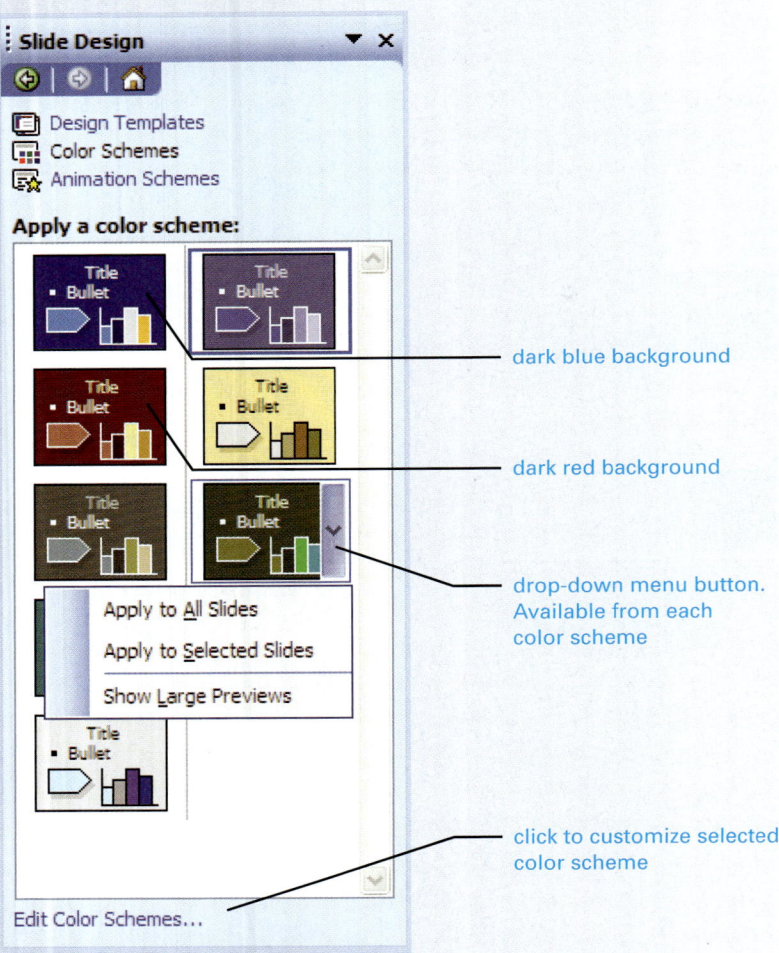

dark blue background

dark red background

drop-down menu button. Available from each color scheme

click to customize selected color scheme

tip: *Pause the cursor over the color scheme to activate the drop-down arrow*

3. Click **Apply to Selected Slides**

4. Use the same methodology to apply the color scheme with the dark red background (row 2, column 1) to slide 4 and the one with the dark blue background (row 1, column 2) to slide 6

A color scheme can be applied to the entire slide show, a single slide, or multiple slides. Select multiple adjacent slides by clicking the first slide and holding the Shift key while clicking the last slide. Select multiple noncontiguous slides by clicking the first slide and then holding the Ctrl key while clicking each of the remaining slides.

Although it is unusual, you can apply color schemes to your notes pages and handouts. Use the Notes view to apply a scheme to notes or use the Handout Master to update handouts (see Figure 6.5). Since notes and handouts are usually printed, a color printer is needed to see the full impact of selected color schemes. When selecting color schemes for printed materials, it is important that you consider that background colors consume large quantities of ink and significantly slow printing time.

Customizing a Color Scheme

The palette of an individual presentation is automatically updated when the color of a font, or other palette object, is changed. The new color appears below the eight colors of the color scheme (slide background, body text, lines, shadows, title text, fills, hyperlinks, and accents) on all color menus. The ability to view colors that have already been applied in a presentation helps you to be consistent.

When you use different colors frequently for a component or two of a Design template, customizing the color scheme simplifies the process and ensures uniformity. Customizing the color scheme is an efficient way to change a color component that does not display well on a monitor or projector throughout a presentation. Color

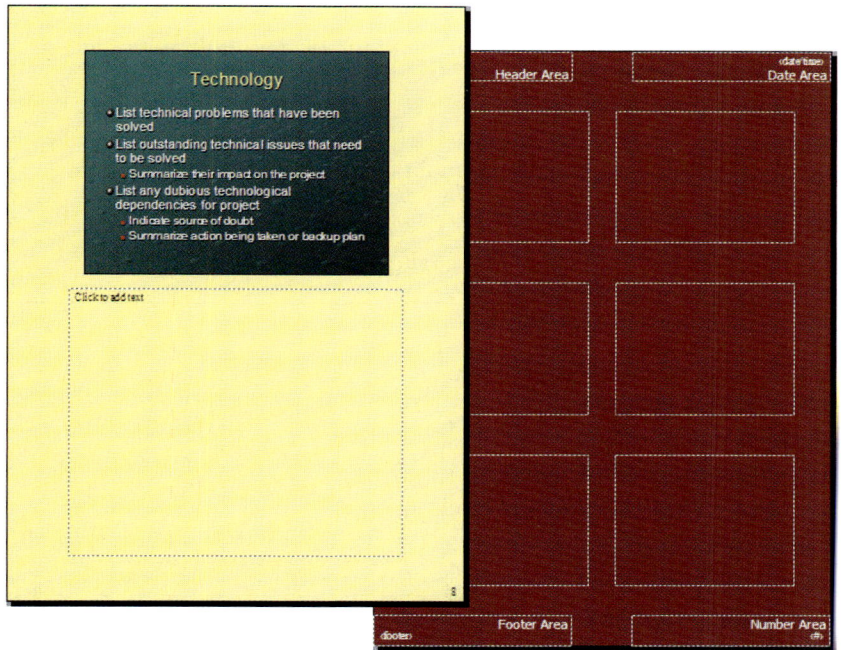

FIGURE 6.5

Color scheme applied to notes and handouts

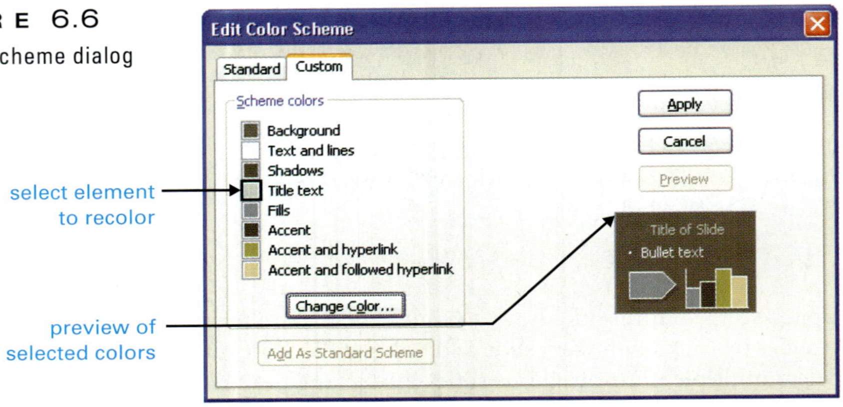

FIGURE 6.6

Edit Color Scheme dialog
box

select element
to recolor

preview of
selected colors

schemes can also be adapted to an event theme that is relevant to a presentation. You
can modify any of the eight template colors using the Color Schemes task pane.

The result of modifying any or all slide colors is a new color scheme. The eight
color scheme elements (slide background, body text, lines, shadows, title text, fills, hyperlinks, and accents) will change or update if a new color scheme is selected, while
other custom colors that have been applied to a presentation will not change (see
Figure 6.6).

task reference   Customize a Color Scheme

- Use the task pane drop-down list to activate the **Slide Design—Color Scheme** panel

- Click the **Edit Color Schemes** link in the Slide Design—Color Scheme panel

- On the **Standard** tab of the Edit Color Scheme dialog box, select the standard color scheme to be customized

- On the **Custom** tab, select the color scheme element to customize and click **Change Color**

  - Use either the Standard or Custom tab of the Background Color dialog box to select a new color

  - Click **OK**

- Repeat the previous step for each element to be customized

- Use the **Preview** button to view the new colors on your slide

- Click **Apply** to permanently apply the changes

Customizing a color scheme:

1. Move to slide 1

2. Use the task pane drop-down list to activate the **Slide Design—Color Scheme**, if necessary

3. Click the **Edit Color Schemes** link, located at the bottom of the task pane

4. Click the **Standard** tab of the Edit Color Scheme dialog box, click the standard color scheme that matches the current slide (dark gray background)

5. Click the **Custom** tab of the Edit Color Scheme dialog box (see Figure 6.6), click the **Title text** check box and click **Change color**

6. Click the **Standard** tab of the Title Text Color dialog box, click the color indicated in Figure 6.7 and click **OK**

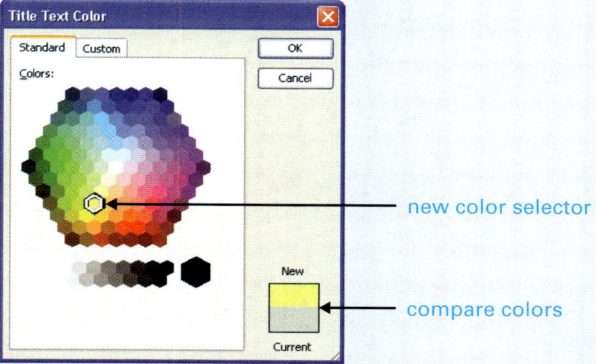

FIGURE 6.7

Selecting a new title color

7. Repeat the process to choose a light blue color for *Text and Lines*

8. Click the **Preview** button to evaluate the impact on your slide

9. Click **Apply** to apply the revised color scheme to the presentation and create a custom scheme

Each time a standard color scheme is modified, a new color scheme is created. A total of 16 color schemes can be stored for each Design template. Custom color schemes display along with the standard schemes in the color gallery in the Slide Design—Color Schemes task pane. Custom schemes are available to any presentation using the Design template that was updated.

Painting and Deleting a Color Scheme

PowerPoint's format painting feature can be used to copy the color scheme from one slide to another slide within a presentation or to copy schemes between presentations. Click the slide with the format that you would like to copy and then activate the Format Painter button of the Standard toolbar. Single-click the button to apply the format to one additional slide, or double-click it to apply the format to multiple slides. The Esc key will cancel format painting initiated by double-clicking. When a color scheme is copied from another presentation, it becomes available in the Slide Design—Color Schemes task pane of the destination presentation.

Color schemes can be deleted from the list of standard schemes using the Edit Color Scheme dialog box. It is important to remove any color schemes that are created by mistake or are not used for another reason. An unnecessary color scheme will be created and deleted to demonstrate this concept.

---

task reference   Delete a Color Scheme

- Use the task pane drop-down list to activate the **Slide Design—Color Scheme** panel
- Click the **Edit Color Schemes** link in the Slide Design—Color Scheme panel
- On the **Standard** tab of the Edit Color Scheme dialog box, select the color scheme to be deleted
- Click the **Delete Scheme** button
- Click **Apply**

Deleting a custom color scheme:

1. Move to slide 1

2. Use the task pane drop-down list to display the **Slide Design—Color Scheme** panel, if necessary

3. Click the **Edit Color Schemes** link

4. Click the **Standard** tab of the Edit Color Scheme dialog box, select the standard color scheme with a dark green background

5. Click the **Custom** tab of the Edit Color Scheme dialog box, click the **Background** element, click **Change Color**, and click the **Standard** tab

6. Choose a bright green, click **OK**, and then click **Apply**

tip: *The bright green color scheme has now been added to the Standard Schemes gallery*

7. Click the **Edit Color Schemes** link to reactivate the Edit Color Scheme dialog box

8. Click the **Standard** tab of the Edit Color Scheme dialog box, select the standard color scheme with a light green background, if necessary (see Figure 6.8)

FIGURE 6.8

Deleting a color scheme

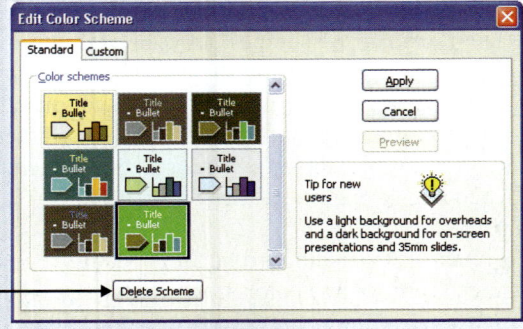

click to delete the selected color scheme

9. Click **Delete Scheme**

10. Click **Apply** to apply the revised color scheme to the presentation and create a custom scheme

You can restore a mistakenly deleted color scheme using the Undo button on the Standard toolbar. Reinstalling PowerPoint may be required to restore standard color schemes once the application has been shut down. Deleting a color scheme makes it unavailable to other presentations using the updated Design template.

help yourself *Click the* Type a Question for help *combo box, type* **remove graphic fill***, and press* **Enter***. Click the hyperlink* **Add, change, or remove a fill** *and then click the hyperlink* **Remove a fill** *to display Help on how you can remove the graphic color or fill from a graphic. Click the Help screen* **Close** *button when you are finished*

Customizing the Color Menus

The eight colors defined by the selected color scheme are automatically applied to the appropriate components of each slide. These colors will display on all color menus. Other colors are added to these menus as you apply them to slide components. Colors added to one of the menus, for example the Font Color menu, will appear on all of the other menus. This feature allows you to apply the same custom color to various objects throughout the presentation.

Adding new colors to the Color menus:

1. Move to slide 2 and select the text box in the top triangle containing "The Future"

tip: *You will need a dotted line selection box around the object or to select the text*

2. Drop down the **Font Color** selections from the Formatting toolbar (see Figure 6.9)

   a. Click **More Colors** to activate the Colors dialog box

   b. Click the **Standard** tab of the Colors dialog box and then click the top left dark blue hexagon

   c. Click **OK**

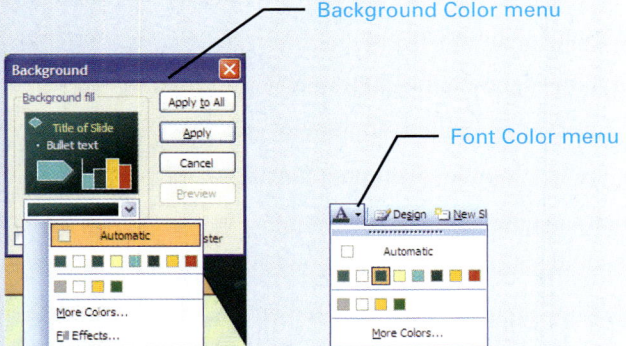

Background Color menu

Font Color menu

FIGURE 6.9
Color menus

3. Select the remaining text boxes in the pyramid and use the Font Color menu to apply the same color from step 2

tip: *Select the first text box with a dotted line selector and then hold the Shift key while selecting the remaining text boxes. The color appears in the line below the eight color scheme colors*

4. Save the presentation

As was previously mentioned, the color menus are palettes that display colors already in use for a presentation. Up to eight custom colors display below the eight colors of the active color scheme. If more than eight custom colors are used in a presentation, the ninth color displays in the first slot replacing the first custom color used. The tenth color will display in the second slot, and so on.

Customizing Slide Backgrounds

Changing the color of a slide background can be accomplished by adjusting the Background component of the color scheme, or using the Background Color menu. The Background Color menu can also be used to change the slide background to a texture, fill pattern, or picture.

Gradient and Texture Backgrounds

Gradient and Texture backgrounds add a depth and professionalism to a presentation. Gradient backgrounds merge two or more colors to create the illusion of light. Gradients and textures can be added using the preset selections or colors from the presentation's color scheme, or they can be completely customized.

---

task reference   Define a Gradient Background

- Right-click on the slide to contain the gradient background
- Click the **Background** pop-up menu option
- Click **Fill Effects**
- Click the **Gradient** tab
- Select the desired gradient effects and click **OK**
- Click either
  - **Apply to All** to set this as the background for all presentation slides
  - **Apply** to set this as the background for the selected slides only

---

Adding a gradient background:

1. Move to slide 3
2. Right-click the slide background and click **Background** from the pop-up menu
3. Drop down the **Color** menu and click **Fill Effects**
4. Click the **Gradient** tab and refer to Figure 6.10 for the settings
   a. Select the **Two colors** option button
   b. Match the Color 1 and Color 2 selections shown in Figure 6.10
   c. Click the **From corner** Shading styles option button
   d. Click **OK**
5. Click **Apply** to apply the gradient to the current slide

FIGURE 6.10
Gradient settings

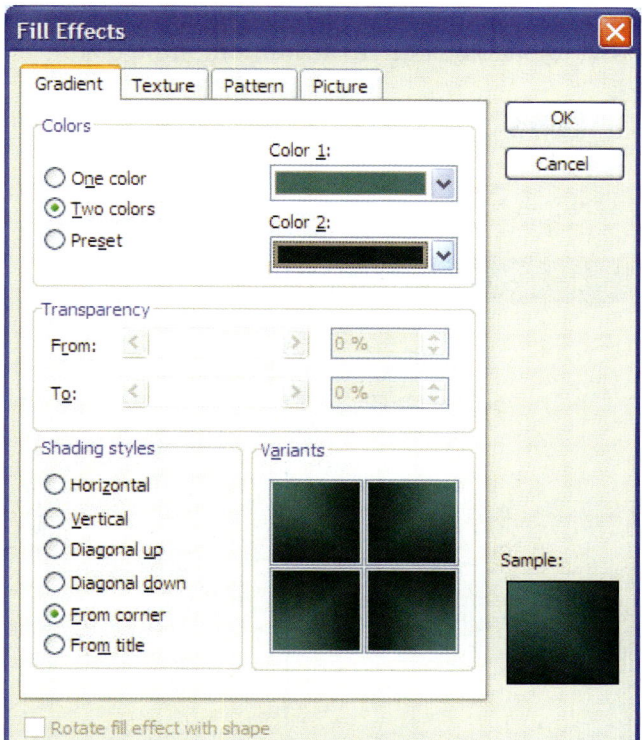

The gradient background just applied should appear behind the graphic of the Digital Dots design template. In this case the gradient effect works well with the template graphic and slide text. Sometimes the result could be too busy for a readable slide, and one solution is to omit the graphic. The Background option of the slide pop-up menu has a check box that will omit any background graphics from the Slide Master.

---

task reference Select a Texture Background

- Right-click on the slide to contain the texture background
- Click the **Background** pop-up menu option
- Click **Fill Effects**
- Click the **Texture** tab
- Select the desired texture and click **OK**
- Click either
  - **Apply to All** to set this as the background for all presentation slides
  - **Apply** to set this as the background for the selected slides only

---

Adding a texture background:

1. Move to slide 2

2. Right-click on the slide background and click **Background** from the pop-up menu

3. Drop down the **Color** menu (the list box on the lower left of the dialog box) and click **Fill Effects**

4. Click the **Texture** tab, click the **Purple mesh** texture (see Figure 6.11), and click **OK**

5. Click **Apply** to apply the texture to the current slide

FIGURE 6.11

Selecting the Purple mesh texture

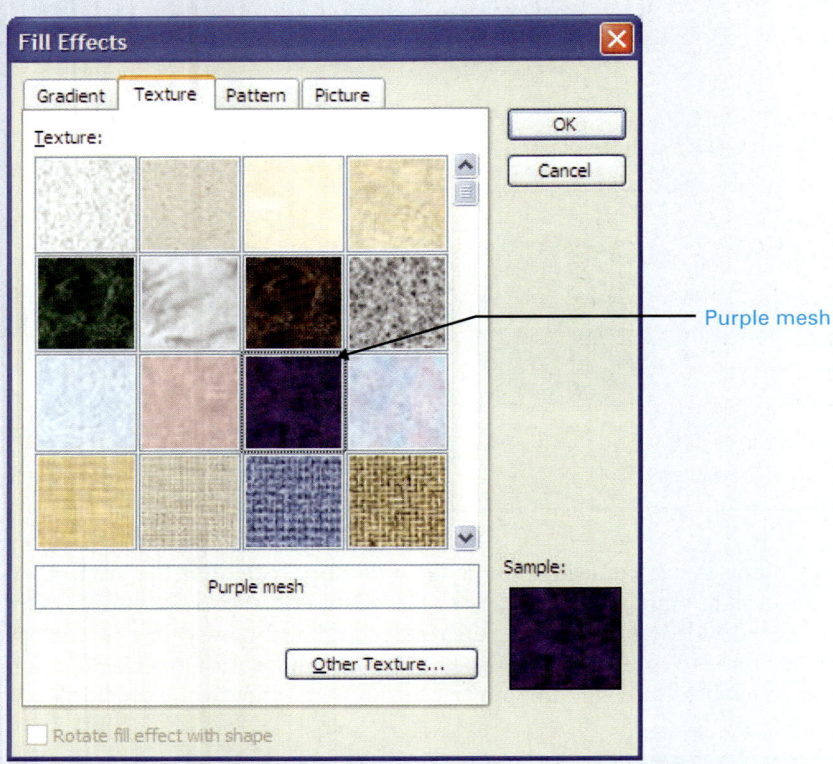

Many of the available textures are busy and can detract from the text in a presentation. Be sure to select textures that are appropriate for your audience and topic, while still providing the high contrast necessary for readable text. When changing the text color does not improve readability, adding a solid panel behind the text will usually allow text to be read. This technique, called *matting*, will be demonstrated with a busy picture background in the next topic.

Picture Backgrounds

Pictures can also be used as slide backgrounds. Appropriate background images typically are related to the presentation topic and will not interfere with the text of the presentation. The Microsoft Clip Organizer contains a few background images. A broader image selection is available from the online gallery, or images from other sources can be used.

task reference   Apply a Picture Background

- Locate and save an appropriate picture
- Right-click on the slide to contain the picture background
- Click the **Background** pop-up menu option
- Click **Fill Effects**
- Click the **Picture** tab
- Click the **Select Picture** button, choose the picture file, click **Insert**, and then click **OK**
- Click either
  - **Apply to All** to set this as the background for all presentation slides
  - **Apply** to set this as the background for the selected slides only
  - **Preview** to evaluate the effect of the background without applying it

Adding a picture background to a slide:

1. Move to slide 1
2. Right-click on the slide background and click **Background** from the pop-up menu
3. Drop down the **Color** menu and click **Fill Effects**
4. Click the **Picture** tab
5. Click the **Select Picture** button, navigate to the files for this chapter, select **pp06SunriseOil.jpg**, click **Insert**, and then click **OK** (see Figure 6.12)

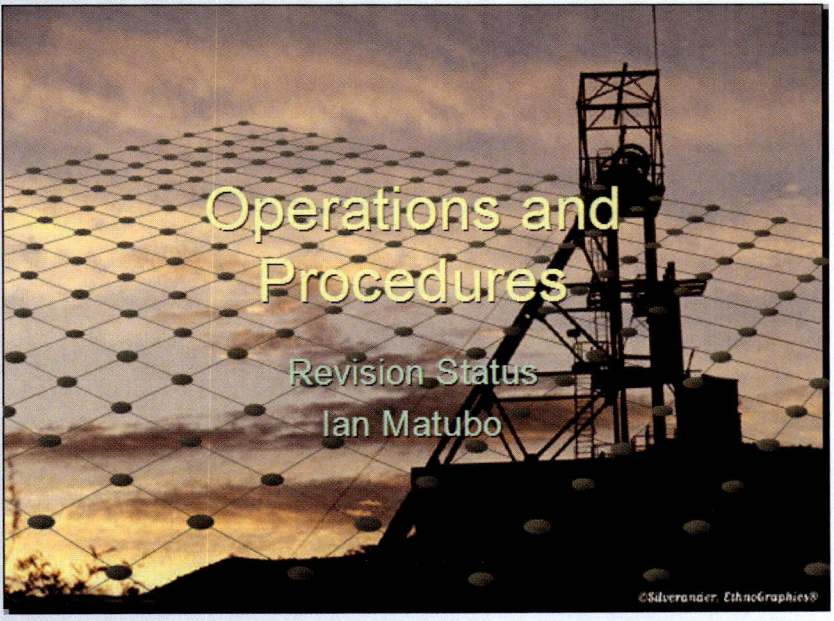

FIGURE 6.12
Title slide with SunriseOil picture background

6. Click **Apply** to apply the picture to the current slide

7. Move to slide 4, repeat steps 2 through 5, but select **pp06Background2.jpg** the background picture, check **Omit background graphics from master**, and click **Apply**

8. Move to slide 5, repeat steps 2 through 6, make **pp06ArtisticBackground.wmf** the background picture, and check **Omit background graphics from master**

9. Adjust the text color in slide 4 and slide 5 to **black**

Any picture format that can be accessed by PowerPoint can be used as a background. Most of the sources already mentioned for graphics have images specifically designed to be used as backgrounds. The images used in the previous steps were downloaded from the Microsoft Media Gallery online.

The fourth slide is still not as readable as Ian would like, so you decide to apply a mat effect behind the text. Matting can be accomplished using shape objects from the Drawing toolbar or by simply formatting each placeholder.

Adding a mat background to the text:

1. Move to slide 4

2. Right-click on the title placeholder and click **Format Placeholder** from the pop-up menu

3. Click the Fill Color list box (at the top of the dialog box) and click the **White** color square

4. Click the Line Color list box and select a dark gray (not black) line color, and set the line weight to **2.5 pt**

5. Click **OK**

6. Repeat steps 3 through 6 for the bulleted list placeholder

7. Use the Formatting toolbar to remove the shadow from all slide text (see Figure 6.13)

tip: *Select the text and click the* **Shadow** $\boxed{\text{S}}$ *button*

When matting text by formatting the placeholder background, select a color that complements the background image on the slide while maintaining high contrast between the mat and text. Adding a line around the mat provides a 3-D effect. Experiment with different line colors and weights until you achieve the desired look. All of the custom background effects that have been applied to slides can also be applied to notes pages.

Pictures as Bullets

You have seen pictures used as bullets in the PowerPoint templates. Custom bullets can be selected to match the theme or color scheme of any presentation. The Clip Organizer contains several images that make suitable bullets, and more are available online.

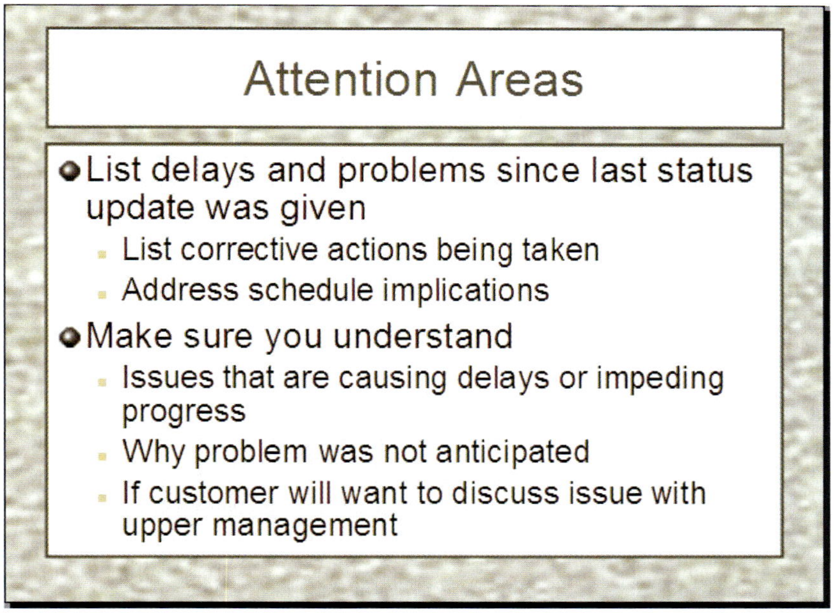

Attention Areas

- List delays and problems since last status update was given
  - List corrective actions being taken
  - Address schedule implications
- Make sure you understand
  - Issues that are causing delays or impeding progress
  - Why problem was not anticipated
  - If customer will want to discuss issue with upper management

FIGURE 6.13
Formatted text placeholders

task reference   **Apply a Picture as a Bullet**

- Select the text or list that will contain the picture bullet
- On the **Format** menu, click **Bullets and Numbering**, and then click the **Bulleted** tab
- On the Bulleted tab, click the **Picture** button
  - Select a picture from the Picture Bullet dialog box
  - Click **OK**

Adding a picture bullet to pp06StatusReport.ppt:

1. Move to slide 5

2. Select the first three bullets by dragging the mouse through the first three bulleted items

3. Click **Format**, click **Bullets and Numbering**, and then click the **Bulleted** tab, if necessary

4. On the Bulleted tab, click the **Picture** button

5. Select the bulleted picture shown in Figure 6.14 (scroll about 1/3 down the list)

6. Click **OK** to apply the picture to the selected text

7. Click **File**, click **Exit**, and click **Yes** when asked if you want to save your changes

POWERPOINT

FIGURE 6.14
Picture bullets

picture bullets

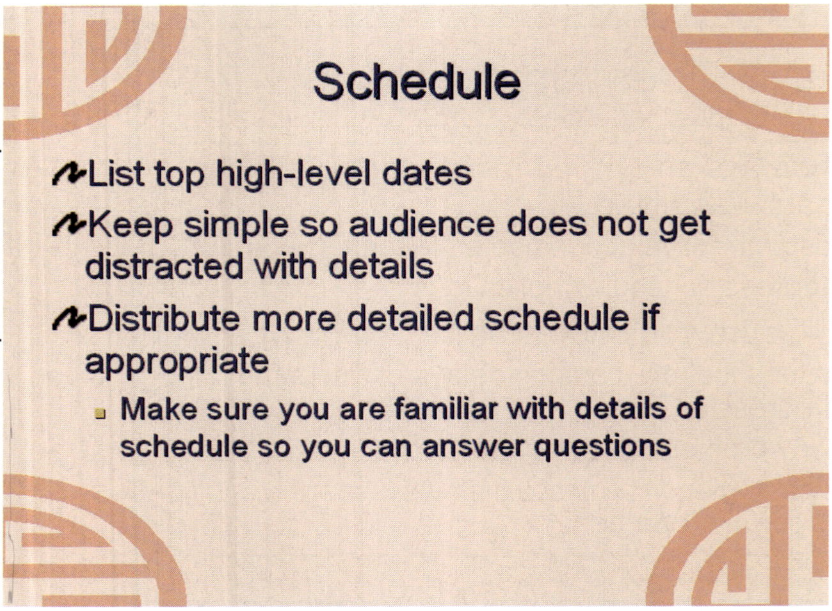

Pictures used as bullets should match the color scheme and topic of the presentation. Custom photographs and scanned images can be used as bullets with the Import button of the Picture Bullet dialog box. Imported images will appear as a choice in the dialog box. Custom bullets set in the Slide Master will be applied to all slides based on that master.

SESSION 6.2 CREATING CUSTOM ART

Shapes, pictures, and clip art are critical components of a compelling presentation. Although large collections of stock artwork are readily available, the ability to create and modify custom images can greatly enhance any slide show.

SESSION 6.1

making *the grade*

1. What are intrinsic color schemes?

2. Assume that you are creating a presentation for parents of brain injured children. The content has three distinct parts: types of injuries, financial resources, and support groups. What color scheme would be appropriate?

3. How many custom colors can be displayed on the Color menu palette?

4. How can you make the text more readable when using pictures, textures, and fill effects on slide backgrounds?

Creating and Modifying Drawing Objects

The Drawing toolbar allows standard objects such as lines, rectangles, and shapes to be drawn, edited, customized, and combined to create complex artwork. Each shape can be resized, rotated, flipped, colored, and combined into complex shapes. To draw an object, select the drawing tool or AutoShape from the Drawing toolbar; then drag on the slide to create the object.

Draw and Format Objects

The Drawing toolbar displays the most commonly used shapes so they can be readily selected. The AutoShapes menu contains the full array of drawing objects categorized as lines, connectors, Basic Shapes, Block Arrows, Flowchart, Stars and Banners, Callouts, and more. Additional shapes can be accessed from the Clip Organizer.

task reference	Using the AutoShape Button of the Drawing Toolbar

- Select the slide that will contain the AutoShape
- Click the **AutoShapes** menu of the **Drawing** toolbar
- Select the shape category and then the shape to be applied
- Click and drag on the slide surface to create the shape

Adding an AutoShape object:

1. Open PowerPoint, open **<yourname>StatusReport.ppt**, and ensure the Drawing toolbar is open
2. Move to slide 10
3. Click **AutoShapes** on the Drawing toolbar, point to **Block Arrows**, and then click **Up Arrow** shape from the first row
4. Click and drag the shape on the bottom right-hand corner of the slide

tip: *You are creating the upward pointing light gray arrow from the figure*

5. With the arrow still selected, click the **Fill Color** tool of the Drawing toolbar and choose a light gray
6. Repeat step 3, but select the downward pointing block arrow from the AutoShapes menu and draw an arrow below the current one

tip: *You are creating the orange arrow in Figure 6.15*

7. Use the **Fill Color** arrow to color the new arrow orange (click **More Fill Colors** on the Fill Color pop-up menu)
8. Press **Ctrl+C** and then press **Ctrl+V** to copy and paste a second orange arrow
9. Use the **Fill Color** arrow to color the copy gold, and then drag it to the location shown in Figure 6.15
10. Create, color, and position the straight left and right pointing arrows
11. Create, color, and position the left and right curved arrows using the corresponding arrows from the Block Arrows collection of the AutoShapes menu

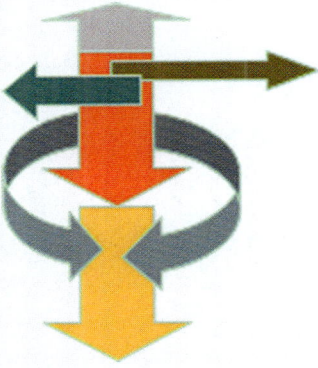

FIGURE 6.15
Block arrow object

The previous steps created and formatted the group of objects that will be used as a single graphic on the Goals slide. To create the final graphic, these individual objects will be combined into one object, rotated, and have 3-D effects applied.

Customizing Objects

All objects from the AutoShapes menu are drawn, colored, and positioned in the same fashion as the arrows manipulated in the previous steps. Each drawn object can be moved, copied, pasted, and resized as you practiced with the arrows. In addition, all objects can be rotated, many objects can contain text, and some objects include *adjustment handles* that can be used to change the object's prominent features.

Text can be added to most objects. Text added to a shape becomes part of the shape and will rotate and flip as those options are applied to the shape. Once a shape has been added to the slide, the shortcut menu contains the Add Text option. Text added to an object can be selected and formatted like any other text on the slide.

task reference	Adding Text to an AutoShape

- Select the AutoShape
- Right-click the **AutoShape** and select **Add Text** from the shortcut menu
- Type and format the text

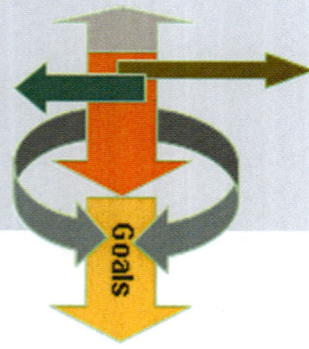

FIGURE 6.16

Text added to a block arrow object

Adding text to an AutoShape object:

1. If you are not already at slide 10, move to it
2. Right-click on the downward pointing gold arrow and click **Add Text**
3. Type **Goals** in the arrow's text box
4. Select the text by pressing **Ctrl+A**, press **Ctrl+B** to bold the text, click the Font Color list box arrow (on the Formatting toolbar), and click the **dark gray** color square

Notice that the text you added to the downward pointing arrow in the previous steps is oriented with the arrow. All drawn objects have a default text orientation that can be adjusted 90 degrees using the formatting options of the object. As a drawn object is rotated, the text will also reorient. In the next steps these techniques will be used to create a graphic slide title.

To add interest to the presentation, Ian would like to use an image to contain the title on slide 8. The ribbon with the title will run down the left edge of the slide.

Rotating text in an AutoShape object:

1. Move to slide 8
2. Select the title placeholder containing the text *Technology* (dotted placeholder, not slashes) and **delete** it
3. Click **AutoShapes** in the Drawing toolbar and click **More AutoShapes**
4. Search for and then click the light blue **Sharp Ribbon** object in the task pane to add it to your slide

tip: *Pause the cursor over the image to see its name*

5. Right-click on the ribbon, click **Add Text**, and type **TECHNOLOGY**

6. Select **TECHNOLOGY** and use Formatting toolbar buttons to center it, and make it **Bold** and **20** point

7. Right-click the ribbon and click **Format AutoShape** from the pop-up menu

8. Click the **Text Box** tab, check both **Resize AutoShape to fit text** and **Rotate text within shape by 90°**, and click **OK**

9. Use the white sizing handles (see Figure 6.17) to narrow the ribbon so that it is one character wide

tip: *The shape should resize, but will not fit completely on the slide until you complete the next series of steps*

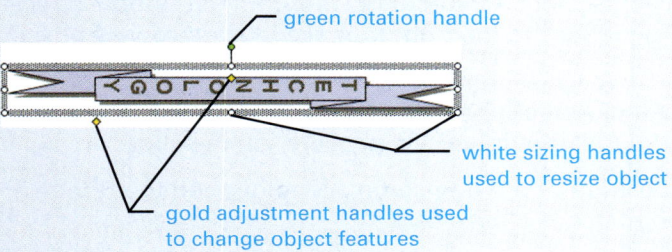

green rotation handle

white sizing handles used to resize object

gold adjustment handles used to change object features

F I G U R E 6.17
Rotated text in a ribbon

Most objects contain eight white resizing handles. The four corner handles can be used to adjust height and width simultaneously, while the remaining handles will only adjust one dimension. The green handle, called the ***rotation handle***, controls the rotation of an object. Clicking and dragging the rotation handle will adjust the orientation of the object on the slide. The TECHNOLOGY ribbon needs to be rotated to a vertical rather than horizontal orientation.

Using the ribbon object's rotation handle:

1. Ensure slide 8 is active

2. Select the **TECHNOLOGY** ribbon by clicking it, if necessary

3. Click and drag the green rotation handle as shown in Figure 6.17 down and to the left until the ribbon is vertical as shown in Figure 6.18

4. Move the ribbon to left side of the slide (see Figure 6.19). (*Hint:* use the keyboard arrow keys to nudge the object in small increments)

5. Click outside the object

F I G U R E 6.18
Rotated ribbon

The gold handles shown in Figure 6.17 are called adjustment handles and will modify the prominent features of an object. For example, the adjustment handles for a block arrow object will change the size of the arrow head, and those of a parallelogram will adjust the wall angle. In the ribbon object, the adjustment handles control how long the ribbon tails are and how far offset the center of the ribbon is from the tails. Adjusting the ribbon will help it to fit on the slide effectively.

anotherway
. . . to Rotate an Object

Rotating an object by 90 degrees to the left or right can also be accomplished using the Draw menu of the Drawing toolbar. From the Draw menu select Rotate or Flip and then use either Rotate Left or Rotate Right to achieve the desired result. This process can be reversed with the Undo menu or repeated to rotate an additional 90 degrees

anotherword   . . . on Rotating Objects

Sometimes the freedom of an object's rotation handle can be difficult to control precisely. Hold down the **Shift** key while rotating to limit the rotation to 15-degree angles, making the rotation process easier to manage

FIGURE 6.19

Adjusting ribbon AutoShape

Adjusting the ribbon object's features:

1. If Slide 8 is not the active slide, move to it

2. Select the **TECHNOLOGY** ribbon by clicking it

tip: *You may need to click the object again to activate the gold adjustment handles*

3. Drag the left golden adjustment handle to the left until the ribbon is rectangular and then drag it back to the right to make it as narrow as possible

4. Drag the right golden adjustment handle up to lengthen the tails of the ribbon and then down until the ribbon fits properly on the slide

5. Adjust the size and position of the bulleted placeholder and the ribbon until their orientation matches Figure 6.19

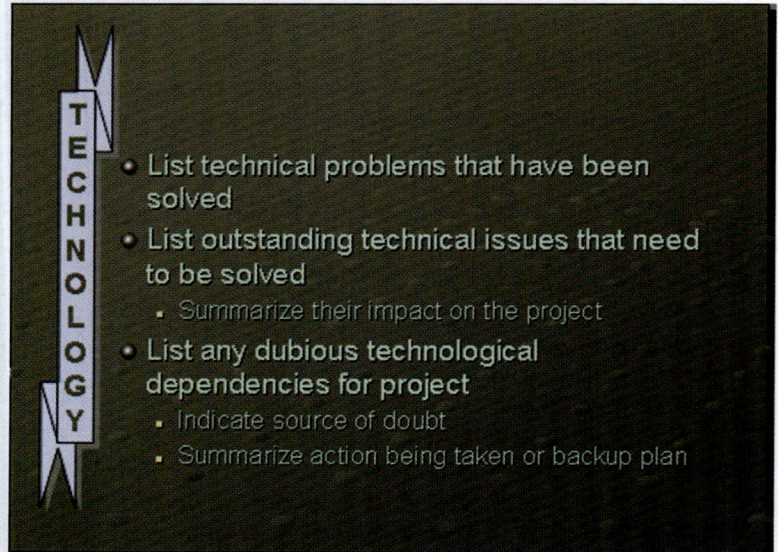

6. Adjust the text color to black if necessary

tip: *Click in the text of the ribbon and then press* **Crtl+A** *to select all the text*

The prominent features of each AutoShape object are different, but the adjustment techniques are the same. The adjustment handles will change the shape of a prominent feature while holding the object size constant. As an adjustment handle is moved, a dotted outline of the object indicates how the object will be changed when the mouse button is released. When you have a concept of the shape that you would like to use, find the AutoShape that is closest to your ideal, and then manipulate the adjustment handles to achieve the desired effect.

Positioning Objects

When two or more objects are placed on a slide, aligning them manually can pose a problem. The Draw menu of the Drawing toolbar has options to position objects relative to each other. Another useful feature allows shapes to be flipped either horizontally or vertically.

Aligning objects:

1. Move to slide 9

2. Use the **More AutoShapes** option of the **AutoShapes** menu to place a Scanner, a Printer, and a Computer with Tower in the top right-hand corner of the slide. Refer to Figure 6.20 for a visual view of these shapes. (Use the **Search for** text box in the Clip Art panel of the task pane)

3. Position the scanner to the left of the computer and the printer to the right with the images overlapping slightly

4. Select all three AutoShape objects by clicking the first object and then holding the **Shift** key while clicking the others

5. Click the **Draw** button of the Drawing toolbar, point to **Align or Distribute**, and then click **Align Middle**. Repeat the process selecting **Align Bottom** to demonstrate alignment differences

6. Click the **Draw** button of the Drawing toolbar, point to **Align or Distribute**, and then click **Distribute Horizontally**

7. Left align the Title placeholder text by clicking the Title placeholder text, pressing **Ctrl+A**, and pressing **Ctrl+L**

8. Adjust the position of the bulleted placeholder and the aligned objects until they are similar to Figure 6.20

9. Save the presentation

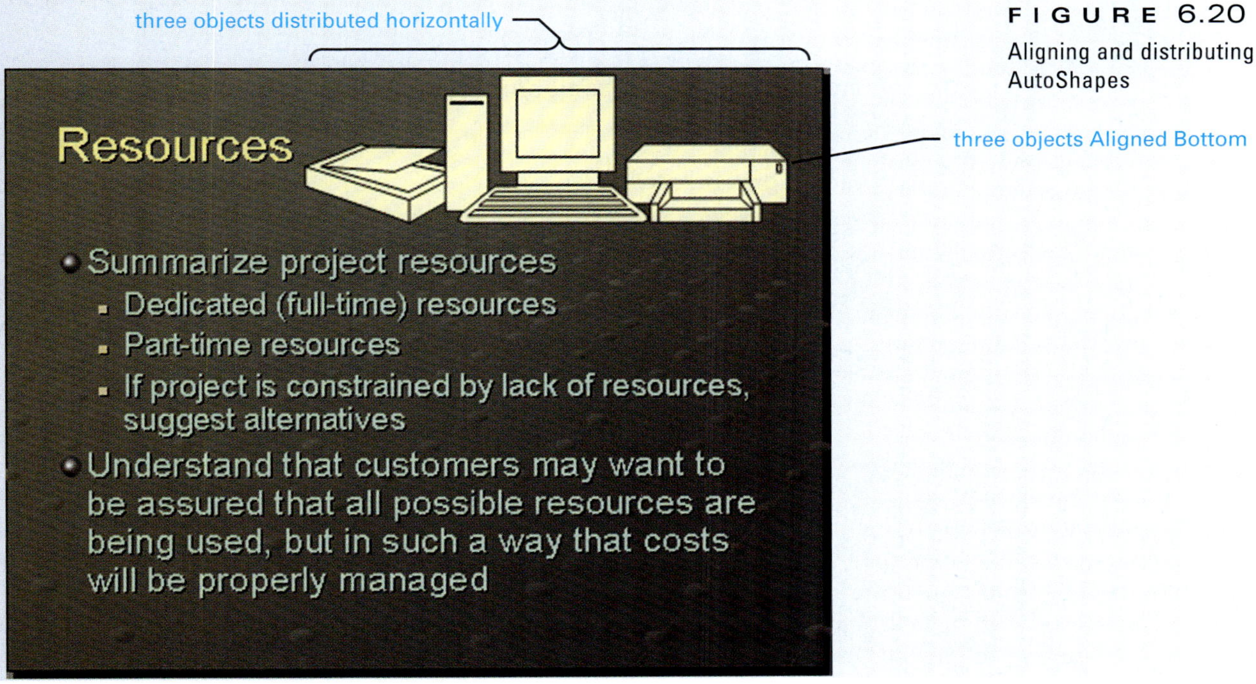

FIGURE 6.20

Aligning and distributing AutoShapes

three objects distributed horizontally

three objects Aligned Bottom

Resources

- Summarize project resources
  - Dedicated (full-time) resources
  - Part-time resources
  - If project is constrained by lack of resources, suggest alternatives
- Understand that customers may want to be assured that all possible resources are being used, but in such a way that costs will be properly managed

POWERPOINT

You may have noticed that there are two alignment groupings from the Align or Distribute menu. The first group includes Align Left, Align Center, and Align Right. These options are to align vertically organized objects. The second group includes Align Top, Align Middle, and Align Bottom. This group is designed to operate on horizontally organized objects. The Distribute Horizontally and Distribute Vertically options are used to evenly distribute selected objects along the horizontal or vertical axis, respectively.

If you prefer to align objects manually, *grids* and *guides* can be helpful. Dotted lines display at regular intervals on each slide when grids are turned on. Grids can be used as visual aids or have the snap-to option activated so that objects align to the nearest grid. The spacing between gridlines can be set from a list of preset measures.

When guides are activated, one horizontal and one vertical line are added to the slide to be positioned as needed to align slide objects. Guides can be moved by dragging. An unwanted guide can be deleted by dragging it off the edge of a slide. New guides are added by holding the CTRL key while dragging an existing guide.

---

task reference   Adding Grids and Guides
                                               to a Presentation

- Use the **Toolbars** option of the **View** menu to activate the **Drawing** toolbar, if it is not already visible

- Click the **Draw** drop-down list of the Drawing toolbar and click **Grid and Guides**

- Adjust the Snap to, Grid, and Guide settings in the Grid and Guides dialog box and then click OK

Using Grid and Guides when drawing:

1. Move to slide 6

2. Click the **Draw** button (Drawing toolbar) and click **Grid and Guides**

3. In the Grid and Guides dialog box check

    a. **Snap objects to grid**

    b. **Display grid on screen**

    c. **Display drawing guides on screen**

4. Click **OK**

5. Drag the vertical guide to **4.53** and the horizontal guide to **1.97**

tip: *Refer to Figure 6.21. The position displays in a pop-up box as you drag. The Snap To Grid feature controls the numbers that appear as you drag and may need to be disabled (see step 3) to get these exact settings*

6. Click the title placeholder and then use the left sizing handle to align it with the vertical guide at 4.53 and then drag the vertical guide to **4.33**

7. Click the **Rectangle** ▢ tool from the Drawing toolbar and draw the trailer of the semi-trailer (see Figure 6.21)

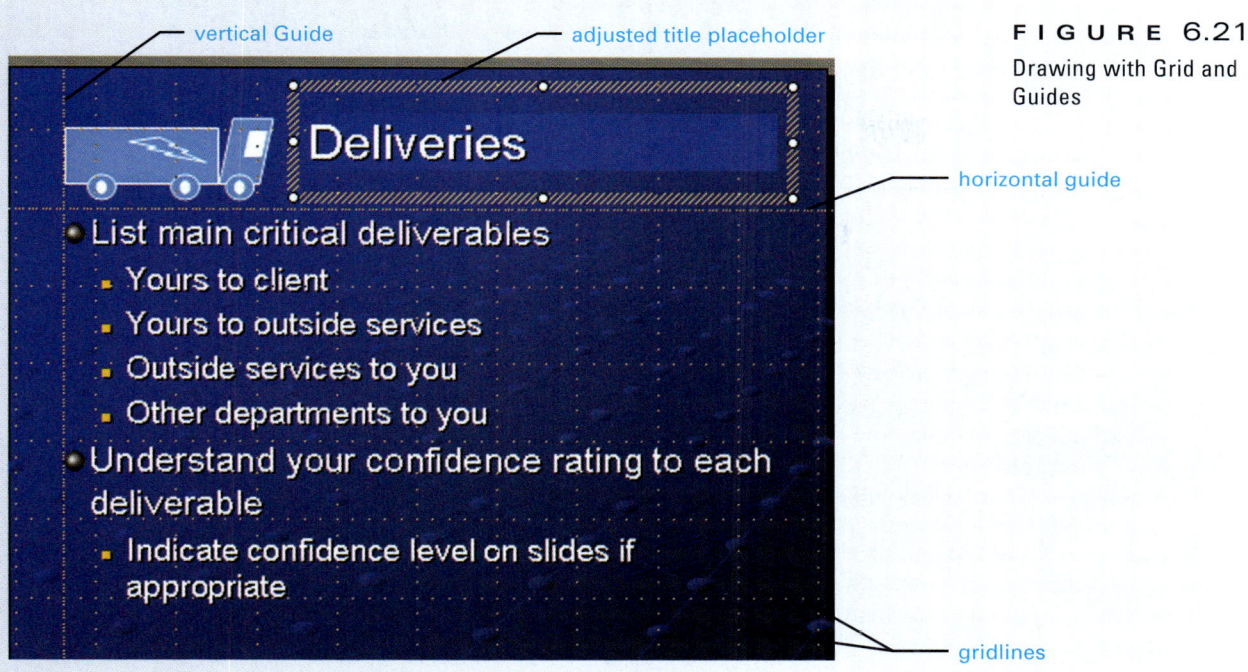

FIGURE 6.21
Drawing with Grid and Guides

vertical Guide

adjusted title placeholder

horizontal guide

gridlines

8. Select the **Parallelogram** from the **Basic Shapes** option of the **AutoShapes** menu and draw the cab of the semitrailer

9. Stack a second smaller parallelogram on the first to make the window. Use the Fill Color ▨ tool of the Drawing toolbar to make this object white

10. Use the Oval ⬭ tool of the Drawing toolbar to draw a tire. Stack a white oval on top of the blue one to complete the tire

tip: *Press **Shift** as you drag the oval to produce a circle*

tip: *With both ovals for one tire selected, use the **Align Middle** and **Align Center** options of the Draw button's Align and Distribute option to center the inner oval inside the outer oval*

11. Repeat step 10 for the remaining wheels (or copy/paste them)

12. Select the **Lightning Bolt** from the **Basic Shapes** option of the **AutoShapes** menu and add it to the trailer of the semitrailer (see Figure 6.21)

The Grid and Guides dialog box allows a designer to choose the alignment options that best suit the situation. By returning to the dialog box, any or all selected options can be reversed. When the snap-to grid option is selected, the grids do not need to be visible for objects to align with the nearest grid. The default is to have snap-to active and both guides and grids hidden. Guides and grids display as slides are developed, but are not visible in Slide Show view and will not print with the presentation.

Using 3-D Effects

Drawn objects can be modified to look three-dimensional. The 3-D options control the depth, rotation, angle, lighting direction, color, and texture of an object. Multiple objects can be selected to apply the same effects to each.

- Select the object(s) that will have 3-D effects
- Choose the desired 3-D effects from the 3-D Style button of the Drawing toolbar

F I G U R E 6.22

Arrows with 3-D effects

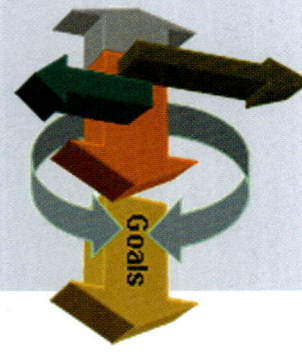

Applying 3-D effects to arrow objects:

1. Move to slide 10

2. Select all of the arrows except the left and right curved arrows, which do not support 3-D effects

tip: *Hold down the Shift key to click additional objects*

3. Click the **3-D Style** button on the Drawing toolbar and try some of the options. When you are finished exploring, click **3D Style 6** (hover over a choice to display its name)

As you just saw, there are 20 predefined 3-D effects that can be added to objects that support 3-D. Not all objects support 3-D effects. If a selected object does not allow 3-D effects, the 3-D Styles will display in gray as an indication that they cannot be applied. When the predefined effects do not match your needs, you can create your own effect using the 3-D Settings toolbox.

Exploring the 3-D Settings toolbox:

1. Move to slide 7

2. Click **AutoShapes**, point to **Stars and Banners**, and click **Explosion 2**

tip: *Pause over the shapes to see their names*

3. Click to the right of the title to add the object to the slide using its default size

4. Right-click the explosion, click **Add Text** from the pop-up menu, and type **$$$**

5. From the Drawing toolbar, open the **3-D Style** options and click **3-D Style 16** as the foundation for the 3-D effect being built

6. Click **3-D Style** on the Drawing toolbar and click **3-D Settings** to open the 3-D Settings toolbar. Refer to Figure 6.23 and

   a. Click the **Tilt Up** button of the 3-D Settings toolbox several times to adjust the length of the explosion's tail

   b. Click the **Tilt Right** option several times to adjust the angle of the explosion's tail to match Figure 6.23

   c. Explore the *Depth and Direction* settings of the 3-D Settings toolbox leaving them at their original settings

d. Use the Lighting options to reverse the angle of light (click the right-center light)

7. Drag the explosion's rotation handle to the right to angle the text to the right

8. Use the top right sizing handle to increase the explosion's dimension

9. Make the dollar signs ($$$) 32 point

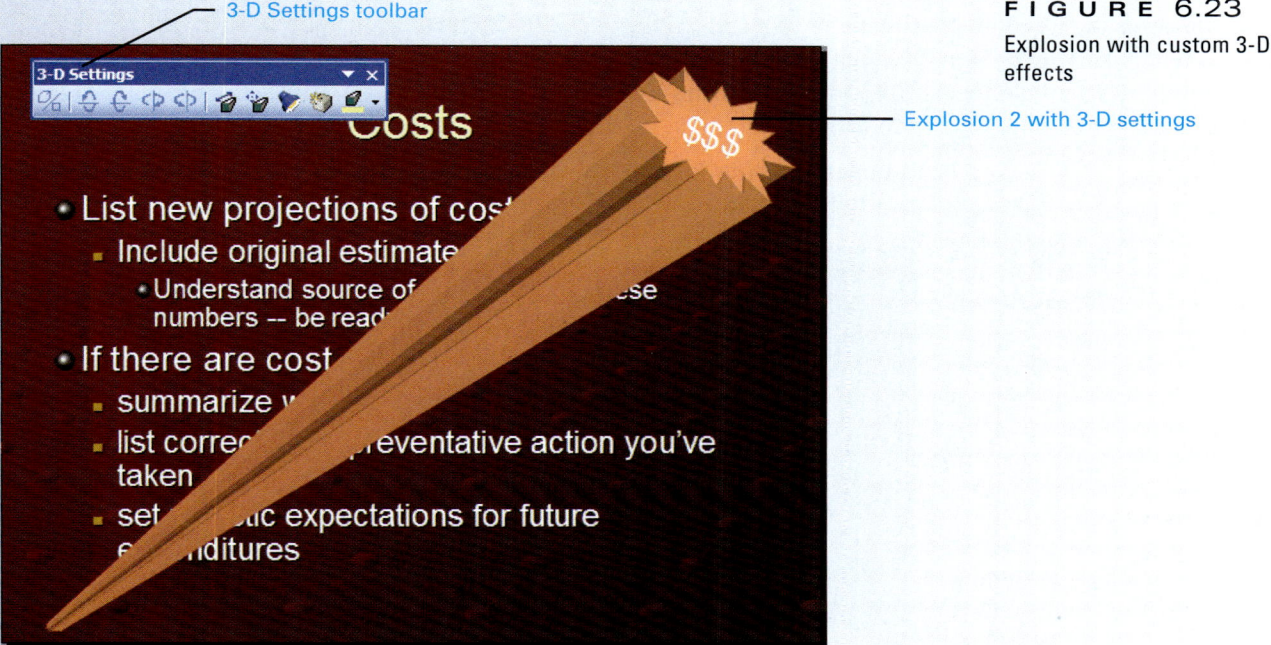

3-D Settings toolbar

F I G U R E 6.23

Explosion with custom 3-D effects

Explosion 2 with 3-D settings

At this point the object created from the explosion is in front of the text on the slide. This situation will be remedied by restacking the objects in later steps.

Editing Objects

Many of the familiar editing techniques can readily be applied to drawn objects. Setting the attributes of text or the background color of an object is the same regardless of the object involved. Drawn objects are selected by clicking and deselected by clicking elsewhere on the slide. Multiple objects can be simultaneously edited.

help yourself *Click the* Type a Question for help *combo box, type* **editing objects***, and press* **Enter***. Click the hyperlink* **Align objects** *and then click the hyperlink* **Align objects relative to the slide** *to review the steps presented in order to align drawing objects. Click the Help screen* **Close** *button when you are finished and close the task pane*

Duplicating Objects

Although you have been duplicating objects for some time, there are details to these operations that have not been addressed. Drawn objects can be deleted, copied, and pasted using the familiar Cut, Copy, and Paste buttons of the Standard toolbar, but other techniques can be more effective. The Edit menu contains a Duplicate option that can be used to copy objects. This menu selection can be accessed with the shortcut keys Ctrl+D.

Duplicating objects:

1. Move to slide 8 and select the **TECHNOLOGY** ribbon

tip: *You may need to click twice to get a dotted-line selection box*

2. Press **Ctrl+D** to create a duplicate

3. Adjust the position of the duplicate to cover the text of the original

4. Press **Ctrl+D** to create a second duplicate and then adjust its position

5. Press **Ctrl+D** to create a third duplicate and then adjust its position. Remember you can use arrow keys to move an object in small increments

6. If necessary, adjust the left margin of the bulleted placeholder so that all of the bullets are visible. Refer to Figure 6.24

FIGURE 6.24

Duplicate ribbons stacked

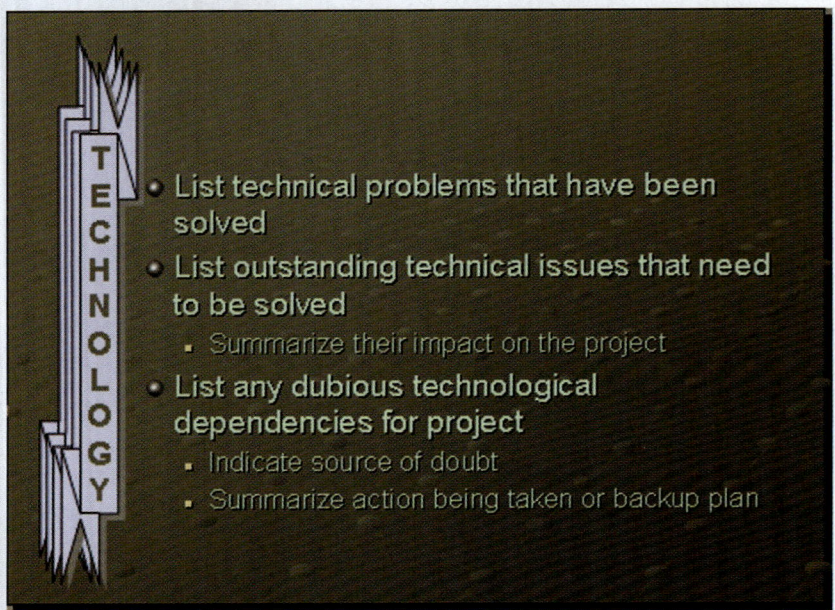

Stacking duplicate objects like the ribbons is a simple way to add interest to a graphic element. Lines are another method for adding interest and can also separate topics on a slide. Creating straight lines can be difficult unless the Shift key is used. The Shift key restricts the movement of an object being drawn or resized to either horizontal or vertical movement. Using the Ctrl key to drag duplicates makes it easier to align them and is faster than using the Office Clipboard buttons (Cut, Copy, and Paste).

Using the Shift and Ctrl keys when drawing and duplicating objects:

1. Move to slide 6

2. Select the **Line** ◥ tool from the Drawing toolbar and hold the **Shift** key while drawing a horizontal line below the semitrailer and slide title

tip: *The Shift key constrains the drawing motion to one direction ensuring a straight line*

3. Hold the **Ctrl** key while dragging the existing line to create a duplicate of the line. Position the duplicate half way up the semi tires. Review Figure 6.25 for a visual view

tip: *When using Ctrl to drag a duplicate object, the pointer has a box and a plus sign to indicate that duplication is active*

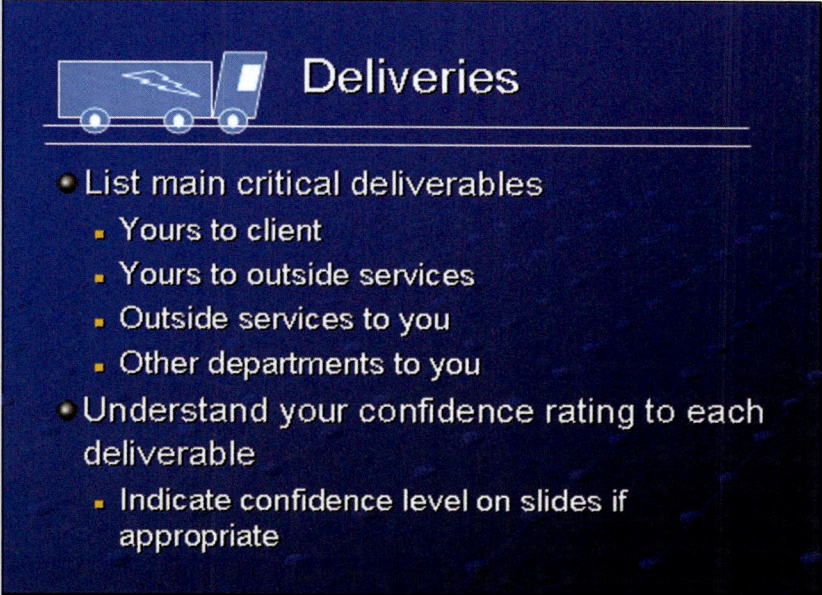

FIGURE 6.25

Lines created using the Shift and Ctrl keys

Ctrl+drag is about the fastest way to create a replica of an object. With multiple objects selected, Ctrl+drag will copy all selected objects simultaneously. Ctrl+click is used to select multiple objects. Clicking outside the multiple selection will deselect everything. Ctrl+clicking an already selected object will deselect just that object.

The work on slide 6 is nearly completed, but the line through the semi's tires needs to be placed in the background.

Changing an Object's Shape

Using AutoShapes to create drawn art often involves trial and error. You may begin with one shape and then decide that another shape is better suited for your purpose. Fortunately PowerPoint provides a menu option for changing a shape. Ian has decided that the lightning bolt emblem on the semi in slide 6 is inappropriate for the audience. You will change it to an inverted moon shape.

Changing the shape of a lightning bolt:

1. If slide 6 is not the active slide, move to it

2. Click the **lightning bolt** on the semitrailer

3. Click **Draw** on the Drawing toolbar, pause the cursor over **Change AutoShape**, pause the cursor over **Basic Shapes**, and then click the **Moon** object

4. With the moon still selected, click **Draw** on the Drawing toolbar, pause the cursor over **Rotate or Flip**, and click **Flip Horizontal**. Refer to Figure 6.26

You can select multiple objects and change them to a new shape. The original objects do not have to be the same shape, but the goal should be to convert all selected objects to the same new object. You have decided that the round inner ring of the semi tires is boring and want to convert all three objects to octagons.

Changing the shape of multiple objects simultaneously:

1. If slide 6 is not the active slide, move to it

2. Use the Zoom box of the Standard toolbar to make the slide 100% or greater so that you can select small objects

3. Deselect any selected objects and then hold the **Ctrl** key while clicking each of the inner white circles on the semi tires

4. With three circles selected, click **Draw** on the Drawing toolbar, hover over **Change AutoShape**, hover over **Basic Shapes**, and then click the **Hexagon** object

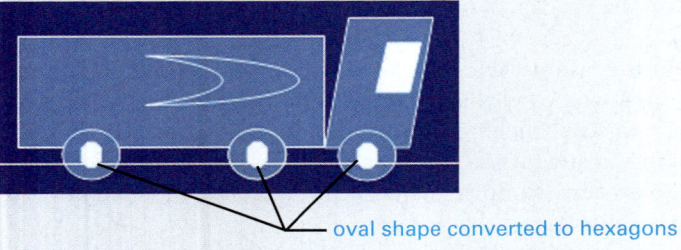

oval shape converted to hexagons

Most of the clip art in the Media Gallery is constructed using objects from the AutoShapes menu. The basic concept is that altering existing shapes to suit the current need is less time intensive than custom drawing each new work. Although the most dramatic changes to an object are accomplished using the techniques already reviewed, there are a few more subtle tricks that can improve the artwork in any presentation.

Other Object Attributes

The attributes of an object determine how it displays on the slide. The graphic attributes include fill, line, shape, and shadow. Text attributes include font, color, embossment, and shadow. All of the features covered for slides in the first session of this chapter are available for individual objects on the slide. Custom colors can be created using the More Fill Colors option of the Fill Color button. The Fill Effects option of the Fill Color button includes gradients, textures, patterns, and pictures that can be added to any object.

Creating and copying object fill effects:

1. Select the **semitrailer**

2. Click the **Fill Color** list arrow (on the Drawing toolbar), and then click **Fill Effects**

3. Click the **Gradient** tab of the Fill Effects dialog box

   a. Click **Two colors**

   b. Set the Shading styles to **Diagonal Up**

   c. Select the bottom left square in the Variant panel

   d. Click **OK**

4. With the trailer selected click the **Format Painter** button of the Standard toolbar and then click the **cab** of the semitrailer

tip: *The cursor will change to a paintbrush when a format can be painted*

5. Select the **inverted moon** on the semitrailer, choose the Fill Color list arrow, and then click **Fill Effects**

6. Click the **Texture** tab of the Fill Effects dialog box, choose the **Bouquet** (it is blue with some pink in it and located in the third row, fourth column) pattern and click **OK**

tip: *The pattern name for the selected texture displays in the box below the textures*

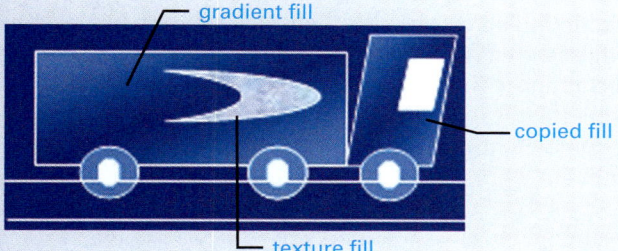

gradient fill
copied fill
texture fill

FIGURE 6.28

Object fill effects

The Format Painter can be used to transfer the formatting of one object to another. Single-clicking the Format Painter allows one object to be painted, while double-clicking will allow multiple objects to be painted. When Format Painter is double-clicked, painting must be turned off by either hitting Esc on the keyboard or clicking the Format Painter button again.

For many audiences and tasks, dramatic formatting is not appropriate. Such simple changes can improve the dynamics of an object without overshadowing other slide elements. The shadow attribute can be used to create a subtle 3-D effect, while line color, style, and weight help to differentiate art components.

Adding shadows and setting line color:

1. Select the **semitrailer**

2. Click the **Shadow Style** button of the Drawing toolbar and click **Shadow Style 2**

3. From the **Shadow Style** button of the Drawing toolbar, click **Shadow Settings** to open the Shadow Settings dialog box

4. With the semitrailer selected, click the **Nudge Shadow Up** button twice and the **Nudge Shadow Right** button five times. Close the Shadow Settings dialog box

5. Select the inverted moon and complete the following

   a. Use the **Line Style** ≣ button of the Drawing toolbar to set the line to **1½ pt**

   b. Use the **Line Color** 🖌 button of the Drawing toolbar to set the line color to the gold used as an accent in the color scheme

6. Save the presentation

FIGURE 6.29

Shadow and line adjustments

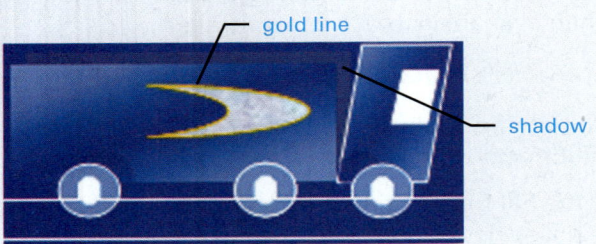

Shadowing can be added to most slide objects such as text characters, AutoShapes, and images. Once a shadow is added to an object, the Nudge features of the Shadow Setting toolbox can be used to adjust the width and length of the shadow. The color and transparency of a shadow can be adjusted in the same fashion. A transparent shadow allows background colors and objects to show through. The Shadow Style button can also be used to remove existing shadow settings.

Objects outside the Slide Area

You can create and manipulate objects in the background portion of the presentation window. Objects outside the slide area provide information to developers since they do not display during a slide show and will not print.

Viewing objects outside the slide area:

1. Move to slide 1

2. Click in the Slide pane, click the Zoom drop-down list arrow, and click **Fit**

3. Notice the notes to developers in the rectangle to the right of the first slide (close the task pane, if it is visible)

The notes from slide 1 of this slide show are part of the AutoContent template that was used to build the presentation. It contains tips for anyone using the template. The rectangle can be edited or deleted to suit your needs. You can add your own background objects by changing the zoom to expose the background and then drawing.

FIGURE 6.30

A rectangle object in the presentation window

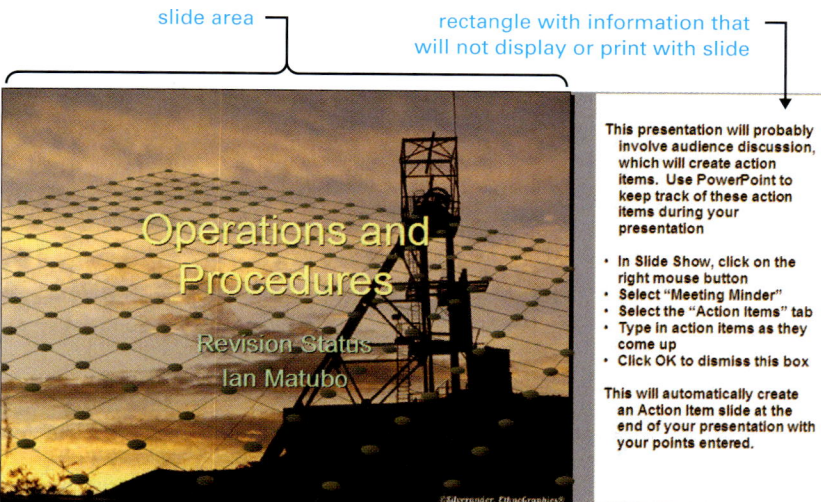

slide area

rectangle with information that will not display or print with slide

Stacking and Grouping Objects

As more and more objects are added to a slide, it becomes critical to control their positioning. The stacking order determines what object(s) display in the foreground and background. Grouping allows multiple objects to be treated as a single object when moving, formatting, and editing.

Controlling Z-Order

To make editing, moving, and combing objects easier, each object added to a presentation is placed in its own layer. The layers stack on top of each other with the first object added being closest to the slide and the last object added the farthest away. This stacking order is also referred to as the *z-order* referencing the z-axis of a three-dimensional chart.

Ideally, each object would be created in the correct order so that it could be freely edited and never touched again. There are a series of Send and Bring options used to control z-order.

---

task reference Changing the Z-Order of an Object

- Select the object(s) to be moved in the stack of objects

- From the Drawing toolbar, click **Draw**, pause over **Order**, and then select the appropriate movement option

---

Changing Z-order of objects:

1. Move to slide 6

   a. Click the line that is in front of the semi tires

   b. Click the **Draw** button of the Drawing toolbar, pause the cursor over **Order**, and click **Send to Back**

2. Move to slide 7

   a. Click the bulleted list placeholder

   b. Click the **Draw** button of the Drawing toolbar, pause the cursor over **Order**, and select **Bring to Front**

3. Move to slide 8

   a. Select any slide object

tip: *You may need to click again to get a dotted-line selection box*

   b. Use the Tab key to move through the slide objects

   c. Use Shift+Tab to move backward through slide objects

F I G U R E 6.31

Bulleted list placeholder brought to front

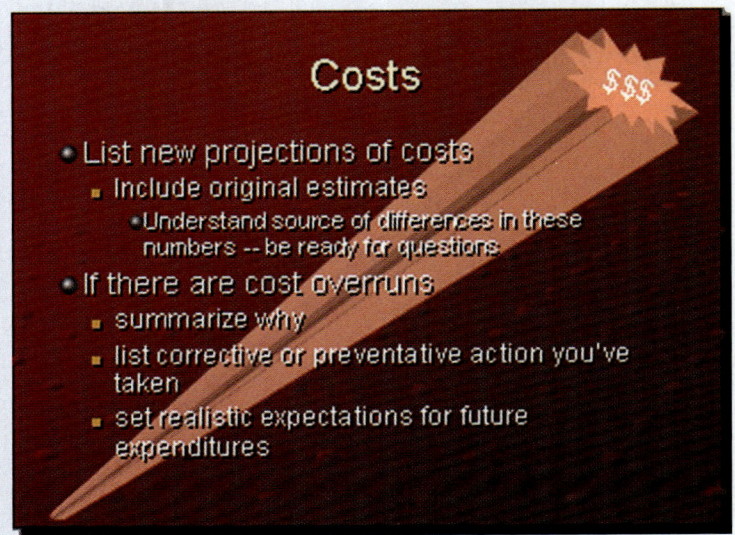

anotherway
. . . to Change Z-Order

The Order menu options can be accessed by right-clicking an object

When ordering objects on a slide, it is important that you remember that each slide element, including text and placeholders, is an object. The Send to Back and Bring to Front options of the Order menu were demonstrated in the previous steps. Regardless of how many layers there are, these options will place the selected object on the bottom or top, respectively. The remaining options of the Order menu will move an object one layer at a time. Bring Forward will move the object one layer toward the top of the stack, while Send Backward will move the object one layer toward the bottom of the stack.

Layering can sometimes make an object difficult to select because it is behind other objects. For example, selecting the second stacked TECHNOLOGY ribbon on slide 8 would be particularly arduous. Sometimes the desired object can be reached by zooming in until each object's borders are distinct. PowerPoint can zoom to 400 percent to support this type of selection. Another option is to move the layers that are in front of the desired object. Depending on the number of layers, this option is also tedious. The Tab and Shift+Tab keys are usually the easiest way to move from object to object on a slide.

Grouping Objects

When objects have been combined or stacked to achieve a desired effect, it is a good idea to finish the process by grouping the discrete objects into one object. *Grouping* ensures that the work is not accidentally ruined by inadvertently moving a component. It also makes moving, copying, editing, and setting attributes much simpler.

---

task reference   **Grouping Objects**

- Select all objects to be grouped
- From the Drawing toolbar, click **Draw** and then select the appropriate grouping (Group, **Ungroup**, or **Regroup**) option

---

Working with grouped objects:

1. Move to slide 6

   a. Select all the objects that make up the tractor and trailer by clicking and dragging a selection box around the semi

tip: *A selection box does not select objects not completely contained in its area. Be sure to include all of the semi parts and exclude both lines and the title placeholder*

   b. Click the **Draw** button of the Drawing toolbar and click **Group**

   c. With the semi group selected, hold down the **Ctrl** key and select both lines

   d. Click the **Draw** button of the Drawing toolbar and click **Group**

   e. With the group selected, click on the inverted moon on the semitrailer (see Figure 6.32)

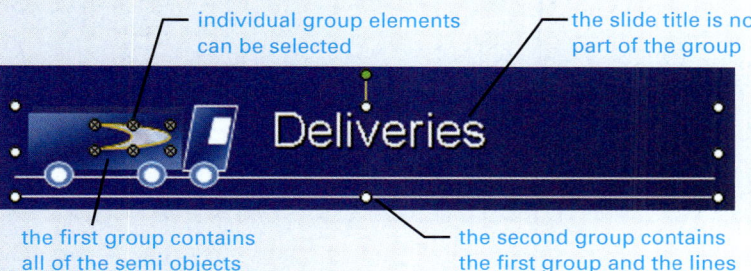

individual group elements can be selected

the slide title is not part of the group

the first group contains all of the semi objects

the second group contains the first group and the lines

FIGURE 6.32

Doubly grouped object with one element selected

tip: *Although we will not set any attributes for the inverted moon, selecting it would allow you to do so*

   f. Click off the group to deselect

2. Move to slide 8

   a. Group all of the TECHNOLOGY ribbons into one object using the techniques from step 1

   b. Use the rotation handle for the group to angle all of the ribbons a few degrees to the left

tip: *If all the ribbons do not rotate, they are not properly grouped. Ungroup, adjust your selection, and then Regroup*

3. Move to slide 9

   a. Select and group the computer equipment clip art

   b. Use the **Fill Color** button of the Drawing toolbar to change the color to the gray brown of the background

    c. Use the **Line Color** button of the Drawing toolbar to match the line color to the title text color

  4. Move to slide 10

    a. Select and group all of the arrows

    b. Use the **Ctrl+drag** method to create a copy of the group

    c. Select the **Goals** text in the copy and delete it

    d. Reduce the size of the copy (drag a corner sizing handle)

    e. Use the rotation handle to rotate the copy to the right (clockwise)

    f. Position the copy to the left of the title

FIGURE 6.33

Copied arrow group

copied, resized, and rotated arrow group →

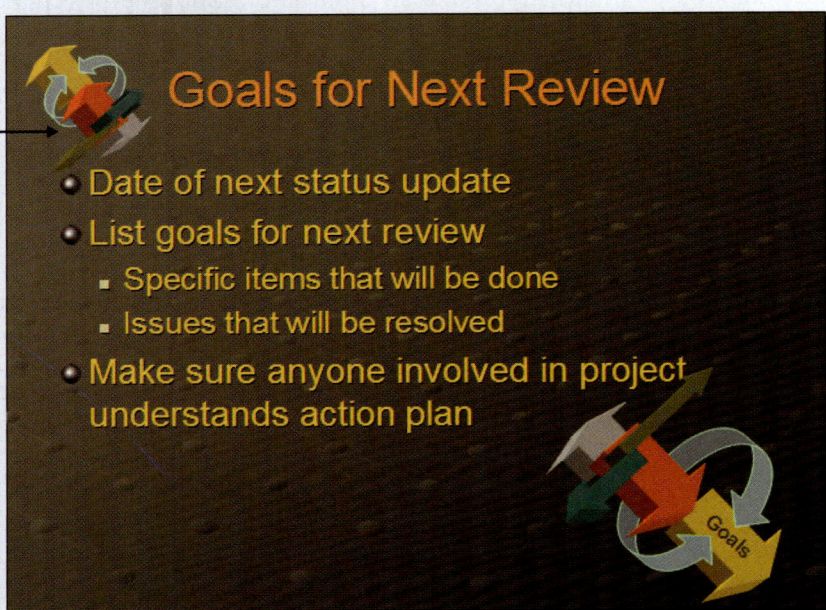

  5. Click **Save** on the Standard toolbar

  6. Close PowerPoint

The attributes of all grouped objects can be changed simultaneously. For example, the same fill or shadow can be applied to all group objects. Flip, resize, rotate, and 3-D effects also work well with groups. Individual objects from a group can be selected without ungrouping to have unique attributes set. Grouped objects can be ungrouped when it is necessary to work exclusively with a single object from the group and re-grouped when those tasks are completed. The Ungroup and Regroup options are available from the Draw menu. A group can be included in other groups to create even more complex objects.

making *the grade*

1. What is the difference between the rectangle shape on the Drawing toolbar and the one available from the Basic Shapes option of the AutoShapes button?

2. How can you create a mirror image of an object?

3. How are adjustment handles valuable?

4. A slide contains three rectangles stacked top to bottom whose left sides need to be aligned. How would you accomplish this?

SESSION 6.3 SUMMARY

Color is a critical component of any presentation. The colors used impact the mood and readability of the presentation. When choosing a color scheme, consider the audience, presentation topic, and how the presentation will be delivered. Projected presentations and kiosks have very different color requirements.

A color scheme is a palette of eight colors used as the presentation default colors for the slide background, body text, lines, shadows, title text, fills, hyperlinks, and accents. Each PowerPoint Design template has a selection of intrinsic color schemes that have been developed by artists. Color schemes can be applied to an entire presentation or to selected slides. New slides and objects created in a presentation follow the active color scheme. You can customize the color of individual objects or the entire color scheme. When custom colors are applied to an object, the new color displays below those of the color scheme in all of the color menus. When a color or colors of a color scheme are customized, a new color scheme is added to the Design template. Deleting a color scheme removes it from the Design template.

Most PowerPoint objects, including slides and AutoShapes, can use special fills such as gradient, texture, and picture. These custom fills add distinction to objects and present a more professional image. Be sure, however, that the fills do not detract from readability or presentation content.

The Drawing toolbar supplies an array of standard objects that can be used to create more complex objects and drawings. Select a drawing tool and then click and drag the shape on a slide. As new objects are added, they are stacked so that the first object is closest to the slide and the last object added is on top. Tab and Shift+Tab usually provide the easiest navigation between stacked slide objects. Objects that will display together should be grouped to avoid accidental alterations to their arrangement.

MICROSOFT OFFICE SPECIALIST OBJECTIVES SUMMARY

- Create and add Office Art elements to slides using the Drawing toolbar—MOS PP035-1-4
- Customize slide backgrounds using bitmaps—MOS PP035-2-3

making the grade *answers*

SESSION 6.1

1. Intrinsic color schemes are the default color palettes assigned to each PowerPoint template. This is in contrast to custom color schemes that can be created by the user.

2. A wide variety of considerations are appropriate for this question. An overall color scheme could include bright primary colors since the presentation is for parents. Some students might feel that bright colors are inappropriate because the children are injured and choose calming pastels. The unique components of the presentation could each have a different color scheme to differentiate them. There is no absolute answer, but it is important to evaluate the impact of color on the topic and audience.

3. 8

4. The most important consideration for readable text is high contrast between the text and background. The size of the text can also have considerable impact on how easily it is read. Busy backgrounds should be matted either by formatting the slide placeholders or by adding a drawing object.

SESSION 6.2

1. Both rectangle shape objects are the same. The most commonly used options are placed directly on the Drawing toolbar for faster access.

2. Use the Draw menu of the Drawing toolbar to access Flip options. Flip Horizontal creates a side-to-side mirror image. Flip Vertical creates a top-to-bottom mirror image.

3. Adjustment handles are visible when an adjustable object is selected. These handles allow you to alter the prominent features of the object. For example, the adjustment handles of block arrows will allow you to change the size of the arrowhead.

4. Select all three rectangles, activate the Draw button of the Drawing toolbar, pause the cursor over Align or Distribute, and click Align Left.

task reference *summary*

Task	Page #	Preferred Method
Select a color scheme	PP 6.4	• Select a Design template • Select the slide(s) the color scheme will be applied to • Use the drop-down menu of the task pane to activate the Slide Design—Color Scheme panel • Click a color scheme
Customize a color scheme	PP 6.8	• Use the task pane drop-down list to activate the **Slide Design—Color Scheme** panel • Click the **Edit Color Schemes** link in the Slide Design—Color Scheme panel • On the **Standard** tab of the Edit Color Scheme dialog box, select the standard color scheme to be customized • On the **Custom** tab, select the color scheme element to customize and click **Change Color** • Use either the Standard or Custom tab of the Background Color dialog box to select a new color • Click **OK** • Repeat the previous step for each element to be customized • Use the **Preview** button to view the new colors on your slide • Click **Apply** to permanently apply the changes

task reference *summary*

Task	Page #	Preferred Method
Delete a color scheme	PP 6.10	• Use the task pane drop-down list to activate the **Slide Design—Color Scheme** panel • Click the **Edit Color Schemes** link in the Slide Design—Color Scheme panel • On the **Standard** tab of the Edit Color Scheme dialog box, select the color scheme to be deleted • Click the **Delete Scheme** button • Click **Apply**
Define a gradient background	PP 6.12	• Right-click on the slide to contain the gradient background • Click the **Background** pop-up menu option • Click **Fill Effects** • Click the **Gradient** tab • Select the desired gradient effects and click **OK** • Click either • **Apply to All** to set this as the background for all presentation slides • **Apply** to set this as the background for the selected slides only
Select a texture background	PP 6.13	• Right-click on the slide to contain the texture background • Click the **Background** pop-up menu option • Click **Fill Effects** • Click the **Texture** tab • Select the desired texture and click **OK** • Click either • **Apply to All** to set this as the background for all presentation slides • **Apply** to set this as the background for the selected slides only
Apply a picture background	PP 6.15	• Locate and save an appropriate picture • Right-click on the slide to contain the picture background • Click the **Background** pop-up menu option • Click **Fill Effects** • Click the **Picture** tab • Click the **Select Picture** button, choose the picture file, click **Insert**, and then click **OK** • Click either • **Apply to All** to set this as the background for all presentation slides • **Apply** to set this as the background for the selected slides only • **Preview** to evaluate the effect of the background without applying it
Apply a picture as a bullet	PP 6.17	• Select the text or list that will contain the picture bullet • On the **Format** menu, click **Bullets and Numbering**, and then click the **Bulleted** tab • On the Bulleted tab click the **Picture** button • Select a picture from the Picture Bullet dialog box • Click **OK**
Using the AutoShape button of the Drawing toolbar	PP 6.19	• Select the slide that will contain the AutoShape • Click the **AutoShapes** menu of the **Drawing** toolbar • Select the shape category and then the shape to be applied • Click and drag on the slide surface to create the shape
Adding text to an AutoShape	PP 6.20	• Select the AutoShape • Right-click the **AutoShape** and select **Add Text** from the shortcut menu • Type and format the text
Adding Grids and Guides to a presentation	PP 6.24	• Use the **Toolbars** option of the **View** menu to activate the **Drawing** toolbar, if it is not already visible • Click the **Draw** drop-down list of the Drawing toolbar and click **Grid and Guides** • Adjust the Snap to, Grid, and Guide settings in the Grid and Guides dialog box, and then click OK

POWERPOINT

task reference *summary*

Task	Page #	Preferred Method
Adding 3-D effects to an object	PP 6.26	• Select the object(s) that will have 3-D effects • Choose the desired 3-D effects from the 3-D Style button of the Drawing toolbar
Changing the Z-order of an object	PP 6.33	• Select the object(s) to be moved in the stack of objects • From the Drawing toolbar, click **Draw**, pause over **Order**, and then select the appropriate movement option
Grouping objects	PP 6.35	• Select all objects to be grouped • From the Drawing toolbar, click **Draw** and then select the appropriate grouping (Group, Ungroup, or Regroup) option

TRUE OR FALSE

1. Color is not a critical component of any presentation.

2. You cannot customize the color of individual objects.

3. Deleting a color scheme removes it from the Design template.

4. Objects that will be displayed together should not be grouped to avoid accidental alterations to their arrangement.

5. The attributes of all grouped objects can be changed simultaneously.

6. 3-D options control the depth, rotation, angle, lighting direction, and color of an object.

FILL-IN

1. Ctrl+_____ can be used to create a duplicate of the selected object.

2. _____ lines can be moved to facilitate object alignment.

3. The _____ (color) handle of an object is used to rotate it.

4. A _____ fill effect merges colors to create the illusion of light.

5. The _____ (color) handles of an object are used to resize it.

MULTIPLE CHOICE

1. A color scheme is a palette of _____ colors used as the presentation default colors.
   a. 4
   b. 6
   c. 8
   d. 10

2. Most PowerPoint objects can use special fills such as:
   a. gradients
   b. texture
   c. picture
   d. all of the above

3. Each object added to a presentation is placed in its own layer. The stacking order is referred to as the:
   a. s-stack
   b. z-stack
   c. z-order
   d. none of the above

4. When trying to draw a straight line using the line tool, you should hold down this key:
   a. Shift
   b. Ctrl
   c. a and b
   d. none of the above

5. Grids can be used as visual aids or have the _____ option activated so that objects align to the nearest grid.
   a. Snap-to
   b. Guides
   c. a or b
   d. none of the above

review of concepts

REVIEW QUESTIONS

Each of the following topics should be addressed in one to three paragraphs.

1. What should be considered when selecting a color scheme and graphics for a retirement planning presentation?

2. Describe how the Format Painter is helpful.

3. How many backgrounds should be used in a single presentation?

4. Discuss techniques that could be used to improve the readability of text on a busy slide background.

5. Discuss how you would locate graphics for an educators' seminar on using PowerPoint in the classroom.

CREATE THE QUESTION

For each of the following answers, create the question.

ANSWER	QUESTION
1. Use the Fill Color button on the Drawing toolbar	_____
2. Select the item and then Ctrl+drag	_____
3. Use the Shift key	_____
4. Format Painter	_____
5. The 3-D Style selected	_____

FACT OR FICTION

1. The slide template of a presentation determines the initial color scheme applied to a slide show. Each Design template, including the blank template, has a default color scheme and several alternate color schemes referred to as intrinsic color schemes.

2. The color scheme selected impacts the personality and readability of the presentation. In general, dark backgrounds are best for printed presentations and light backgrounds work best for on-screen or projected presentations.

3. PowerPoint's Format Painting feature can be used to copy the color scheme from one slide to another slide within a presentation or to copy schemes between presentations.

4. The AutoShapes menu contains the full array of drawing objects categorized as lines, connectors, basic shapes, block arrows, flowchart, stars and banners, callouts, and more. Additional shapes can be accessed from the Clip Organizer.

5. The Grid and Guides dialog box allows a designer to choose the alignment options that best suit the situation. By returning to the dialog box, any or all selected options can be reversed. When the Snap-to Grid option is selected, the grids do not need to be visible for objects to align with the nearest grid.

1. Story Weavers

This nonprofit organization teaches others how to tell a story in a way that captivates an audience. From scary to hilarious topics, Story Weavers teaches others to hold audiences in the palm of their hands even with the driest of material. Audiences cry for more! Story Weavers' instructors are retired drama teachers, playwrights, authors, and fine arts directors—those who work with the written and acted word. Schools, libraries, private parties, and churches are popular recipients of Story Weavers' services. You have been asked to prepare a PowerPoint presentation to publicize Story Weavers.

1. Start PowerPoint and open **pp06StoryWeavers.ppt**

2. On slide 1, create a web and spider similar to that shown in Figure 6.34

   a. Right-click on the first slide, select **Background**, check **Omit background graphics from master**, and click **Apply**

   b. Using the **Line** tool from the Drawing toolbar, create a spider web

   c. Use the **Oval** tool to create a body and head for a spider. Use the Fill tool to fill the spider in dark gray

   d. Use the **Arc** Basic Shape to create curved spider legs. You will need to flip four of the legs

   e. Select the spider components, right-click, and group them into a single object

   f. Select all of the web and spider components, right-click, and group them into a single object

   g. Add another relevant graphic to the slide

3. Copy the spider and web to the Clipboard

   a. Use the **View** menu to open the Slide Master

   b. Paste the spider and web on the Slide Master (not the Title Slide Master)

   c. Right-click on the graphic and use the Format Graphic option to change the image color to medium gray

   d. Place a second copy of the recolored image near the center of the slide

   e. Artistically arrange the images and **Close Master View**

4. Add relevant graphics to slides 2 through 7. Arrange the graphics to appear as part of the background. For example, place the image over one of the spiders

5. Copy two extra webs to the final slide of your screen and change the color of each new spider by adding a Texture Fill effect

6. Save the presentation as **<yourname>StoryWeavers.ppt**

FIGURE 6.34

Spider and web on the opening slide

PP 6.43

2. Four-Wheelin'

Colorado Four-Wheelin' is owned and operated by Trevor Aaron, a 4x4 driver training specialist. The main focus of Colorado Four-Wheelin' is education, safety, trail etiquette, and environmental awareness for all users of 4-wheel drive vehicles.

Clients travel on a variety of trails, from rocky to muddy to sandy, through hill and dale, and enjoy spectacular high mountain and desert scenery while Trevor shares his lifetime of back country adventure skills and 4-wheeling expertise. Clients also learn how to get there and back, how to negotiate the various types of terrain, all recovery techniques, suggested on-vehicle equipment, maintenance techniques, and what is needed to know about safe off-highway driving. Trevor has asked you to prepare a PowerPoint presentation to publicize Colorado Four-Wheelin's services.

1. Start PowerPoint and open **pp06FourWheelin.ppt**

2. On slide 1, create a sketch of a small mountain range with snow covering the middle peak similar to that shown in Figure 6.35

    a. Right-click on the first slide, select **Background**, check **Omit background graphics from master**, and click **Apply**

    b. Using the **Line** tool from the Drawing toolbar, create a mountain range with three peaks, the middle one taller than the other two

    c. Using the **AutoShapes** feature, select the **Basic Shapes** option, and then use the **Isosceles Triangle** shape tool to create the shape for the snow peak. Use the Fill tool to fill the snow in white

    d. Select all the line components, right-click, select **Format AutoShape**, and set the Line Weight to **1 pt**

    e. Select the mountain components, right-click, and group them into a single object

    f. Add another relevant graphic to the slide

3. Copy the mountain peaks to the Clipboard

    a. Use the **View** menu to open the Slide Master

    b. Paste the mountain peak on the Slide Master (not the Title Slide Master) in the lower right-hand corner

    c. **Close Master View**

4. Add relevant graphics (photographs are preferred) to each of the other slides.

    a. Use the **Shadow Style** option, then select **Shadow Style 2**

    b. Change the shadow color to black and adjust the depth of the shadow so that it is fairly faint

    c. Repeat the above two steps for all the added graphical pictures inserted in step 3

5. Save the presentation as **<yourname>FourWheelin.ppt**

FIGURE 6.35
Four-Wheelin' opening slide

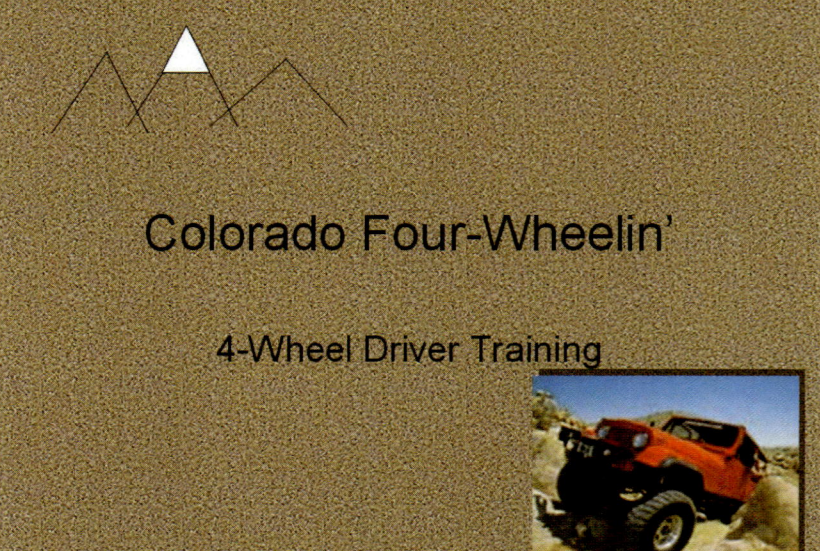

challenge

1. Preview Specialists

Across America before each movie shows, a "captive audience" sits. Usually the viewer sees a slide show of ads for local businesses. Some theaters run quizzes to engage the audience. However, frequently these presentations show little design aptitude, and many times they are quite ignored. Using market research, Preview Specialists discovered that audiences prefer preshows that provide information about current local events. With this technique in mind, the Preview Specialists' shows have been distributed across the United States tailored to each community, at the major movie chains. You have been asked to create such a presentation for your locale.

1. Open PowerPoint and select a blank screen

2. Save your presentation as **<yourname>PreviewSpecialists.ppt**

3. Title your presentation "Events in <name of your city or state>" and subtitle text "What To Do and See"

4. Locate a photograph to use as the background for this slide and apply it. Adjust the text color, size, and font to achieve optimal readability

5. Create at least five additional slides using photos you own or have found; select activities characteristic to your community

   a. Add titles and information for each slide to highlight the activity

   b. Include slides about local sports, social events, and culture

   c. Demonstrate matting on at least one of the slides

6. Select animations for the information and Slide Transitions

7. Choose a sound or sounds to punctuate the slides

8. Set the show to run continuously

9. Preview your presentation, make adjustments, and save it again

FIGURE 6.36

Sample opening slide

FIGURE 6.37

Sample matting

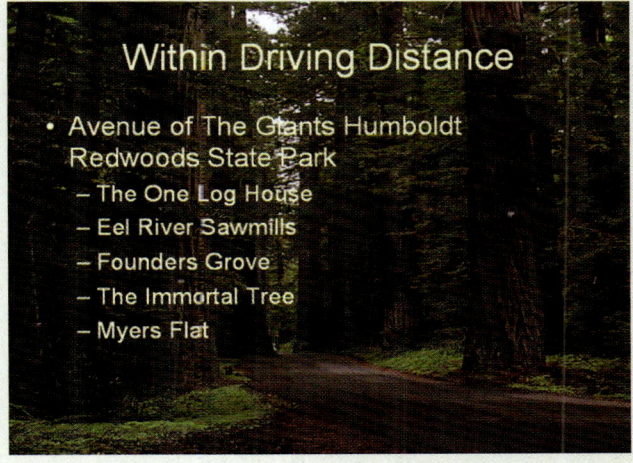

2. So . . . You Want to Be a Doctor?

Many people think that becoming a doctor is difficult. Others have some sense that becoming a physician takes many years and is expensive. Most people realize that being a physician is difficult yet rewarding. All these people are correct. Becoming a physician is a long, arduous, expensive process that can only be accomplished with great dedication.

Before starting the process of becoming a physician (or any profession) individuals must do some honest soul-searching. First of all, there must be an awareness of the time commitment involved in becoming a physician. Medicine is a career that requires many years of preparation. Generally most people graduate college at age 22 and medical school at 26. Then after three years of internship and residency, many physicians begin their career at age 29. However, the training for some specialties can last until the physician's early to mid-30s.

You have been asked to assist with a brief informational presentation for a group of prospective medical students.

1. Start PowerPoint and open **pp06Doctor.ppt**

2. Change the color scheme from green and blue to gold and orange. This includes the textual elements as well

3. Locate an image to use as the background for the title slide. Make sure you select something that will be aesthetically pleasing and that complements the new color scheme

4. Repeat step 3 for each one of the additional slides using images from **Clips Online**

5. Add a shadow style to each of the slide titles. Make the shadow color the same color as the body text for optimal color balance

6. Select animations for the information and Slide Transitions. Set the Slide Transition to move to the next slide automatically after seven seconds

7. Choose a sound or sounds to punctuate a few of the slides

8. Set the show to run continuously

9. Preview your presentation and make any needed adjustments

10. Save the presentation as **<yourname>Doctor.ppt**

FIGURE 6.38
Doctor opening slide

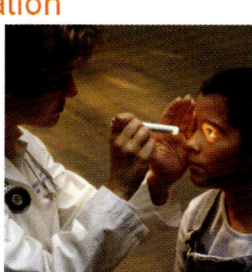

e-business

1. Trekking Assistant

Trekking is a getaway vacation involving slow, prolonged travel by foot, ox, or other beast of burden. Trekking Assistant (TA) is a full-service trekking administrator. Working closely with clients TA is able to plan treks of any length through hundreds of locations around the world. TA provides carefully planned routes with detailed maps and orienting photographs. After the route is determined, TA identifies and provides equipment, food, and porters, if desired. The cache areas are mapped, and all supplies are transported to cache sites. Once the trek is in progress, TA makes sure all goes smoothly. Clients can be as involved in their planning as they choose. You have been asked to prepare a PowerPoint kiosk presentation about the services offered by Trekking Assistant. The kiosk will be distributed at recreational and sporting goods stores, travel agencies, malls, and posted to the TA Web site.

1. Start PowerPoint and open **pp06TrekkingAssistant.ppt**

2. Use your favorite search engines to find 10 pictures of locations suitable for trekking (mountains, forests, deserts, and so on). Some of the pictures should include people walking. Images of pack animals could also be appropriate (see Figure 6.39)

3. On slide 1, insert a background picture with blue sky. Use the Cloud Callout from the AutoShapes menu to create a mat for the slide title. Send the cloud behind the text. Use the gold adjustment handle and sizing handles to adjust the shape as necessary

4. For slides 2 through 9
   a. Apply one of the background pictures
   b. Use matting techniques to make the slide text stand out without obscuring the photograph
   c. Customize slide colors as needed to obtain optimal visual impact and readability

5. Set slide transitions with varying delays depending on the slide content. Be sure to set the show to loop continuously

6. Preview the slide show, make any needed adjustments, and save as **<yourname>TrekkingAssistant.ppt**

FIGURE 6.39
Sample Trekking Assistant slide

2. Wheel Women

Wheel Women is a nonprofit organization run by women who have created a nationwide network of public bike paths. Wheel Women have established PathLink.com, which is dedicated to providing detailed, up-to-date information on path access, services, and activities. PathLink.com helps interested bikers take advantage of trails for pleasure, exercise, and transportation anywhere around the country. Through its extensive network of local paths, databases of current path reviews and contacts, and interactive, consumer-friendly path information resources, PathLink.com is a primary resource for bike path activities and travel.

PathLink.com is the nation's largest bike path organization with more than 100,000 members and supporters who believe in the bike path mission of building and maintaining paths. Wheel Women are dedicated to connecting people and communities by creating a nationwide network of these public paths from former rail lines and connecting corridors. You have been asked to create a PowerPoint presentation to publicize PathLink.com.

1. Start PowerPoint and open **pp06WheelWomen.ppt** (see Figure 6.40)

2. Use your favorite search engines to find eight pictures of images suitable for biking. Most of the pictures should include people biking

3. On slide 1, insert a background picture with blue sky. Use the Cloud Callout from the AutoShapes menu to create a mat for the slide title. Send the cloud behind the text. Use the gold adjustment handle and sizing handles to adjust the shape as necessary.

4. For slides 2 through 7
   a. Apply one of the background pictures
   b. Use matting techniques to make the slide text stand out without obscuring the photograph
   c. Customize slide colors as needed to obtain optimal visual impact and readability

5. Set Slide Transitions with varying delays depending on the slide content. Be sure to set the show to loop continuously

6. Save the presentation as **<yourname>WheelWomen.ppt**

FIGURE 6.40
Wheel Women opening slide

1. World Horizons

History is usually taught by exploring an event as it occurs across time. For example, students are exposed to a civilization as it progresses century after century. Events or cultures unrelated to that civilization are minimized. World Horizons is a Web site that doesn't ignore this discrepancy. Students can now discover the world concurrently rather than in date-oriented fashion. When a student enters a year or range of years, the Horizon Timeline for that time period is displayed. Major events in history, literature, religion, visual arts, music, science, and daily life across all cultures are represented on the time line. Each event is hot-linked to an encyclopedic reference. Other links are also available by category. At World Horizons' inception a handful of schools subscribed to its services. Now, two years later, World Horizons is available in 90 percent of the schools in the United States and internationally in 23 countries. You have been asked by World Horizons to prepare a presentation that will be used at educational conventions to inform teachers of World Horizons' subscription service.

1. Start PowerPoint and open **pp06WorldHorizons.ppt**

2. Move to slide 1
   a. Place an image of a globe in the center of the slide using images from Clips Online
   b. Make the globe as large as possible without hanging off the slide and send it behind the slide text

tip: *You may need to recolor the image to match the presentation. Right-click, choose Format object, and use the Recolor button. Customizing the color scheme may also be necessary to improve readability*

3. Move to slide 2 and create two images
   a. Use multiple block arrows with 3-D effects to represent longitude. Group the component parts and animate it to load with the "Teaching is" text
   b. Use multiple block arrows with 3-D effects to represent both latitude and longitude. Group the component parts and animate it to load with the "History is" text

4. Use a search engine such as Google to locate a picture of a solar eclipse and use this image as a background on slide 3

5. Create a representative time line on slide 4. Use a double-headed horizontal arrow across the width of the slide. Adjust the line weight to 10 pt. Select a color to match the slide's colors. Add six or seven oval callouts from the AutoShapes menu to indicate how historical data would be displayed. Group all of the objects into a single image

6. Locate or create art to illustrate the remaining slides

7. Preview the presentation, make any needed adjustments, and save as **<yourname>WorldHorizons.ppt**

FIGURE 6.41
Globe background

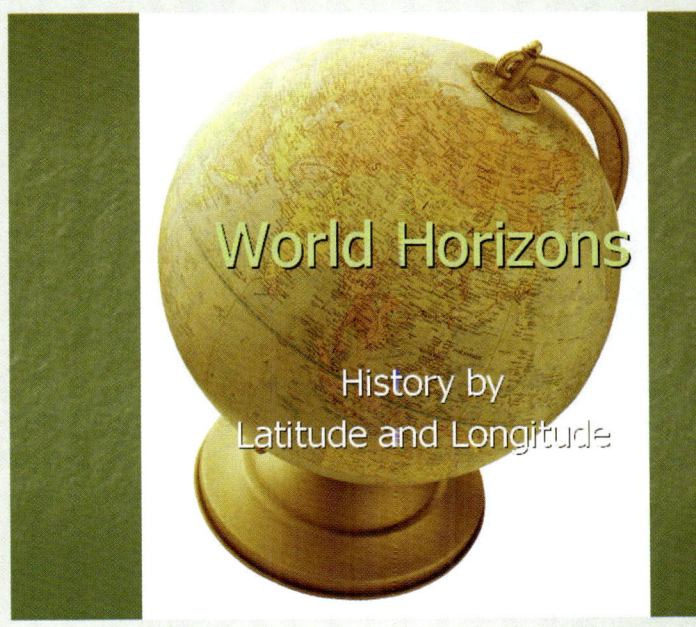

2. CollegeAdmissions.com

Applying to college can be a very imposing and intimidating experience for both high school students and their parents. At CollegeAdmissions.com, they employ a staff of former admissions officers from top universities around the country. By matching students with the right counselor, they help meet family needs and offer step-by-step assistance throughout the entire admissions process.

1. Start PowerPoint and open **pp06CollegeAdmissions.ppt**

2. Move to slide 1
   a. Place an image of a desk in the center of the slide
   b. Make the desk as large as possible without hanging off the slide of the title text and send it behind the slide text

tip: *You may need to recolor the image to match the presentation. Right-click, choose Format object, and use the Recolor button. Customizing the color scheme may also be necessary to improve readability*

3. Move to slide 2 and create a quad arrow with 3-D effects. Place the image in the lower right-hand corner and rotate the image 314 degrees. Animate it to load with the bulleted text

4. Move to slide 3 and insert an image (clip art is fine) that represents writing and use this image as a background

tip: *You may need to recolor the image to match the presentation. Right-click, choose Format Object, and use the Recolor button. Customizing the color scheme may also be necessary to improve readability*

5. Create a representative timeline on slide 4
   a. Use a double-headed vertical arrow ("Double Arrow under Lines selection) about the height of the text. Make the line weight 2 pt. Add four Callouts from the AutoShapes menu to indicate each major bullet point. Use "Line Callout 2 (Accent Bar)." Create a text box within each callout with the major bullet point text. Recolor images to your liking. Group all of the objects into a single image

6. Locate or create art to illustrate the remaining slides. Add Custom Animations for effect

7. Preview the presentation, and make any needed adjustments

8. Save the presentation as **<yourname>CollegeAdmissions.ppt**

FIGURE 6.42
College Admissions opening slide

around the world

1. Arrow Briefings

Arrow Briefings (AB) produces efficiency products to assist executives in improving productivity. While Arrow Briefings produces tangible products such as extremely rapid Internet access and a user-friendly operating system for their computers, the most valuable product is their two-day seminar teaching patented techniques to improve the decision-making process. Arrow Briefings' clients are top executives of businesses from all over the world. All are Fortune 500 companies.

The seminar is always located in an elegant hotel. Here all the trimmings are provided, down to meals on fine china. Topics include studies on the effects of productivity, how professionals spend (or waste) their time, human factors in productivity, effectiveness of corporate executives in decision making, communicating decisions in today's complex world, and AB's state-of-the-art technology. You have been asked to prepare a PowerPoint presentation at conventions that will introduce the seminar to executives.

1. Start PowerPoint and open **pp06ArrowBriefings.ppt**

2. Save the presentation as **<yourname>ArrowBriefings.ppt**

3. Select the light blue color scheme for this template

FIGURE 6.43

Sample Arrow Briefings slide

4. Use shapes from the Drawing toolbar to create a logo for the company. Include the company name. Use shadow and 3-D effects. Group the finished logo into one object (see Figure 6.43)

5. Position the logo on the slide 1

6. Use AutoShapes to create a moon and stars on the second slide. Arrange and color artistically and then group the finished work

7. Use a lightning bolt with other graphics to illustrate slide 3. Add a custom fill to the lightning bolt

8. Apply a Texture background to slide 4. Mat text and/or customize colors to obtain optimal readability. Place a reduced size logo on this slide

9. Apply a picture background to slide 5 reflecting leisure activities. Mat text and /or customize colors to obtain optimal readability

10. Use stacked ovals to create a target on slide 6. The largest circle is white, the next is red, and the center is black. Align the centers of the circles. Draw an arrow approaching the bull's-eye. Group the component parts into one object

11. Add effective graphics to each of the remaining slides

12. Set slide transitions and use Custom Animations for graphics

13. Test your presentation, make needed adjustments, and save it again

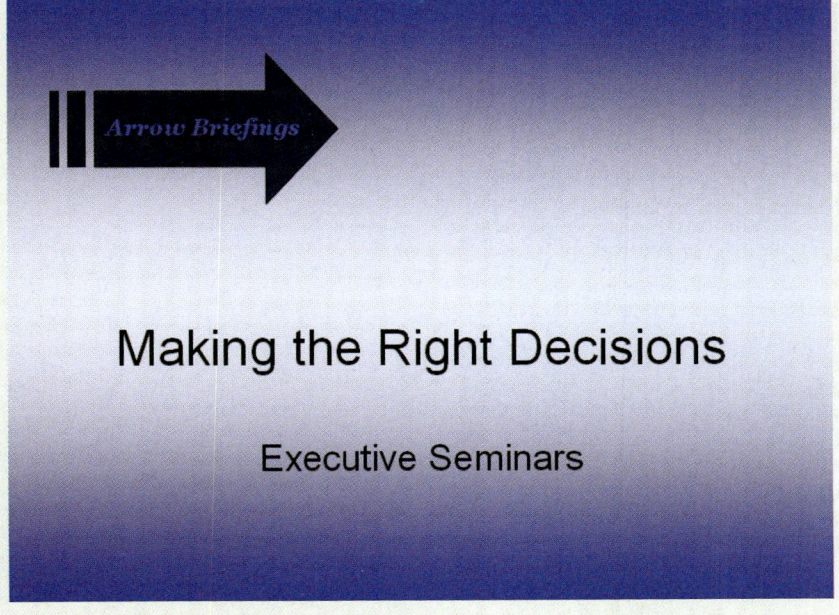

2. WorldGenes.com

WorldGenes.com is the leading network for connecting families and generations on the Web, and is the largest and most active online community of its kind. Consistently ranked among the top 15 Internet properties worldwide in both page views and "stickiness," the WorldGenes.com network of sites is a key online destination for those interested in family history. The company's business model takes advantage of its leading position as a premier source for content, community, and commerce. Revenue drivers include premium subscription services, e-commerce opportunities, and advertising and sponsorship agreements.

1. Start PowerPoint and open **pp06WorldGenes.ppt**

2. Use shapes from the Drawing toolbar to create a logo for the company. Include the company name. Use shadow and 3-D effects. Group the finished logo into one object

3. Position the logo on slide 1 (see Figure 6.44)

4. Use AutoShapes to create a spiral arrow on slide 2 starting with the second-level bullet and going down to the last one. Arrange and color to complement the slide design and then group the finished work

5. Use a tree image with other graphics to illustrate slide 3. Add a custom fill to the tree and other graphical images

6. Apply a Pattern background to slide 4. Customize colors to obtain optimal readability. Place a reduced size logo on this slide

7. Apply a picture background to slide 5 reflecting a calendar image. Customize colors to obtain optimal readability

8. Set Slide Transitions and Custom Animations for the bulleted items and graphics

9. Test your presentation, and make needed adjustments

10. Save the presentation as **<yourname>WorldGenes.ppt**

FIGURE 6.44
WorldGenes.com opening slide

Montgomery-Wellish Foods, Inc.

One of the first lessons the new Montgomery-Wellish trainees learn is to pick a product and follow it throughout its life cycle. There are several steps to a product's life cycle. The trainee receives a request to buy food from a producer. A number of cases or palettes are purchased. The goods are then shipped to MWF's warehouse. Once there, the warehouse is responsible for placing the goods in storage and then sending the goods out to the supermarkets. The trainee not only authorizes the purchase of the product but also is responsible for tracking the shipment every step of the way. If the food isn't available to the supermarket in a timely fashion (e.g., for seasonal display), supermarkets may not purchase from MWF at a later date. Mary Einhorn has been charged with tracking spices. Mary's data show that there are delays in the shipping and handling of spices all along the way. You have been asked to prepare a PowerPoint presentation that illustrates Mary Einhorn's tracking of spices, which she will present to the trainees.

1. Start PowerPoint and open **pp06MWFTracking.ppt** (see Figure 6.45)
2. Use various gradient combinations of the presentation color scheme to vary the background of slides 2 through 8 while maintaining a consistent look

3. Add pictures of herbs and spices to the first slide
4. Search for art that will enhance each of the remaining slides
5. Title the sixth slide Transport Timetable Averages. Construct a chart (graph) that shows the expected time and actual time in days for delivery to the warehouse, storage processing time, and delivery to the market, using data from the next figure. Title the chart **Shipping and Handling Days January–June 2004**
6. Set custom animation for the title, bulleted text, and chart. Establish Slide Transitions
7. Preview your presentation, make adjustments, and save it as **<yourname>MWFTracking.ppt**

FIGURE 6.45

Sample opening slide

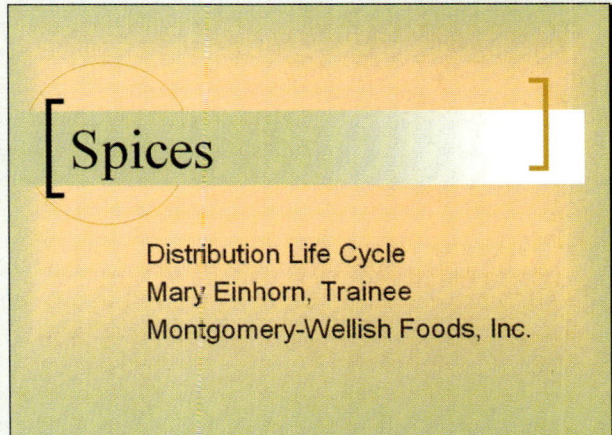

FIGURE 6.46

Chart data

Shipping to Warehouse		Storage		Delivery to Market	
Expected	Actual	Expected	Actual	Expected	Actual
3	5	.5	1.5	1	2.5

1. Usefulness of Sound Clips

Establish some guidelines for the use of sound clips in presentations. Some people feel that sound clips are a distraction to the presentation, while others consider sound clips to be helpful. Explain the reasons for your guidelines.

2. Using Specialized Animations

Rehearsing a presentation thoroughly before attempting to present it to its intended audience is very important. Discuss ways in which you would rehearse the presentation. What are the advantages of rehearsing it before a live audience of family or friends?

7

Internet/ Intranet Presentations

did you know?

vanilla *is the extract of fermented and dried pods of several species of orchids.*

if *the sun stopped shining suddenly, it would take eight minutes for people on earth to be aware of the fact.*

almonds, *peaches, and apricots belong to the rose family.*

the *oldest living thing in existence is a bristlecone pine in the White Mountains of California, dated to be 4,600 years old.*

ten *inches of snow equals one inch of rain in water content.*

the *first woman to qualify for the Indianapolis 500 was Janet Guthrie in 1977.*

one *organ donor can save up to _____ lives.*

Chapter Objectives

- **Add hyperlinks to slides—MOS PP035-4-1**
- **Save a presentation as a Web page (publish)—MOS PP035-4-6**
- **Manage files and folders for presentations—MOS PP035-4-6**

Using PowerPoint to Build a Donor Information Kiosk

Lauda Simmons is the coordinator of several donor organizations in the southern United States. These organizations are responsible for tracking the need for donated organs and tissue, educating the public about these needs, and coordinating the donation process.

Lauda spends a considerable amount of her time speaking at public events to promote organ and tissue donation. She has a PowerPoint presentation that she typically modifies to suit the technical understanding of the audience. For example, when speaking to the general public, the presentation typically contains very few medical terms, but when speaking to the medical or legal community, the terms and definitions must be included.

Keeping multiple copies of the presentation and updating each time she speaks is becoming tedious and too time-consuming. Lauda has asked you to help her create an interactive presentation that will allow her to choose what content to include in her production as the slide show is running. She envisions a linked slide show that contains all of the information that she might need to address. As she is speaking, she would like to be able to choose or ignore links based on audience interest and available time.

FIGURE 7.1
Organ Donor presentation links

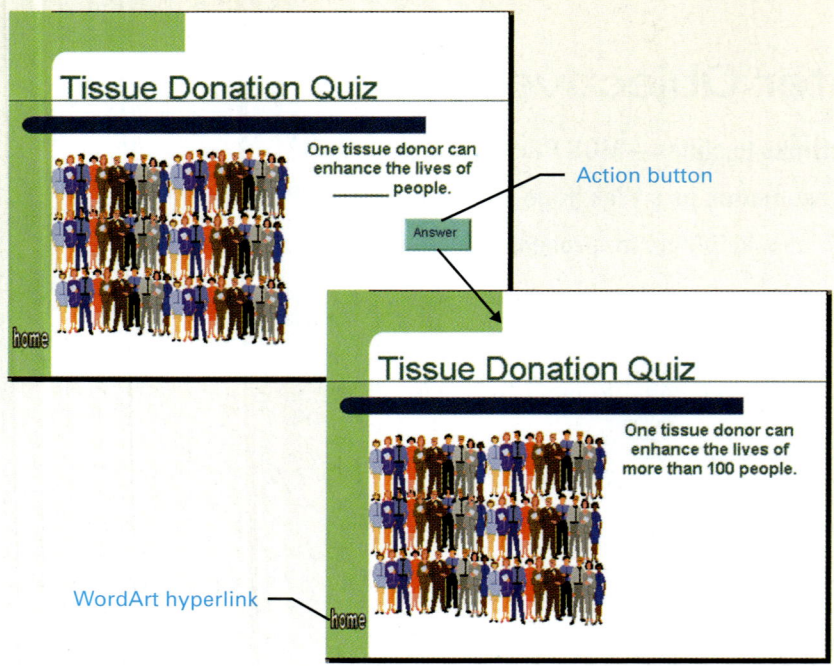

Lauda would also like to promote organ and tissue donation to a wider audience than just those she can personally present to. The organization she represents has a Web site that is currently used to promote the organization. Lauda would like to put a version of her presentation on the Web site to more specifically address the information needs of potential organ and tissue donors.

Finally, Lauda believes that a Web site could be used by hospital personnel like an informational kiosk. Because the presentation would be Web-based, there would be no need for a dedicated computer. The kiosks would not replace the medical professional speaking to family members, but could serve as on-demand reinforcement of information provided at a very stressful time.

SESSION 7.1 INTERACTIVE PRESENTATIONS

The linear presentations that have been developed up to this point are very effective for short speaker-led slide shows or any presentation that is always run from beginning to end. Linear presentations make use of the basic navigation provided by PowerPoint. Such a presentation can move forward and backward one slide at a time or use pop-up menus and shortcuts to move to a specific slide. By contrast, interactive presentations allow the order of a slide show to be determined by the viewer. Interactive slide shows are effective as kiosks, Web sites, and presentations that change based on the audience.

Adding Navigation to Your Presentation

Before adding nonlinear navigation to Lauda's Organ Donor presentation, you will need to review the slides and evaluate how well they work with PowerPoint's default navigation features. PowerPoint's native navigation methods are outlined in Figure 7.2. Although it is possible to move to any slide without using special features, the way to accomplish such movement is not intuitive to a novice user and can be visually disturbing to an audience.

Slide Show Navigation	
Go to the next slide	Click the mouse
	Press Spacebar or Enter
	Right-click, and on the shortcut menu, click Next
Go to the previous slide	Press Backspace
	Right-click, and on the shortcut menu, click Previous
See a specific previously viewed slide	Right-click, point to Go on the shortcut menu, and then click Previously Viewed
Go to a specific slide	Type the slide number, and then press Enter
	Right-click, point to Go on the shortcut menu, then point to By Title, and click the slide you want

FIGURE 7.2
Slide show navigation

Navigating PP07OrganDonor:

1. Start PowerPoint and open **pp07OrganDonor.ppt**

2. Click the **Slide Show** button to run the show (or press **F5**)

3. Press the **Spacebar** to advance one slide and then press the **Spacebar** again after the slide's animations have completed

4. Press **Enter** to advance one slide and then press **Enter** again when the slide animations are completed

5. Press **Backspace** to move back one animation and then continue pressing Backspace until you are on the first slide

   tip: *You will need to backspace twice for slides containing animations—once to move to the slide and the second time to initiate the animation*

6. Type **9** and press **Enter** to move to slide 9

7. Type **5** and then press **Enter** to move to slide 5

   tip: *Either the Slide Navigator or By Title option of the Go menu is appropriate*

8. Use **Esc** to end the slide show

Nonlinear navigation is added to a presentation using hyperlinks and action buttons. These features provide an intuitive way for users to move directly to materials of interest. Each hyperlink or action button is linked to a specific slide, another slide show, a Web page, or a file. Presentations with links are typically hierarchical in structure with several paths the user can choose. The audience may view every slide in the presentation, or just those of current interest.

Designing Hierarchical Presentations

When you are accustomed to creating linear presentations, it is important to take some time to review the design of nonlinear presentations. Nonlinear presentations are usually hierarchical with several branches or fingers that the viewer can follow. If you have visited Web sites, you are familiar with the methodology. By clicking, you can choose what topic(s) to view and how much to view about it.

Hierarchical structures typically have a menu page of topics with each topic having additional options for as many levels as are necessary for the materials. The menu may be the opening page or can follow introductory materials. Any page layout that provides the user with clickable options can be considered a menu. Figure 7.3 shows the hierarchical structure that will be applied to the Organ Donor presentation.

The hierarchy chart in the previous figure effectively defines the paths that should be available to the viewer when moving through the presentation. To determine an appropriate structure, review the slides of a presentation and group them by topic. Each topic will become a menu item on the opening slide. Repeat this process for the slides in each topic to determine what lower level links will need to be added.

After establishing the slide hierarchy, it is time for you to determine the direction of navigation. The arrow heads in the previous figure represent the direction of navigation. It is rare to have a hierarchy that can only be navigated from top to bottom. It is common to allow the user to return to the menu from every slide, but sometimes additional movement between slides and topics is desirable. For the Organ Donor presentation, Lauda would like to be able to access the menu from every slide but have linear progression through each topic.

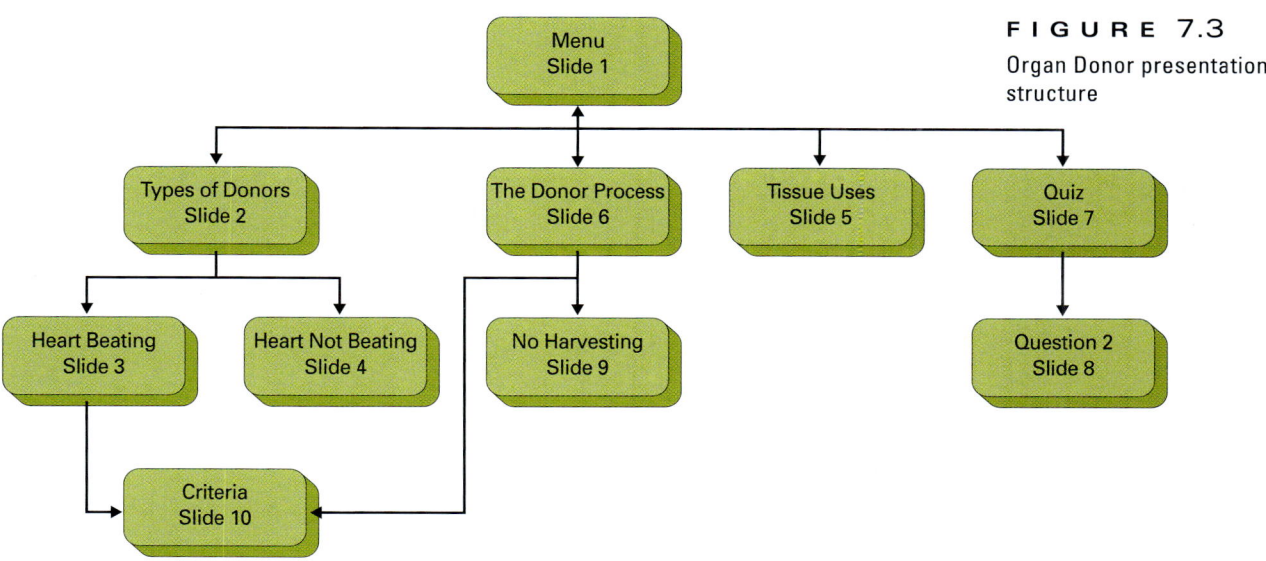

FIGURE 7.3
Organ Donor presentation structure

Slides 2 through 10 will be able to return directly to the menu

Creating Hyperlinks

A *hyperlink* is a connection from one slide in a presentation to another location. The other location can be another slide in the current presentation, a slide in another presentation, a file, a Web page address, or an e-mail address. The hyperlink can be any text or object on the slide including a clip art, WordArt, graph, or image. Hyperlinks are not active in any of the PowerPoint views used to develop slide shows, but become clickable when the show is run.

When a link to another PowerPoint slide is clicked, the slide is displayed as part of the PowerPoint presentation. If the link is to a Web page and an active Internet connection is available, the page will open in your default browser. Links to other types of files will open in the source application.

Adding hyperlinks to an Internet resource like a Web page or e-mail address is simple. Just type the address, called a **uniform resource locator** (URL), of a Web page or an e-mail address as part of the content of a slide; PowerPoint automatically creates a hyperlink to those external locations. This is because Internet addresses contain all of the information needed to locate a particular Web page or e-mail account. Other types of hyperlinks must be specifically defined. You will begin this process by building the opening page for Lauda's presentation, which will contain links to Web resources and specific locations within the slide show.

---

task reference — Insert a Hyperlink

- Select the object that will initiate the hyperlink. The object can be text, WordArt, a graphic, or any other clickable object
- Click the **Insert Hyperlink** button on the Standard toolbar
- Select the location of the link and then set the link options

---

Building the PP07OrganDonor opening page:

1. Move to slide 1

2. Add a Textbox 🖺 to the bottom right of the slide as shown in Figure 7.4 by dragging it from the Drawing toolbar

   a. Type **www.organdonor.com**

   b. Press **Enter** and type your e-mail address (if you don't have an e-mail address, use *yourname@emailserver.edu*)

3. Select the subtitle placeholder containing Lauda's name and type the following text in its place

   Types of Donors

   The Donor Process

   Tissue Uses

   Quiz

4. Adjust the subtitle placeholder as needed (drag the textbox) to match your positioning of the menu items to the figure

5. Select the **Types of Donors** text

   a. Click the **Insert Hyperlink** 🖳 button in the Standard toolbar

   b. Click the **Place in This Document** option

   c. Select 2. **Categories of Donors** in the left panel and click **OK**

tip: *The Types of Donors text is now formatted as a hyperlink. The link will not become active until the slide show is run*

6. Repeat actions outlined in step 5 to

   a. Link **The Donor Process** to slide 6

   b. Link **Tissue Uses** to slide 5

   c. Link **Quiz** to slide 7

7. Save your changes as **<yourname>OrganDonor.ppt**

8. Press **F5** to test each of the links

9. Press **Esc** to end the slide show

Referring to Figure 7.3, notice that the first level of downward links from the hierarchy chart has now been added to your presentation. It is easiest to add one level of links and test them before adding the next level of links. For the menu, specific text was created to be used as the link text. The next level of links uses existing slide content as the link text.

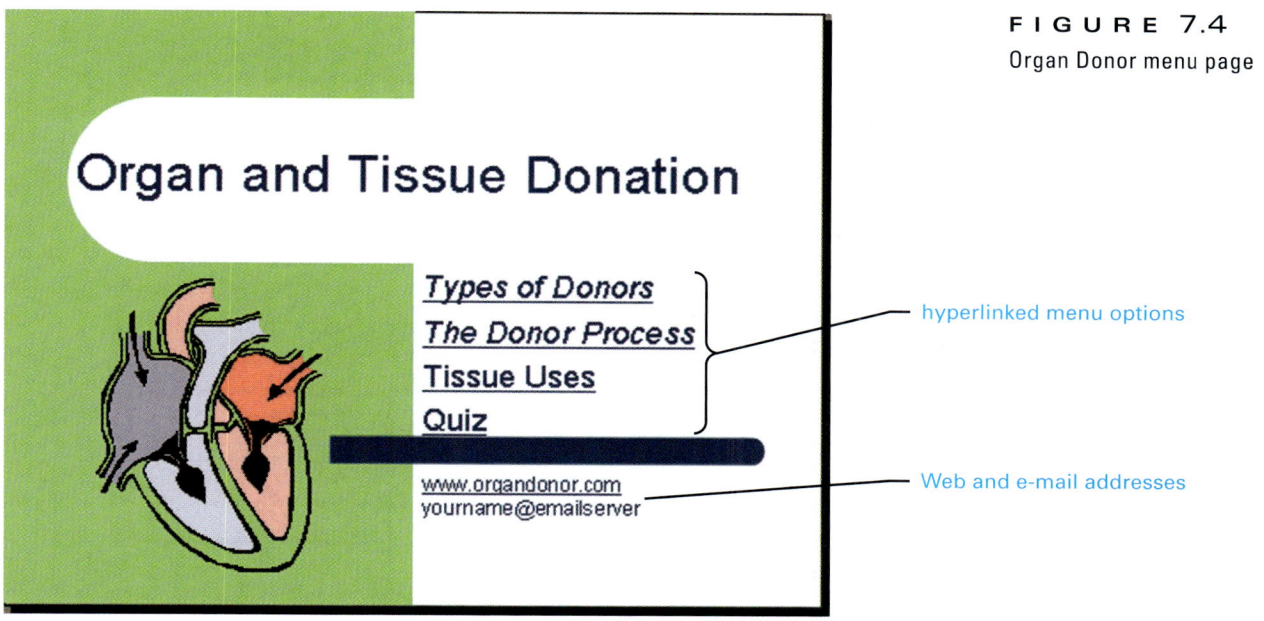

FIGURE 7.4
Organ Donor menu page

Building second-level links:

1. Move to slide 2

2. Select **Heart Beating**, click the **Insert Hyperlink** button, and add a hyperlink to slide 3

3. Select **Non-Heart Beating**, click the **Insert Hyperlink** button, and add a hyperlink to slide 4

4. Select **Brain Death**, click the **Insert Hyperlink** button, and add a hyperlink to slide 10

5. Move to slide 6

6. Select **Brain Death** in the first bullet, click the **Insert Hyperlink** button, and add a hyperlink to slide 10 (see Figure 7.5)

7. Move to slide 4, select **Only**, remove the underline (click the **Underline** button on the Formatting toolbar to toggle it off), and add italic formatting

8. Press **F5** to test the new links

9. Press **Esc** to end the slide show

Underlining and color are both used to indicate text that can be clicked. The visited and unvisited text hyperlink colors are set by the active color scheme. Other hyperlinked objects like pictures, WordArt, or shapes are not formatted to indicate that they are hyperlinked.

POWERPOINT

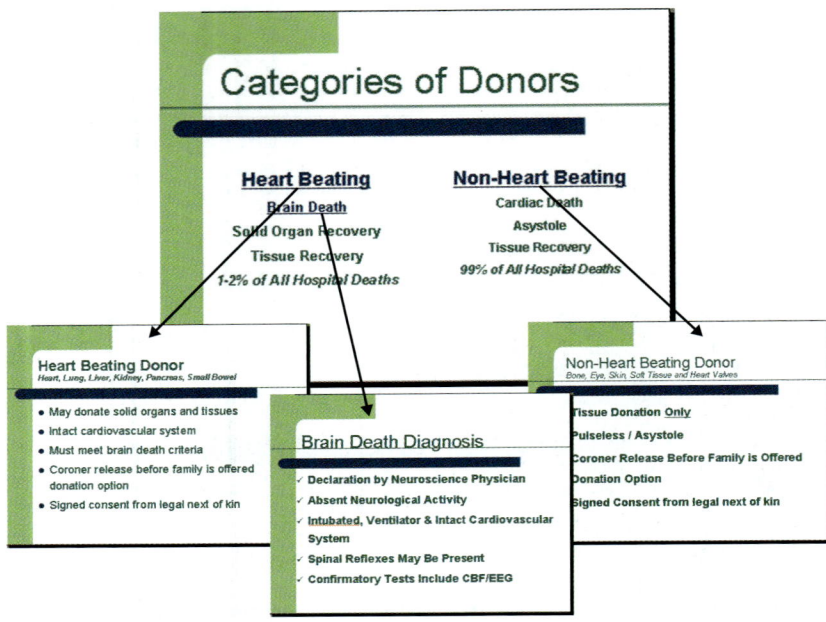

You removed the underline from *Only* in the previous steps because it confuses users to have underlines used for emphasis in a presentation also containing hyperlinks. Although the mouse pointer changes to a pointing finger when it is over a clickable object, many users don't notice this change and will try to click any underlined text. Try to make navigation as intuitive as possible to avoid confusing users.

Since hyperlinks can be applied to any text or object, text, shapes, tables, graphics, and pictures can link to other locations. Although clicking is the most common way to initiate a link, other actions, like pausing over a link, can be used to start the action. When linking compound objects like text within a shape or grouped objects, each component can have a unique link attribute set. Editing a hyperlinked object does not impact the hyperlink, but deleting a hyperlinked object removes the associated hyperlink.

help yourself *Click the* Type a Question for help *combo box, type* **hyperlink**, *and press* **Enter**. *Click the hyperlink* **Create a hyperlink** *in the Search Results panel and then click the hyperlink* **Create a hyperlink to a custom show or a location in the current presentation** *to display help on how you can create a hyperlink to another slide in your presentation. Click the Help screen* **Close** *button when you are finished. Close the task pane*

Using the Insert Hyperlink Dialog Box

The Insert Hyperlink dialog box has already been used to add hyperlinks to the Organ Donor slide show, but a closer look at its capabilities is warranted. In the original evaluation of the donor presentation, a reference to brain death on slide 3 was missed. That text needs to be linked to the brain death criteria on slide 10.

Exploring the Insert Hyperlink dialog box:

1. Move to slide 3

2. Select **Brain Death** in the third bulleted item and click the **Insert Hyperlink** button

3. Click **Existing File or Web Page** in the *Link to* panel on the left side.

FIGURE 7.6
Insert Hyperlink dialog box

link text

add text that will display when
the user hovers over the link

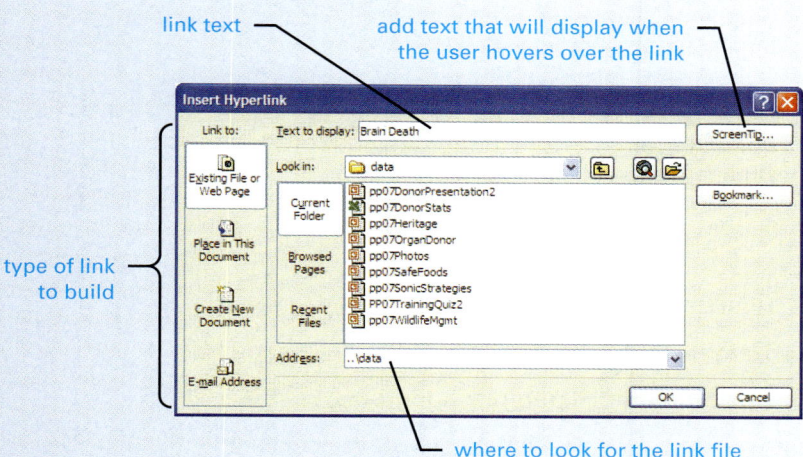

type of link
to build

where to look for the link file

tip: *Notice that Current Folder is the default selection, so the display represents the files and folders in the current folder*

4. Click **Browsed Pages**

tip: *A list of Web addresses that have been visited with the default browser on your computer will be displayed. This methodology avoids typing errors when entering URLs*

5. Click **Recent Files** for a listing of the most recently opened files on your computer

6. Click **E-mail Addresses** in the *Link to* panel and notice the display of recent e-mail addresses

7. Click **Create New Document** and review the options for creating a new document

tip: *You can use new documents to record information being gathered during the presentation*

8. Click **Place in This Document**, set the link to slide 10, and click **OK**

9. Press **Shift+F5** to test the new link on the current slide

10. Press **Esc** to end the slide show

When an e-mail or Web address is known, it is convenient to just type it in and let PowerPoint take care of making the link. This method was demonstrated on the first slide of Organ Donor. When a site has been visited but the URL was not committed to memory, the Insert Hyperlink dialog box will display a selectable list of recently viewed addresses. Similarly, the Current Folder and Recent Files selections display files for you to select from.

Changes can be made to an existing hyperlink by selecting the link and clicking the Insert Hyperlink button. This action opens the Edit Hyperlink dialog box. Lauda would like Screen Tips added to some of the hyperlinks in the presentation.

Setting Screen Tip text:

1. Move to slide 3 if necessary

2. Select the **Brain Death** hyperlink in the third bulleted item and click the **Insert Hyperlink** button

tip: *Notice that the hyperlink is not active in Design Views, and you can select it like any other slide text*

3. Click the **ScreenTip** button

4. Type **View Brain Death Diagnosis** (see Figure 7.7) and click **OK**

5. Click **OK** to close the Edit Hyperlink dialog box

FIGURE 7.7

Setting a ScreenTip

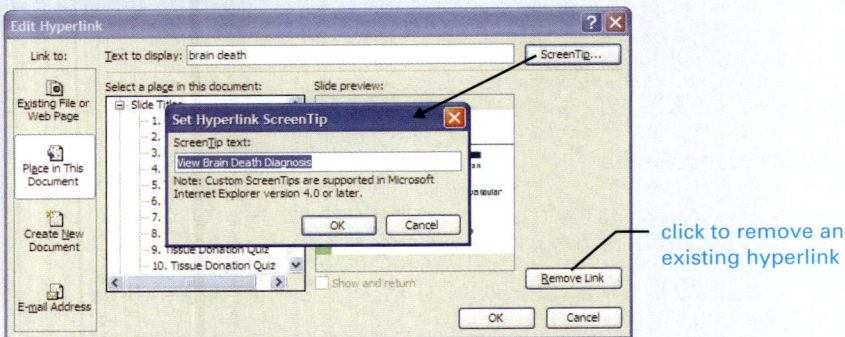

6. Run the presentation from slide 3 (press **Shift+F5**) and hover the cursor over the Brain Death link to view the ScreenTip

7. Use **Esc** to end the show

You probably noticed that the Edit Hyperlink dialog box is very similar to the Insert Hyperlink dialog box. The most significant difference is the Edit Hyperlink option for removing the hyperlink while leaving the hyperlinked object intact. The Edit Hyperlink dialog box can also be used to update link text and change the link address.

When presentations are moved to a new computer, it is common to have **broken hyperlinks**. It is always best that you test all hyperlinks before running a slide show, but this is critical if the show has been moved to a new folder or computer. A broken hyperlink is one that has an invalid destination causing an error to display when it is clicked. The cause might be as simple as a URL that you mistyped, or a hyperlink to a destination that you may have moved or deleted. Update broken hyperlinks with the Edit Hyperlink features just discussed.

Noticeably absent from the Edit Hyperlink dialog box is the ability to change the color of the hyperlinks. That is because hyperlinks are controlled by the eight colors of the color scheme. Updating the colors of the color scheme is the only way to change hyperlink colors.

Hyperlinking Other Objects

All other linking methods are based on hyperlinks. The first step is to build the object that will be used to initiate the link. Once an object is built, it is made clickable by adding a hyperlink to it.

Placing Links on the Slide Master

The original hierarchy designed for the Organ Donor presentation noted that slides 2 through 10 were to provide navigation back to the menu. The first slide in a presentation is often referred to as the home slide. Lauda would like to use WordArt to create a navigation icon for this purpose. This icon will be placed on the Slide Master so that it will appear on all slides that do not use the Title Slide format.

Adding a link to the Slide Master:

1. Click **View**, point to **Master**, and click **Slide Master**

2. Select the Slide Master (with the bulleted list), *not* the Title Master

3. Click the **Insert WordArt** button on the Drawing toolbar

   a. Select the top-left style and click **OK**

   b. Type **home** and click **OK**

   c. Position and size the WordArt to match Figure 7.8

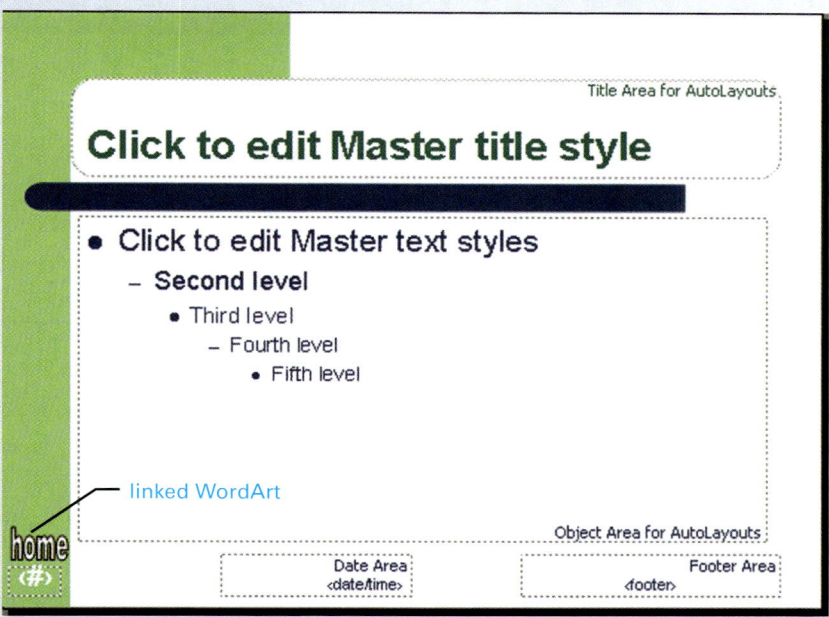

FIGURE 7.8
WordArt link added to
Slide Master

4. With the WordArt still selected

   a. Click the **Insert Hyperlink** button, select **Place in This Document** and then click **1. Organ and Tissue Donation**

   b. Click the **ScreenTip** button, type **Return to menu slide**, and click **OK**

   c. Click **OK** to close the Insert Hyperlink dialog box

   d. Click **Close Master View** on the Slide Master View toolbar

5. Run the presentation and test the *home* links on several slides

6. Use **Esc** to end the slide show

7. Press the **Save** button to save your altered presentation

Any object placed on a Slide Master will appear on all slides in the presentation based on that master. The Home link could have been text or any other object placed on the master. If your presentation uses multiple templates, each set of masters would need to be updated to place an item on all pages.

Using Action Buttons

Action buttons are ready-made buttons that can be placed on a slide to intuitively control slide progressions. Once the button is placed on a slide, it is assigned a hyperlink that controls its action. Action buttons are available from the AutoShapes menu of the Drawing toolbar and are added to a slide by selecting the button and then clicking and dragging it onto the slide. Action buttons are effective when a simple pictorial interface is needed for moving between slides, playing movies, and playing sounds.

Lauda would like to use Action buttons for the navigation in the quiz component of Organ Donor. The plan is to add a few more questions and make the quiz more interactive. The first step of this process is to duplicate each quiz slide and remove the answer from the first slide. Action buttons will be added to the question slide so the user can see the answer and move to the next question.

---

task reference   Create and Link an Action Button

- Select the slide to contain the Action button

- If needed, use the View menu to activate the Drawing toolbar

- Click the **AutoShapes** button of the Drawing toolbar, pause over **Action Buttons**, and click the desired button

- Click and drag the button on the slide surface

- Click the Action button and follow the steps to set a hyperlink

---

Adding Action buttons:

1. Move to slide 7 if necessary

2. Click **Edit** and then click **Duplicate** to create a copy of this slide

3. Return to slide 7, delete the answer text in the bottom of the slide, and reduce the size of the question placeholder

4. Click **AutoShapes** on the Drawing toolbar, point to **Action Buttons**, then click the **Custom** (blank) Action button, and draw it on the slide using Figure 7.9 as your guide

5. On the Mouse Click tab of the Action Settings dialog box, click the **Hyperlink to** option button, then select **Next Slide** and click **OK**

6. Type **Answer** in the action button

7. Move to slide 8, delete the answer text, and replace the underline with **up to 8**. Reduce the size of the text box

8. Click **AutoShapes**, point to **Action Buttons**, click the **Forward or Next** action button, drag it to the slide, fill in the Action Settings dialog box to **Hyperlink to Next Slide** and click **OK**

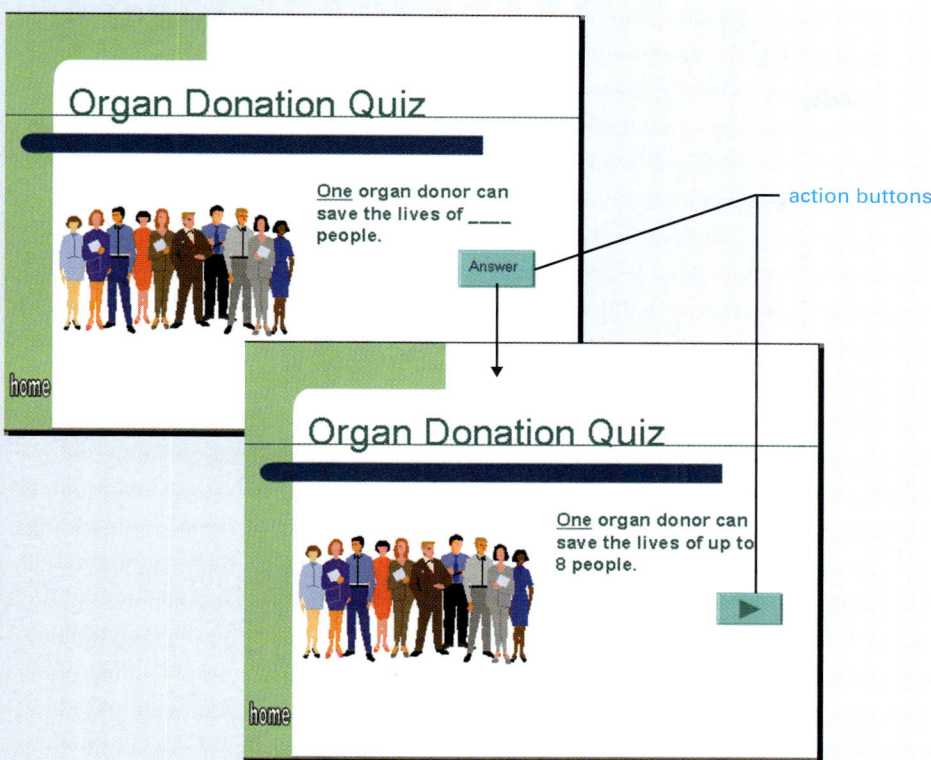

FIGURE 7.9

Action buttons with hyperlinks

9. Repeat steps 2 through 5 to duplicate, edit, and add Action buttons to slide 9

tip: *You can copy and paste Action buttons that suit your needs*

10. Move to slide 10 and replace the underline with **more than 100**

11. Run the slide show from slide 7 (press **F5**, type **7**, and press **Enter**) and test the Action buttons

12. Press **Esc t**o end the slide show

If you make a mistake when attaching a hyperlink to an object such as WordArt or an Action button, use the Insert Hyperlink button to open the Edit Hyperlink dialog box and make adjustments. When using objects other than text for a hyperlink, there are no visual indications to the user like the change in text color and underline used for text links. It is important that hyperlinked objects look clickable. Clickable objects can be distinguished by color, background, and position on the slide. In general, buttons should be placed on the bottom or down the left of the slide.

Linking to External Resources

One of the most powerful features of hyperlinked presentations is the ability to draw in external resources as you need them. When linking to an external resource, its location is described with a uniform resource locator (URL). When the hyperlink is to a page or file on your local computer or network, the location is represented by the path to the file. The path contains the drive name and all of the folders that must be opened to reach the file. For example, C:\My Documents\Presentation\Notes.doc describes the location of the Word file, Notes.doc, as being on the C: drive in the Notes folder, which can be found in the My Documents folder. Similarly www.microsoft.com describes the default Web page (since no filename is included) found on the Microsoft.com server.

The hyperlinks that are connected to resources outside a slide show can use either absolute or relative paths. ***Absolute links*** state all of the information required to find the resource, so for a file it would contain the drive, path, and filename. ***Relative links*** usually don't include a drive and path, but depend on the file being in the same folder as the presentation or in a folder that has been specified as the hyperlink base.

Relative linking allows you to move the presentation and base folder to another computer without breaking any links. When delivering a presentation from a stand-alone computer, it is best that you place all linked files in the same folder as your presentation. If you move your presentation to another computer, you must move all of the linked files as well.

When your presentation is stored on a server with links to several files, it is a good practice to put the files in a common location on a server and set a ***hyperlink base***. If the server URL changes, updating the hyperlink base will repair any broken links without editing each link. If you need this feature, please refer to PowerPoint Help for instructions.

When presenting to certain audiences, Lauda has found that she likes to use slides from some of her other presentations. In the past she has stopped the current slide show and opened another to retrieve the data. To avoid this juggling, she wants to place links to other shows in the Organ Donor presentation.

Linking to another PowerPoint file:

1. Move to slide 5

2. Build a WordArt object with the first style from the style gallery. The text should be **case**

3. Position the new WordArt object above the home object as shown in Figure 7.10. Resize it to match Figure 7.10

tip: *The home object is on the Slide Master and cannot be manipulated from slide 5*

4. Select the **case** WordArt object

   a. Click the **Insert Hyperlink** button

   b. Click **Existing File or Web page**

   c. Click **Current Folder** and navigate to and then click **pp07DonorPresentation2.ppt**

   d. Click the **Bookmark** button, select slide 4 of the presentation, and click **OK**

   e. Click **OK** again to exit the Insert Hyperlink dialog box

5. Run the slide show by pressing **Shift+F5** to display slide 5 in the slide show and test the *case* link

6. Press **Esc** to end the pp07DonorPresentation2.ppt slide show

7. Press **Esc** again to end your slide show

The **bookmark** created in the previous steps is similar to a bookmark left in a book to mark your place, but this one keeps track of which slide to display when the hyperlink is clicked. With the slide show running you clicked the case link causing pp07DonorPresentation2 to open as a separate presentation. The bookmark caused

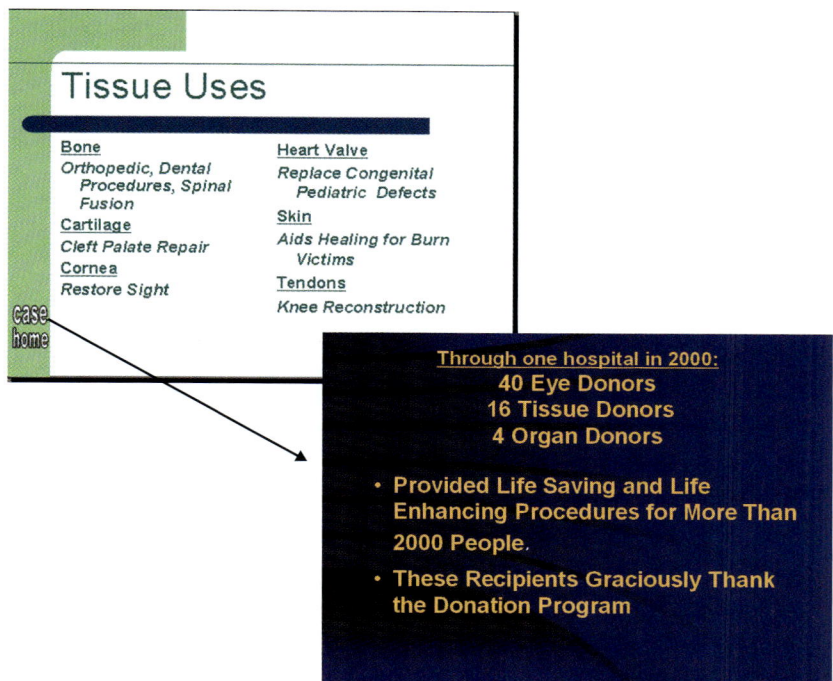

slide 4 to be active when the presentation opened, but navigation can be used to move to any slide in the presentation. Since two slide shows were open, both needed to be closed.

Links can also open files of other types. Lauda has created a chart in Excel that she would like to access from a link in the slide show.

Linking to an Excel file:

1. Move to slide 2

2. Build a WordArt object with the first style from the style gallery containing the text **chart** (click the **Insert WordArt** button on the Drawing toolbar)

3. Position and resize the new WordArt object above the home object as shown in Figure 7.11

tip: *The home object is on the Slide Master and cannot be manipulated from slide 2*

4. Select the **chart** WordArt

   a. Click the **Insert Hyperlink** button on the Standard toolbar

   b. Click **Existing File or Web page** in the *Link to* list

   c. Click **Current Folder**, navigate to the Excel file **pp07DonorStats.xls**, and click the filename

   d. Click **OK**

5. Press **Shift+F5** to run the slide show from slide 2 and click the **Chart** hyperlink to test it

6. Close Excel by clicking **File** and then clicking **Exit**

FIGURE 7.11

Hyperlink to an Excel file

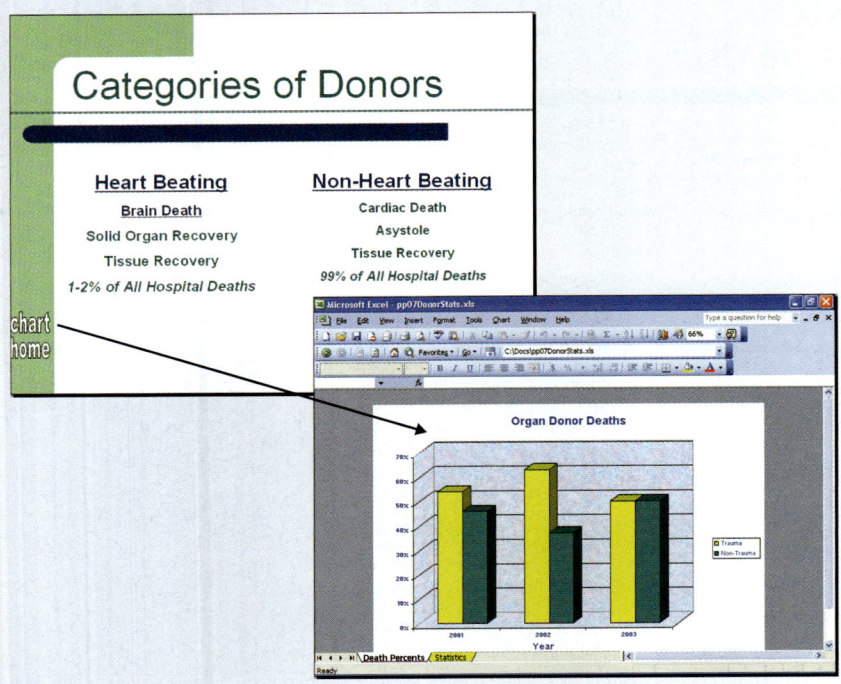

7. Press **Esc** to end the slide show

8. Save the presentation (click **File**, click **Save**)

9. Close PowerPoint

You can use the hyperlink to open files created in any application. When a link to a file created in another application is clicked, the native application is opened to display the file. For this to work properly, the file type must be recognized by Windows. Any needed operations can be performed in the native application before closing it. Lauda is happy with the presentation and understands how to add more links to external documents as she needs them.

SESSION 7.1

making *the grade*

1. What are the advantages of using nonlinear navigation?

2. What objects can have hyperlinks added to them?

3. How do you remove a hyperlink but leave the object?

4. Where can a hyperlink take you?

SESSION 7.2 USING POWERPOINT TO PUBLISH WEB PAGES

PowerPoint makes creating a Web publication as easy as building a speaker-led presentation. Web presentations can be designed specifically for Web publication, or an existing presentation can be converted to a Web format. Even though Web publishing is easy, there is some Web-specific knowledge necessary to fully control the published results.

Preparing for Web Publishing

Web formatted documents, called **Web pages**, rely mostly on **hypertext markup language (HTML)**, a scripting language that describes how to format the content of the page. **HTML tags** are enclosed in $<>$ throughout page content describing how the browser will display the content. For example $$Hello$$ would cause the browser to bold the text between the tags, resulting in **Hello**. Using PowerPoint, Web pages can be created without knowing HTML, because it is generated without user intervention. At least some HTML skill is needed to maintain and customize the generated pages. There are many good HTML tutorials available on the World Wide Web.

Publishing Web Pages

The motivations for publishing PowerPoint presentations as Web pages are as varied as the people and organizations using this feature. Published pages provide an easy way to share documents without face-to-face contact. Web pages can be viewed using any browser, making a presentation more portable. Pages can be published to either an intranet or the Internet. **Intranets** are networks serving an organization and are used to share documents within that organization. The **Internet** is a worldwide network of computers used to support the **World Wide Web** (WWW), a network of Web documents, and other services such as e-mail. Although World Wide Web sites can be secured to restrict access, they are generally intended to reach a larger audience than intranet publications.

Publishing a presentation involves creating the presentation, converting the presentation to a Web format, and then placing the files on a shared server. A server is a computer that provides services to a network. A shared server can be a **local server**, meaning that it provides services within an organization, or a **Web server** that provides computing services to access the World Wide Web. Publishing a presentation to a local server makes the content available locally, while publishing to a Web server makes the presentation available from the Internet. The steps to create the Web pages are the same, regardless of where the converted files are placed.

Navigation is a critical element of any Web presentation. To avoid mystery navigation, PowerPoint adds a **navigation bar** to all Web publications. PowerPoint's navigation bar provides linear movement through pages, while a hierarchical structure like that built for Organ Donor in the previous session is usually better suited to Web presentations.

Speaker's notes are visible in a Web publication and can be used to provide slide captions and explanatory notes. Depending on the browser being used, animations, movies, and sound files will play. Sound files can be used to narrate a Web presentation in a manner similar to that explored for a standalone kiosk.

Selecting a Web Browser

A **Web browser** is the software application used to view Web pages. The browser reads and interprets HTML and other scripting languages to determine how the page content should visually appear on the screen. The two most popular browsers are Microsoft Internet Explorer and Netscape Navigator. Many **Internet service providers (ISPs)** provide a custom browser highlighting their Web services. America On Line (AOL) and AT&T@Home are examples of ISPs with custom browsers.

The browser used by those viewing your published pages has an impact on how well the presentation works. PowerPoint is a Microsoft product, and the HTML code that it generates is optimized for Microsoft Internet Explorer 4.0 or above. This format provides the best fidelity, fastest performance, and smallest file size. During the publication process, a selection is available to save files for other browsers, but the result is larger files and slower performance. Additionally, not all of the browsers support all of the features published by PowerPoint. For example, older versions of Internet Explorer and all versions of Netscape Navigator will not display slide animations, transitions, sounds, or movies. If all of these features are needed, it is best to encourage your audience to use the current version of Internet Explorer.

Creating a Personal Web Page

There are several ways to create a Web site using PowerPoint. Choose the method that best suits your skills and goals. The AutoContent Wizard can be used to create any of the standard presentations supported as Web pages. When Web page is chosen as the output type, the Wizard will automatically select a color scheme appropriate for Web browsing. The AutoContent Wizard also has a template that can be used to create a Group home page. This template is designed to allow a group of people working on a project or projects to update Web pages to reflect project status.

Microsoft provides a Wizard that will publish your site on an organizational server or to a number of popular ISPs. The Wizard is initiated from the New Document task pane in any Office application. Since this Wizard is available from any Office application, it can publish content from any Office application to the Web. You must have an account with the ISP before Web pages can be stored to their server.

---

task reference   **Build an AutoContent Web Page**

- In the PowerPoint open the New Presentation task pane, select **From AutoContent wizard**

- Read the introductory screen and click **Next**

- Choose the type of presentation you would like to develop and click **Next**

- Select **Web presentation** and click **Next**

- Enter the Presentation title and Footer information and click **Next**

- Click **Finish**

FIGURE 7.12

New Presentation task pane

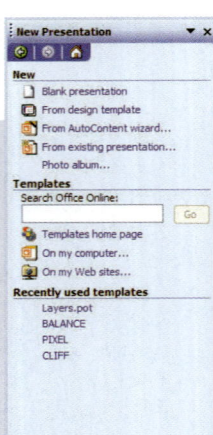

The simplest way to create a Web page is to use the Save As option of the File menu. If direct access to a file or network server is available, the files can be stored in a shared location using the Save As process. If direct access is not available, *file transfer protocol (FTP)* software can be used to place a copy of the Web files on the appropriate server.

Building your home page:

1. Launch PowerPoint, if necessary, and close any open presentations

2. On the **File** menu click **New** to open the New Presentation task pane (see Figure 7.12)

3. Click **From design template** in the New Presentation task pane

4. Click the **Textured** template

tip: *Hover the cursor over each template to see its name*

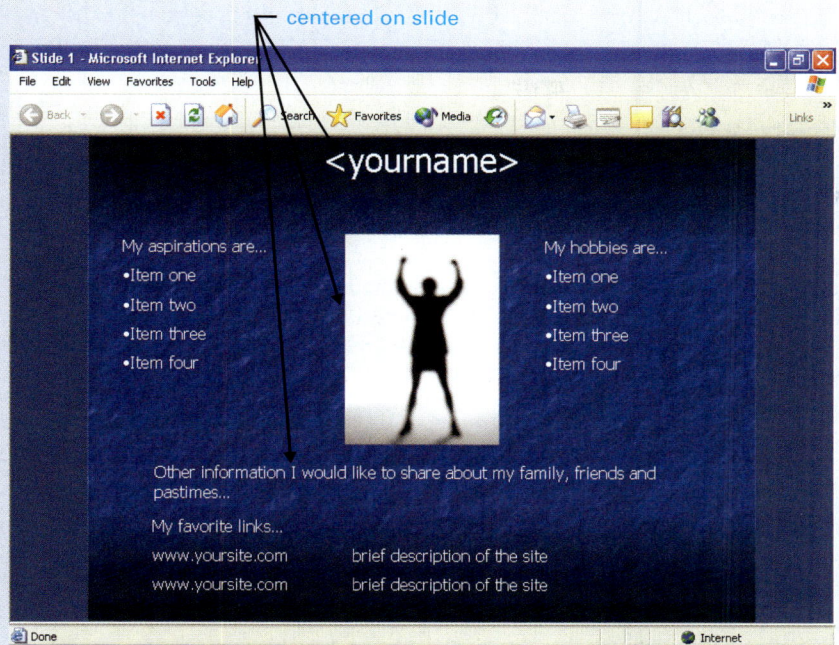

5. Click the drop-down arrow at the top of the task pane and click **Slide Layout.** Click the **Blank** layout

6. Refer to Figure 7.13 as you use the Drawing toolbar to do the following:

   a. Add a text box. Type your name in the text box, position it as shown, center the text in the text box, center the text box (left to right) on the slide, and size the characters to 36 point Tahoma

   b. Add another text box. **Type My aspirations are . . . ,** press **Enter,** click the **Bullets** ☰ button on the Formatting toolbar, and type at least four aspirations, pressing **Enter** after each

   c. Use the **Insert Picture** 🖼 button of the Drawing toolbar to insert a picture of yourself. If you don't have a digital image of yourself, the image shown is in the Clip Organizer (business women in the photographs media type)

   d. Copy and paste the bulleted list text box and then edit the text to read **My hobbies are . . .** Edit the bullets to reflect your hobbies and areas of interest

   e. Add a third text box and type any other information you would like to share about yourself

   f. Add a fourth text box and enter at least two Web URLs and descriptions for sites you like to visit

7. Use the **Align or Distribute** options of the **Draw** menu on the Drawing toolbar to align your objects

8. Click **File** and click **Web Page Preview**

POWERPOINT

tip: *The page will display in your default browser. If your browser is not Internet Explorer 4.0 or above, your results may be very different. Visit www.microsoft.com to download the latest Internet Explorer version*

9. Close the browser window

10. Save your presentation as **<yourname>PersonalHomePage**

In the previous steps you were able to preview your work in the browser as it was being developed, but the presentation is still in PowerPoint format. Before placing the files on a server, they must be converted to HTML format that can be understood by all browsers. PowerPoint converts slides to Web format when you click Save As Web Page on the File menu.

Saving your presentation as a Web page:

1. Click **File** and then click **Save as Web Page**

2. In the Save As dialog box

    a. Click the **Create New Folder** 🗀 button and name the folder **PowerPointWeb**

    b. Name the file **<yourname>PersonalHomePage**

    c. Verify that the **Save As type** is Web Page (*.htm,*.html)

    d. Click **Save**

3. Minimize PowerPoint and use Windows Explorer to move to the folder PowerPointWeb

4. Compare your results with Figure 7.14

FIGURE 7.14

Files created by *Save as Web Page* command

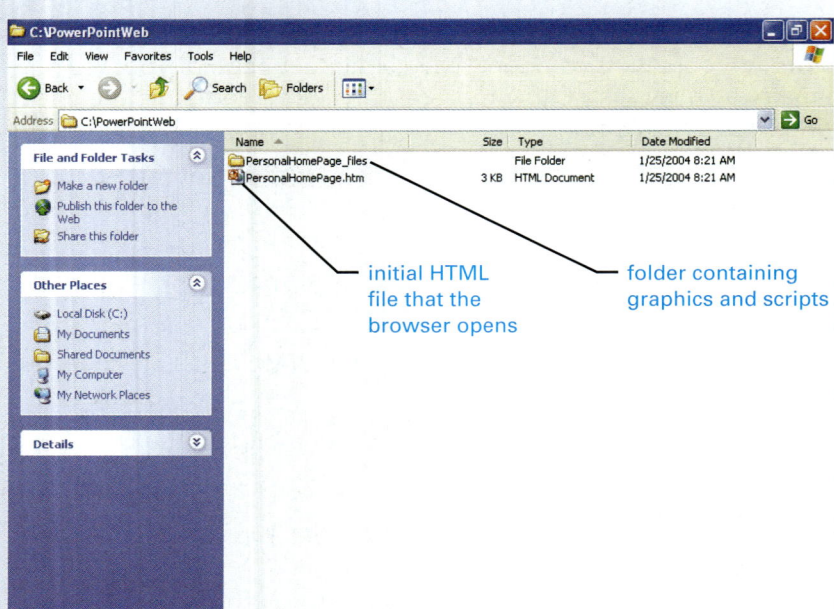

initial HTML file that the browser opens

folder containing graphics and scripts

5. Double-click on the file **<yourname>PersonalWebPage.htm** to open it in your browser

6. Close the browser window when done examining the Web page, and close Windows Explorer

7. Close the presentation leaving PowerPoint open

The Save As Web Page process creates files with .htm extensions that can be opened by Web browsers. The .htm extension indicates that the file is in HTML format. Other files, such as the graphics in the presentation and a style sheet, are stored in a folder. The folder carries the name of the presentation plus _files. For this presentation to work from a server, the .htm file and the associated folder with all of its files must be on the server.

---

anotherword   ... on Creating Web Pages Stored in a
                                    Single File from PowerPoint Slides

After clicking **File, Save As Web Page,** you can create a one-file Web page from any PowerPoint presentation by selecting **Single File Web Page (*.mht; *.mhtml)** from the *Save as type* list of the Save As dialog box. The resulting file has the file extension .mht and is more compact and easier to manage than the myriads of files produced by selecting **Web Page (*htm; *.html)** option of the *Save as type* list box. Currently, only Internet Explorer can properly render a one-file Web page saved with the file extension .mht

---

PowerPoint does not provide a way to directly edit any of the files created in the Save As Web Page process. The .htm file can be edited in any text editor, such as Notepad, or in a code generator such as Microsoft Front Page. PowerPoint can open the .htm file as a presentation so that it can be edited and the Save As Web Page process repeated to replace the original files.

Saving Existing Presentations as Web Pages

When saving a multi-slide presentation in HTML format, a Web site with a home page is created. A **Web site** is a group of organized Web pages that cover a topic area and are stored in a specific electronic location. Typically the **home page** is the opening page of the site and contains general information about the site and navigational links to access the various topics. Each slide becomes a page in the Web site.

The Organ Donor presentation built in Session 7.1 was designed to be placed on a shared server in HTML format. Since there are 10 slides in the presentation, there will be 10 Web pages created in the Save As Web Page operation. By default, PowerPoint creates the presentation with frames. On the Web, **frames** allow multiple Web pages to display simultaneously. Frames are similar to the panels in the PowerPoint development environment.

help yourself *Click the* Type a Question for help *combo box, type* **web page**, *and press* **Enter**. *Click the hyperlink* **About publishing a presentation to the Web** *and review all the options available for saving and publishing a PowerPoint presentation on the Web. Click the Help screen* **Close** *button when you are finished*

task reference	Preview a Presentation as a Web Site

- Open the presentation in PowerPoint
- Select **Web Page Preview** from the **File** menu

Previewing the Organ Donor Web site:

1. With PowerPoint running, click **File** and then click **Open**

2. Use the Open dialog box to navigate to **<yourname>OrganDonor.ppt** and open it

3. Click in the Notes pane of the first slide and type **Click underlined text**

tip: *Notes must be present for the Notes pane to display in your Web presentation*

4. Click **File** and click **Web Page Preview** (see Figure 7.15)

5. Click the links in the Navigation frame to display several presentation slides

6. Close the browser window

FIGURE 7.15

Web Page Preview

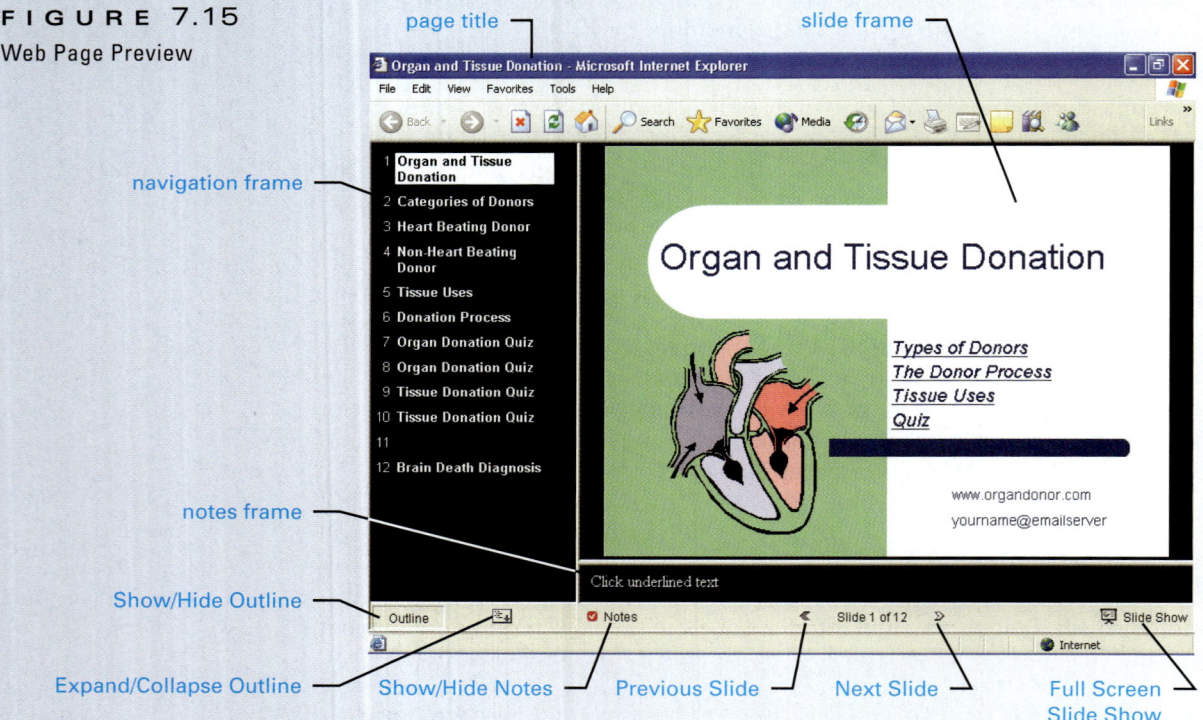

The Web Page Preview displays a Web site as it would appear created with the default settings. When there are multiple slides in the presentation, a navigation frame is created displaying the title of each slide. The notes frame will display when there are notes in the Notes panel of the presentation. The navigation bar across the bottom of the presentation allows the viewer to customize the display to suit his or her needs.

---

task reference   Save a Presentation in
                                              Web Format

- Open the presentation in PowerPoint
- From the **File** menu select **Save as Web Page**
- Click **Publish** to customize the Save As settings
- Click **Publish** when the settings are complete

Creating the Organ Donor Web site:

1. Click **File**, click **Save as Web Page** and navigate to the folder where you want to store your Web page(s) (see Figure 7.16)

2. Click the **Publish** button to open the *Publish as Web Page* dialog box

   a. Click the **Web Options** button

      i. On the General tab, unclick **Add slide navigation controls**

      ii. Click **Show slide animation while browsing**

      iii. Click the **Browsers** tab and click **Microsoft Internet Explorer 5.0 or later** as the target browser (see Figure 7.17)

      iv. Click **OK**

   b. Click the **Change** button to the right of *Page title*, type your first name in front of *Organ and Tissue Donation,* and click **OK**

   c. Check **Open published Web page in browser**

   d. Click the **Publish** button

3. Use the links to navigate through the presentation

4. Close the browser. Your PowerPoint presentation reappears

FIGURE 7.16

Save as Web Page dialog box

FIGURE 7.17

Web Options dialog box

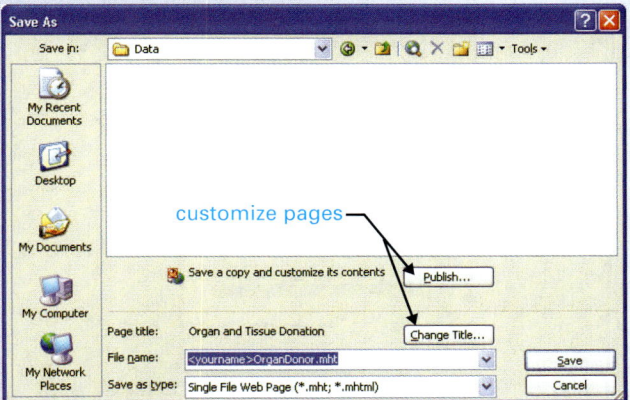

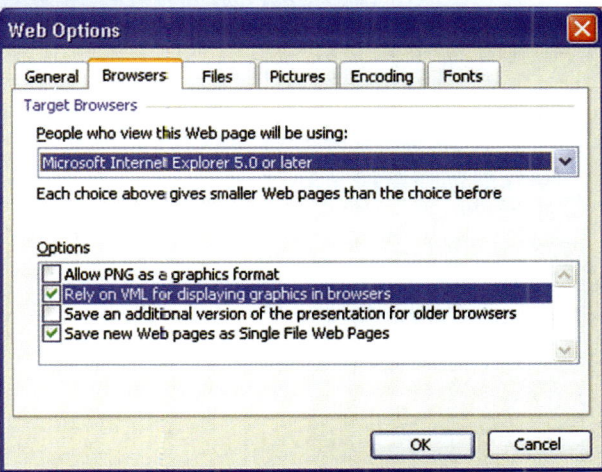

another way
. . . to Show the
Web Toolbar

Right-clicking any toolbar will open the list of available toolbars. Clicking Web in this list will show the Web toolbar. Repeating the process will hide the Web toolbar again

By customizing the publication settings, the Web presentation was optimized for a specific browser. Optimizing for newer browsers results in smaller file sizes, but the pages will not view appropriately on older browsers. Optimize for the oldest browser in use by your intended audience.

The customization process also allows adjustments to be made for your intended audience and presentation style. For instance, the default Save As Web Page options do not display slide animations or transitions. By clicking that option, the final product includes all animation that would play if the presentation were run in PowerPoint. The title of the presentation can also be customized. The title may seem insignificant, but this text displays in the Title bar of the browser when the page is open. If a site is stored in a browser history or favorites list, the title text is what displays, so it is important for the title to be descriptive.

Web Access from PowerPoint

Like all Microsoft Office applications, PowerPoint supports Internet and intranet browsing without opening another application. If you have access and permission on the local network to allow it, the Web toolbar has many of the same features as Internet Explorer.

---

task reference   **Showing the Web Toolbar**

- Click the **View** menu
- Pause over **Toolbars** and click **Web**

Using PowerPoint's Web toolbar:

1. On the **View** menu, pause over **Toolbars** and click **Web** (see Figure 7.18)

tip: *You must have Internet access to complete the remaining steps*

FIGURE 7.18
PowerPoint Web toolbar

Web toolbar

Favorites list

show or hide other toolbars

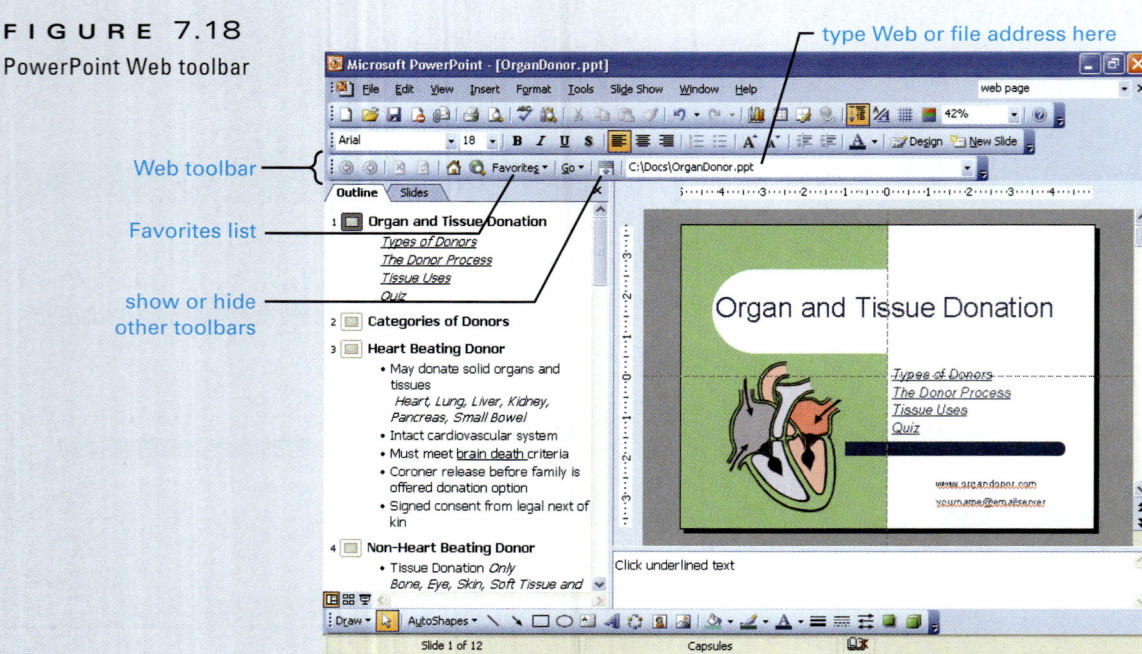

2. Click the **Show Only Web Toolbar** 🖼 button on the Web toolbar

3. Drop down the address bar list by clicking the down arrow on its right and then select an address to visit

tip: *The most recently viewed Web addresses should display*

4. Select the address currently in the address bar, type **www.microsoft.com** over the selection, and press **Enter** to visit the Microsoft Web site in your current browser. Close your browser

5. Drop down the **Favorites** Favorites ▾ list and select one of the sites to visit

tip: *If you have not added addresses to your Favorites list, nothing will display*

6. Click the **Go** Go ▾ button

7. Click the Start Page button. Then, close the browser

8. Click the **Favorites** button, then click **Add to Favorites**, select a Favorites category, and then click **Add** to add the open file to your Favorites list for quick future access

9. Use the **Show Only Web Toolbar** 🖼 button to display the Standard and Formatting toolbars

10. Click **View** and then click **Web** to remove the Web toolbar

Adding a presentation to the Favorites list is an easy way to find it again. The Favorites list is also a good place to store Web sites that need to be available for a presentation. It is important to have valid addresses to avoid broken links.

Getting Help on the Web

The Ask a Question box and the Office Assistant are the most common tools used to look up helpful information about a task. Both of these tools are search engines that use the Help files installed with PowerPoint. The latest tools for PowerPoint and other Office applications can be found on the Microsoft Web site. Additionally there are tips, techniques, free stuff, product news, answers to frequently asked questions (FAQ), and online support for licensed Microsoft products.

---

task *reference*   Accessing Microsoft Online Support

- Click the **Help** menu
- Click **Microsoft Office Online**

Accessing Microsoft Office on the Web:

1. Verify that PowerPoint is running

tip: *You must have Internet access to complete the remaining steps*

2. Click **Help** and then click **Microsoft Office Online**

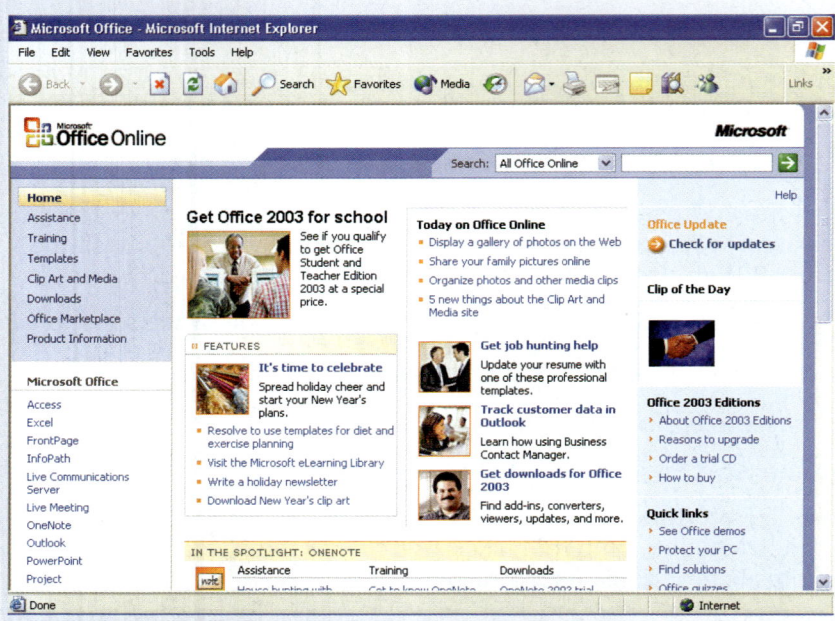

3. Explore the available resources

4. Close the browser window

5. Save your presentation and then close PowerPoint

Microsoft is known for frequent updates to its site, so the pages you visit may look different from the figure and from any previous visits. Even though the look and organization change, extensive online support for all licensed copies of Microsoft products will be available. The support Web site is the best place to get up-to-date information about products as well as tips and techniques.

S E S S I O N   7 . 2

making *the grade*

1. Why use PowerPoint to create Web pages?

2. How would you choose whether to publish your Web pages on the Internet or an intranet?

3. What browser is most effective for viewing PowerPoint Web publications?

4. How do you update Web pages published from PowerPoint?

SESSION 7.3 SUMMARY

Interactive presentations are typically hierarchical in structure. The opening page or home page outlines the viewing options as hyperlinks. Hyperlinks are clickable objects that allow the user to click and move to another slide in the current document, a slide in another presentation, a file, or any Web resource. Most commonly the hyperlinks on the opening page will move to a topic overview that presents linear navigation through the pages of topical material. The user should be able to return to the opening page from at least some of the other presentation pages.

Before a hyperlink can be set, the hyperlink object must be built. Hyperlink objects can be any clickable object like text, WordArt, charts, graphs, Action buttons, and images. Hyperlinks are created by selecting the link object and then using the Insert Hyperlink button on the Standard toolbar to set the link attributes. The Insert Hyperlink button can also be used to edit an erroneous hyperlink or delete a link that is no longer needed.

Hyperlinks to Web addresses are called uniform resource locators and can be added to a presentation by typing the address. Hyperlink colors are controlled by the color scheme of the project. Links placed on the Slide Master will be active on all slides using that master.

A presentation created in PowerPoint can be saved in HTML format and published on an intranet or the Internet. HTML uses tags contained in <> to control the display of a page in the Web browsers. Once a presentation is in HTML format, it can be moved to a server so that it can be shared. The presentation must be placed on a Web server to make it available through the World Wide Web.

MICROSOFT OFFICE SPECIALIST OBJECTIVES SUMMARY

- Add hyperlinks to slides—MOS PP035-4-1
- Save a presentation as a Web page (publish)—MOS PP0035-4-6
- Manage files and folders for presentations—MOS PP0035-4-6

making the grade *answers*

SESSION 7.1

1. Nonlinear navigation groups areas of the presentation by topic so the viewer can choose what to view. A presenter using a nonlinear presentation can choose how much to include on each topic as the presentation progresses.

2. Any clickable object such as text, graphics, charts, WordArt, and images can contain hyperlinks.

3. Select the object, click the Insert Hyperlink button, and then click the Remove Hyperlink button.

4. Hyperlinks can take you to another page in the current document, to another local document, or to Web resources.

SESSION 7.2

1. If you are familiar with PowerPoint, it is simple to create a presentation and save it in a Web format. Additionally, publishing to the Web is a good way to share the content of your presentation with a wider audience and Web pages are highly portable.

2. The intended audience determines where it is appropriate to publish. Intranets are typically for publications within an organization, while the Internet is for a broader audience.

3. Microsoft Internet Explorer 4.0 or higher provides the best browsing results.

4. PowerPoint does not have any facilities for directly editing the generated HTML. The only way to make changes from PowerPoint is to open the HTML file, edit it as a presentation, and then resave it to a Web format. You can also use a dedicated editor like Front Page.

task reference *summary*

Task	Page #	Preferred Method
Insert a hyperlink	PP 7.5	• Select the object that will initiate the hyperlink. The object can be text, WordArt, a graphic, or any other clickable object • Click the **Insert Hyperlink** 🖳 button on the Standard toolbar • Select the location of the link and then set the link options
Create and link an Action button	PP 7.12	• Select the slide to contain the Action button • If needed, use the View menu to activate the Drawing toolbar • Click the **AutoShapes** button of the Drawing toolbar, pause over Action buttons, and select the desired button • Click and drag the button on the slide surface • Click the Action button and follow the steps to set a hyperlink
Build an AutoContent Web page	PP 7.18	• In the PowerPoint open the New Presentation task pane, select **From AutoContent wizard** • Read the introductory screen and click **Next** • Choose the type of presentation you would like to develop and click **Next** • Select **Web presentation** and click **Next** • Enter the Presentation title and Footer information and click **Next** • Click **Finish**
Preview a presentation as a Web site	PP 7.22	• Open the presentation in PowerPoint • Select **Web Page Preview** from the **File** menu
Save a presentation in Web format	PP 7.23	• Open the presentation in PowerPoint • From the **File** menu select **Save as Web Page** • Click **Publish** to customize the Save As settings • Click Publish when the settings are complete
Showing the Web toolbar	PP 7.24	• Click the **View** menu • Pause over **Toolbars** and click **Web**
Accessing Microsoft online support	PP 7.25	• Click the **Help** menu • Click **Microsoft Office Online**

TRUE OR FALSE

1. Interactive presentations are typically not hierarchical in nature.

2. Hyperlinks are clickable objects that allow the user to only access files on the Internet.

3. Web addresses are also called uniform resource locators.

4. A presentation created in PowerPoint can be saved in HTML format without any other filter or application.

5. HTML uses tags contained in <% %> to control the display of a Web page.

FILL-IN

1. The most widely used scripting language to create Web pages is _____.

2. A hyperlink with a _____ is used to open to a specific location in the hyperlinked document.

3. Typing a _____ on a PowerPoint slide will automatically create a hyperlink.

4. _____ and _____ are used to add non-linear navigation to a presentation.

5. Hyperlinks placed on the _____ are available to all slides.

MULTIPLE CHOICE

1. A hyperlink can be any text or object on a slide including:
   a. clip art
   b. WordArt
   c. graph
   d. all of the above

2. A Web address is also referred to as a(an):
   a. HTTP
   b. URL
   c. HTML
   d. none of the above

3. _____ are ready-made buttons that can be placed on a slide to control slide progressions.
   a. Radio buttons
   b. Action buttons
   c. both a and b
   d. none of the above

4. The _____ is a network of Web documents.
   a. WWW
   b. Internet
   c. intranet
   d. all of the above

5. A(An) _____ is a group of organized Web pages that cover a topic area stored in a specific electronic location.
   a. Internet
   b. WWW
   c. Web site
   d. all of the above

review of concepts

REVIEW QUESTIONS

Each of the following topics should be addressed in one to three paragraphs.

1. Discuss the various native navigation options available in PowerPoint.

2. Discuss how custom navigation is added to a PowerPoint presentation.

3. How do you determine what custom navigation to add to a presentation?

4. What information must be provided for a functioning hyperlink?

5. How do you determine what HTML format to use when creating Web pages from a PowerPoint presentation?

CREATE THE QUESTION

For each of the following answers, create the question.

ANSWER	QUESTION
1. Any clickable object	_____
2. URL	_____
3. Esc	_____
4. Place the link on the Slide Master	_____
5. A link that includes all information needed to find a resource	_____

FACT OR FICTION

1. Nonlinear navigation is added to a presentation using hyperlinks and Action buttons. These features provide an intuitive way for users to move directly to materials of interest.

2. A hyperlink is a connection from one slide in a presentation to another slide in the current presentation, a slide in another presentation, a file, a Web page address, or an e-mail address. The hyperlink can be any text or object on the slide including a clip art, WordArt, graph, or image.

3. When presentations are moved to a new computer, it is common to have broken hyperlinks. A broken hyperlink is one that has an invalid destination causing an error to display when it is clicked. The cause might be as simple as a URL that was mistyped, or a hyperlink to a destination that was moved or deleted.

4. The motivations for publishing PowerPoint presentations as Web pages are as varied as the people and organizations using this feature. Published pages provide an easy way to share documents without face-to-face contact.

5. The AutoContent Wizard can be used to create any of the standard presentations supported as Web pages. When Web page is chosen as the output type, the Wizard will automatically select a color scheme appropriate for Web browsing.

1. Wildlife Management Associates

Wildlife Management Associates (WMA) contracts with the U.S. Fish and Wildlife Department to perform population counts and assess the health of wildlife. WMA has put together a presentation that illustrates their study areas and the results of their assessments. The best approach is an interactive presentation with the following menu items: Home, Assessments, About Us, Fish Program, and Contact Us (see Figure 7.20). WMA has provided you with a map of the presentation and a Word document to help you understand its layout and text. For now you will develop the Aquatic Division's assessment of Colorado Brook Trout population. Although the other divisions only have data pending, you will still create the pages. At a later date, the data can be added.

1. Start PowerPoint and open **pp07WildlifeMgmt.ppt**

2. Save the presentation as **<yourname>WildlifeMgmt.ppt**

3. Open the Slide Master

   a. In the lower left corner create a text box containing the word *Home* in 20 point Tahoma bold

   b. Use the Fill option in the Format Text Box dialog box to set a two-color (dark blue and white) vertical gradient fill for the text box

   c. Set the text box (not the text) as a hyperlink to slide 1

   d. Close the Slide Master view

4. Use the techniques outlined in step 3 to create Assessments, About Us, Fish Program, and Contact Us buttons on slide 1. Arrange the buttons as shown in Figure 7.21

   a. Hyperlink the *Assessments* text box to slide 2

   b. Hyperlink the *About Us* text box to slide 9

   c. Hyperlink the *Fish Program* text box to slide 7

   d. Hyperlink the *Contact Us* text box to slide 8

5. Move to slide 2

   a. Hyperlink the text *Aquatic Division* to slide 3

   b. Hyperlink *Avian Division* to slide 5

   c. Hyperlink *Mammalian Division* to slide 6

   d. Copy the relevant navigation buttons from slide 1

6. Move to slide 3, copy the navigation buttons from slide 1, and create a Next button linked to slide 4

7. Move to slide 4, copy the navigation buttons from slide 1, and add a Back button linked to slide 3

8. Add the navigation buttons to the remaining slides

9. Be sure to exclude the particular navigation button that pertains to each slide. For example, omit the *About US* button on the About Us slide

10. Test the presentation, make any needed adjustments, and save the presentation again

FIGURE 7.20

Wildlife Management site map

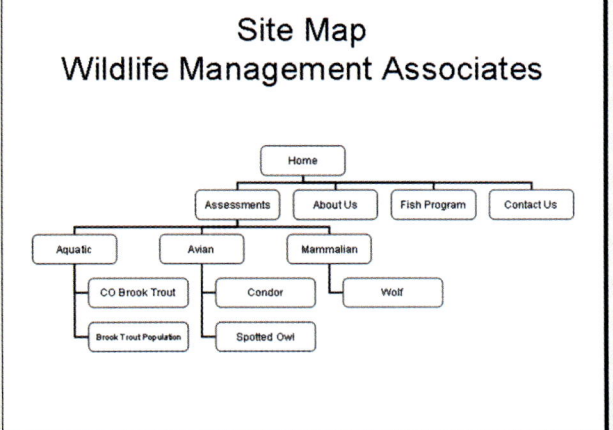

FIGURE 7.21

Wildlife Management navigation buttons

2. Building a Future (BUFF)

Operation Building a Future (BUFF) seeks active involvement in the education of students in secondary schools across the nation. BUFF members work with students to close the gap between theory in the classroom and practical application in public and private sectors. The BUFF organization has just developed an Engineer & Construction camp designed to provide high school students with an excellent opportunity to gain hands-on experience in engineering and construction skills in an outdoor environment in Denver, Colorado. This one-week program is supervised by professional engineers. The campers live, eat, and learn engineering skills at this world-class facility.

BUFF members mentor individual students and offer projects and competitions to make the experience of learning relevant to the practical aspects of engineering, technology, and related fields. BUFF member firms provide work–study opportunities and intern programs to emerging professionals, as well as partner with local school districts to acquaint junior and senior high school students with the rewards of careers in technical professions. You have been assigned by the BUFF outreach coordinator to edit a PowerPoint presentation that provides students with information about the Engineer and Construction camp.

1. Start PowerPoint and open **pp07BUFF.ppt**

2. Save the presentation as **<yourname>BUFF.ppt**

3. Open the Slide Master
   a. Create a text box containing the word **Home** in 18 point Arial bold. Center the text within the text box
   b. Use the Fill option in the *Format Text Box* dialog box to set the fill color to khaki for the text box and the line color to black
   c. Set a hyperlink to slide 1 for the text box (not the text)
   d. Close the Slide Master view

4. Move to slide 1. Use techniques outlined in step 3 to create Information, Selection, Application, and Schedule buttons. Do not bold the text. Arrange the buttons as shown in Figure 7.22
   a. Hyperlink the *Information* text box to slide 3
   b. Hyperlink the *Selection* text box to slide 4
   c. Hyperlink the *Application* text box to slide 5

d. Hyperlink the *Schedule* text box to slide 6

5. Copy and paste the buttons from slide 1 to the rest of the slides. Be sure to exclude the appropriate button on each slide. For example, omit the *Application* button on the Application slide, and so on

6. Move to slide 2
   a. Using the AutoShape feature, select the block arrows and choose a left arrow. Place the left arrow on the left-hand side of the Home button. Change the fill color to the khaki color for symmetry
   b. Using the AutoShape feature again, select the block arrows and choose the right arrow. Place the right arrow on the right-hand side of the Schedule button
   c. Hyperlink the left arrow to the previous slide
   d. Hyperlink the right arrow to the next slide
   e. Select both the left arrow and right arrow object and copy them to the Clipboard

7. Move to slide 3 and paste the arrows that you copied from slide 2

8. Repeat step 7 for slides 4, 5, 6, 7, and 8

9. On slide 8, remove the right arrow

10. Test the presentation, make any needed adjustments, and save the presentation again

FIGURE 7.22
BUFF opening slide

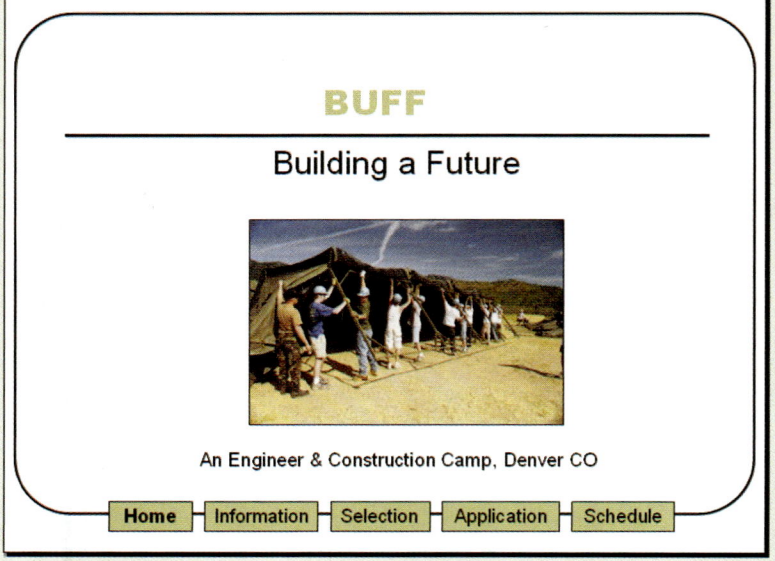

1. Safe Foods

Safe Foods is an informational Web site designed to educate the consumer about food preparation and handling. It provides links to other Web sites about eating foods safely. In addition, at the Safe Foods site you can document a possible food poisoning episode through a hyperlink to a Word document. The viewer can print the online form, fill in the information, and mail or fax it back to Safe Foods. You have been asked to prepare this Web site.

1. Start PowerPoint and open **pp07SafeFoods.ppt**

2. Save the presentation as **<yourname>SafeFoods.ppt**

3. Refer to Figure 7.23 for the overall site organization and navigation

4. On slide 1 create three navigation buttons using text boxes with 14-pt Verdona, yellow text on a brown background

   a. Hyperlink the *Safe Handling* button to slide 2

   b. Hyperlink the *Register Poisoning* button to slide 10

   c. Hyperlink the *Other Site References* button to slide 9

5. On slide 2

   a. Hyperlink the *Traveling* text to slide 3

   b. Hyperlink the *In the kitchen* text to slide 4

   c. Hyperlink the *Restaurants* text to slide 5

   d. Hyperlink the *Preparing Food* text to slide 6

6. Add a **Home** button to slides 2 through 10 using the Slide Master for non title slides 2–10. Place the button in the lower right corner of the Slide Master

7. Add the **Next** buttons to the first three slides in the Safe Handling Tips sequence (refer to Figure 7.23)

8. Use your favorite search engine to locate five Web sites to be included on slide 9. Add the URLs to the slide

9. Test the presentation, make any needed adjustments, and save the presentation

10. Save the presentation as a single-file (.mht) Web page

    a. Suppress PowerPoint navigational controls using the Web Options button from the Publish dialog box

    b. Set the title to **Safe Food Handling and Preparation**

    c. When the *Publish as Web Page* dialog box reappears, click the **Browse** button next to the *File name* text box, click the **Save as type** list box, click **Single File Web Page (*.mht; *.mhtml)**, navigate to the folder where you want to store your single-page Web page, and click **OK**. Click the **Publish** button in the *Publish as Web Page* dialog box

    d. Test the result using Microsoft Internet Explorer

11. Save your presentation again

FIGURE 7.23

Safe Foods Site Map

FIGURE 7.24

Safe Foods opening page with navigation buttons

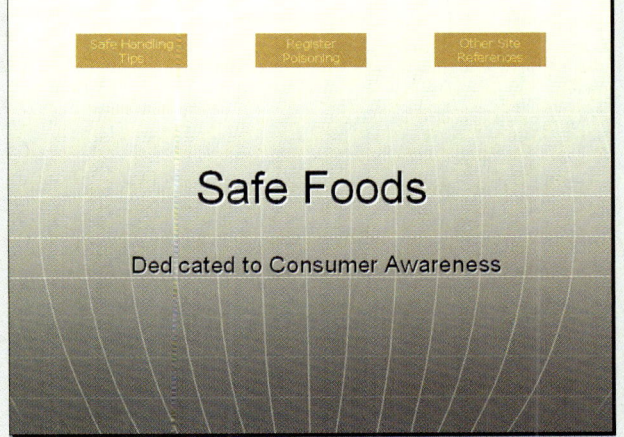

2. Foothills Golf Course

The Foothills Golf Course is a new, beautiful, and challenging nine-hole golf course located in the peaceful confines of Highlands Ranch, Colorado. With the Rocky Mountain foothills as a scenic backdrop and the western open range surrounding the golf course, you couldn't ask for a more picturesque and enjoyable setting.

The nine-hole course plays to a formidable par 60 (combined par for white and blue tees). Available practice facilities include a night-lighted driving range (with six target greens), a sand bunker, and a grass teeing area. There are also putting and chipping greens available at no charge. The course includes a full-service pro shop and restaurant facilities. The course is open to the public, with preferential rates and availability of tee times for Highlands Ranch residents. You have been asked to make some modifications to an existing PowerPoint presentation and then prepare a Web site.

1. Start PowerPoint and open **pp07FoothillsGolf.ppt**

2. Save the presentation as **<yourname>FoothillsGolf.ppt**

3. On slide 1 create eight navigation buttons from text boxes whose fill color matches the scheme color (sea green) and whose text is black. Place the buttons in four rows of two just below the horizontal line. Align the buttons

   a. Hyperlink the *General Information* button to slide 2

   b. Hyperlink the *Contact Information* button to slide 3

   c. Hyperlink the *General Green Fees* button to slide 4

   d. Hyperlink the *Policies and Procedures* button to slide 5

   e. Hyperlink the *Course Photos* button to slide 6

   f. Hyperlink the *Resident Permit* button to slide 7

   g. Hyperlink the *Tournaments* button to slide 8

   h. Hyperlink the *Directions to Course* button to slide 9 (see Figure 7.25)

4. On slide 2 at the bottom of the slide

   a. Add a *Previous* button using an arrow (from the Block Arrows collection of the AutoShapes button) with text; hyperlink that to the previous slide. Place it in the lower left of the slide

   b. Add a *Next* button using an arrow with text; hyperlink that to the next slide. Place it in the lower right of the slide

   c. Add a *Home* button using an AutoShape of your choice and text; hyperlink that to slide 1. Place it in the bottom, center of the slide

5. Group all the elements that you created in step 3, copy them to the Clipboard, and paste them on slides 3 through 9

   a. Remove the Next button and text from slide 9

6. Test the presentation, make any needed adjustments, and save the presentation again

7. Save the presentation as a Single-File Web page (.mht) named **<yourname>FoothillsGolf.mht**

   a. Suppress PowerPoint navigational controls using the Web Options button from the Publish dialog box

   b. Set the title to **Highlands Ranch Golf Course**

8. Test the result using Microsoft Internet Explorer

FIGURE 7.25

Foothills Golf Course opening slide

e-business

1. Chuska Photos

For years Harold Chuska has traveled around the world capturing photographs of nature, people, and places. His photographs have consistently won top prizes in photography contests. Now he has decided to set up an interactive kiosk that will provide a taste of his photography. Chuska wishes to start locally, and then expand later to the Web. With luck, he will be able to sell his photographs and finance additional trips around the world. You have been asked to prepare the kiosk presentation that will appear in malls in Chuska's home city.

1. Start PowerPoint and open **pp07Photos.ppt**

2. Save the presentation as **<yourname>Photos.ppt**

3. Create four Custom Action Buttons on the first slide. Select each button and label them Nature, People, Contact Me, and Places. Make the button text Comic Sans MS, 28 point, bold. Place the buttons at the tip of each arrow (see Figure 7.26)

   a. Hyperlink the *Nature* button to slide 4
   b. Hyperlink the *People* button to slide 3
   c. Hyperlink the *Contact Me* button to slide 2
   d. Hyperlink the *Places* button to slide 5

4. On slide 4 arrange three to five thumbnail (reduced-size) nature photographs that you have located (look in the ChuskaPhotos folder)

   a. Place full-size versions of each of these photographs on separate slides
   b. For each thumbnail photograph, create a new corresponding slide that displays the full-size photograph
   c. Hyperlink each thumbnail photograph on slide 4 to the corresponding slide containing the full-size photograph
   d. On each slide with a full-size photograph, place a *Back* button that returns to slide 4

5. On slide 3 arrange three to five thumbnail (reduced-size) photographs of people that you have located. Use the techniques from step 4 to create links from the thumbnail photographs to their full-size versions and back

6. On slide 5 arrange three to five thumbnail (reduced-size) places photographs that you have located. Use the techniques from step 4 to create links from the thumbnail photographs to their full-size versions and back

7. Create and add a *Home* button to every slide but slide 1. Hyperlink each Home button to slide 1

8. Test your presentation, make any needed adjustments, and save it again

9. Save the presentation as a Single File Web Page:

   a. Click the **Web Options** button in the Publish dialog box. Click the **General** tab and be sure to clear the **Add slide navigation controls** check box
   b. Set the Page title to **Chuska Photos**
   c. Click **Publish**
   d. Test the result using Microsoft Internet Explorer
   e. Save the Web page as **<yourname>Chuska.mht**

FIGURE 7.26
Chuska Photos opening slide

2. Wild Wild West Web Hosting

Wild Wild West Web Hosting, a national leader in Internet commerce and infrastructure, is launching a Web hosting initiative to help small- and medium-sized businesses create an Internet presence. Wild Wild West Web Hosting will provide the Internet infrastructure, services, and e-commerce expertise necessary for these businesses to grow and serve their customers on the Web.

Web hosting allows businesses to set up and run Web sites on servers housed in a separate, secure, high-end data center. Through Web hosting, companies outsource the servers that run their e-businesses but maintain access to their site's information and content. The general partners of Wild Wild West Web Hosting have asked you to create a presentation for an informational kiosk that will be on display in many of the major airport hubs through the United States.

1. Start PowerPoint and open **pp07WildWest.ppt**

2. Save the presentation as **<yourname>WildWest.ppt**

3. On slide 1, create four Custom Action buttons at the bottom of the slide using the default format settings. Select each button and type to add a label. Label the buttons About Us, Hosting Plans, Domain Names, and Search Engines. Make the button text Garamond, 20 point, bold. Add a Next button hyperlinked to the next slide

   a. Hyperlink the *About Us* button to slide 2

   b. Hyperlink the *Hosting Plans* button to slide 4

   c. Hyperlink the *Domain Names* button to slide 7

   d. Hyperlink the *Search Engines* button to slide 8

4. Move to slide 4

   a. Select the text *Starter Plan* and hyperlink to slide 5

   b. Select the text *150MB Plan* and hyperlink to slide 6

5. Move to slide 7. Select the text *www.networksolutions.com* and hyperlink it to the Internet address http://www.networksolutions.com

6. Create and add a Next, Previous, and Home button to every slide but slide 1, using the same formatting and positioning as in step 3. Hyperlink each of the buttons to the appropriate next, previous, or home slide. Remove the Next button from slide 8

7. Test your presentation, make any needed adjustments, and save as a Single File Web Page

   a. Click the Web Options dialog box in the Publish dialog box. On the General tab, be sure to de-select Add slide navigation controls

   b. Set the Page title to **Wild Wild West Web Hosting**

   c. Click Publish

   d. Test the result using Microsoft Internet Explorer

   e. Save the Web page as **<yourname>WildWest.mht**

FIGURE 7.27
Wild Wild West Web Hosting opening slide

1. Heritage Conversations

What if you had a tool to help you understand and learn about your grandparents? And in doing so you learned a lot about yourself. That's the premise for Heritage Conversations. This company publishes a book with questions, worksheets, and helpful suggestions to make the interviewing process with your grandparent successful. Heritage Conversations' Web site lets others know about its product. You have been asked to build this Web site using PowerPoint.

1. Start PowerPoint and open **pp07Heritage.ppt**

2. Save the presentation as **<yourname>Heritage.ppt**

3. Review the site map on slide 2 to understand the navigational structure you will build

4. Add slide 9 with a Blank layout. This slide will be used as a work space to create buttons and then delete them

   a. Click the **Custom** button from the Action buttons selection of the AutoShapes menu on the Drawing toolbar to create (create one, clone eight others) nine buttons. Make them 0.5″ high by 1.6″ wide. (Double-click and then click the **Size** tab)

   b. Click each button and type one of the following labels: **Home, Next, Back, Conversations, Publications, Readers Share, About Us, Contact Us,** and **Site Map**

   c. Place the Next button on the lower right-hand corner of the Conversations slide and hyperlink it to the next slide

   d. Place the Back button on the lower right-hand corner of the Sample Questions slide and hyperlink it to the previous slide

   e. Place the Site Map button on the lower right-hand corner of slide 1 and hyperlink it to the second slide

   f. Place the six remaining buttons down the left-hand side of both the Title Master and Slide Master. Use distribution and alignment options to adjust their position. Hyperlink each appropriately

   g. Delete slide 9

5. Visit each slide and adjust content as necessary for readability and alignment

6. On slide 3 adjust the e-mail Screen Tip to read **Email Heritage Conversations** and the Web site Screen Tip to read **Visit Heritage Conversations home page**

7. Use your favorite search engine to locate at least two Web sites appropriate for slide 5. Add the URLs to the slide, and add an appropriate ScreenTip for each link

8. Test the presentation, make any needed adjustments, and save the presentation

9. Save the presentation as a single-file Web page (.mht)

   a. Suppress PowerPoint navigational controls using the Web Options button from the Publish dialog box

   b. Set the title to **Heritage Grandparent Conversations**

   c. Test the result using Microsoft Internet Explorer

   d. Save the page as **<yourname>Heritage.mht**

FIGURE 7.28

Heritage Conversations opening page

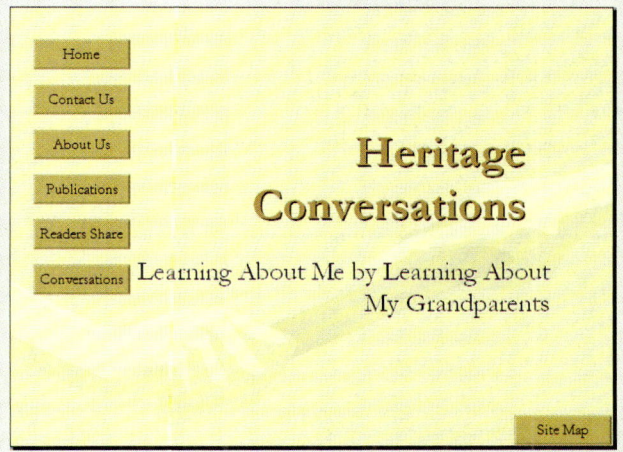

2. e-DEV

e-DEV is the leading provider of technical information and services that enable corporate application development teams to efficiently conquer development challenges and keep projects moving. They are committed to leading the market by offering customers timely, vital resources and superior services designed to enhance their efforts of applying new technologies and techniques.

e-DEV provides the international developer community with the most comprehensive information available on software development for corporate applications. Their network consists of sites that are leaders in their respective vertical markets, such as Windows and Web development, .NET, Java, XML, C/C++, Visual Basic, Database, and Wireless.

1. Start PowerPoint and open **pp07eDEV.ppt**. Immediately save it as **\<yourname\>eDEV.ppt**

2. Edit the Title Master and insert hyperlinks to the appropriate slides according to the button titles

3. On the Slide Master use the block arrows from the AutoShapes menu on the Drawing toolbar to create two buttons as follows:

    a. Create a right arrow in the lower right-hand corner of the slide and type **Next** for a label. Create a hyperlink that goes to the next slide

    b. Create a left arrow in the lower right-hand corner of the slide to the left of the right arrow you created above. Type **Back** for a label. Create a hyperlink that goes to the previous slide (see Figure 7.29)

    c. Copy the buttons that you created in step 2 and place them on the left-hand side of the slide, aligned vertically beginning with "Home" and ending with "Wireless"

4. Visit each slide and adjust content as necessary for readability and alignment. Remember to use the Draw menu (Align or Distribute) to align buttons or other objects

5. Test the presentation and its hyperlinks (see Figure 7.29), make any needed adjustments. Save the presentation again

6. Save the presentation as a single-file Web page (*mht)

    a. Suppress PowerPoint navigational controls using the Web Options button from the Publish dialog box

    b. Set the title to **e-DEV Solutions**

    c. Test the resulting Web page using Microsoft Internet Explorer. Be sure to test all the links

    d. Save the Web page as **\<yourname\>eDEV.mht**

FIGURE 7.29

e-DEV About Us page

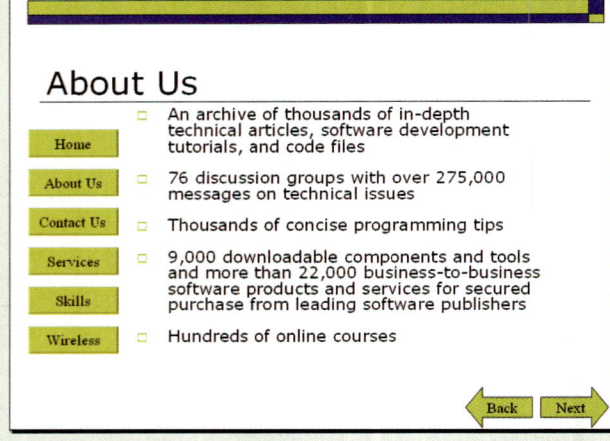

around the world

1. Sonic Strategies

Sonic Strategies manufactures and sells the Sonic 5 throughout the world. The Sonic 5 device identifies anything in the atmosphere of import: comets, meteors, catastrophic weather, or explosions are some examples. The device produces an infrasound wave of low frequency into the atmosphere. When it encounters compressed air, it returns a frequency wave. Each atmospheric event has its own characteristic wave shape. The wave data are recorded, entered into a database, and returned to Sonic Strategies' database headquarters for analysis. The resulting assessment is distributed to governmental agencies such as NASA, NCAR, and the Department of Defense. Monitoring of the Sonic 5 outside the United States occurs through Sonic Strategies' International Division. International teams are located on all seven continents. Sonic Strategies wants the international teams to preview the Sonic 9 that will replace the Sonic 5 next year. You have been asked to prepare a PowerPoint presentation for the teams.

1. Start PowerPoint and open **pp07SonicStrategies.ppt**

2. Save the presentation as **<yourname>SonicStrategies.ppt** in a folder named **SonicStrategies**

3. Use the **Oval** tool of the Drawing toolbar (in Basic Shapes of the AutoShapes collection) to create four buttons on the home page. Make the ovals 1.00″ high by 2.00″ wide (see Figure 7.30)

   a. Apply **Shadow Style 4** from the Shadow Style menu of the Drawing toolbar to each oval

   b. Type one of the following labels on each button. Bold the text and use Enter to cause each word to be on a new line

   - U.S. Division
   - Int'l Division
   - Specs
   - Training

4. Hyperlink each of the buttons as follows

   a. *U.S. Division* to slide 2

   b. *Int'l Division* to slide 3

   c. *Specs* to slide 4

   d. *Training* to slide 5

5. Create and place a Home button on all slides except the title slide. Hyperlink this button to return to the first slide. (*Hint:* Copy one of the ovals on the first slide, paste it onto slide 2, adjust its position on the slide, and change its hyperlink to go to "First Slide." Then, copy it to the clipboard and then paste it repeatedly onto slides 3 through 5. Pasting this way will place the button in the same exact position on each slide)

6. Test your presentation, make any needed adjustments, and save it again

7. Save the presentation for Web delivery as a single-file Web page

   a. Suppress PowerPoint navigational controls using the Web Options button from the Publish dialog box

   b. Set the title to **Announcing the Sonic 9**

   c. Test the result using Microsoft Internet Explorer

8. Print the PowerPoint presentation as 6 slides-per-page handouts. (Place your name in the heading)

F I G U R E 7.30
Sonic Strategies opening page

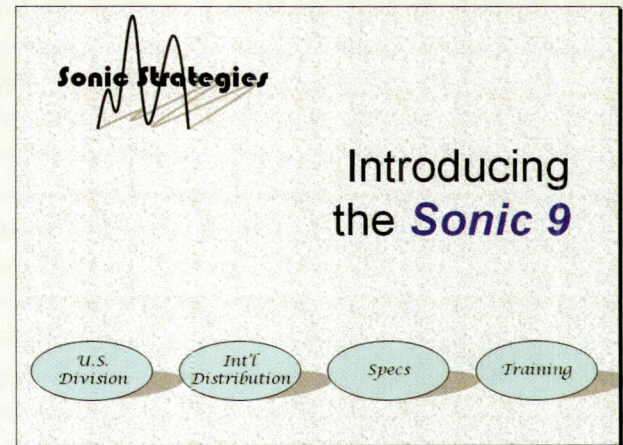

2. AirFares

AirFares.com is a premier comparison airfare shopping destination that helps people make more informed travel purchase decisions. AirFares uses Virtual Agent™ technology to create "intelligent agents" trained by the company's team of shopping experts to collect information from virtually every online travel resource. The result is the best pricing information across the Web.

1. Start PowerPoint, open **pp07AirFares.ppt**

2. On the Title Master slide, use the **Oval** tool of AutoShapes on the Drawing toolbar to create five circular buttons. Try to create some symmetry with the circles used for the design background. (You can create circles by holding the Shift key and drawing the oval)

   a. Apply **Shadow Style 17** from the Shadow Style menu of the Drawing toolbar to each. Make the image color match the design. Align the buttons of the circles and place them near the bottom of the slide

   b. Type one of the following labels on each button. Make sure that you make the ovals (see Figure 7.31) the correct colors

      • Priceline (blue circle)

      • Expedia (tan circle)

      • Hotwire (blue circle)

      • TravelNow (tan circle)

      • OneTravel (blue circle)

3. Insert hyperlinks to the appropriate slides according to the button titles

4. Create and place a Home button on all slides except the title slide (*Hint:* create it on the Slide Master). Hyperlink this button to return to the first slide. Place the blue button in the lower right corner

5. Move to slide 2 and turn the text *Priceline.com* in the first bullet into a Web link pointing to www.priceline.com

6. Repeat step 5 for slides 3 through 6, creating links for the text as follows:

   • Expedia.com   www.expedia.com

   • Hotwire.com   www.hotwire.com

   • TravelNow.com   www.travelnow.com

   • OneTravel.com   www.onetravel.com

7. Test your presentation, make any needed adjustments, and save as **<yourname>AirFares.ppt**

8. Save the presentation as a one-file Web page (*.mht)

   a. Suppress PowerPoint navigational controls using the Web Options button from the Publish dialog box

   b. Set the title to **Online Airfares**

   c. Test the result using Microsoft Internet Explorer

9. Print the first Web page, and then print the PowerPoint presentation (with your name in the header) as a six slides per page handout

FIGURE 7.31

AirFares.com opening slide

running project

Montgomery-Wellish Foods, Inc.: Understanding Critical Time Lines

Well-designed and implemented training materials are critical to the success of MWF employees. Time lines are a particularly difficult concept for trainees. Daniel Wellish has developed the skeleton for a PowerPoint slide show to present time lines and quiz trainees in the following areas: Order Confirmation, Warehouse Stocking and Transport, and Foreign Shipments. You have been asked to complete this PowerPoint presentation.

1. Start PowerPoint and open **pp07MWFTraining.ppt**

2. Save the presentation as **<yourname>MWFTraining.ppt**

3. Use the Rectangle tool to create seven buttons to navigate this presentation
   a. Type the following headings in each of seven buttons
      - Home
      - Order
      - Order Quiz
      - Foreign
      - Foreign Quiz
      - Warehouse
      - Warehouse Quiz
   b. Arrange the buttons as shown in Figure 7.32
   c. Hyperlink as follows
      - Home to slide 1
      - Order to slide 2
      - Order Quiz to slide 3
      - Foreign to slide 7
      - Foreign Quiz to slide 8
      - Warehouse to slide 11
      - Warehouse Quiz to slide 12
   d. Group the buttons and use Copy and Paste to place them in the Slide Master. Verify that they display correctly on all of the slides

4. Create **Try Again** and **Next Question** buttons to be used in the quiz portion of the presentation

5. On slide 3 hyperlink as follows:
   a. Hyperlink the 2 hours text to slide 4
   b. Hyperlink the 4 hours text to slide 5
   c. Hyperlink both the 8 hours and 12 hours text to slide 6

6. Add Try Again buttons to bottom right-hand side of slides 4 and 6 that return the trainee to slide 3 for another try

7. Add a Next Question button to the bottom of slide 12 that hyperlinks to slide 13

8. The rest of the hyperlinks have already been constructed. Test your presentation, make any needed adjustments, and save it

9. Save the presentation as a Single-File Web Page (*.mht)
   a. Suppress PowerPoint navigational controls using the Web Options button from the Publish dialog box
   b. Set the title to **Time Lines Quiz**
   c. Test the result using Microsoft Internet Explorer

10. Print the PowerPoint presentation, and print the first page of the Web version

F I G U R E 7.32

Training Quiz opening page

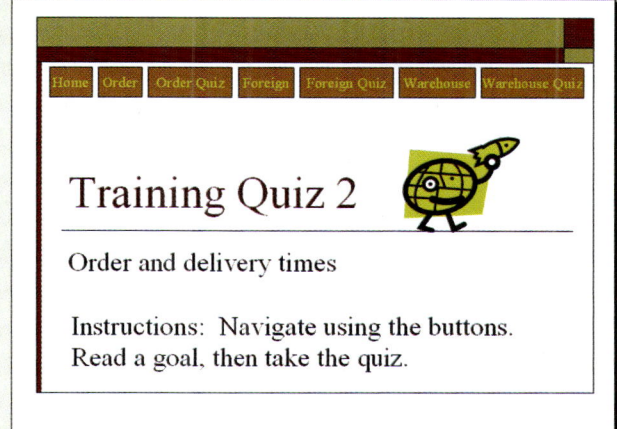

1. Action Buttons

Discuss how well-designed and implemented Action buttons can really enhance a presentation. Discuss the importance of creating hyperlinks using Action buttons so the presentation viewer can move backward and forward through the slides.

2. Creating a Web Page

You can use the Web to give others access to your presentation by publishing it to a Web server or another computer that is accessible to those you want to view the presentation with a Web browser. Discuss the advantages and disadvantages of using PowerPoint as your main tool for creating a Web page.

PowerPoint Power Features

did you know?

the *first true calculator, the abacus, originated in China during the sixth century B.C.*

the *last thing to happen is the ultimate. The next-to-last is the penultimate, and the second-to-last is the antepenultimate.*

the *plastic things on the end of shoelaces are called aglets.*

the *"O" when used as a prefix in Irish surnames means "descendant of."*

every *human spent about half an hour as a single cell.*

the *blood of mammals is red, the blood of insects is yellow, and the blood of lobsters is blue.*

of *the Atlantic and Pacific oceans, which is saltier?*

Chapter Objectives

- Set up presentations for remote delivery—MOS PP03S-4-5
- Deliver presentations—MOS PP03S-4-4
- Work with embedded fonts
- Use Package for CD
- Use workgroup collaboration—MOS PP03S-3

Collaborating and Sharing the PhonePerformance Presentation

Parks Industries is a large privately held company that produces consumer plastics. The publicly marketed products include everything from plastic dinnerware to skateboard wheels. One of the company's divisions also produces custom molded plastic parts used in manufacturing.

The various manufacturing facilities used to produce different types of plastic products are scattered throughout the Midwest. In the past, each site has had a manager who coordinated all local operations including computing and telephone services. As the company has grown and competition on the plastics arena has become intense, the need to share resources and reduce overhead has become critical to the success of Parks.

Walter Pauls is the son of the founder and current CEO. Each of the remote production facilities is managed by a division president who is also a family member. As one of the initiatives to consolidate efforts and reduce costs, Parks executive officers decided to standardize computing services and implement a central phone system that would meet all of their needs while reducing overhead.

FIGURE 8.1

PowerPoint Web communication

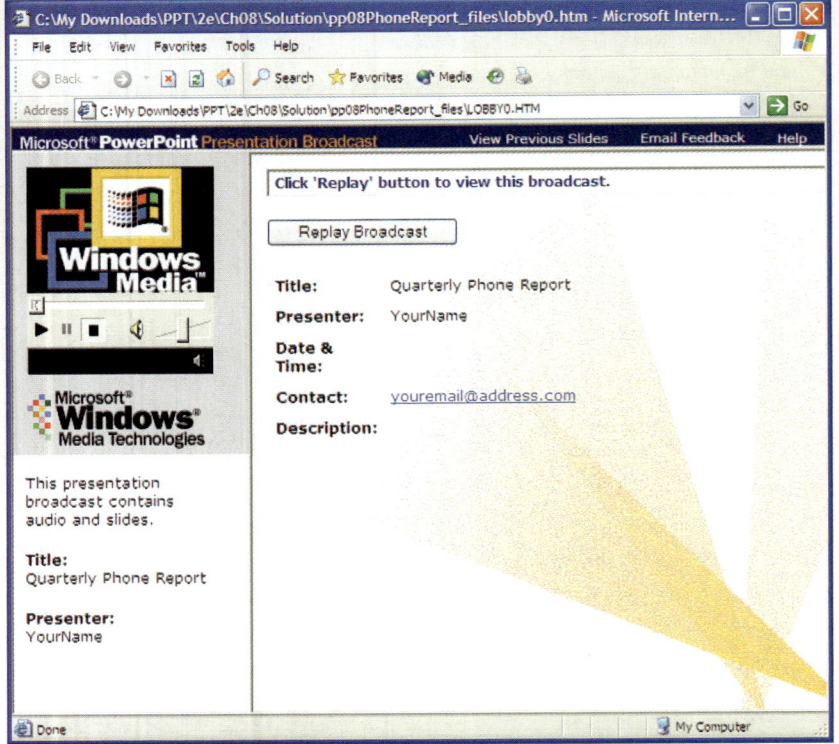

Computer Services elected to use Microsoft products across the board. Each site has a Microsoft NT network with all of the features needed to support the workgroup capabilities of Microsoft Office products. The various sites are also connected so that Microsoft Outlook can be used to coordinate planning, set appointments, share client contact files, and send e-mail.

Catherine Witt has been charged with coordinating the phone efforts among the various locations and reporting back to the executive officers in their monthly meeting. She has created a PowerPoint presentation to use in reporting and has asked you to help implement all of the necessary features. She will need PowerPoint collaboration features to retrieve comments from the phone system managers at the remote sites and incorporate them into the presentation for the executives. To accomplish this reporting task, it is essential to understand how PowerPoint can be used to share documents, collaborate effectively, take a presentation on the road, and add custom functionality.

SESSION 8.1 POWERPOINT POWER USER FEATURES

Many presentations are developed on one computer and presented on another. PowerPoint's viewer will allow slide shows to display on a computer that does not have PowerPoint, while the Package for CD Wizard prepares the presentation for travel.

Taking Your Show on the Road

There are many things to consider when moving a PowerPoint presentation from the development computer to another environment. For a successful presentation, it is critical that you move all files required to run the slide show to the new computer and prepare a backup plan. Catherine has developed the presentation on her desktop computer and will need to run it on a laptop for the presentation to the Parks executives.

Backup Planning

It is easy to overlook backup plans when preparing to present, but plans are essential to a successful show. In most instances everything will run smoothly, but spending a little time planning for difficulties can ensure a smooth show even when things go wrong.

Any component that is critical for the show should be considered when backup planning. It is always a good idea to have a second copy of your presentation files on a separate media. A second computer capable of running the slide show and extra projector bulbs are a must. You can place copies of the files on the backup computer if the original presentation fails. Having a spare projector bulb, and knowing how to replace the bulb, allows the completion of repairs that would otherwise have to wait for a technician. For critical projected presentations, consider having additional projector units available. Sometimes scheduling a backup speaker is also a good idea. The importance of the presentation determines how much effort should be spent ensuring success.

Whenever possible you should arrive at the presentation site early enough to test all of the equipment, preview the presentation colors, and ensure proper visibility for all attendees. In most instances, improperly functioning equipment will be discovered and can be repaired before the presentation should start.

Introducing the PowerPoint Viewer

When preparing to take a presentation on the road, you must decide whether or not to use the Microsoft *PowerPoint Viewer.* The viewer is a software program that will run PowerPoint presentations on computers that do not have PowerPoint installed. If the viewer is installed on your computer, it can be added to the presentation in the packaging process.

The viewer is stored in the file Ppview.exe, is distributed at no cost, and will operate files created in either PowerPoint for Windows or PowerPoint for the Macintosh. As a backup, the viewer can also be downloaded at no cost from the Microsoft Office Web site.

Using the Package for CD Wizard

When taking a presentation on the road, you will find that the most effective way to ensure that it will run properly on another computer is to use the Package for CD. The Package for CD packages all of the required files into one file that can be placed on a CD. In the packaging process, there are options to include any linked files and embed TrueType fonts. Embedding the fonts ensures that the fonts used by your presentation are available when running on a different computer.

---

task *reference*   **Package a Presentation**

- Open the presentation to be packaged
- If you are saving the presentation to a storage media, insert it
- Click the **File** menu and then **Package for CD**
- Make appropriate selections on each screen
    - Clicking **Add Files** will allow you to package multiple presentations
    - Use the **Options** button to include the Microsoft PowerPoint viewer in the package.

Packaging pp08PhoneReport:

1. Start PowerPoint and open **pp08PhoneReport.ppt**

2. Click the **File** menu and then click **Package for CD** to start the Package for CD Wizard

FIGURE 8.2

Package for CD opening page

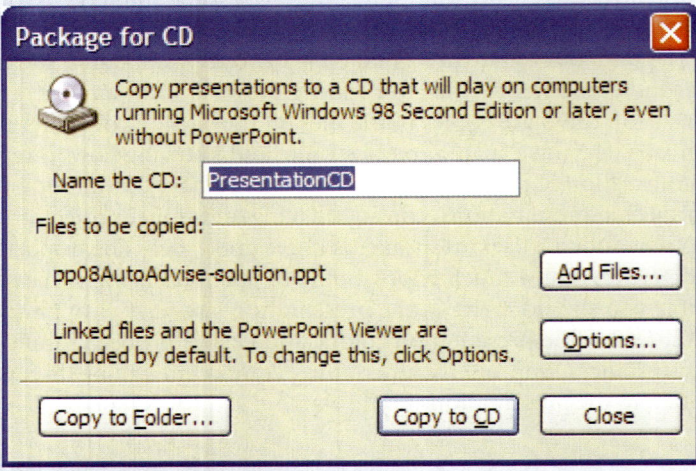

3. Click **Options**

4. Click **PowerPoint Viewer** to place a checkmark in it, if necessary

5. Click **Linked Files** and **Embed TrueType fonts** to place checkmarks in them (see Figure 8.3) and then click **OK**

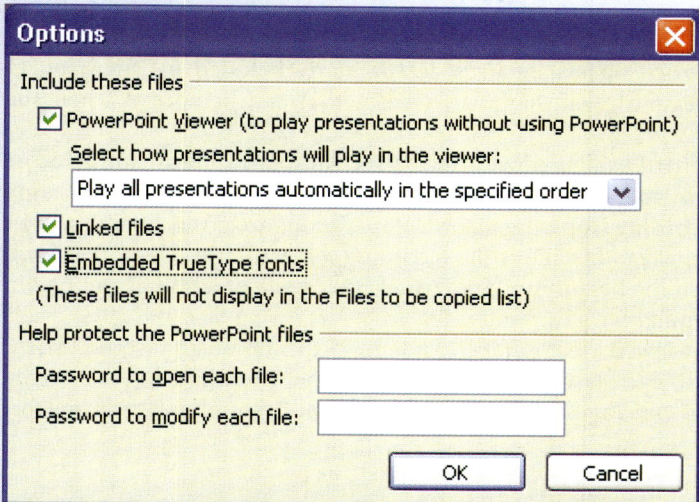

F I G U R E 8.3

Including the Microsoft PowerPoint Viewer

6. Click **Copy to Folder**, click the **Browse** button to navigate to the folder where you want to store your presentation, and type a folder name in the *Folder name* text box. Click **Continue** if you receive a warning message

7. Click **OK**

8. Click **Close** in the Package for CD dialog box

9. Close PowerPoint

Reviewing pp08PhoneReport:

1. Verify that PowerPoint is closed

2. Use Windows Explorer to locate the packaged presentation folder in which you saved your presentation in previous steps

3. Double-click **pptview.exe** (if necessary, click **Accept** if the PowerPoint Viewer license agreement appears)

4. Click **pp08PhoneReport.ppt** in the Microsoft Office PowerPoint Viewer dialog box, and click **Open**

5. Use standard PowerPoint navigation to move through the presentation

tip: *The viewer automatically closes when the slide show is ended*

6. If the dialog box reappears after you close the presentation, click the **Cancel** button

Right-clicking on a PowerPoint file in Windows Explorer will display both Show and Open options in the pop-up menu. Selecting Show will run the presentation in the viewer while Open will open the file in PowerPoint.

Automating Tasks with Macros

A *macro* can be created in any Microsoft Office product to store common tasks. Macros are recorded commands that are stored in a Microsoft Visual Basic module attached to the presentation. Macros should be created for frequently repeated operations to save time and reduce errors. Special security features are included in Microsoft Office System 2003 to safeguard against macro viruses that can be spread when sharing macros.

Macros are recorded using a process that is similar to creating an audio recording. Once recording starts, all keyboard and mouse operations performed on the computer are stored. When recording stops, the recorded operations are given a name so they can be replayed. If you make a mistake while recording a macro, it is usually easiest to re-record the steps from the beginning. The Visual Basic code of a macro can be directly edited, if you are familiar with the language.

Catherine has reviewed the PhonePerformance presentation and would like the letter grades assigned to each task to stand out more. She would like to see a larger text size and yellow text color. You will build a macro to simplify applying the same formats multiple times.

---

task reference   Record and Play a Macro

- Click **Tools**, point to **Macro**, then click **Security**, and select appropriate Security Level settings and add Trusted Sources

- Click **Tools**, point to **Macro**, then click **Record New Macro**

  - Select the storage location for the macro, enter the macro name in the Macro name box, and click **OK** to begin recording

  - Perform the actions to be recorded

- Click **Stop Recording** on the Stop Recording toolbar

Recording a macro to format text:

1. Start PowerPoint, open **pp08PhoneReport.ppt**

2. Move to slide 4 and select the **F** rating of the Appointment notification system bullet

3. Click **Tools**, point to **Macro**, then click **Security**, read about the security setting, click the **Medium** setting option button, and click **OK**

4. Click **Tools**, point to **Macro**, then click **Record New Macro**

   a. Name the macro **GradesFormat**

   b. In the Description box, replace all text with **Recorded by <yourname>**, substituting your first and last names for "<yourname>"

   c. Click **OK**

5. Click the **Font Size** drop-down arrow on the Formatting toolbar and click **28**, click the **More Colors** option on the Font Color drop-down to set the text color to **yellow**, and click **OK**

6. Click the **Stop Recording** 🔲 button in the Stop Recording toolbar

PowerPoint recorded this macro so all the keystrokes and commands you invoked to apply the formatting characteristics are captured. Then, you can simply replay the macro to repeat the steps to another section of text in the PowerPoint slide whenever needed. Unfortunately, the macro, which is a series of VBA (Visual Basic for Applications) lines of code, contains one code line that instructs the macro is to go to a particular place in the PowerPoint slide—the character F in the first bullet point—and apply the formatting. Because you want to apply the formatting to any text in the presentation, you must generalize the macro by eliminating one code line. One way to eliminate the lines is to edit the macro and type an apostrophe on the left end of the code line. Doing so turns it into a comment and eliminates its effect whenever you run the macro.

Editing a macro:

1. With the fourth slide of the presentation **pp08PhoneReport.ppt** still active, click **Tools**, point to **Macro**, and click **Macros**. The Macro dialog box reappears

2. Ensure that macro name *GradesFormat* is selected and then click **Edit**. The Microsoft Visual Basic window opens, revealing VBA code in the right panel. Observe that the first code line below the comment Recorded by (in green to indicate a comment) begins with "ActiveWindow.Selection.ShapeRange..."

3. Click anywhere on the line and to the left of the text *ActiveWindow.Selection.ShapeRange*, type an apostrophe ('), and press the **down arrow** key to move the insertion point to the next code line. Observe that the line above turns green to indicate it is now a comment—a line ignored whenever the macro runs

4. Press **Alt+Q** to close the VBA window and return to PowerPoint

You have modified and saved the GradesFormat macro. Now, you can run it anytime you want to apply the same formats you applied earlier to the Appointment Notification System grade in the first bullet point of slide 4.

Running a macro to format text:

1. Select the **D** score in the Call Management line (the second bullet on slide 4), click **Tools**, point to **Macro**, and click **Macros**

2. In the Macro dialog box, verify that **GradesFormat** is selected (see Figure 8.4). Click **Run** to run the macro. The PowerPoint macro formats the character just like it did when you recorded it

FIGURE 8.4

The Macro dialog box

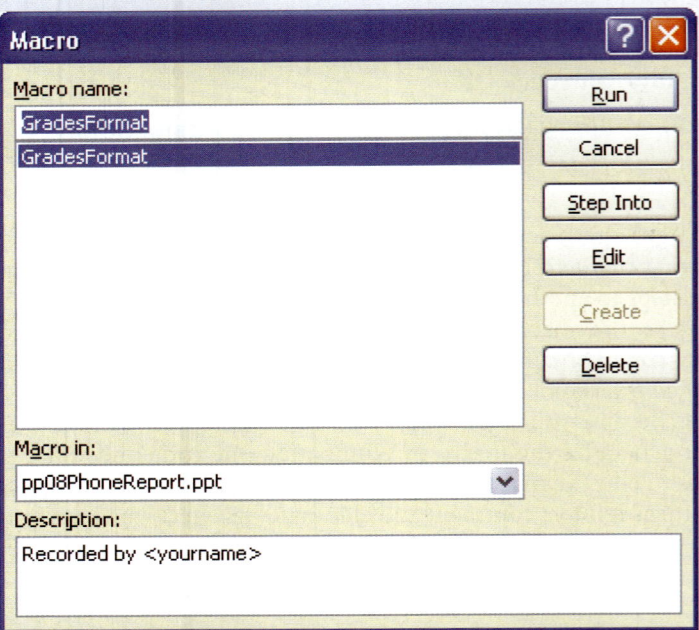

3. Select **B** in the Disaster Recovery (3rd) bullet point, press **Alt+F8** (a shortcut to the Macros dialog box), verify that **GradesFormat** is selected (see Figure 8.4), and click **Run**

4. Click anywhere to deselect the grade

5. Save your presentation. PowerPoint automatically saves the macro along with the presentation

You can record macros for any combination of mouse and keyboard operations that you frequently perform and then store with a particular presentation or share across presentations. Macro names must begin with a letter and cannot contain spaces. Macros can be edited as well as run from the Macro dialog box. Macros are often contained in PowerPoint files from other people or add-in software used to expand Office functionality.

A *macro virus* is a computer virus stored in a macro, an add-in, or template. Such viruses are spread by sharing files containing macros. Although virus protection software can isolate and reverse the damage of most macro viruses when their virus profiles are regularly updated, there is no guarantee. Microsoft Office System 2003 provides *macro security levels* and *digital signatures* to further reduce the risk of macro virus infection. Both are controlled from the Security option of the Macro menu demonstrated in the previous steps.

When Office 2003 is installed, the default macro security level is High. With this setting only macros that have been digitally signed and that appear on the trusted source list can be run. Unsigned macros are disabled, and the file is opened without a warning message. The security level can be adjusted to medium or low. The medium setting will display the message shown in Figure 8.5 when questionable macros are encountered. The low setting enables all macros without verifying sources.

help yourself Click the Type a Question for help *combo box, type **macros**, and press* **Enter**. *Click the hyperlink* **Create a macro** *and then click the hyperlink* **Record a macro** *to display help on recording a macro. Click the Help screen* **Close** *button when you are finished, and close the task pane*

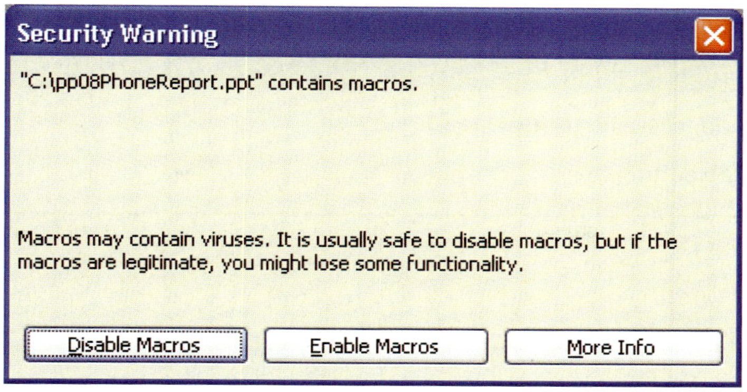

FIGURE 8.5
Enabling macros

Security Warning

"C:\pp08PhoneReport.ppt" contains macros.

Macros may contain viruses. It is usually safe to disable macros, but if the macros are legitimate, you might lose some functionality.

| Disable Macros | Enable Macros | More Info |

Digital signatures are used to verify the source of a macro and that it has not been tampered with. When a file or an add-in containing a digitally signed macro is opened, the digital signature appears on the computer monitor as a certificate. The certificate names the macro's source, plus additional information about the identity and integrity of that source. A digital signature does not necessarily guarantee the safety of a macro, so users must still decide whether to trust a macro that has been digitally signed. For example, don't trust unknown sources, but macros signed by someone known or by a well-established company are probably safe. When unsure about a file or add-in that contains digitally signed macros, carefully examine the certificate before enabling macros or, to be even safer, disable the macros. If there are individuals and organizations that can always be trusted, they can be added to the list of trusted sources when a file is opened or add-in loaded.

You learned about running macros from the Tools menu in the previous steps, but doing so does not save enough keystrokes to make creating macros for simple operations effective. Faster access to macros is provided by assigning the macro to a toolbar button, a keyboard shortcut, or an object in a presentation.

Modifying Menus and Toolbars

Like all Office applications, PowerPoint can be completely customized to suit the work habits of each user. Using the Customize option of the Tools menu, the content and placement of each toolbar can be adjusted, or new custom toolbars developed. Since the Standard and Formatting toolbars are frequently used, most users choose not to customize them to avoid confusion.

Standard Menus and Toolbars

All Microsoft Office applications provide menus and toolbars as the primary method for users to control the application. Most users view menus and toolbars as different tools, but both are actually toolbars. A toolbar can contain buttons, menus, or a combination of the two.

Microsoft Office System 2003 menus and toolbars automatically customize themselves based on how they are used. When an application is first used, only the most basic commands appear on the menus. Full menus appear after a short delay or by clicking the downward-pointing arrows at the bottom of the menu. Once a menu is expanded, all menus remain expanded until a command is selected. The selected command is added to the short version of the menu. Infrequently used commands are removed from the short menu.

When you first use an Office application, multiple toolbars share the same row without room to display all of the buttons. Since there is not enough space to display all of the buttons, only the most recently used buttons will display. Complete toolbars are available by clicking the right-pointing chevrons on the right end of the toolbar. The settings that control how Microsoft Office customizes menus and toolbars can be adjusted from the Customize option of the Tools menu.

<table>
<tr><td>**task reference**</td><td>**Personalize Menu and Toolbar Settings**</td></tr>
</table>

- On the **Tools** menu, click **Customize**
- Adjust Options tab settings

Personalizing menu and toolbar settings:

1. Verify that PowerPoint is running. There is no need to have a particular presentation open for this operation

2. Click **Tools** and then click **Customize**

3. If necessary, select the **Options** tab on the Customize dialog box

4. Click **Show Standard and Formatting toolbars on two rows**, if necessary, to place a checkmark there

5. Click the **Always show full menus** check box, if necessary, to place a checkmark in that check box (see Figure 8.6)

FIGURE 8.6

The Customize dialog box

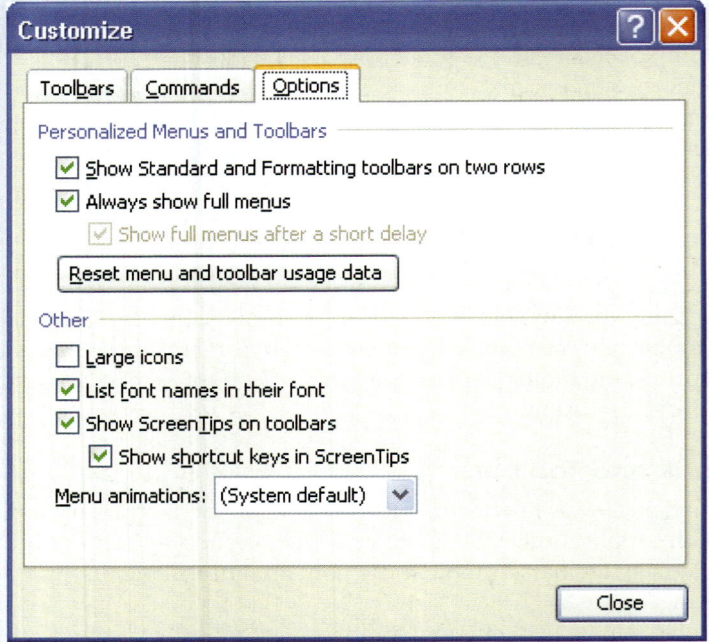

6. Click the **Large icons** check box

tip: *You should be able to see the icons increase in size behind the dialog box*

7. Uncheck **Large icons** to clear the checkmark

8. Click **Close**

The Customize dialog box settings impact the behavior of menus and toolbars throughout all Microsoft Office System applications. The *Reset menu and toolbar usage data* button restores the menus and toolbars to their installed settings by deleting the user history. A new user history will be created as you use the applications. The *Show Standard and Formatting toolbars on two rows* check box takes up more screen real estate, but ensures that all buttons you use show. The *Always show full menus* option checked in the steps stops Office from customizing menus based on use. When this is clicked, all menu items always appear when you click a menu.

Custom Toolbars

You can customize menus and toolbars by adding and removing buttons and menus or even creating completely new toolbars. The menu bar and any toolbar are updated following the same procedures. Options added to menus or toolbars can be attached to either existing PowerPoint commands or macros that you create.

---

task reference   Customize an Existing Toolbar

- Click the **Toolbar Options** downward-pointing arrow at the right end of the toolbar
- Point to **Add or Remove Buttons**, click **Customize**, and click the **Commands** tab
- In the **Categories** box select the type of command to be added. For example, Macros
- From the **Commands** box, click and drag the command to a toolbar

---

Adding the GradesFormat macro to the Formatting toolbar:

1. Verify that PowerPoint is running with **pp08PhoneReport.ppt** open
2. On the Formatting toolbar, click the **Toolbar Options** arrow (downward-pointing arrow at the right end of the toolbar)
3. Point to **Add or Remove Buttons**, and then click **Customize**
4. Click the **Commands** tab, if necessary, to activate it
5. In the Categories box click **Macros**
6. Click and drag **GradesFormat** from the Commands box to the Formatting toolbar (see Figure 8.7)
7. Click the **Close** button on the Customize dialog box

Some security-conscious organizations often restrict the ability of their members to customize toolbars. If you were unable to complete these steps, it may be because customization has been disabled. The GradesFormat button acts like the toolbar's intrinsic buttons; select text and click the button to activate the GradesFormat macro.

FIGURE 8.7

The GradesFormat macro
on the Formatting toolbar

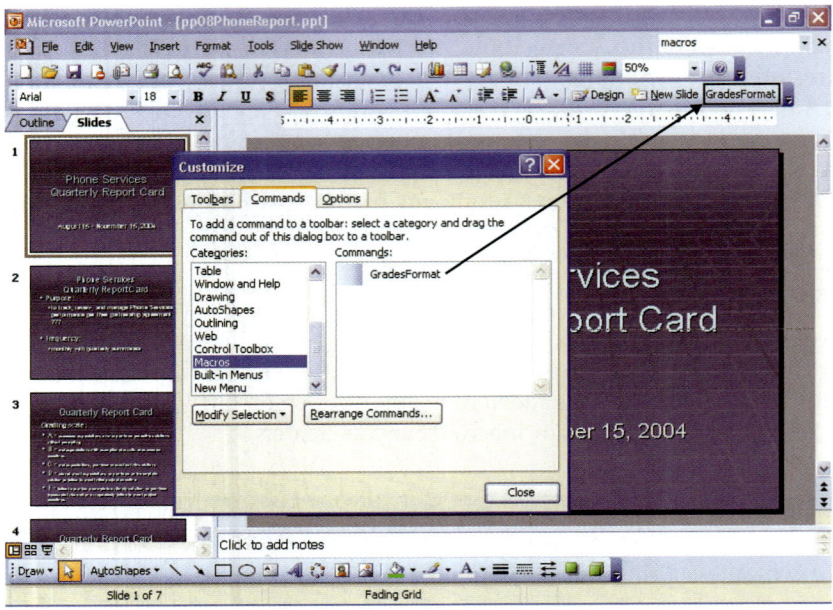

Removing the GradesFormat button from the Formatting toolbar:

1. On the Formatting toolbar, click the **Toolbar Options** downward-pointing arrow at the right of the toolbar

2. Point to **Add or Remove Buttons**, and then click **Customize**

3. Click the **Toolbars** tab

4. Select the **Formatting** toolbar (click the name, not the check box)

5. Click the **Reset** button

6. Click **OK** when asked to reset the Format toolbar settings

7. Click **Close**

As mentioned before, it is best to create custom toolbars to hold your favorite commands and macros. Creating a custom toolbar avoids the confusion of customizing the Standard or Formatting toolbars, while allowing commonly used tasks to be readily available.

Creating the Custom Formats toolbar:

1. Click **Tools**, click **Customize**

2. Click the **Toolbars** tab

3. Click the **New** button

4. Name the new toolbar **Custom Formats** and click **OK**

5. Reposition the Customize dialog box, if necessary, so the new toolbar is visible. Adjust the new toolbar's position so that commands can be dragged from the dialog box to the toolbar

tip: *The Custom Formats toolbar will not contain any buttons and is usually floating near the center of the screen*

6. Click the **Commands** tab of the Customize dialog box

7. In the Categories box click **Macros**

8. Click and drag **GradesFormat** from the Commands box to the Custom Formats toolbar

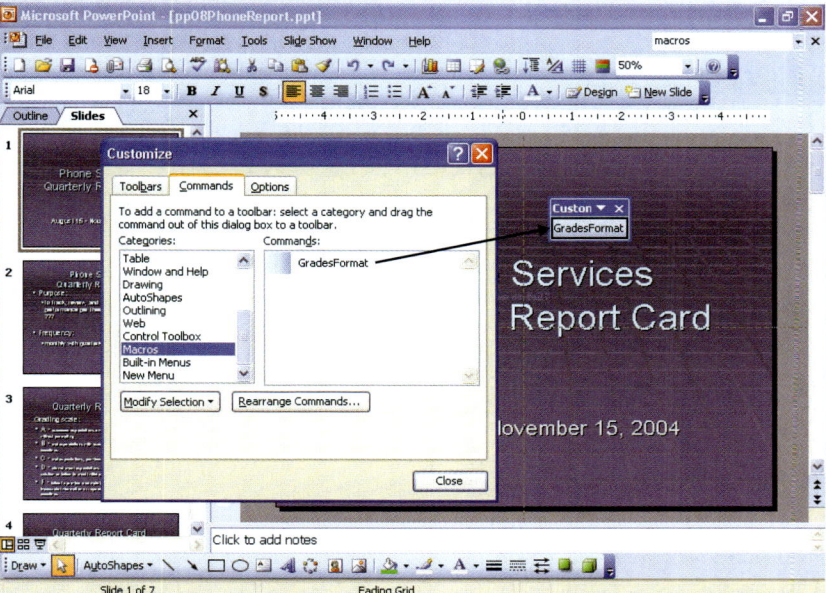

FIGURE 8.8

Dragging GradesFormat to the Custom Formats toolbar

9. Click the **Close** button on the Customize dialog box

10. Move to slide 4, select the **F** grade for PBX Upgrades, and click the **GradesFormat** button of the Custom Formats toolbar

    Repeat step 10 for the remaining grades on slides 4, 5, 6, and 7. Do not use this format for the *Overall* scores on each slide

11. Save the presentation

Adding macros to toolbar buttons is the most effective way to save keystrokes and maintain consistency. Any number of buttons and menus can be added to a custom toolbar. Like built-in toolbars, custom toolbars can be moved and anchored to any window edge. When the toolbar is no longer functional, the Toolbars tab of the Customize dialog box contains a Delete button.

Revising PowerPoint Settings

Many of the ways to customize PowerPoint have been addressed as each related topic was covered. The most common place to adjust settings is the Options selection of the Tools menu. Properties of individual PowerPoint files can be adjusted from the Properties option of the File menu.

Changing PowerPoint Defaults

The Options selection of the Tools menu is a multi-tabbed dialog box with settings to control the behavior of most critical PowerPoint operations. This dialog box contains options to control save, print, view, security, edit, spelling, and style. It is not possible in a text of this nature to cover every customization situation, so this review is intended to point you in the right direction to find the necessary options.

Exploring the Options dialog box:

1. Click **Tools** and then click **Options**
2. Click the **Save** tab and examine the available options (see Figure 8.9)

FIGURE 8.9

Exploring the Options dialog box

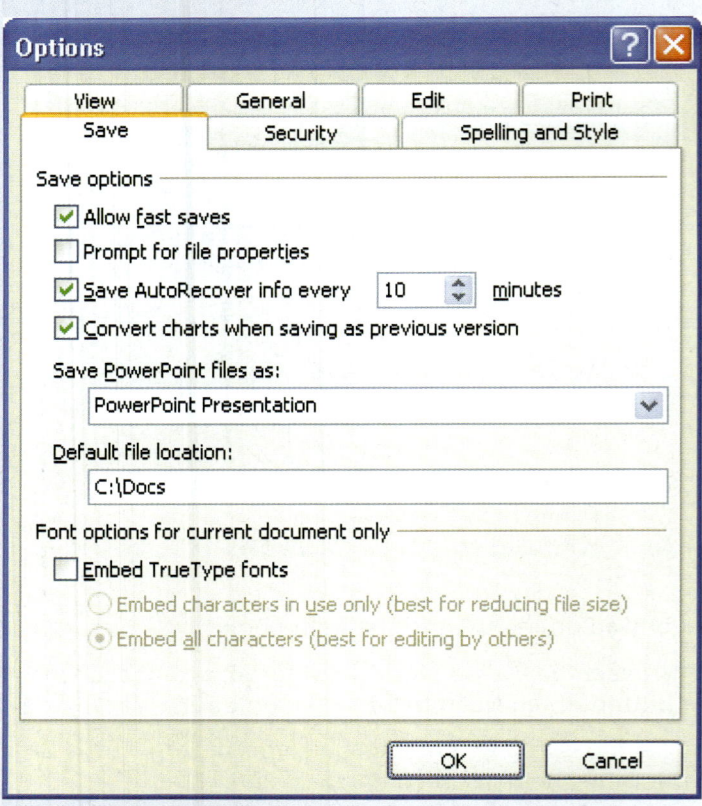

3. Click the **Security** tab and examine the available options
4. Click the **Spelling and Style** tab and examine the available options
5. Click the **View** tab and examine the available options
6. Click the **General** tab and examine the available options
7. Click the **Edit** tab and examine the available options
8. Click the **Print** tab and examine the available options
9. Click **OK**

All Microsoft Office System applications use the Customize option of the Tools menu to control toolbars and the Options choice to control other critical operations.

Customizing File Properties

Each Office file is saved with properties including the author, file type, and file size. Pausing the cursor over a filename in Windows Explorer will display the author and file size properties. Other properties are maintained and can be customized.

Exploring the File Properties dialog box:

1. Click **File** and then click **Properties**, and then click the **General** tab

2. Review contents of the General tab

3. Click the **Statistics** tab and review the contents

4. Click the **Contents** tab and review its contents

5. Click the **Summary** tab

   a. Update the title to reflect the current month and the title **Phone Report**

   b. Click the **subject** text box, select all of its contents, and type **Unsatisfactory phone support services**

   c. Click the **Author** text box and type your full name

   d. Type your instructor's name in the Manager text box

6. Click **OK**

7. Save your presentation

Most users don't override the default settings for author and title. The other settings on the Summary tab can be very useful for published or shared presentations. The Custom tab contains settings for adding the names of reviewers, checking out files, and adding custom comment fields.

Enhancing PowerPoint with Add-Ins

Add-ins are additional software programs that augment the capabilities of an existing application like PowerPoint. Many add-ins are available from the Microsoft Office Web site, while others can be obtained from third-party vendors. Visual Basic for Applications can also be used to write add-ins. All PowerPoint add-ins have the file extension .ppa.

Loading Add-Ins

Add-ins can be as simple as expanded templates and Help files, or they can include complex programming like the kiosk creator or interactive Web add-in. Visit www.microsoft.com, go to the PowerPoint home page, and look through the PowerPoint downloads for add-ins. Currently the site has more than 50 add-ins available at no charge. The exact installation process varies from add-in to add-in, but the general process is reflected in the following steps.

Loading an add-in:

1. Visit www.microsoft.com, locate a PowerPoint add-in, and download it. Locate the Microsoft Producer for Microsoft Office PowerPoint 2003, for example

2. Place the add-in file on a disk available to your system

3. Verify that PowerPoint is open. No particular file is needed for this operation

4. Click **Tools** and then click **Add-Ins** (see Figure 8.10)

FIGURE 8.10

Add-Ins dialog box

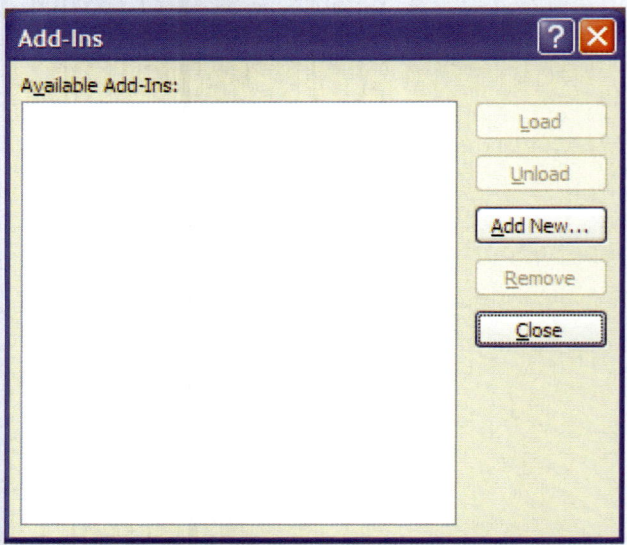

5. If the add-in to be loaded is in the Available Add-Ins list, select it, and click the **Load** button. Otherwise use the **Add New** button to locate the add-in file

6. Click **OK**

The features of the add-in are available when the load operation is completed. How the features are accessed varies from add-in to add-in. Additional templates and Help files simply display with the built-in versions. Others may be accessed from custom menus and toolbars. Read the available documentation for details on a specific add-in.

Unloading Add-Ins

In general, add-ins should be loaded, used, and then unloaded unless the features are needed on a continual basis. Unloading an add-in does not remove the file from the computer, but stops it from loading with PowerPoint. Unloading saves memory and improves application performance.

Unloading an add-in:

1. Verify that PowerPoint is open. No particular file is needed for this operation

2. Click **Tools**, click **Add-Ins**, and click the add-in

3. Click **Unload**

tip: *Clicking Remove will cause the add-in not to show in the list*

4. Click **OK**

5. Click **Save** on the Standard toolbar, and then close PowerPoint

Since the unload process does not remove the add-in from your computer, it can be reloaded whenever it is needed. Add-ins that will not be used again should be removed, and then the install file deleted from the disk.

---

making *the grade*

1. Discuss the importance of creating presentation backups.

2. Why use the PowerPoint Viewer?

3. What is the advantage of packaging a presentation before it is delivered?

4. Explain the advantage of using macros. Of attaching macros to toolbar buttons.

5. What is the difference between settings in the Customize dialog box and the Options dialog box?

SESSION 8.2 SHARING PRESENTATIONS

When creating a presentation needs to be a team effort or a presentation must play simultaneously in diverse locations, the workgroup and integration features of PowerPoint provide the necessary functionality. In the previous chapter we began to look at using Web publishing to share documents. Besides publishing in Web format, presentations can also be sent via e-mail and broadcast during an online meeting. When using a computer attached to a network or the Internet, a presentation can be run on any computer on that network.

Understanding Online Collaboration Tools

A presentation being created by multiple people must support gathering team member input and tracking comments. Software that supports such collaboration is called *workgroup software*. There are several ways that e-mail can be used to collaborate.

Sending a Presentation for Review via E-Mail

The simplest ways to share any document is to give it to reviewers on a disk or send it as an e-mail attachment. Almost any e-mail software will support attaching files, but the exact methodology will vary from package to package. Simply sending a PowerPoint file on disk as an attachment has the disadvantage of requiring one of the team members to coordinate the review process, collect suggestions, and apply updates to the original presentation.

Before you send a presentation to others on a disk or as a simple e-mail attachment, it is important to take care of any linked files. Linked files include any large sound files that the presentation plays and non-Internet files that the presentation needs to run effectively. If linked files are not changed to embedded files, they must be transported with the presentation.

Parks Industries' PhoneReport does not contain any linked files, so no special processing to deal with links is needed. The presentation does need input from each of the phone system managers at the remote sites before it can be finalized. To simulate this process, you will create two review files that could be distributed to reviewers, edit the files yourself, and then merge the updates with the original file.

---

task reference   Prepare a Presentation for Review

- Open the presentation to be reviewed
- For each reviewer:
  - Click **Save As** on the **File** menu
  - Change the name in the **File name** box to indicate whose review copy it is
  - Change the **Save as type** to **Presentation for Review**
  - Click **Save**
- Distribute the files to reviewers on disk or as e-mail attachments

---

Reviewing the phone report presentation:

1. Open PowerPoint and then open **pp08PhoneReport.ppt**. Click the **Enable Macros** button when the Security Warning dialog box appears

2. Click **File** and then click **Save as**

3. Type **Reviewer1PhoneReport** in the File name text box, click the **Save as type** list box, click **Presentation for Review (*.ppt)**, and click the **Save** button

tip: *Notice that the filename in the Title bar does not change as it would with a typical Save as operation*

4. Click **File**, click **Save as**, type **Reviewer2PhoneReport** in the File name text box, click the **Save as type** list box, click **Presentation for Review (*.ppt)**, and click the **Save** button

5. Open **Reviewer1PhoneReport.ppt**

   a. Click **No** when the dialog box to merge changes appears

   b. Click **Enable Macros** when the Security Warning dialog box appears

   c. Type your name in the line above the date on the first slide

   d. Move to slide 2 and change **???** to **with Parks Industries**

   e. Close the presentation and save your changes

6. Open **Reviewer2PhoneReport.ppt**

   a. Click **No** when the dialog box to merge changes appears

   b. Click **Enable Macros** when the Security Warning dialog box appears

   c. Type **Walter Pauls** in the line above the date on the first slide

   d. Move to slide 2 and change **???** to **with Parks Industries**

   e. Close the presentation and save your changes

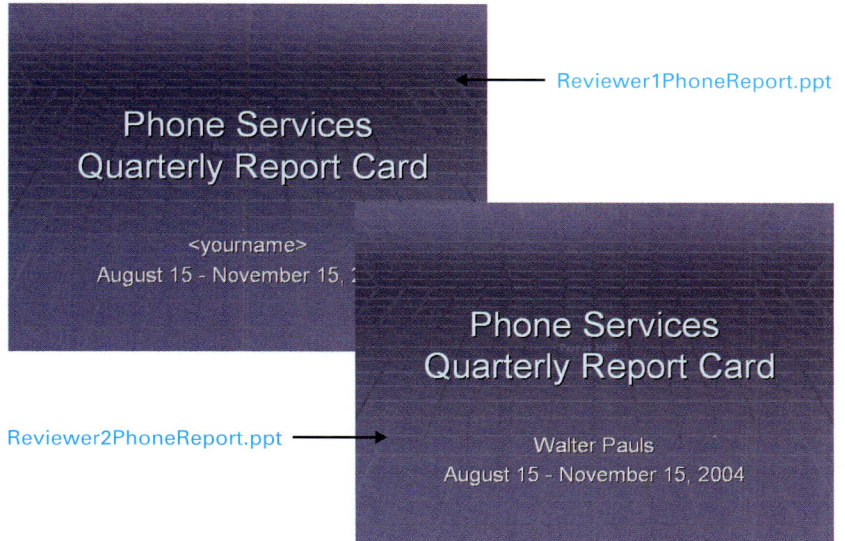

F I G U R E 8.11
Reviewer changes

Once all review copies have been created, they can be distributed to the intended reviewers as an attachment in any e-mail program or on disk. As was demonstrated in the steps, each reviewer can open their copy of the file, make changes, and then return the file to the coordinator. The coordinator is responsible for distributing the review files, ensuring that the reviewed files are returned, and accepting/rejecting reviewers' suggestions.

Comparing and merging reviews:

1. Verify that **pp08PhoneReport.ppt** is open

2. Click **Tools** and then select **Compare and Merge Presentations**

3. Click **Reviewer1PhoneReport.ppt**, then hold the **Ctrl** key to click **Reviewer2PhoneReport.ppt**, and click the **Merge** button

4. Move to slide 1, and then click the **Gallery** button. In the Revisions pane click the slide with your name (see Figure 8.12)

5. Move to slide 2 and click the lower slide in the Gallery to apply its revisions

6. Click the **End Review** button on the Reviewing toolbar

7. Read the warning and click **Yes**

8. Click **Save** on the Standard toolbar

When you click the End Review button, PowerPoint disables the ability to combine revisions from the reviewer file. Many of the review tools are not available with simple attached e-mail files. Full reviewing functionality is available to users of Microsoft Outlook.

FIGURE 8.12

Viewing revisions

Reviewing with Microsoft Office Outlook 2003

Microsoft Office Outlook 2003 is software designed to coordinate workgroup activities by providing e-mail, calendars, contacts, and other shared and personal support. If all parties involved in the collaboration are using Microsoft Outlook, features for coordinating and tracking the presentation review are available. When PowerPoint is used to send a presentation for review through Outlook, other team members can add comments and make changes in their personal review copy of the presentation. The reviews are returned to the author, who combines them with the original file and then uses reviewing tools to apply or reject suggested updates.

Outlook will automatically generate a review request e-mail message with appropriate text, create a follow-up flag, and track changes made by reviewers. Some of this functionality is available using other 32-bit e-mail programs compatible with the Messaging Application Programming Interface (MAPI).

Parks Industries has implemented all of the Microsoft product features needed to collaborate using Outlook. Since it is anticipated that the reader does not have all of these features and there is no actual Phone Services group to interact with, this topic includes discussion and Task References to indicate how each task could be completed, but steps are not included for the reader to follow.

---

task reference   **Use Outlook to Send a Presentation for Review**

- Open the presentation to be reviewed

- On the **File** menu, point to **Send To**, and then click **Mail Recipient (for Review)**

- In the e-mail that opens enter the To and Cc e-mail addresses of your reviewers

- Click **Send**

Mailing a presentation for review:

NOTE: *You must be running Microsoft Office Outlook 2003 to complete the steps*

1. Click the **File** menu, point to **Send To**, and then click **Mail Recipient (for Review)** (see Figure 8.13)

2. Enter your e-mail addresses

tip: *In an actual review process you would enter the e-mail addresses of the reviewers*

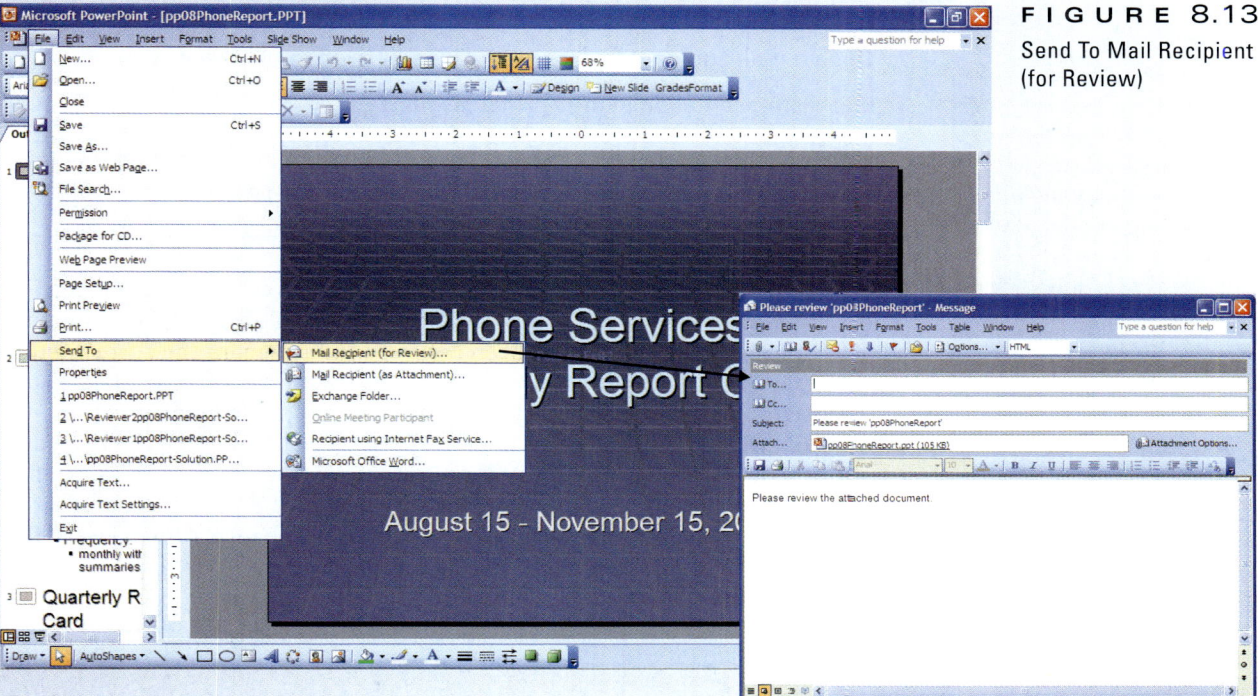

FIGURE 8.13

Send To Mail Recipient (for Review)

3. Set any other desired options

4. Click **Send** on the E-mail toolbar

Microsoft Office Outlook 2003 provides an array of e-mail options that can be useful when tracking revisions. A pivotal feature of Outlook is the address book. Besides being able to keep individual information in the address book, e-mail lists and groups can be created so that clicking one address book entry sends e-mails to all members of that group. Other valuable options include:

- Setting the importance level from low to high
- Flags to remind yourself to follow up and reviewers to respond by a specific due date
- The ability to mark the message private, personal, or confidential. Private messages cannot be modified after they are sent
- Adding security to messages
- Tracking messages and replies
- Delaying message delivery or causing the message to expire on a specified date

POWERPOINT

Deadlines and follow-ups are particularly useful in review cycles. They help to keep the project on track without further intervention by the coordinator. If you are not familiar with these features, please refer to Outlook's Help facilities for further information.

The reviewers will receive e-mail with an individual copy of your presentation attached. When a reviewer opens the e-mail, he or she will be able to double-click the attachment to open the document and add comments. Once a reviewer's changes and comments are complete, their copy of the presentation is returned to you.

---

task reference   Review a Presentation Sent with Outlook

- Open e-mail and double-click on the presentation to be reviewed
- Edit the presentation in the normal fashion
- Use the Comments button of the Reviewing toolbar to add comments
- From the **File** menu click **Send**, and then click **Original Sender**

Using *Return To Original Sender* has some advantages over using the standard reply or forward e-mail buttons. Return To Original Sender automatically generates the e-mail text indicating that the file has been reviewed. Additionally, the correct return address and file attachment are ensured. The review request e-mail can be deleted, saved, or moved to a specific folder, just like any other e-mail (see Figure 8.14).

When you, the originator, receive the reviewers' e-mails, combine their updated presentations with your original presentation so that you can see everything at once. Each reviewer's comments and changes are identified in your presentation by a color-coded comment or a change icon with a description of the change. All reviewers' files do not need to be available to begin this process since additional reviewed presentations can be combined with the original presentation until the review is ended.

---

task reference   Use Outlook to Combine Reviewed Presentations

- Open the Outlook e-mail containing the reviewed presentation
- Double-click the attached reviewed presentation
- Click **Yes** in the alert box so that PowerPoint will automatically combine the reviewed presentation with your original presentation
- Close the e-mail and repeat the process for any other reviews

---

As the author of the slide show, it is up to you to make the final edit of the presentation. Comments and changes from reviewers can be ignored, applied individually, by slide, or by reviewer. If reviewers have made conflicting changes, the various updates are displayed and the coordinator must select which changes to apply.

Changes made by reviewers and combined with the original presentation will display as a change icon on the original presentation slide or in the Revisions pane of the task panel. There are several effective ways to view, evaluate, and apply changes. Moving through the combined presentation one slide at a time displays what each reviewer suggested about each slide. Alternatively a single reviewer can be selected from the Reviewers list of the Reviewing toolbar to follow just one person's comments. The Next

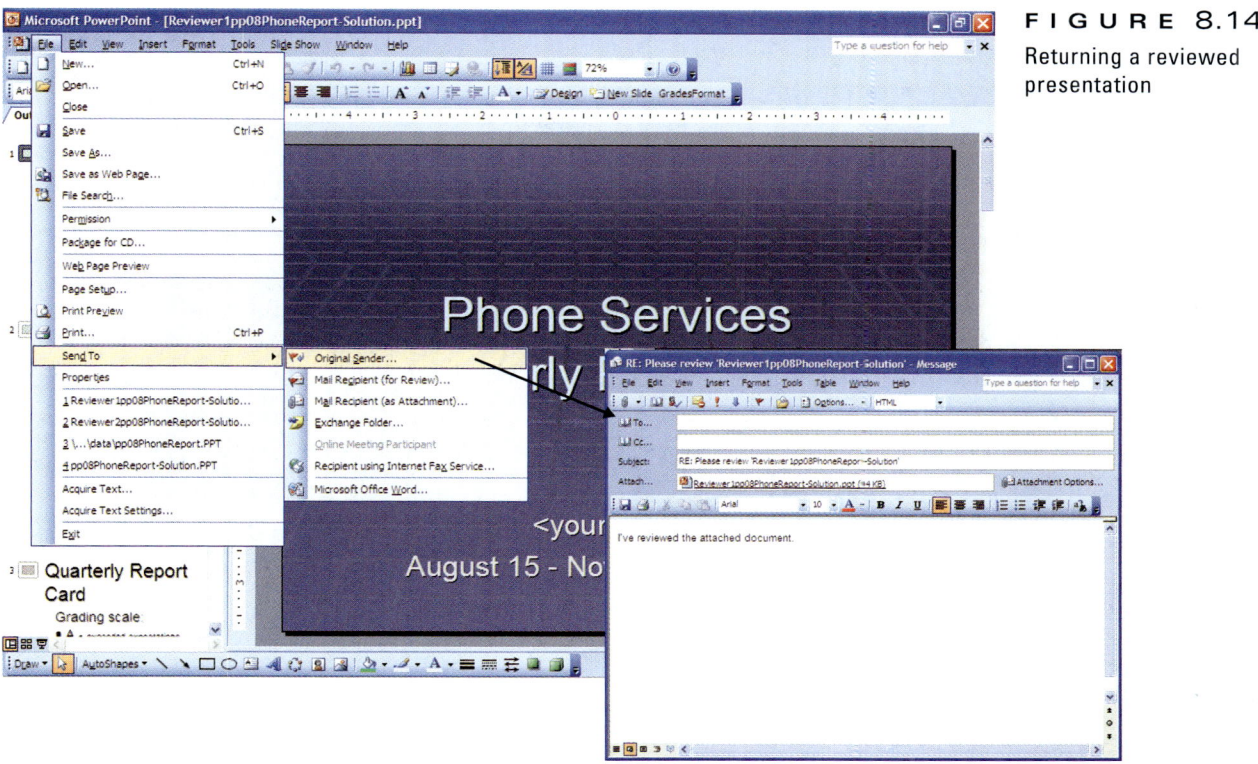

FIGURE 8.14
Returning a reviewed
presentation

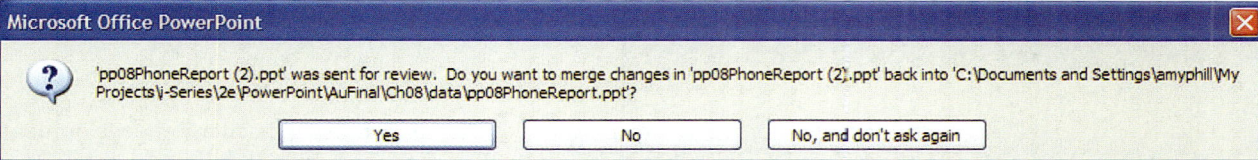

FIGURE 8.15
Combining reviewed
presentations

Item and Previous Item buttons of the Reviewing toolbar will move from comment to comment in the presentation. The Apply and Unapply buttons are used to make and unmake the suggested changes to the original presentation.

When working through the combined presentation, changes that won't be applied can be deleted. To remove unwanted icons from the combined presentation, select them and click the Delete button. Removing unneeded icons unclutters the slide and allows the originator to concentrate on issues that need to be addressed. The check boxes representing each task performed by each reviewer can be checked and unchecked to indicate which revisions to retain. When multiple reviewers have made conflicting changes, click Multiple Reviewers and select the changes to retain.

If any presentation reviewers made changes to the Slide Master, those suggestions must be reviewed separately. Use the View menu to open the Slide Master so that reviewer notes will display. Apply or ignore Slide Master updates as you would any other update and then close the view.

When all desired reviews have been applied, end the review. Once the review is ended, it will not be possible to combine any more reviewed presentations with the original presentation.

---

task reference — End a Review

- On the Reviewing toolbar, click **End Review**

FIGURE 8.16

Applying reviewer suggestions

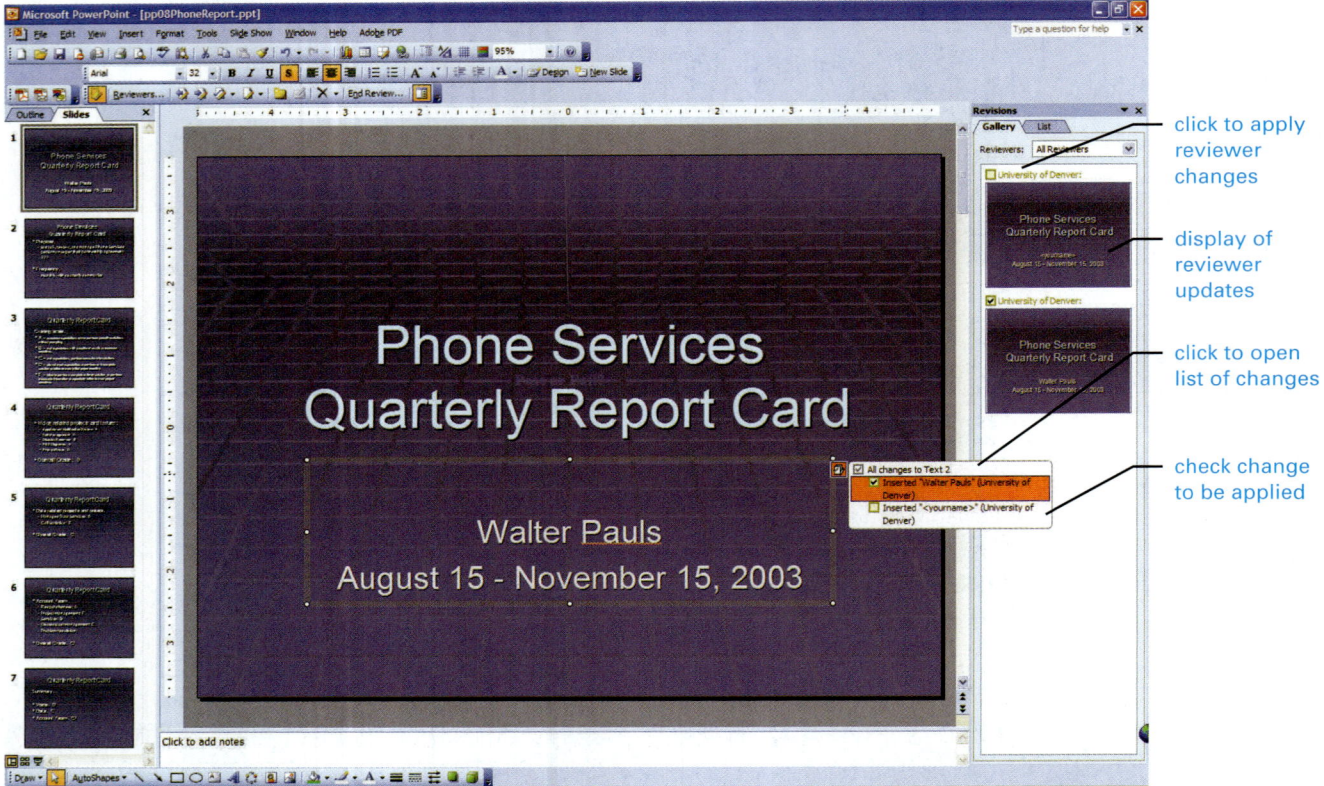

Often multiple review cycles are required to complete presentation development. The completed cycle should be ended and another one begun each time feedback is solicited. By combining the power of multiple Microsoft applications, coordinating a review cycle is greatly simplified. This scenario assumes that Outlook has been installed with the configuration options necessary to support online collaboration.

Web Broadcasting

Complete presentations including video and audio narration can be delivered over the World Wide Web. Web broadcasts can be live or recorded. Recorded broadcasts can be rebroadcast at scheduled times or configured for on-demand viewing. Web broadcasts are ideal for large geographically dispersed audiences or when multiple conference rooms are required to handle the volume of people.

help yourself *Click the* Type a question for help *combo box, type* **web broadcasting**, *and press* **Enter**. *Click the hyperlink* **About presentation broadcasting** *and review all the options available for broadcasting a presentation on the Web. Click the Help screen* **Close** *button when you are finished, and close the task pane*

Viewing a Web Broadcast

The contents of a Web broadcast are saved in HTML format so that viewers need a Web browser to view the presentation. Microsoft Internet Explorer 5.1 or later is the recommended browser since it supports all the features that might be included in a broadcast. The viewer must know how to access the server where the broadcast is stored.

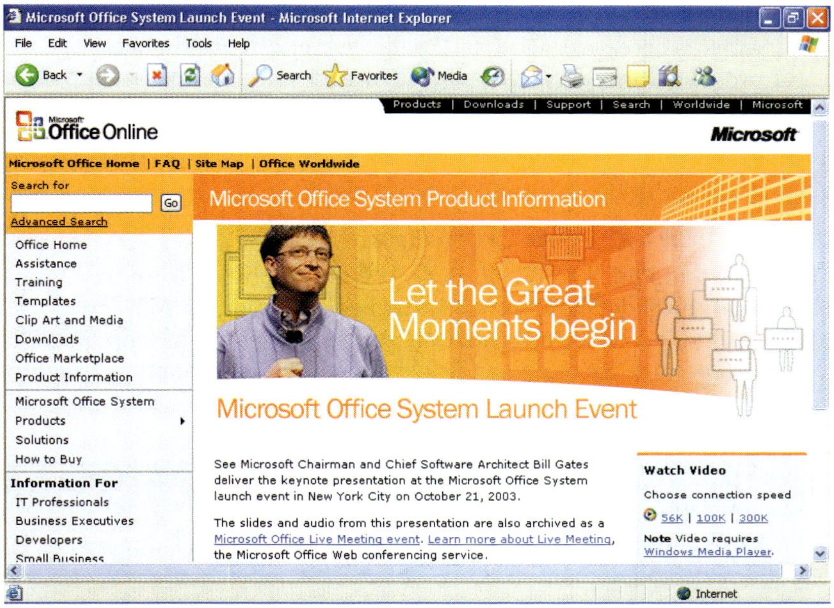

FIGURE 8.17

Web broadcast

Web broadcasts are similar in appearance to presentations saved as Web pages. The broadcast consists of multiple frames as follows:

- The current slide displayed in a browser frame
- A clickable table of contents so the audience can view previous slides or skip ahead
- Live video displayed in its own browser frame
- Audience tools like Help, E-mail, and View Previous

Most business presentations using Web broadcasting are initiated via e-mail. The participant receives an e-mail with the broadcast time and URL. It is best to join a live broadcast early to verify the URL and check for any last-minute changes.

---

task reference   **View a Web Broadcast**

- To view a live broadcast, open the e-mail with the broadcast invitation and click the URL

- To view a recorded broadcast, go to the start page provided by the presenter and click **Replay Broadcast**

Preparing for Web Broadcast

Web broadcasts should be set up and tested well in advance of the scheduled presentation delivery. In most situations, the presenter is responsible for organizing and delivering the broadcast. Setting up small-group presentations on a local intranet or the Internet does not require much technical expertise and can usually be completed by the presenter alone.

The minimum requirements for Web broadcasting are PowerPoint 2002 and Internet Explorer 5.1 or later. If the live broadcast is to contain audio, video, or both, a video camera and microphone must be properly connected to the presentation computer. Microsoft Outlook or another e-mail client will be needed to distribute the live broadcast invitations. PowerPoint creates e-mail invitations during the online broadcast setup process.

For a successful presentation involving 10 or more audience computers, Microsoft Windows Media Server is necessary. Microsoft Media Server can be purchased and locally installed, or provided through a third party. Whether these services are provided locally or through a service provider, the setup will require additional time and coordination before the presentation can be delivered. See the *Tips for broadcasting* Help topic for more broadcasting resources.

Setting Up a Recorded Web Broadcast

All of the PowerPoint setup for an online broadcast is accomplished from the Online Broadcast selection of the Slide Show menu. As has been mentioned, Web broadcasts can be recorded for later delivery or presented live. Live broadcasts can begin immediately or be scheduled for later. Each of these delivery methodologies requires a slightly different setup.

---

task reference   Set Up a Recorded Web Broadcast

- Open the presentation to be broadcast on a computer with functioning audio and/or video equipment
- On the **Slide Show** menu, point to **Online Broadcast** and select **Record and Save a Broadcast**
- Complete the information for the broadcast lobby
- Click **Settings** and update the audio/video, presentation display, speaker notes, and file location
- Click **OK**
- Click **Record** to prepare the presentation for recording
- Click **Start** to begin recording the broadcast
  - Narrate each slide speaking clearly and staying positioned in front of the camera, if there is one
  - Click to progress to the next slide
- When you have recorded through all of the slides in the presentation, you will be presented with an option to Replay the Broadcast
- Move all broadcast files to a shared folder on your intranet or to the Internet and notify your audience of the location

---

Recording the pp08PhoneReport Web broadcast:

1. Open **pp08PhoneReport.ppt**, if necessary

2. Click **Slide Show**, point to **Online Broadcast**, and select **Record and Save a Broadcast**

3. Change the Title to **Quarterly Phone Report**, insert your name as the speaker, and place your e-mail address in the Email text box

4. Click the **Settings** button

   a. Select the Audio/Video setting appropriate for your computer

tip: *Be sure to use the Test button if you are using either audio or video*

b. Click **Display speaker notes with the presentation**

c. Change the *Save broadcast files in* location to reflect where you are storing your work

d. Click **OK**

5. Click the **Tips for Broadcast** button, review the tips, and then close the window

6. Click **Record**, wait for the presentation to be prepared, perform any requested checks, and then click **Start**

7. Click through the presentation reading highlights of the slide content for audio and video presentation

tip: *When you click to end the presentation, PowerPoint saves the broadcast and displays a dialog box with an option to view the broadcast*

8. Click the **Replay Broadcast** button and watch the show

tip: *If you included audio or video, you should see and hear it as the presentation plays*

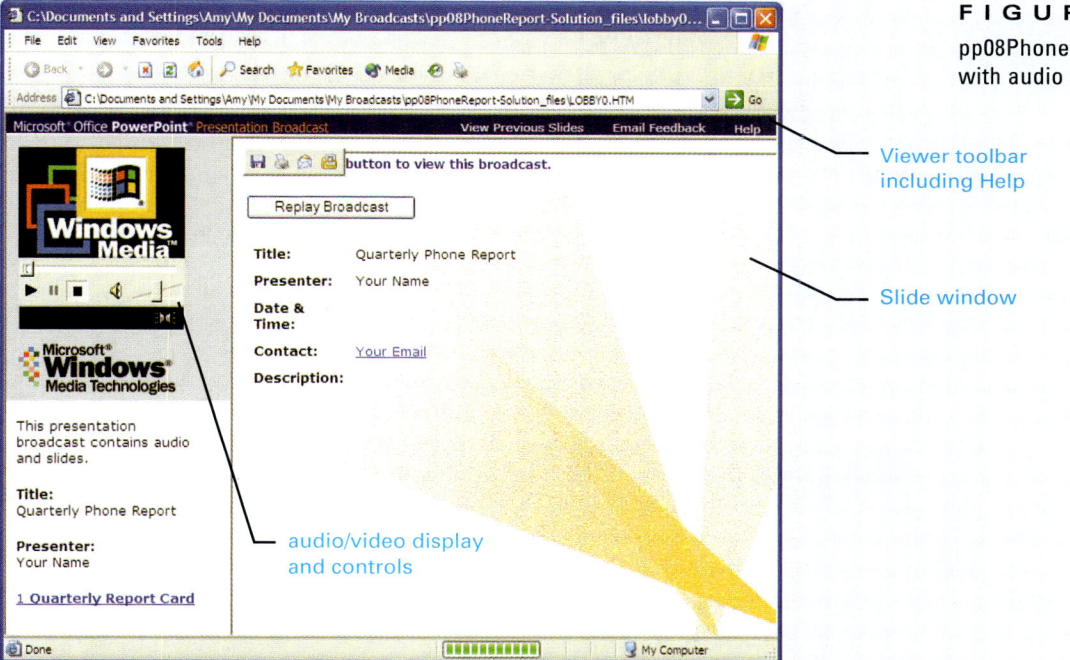

FIGURE 8.18

pp08PhoneReport lobby with audio recorded

9. Close the Web browser window when you are done viewing the broadcast

---

anotherword   . . . **on Broadcast Settings**

In these steps, you used the Settings button to set options for the presentation media, display, and storage location. These options are available on the Presenters tab of the Broadcast Settings dialog box. The Advanced tab of this dialog box can be used to set up Windows Media Encoder, a chat room URL, or Windows Media Services. These options use the resources of other computers and the network that must be set up by a technician

F I G U R E 8.19

Setting up a live broadcast

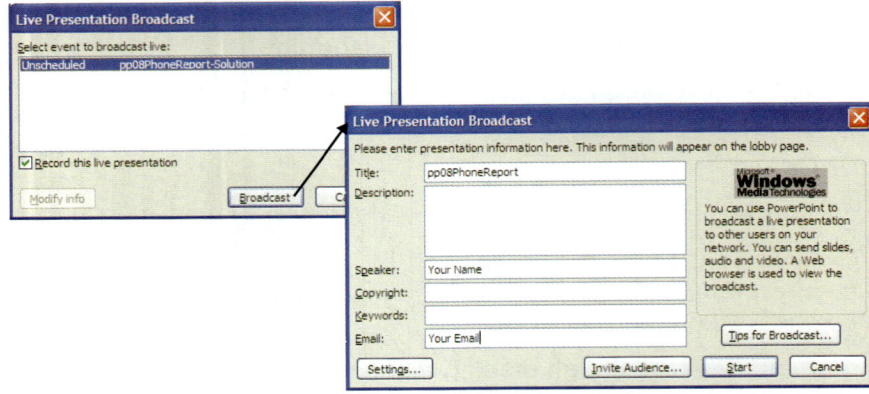

In the preceding steps the recorded broadcast was saved locally but the files can still be moved to a shared location for audience browsing. During the recording process, Microsoft PowerPoint creates the opening or lobby page using the name of the PowerPoint presentation with the .htm file extension of an HTML file. All of the pages of the presentation, graphics, audio, and video files are stored in a folder with the same name as the presentation plus _files. The .htm file and the folder of supporting files must be moved or copied to the same location for the broadcast to work correctly.

Setting Up a Live or Scheduled Web Broadcast

A live Web broadcast is viewed by the audience at the same time that it is being produced by the speaker. Viewing and creating the broadcast are very similar to the experience of creating a recorded broadcast, but the setup is somewhat different. An unscheduled live broadcast can be started at any time, but you are responsible for inviting and organizing the participants. A scheduled broadcast will use your e-mail software to invite people you select to the future event.

As with recorded presentations, functioning audio and video equipment are required to include those components in your broadcast, and broadcasting to 10 or more computers requires additional resources. Live presentations must be saved to a shared intranet or Internet drive as they are created so that the audience can view them.

---

task reference   **Start a Live Web Broadcast**

- Open the presentation to be broadcast on a computer with functioning audio and/or video equipment

- On the **Slide Show** menu, point to **Online Broadcast** and select **Start Live Broadcast Now**

- In the Live Presentation Broadcast dialog box, select the presentation, check the record option if you want a recorded copy for on-demand viewing, and click **Broadcast**

- Enter the information to create the lobby

- Click **Settings** and update the audio/video, presentation display, speaker notes, and file location. A shared file location must be specified to continue

- Click **OK**

- If you want to invite participants, click **Invite Audience** to send e-mails

- Click **Start** to begin recording the broadcast

- Click **Start** again to begin streaming audio and video

It is wise to check the settings prior to each broadcast, because they apply to all broadcasts from a particular computer, not just to the current broadcast. The actual presentation of a scheduled broadcast is initiated using the live broadcast procedure just explored. Scheduled presentations will be listed in the selection box of the opening Live Presentation Broadcast dialog box. The steps to scheduling a broadcast should be completed a week or more before the broadcast to verify hardware and accommodate participants' needs.

---

task reference   Schedule a Live Web Broadcast

- Open the presentation to be broadcast on a computer with functioning audio and/or video equipment

- On the **Slide Show** menu, point to **Online Broadcast** and select **Schedule a Live Broadcast**

- Enter the information to create the lobby

- Click **Settings** and update the audio/video, presentation display, speaker notes, and file location. A shared file location must be specified to continue

- Click **OK**

- Click **Schedule** in the Schedule Presentation Broadcast dialog box

---

Live Web broadcasts are an effective way to communicate across distances to multiple concurrent audiences. Saving the live presentation allows participants to review its content and those who were unable to attend the live broadcast the ability to participate.

Making Online Meetings Work for You

PowerPoint presentations can be shared online using Microsoft NetMeeting. All computers participating in an online meeting must be connected to a network and have NetMeeting installed and properly configured. Such online meetings are called ***collaborative meetings*** and are usually conducted when members of an organization are unable to convene at a central location.

The act of initiating an online meeting automatically starts NetMeeting in the background. NetMeeting is capable of delivering the presentation and allowing the distributed audience to exchange information in real time (as if everyone were in the same room). ***Chat*** can be used to send text messages, and the ***Whiteboard*** is visible to all users. Collaboration settings will allow multiple audience members to work in Chat or on the Whiteboard simultaneously. Only one user at a time can work on the presentation, however.

Scheduling Online Meetings

Online meeting attendees can have the role of either host or participant. All meeting participants must have access to a server that will be used to present the meeting. Only the meeting host needs to have the shared document and its host application installed.

Online meetings can be scheduled in advance or started immediately. All participants can see a shared document such as a PowerPoint presentation, but the host has control of who can update the document. As the host makes changes to the document, other meeting attendees can watch the work. When attendees are updating a document, the host cannot use the pointer for any purpose. Multiple attendees can use Chat and the Whiteboard at any time during the meeting.

task *reference*	Host an Online Meeting with PowerPoint

- Open the presentation to be broadcast on a computer with functioning audio and/or video equipment
- On the **Tools** menu, point to **Online Collaboration** and select either **Meet Now** or **Schedule Meeting**
- Complete the NetMeeting dialog box and click **OK**
- On the Online Meeting toolbar, click **Call Participant** and use the Find Someone dialog box to invite attendees
- Participate in the meeting
- On the Online Meeting toolbar, click **End Meeting**

Only the host of a meeting can use the Online Meeting toolbar to invite attendees, open the Whiteboard, or initiate Chat. Once a participant has joined a meeting, they can see the shared document, use the Whiteboard and Chat if they are open, and use the End Call option of the Online Meeting toolbar to leave the meeting.

Collaborating on the Web

Microsoft Office also provides tools for collaborating on the Web. Some Web collaboration features will work on a network that supports Microsoft Office Server Extensions, but many require a server running Microsoft SharePoint Team Services. The network administrator can tell you whether these services are available to you.

Web discussions can be used to add comments to any document that can be opened with a Web browser. The discussions are threaded and display with the page in the browser. Anyone with permission to discuss a document can use the Web Discussion button on the toolbar to add general discussions about the entire document or online discussions about a particular paragraph. These discussions are asynchronous

FIGURE 8.20

Initiating an online meeting

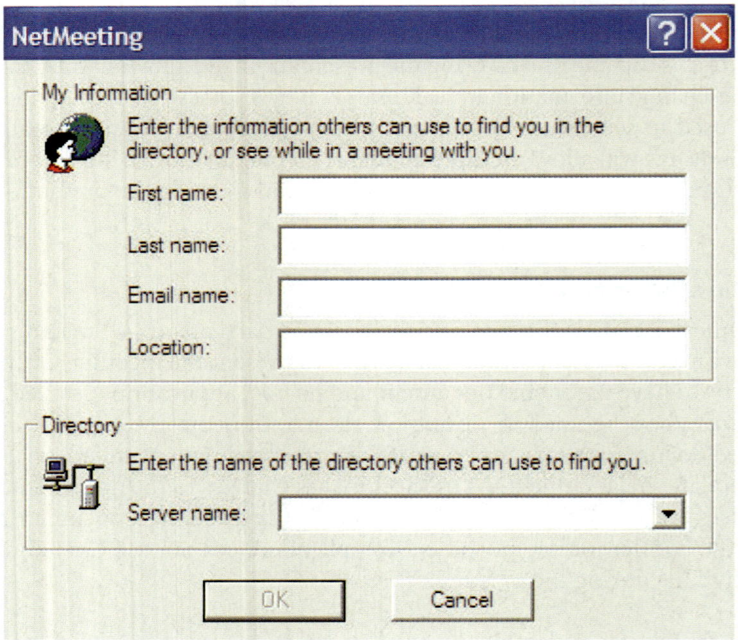

so that participants do not have to be online simultaneously. The Web Discussions toolbar is available in Microsoft Internet Explorer 4.0 and later.

Team Web sites are designed to help groups share files, participate in discussions, and communicate effectively from the Web. Although these sites are built and accessed from Microsoft Office products, Microsoft SharePoint Team Services software must be installed on a network supporting team Web sites.

If the support software is functioning properly, creating a team Web site is simple. The New File task pane of any Microsoft Office product contains an Add Network Place link that initiates a Wizard. A basic team site can be functioning in a few minutes. A team Web site can contain:

- Libraries of documents to share
- Discussion boards for team communication
- Web document discussions
- Announcements
- Upcoming events
- Surveys to gather data
- Shared favorites listing Web sites of interest
- Custom lists for any purpose
- Subscriptions to notify members of file and folder changes

Team Web sites can be created from any Office application and easily customized using Microsoft Front Page. Each team member is assigned a role that determines what operations they can perform. The SharePoint team member Web site roles are:

- Browser—A member who can view pages, documents, and Web document discussions
- Discussion Participant—A member who can view pages and documents and participate in Web document discussions
- Author—A team member who can view pages, participate in Web document discussions, and modify pages, documents, or tasks
- Advanced Author—A team member who can create content, contribute to Web document discussions, change themes and borders, and update hyperlinks
- Content Manager—The team member responsible for advanced authoring tasks like managing subscription lists and Web document discussions
- Administrator—The network person responsible for managing server settings and accounts

Team Web sites are ideal for communicating information to a geographically dispersed group of people, or facilitating discussions and documenting project progress.

making the grade

SESSION 8.2

1. Why is a simple e-mail attachment not the most effective way to send a presentation to a reviewer?

2. T F A review must be ended before applying the reviewer suggestions.

3. How are reviewer suggestions represented in the original file?

4. What is needed for a successful Web broadcast?

POWERPOINT

SESSION 8.3 SUMMARY

When creating a presentation, it is important to consider storing backups of the involved files. Backups can be simple copies of the files on a separate media. If the presentation is critical, multiple backups can be created and one stored off-site. Backups are used to restore files that become damaged due to user error or mechanical failure.

PowerPoint contains many features to make presenting on the road easier. The PowerPoint viewer will allow a presentation to be run on a computer that does not have PowerPoint installed. The Package for CD Wizard will consolidate and package all project files for transport. The PowerPoint Viewer is automatically packaged with the files.

Macros are recorded mouse and keyboard operations that can be replayed any time the actions need to be repeated. Microsoft Office System 2003 provides added security features including security levels and digital signatures to help protect against macro viruses. Toolbars and menus can be customized to contain options configured by the user including macros.

The default behavior of Microsoft Office System 2003 applications is updated from the Options selection of the Tools menu. Updatable categories include Print, Edit, Save, and Security.

Add-ins are special software that enhance the capabilities of an application like PowerPoint. PowerPoint add-ins can be found on the Microsoft Office Web page or from third-party vendors.

Collaborative or workgroup tools support groups of people working together. These tools range from the ability to control and track presentation review cycles to creating complex Web sites. Web broadcasts are used to present recorded presentations with audio and video over the Internet. Such broadcasts can be live or stored for on-demand review.

MICROSOFT OFFICE SPECIALIST OBJECTIVES SUMMARY

- Set up presentations for remote delivery—MOS PP035-4-5
- Deliver presentations—MOS PP035-4-4
- Work with embedded fonts
- Use Package for CD
- Use workgroup collaboration— MOS PP035-3

making the grade *answers*

SESSION 8.1

1. A backup copy of a presentation should be stored on a different media and, for critical files, in a different location. Backups are important to protect against accidental user errors like mistake updates to the file as well as mechanical failures like a bad disk drive.

2. The PowerPoint viewer is software that can be bundled with a presentation to allow it to run on any computer. PowerPoint does not have to be installed on the presentation computer when the viewer is used.

3. Packaging is the simplest way to ensure that all necessary files including fonts, graphics, and sounds are transported. It will also place files that are too large for a single disk on multiple disks and can be used to include the PowerPoint viewer in the package.

4. Macros store keystrokes and mouse operations to complete a task. Once these are stored, running the macro will repeat them, saving time and ensuring continuity. More interface steps are saved by attaching a macro to a toolbar button where it is activated in one mouse click rather than stepping through the Tools menu options.

5. The Customize dialog box is used to set options for toolbars and menus. The Options dialog box changes default settings of the application related to print, save, editing, and other common tasks.

SESSION 8.2

1. Simple e-mail attachments do not have any services to track or remind reviewers.

2. False. Once the review has been terminated, no more revisions can be applied to the original file.

3. Reviewer suggestions appear as icons in the original file with the details in the task pane.

4. The minimum requirements for Web broadcasting are PowerPoint 2002 and Internet Explorer 5.1 or later. If you want to broadcast live with audio, video, or both, you will need a video camera and microphone properly connected to your presentation computer.

task reference *summary*

Task	Page #	Preferred Method
Package a presentation	PP 8.4	• Open the presentation to be packaged • If you are saving the presentation to a storage media, insert it • Click the **File** menu and then **Package for CD** • Make appropriate selections on each screen • Clicking **Add Files** will allow you to package multiple presentations • Use the **Options button** to include the Microsoft PowerPoint viewer in the package
Record and play a macro	PP 8.6	• Click **Tools**, point to **Macro**, then click **Security**, and select appropriate Security Level settings and add Trusted Sources • Click **Tools**, point to **Macro**, then click **Record New Macro** • Select the storage location for the macro, enter the macro name in the Macro name box, and click **OK** to begin recording • Perform the actions to be recorded • Click **Stop Recording** on the Stop Recording toolbar
Personalize menu and toolbar settings	PP 8.10	• On the **Tools** menu, click **Customize** • Adjust Options tab settings

task reference *summary*

Task	Page #	Preferred Method
Customize an existing toolbar	PP 8.11	• Click the **Toolbar Options** arrow at the right end of the toolbar • Point to **Add or Remove Buttons**, click **Customize**, click the **Commands** tab • In the **Categories** box select the type of command to be added. For example, Macros • From the **Commands** box, click and drag the command to a toolbar

Prepare a presentation for review	PP 8.18	• Open the presentation to be reviewed
		• For each reviewer:
		  • Click **Save As** on the **File** menu
		  • Change the name in the **File name** box to indicate whose review copy it is
		  • Change the **Save as type** to **Presentation for Review**
		  • Click **Save**
		• Distribute the files to reviewers on disk or as e-mail attachments

Use Outlook to send a presentation for review	PP 8.20	• Open the presentation to be reviewed • On the **File** menu, point to **Send To** and then click **Mail Recipient (for Review)** • In the e-mail that opens, enter the To and Cc e-mail addresses of your reviewers • Click **Send**
Review a presentation sent with Outlook	PP 8.22	• Open e-mail and double-click on the presentation to be reviewed • Edit the presentation in the normal fashion • Use the Comments button of the Reviewing toolbar to add comments • From the **File** menu click **Send**, and then click **Original Sender**
Use Outlook to combine reviewed presentations	PP 8.22	• Open the Outlook e-mail containing the reviewed presentation • Double-click the attached reviewed presentation • Click **Yes** in the alert box so that PowerPoint will automatically combine the reviewed presentation with your original presentation • Close the e-mail and repeat the process for any other reviews
End a review	PP 8.23	• On the Reviewing toolbar, click **End Review**
View a Web broadcast	PP 8.25	• To view a live broadcast, open the e-mail with the broadcast invitation and click the URL • To view a recorded broadcast, go to the start page provided by the presenter and click **Replay Broadcast**

Set up a recorded Web broadcast	PP 8.26	• Open the presentation to be broadcast on a computer with functioning audio and/or video equipment
		• On the **Slide Show** menu, point to **Online Broadcast** and select **Record and Save a Broadcast**
		• Complete the information for the broadcast lobby
		• Click **Settings** and update the audio/video, presentation display, speaker notes, and file location
		• Click **OK**
		• Click **Record** to prepare the presentation for recording
		• Click **Start** to begin recording the broadcast
		  • Narrate each slide speaking clearly and staying positioned in front of the camera, if there is one
		  • Click to progress to the next slide
		• When you have recorded through all of the slides in the presentation, you will be presented with an option to Replay the Broadcast
		• Move all broadcast files to a shared folder on your intranet or to the Internet and notify your audience of the location

task reference *summary*

Task	Page #	Preferred Method
Start a live Web broadcast	PP 8.28	• Open the presentation to be broadcast on a computer with functioning audio and/or video equipment • On the **Slide Show** menu, point to **Online Broadcast** and select **Start Live Broadcast Now** • In the Live Presentation Broadcast dialog box, select the presentation, check the record option if you want a recorded copy for on-demand viewing, and click **Broadcast** • Enter the information to create the lobby • Click **Settings** and update the audio/video, presentation display, speaker notes, and file location. A shared file location must be specified to continue • Click **OK** • If you want to invite participants, click **Invite Audience** to send e-mails • Click **Start** to begin recording the broadcast • Click **Start** again to begin streaming audio and video
Schedule a live Web broadcast	PP 8.29	• Open the presentation to be broadcast on a computer with functioning audio and/or video equipment • On the **Slide Show** menu, point to **Online Broadcast** and select **Schedule a Live Broadcast** • Enter the information to create the lobby • Click **Settings** and update the audio/video, presentation display, speaker notes, and file location. A shared file location must be specified to continue • Click **OK** • Click **Schedule** in the Schedule Presentation Broadcast dialog box
Host an online meeting with PowerPoint	PP 8.30	• Open the presentation to be broadcast on a computer with functioning audio and/or video equipment • On the **Tools** menu, point to **Online Collaboration** and select either **Meet Now** or **Schedule Meeting** • Complete the NetMeeting dialog box and click **OK** • On the Online Meeting toolbar, click **Call Participant** and use the Find Someone dialog box to invite attendees • Participate in the meeting • On the Online Meeting toolbar, click **End Meeting**

POWERPOINT

TRUE OR FALSE

1. When creating a presentation, it is important to consider storing a backup of the file.

2. PowerPoint presentations cannot be viewed on computers if they do not have a copy of the PowerPoint application.

3. Macros can only record keyboard operations that can be repeated.

4. Add-ins are special features to enhance the performance of the macros.

5. You need a special server to use the Web broadcast feature in PowerPoint.

6. Toolbars and menus can be customized to contain options configured by the user including macros.

FILL-IN

1. Web-based meetings using Microsoft NetMeeting are called _____.

2. A _____ is created in Notepad to control the order that presentations will play in the PowerPoint Viewer.

3. _____ are recorded mouse and keyboard actions that can be replayed.

4. A _____ is a plan to handle things that could go wrong while presenting.

5. The default Office security level setting is _____.

MULTIPLE CHOICE

1. This PowerPoint feature allows you to take a presentation on the road to ensure the most effective way it will run properly on another computer:
   a. PowerPoint Viewer
   b. Package for CD
   c. Save as Web Page
   d. all the above

2. A _____ is a recorded command stored in a Microsoft Visual Basic module.
   a. Package for CD
   b. macro
   c. custom toolbar
   d. none of the above

3. _____ are additional software programs that augment the features of the existing PowerPoint application.
   a. Add-ins
   b. Macros
   c. both a and b
   d. none of the above

4. A complete presentation including video and audio narration can be delivered over the Web. This is called _____.
   a. broadcasting
   b. Web broadcasting
   c. online broadcasting
   d. all of the above

5. _____ is referred to as sharing a document online such as a PowerPoint presentation.
   a. Online collaboration
   b. Online broadcasting
   c. Whiteboard
   d. all of the above

review of concepts

REVIEW QUESTIONS

Each of the following topics should be addressed in one to three paragraphs.

1. Explain how digital signatures help to protect against macro viruses.

2. Where would you go to customize PowerPoint and what types of things can be customized?

3. Discuss the benefits of using macros.

4. Why do linked files used in a presentation need to be moved with it?

5. How are the comments from various reviewers differentiated in a routed file?

CREATE THE QUESTION

For each of the following answers, create the question.

ANSWER	QUESTION
1. PowerPoint Viewer	_____
2. Linked file and fonts	_____
3. Controls the behavior of menus and toolbars throughout Office	_____
4. Digital signatures	_____
5. Add-ins	_____

FACT OR FICTION

1. When preparing to take a presentation on the road, you must decide whether or not to use the Microsoft PowerPoint Viewer. The viewer is a software program that will run PowerPoint presentations on computers that do not have PowerPoint installed.

2. A macro can be created in any Microsoft Office product to store common tasks. Macros are recorded commands that are stored in a Microsoft Visual Basic module attached to the presentation.

3. The Options selection of the Tools menu is a multi-tabbed dialog box with settings to control the behavior of most critical PowerPoint operations. This dialog box contains options to control save, print, view, security, edit, spelling, and style.

4. The contents of a Web broadcast are saved in HTML format so that viewers need a Web browser to view the presentation. Microsoft Internet Explorer 5.1 or later is the recommended browser since it supports all of the features that might be included in a broadcast.

1. Triathlon Training Part I

Meghan Owens is a personal trainer who specializes in exercise and nutrition programs for competitive athletes. She is a successful triathlon competitor who has trained several winning triathletes. Meghan has firsthand knowledge of what strategies work best in the months before a competition—nutrition, swimming, biking, and running. It is important for trainers to understand the unique nature of this training, so a new qualification in triathlon is being offered to degreed personal trainers. Meghan has been asked to present an overview of the program, which will be placed on the Web and used to market the new qualification to the trainers. The same program will be used to open each seminar where Meghan is the keynote speaker. She has developed a draft PowerPoint presentation, but needs help obtaining feedback on the content, preparing it for delivery, and setting up the broadcast.

1. Start PowerPoint and open **pp08Triathlon.ppt**

2. Save the presentation as **<yourname>Triathlon.ppt**

3. Use the **Package for CD** option of the **File** menu to package Meghan's presentation for travel on a floppy disk in a folder called *Presentation*

4. Create a backup of the package files

5. Move the presentation on another computer to verify that it will work when ported

6. Meghan has decided that some presentation graphics need to be adjusted. Develop a macro activated by a button on a Custom toolbar

   a. On slide 1 select the graphic of swimmers

   b. Click **Tools**, point to **Macro**, and click **Record New Macro**

      i. Name the macro **PhotoAdjust**, type your name in the Description, and click **OK**

      ii. Right-click on the selected swimmers and click **Format Object**

      iii. On the Picture tab set the Brightness to **40**, the Contrast to **70**, and click **OK**

      iv. Click off the object to deselect it

      v. Stop recording

   c. Use the **Customize** option of the **Tools** menu to create a new toolbar

      i. Select **New** on the **Toolbars** tab of the **Customize** menu

      ii. Name the toolbar **<yourname>** and click **OK**

      iii. On the **Commands** tab of the **Customize** dialog box, select **Macros** and then click and drag the **PhotoAdjust** command to your new toolbar

   tip: *You may need to move the Customize dialog box to see the new toolbar*

      iv. Close the Customize dialog box

   d. Move to slide 2 and use the PhotoAdjust button to modify each color graphic (see Figure 8.21)

   e. Use the Customize dialog box to remove the new toolbar from your computer

   f. Save the presentation again

7. Print the macro code:

   a. Click **Tools**, point to **Macro**, and click **Macros**

   b. Click the **PhotoAdjust** name in the Macro name box and then click the **Edit** button

   c. Click **File** on the Visual Basic menu bar, click **Print**, and click **OK**

   d. Press **Alt+Q** to close the Visual Basic window and return to the presentation

FIGURE 8.21

New toolbar with PhotoAdjust button

new toolbar with PhotoAdjust button —

2. Auto Advice Part I

Next to a home, a car is perhaps the largest purchase that we make. Unfortunately, unlike a home, cars do not appreciate in value; they depreciate. With the average cost of a car well over $20,000, it is more important than ever to buy smart.

Traditionally, dealers have sought to maximize their profit by keeping most of the figures in a deal hidden. In this way dealers charge customers whatever they can convince them to pay for a car. Because of the complexity of a transaction filled with many variables (trade-in value, interest rate, different loan terms, multiple fees) buyers often didn't even know how much they were really paying for the car.

But in the late 1990s, Web sites began publishing the invoice prices of cars while also reaching a larger segment of the car-buying public. This neutralized the car salesman's most powerful weapon: confusion. A smart shopper could find the invoice price of the car he or she wanted to buy, add a 2 to 3 percent profit, and make a take-it-or-leave-it cash offer.

Auto Advice is a free service to consumers who want inside secrets, tips, and facts about auto buying, invoice price, rebates, and trade-ins as well as advice on how to save money on financing, insurance, warranties, and much more. You have been asked to assist with a draft PowerPoint presentation, prepare it for delivery, and set up a Web broadcast.

1. Start PowerPoint and open **pp08AutoAdvice.ppt**

2. Save the presentation as **<yourname>AutoAdvice.ppt**

3. Use the **Package for CD** option of the **File** menu to package the presentation for travel on a floppy disk in a folder whose name is <yourname> (substitute your last name for "<yourname>")

4. Create a backup of the packaged file and its folder

5. Port the presentation on another computer to verify that it will work when exported

6. You will need to adjust some presentation graphics. Develop a macro activated by a button on a Custom toolbar
   a. On slide 2 select the clip art of the automobile in the upper right-hand corner (see Figure 8.22)
   b. Click **Tools**, point to **Macro**, and click **Record New Macro**
      i. Name the macro **GraphicHighlight**, and ensure that the macro is stored with the AutoAdvice presentation
      ii. Type your name in the Description text box, and click **OK**
      iii. Right-click the selected object and click **Format Picture**
      iv. Click the **Picture** tab, set the Brightness to **40**, the Contrast to **40**, and click **OK**
      v. Click off the object to deselect it
      vi. Click the **Stop recording** button
   c. Click **Tools** and click **Customize** to create a new toolbar
      i. Click the **New** button on the **Toolbars** tab of the Customize dialog box
      ii. Name the toolbar **<yourname>** and click **OK**
      iii. Click the **Commands** tab of the Customize dialog box, click **Macros** and then click and drag the **GraphicHighlight** command to your new toolbar
      iv. Close the Customize dialog box by clicking the **Close** button
   d. Move to the remaining slides and use the GraphicHighlight button to modify each color graphic in the upper right-hand corner
   e. Use the Customize dialog box to remove the new toolbar from your computer

7. Print the macro code:
   a. Click **Tools**, point to **Macro**, and click **Macros**
   b. Click the **GraphicHighlight** name in the Macro name box, and click the **Edit** button
   c. Click **File** on the Visual Basic menu bar, click **Print**, and click **OK**
   d. Press **Alt+Q** to close the Visual Basic window and return to the presentation

8. Save the presentation

FIGURE 8.22

Auto Advice screen shot

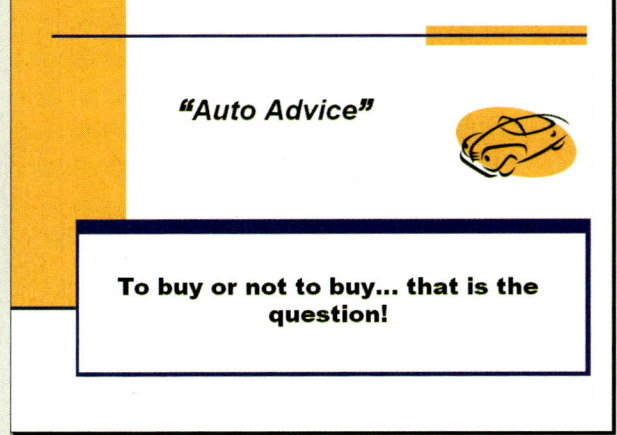

1. Triathlon Training Part II

Meghan Owens' triathlon slide show was introduced in the Practice project for this chapter.

1. Start PowerPoint and open **pp08TriathlonBroadcast.ppt**

2. Prepare this presentation for review by saving two review formatted copies. Name the first copy **TriathlonReviewer1.ppt** and the second **TriathlonReviewer2.ppt**

   a. Close **pp08TriathlonBroadcast.ppt**

   b. Pretend that you are Reviewer 1 and open that presentation. Click **No**. On slide 2 add a bullet **Begin nutritional regimen**. Close and save the presentation

   c. Move to slide 6 and change the third bullet point (*Set aside a rest day a week*) to **Take one day off each week to rest**. Close and save the presentation.

   d. Reopen **<yourname>TriathlonBroadcast.ppt** you created in the Practice problems

   e. Click **Compare and Merge Presentations** from the **Tools** menu. Review the suggested changes, but do not apply any. Save the merged presentation as **<yourname>TriathlonMerge.ppt** and close it

   f. Do not end the review so that your instructor can evaluate the reviews

   g. Close the presentation

3. Record and save a Web broadcast. You will need the ability to record sounds to successfully complete this broadcast

   a. Open **pp08TriathlonBroadcast.ppt**

   b. Use the Notes pane to create a short script for each slide of the presentation. You will need to print this before recording

   c. Complete the setup necessary to record and save a Web broadcast with audio (video can be used if your computer has the appropriate hardware). (Click **Slide Show**, point to **Online Broadcast**, and click **Record and Save a Broadcast**)

      i. Create a folder **<yourname>TriathlonTraining** and set the Web broadcast to save there

      ii. Set the title to **Training Triathletes**

      iii. List **Meghan Owens** as the speaker

      iv. Insert your e-mail address

      v. Click the **Settings** button. Display the speaker notes

   d. Record the Web broadcast and replay it to verify your work. Rerecord if needed

4. Close and Save your presentation

FIGURE 8.23

Triathlon Training Part II

2. Auto Advice Part II

The Auto Advice slide show was introduced in Practice problem 2 of this chapter. If you did not complete that Practice problem, please do so before starting this problem.

1. Start PowerPoint and open **<yourname>AutoAdvice.ppt** (click **Enable Macros** when the dialog box appears requesting your input)

2. Prepare the presentation for review by saving a re-view formatted copy: Click **File**, click **Save As**, type **Reviewer1AutoAdvice.ppt** in the *File name* list box, select **Presentation for Review** from the *Save as type* list box, and click the **Save** button

3. Repeat step 2 for the second reviewer, but this time name the file **Reviewer2AutoAdvice.ppt**

4. Close **<yourname>AutoAdvice.ppt**

5. Pretend that you are Reviewer 1 by opening **Reviewer1AutoAdvice.ppt** (Click **No** when asked if you want to merge changes. Click **Enable Macros** when prompted)

   a. On slide 2, highlight the text **kbb.com** and then create a hyperlink to http://www.kbb.com

   b. Highlight the text **edmunds.com** and then cre-ate a hyperlink to http://www.edmunds.com

   c. Click **File**, click **Close**, and click **Yes** when asked if you want to save your presentation

6. Pretend that you are Reviewer 2 by opening **Reviewer2AutoAdvice.ppt** (Click **No** when asked if you want to merge changes. Click **Enable Macros** when prompted)

   a. Move to slide 3, change **25–40%** to read **20–35%**

   b. Click **File**, click **Close**, and click **Yes** when asked if you want to save your presentation

7. Reopen **<yourname>AutoAdvice.ppt** (Click **Enable Macros** when prompted)

8. Click **Tools**, click **Compare and Merge Presentations**, click **Reviewer1AutoAdvice.ppt**, press the **Shift** key, click **Reviewer2AutoAdvice.ppt**, and click the **Merge** button

9. Review the changes and click the Apply each change, in turn, to the presentation, and save the presentation as **<yourname>AutoAdvicePartIIMerge.ppt** and close it

10. Open **<yourname>AutoAdvicePartIIMerge.ppt** and save it as **<yourname>AutoAdviceBroadcast.ppt**

11. Next, you will record and save a Web broadcast. You *do not* need to be able to record sounds to complete this exercise

    a. Open **<yourname>AutoAdviceBroadcast.ppt**

    b. Create a folder called **<yourname>AutoAdviceBroadcast** in which you will save your broadcast

    c. Click **Slide Show**, point to **Online Broadcast**, click **Record and Save a Broadcast**

    d. Title the presentation **Auto Advice**

    e. Type **Meghan Owens** in the Speaker text box, enter your e-mail address in the Email text box, and click the **Record** button

    f. Click **OK** on the Microphone Check dialog box, and click the **Start** button to begin

    g. Click the mouse and pace the presentation as you would in a live presentation. Click the black "end of presentation" screen to proceed

    h. Click the **Continue** button when the Congratulations! message appears, and close the presentation

12. Try out your broadcast: Open the **<yourname>AutoAdviceBroadcast** folder and then double-click **AutoAdviceBroadcast.htm** (see Figure 8.24)

FIGURE 8.24

Auto Advice broadcast page

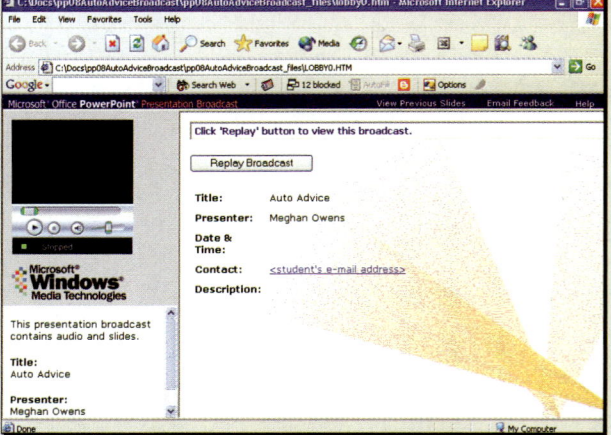

1. Balloon Adventures

Balloon Adventures was introduced in Chapter 4 where the assignment was to create a presentation that would later be converted to a Web kiosk. The kiosk has been updated with content from the remaining chapters and is now ready to be placed on the Web as a recorded Web broadcast. Additionally, the presentation needs to be packaged so that it can be transported and used as a speaker-led presentation at various gatherings where Balloon Adventures' services can be marketed.

1. Start PowerPoint and open **pp08BalloonAdventures.ppt**

2. Save the presentation as **<yourname>BalloonAdv.ppt**

3. Review the slides to familiarize yourself with their content

4. Record and save a Web broadcast. You will need the ability to record sounds to successfully complete this broadcast

   a. Use the Notes pane to create a short script for each slide of the presentation. You will need to print this before recording

   b. Complete the setup necessary to record and save a Web broadcast with audio (video can be used if your computer has the appropriate hardware)

      i. Create a folder called **<yourname>BalloonAdv** in preparation to save the Web broadcast

      ii. Set up the broadcast: Click **Slide Show**, point to **Online Broadcast**, and click **Record and Save a Broadcast**

      iii. Type **Come Fly With Us** in the Title text box, press **Tab** and type **Balloon Adventures online brochure** in the Description box, press **Tab**, and type **Glenn Bachmann** in the speaker box

      iv. Press **Tab** and type **Balloon Adventures** in the Copyright box, press **Tab** *twice* and type your e-mail address in the Email box

      v. Click the **Settings** button, click the **Browse** button in the File location section of the Broadcast Settings dialog box, navigate to the folder you created called **<yourname>BalloonAdv**, and click the **Select** button

      vi. Click the **Audio only** option button, and clear the **Display speaker notes with the presentation** check box, and click **OK**

   c. Click the **Record** button, follow the instructions for the Microphone check, and then click Start to begin recording the presentation. Click the mouse to display the slides at a comfortable rate. Speak into the microphone to record your comments along with the slide display. Click the mouse on the final black screen, and then click the **Continue** button to save the broadcast

5. Use Windows Explorer to locate your Web broadcast whose opening page is called **<yourname>BalloonAdventures.htm**. Double-click the file to display the opening Web broadcast presentation page (see Figure 8.25)

6. Print the opening page, which contains your e-mail address, to demonstrate that you have created the Web broadcast

7. Collaborate with two of your classmates to create a presentation review. Save review copies and distribute them to your classmates, who must make comments. Merge the review files with your original presentation

8. Use the Package to CD Wizard to package this presentation and place it on a disk

9. Close and save your presentation

FIGURE 8.25

Balloon Adventures opening screen

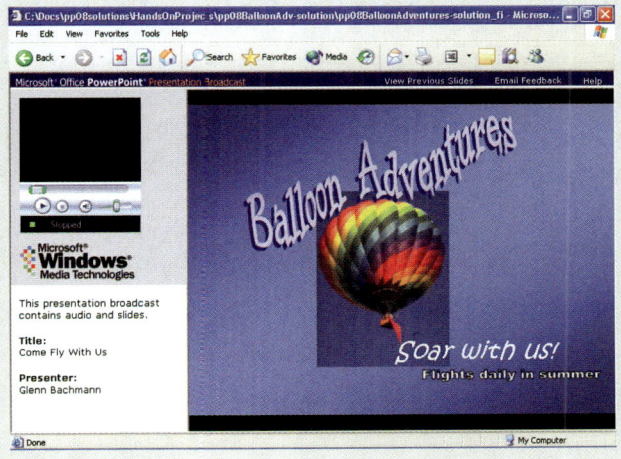

2. Brew HA-HA!

The Foothills Brewing Company was introduced in Chapter 5 where the assignment was to create a presentation that added various transitions and effects. The content of that file has been updated with some features from the remaining chapters and is now ready to be placed on the Web as a recorded Web broadcast. Additionally, the presentation needs to be packaged so that it can be transported and used as a speaker-led presentation at various gatherings where Foothills Brewing Company can peddle their wares.

1. Start PowerPoint and open **pp08BrewHAHA.ppt**

2. Save the presentation as **<yourname>BrewHAHA.ppt**

3. Review the slides to refamiliarize yourself with the content

4. Record and save a Web broadcast. You will need the ability to record sounds to successfully complete this broadcast

    a. Use the Notes pane to create a short script for each slide of the presentation. You will need to print this before recording

    b. Complete the setup necessary to record and save a Web broadcast with audio (video can be used if your computer has the appropriate hardware)

        i. Create a folder called **<yourname>FoothillsBrew** in preparation to save the Web broadcast

        ii. Set up the broadcast: Click **Slide Show**, point to **Online Broadcast**, and click **Record and Save a Broadcast**

        iii. Type **Foothills Brewing Company** in the Title text box, press **Tab** and type **Brew HA-HA Web broadcast and traveling brochure** in the description box, press **Tab**, and type your name in the Speaker box

        iv. Press **Tab** and type **Foothills Brewing Company** in the Copyright box, press **Tab** *twice* and type your e-mail address in the Email box

        v. Click the **Settings** button, click the **Browse** button in the File location section of the Broadcast Settings dialog box, navigate to the folder you created called **<yourname>FoothillsBrew**, and click the **Select** button

        vi. Click the **Audio only** option button, and clear the **Display speaker notes with the presentation** check box, and click **OK**

    c. Click the **Record** button, follow the instructions for the Microphone check, and then click Start to begin recording the presentation. Click the mouse to display the slides at a comfortable rate. Speak into the microphone to record your comments along with the slide display. Click the mouse on the final black screen, and then click the **Continue** button to save the broadcast

5. Use Windows Explorer to locate your Web broadcast whose opening page is called <yourname>BrewHAHA.htm. Double-click the file to display the opening Web broadcast presentation page (see Figure 8.26)

6. Print the opening page, which contains your e-mail address, to demonstrate that you have created the Web broadcast

7. Collaborate with two of your classmates to create a presentation review. Save review copies and distribute them to your classmates, who must make comments. Merge the review files with your original presentation

8. Use the Package to CD Wizard to package this presentation and place it on a disk

9. Save the presentation again

FIGURE 8.26

Brew HA-HA Web broadcast opening slide

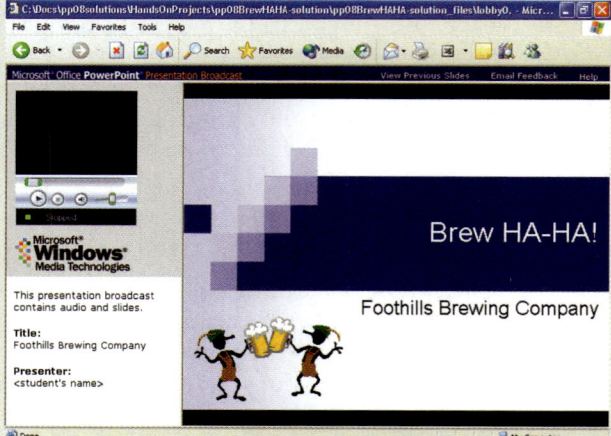

1. Culinary Arts Referrals

This online referral service is headed by Sarah Silverman and opened last year in Colorado to provide evaluation and ranking of culinary arts programs nationwide. The service is funded by subscription. Each evaluated school subscribes to the service and is listed in Culinary Arts reports. The schools are ranked based on the number of kitchens, faculty, and classes given each year. You will be using PowerPoint to create a Web broadcast for potential subscribers.

1. Start PowerPoint and open **pp08CulinaryArts.ppt**

2. Add **Prepared by: <yourname>** as a footer for every slide in the presentation

3. Use your favorite Web search engine to locate the *Atlantic Culinary Academy* and the *Cooking and Hospitality Institute of Chicago.* Document the number of kitchens, the number of faculty, the number of classes they offer, and whether or not they sell products

4. On slide 3 add the names and URLs for the cooking schools you located on the Web

5. Add the kitchen data you researched to the table on slide 4

6. Add the faculty data you located to the table on slide 5

7. Update the graph on slide 6 with the data about the number of classes offered

8. Update slide 7 with your research on products

9. On slide 8, write a short referral to a particular school based on an analysis of your research

10. Save the presentation as **<yourname>CulinaryArts.ppt**

11. Record and save a Web broadcast. You will need the ability to record sounds to successfully complete this broadcast

    a. Use the Notes pane to create a short script for each slide of the presentation. You will need to print this before recording

    b. Complete the setup necessary to record and save a Web broadcast with audio (video can be used if your computer has the appropriate hardware)

    i. Create a folder called **<yourname>CulinaryArts** in preparation to save the Web broadcast

    ii. Set up the broadcast: Click **Slide Show**, point to **Online Broadcast**, and click **Record and Save a Broadcast**

    iii. Type **Evaluating Culinary Arts Education** in the Title text box, press **Tab** twice and type **Sarah Silverman** in the Speaker box

    iv. Press **Tab** and type **Culinary Arts Referrals** in the Copyright box, press **Tab** twice and type your e-mail address in the Email box

    v. Click the **Settings** button, click the **Browse** button in the File location section of the Broadcast Settings dialog box, navigate to the folder you created called **<yourname>CulinaryArts**, and click the **Select** button

    vi. Click the **Audio only** option button, and clear the **Display speaker notes with the presentation** check box, and click **OK**

    c. Click the **Record** button, follow the instructions for the Microphone check, and then click Start to begin recording the presentation. Click the mouse to display the slides at a comfortable rate. Speak into the microphone to record your comments along with the slide display. Click the mouse on the final black screen, and then click the **Continue** button to save the broadcast

12. Use Windows Explorer to locate your Web broadcast whose opening page is called **<yourname>CulinaryArts.htm**. Double-click the file to display the opening Web broadcast presentation page

13. Print the opening page, which contains your e-mail address, to demonstrate that you have created the Web broadcast

14. Collaborate with two of your classmates to create a presentation review. Save review copies and distribute them to your classmates, who must make comments. Merge the review files with your original presentation

15. Close and save your presentation

2. Internet2

Internet2 is a consortium of over 200 universities that are working with industry and government in search of revolutionary new possibilities for the Internet. As a public relations officer with this non-profit organization, your job is to promote Internet2 in various academic and commercial settings. Next summer, representatives from Internet2 will attend a large academic computing conference. You have been assigned to create an informational CD for the conference that will be distributed to those who would like to know more about the project.

1. Start PowerPoint and open **pp08Internet2.ppt**, and save it as **<yourname>Internet2.ppt**

2. Add **Prepared by: <yourname>** as a footer for the entire presentation (see Figure 8.27)

3. Use your favorite Web search engine to locate the Internet2 homepage. Enter the Web address on slides 5 and 6 in the spaces provided and then hyperlink the addresses to the home page

4. In the *About Us* section of the Internet2 Web site, find the three stated goals of the organization. Additionally, find five universities that are members of Internet2

5. On slide 2, list the three goals of Internet2

6. On slide 4, list five participating universities, linking the names of the universities to their respective home pages

7. At the bottom of slide 6, create a textbox hyperlinked to the *About Us* section of the Web site: Use a white **Fill** with **No Line**, 25 point Arial. Type the text **Click here for more information**

8. Recipients of the informational CD may not have access to PowerPoint, so you must package the presentation using the **Package for CD** feature found on the File menu

   a. Create a folder entitled **Internet2InfoCD**

   b. In PowerPoint, click **File**, and then click **Package for CD**

   c. In the dialog box that appears, name the CD **Internet2Info**

   d. Because you may not have access to a CD burner, click **Copy to Folder** and then click **Browse**. Navigate to the **Internet2InfoCD** folder that you just created and click **OK**

   e. Click **Close**

9. Close PowerPoint and save your presentation

F I G U R E 8.27

Internet2 opening screen

Holistic Health Services

Holistic Health Services is an organization that markets alternative health products through local vendors around the world. Its products include herbal and medicinal remedies, and alternative health books. Terri Lane, the director of Sales, has asked you to prepare a PowerPoint presentation for the Quarterly Sales Meeting. Terri is pleased with the improvement in this quarter's results. She believes the success is due in part to a better allocation of her sales reps' time. Travel is being reduced by holding online meetings, and support staffs have been employed to complete much of the paperwork, thereby freeing up the sales reps to focus on clients.

1. Start PowerPoint and open **pp08HolisticHealth.ppt**

2. Save the presentation as **<yourname>HolisticHealth.ppt**

3. Review the slides to familiarize yourself with their content

4. Record and save a Web broadcast. You will need the ability to record sounds to successfully complete this broadcast

   a. Use the Notes pane to create a short script for each slide of the presentation. You will need to print this before recording

   b. Complete the setup necessary to record and save a Web broadcast with audio (video can be used if your computer has the appropriate hardware)

      i. Create a folder called **<yourname>HolisticHealth** in preparation to save the Web broadcast

      ii. Set up the broadcast: Click **Slide Show**, point to **Online Broadcast**, and click **Record and Save a Broadcast**

      iii. Type **Holistic Health Sales Report** in the Title text box, press **Tab** and type **U.S. 4th to 3rd Quarter Comparison**, press **Tab**, and type **Terri Lane** in the Speaker text box

      iv. Press **Tab** and type **Holistic Health Services**, press **Tab** *twice* and type your e-mail address in the Email box

      v. Click the **Settings** button, click the **Browse** button in the File location section of the Broadcast Settings dialog box, navi-

gate to the folder you created called **<yourname>HolisticHealth**, and click the **Select** button

      vi. Click the **Audio only** option button, and clear the **Display speaker notes with the presentation** check box, and click **OK**

   c. Click the **Record** button, and then click the mouse to display the slides at a comfortable rate. Speak into the microphone to record your comments along with the slide display, click the mouse on the final, black screen, and click the **Continue** button to save the broadcast

5. Use Windows Explorer to locate your Web broadcast whose opening page is called **<yourname>HolisticHealth.htm**. Double-click **<yourname>HolisticHealth.htm** to display the opening Web broadcast presentation page (see Figure 8.28)

6. Print the opening page, which contains your e-mail address, to demonstrate that you have created the Web broadcast

7. Collaborate with two of your classmates to create a presentation review. Save review copies and distribute them to your classmates, who must make comments. Merge the review files with your original presentation

8. Use the Package to CD Wizard to package this presentation and place it on a CD

9. Close and save your presentation

FIGURE 8.28

Holistic Health opening screen

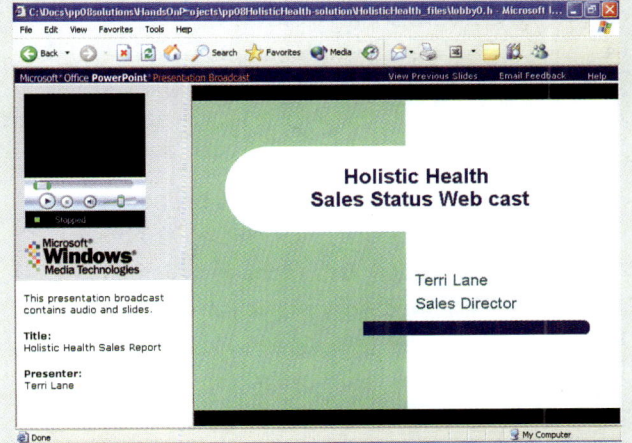

LEVEL THREE

CHAPTER EIGHT

running project

Montgomery-Wellish Foods, Inc.: Presentation Skills

In Chapter 4, you developed a slide show covering the important skills a trainee needs to acquire in order to present effectively. Daniel Wellish believes presentation skills are the single most important attribute a trainee can learn. Managers, by nature, are people-oriented and must use their skills not just to prepare reports but to inspire, inform, and persuade. To the degree they can communicate clearly and cogently, they will be successful. Daniel has asked you to prepare a PowerPoint presentation outlining the skills necessary for successful Web broadcasts to the new trainees. (The custom animations are absent in this version of the presentation.)

1. Start PowerPoint and open **pp08MWFWebPresentation.ppt**
2. Save the presentation as **<yourname>WebPresentation.ppt**
3. Review the slides to familiarize yourself with their content
4. Record and save a Web broadcast. You will need the ability to record sounds to successfully complete this broadcast
   a. Use the Notes pane to create a short script for each slide of the presentation. Print this before recording your Web broadcast
   b. Complete the setup necessary to record and save a Web broadcast with audio (video can be used if your computer has the appropriate hardware)
      i. Create a folder called **<yourname>MWF** in preparation to save the Web broadcast
      ii. Set up the broadcast: Click **Slide Show**, point to **Online Broadcast**, and click **Record and Save a Broadcast**
      iii. Type **Web Broadcasting Skills** in the Title text box, press **Tab** and type **How to be an Effective Presenter**, press **Tab**, and type **Daniel Wellish** in the Speaker text box
      iv. Press **Tab** and type **Montgomery-Wellish Foods**, press **Tab** *twice* and type your e-mail address in the Email box
      v. Click the **Settings** button, click the **Browse** button in the File location section of the Broadcast Settings dialog box, navigate to the folder you created called **<yourname>MWF**, and click the **Select** button
      vi. Click the **Audio only** option button, and clear the **Display speaker notes with the presentation** check box, and click **OK**
   c. Click the **Record** button and then click the mouse to display the slides at a comfortable rate. Speak into the microphone to record your comments along with the slide display. Click the mouse on the final black screen, and then click the **Continue** button to save the broadcast
5. Use Windows Explorer to locate your Web broadcast whose opening page is called **<yourname>MWFWebPresentation.htm**. Double-click the file **<yourname>MWFWebPresentation.htm** to display the opening Web broadcast presentation page
6. Print the opening page, which contains your e-mail address, to demonstrate that you have created the Web broadcast
7. Collaborate with two of your classmates to create a presentation review. Save review copies and distribute them to your classmates, who must make comments. Merge the review files with your original presentation
8. Use the Package for CD Wizard to package this presentation and place it on a disk. Create a backup
9. Close and save your presentation

1. Taking Your Show on the Road

Discuss the importance of being able to take your PowerPoint show on the road. Consider not being able to have your own laptop or desktop system available when you need to make an important presentation. What advantages does Package for CD have that PowerPoint viewer doesn't? Does this have a true impact on taking your show on the road?

2. Sharing Presentations

Identify what a team requires in order to play a presentation simultaneously at diverse locations. What is necessary for proper functionality and synchronization of the presentation? What control does the developer of the presentation have over the distribution of the presentation?

know?

did you

Picasso *could draw before he could walk and his first word was the Spanish word for pencil.*

the *largest statue in the world is Mount Rushmore, the heads of four U.S. presidents carved into the Black Hills near Keystone. The heads are 18 m (60 ft) tall.*

to *win a gold disc, an album needs to sell 100,000 copies in Britain and 500,000 in the United States.*

the *can opener was invented 48 years after cans were introduced.*

traffic *jams of New York, San Francisco, and Paris are well known—beaten only by those in Seattle, where a driver annually spends 59 hours a year stuck in traffic.*

75 *percent of wild birds die before they are six months old.*

Appendix Objectives

- Use IF . . . THEN statements in a mail merge to locate specific records for a form letter
- Analyze Access queries and records with an Excel spreadsheet
- Export an Access query to a Word document
- Copy the contents of an Access query and paste the results in a PowerPoint presentation
- Create a Pivot Table in Excel and copy results into a Word document
- Establish an AutoFilter in Excel and link results to an Access database
- Use the Goal Seek function in Excel and copy results to a Word document

University of Denver Lacrosse Team Donors

The coaching staff at the University of Denver has started their fund-raising season. Abby Burbank, the head women's lacrosse coach, has kept busy during the season contacting people who have contributed to her program in the past—alumnae, fans, parents, and others. She has created a main document to send to those past contributors trying to solicit continued support for this year. Abby also realizes that she needs to identify the alumnae in a letter to include a special note just for them. Using data stored in a Microsoft Access database, she will need to merge that data source with a preformatted Microsoft Word document in order to create a mail merge to send the letters. Luckily Abby has just learned how to use the IF . . . THEN . . . ELSE function with mail merge in order to specify criteria for her letters to the alumnae.

Once the letters have been completed, Coach Burbank wants to make some calculations on the donations her lacrosse program has received. Since she is more familiar with using Excel for this function, Abby will create a query of the donations with specific records in Access and analyze those data in an Excel spreadsheet.

In addition to using Excel for calculations, Abby will need to use similar data from an Access database for use in a Word document for future documentation. Her task with these data will be to export the donor information data from Access to a PowerPoint presentation she will make to the athletics administration. At the end of her presentation, Abby knows that she will have to submit a report of the donor information. Coach Burbank will create a Pivot Table to organize, summarize, and analyze the data and then link that information to a Word document to be sent to the athletics director.

Since Abby has a long list of possible donors in an Excel spreadsheet, she will want to transfer those data to an Access database for further analysis. She will use the AutoFilter function to select out those individuals who have already made a donation this year and copy that information into a new database. Once that process is complete, the last task that Abby needs to fulfill with her fund-raising is for her team to sell T-shirts. In order to meet her goal of $10,000, Abby will use the Goal Seek function in Excel to calculate how many T-shirts she and her team will have to sell if the selling price is $8.00 per shirt.

In the appendix entitled "Integration I," you learned that *linking* and *embedding* a file are two very different processes, each providing a different function. Linking an object is beneficial when you need to keep data in your documents up-to-date by creating a link to the source file. Embedding objects is a good idea when you don't need to maintain a link but want to have the ability to edit the object within your document. However, with *static copying*, the data that you insert become an integral part of the receiving document and retain no link or connection with the document or program from which they came.

This appendix describes the advanced functions of integrating Microsoft Office applications with one another. More specifically, you will focus much of your attention on Microsoft Office Access 2003 and learn the different ways of exchanging data with the separate Office applications. You will use the link, embed, and static copy functions and a few built-in tools to move data from one application to another with the ability to edit the data within the receiving document.

Of all the Office applications, Access seems to be the one that most people are intimidated with using. However, you will see throughout the practice tasks that the overall effect of sharing data with Word, Excel, PowerPoint, and Access is rather simple.

SESSION 1.1 ADVANCED MAIL MERGE WITH WORD AND ACCESS

In appendix Integration I, you learned how to use the basic functions of the Mail Merge Wizard to create form letters, mailing labels, envelopes, and directories, as well as mass e-mail and fax distributions. You learned that to complete the basic process, you had to

- Open or create a main document
- Open or create a data source with individual recipient information
- Add or customize merge fields in the main document
- Merge data from the data source into the main document to create a new, merged document

Word offers a number of preset *merge fields* you can insert by pointing and clicking. You can further personalize your main document by adding address or database fields. Here are some examples of using fields to control how Word merges data:

- ASK and FILLIN fields display a prompt as Word merges each data record with the main document. Your response is printed in the specific form letter, contract, or other merged document resulting from the data record
- IF (If . . . Then . . . Else . . .) fields print information only if a condition you have specified is met. For example, you can use an IF field to locate specific data that fit a particular criterion that you are able to define within the Mail Merge Wizard
- SET (Set Bookmark) fields allow you to assign text, a number, or other information to a bookmark. You can use the information multiple times in the merged documents. If the information changes, then you can edit the SET field once rather than searching through the main document and changing each occurrence

In addition to merge fields, you can insert fields into the main document to customize your mail merge documents even more. In this lesson, you'll learn how to insert the most commonly used fields: the IF–THEN–ELSE statement. An IF–THEN–ELSE field compares the information in the data source to a value you specify and inserts one piece of text if the comparison is true and another piece of text if the comparison is false. Mass-producing letters has always been an important application of word processing and a database. Mail merging has usually meant creating printed material such as letters or invoices, but recently, users have started to use mass-customized e-mails as well.

Microsoft has an obvious advantage with this kind of application, since Word and Access are bundled together with the Microsoft Office 2003 Professional Suite. Word can import native Access data automatically, or you can choose a selection of merge data for export within Access. You also can restrict the fields available for inclusion in mail merge documents once the process begins.

Merging is clearly a straightforward activity using Access, but it's worth noting that it's Word, not Access, that is doing virtually all the work.

---

task reference — Inserting Merge Fields into a Word Document

- Click **View**, click **Toolbars**
- Select **Mail Merge**
- Click **Insert Merge Fields** icon
- Insert **Merge Fields**

Because you had already entered the "Address" («AddressBlock») and "Greeting" («GreetingLine») tag, you do not have to use the Mail Merge Wizard for this task. Instead, you will rely on the Mail Merge Taskbar to assist with inserting other fields from the database and creating a query using the IF–THEN–ELSE function to develop a customized letter.

Inserting Merge Fields

1. Open Microsoft Office Word 2003, click **File**, and then click **Open**. In the Open Document window pane, select the file **int02Merge.doc**. (Click **yes** if asked to open the document with a SQL command)

2. In Microsoft Word, make sure that the Mail Merge toolbar is active. To do this, click **View**, select **Toolbars**. **Mail Merge** should have a check next to it. If not, select **Mail Merge**

3. Place your insertion pointer between "**Your**" and "**donation**" in the second sentence of the first paragraph. You are ready to insert another field here

4. Click the **View Merged Data** button if the letter displays field values rather than field tags (GreetingLine, for example). Click the **Insert Merge Fields** icon (see Figure 1.1) on the Mail Merge toolbar. The Insert Merge Field dialog box appears

FIGURE 1.1

Insert Merge Fields button

Insert Merge Fields button —

5. Select **PledgeAmount** from the list of fields (see Figure 1.2), click the **Insert** button, and click **Close**

6. The «PledgeAmount» tag appears. Add a **space** between «PledgeAmount» and "donation." Place the "**$**" symbol in front of the «PledgeAmount» tag (see Figure 1.3)

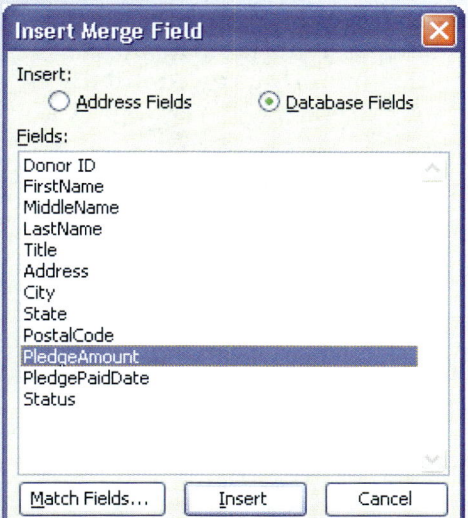

List of fields available
from the attached
database

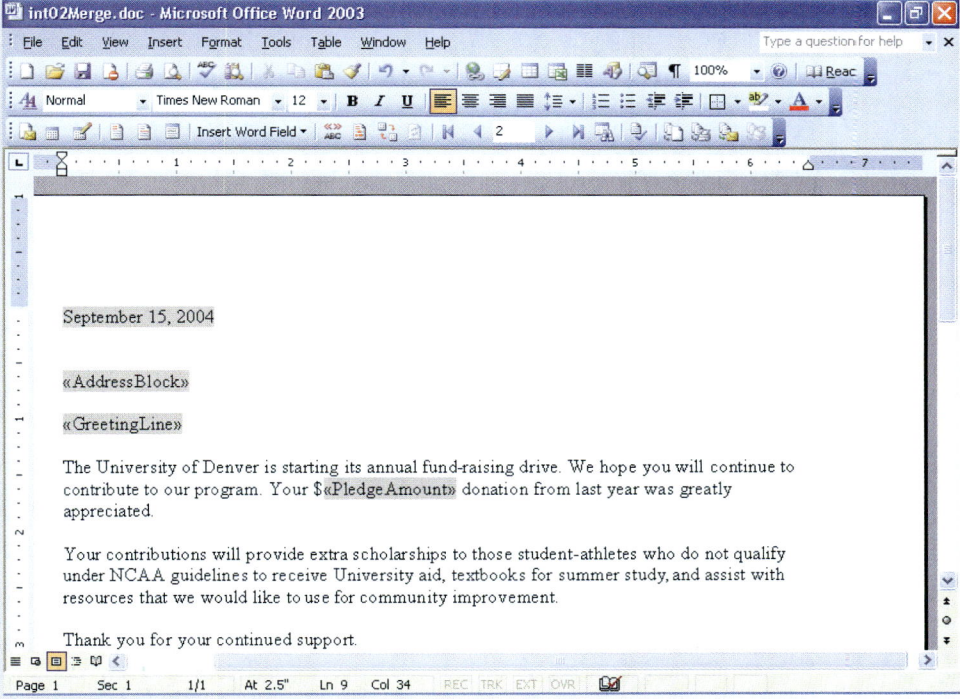

F I G U R E   1.3

PledgeAmount field in
place

7. Place your insertion point at the beginning of the last paragraph in front
of "Thank you…"

8. Click the **Insert Word Field** button on the Mail Merge toolbar. A
drop-down menu appears, listing the word field choices. Click
If . . . Then . . . Else. You will now need to define some criteria for the
query

9. In the Field name box, click the Field name list arrow, scroll the list to
the bottom, and click **Status.** Set the Comparison box to **Equal to,** and
in the Compare to box, type in **Alumna**

10. In the **Insert this text** box, type in **"As an Alumna of the Women's Lacrosse team, you know just how important fund-raising is to our overall development and success. Anything that you can contribute is greatly appreciated."** (See Figure 1.4)

F I G U R E   1.4

Insert Word Field criteria

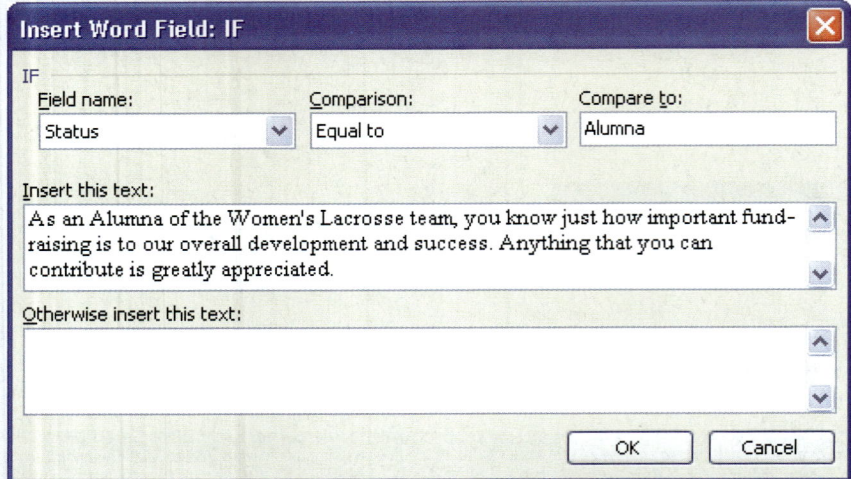

11. Click **OK**

12. Click the **View Merged Data** button on the Mail Merge toolbar (see Figure 1.5)

F I G U R E   1.5

View Merged Data button

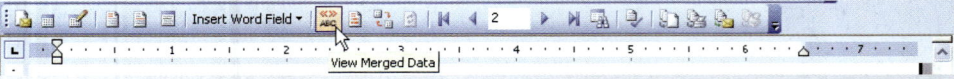

13. Click the **Next Record** button several times to view the different records from the data source (see Figure 1.6)

F I G U R E   1.6

Next Record button

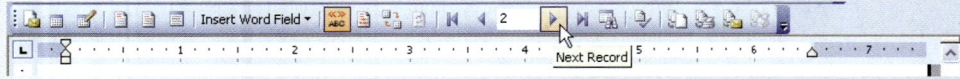

14. Click the **Merge to New Document** button on the Mail Merge toolbar. The Merge to New Document dialog box appears (see Figure 1.7)

F I G U R E   1.7

Merge to New Document

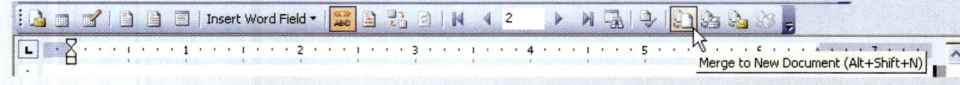

15. Make sure **All** is selected and click **OK**

16. Word merges the main document and the Microsoft Access database information into a new document (see Figure 1.8)

17. Click **File**, click **Close**, and click **No** to close the merged letters without saving them

18. Click **File**, click **Save As**, type **<yourname>MergeComplete** in the File name box, and click **Save**

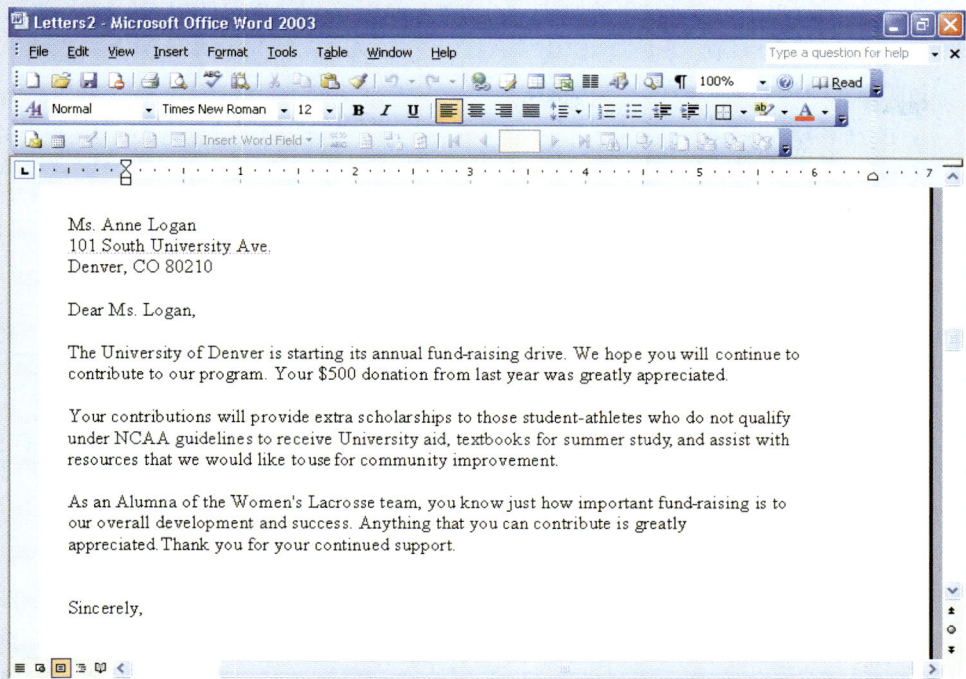

19. Select **File** from the menu bar and click **Exit**

Word enables you to use data you've entered and organized in other programs—such as Microsoft Access, Microsoft Excel, other database programs, or compatible e-mail utilities—to serve as the source for your mail merge.

making the grade

SESSION 1.1

1. Must you use the Mail Merge Wizard to insert criteria for additional fields in a form letter?

2. What is the difference between Insert Merge Fields and Insert Word Field?

3. What mail merge feature allows you to view different records from the data source in your mail merge main document?

SESSION 1.2 ANALYZING ACCESS RECORDS WITH EXCEL

Microsoft Office Access 2003 is capable of performing calculations on groups of records; however, that function is best suited for Microsoft Office Excel 2003. An Excel spreadsheet is similar to an Access datasheet in many ways; however, when you want to easily perform calculations on data, Excel would be your better solution. Access, on the other hand, is better suited for creating and storing data in tables, forms, reports, and queries. In this session, you will understand the need to use both applications and how they can share informational resources in analyzing records from Access with Excel.

<table>
<tr><td>**task** reference</td><td>Analyzing Records with Access and Excel</td></tr>
</table>

- Open the database
- Click the **Queries** tab
- Click a query
- Click **Tools**
- Point to **Office Links**
- Click **Analyze It with Microsoft Office Excel**

Analyzing records with Access and Excel

1. Click **File** from the Access menu bar, then select **Open**, select the database **int02MergeData.mdb**

2. Click the **Queries** tab and double-click **qryAmountReceived**

FIGURE 1.9

Amount received query

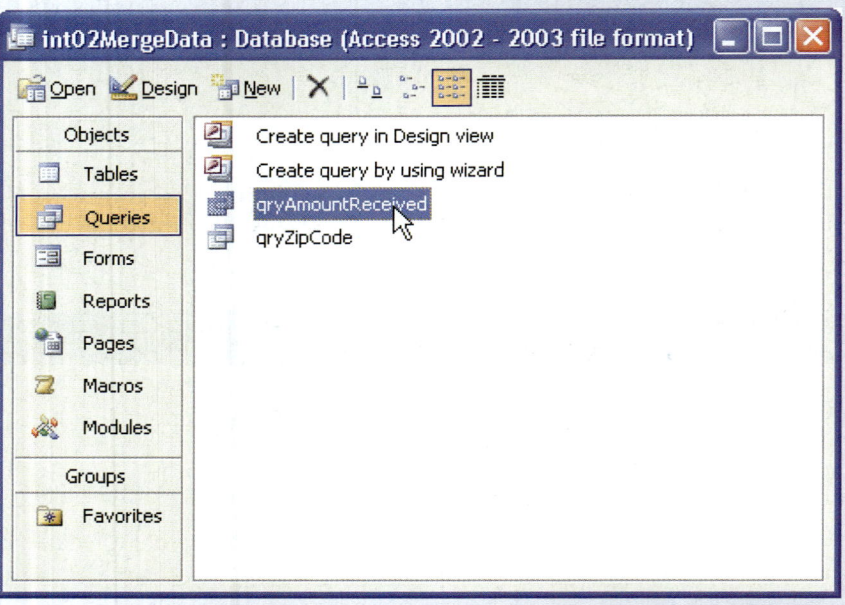

3. Click **Tools** on the menu bar, point to **Office Links**, and click **Analyze It with Microsoft Office Excel** (see Figure 1.10)

4. Wait a few seconds while Access opens Excel with the queried data, and then click the **Microsoft Office Excel** button in the Taskbar

5. Click cell **I8**, type **=SUM(I2:I7)**, and press **Enter**. You will see the total amount received from all donors

6. Click **File** from the Excel menu bar and click **Exit**. There is no need to save your results. (Leave Access running for work in the next session)

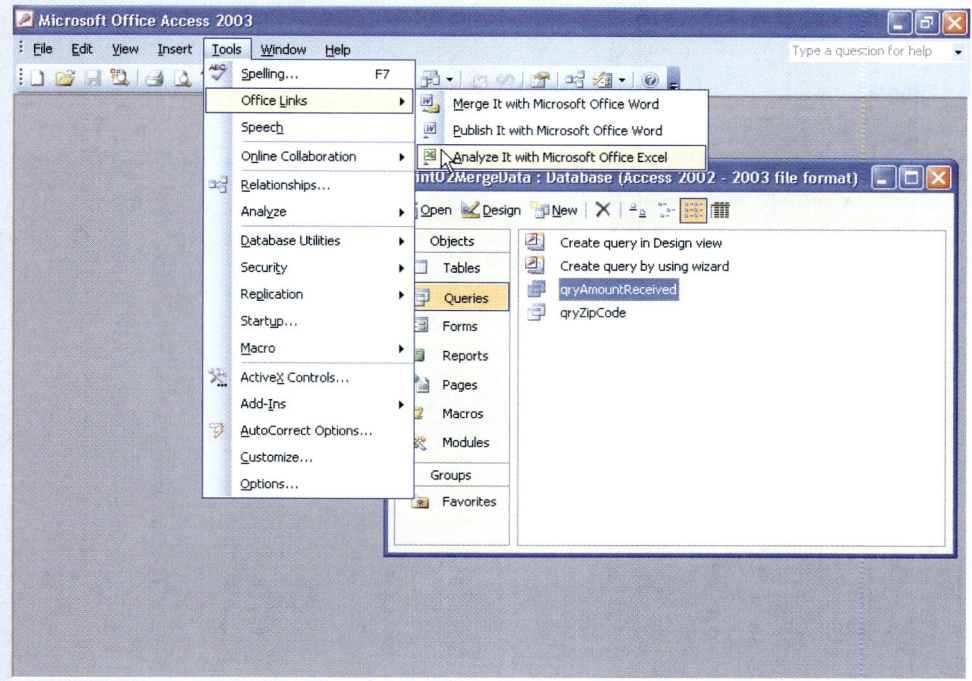

FIGURE 1.10

Analyze with Excel

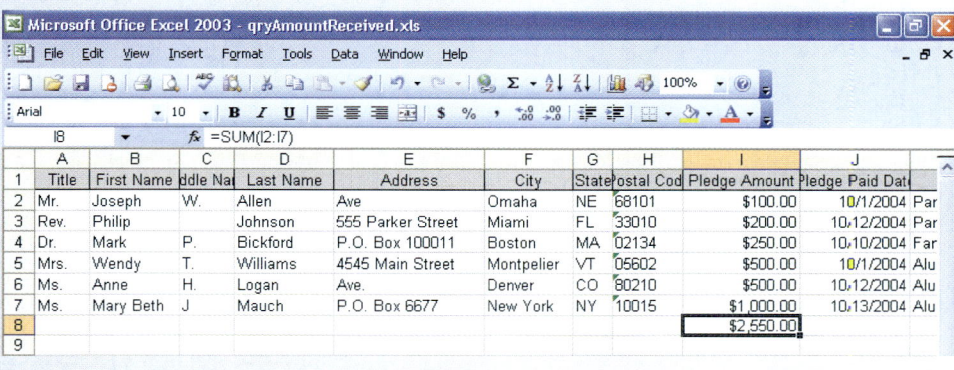

FIGURE 1.11

Excel displaying data from an Access query

SESSION 1.2

making the grade

1. What are the steps involved in analyzing data from Access using Excel?

2. What is the function in Access that allows you to share data with Excel?

SESSION 1.3 EXPORTING AN ACCESS QUERY TO WORD

You are able to use almost the same process exporting records from an Access table or query to Word that you used in Session 1.2 with Access and Excel. You can transfer records by using the simple copy and paste commands or by using the Publish It with Microsoft Office Word command in Access. When records are transferred from Access to Word, they are formatted with the document as a Word document.

task reference Exporting an Access Query to Word

- Open the database
- Click the **Queries** tab
- Click the query you want to export
- Click **Tools**
- Point to **Office Links**
- Click **Publish It with Microsoft Office Word**

Exporting an Access query to Word

1. Ensure the int02MergeData database is still open
2. Click the **Queries** tab and click **qryZipCode** (see Figure 1.12)

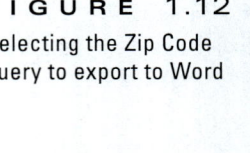

FIGURE 1.12

Selecting the Zip Code query to export to Word

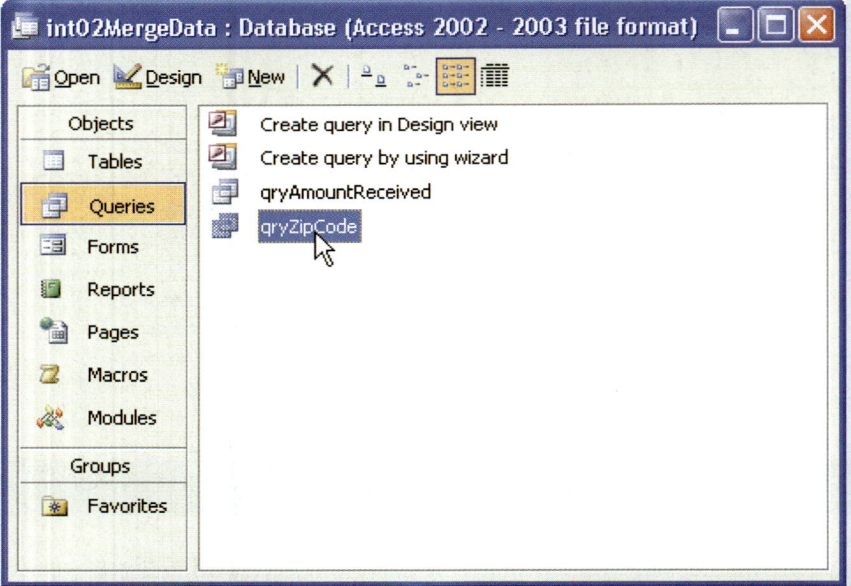

3. Click **Tools**, point to **Office Links**, and click **Publish It with Microsoft Office Word**
4. Wait a few seconds while Access opens Word with the queried data
5. You may have to make some minor adjustments to the margins to allow all the data to fit your screen
6. Click **File** from the Word menu bar and click **Exit**. There is no need to save your results. (Leave Access running)

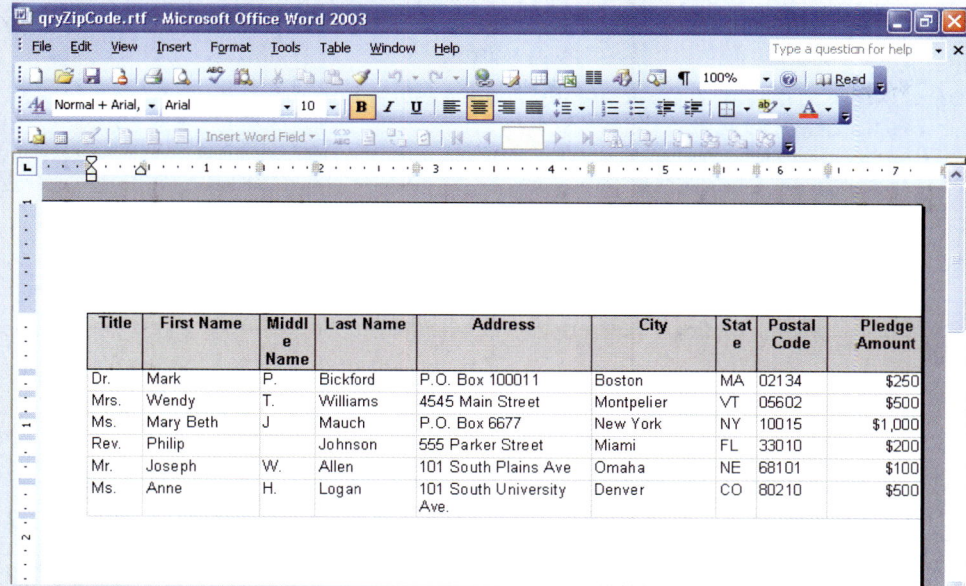

FIGURE 1.13
A Word document with imported Access data

making *the grade*

1. What are the steps involved in exporting a query from Access into Word?

2. What is the function in Access that allows you to share data with Word?

SESSION 1.4 EXPORTING ACCESS RECORDS TO POWERPOINT

In this session you will learn how to copy and paste an Access query into a PowerPoint presentation. You will not use the same methods used in the previous sessions; rather you will learn to use the static copy and paste functions within Access and PowerPoint.

task reference — Exporting Records with Access and PowerPoint

- Open the database
- Open a PowerPoint presentation
- Select all the records from a database table
- Paste records into the PowerPoint slide

Pasting records from Access to PowerPoint

1. Ensure int02MergeData is still open in Access

2. Launch PowerPoint, click **File** from the PowerPoint menu bar, click **Open**, and locate the file **int02Contributors.ppt**

3. In Access, click the **Queries** tab, if necessary, and double-click **qryAmountReceived**

4. Press **Ctrl+A** to select all the records in this query. Then press **Ctrl+C** to copy that selection to the Clipboard

5. Switch to **PowerPoint**, position the insertion pointer inside slide number **4**

6. Press **Ctrl+V**, (or click **Edit** and select **Paste**) to paste the copied query

7. Click the table object and use the selection handles to make adjustments and to arrange the copied data onto the slide (see Figure 1.14)

FIGURE 1.14

PowerPoint and
Access data

Contributions to date...

Title	First Name	Middle Name	Last Name	Address	City	State	Postal Code	Pledge Amount	Pledge Paid Date	Status
Mr.	Joseph	W.	Allen	101 South Plains Ave	Omaha	NE	68101	$100.00	10/1/2004	Parent
Rev.	Philip		Johnson	555 Parker Street	Miami	FL	33010	$200.00	10/12/2004	Parent
Dr.	Mark	P.	Bickford	P.O. Box 100011	Boston	MA	02134	$250.00	10/10/2004	Fan
Mrs.	Wendy	T.	Williams	4545 Main Street	Montpelier	VT	05602	$500.00	10/1/2004	Alumna
Ms.	Anne	H.	Logan	101 South University Ave.	Denver	CO	80210	$500.00	10/12/2004	Alumna
Ms.	Mary Beth	J	Mauch	P.O. Box 6677	New York	NY	10015	$1,000.00	10/13/2004	Alumna

8. Select **File** from the Excel menu bar and click **Exit**. There is no need to save your results

9. Close the query and close Microsoft Office Access

SESSION 1.4

making *the grade*

1. What are the steps involved in exporting a query from Access into a PowerPoint presentation?

2. What are the functions in Access that allow you to share data with a PowerPoint presentation?

SESSION 1.5 LINKING AN EXCEL PIVOT TABLE TO A WORD DOCUMENT

Creating a Pivot Table in Excel is usually the best way to organize, summarize, and analyze list data. A *Pivot Table* is an organization and analysis tool that displays the fields and records in your list in new format for further analysis. Pivot Tables are easy to create in Excel by using a Wizard on the Data menu. The Wizard will ask you which fields you want to include in the Pivot Table, how you want your Pivot Table organized, and which calculations your Pivot Table should perform. Using the PivotTable Wizard also will allow you to create Pivot Charts, which will not be covered in this session.

Why organize list data into a Pivot Table? There are three key reasons for organizing data into a Pivot Table:

- To summarize the data contained in a lengthy list into a compact format
- To find relationships within the data that are otherwise hard to see because of the amount of detail
- To organize the data into a format that's easy to chart

In this session, you will create a Pivot Table first and then link that element to a Microsoft Word document.

Creating a Pivot Table and placing it on the Clipboard

1. Launch Microsoft Office Word, click **File** on the menu bar, click **Open**, locate and click the file **int02PivotTable.doc**, and click the **Open** button to open the document

2. Launch Microsoft Office Excel, click **File** on the menu bar, click **Open**, locate and click the file **int02PivotTableData.xls**, and click the **Open** button to open the workbook

3. If necessary, click the **Current Donors** worksheet tab to display that worksheet. Click and drag the cell range **A3:I13** (see Figure 1.15)

4. Click **Data** on the menu bar and then click **PivotTable and PivotChart Report**. Excel opens the first of three dialog boxes to help you create a Pivot Table (see Figure 1.16)

5. Click the **Microsoft Office Excel list or database** option button, if it is not already selected, and click **Next**

6. PivotTable step 2 appears and indicates the Excel cell range you selected for the Pivot Table. Because this is correct (see Figure 1.17), click **Next** to proceed to the last Pivot Table step

7. Click, if necessary, the **New worksheet** option button in the step 3 dialog box, and then click **Finish**

8. A new worksheet appears with the initial layout of your PivotTable (see Figure 1.18)

9. Drag the **Region** field button from the PivotTable Field List to the **Drop Row Fields Here** area of the PivotTable

10. Drag the **Status** field button from the PivotTable Field List to the **Drop Column Fields Here** area of the PivotTable

F I G U R E   1.15

Selecting Excel data

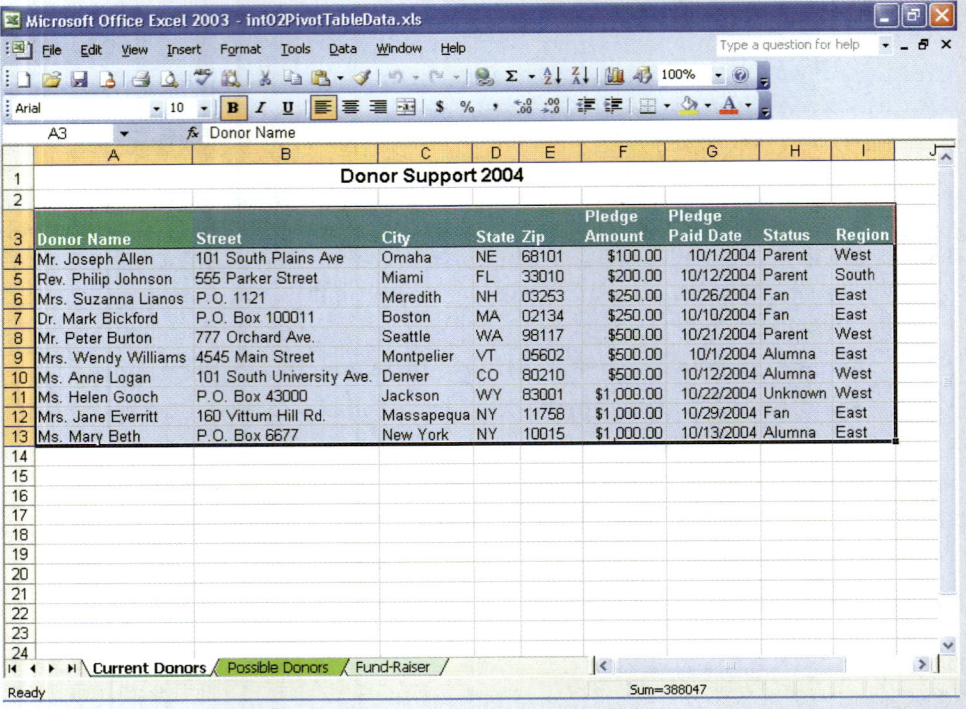

F I G U R E   1.16

Pivot Table Wizard step 1

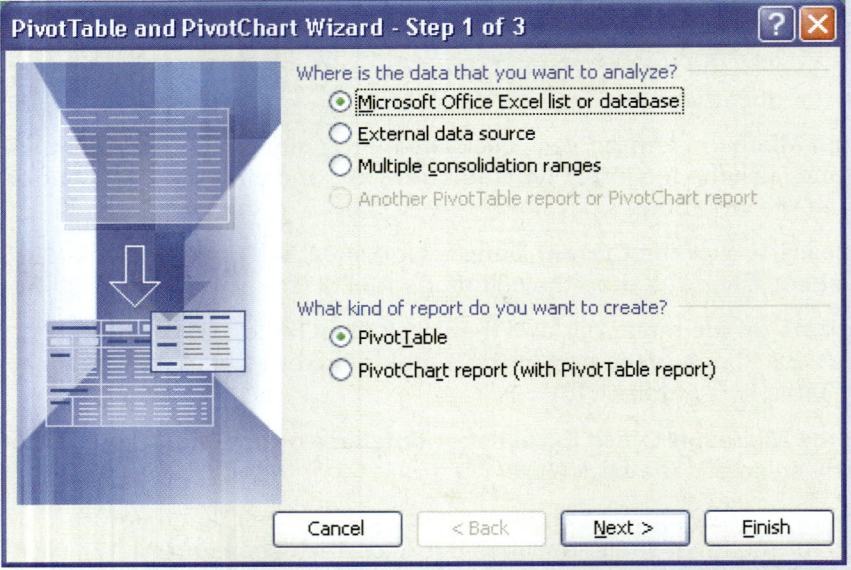

11. Drag the **Pledge Amount** field button from the PivotTable Field List to the **Drop Data Items Here** area of the PivotTable (see Figure 1.19)

12. Format the Pledge Amount field: Click the **PivotTable** button in the PivotTable toolbar, click **Field Settings**, the **Number** button on the Pivot Table Field dialog box, click **Currency** in the Category list, click **OK** to close the Format Cells dialog box, and click **OK** to close the PivotTable Field dialog box. Excel formats the data entries

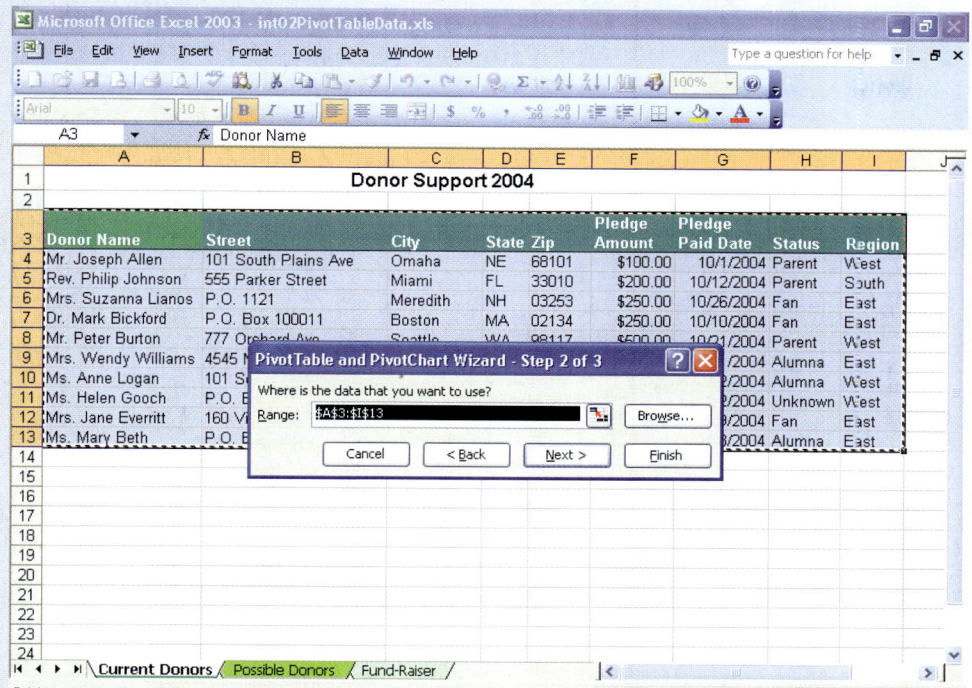

FIGURE   1.17
Pivot Table Wizard step 2

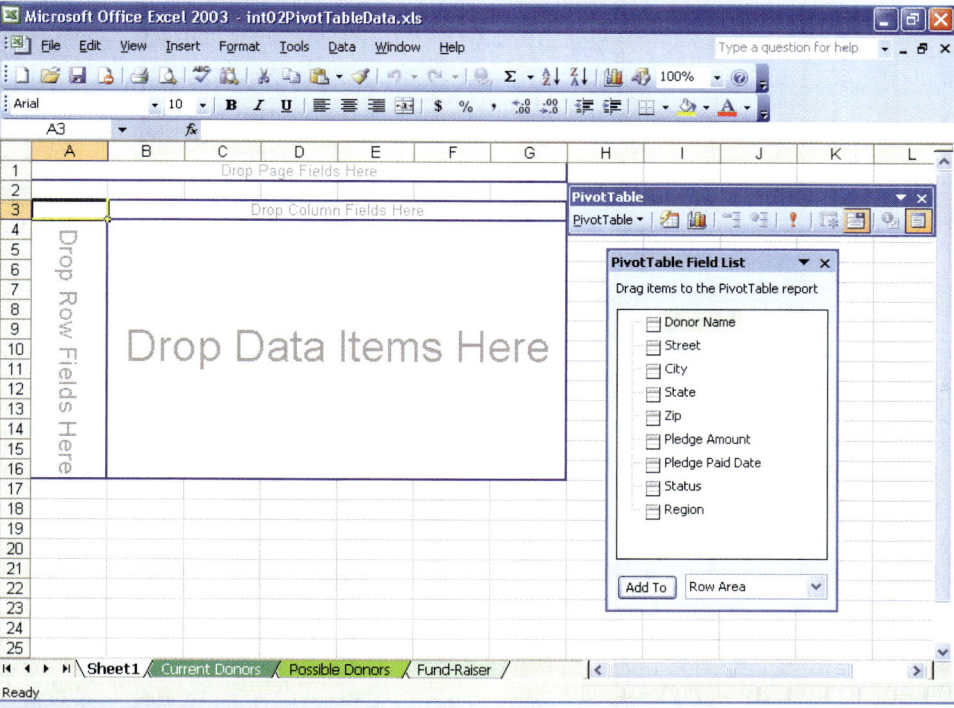

FIGURE   1.18
Pivot Table shell

13. Right-click any data value in the Pivot Table, point to **Select**, and click
Entire Table (see Figure 1.20)

14. Click **Edit** on the menu bar and click Copy. Excel copies the Pivot Table
to the Clipboard

FIGURE 1.19

Pivot Table with Pledge
Amount in the data area

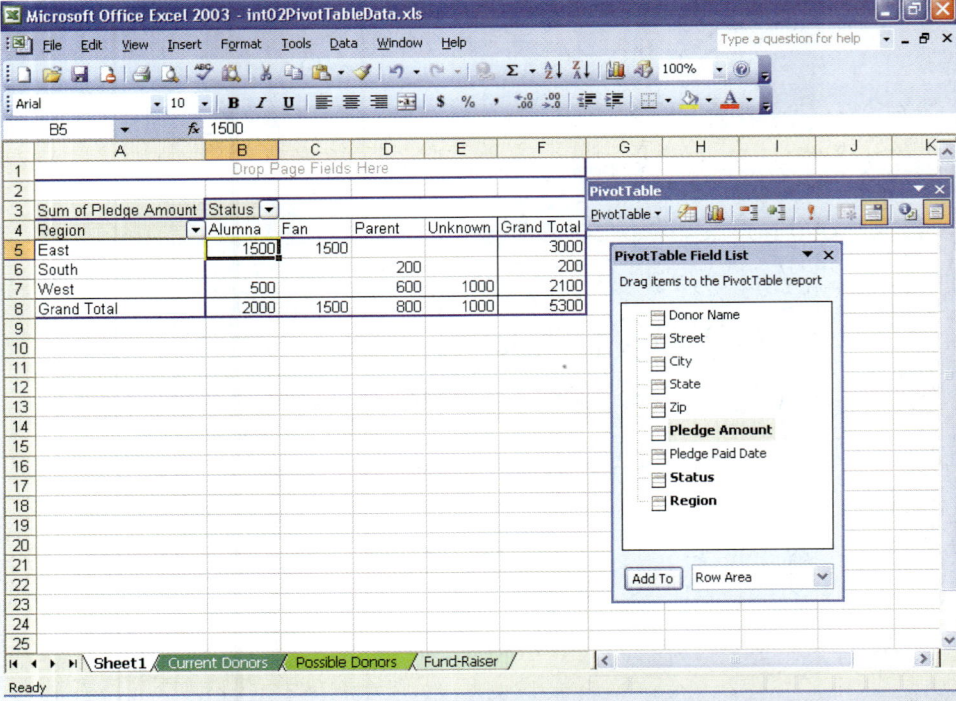

FIGURE 1.20

Selecting the Pivot Table
before pasting it into a
Word document

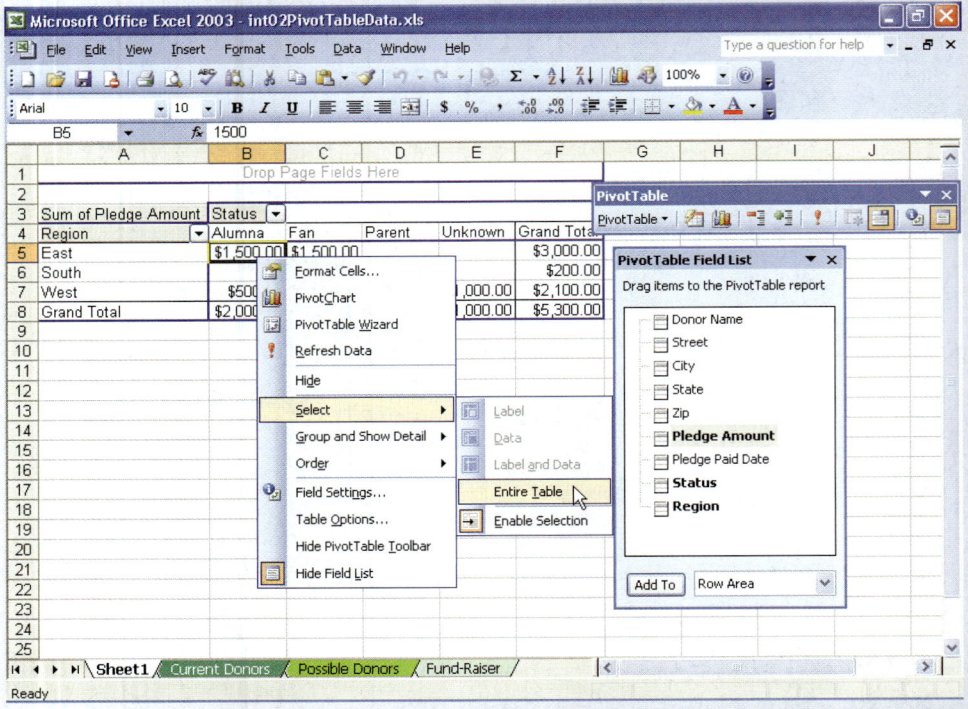

Now you are ready to copy the Pivot Table from the Clipboard to Word. Execute the following steps.

Pasting a Pivot Table from the Clipboard into a Word document

1. Click the Taskbar button corresponding to the Word document you opened in step 1 in the previous series of steps. Word displays a document

2. Click in the text **[Object goes here . . .]** to establish the insertion point

3. Click **Edit** on the menu bar and click **Paste Special**. The Paste Special dialog box appears

4. Click **Microsoft Office Excel Worksheet Object** in the list, click the **Paste Special** option button (see Figure 1.21), and click **OK** to complete the paste special operation. The Pivot Table appears in the Word document

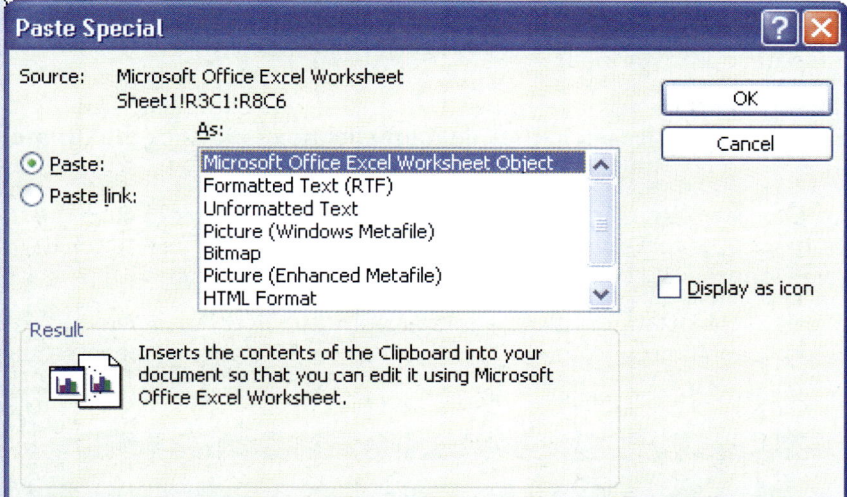

FIGURE 1.21
Paste Special dialog box

5. Select the text **[Object goes here . . .]** and press the Delete key to delete it

6. Click **File**, click **Save As**, and save the document as **<yourname>PivotTable2.doc**. Close Word; close Excel without saving the workbook

---

making the grade

1. What are the steps involved in creating a Pivot Table?

2. What functions do you use to link a Pivot Table to a Microsoft Word document?

SESSION 1.6 FILTERING AN EXCEL SPREADSHEET AND EXPORTING IT TO ACCESS

A list is essentially a database, but because lists are stored in Excel workbooks and not in formatted files created by database programs such as Microsoft Access, Microsoft has chosen to use the word "list" as the preferred term. The lists that you create in Excel will be fully compatible with Access. When you want to hide all the records (rows) in your list except those that meet certain criteria, you can use the **AutoFilter** command on the Filter submenu of the Data menu. The AutoFilter command places a drop-down list at the top of each column in your list (in the heading row). To display a particular group of records, select the criteria that you want in one or more of the drop-down lists.

Creating an Access database from an Excel list

1. Launch Access and then click **File** on the menu bar, click **New**, and click **Blank database** in the New File panel of the task pane. The File New Database dialog box appears

2. Navigate to the folder where you want to save your database, type **<yourname>Excel2Access** in the File name list box, and click the **Create** button

3. Launch Excel and then click **File** on the menu bar, click **Open**, click the workbook **int02PivotTableData.xls**, and click the **Open** button. Click the **Possible Donors** worksheet tab to make it the active worksheet

4. Click cell **A3**, click **Data** on the menu bar, point to **Filter**, then click **AutoFilter**. Each column heading now displays a list arrow (see Figure 1.22)

FIGURE 1.22

Excel AutoFilter

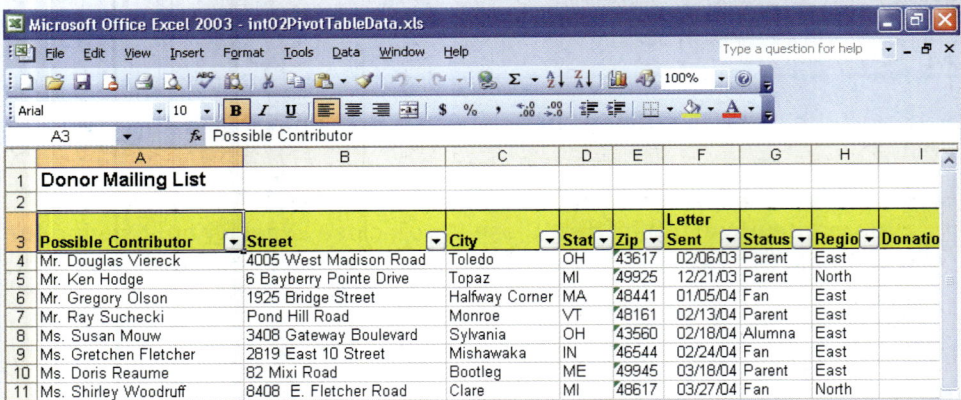

5. Click the **Donations** list arrow and then click **(Blanks)** to hide all rows except those who have not made a donation

6. Select the range **A3:I41**. Click the **Name** box at the left end of the formula bar, type **DonorFilter**, and press **Enter** (see Figure 1.23)

7. Click **Data** on the menu bar, point to **Filter**, then click **AutoFilter** to clear the AutoFilter

8. Click **File**, click **Exit**, and click **Yes** when Excel asks you if you want to save your changes

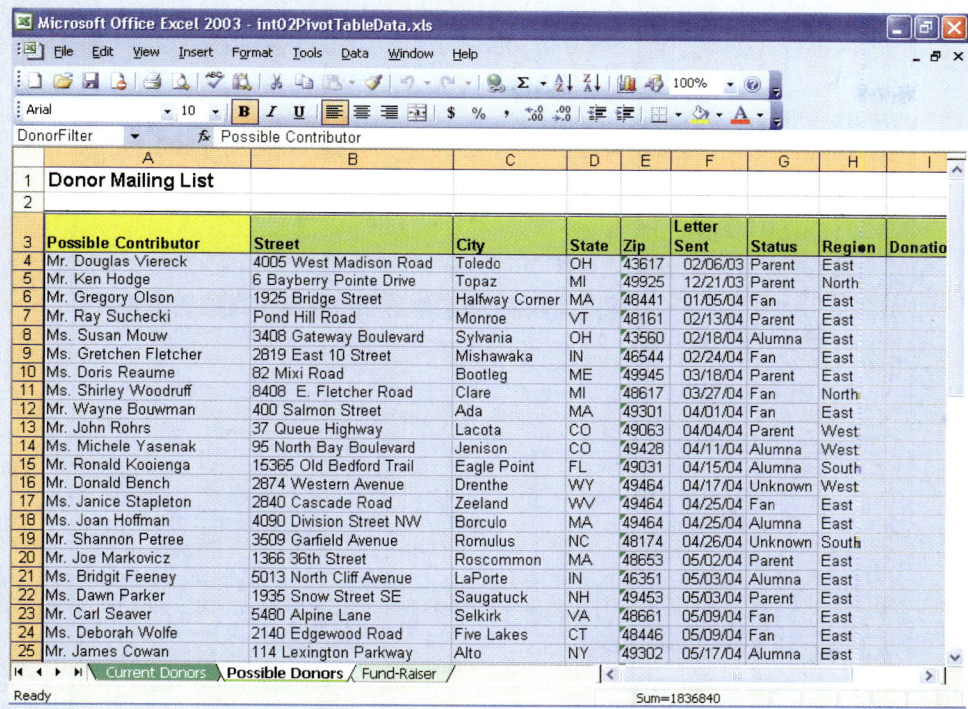

FIGURE 1.23
Naming a cell range

9. Switch to Microsoft Access, select **Tables** under the *Objects* category, click **New** in the Database window, click **Import Table**, and click **OK**

10. In the *Files of type* drop-down box click **Microsoft Excel (*.xls)**. Using the *Look in* list box, navigate to and then click **<yourname>Excel2Access** (see Figure 1.24), and then click **Import**. The Import Spreadsheet Wizard dialog box appears

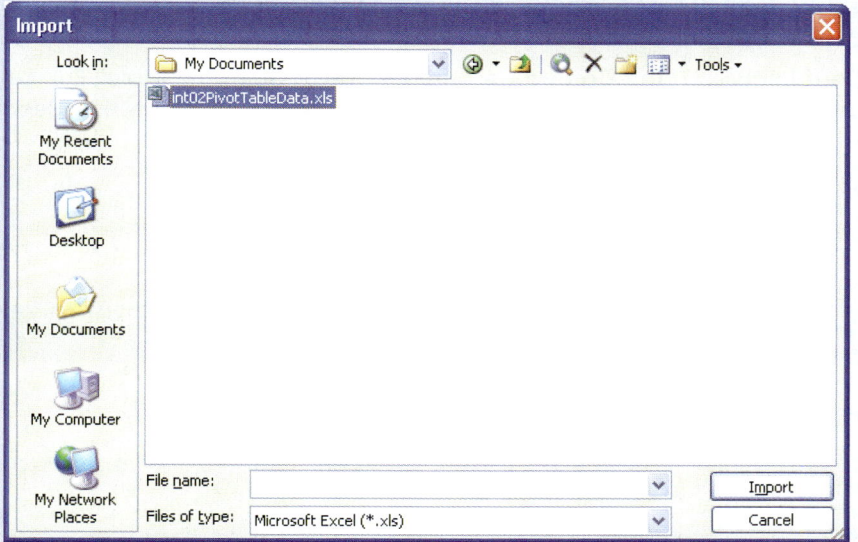

FIGURE 1.24
Import dialog box

11. Click the **Show Named Ranges** option button

tip: *Click **OK** if a message appears indicating Access cannot find the object "Possible Donors$"*

12. Click the **DonorFilter** entry (see Figure 1.25), and click **Next**

FIGURE **1.25**

Selecting the *DonorFilter* range name

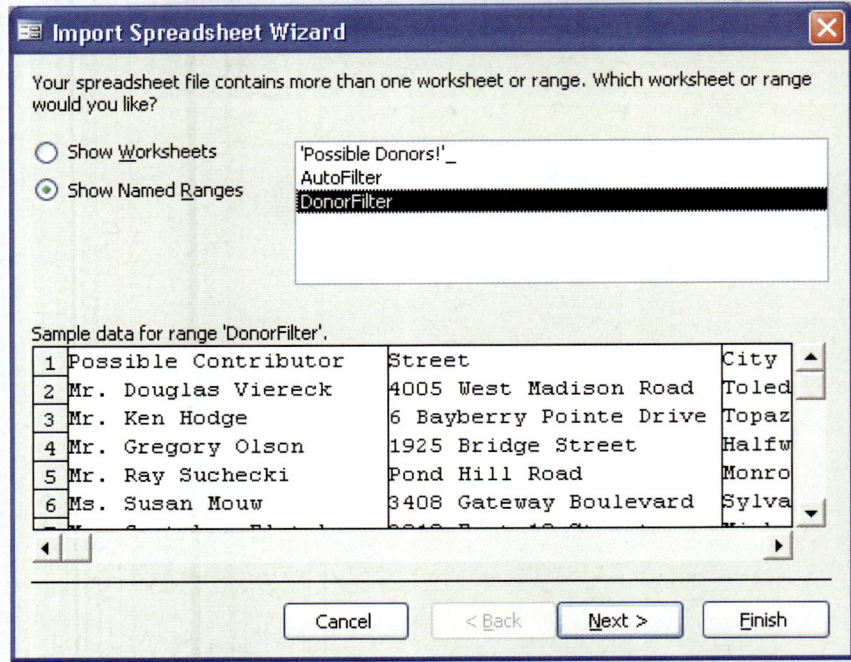

13. Ensure the *First Row Contains Column Headings* check box has a check-mark (click it, if it doesn't), and then click **Next**

14. Click the **New Table** option button, if necessary, and then click **Next**

15. Click **Finish** to complete the import procedure, and click **OK** to acknowledge the Import Spreadsheet Wizard's message

16. Double-click on the **DonorFilter** table name to open the table. The column headings in Excel have become the field names in Access (see Figure 1.26)

17. Select **File** on the menu bar and click **Exit** to close Access

SESSION 1.6

making *the grade*

1. What are the steps involved in creating an AutoFilter list with Excel?

2. What functions do you use to export an AutoFilter list to a Microsoft Access database?

FIGURE 1.26

DonorFilter table

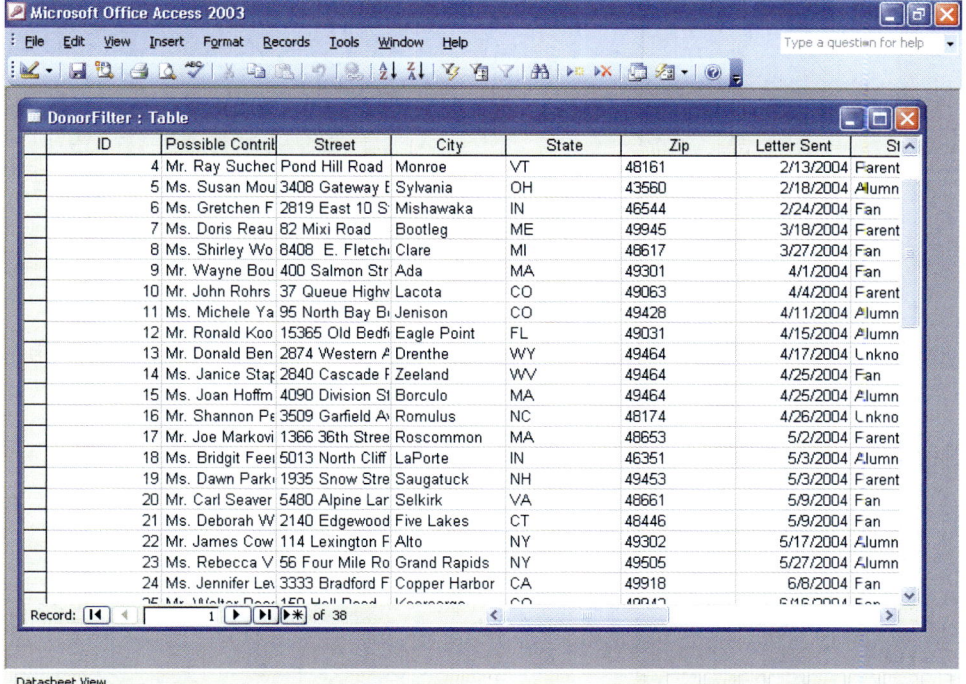

SESSION 1.7 EMBEDDING A GOAL SEEK WORKSHEET IN A WORD DOCUMENT

When you use the *Goal Seek* command, Excel changes the value in one cell until the value in a second cell reaches a number that you desire. For instance, if you had a spreadsheet that calculated class profit from a variety of inputs, including student enrollment numbers, teacher salary, and facility charges, you might use Goal Seek to define your break-even course price. You would tell the computer to change the class price until Profit was zero (break-even), and you would do that using the Goal Seek function.

In order to use Goal Seek, you will need to set up your worksheet to contain the following:

- A formula that calculates your goal
- An empty cell for the missing number that will get you to the desired result
- Any other values required in the formula

When the Goal Seek command starts to run, it repeatedly tries new values in the variable cell to find a solution. This process is called *iteration*, and it continues until Excel has run the problem 100 times or has found an answer within 0.001 of the target value you specified. (You can adjust these iteration settings by choosing Tools, Options and adjusting the Iteration options in the Calculations tab.) Because it calculates so fast, the Goal Seek command can save you significant time and effort over trying one number after another in the formula.

Using Goal Seek to forecast and embedding the worksheet in Microsoft Word

1. Open Excel, click **File** from the Excel menu bar, click **Open**, and then select the database **int02PivotTableData.xls**. Click the **Fund-Raiser** tab

2. Open Word, click **File** from the Word menu bar, click **Open**, and then locate and open the file **int02Link2GoalSeek.doc**

3. Click the Excel button in the Taskbar to make the worksheet active

4. Click **Tools** on the menu bar and click **Goal Seek**. The Goal Seek dialog box will appear with three boxes. In the **Set cell** box type **D5**, which is the cell where you want to specify the ending value. Press **Tab**

5. In the second box, type in **10000**. Press **Tab**

6. In the third box, type **D4**, the cell you want to modify so that your first cell will reach its target (see Figure 1.27). Click **OK**. Click **OK** in the Goal Seek Status dialog box

FIGURE 1.27

Using Goal Seek to find a solution

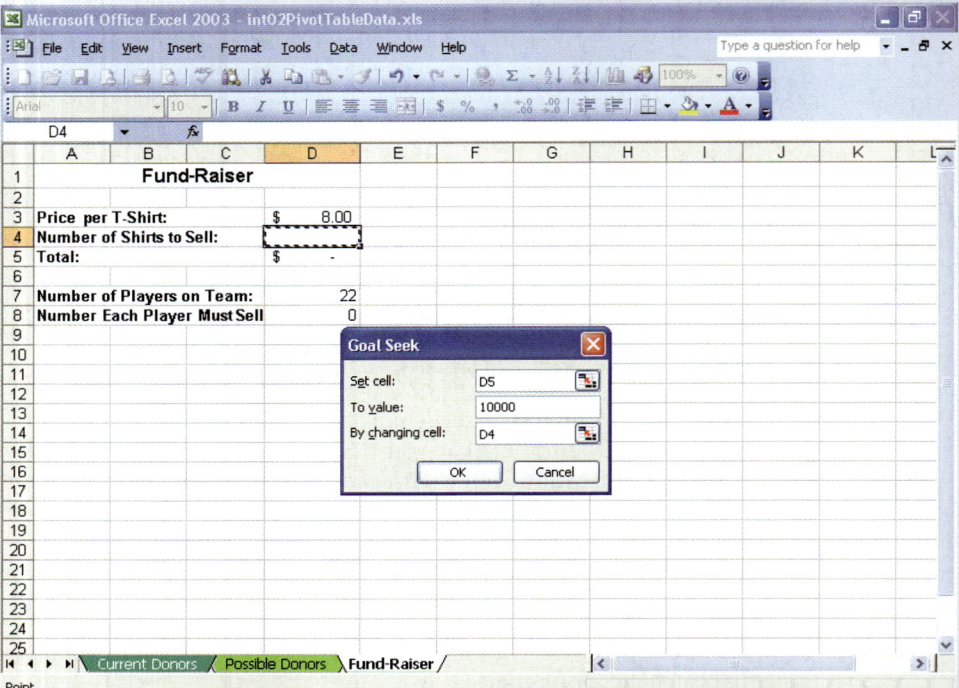

7. Select cell range **A1** to **D8** (click cell A1 and drag through cell D8)

8. Press **Ctrl+C** to copy the selection to the Clipboard

9. Switch to Word, position the insertion pointer to the left of the text **[Object goes here . . .]**

10. Click **Edit** on the menu bar and click **Paste Special**. The Paste Special dialog box opens. Make sure that the **Paste** radio button is selected. In the **As** drop-down box select **Microsoft Office Excel Worksheet Object** (see Figure 1.28). Click **OK**

11. Highlight **[Object goes here . . .]** and delete it (see Figure 1.29)

12. Close Excel and then close Word

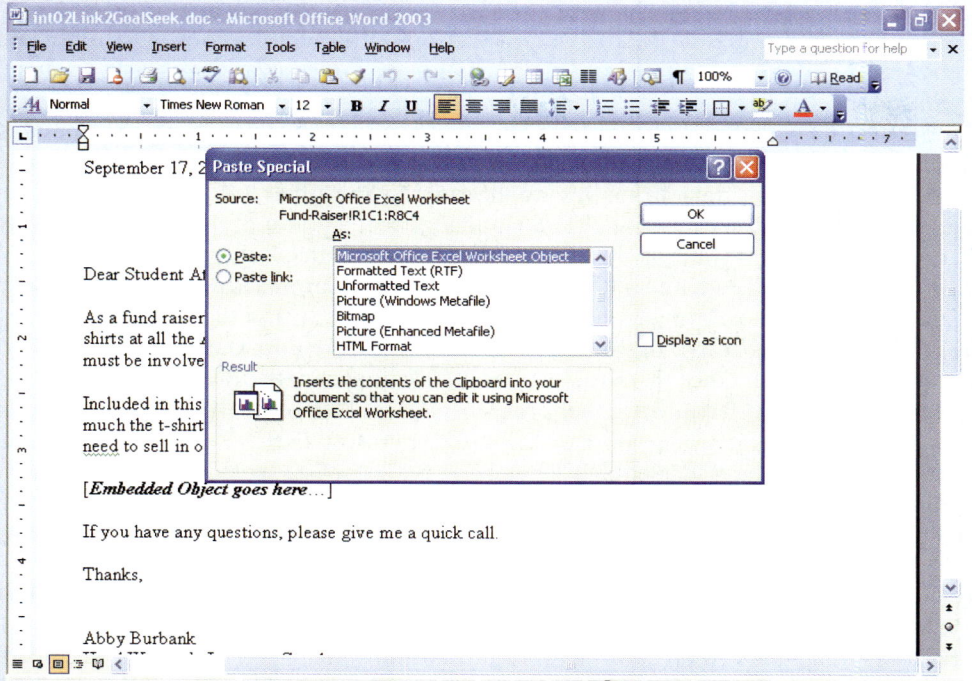

FIGURE 1.28

Embedding an Excel cell range into a Word document

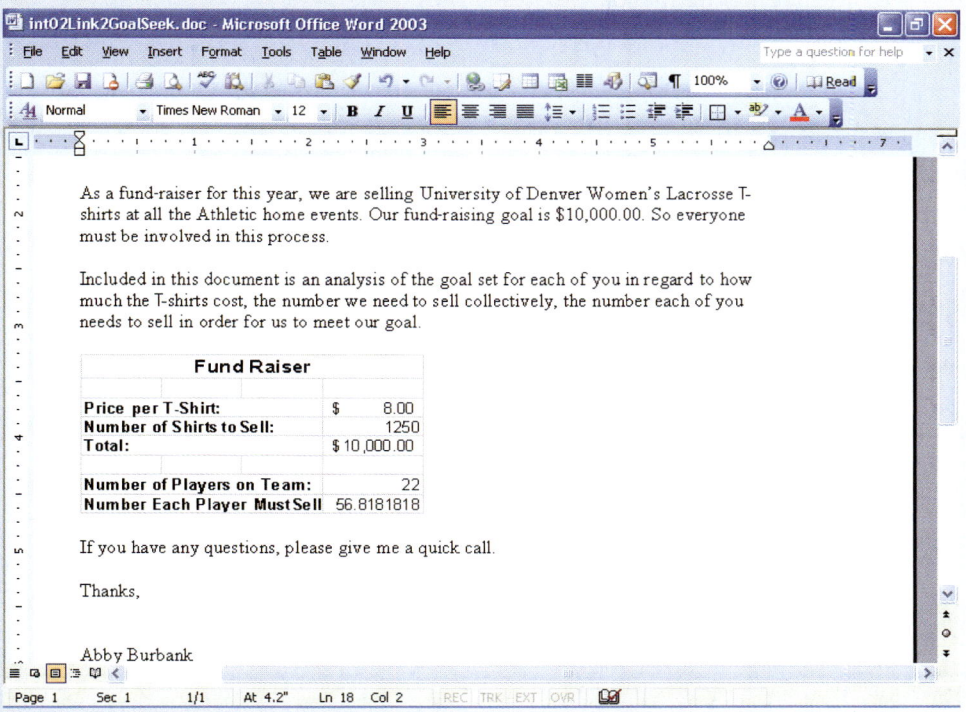

FIGURE 1.29

Word document with Excel embedded object

---

making *the grade*

1. What are the steps involved in using the Goal Seek function in Excel?

2. What functions do you use to embed spreadsheet data in a Microsoft Word document?

SESSION 1.8 SUMMARY

Electronically sharing the data among the various Office applications saves time and energy. The Microsoft Office suite of applications includes a variety of ways to share data among programs. The use of the static copy function and a few built-in tools with some of the Microsoft Office applications allows you to move data from one application to another. Although Microsoft Office Access can sometimes appear to be intimidating, exchanging data from this application to the other Office applications is relatively easy and very functional. Fully utilizing the full power of the Microsoft Office applications will get your job done more efficiently and effectively.

Organizing list data into a Pivot Table allows you to summarize the data contained in a lengthy list into a compact format, find relationships within the data that are otherwise hard to see because of the amount of detail, and organize the data into a format that's easy to chart. Once this simple function is completed, the Pivot Table can easily be linked or embedded into another program, such as Microsoft Office Word.

There are times when you can think of Microsoft Office Excel as a database. Creating a list in Excel is essentially a database; however, lists are stored in Excel workbooks and not in formatted files created by database programs. Massaging data in Excel can be a more intuitive process, but you are able to sort and create Excel lists and export those data directly into a database for further analysis.

Using the Goal Seek command, Excel changes the value in one cell until the value in a second cell reaches a number that you desire. This is an effective analysis tool to use for forecasting that can save you significant time and effort. Excel allows you to embed or link a Goal Seek worksheet to a Word document or other Microsoft applications using the Paste Special command.

task reference summary

Task	Page #	Preferred Method
Inserting Merge Fields into a Word document	INT 1.4	• Click **View**, click **Toolbars**, select **Mail Merge** • Click **Insert Merge Fields** icon • Insert **Merge Fields**
Analyzing records with Access and Excel	INT 1.8	• Click **Queries**, double-click a query • Click **Tools**, point to **Office Links**, click **Analyze It with Microsoft Office Excel**
Exporting an Access query to Word	INT 1.10	• Open the database • Click **Queries**. Click the query you want to export • Click **Tools**, point to **Office Links**, click **Publish It with Microsoft Office Word**
Exporting records with Access and PowerPoint	INT 1.11	• Open the database • Open a PowerPoint presentation • Select all the records from a database table • Paste records into the PowerPoint slide

FILL-IN

1. There are three basic ways to exchange data among the Office applications: _____, _____, and _____.

2. _____ function allows you to define some criteria for a mail merge.

3. You use the _____ function in Access to share data records with Excel.

4. _____ is the function in Access to share data records with Word.

5. You use the _____ function and the _____ function to copy data records from Access to a PowerPoint presentation.

6. A _____ is created to better organize, summarize, and analyze list data.

7. In Excel, you can use the _____ function to select out specific records from a list.

8. You use the _____ function in Excel to calculate what-if analysis.

review of concepts

REVIEW QUESTIONS

1. Discuss the difference between static copying, linking data, and embedding data.

2. Explain some of the major tasks involved in using the IF . . . THEN . . . ELSE function with mail merge.

3. List the steps involved when using the data from an Access query in an Excel spreadsheet.

4. Explain the steps involved when using the data from an Access query in a Word document.

5. List the multiple ways you can copy data from an Access query and paste them into a PowerPoint presentation.

6. What are the major benefits of using a Pivot Table in Excel?

7. List the steps involved in using the custom AutoFilter in Excel.

8. What is the main purpose of using the Goal Seek function in Excel?

CREATE THE QUESTION

For each of the following answers, create an appropriate, short question.

ANSWER	QUESTION
1. You use this function to insert data from an external source in a mail merge.	_____
2. You use this function to insert data that will not retain their connection with the source program or the source document.	_____
3. The shortcut keys that allow you to copy static data from a file.	_____
4. The short cut keys that allow you to paste static data to a file.	_____
5. The function in Excel that organizes, summarizes, and analyzes list data.	_____
6. You use this function in Excel to specify certain criteria in a query for a list.	_____
7. This function in Excel is an iterative process that creates a What-If analysis.	_____

1. Creating an Analysis Sheet from an Access Database

The manager of Tom's Volvo needs a sales analysis worksheet developed from an Access database. You have been asked to export the data for all the cars that Tom's currently has in a database file and to analyze the data in Excel.

1. Launch Microsoft Office Access and open the file **int02TomsVolvo.mdb**

2. Click the **Tables** tab in the Database window, if necessary, and then click **tblCars** to select, but not open, that table

3. Click **Tools** on the menu bar, point to **Office Links**, and click **Analyze It with Microsoft Office Excel**. The database table opens in an Excel worksheet (see Figure 1.30)

4. Click cell **E28**, type **Total**, and press **Enter**

5. Click cell **F28**, type **=SUBTOTAL(9,F2:F26)**, and press **Enter**. The formula displays the total cost of all cars, $759,745

6. Click cell **F2**, click **Data**, point to **Filter**, and click **AutoFilter**

7. Click **View** on the menu bar, click **Header and Footer**, click the **Custom Header** button, click in the **Right** section, type your first and last names, click **OK**, and click **OK** again to close the Page Setup dialog box

8. Click the AutoFilter list arrow in column D, corresponding to *Year*, and click **2002** from the list

9. Click **File** on the menu bar, click **Print**, and click **OK** to print the 2002 Volvos available

10. Click the AutoFilter list arrow in column D, corresponding to *Year*, click (**All**) from the list, click the AutoFilter list arrow in column E, LocCode, and click **S**. A list of all cars in that region appears

11. Click **File** on the menu bar, click **Print**, and click **OK** to print your workbook

12. Click **File**, click **Exit**, and click **No** when asked if you want to save changes to tblCars.xls

13. Reopen the Access window by clicking its button on the Taskbar. Then, click **File**, and click **Exit** to close Access

FIGURE 1.30

Excel worksheet exported from an Access database

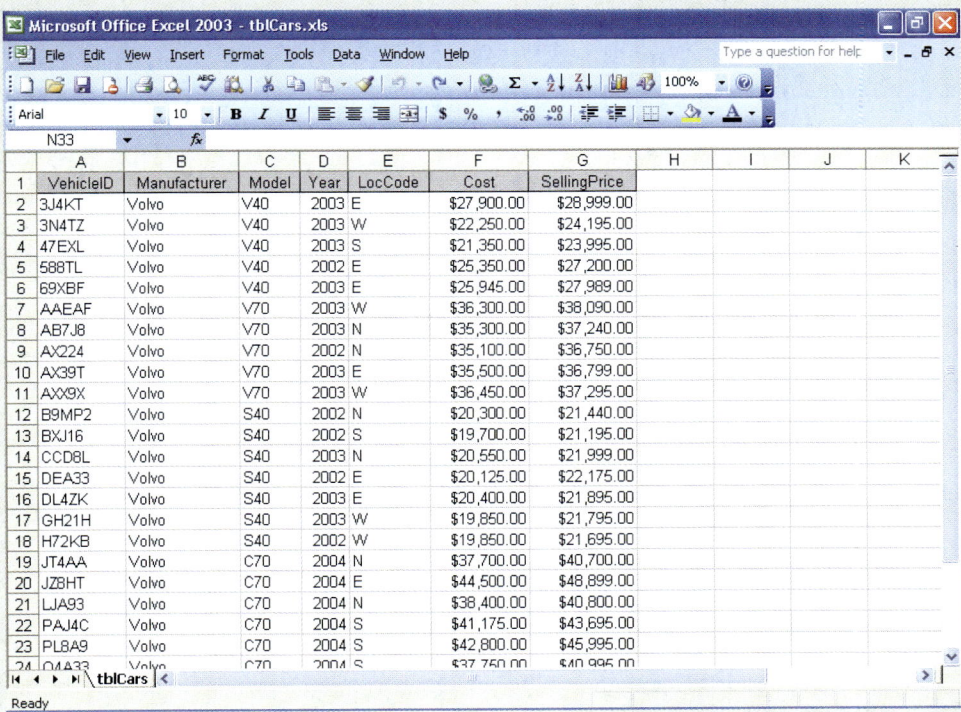

2. Importing an Excel Spreadsheet into an Access Database

Your best friend, Juan, has just asked you to create a database file from a personal Excel spreadsheet. Juan has been documenting his musical purchases for the past 6 months in Excel, but now, he realizes that a database would be a better solution to keep track of these data. You need to help Juan with the task of exporting these data to an Access database.

1. Launch Microsoft Office Access. Then, click **File** on the menu bar, click **New**, and click **Blank database** in the task pane

2. Using the *Save in* list box, navigate to the folder in which you want to save your new database, drag the mouse across the name in the *File name* list box, type <**yourname**>**Music**, and click the **Create** button to create a new, blank database

3. Click the **Tables** tab in the Database window, if necessary, and then click the **New** button

4. Click **Import Table** from the list of choices in the New Table dialog box, and click **OK**

5. Click the **Files of type** list box, scroll it until you see the list entry *Microsoft Excel (*.xls)*, and click **Microsoft Excel (*.xls)**

6. Using the *Look in* list box, navigate to the window containing the file **int02Music.xls**, click **int02Music.xls**, and click the **Import** button. Access displays the Import Spreadsheet Wizard dialog box (see Figure 1.31)

7. Click the **Show Worksheets** option button, if necessary, and click **Next**

8. Ensure the *First Row Contains Column Headings* check box contains a checkmark and then click **Next**

9. Click the **In a New Table** option button, if necessary, and click **Next**

10. Click **Next** again. Click the **No primary key** option button, and click the **Next** button

11. In the *Import to Table* list box, type **tblMusic** and click the **Finish** button

12. Click **OK** to acknowledge the successful import operation. The Access database window is available

13. Double-click the **tblMusic** table name to open it

14. Press **Ctrl+P** to open the Print dialog box, click the **Pages** option button in the Print Range panel of the Print dialog box, type **1**, press **Tab**, type **1**, and click **OK** to print the first page of the tblMusic table. Remember to write your name on the printout

15. Click **File** on the menu bar, and click **Close** to close Access and the database

FIGURE 1.31

Importing an Excel worksheet into an Access database

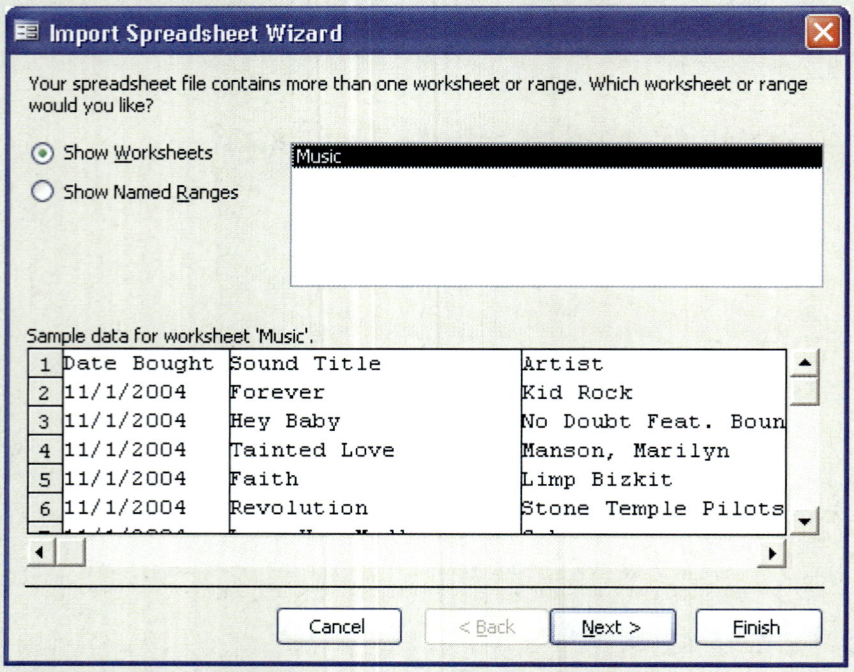

challenge

1. Creating a PowerPoint Slide Show from a Word Document

Measuring People Responses, a Bedford, Massachusetts, research think tank, conducted a study to compare Microsoft Office XP with Microsoft Office 2003. They published their study online and have provided an outline of that study in a Word-formatted document called **int02Comparison.doc**. Convert the Word document into a PowerPoint slide presentation. Immediately save the fledgling PowerPoint presentation as **<your-name>Comparison2.ppt**. Delete any blank slides. (Sometimes the first slide is blank.) Once you have created the initial presentation from the Word document, run the presentation through the PowerPoint style checker to ensure that all slide titles use sentence case and all body text follows sentence case without punctuation. (*Hint:* Tools, Options, Spelling and Style, Check style.) Reformat the PowerPoint presentation by applying the Capsules template. (*Hint:* Open the task pane, click the list arrow at the top of the task pane, and click Slide Design. Then, hover the mouse over each design, in turn, until the ToolTip displays *Capsules.pot.*) Place your name in the Notes and Handouts header, and print three-per-page handouts and choose **Grayscale** in the Print dialog box. (In the Print dialog box, click the **Print what** list box and click **Handouts**; click **Grayscale** in the Color/grayscale list box.)

2. Analyzing Sales in Excel with Access Data

Milton Windy has stored sales information detailing sales by salesperson in an Access database query called qrySalesByEmployee. Milton wants you to import the Access data created by that query into an Excel workbook and perform some calculations. The query displays the state in which a sale has been made, the salesperson's name, the amount of the sale, and the gender of the salesperson making the sale. Milton wants to sum sales by state and gender within state. You will use an Excel Pivot Table to provide the summary information that Milton wants. Begin by opening the Access database file called **int02SalesAnalysis.mdb**. Export the query qrySalesByEmployee to Excel. Close the Access database and open the Excel workbook that Access created called qrySalesByEmployee.xls. Save it as **<yourname>SalesAnalysis.xls**. Create a Pivot Table using the Pivot Table Wizard (click Data, click Pivot Table and Pivot Chart Report). Place *Employee* in the Row area, *State* in the Page area, and *SaleAmount* in the Data area of the Pivot Table layout. Create the Pivot Table on its own worksheet. Once Excel creates the Pivot Table, click its worksheet tab, place your name in the worksheet header, and print the Pivot Table worksheet. Save the workbook again.

did you
know?

"logizomechanophobia" *is the technical term used to describe someone who has a fear of computers or machines.*

all *polar bears are left-handed.*

the *act of flicking one's finger is called a "fillip."*

a *United States nickel is made up of 75 percent copper and only 25 percent actual nickel.*

Appendix Objectives

- **Open and close Visual Basic**
- **Familiarize yourself with the Visual Basic environment and its components**
- **Learn the structure of a Visual Basic program**
- **Save your Visual Basic project**
- **Open an existing Visual Basic project**

appendix case

VanBuren Computer Supply

VanBuren Computer Supply is a store that sells assembled computer systems as well as miscellaneous parts and supplies. The store began as a small shop, but due to the demand of personal computers over the years, it has grown into a large store with a full sales staff. As their business has grown, on-hand inventory has increased substantially, and the owners have had some trouble keeping count of remaining stock. This caused them to run out of inventory unexpectedly, as well as order insufficient amounts of new inventory from their suppliers.

Given their problems with inventory management, Tom and Vicki have decided to come up with a solution that will fit into their current workflow pattern. They determined that they needed a computer program that could itemize every unit sold and then provide this information in a printed detail. Since Tom has some background with computer programming, he insisted that he tackle the project himself. Before diving straight into developing an application, Tom thought that it would be wise to begin with a small portion of the program so that he can learn how development in Visual Basic is accomplished.

FIGURE 1.1

The default Visual Basic desktop

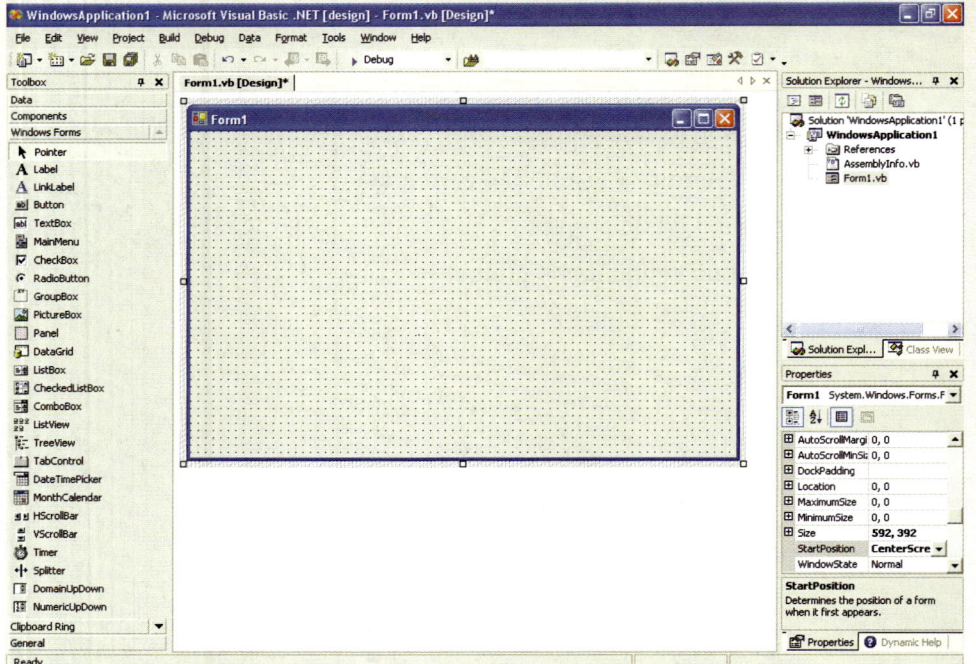

SESSION 1.1 INTRODUCTION TO VISUAL BASIC

This session will teach you the basics of getting started with Visual Basic, including opening and closing the program and examining the layout and composition of the Visual Basic environment. Additionally, you will learn some of the concepts of Visual Basic development and how they come into play in your applications.

WELCOME TO VISUAL BASIC DEVELOPMENT

Visual Basic has become a very popular language used to write *GUI* (graphical user interface) programs that operate in Microsoft Windows. More than likely, if you are familiar with Windows applications, you are familiar with the building blocks, or *controls*, with which you will construct your Visual Basic applications, such as buttons, menu bars, text boxes, and so forth. These controls will be grouped together and placed in special windows called *forms*. These forms can be grouped together, along with the code that provides the functionality to the forms, in various ways to create an entire application.

Traditional programming languages of the past have been structured in such a way that they follow the programmer's commands in a sequential manner, from one to the next. These languages were said to be *procedural*. They created programs that followed a rigid flow—the order of execution relied entirely on how the code was written. However, a trend developed not long ago in the programming world where applications were no longer restricted to a set sequence of events. On the contrary, this new breed of application responded to the user and his or her actions. These new programs and languages are referred to as *event-driven*. In an event-driven application, different parts of the program's code are executed depending on what events the user might trigger. From a development standpoint, programmers now create procedures that respond to events, instead of directing the user to respond to the program.

STARTING VISUAL BASIC

One evening after work, Tom sits down in front of his home PC and decides to experiment with Visual Basic. He decides that the first thing he should do is to start up the program and familiarize himself with the layout of the environment and its tools. Once he has an understanding of how to go about starting a project, then he can explore the various tools needed to create his application's splash screen.

Starting Visual Basic

1. Click the **Start** button on your Windows Taskbar

2. On the **Start** menu, point to **Programs**, and then point to **Microsoft Visual Studio .NET 2003**

3. From the menu, select **Microsoft Visual Studio .NET 2003**

4. The Visual Basic splash screen will appear momentarily and then you will see the Visual Basic desktop on your screen

5. Click **File**, then point to **New**, and click **Project** to display the New Project dialog box. Your screen should resemble the one pictured in Figure 1.2

6. Click the Windows Application icon in the New Project dialog box

7. Click the **OK** button

VB 1.3

VISUAL BASIC

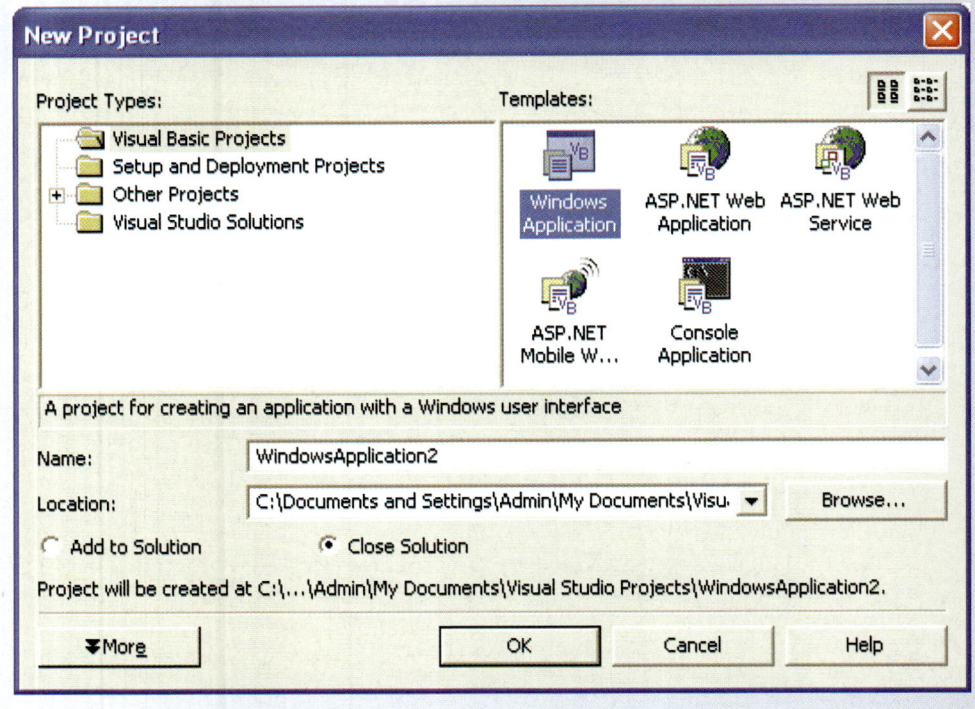

THE NEW PROJECT WIZARD

The New Project Wizard gives users a simplified way to select which kind of project
they would like to work on in Visual Basic. If you would like to bypass this Wizard, simply click on the Cancel button. Most often, if you are beginning a new project, you will
want to click Windows Application.

THE VISUAL BASIC DESKTOP

Once you have gotten past the New Project Wizard, you are presented with the Visual
Basic desktop. At first glance, there seems to be an overwhelming amount of screen
components and information. However, once these items are explained in detail, you
will see that everything on the screen is grouped by function, and this screen arrangement actually offers an optimized workflow. There are five basic areas of the Visual
Basic development screen: the Main window, the Form window, the toolbox, the
Project Explorer, and the Properties window.

THE MAIN WINDOW

The *Main window* (see Figure 1.3) is the topmost area on the screen. It contains the
Visual Basic Title bar, the menu bar, and the Standard toolbar. If you are familiar with
Windows-style applications, then these elements should be familiar to you as well. The
Title bar displays the name of the project you are working with, the name of the application you are working in (Visual Basic .NET), and the current status of Visual Basic,
displayed in square brackets. In this case, you are just starting a new project, so your
project is in *design time*. This means that Visual Basic is ready for you to begin editing
your application. Alternatively, the Title bar could indicate that your project is in *run
time,* which means that your application is running and is ready to be tested and

interacted with. Also, when problems arise with your code, and Visual Basic cannot execute a particular statement, your project may be placed into *break time*. Break time is a special mode that allows you to view your troublesome code and make corrections while your application is paused momentarily.

The *menu bar*, located below the Title bar, shows you the various commands available for you to use while designing your application. Finally, the *Standard toolbar* provides shortcuts, in the form of icons, to the most commonly used items in the menu bar.

THE FORM WINDOW

The *Form window* (see Figure 1.4) is where you do the actual designing of your application and user interface for your Visual Basic program. Just as Visual Basic assigned the generic name "Form1" for your new project, Visual Basic also assigns the first form in your new project the name "Form1." It is in this window that you will lay out the controls that define what your Visual Basic application does and how it will interact with your users.

THE TOOLBOX

The *toolbox* (see Figure 1.5), located on the left side of the Visual Basic desktop by default, contains an array of controls available for you to use when designing your application in the Form window. Note that depending upon which version of Visual Basic you have, your toolbox may differ slightly from that shown in Figure 1.5. For a description of each item in the toolbox, hover your mouse over the icon and a tooltip will appear describing it.

F I G U R E   1.5

The Toolbox window

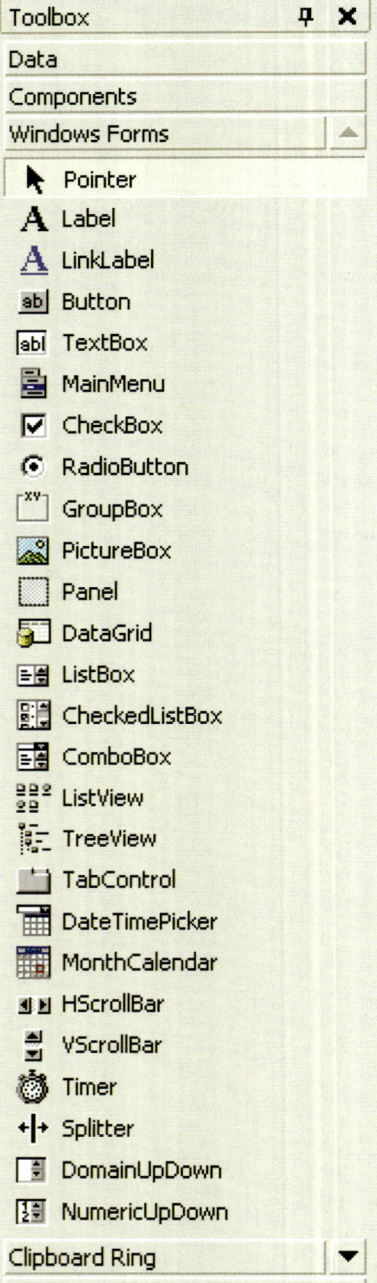

F I G U R E   1.5

The Toolbox window

F I G U R E   1.6

The Solution Explorer window

F I G U R E   1.7

The Properties window

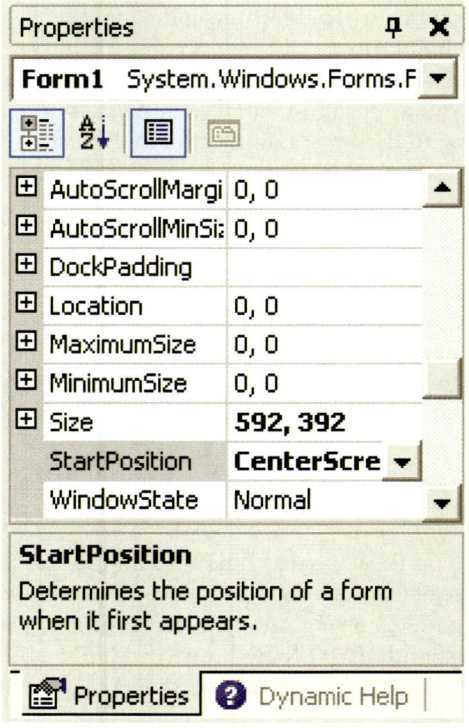

THE SOLUTION EXPLORER

The *Solution Explorer* window (see Figure 1.6) displays a hierarchical tree view of your project and the files that it contains. You use this window to see, at a glance, with which object of your project you are working on, and it provides a simple navigation between objects. As with other tree structures in Windows, the sections of the tree can be collapsed and expanded by clicking the expand and collapse, (plus and minus signs) at each level. Under the Title bar are three icons. On the left is the View Code icon, which, when pressed, opens a new window that displays the code that supports the currently selected object in either the Solution Explorer or the Form window. To the right of the View Code icon is the View Object icon, which opens the Form window and brings it to the front of the desktop. Finally, on the right-hand side of these icons is the Toggle Folders icon. When toggled on, this button displays the objects of your application as items beneath categorized yellow folders.

THE PROPERTIES WINDOW

The *Properties* window (see Figure 1.7) displays a list of design time attributes associated with the object or control currently selected in the Form window or Solution Explorer window. The Title bar of this window displays the name of the object that is being edited. Below the Title bar is a drop-down box that allows you to select for which element of the form you would like to see properties. This is an alternative to selecting an object in the Form window itself to change focus. Beneath this drop-down box is the text area that contains the actual properties that you can modify at design time.

SAVING YOUR PROJECT

It is very important to save your Visual Basic projects so that they are not lost when you shut off your computer, close Visual Basic, or perhaps have a loss of power unexpectedly. A good rule of thumb: whenever you get a new piece of your form placed just the way you like it, or get a particularly troublesome piece of code working properly, save your project so that your most recent milestone is not lost. As an additional benefit, if you follow this saving strategy, you can easily open your saved project and return your project to a known working state, in case you inadvertently add new bugs since you last saved your work! Experiment as you learn Visual Basic and find a saving strategy that fits into your workflow.

When you save your Visual Basic project, you are actually saving more than one file. First, you will save the form that you are currently editing. Then you will save the project file itself. Recall that a project can contain many different forms, and an application with any amount of complexity will surely have more than one form in it. The job of a project file is to keep track of all of the forms contained in a project. Due to the way that Visual Basic saves your projects, it is recommended that you begin each new project by creating a new folder for it, and saving all of your forms and your project file in this new folder.

---

task reference   Saving Your Visual Basic Project

- Select **File** from the menu bar, and then select **Save Form1 As**

- In the Save File As dialog box that pops up, create a new folder to hold your project files. Once created, open your new folder

- In the File name text box, enter a name for your form

- Click the **Save** button

- Select **File** from the menu bar, and select **Save All**

Tom decides that since he has a new, blank project with a blank form open, he might as well practice saving his files so that he understands how to do this later.

Saving your Visual Basic project

1. In the Visual Basic window, click **File** from the menu bar. Select **Save Form1.vb As** from the File menu (see Figure 1.8). The Save File As dialog box will now appear on your screen

2. **Type a name** for your folder and press **Enter** on your keyboard. **Double-click** on the new folder to open it

3. **Double-click** your mouse in the *File name* text box and type a new name for your form (see Figure 1.9)

4. Click the **Save** button to save your form

FIGURE 1.8

Saving the form file

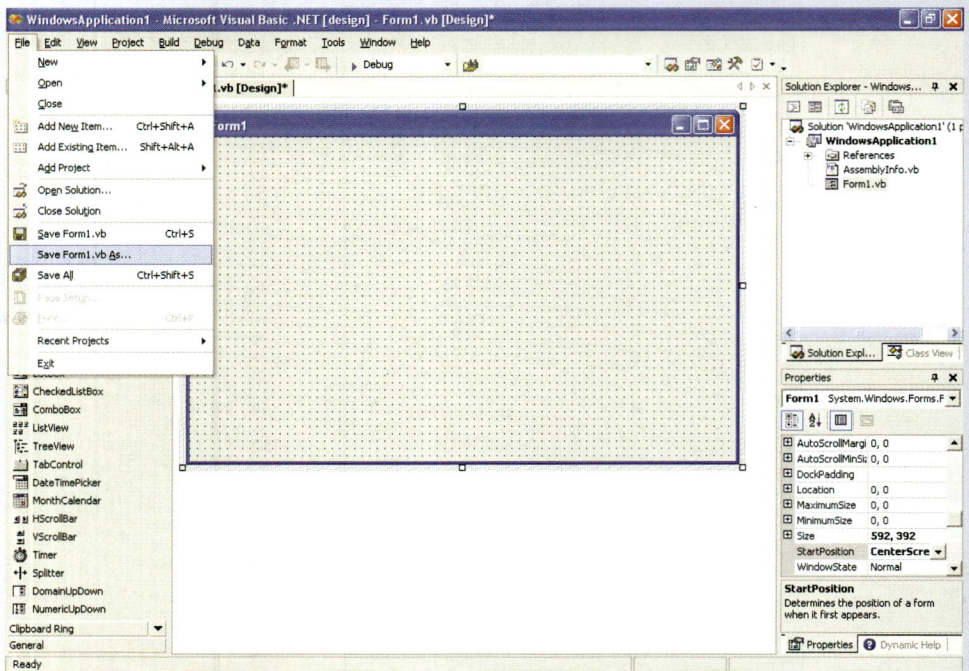

FIGURE 1.9

Save File dialog box

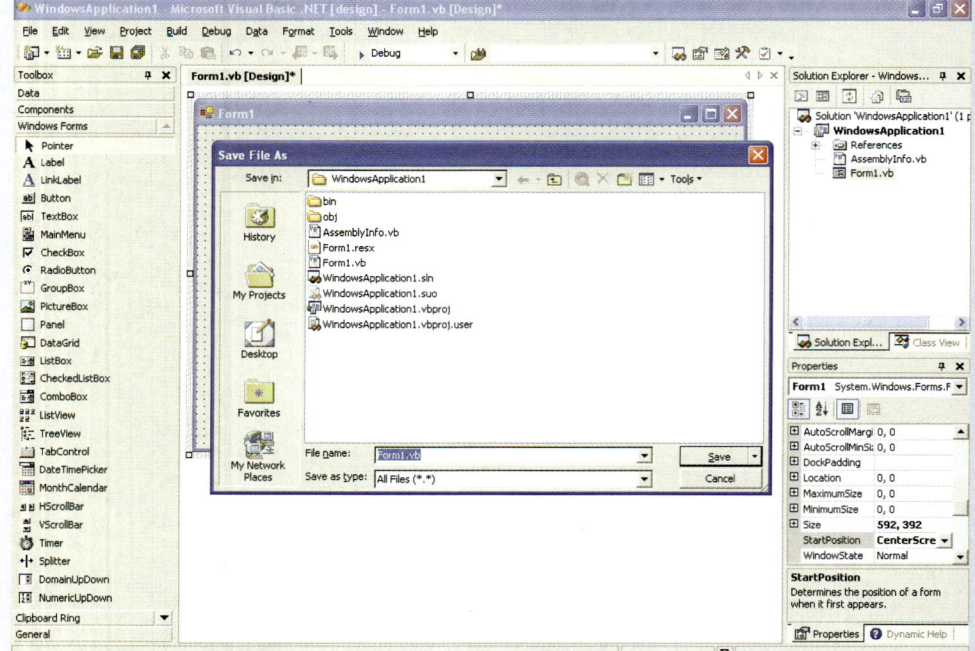

anotherway
. . . to Save Your
Visual Basic Project

To save both your
form and your
project at the same
time, select **Save All**
from the File menu.
This will prompt you
to save your form
first, then the project

5. Select **File** again, from the Visual Basic Main window, and then select
   Save All

6. Click **File** and then click **Close Solution** to close your new project

Once you have saved your project initially, you can simply click the Save Project icon in the Visual Basic Standard toolbar.

OPENING AN EXISTING PROJECT

Of course, if you save a project, you are going to want to open it again at some point in the future. Opening a saved project requires much less work than saving a new project. Tom decides to practice opening a saved project as well, and chooses to reopen the project he just saved.

---

task reference — **Opening a Saved Visual Basic Project**

- Select **File** from the *menu bar*, and then select **Open**, and finally select **Project** . . .

- Locate your project in the *file list box*

- Select your project in the *file list box* and click the **Open** button

---

Opening a saved Visual Basic project

1. Select **File** from the menu bar, click **Open**, then click **Project**. The Open Project dialog box will appear on your screen

2. Use the controls in the Open Project dialog box to locate your project file in the *file list box*

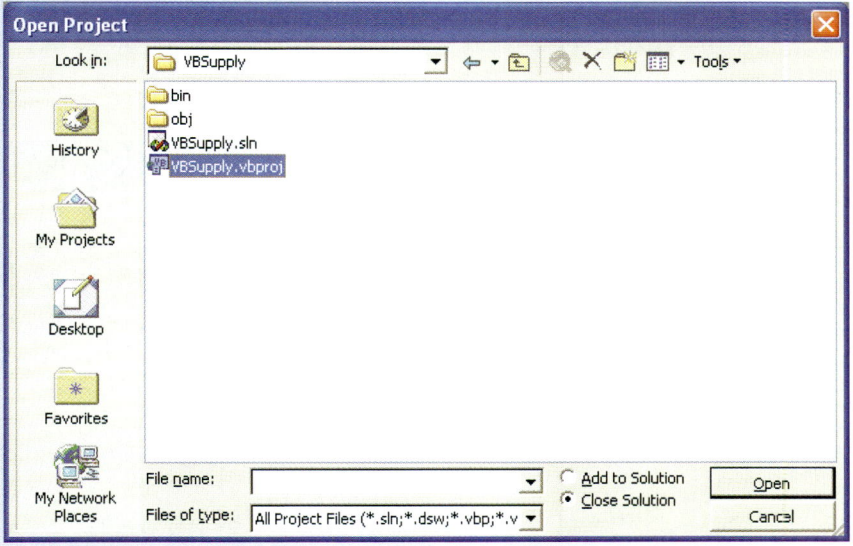

FIGURE 1.10

Open Project dialog box

3. Once you have located your project file, click it to select it, and then click the **Open** button to open the saved project

4. If you do not see anything in the Form window, locate the Project Explorer window, click the form you wish to view from the tree, and click the **View Designer** button. Your form should then appear

making *the grade*

1. _____ are considered to be the building blocks of a Visual Basic application.

2. A program that responds to a user's requests, instead of following a strict sequence of operations, is called a(n) _____ program.

3. The _____ is the area of the Visual Basic desktop that contains a palette of controls at your disposal.

4. If Visual Basic is ready for you to edit your project, it is said to be in _____ time.

SESSION 1.2 SUMMARY

Visual Basic is a tool that is used to create GUI applications for the Windows environment. The basic components of any Visual Basic application are called controls. Controls are grouped together and placed on forms to accomplish a common functional goal, such as gathering information or providing user feedback. Visual Basic is one of a breed of new languages that supports a modern paradigm of programming called event-driven programming, which responds to user events rather than a set order of execution.

When saving your project, Visual Basic places each project in its own folder in your disk, so that all files are kept in the same location, avoiding any confusion. Thereafter, projects can be saved quickly by pressing the Save All icon in the Standard toolbar. Develop a saving strategy that fits into your workflow and follow it. Visit the series Web site at www.mhhe.com/i-series/ for more information.

task reference *summary*

Task	Page #	Preferred Method
Project, saving	VB 1.7	• Click **File**, click **Save <form name> As . . .** , type form name, click the **Save** button • Click **File**, click **Save All**
Project, opening	VB 1.9	• Click **File**, click **Open**, **Project . . .** , and select project from list; click **Open**

FILL-IN

1. _____ is the mode of Visual Basic where you edit your forms.

2. Forms are edited in the _____ window.

3. A _____ is a computer's way of presenting information graphically to a user.

4. The area of the Visual Basic desktop that contains the menu bar and Standard toolbar is the _____.

5. The _____ is where you would edit the characteristics of a control.

6. When a Visual Basic program is paused so that users can view and correct malfunctioning code, it is said to be in _____ time.

REVIEW QUESTIONS

1. Identify the five main areas of the Visual Basic desktop. Write out a short description of what is contained in each area.

2. Describe the difference between procedural and event-driven programming methodologies.

3. List the three modes of Visual Basic, and describe what would be happening in each mode.

4. Outline the basic steps of saving your project for the first time.

CREATE THE QUESTION

For each of the following answers, create an appropriate, short question.

ANSWER

1. This area of the Visual Basic desktop contains a palette of tools and controls used in building your application.

2. This Wizard presents users with a list of types of projects to open.

3. This is a shortcut to saving your project, found in the Standard toolbar.

4. This Visual Basic element contains a collection of controls used to build your application.

QUESTION

_____

_____

_____

_____

1. Reviewing the Modes of Visual Basic

Angel is a student in a Visual Basic class, and she has been given an assignment to read a chapter in her textbook and give a quick nutshell overview of the different modes of Visual Basic—design time, run time, and break time. All that is required of her is to create a basic outline of what these different modes mean, and why they exist in Visual Basic. Write a brief description of these modes.

2. Reviewing File Operations in Visual Basic

Leia, another Visual Basic student, has been asked by her instructor to prepare a discussion on the virtues of saving your work and to briefly describe how to save projects in Visual Basic. Write a short discussion about why saving your files is important and how to go about saving your project.

Writing Visual Basic Applications

did you know?

bees *have five eyes: three small ones on the top of their head and two larger ones in front.*

Abraham *Lincoln was a licensed bartender and part owner of a saloon in Springfield, Illinois, in 1833.*

red *algae gives the Red Sea its color.*

the *Statue of Liberty has a four-foot-long nose.*

Appendix Objectives

- **Create and execute a simple Visual Basic program**
- **Learn how controls and code interact**
- **Modify properties of controls**

VanBuren Computer Supply

Recall from the last appendix that Tom and Vicki have problems tracking their inventory for VanBuren Computer Supply. After thinking about possible solutions, they decided upon creating a cashiering application that can assist them in tracking how much inventory they sell each day. And since Tom has some background with computer programming, he has taken on the role of lead developer for this project. To begin, he sat down with Visual Basic and studied the layout of the programming environment so that he would understand the tool very well before beginning any actual work. Now that Tom has become familiar with the Visual Basic environment, he is ready to begin creating his application. He decides that he would like their application to contain a splash screen that appears while the program is starting up. The splash screen displays the VanBuren company logo and provides a copyright notice.

Once the splash screen is complete, Tom proceeds to develop his inventory-tracking program. He hopes that it alleviates his problem with lost time and money due to over- and understocking. The program generates an itemized detail of each

FIGURE 2.1
Completed application screen

sale, as well as generating internal records used to track inventory status. At the end of each day, Tom and Vicki collect these receipts and use them to calculate the total items sold and how much money they received. The finished application is shown in Figure 2.1.

SESSION 2.1 GETTING STARTED: YOUR FIRST VISUAL BASIC PROGRAM

In this session, you will learn about Tom's first project: creating a splash screen for VanBuren Computer Supply's sales tracking application. You will learn how to place controls onto a form and modify the properties of the controls. Additionally, you will learn how to place your form in its default starting position and test it to view your final results.

STARTING YOUR FIRST PROJECT

Begin a new project by selecting File from the menu bar, and then selecting New. If you look closely at the Form Layout window, you will notice that there are small white boxes surrounding the form (see Figure 2.2). These boxes, called *sizing handles*, are used to set the size of an object horizontally and vertically. The handles on the sides of an object resize in a single direction, and the handles on corners of objects allow you to stretch an object horizontally and vertically at the same time. Experiment with the sizing controls now.

FIGURE 2.2

Form being resized

Resizing a Visual Basic form

1. Locate the form's lower-right-hand corner sizing handle. Place your mouse cursor over the handle until it becomes a double arrow

2. Click and drag the sizing handle outwards until the form is sized to your liking

3. Release the mouse button

FIGURE 2.3

Selecting a tool

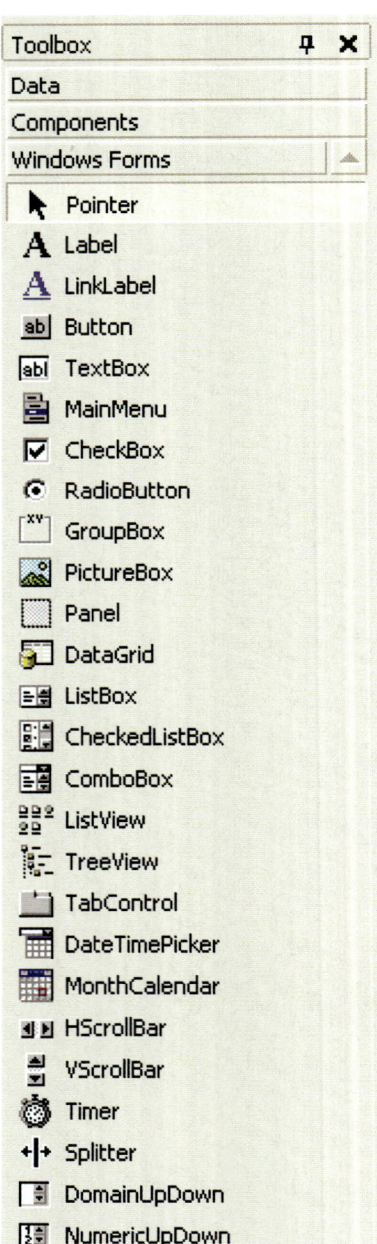

Now that your form is resized to give you more working area, the next step is to add controls to the form.

WORKING WITH CONTROLS

Recall from Session 1.1 that all of the controls that you will use are stored in the Toolbox window, which is located on the left-hand side of your screen by default. Before you can place any controls onto your form, you first must select the control from the toolbox by clicking on its icon (see Figure 2.3). Your selection will then become the active tool, and any changes you make to your form will be related to that tool.

Once you have selected the control you want to use in your form, you must then draw the control onto your form. To draw a control, move your mouse pointer back into the Form window, and notice that your mouse cursor now changes to a cross hair. When you draw a control on a form, you position the mouse in the upper-left-hand corner of where you want the control to be, click the left mouse button, and drag a region the size of the final control on your form. Visual Basic will draw the control onto the form to your specifications. An alternative method to drawing your control onto your form is to double-click on the control in the toolbox, which will insert your control in the center of your form and to a default size. You can fine-tune the position and size of all controls later by dragging them around with the pointer tool in your toolbox.

ADDING AN IMAGE TO YOUR FORM

The first control you will use is the PictureBox control. It is used to insert a graphic onto your form. Let's practice adding controls by creating an image on this form.

---

task reference   Adding a Control to a Form

- Locate and click the control you need from the Toolbox window
- Drag a rectangle in the position where you want your control to be placed, and to the necessary size
- Release the mouse button
- Make any necessary modifications to the properties of the control

Adding an image to a form

1. Locate and **click** the PictureBox control in the Toolbox window

2. Position your mouse cursor in the upper-left corner of the Form window

3. Drag your mouse cursor toward the lower-right corner of the Form window, filling about two-thirds of the form (see Figure 2.4)

4. Release the mouse button. Visual Basic will display a dashed-outline box, indicating that an image will appear in this space

FIGURE 2.4

Blank Image control

After placing your PictureBox control onto your form, you must now edit the properties of the image to tell Visual Basic which image it should place on the form and describe how the image should be displayed.

CONTROLS AND PROPERTIES

Every control in the toolbox, except for the pointer tool, has a set of ***properties*** that are used to describe the control that you place on your form. These properties describe the appearance, behavior, and position of your controls. They can be edited using the Properties window, located on the right-hand side of the Visual Basic desktop by default.

To demonstrate how properties affect controls, experiment by changing the appearance of the image that you just created. Initially, Visual Basic does not know which image you want loaded into the space defined by the Image control. You must set the control's Image property to point to a file.

Defining the Picture property of an image

1. Place your data disk in the appropriate drive on your computer

2. Make sure that your new image is selected on your form by clicking it. The Title bar of the Properties window should now indicate which object you have selected, "**PictureBox1**"

3. If the Alphabetic button is not selected in the Properties window, click it. In the Properties section, locate the item labeled Image. It will be highlighted by default (see Figure 2.5)

FIGURE 2.5

Changing the Picture property

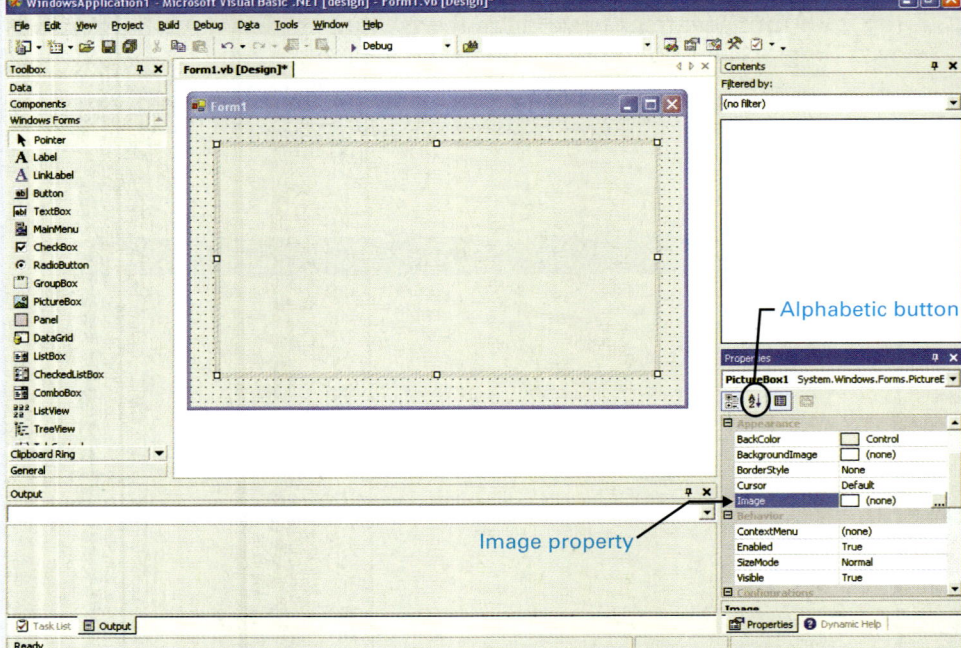

4. Click your mouse in the next cell to the right of the Image property, which should display "(None)" at this point. When you click in this cell, a button with an ellipsis will appear. **Click** this button now to open the Open dialog box

5. Use the tools in the Open dialog box to locate the file **VCS_Logo.gif** on your data disk (see Figure 2.6)

6. Select the file in the file list box and click **Open**. The VanBuren Computer Supply logo will appear within the Image control on your form

7. If necessary, use the sizing handles of the Image control so you can see all of the logo (see Figure 2.7)

You have now successfully added your first control and have adjusted its properties to display any image to your liking. Your form should resemble the one shown in Figure 2.7. If you would like, take time to add a couple of more images to your form so that you get used to the process. But what if you want to remove some of these images from your form?

DELETING A CONTROL

Select the control you would like to modify or delete by clicking it in the Form window. You will know that your control is selected when you see its sizing handles appear. To delete the control, press the Delete key on your keyboard. Alternatively, you may right-click on the control in the Form window and a context-sensitive menu will appear. In this menu, you can then select the Delete option.

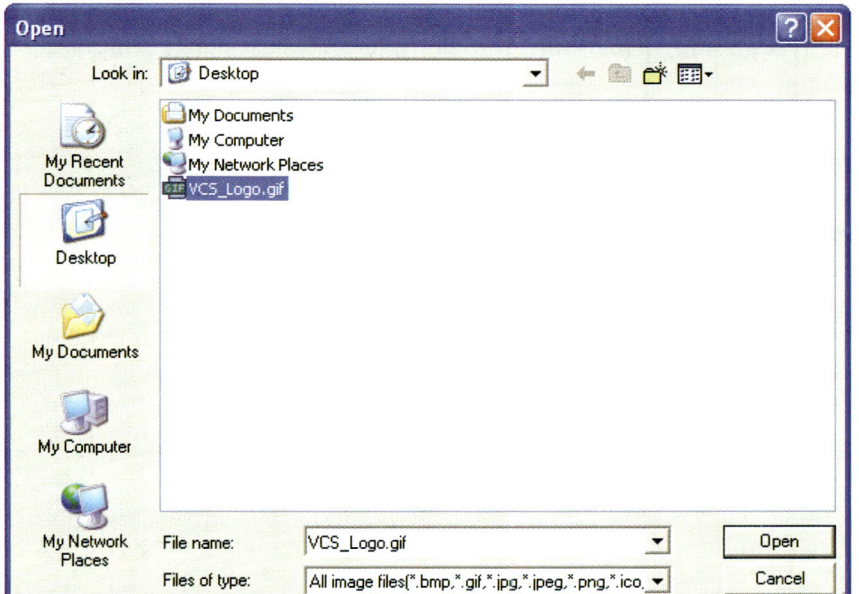

FIGURE 2.6

Selecting an image file

FIGURE 2.7

Complete addition of image

THE LABEL CONTROL

On his splash screen, Tom also would like a copyright notice to appear. Since that means adding text to this form, we need to add a ***Label control*** to this form. A Label control is used in Visual Basic to display static text, meaning that it is text that is not meant to change. Let's discover how to add Tom's copyright notice to this splash screen using a Label control.

Adding a Label control to a form

1. Select the Label control from the Toolbox window

2. Move the mouse cursor back into the Form window

3. Click and drag a box on the form to contain your label. A default label will appear on the form with the text Label1 pre-entered into it

4. Drag the sizing handles of the label control so that it stretches from the left-hand edge of the form to the right-hand edge

5. In the Properties window, locate the Text property in the Properties list. Double-click in the cell to the right to select the **Label1** text

6. Type the following into this cell: **Copyright 2003 Tom VanBuren**

7. Press **Enter** to make the change to the Text property for this Label control

8. Locate the TextAlign property of the label. In the cell to the right, you will see a drop-down list, allowing you to choose from a list of alignment styles for this label

9. Click the down arrow for the list box to display the other options, and click the **Center** option. The drop-down box will collapse, and your selection will be displayed next to the TextAlign property

F I G U R E   2.8

Setting the label properties

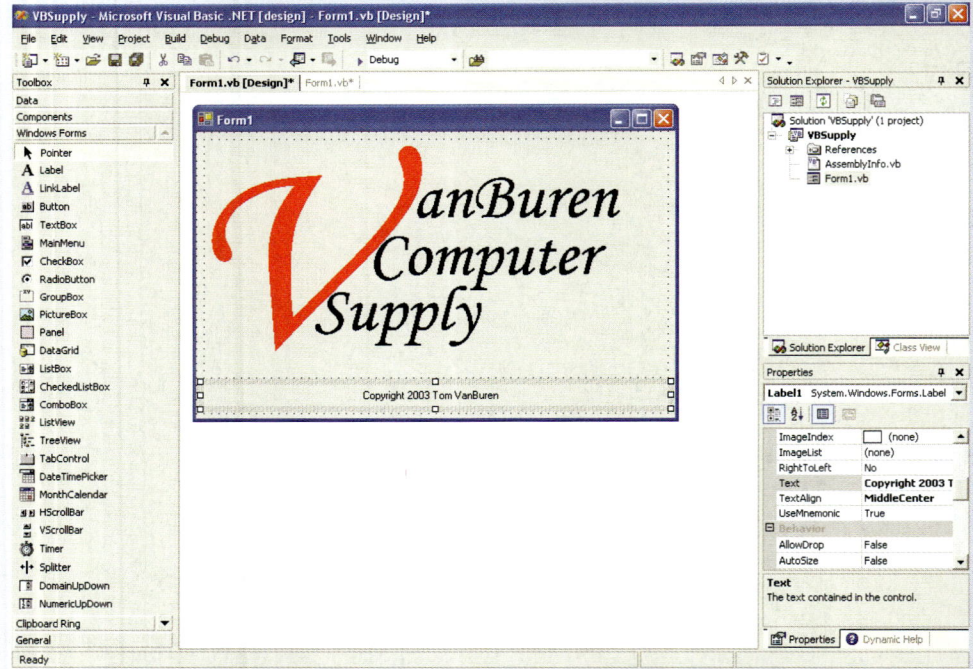

10. Click anywhere outside of the TextAlign property's drop-down box to finalize this change

THE TEXT PROPERTY

In the previous step, you modified the ***Text property*** of the Label control to change the text that the label displays on your form. As it turns out, the Text property is used by many other controls, including Visual Basic forms themselves. Setting a form's Text property (see Figure 2.9) will change the text that appears in the Title bar of the window that holds the form. For example, your form will display a generic message by default, most likely "Form1." It is generally considered good practice to change this text to a more meaningful value.

TESTING YOUR FORM

The Visual Basic environment lets you test your forms whenever you like while you are designing them, to aid development. To test your form at any time, simply press the Start button on the Visual Basic Standard toolbar. This will place your project into run time, and you can interact with your form as you would when it is actually run. To stop your application, either press the Close Window button in the upper-right-hand corner or press the Stop button in Visual Basic's toolbar.

If you wish to do so, save your project following the directions in Session 1.1. Make a note of where you store your project on your computer's disk drive so you may retrieve it later.

FIGURE 2.9

Modifying a form caption

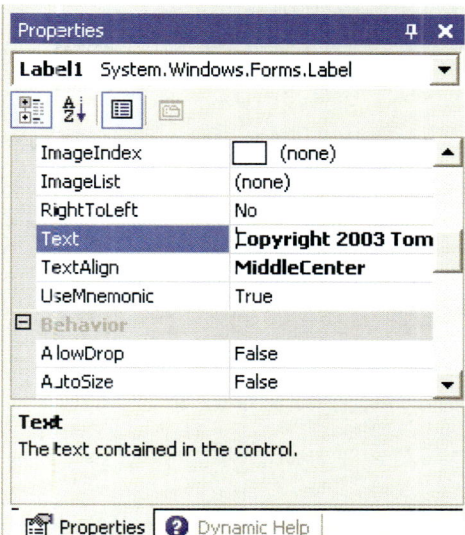

SESSION 2.1

making *the grade*

1. _____ is/are used to resize a control or form.

2. After placing a control on a form, you generally edit its _____ to affect its appearance and behavior.

3. Changing the _____ property of a form will change the text that it displays in its Title bar.

4. In order to remove a control from a form, select it and press _____ on your keyboard.

5. To test your form, press the _____ button to execute it.

SESSION 2.2 GOING FURTHER: A LARGER EXAMPLE

This session will introduce you to more of the commonly used Visual Basic controls and show you how to put them to use in an actual application. You will gain exposure to more complex forms, writing code, and linking to the first form completed in Session 2.1 (see Figure 2.10). Finally, you will compile your application into an executable file and exit Visual Basic.

Now that Tom has completed his splash screen, he wants to continue on to making the sales tracking portion of the program. He opens his splash screen project back into Visual Basic and begins from here. If you do not have the splash screen project open, open it now. It's time to get to work learning Visual Basic. One of the best ways to learn Visual Basic is to learn by doing, so let's follow along with Tom as he builds his application.

Developing Visual Basic projects can be broken down into three basic steps: designing the user interface, laying out the user interface, and writing the code behind the user interface. In general, the development process goes the smoothest if the steps are followed in this order. Let's take a look at what is involved in each step.

FIGURE 2.10

Running your Visual Basic
project

DESIGNING THE USER INTERFACE

The first step to almost any successful project is great planning. The same holds true for a Visual Basic project. Just as an architect draws up a blueprint before any building begins on a house, it is important for you as the programmer to draw up a blueprint of your own that details what your **user interface** will look like. The term *user interface* describes the screen of information you present to your users and the tools you provide for them to interact with your application. The design of your user interface should reflect the goals of the application you are creating. This is where user input is invaluable. It is extremely important that your application meets the user's requirements, and the best way to ensure this is to involve the user in the planning process.

Designing a successful user interface involves asking questions about the goal of your program. One such question may be, "What information will I need to gather from the user?" Another question might be, "What information needs to be displayed on the screen?" As you begin to answer these kinds of questions, you will discover what controls are necessary in your form. Refer to Figure 2.11 for a list of common tasks and the appropriate controls to use to complete these tasks.

Once you have an idea of what controls need to be included, it is common practice to create a sketch of how you will lay out your user interface. Your sketch may be as simple as a group of boxes drawn on a sheet of paper, or it may be a fully labeled diagram of what your finished screen will look like. The important thing is that you define what controls will go where. Figure 2.12 shows Tom's sample sketch of his user interface.

LAYING OUT THE USER INTERFACE

Earlier in Session 2.1 you were given a chance to lay out a simple form. You learned how to select controls from the toolbox and place them onto your form. Once you placed the controls onto your form, you modified some properties of the controls to alter their appearance and/or behavior. Laying out your user interface requires that you repeat this procedure many times over until each control you drew in your sketch is placed onto your form. All that you need to do is familiarize yourself with each of the controls, what they do, how they work, and what their properties change. Tom has provided us with a

FIGURE 2.11
Controls grouped by task

Task	Commonly Used Control
Gathering typed user input	Text box
Providing a selection of options	Check box Radio button Combo box List box
Displaying text information	Label Text box
File navigation	Drive list box Dir list box File list box
Miscellaneous visual elements	Picture box Frame Horizontal scroll bar Vertical scroll bar

FIGURE 2.12
User interface sketch

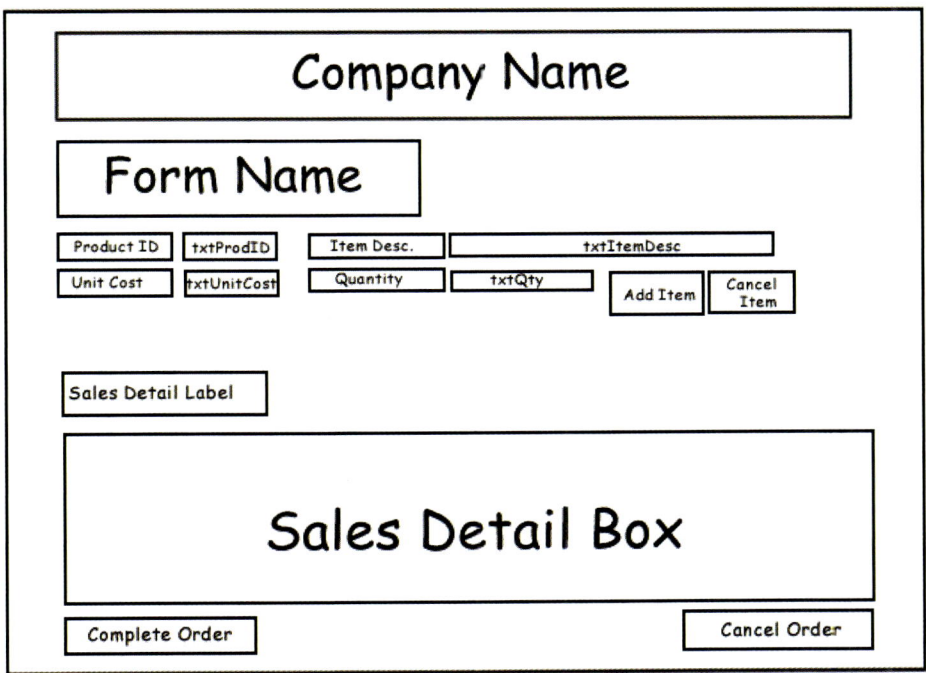

nearly complete copy of his order entry form. His form is missing two text boxes that you need to add. Let's open his file and finish it for him.

Reopening Tom's partial form

1. Make sure that your data disk is placed in the appropriate drive in your computer

2. Locate and open the project **frmOrder.sln** on your data disk

3. Double-click the name of the form in the Project Explorer window to open the form

4. Select **Save frmOrder.vb As** from the File menu to save the form as **frmEntry.vb** to your computer's hard drive

FIGURE 2.13

Tom's nearly complete form

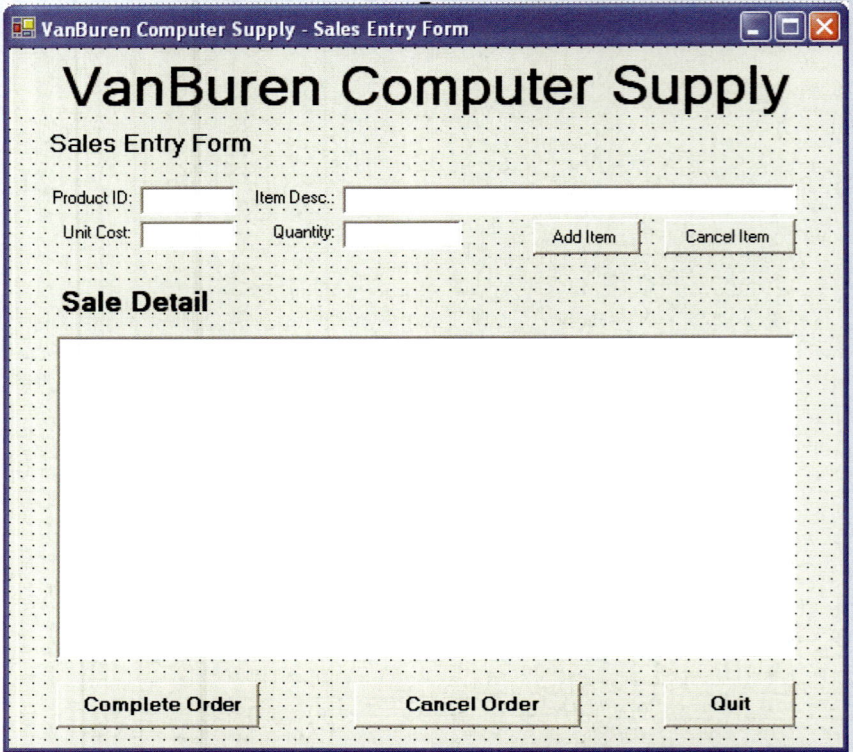

Both of the missing controls on Tom's order entry form are text boxes. A **text box** provides a space for users to type data onto a form. Text boxes can contain a value in them by default, which is stored in the control's Text property, and will accept any number of characters in them unless the number in its MaxLength property is changed. Also, text boxes contain another property called a TabIndex, which defines the order in which the controls will be activated as the user presses the Tab key when filling out the form. This becomes important when you want to lead the user through a logical order of data entry, so we will fix this property as well. We also will add the missing Product ID text box by placing the control on the form and setting its properties.

Adding a Text Box control to the form

1. Select the Text Box control in the Toolbox window

2. Just as you did on the splash screen, drag a Text Box control to the form directly above and the same size as the Unit Cost field. Notice that default text is placed into the box

3. Locate the Text property in the Properties window. Delete the contents of the property by double-clicking the value **TextBox1** and pressing **Delete** on your keyboard

4. Locate the MaxLength property. Replace the property's value by double-clicking in the value cell and type **6**

5. Locate the Name property (the first property in the Alphabetic list) in the Properties window. Change this control's name by double-clicking the property and typing **txtProdID**

6. Locate the TabIndex property of the Text Box control. Change this property by double-clicking it and typing **1**

This leaves one more missing text box: the quantity box. Tom was able to tell us that VanBuren Computer Supply does not sell more than 999 units of any item at one time. Therefore, we know that we can limit the length of the quantity text box to three characters. He also has determined that the Name property of the control must be set to "txtQty," and that the text box should not contain any text by default. That gives us enough information to add the final text box on the form. Refer to Tom's sketch for the placement of this box. Add it now.

Adding the quantity text box to the form

1. Drag a Text Box control onto the form directly beneath the *Item Desc* text box

2. Delete the contents of the control's Text property

3. Locate the control's Name property and type **txtQty**

4. Locate the control's MaxLength property and type **3**

5. Locate the control's TabIndex property and type **4**

6. Click the **Save All** button on the toolbar to save all your changes

Now that the remaining controls have been placed on the form, it should look like the form shown in Figure 2.1. It's a good idea to test your project. If all of the properties of your controls have been set properly, Visual Basic will not display any error messages when you test your form.

WRITING THE CODE FOR YOUR INTERFACE

As you know by now, Visual Basic is an event-driven programming language, which means that programs consist of events that trigger procedures, and the actual procedures themselves. When you write code for a Visual Basic program, you will be writing pieces of code called *event handlers*, which are sections of code that respond to events. You also may write procedures that are not related directly to any event, but those procedures are outside of the scope of this appendix.

Tom was able to figure out how to write the code that makes his order entry form work as he intended. However, one small piece of code he didn't yet write is the event handler for a button he added to his splash screen. Tom thought he would place a button that users would press on the splash page so that it does not disappear before anyone has a good look at it. We have access to this file as well. Let's open his splash screen form, add it to our existing project, and complete Tom's application.

Opening Tom's nearly complete splash page

1. Make sure that your data disk is placed in the appropriate drive in your computer

2. Locate and open the file **frmSplash.sln** on your data disk

3. Double-click the name of the form in the Project Explorer window to open the form

4. Select **Save frmSplash.vb As** from the File menu to save the form as **frmSplsh.vb** to your computer's hard drive (omit the letter "a" from the name)

5. If it is not displayed, open the splash page form by double-clicking it in the Project Explorer window

FIGURE 2.14

Partially complete splash screen

You will notice that Tom has placed an OK button at the bottom of the splash screen that, when pressed, should close the splash screen and open the order entry form. What kind of code does this involve? It means that we must write an event handler that can respond to the OK button being pressed. The event handler will tell the splash screen to hide itself, and will ask the order entry form to show itself.

Visual Basic, like many other newer programming languages such as C/C++ and Java, supports development using a concept known as *object-oriented programming*. Just as forms and controls can be considered the basic pictorial building blocks of a Visual Basic application, an *object* is considered the basic building block in your Visual Basic application's code. Every object, whether it is visual or code, has properties that describe the object to which it belongs. You should now be familiar with the various properties of some of Visual Basic's controls. However, every object will have certain *methods* associated with it as well. Methods are groups of instructions that describe an action that the object can perform. Some examples of methods include **Focus, Resize**, and **Close**. An easy way to think about object-oriented programming is to relate everything to grammar. Objects (or controls) can be considered the "things" of an application, or, in other words, the nouns. Properties act as adjectives of nouns, describing them further to Visual Basic. Methods can be considered the verbs of the programming world, naming the actions that the objects (or nouns) take.

Now that you know what objects, properties, and methods are, how do you write code that uses them? When you are writing code and would like to name an object on your form, you can use the name specified in the object's Name property. For example, in Tom's splash page, he named the button "OKButton." So, in your event handler, you would type "OKButton" to name this button in your code. But naming an object does not cause anything to happen in your code. If you want some action to take place, you must ask an object to execute one of the methods that it understands, or change one of its properties. When you want to refer to a method or property of an object, you use something called **dot notation**. If you wanted to ask a form to print itself, for example, you would write "MyForm.PrintForm" in your code (without the quotes). The left side of the dot names an object, and the right side refers to a method or property.

Given this knowledge of objects and dot notation, how do we put this to use in Tom's splash page? As was mentioned earlier, you must ask the splash page form to hide itself, and ask the order entry form to show itself. This means that the names of the forms will be the nouns to which you need to refer. Visual Basic forms have built-in methods that have been written to hide and show forms. They are called "Hide" and "Show." Use this information to write the event handler for the OK button.

Coding the event handler for the OK button

1. In the frmSplash form, locate the **OK** button and double-click it. This will open the Code window and position your cursor at the event handler that handles the button click event

2. Type **Me.Hide** in the Code window and press **Enter** to move to the next line of your code. Visual Basic will interpret the code you just typed to make sure it is error free

3. Create a new instance of the order entry window by typing **Dim OrderForm As NewfrmOrderEntry** and pressing **Enter**

4. Type **OrderForm.Show** in the Code window and press **Enter** to accept this last line of code

Before you run this application to see if it functions, make sure that the correct screen appears first, since that was the point of the splash screen. This can be accomplished by designating which object in your project is loaded first (see Figure 2.16).

Selecting your project's startup object

1. Click **Project** on the Visual Basic menu bar, then click the **Properties** option at the bottom of the menu (see Figure 2.15). This will open a dialog box similar to the one shown in Figure 2.17

2. In the General area of this window, there is a drop-down box labeled Startup object (see Figure 2.17). Click the Startup object list arrow and select the **frmSplash** object from the list

3. Click the **OK** button

4. Click the **Save All** button to save your changes

FIGURE 2.15

OK button event handler code

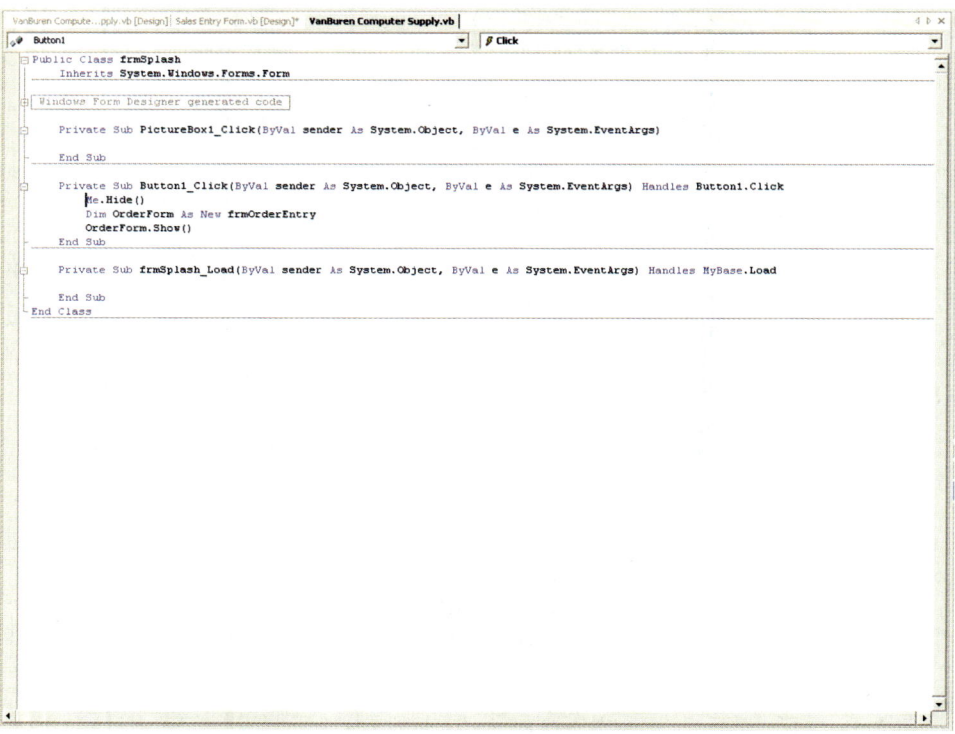

FIGURE 2.16

Project options menu item

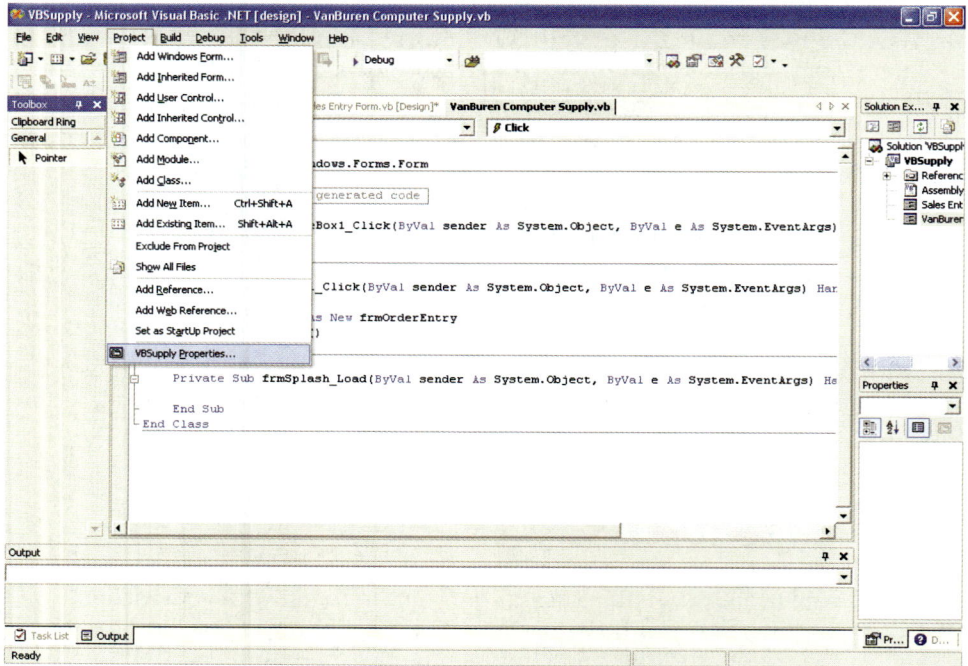

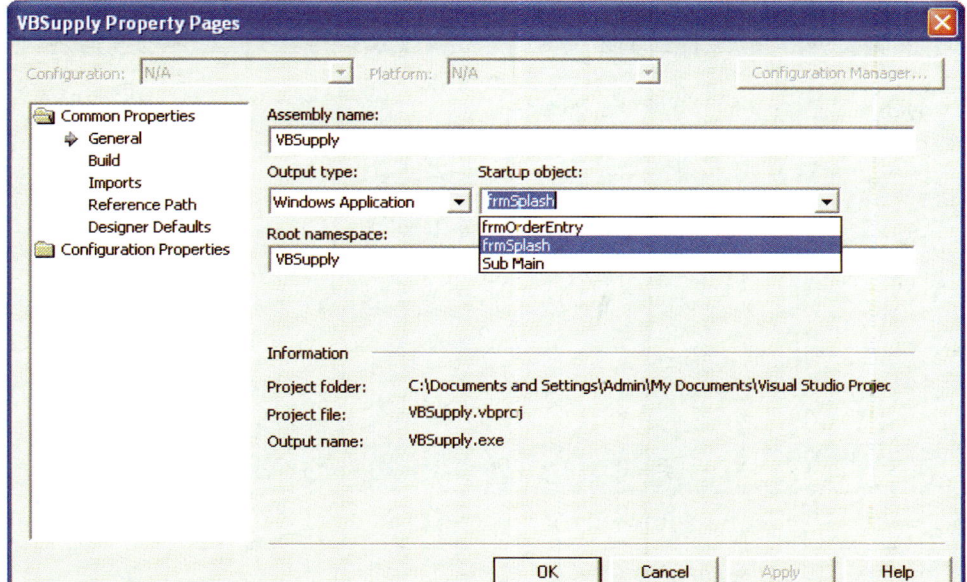

making *the grade*

1. The three steps involved in creating a Visual Basic application are
_____, _____, and _____.

2. _____ is a control/are controls used to provide a space for users to type input on a form.

3. A piece of code that executes in response to a user interacting with a form control is called a/an _____.

SESSION 2.3 SUMMARY

Designing a Visual Basic application consists of three basic steps: designing the user interface, laying out the user interface, and writing the code to support the interface. In order to determine what controls are necessary for your project, you must gather the user's requirements and analyze them to determine what tasks the program must complete. Once you have a list of tasks for your program, determine which controls can be used to complete those tasks.

Controls are placed on a form by first selecting a tool from the Toolbox window. Then, in the Form window, drag with the mouse to draw a bounding box to contain your control. Visual Basic will place a generic control onto the form inside of your bounding box. Then, customize each control by modifying its properties.

Writing code for Visual Basic projects is an easy process that relies on an understanding of object-oriented programming. Objects refer to any nouns in your project (forms, controls, etc.). Properties are the adjectives that describe the appearance and behavior of objects. Methods are the verbs of your program, describing the steps involved in each action that an object can support to execute.

In order to complete your application and distribute it in a format that is usable by most computer users, you should compile your project to output it in a language common to all PCs.

making the grade *answers*

SESSION 2.1

1. Sizing handles

2. properties

3. text

4. delete

5. start

SESSION 2.2

1. designing the user interface, laying out the user interface, writing the code behind the user interface

2. A text box

3. event handler

task reference *summary*

Task	Page #	Preferred Method
Controls, adding to form	VB 2.4	• Click the control you need from the Toolbox window • Drag a rectangle on the form to enclose the control • Release the mouse button • Modify the control parameters to your needs

FILL-IN

1. The _____ control is used to display static text in your Visual Basic program.

2. Drag the _____ of an object to resize it.

3. _____ describe the appearance, behavior, and position of the controls in your Visual Basic program.

4. One control that lets users type text into your program is the _____.

5. An _____ is a piece of code that is executed when a user triggers a specific event.

6. Modifying the Caption property of a form will cause it to display your text in its _____.

REVIEW QUESTIONS

1. Suppose you are creating an order entry screen that will consist of a customer's contact information (name, phone number, address, etc.). Create a list of controls that you would place on the form to accomplish this task. For each control, indicate which kind of control, what task it accomplishes, and any specific properties of the control you would modify (i.e., MaxLength of a text box, Alignment of a label, etc.). Don't forget about buttons that may be necessary to complete the form and tell the computer to accept the user's input.

2. Briefly discuss the three steps involved in the creation of a Visual Basic project.

3. Describe the purpose of the TabIndex property of a control. What does it do? Why is it important?

4. Outline the basic steps you would take to add a Label control to your form. What are some properties of this control that you might modify?

CREATE THE QUESTION

For each of the following answers, create an appropriate, short question.

ANSWER	QUESTION
1. This is a section of code that executes based on a user-triggered event.	_____
2. You must first save the form you are editing, and then the project. Subsequent saves merely require you to save each piece separately.	_____
3. You must grab the object's sizing handles and drag them.	_____
4. These are groups of instructions that are grouped together. Consider them the verbs of an object.	_____
5. This is the option you would most often select from the New Project window when starting a new project.	_____
6. To do this, simply select the object you wish to edit and press Delete on your keyboard.	_____

1. Creating a Customer Information Screen

You have been hired as a freelance developer to create a customer information entry screen for Fast Floral, your neighborhood florist shop. They would like a program that will allow them to type in a customer's name and address, which will then be placed into a database for use in direct mailings at a later date. Currently, you are working on creating their user interface. Create a simple entry screen that will allow them to capture the information they require.

1. Open Visual Basic and begin a new project

2. If necessary, resize your form by dragging its sizing handles

3. Beginning with the Name field, select the label tool from the toolbox and create a small label on your form. Modify the label's Text property by typing **Name** in as the value, set the label's TextAlign property to right justify, and set the TabIndex to **0**

4. Repeat this process for the following fields: Address, City, State, Zip. Set each text box's TabIndex one value higher than the last box's value. Arrange the labels on your form in a vertical fashion, each field below the next

5. Select the Text Box control from your toolbox. For each label you just created, **draw a box** on the screen, directly to the right of the label. Be sure to make the horizontal length of the text boxes appropriate for each field of information. Also, delete the contents of their Text property. When finished, select the Pointer tool

6. For the Name, Address, and City text boxes, select each and modify their MaxLength to be **25**. Similarly, set the State field's text box to have a MaxLength of **2** and Zip's MaxLength to **6**

7. Select your form and change its Caption property by typing **Fast Floral—Add New Customer** in the property's value cell

8. Select the Button tool. Drag a button onto the form and modify its Caption property to read **Add Customer**. Create another button and make its Caption read **Cancel**

9. **Drag** the buttons so that they sit side by side at the bottom of the form

10. Click the **Save** button on the Standard toolbar to save your new form

2. Creating a Flash Card Program

You have been commissioned by FGNB Publishers to create a study program for their upcoming Spanish textbook. They are looking for an application that can display a Spanish word and give the student two buttons to choose from, each with a different English translation on it. A correct choice will yield a positive response, and an incorrect one will produce a negative response. Before producing the actual application, the project manager at FGNB has requested that you send them a mockup of the actual program for them to review.

1. If necessary, start Visual Basic and open a new project

2. **Select** the Label tool from the toolbox. Create a label on the form and make its Caption property read **Translate the following word into English**

3. Create another text label that reads **Queso**. This will be the Spanish word to translate

4. Directly below the Queso label, create two more labels that read **Correct** and **Incorrect**. Set both of their Visible properties to False

5. In each of the labels' Font properties, enter a size of **14**, and change their TextAlign property to MiddleCenter

6. Using the Button tool, draw two buttons on the form. Modify their Caption properties to read **Cheese** and **Pants**

7. **Double-click** the **Cheese** button. When the Code window appears, type the following code on two separate lines:

   ```
   Label4.Visible = False
   Label3.Visible = True
   ```

8. Return to the Form window. **Double-click** on the **Pants** button. Type the following Code into the code window:

   ```
   Label3.Visible = False
   Label4.Visible = True
   ```

9. Set the caption of the form to read **Vocab Quiz**

10. Click the **Save** button on the Standard toolbar to save your new form

challenge!

1. Creating a Software Installation Program

Peter is a new hire at Horizon Software. He has been instructed to create an installation program for their new software product. Peter knows that he wants to first create a mockup of the functionality that will be included in the installation utility. It will need to have two Visual Basic forms, one to let users indicate the filepath where they would like their program installed and one screen to set some options. On the options screen, give the users two options that they can select or deselect in a toggle fashion. One option is to run the program after it has been installed and the other is whether or not to display the Read Me file to the user after installation. Be sure to place buttons on the forms that allow you to move to the next screen, cancel the installation, and begin the installation.

reference 1

Word *File Finder*

Location in Chapter	Data File to Use
CHAPTER 5	
Session 5.1	
Adding a masthead	wd05Email.doc
Adding a reverse to the masthead	wd05Email.doc
Changing the font in the masthead	wd05Email.doc
Inserting a pull quote	wd05Email.doc
Adding a dropped-capital letter to Tim's newsletter	wd05Email.doc
Session 5.2	
Adding columns to Tim's document	wd05Email.doc
Changing the width of Tim's columns	wd05Email.doc
Session 5.3	
Inserting additional columns in Tim's document	wd05Email.doc
Inserting a clip art in Tim's document	wd05Email.doc
Wrapping text around Tim's graphic	wd05Email.doc
Inserting a text box	wd05Email.doc
Hands-On Projects	
Practice Exercise 1	
Practice Exercise 2	wd05Dogs.doc
Challenge Exercise 1	wd05Environment.doc
Challenge Exercise 2	wd05Tours.doc
E-Business Exercise 1	wd05Candy.doc
E-Business Exercise 2	
On the Web Exercise 1	
On the Web Exercise 2	
Around the World Exercise 1	wd05Travelight.doc
Around the World Exercise 2	wd05Directory.doc
Running Project	wd05KasotaNewsPrintMe.doc wd05KasotaNews.doc

REF 1.1

Location in Chapter	Data File to Use
CHAPTER 6	
Session 6.1	
Creating a data source and entering data	wd06Napeletter.doc
Setting up merge for the NAPE letters	wd06Napeletter.doc
Session 6.2	
Creating mailing labels for letters to NAPE members	wd06Napeletter.doc
Creating a directory	wd06Napeletter.doc
Sorting by zip code	wd06Napeletter.doc
Session 6.3	
Embedding a worksheet into Word	wd06Contest.doc
Creating a directory by querying an Excel worksheet	wd06Contest.doc
Hands-On Projects	
Practice Exercise 1	wd06NapeYou.doc
Practice Exercise 2	wd06NapeNamesComplete.doc
Challenge Exercise 1	wd06Steakhouse.doc
Challenge Exercise 2	wd06NapeMeeting.doc
E-Business Exercise 1	wd06AssignMain.doc
E-Business Exercise 2	wd06Sales.doc
On the Web Exercise 1	
On the Web Exercise 2	
Around the World Exercise 1	
Around the World Exercise 2	
Running Project	wd06Scholarship.doc
CHAPTER 7	
Session 7.1	
Assigning outline levels to Applied Animal Nutrition lecture	wd07Lecture.doc
Sending a lecture outline to PowerPoint	wd07Lecture.doc
Session 7.2	
Saving a Word document as a Web page	wd07Petfood.doc
Saving and viewing a Word document as a Web page	wd07Petfood.doc
Session 7.3	
Using the Document Map	wd07Lecture.doc

Location in Chapter	Data File to Use
Adding a Bookmark	wd07Lecture.doc
Creating a hyperlink to a different Web site	wd07Lecture.doc
Hands-On Projects	
Practice Exercise 1	wd07Lecture2.doc
Practice Exercise 2	wd07Menu.doc
Challenge Exercise 1	
Challenge Exercise 2	wd07HowTo.doc
E-Business Exercise 1	wd07Ecommerce.doc
E-Business Exercise 2	wd07EcommerceWeb.doc
On the Web Exercise 1	
On the Web Exercise 2	
Around the World Exercise 1	
Around the World Exercise 2	
Running Project	wd07Presentation.doc
CHAPTER 8	
Session 8.1	
Creating a master document from a file	wd08KranMain.doc
Renaming subdocuments to preserve the original files	wd08KranPart2.doc wd08KranPart3.doc
Inserting a file as a subdocument of a master document	wd08KranMain.doc wd08KranPart2.doc wd08KranPart3.doc
Opening a master document	wd08KranMain.doc wd08KranPart2.doc wd08KranPart3.doc
Session 8.2	
Moving to a subdocument from a master document	wd08KranMain.doc wd08KranPart2.coc wd08KranPart3.coc
Session 8.3	
Numbering front matter pages	wd08KranMain.coc
Hands-On Projects	
Practice Exercise 1	wd08Worksheet1.doc wd08Worksheet2.doc wd08Worksheet3.doc
Practice Exercise 2	wd08Listproc.doc

Location in Chapter	Data File to Use
Challenge Exercise 1	wd08Pakistan1.doc wd08Pakistan2.doc wd08Pakistan3.doc
Challenge Exercise 2	wd08ScholarshipErrata.doc wd08ScholarshipFunding.doc wd08ScholarshipList.doc
E-Business Exercise 1	wd08GlobusPartA.doc wd08GlobusPartB.doc wd08GlobusPartC.doc
E-Business Exercise 2	wd08Trinidad.doc
On the Web Exercise 1	
On the Web Exercise 2	
Around the World Exercise 1	wd08Austen.doc
Around the World Exercise 2	
Running Project	wd08Kasota.doc

Excel *File Finder*

Location in Chapter	Data File to Use
CHAPTER 5	
Session 5.1	
Opening the Employee worksheet and saving it under a new name	ex05Employee.xls
Freezing label rows and employee name columns	Employee1.xls
Session 5.2	
Filtering a list with the AutoFilter command	Employee2.xls
Session 5.2	
Creating the pivot table layout	Employee3.xls
Hands-on Projects	
Practice Exercise 1	ex05Fairmont.xls
Practice Exercise 2	ex05Grades.xls
Challenge Exercise 1	ex05Shores.xls
Challenge Exercise 2	ex05Doctors.xls
E-Business Exercise 1	ex05Service.xls
E-Business Exercise 2	ex05FuturesTrading.xls
On the Web Exercise 1	(new file)
On the Web Exercise 2	ex05Salaries.xls
Around the World Exercise 1	ex05Tennis.xls
Around the World Exercise 2	ex05Varoom.xls
Running Project	ex05ProGolf.xls
CHAPTER 6	
Session 6.1	
Opening the Loan Analysis workbook and saving it under a new name	ex06CalsCars.xls
Entering input values in the Assumptions area	CalsCars1.xls
Session 6.2	
Writing the PMT function	CalsCars2.xls
Hands-on Projects	
Practice Exercise 1	ex06Savings.xls
Practice Exercise 2	ex06CarLoan.xls

REFERENCE

Location in Chapter	Data File to Use
Challenge Exercise 1	ex06Desserts.xls
Challenge Exercise 2	ex06Shipping.xls
E-Business Exercise 1	ex06Leitman.xls
E-Business Exercise 2	ex06Avocado.xls
On the Web Exercise 1	ex06Conservative.xls
On the Web Exercise 2	ex06Stocks.xls
Around the World Exercise 1	ex06AbroadCosts.xls
Around the World Exercise 2	ex06Marathon.xls
Running Project	ex06ProGolf.xls
CHAPTER 7	
Session 7.1	
Copying the Van Buren worksheet to the BECO master workbook	ex07Beco.xls, ex07VanBuren.xls
Copying the West Lafayette worksheet to the BECO master workbook	Beco2.xls, ex07WestLafayette.xls
Session 7.2	
Opening the Danielli workbook	ex07Danielli.xls
Opening the BECO workbook and entering a link formula	Danielli3.xls, Beco3.xls
Redirecting link references to a renamed supporting workbook	Beco3.xls, Acquisition.xls
Hands-on Projects	
Practice Exercise 1	ex07ReedReps.xls
Practice Exercise 2	ex07DelzuraHawthorne.xls, ex07DelzuraPortland.xls, ex07DelzuraMain.xls
Challenge Exercise 1	ex07Kelleher.xls
Challenge Exercise 2	ex07Robot.xls, ex07RobotPets.xls
E-Business Exercise 1	ex07AIFlorida.xls, ex07AIGeorgia.xls, ex07AILouisiana.xls
On the Web Exercise 1	ex07LawSchools.xls
Around the World Exercise 1	ex07Wilton.xls
Around the World Exercise 2	ex07JumpStart.xls, ex07Tokyo.xls, ex07Beijing.xls
Running Project	ex07ProGolf.xls

Location in Chapter	Data File to Use
CHAPTER 8	
Session 8.1	
Opening the Nivaca workbook and displaying the Formula Auditing toolbar	ex08Nivaca.xls
Tracing the precedent cells for a formula	<yourname>Nivaca2.xls
Session 8.2	
Establishing a shared Nivaca workbook	<yourname>Nivaca2.xls
Opening the shared and modified Nivaca workbook	ex08NivacaShared.xls
Reviewing others' comments	<yourname>Nivaca3.xls
Session 8.3	
Opening the Nivaca workbook and saving it under a new name	<yourname>Nivaca3.xls
Hiding select cells' formulas	<yourname>Nivaca4.xls
Reviewing a noninteractive Web workbook page	NivacaSales.mht
Performing what-if analysis with an interactive Web workbook	NivacaSalesInteractive.mht
Hands-on Projects	
Practice Exercise 1	ex08ScripVantage.xls
Practice Exercise 2	ex08Grimwald.xls
Challenge Exercise 1	ex08PrinterTCO.xls
Challenge Exercise 2	ex08GradeCalc.xls
E-Business Exercise 1	ex08IncredibleCheesecake.xls
E-Business Exercise 2	ex08LathramInvoice.xls
On the Web Exercise 1	ex08ExoticFruit.xls
On the Web Exercise 2	ex08Sunny.xls
Around the World Exercise 1	ex08AfricanCoffee.xls
Running Project	ex08ProGolf.xls

REFERENCE

Access *File Finder*

Location in Chapter	Data File to Use
CHAPTER 5	
Session 5.1	
Creating the Customer form in Design View	ac05KoryoKicks.mdb
Adding content to the Form Header	ac05KoryoKicks.gif
Session 5.2	
Customizing the Customer AutoReport	ac05KoryoKicks.mdb
Adding the Report Header to the Customer report	ac05KoryoKicks.gif
Hands-on Projects	
Practice Exercise 1	ac05Cyberia.mdb ac05Cyberia.tif
Practice Exercise 2	ac05GradeBook.mdb ac05GradeBookLogo.gif
Challenge Exercise 1	ac05CyberiaChallenge.mdb ac05Cyberia.tif
Challenge Exercise 2	ac05GradeBookChallenge.mdb ac05GradeBookLogo.gif
E-Business Exercise 1	ac05SportsPix.mdb ac05SportsPix.tif
E-Business Exercise 2	ac05NMOEnergy.mdb ac05NMOLogo.gif ac05DiamondBullett.emf
On the Web Exercise 1	ac05TerraPatrimonium.mdb ac05TerraPatrimonium.tif
Around the World Exercise 1	ac05Seminars.mdb ac05TechRocks.tif
Running Project	ac05TnT.mdb ac05TnT.tif
CHAPTER 6	
Session 6.1	
Viewing KoryoKicks relationships	ac06KoryoKicks.mdb
Session 6.2	
Creating a multitable query, InvoiceJoin	ac06KoryoKicks.mdb
Creating a logo and title for the InvoiceJoinWithCalc report	ac06KoryoKicksLogo.gif

Location in Chapter	Data File to Use
Hands-on Projects	
Practice Exercise 1	ac06AltamonteBcosters.mdb
Practice Exercise 2	ac06NMOEnergy.mdb
Challenge Exercise 1	ac06AltamonteBcosters.mdb
Challenge Exercise 2	ac06NMOEnergy.mdb
E-Business Exercise 1	ac06CurbsideRecycling.mdb
E-Business Exercise 2	ac06CommunityHospital.mdb ac06Nurse.gif
On the Web Exercise 1	ac06Software.mdb
Around the World Exercise 1	ac06Seminars.mcb
Running Project	ac06TnT.mdb
CHAPTER 7	
Session 7.1	
Customizing the Customer table input masks	ac07KoryoKicks.mdb
Session 7.2	
Splitting the KoryoKicks database	ac07KoryoKicks.mdb
Hands-on Projects	
Practice Exercise 1	ac07AltamonteBoosters.mdb
Practice Exercise 2	ac07BBsShoes.mdb
Challenge Exercise 1	ac07AltamonteBoosters.mdb
Challenge Exercise 2	ac07HealthCare2Go.mdb
E-Business Exercise 1	ac07CurbsideRecycling.mdb
E-Business Exercise 2	ac07SportBabies.mdb
On the Web Exercise 1	ac07Software.mdb
Around the World Exercise 1	ac07SSeminars.mdb
Running Project	ac07TnT.mdb
CHAPTER 8	
Session 8.1	
Creating a report with a chart	ac08KoryoKicks.mdb
Linking a Word document to the OrdersByStateChart report	ac08OrdersAnalysis.doc
Importing ac08NewCustomerContacts.mdb	ac08NewCustomerContacts.mdb
Importing ac08Importers.xls	ac08Importers.xls

REFERENCE

Location in Chapter	Data File to Use
Session 8.2	
Exporting Importers.html	ac08KoryoKicks.mdb
Adding an Image to ImportersDataAccess.htm	ac08Warrior.gif
Importing WebImporters.htm as an Access table	ac08WebImporters.htm
Entering and repairing a hyperlink in WebImporters	ac08KoryoKicksHome.htm
Hands-on Projects	
Practice Exercise 1	ac08AltamonteBoosters.mdb
Practice Exercise 2	ac08ScaleModels.mdb
Challenge Exercise 1	ac08AltamonteBoosters.mdb ac08AltamonteSummary.doc
Challenge Exercise 2	ac08ScaleModels.mdb ac08ScaleModel.gif
E-Business Exercise 1	ac08CurbsideRecycling.mdb ac08Competition.xls
E-Business Exercise 2	ac08xXtreMeSportz.mdb ac08xXtreMeSportzLinks.xls ac08xXtreMeSportz.gif
On the Web Exercise 1	ac08Software.mdb ac08SoftwareTitles.xls
Around the World Exercise 1	ac08Seminars.mdb ac08Seminars.gif
Running Project	ac08TnT.mdb

PowerPoint *File Finder*

Location in Chapter	Data File to Use
CHAPTER 5	
Hands-on Projects	
Practice Exercise 1	pp05HeapCollectors.ppt
Practice Exercise 2	pp05AirTraffic.ppt
Challenge Exercise 1	pp05PlazaMall.ppt
Challenge Exercise 2	pp05BrewHAHA.ppt
E-Business Exercise 1	pp05ExoticFlora.ppt
E-Business Exercise 2	pp05e-Business.ppt
On the Web Exercise 1	pp05EUCurrency.ppt
On the Web Exercise 2	pp05HummerGear.ppt
Around the World Exercise 1	pp05GoldenGlobe.ppt
Around the World Exercise 2	pp05USGTF.ppt
Running Project	pp05MWFoodsPresentation.ppt
CHAPTER 6	
Hands-on Projects	
Practice Exercise 1	pp06StoryWeavers.ppt
Practice Exercise 2	pp06FourWheelin.ppt
Challenge Exercise 1	(new file)
Challenge Exercise 2	pp06Doctor.ppt
E-Business Exercise 1	pp06TrekkingAssistant.ppt
E-Business Exercise 2	pp06WheelWomen.ppt
On the Web Exercise 1	pp06WorldHorizons.ppt
On the Web Exercise 2	pp06CollegeAdmissions.ppt
Around the World Exercise 1	pp06ArrowBriefings.ppt
Around the World Exercise 2	pp06WorldGenes.ppt
Running Project	pp06MWFTracking.ppt
CHAPTER 7	
Hands-on Projects	
Practice Exercise 1	pp07WildlifeMgmt.ppt
Practice Exercise 2	pp07BUFF.ppt

REFERENCE

Location in Chapter	Data File to Use
Challenge Exercise 1	pp07SafeFoods.ppt
Challenge Exercise 2	pp07FoothillsGolf.ppt
E-Business Exercise 1	pp07Photos.ppt
E-Business Exercise 2	pp07WildWest.ppt
On the Web Exercise 1	pp07Heritage.ppt
On the Web Exercise 2	pp07eDEV.ppt
Around the World Exercise 1	pp07SonicStrategies.ppt
Around the World Exercise 2	pp07AirFares.ppt
Running Project	pp07MWFTraining.ppt
CHAPTER 8	
Hands-on Projects	
Practice Exercise 1	pp08Triathlon.ppt
Practice Exercise 2	pp08AutoAdvice.ppt
Challenge Exercise 1	pp08TriathlonBroadcast.ppt
Challenge Exercise 2	<yourname>AutoAdvice.ppt
E-Business Exercise 1	pp08BalloonAdventures.ppt
E-Business Exercise 2	pp08BrewHAHA.ppt
On the Web Exercise 1	pp08CulinaryArts.ppt
On the Web Exercise 2	pp08Internet2.ppt
Around the World Exercise 2	pp08HolisticHealth.ppt
Running Project	pp08MWFWebPresentation.ppt

reference 2

Word *Microsoft Office Specialist Certification Guide*

Microsoft Office Specialist Objective	Task	Session Location	End-of-Chapter Location
CHAPTER 5	**Desktop Publishing**		
WW03S-3-3	Apply and format columns	5.2	5.22
WW03E-2-4	Summarize document content using automated tools	5.3	5.22
CHAPTER 6	**Merging Documents and Object Linking and Embedding**		
WW03E-2-6	Merge letters with other data sources	6.2	6.24
WW03E-2-7	Merge labels with other data sources	6.2	6.24
WW03E-1-4	Insert and modify objects	6.3	6.24
CHAPTER 7	**Outlines, PowerPoint, and Web Pages**		
WW03S-2-2	Create bulleted lists, and numbered lists and outlines	7.1	7.24
WW03S-5-4	Save documents in appropriate formats for different uses	7.2	7.24
WW03S-5-6	Preview documents and Web pages	7.2	7.24
WW03S-2-3	Insert and modify hyperlinks	7.3	7.24
WW03E-2-8	Structure documents using XML	7.2	7.24
WW03E-4-2	Publish and edit Web documents in Word	7.2	7.24
WW03E-2-5	Use automated tools for document navigation	7.3	7.24
CHAPTER 8	**Creating and Managing Long Documents**		
WW03E-3-5	Create and manage master documents and subdocuments	8.1	8.43
WW03E-3-3	Create and modify document indexes and tables	8.3	8.43
WW03E-3-4	Insert and modify endnotes, footnotes, captions, and cross-references	8.3	8.43

REF 2.1

REFERENCE

Excel Microsoft Office Specialist Certification Guide

Microsoft Office Specialist Objective	Task	Session Location	End-of-Chapter Location
CHAPTER 5	**Exploring Excel's List Features**		
XL03S-1-2	Navigate to specific cell content	5.1	EX 5.52
XL03S-2-1	Filter lists using AutoFilter	5.2	EX 5.52
XL03S-2-2	Sort lists	5.1	EX 5.52
XL03S-5-6	Customize Window layout	5.1	EX 5.52
XL03E-1-1	Use subtotals	5.2	EX 5.52
XL03E-1-2	Define and apply advanced filters	5.2	EX 5.52
XL03E-1-3	Group and outline data	5.2	EX 5.52
XL03E-1-5	Create and modify list ranges	5.1	EX 5.52
XL03E-1-8	Create PivotTable and PivotChart reports	5.3	EX 5.52
XL03E-1-14	Define, modify, and use named ranges	5.3	EX 5.52
XL03E-2-2	Use conditional formatting	5.2	EX 5.52
CHAPTER 6	**Employing Functions**		
XL03S-2-3	Insert and modify formulas	6.1	EX 6.34
XL03S-2-4	Use statistical, date and time, financial, and logical functions	6.2	EX 6.34
XL03E-1-4	Use data validation	6.1	EX 6.34
XL03E-1-9	Use Lookup and Reference functions	6.1	EX 6.34
XL03E-1-14	Define, modify, and use named ranges	6.1	EX 6.34
CHAPTER 7	**Developing Multiple Worksheet and Workbook Applications**		
XL03S-3-4	Format worksheets	7.1	EX 7.39
XL03S-5-4	Organize worksheets	7.1	EX 7.39
XL03S-5-6	Customize Window layout	7.1	EX 7.39
XL03S-5-7	Set up pages for printing	7.1	EX 7.39
XL03E-1-14	Define, modify, and use named ranges	7.2	EX 7.39
XL03E-4-4	Create and edit templates	7.1	EX 7.39
XL03E-5-3	Modify Excel default settings	7.2	EX 7.39

Microsoft Office Specialist Objective	Task	Session Location	End-of-Chapter Location
CHAPTER 8	**Auditing, Sharing, Protecting, and Publishing Workbooks**		
XL03S-3-4	Format worksheets	8.1	EX 8.43
XL03S-4-1	Insert, view, and edit comments	8.2	EX 8.43
XL03S-5-3	Create and modify hyperlinks	8.2	EX 8.43
XL03E-1-11	Trace formula precedents, dependents, and errors	8.1	EX 8.43
XL03E-1-12	Locate invalid data and formulas	8.1	EX 8.43
XL03E-3-1	Protect cells, worksheets, and workbooks	8.3	EX 8.43
XL03E-3-2	Apply workbook security settings	8.3	EX 8.43
XL03E-3-3	Share workbooks	8.2	EX 8.43
XL03E-3-5	Track, accept, and reject changes to workbooks	8.2	EX 8.43
XL03E-4-3	Publish and edit Web worksheets and workbooks	8.3	EX 8.43

REFERENCE

Access *Microsoft Office Specialist Certification Guide*

Microsoft Office Specialist Objective	Task	Session Location	End-of-Chapter Location
CHAPTER 5	**Customizing Forms and Reports**		
AC03S-1-9	Changing form properties	5.1	AC 5.42
AC03S-1-9	Repositioning Customer form controls	5.1	AC 5.42
AC03S-1-11	Customizing the Customer AutoReport	5.2	AC 5.42
AC03S-1-11	Building the Customer report in Design View	5.2	AC 5.42
AC03S-1-11	Editing label captions	5.2	AC 5.42
AC03S-1-11	Aligning Customer report controls	5.2	AC 5.42
AC03S-1-11	Adding the Customer report date and time	5.2	AC 5.42
AC03S-3-2	Creating the Customer form in Design View	5.1	AC 5.42
AC03S-3-2	Changing labels	5.1	AC 5.42
AC03S-3-2	Changing text boxes	5.1	AC 5.42
AC03S-3-2	Adding Form Header/Footer	5.1	AC 5.42
AC03S-3-2	Adding content to the Form Header	5.1	AC 5.42
AC03S-3-3	Adding page numbers to the Customer report	5.2	AC 5.42
AC03S-3-3	Adding the Report Header to the Customer report	5.2	AC 5.42
AC03S-3-3	Adding separators to the Customer report	5.2	AC 5.42
AC03S-3-3	Adding a report total (Count) to the Customer report	5.2	AC 5.42
AC03S-3-3	Adding Sorting and Grouping to the Customer report	5.2	AC 5.42
AC03S-3-3	Adding State Header and Footer content	5.2	AC 5.42
AC03S-3-3	Hiding duplicate State values	5.2	AC 5.42
AC03S-3-5	Finding form records	5.1	AC 5.42
AC03S-3-5	Filtering form records	5.1	AC 5.42
AC03S-4-2	Querying an Open Form	5.1	AC 5.42

Microsoft Office Specialist Objective	Task	Session Location	End-of-Chapter Location
AC03S-4-2	Customizing the Customer AutoReport	5.2	AC 5.42
AC03S-4-2	Building the Customer report in Design View	5.2	AC 5.42
AC03S-4-2	Previewing and printing reports	5.2	AC 5.42
CHAPTER 6	**Defining Table Relationships**		
AC03S-1-5	Viewing KoryoKicks relationships	6.1	AC 6.39
AC03S-1-5	Viewing KoryoKicks relationship properties	6.1	AC 6.39
AC03S-1-5	Building a one-to-one relationship	6.1	AC 6.39
AC03S-1-5	Deleting a table and its associated relationships	6.1	AC 6.39
AC03S-1-5	Building a one-to-many relationship	6.1	AC 6.39
AC03S-1-6	Viewing KoryoKicks relationship properties	6.1	AC 6.39
AC03S-4-1	Viewing KoryoKicks object dependencies	6.2	AC 6.39
CHAPTER 7	**Maintaining Databases**		
AC03S-1-4	Customizing the Customer table input masks	7.1	AC 7.35
AC03S-1-4	Customizing the Order.OrderDate field format	7.1	AC 7.35
AC03S-1-4	Adding default values to the KoryoKicks database	7.1	AC 7.35
AC03S-1-4	Requiring fields in the KoryoKicks database	7.1	AC 7.35
AC03S-1-4	Adding field validation to the KoryoKicks database	7.1	AC 7.35
CHAPTER 8	**Integrating with Other Applications**		
AC03S-1-12	Using the Page Wizard to create ImportersDataAccess.htm	8.2	AC 8.46
AC03S-1-12	Adding scrolling text to ImportersDataAccess.htm	8.2	AC 8.46
AC03S-1-12	Adding an Image to ImportersDataAccess.htm	8.2	AC 8.46
AC03S-1-12	Applying a Theme to ImportersDataAccess.htm	8.2	AC 8.46
AC03S-2-3	Linking a Word document to the OrdersByStateChart report	8.1	AC 8.46

REFERENCE

Microsoft Office Specialist Objective	Task	Session Location	End-of-Chapter Location
AC03S-2-3	Embedding a Word document in the OrdersByStateChart report	8.1	AC 8.46
AC03S-2-3	Importing ac08NewCustomerContacts.mdb	8.1	AC 8.46
AC03S-2-3	Linking ac08NewCustomerContacts.mdb	8.1	AC 8.46
AC03S-2-3	Importing ac08Importers.xls	8.1	AC 8.46
AC03S-2-3	Importing WebImporters.htm as an Access table	8.2	AC 8.46
AC03S-2-3	Confirming the import	8.2	AC 8.46
AC03S-4-4	Exporting ProductByStateCrosstab.rtf	8.1	AC 8.46
AC03S-4-4	Exporting OrderData.xls	8.1	AC 8.46
AC03S-4-4	Exporting Importers.html	8.2	AC 8.46

PowerPoint *Microsoft Office Specialist Certification Guide*

Microsoft Office Specialist Objective	Task	Session Location	End-of-Chapter Location
CHAPTER 5	**Creating a Multimedia Presentation**		
PP03S-2-5	Apply Slide Transitions	5.1	PP 5.31
PP03S-1-5	Insert objects	5.1	PP 5.31
PP03S-4-3	Rehearse timings	5.1	PP 5.31
PP03S-2-2	Format pictures, shapes, and graphics	5.2	PP 5.31
CHAPTER 6	**Color Schemes and Drawing**		
PP03S-2-3	Formatting slides	6.1	PP 6.37
PP03S-2-2	Format pictures, shapes, and graphics	6.2	PP 6.37
CHAPTER 7	**Internet/Intranet Presentations**		
PP03S-4-2	Set up slide shows for delivery	7.1	PP 7.27
PP03S-4-6	Save and publish presentations	7.2	PP 7.27
CHAPTER 8	**PowerPoint Power Features**		
PP03S-4-5	Prepare presentations for remote delivery	8.1	PP 8.32
PP03S-3-1	Track, accept, and reject changes in a presentation	8.2	PP 8.32
PP03S-3-2	Add, edit, and delete comments in a presentation	8.2	PP 8.32
PP03S-3-3	Compare and merge presentations	8.2	PP 8.32

REFERENCE

reference 3

Word *Task Reference Summary*

Task	Page #	Preferred Method
Adding a dropped-capital letter	WD 5.8	• Click immediately before the text where you want the drop cap to appear • On the **Format** menu, click on the **Drop Cap** command to view the dialog box • Click the position icon for **Dropped** • Choose the font, lines to drop, or distance from text • Click **OK**
Turning on readability statistics	WD 5.9	• On the **Tools** menu, click **Options**, and then click the **Spelling & Grammar** tab • Select the **Check grammar with spelling** check box • Select the **Show readability statistics** check box, and then click **OK** • On the **Standard** toolbar, click **Spelling and Grammar** • When Microsoft Word finishes checking spelling and grammar, it displays information about the reading level of the document
Setting up columns	WD 5.10	• Switch to **Print Layout view** • To format the entire document in columns, click **Select All** on the **Edit** menu or • To format part of the document in columns, select the text or • To format existing sections in columns, click in a section or select multiple sections • On the Standard toolbar, click **Columns** button • Drag to select the number of columns you want • To set exact column widths and spacing, follow steps 1 and 2 • Click **Columns** on the **Format** menu, and select the options you want
Changing the width of columns	WD 5.11	• Click on the **Format** menu and click **Columns** • Set the column widths in the dialog box • Click **OK**
Forcing the start of a new column	WD 5.12	• Switch to **Print Layout view** • Click where you want to start the new column • On the **Insert** menu, click **Break** • Click **Column break**
Displaying multiple column format on the same page	WD 5.13	• Select the text that will appear in the columns • Choose the **Columns** option from the **Format** menu • In the **Number of Columns** field, specify the number of columns you desire • In the **Apply to** box, make sure it says **Selected Text** • Click your mouse on **OK**
Changing the number of columns	WD 5.14	• On the **Format** menu, click on **Columns** to view the columns dialog box • Enter in the number of columns • Click **OK**
Inserting a clip art	WD 5.17	• On the **Insert** menu, point to **Picture**, and click **Clip Art** • In the task pane in the **Search** text box, type a word or phrase that describes the image you want or leave the Search text box blank to display all clip art images or • In the **Search in** box, click the arrow and select the collections you want to search

Task	Page #	Preferred Method
		or • In the **Results should be** box, click the arrow and select the check box next to the types of clips you want to find • Click **Search**
Wrapping text	WD 5.17	• Click on the graphic where you want to wrap the text • Click on the Format menu, click Picture • Click on the **Layout** tab and select a Wrapping style • Click **OK**
Adding bullets or numbers	WD 5.19	• **Select** the items you want to add bullets or numbers • On the Formatting toolbar, do one of the following: • To add bullets, **click** Bullets button or • To add numbering, **click** Numbering button
Adding borders and shading	WD 5.19	• Select the column where you want to apply a border or shading • On the **Format** menu, click **Borders and Shading** • Select the **Borders** tab and apply the desired border or • Select the **Shading** tab and apply the desired shading
Inserting an AutoShape	WD 5.20	• On the Drawing toolbar, click **AutoShapes**, point to a category, and then click the shape you want • To insert a shape with a predefined size, click the document • To insert a different size, drag the shape to the size you want • To maintain the shape's width-to-height ratio, hold down **Shift** while you drag the shape • To add color, change borders, rotate, add shadow, or 3-D effects select the object, and then use the buttons on the Drawing toolbar
Creating a Text Box	WD 5.20	• On the Drawing toolbar, click the **Text Box** button • To insert a text box with a predefined size, click the document • To insert a text box with a different size, drag its sizing handles until the text box is the size you want • To maintain the text box's width-to-height ratio, hold down **Shift** while you drag the sizing handles • Position the text box by dragging it to the location you want
Using the Mail Merge Wizard	WD 6.4	• To start the Mail Merge Wizard in the task pane, click **Tools, Letters and Mailings, Mail Merge** • Indicate which type of document by clicking to select **Letters, E-mail messages, Envelopes, Labels**, or **Directory** • Determine where the document will be found—a new one, a template, or one already saved • Continue following steps at the bottom of the task pane
Creating a data source with Mail Merge Wizard	WD 6.7	• Click **Tools, Letters and Mailings, Mail Merge** • Select document type • Click **Next: Starting document** • Select type of starting document • Click **Next: Select recipients** • Select **Type a new list** • Click **Create** • Click **Customize** to remove fields • Enter data • Click **Close** when all data have been entered into the fields • Provide filename for data source

Task	Page #	Preferred Method
Inserting merge fields	WD 6.8	• Click **View, Toolbars, Mail Merge** • On the Mail Merge toolbar, click **Insert Merge Fields** button • Select the fields and click **Insert** or • Using the Mail Merge Wizard, open the **Merge Field dialog box** • Click **Insert** • Click **Close**
Creating mailing labels	WD 6.11	• Open a new blank document • Click **Tools, Letters and Mailings, Mail Merge** • Select **Labels** as the document type from the merge task pane • Click **Next: Starting document**, click **Label Options** • From the Label Products drop-down list of the Label Information section, select the correct label • Click **OK** • Click **Next: Select recipients** and select the data source • Follow the remaining task pane instructions for creating labels
Creating a directory	WD 6.14	• Open a new blank document and click **Tools, Letters and Mailings, Mail Merge, Directory** • Click **Next: Select starting document; Use the current document** • Click **Next: Select recipients** • Click **Use an existing list**, and click **Browse** • Locate the data source file and click **Open**; click **OK**; click **Next: Arrange your directory**, and click **More items** • Using the Insert Merge Field dialog box, insert the fields; click **Next: Preview your directory**, click **Complete the merge**, select **To a new document** • Select **All** on the **Merge to a New Document** dialog box • Click **OK**
Creating a linked object from an existing file	WD 6.18	• Click in the document where you want to place the linked object • On the **Insert** menu, click **Object**, and then click the **Create from File** tab • In the File name box, type the name of the file you want to use to create a linked object, or click **Browse** to select from a list • Select the **Link to file** check box • Click **OK**
Creating an embedded object from an existing file	WD 6.19	• Click in the document where you want to place the embedded object • On the **Insert** menu, click **Object**, and then click the **Create from File** tab • In the File name box, type the name of the file you want to use to create an embedded object, or click **Browse** to select from a list (make sure there is no checkmark in the **Link to file** check box) • Click **OK**
Creating a directory by querying Excel	WD 6.21	• Open a new blank document and click **Tools, Letters and Mailings, Mail Merge, Directory** • Click **Next: Starting document** and click **Use the current document** • Click **Next: Select recipients** and select **Use an existing list** • Click **Browse** • Select the file and click **Open**; click **OK** • Click **Edit recipient list**; click the arrow next to the appropriate header button • Click **(Advanced . . .)** and then click the tab for **Filter Records** • Complete the Field box for comparisons • Click **Arrange directory**
Organizing a new document using the Outline view	WD 7.4	• In a new document, switch to **Outline** view • Type each heading, and press **Enter** (Word formats the headings with the built-in style Heading 1) • To assign a heading to a lower level and apply the corresponding heading style, drag the heading's plus (1) or minus (2) or outline symbol to the right

Task	Page #	Preferred Method
		• To *promote* a heading to a higher level, drag the symbol to the left • To move a heading to a different location, drag the symbol up or down (the subordinate text under the heading moves with the heading) • After organizing the outline, switch to **Normal** view or **Print Layout** view to add detailed body text and graphics
Assigning outline levels to a paragraph	WD 7.7	• Switch to **Print Layout** view • Select a paragraph you want to assign an outline level to • On the Format menu, click **Paragraph**, and then click the **Indents and Spacing** tab • In the **Outline level** box, click the level you want
Creating an outline numbered list	WD 7.8	• On the Format menu, click **Bullets and Numbering**, and then click the **Outline Numbered** tab • Click a list format that does not contain the text Heading 1, and then click **OK** • Type the list, pressing **Enter** after each item • To *demote* the item to a lower numbering level, click anywhere in the item, and click **Increase Indent** on the Formatting toolbar • To promote the item to a higher numbering level, click anywhere in the item, and click **Decrease Indent** on the Formatting toolbar
Creating a PowerPoint slide show	WD 7.9	• Open the document with the outline that you want to use to create a PowerPoint presentation • On the File menu, point to **Send To**, and then click **Microsoft PowerPoint**
Using the Web page template	WD 7.12	• On the File menu, click **New** • In the New Document task pane, under templates, click **On Your Computer** • Click the **Web Page** template • To create a blank Web page, on the File menu, click **New** • Under New in the New Document task pane, click **Web Page**
Saving a Web page from a Word document	WD 7.13	• On the File menu, click **Save as Web Page** • If you want to save the document in a different folder, locate and open the folder • In the File name box, type a name for the document • Click **Save**
Viewing a document as a Web page	WD 7.16	• Click on the View menu and select **Web Layout** or • Click **Web Layout view** on the buttons in the lower left of the document screen
Viewing the Document Map	WD 7.18	• On the menu bar, click **View, Document Map** to show the Document Map pane • To move through the document, click on any titles shown in the Document Map • Click **View, Document Map** again to turn off the Document Map
Adding a Bookmark	WD 7.20	• Select an item you want a Bookmark assigned to, or click where you want to insert a Bookmark • On the Insert menu, click **Bookmark** • Under Bookmark name, type or select a name • Click **Add** • To go to a Bookmark, click **Edit, Go To, Bookmark** and then select the name of the Bookmark
Creating a hyperlink within a document	WD 7.21	• Click **Insert** on the menu bar, and select **Hyperlink** or **Ctrl+K** • In the Insert Hyperlink dialog box, decide what you are linking • Select the correct **Link to**: Existing File or Web Page, Place in this Document, Create New Document, or E-mail Address

Task	Page #	Preferred Method
		• Choose or type the address text will link to • Click **OK**
Editing a hyperlink	WD 7.23	• Right-click on the hyperlink • Select **Hyperlink, Edit Hyperlink** • Make changes in the Edit Hyperlink dialog box • Click **OK** or • Click the **Remove Link** button
Creating a master document	WD 8.6	• Open in the usual way the document that is to be the master document. Display nonprinting characters by clicking the **Show/Hide** button on the Standard toolbar, click **View** on the menu bar, and then click **Outline**. If necessary, click the **Master Document View** button on the Outlining toolbar to display the Outlining toolbar
Moving to a subdocument from a master document	WD 8.11	• Press and hold the **Ctrl** key, click the subdocument hyperlink in the master document
Expanding a subdocument within a master document	WD 8.12	• Ensure that the master document is open in Master Document View, change to Outline view by clicking **View** and then clicking **Outline**, if necessary. Place the insertion point at the beginning of the document. Click the **Expand Subdocuments** button on the Outlining toolbar
Splitting a subdocument into two subdocuments	WD 8.15	• Ensure that the document you are about to split is in Master Document View, click **View** on the menu bar and then click **Outline** to display the subdocument in Outline view • Click the **Show Level** list box arrow and click **Show All Levels** in the list to ensure that all headings and subheadings appear, create a new Heading 1 heading at the point where you want to make the split or raise an existing heading to a Heading 1 level, click the outline marker of the Heading 1 where you want to split the subdocument, and click the **Split Subdocument** button on the Outlining toolbar
Merging subdocuments	WD 8.17	• Ensure that the document you are about to split is in Master Document View, click **Expand Subdocuments** button on the Outlining toolbar, ensure the subdocuments you want to merge are adjacent to one another, click the **Subdocument icon** of the first subdocument, press and hold down the **Shift** key, click **Subdocument icon** of the second subdocument, and release the **Shift** key, and click the **Merge Subdocument** button on the Outlining toolbar
Removing a subdocument	WD 8.20	• Ensure that the subdocument you are about to remove is expanded in the master document, click the subdocument's Subdocument icon to select the subdocument, click the Remove Subdocument button on the Outlining toolbar, and then click anywhere in the master document text to deselect the highlighted text section
Renaming a subdocument	WD 8.21	• Ensure that the master document is open in Master Document View, collapse all subdocuments by clicking the **Collapse Subdocuments** button on the Outlining toolbar, press and hold the **Ctrl** key, click the subdocument link for the document you want to rename, and release the **Ctrl** key. When the subdocument opens in its own window, click **File** on the menu bar, click **Save As**, type the new subdocument name in the File name text box, and click the **Save** button. Click **File** and then click **Close** to close the subdocument
Printing a master document	WD 8.22	• Open the master document. If necessary, expand the subdocuments by clicking the **Expand Subdocuments** button, click **View** on the menu bar and then click **Print Layout**, click **File** on the menu bar, click **Print**, and click **OK**

Task	Page #	Preferred Method
Marking index entries and subentries	WD 8.28	• Select the word or phrase you want to mark as an index entry, or place the insertion point where you want to add a new word or phrase, not found in the text, as an index entry, click **Insert**, on the menu bar, point to **Reference**, click **Index and Tables**, click the **Index** tab, and then click the **Mark Entry** button. Ensure the Current page option, in the Options panel, is selected. If needed, type an index word or phrase in the Main entry text box, and then type an optional word or phrase in the Subentry text box, click the **Mark** button to mark the single occurrence or click the **Mark All** button to mark every occurrence of the selected word or phrase in the document. Click the **Close** button to close the dialog box
Marking a cross-reference index entry	WD 8.31	• Type the text for the index entry, or position the insertion point in the document, press **Alt+Shift+X** to display the Mark Index Entry dialog box, type the Main entry text. Optionally, type a subentry index term in the Subentry text box, click the **Cross-reference** option, type the cross-reference entry you want to refer readers to following the word *See* in the cross-reference text box, and then click the **Mark** button
Marking a page range index entry	WD 8.33	• Select a range of pages, several paragraphs, a section, or a chapter, for example. Click **Insert** on the menu bar, click **Bookmark**, type the Bookmark name, and then click the **Add** button, press **Alt+Shift+X** to open the Mark Index Entry dialog box, if necessary, click the **Page range** option button, click the Bookmark list arrow, and click the Bookmark name you created above. Click the **Mark** button
Deleting an index entry	WD 8.34	• Display a document in Normal view, and click the **Show/Hide** button on the Standard toolbar to reveal the document's hidden codes, drag the mouse across the entire index entry field, including the curly braces, that you want to delete, press the **Delete** key
Generating an index	WD 8.36	• Place the insertion point where you want to create the index, click **Insert** on the menu bar, point to **Reference**, and click **Index and Tables**, and click **OK**
Updating an index	WD 8.39	• Mark any new index entries you want to add to an index, click anywhere within the index, and press **F9**
Creating a table of contents	WD 8.40	• Place the insertion point where you want to add the table of contents, click **Insert** on the menu bar, point to **Reference**, and click **Index and Tables**, click the **Table of Contents** tab, select any options, and click **OK**

Excel *Task Reference Summary*

Task	Page #	Preferred Method
Freezing rows and columns	EX 5.5	• Select cell at upper-left corner • Click **Window**; click **Freeze Panes**
Adding a record to a list using a data form	EX 5.6	• Click list cell, click **Data**, click **Form** • Click **New**, type values in fields, press **Enter**, and click **Close**
Deleting a record from a list with a data form	EX 5.9	• Click list cell, click **Data**, click **Form** • Click **Criteria** button, click **Find Next** as needed, click **Delete**, and click **OK**
Sorting a list on one column	EX 5.12	• Click cell in list • Click the **Sort Ascending** or **Sort Descending** button
Sorting a list on more than one field	EX 5.13	• Click list cell, click **Data**, click **Sort** • Specify Sort by and Ascending/Descending options • Repeat for up to two **Then by** fields • Click **OK**
Creating a custom sort order	EX 5.15	• Click **Tools**, click **Options**, click **Custom Lists** tab • Click **NEW LIST**, type each new member of the list in order • Click the **Add** button and click **OK**
Filtering a list with AutoFilter	EX 5.19	• Click list cell, click **Data** • Click **list arrow** on filtering column, click filter value from list
Clearing all AutoFilter filtering criteria	EX 5.21	• Click **Data**, point to **Filter** • Click **Show All** to remove all existing filters
Subtotaling a list's entries	EX 5.23	• Sort list by grouping column • Click a cell inside the list • Click **Data**, click **Subtotals** • Choose group column, choose aggregate function • Click **OK**
Displaying row or column headings on each page	EX 5.27	• Click **File**, click **Page Setup**, click the **Sheet** tab • Click **Collapse** dialog button on the **Specify Rows to repeat at top** or the **Specify Columns to repeat at left** • Specify row(s) or column(s) • Click **OK**
Applying a conditional format to cells	EX 5.30	• Click cell range to conditionally format • Click **Format**, click **Conditional Formatting**, specify criteria • Click **Format** button on the Conditional Formatting dialog box and specify formatting options • Click **OK** • Click **OK**
Creating a pivot table with the PivotTable Wizard	EX 5.35	• Click **Data**, click the **PivotTable and PivotChart Report** • Specify the data's location • Select the **PivotTable** option and click the **Layout** button • Design pivot table layout by selecting row, column, data, and page fields and click **OK** • Designate location for pivot table as separate page or object on worksheet, click the **Finish** button

REFERENCE

Task	Page #	Preferred Method
Selecting pivot table fields	EX 5.38	• Click and drag selected field(s) to summarize to Data Items area • Click and drag field buttons to Column, Row, and Page fields
Formatting pivot table fields	EX 5.40	• Select any cell in the pivot table data item area • Open the PivotTable toolbar, click **Field Settings**, and click the **Number** button • Select a format from the Category list and make associated format choices • Click **OK** to close the Format Cells dialog box and then click **OK** to close the PivotTable Field dialog box
Naming a cell or cell range	EX 6.12	• Select the cell or cell range you want to name • Click the **Name box** in the formula bar • Type the name and press **Enter**
Deleting a name	EX 6.14	• Click **Insert**, point to **Name**, and then click the **Define** button • Click the name in the *Names in workbook* list that you want to delete • Click the **Delete** button and then click the **OK** button
Using the VLOOKUP function	EX 6.19	• Create a lookup table and sort the table in ascending order by the leftmost column • Place in columns to the right of the search columns values you want to return as answers • Write a VLOOKUP function referencing a cell containing the lookup value, the lookup table, and the column containing the answer
Deleting a worksheet	EX 7.6	• Right-click the tab of the worksheet to delete • Click **Delete** on the shortcut menu
Saving a Workbook as a Template	EX 7.7	• Activate the workbook you want to save as a template, click **File** and then click **Save As** • Type the template name in the File name list box, click the **Save as type** list box, scroll the list box to locate and then click **Template (*.xlt)**, and click **Save** button
Copying worksheets from other workbooks	EX 7.8	• Open the master workbook—the workbook into which you want to copy worksheets from other workbooks • Open all other workbooks containing worksheets you want to copy to the master workbook • In any of the open Excel workbooks, click **Window**, click **Arrange**, click the **Tiled** option button, and click **OK** • Press and hold the **Ctrl** key, and then click and drag to the master workbook the tab of the worksheet you want to copy • Release the mouse when the down-pointing arrow is in the correct tab location in the master workbook, and then release the **Ctrl** key
Grouping contiguous worksheets	EX 7.13	• Click the worksheet tab of the first worksheet in the group • Use the tab scrolling buttons if necessary to bring the last worksheet tab of the proposed group into view • Hold down the **Shift** key and click the last worksheet tab in the group
Grouping noncontiguous worksheets	EX 7.13	• Click the worksheet tab of the first worksheet you want in the group • Press and hold the **Ctrl** key and then click each worksheet you want to include in the group • When you are done, release the **Ctrl** key
Ungrouping worksheets	EX 7.14	• Click the worksheet tab of any worksheet not in the worksheet group • If all worksheets in the workbook are grouped, right-click any worksheet tab and click **Ungroup Sheets** from the shortcut menu

Task	Page #	Preferred Method
Writing a formula containing a 3-D reference	EX 7.23	• After clicking the cell where you want the formula to appear, type **=**, type a function name, and type the left parenthesis. If no function is needed, then type **=** • Click the sheet tab of the worksheet containing the cell or cell range you want to reference • If a worksheet range is needed, then press and hold the **Shift** key and click the last worksheet tab in the range • Click the cell or cell range you want to reference • Complete the formula (type a concluding right parenthesis for a function, for instance) and then press **Enter**
Printing multiple worksheets	EX 7.27	• Group the worksheets you want to print by pressing **Ctrl** and then clicking the worksheet tabs or pressing **Shift** and clicking the first and last worksheets in a contiguous group • Click **File**, click **Print**, ensure the **Active sheet(s)** option button is selected, and click **OK**
Deleting an Excel Template	EX 7.28	• Click **File** on the menu bar, click **New**, and click **On my computer** in the Templates panel of the task pane • Right-click the template which you want to delete, and click **Delete**, and click **OK** when asked if you want to send the template to the Recycle Bin
Building link references by pointing	EX 7.30	• Open the supporting workbook • Make active the workbook to contain the link reference and the cell to contain the link reference • Type the formula up to the point in which you reference the cell or cell range in another workbook • Click the Taskbar button corresponding to the supporting workbook to make it active • Click the worksheet tab containing the cell or cell range to reference • Click the cell or drag the cell range of the cell(s) you want to reference and press **Enter**
Opening a supporting workbook from a dependent workbook	EX 7.35	• Open the dependent workbook containing the link reference • Click **Edit** and then click **Links** • Click the name of the supporting workbook you want to open from the Links list • Click the **Open Source** button
Tracing precedent or dependent cells	EX 8.5	• Select the cell whose formula you want to trace • Click the **Trace Precedents (Trace Dependents)** button on the Formula Auditing toolbar to display tracer arrows pointing to the formula's precedent (dependent) cells
Tracing errors	EX 8.12	• Click the cell displaying an error value • Click the **Trace Error** button on the Formula Auditing toolbar • Follow any tracer arrows back to the error source
Finding subtle errors	EX 8.14	• Click the worksheet tab of the worksheet whose integrity you want to check • Click the **Error Checking** button on the Formula Auditing toolbar • Use the options available in the Error Checking dialog box to correct the errant formula or • Click the Next button to go to the next suspicious formula
Tracking worksheet changes	EX 8.20	• Click **Tools** • Point to **Track Changes** • Click **Highlight Changes** • Click the list arrow next to the When check box • Click one of the available time periods

Task	Page #	Preferred Method
		• Click the list arrow next to the Who list box • Click one of the available names whose changes you want to track • Click the **Where** reference box and indicate which part of the workbook you want to review changes • Click the **List changes on a new sheet** check box to collect • Display the changes on a separate worksheet • Click **OK** to finalize your choices
Accepting and rejecting suggested changes to cells	EX 8.22	• With a shared workbook open, click **Tools** • Point to **Track Changes** • Click **Accept or Reject Changes** • Click the list arrow next to the When check box • Click one of the available time periods • Click the list arrow next to the Who list box • Click one of the available names whose changes you want to accept or reject • Click the **Where** reference box and indicate which part of the workbook you want to review changes • Click **OK** to finalize your choices
Merging multiple versions of the same workbook	EX 8.24	• Open the workbook into which you want to merge changes • Click **Tools** on the menu bar and click **Compare and Merge Workbooks** • Press and hold the **Ctrl** key and click each workbook listed in the *Select Files to Merge Into Current Workbook* dialog box that you want to merge, and click **OK**
Hiding a worksheet	EX 8.26	• Click the worksheet tab of the worksheet you want to hide • Click **Format**, point to **Sheet** • Click **Hide**
Unhiding a worksheet	EX 8.27	• Click **Format**, point to **Sheet** • Click **Unhide** • In the Unhide dialog box, click the name of the worksheet you want to unhide from the list • Click **OK**
Unlocking cells	EX 8.28	• Select the cell or cell range you want to be unlocked • Click **Format**, click **Cells** • Click the **Protection** tab • Click the **Locked** check box to clear its checkmark • Click **OK**
Enabling worksheet protection	EX 8.29	• Select the worksheet on which you want to enable protection • Click **Tools**, point to **Protection** • Click **Protect Sheet**. Optionally enter (and remember) a password twice • Click **OK**
Protecting a workbook	EX 8.30	• Click **Tools**, point to **Protection** • Click **Protect Workbook** • Check or clear check boxes to set options as needed, type an optional password • Click **OK** • If you entered a password, then you are asked to retype it and then click **OK**
Publishing an Excel workbook as a noninteractive Web page	EX 8.33	• Click **File** • Click **Save as Web Page** • In the Save As dialog box, click **Entire Workbook** and clear the **Add interactivity** check box • Type a filename in the Filename list box • Optionally, click the **Change Title** button, type a new Web page title, and click **OK**, and click **Save**

Task	Page #	Preferred Method
Publishing an Excel workbook as an interactive Web page	EX 8.35	• Click **File** • Click **Save as Web Page** • In the Save As dialog box, click **Entire Workbook** and check the **Add interactivity** check box • Click the **Publish** button • Click the **Choose** list box and select the portions of the workbook you want to publish • Click the **Change** button to change the Web page title • Click the **Browse** button to specify a filename and folder location • Click the **AutoRepublish every time this workbook is saved** check box (placing a checkmark in it) • Click the **Open published web page in browser** check box (placing a checkmark in it) • Click the **Publish** button

Access Task Reference Summary

Task	Page #	Preferred Method
Open a new form in Design View	AC 5.6	• In the Database Window of an open database, click the **Forms** object • Click the **New** button on the Database Window toolbar • In the New Form dialog box, click **Design View** • Select the table or query that will be the record source for the form and click **OK**
Select and move form controls	AC 5.9	• Select the control to be operated on by clicking it. The Shift key can be used to select multiple controls • Drag the control(s) to the new location. Use the large move handle to independently move components of a bound control
Set control properties	AC 5.11	• Right-click the control to open the pop-up menu • Select **Properties** from the pop-up menu • Select the appropriate Properties tab (usually Format) • Navigate to the property and change its setting
Show Form Headers and Footers	AC 5.15	• Open a form in Design View • Select **Form Header/Footer** from the **View** menu
Add Toolbox controls to a design	AC 5.16	• Open a form or report in Design View • If necessary, activate the toolbox using the **Toolbox** button on the Form Design toolbar • Verify that the Toolbox **Control Wizards** button is depressed (a blue outline will show around it) • Click the Toolbox control that is to be added to the form • Click in the Form section that will contain the control • Set the control's properties using the Properties pages activated with the Properties button
Query an open form with a saved filter	AC 5.21	• Open a form in Form View • Click the **Filter By Form** button • Click the **Load From Query** button • Select the query to be applied and click **OK** • Click the **Apply Filter** button
Create a report in Design View	AC 5.27	• In the Database Window click the **Reports** object and click the **New** button • Click **Design View** as the way to develop the report, select the record source from the drop-down list, and click **OK**
Add page numbers to a report in Design View	AC 5.32	• Display the report in Design View • Choose **Page Numbers** from the **Insert** menu • Select the formatting, position, and alignment options that you want and click **OK**
Control Sorting and Grouping in a report	AC 5.37	• Display the report in Design View • Click the **Sorting and Grouping** button on the toolbar • Use the Field/Expression drop-down list box to select each field that you want to use to sort or group data. Each selected Field/Expression will be on a different line of the grid • Select the Sort order for each Field/Expression listed. The order of multiple fields determines their priority in the sort • Select the grouping option(s) for each field • Close the Sorting and Grouping dialog box • Add the necessary controls and content to any Group Headers and Footers created

Task	Page #	Preferred Method
View table relationships	AC 6.4	• Click the **Relationships** button on the Database toolbar • If relationships exist, they will be displayed. If there are no current relationships, you can add tables and build relationships between them
View relationship properties	AC 6.6	• Click the **Relationships** button on the Database toolbar • If relationships exist, they will be displayed. If there are no current relationships, you can add tables and build relationships between them • Double-click the relationship line that you would like to view • The Edit Relationships dialog box displays the properties of that relationship
Create a relationship	AC 6.8	• Click the **Relationships** button on the Database toolbar • If relationships exist, they will be displayed • Click the **Show Table** button on the toolbar • Select the table that you want to relate and click the **Add** button. Repeat this process for each table to be related • When you have added all of the necessary tables, click **Close** • Click the primary table field of the relationship and drag to the secondary field to initiate the relationship • Select the Referential Integrity options in the Edit Relationships dialog box • Click **OK** to close the Edit Relationships dialog box • Repeat this process for any other relationships to be built • Close the Relationships window
Index a table field	AC 6.13	• Open the table in **Design View** • Select the field to be indexed from the Field Name column • Set the Indexed field property to **Yes (Duplicates OK)** or **Yes (No Duplicates)** • Close the table design and save the changes
Delete an index	AC 6.14	• Open the table in **Design View** • Select the field whose index is to be removed from the Field Name column • Set the Indexed field property to **No** (this does not impact the field or its data) • Close the table design and save the changes
View the indexes of a table	AC 6.14	• Open the table in **Design View** • Click the **Indexes** button of the toolbar • Click an index to review its properties
Viewing object dependencies	AC 6.37	• Open the task pane and use the drop-down arrow to select **Object Dependencies** • In the dependency pane • Review the list of objects that use the selected object • To view the list of objects that are being used by the selected object, click **Objects that I depend on** at the top of the pane • To view dependency information for an object listed in the pane, simply click on the expand icon (+) next to it
Controlling blank data values	AC 7.11	• Open the table in Design View • Click the field whose blank values you would like to control • Set Required to **Yes** to disallow blank values (Allow Zero Length should be set to No)
Defining field validation rules	AC 7.14	• Open the table in Design View • Click the field that will be monitored by the validation rule • Select the **Validation Rule** property for that field • Type the validation expression or use the Expression Builder by clicking the ellipsis to the right of the Validation Rule text box

Task	Page #	Preferred Method
		• Click the Validation Text property box for the same field and enter the text that is to display when the validation rule is broken • Save the table update • If the validation rule has been set for a field that already contains data, Access will ask if you want to apply the new rule to existing data • If there are no existing data in the field, there will be no prompt
Splitting a database	AC 7.16	• Back up the database • On the Tools menu, point to **Database Utilities**, and then click **Database Splitter** • Follow the Database Splitter Wizard instructions
Optimizing database objects	AC 7.18	• Open the database to be optimized • Click the **Tools** menu, then **Analyze**, and then **Performance** • Select the tab for the database object (table, query, report, form, etc.) that you would like to analyze • Click the check box of each object to be evaluated or click Select All to select all objects in the list • Select objects from other tabs if desired • Click **OK** • Review and apply results as needed
Replicating a database	AC 7.20	• Open the database to be replicated • Remove any password protection and ensure that the database is not open by any other users • On the **Tools** menu, point to **Replication**, and then click **Create Replica** • Click **Yes** when prompted with: The database must be closed before you can create a replica • Answer **Yes** when prompted with: Converting a database into a Design Master results in changes . . . • In the Location of New Replica dialog box • Navigate to the location for the replica • Set the **Priority** • Check the **Prevent deletes** check box to prevent record deletions in the replica • In the Save as type box, select the replica visibility • Click **OK**
Synchronizing replicated databases	AC 7.23	• Open the replica to be synchronized • On the **Tools** menu, point to **Replication**, and then click **Synchronize Now** • Select the other replica set member to be synchronized from the Directly with Replica drop-down list box • Click **OK** • Respond **Yes** when prompted to close the database for synchronization • Respond **OK** when notified that the process has been completed
Hiding a database	AC 7.26	• Open Windows Explorer • Navigate to the file to be hidden • Right-click on the file to be hidden • Click the **Properties** option • Click the **Hidden** attribute • Click **OK**
Encoding a database	AC 7.28	• Open Access with no open database • Open the **Tools** menu, pause over **Security**, and click **Encode/Decode Database . . .** • Enter a folder and a name for the database to be encoded and click **OK** • Enter a folder and name for the encoded database and click **Save**

Task	Page #	Preferred Method
Password protecting a database	AC 7.29	• Open Access with no open database • Click the **Open** button on the Database toolbar • Navigate to the folder and select the file to be password protected • Click the Open button's list arrow and select **Open Exclusive** • Open the **Tools** menu, pause over **Security**, and then click **Set Database Password** • Type the password in the Password text box, repeat the same password in the Verify text box, and then press **Enter**
Setting user-level security	AC 7.32	• Open the Access database to be secured • On the **Tools** menu, pause over **Security** and then click **User-Level Security Wizard** • Follow the Wizard instructions
Create a Microsoft Graph	AC 8.4	• Click the **Reports** object in the Database Window • Click **New** to activate the New Report dialog box • Select **Chart Wizard**, use the drop-down list to select the query or table containing the data to be charted, and then click **OK** to initiate the Chart Wizard • Follow the instructions to select the field(s) with the data to be charted, select the chart type, specify the layout, and add a chart title
Importing with an unbound object frame on a form or report	AC 8.11	• Open the Design View of the form or report to contain the imported object • Click the **Unbound Object Frame** tool in the toolbox • Click and drag the area on the form or report that will contain the object • In the Microsoft Access dialog box • Click **Create From File** • Browse to the file for import • Click the Link check box to create a linked object or leave it unclicked to create an embedded object • Click **OK**
Import or link to another Access database	AC 8.16	• Open the Access database that is to contain the imported data • Open the **File** menu, point to **Get External Data**, and then do one of the following: • Click **Import** to create Access tables from the external data • Click **Link Tables** to create links to tables that remain in the source location • In the Import or Link dialog box • Use the Files of Type drop-down list to select **Microsoft Office Access (*.mdb, *.mda, *.mde)** as the type of file to be linked or imported • Use the Look in box to select the drive, folder, and filename of the file to be imported or linked • Select the import tables and click **Import**
Import or link to an Excel spreadsheet	AC 8.18	• Open the Access database that is to contain the imported data • Open the **File** menu, point to **Get External Data**, and then click **Import** • Click **Import** to create Access tables from the external data • Click **Link Tables** to create links to tables that remain in the source location • In the Import or Link dialog box • Use the Files of Type drop-down list to select **Microsoft Excel (*.xls)** as the type of file to be linked or imported • Use the Look in box to select the drive, folder, and filename of the file to be imported or linked • Follow the Import Spreadsheet Wizard instructions

REFERENCE

Task	Page #	Preferred Method
Export an Access object to Microsoft Word	AC 8.22	• Open the Access database with the object to be exported • Select the object to be exported in the Database Window (it is best to preview the object before exporting) • Open the **Tools** menu, point to **Office Links**, and then either • Select **Merge It with Microsoft Word** to use an Access table or query as the data source for a Word merge document or • Select **Publish It with Microsoft Word** to create an .rtf file in the default database folder (usually C:\ My Documents or the folder containing the database) with the same name as the exported object
Export an Access object to an Excel spreadsheet	AC 8.23	• Open the Access database that contains the data to be exported • Select the object to be exported in the Database Window (it is best to preview the object before exporting) • Open the **Tools** menu, point to **Office Links**, and then click **Analyze It with Microsoft Excel**
Export an Access object to a static HTML page	AC 8.26	• Open the Access database that contains the data to be exported • Select the object to be exported in the Database Window (it is best to preview the object before exporting) • Open the **File** menu and click **Export** • In the Export To dialog box • Use the Save In box to select the drive and folder for the Web page • Set the Save As Type to **HTML Documents (*.html; *.htm)** • In the File Name box, enter the name for the Web page (it is best not to use spaces in these names) • **Save Formatted** should be clicked to retain the formatting applied to the datasheet in Access and activate the next two options • Check **AutoStart** to display the page in your default browser • In the HTML Output Options dialog box • Apply an HTML template to standardize formatting (Optional) • Click **OK**
Use Internet Explorer to view a static HTML page	AC 8.28	• Open Access • From the **View** menu, pause over **Toolbars** and then click **Web** • On the Web toolbar, drop down the **Go** list and select **Open Hyperlink** • Click the **Browse** button in the Open Internet Address dialog box • Use the Browse dialog box to navigate to the file to be viewed • Select the file and click **Open** • Click **OK**
Use the Page Wizard to create a Data Access Page	AC 8.30	• Open the database containing the data for the Data Access Page • Click the **Pages** object in the Database Window • Double-click **Create data access page by using wizard** • Follow the Wizard instructions
Repair broken Data Access Page links	AC 8.38	• Open the Data Access Page with a broken database link in Design View • Click **Update Link** in the informational dialog box • Navigate to the network folder containing the Data Access Page • Select the page and click **OK** • Click **OK** in the dialog box explaining that the connection needs to be repaired • On the right-hand side of the Data Access Page Design View, click the **Page connection properties** option in the Field List Window • On the Connection tab, click the ellipsis (…) and update the database name • Click **Open** • Click the **Test Connection** button • When the test works, click **OK** • Click **OK** again to end the update

Task	Page #	Preferred Method
Importing an HTML document as an Access table	AC 8.39	• Open the database to hold the imported table • Verify that the layout of the data to be imported is either a list or a table • On the **File** menu, point to **Get External Data**, and then click **Import** • Select the HTML file for import and click **Import** (be sure to set the Files of Type to HTML documents) • Complete the Wizard dialog boxes

Construct a Web page or file hyperlink	AC 8.43	• Open the form, report, or Data Access Page in Design View
		• Click the Insert Hyperlink button in the toolbox and drag the display area on the form, report, or Data Access Page
		• In the Insert Hyperlink dialog box
		  • Select the type of object to **Link to** (Existing File or Web Page, Object in This Database, Create New Page, or E-Mail Address)
		  • Enter the **Text to display** for the hyperlink (if this is blank, the URL will display)
		  • Enter the **Screen Tip text** (if this is blank, the URL displays when the user pauses the cursor over the link)
		  • In the Address box, type or browse to the path of a file or a URL
		• Click **OK**

PowerPoint Task Reference Summary

Task	Page #	Preferred Method
Apply a slide transition	PP 5.3	• Select the slide(s) the transition will be applied to. If no slide(s) is selected, the transition will be applied to all slides • From the **Slide Show** menu select **Slide Transition** • Select a transition effect
Set slide timing while rehearsing	PP 5.6	• Activate the timing feature • On the **Slide Show** menu, click **Set Up Show** • Under **Advance slides**, click **Use timings, if present** • Set the time for each slide • On the **Slide Show** menu click **Rehearse Timings** • Rehearse the show to set timings automatically as you advance • At the end of the show, click **Yes** to accept automatic timings or **No** to start again
Adding custom animations to text	PP 5.7	• In Normal view, select the text object to be animated • From the task pane drop-down list select **Custom Animation** • In the Custom Animation task pane click **Add Effects** and select the desired effect(s)
Animating a chart or diagram	PP 5.13	• In Normal view, select the object to be animated • From the task pane drop-down list select **Custom Animation** • To animate the whole object, in the Custom Animation task pane click **Add Effects** and select the desired effect(s) • To animate individual chart elements • In the Custom Animation task pane, select the animation applied to the chart • Click the down arrow and select **Effect Options** • On the Chart Animation or Diagram Animation tab, select an option from the Group Diagram list
Inserting a media clip	PP 5.15	• In Normal view, move to the slide that will contain the clip • Use the Slide Layout panel of the task pane to select a layout with a media placeholder • Click the **Insert Media Clip** icon • Browse through the available selections until you find a clip that you want, click the clip, and click **OK** • Use Slide Show view to preview the media clip
Hide a slide	PP 5.17	• Select the slide to hide on the Slides tab in Normal view • Click **Slide Show** and then click **Hide Slide**
Create a self-running presentation	PP 5.18	• Click **Slide Show** and then click **Set Up Show** • Click **Loop continuously until 'Esc'**
Insert a sound clip	PP 5.19	• Click **Insert**, pause over **Movies and Sounds** and click • **Sound from Media Gallery** to insert a sound stored in the Microsoft Media Gallery • **Sound from File** to insert a sound that you have stored in a file on your computer • **Play CD Audio Track** to play a specific track from the CD loaded in your CD tray • **Record Sound** to record your own sound or narration • Right-click on the sound icon and use the Edit Sound Object options to customize the sound settings • Use the Reorder buttons on the Custom Animation panel of the task pane to control the play order of the sound

Task	Page #	Preferred Method
Add sound to a transition or animation	PP 5.21	The transitions and animations must be set before sounds can be added to them • Move to the slide where sounds will be added to transitions and/or animations • Activate the task panel pane for Slide Transitions to add a sound to a transition or Custom Animations to add a sound to an animated object • Use the sound drop-down list to select the sound
Select a color scheme	PP 6.4	• Select a Design template before choosing a color scheme • Select the slide(s) the color scheme will be applied to • Use the drop-down menu of the task pane to activate the Slide Design—Color Scheme panel • Click a color scheme
Customize a color scheme	PP 6.8	• Use the task pane drop-down list to activate the **Slide Design—Color Scheme** panel • Click the **Edit Color Schemes** link in the Slide Design—Color Scheme panel • On the **Standard** tab of the Edit Color Scheme dialog box, select the standard color scheme to be customized • On the **Custom** tab, select the color scheme element to customize and click **Change Color** • Use either the Standard or Custom tab of the Background Color dialog box to select a new color • Click **OK** • Repeat the previous step for each element to be customized • Use the **Preview** button to view the new colors on your slide • Click **Apply** to permanently apply the changes
Delete a color scheme	PP 6.10	• Use the task pane drop-down list to activate the **Slide Design—Color Scheme** panel • Click the **Edit Color Schemes** link in the Slide Design—Color Scheme panel • On the **Standard** tab of the Edit Color Scheme dialog box, select the color scheme to be deleted • Click the **Delete Scheme** button • Click **Apply**
Define a gradient background	PP 6.12	• Right-click on the slide to contain the gradient background • Click the **Background** pop-up menu option • Click **Fill Effects** • Click the **Gradient** tab • Select the desired gradient effects and click **OK** • Click either • **Apply to All** to set this as the background for all presentation slides • **Apply** to set this as the background for the selected slides only
Select a texture background	PP 6.13	• Right-click on the slide to contain the texture background • Click the **Background** pop-up menu option • Click **Fill Effects** • Click the **Texture** tab • Select the desired texture and click **OK** • Click either • **Apply to All** to set this as the background for all presentation slides • **Apply** to set this as the background for the selected slides only
Apply a picture background	PP 6.15	• Locate and save an appropriate picture • Right-click on the slide to contain the picture background • Click the **Background** pop-up menu option • Click **Fill Effects** • Click the **Picture** tab • Click the **Select Picture** button, choose the picture file, click **Insert**, and then click **OK**

Task	Page #	Preferred Method
		• Click either • **Apply to All** to set this as the background for all presentation slides • **Apply** to set this as the background for the selected slides only • **Preview** to evaluate the effect of the background without applying it
Apply a picture as a bullet	PP 6.17	• Select the text or list that will contain the picture bullet • On the **Format** menu, click **Bullets and Numbering**, and then click the **Bulleted** tab • On the Bulleted tab click the **Picture** button • Select a picture from the Picture Bullet dialog box • Click **OK**
Using the AutoShape button of the Drawing toolbar	PP 6.19	• Select the slide that will contain the AutoShape • Click the **AutoShapes** menu of the **Drawing** toolbar • Select the shape category and then the shape to be applied • Click and drag on the slide surface to create the shape
Adding text to an AutoShape	PP 6.20	• Select the AutoShape • Right-click the **AutoShape** and select **Add Text** from the shortcut menu • Type and format the text
Adding Grids and Guides to a presentation	PP 6.24	• Use the **Toolbars** option of the **View** menu to activate the **Drawing** toolbar, if it is not already visible • Click the **Draw** drop-down list of the Drawing toolbar and click **Grid and Guides** • Adjust the Snap to, Grid, and Guide settings in the Grid and Guides dialog box, and then click OK
Adding 3-D effects to an object	PP 6.26	• Select the object(s) that will have 3-D effects • Choose the desired 3-D effects from the 3-D Style button of the Drawing toolbar
Changing the Z-order of an object	PP 6.30	• Select the object(s) to be moved in the stack of objects • From the Drawing toolbar, click **Draw**, pause over **Order**, and then select the appropriate movement option
Grouping objects	PP 6.35	• Select all objects to be grouped • From the Drawing toolbar, click **Draw** and then select the appropriate grouping (Group, Ungroup, or Regroup) option
Insert a hyperlink	PP 7.5	• Select the object that will initiate the hyperlink. The object can be text, WordArt, a graphic, or any other clickable object • Click the **Insert Hyperlink** button on the Standard toolbar • Select the location of the link and then set the link options
Create and link an Action button	PP 7.12	• Select the slide to contain the Action button • If needed, use the View menu to activate the Drawing toolbar • Click the **AutoShapes** button of the Drawing toolbar, pause over Action buttons, and select the desired button • Click and drag the button on the slide surface • Click the Action button and follow the steps to set a hyperlink
Build an AutoContent Web page	PP 7.18	• In the PowerPoint open the New Presentation task pane, select **From AutoContent wizard** • Read the introductory screen and click **Next** • Choose the type of presentation you would like to develop and click **Next** • Select **Web presentation** and click **Next** • Enter the Presentation title and Footer information and click **Next** • Click **Finish**
Preview a presentation as a Web site	PP 7.22	• Open the presentation in PowerPoint • Select **Web Page Preview** from the **File** menu

Task	Page #	Preferred Method
Save a presentation in Web format	PP 7.23	• Open the presentation in PowerPoint • From the **File** menu select **Save as Web Page** • Click **Publish** to customize the Save As settings • Click Publish when the settings are complete
Showing the Web toolbar	PP 7.24	• Click the **View** menu • Pause over **Toolbars** and click **Web**
Accessing Microsoft online support	PP 7.25	• Click the **Help** menu • Click **Microsoft Office Online**
Package a presentation	PP 8.4	• Open the presentation to be packaged • If you are saving the presentation to a storage media, insert it • Click the **File** menu and then **Package for CD** • Make appropriate selections on each screen • Clicking **Add Files** will allow you to package multiple presentations • Use the **Options button** to include the Microsoft PowerPoint viewer in the package
Record and play a macro	PP 8.6	• Click **Tools**, point to **Macro**, then click **Security**, and select appropriate Security Level settings and add Trusted Sources • Click **Tools**, point to **Macro**, then click **Record New Macro** • Select the storage location for the macro, enter the macro name in the Macro name box, and click **OK** to begin recording • Perform the actions to be recorded • Click **Stop Recording** on the Stop Recording toolbar
Personalize menu and toolbar settings	PP 8.10	• On the **Tools** menu, click **Customize** • Adjust Options tab settings
Customize an existing toolbar	PP 8.11	• Click the **Toolbar Options** arrow at the right end of the toolbar • Point to **Add or Remove Buttons** and then click **Customize** • In the **Categories** box select the type of command to be added. For example, Macros • From the **Commands** box, click and drag the command to a toolbar
Prepare a presentation for review	PP 8.18	• Open the presentation to be reviewed • For each reviewer: • Click **Save As** on the **File** menu • Change the name in the **File name** box to indicate whose review copy it is • Change the **Save as type** to **Presentation for Review** • Click **Save** • Distribute the files to reviewers on disk or as e-mail attachments
Use Outlook to send a presentation for review	PP 8.20	• Open the presentation to be reviewed • On the **File** menu, point to **Send To** and then click **Mail Recipient (for Review)** • In the e-mail that opens, enter the To and Cc e-mail addresses of your reviewers • Click **Send**
Review a presentation sent with Outlook	PP 8.22	• Open e-mail and double-click on the presentation to be reviewed • Edit the presentation in the normal fashion • Use the Comments button of the Reviewing toolbar to add comments • From the **File** menu click **Send**, and then click **Original Sender**
Use Outlook to combine reviewed presentations	PP 8.22	• Open the Outlook e-mail containing the reviewed presentation • Double-click the attached reviewed presentation • Click **Yes** in the alert box so that PowerPoint will automatically combine the reviewed presentation with your original presentation • Close the e-mail and repeat the process for any other reviews
End a review	PP 8.23	• On the Reviewing toolbar, click **End Review**

Task	Page #	Preferred Method
View a Web broadcast	PP 8.25	• To view a live broadcast, open the e-mail with the broadcast invitation and click the URL • To view a recorded broadcast, go to the start page provided by the presenter and click **Replay Broadcast**
Set up a recorded Web broadcast	PP 8.26	• Open the presentation to be broadcast on a computer with functioning audio and/or video equipment • On the **Slide Show** menu, point to **Online Broadcast** and select **Record and Save a Broadcast** • Complete the information for the broadcast lobby • Click **Settings** and update the audio/video, presentation display, speaker notes, and file location • Click **OK** • Click **Record** to prepare the presentation for recording • Click **Start** to begin recording the broadcast • Narrate each slide speaking clearly and staying positioned in front of the camera, if there is one • Click to progress to the next slide • When you have recorded through all of the slides in the presentation, you will be presented with an option to Replay the Broadcast • Move all broadcast files to a shared folder on your intranet or to the Internet and notify your audience of the location
Start a live Web broadcast	PP 8.28	• Open the presentation to be broadcast on a computer with functioning audio and/or video equipment • On the **Slide Show** menu, point to **Online Broadcast** and select **Start Live Broadcast Now** • In the Live Presentation Broadcast dialog box, select the presentation, check the record option if you want a recorded copy for on-demand viewing, and click **Broadcast** • Enter the information to create the lobby • Click **Settings** and update the audio/video, presentation display, speaker notes, and file location. A shared file location must be specified to continue • Click **OK** • If you want to invite participants, click **Invite Audience** to send e-mails • Click **Start** to begin recording the broadcast • Click **Start** again to begin streaming audio and video
Schedule a live Web broadcast	PP 8.29	• Open the presentation to be broadcast on a computer with functioning audio and/or video equipment • On the **Slide Show** menu, point to **Online Broadcast** and select **Schedule a Live Broadcast** • Enter the information to create the lobby • Click **Settings** and update the audio/video, presentation display, speaker notes, and file location. A shared file location must be specified to continue • Click **OK** • Click **Schedule** in the Schedule Presentation Broadcast dialog box
Host an online meeting with PowerPoint	PP 8.30	• Open the presentation to be broadcast on a computer with functioning audio and/or video equipment • On the **Tools** menu, point to **Online Collaboration** and select either **Meet Now** or **Schedule Meeting** • Complete the NetMeeting dialog box and click **OK** • On the Online Meeting toolbar, click **Call Participant** and use the Find Someone dialog box to invite attendees • Participate in the meeting • On the Online Meeting toolbar, click **End Meeting**

glossary

1.5 line spacing: Line spacing that is one-and-one-half times that of single line spacing.

Action: A field that asks the user to take a particular action.

At least line spacing: Minimum line spacing that Word can adjust to accommodate larger font sizes or graphics.

At line spacing: Amount of line spacing selected by the user.

AutoComplete: A feature that attempts to anticipate words you are entering and completes them for you.

AutoCorrect: Automatically corrects common errors while you type.

AutoCorrect: A feature that catches errors in spelling, capitalization, and spacing.

AutoMacro: A macro that runs automatically whenever Word carries out particular activities such as starting Word, opening a new document, opening an existing document, closing a document, and exiting Word.

AutoShape: A group of ready-made shapes that include such basic shapes as rectangles and circles, plus a variety of lines and connectors, block arrows, flowchart symbols, stars and banners, and callouts.

AutoText: Allows you to insert text or graphics into documents quickly and with a minimum of keystrokes.

Back matter: Typically contains appendices and an index.

Backspace key: Moves the cursor to the left while deleting a single character one space at a time.

Balloon: A way of displaying comments in the margin in Print Layout view.

Boilerplate: A unit of writing that can be reused over and over with little or no change.

Bookmark: An electronic placeholder for Word documents.

Bookmark: A location or selection of text named for reference purposes. Word marks the location with the name you specify. Bookmarks are more than placeholders. For example, you can use them to create and number cross-references.

Border: Outside edges of a table.

Calculation: A type of text form field that calculates numbers based on formulas and cannot be modified by form users.

Cascading style sheet (CSS): Part of a Web page that defines styles controlling the way a Web page or a part of a Web page appears in a browser. Microsoft Office stores embedded style sheets at the top of each Web page.

Case: Refers to whether the text is in uppercase (all capital letters), lower case (all small letters), or a mix of the two.

Cell: Area at the intersection of a row and column.

Cell padding: Spacing between the boundary or the cell and the text inside the cell.

Changed line: The vertical line Word inserts in the left margin to mark text lines containing changes.

Character style: Include any of the option available from the Font dialog box, such as bold, italic, and small caps.

Check box: A form field providing a "yes" or "no" response.

Click and Type: A feature that allows quick insertion of text in a document.

Clip art: A stored image that you can insert into a Word document.

Collapse(ing): Make lower levels of an outline invisible in the Outline View.

Comment: Word note attached to a document that also contains the author's initials and a number.

Continuous section break: Inserts a section break and starts the new section on the same page.

Current Date: A form field that displays the current date and cannot be modified by form users.

Current Time: A form field that displays the current time, which cannot be modified by form users.

Data document: File contains the unique information for each record and merged with the main document to create the customized form letter or mailing list (see *data source*).

Data field: Category of information in a data source; corresponds to one column of information in the data source; name of each data field is listed in the header row of the data source, for example "Zip" and "First_Name"; can contain only letters, numbers, and the underscore character (_); cannot have more then 40 characters and cannot contain spaces.

Data record: Complete set of related information in a data source; corresponds to one row of information in the data source, for example all information about one client in a client mailing list.

Data source: A file that contains the information that varies with each record to be merged into a main document.

Date: A text form field that requires the user to type a date form.

Delete key: Moves the cursor to the right while deleting a single character one space at a time.

Demote: Move down the outline level to a lower level.

Desktop publishing: The combination of text and graphics to produce a high quality, professional-looking document.

Directory: A single document containing a catalog or printed list of address; generated using the merge feature.

Distribution list: A small piece of paper containing the list of people involved in the review and revision of a document.

Document Map: Provides a quick outline-type overview of the document's organization, showing the headings arranged hierarchically in a narrow, scrollable pane on the left side of the screen.

Document Map: Outline-type overview of the document's organization, showing the headings arranged hierarchically in a narrow, scrollable pane.

EOB 1.1

Document window: Where you will enter text, tables, charts, and graphics.

Double line spacing: Twice that of single line spacing.

Drag: To hold down on the left mouse button and move the mouse pointer across text or to move toolbars and scroll bars.

Drawing canvas: An area upon which you can draw multiple shapes; shapes contained within the drawing canvas can be moved and resized as a unit.

Drawing object: AutoShapes, curves, lines, and WordArt that are part of a Word document.

Drawing toolbar: Toolbar containing buttons for Draw, Rotate, AutoShapes, Line, Arrow, Rectangle, Oval, Text Box, Insert WordArt, Insert Clip Art, Fill Color, Line Color, Font Color, Line Style, Dash Style, Arrow Style, Shadow, and 3-D.

Drop down: A form field that displays a list of choices.

Dropped-capital letter: A large capital letter at the beginning of a paragraph used to capture the reader's attention and emphasize the associated text.

Embedded object: Information (the object) inserted into a file (the destination file).

End mark: Used to indicate the end of a row or a cell (_); viewed when the Show/Hide button (¶) is clicked.

Endnote: References or explanations that typically appear at the end of a document.

Even-page section break: Inserts a section break and starts the new section on the next even-numbered page.

Exactly line spacing: Fixed line spacing that Word does not adjust.

Expand (subdocument): When Word replaces a link in the master document with the text from the subdocument.

Expand(ing): Make lower levels of an outline visible in the Outline View.

Field code: A placeholder inserted in a Word document that allows you to enter variable data, as for input from the document's reader, or launch another application.

Field identifier: The curly braces that begin and end the entire field code.

Field instruction: Any text you want to display as a user prompt, a phrase or value, or a bookmark to insert.

Field name: The name of the inserted field.

Field switch: An option you establish to specify the exact way Word is to display or format a field.

Field(s): See *data field*.

File Transfer Protocol (FTP): Transfers files between computers.

Fill: Color, pattern, or image inside a drawing object.

Find: Allows you to find any particular word or phrase in a document.

First line indent: Often used to indicate the first line of a new paragraph.

Font: Overall design for a set of characters.

Footer: Displayed and printed in the margin at the bottom of a page.

Footnote: References or explanations at the end of a page in a document.

Form field: The special codes that store a particular type of information that holds a name, a numeric value, a date, or provides a list of possible choices.

Formatting: Changes the look of a single letter, word, or a whole series of words.

Formatting toolbar: Normally appears below the Standard toolbar and contains buttons that change the appearance of text in a document, for example, bold, italicize, underline, justify, number, or bullet text.

Frame: The named sub-window of a frames page. The frame appears in a Web browser as one of a number of window regions in which pages can be displayed. The frame can be scrollable and resizable, and it can have a border.

Front matter: The first several pages containing a title page, table of contents, preface, acknowledgments, and so on.

Graphic filter: Allow images with different formats imported into Word.

Grid: An invisible set of horizontal and vertical lines that determine the organization of a newsletter.

Gridlines: Lines separating rows and columns in a table.

Gutter space: Simply the white space between columns.

Hanging indent: Occurs when the first line or phrase is against the left margin and the remaining text is indented a set amount from the left margin.

Hard page break: Inserted manually at a specific point.

Header: Displayed and printed in the margin at the top of a page.

Header row: First row of the data source.

Help: An arbitrarily long message that appears in a dialog box when a form user presses the F1 function key.

Highlighted text: Text selected by the user that is marked with a colored background and white lettering.

Highlighting: A transparent colored bar over selected text.

Horizontal ruler: A bar marked off in units of measure (such as inches) that is displayed across the top of the document window.

HTML tags: Contain all the information you'd like to include in your Web page.

Hyperlink: Colored and underlined text or a graphic that you click to go to a file, a location in a file, an HTML page on the World Wide Web, or an HTML page on an intranet.

HyperText Markup Language (HTML): HyperText Markup Language tells browser software how to display text and other objects on the World Wide Web.

HyperText Transfer Protocol (HTTP): The protocol used by the World Wide Web.

Icon: A small button on the toolbar that executes a command when the button is clicked.

Index: A listing of key word locations placed at the end of a long document.

Index: Lists the words and phrases that occur in a document along with page numbers on which they appear.

Insert Symbol command: Allows you to enter symbols into your documents.

Insertion Point: Indicates the position where you will be entering text.

Intranet: A network within an organization that uses Internet technologies such as the HTTP or FTP protocol.

Landscape: Orientation of text and graphics on the width of a page.

Layout: Displays how the document is going to look.

Line spacing: Determines the amount of vertical space between lines of text.

Link bar: A collection of graphic or text buttons representing hyperlinks to pages within your Web site and to external sites.

List box: (see Drop-down form field).

Looping: To execute a section of code repeatedly until a particular condition arises signaling that the process should halt.

Macro: A recording of the keystrokes, menu clicks, and command clicks that Word records as you perform a sequence of activities, which you can play back repeatedly.

Main document: In a mail-merge operation, the document that contains the text and graphics that are the same for each version of the merged document, for example, the return address or salutation in a form letter.

Margin: Blank spaces around the edges of a document.

Marker: A field code that marks an item for a particular purpose, such as an index term.

Master document: A file containing links to individual files that make up a larger document.

Masthead: The identifying information found at the top of a newsletter containing information such as the date of publication, title, and volume or number of the newsletter.

Menu bar: A horizontal menu that appears on top of the window.

Merge (subdocuments): Combining into one document two adjacent subdocuments.

Merge field(s): A placeholder that is inserted in the main document; for example, <<City>> to have Word insert a city name, such as "New York," that is stored in the City data field in the main document.

Merge or Merging: A process that uses a main document with text common to all final documents and inserts data from a data source to supply text uncommon in each document.

Merging cells: Takes two or more cells and merges them into one cell.

Module: A collection of VBA macros or subroutines.

Mouse pointer: Indicates the current position of the mouse as you move around the screen.

Multiple line spacing: Increased or decreased by a percentage specified by the user.

Multiple versions: Consists of the original document and the differences between versions stored in a single file.

Negative indent: Text extends beyond the horizontal margin set for the rest of the text.

Nested table: Table inside of the cell of another table.

Next page section break: Inserts a section break and starts the new section on the next page.

Nonbreaking hyphen: Prevents a hyphenated word from breaking if it falls at the end of a line.

Nonbreaking space: Prevents a line break between two words.

Nonprinting characters: Text not visible in a document such as spaces, tabs, and paragraph marks.

Number: A type of text form field that accepts only numbers in a text form field.

Numeric picture: A series of symbols and digits that specifies the format and content of the number.

Objects: A table, chart, graphic, equation, or other form of information.

Odd page section break: Inserts a section break and starts the new section on the next odd-numbered page.

Office Assistant: Provides a wide variety of help and tips on Word features and functions.

Onscreen form: A Word template containing special codes in which anyone reading the document can insert information.

Optional hyphen: Used to control where a word or phrase breaks if it falls at the end of a line.

Orientation: Flow of text or graphics across the width or length of a page.

Orphan: Occurs when the first line of a paragraph is printed by itself at the bottom of a page.

Paragraph style: Includes character and paragraph formatting, tab settings, paragraph positioning, borders, and shading.

Picture: Graphics created from another file using different software.

Portrait: Orientation of text and graphics on the length of a page.

Print dialog: Allows you to select a number of printing options.

Print Preview: Displays text and graphics as they will appear when printed on paper.

Promote: Move up one level in the outline levels.

Project: Holds one or more VBA modules.

Promote (heading): Reformat the text to a higher level heading (lower number).

Prompt: A very short text phrase, appearing in the status bar, which provides insights about the selected form field.

Protect: This prevents anyone from modifying a document without revision marks appearing.

Protect: An action that locks the fields in place so that no one can make changes to the field formats or other form field specifications.

Pull quote: Phrase or sentence pulled out of the main text and enlarged and typically used to emphasize a key point.

Query: A means of finding all the records stored in a data source that fit a set of criteria you name.

Record: See *data record*.

Redo: Repeats recent actions, such as typing and formatting.

Regular: A type of text form field that includes text, number, symbols, and spaces.

Replace: Allows you to replace any particular word or phrase in a documents with a new word or phrase.

Result: A field code produces the answer to a calculation or causes a file-retrieval.

Reverse: Light text on a dark background and typically used to emphasize specific text.

Revision mark: It shows where a reviewer has inserted, deleted, or moved text or graphics.

ScreenTip: It appears in a small, yellow box near the mouse pointer whenever you hover the mouse over a toolbar button.

Scroll bar: Shaded bars along the right side and bottom of a document window that allow scrolling to another part of a document by dragging the box or clicking the arrows.

Scrolling: Moving left and right and up and down through a document.

Section break: Stores the formatting elements, such as the margins, page orientation, headers and footers, and sequence of page numbers for a specific area of a document.

Selection: A branching statement that evaluates a condition and then takes one of several alternative actions based on the result of the condition.

Separator character: Characters such as paragraph marks (¶), tabs (→), or commas you choose to indicate where you want text to separate when you convert a table to text, or where you want new rows or columns to begin when you convert text to a table.

Shortcut menu: A menu that shows a list of commands relevant to a particular item; evoked with the right click of a mouse button.

Single line spacing: Accommodates the largest font in that line, plus a small amount of extra space.

Sizing handle: Square handle that appears at each corner and along the sides of the rectangle that surrounds a selected drawing object; drag a sizing handle to resize an object.

Soft page break: Inserted automatically at a point determined by Word.

Sort: Arrange data numerically or alphabetically or by some other criteria common to the records.

Split: Dividing a subdocument into two subdocuments.

Splitting cells: Takes on cell and splits it into two or more cells.

Standard toolbar: Normally appears below the menu bar and contains buttons representing the most popular commands such as Open, Save, Print, Cut, and Paste.

Status bar: Normally appears at the bottom of the window and displays information about a command or a toolbar button, an operation in progress, or the location of the insertion point.

Style: A set of formatting characteristics identified by name that you can apply to text in your document to quickly change its appearance.

Style Gallery: Allows copying of the style formatting from the new template into the active document, only replacing the style definitions.

Style reference: A field (named StyleRef) that is formatted with a style and that is inserted in the document where a special style reference field code appears.

Subdocument: A file which is part of the master document.

Subentry: A secondary topic you use to narrow the search of a specific topic.

Tab stops: Insert a space for formatting text, as in indenting a line or block of text.

Table move handle: Used to drag a table to another location by holding down the right mouse button.

Table of contents: Lists the important headings that appear in your document and the pages on which they appear.

Table resize handle: Used to enlarge or reduce a table by clicking and holding down the right mouse button.

Task pane: A dockable dialog window that provides a convenient way to use a command, gather information, and modify a document.

Template: A collection of styles, keyboard assignments, and toolbar assignments saved to a file.

Text: A form field that allows a user to type text, numbers, symbols, or perform calculations.

Text box: Movable, resizable container for text or graphics.

Text wrapping: Determines the way text is positioned around a graphic.

Theme: A set of unified design elements that provide a look for your document using color, fonts, and graphics.

Title bar: The area displaying the current document name and the program.

Track changes: Tools that color-code the modifications by reviewer, making it easy to determine who made each suggested change.

Typography: Refers to the style and appearance of printed text.

Typography: The style and appearance of printed matter or the arrangement of composed type.

Undo: Allows you to undo your last change.

Visual Basic Editor: A programming environment used to create, manage, and modify Office macros.

Voice comment: A recording you make and attach to a document.

Web browser: Software that interprets HTML files, formats them into Web pages, and displays them. A Web browser, such as Microsoft Internet Explorer, can follow hyperlinks, transfer files, and play sound or video files that are embedding in Web pages.

Web page: Text file with HTML code, pictures, and other components capable of being interpreted by a Web browser.

Widow: Occurs when the last line of a paragraph is printed by itself at the top of a page.

Word-processing software: Helps you create papers, letters, memos, and other basic documents.

Word wrap: Flow of text between the right and left margins without pressing Enter.

WordArt: Text created with special effects by inserting a Microsoft Office drawing object.

Wrapping: How text flows around an image.

glossary

Absolute cell reference: A cell reference in which a dollar sign ($) precedes both the column and row portions of the cell reference.

Activating (toolbar): Making a toolbar appear on the desktop.

Active cell: The cell in which you are currently working.

Active sheets: Sheets that are selected.

Alignment: The position of the data relative to the sides of a cell.

Amortization: The process of distributing periodic payments over the life of a loan.

Amortization schedule: Lists the monthly payment, the amount of the payment applied toward reducing the principal (loan amount), and the amount of the payment that pays the interest due each month.

Argument list: The collection of cells, cell ranges, and values listed in the comma-separated list between a function's parentheses.

Argument list, function: The data that a function requires to compute an answer in which commas separate individual list entries.

Arguments: A list of zero or more items enclosed in parentheses and following the function name.

Arguments, function: They specify the value that the function uses to compute an answer, and comprise the argument list that can be values, cell references, expressions, a function, or an arbitrarily complex combination of the preceding that results in a value.

Ascending order: Arranges text values alphabetically from A to Z, arranges numbers from smallest to largest, and arranges dates from earliest to most recent.

Assumption cells: Cells upon which other formulas depend and whose values can be changed to observe their effect on a worksheet's entries.

Attached text: Chart objects such as X-axis title, Y-axis title, and tick marks.

AutoComplete: Excel offers to fill in the remainder of the cell with information that matches your partial entry from another cell in the same column.

Axis: Line that contains a measurement by which you compare plotted values.

Bottom margin: The area at the bottom of the page between the bottom-most portion of the print area and the bottom edge of the page.

Categories: Organizes values in a data series.

Category names: Correspond to worksheet text you use to label data.

Cell: The Excel worksheet element located at the intersection of a row and a column and identified by a cell reference.

Cell border: A format that applies lines of various types to one or more edges of cells (left, right, top, bottom) of the selected cell(s).

Cell contents: The text, formulas, or numbers you type into a cell.

Cell range: One or more cells that form a rectangular group.

Cell reference: A cell's identification consisting of its column letter(s) followed by its row number.

Chart area: The area in which all chart elements reside.

Chart sheet: Chart on a separate sheet.

Chart title: Labels the entire chart.

Charts: Sometimes called graphs, they are a graphical representation of data.

Client: The program that receives the information copied from another program.

Column field: A pivot table field that summarized data horizontally by groups.

Comments: Worksheet cell notes that are particularly helpful to indicate special instructions about the contents or formatting of individual cells.

Compound document: A document containing linked and embedded data drawn from several sources.

Conditional test: An equation that compares two values, functions, formulas labels, or logical values.

Consolidate: Summarizing data from multiple worksheets.

Consolidation worksheet: *See* Summary worksheet.

Container or container program: *See* Client.

Custom sorting series: An ordered list you create to instruct Excel in what order to sort rows containing the list items.

Data fields (pivot table): Numeric data that appears in the pivot table's central position and is summarized.

Data form: A dialog box displaying one row of a list in text boxes in which you can add, locate, modify, or delete records.

Data label: The value or name assigned to an individual data point.

Data marker: A graphic representation of the value of a data point in a chart.

Data points: The values that comprise a data series.

Data series: The set of values that you want to chart.

Date constant: A date such as 12/12/2003.

Dependent cell: A cell that uses the value of the active cell in its formula.

Dependent workbook: A workbook containing a link to a supporting worksheet.

Descending order: Arranges text values alphabetically from Z to A, arranges numbers from largest to smallest, and arranges dates from most recent to earliest.

Disintermediation: Eliminating the often expensive intermediary in a transaction.

Dock (toolbar): Toolbar adheres to one of the four edges of the window.

Drilling down: Entering data in the same cell of several workbooks simultaneously.

Drop shadow: The shadow that is cast by an object.

Dynamic link: *See* link.

Editing: Modifying the contents of a cell.

Embedded chart: Chart on a worksheet near the data you are charting.

Embedding: Placing a copy of an object from one program within another program's file.

Error indicator: A small triangle, which appears in the upper-left corner of a cell whenever Excel finds a formula that breaks one of its internal rules for valid formulas.

Error value: A special Excel constant that indicates something is wrong with the formula or one of its components.

Exact match criteria: Criteria in which a row's field exactly matches a particular filter value.

External reference: *See* Link.

Field: Each column of a list of related information describing some characteristic of the object, person, or place.

Filter: Selection criteria applied to a merge operation to restrict the source data records chosen to those that satisfy the criteria.

Filtering: A list displaying only records that match particular criteria and hiding the rows that do not.

Fixed pitch (font): Every character is the same width.

Floating (toolbar): Toolbar that can appear anywhere on the work surface.

Font: The combination of typeface and qualities including character size, character pitch, and spacing.

Footer: Text that appears automatically at the bottom of each printed page in the footer margin.

Format: Cosmetic changes to a worksheet that make the text and numbers appear different.

Formatting: The process of altering the appearance of data in one or more worksheet cells.

Formula: An expression that begins with an equals sign and consists of cell references, arithmetic operators, values, and Excel built-in functions (see Chapter 6) that result in calculated value.

Formula Auditing mode: When Excel displays all of the worksheet's formulas on screen rather than the values they represent.

Formula bar: Appears below the menu bar and displays the active cell's contents.

Function: A built-in or prerecorded formula that provides a shortcut for complex calculations.

General (format): Formatting that aligns numbers on the right side of a cell, aligns text on the left side, indicates negative numbers with a minus sign on the left side of a number, and displays as many digits in a number as a cell's width allows.

Gridlines: Extensions of tick marks that help identify the value of the data markers.

Grouping: Joining two objects into one object.

Header: Text that appears automatically at the top of each printed page in the header margin.

Headings row: The list row containing the column headings appearing at the top of the list.

Hide (data): Reduce a row's height to zero.

Interactive Web page: A spreadsheet component enabled within the Web page.

Label text: Chart text such as tick mark label, category axis labels, and data series names.

Landscape: Print orientation in which the width is greater than the length.

Left margin: Defines the size of the white space between a page's left edge and the leftmost edge of the print area.

Legend: Indicates which data marker represents each series when you chart multiple series.

Link: Formulas that reference cells in other worksheets.

Link or linking: To paste a copy of an object into a document in such a way that it retains its connection with the original object. Updates to the original object appear automatically in the documents in which they are pasted.

List: A collection of data arranged in columns and rows in which each column displays one particular type of data.

List definition table: A table with column names and their definitions.

Lookup function: Uses a search value to search a table—a range of cells—for a match or close match and then return a value from the table as a result.

Lookup table: The table that a lookup function searches.

Lookup value: The value being used to search a lookup table.

Main document: The document containing merge fields from which merged documents are created.

Mathematical operator: A symbol that represents an arithmetic operation.

Menu bar: Contains Excel menus.

Merge field: A special tag placed in a document into which an actual field value from a source data file is substituted.

Mixed cell reference: A cell reference in which either the column or the row is never adjusted if the formula containing it is copied to another location.

Model row: Contains distinct formulas that you can copy to other rows and not have to modify any copied cell formulas afterward.

Mouse pointer: Indicates the current position of the mouse.

Name box: Appears on the left of the formula bar and displays either the active cell's address or its assigned name.

Noninteractive Web page: Web pages created from an Excel workbook in HTML format that allows users to view the entire Excel workbook but not change anything in it.

Object linking and embedding: A technology developed by Microsoft that enables you to create objects with one application and then link or embed them in a second application.

Page field: A pivot table field that filters the entire PivotTable report to display data for a single item or all the items.

Paste: Placing information into one document that is copied from another document.

Path: The disk drive and folders that lead to a referenced workbook.

Pitch: The number of characters per horizontal inch.

Pivot table: An interactive table enabling you to quickly group and summarize large amounts of data.

Plot area: Rectangular area bounded by the X-axis on the left and the Y-axis on the bottom.

Point: The height of characters in a typeface; equal to 1/72 of an inch.

Pointing: Using the mouse to select a cell range while writing a formula.

Portrait: Print orientation in which the length is greater than the width.

Positional arguments: Arguments whose position in the argument list is important and inflexible.

Precedence order: Determines the order in which to calculate each part of the formula—which mathematical operators to evaluate first, which to evaluate second, and so on.

Precedent cell: A cell upon which a formula depends.

Primary sort field: The first sort field of multiple sort fields required to reorder a list.

Principal: Amount of money borrowed.

Properties dialog box: Contains several text boxes that you can fill in with helpful information including the fields Title, Subject, Author, Manager, Company, Category, Keywords, and Comments.

Proportional (font): Each character's pitch varies by character.

Protect (worksheet): Excel disallows modifications to cells or new values in cells.

Prototype: A proposed worksheet model.

Query: *See* Filter.

Range errors: Values that are either too large or too small (negative or too close to zero, for example) that do not make sense in the context of the application.

Range finder: A feature that color-codes an outline surrounding each cell referenced by a formula.

Range name: A name that you assign to a cell or cell range that can replace a cell address or cell range in expressions or functions.

Rate: Percentage interest rate.

Record: Each row of a list containing the fields that collectively describe a single object, person, or place.

Reference: A link to an object identifying the filename and its location.

Refresh (pivot table): Make Excel recalculate the values in the pivot table based on the data list's current values.

Relational operator: Compares two values and the result in either true or false.

Relational operator: Compares two parts of a formula.

Relative cell reference: Cell references in formulas that change when Excel copies them to another location.

Right margin: Defines the white space between the print area's rightmost position and the right edge of a printed page.

Row field: A pivot table field that summarizes data vertically by groups.

Search criteria: Values that the data form should match in specified data form fields.

Secondary sort field: The field used to break ties on a group of matching primary sort field values.

Selection handles: Small, white squares that appear around an object that is selected.

Series in: Option that establishes the way the data series is represented—either by rows or by columns.

Server: The program from which you copy information pasted into another program.

Shared workbook: An Excel workbook that more than one person can open, modify, and save.

Sheet tab: Contains the sheet's name.

Sheet tab scroll buttons: The buttons you click to scroll through an Excel workbook's sheet tabs.

Sizing handles: *See* Selection handles.

Sort field: The field or fields you use to sort a list.

Sort key: *See* Sort field.

Source cell(s): The copied cell(s).

Source program: *See* Server.

Spreadsheet: A popular program used to analyze numeric information and help make meaningful business decisions based on the analysis.

Stacked bar chart: A subtype of the bar chart, combines the data markers in a data series together to form one bar, placing each marker at the end of the preceding one in the same data series.

Standard toolbar: Contains buttons that execute popular menu bar commands such as Print, Cut, and Insert Table.

Status bar: Bar appearing at the bottom of the display that shows general information about the worksheet and selected keyboard keys.

Summary worksheet: Contains a digest or synopsis of the information contained in the individual worksheets.

Supporting workbook: A workbook containing a worksheet to which a link formula refers.

Supporting worksheets: Worksheets that are referenced by other worksheets.

Syntax: Rules governing the way you write Excel functions.

Target cell(s): The cell or cells to which the contents are copied.

Task pane: A dialog window that provides a convenient way to use commands, gather information, and modify Excel documents.

Term: Time period over which you make periodic payments.

Text (entry): Any combination of characters that you can type on the keyboard including symbols.

Text box: A rectangular-shaped drawing object that contains text.

Three-dimensional formulas: Formulas that reference other worksheets in the current workbook.

Tick marks: Small lines, similar to marks on a ruler, which are uniformly spaced along each axis and identify the position of category names or values.

Tie (sort): Exists when one or more records have the same value for a field.

Time value of money: $100 today is more valuable than $100 is next year.

Top margin: The area between the top of page and topmost edge of the print area.

Tracer arrow: Displays the relationship between the active cell and another cell related to it.

Two-dimensional formulas: Formulas that reference cells on a single worksheet.

Unattached text: Chart objects such as comments or text boxes.

Unlocked: An attribute of a cell that leaves it unprotected.

Value (entry): Numbers that represent a quantity, date, or time.

What-if analysis: Making changes to spreadsheets and reviewing their effect on other values.

Wild card character: A special character that stands for zero or more characters.

Workbook: A collection of one or more individual worksheets.

Workbook window: The document window open in Excel.

Worksheet: They resemble pages in a spiral-bound workbook like the ones you purchase and use to take class notes.

Wrap text: Formatting that continues long text on multiple lines within a cell.

X-axis: Contains markers denoting category values.

X-axis title: Briefly describes the X-axis categories.

Y-axis: Contains the value of data being plotted.

Y-axis title: Identifies the values being plotted on the Y-axis.

glossary

=Count(): A predefined function that returns a count of values. Format: =Count(fieldname).

=Max(): A predefined function that returns the maximum value for a field. Format: =Max(fieldname).

=Min(): A predefined function that returns the minimum value from a group of values. Format: =Min(fieldname).

=Now(): A predefined function that returns the current date and time from the system clock.

=Sum(): A predefined function that returns the sum of a group of values. Format: =Sum(fieldname).

Absolute address: An address to a Web page, local file, or other object that contains values for every address component. Moving files will cause an absolute address to be invalid.

Access Window: The main window of the Microsoft Access user interface. Other windows display inside it.

Action queries: Queries that update the data in a database in some fashion. For example, to delete a group of records that meet a criterion, to update a group of records, to add records to an existing table, or to add records to a new table.

Active Server Page: A Web page designed to display up-to-date read-only data. The data are selected by the server and displayed in a table format. Opening or refreshing an ASP file from a Web browser causes the page to be dynamically created from current values and sent to the browser.

Advanced Filter/Sort: The most comprehensive filtering method that presents a grid of the table being filtered and allows you to enter record selection criteria.

Aggregate function: Access predefined calculations used to summarize groups of data (e.g., Sum and Avg).

Alternate keys: A table field that could have been assigned as the primary key but was not.

And: The logical operator that combines two conditions that must both be true to retrieve a record.

Back-end: The centralized data storage of a split database.

Between: The relational operator used to select records whose values fall between the stated upper and lower bounds. For example, Between 14 and 18.

Bound control: A control that will display data values from the record source. Text boxes are typically bound to a field from a table.

Calculated control: A control that contains an expression whose results display in the control. For example, a text box containing the expression =Now() will display the date/time retrieved from the system clock.

Calculated field: A field of a query that contains an expression.

Candidate key: Each table field that could be defined as the primary.

Caption: The table field property that determines what displays as the label for the field in Datasheet and other views.

Cascade Delete Related Records: Referential Integrity setting that causes the related records to be deleted when a primary record is deleted.

Cascade Update Related Fields: Referential Integrity setting that causes an update in the primary table to also be applied to the related table.

Chart: A graphical representation of numeric data. For example, a pie chart.

Chart Wizard: An Access Wizard that walks you through the process of creating a chart based on table data.

Client/server databases: DBMSs that are designed to support multiple users in a networked environment.

Compact on Close: The database option that causes a database to automatically compact each time it is closed.

Compacting: The process of removing excess space from a database.

Composite key: The result of multiple attributes being combined for the primary key.

Concatenate: The act of joining one string value to another string value using the ampersand (&) operator.

Condition: The method of entering selection criteria using operators such as >, <, >=, <=, and <>.

Conflict Viewer: Access tool used to resolve synchronization conflicts in replication sets.

Control Wizards: A group of Wizards that walk the user through the creation properties for complex controls, for example, the Image Control Wizard.

Crosstab Queries: Queries that are used to analyze data by grouping data and calculating values for each group.

Crosstab Query: A query format that allows data to be tabulated by two variables: a row header and a column header.

Custom report: A report that contains features not available in the Report Wizard.

Data access language (DAL): RDBMS language for rapidly retrieving and organizing stored data. SQL is the standard.

Data Access Pages: Web pages that allow a Web browser to be used to view and update table data via a live connection to the data in your database.

Data definition language (DDL): The language provided by RDBMS for structuring the data tables and their relationships.

Data integrity: A term used to describe the reliability of data.

Data redundancy: Storing the same data such as a customer's last name multiple times. Redundant data increase the likelihood that data will not be updated properly in all locations and so reduce data integrity.

Data type: The table field property that determines what type of data it can store and how much storage space it will require.

Data validation rules: Rules that verify data entered are within appropriate bounds. For example, Gender should contain only M for male or F for female.

Data value: The intersection of a table row and column containing data pertaining to one attribute of one entity.

Database: A file that organizes Access objects (tables, queries, forms, reports, and so on) that are related to each other.

Database management system (DBMS): The software used to store data, maintain those data, and provide easy access to stored data.

Database Window: The window displaying an open Access database.

Datasheet View: The default grid layout used to display Access table data.

Default Value: The table field property that determines the value that will automatically be loaded for the field in a new record. The user can overtype the default value.

Design grid: The form used to specify fields and criteria in a query.

Design Master: The original database of a replica set that keeps track of all replicas.

Design View: The view of an object that is used to change the structure of the object.

Detect and Repair: A facility to detect and repair problems with Office software.

Direct synchronization: The synchronization method used when the replica set shares a network and can directly connect to each other.

Domain: All valid entries for one table attribute (column).

Embedded: A distinct copy of an object placed in a destination document that retains a link to the program that developed them, called the source program. Double-clicking an embedded object will open the source program in edit mode.

Encoding: A method of coding a file so that it is indecipherable without the conversion algorithm.

Entity: A person, place, object, idea, or event about which data are being collected.

Exclusive: A type of database access that locks out all other users. Use the Open button drop-down list to access this mode.

Explicit permissions: Those permissions granted directly to a user account.

Expression Builder: A tool for building expressions by selecting fields from tables, operators, and other calculation components.

Extranet: A combination of Internet and intranet technologies capable of securing and sharing data and information both locally and via the World Wide Web.

Field: A table column representing a unique property of an entity such as LastName, BirthDate, or Quantity; it can also be referred to as an attribute.

Field list: The listing of fields for a table used to select fields to be included in a query.

Field Name: The attribute of a table field that identifies it and is used to refer to it in queries, forms, reports, and modules.

Field selector: The button containing the field name that can be used to select an entire column of a datasheet.

Field Size: The table field property that determines the maximum value that the field can store, how much space is required to store it, and how fast it can be processed.

Filter by Form: A method of filtering or selecting records using an empty version of the current datasheet where you can type match values.

Filter by Selection: The simplest type of filter, which selects records that match the datasheet value you have selected.

Filter Excluding Selection: A method of selecting records that do not meet the stated criteria.

Filter for Input: A filter initiated from the pop-up menu that provides a text box for entering record selection criteria.

Foreign key: The value used to match the attributes from one table to those in another table.

Form: A user-friendly way to view and update data on a computer screen.

Form Detail section: The area of a form design that specifies what the form will display—typically fields from the record source.

Form Footer section: The area of form design that specifies what will display at the bottom of each form and at the end of each form print.

Form Header section: The area of form design that specifies what will display at the top of each form and at the beginning of each form print.

Form View: The view used to manipulate data in a form.

Form Wizard: An Access Wizard that walks you through the process of building a form by selecting fields from multiple tables and queries.

Format: The field property of a table definition that controls how data display to the user after they have been entered.

Format Painter: A tool available on the Standard toolbar that will pick up formatting applied to text and allow you to paint it onto other text.

Freezing columns: Keeping the leftmost columns of a datasheet on the screen when scrolling through columns to the right. The leftmost columns would scroll off of the screen if they were not frozen.

Front-end: In a split database, this is the part that is customized for each user.

Global chart: A type of chart that is based on all of the available data. Totals or averages from the data are usually charted.

Group by: Option used to set a field or fields that will be used to calculate subtotals.

Groups bar: A bar in the Access Database Window to allow users to group database objects for easier manipulation.

Group Header/Footer sections: The sections of report design that define what appears before and after each group of records. The header typically identifies the group and the footer typically contains group calculations.

Handles: The squares that appear on the borders of selected objects like a text box. When handles of different size are present, the large handle is used to move and the smaller handles are used to resize.

HTML: *See* Hypertext Markup Language.

Hyperlink: A link between two objects that allows the user to navigate from object to object. Text hyperlinks are usually underlined and a different color. When the cursor is over a hyperlink, it changes to a pointing hand.

Hypertext Markup Language: A tag-based language used to create and link Web pages for delivery on a local computer, the Internet, an intranet, or an extranet.

Implicit permissions: Those permissions inherited from the group to which the user belongs.

Imported: A document or object from another source that has been inserted into an Access container such as a table and is no longer associated with the original.

In: The relational operator used to select records whose values match those listed. For example, In ("CO", "IN", "CA").

Index: Used to speed data access and sorting by allowing direct access to a specific value. Works like the index of a book.

Indexed: The field property of a table definition that determines whether or not this field indexes the table.

Inner join: A type of table relationship that creates rows in the query answerset when the related fields have matching values.

Internet: A worldwide network of computers used to distribute and share data and information.

Internet Service Provider: A company that provides access to Internet services for its customers.

Intranets: A local network used to share data and information using Web pages and other Internet technologies.

Joining: The process of using a foreign key from one table to link to the data in another table.

Label control: A control that is used to display unchanging text in a form or report.

Left outer join: A type of table relationship that creates rows in the query answerset for all of the records in the first (left) table and adds the data from the second table when the related fields have matching values.

Like: The relational operator used to select records using wild cards (*, ?, #).

Linked: A picture of an object displays in the destination document but there is only one copy of the object, which can be maintained only from the source program.

Lookup field: A tool to ease data entry by listing valid values from a related table. Lookup fields are created using a Wizard in table Design View.

Macros: Used to automate repetitive database tasks using a series of actions; a self-contained instruction or command.

Main form: The outer form in a main form/subform pair. The main form typically displays data from the primary table and a subform displays related records.

Many-to-many: A table relationship that exists when one row in the first table matches with multiple rows in the second table and one row in the second table matches with multiple rows in the first table. Many-to-many relationships can't be directly modeled in relational databases, but are broken into multiple one-to-many relationships (abbreviated M:N or ∞:∞).

Microsoft Graph: The application that is used by the Chart Wizard to create a chart.

Module: A collection of Visual Basic statements and procedures that are organized and stored together to be accessed as a unit.

Move handle: When multiple sizes of handles appear on an object, the larger handle is referred to as the Move handle and will allow this object to move independently of other objects.

Not: The logical operator that negates the condition that it precedes.

Null: A field is said to be null or contain null values when nothing has been entered. This is used to differentiate between spaces and nothing entered in a field.

Object: Virtually anything—traditional data, a moving image, people talking, a photograph, narrative, text, music, or any combination.

Object bar: A bar displaying icons in the Access Database Window for each of the objects that can be created for a database.

Object linking and embedding: The Microsoft technology that allows objects to be placed in other objects. Such objects are either linked to the source object or embedded with no link to the source.

OLE: See Object linking and embedding.

One-to-many: The table relationship that exists when one row of the first table matches to multiple rows in the second table (abbreviated 1:M or 1:∞).

One-to-one: The table relationship that exists when one row of the first table matches to one and only one row of the second table and both tables have the same primary key (abbreviated 1:1).

Optimizing: A series of performance-enhancing operations that will result in a more efficient database.

Or: The logical operator that combines two conditions when either one or both of the conditions can be true to retrieve a record.

Owner: The user who created a database object is the owner of that object and has all security rights to that object.

Page Header/Footer sections: The sections of report design that define what appears at the top and bottom of each report page.

Parameter query: A query that prompts the user for criteria that will be used in selecting data from the database.

Password: A password is used to allow only authorized users to access a database.

Permissions: Permissions establish the level of access a user has to a specific object. The level of permission determines whether the user can see, update, print, modify, and perform other operations on an object.

Personal databases: Systems like Microsoft Access that work best in single-user environments.

Primary key: A table field or fields that uniquely and minimally identifies an entity.

Primary sort: The first field that is used to order rows of data.

Primary table: The table on the one side of a one-to-many relationship.

Properties: The attributes of an object like a Label control that determine what is displayed and how it is formatted. Properties are set using the Properties pages.

Properties pages: A tabbed dialog box that displays all of the properties that can be set for an object.

Query Questions that are posed to a relational database using *Structured Query Language (SQL)*.

Read-Only: A type of database access that will not allow updates to the database. Use the Open button drop-down list to access this mode.

Record: One row in a relation (table) representing the unique data for one *entity* (person, place, object, idea, or event); it also can be referred to as a tuple.

Record-bound chart: A type of chart that reflects the data of the current record and changes when another record is active.

Record Navigation toolbar: A toolbar on a Data Access Page that will allow you to save edits, delete records, move through the records, and other maintenance tasks.

Record selector: The buttons to the left of records in Datasheet View used to select a row.

Record source: The source of data for an object like a form or report. Tables and queries are valid record sources.

Related table: The table on the many side of a one-to-many relationship.

Relational database: A collection of data relations defined using related tables.

Relational database management systems (RDBMS): A type of DBMS that stores data in interrelated tables. Tables are related by sharing a common field.

Relational operator: The operators (>, < >=, <=, <>) used to set conditions in queries.

Relationships window: The window used to set or edit table relationships. Accessed using the Relationships button on the toolbar.

Relative address: An address to a Web page, local file, or other object that does not contain all of the address components. The missing components are assigned the values of the current object.

Repair: The process of fixing errors in the structure of database objects.

Replica: A copy of a database that must be synchronized with the Design Master to maintain accuracy among all of the replicas.

Replica set: The Design Master and all of its replicas.

Report: RDBMS object used to format data for printing.

Report Detail section: The section of report design that specifies what is to display on each detail line—typically fields from the record source.

Report Header/Footer sections: The sections of report design that define what will appear at the beginning and end of a report. The Report Header usually contains the report title and the Report Footer usually contains grand totals.

Required: The table field property that determines whether or not the user must enter a value in this field.

Right outer join: A type of table relationship that creates rows in the query answerset for all of the rows in the second (right) table and adds the data from the first (left) table when the related fields have matching values.

Secondary sort: The second field that is used to order rows of data.

Select queries: The most common type of query used to retrieve (select) data from one or more tables.

Selection Bar: The bar that separates the sections of a report or form and contains the section name. This bar is used to select and resize the section.

Shared: A type of database access that allows multiple users to be logged on to the same database simultaneously. The default open mode.

Sizing handle: The small squares that appear on the borders of the object that is selected. These handles can be dragged to resize the object.

Sort Ascending: Toolbar button used to cause an ascending sort based on the selected column(s).

Sort Descending: Toolbar button used to cause a descending sort based on the selected column(s).

Static HTML: Web pages used to publish a snapshot of the data, which have to be updated manually.

Structured Query Language (SQL): The language used to pose questions or queries to a relational database; SQL has been standardized by the American National Standards Institute (ANSI).

Subdatasheet: A small datasheet that presents over the main datasheet to display related data. Activated by clicking the plus (+) sign on the main datasheet.

Subform: The inner form in a main form/subform pair. The main form typically displays data from the primary table and the subform displays related records.

Synchronization: The process of retrieving updates from replicas and applying them to the members of the replica set so that they all reflect the same data, queries, forms, and reports.

Table: Rows and columns used to store data in a relational database management system.

Tags: HTML instructions that are enclosed in <> such as <bold> or <p>.

Text Box control: The control used to display values from a record source or the result of an expression.

Unbound control: A control that is not tied to a record source and so its content does not change from record to record.

Uniform Resource Locator: The address that identifies an object on a computer. An Internet address consists of the protocol, server address, path, and file name.

URL: See Uniform Resource Locator.

User-level security: Complex security such as that found on larger computers. Users belong to user groups that carry permissions for levels of access to each database object.

Validation: The table field property that contains the rule or rules that govern what data are acceptable for that field of a table.

Web browser: The software that allows you to view Internet documents. For example, Microsoft Internet Explorer.

Web servers: Computers that store documents for Internet distribution.

Wizards: Provide the user with step-by-step instructions on common tasks such as creating simple queries, forms, and reports.

World Wide Web: A network of linked documents made available through the Internet.

WWW: See World Wide Web.

Z-order: The order that objects are placed on the screen controlling which object is in the foreground when objects are stacked. Use the Order option of the popup menu to change this.

Zero-length strings: Entered as " ", this indicates that the field is not supposed to contain data.

Zoom box: An enlarged area for entering long expressions activated by pressing Ctrl+F2.

glossary

Absolute links: Links that contain complete addresses to the resource.

Action buttons: Ready-made buttons used to provide navigation such as next, previous, first, and last. The action is controlled by adding a hyperlink.

Adjustment handles: The gold handles of a selected object that allow the prominent feature of the object to be adjusted. Not all objects can be adjusted.

Animation: Motion added to a presentation object.

Animation Schemes: Preset combinations of Slide Transitions and text animations.

AutoContent Wizard: A Wizard that will create a presentation with suggested content based on a series of questions answered by the user.

AutoCorrect: The facility that makes corrections to common mistakes as you type.

AutoFit: The facility that causes text to reduce its size to fit within a placeholder.

Backspace: The keyboard key used to move backward through text deleting one character to the left of the cursor for each backspace.

Bitmap: A type of image composed of small dots of color. Also called a raster image.

Blank presentation: One method of creating a new presentation. When this option is used, the presentation has no background or color selections applied.

Bold: Text property that causes text to appear darker.

Bookmark: Used to mark a specific page or location within a file for linking.

Broken hyperlinks: Hyperlinks that do not work because the document is not at the indicated address.

Chat: Real-time Web-based communication that is typically accomplished by typing messages, but can include voice communication.

Clip art: Drawings that can be added to documents, including those in the Microsoft Media Gallery.

Clip Organizer: *See* Microsoft Clip Organizer

Collaborative meetings: Usually online meetings used to facilitate collaboration of groups who can't have face-to-face meetings due to time or geographic constraints.

Color scheme: The palette that controls default color values for the slide background, body text, lines, shadows, title text, fills, hyperlinks, and accents.

Control boxes: The gray boxes above and to the left of the cells in a datasheet that are used to select rows and columns.

Copy: Placing a duplicate of the selection on either the Windows Clipboard or the Office Clipboard so that it can be pasted in another location. This can be accomplished using the Standard toolbar's Copy button or from the Edit menu. *See also* Cut and Paste.

Copyright law: The laws that give the person who owns a work the rights to control how the work is used.

Custom Animation: The pane of the task panel that allows you to fully control object animation in a presentation.

Cycle diagram: One of the diagrams available in Microsoft PowerPoint that is used to show cyclical processes such as the water cycle.

Data series: The numbers of one group to be graphed in the same color or line. For example, the total sales values for each month of the year would be a data series.

Data value: The contents of one cell in a datasheet.

Datasheet: The rows and columns that hold the data for Microsoft Graph.

Default view: The view that will be used to open presentations. Set with the View tab of the Tools/Options menu.

Del: The keyboard key used to delete the character to the right of the cursor.

Design template: Templates that contain backgrounds and color selections that can be applied to a new or existing presentation.

Digital signatures: Information embedded in a file identifying the creator and the validity of the source. Digital signatures present as certificates to allow the user to decide whether or not to trust this source.

Dimming effect: The animation effect that causes an animated object to change color after the animation.

Dotted-line selection box: Selection border indicating that an object can be operated.

Drawing: Toolbar containing graphic objects that normally appear at the bottom of a screen.

Drawing toolbar: The toolbar with tools to draw lines, shapes, and other graphic objects. Typically displayed at the bottom of the screen.

Drawn pictures: A type of image created using calculated shapes so that they have small file sizes and resize well. Also called vector graphics.

Embedded: A method of placing a copy of an image or other objects into a document with no connection to the original file.

Embedded: When a file created in an external application is stored in PowerPoint, for example, an embedded voice narration file.

Expand All button: The toolbar button used to expand and collapse outlines.

Export: Sending data from the current application to another application. For example, using the Send To option of the File menu to send a PowerPoint outline to Word.

File converters: Programs that convert documents created in one application so that they are compatible with another. For example, converting a PowerPoint outline to Word format.

File transfer protocol (FTP): Software applications used to move files from a local computer to a Web server.

Font: The typeface property of text.

Footer: Content to print in the bottom margin of a document.

Format Painter: Tool used to copy formats from text to be painted on other selections.

Formatting toolbar: The toolbar with options to format text, graphics, and slides.

Frames: A Web page that has multiple windows. Each window is a frame and displays a different HTML document.

Grayscale: A printing option that will print a color presentation in shades of gray.

Grids: Evenly spaced lines that display on the slide to help size and align objects. Grids are controlled from the Draw menu of the Drawing toolbar and do not display or print with the slide show.

Grouping: The ability to combine multiple objects into a single object. Grouped objects can be manipulated as one object, or each component can have individual properties set.

Guides: User positioned lines that display on the slide to help size and align objects.

Hanging indent: A style of paragraph indention where the first line is farther left than the rest of the paragraph.

Header: Content to print in the top margin of a document.

Home page: The opening page of a Web site that typically contains a list of available services, topics, and features.

HTML: *See* hypertext markup language.

HTML tags: HTML instructions enclosed in <> such as <b> or <i>.

Hyperlink: A clickable object that links to another point in the current document or to another document.

Hyperlink base: The common location used for all linked files of a project.

Hypertext markup language: A tag-based language used to describe to browsers how a Web page should be displayed. For example, <i>Hello</i> would display *Hello*.

Importing: Moving content from another application into the current document.

Indent markers: Markers on the rule that control the placement of bullets and text.

Internet: A network of privately owned computers designed to share documents and services worldwide.

Internet search engine: Any of a group of Web products designed to search the Web based on the criteria that you enter, for example, Yahoo!, WebCrawler, AskJeeves, and so on.

Internet service providers (ISPs): Organizations that provide access to the Internet and Web services.

Intranets: Networks providing services within an organization similar to those provided by the Internet.

Intrinsic color schemes: Color schemes that are shipped with a particular PowerPoint template.

Intrinsic sounds: Sounds that ship as part of the Microsoft Office Media Gallery.

ISP: *See* Internet service providers.

Italic: Text property used for emphasis resulting in right-slanting text.

Keywords: Descriptive words used to locate clips in the media gallery.

Kiosk: A self-running slide show that can include Custom Animations, a recorded narration, and protects against presentation update.

License agreement: A legal agreement that outlines how copyrighted materials can be used.

Linked: When a link to an external file is used to display its contents in a PowerPoint presentation. For example, a linked voice narration file is separate from the presentation. A method of displaying images and other objects in a document using a link to the original file.

Local server: A computer providing services to an organization's local area network.

Macro: A facility used to store keystrokes and mouse operations so they can be replayed.

Macro security levels: Microsoft Office security features designed to verify the source of macros and reduce the risk of macro viruses.

Macro virus: A computer virus stored in a macro and spread by sharing the infected file.

Matting: Placing a solid background behind text to differentiate it more clearly from a busy background.

Media clip: Members of the Microsoft Media Gallery including sounds, animations, movies, pictures, and clip art.

Meeting Minder: Allows the presenter to take notes and track action items during a presentation.

Microsoft Clip Organizer: A collection of media clips (pictures, clip art, sounds, and animations) that installs with Office.

Navigation bar: Navigation controls such as next and previous added to a presentation saved as a Web page.

Normal view: The view most often used to develop presentations consisting of the Outline, Slide, and Notes panes.

Notes pane: The Normal view pane that allows you to add notes to a slide that will not be seen as part of the presentation. Typically these are printed as speaker's notes.

Object: Anything that can be manipulated on a slide.

Organization chart: One of the diagrams available in Microsoft PowerPoint that is used to show hierarchical relationships such as the management structure of an organization.

Outline pane: The Normal view pane that contains the Outline and Slides tabs. It is most often used to enter and edit text.

Outline view: A customization of PowerPoint's Normal view featuring the Outline pane.

Outlining toolbar: A special PowerPoint toolbar designed to work with outlines. Activate it from the View/Toolbars menu.

Package for CD: The PowerPoint facility used to prepare presentations for transport. It ensures that all necessary files, including fonts and the viewer, are packaged.

Page orientation: Setting that controls whether output is printed in landscape or portrait.

Page Setup: The dialog box used to select page orientation, slide number, and slide size when printing a presentation.

Palette: The selection of available colors that displays on color menus. Custom colors can be added to the palette.

Paste: The paste operation places the contents of the clipboard at the active cursor location. *See also* Copy and Paste.

Pen tool: Tool available during a presentation to annotate slides.

Playlists: The instructions followed by the PowerPoint viewer to play multiple presentations sequentially.

Point size: The height measurement of text size.

PowerPoint viewer: A software application used to display PowerPoint presentations on computers without PowerPoint loaded. The viewer is also capable of sequentially playing multiple presentations based on a playlist.

Print dialog box: The dialog box accessed from the File menu to select and customize printer options.

Print Preview: A "what you see is what you get" (wysiwyg) environment displaying documents exactly as they will print.

Print range: The page or pages to be printed as defined in the Print dialog box.

Properties: Settings that control how an object looks or behaves like font. The attributes that can be set to control object behavior, for example, the speed and type of transition.

Pyramid diagram: One of the diagrams available in Microsoft PowerPoint that is used to show foundational relationships like progressive levels of mathematics.

Radial diagram: One of the diagrams available in Microsoft PowerPoint that is used to show multiple relationships to a central element like multiple reports generated from the same data.

Raster image: A type of image composed of small dots of color. Also called a bitmap.

Redo: A button on the Standard toolbar that will reinstate actions that have been undone. *See also* Undo.

Regroup: Causing ungrouped objects to become a group or single object again.

Relative links: Links that use a default value for part of the resource address. For example, when only a filename is included, the drive, path, and folder of the current file is assumed to complete the address.

Rich text format: A file format commonly used in word processing applications capable of storing text, graphics, and their formats.

Rotation handle: The green handle above a selected image that will allow you to rotate the image.

Screen Tips: Text descriptions of screen elements that appear when the mouse pointer is paused over them.

Shadow: Property that places a shadow on a character.

Shapes tool: Tools on the Drawing toolbar used to place shapes like rectangles on a slide.

Sizing handles: White circles in a selection border that can be used to resize an object.

Slanted-line selection box: Selection border indicating that the contents of an object can be edited.

Slide layout: A pattern of text and media that control what can be entered on a slide. Slide layout is selected from the Slide Layout panel of the task pane and can be updated at any time.

Slide Master: Sets the formats, placeholders, and backgrounds that will be used as the presentation default.

Slide pane: The pane of Normal view that displays a slide as it will appear during the presentation. Most often used to add and modify media elements of a presentation.

Slide placeholders: The areas where text or media can be entered on a slide. Slide layout controls what placeholders are visible on a particular slide.

Slide Show view: The view used to preview a presentation. Each slide fills the screen. No editing is possible in this view.

Slide Sorter view: The view consisting of thumbnails of the presentation. Ideal for reorganizing the slides and adding transitions and animations.

Slide timings: The time that a slide will remain on the screen when the slide show is set to advance using timings. Timings can be set manually or while rehearsing the show.

Slide Transition: The visual effect like dissolve or fade that ushers a slide onto the screen.

Slide Transition: Controls how a slide enters and leaves the screen.

Slides tab: The tab that displays thumbnails of the presentation in the Outline pane of PowerPoint's Normal view.

Slide-title master pairs: The two slides that make up the slide master—the title slide and the body slide master.

Spelling Checker: Facility that places red wavy underlines under words that are not found in the dictionary.

Standard toolbar: The toolbar that is common to most Windows applications with options to save, print, cut, copy, and paste.

Style Checker: Facility that warns the developer of style rules violations.

Style rules: Style rules set the parameters for punctuation, fonts, number of bullets, and so on, that are used by the Style Checker to review the style of a presentation.

Target diagram: One of the diagrams available in Microsoft PowerPoint that is used to show steps toward a goal.

Task pane: A window used to access important tasks conveniently without leaving your document.

Text animation: Effects that control how text enters and leaves a slide.

Text box: The object that holds text and is added to a slide from the Drawing toolbar.

Title Master: The master that sets the default format for title slides.

Toggle button: Buttons that apply and remove properties. For example, the Bold button on the toolbar.

Toolbar: A horizontal or vertical ribbon of icons used to accomplish application tasks like save a file, change the font, and adjust paragraph indentation.

Transparencies: Printing on transparent slides to be used with an overhead projector.

Underline: A format that applies an underline to the selected text.

Undo: A button on the Standard toolbar that will allow you to reverse up to 20 actions. *See also* Redo.

Ungroup: Returning a grouped object to its original state of individual objects.

Uniform resource locator: The address of a Web page or other Web resource.

URL: *See* Uniform resource locator

Vector graphics: A type of image created using calculated shapes so that they have small file sizes and resize well. Also called drawn pictures.

Venn diagram: One of the diagrams available in Microsoft PowerPoint that is used to show overlapping relationships like two sets of data that share some values.

View: The current view controls what panes and operations can be accomplished. Normal, Slide Sorter, and Slide Show views are each designed to support a specific part of presentation development.

View toolbar: The toolbar used to move between PowerPoint views. Typically displayed at the bottom of the Outline pane in Normal view.

Web browser: Software application like Microsoft Internet Explorer and Netscape Navigator used to view Web pages.

Web discussions: A Web-based forum used to discuss Web pages viewed in Microsoft Internet Explorer 4.0 or later and set to allow discussion. Participants must have permission to join the discussion.

Web pages: Pages formatted with HTML for delivery through the World Wide Web or a local intranet.

Web server: A computer that provides access to and from the World Wide Web and Internet.

Web site: A group of Web pages published to be used together. A home page typically provides a starting point with a menu of available topics.

Whiteboard: A Web-based writing space used to present information to a group like a whiteboard in a classroom.

Workgroup software: A category of software designed to facilitate working in groups, for example, software to manage a review cycle or track edits to a shared document.

World Wide Web: A worldwide network of hyperlinked documents.

X-axis: The axis of a chart that identifies the data values of a series. For example, the days of the week. Usually the horizontal axis.

Y-axis: The axis of a chart that quantifies the values being charted.

Z-order: The order that objects are stacked as they are added to a slide. The first object added is closest to the slide.

index

index

index

index

index